Principles
of
Managerial
Finance

First Canadian
Edition

Principles of Managerial Finance

First Canadian Edition

Lawrence J. Gitman

San Diego State University

Sean Hennessey

University of Prince Edward Island

PEARSON

Addison Wesley

Toronto

National Library of Canada Cataloguing in Publication

Gitman, Lawrence J.
    Principles of managerial finance / Lawrence J. Gitman, Sean M. Hennessey. — Canadian ed.

Includes index.
ISBN 0-321-11535-X

1. Corporations—Finance. 2. Business enterprises—Finance.
I. Hennessey, Sean M. II. Title.

HG4026.G58 2004   658.15   C2002-905906-2

0-321-11535-X

Vice President, Editorial Director: Michael J. Young
Acquisitions Editor: Gary Bennett
Marketing Manager: Deborah Meredith
Developmental Editor: Meaghan Eley
Production Editor: Richard di Santo
Copy Editor: Tally Morgan
Production Coordinator: Janette Lush
Page Layout: Hermia Chung
Permissions and Photo Research: Amanda McCormick
Art Director: Mary Opper
Cover Design: Alex Li
Cover Image: Charly Franklin/Getty Images/Taxi

Statistics Canada information is used with the permission of the Minister of Industry, as Minister responsible for Statistics Canada. Information on the availability of the wide range of data from Statistics Canada can be obtained from Statistics Canada's Regional Offices, its World Wide Web site at http://www.statcan.ca, and its toll-free access number 1-800-263-1136.

1 2 3 4 5   08 07 06 05 04 03

Printed and bound in the United States of America.

*Dedicated to the memory
of my mother, Dr. Edith Gitman,
who instilled in me the importance
of education and hard work.*

Lawrence J. Gitman

*To Roberta, my wife and best friend,
our son Liam,
and my parents, Aletha and Michael.*

Sean Hennessey

Brief Contents

Contents

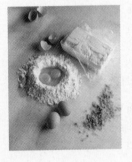

Part 5   *Long-Term Investment Decisions*   *549*

Part 6   *Working Capital Management 661*

Part 7   *Special Topics in Managerial Finance*   *743*

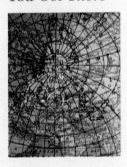

Preface

The desire to write the first Canadian edition of *Principles of Managerial Finance* came out of our experiences teaching the introductory managerial finance course. When we began teaching full time, we were not very far removed from our own undergraduate studies and therefore could appreciate the difficulties some of our students were having with the textbooks we were using. They wanted a book that spoke to them in plain English. They wanted a book that tied concepts to reality. They also wanted not just descriptions, but demonstrations of concepts, tools, and techniques.

In writing this text, our goal was to provide students with a resource that presents the principles of Canadian managerial finance with clarity. This goal is accomplished through a student-focused writing style based on clearly defined learning goals, a chapter-opening picture box that provides an overview of the key ideas covered in the chapter, the use of numerous examples, ties to the practice of finance, examples of how finance is integrated with other functional areas, links to important Web sites, succinct end-of-chapter summaries tied to the chapter's learning goals, self-test problems, numerous end-of-chapter problems, cases, and engaging Web exercises.

This text provides students with a total package that reduces the stress of learning managerial finance. Some readers have even suggested the text makes the learning of managerial finance "fun." In satisfying the needs of students, we believe we have satisfied the needs of instructors as well. Readers will note that the text is firmly grounded in the theory and practice of finance and is user-friendly at the same time.

The text uses plain English, ties concepts to reality, and demonstrates concepts, tools, and techniques. It incorporates a proven learning system that integrates pedagogy with concepts and practical applications. It concentrates on the concepts, techniques, and practices that students require to make managerial financial decisions in an increasingly competitive and international business environment. The strong pedagogy and generous use of examples and practical applications make the textbook an easily accessible resource for students of all abilities.

This first Canadian edition of *Principles of Managerial Finance* presents important current and emerging issues and techniques affecting the practice of financial management while focusing on the practical application of the concepts. The goal throughout the text is to present the material in an engaging, easy to read, and understandable style. The use of colour and the eye-catching, pleasing design are sure to appeal to readers.

Intended Audience

This text has been designed, developed, and written for a first course in managerial or corporate finance. The typical student will not have previously taken a course in finance, and the text is written assuming no previous knowledge of finance. Since the first finance course is part of a core business program, the text is intended for all students: finance majors and non-majors alike. It is an ideal text for self-study or a Web-based course given its direct style and focus on examples.

The text is a self-contained resource in finance. It assumes some familiarity with basic accounting and time value of money concepts, but these topics are reviewed in chapters dedicated to these important foundation concepts. Students do require basic mathematical skills. Students with very different backgrounds and abilities will find the text very accessible and easy to understand. Again, this is due to the clear writing style and the regular use of examples that make learning finance concepts easier.

This text will become an important part of the student's reference library that will be referred to in later courses in the business program and later in business life. From the classroom to the office, the first Canadian edition of *Principles of Managerial Finance* will help readers get to where they want to go.

Distinguishing Features of the Book

Numerous features distinguish the first Canadian edition of *Principles of Managerial Finance* from its many competitors. Among them are the book's flexible organization, proven teaching/learning system, strong ties to practice, and text organization.

Flexible Organization

The text's organization conceptually links the firm's actions and its value as determined in the securities markets. Each major decision area is presented in terms of both risk and return factors and their potential impact on the owners' wealth, as reflected by share value.

In organizing each chapter, we have adhered to a managerial decision-making perspective. That is, we have described a concept such as present value or operating leverage and have also related it to the financial manager's overall goal of wealth maximization. Once a particular concept has been developed, its application is illustrated by an example. The student is not left with just an abstract definition or discussion, but truly senses the related decision-making considerations and consequences.

The first Canadian edition of *Principles of Managerial Finance* contains 17 chapters, in seven parts. For an overview of the book's part and chapter organization, see the Brief Contents listing on page vii. Although the text is sequential, instructors can assign almost any chapter as a self-contained unit. Where necessary, students are directed to specific pages in earlier or later chapters where important concepts for the issue under consideration are discussed. This flexibility enables instructors to customize the text to various teaching strategies and course lengths.

Proven Teaching/Learning System

Feedback from readers has praised the effectiveness of the book's teaching/learning system. The system is driven by a set of carefully developed learning goals that help guide and organize student reading and study. In addition, numerous other features facilitate teaching and reinforce student learning to promote achievement of the learning goals. Each of the system's key elements is described in what follows.

 Learning Goals   The teaching/learning system is anchored in a set of six proven *Learning Goals* (LGs) per chapter. Marked by a special icon, shown here in the margin, the learning goals are listed at the start of each chapter, tied to first-level headings, reviewed point by point at the chapter's end, and noted in assignment material and supplements. These goals focus student attention on what material needs to be learned, where it can be found in the chapter, and whether it has been mastered by the end of the chapter. In addition, instructors can easily build lectures and assignments around the LGs.

Example Method   The *Example Method* is an important component of the teaching/learning system because it infuses practical demonstrations into the learning process. Seeing a financial concept or technique applied in a realistic example provides students with immediate reinforcement that helps cement their understanding of that concept or technique. Where applicable, the solution of each example shows the use of timelines, tables, and financial calculators. Calculator keystrokes of inputs, functions, and outputs are highlighted in discussions and examples of time value techniques in Chapter 5 and in the application of those techniques in subsequent chapters. Appendix A contains financial tables and notes the basic calculator keystrokes for the most popular financial calculators.

Key Equations   Key equations are printed in blue throughout the text to help students identify the most important mathematical relationships. The variables used in these equations are for listed on page xxxiv for convenience.

Marginal Glossary   Throughout the text, key terms and their definitions appear in the text margin when they are first introduced.

Marginal Hints   Marginal *Hints* add useful pieces of information to enrich the text discussion and assist student learning.

International Coverage   Discussions of international dimensions of chapter topics are integrated throughout the book. For example, Chapter 7 discusses the risks and returns associated with international diversification. Similarly, Chapter 13 addresses the international aspects of capital budgeting and long-term investments. In each chapter in which international coverage is included, the international material is integrated into chapter learning goals as well as the end-of-chapter summary and problem material.

Review Questions   *Review Questions* appear at the end of each section of the chapter (positioned before the next first-level heading) and are marked with a special design element. As students progress through the chapter, they can test their understanding of each key concept, technique, and practice before moving on to the next section.

Summary   End-of-chapter summaries are keyed to the learning goals, which are restated for reinforcement at the beginning of each *Summary* paragraph. The learning-goal-driven summary facilitates the student's review of the key material that was presented to support mastery of the given goal.

Self-Test Problems   At the end of most chapters, one or more *Self-Test Problems* are included. Each problem is keyed to the appropriate learning goal. Appendix B contains all worked-out solutions to Self-Test Problems in one location. These demonstration problems with solutions help to strengthen the student's understanding of the topics and the techniques presented.

Chapter Problems   A comprehensive set of *Problems,* containing more than one problem for each concept or technique, provides students with multiple self-testing opportunities and gives professors a wide choice of assignable material. There are literally hundreds of problems graded at various difficulty levels—warm-up, intermediate, and challenge—to indicate the amount of work that should be involved in solving each problem. Some of the end-of-chapter problems are captioned "integrative" because they tie together related topics. All problems are keyed to the learning goals. The depth of problems is particularly impressive in chapters where instructors and students want choice. These include Chapter 2, on the review of financial statements, Chapter 5, the time value of money, Chapter 7, on valuation of financial securities, Chapter 9, on cost of capital, Chapter 16, on capital budgeting, and Chapters 14 and 15, on working capital management. The impressive selection of interesting problems sets this text apart from its many competitors. Guideline answers to selected end-of-chapter problems appear in Appendix C.

Chapter Cases   Chapter *Cases* enable students to apply what they've learned in the chapter to realistic situations. Each case integrates all or a number of the chapter's learning goals. For example, at the end of Chapter 8 ("Valuation of Financial Securities"), students are asked to assess the impact of a proposed risky investment on the value of a firm's long-term debt and common shares. These end-of-chapter cases help strengthen a practical understanding of financial tools and techniques without the added expense of a separate casebook.

Web Exercises   A minimum of three *Web Exercises* follow the end-of-chapter cases. The Web provides a wealth of information regarding managerial finance and these exercises link chapter topics to related sites on the Internet. Once students access the Web sites, they use the information found there to answer various questions. These exercises will capture student interest in using the Internet while educating them about finance-related sites. There are also practical applications of chapter concepts that complement the In Practice boxes found in every chapter.

End-of-Part Cases   At the end of six of the book's seven parts are Integrative Cases that challenge students to use what they have learned in a realistic business context. At the end of Part 4, for example, students can apply a variety of concepts from Chapters 9 through 11 to assess and make recommendations with regard to an apparel company's capital structure, cost of capital, and dividend policy.

Contemporary Design   A vibrant, contemporary design, with pedagogical use of colours in charts and graphs, draws the reader's attention to features of the learning system. Bars of data are highlighted with colour in tables and then graphed in the same colour so that visual learners can immediately see relationships among data. Additionally, new attention-getting photographs and related short vignettes at the beginning of each chapter connect to key points in the chapter.

Strong Ties to Practice

A variety of features are used in the book to anchor student understanding in the operational aspects of topics presented. Many textual discussions present practical insights and applications of concepts and techniques. In addition, a number of special features are used both to assure realism and to stimulate student interest.

Cross-Disciplinary Focus   We have included an element that helps students understand the importance of the chapter material in relation to other major business disciplines. Throughout the book, *Career Keys* are placed in the margins to indicate the benefit or interactions that those in other disciplines would have with the topic covered at that point in the text. This feature allows students who are not finance majors to see how various finance topics relate to their chosen business major. In addition, this element gives students a better appreciation for the numerous cross-disciplinary interactions that routinely occur in business.

In Practice   Each chapter contains two *In Practice* boxes which offer insight into important topics in finance through experiences of individuals and of real companies, both large and small. There are 34 In Practice boxes included in the text. These are wide-ranging in scope but share the distinction of providing practical applications of chapter concepts through the actions of a real company. Also, they are focused on events relating to managerial finance that primarily took place in Canada during the year 2002. A number of these also focus on timely issues such as corporate governance and on the impact of the Kyoto Treaty on Canadian companies.

For example, in Chapter 16, BCE's repurchase of the 20 percent share in Bell Canada through a unique type of call option is discussed. In Chapter 17, the operation of Export Development Canada is explained, as is their large loan exposure to two Canadian companies. In Chapter 8, two methods of valuing a business are considered, a Web site providing information regarding businesses currently for sale is introduced, and the valuation of a number of businesses currently for sale are considered. In Chapter 6, Bombardier's two classes of common shares are summarized and the benefits of the share structure to the Bombardier family and to public shareholders are considered.

Each chapter has interesting and engaging *In Practice* boxes and this sets the text apart from its competitors. Note on page xxxiii, the long list of real companies discussed in the text. The focus on the practice of managerial finance is real and intense, and is seen throughout the text. All of the In Practice boxes provide students with a solid grounding in the practice of finance in the real world. Consistent exposure to current practical applications throughout the text enable students to walk away from the book and onto the job well-prepared with forward-looking, practical insight, rather than merely a conceptual grasp of the finance function.

Organization of the Text

In writing the first Canadian edition of *Principles of Managerial Finance*, our objective was to design a text that was extremely flexible for instructors and students. The text has 17 chapters in seven parts but is designed so instructors can assign almost any chapter as a self-contained unit. This adaptability means that the content can be arranged to meet individual needs. For example, a subset of chapters and/or parts of chapters can be used for a single course in managerial or corporate finance or the total text can be used for a finance course taught over two semesters. There is an abundance of content, review questions, problems, cases, and Web exercises that allow an instructor to present an overview of a topic or very detailed coverage. Instructors have control over the topics covered, their sequence, and the depth of coverage.

Part 1 of the text provides an introduction to managerial finance. Chapter 1 is an overview of the topic including a description of the major areas of finance, the managerial finance function in particular, the goal of a corporation, and a brief overview of financial markets. Distinguishing features of this chapter include: 1) coverage of the career opportunities in various areas of finance; 2) the relationships of the finance function to other functions; 3) a discussion of the key activities of the finance manager; and 4) a timely discussion of corporate governance and the agency problem with practical examples of these issues.

Chapter 2 summarizes key accounting concepts that students must know in order to understand the discipline of managerial finance. Distinguishing features of this chapter include: 1) a comprehensive review of financial statements with a focus on the importance of cash flows; 2) a detailed summary of corporate taxation issues; 3) an easy-to-follow six-step process to complete a statement of cash flows; 4) discussion of a company's annual report focusing on the various parts of the report; and 5) an introduction, early in the text, to key financial concepts and the "language of finance."

Part 2 of the book presents the topics of financial analysis and planning. These two chapters are strongly linked as financial forecasting builds on the strengths and weaknesses uncovered in a ratio analysis. Chapter 3 considers financial statement or ratio analysis. The focus of the chapter is on using the four categories of ratios to uncover a company's financial strengths and weaknesses. Distinguishing features of this chapter include: 1) two samples of real industry ratios from D&B Canada based on data for 1999 to 2001; 2) a unique approach to the presentation of activity ratios, focusing on days not turnovers; 3) presenting an approach that illustrates the impact of leverage on measures of profitability; 4) a comprehensive approach to the discussion of the DuPont system of analysis; and 5) a discussion of the meaning of the ratios that is more complete than is normally found in most managerial finance texts.

Chapter 4 considers financial planning and forecasting. The chapter discusses the financial planning process, as well as the fundamentals and approaches to preparing the pro forma financial statements. Distinguishing features of this chapter include: 1) the location of this topic follows logically from the results of a ratio analysis; 2) extensive coverage of the cash budget recognizes the importance of this statement to providers of financing; and 3) extensive coverage of more realistic methods to forecast the income statement and balance sheet which is often missing in other texts.

Part 3 of the book consists of four chapters that consider important concepts in managerial finance. Chapter 5 provides coverage of time value of money concepts. Distinguishing features of this chapter include: 1) extensive use of time lines and detailed coverage of how to use financial tables and calculators, using "calculator use" illustrations, to solve time value problems; 2) coverage of time value topics that are missing from some books including the method to calculate growth rates when multiple years of data are provided, illustrations of the benefit of early investment for savers, and early repayment of loans for those borrowing; and 3) a wealth of problems at various levels considering all aspects of time value—a powerful resource for students who have not seen this topic before.

Chapter 6 provides an extensive overview of financial markets, institutions, and securities. Distinguishing features of this chapter include: 1) extensive discussion of the general concept of financial markets, how they work, the participants, and the classification of the markets—topics that many students have not seen before; 2) the chapter is organized based on the financial securities that trade in the money and capital markets; 3) a detailed discussion of the characteristics of preferred shares, a security that is widely used by Canadian corporations; 4) consideration of the trading of common and preferred shares in Canada with an overview of the possible "hollowing out" of corporate Canada; and 5) extensive discussion of underwriting in Canada providing a step-by-step overview of the underwriting process.

Chapter 7 discusses the important financial concept of risk and return—a trade-off associated with the financial decisions made by both businesses and individuals. Distinguishing features of this chapter include: 1) the easy-to-understand approach used to define, explain, and expand upon the concepts of risk and return; 2) the clear discussion of the correlation between the returns on assets and its impact on risk and return; and 3) the derivation of beta, the CAPM, and the SML from the earlier discussion of risk and return concepts.

Chapter 8 discusses valuation fundamentals and the concepts and procedures for valuing long-term debt securities and common and preferred shares. Distinguishing features of this chapter include: 1) the opening coverage of yields and required rates of return on financial securities that set the foundation for valuation concepts; 2) consideration of the term structure of interest rates, an important consideration in long-term debt valuation; 3) discussion of four common share valuation techniques presenting a range of approaches that illustrates that the valuation of common shares is complex and that no one approach will work in practice; and 4) extensive coverage of the valuation of preferred shares and the impact Canadian taxation has on security returns.

The topics in Part 4 follow from those in Part 3, but this is not a required sequence. With an understanding of valuation fundamentals and techniques, readers can consider long-term financial decisions, the focus of Part 4. Chapter 9 discusses the extremely important financial concept of cost of capital. Distinguishing features of this chapter include: 1) the immediate discussion of the purpose and importance of calculating the cost of capital; 2) an early overview of the basic concept including an easy-to-understand rationale for calculating the weighted average cost of capital; 3) a focused discussion of the cost of common equity on reinvested profits, the year's contribution to retained earnings; and 4) a practical application of cost of capital for Brascan Corporation illustrating how a company attempts to minimize their cost of capital and how this is a benefit to the company and its shareholders.

Chapter 10 considers leverage and the firm's capital structure. Distinguishing features of this chapter include: 1) the introduction of the concept of leverage as part of breakeven analysis and the illustration of leverage through easy-to-picture images; 2) the calculation of breakeven is reduced to one easy to use formula; 3) the debt and times interest earned ratios for numerous Canadian industries is provided and the discussion of the data illustrates the concept that the optimal capital structure varies across industries; and 4) international capital structure considerations are reviewed and, again, readers see that capital structure decisions vary not just across industries but also across countries.

Chapter 11 discusses the fundamentals and relevance of dividends. Distinguishing features of this chapter include: 1) expanded coverage of Canadian dividend reinvestment and share purchase plans including the benefits these plans provide to both investors and companies; 2) full coverage of share repurchases including three types of share repurchase programs and the reasons companies repurchase their own shares; and 3) a practical example of dividend policy in Canada.

Part 5 of the text concerns long-term investment decisions. Chapter 12 discusses the principles and techniques of capital budgeting. Distinguishing features of this chapter include: 1) the early introduction of NPV analysis comparing the cost and value of a project; application of this approach is emphasized in the remainder of the chapter; 2) a comprehensive discussion of the various components that determine the cash inflows for a project; 3) a novel approach illustrating that cash flows should be split into their various components when calculating the NPV of a project; and 4) the use of the NPV profile approach to illustrate IRR and to explain why differences in ranking can occur with the NPV and IRR techniques.

Chapter 13 considers the concept of project risk and the techniques that can be used to evaluate projects that have a different level of risk from the company. Other issues in capital budgeting are also covered. Distinguishing features of this chapter include: 1) introducing the concept of risk in capital budgeting; 2) the early discussion indicating that a sensitivity analysis of all capital budgeting projects should be completed since positive NPV projects for most firms are limited; 3) examples of capital budgeting projects that turned out very wrong for two Canadian companies since the risks of the projects were not properly evaluated; 4) the discussion of the uncertainty created by the Kyoto Treaty for Canadian oil companies; and 5) illustrating how a risk index, rather than beta, can be used to calculate risk-adjusted discount rates for risky projects.

Part 6 of the text discusses working capital management. Chapter 14 provides an overview of working capital management and discusses the management of current assets. Distinguishing features of this chapter include: 1) the early recognition that management of working capital, current assets and current liabilities, is a vital task for many businesses; 2) providing data for Canadian companies that support this general statement; 3) illustrating that the cash conversion cycle is based on the three activity ratios calculated in Chapter 3; 4) demonstrating how credit applicants can be evaluated using information from credit agencies such as D&B Canada; and 5) supplying links to Web sites that provide samples of the information that is available from D&B Canada.

Chapter 15 considers current liability management, particularly the management of accounts payable, short-term loans, and lines of credit. Distinguishing features of this chapter include: 1) the discussion of a method to calculate the annual cost of discounted financial securities such as commercial paper and banker's acceptances; and 2) discussion and practical examples of securitization of accounts receivable as a method to raise short-term financing.

Part 7 covers two special topics in managerial finance. Chapter 16 considers hybrid and derivative securities: leasing, convertible securities, warrants, and options. Distinguishing features of this chapter include: 1) a clear discussion of the cash flows that should be considered and the discount rate that should be used to evaluate a lease; 2) the presentation of the lease-versus-purchase analysis as an extension of a capital budgeting analysis; 3) a clear discussion of options indicating the relevant position of both buyers and sellers of calls and puts; and 4) a discussion of option trading in Canada providing clear examples of what can occur when call and put options are purchased.

Chapter 17, an overview of international managerial finance, concludes Part 7 and the text. Distinguishing features of this chapter include: 1) a discussion of the major trading blocks in the world, particularly NAFTA, the European Union, and the emerging Free Trade Area of the Americas (FTAA), and the impact these may have on Canadian MNCs; 2) an overview of the ways an MNC can set up operations in a foreign country; 3) consideration of the tax issues a Canadian MNC may face when they establish a foreign operation; and 4) a discussion of the Opacity Index and how it could be used by a Canadian MNC to evaluate the risk associated with operating in a foreign country.

Supplements to the Textbook

This first Canadian edition of *Principles of Managerial Finance* provides a range of useful supplements for both instructors and students.

Teaching Tools for Instructors

Instructor's Resource Disk   The key teaching tools available to instructors—the Instructor's Resource Manual, Pearson TestGen and PowerPoint Presentations—are all exclusively contained within the *Instructor's Resource Disk*, compatible with both Windows and Macintosh systems.

Instructor's Resource Manual   This comprehensive resource available exclusively on the Instructor's Resource Disk pulls together the teaching tools so that instructors can use the textbook easily and effectively in the classroom. Each chapter provides an overview of key topics and detailed solutions to all review questions, end-of-chapter problems, and chapter cases. At the end of the manual are practice quizzes and solutions.

Test Item File   The *Test Item File* contains 2,500 questions made up of a mix of true/false, multiple choice, and essay questions. For quick test selection and construction, each chapter features a handy chart for identifying type of question, skill tested by learning goal, and level of difficulty.

Pearson TestGen   The *Pearson TestGen* is a special computerized version of the Test Item File that enables instructors to view and edit the existing questions, add questions, generate tests, and print the tests in a variety of formats. Powerful search and sort functions make it easy to locate questions and arrange them in any order desired. TestGen also enables instructors to administer tests on a local area network, have the tests graded electronically, and have the results prepared in electronic or printed reports. Issued on the Instructor's Resource Disk, the Pearson TestGen is compatible with both Windows and Macintosh systems.

PowerPoint Presentations   Available exclusively on the Instructor's Resource Disk, this presentation combines lecture notes with art from the textbook. The lecture presentations for each chapter can be viewed electronically in the classroom or can be printed as black-and-white transparency masters.

Learning Tools for Students

Companion Website   Beyond the book itself, students have access to the *Companion Website*, located at **www.pearsoned.ca/gitman**. The site contains valuable links, self-assessment quizzes, threaded discussion boards, and much more. The site will be updated on a regular basis, so check frequently for new features.

Study Guide   The *Study Guide* is an integral component of the teaching/learning system, offering many tools for studying finance. Each chapter contains the following features: chapter summary enumerated by learning goals; topical chapter outline, also broken down by learning goals for quick review; sample problem solutions; study tips; a full sample exam with answers at the end of the chapter; and thumbnail printouts of the PowerPoint Presentations to facilitate classroom note taking.

A Note to Students

In writing this text, our goal was to provide students with a resource that clearly presents the principles of Canadian managerial finance. The text is user-friendly and provides a total package that reduces the stress of learning managerial finance. We use plain English, tie concepts to reality, and demonstrate concepts, tools, and techniques. The book incorporates a proven learning system that integrates pedagogy with concepts and practical applications.

We have worked hard to present the most important concepts and practices of managerial finance in a clear and interesting way.

 Each chapter begins with a photo and short paragraph that introduce a key idea of the chapter. These brief introductions won't take long to read, but they will give you a useful preview of the chapter topic. You will also find at the beginning of each chapter a list of six *Learning Goals*. Marked by a special icon, shown here in the margin, the Learning Goals are tied to first-level headings in the chapter and are reviewed point by point in the end-of-chapter summary. These goals will help you focus your attention on what material you need to learn, where you can find it in the chapter, and whether you've mastered it by the end of the chapter.

Other features are included to support your learning experience. At the end of each major text section are a set of *Review Questions*. Although it may be tempting to rush past these questions, try to resist doing so. Pausing briefly to test your understanding of the key concepts, techniques, and practices in the section you've just read will help you cement your understanding of that material.

Other features in the body of each chapter are intended to motivate your study. *In Practice* boxes offer practical insights into the topic at hand through real company experiences. Some provide applications of the chapter material to typical personal financial situations, and others relate specifically to small businesses. Both these types of special applications are marked by headings. *Career Keys,* set in the margins, help you understand the importance of the material being covered to business majors other than finance. After all, managerial finance is an essential component not just in the business curriculum or in professional training programs, but in your daily job activities, *regardless of your major*. Other marginal items are *Hints* and *Key Terms*. Hints are just what their name implies—ideas and comments that help clarify important concepts. Key Terms and their definitions also appear in the margin when they are first introduced. These terms are the basic vocabulary of finance; you should be sure you know the key terms in any section of the text covered in your coursework.

We are striving daily to keep apace of your needs and interests, and value your ideas for improving the teaching and learning of finance. If you wish to write to us about anything in the book, please see the content information in the "Request for Feedback" section below. We wish you all the best in both your academic and professional careers.

Acknowledgements

Writing a textbook is a lengthy and complicated process that is achievable only with the co-operation and hard work of many people. We would like to thank colleagues, editors, research assistants, administrative support, students, and family for the incredible amount of help and support we received while completing the text.

First, Pearson Education Canada sought the opinion and advice of many excellent reviewers, all of whom strongly influenced various aspects of this text. We value the many comments and suggestions we received that helped us improve the content, organization, discussion, and flow of the book. Your efforts helped with the student-focused, user-friendly writing style of the text. The following reviewers provided extremely useful comments, and we are extremely grateful for your efforts:

Ben Amoako-Adu, *Wilfrid Laurier University*
Larry Bauer, *Memorial University of Newfoundland*
Trevor Chamberlain, *McMaster University*
Phil Cyrenne, *University of Winnipeg*
Alex Faseruk, *Memorial University of Newfoundland*
Ken Hartviksen, *Lakehead University*
Greg Hebb, *St. Mary's University*
Kurt Loescher, *University of Saskatchewan*
Jacques Schnabel, *Wilfrid Laurier University*
David Strangeland, *University of Manitoba*
Nancy Tait, *Sir Sanford Fleming College*
Francis Tapon, *University of Guelph*
Ganesh Vaidyanathan, *University of Saskatchewan*

A number of other people made important contributions to the text. Four research assistants, Paul Murphy, Kim Tran, Craig St. Germain and Crystal MacLeod, helped with various aspects of the text including checking problems, updating tables and figures, and collecting articles for the *In Practice* boxes. Michael Hennessey read various drafts of chapters and provided editorial advice; I wish to thank him for his ongoing support.

Special thanks for the excellent administrative support provided by Edith MacLauchlan and Mollie Cooke. Your good-natured response to my request, "I need this yesterday," is well appreciated. I am still amazed at the number of times your were able to "turn the work around" in short order. Without your cooperation and hard work, this text would not have been finished in time.

The publishing team at Pearson Education Canada deserve a tremendous amount of credit for the effort devoted to the text. The time lines were incredibly tight on this book and the top-notch group of people at Pearson helped bring it all together to produce the excellent product you are now holding. Sincere thanks to Gary Bennett, Dave Ward, Meaghan Eley, Laurie Goebel, Richard di Santo, Söğüt Güleç, Tally Morgan, Marisa D'Andrea, and to the others who worked on the text. We appreciate the inspiration, team-work, and organized effort that helped pull this text together on a remarkably tight schedule. We particularly appreciated the team's ability to juggle deadlines with much grace and understanding.

Special thanks go to our many students who, over the years, helped to teach us the best way of teaching managerial finance. Individual contributions of students are too numerous to mention here.

Finally, we would also like to thank Roberta and Liam Hennessey for patiently providing support, understanding, and good humour throughout the writing process.

Request for Feedback

As we designed and wrote this text, we took great care to present the material in the best possible manner and make the text as user-friendly as possible. One aspect of this process was to ensure that there were no errors in the content or in the solutions to problems. Our goal is to provide instructors and students with the best Canadian managerial finance textbook available on the market. If you have any comments on the text and its package of material, either positive or negative, please write to us.

We invite colleagues to relate their classroom experiences with the book or students to indicate whether the book has achieved the goal of clear presentation of material. Compliments or constructive criticism alike will help us improve the textbook and the teaching/learning system still further. Please write to: Sean Hennessey, School of Business Administration, University of Prince Edward Island, 550 University Avenue, Charlottetown, PE C1A 4P3. You can also e-mail Sean Hennessey at **hennessey@upei.ca**.

Lawrence J. Gitman
Sean Hennessey

List of Companies

Frequently Used Symbols and Abbreviations

ACH	Automated Clearinghouse		DRIPs	Dividend Reinvestment Plans
AcSB	Accounting Standards Board		DSO	Days' Sales Outstanding
ADRs	American Depository Receipts		DTC	Depository Transfer Cheque
AF_j	Amount of Funds Available from Financing Source j at a Given Cost		DTL	Degree of Total Leverage
			DVM	Dividend Valuation Model
ANPV	Annualized Net Present Value		e	Exponential Function = 2.7183
A/P	Accounts Payable		EAC	Earnings Available for Common Shareholders
APR	Annual Percentage Rate		EAR	Effective Annual Rate
A/R	Accounts Receivable		EBIT	Earnings Before Interest and Taxes
ARR	Average Rate of Return		EBT	Earnings Before Taxes
b	Beta Coefficient		EFR	External Financing Required
b_j	Beta Coefficient or Index of Nondiversifiable Risk for Asset j		EMH	Efficient Market Hypothesis
			EOQ	Economic Order Quantity
b_p	Portfolio Beta		EPS	Earnings Per Share
B_0	Value of a Bond		EVA	Economic Value Added
bp	Business Risk Premium		FC	Fixed Operating Cost Per Unit
BP_j	Break Point for Financing Source j		FDI	Foreign Direct Investment
CAPM	Capital Asset Pricing Model		FLM	Financial Leverage Multiplier
CCA	Capital Cost Allowance		fp	Financial Risk Premium
CCC	Cash Conversion Cycle		FTAA	Free Trade Area of the Americas
CCPC	Canadian-Controlled Private Corporation		FV	Future Value
CDCC	Canadian Derivatives Clearing Corporation		FVA_n	Future Value of an n-Year Annuity
CE	Certainty Equivalent		$FVIF_{k,n}$	Future Value Interest Factor
CEO	Chief Executive Officer		$FVIFA_{k,n}$	Future Value Interest Factor for an Annuity
CF	Cash Flow		g	Growth Rate
CFO	Chief Financial Officer		GAAP	Generally Accepted Accounting Principles
CICA	Canadian Institute of Chartered Accountants		GATT	General Agreement on Tariffs and Trade
COGS	Cost of Goods Sold		GDP	Gross Domestic Product
CV	Coefficient of Variation		IOS	Investment Opportunities Schedule
D_p	Preferred Stock Dividend		I	Interest Payment
D_t	• Per-Share Dividend Expected at the end of Year t		IC	Incremental Cost
			ICF	Incremental Cash Inflow
	• Depreciation Expense in Year t		IP	Inflation Premium
DBRS	Dominion Bond Rating Service		IPO	Initial Public Offering
DFL	Degree of Financial Leverage		IRR	Internal Rate of Return
DOL	Degree of Operating Leverage		ITC	Investment Tax Credit

JIT	Just-In-Time System		PV	Present Value
k	• Actual, Expected, or Required Rate of Return		PVA_n	Present Value of an n-Year Annuity
	• Annual Rate of Return		$PVIF_{k,n}$	Present Value Interest Factor for a Single Amount Discounted at k Percent for n Periods
	• Cost of Capital			
k_a	Weighted Average Cost of Capital		$PVIFA_{k,n}$	Present Value Interest Factor for an Annuity When Interest is Discounted Annually at k Percent for n Periods
k_d	Required Rate of Return on a Bond			
k_{eff}	Effective Interest Rate			
k_i	Return for the ith Outcome		$PVIFA_{k,\infty}$	Present Value Interest Factor for a Perpetuity When Interest is Discounted Annually at k Percent
k_j	Required Return on Asset j			
k_l	Specific (or Nominal) Rate of Return			
k_m	Market Return; Return on the Market Portfolio of Assets		Q	Sales Quantity in Units
			r_l	Risk-Free Cost of the Given Type of Financing, l
k_n	Cost of a New Issue of Common Shares		R_F	Risk-Free Rate of Return
k_p	Portfolio Return		RADR	Risk-Adjusted Discount Rate
k_r	Cost of Reinvested Profits		ROA	Return on Total Assets
k_s	Required Return on Common Stock		ROE	Return on Equity
LIBOR	London Interbank Offered Rate		ROI	Return on Investment
m	Number of Times Per Year Interest is Compounded		RP	Risk Premium
			SCF	Statement of Cash Flows
M	Par Value of a Bond		SML	Security Market Line
M/B	Market/Book Ratio		SPPs	Share Purchase Plans
MCC	Marginal Cost of Capital		t	Time
MD&A	Management's Discussion and Analysis		T	Tax Rate
MNC	Multinational Company		TIE	Times Interest Earned
MRP	Materials Requirement Planning System		TSOR	Term Structure of Interest Rates
n	• Life of Project in years		TSX	Toronto Stock Exchange
	• Number of Outcomes Considered		UCC	Undepreciated Capital Cost
	• Number of Periods—Typically, Years		V	Value of an Asset
	• Number of Years to Maturity		VAR	Value-At-Risk Approach
N_d	Net Proceeds from the Sale of Debt (Bond)		VC	Variable Operating Cost Per Unit
N_n	Net Proceeds from the Sale of New Common Stock		w_i	Proportion of Long-Term Debt in Capital Structure
N_p	Net Proceeds from the Sale of the Preferred Stock		w_j	• Proportion of Portfolio's Total Dollar Value Represented by Asset j • Capital Structure Weight for Financing Source j
NAFTA	North American Free Trade Agreement			
NIAT	Net Income After Taxes			
NPV	Net Present Value		w_p	Proportion of Preferred Equity in Capital Structure
OC	Operating Cycle			
OCS	Optimal Capital Structure		w_s	Proportion of Common Equity in Capital Structure
OPEC	Organization of Petroleum Exporting Countries			
P	Price (or Value) of Asset		WACC	Weighted Average Cost of Capital
P_t	Price (or Value) of Asset at Time t		YTM	Yield To Maturity
P/E	Price/Earnings Ratio		ZBA	Zero-Balance Account
PI	Profitability Index		α_t	Certainty Equivalent Factor in Year t
PMT	Amount of Payment		σ	Standard Deviation
POP	Prompt Offering Prospectus System		σ_k	Standard Deviation of Returns
Pr	Probability		Σ	Summation Symbol

A Great Way to Learn and Instruct Online

The Pearson Education Canada Companion Website is easy to navigate and is organized
to correspond to the chapters in this textbook. Whether you are a student in the classroom
or a distance learner you will discover helpful resources for in-depth study and research
that empower you in your quest for greater knowledge and maximize your potential for
success in the course.

Companion
Website

[www.pearsoned.ca/gitman]

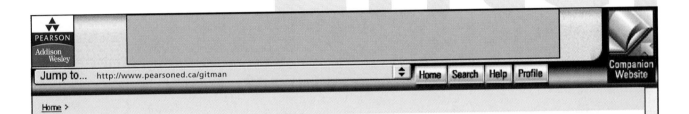

Jump to...   http://www.pearsoned.ca/gitman   Home Search Help Profile

Companion
Website

Home >

Pearson AW Companion Website

Principles of Managerial Finance, First Canadian Edition,
by Gitman and Hennessey

Student Resources

The modules in this section provide students with tools for learning course material.
Some of these modules will be the following:

- Learning Goals
- Destinations
- Quizzes
- Internet Exercises
- Glossary

In the quiz modules students can send answers to the grader and receive instant
feedback on their progress through the Results Reporter. Coaching comments and
references to the textbook may be available to ensure that students take advantage
of all available resources to enhance their learning experience.

Instructor Resources

This module links directly to additional teaching tools. Downloadable PowerPoint
Presentations and an Instructor's Manual are some of the materials that are
available in this section.

Introduction to Managerial Finance

Overview of Managerial Finance

LG1 Define *finance* and describe its three major areas—financial markets, financial services, and managerial finance—and the career opportunities within them.

LG2 Review the basic forms of business organization and their respective strengths and weaknesses.

LG3 Describe the managerial finance function and differentiate managerial finance from the closely related disciplines of economics and accounting.

LG4 Identify the key activities of the financial manager within the firm.

LG5 Explain why wealth maximization, rather than profit maximization, is the firm's goal and how economic value added (EVA), a focus on stakeholders, and ethical behaviour relate to its achievement.

LG6 Discuss the agency issue as it relates to owner wealth maximization.

1.1 Finance as an Area of Study

The field of finance is broad and dynamic. It directly affects the lives of every person, organization, and branch of government in a country. There are many areas for study, and a large number of career opportunities are available in the field of finance.

What Is Finance?

finance
The knowledge, science, techniques, and art of managing money.

Finance is the management of money—more specifically, the knowledge, science, techniques, and art associated with the management of capital. Virtually

2

The Balance of Power

MOST BUSINESSES ARE STRUCTURED like pyramids—with power to set policies concentrated at the top and spreading toward the bottom where day-to-day operations are carried out. However, the ultimate authority over all management of the organization resides in the owners of a corporation—its common shareholders. The goal of the business organization, and the goal of its financial managers, is to achieve the objectives of the firm's owners. This chapter will explain corporate organization and the managerial finance function within the organization. It also will explore the key goal of the firm's owners—to maximize shareholder wealth—and the role of the financial manager in meeting that goal.

all individuals and organizations earn or raise money and spend or invest money. Finance is concerned with the process, institutions, markets, and instruments involved in the transfer of money among and between individuals, businesses, and governments. As such, it directly affects every individual, organization (public and private, for-profit and not-for-profit), and branch of government in the country. An understanding of finance will benefit most adults by allowing them to make better personal financial decisions. Those who work in financial jobs will benefit from an understanding of finance by being able to interface effectively with the firm's financial personnel, processes, and procedures.

Finance is closely related to economics and accounting. Individuals and organizations operate within the national and international economic environments, so broad macro-economic variables have a major impact on business. Accounting is the language of finance. A solid and complete understanding of the language of accounting and the financial statements is vital for a student of finance.

Major Areas and Employment Opportunities in Finance

Finance is a discipline with many sub-branches and one or more of these impact most Canadians on a daily basis. There are three major but interrelated areas of finance: financial markets, financial services, and managerial or corporate finance. Each of these areas is discussed below. Often, a good way to introduce a business discipline is to discuss the types of career opportunities available in the field. A brief discussion of employment opportunities available in each of these areas of finance is provided in the following section.

Financial Markets

financial markets
Provide a forum where savers of funds and users of funds can transact business.

Financial markets is a branch in the study of macroeconomics. **Financial markets** provide a forum where *savers of funds* and *users of funds* can transact business. These two groups must be able to make an exchange that is expected to be beneficial to both parties. Individuals, governments, and business organizations are all involved in financial markets. In financial markets, cash moves from savers to users, and users provide a financial security in return. For financial markets to work, **financial institutions** are necessary. These are intermediaries that allow for the efficient and low cost transfer of the savings of individuals, governments, and business for financial securities. Intermediaries include institutions such as banks and investment dealers. Investment management is a major part of this area of finance.

financial institutions
Intermediaries that allow for the efficient transfer of the savings of individuals, governments, and business for financial securities.

Numerous career opportunities are available in this area, including the trading of financial securities such as common and preferred shares, bonds and debentures, foreign exchange, commodities, derivatives, and treasury bills. In addition, banks, investment dealers and other financial intermediaries offer thousands of jobs to business graduates each year. Other opportunities are available in the regulation of financial markets with organizations such as the Bank of Canada or the Ontario Securities Commission. For more information regarding a career in this branch of finance visit the following Web sites: **www.osc.gov.on.ca/en/about.html, www.bankofcanada.ca/en**, or **www.streetjobs.com**.

Financial Services

financial services
The part of finance concerned with design and delivery of advice and financial products to individuals, business, and government.

Financial services is the area of finance concerned with the design and delivery of advice and financial products to individuals, business, and government. Financial institutions such as banks, trust companies, investment dealers and brokers, personal financial planners, mutual fund companies, life and property insurance companies, mortgage brokers, and real estate companies, together with the professional organizations that support these institutions and the regulators that oversee the operation of the financial institutions, are all major participants in this sub-branch of finance. Financial services involve a variety of interesting career opportunities within the areas of banking and related institutions, personal financial planning, investments, real estate, and insurance. Career opportunities available in each of these areas are described at **www.careers-in-finance.com**. This Web site is included as one of the Web Exercises: Links to Practice at the end of the chapter.

Managerial Finance

managerial finance
Concerns the duties of the financial manager in the business firm.

financial manager
Actively manages the financial affairs of any type of business, whether financial or nonfinancial, private or public, large or small, profit-seeking or not-for-profit.

Managerial finance is concerned with the duties of the financial manager in the business firm. **Financial managers** actively manage the financial affairs of many types of business—financial and nonfinancial, private and public, large and small, profit-seeking and not-for-profit. They perform such varied financial tasks as evaluating financial strengths and weaknesses, planning and forecasting the need for financing, managing the daily financial activities such as extending credit, collecting receivables, buying inventory, and paying suppliers to ensure sufficient cash is on hand to maintain operations, evaluating proposed large expenditures, and raising money to fund the firm's operations. In recent years, the changing economic and regulatory environments have increased the importance and complexity of the financial manager's duties. As a result, many top executives in industry and government have come from the finance area.

Another important recent trend has been the globalization of business activity. Canadian corporations have dramatically increased their sales, purchases, investments, and fund raising in other countries, and foreign corporations have likewise increased these activities in Canada. These changes have created a need for financial managers who can help a firm to manage cash flows in different currencies and protect against the risks that naturally arise from international transactions. Although this need makes the managerial finance function more complex, it can also lead to a more rewarding and fulfilling career.

The Study of Managerial Finance

An understanding of the theories, concepts, techniques, and practices presented throughout this text will fully acquaint you with the financial manager's activities and decisions. Because most business decisions are measured in financial terms, the financial manager plays a key role in the operation of the firm. People in all areas of responsibility—accounting, information systems, management, marketing, operations, and so forth—need a basic understanding of the managerial finance function.

All managers in the firm, regardless of their job descriptions, work with financial personnel to justify manpower requirements, negotiate operating budgets, deal with financial performance appraisals, and sell proposals based at least in part on their financial merits. Clearly, those managers who understand the financial decision-making process will be better able to address financial concerns and will therefore more often get the resources they need to accomplish their own goals. Throughout the text, "career keys" are positioned in the text margin. These are brief discussions (preceded by the icon ○–▼) that highlight the relationship between the topic being discussed and one or more nonfinancial area of business responsibility. These marginal notes should help you understand some of the many interactions between managerial finance and other business careers.

As you study this text, you will learn about the career opportunities in managerial finance. Some of these are briefly described in Table 1.1. Although this

TABLE 1.1	Career Opportunities in Managerial Finance
Position	Description
Financial analyst	Primarily responsible for preparing and analyzing the firm's financial plans and budgets. Other duties include financial forecasting, performing financial ratio analysis, and working closely with accounting.
Capital budgeting analyst/manager	Responsible for the evaluation and recommendation of proposed asset investments. May be involved in the financial aspects of implementation of approved investments.
Project finance manager	In large firms, arranges financing for approved asset investments. Coordinates consultants, investment bankers, and legal counsel.
Cash manager	Responsible for maintaining and controlling the firm's daily cash balances. Frequently manages the firm's cash collection, short-term investment, transfer, and disbursement activities and coordinates short-term borrowing and banking relationships.
Credit analyst/manager	Administers the firm's credit policy by analyzing or managing the evaluation of credit applications, extending credit, and monitoring and collecting accounts receivable.
Pension fund manager	In large companies, responsible for coordinating the assets and liabilities of the employees' pension fund. Either performs investment management activities or hires and oversees the performance of these activities by a third party.

text focuses on profit-seeking firms, the principles presented here are equally applicable to public and not-for-profit organizations. The decision-making principles developed in this text can also be applied to personal financial decisions. We hope that this first exposure to the exciting field of finance will provide the foundation and initiative for further study and possibly even a future career.

? Review Questions

1–1 What is *finance*? Explain how this field affects the lives of everyone and every organization.

1–2 What is the *financial markets* area of finance?

1–3 What is the *financial services* area of finance?

1–4 Describe the field of *managerial finance*. Why is the study of managerial finance important regardless of the specific area of responsibility one has within the business firm?

1.2 Basic Forms of Business Organization

The three basic legal forms of business organization are the *sole proprietorship*, the *partnership*, and the *corporation*. The sole proprietorship is the most common form of organization. However, the corporation is by far the dominant form with respect to sales, assets, and profits. Corporations are given primary emphasis in this textbook.

Sole Proprietorships

sole proprietorship
A business owned by one person and operated for his or her own profit.

A **sole proprietorship** is a business owned by one person who operates it for his or her own profit. A large majority of all business firms are sole proprietorships. The typical sole proprietorship is a small business, such as a bike shop, hair salon, personal trainer, or plumber. Typically, the proprietor, along with a few employees, operates the proprietorship. He or she normally raises capital from personal resources or by borrowing and is responsible for all business decisions. The sole proprietor has **unlimited liability;** his or her total wealth, not merely the amount originally invested, can be taken to satisfy creditors. The majority of sole proprietorships are found in the wholesale, retail, service, and construction industries. The key strengths and weaknesses of sole proprietorships are summarized in Table 1.2.

unlimited liability
The condition of a sole proprietorship (or general partnership) allowing the owner's total wealth to be taken to satisfy creditors.

Partnerships

partnership
A business owned by two or more people and operated for profit.

A **partnership** consists of two or more owners doing business together for profit. Partnerships, which account for a small percentage of all businesses, are typically larger than sole proprietorships. Finance, insurance, accounting, and real estate

---

TABLE 1.2	**Strengths and Weaknesses of the Basic Legal Forms of Business Organization**		
	Legal form		
	Sole proprietorship	Partnership	Corporation
Strengths	Owner receives all profits (as well as losses) Low organizational costs Income included and taxed on proprietor's personal tax return Independence Secrecy Ease of dissolution	Can raise more funds than sole proprietorships Borrowing power enhanced by more owners More available brain power and managerial skill Income is split according to the partnership contract and taxed as personal income	Owners have *limited liability*, which guarantees that they cannot lose more than they invested Can achieve large size due to sale of common shares Ownership (shares) is readily transferable Long life of firm Can hire professional managers Has better access to financing Receives certain tax advantages
Weaknesses	Owner has *unlimited liability*— total wealth can be taken to satisfy debts Limited fund-raising power tends to inhibit growth Proprietor must be jack-of-all-trades Difficult to give employees long-run career opportunities Lacks continuity when proprietor dies	Owners have *unlimited liability* and may have to cover debt of other partners Partnership is dissolved when a partner dies Difficult to liquidate or transfer partnership	Taxes generally higher, because corporate income is taxed and dividends paid to owners are also taxed More expensive to organize than other business forms Subject to greater government regulation If publicly traded, lacks secrecy, since shareholders must receive financial reports

firms are the most common types of partnerships, with some of these businesses often having large numbers of partners.

Most partnerships are established by a written contract known as a **partnership agreement.** In a *general partnership*, all partners have unlimited liability, and each *general partner* is legally liable for all of the debts of the partnership. To avoid this disadvantage, a **limited partnership** can be formed. Under this arrangement, there are one or more general partners with unlimited liability and one or more *limited partners* with limited liability. These partners are only responsible for the funds they invested in the business. Limited partners are not allowed to be involved in the management of the business; they are passive investors. Limited partnerships are common in real estate development, with the limited partners providing the cash and the general partner(s) developing the property. Strengths and weaknesses of partnerships are summarized in Table 1.2.

Corporations

A **corporation** is an artificial entity created by law. Often called a "legal entity," a corporation has the powers of an individual in that it can sue and be sued, make and be party to contracts, and acquire property and incur debts in its own name. Although a minority of all businesses are incorporated, the corporation is the dominant form of business organization. It accounts for nearly all of the assets owned and sales and profits generated by all businesses in Canada. While some people in a community may know of the local electrician or law firm, most Canadians and many people around the world know of Canadian corporations such as Nortel Networks, Bombardier, Molson, Bell Canada Enterprises (BCE), or the Royal Bank. Corporations are involved in all types of businesses. At one time, goods-producing corporations accounted for a majority of corporate activity in Canada. Over the last 30 years, however, the service sector has experienced tremendous growth and now accounts for a significant majority of total corporate sales, profits, and total assets. The key strengths and weaknesses of large corporations are summarized in Table 1.2.

The owners of a corporation are its **shareholders,** whose ownership or "equity" is evidenced by *common shares.*[1] This form of ownership is defined and discussed in Chapter 6; at this point suffice it to say that **common shares** are the purest and most basic form of corporate ownership. Shareholders expect to earn a return by receiving **dividends**—periodic distributions of earnings—or by realizing gains through increases in share price. As noted in the upper portion of Figure 1.1, the shareholders vote periodically to elect the members of the board of directors and to amend the firm's corporate charter.

The **board of directors** has the ultimate authority in guiding corporate affairs and in making general policy. The board of directors is headed by the chair. For most corporations, the chair of the board is normally the company's CEO, the founding CEO, or a well respected business person with a long association with the company. The directors include key corporate personnel as well as outside individuals who typically are successful businesspeople and executives of other

partnership agreement
The written contract used to formally establish a business partnership.

limited partnership
A partnership with one or more general partners with unlimited liability and one or more limited partners with limited liability.

corporation
A business entity created by law (often called a "legal entity").

▮ Hint
For many small corporations, as well as small proprietorships and partnerships, there is no access to financial markets. In addition, whenever the owners make a loan, they usually must provide a personal guarantee.

shareholders
The owners of a corporation, whose ownership or "equity" is evidenced by either *common shares* or *preferred shares.*

common shares
The purest and most basic form of corporate ownership.

dividends
Periodic distributions of earnings to the shareholders of a firm.

board of directors
Group elected by the firm's shareholders and having ultimate authority to guide corporate affairs and make general policy.

---

1. Corporations may also have preferred shares but preferred shareholders are not owners. There are no ownership rights attached to preferred shares. Some corporations do not have shareholders but rather have "members" who often have rights similar to those of shareholders—they are entitled to vote and receive dividends. Examples include cooperatives, credit unions, mutual insurance companies, and many charitable organizations.

FIGURE 1.1   Corporate Organization

The general organization of a corporation and the finance function (which is shown in yellow).

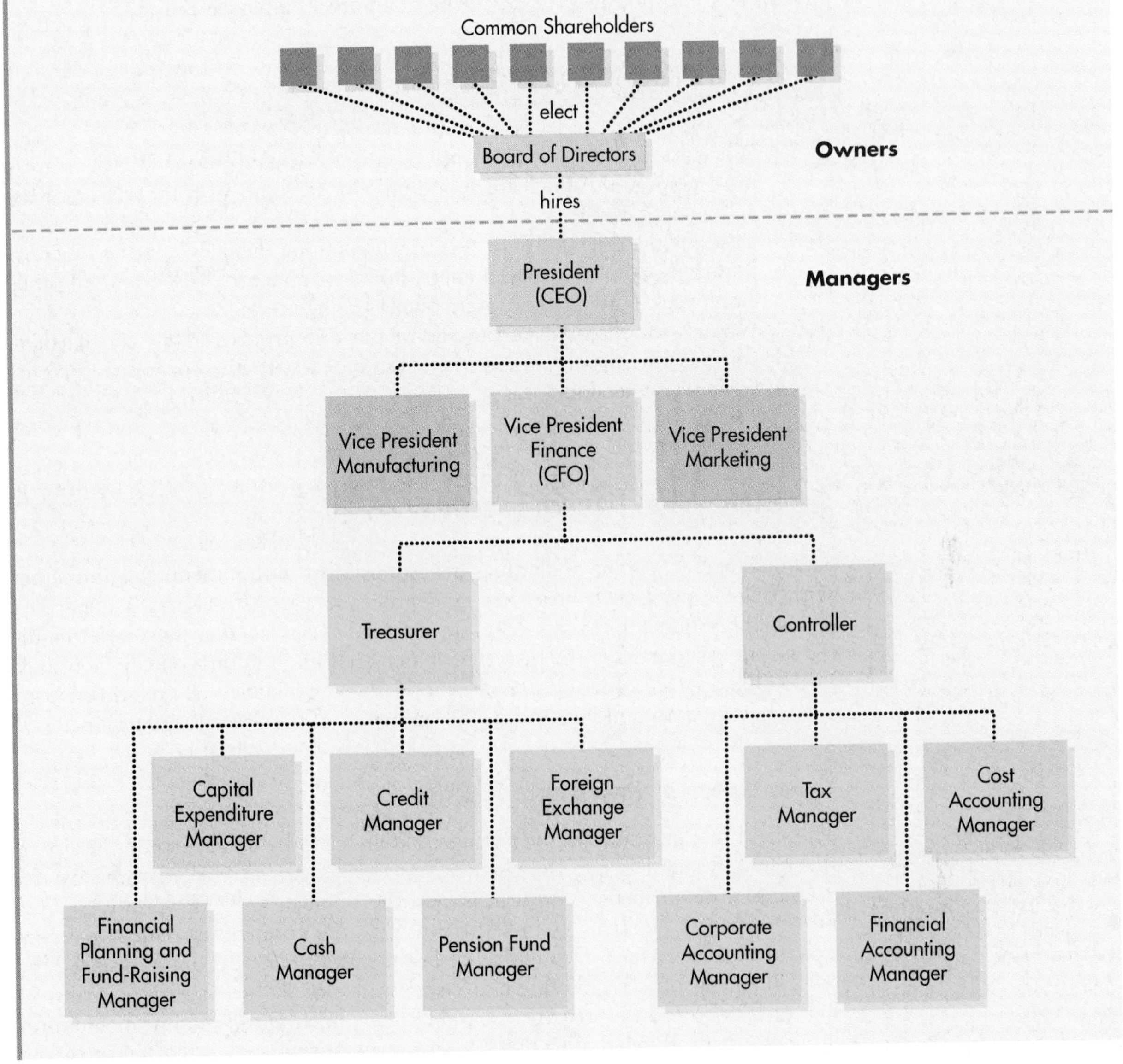

Common Shareholders

elect

Board of Directors — **Owners**

hires

President (CEO) — **Managers**

Vice President Manufacturing

Vice President Finance (CFO)

Vice President Marketing

Treasurer

Controller

Capital Expenditure Manager

Credit Manager

Foreign Exchange Manager

Tax Manager

Cost Accounting Manager

Financial Planning and Fund-Raising Manager

Cash Manager

Pension Fund Manager

Corporate Accounting Manager

Financial Accounting Manager

president or chief executive officer (CEO)
Corporate official responsible for managing the firm's day-to-day operations and carrying out the policies established by the board of directors.

major organizations. Outside directors for major corporations are typically paid an annual fee (retainer) of $10,000 to $20,000 or more plus fees for attending board meetings, and are frequently granted options to buy a specified number of the firm's common shares at a stated—and often attractive—price.

The **president or chief executive officer (CEO)** is responsible for managing day-to-day operations and carrying out the policies established by the board. The CEO is required to report periodically to the firm's directors. It is important to note the division between owners and managers in a large corporation, as shown by the dashed horizontal line in Figure 1.1. This separation and some of the issues surrounding it will be addressed in the discussion of *the agency issue* later in this chapter. Also note that while the board of directors hires the CEO and, depending on the company, possibly the various vice presidents, these senior managers are responsible for the hiring of all other employees.

? Review Questions

1–5   What are the three basic forms of business organization? Which form is most common? Which form is dominant in terms of total sales, profits, and assets? Why?

1–6   Describe the role and basic relationship among the major parties in a corporation—common shareholders, board of directors, CEO, and all other employees. How are corporate owners compensated?

1–7   What is the major disadvantage of the sole proprietorship and partnership? Is this disadvantage truly eliminated with the corporate form of business ownership?

1.3 The Managerial Finance Function

As noted earlier, people in all areas of responsibility within the firm will interact with finance personnel, processes, and procedures to get their jobs done. For financial personnel to make useful forecasts and decisions, they must talk to individuals in other areas of the firm. The managerial finance function can be broadly described by considering its role within the organization, its relationship to economics and accounting, and the key activities of the financial manager.

Organization of the Finance Function

Career Key
Management will define the tasks that will be performed by the finance department. It will also choose how the finance function fits within the total structure of the firm.

treasurer
The officer responsible for the firm's financial activities such as financial planning and fund raising, making capital expenditure decisions, and managing cash, credit, the pension fund, and foreign exchange.

controller
The officer responsible for the firm's accounting activities, such as corporate accounting, tax management, financial accounting, and cost accounting.

The size and importance of the managerial finance function depend on the size of the firm. In small firms, the finance function is generally performed by the accounting department. As a firm grows, the finance function typically evolves into a separate department linked directly to the company president or chief executive officer (CEO) through a vice president of finance, commonly called the chief financial officer (CFO). The lower portion of the organizational chart in Figure 1.1 showed the structure of the finance function in a typical medium-to-large-size firm. Reporting to the vice president of finance are the treasurer and the controller. The **treasurer** is commonly responsible for handling financial activities, such as financial planning and fund raising, making capital expenditure decisions, managing cash, managing credit activities, managing the pension fund, and managing foreign exchange. The **controller** typically handles the accounting activities, such as corporate accounting, tax management, financial accounting, and cost accounting. The treasurer's focus tends to be more external, whereas the controller's focus is more internal. *The activities of the treasurer, or financial manager, are the primary concern of this text.*

If international sales or purchases are important to a firm, it may well employ one or more finance professionals whose job is to monitor and manage

Hint
A *controller* is sometimes referred to as a *comptroller*. Not-for-profit and governmental organizations frequently use the title of comptroller.

foreign exchange manager
The manager responsible for monitoring and managing the firm's exposure to loss from currency fluctuations.

the firm's exposure to loss from currency fluctuations. A trained financial manager can "hedge," or protect against, this and similar risks, at reasonable cost, using a variety of financial instruments. These **foreign exchange managers** (or traders) typically report to the firm's treasurer.

Relationship to Economics

The field of finance is closely related to economics. Financial managers must understand the economic framework and be alert to the consequences of varying levels of economic activity and changes in economic policy. They must also be able to use economic theories as guidelines for efficient business operation. Examples include supply-and-demand analysis, profit-maximizing strategies, and price theory. A primary economic principle used in managerial finance is **marginal analysis,** the principle that financial decisions should be made and actions taken only when the added benefits exceed the added costs. Nearly all financial decisions ultimately come down to an assessment of their marginal benefits and marginal costs. A basic knowledge of economics is therefore necessary to understand both the environment and the decision techniques of managerial finance.

marginal analysis
Economic principle that states that financial decisions should be made and actions taken only when the added benefits exceed the added costs.

Example ▼ Jamie Teng is a financial manager for Nord Department Stores—a large chain of upscale department stores operating primarily in western Canada. She is currently trying to decide whether to replace one of the firm's on-line computers with a new, more sophisticated one that would both speed processing time and handle a larger volume of transactions. The new computer would require a cash outlay of $80,000, and the old computer could be sold to net $28,000. The total benefits from the new computer (measured in today's dollars) would be $100,000, and the benefits over a similar time period from the old computer (measured in today's dollars) would be $35,000. Applying marginal analysis to this data, we get

Benefits with new computer	$100,000	
Less: Benefits with old computer	35,000	
(1) Marginal (added) benefits		$65,000
Cost of new computer	$ 80,000	
Less: Proceeds from sale of old computer	28,000	
(2) Marginal (added) costs		52,000
Net benefit [(1) − (2)]		$13,000

Because the marginal (added) benefits of $65,000 exceed the marginal (added) costs of $52,000, the purchase of the new computer to replace the old one is recommended. The firm will experience a net benefit of $13,000 as a result of this ▲ action.

Relationship to Accounting

The firm's finance (treasurer) and accounting (controller) activities, shown in the lower portion of Figure 1.1, are closely related and generally overlap. Indeed, managerial finance and accounting are not often easily distinguishable. In small firms the controller often carries out the finance function, and in large firms many accountants are closely involved in various finance activities. However, there are two basic differences between finance and accounting; one relates to the emphasis on cash flows and the other to decision making.

Emphasis on Cash Flows

The accountant's primary function is to develop and provide data for measuring the performance of the firm, assessing its financial position, and paying taxes. Using certain standardized and generally accepted principles, the accountant prepares financial statements that recognize sales revenue and the expenses that were incurred to generate the sales, at the time of sale. This approach is referred to as the **accrual basis**.

accrual basis
Recognizes sales revenue at the time of sale and the expenses incurred to generate the sales.

The financial manager, on the other hand, places primary emphasis on *cash flows*, the intake and outgo of cash. He or she maintains the firm's solvency by planning the cash flows necessary to satisfy its obligations and to acquire assets needed to achieve the firm's goals. The financial manager uses this **cash basis** to recognize the revenues and expenses only with respect to actual inflows and outflows of cash. Regardless of its profit or loss, a firm must have a sufficient flow of cash to meet its obligations as they come due. It is not uncommon for profitable firms still to experience financial problems due to holding insufficient amounts of cash.

cash basis
Recognizes revenues and expenses only with respect to actual inflows and outflows of cash.

Example ▼ Peakes Quay, Inc., a small yacht dealer, in the calendar year just ended sold one yacht for $100,000; the yacht was purchased during the year at a total cost of $80,000. Although the firm paid in full for the yacht during the year, at year end it has yet to collect the $100,000 from the customer. The accounting view and the financial view of the firm's performance during the year are given by the following income and cash flow statements, respectively.

Accounting (accrual basis) view		Financial (cash basis) view	
Income Statement Peakes Quay, Inc. for the year ended 12/31		**Cash Flow Statement** Peakes Quay, Inc. for the year ended 12/31	
Sales revenue	$100,000	Cash inflow	$ 0
Less: Costs	80,000	Less: Cash outflow	80,000
Net profit	$ 20,000	Net cash flow	($80,000)

In an accounting sense Peakes Quay is profitable, but it is a financial failure in terms of actual cash flow. Its lack of cash flow resulted from the uncollected account receivable of $100,000. Without adequate cash inflows to meet its obligations the firm will not survive, regardless of its level of profits. ▲

The preceding example shows that accrual accounting data do not fully describe the circumstances of a firm. Thus, the financial manager must look beyond financial statements to obtain insight into developing or existing problems. The financial manager, by concentrating on cash flows, should be able to avoid insolvency and achieve the firm's financial goals. It is also worth noting that the financial manager measures cash flow on an after-tax basis.

Decision Making

We come now to the second major difference between finance and accounting: decision making. Whereas accountants devote most of their attention to the collection and presentation of financial data, financial managers evaluate the accounting statements, develop additional data, and make decisions based on their assessment of the associated returns and risks. Accountants provide consistently developed and easily interpreted data about the firm's past, present, and future operations. Financial managers use these data, either in raw form or after adjustments and analyses, as inputs to the decision-making process. Essentially, finance takes over where accounting leaves off. Accounting focuses on information collection and generation. Finance uses information to make decisions. This is a good way to distinguish between the two disciplines.

Key Activities of the Financial Manager

The financial manager's primary activities are (1) performing financial analysis and planning, (2) making investment decisions, and (3) making financing decisions. Figure 1.2 relates each of these financial activities to the firm's balance sheet. Although investment and financing decisions can be conveniently viewed in terms of the balance sheet, these decisions are made on the basis of their cash flow effects. This focus on cash flow will become clearer in later chapters.

Performing Financial Analysis and Planning

Financial analysis and planning is concerned with (1) monitoring the firm's financial condition, (2) evaluating the need for increased (or reduced) productive capacity, and (3) determining what financing is required. Monitoring the firm's *working capital* position is a vital aspect of financial analysis and a day-to-day

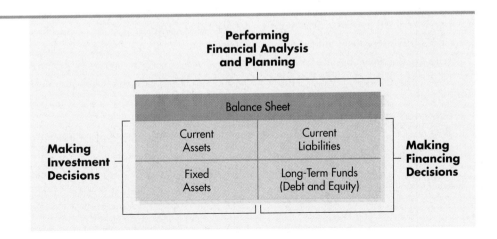

FIGURE 1.2

Financial Activities
Key activities of the financial manager

activity that ensures the company survives and grows. Working capital is the firm's level of current assets, such as accounts receivable and inventory, and the use of current liabilities, such as accounts payable and short-term loans. These functions encompass the entire balance sheet as well as the firm's income statement and other financial statements. Although this activity relies heavily on accrual-based financial statements, its underlying objective is to assess the firm's cash flows and develop plans that ensure adequate cash flow to support goal achievement.

Making Investment Decisions

Investment decisions determine both the mix and the type of assets found on the left-hand side of the firm's balance sheet. *Mix* refers to the number of dollars of current and fixed assets. Once the mix is established, the financial manager attempts to maintain optimal levels of each type of current asset. The financial manager also decides which fixed assets to acquire and when existing fixed assets

IN PRACTICE

Being a CFO

Wanted: Physically fit thinker with excellent operational, technical, interpersonal, and leadership skills to maintain company's infrastructure and achieve management's strategic goals. Must have extensive knowledge of accounting and finance, endurance to deal with skeptics and the stress of rising workloads, and the ability to respond to and anticipate a changing business environment.

What does it take to be a successful chief financial officer (CFO)? Obviously, a thorough knowledge of both accounting and finance is a prerequisite, but what else is important? An undergraduate degree and often graduate education in business (MBA) are starters. An accounting designation helps, but CFOs are no longer viewed just as bean counters making sure that debits equal credits and that income exceeds expenses. These days, CFOs are expected to have a full-spectrum perspective of the nature of the company.

No longer just focused on finance, CFOs are key members of the executive team setting the company's overall financial strategy and participating in senior management activities. Successful CFOs share common abilities and responsibilities. Key abilities include: analytical thinking, strategic planning, creativity, leadership, interpersonal skills, and general management experience. CFOs are responsible for implementing management information systems, reviewing operational and acquisition strategies, raising external financing, managing cash, and communicating with investors and other members of senior management. They interact with all functional areas of a business on a daily basis.

According to a study by Robert Half International Inc., the future of the profession lies in technology, specifically, expertise in information technology and experience in the emerging technology environment. Increasingly, CFOs and their department are becoming more involved with their company's technology ventures and with e-commerce. Another trend in the profession is the rise of female CFOs, a trend that is concurrent in other management-level positions. Jill

▶

need to be modified, replaced, or liquidated. The process of planning and analyzing the investment in fixed assets is referred to as capital budgeting. Investment decisions are important because they affect the firm's success in achieving its goals.

Making Financing Decisions

Financing decisions deal with the right-hand side of the firm's balance sheet and involve two major areas. First, the most appropriate mix of short-term and long-term financing must be established. A second and equally important concern is which individual short-term or long-term sources of financing are best at a given point in time. The two long-term financing choices are debt and equity capital. Many of these decisions are dictated by necessity, but some require in-depth analysis of the financing alternatives, their costs, and their long-run implications. The mix of short- and long-term financing and the mix of debt and equity financing used is the company's **capital structure**. Again, it is the effect of these decisions on the firm's goal achievement that is most important.

capital structure
The mix of short- and long-term financing and the mix of debt and equity financing used by a company.

IN PRACTICE

(Continued)

Denham, Senior Executive Vice President of CIBC, and Sherry Cooper, Chief Economist of BMO Nesbitt Burns (both of whom have backgrounds rooted in finance) are two of the most influential female figures in Canadian business.

Jill Denham is a Harvard MBA who was president of CIBC's merchant banking operations, then a senior executive at CIBC Wood Gundy's operation in London, before being appointed to corporate banking, the division that lends money mainly to mid-sized companies, to bring "more discipline" to the business. Later she was given responsibility for e-commerce initiatives. Her latest position is senior executive vice president of retail and small-business banking where she is responsible for what goes on in all of CIBC's 1,150 branches!

Like Denham, Sherry Cooper is another major player in banking. After working at the U.S. Federal Reserve Board for five years, she became the first female director of an investment dealer on Bay Street. Ms. Cooper, now chief economist of BMO Nesbitt

Burns, provides economic and market analysis for the Bank and its subsidiaries. She is one of Canada's most well-known economists, mostly because of her exceptional financial skills and her ability to analyze, communicate, and bring economics to life. She's driven. She wakes at 4:40 a.m., reads three newspapers, and is at work before 7 a.m. She often gives speeches after work. "I work like a demon, I really do. But that is because I love my job. That's the ultimate driver of my success."

REFERENCES: Paul Vieira, "Power Company CEO Heads the Power 50," *National Post*, May 6, 2002; Derek DeCloet, "Ms. Fix-it to the Rescue," *National Post*, May 6, 2002; Jacqueline Thorpe, "Jazzing Up the 'Dismal Science,'" *National Post*, May 6, 2002; Rob Snow, "Get Smart: A Top CFO is a Lot More Than a Wizard with Numbers and Keeper of the Corporate Vault," *Atlantic Progress* magazine, November 2001; Stephen Taub, "The CFO of the Future," CFO.com, June 29, 2001. See: www.cfo.com/article/1,5309,3885|||9,00.html.

? Review Questions

1–8 What financial activities does the treasurer, or financial manager, perform in the mature firm?

1–9 Explain why the financial manager should possess a basic knowledge of economics. What is the primary economic principle used in managerial finance?

1–10 What are the major differences between accounting and finance with respect to: (a) emphasis on cash flows; (b) decision making?

1–11 What are the three key activities of the financial manager? Relate them to the firm's balance sheet.

1.4 Goal of the Financial Manager

As noted earlier, the owners of a corporation are normally distinct from its managers. Actions of the financial manager should be taken to achieve the objectives of the firm's owners, its common shareholders. In most cases, if financial managers are successful in this endeavour, they will also achieve their own financial and professional objectives. So, financial managers need to know the objectives of the firm's owners. Many people believe that the owner's objective is always to maximize profit. Let's begin by looking at that goal.

Maximize Profit?

earnings per share (EPS)
The amount earned during the accounting period on each outstanding common share, calculated by dividing the period's total earnings available for the firm's common shareholders by the number of common shares outstanding.

To achieve the goal of profit maximization, the financial manager takes only those actions that are expected to contribute to the firm's overall profits. For each alternative being considered, the financial manager would select the one that is expected to result in the highest monetary return. Corporations commonly measure profits in terms of **earnings per share (EPS)**, which represent the amount earned during the accounting period on each outstanding common share of the corporation. EPS are calculated by dividing the period's total earnings available for the firm's common shareholders by the number of common shares outstanding.

Example ▼ Nick Dukakis, the financial manager of Neptune Manufacturing, a producer of marine engine components, is attempting to choose between two major investments, X and Y. Each is expected to have the following earnings per share effects over its 3-year life.

| | Earnings per share (EPS) | | | |
Investment	Year 1	Year 2	Year 3	Total for years 1, 2, and 3
X	$1.40	$1.00	$ .40	$2.80
Y	.60	1.00	1.40	3.00

Based on the profit-maximization goal, investment Y would be preferred over investment X, because it results in higher total earnings per share over the 3-year period. ▲

But, profit maximization is not a reasonable goal. It fails for a number of reasons: it ignores (1) the timing of returns, (2) cash flows available to common shareholders, and (3) risk.[2]

Timing

Because the firm can earn a return on funds it receives, *the receipt of funds sooner rather than later is preferred.* In our example, in spite of the fact that the total earnings from investment X are smaller than those from Y, investment X provides much greater earnings per share in the first year. The larger returns in year 1 could be reinvested to provide greater future earnings. Timing issues are considered through time value of money calculators. Chapter 5 is devoted to time value calculation.

Cash Flows

Profits do *not* necessarily result in cash flows available to the common shareholders. Owners receive cash flow either in the form of cash dividends paid them or the proceeds from selling their shares for a higher price than initially paid. A greater EPS does not necessarily mean that a firm's board of directors will vote to increase dividend payments.

Furthermore, a higher EPS does not necessarily translate into a higher share price. Firms sometimes experience earnings increases without any correspondingly favourable change in share price. Only when earnings increases are accompanied by increased future cash flows would a higher share price be expected. For example, a firm in a highly competitive technology-driven business could increase its earnings by significantly reducing its research and development expenditures. As a result the firm's expenses would be reduced, thereby increasing its profits. But because of its lessened competitive position, the firm's share price would drop, as many well-informed investors sell their shares in recognition of lower future cash flows. In this case, the earnings increase was accompanied by lower future cash flows and therefore a lower share price.

Risk

risk
The chance that actual outcomes may differ from those expected.

⑂ Hint
This is one of the most important concepts in the book. Investors who seek to avoid risk will always require a bigger reward for taking bigger risks.

Profit maximization also disregards **risk**—the chance that actual outcomes may differ from those expected. A basic premise in managerial finance is that a trade-off exists between return (cash flow) and risk. *Return and risk are in fact the key determinants of share price, which represents the wealth of the owners in the firm.*

Cash flow and risk affect share price differently: Higher cash flow is generally associated with a higher share price. Higher risk tends to result in a lower share price because the shareholders must be compensated for the greater risk. For example, if a lawsuit claiming significant damages is filed against a company, its share price typically will immediately drop. This occurs not because of any near-term cash flow reduction, but rather in response to the firm's increased risk—

---

2. Another criticism of profit maximization is the potential for profit manipulation through the creative use of elective accounting practices. This has become a widespread complaint of common shareholders in both Canada and the United States.

there's a chance that the firm will have to pay out a large amount of cash some time in the future to eliminate or fully satisfy the claim. Simply put, the increased risk reduces the firm's share price. In general, individuals are risk-averse—that is, they want to avoid risk. When risk is involved, they expect to earn higher rates of return on investments of higher risk and lower rates on lower-risk investments. The key point, which will be fully developed in Chapter 7, is that differences in risk can significantly affect the value of an investment.

Because profit maximization does not achieve the objectives of the firm's owners, it should *not* be the goal of the financial manager.

Maximize Shareholder Wealth

The goal of the firm, and therefore of all managers and employees, is *to maximize the wealth of the owners for whom it is being operated.* The wealth of corporate owners is measured by the price of the common shares, which in turn is based on the timing of returns (cash flows), their magnitude, and their risk. The goal is to maximize the value of the common shareholders' total interest in the company. This is measured by multiplying the total number of common shares outstanding by the common share price.

When considering each financial decision alternative or possible action in terms of its impact on the firm's share price, *financial managers should accept only those actions that are expected to increase share price.* (Figure 1.3 depicts this process.) Because share price represents the owners' wealth in the firm, share-price maximization is consistent with owner-wealth maximization. Note that *return (cash flows) and risk are the key decision variables in the wealth maximization process.* It is important to recognize that earnings per share (EPS), because they are viewed as an indicator of the firm's future returns (cash flows), often appear to affect share price. Two important issues related to share-price maximization are economic value added (EVA) and the focus on stakeholders.

economic value added (EVA)
A popular measure, used by many firms to determine whether an investment contributes positively to the owners' wealth; calculated by subtracting the cost of funds used to finance an investment from its after-tax operating profits.

Economic Value Added (EVA)

Economic value added (EVA) is a popular measure used by many firms to determine whether an investment—proposed or existing—positively contributes to the owners' wealth. EVA is calculated by subtracting the cost of funds used to finance an investment from its after-tax operating profits. Investments with posi-

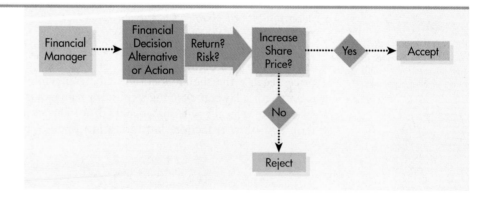

FIGURE 1.3

Share Price Maximization

Financial decisions and share price

tive EVAs increase shareholder value and those with negative EVAs reduce shareholder value. Clearly, only those investments with positive EVAs are desirable. For example, the EVA of an investment with after-tax operating profits of $410,000 and associated financing costs of $375,000 would be $35,000 (i.e., $410,000 − $375,000). Because this EVA is positive, the investment is expected to increase owner wealth and is therefore acceptable. Of course, in practice numerous accounting and financial issues would be involved in estimating both the after-tax operating profits attributable to the given investment and the cost of funds used to finance it.

The growing popularity of EVA is due to both its relative simplicity and its strong link to owner wealth maximization. Advocates of EVA believe it exhibits a strong link to share prices—positive EVAs are associated with increasing share prices, and vice versa. While EVA analysis is very popular in the United States, only a handful of companies in Canada have attempted to implement the technique. Two of these companies are Domtar, the third largest manufacturer of business, printing and publishing, and technical and specialty paper in North America, and Alcan, the second largest aluminum company in the world. Coca-Cola is a long-time user of EVA. The former CEO of the company has stated: "You only get rich if you invest money at a higher rate of return than the cost of that money to you." This comment illustrates the simplicity of the concept.

Given that highly successful firms such as Coca-Cola use and widely tout the effectiveness of EVA in isolating investments that create shareholder value, it is surprising that more Canadian companies are not using the technique to help make investment decisions. While EVA is popular among some companies, it is important to note that it is simply a repackaged application of a standard investment decision-making technique called *net present value (NPV)*, which is described in detail in Chapter 12. What's important at this point is to recognize that useful tools, such as EVA, are available for operationalizing the owners' wealth maximization goal, particularly when making investment decisions.[3]

What About Stakeholders?

stakeholders
Groups such as employees, customers, suppliers, creditors, owners, and others who have a direct economic link to the firm.

Although shareholder wealth maximization is the primary goal, in recent years many firms have broadened their focus to include the interests of *stakeholders* as well as shareholders. **Stakeholders** are groups such as employees, customers, suppliers, creditors, owners, and others who have a direct economic link to the firm. Employees are paid for their labour, customers purchase the firm's products or services, suppliers are paid for the materials and services they provide, creditors provide debt financing that is to be repaid subject to specified terms, and owners provide equity financing for which they expect to be compensated. A firm with a *stakeholder focus* consciously avoids actions that would prove detrimental to stakeholders. The goal is not to maximize stakeholder well-being but to preserve it.

The stakeholder view does not alter the shareholder wealth maximization goal. Such a view is often considered part of the firm's "social responsibility" and

3. For a good overview of EVA (including a video on the concept), see Stern Stewart & Co's Web site at: www.sternstewart.com or Brian A. Schofield, "EVAluating Stocks," *Canadian Investment Review*, Spring, 2000; available at: www.investmentreview.com/archives/spring00/stocks.html.

is expected to provide maximum long-run benefit to shareholders by maintaining positive stakeholder relationships. Such relationships should minimize stakeholder turnover, conflicts, and litigation. Clearly, the firm can better achieve its goal of shareholder wealth maximization with the cooperation of—rather than conflict with—its other stakeholders.

The Role of Ethics

In recent years, the ethics of actions taken by certain businesses have received major media attention. For example, Nexfor has implemented an environmental management system that: (1) ensures that their lumber and pulp and paper operations have minimal environmental impact, (2) strives for sustainable forestry, (3) regularly evaluates performance, (4) communicates with stakeholders, including employees, shareholders, the communities in which the company operates, and the government, (5) supports environmental research and implements findings, and (6) audits the environmental impact of their operations. This system ensures that Nexfor fully complies with all environmental regulations. Bombardier allocates approximately 3 percent of its earnings before taxes to the J. Armand Bombardier Foundation. For the three fiscal years from 2000 to 2002, this implied a total contribution of about $92 million. The Foundation supports a significant number of social welfare organizations and provides major funding for education, health, culture, and social development. In the 2002 fiscal year, the foundation made donations worth nearly $10 million to various fields.

ethics
Standards of conduct or moral judgment.

Clearly, these and other similar actions have raised the question of **ethics**— standards of conduct or moral judgment. Today, the business community in general and the financial community in particular are developing and enforcing ethical standards. Credit for this is primarily due to the increased public awareness resulting from the widespread publicity surrounding major ethical violations and their perpetrators. The goal of these ethical standards is to motivate business and market participants to adhere to both the letter and the spirit of laws and regulations concerned with business and professional practice.

It can be argued that a business enterprise actually strengthens its competitive position by maintaining high ethical standards. A logical way to encourage ethical business behaviour is for firms to adopt a business code of ethics. Many Canadian companies have done this and highlights of the ethical code are often included in the company's *annual report*, the report to common shareholders that summarizes and documents the firm's financial activities during the past year. In addition, it is now common to see advertisements in newspapers and magazines or on television that explain what a company is doing to be a "good corporate citizen."

These initiatives may have been motivated by the downfall of numerous companies in 2002 over ethical violations. Companies such as Enron, WorldCom, Tyco, Adelphia, ImClone, Dynegy, and Global Crossing all suffered huge financial losses and, in some cases, bankruptcy over corrupt actions. Many other companies were tarnished over claims of unethical accounting practices. Business ethics is associated with the struggle to curtail corporate power, particularly the power of the CEO. Ethical behaviour helps balance the two major pulls of capitalism: efficiency and greed. Business ethics is the subject of the In Practice reading on page 27.

Considering Ethics

Robert A. Cooke, a noted ethicist, suggests that the following questions be used to assess the ethical viability of a proposed action.[4]

1. Is the action or anticipated action arbitrary or capricious? Does it unfairly single out an individual or group?
2. Does the action or anticipated action violate the moral or legal rights of any individual or group?
3. Does the action or anticipated action conform to accepted moral standards?
4. Are there alternative courses of action that are less likely to cause actual or potential harm?

Clearly, considering such questions before taking an action can help to ensure its ethical viability. Specifically, Cooke suggests the impact of a proposed decision should be evaluated from a number of perspectives before it is finalized:

1. Are the rights of any stakeholder being violated?
2. Does the firm have any overriding duties to any stakeholder?
3. Will the decision benefit any stakeholder to the detriment of another stakeholder?
4. If there is detriment to any stakeholder, how should this be remedied, if at all?
5. What is the relationship between shareholders and other stakeholders?

Today, more and more firms are directly addressing the issue of ethics by establishing corporate ethics policies and guidelines and by requiring employee compliance with them. Frequently, employees are required to sign a formal pledge to uphold the firm's ethics policies. Such policies typically apply to employee actions in dealing with all corporate stakeholders, including the public at large. Many companies require employees to participate in ethics seminars and training programs that convey and demonstrate corporate ethics policy.

Ethics and Share Price

The implementation of a proactive ethics program is believed to enhance corporate value. An ethics program can produce a number of positive benefits: reduce potential litigation and judgment costs; maintain a positive corporate image; build shareholder confidence; and gain the loyalty, commitment, and respect of all of the firm's stakeholders. Such actions, by maintaining and enhancing cash flow and reducing perceived risk (as a result of greater investor confidence), are expected to positively affect the firm's share price. *Ethical behaviour is therefore viewed as necessary for achievement of the firm's goal of owner wealth maximization.*[5]

---

4. Robert A. Cooke, "Business Ethics: A Perspective," in *Arthur Andersen Cases on Business Ethics* (Chicago: Arthur Andersen, September 1991), pp. 2 and 5.

5. For an excellent discussion of how corporations can maximize wealth in an ethical manner, see: Donald R. Chambers and Nelson J. Lacey, "Corporate Ethics and Shareholder Wealth Maximization," *Financial Practice and Education* (Spring/Summer), 1996, pp. 93–96. For more on business ethics and ethical leadership, see the following Web site: www.economist.com/globalExecutive/education/executive/displayStory.cfm?story–id=1312952

FIGURE 1.4

The Financial Goal
Maximize shareholder
wealth

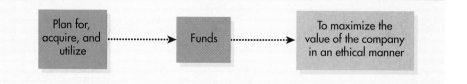

So, What Is the Financial Goal of a Company?

This section of the chapter considers the financial goal of a company. When you think about possible financial goals a company could pursue, items such as the following may come to mind:

- maximize sales
- maximize cash flow
- maximize market share
- maximize profits
- minimize costs
- maximize number of customers
- maximize return on sales, investment, or shareholders' equity
- ensure earnings stability
- achieve a certain level of sales, profits, market share, or return

By this point, it is clear that the only financial goal a company should be concerned with is to maximize shareholder wealth. This is the value of the company to the owners—the common shareholders. Shareholder wealth is a function of the number of common shares multiplied by the price of the common shares. The goal of financial management should be to maximize the value of the outstanding common shares while treating all stakeholders equitably. This is depicted in Figure 1.4.

? Review Questions

1–12   For what three basic reasons is profit maximization inconsistent with wealth maximization?

1–13   What is *risk?* Why must risk as well as return be considered by the financial manager when evaluating a decision alternative or action?

1–14   What is the goal of the firm and therefore of all managers and employees? Discuss how one measures achievement of this goal.

1–15   What is *economic value added (EVA)?* How is it used? Why is it currently quite popular?

1–16   Describe the role of corporate ethics policies and guidelines, and discuss the relationship that is believed to exist between ethics and share price.

1.5 The Agency Issue

We have seen that the goal of the financial manager should be to maximize the wealth of the owners of the firm. Thus management can be viewed as *agents* of the owners who have hired them and given them decision-making authority to manage the firm for the owners' benefit. Technically, any manager who owns less than 100 percent of the firm is to some degree an agent of the other owners. (This separation of owners and managers is shown by the dashed horizontal line in Figure 1.1.)

In theory, most financial managers would agree with the goal of owner wealth maximization. In practice, however, managers are also concerned with their personal wealth, job security, lifestyle, and fringe benefits, such as posh offices, country club memberships, and limousines, all provided at company expense. Such concerns may make managers reluctant or unwilling to take more than moderate risk if they perceive that too much risk might result in a loss of job and damage to personal wealth. The result of such a "satisficing" approach (a compromise between satisfaction and maximization) is a less-than-maximum return and a potential loss of wealth for the owners.

■ Hint
An investment advisor (stockbroker) has the same issue. If she gets you to buy and sell more stock, it's good for *her*, but it may *not* be good for you.

Resolving the Agency Problem

agency problem
The likelihood that managers may place personal goals ahead of corporate goals.

From this conflict of owner and personal goals arises what has been called the **agency problem**—the likelihood that managers may place personal goals ahead of corporate goals.[6] Two factors—corporate governance and market forces—serve to prevent or minimize agency problems.

Corporate Governance

corporate governance
The set of actions and procedures common shareholders use to ensure they receive a reasonable return on their investment in the company.

publicly traded
Companies whose common shares are listed and trade on a stock exchange.

Corporate governance is the set of actions and procedures common shareholders use to ensure they receive a reasonable return on their investment in the company. The most obvious example of corporate governance is the company's board of directors. Most large companies whose common shares are listed and trade on a stock exchange (**publicly traded**) have millions, in some cases billions of common shares outstanding and tens of thousands of common shareholders. Some of these shareholders are large, owning tens of thousands of shares; some are very small, owning 300 or fewer shares. For example, BCE has about 810 million common shares outstanding and over 180,000 common shareholders. Obviously, the owners of BCE cannot be actively involved in the affairs of the company. The shareholders elect a small group of people, the Board of Directors, to represent their interests to senior management. The board hires the CEO and other senior managers. The board is then responsible to ensure that the senior managers act in the owners' best interests.

For publicly traded companies in Canada, a system of corporate governance based on the duties and responsibilities of the board must be in place and fully documented. Each year, companies are required to disclose this information to shareholders. The disclosure generally includes a statement to the effect that the company's approach to corporate governance is to ensure that the business

6. The agency problem and related issues are addressed in the following papers: Michael C. Jensen and William H. Meckling, "Theory of the Firm: Managerial Behavior, Agency Costs, and Ownership Structure," *Journal of Financial Economics*, 3 (1976), pp. 305–360 and Michael C. Jensen, "Agency Costs of Free Cash Flow, Corporate Finance, and Takeover," *American Economic Review*, 76 (1986), pp. 323–329. For a detailed discussion and practical application of agency issues in Canada, see: Sean Hennessey, "Financial Theories in Practice: The Surprising Case of the Air Canada, Canadian Airlines, Onex Affair," or "A Remarkably Futile Record," *National Post*, December 15, 2001, both available at: **www.upei.ca/~sbusines/faculty/hennessey/research.**

affairs of the company are managed to enhance shareholder value. Usually, a lengthy list of guidelines is provided that indicate the governance process. An all-inclusive statement to the effect that the board assumes responsibility for the stewardship of the company usually heads the list. While boards directly represent shareholders' interests to management and are meant to help solve the agency problem in managing public companies, agency issues may also affect the performance of the board of directors.

For example, in Canada, corporate boards seem to be drawn from the same small subset of people. Boards have been described as: "a close-knit fraternity of perhaps 100 peripatetic directors, each serving on between five and 15 boards. It's still a fairly closed network, you might call it stacking the deck."[7] Board memberships are lucrative and membership is often tied to the ability to work with the CEO. The CEO often serves on other companies' boards. It's a system where being critical of senior management may be very difficult. There may be an element of people helping each other to "get the cookies out of the jar." The effectiveness of corporate boards may be hampered by a "culture of seduction." Directors are wooed with perks such as access to corporate jets, first class travel, contributions to their favourite charities, and consulting contracts. It may be that for some companies, the board of directors puts management's interest ahead of the goal of maximizing shareholder wealth.

There are three additional very direct and focused corporate governance procedures that can prevent or minimize agency problems. These are sometimes referred to as **agency costs**, since shareholders incur a direct, often high cash cost. The three costs are discussed below.

agency costs
Costs borne by shareholders to prevent or minimize agency problems and to contribute to the maximization of shareholders' wealth.

1. *Monitoring expenditures* prevent satisficing (rather than share-price-maximizing) behaviour by management. These outlays pay for audits and control procedures that are used to assess and limit managerial behaviour to those actions that tend to be in the best interests of the owners.

2. *Bonding expenditures* protect against the potential consequences of dishonest acts by managers. Typically, the owners pay a third-party bonding company to obtain a **fidelity bond.** This bond is a contract under which the bonding company agrees to reimburse the firm for up to a stated amount if a bonded manager's dishonest act results in financial loss to the firm.

3. *Structuring expenditures* are the most popular, powerful, and expensive agency costs incurred by firms. They result from structuring managerial compensation to correspond with share price maximization. The objective is to give managers incentives to act in the best interests of the owners and to compensate them for such actions. In addition, the resulting compensation packages allow firms to compete for and hire the best managers available. Compensation plans can be divided into two groups—incentive plans and performance plans.

fidelity bond
A contract under which a bonding company agrees to reimburse a firm for up to a stated amount if a bonded manager's dishonest act results in a financial loss to the firm.

incentive plans
Management compensation plans that tend to tie management compensation to share price; most popular incentive plan involves the grant of *stock options.*

stock options
An incentive allowing managers to purchase common shares at the market price set at the time of the grant.

Incentive plans tend to tie management compensation to share price. The most popular incentive plan is the granting of **stock options** to management. These options allow managers to purchase common shares at the market price set at the time of the grant. If the market price rises, they will be rewarded by

7. See: David Olive, "CEOs Not Sharing Investors' Pain: Compliant Boards Find a Way to Prop Up Executive Pay," *National Post*, May 22, 2001.

being able to resell the shares subsequently at the higher market price. Although in theory these options should motivate, they are sometimes criticized because positive management performance can be masked in a poor stock market in which share prices in general have declined due to economic and behavioural "market forces" outside of management's control. The reverse is also true.

performance plans

Plans that compensate managers on the basis of proven performance measured by EPS, growth in EPS, and other ratios of return. *Performance shares* and/or *cash bonuses* are used as compensation under these plans.

performance shares

Common shares granted to management for meeting stated performance goals.

cash bonuses

Cash paid to management for achieving certain performance goals.

The use of **performance plans** has grown in popularity in recent years due to their relative independence from market forces. These plans compensate managers on the basis of their proven performance measured by earnings per share (EPS), growth in EPS, and other ratios of return. **Performance shares,** common shares granted to management as a result of meeting the stated performance goals, are often used in these plans. Another form of performance-based compensation is **cash bonuses,** cash payments tied to the achievement of certain performance goals. Under performance plans, management understands in advance the formula used to determine the amount of performance shares or cash bonus it can earn during the period. In addition, the minimum benefit (typically, $0) and maximum benefit available under the plan are specified.[8]

Market Forces

When shareholders can freely trade their common shares in efficiently operated markets, the mechanism of market pricing allows shareholders to "vote" on managements' actions, thereby minimizing agency costs and encouraging acceptable performance. If a company's financial performance is poor, shareholder "voting" in the stock market will result in the common share price declining. When this happens, shareholder wealth will be reduced, not maximized, and the board of directors should question the poor corporate performance. Stock options provided to managers will lose value. With this series of events, changes should occur, either with the strategic direction of the company, the tactics the company is using to meet their goals, or with senior management. The ultimate power of the board (shareholders) is to fire underperforming managers.

In addition, in Canada, institutional investors, such as mutual funds, pension funds, and life insurance companies, often own a majority of the common shares of publicly traded companies. These types of investors, with large blocks of common shares in many companies, will watch the performance of these companies very closely. Poor financial performance may provoke these large shareholders to attempt to gain control of the board and fire underperforming managers, replacing them with more competent managers. Note that the formal mechanism through which these shareholders act is by voting their shares in the election of directors, who are empowered to hire and fire operating management. In addition to their legal voting rights, large shareholders are able to communicate with and exert pressure on management to perform or be fired.

This type of behaviour is referred to as shareholder activism. In the United States, large shareholders are very active in ensuring acceptable company performance. In Canada, shareholder activism is very rare, even in cases where institutional investors own a large majority (more than 70 percent) of the common

---

8. For an excellent discussion of corporate governance, including ways to improve the standards and practices of governance, see: Anthony Atkinson and Steve Salterio, "Shaping Good Conduct: The Search for More Effective Systems of Corporate Governance Has Created a Unique Opportunity for Strategic Financial Management Professionals," *CMA Management*, 75 (10), February 2002, pp. 19–23.

shares of a company and company performance is poor. The reason for the lack of shareholder activism in Canada is not clear.

Another market force that has in recent years threatened management to perform in the best interests of shareholders is the possibility of a *hostile takeover*. A **hostile takeover** is the acquisition of the firm (the *target*) by another firm or group (the *acquirer*) that is not supported by management. Hostile takeovers typically occur when the acquirer feels that the target firm is being poorly managed and, as a result, is undervalued in the marketplace. The acquirer believes that by acquiring the target at its current low price and restructuring its management, operations, and financing, it can enhance the firm's value—that is, its share price. Although techniques are available for defending against a hostile takeover, the constant threat of a takeover often motivates management to act in the best interests of the firm's owners.

hostile takeover
The acquisition of the firm (the *target*) by another firm or group (the *acquirer*) that is not supported by management.

The Current View on Incentive Plans

Although experts agree that an effective way to motivate management is to tie compensation to performance, the execution of many compensation plans has been closely scrutinized in recent years. Shareholders, both individuals and institutions, have publicly questioned the appropriateness of the multimillion-dollar compensation packages (including salary, bonus, and long-term compensation) that many corporate executives receive. For example, based on a Financial Post, William M. Mercer survey of executive compensation,[9] the three highest paid CEOs in 2001 were: Travis Engen of Alcan Aluminium Ltd., who earned $18.5 million; Jean Monty of BCE, who earned $18.4 million; and Frank Dunn of Nortel Networks Corporation, who earned $18.2 million.

The top ten CEOs had total compensation packages of $140.4 million in 2001 versus $188.8 million in 2000. The much higher level in 2000 was due to John Roth of Nortel Networks Corporation, who earned $70.8 million. Even though total compensation decreased, the median compensation paid to the CEOs of Canada's top 60 companies increased over 18 percent to $4.37 million.

The study also revealed that long-term compensation, like grants of stock options, accounted for $2.67 million or 61 percent of total pay, an increase of 65 percent over 2000. For a recent listing of the 50 best paid executives (not just CEOs) in Canada, see the following Web site: **top1000.robmagazine.com/2002/executives/executives.htm**.

Although these sizable compensation packages may be justified by significant increases in shareholder wealth, recent studies have failed to find a strong relationship between CEO compensation and share price. The publicity surrounding these large compensation packages (without corresponding share price performance) has had little impact to date in reducing the level of executive compensation. Contributing to this publicity is the requirement that publicly traded companies disclose to shareholders and others both the amount of and method used to determine compensation to their highest paid executives. At the same time, new compensation plans that better link management performance with regard to shareholder wealth to its compensation are expected to be developed and implemented.

---

9. See: "Executive Pay Jumps 18% on Option Grants," *National Post*, July 22, 2002, p. FP1.

Unconstrained, managers may have other goals in addition to share price maximization, but much of the evidence suggests that share price maximization—the focus of this book—is the primary goal of most firms.

IN PRACTICE

Agency Issues and Ethics

Management operates a company on behalf of the common shareholders. This can create agency issues and also ethical dilemmas. Does management run a company to achieve the goal of maximizing shareholders wealth in an ethical manner? For the large majority of companies the answer is yes, but for some, the actions of management fail to meet one or both parts of the goal. Enron is a name that will be long associated with a failure to achieve both parts of the goal.

In December 2001, Enron filed for bankruptcy. With about $50 billion in assets and more than $40 billion in debt, Enron was the largest bankruptcy in history. Investors in Enron, including thousands of employees, lost billions. This was a shocking ending for the company since through the 1990s, Enron had reinvented itself, completely reorganizing and developing new products and markets. Enron was rewarded for this transformation with a soaring share price and recognition from *Fortune* magazine, for six successive years, as "the most innovative firm in America." The company became one other managers wanted to emulate.

But, by mid-2001, dirty secrets started to be uncovered. The financial data that the company released to the public was incorrect. It turned out that through illegal accounting practices, Enron was hiding a huge debt load and inflating both sales and profits. In addition, senior managers were making millions on these illegal schemes while the company was losing billions. As the investigation evolved, it was discovered that Enron's auditor, Arthur Andersen, the independent firm that ensures a company's financial reports are legal, was hiding these shady accounting practices and shielding senior management's involvement.

In addition, Arthur Andersen was shredding tonnes of paper documenting the affair. Enron's board of directors, the group that represents shareholders' interests to senior management, was accused of fiddling while the company self-destructed. The Enron debacle has become the headline for failure to maximize shareholder wealth and for unethical behaviour. Enron's management and auditors lied to shareholders, obviously violating their obligations.

Enron, however, is not the first company to violate their ethical responsibilities to shareholders and other stakeholders. Michael Milken and Ivan Boesky were convicted of insider trading in the great junk bond trading scandal of the late 1980s and were sentenced to jail and fines as high as $600 million. Waste Management and Sunbeam Corporation were also discovered to have inflated their profits, misleading investors. Ironically, Arthur Andersen was the auditor for both companies. Sunbeam Corporation is now bankrupt. For Waste Management, it has been alleged that six former top executives perpetuated a "massive financial fraud. For years, the six executives cooked the books, enriched themselves, preserved their jobs, and duped unsuspecting shareholders. Their fraudulent conduct was driven by greed and a desire to retain their corporate positions and status in the business and social communities," said one of the investigators.

Canada is not immune from these types of transgressions. Some Canadian examples include Livent and former CEO Garth Drabinsky, who have been accused of overstating Livent's earnings with a series of accounting tricks; Cinar Corporation, and the company's two founders, who have been accused of diverting

▶

IN PRACTICE

(Continued)

US$122 million of company funds to offshore investments; and Michael Cowpland, the founder and the former CEO of Corel Corporation, who was charged with insider trading involving the $20.4 million sale of Corel stock. But the most notorious example is Bre-X.

In 1997 it was discovered that Bre-X Minerals had falsified gold samples. Rather than millions of ounces of gold and the richest gold mine in the world, as the falsified samples suggested, the "gold" deposit in the jungles of Indonesia contained virtually no gold. As soon as news of the fraud was reported, Bre-X's share price declined over 90 percent from a high price of $280 per share. A company that at one point was valued at over $6 billion was reduced to nothing within a few days.

These episodes may suggest that unethical behaviour is rampant in corporate North America. This, of course, is not the case. There are over 10,000 publicly traded companies in North America and the vast majority of managers act ethically and in the owners' interests. But, in all areas where large sums of money are involved, abuses can occur and, as we have seen, managers can act in their own interests.

REFERENCES: Derek DeCloet, "Canadian Regulators Can't Even Confiscate Ill-gotten Gains," *National Post*, March 29, 2002; John Gray, "Home-grown Accounting Scandals," *Canadian Business*, April 1, 2002; Susan Cornwell, "U.S. Senate Condemns Enron Board," *National Post*, May 8, 2002; "Former Corel CEO Hit with Insider Trading Fine," Reuters, February 11, 2002. Available at: www.news.com/2100-1040-834304.html; Al Rosen, "Easy Prey," *Canadian Business*, April 16, 2001.

? Review Questions

1–17 What is the *agency problem?* Define and discuss *corporate governance.* Define *agency costs*, and explain why firms incur them. How do market forces act to prevent or minimize the agency problem?

1–18 Describe and differentiate between *incentive* and *performance* compensation plans.

1.6 Using This Text

The text's organization links the firm's activities to its value, as determined in the securities markets. The activities of the financial manager are described in six parts:

Part 1: Introduction to Managerial Finance
Part 2: Financial Analysis and Planning
Part 3: Important Financial Concepts
Part 4: Long-Term Financing Decisions
Part 5: Long-Term Investment Decisions
Part 6: Working Capital Management
Part 7: Special Topics in Managerial Finance

Each major decision area is presented in terms of both return and risk factors and their potential impact on the owners' wealth. Coverage of international events and topics is integrated into the chapter discussions. A separate international managerial finance chapter is also included.

The text has been developed around a group of about 102 learning goals—an average of 6 per chapter. Mastery of these goals results in a broad understanding of the theories, concepts, techniques, and practices of managerial finance. These goals have been carefully integrated into a learning system. Each chapter begins with a numbered list of learning goals. Next to each major text heading is a *toolbox*, which notes by number the specific learning goal(s) addressed in that section. At the end of each section of the chapter (positioned before the next major heading) are review questions that test your understanding of key theories, concepts, techniques, and practices in that section. At the end of each chapter, the chapter summaries, self-test problems, and problems are also keyed by number to each chapter's learning goals. By linking all elements to the learning goals, the integrated learning system facilitates the mastery of those goals.

Each chapter ends with a case that integrates the chapter materials, and each part ends with an integrative case that ties together the key topical material covered in the chapters within that part. Both the chapter-end and part-end cases can be used to synthesize and apply related concepts and techniques.

SUMMARY

 Define *finance* and describe its three major areas—financial markets, financial services, and managerial finance—and the career opportunities within them. Finance, the art and science of managing money, affects the lives of every person and every organization. Financial markets provide a forum where savers of funds and users of funds transact business. Career opportunities available include the trading of financial securities and work with the financial intermediaries that allow the markets to function and the organizations that regulate the markets. Financial services involve the design and delivery of financial products. Major opportunities in financial services exist within banking and related institutions, personal financial planning, investments, real estate, and insurance. Managerial finance, concerned with the duties of the financial manager in the business firm, offers numerous career opportunities such as financial analyst, capital budgeting analyst/manager, project finance manager, cash manager, credit analyst/manager, and pension fund manager. The recent trend toward globalization of business activity has created new demands and opportunities in managerial finance.

 Review the basic forms of business organization and their respective strengths and weaknesses. The basic forms of business organization are the sole proprietorship, the partnership, and the corporation. Although there are more sole proprietorships than any other form of business organization, the corporation is dominant in terms of business sales, profits, and assets. The owners of a corporation are its common shareholders. Shareholders expect to earn a return by receiving dividends or by realizing gains through increases in share price. The key strengths and weaknesses of each form of business organization are summarized in Table 1.2.

 Describe the managerial finance function and differentiate managerial finance from the closely related disciplines of economics and accounting. All areas of responsibility within a firm interact with finance personnel, processes, and procedures. In large firms, the managerial finance function might be handled by a separate department headed by the vice president of finance (CFO), to whom the treasurer and controller report; in small firms, the finance function is generally performed by the accounting department. The financial manager must understand the economic environment and relies heavily on the economic principle of marginal analysis when making decisions. Financial managers use accounting data but differ from accountants, who devote primary attention to accrual methods and to gathering and presenting data, by concentrating on cash flows and decision making.

 Identify the key activities of the financial manager within the firm. The three key activities of the financial manager are (1) performing financial analysis and planning, (2) making investment decisions, and (3) making financing decisions.

 Explain why wealth maximization, rather than profit maximization, is the firm's goal and how economic value added (EVA), a focus on stakeholders, and ethical behaviour relate to its achievement. The goal of the financial manager is to maximize the owners' wealth (dependent on share price) rather than profits, because profit maximization ignores the timing of returns, does not directly consider cash flows, and ignores risk. Because return and risk are the key determinants of share price, both must be assessed by the financial manager when evaluating decision alternatives or actions. EVA is a popular measure used to determine whether an investment positively contributes to the owners' wealth. The wealth maximizing actions of financial managers should be consistent with the preservation of the wealth of *stakeholders*, groups such as employees, customers, suppliers, creditors, owners, and others who have a direct economic link to the firm. Positive ethical practices by the firm and its managers are believed to be necessary for achievement of the firm's goal of owner wealth maximization.

 Discuss the agency issue as it relates to owner wealth maximization. An agency problem results when managers as agents for owners place personal goals ahead of corporate goals. Corporate governance is the set of actions and procedures common shareholders use to ensure they receive a reasonable return on their investment in the company. For publicly traded companies, a system of corporate governance based on the duties and responsibilities of the company's board of directors is used. Agency issues may also affect the performance of the board of directors, however. Three additional very direct and focused corporate governance procedures can prevent or minimize agency problem. These agency costs are monitoring, bonding, and structuring expenditures. In addition, market forces, both activism on the part of shareholders, particularly large institutional investors, and the threat of hostile takeover, tend to act to prevent or minimize agency problems.

SELF-TEST PROBLEM   (Solution in Appendix B)

 ST 1–1 **Goals of a company** Liam Murphy, financial analyst with Doyle Power Supply, is evaluating two different projects that the firm could implement. Doyle Power Supply's current earning per share (EPS) are $1.63, the company has 10,000,000 common shares outstanding, and the compamy's common shares are trading for $19.50 per share.

   If Doyle implements project 1, the firm will issue 1,000,000 common shares, the total increase in EPS will be $1.32 (in today's dollars), and the firm's share price will increase to $28.00. If project 2 is implemented, the firm will issue 1,800,000 common shares, the total increase in EPS will be $1.19 (in today's dollars), and Doyle's common share price will increase to $26.50.
   a. If profit maximization was Doyle Power Supply's goal, which project should Liam Murphy recommend? Why?
   b. If share price maximization was Doyle Power Supply's goal, which project should Liam Murphy recommend? Why?

c. If the maximization of common shareholder wealth was Doyle Power Supply's goal, which project should Liam Murphy recommend? Why?

d. As Liam Murphy, which project would you recommend? Why?

e. Why might project 2 be the better project, even though it results in lower EPS and a lower share price? Explain.

PROBLEMS

WARM-UP   **1–1** **Liability comparisons**   Meredith Harper has invested $25,000 in Southwest Development Company. The firm has recently declared bankruptcy and has $60,000 in unpaid debts. Explain the nature of payments, if any, by Ms. Harper in each of the following situations.

a. Southwest Development Company is a sole proprietorship owned by Ms. Harper.

b. Southwest Development Company is a 50–50 partnership of Ms. Harper and Christopher Black.

c. Southwest Development Company is a corporation.

INTERMEDIATE

1–2 **The managerial finance function and economic value added (EVA)**   Ken Allen, capital budgeting analyst for Bally Gears, Inc., has been asked to evaluate a proposal. The manager of the automotive division believes that replacing the robotics used on the heavy truck gear line will produce total benefits of $560,000 (in today's dollars) over the next 5 years. The existing robotics would produce benefits of $400,000 (also in today's dollars) over that same time period. An initial cash investment of $220,000 would be required to install the new equipment. The manager estimates that the existing robotics can be sold for $70,000. Show how Ken will apply marginal analysis techniques to determine the following:

a. The marginal (added) benefits of the proposed new robotics.

b. The marginal (added) cost of the proposed new robotics.

c. The net benefit of the proposed new robotics.

d. What should Ken Allen recommend that the company do? Why?

e. What factors besides the costs and benefits should be considered before the final decision is made?

f. Now assume that the additional yearly after-tax operating profits associated with the new robotics equipment is expected to be $28,875. The new equipment will cost $220,000 and Bally's cost of financing is 13.6 percent. Using an economic value added analysis, should Bally Gears replace the robotics equipment?

WARM-UP **1–3** **Accrual income versus cash flow for a period**   Thomas Book Sales, Inc., supplies textbooks to college and university bookstores. The books are shipped with a proviso that they must be paid for within 30 days, but can be returned for a full refund credit within 90 days. In 2003, Thomas shipped and billed book titles totalling $760,000. Collections, net of return credits, during the year totalled $690,000. The company spent $300,000 acquiring the books that it shipped.

a. Using accrual accounting and the preceding values, show the firm's income for the past year.

    b. Using cash accounting and the preceding values, show the firm's cash flow for the past year.

    c. Which of these statements is more useful to the financial manager? Why?

INTERMEDIATE   **LG6**   **1–4** **Identifying agency problems, costs, and resolutions** Explain why each of the following situations is an agency problem and what costs to the firm might result from it. Suggest how the problem might be dealt with short of firing the individual(s) involved.

    a. The front desk receptionist routinely takes an extra 20 minutes of lunch to take care of her personal errands.

    b. Division managers are padding cost estimates in order to show short-term efficiency gains when the costs come in lower than the estimates.

    c. The firm's chief executive officer has secret talks with a competitor about the possibility of a merger in which (s)he would become the CEO of the combined firms.

    d. A branch manager lays off experienced full-time employees and staffs customer service positions with part-time or temporary workers to lower employment costs and raise this year's branch profit. The manager's bonus is based on profitability.

CASE   **CHAPTER 1**   **Assessing the Goal of Sports Products, Inc.**

Loren Seguara and Dale Johnson both work for Sports Products, Inc., a major producer of boating equipment and accessories. Loren works as a clerical assistant in the Accounting Department, and Dale works as a packager in the Shipping Department. During their lunch break one day, they began talking about the company. Dale complained that he had always worked hard trying not to waste packing materials and efficiently and cost-effectively performing his job. In spite of his efforts and those of his co-workers in the department, the firm's stock price had declined nearly $2 per share over the past 9 months. Loren indicated that she shared Dale's frustration, particularly because the firm's profits had been rising. Neither could understand why the firm's stock price was falling as profits rose.

Loren indicated that she had seen documents describing the firm's profit-sharing plan under which all managers were partially compensated on the basis of the firm's profits. She suggested that maybe it was profit that was important to management, because it directly affected their pay. Dale said, "That doesn't make sense, because the shareholders own the firm. Shouldn't management do what's best for shareholders? Something's wrong!" Loren responded, "Well, maybe that explains why the company hasn't concerned itself with the share price. Look, the only profits shareholders receive are in the form of cash dividends, and this firm has never paid dividends during its 20-year history. We as shareholders therefore don't directly benefit from profits. The only way we benefit is for the share price to rise." Dale chimed in, "That probably explains why the firm is being sued by provincial and federal environmental officials for dumping pollutants in the river adjacent to the plant. Why spend money for pollution controls? It increases costs, lowers profits, and therefore lowers management's earnings!"

Loren and Dale realized that the lunch break had ended and they must quickly return to work. Before leaving, they decided to meet the next day to continue their discussion.

Required

a. What should the management of Sports Products, Inc., pursue as its overriding goal? Why?

b. Does the firm appear to have an *agency problem?* Explain.

c. Evaluate the firm's approach to pollution control. Does it seem to be *ethical?* Why might incurring the expense to control pollution be in the best interests of the firm's owners in spite of its negative impact on profits?

d. On the basis of the information provided, what specific recommendations would you offer the firm?

WEB EXERCISES   LINKS TO PRACTISE

Visit the following Web sites and complete the suggested exercises. These exercises will allow you to review practical applications of the chapter topics as well as explore the wealth of information regarding managerial finance that is available on the Internet.

   www.careers-in-finance.com

1. What are the main areas for careers in finance according to this Web site? What major areas seem to be missing?

2. Click on corporate finance. Describe what a career in corporate finance might entail.

3. Review the list of skills and talents required for a job in corporate finance. What do you think are the five most important skills to have? Do you posses these?

4. Review the list of job options. Which of these types of jobs, if any, appeal to you?

5. What are the starting salary ranges for: a rookie financial analyst, credit manager, tax manager, treasurer, CFO?

6. What are five facts and trends for careers in corporate finance?

7. Follow the link for job listings. Select on a job category that might be of interest to you and click on Find Jobs. Summarize the job description and state the salary if provided.

 www.teachmefinance.com

Review the main topics covered on the Web sites. Which topics were covered in this chapter? Follow the link for three other topics for an overview of the topic that will be covered in managerial finance. Bookmark this Web site, as you may regularly wish to review the material.

 www.tse.com/en

What is the Toronto Stock Exchange? What happens at the Toronto Stock Exchange? What is the S&P/TSX Composite Index and what is the current level of the index? How do companies get listed on the Toronto Stock Exchange and what are the benefits of listing? Provide the names of five recently listed companies.

2

Financial Statements, Cash Flows, Taxes, and the Language of Finance

LEARNING GOALS

LG1 Review the characteristics, format, key components, and relationships between the income statement, balance sheet, statement of retained earnings, and statement of cash flows.

LG2 Analyze a company's cash flows and develop and interpret the statement of cash flows.

LG3 Introduce the basics of corporate taxation in Canada.

LG4 Understand how the tax deductibility of expenses reduces their actual, after-tax cost to a profitable company.

LG5 Discuss and illustrate Capital Cost Allowance (CCA), the tax version of amortization, and how CCA increases a company's cash flows.

LG6 Review the information provided in a publicly traded company's annual report to shareholders.

LG7 Discuss some key concepts in finance and review the language of finance.

2.1 The Four Principal Financial Statements

One of the chief objectives of this chapter is to provide an understanding of the information presented in the financial statements developed by companies. The Canadian Institute of Chartered Accountants (CICA) has developed a set of accounting standards that specify the four financial statements that companies must develop and how information is to be presented and disclosed in the financial statements. The CICA's objective is to ensure companies provide information that meets the needs of users of financial statements. In this chapter, we use the four financial statements from the 2002 annual report of a hypothetical

The Language of Finance

The language of, and many concepts studied in, finance logically flow from an understanding of accounting. It is often said that accounting provides the basis for the language of finance. Financial statements provide the foundation data for many topics in finance. To avoid difficulties in managerial finance, it is important to know the "language" of the discipline. You must understand and be able to apply concepts such as reinvested profits, earnings available for common shareholders, dividends, shareholders' equity, cash flow, working capital, amortization, and earnings per share. The purpose of this chapter is to review the content and format of the four basic financial statements and the relationships between the statements, to examine a company's cash flow, to discuss corporate taxation, and to introduce some key terms and concepts in finance.

company, Baker Corporation, to illustrate and describe the statements. This chapter also discusses the relationships between the four financial statements.

Income Statement

income statement
Provides a financial summary of the firm's operating results for a specified period.

The **income statement** provides a financial summary of the firm's operating results for a specified period. Most common are income statements covering a 1-year period ending at a specified date, ordinarily December 31 of the calendar year. Many large firms, however, operate on a 12-month financial cycle, or *fiscal year*, that ends at a time other than December 31. Monthly income statements are

amortization
The systematic expensing of a portion of the cost of a fixed asset against sales.

typically prepared for use by management, and quarterly statements must be made available to the shareholders of publicly owned corporations.

Table 2.1 presents Baker Corporation's income statement for the year ended December 31, 2002. The statement begins with *sales revenue*—the total dollar amount of sales during the period—from which the *cost of goods sold* is deducted. Cost of goods sold (COGS) is the total direct cost of producing or purchasing the product sold. COGS is normally the total of direct materials, direct labour, and direct factory overhead. The difference between sales revenue and COGS is gross margin. For Baker Corporation, the resulting gross margin of $700,000 represents the amount remaining to satisfy operating, financial, and tax costs after meeting the costs of producing or purchasing the products sold. Next, *operating expenses,* which include selling expense, general and administrative expense, and amortization expense, are deducted from gross margin.

Amortization is the systematic expensing of a portion of the cost of a fixed asset against sales. This expense is associated with capital assets, assets that are expected to have a life greater than one year. Expenditures on these assets are not expensed; rather, they are capitalized and the expenditure is written off over time via the amortization expense.[1] The resulting *operating earnings* of $370,000 represent the profits earned from producing and selling products; this amount does not consider financial and tax costs. (Operating earnings are often called *earnings before interest and taxes,* or *EBIT.*)[2] Next, the financial cost—*interest expense*—is subtracted from operating earnings to find *earnings before taxes (EBT).* After subtracting $70,000 in 2002 interest, Baker Corporation had $300,000 of earnings before taxes.

After the appropriate tax rates have been applied to before-tax earnings, taxes are calculated and deducted to determine *net income* (or *earnings*) *after taxes* (NIAT). Baker Corporation's net income after taxes for the 2002 fiscal year was $180,000. With the NIAT, Baker Corporation may pay dividends to shareholders or reinvest the profits back into the company. A company can have two types of shareholders: preferred and common. Dividends must be paid to preferred shareholders before common shareholders receive any income. Baker Corporation has preferred shareholders so the dividends due on the preferred shares must be subtracted from NIAT to arrive at *earnings available for common shareholders (EAC).* All income after all expenses and preferred share dividends have been paid belongs to the common shareholders. Shareholders can receive the benefit of the EAC in two ways. First, the company can directly pay the EAC as *common share dividends.* In this way, the EAC provides a direct cash payment to common shareholders. Second, any EAC not paid to shareholders, by default, is reinvested back into the company.

After reading the previous paragraph, you may be wondering how reinvesting a portion of the profits is a benefit to common shareholders. Since the EAC belong to the common shareholders, why doesn't the company pay all of it to common shareholders as dividends? It is easy to see the benefit of receiving a cash payment to common shareholders, but how are *reinvested profits* a benefit?

---

1. Amortization is the term used in this book to describe this expense. This is the case since in 1990, the CICA recommended that "amortization" replace the term "depreciation." In practice, amortization is often included within COGS. In this book, however, amortization will be shown as an operating expense in order to be able to highlight its impact on cash flows.

2. In practice, EBITDA is often used to measure operating earnings. This means earnings before interest, taxes, depreciation, and amortization.

TABLE 2.1	Baker Corporation Income Statement ($000) for the Year Ended December 31, 2002		

Sales revenue			$1,700
Less: Cost of goods sold			1,000
Gross margin			$ 700
Less: Operating expenses			
Selling expense		$ 80	
General and administrative expense		150	
Amortization expense		100	
Total operating expenses			330
Operating earnings (EBIT)			$ 370
Less: Interest expense[a]			70
Earnings before taxes			$ 300
Less: Taxes (rate = 40%)			120
Net income after taxes			$ 180
Less: Preferred share dividends			10
Earnings available for common shareholders (EAC)			$ 170
Earnings per share (EPS)[b]			$ 1.70

[a]Interest expense includes the interest component of the annual financial lease payment as specified by the Accounting Standards Board (AcSB).

[b]Calculated by dividing the earnings available for common shareholders by the number of shares of common shares outstanding ($170,000 ÷ 100,000 shares = $1.70 per share).

A company will grow over time. In order to support growth, a company requires money. Some, or all, of the EAC is retained by all companies to provide money needed to support current and future growth. A growing company should have higher net income (and EAC) in future years. If so, the value of the company will increase and so too will shareholder wealth.

A key financial item reported by corporations is *earnings per share (EPS)*. EPS is calculated by dividing EAC by the number of common shares outstanding. EPS represents the amount earned on each outstanding common share during the period of time covered by the income statement. For the 2002 fiscal year, Baker Corporation EAC was $170,000. Assuming Baker had 100,000 common shares outstanding, this EAC represents earnings of $1.70 for each common share. Note that the income statement does not indicate whether Baker Corporation paid common share dividends. To determine the dollar amount of dividends paid, the balance sheet can be used.

Example ▼ Auto Corp's net income after tax for the 2003 fiscal year was $68,400,000. Auto Corp has 85,942,000 common shares outstanding. The company paid $9,100,000 of preferred share dividends and $23,200,000 of common share dividends. Earnings available for common shareholders were $59,300,000 ($68,400,000 − $9,100,000), EPS were $0.69 ($59,300,000 ÷ 85,942,000), and reinvested profits were $36,100,000 ($59,300,000 − $23,200,000). The reinvested profits are a source of financing that is used to invest in assets. The assets are required to support increasing sales. When sales increase, so too should profits. When profits increase, the value of common shares increase.

Balance Sheet

balance sheet
Summary statement of the firm's financial position at a given point in time.

The **balance sheet** presents a summary statement of the firm's financial position at a given point in time. The statement balances the firm's *assets* (what it owns) against its financing, which can be either *debt* (what it owes) or *equity* (what was provided by owners). Baker Corporation's balance sheets on December 31 of 2001 and 2002 are presented in Table 2.2. They show a variety of asset, liability (debt), and equity accounts. The basic balance sheet identity or equation is assets = liabilities + equity, A = L + E. This concept is depicted in Figure 2.1. An important distinction is made between short-term and long-term assets and liabilities. The **current assets** and **current liabilities** are *short-term* assets and liabilities. This means that they are expected to be converted into cash (current assets) or paid (current liabilities) within 1 year or less. Managing the level of current assets and the use of current liabilities is termed *working capital management.* All other assets and liabilities, along with shareholders' equity, which is assumed to have an infinite life, are considered *long-term,* or *fixed,* because they are expected to remain on the firm's books for 1 year or more.

Hint
The balance sheet identity or equation is A = L + E, assets = liabilities + equity.

current assets
Short-term assets, expected to be converted into cash within 1 year or less.

current liabilities
Short-term liabilities, expected to be paid within 1 year or less.

As is customary, the assets are listed beginning with the most liquid down to the least liquid. Current assets therefore precede fixed assets. Cash is listed first since it is the most liquid asset—it is cash! *Marketable securities* held by the company represent very liquid short-term investments, such as Government of Canada Treasury bills or term deposits issued by a chartered bank or trust company. Because of their highly liquid nature, marketable securities are frequently viewed as a form of cash. *Accounts receivable* are the total credit sales made by the company that are uncollected as of the date of the balance sheet. *Inventories* include raw materials, work in process (partially finished goods), and finished goods held by the firm. The entry for *gross fixed assets* is the original cost of all fixed (long-term) assets owned by the firm.[3] *Net fixed assets* represent the difference between gross fixed assets and *accumulated amortization*—the running total of the amortization expense recorded each year. For example, the amortiza-

FIGURE 2.1
Basic Balance Sheet Equation
A = L + E

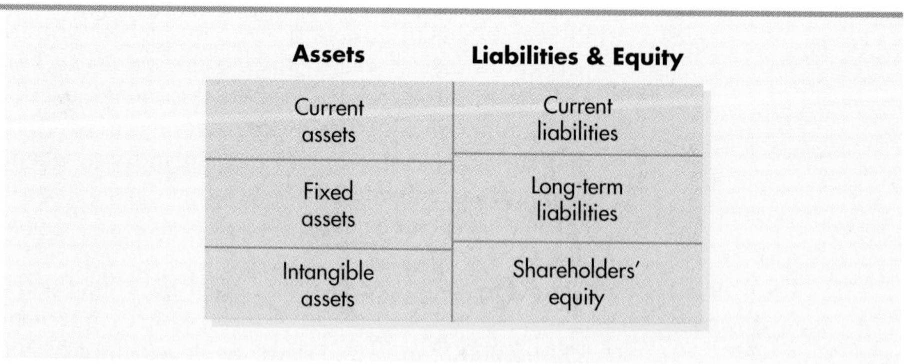

3. For convenience the term *fixed assets* is used throughout this text to refer to what, in a strict accounting sense, is captioned "property, plant, and equipment." This simplification of terminology permits certain financial concepts to be more easily developed.

TABLE 2.2	Baker Corporation Balance Sheets ($000)		
		December 31	
Assets		2001	2002
Current assets			
Cash		$ 300	$ 400
Marketable securities		200	600
Accounts receivable		500	400
Inventories		900	600
Total current assets		$1,900	$2,000
Gross fixed assets (at cost)			
Land and buildings		$1,050	$1,200
Machinery and equipment		800	850
Furniture and fixtures		220	300
Vehicles		80	100
Other (includes certain leases)		50	50
Total gross fixed assets (at cost)		$2,200	$2,500
Less: Accumulated amortization		1,200	1,300
Net fixed assets		$1,000	$1,200
Total assets		$2,900	$3,200
Liabilities and shareholders' equity			
Current liabilities			
Accounts payable		$ 500	$ 700
Line of credit		700	600
Accruals		200	100
Total current liabilities		$1,400	$1,400
Long-term debt		$ 400	$ 540
Total liabilities		$1,800	$1,940
Shareholders' equity			
Preferred shares (4,000 shares outstanding)		$ 100	$ 100
Common shares (95,000 shares outstanding in 2001, 100,000 in 2002)		500	560
Retained earnings		500	600
Total shareholders' equity		$1,100	$1,260
Total liabilities and shareholders' equity		$2,900	$3,200

tion expense recorded by Baker Corporation for the 2002 fiscal year was $100,000 (see Table 2.1). The accumulated amortization as of the beginning of the 2002 fiscal year was $1,200,000. The $100,000 charge for 2002 is added to this amount to calculate accumulated amortization for 2002.

Although not shown in Table 2.2, it is common to also see **intangible assets** on a balance sheet. Intangible assets cannot be seen or touched, but are valuable.

intangible assets
Assets that cannot be seen or touched, but are valuable to a company. Examples include the value of trademarks, patents, franchise rights, and goodwill.

IN PRACTICE

Reporting Profits

How should corporate earnings (profit) be measured and reported? Based on the discussion in the chapter, it seems fairly clear that a company's net income after tax is the measure of corporate earnings. NIAT is simply the difference between sales and all expenses incurred to earn the sales and taxes. This is the basis for earnings reported using Generally Accepted Accounting Principles (GAAP), the guidelines used to prepare financial reports.

Beginning in the late 1990s in North America, however, an approach known as "pro forma" accounting became a common way for companies to report earnings. These earnings are known as "cash or pro forma earnings." These new earnings measures were not recognized by GAAP but their use generally allowed companies that were losing money or not growing earnings quickly enough, when earnings were calculated using GAAP, to report positive results. This is accomplished by ignoring certain expenses and charges.

For example, Nortel Networks, the large Canadian technology company, reports "pro forma net earnings." For the 2001 fiscal year, pro forma net earnings were a loss of US$4.5 billion. But this measure omitted expenses such as amortization of intangibles and special charges. When these expenses were included, as is required under GAAP, Nortel's net income was a US$24.3 billion loss. Toronto-Dominion Bank (TD), one of the big five Canadian banks, reports "operating cash earnings." This measure excludes expenses like restructuring costs and the amortization of goodwill associated with acquisitions. The impact of these exclusions is quite significant. For the 2001 fiscal year, TD reported "operating cash earnings" of $2.158 billion. Net income after tax based on GAAP, however, was much lower, at only $1.383 billion. While both companies reported both numbers in their annual reports, the companies focused on the pro forma number and it became the basis for earnings reports.

Arthur Levitt, the former chair of the U.S. Securities and Exchange Commission, the body that regulates the sale and listing of financial securities, described "cash earnings" as "everything but the bad stuff accounting." While it may seem clear how corporate profits should be measured, users of financial statements must understand how the data is actually presented and be wary.

REFERENCES: Nortel Networks Corporation, 2001 Annual Report; Toronto-Dominion Bank, 2001 Annual Report; "Telling Only Half the Story," *National Post*, February 22, 2002; "TD goes for the cash return," *National Post*, March 29, 2002.

---

goodwill
The amount paid for a business in excess of the value of the assets acquired.

! Hint
Another interpretation of the balance sheet is that on one side are the assets that have been purchased to be used to increase the profit of the firm. The other side indicates how these assets were acquired, either by borrowing or by investing the owners' money.

In some cases, they are some of the most valuable assets owned by a company. Examples of intangibles include the value of trademarks, patents, franchise rights, and goodwill. **Goodwill** is created only when a business is purchased and the amount paid for the business is greater than the value of the assets acquired. The premium paid is an asset termed goodwill. All intangible assets except goodwill are amortized over time as their value declines.

Like assets, the liabilities and equity accounts are listed on the balance sheet from short-term to long-term. Current liabilities are amounts the company must repay within the year. *Accounts payable* are credit purchases made by the company that are unpaid as of the date of the balance sheet. A *line of credit* is a borrowing arrangement between a chartered bank and a company that allows the company to borrow up to a maximum amount at any time. The line of credit is generally repayable on the demand of the bank. The *interest rate* charged on the line of credit is based on the prime rate plus a premium that accounts for the risk the borrower may not repay the amount borrowed. The difference between the interest rate on a loan and the prime rate is the *spread* on the loan. *Notes payable* is another form of short-term loan. It is standard practice to also include in current liabilities the current portion of long-term debt the company must repay over the coming year. *Accruals* are amounts the company owes for a service received or an obligation incurred, but for which payment has not yet been made. (Examples of accruals include taxes due the government and wages due employees.) *Long-term debt* represents debt for which payment is not due in the current year. Common examples of long-term debt are term loans, bonds, and debentures.

Shareholders' equity represents the amount of money invested in the company by the shareholders. The *preferred share entry* shows the total amount raised from the sale of preferred shares ($100,000 for Baker Corporation). Preferred shares are sold for a certain amount, which is sometimes referred to as the "stated value." The **stated value** is an arbitrary amount set by the company when the preferred shares are initially sold to investors. Usual values are $10, $20, $25, and $50 per share. The stated value indicates the actual value of the shares when they are sold. For Baker Corporation, $100,000 of preferred share financing was raised, and from the balance sheet we know 4,000 shares are outstanding. The stated value of the preferred shares was $25 per share ($100,000 ÷ 4,000 shares). Recall from the income statement that Baker Corporation paid preferred share dividends of $10,000. This is $2.50 per share ($10,000 ÷ 4,000 shares). Therefore, the preferred share dividend was 10 percent of the stated value. Preferred shareholders have no ownership interest in the firm. These shareholders are "preferred" in two ways: first, they are entitled to receive dividends before common shareholders; second, if the company goes bankrupt, preferred shareholders receive any payments prior to common shareholders.

Common equity indicates the total investment made by the company's owners. **Common equity** consists of two components: the value of common shares and retained earnings. The entry for **common shares** reflects the total proceeds received from the sale of common shares since the company was formed. This is the amount common shareholders paid when the common shares were sold. As of December 31, 2001, Baker Corporation had sold 95,000 common shares, raising $500,000 of financing. On average, common shareholders paid $5.26 per common share. This does not mean that all of the common shares were sold at the same time, simply that since Baker Corporation was formed, 95,000 common shares have been sold and that $500,000 of financing has been received by the company. During the 2002 fiscal year, Baker Corporation sold 5,000 additional common shares, raising $60,000 of financing. The shares were sold for an average of $12 per share. In Canada, common shares generally have no par value.

Retained earnings represent the running total of all earnings, net of dividends, that have been retained and reinvested in the firm since its inception. It is important to recognize that retained earnings *are not cash* but rather have been utilized to finance the firm's assets. The current year's contribution to retained earnings is termed *reinvested profits*.

---

stated value
The actual value of preferred shares when originally sold to investors.

common equity
The total investment made by the company's owners consisting of the value of common shares plus retained earnings.

common shares
The total proceeds received from the sale of common shares since the company was formed.

retained earnings
The running total of all earnings, net of dividends, that have been retained and reinvested in the firm since its inception.

book value
The total value of common equity at the date of the balance sheet. Book value per share is book value divided by the number of common shares outstanding.

Book value is the total value of common equity as of the date of the balance sheet. Common equity normally consists of the value of common shares plus retained earnings. Book value is sometimes referred to as *net worth*. It can be calculated as $E = A - L$. Instead of total book value, book value per share is often used. Book value per share is total book value divided by the number of common shares outstanding. For Baker Corporation, *book value per share* as of December 31, 2002 is $11.60 ($560,000 + $600,000) / (100,000 common shares).

Baker Corporation's balance sheets show that the firm's total assets increased from $2,900,000 in 2001 to $3,200,000 in 2002. The $300,000 increase was due primarily to the $200,000 increase in net fixed assets. The asset increase in turn appears to have been financed primarily by an increase in long-term debt and common equity, both common shares and reinvested profits. Better insight into these changes can be derived from the statement of cash flows, which we will discuss shortly.

Refer again to Figure 2.1, the basic balance sheet equality. Note that the respective percentages of the various accounts will vary by type of company. Companies in the retail or service sectors carry large amounts of current assets and relatively low investment in fixed assets. Industrial companies have a large investment in fixed assets. Technology companies often have large amounts of intangible assets on their balance sheets. How companies finance their assets (the combination of current and long-term liabilities and equity) also varies by company.

Example ▼ Viat Corporation has current assets of $321,000, fixed assets of $78,000, and intangible assets of $14,000. Viat's long-term debt is $41,000, the value of their common shares is $22,000, while retained earnings total $111,000. What are Viat Corporation's current liabilities?

Since total assets are $413,000, liabilities and equity must also total this amount. Long-term debt is $41,000, while total common equity is $133,000. Therefore, current liabilities must be $239,000. Note that the majority of Viat Corporation's assets are current. The company also uses a large amount of current liabilities to finance assets.

▲

Statement of Retained Earnings

statement of retained earnings
Details the change in retained earnings from the beginning to the end of the fiscal year.

The **statement of retained earnings** details the change in retained earnings from the beginning to the end of the fiscal year. Changes in retained earnings is based on net income after tax. Recall, with NIAT, a company can pay dividends (preferred and/or common) and/or reinvest the net income back into the company. Profits reinvested flow to retained earnings. For Baker Corporation, retained earnings at the beginning of the 2002 fiscal year (which is the same as the end of the 2001 fiscal year) was $500,000. By the end of 2002, the balance was $600,000. What happened? Table 2.3 presents the statement for Baker Corporation for the year ended December 31, 2002. A review of the statement shows that the company began the year with $500,000 in retained earnings and had net income after taxes of $180,000, from which it paid a total of $80,000 in dividends, resulting in year-end retained earnings of $600,000. Thus, the net increase for Baker Corporation was $100,000 ($180,000 net income after taxes minus $80,000 in dividends) during 2002.

TABLE 2.3	**Baker Corporation Statement of Retained Earnings ($000) for the Year Ended December 31, 2002**		
Retained earnings balance (January 1, 2002)			$500
Plus: Net income after taxes (for 2002)			180
Less: Cash dividends (paid during 2002)			
Preferred shares		($10)	
Common shares		(70)	
Total dividends paid			(80)
Retained earnings balance (December 31, 2002)			$600

Statement of Cash Flows

statement of cash flows (SCF)
Provides a summary of the firm's operating, investment, and financing cash flows and reconciles them with changes in its cash and marketable securities during the period of concern.

The fourth financial statement companies must complete is the **statement of cash flows (SCF)**. The SCF provides a summary of inflows and outflows of cash over the same period of time as the balance sheet, typically the fiscal year. The SCF, which prior to 1998 was termed the statement of changes in financial position (SCFP), provides insight into the firm's operating, investment, and financing cash flows and reconciles them with changes in its cash and marketable securities during the period of concern. Since understanding cash flows is vital, the following section fully discusses the concept and presents the process used to develop and analyze a statement of cash flows.

? Review Questions

2–1   What are the characteristics of and what are the main items shown on (a) income statement; (b) balance sheet; and (c) statement of retained earnings? Describe each of the statements.

2–2   Discuss the relationships between the four financial statements discussed in this section of the chapter.

2.2 Completing and Analyzing a Statement of Cash Flows

The statement of cash flows (SCF) documents and details the change in a company's cash and marketable securities over an accounting period, normally a fiscal year. Therefore, as you prepare an SCF, keep in mind that you know the correct answer before you complete the statement. The correct answer is simply the change in cash (and marketable securities), as shown on the balance sheet, from one fiscal year (e.g., 2001) to the next (e.g., 2002).

E x a m p l e ▼ Consider Table 2.2. Here we see that from the 2001 to the 2002 fiscal year for Baker Corporation, cash increased by $100,000 while marketable securities increased by $400,000, a total change of $500,000. Therefore, the SCF for Baker Corporation for the 2002 fiscal year *must* show cash and marketable securities ▲ increasing by $500,000.

Before completing the statement of cash flows for Baker Corporation, however, we will discuss how cash flows through a firm and the classification of cash inflows and outflows.

The Firm's Cash Flows

Hint

Remember that, in finance, cash is king. Income statement profits are good, but they do not pay the bills nor do asset owners accept them in place of cash.

Figure 2.2 illustrates the firm's cash flows. Note that marketable securities, because of their highly liquid nature, are considered the same as cash. Both cash and marketable securities represent a reservoir of liquidity that is *increased by*

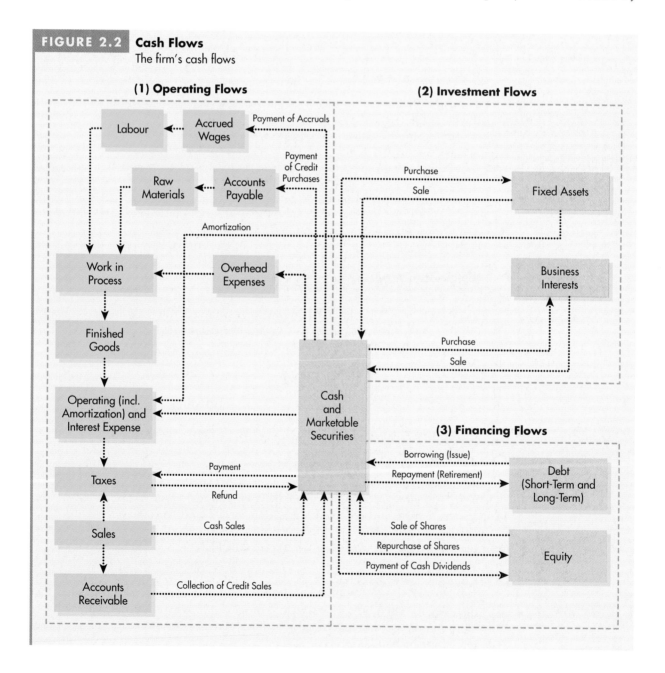

FIGURE 2.2 **Cash Flows**
The firm's cash flows

operating flows
Cash flows directly related to production and sale of the firm's products and services.

investment flows
Cash flows associated with purchase and sale of both fixed assets and business interests.

financing flows
Cash flows that result from debt and equity financing transactions; include issue and repayment of debt, cash inflow from the sale of stock, and cash outflows to pay cash dividends or repurchase stock.

cash inflows and *decreased by cash outflows.* Also note that the firm's cash flows have been divided into (1) operating flows, (2) investment flows, and (3) financing flows. The **operating flows** are cash inflows and outflows directly related to production and sale of the firm's products and services. These flows capture the income statement and changes in current assets and current liabilities (excluding cash and the line of credit) that occurred during the period. **Investment flows** are cash flows associated with purchase and sale of both fixed assets and business interests. Clearly, purchase transactions would result in cash outflows, whereas sales transactions would generate cash inflows. The **financing flows** result from debt and equity financing transactions. Incurring and repaying either short-term debt (line of credit) or long-term debt would result in a corresponding cash inflow or outflow. Similarly, the sale of stock would result in a cash inflow; the payment of cash dividends or repurchase of stock would result in a financing outflow. In combination, the firm's operating, investment, and financing cash flows during a given period will affect the firm's cash and marketable securities balances.

Classifying Inflows and Outflows of Cash

The statement of cash flows in effect summarizes the inflows and outflows of cash during a given period. (Table 2.4 classifies the basic inflows and outflows of cash.) For example, if a firm's accounts payable increased by $1,000 during the year, this change would be an *inflow of cash.* An increase in payables does not result in an inflow in the sense that the firm receives cash. Rather, an increase in payables (or any current liability) means the firm has not paid for a purchase, thereby indirectly providing an inflow. If inventory increased by $2,500, this change would be an *outflow of cash.* The firm acquired inventory resulting in an outflow of cash.

A few additional points can be made with respect to the classification scheme in Table 2.4:

1. A *decrease* in an asset, such as accounts receivable, is an *inflow of cash* because cash that has been tied up in the asset is released and can be used for some other purpose, such as repaying a loan. On the other hand, an *increase* accounts receivable is an *outflow of cash,* because cash is not collected for a sale and is tied up in receivables.
2. Net income after tax is a basic source of cash for a company. But note, non-cash expenses like amortization were deducted when calculating net income.

TABLE 2.4 The Inflows and Outflows of Cash	
Inflows	**Outflows**
Decrease in any asset	Increase in any asset
Increase in any liability	Decrease in any liability
Net income after taxes	Net loss
Amortization and other non-cash expenses	Dividends paid
Sale of shares	Repurchase or retirement of shares

Therefore, for the SCF, these non-cash deductions must be added back to NIAT to determine net cash from operations:

Net cash flow from operations = net income after taxes + non-cash expenses

Note that a firm can have a *net loss* (negative net income after taxes) and still have positive cash flow from operations when non-cash expenses during the period are greater than the net loss. In the statement of cash flows, net income after taxes (or net losses) and non-cash expenses are therefore treated as separate entries.

3. Because amortization is treated as a separate source of cash, only *gross* rather than *net* changes in fixed assets appear on the statement of cash flows. This treatment avoids the potential double counting of amortization.

4. Direct entries of changes in retained earnings are not included on the statement of cash flows. Instead, entries for items that affect retained earnings appear as net income or losses after taxes and dividends are paid.

🔑 Career Key

The cash flow from operations is the concern and responsibility of both *operations* and *financial* personnel. The cash from operations must be positive (operating cash inflows > operating cash outflows) for the firm to survive in the long run.

Developing the Statement of Cash Flows

The statement of cash flows (SCF) can be developed by following a six step process.

Step 1 is to note the correct answer. Remember, when preparing a SCF, you always know the final answer before you begin the process. The bottom line answer is the change in cash (and marketable securities) from the previous year's to the current year's balance sheet. As noted on page 43, for Baker Corporation for the 2002 fiscal year, the SCF *must* show cash and marketable securities increasing by $500,000. The real question that is being answered with the SCF is, *What happened to cash?* Overall, cash changed by a certain amount. The SCF illustrates the inflows and outflows that resulted in the change. The SCF takes information from the income statement and balance sheet and puts it in a format that explains the change in cash.

Step 2 is to calculate net cash from operations. This is based on the income statement. Start with net income after tax. Add to that amortization, the non-cash expense that was deducted from sales to determine net income. This equals net cash from operations.

Example ▼ Baker Corporation's income statement for the 2002 fiscal year (Table 2.1) indicates that NIAT was $180,000 while amortization was $100,000. Net cash from operations is the sum of these two amounts, or $280,000. This is illustrated in ▲ Table 2.5, Baker Corporation's statement of cash flows for the 2002 fiscal year.

Step 3 is to determine the total changes in non-cash working capital accounts. Recall, working capital refers to current assets and current liabilities. For this step, exclude cash (and marketable securities) and current liabilities with a direct cost of financing, accounts such as a line of credit or current portion of long-term debt. Start with the first non-cash current asset. Refer to Table 2.4. If a current asset increases, this is a use of cash. A decrease is a source. The opposite holds for current liabilities.

Example ▼ Review Baker Corporation's balance sheets. Receivables decreased by $100,000 from 2001 to 2002. The company is collecting cash for credit sales in a more timely manner, therefore providing a source of cash. Inventories decrease by $300,000. Baker is selling inventory more rapidly, providing a source of cash. Move on to current liabilities. Accounts payable increase. Baker is making purchases, but not paying for them. This is an indirect source of cash. The line of credit is a costly form of financing and will be considered elsewhere in the SCF. Accruals decrease, Baker is paying off expenses. This is a use of cash. These four items constitute changes in non-cash working capital items. The net impact is a

▲ $500,000 source of cash (see Table 2.5).

Cash from operating activities is the combination of the net cash from operations and the changes in non-cash working capital items. For Baker Corporation, this is $780,000 (see Table 2.5).

TABLE 2.5	Baker Corporation Statement of Cash Flows ($000) for the Year Ended December 31, 2002

A.	**Cash flow from operating activities**			
	NIAT[a]		$180	
Step 2	Plus: Non-cash expense (amortization)		100	
	Net cash from operations		280	
	Plus: Changes in non-cash working capital accounts			
	Decrease in accounts receivable	$100		
	Decrease in inventory	300		
Step 3	Increase in accounts payable	200		
	Decrease in accruals	(100)[b]	500	
	Cash flow from operating activities			$780
B.	**Cash flow from investing activities**			
	Increase in land and buildings		(150)	
	Increase in machinery and equipment		(50)	
Step 4	Increase in furniture and fixtures		(80)	
	Increase in vehicles		(20)	
	Cash flow from investing activities			(300)
C.	**Cash flow from financing activities**			
	Decrease in line of credit		(100)	
	Increase in long-tem debt		140	
Step 5	Increase in common shares[a]		60	
	Payment of preferred dividend[a]		(10)	
	Payment of common dividend		(70)	
	Cash flow from financing activities			20
	Increase in cash and marketable securities during year			500
Steps 1 and 6	Cash and marketable securities at beginning of year			500
	Cash and marketable securities at end of year			$1,000

[a]Note that the change in retained earnings is excluded from the SCF. This change is indirectly considered through the combination of net income after tax and the preferred and common share dividends.

[b]It is customary to use parentheses to denote negative numbers, which in this case is a cash outflow.

Remember for the SCF, both of the main financial statements, the income statement and the balance sheet, are analyzed. This section of the statement has considered most of the income statement, the current assets, and the current liabilities. The remaining sections of the SCF must consider changes in the other items: fixed assets, liabilities with a direct cost, and equity.

Step 4   is to determine cash flow from investing activities. For this step, focus on the gross amount of fixed assets on the balance sheet. Note that the accumulated amortization account is not considered. This is the case since the change in accumulated amortization is the current year's amortization expense and this amount was already considered in Step 2.

Example ▼ Review Baker Corporation's balance sheets (Table 2.2). The gross value of each of the assets with the exception of "other" increased. Each of these changes is a use of cash. The total increase in assets is $300,000. Each of the changes are ▲ reflected on Baker Corporation's SCF for the 2002 fiscal year.

Step 5   is to determine cash flow from financing activities. For this step, focus on the changes in liabilities with a direct cost (both short- and long-term) and equity.

Example ▼ Consider Baker Corporation's balance sheets (Table 2.2). The line of credit decreased by $100,000. Baker repaid a portion of the debt and this is a use of cash. Long-term debt increased by $140,000. The company issued long-term debt raising capital, a source of cash. Preferred equity did not change. Common shares increased by $60,000. As previously discussed, Baker Corporation sold 5,000 common shares to raise financing. Obviously, this is a source of cash. Retained earnings increased by $100,000. Baker reinvested a portion of their NIAT. This appears to be a source of cash, but remember—profits have already been considered in Step 2.

Baker Corporation's NIAT was the first item considered on the SCF. Baker's NIAT was $180,000, yet the change in retained earnings was only $100,000. What happened? Remember, with NIAT a company can pay dividends (both preferred and common) or reinvest. Baker Corporation paid dividends of $80,000 ($10,000 preferred plus $70,000 common) and reinvested the difference. Since the $180,000 was considered in cash flows from operations, dividends must be considered cash outflows from financing activities. This analysis is reflected on Baker Corporation's SCF for 2002. To determine total dividends paid, use the following equation:

▲

Total dividends = NIAT − change in retained earnings

Step 6   is to combine the cash flows from the three sources to determine the change in cash (and marketable securities). In this case, cash and marketable securities increased by $500,000. Compare this with the answer reached in Step 1 of the analysis. Here we noted that cash and marketable securities increased by $500,000. Therefore, we know the SCF is correct. To complete the statement, it is usual to also show cash (and marketable securities) at the beginning and end of the period on the SCF. These are the amounts of cash on the balance sheet. This is included on Baker Corporation's SCF.

Interpreting the Statement

The statement of cash flows allows the financial manager and other interested parties to analyze the firm's cash flow. The manager should pay special attention to both the major categories of cash flow and the individual items of cash inflow and outflow, to assess whether any developments have occurred that are contrary to the company's financial policies. In addition, the statement can be used to evaluate progress toward projected goals. This statement does not match specific cash inflows with specific cash outflows, but it can be used to isolate inefficiencies. For example, increases in accounts receivable and inventories resulting in major cash outflows may signal credit or inventory problems, respectively.

In addition, the financial manager can prepare a statement of cash flows developed from projected, or pro forma, financial statements. This approach can be used to determine whether planned actions are desirable in view of the resulting cash flows.

Example ▼ Analysis of Baker Corporation's statement of cash flows in Table 2.5 does not seem to indicate the existence of any major problems for the company. Its $780,000 of cash provided by operating activities plus the $20,000 provided by financing activities were used to invest an additional $300,000 in fixed assets and to increase cash and marketable securities by $500,000. The individual items of cash inflow and outflow seem to be distributed in a fashion consistent with prudent financial management. The firm seems to be growing: Less than half of its earnings ($80,000 out of $180,000) was paid to shareholders as dividends, and gross fixed assets increased by three times the amount of historic cost written off through amortization expense ($300,000 increase in gross fixed assets versus $100,000 in amortization expense). Major cash inflows were realized by decreasing accounts receivable and inventories (suggesting good management of current assets) and increasing accounts payable, providing a source of financing. The major outflows of cash were to increase cash and marketable securities by $500,000 and thereby improve liquidity and increase fixed assets by $300,000. Note that this latter investment was financed with $100,000 of reinvested profits, $100,000 of long-term debt and common share financing, and $100,000 of amortization. Financing fixed assets with long-term sources of financing is good financial practice. Overall, Baker Corporation's SCF tends to support the fact
▲ that the firm was well managed financially during the period.

An understanding of the basic financial principles presented throughout this text is a prerequisite to the effective interpretation of the statement of cash flows.

? Review Questions

2–3   Describe the overall cash flow through the firm in terms of: (**a**) operating flows; (**b**) investment flows; and (**c**) financing flows.

2–4   Consider changes in specific asset, liability, and equity accounts. Is the change a cash inflow or outflow? Discuss.

2–5   Describe the first four steps in developing the statement of cash flows. How are changes in fixed assets and accumulated amortization treated on this statement?

2–6   What inputs to the statement of cash flows are obtained from the income statement? Explain how the income statement and balance sheet can be used to determine dividends for the period of concern. What other methods can be used to obtain the value of dividends?

2–7   Why are cash and marketable securities the only current assets, and short-term debt with a direct cost the only current liabilities excluded from the change in the non-cash working capital items section on the SCF?

2–8   How can the accuracy of the final statement balance, "net increase (decrease) in cash and marketable securities," be conveniently verified on the SCF?

2–9   How is the statement of cash flows interpreted and used by the financial manager and other interested parties?

   **2.3 Taxation of Business Income**

Businesses, like individuals, must pay taxes on income. Before calculating taxes, businesses can deduct all direct, operating, and financial expenses from sales to arrive at *earnings before taxes (EBT)*. The EBT of sole proprietorships and partnerships is taxed as the income of the individual owners, whereas corporations are viewed as separate legal entities and their EBT is subject to corporate taxes.

Corporations can earn four types of income: active business income, passive income, dividends from other corporations, and capital gains. **Active business income** is income derived from normal business activities—selling a product or a service. **Passive income** is income derived from the property of the corporation such as royalties, rent, interest, or dividends. If the large majority of a firm's income is passive, the company is not considered an active business and is taxed at the highest corporate tax rate. Dividends received from investments in preferred and common shares of other corporations, **intercorporate dividends**, are included as income *but* if the dividends are received from a taxable Canadian corporation, the full amount of the dividend is not taxable. Therefore, the net tax impact of such dividends is nil. This is the case since the income that generates the dividend was already taxed.

Capital gains are generated when a company sells a capital asset for more than its initial purchase price. **Capital assets** include fixed assets that are amortized, land, and financial assets such as common shares, preferred shares, and fixed income securities like bonds. The capital gain is the difference between the selling price and the purchase price. As well, any costs incurred to sell the asset may also be deducted. Capital losses are the opposite of capital gains and are netted against capital gains to determine *net capital gains*. Note, though, that a company cannot claim a capital loss on fixed assets that are amortized. Only 50 percent of net capital gains are taxable. This amount is termed the **taxable capital gain** and is included as income. This capital gains inclusion rate, like all tax regulations, is subject to change and, in fact, it has been changed a number of times over the past 20 years.

active business income
Income derived from the normal business activities of the corporation.

passive income
Income derived from the property of the corporation such as royalties, rent, interest, or dividends.

intercorporate dividends
Dividends received by a corporation from investments in common and preferred shares held in other corporations.

capital gain
The positive difference between the selling price of a capital asset and the asset's original cost plus the costs incurred to sell the asset.

capital asset
A fixed asset that is amortized; land; or financial asset (common shares, preferred shares, and fixed income securities like bonds) held by a corporation.

taxable capital gain
The percentage of net capital gains (the difference between capital gains and losses) that are included as taxable income, currently 50 percent.

Corporate Tax Rates

For corporate tax purposes in Canada, there are two distinct types of corporations: non-manufacturing (general) companies and companies engaged in manu-

Canadian-controlled private corporation (CCPC)
A small corporation whose first $200,000 of taxable income qualifies for the small business deduction offered by the federal government.

facturing and processing. In addition, a company may be a **Canadian-controlled private corporation (CCPC)**, a small corporation whose first $200,000 of taxable income qualifies for a lower tax rate. A CCPC is classified either as a manufacturer and processor or as a non-manufacturing CCPC. Table 2.6 provides the federal tax rate, the provincial tax rates for the ten provinces and three territories, and the combined federal and provincial tax rates for the two types of corporations for the 2001 calendar year. Federal and provincial governments regularly change corporate tax rates. The changes that were announced while this book was being written are reflected in the following discussion. It is highly likely, however, that some of the rates in Table 2.6 will change for the calendar years beginning in 2003.

For the 2001 calendar year, the basic federal tax rate was 38 percent. The federal government allows a 10 percent tax rate reduction for all income earned in a province but then charges a 4 percent surtax on this net rate which makes the effective general (non-manufacturing) federal tax rate 29.12% [i.e., (38% − 10%) × 1.04]. Over the four calendar years beginning in 2001, the general (non-manufacturing) federal rate will fall by 7 percent. For 2001, the general rate falls 1 percent to 28.12 percent. The general federal rate then declines 2 percent each year for the following three years, resulting in general federal tax rates of 26.12 percent for 2002, 24.12 percent for 2003, and 22.12 percent for 2004. Each province in Canada then levies its own tax on the corporation to arrive at the general (non-manufacturing) rates shown in the first numeric column in Table 2.6. The provincial rates range from a low of 13.62 percent in Ontario to a high of 17 percent in Saskatchewan and Manitoba.

Deductions from the Federal Tax Rate

manufacturing and processing deduction
A 7 percent reduction from the general federal tax rate that the government allows manufacturing companies.

The federal government allows three tax rate deductions for certain types of businesses. The first, the **manufacturing and processing deduction**, allows manufacturing and processing businesses a 7 percent reduction from the effective general federal tax rate of 29.12 percent. This reduces the rate for manufacturers to 22.12 percent. This is reflected in the second numeric column in Table 2.6. There is no limit to the amount of taxable income that qualifies for this deduction. As is clear from this column in the table, some provinces also provide a manufacturing and processing deduction. Note the implication of the gradual 7 percent reduction in the general (non-manufacturing) rate. By January 1, 2004, the non-manufacturing and manufacturing federal tax rates will be the same (assuming no other changes in tax regulation occur before then). In other words, the government is gradually phasing out the manufacturing and processing deduction and by 2004, it will no longer exist.

small business deduction
A 16 percent reduction in the general federal tax rate that the government allows CCPCs.

A second deduction is the **small business deduction** of 16 percent applicable to Canadian-controlled private corporations. The 16 percent reduction only applies to the first $200,000 of taxable income and is reduced for corporations with taxable capital of more than $10 million. The impact of this reduction is reflected in the third numeric column of Table 2.6.

CCPC rate reduction
A 7 percent reduction in the general federal tax rate for CCPCs on taxable income of between $200,000 and $300,000.

The third deduction is the **CCPC rate reduction** of 7 percent that applies to taxable income of between $200,000 and $300,000. This 7 percent deduction from the general federal tax rate applies to both non-manufacturing and manufacturing companies. The combined federal and provincial rate for this deduction differs depending on whether the company is a manufacturer or non-manufacturer since some provinces provide a manufacturing deduction. The combined tax rates on this level of taxable income for a CCPC are provided in the final two columns of Table 2.6.

TABLE 2.6	Corporate Tax Rate Schedule for the 2001 Calendar Year (%)

| | | | Canadian-controlled private corporations | | |
| | | | | $ 200,000 to $300,000 | |
	General (non M & P)	Manufacturing and processing	Up to $200,000	M & P	Non M & P
	(1)	(2)	(3)	(4)	(5)
Panel A: federal rate	28.12	22.12	13.12	22.12	22.12
Panel B: provincial rates					
British Columbia	16.50	16.50	4.50	16.50	16.50
Alberta	13.99	13.75	5.25	7.34	7.59
Saskatchewan	17.00	10.00	6.99	10.00	17.00
Manitoba	17.00	17.00	6.00	17.00	17.00
Ontario	13.62	11.75	6.37	6.37	6.37
Quebec	16.51	9.04	9.04	9.04	9.04
New Brunswick	16.00	16.00	4.00	4.00	4.00
Nova Scotia	16.00	16.00	5.00	16.00	16.00
P.E.I.	16.00	7.50	7.50	7.50	16.00
Newfoundland and Labrador	14.00	5.00	5.00	5.00	14.00
Northwest Territories	14.00	14.00	5.00	14.00	14.00
Nunavut	14.00	14.00	5.00	14.00	14.00
Yukon	15.00	2.50	6.00	2.50	15.00
Panel C: combined rates					
British Columbia	44.62	38.62	17.62	38.62	38.62
Alberta	42.11	35.87	18.37	29.46	29.71
Saskatchewan	45.12	32.12	20.11	32.12	39.12
Manitoba	45.12	39.12	19.12	39.12	39.12
Ontario	41.74	33.87	19.49	28.49	28.49
Quebec	44.63	31.16	22.16	31.16	31.16
New Brunswick	44.12	38.12	17.12	26.12	26.12
Nova Scotia	44.12	38.12	18.12	38.12	38.12
P.E.I.	44.12	29.62	20.62	29.62	38.12
Newfoundland and Labrador	42.12	27.12	18.12	27.12	36.12
Northwest Territories	42.12	36.12	18.12	36.12	36.12
Nunavut	42.12	36.12	18.12	36.12	36.12
Yukon	43.12	24.62	19.12	24.62	37.12

NOTE: Panel A provides the federal tax rate; Panel B, the provincial tax rates; while Panel C provides the combined tax rates. Panel C is the overall tax rate for a corporation located in each province.

SOURCE: Tax Facts and Figures for Individuals and Corporations: 2001, PriceWaterhouseCoopers, June 2001. Available at: **www.pwcglobal.com/ ca/eng/main/home/index.html**. Used by permission.

As is clear from this discussion, corporate taxation is complex, with both levels of government building incentives into the system for various types of companies. In addition, many provincial incentives for various corporations are not included in this discussion.

E x a m p l e ▼ Webster Manufacturing's total sales for the fiscal year ending December 31, 2001, were $1,643,200. Direct costs of sales were $1,035,300, operating costs totalled $389,600, while interest payments amounted to $22,800. Webster Manufacturing is a CCPC based in Manitoba. The amounts of federal, provincial, and total taxes Webster will pay for the 2001 fiscal year are calculated below:

	Basic	With capital gain
Sales	$1,643,200	
COGS	1,035,300	
Gross margin	607,900	
Operating expenses	389,600	
EBIT	218,300	
Interest	22,800	
Taxable income	$ 195,500	$221,000 (plus 25,500 taxable capital gain)
Federal taxes: up to $200,000 (13.12%)	$ 25,650	$ 26,240
Between $200,000–$300,000: (22.12%)		4,645
Provincial taxes (6%, 17%)	11,730	15,570 (6% on 1st $200K, 17%
Total taxes	$ 37,380	$ 46,455 on > $200K)
Non-taxable portion of capital gain		$ 25,500
NIAT	$ 158,120	$200,045

Now assume that Webster Manufacturing's controller just realized that the company had also received $31,210 of dividends from Rogers Industries, a taxable Canadian company, on December 31, 2001. Also, on March 31, 2001, Webster sold land that was originally purchased for $32,500 for $86,900. Real estate fees associated with the sale were $3,400. Do these transactions affect the above calculations? The dividends have no impact on the calculation of tax, since they were received from a taxable Canadian corporation. The net impact on taxable income, taxes, and NIAT is nil.

The sale of land results in a capital gain of $51,000 ($86,900 − $32,500 − $3,400).[4] Only one half (50%) of this gain is taxable. Therefore, the net impact would be that taxable income increases by $25,500 to $221,000. Now Webster Manufacturing's taxable income is above $200,000 so federal taxes must be calculated on two amounts: the first $200,000 and then the remaining $21,000. Provincial taxes are based on the total taxable income with the rates taken from Panel B in Table 2.6. Federal taxes total $30,885, while provincial taxes are
▲ $15,570.

---

4. Land is not amortized. Only buildings or structures that are put on the land are amortized.

Tax-Deductible Expenses

In calculating their taxes, corporations are allowed to deduct operating expenses, as well as interest expense. The tax deductibility of these expenses reduces their after-tax cost. The following example illustrates the benefit of tax deductibility.

Example ▼ Companies X and Y each expect in the coming year to have earnings before interest and taxes of $200,000. Company X during the year will have to pay $30,000 in interest; Company Y has no debt and therefore will have no interest expense. Calculations of the earnings after taxes for these two firms are as follows:

	Company X	Company Y
Earnings before interest and taxes	$200,000	$200,000
Less: Interest expense	30,000	0
Earnings before taxes	$170,000	$200,000
Less: Taxes (40%)	68,000	80,000
Net income after taxes	$102,000	$120,000
Difference in earnings after taxes	$18,000	

The data demonstrate that whereas Company X had $30,000 more interest expense than Company Y, Company X's net income after taxes are only $18,000 less than those of Company Y ($102,000 for Company X versus $120,000 for Company Y). This difference is attributable to the fact that Company X's $30,000 interest expense deduction provided a tax savings of $12,000 ($68,000 for Company X versus $80,000 for Company Y). This amount can be calculated directly by multiplying the tax rate by the amount of interest expense (0.40 × $30,000 = $12,000). Similarly, the $18,000 *after-tax cost* of the interest expense can be calculated directly by multiplying one minus the tax rate by the amount of ▲ interest expense [(1 − 0.40) × $30,000 = $18,000].

The tax deductibility of certain expenses reduces their actual (after-tax) cost to the profitable firm. Note that both for accounting and tax purposes *interest is a tax-deductible expense, whereas dividends are not.* Because dividends are not tax deductible, their after-tax cost is equal to the amount of the dividend. Thus, a $30,000 cash dividend would have an after-tax cost of $30,000.

Amortization

Other types of tax-deductible expenses also provide a benefit to a company. Recall the statement of cash flows. One of the major components of cash flows from operations was the non-cash expense amortization. Amortization is the systematic expensing of a portion of the cost of a fixed asset against sales. This expense is associated with capital assets, assets that are expected to have a life greater than one year and whose value is expected to decline through use and/or obsolescence. Expenditures on these assets are not expensed, rather they are capitalized and the expenditure is written off over time via the amortization expense.

This yearly expense: (1) allocates the cost of the asset over its useful life; and (2) recognizes that the asset has declined in value.

Example ▼ Ratheson Ltd. purchases a new machine for $100,000 that has an expected life of 10 years. A simple way to calculate amortization is the straight-line method. With this method, amortization is based on the cost of the asset divided by the expected life of the asset (in years). For Ratheson Ltd., the yearly amortization ▲ would be $10,000 ($100,000 ÷ 10 years).

Capital Cost Allowance (CCA)

capital cost allowance (CCA)
The tax term for amortization. Companies must use the CCA method for tax purposes.

The amortization expense may be used for financial reporting purposes; however, for tax purposes, the Canada Customs and Revenue Agency (CCRA) requires companies to use **capital cost allowance** (CCA). CCA is simply the tax version of amortization. Because the objectives of financial reporting are sometimes different from those of tax legislation, a firm often will use different amortization methods for financial reporting than those required for tax purposes. Tax laws are used to accomplish economic goals such as providing incentives for business investment in certain types of assets, whereas the objectives of financial reporting are quite different. Keeping two different sets of records for these two different purposes is legal and is a practice of all corporations. CCA is explored in more detail in Chapter 12.

non-cash expense
Expenses deducted from sales on the income statement that do not involve an actual outlay of cash during the period.

The benefit to a company of amortization (CCA) is associated with the concept of cash flows discussed in this chapter and in Chapter 1. Recall from Chapter 1 that the primary emphasis of financial management is on cash flows, not profits. Amortization (CCA) is deducted from sales when calculating taxable income. *But*, as a **non-cash expense**, the deduction does not involve an actual outlay of cash during the period, it reduces taxes but no cash has actually been used. Amortization (CCA) reduces net income (profits) but increases cash flow.

Example ▼ Consider two companies A and B, with the same income before amortization and taxes. Company A has an amortization (CCA) expense of $80,000; Company B does not. What are the two companies' NIAT and cash flows?

	Company A	Company B
Income before amortization and taxes	$400,000	$400,000
Amortization	80,000	0
Earnings before taxes	$320,000	$400,000
Taxes (32%)	102,400	128,000
Net income after taxes	$217,600	$272,000
Cash flow	$297,600	$272,000

What is the benefit of amortization (CCA)? Since Company A has lower NIAT than does B, isn't B in a better financial position? It depends on what is being measured. Company A has a lower NIAT *but only because* the company was able to deduct the non-cash expense. The benefit of the non-cash expense is the reduction in taxes. Note that Company A pays $25,600 less in taxes than

tax shield
The tax savings associated with being able to claim non-cash expenses like amortization (CCA).

does Company B. Company A's ability to claim the non-cash expense actually benefitted the company—the company paid lower taxes. These lower taxes provide a benefit in terms of higher cash flows. The amortization (CCA) expense provides a **tax shield**, tax savings associated with being able to claim non-cash expenses, that adds to a company's cash flow. The tax shield is calculated as: (non-cash expense × tax rate). Cash flows can be calculated in two ways:

(1) NIAT + non-cash expense;

(2) (income before amortization and taxes) × (1 − T) + (Amortization × T), where T is the company's tax rate.

For Company B, the cash flow is the same as NIAT, since there was no non-cash expense. For Company A the cash flow was $297,600. This could be calculated as:

(1) $217,600 + $80,000 = $297,600;

▲ (2) $400,000 × (1 − 0.32) + $80,000 (0.32) = $272,000 + $25,600

For Baker Corporation, discussed earlier in this chapter, net cash from operations for 2002 totalled $280,000. Using the above equations, this is calculated as: (3) cash flows = $180,000 + $100,000 = $280,000; (4) cash flow = ($300,000 + $100,000) × (1 − 0.40) + $100,000 (0.40) = $240,000 + $40,000 = $280,000.

? Review Questions

2–10   Briefly define active and passive income and capital gains and describe the tax treatment of each.

2–11   Why does the federal government allow a corporation to exclude from taxable income dividends received from taxable Canadian corporations?

2–12   Why might certain provinces have lower corporate tax rates than others?

2–13   What deduction from the general federal tax rate does the federal government provide manufacturing and processing businesses? Why would the government provide this deduction to a manufacturing and processing business, but not a service business?

2–14   What deduction from the general federal tax rate does the federal government provide small businesses? Why would the government provide this deduction to a small business?

2–15   Discuss the changes in the general federal tax rate that will occur over the four years from 2001 to 2004. What is the impact of these changes? Discuss the change in federal government thinking that these changes imply.

2–16   What benefit results from the tax deductibility of certain corporate expenses? Consider items such as amortization, interest, and dividend payments.

2-17   In what sense does amortization act as a cash inflow? How can NIAT be adjusted to determine net cash from operations?

2.4 The Annual Report

Every corporation has many and varied uses for the standardized records and reports of its financial activities. On a regular basis, financial statements are prepared for internal purposes. Management uses these statements to monitor the company's performance looking for ways to build on strengths and reduce weaknesses. Ensuring the company is generating sufficient cash flow to meet ongoing obligations is a key task for the financial managers. Periodically, reports must be prepared for regulators, creditors (lenders), and owners.

Regulators, such as provincial securities commissions and stock exchanges, enforce the accurate disclosure of corporate financial data. Creditors use financial data to evaluate the firm's credit-worthiness or ability to meet scheduled debt payments. Owners use financial data to judge whether management is running the company to benefit shareholders and to decide whether to buy, sell, or hold its shares. Management must be concerned with regulatory compliance and ensure the company's creditors and owners are satisfied with the financial performance of the company.

generally accepted accounting principles (GAAP)
The practice, procedure, and standards used to prepare and maintain financial records, reports, and statements.

The guidelines used to prepare and maintain financial records, reports, and statements are known as **generally accepted accounting principles** (GAAP). These accounting standards specify how transactions and other events are to be recognized, measured, presented, and disclosed in financial statements. The objective of such standards is to meet the needs of users of financial statements by providing the information needed to make informed decisions. The Canada Business Corporations Act and provincial corporations and securities legislation generally require companies to prepare financial statements for their shareholders in accordance with GAAP. The **Accounting Standards Board** (AcSB), part of the Canadian Institute of Chartered Accountants (CICA), is the accounting profession's rule-setting body that authorizes accounting practices and principles.

Accounting Standards Board (AcSB)
The accounting profession's rule-setting body, part of the CICA, that authorizes generally accepted accounting principles (GAAP).

annual report
The report that corporations must provide to common shareholders that summarizes and documents the firm's financial activities during the past year.

Companies must provide a report to shareholders each year that summarizes and documents for shareholders the company's financial activities during the year. This official report is known as the **annual report**. Annual reports for Canadian companies that are publicly traded are often lengthy documents providing many photos together with comments from management and, of course, the companies' financial statements. Publicly traded companies are those whose common shares are listed and traded on a stock exchange. The best known stock exchange in Canada is the Toronto Stock Exchange (TSX). A typical annual report provides the following types of information to shareholders.

Letter to Shareholders

letter to shareholders
Typically, the first element of the annual report following a summary of the company's financial performance for the year, and the direct communication from senior management to the firm's owners.

The **letter to shareholders**, typically found after a summary of the company's financial performance for the year, provides direct communication from senior management to the company's common shareholders. Generally, the letter is from the company's CEO or the chair of the company's board of directors, the group that represents the shareholders to senior management. The letter describes the events that senior management considers to have had the greatest impact on the firm during the year. In addition, the letter generally discusses management philosophy, strategies, and actions as well as plans for the coming year and their anticipated effects on the firm's financial condition. The letter could be viewed as a summary of the annual report, providing an overview of the company's performance and key actions taken during the previous fiscal year as well as the organization's overall plans for the future. The letter, generally, tries to present a positive image for the company putting the previous fiscal year's performance in as positive a light as possible.

Management's Discussion and Analysis

Management's Discussion and Analysis (MD&A)
MD&A is a supplemental report that allows the reader to look at the company through the eyes of management by providing a current and historical analysis of the business of the company.

Since 1989, all Canadian annual reports must contain a section termed **Management's Discussion and Analysis (MD&A)** of financial performance. MD&A is a supplemental section that analyzes and explains the company's financial results. The intent of the MD&A disclosure requirement is to give the reader the opportunity to look at the company through the eyes of management by providing a current and historical analysis of the business of the company. For the report, management is required to discuss recent financial results and the dynamics of the business and to analyze the financial statements. The report also reviews significant developments that affected the company's performance. Coupled with the financial statements, this information enables readers to better assess the company's performance, position, and future prospects.

MD&A must provide an analysis of the company's financial condition, cash flows, and results of operations for the most recently completed fiscal year, and a comparison to the previous year. The company is expected to describe trends, discuss results for separate business units, consider internal factors and external economic and industry factors affecting the company, explain changes in the company's financial condition and results of operation, and discuss and explain major changes in the direction of the business.

For financial condition, the focus of MD&A is on material information on operations with particular emphasis on liquidity, capital resources, and known trends, commitments, and events. MD&A discusses the ability of the company to generate adequate amounts of cash needed to support planned growth. Qualitative and quantitative risk factors that are expected to affect the company's business, financial condition, or results of operations must be considered. Planned capital expenditures for the upcoming fiscal year must be described and the anticipated cost and source of the funds indicated.

Financial statements are a necessary but insufficient means for measuring and reporting on overall performance. MD&A provides management the opportunity to flesh out and explain the nature of the company, its financial performance, research and development activities, and plans for the future. The report is an opportunity for the company to communicate with those who assess the company's value in the financial markets and is a critical component of a company's annual report. Essentially, this section of the annual report gives management the opportunity to present any type of relevant information they wish.

Financial Statements

Following the first two sections will be the four key financial statements required by regulators and discussed in Section 2.1: the income statement, balance sheet, statement of retained earnings, and statement of cash flows. Annual reports must contain the four financial statements for at least the two most recent years of operation, although many companies provide up to ten years of historical results. Prior to the financial statements are two short reports. The first is "Management's Report" outlining management's responsibility for preparing the annual report. Following this is the "Auditors' Report" describing how the auditor completed the audit of the company's financial records. The auditor must also indicate whether the financial statements presented are "free of material misstatement" and fairly present the financial position of the company.

Following the financial statements are the *Notes to Financial Statements*, an important source of information on the accounting policies, procedures, calculations, and transactions underlying entries in the financial statements. The notes to the financial statements are an integral part of the financial statements. After the notes, selected financial data for the most recent eight quarters are also included, as are historical financial data for the past five to ten years. The historic data are often a summary of key operating statistics and financial ratios (discussed in Chapter 3). Graphs of key variables and ratios are also commonly included in this section of the annual report.

Summary

Companies should view their annual report not as a requirement, but as an important vehicle for influencing readers' perceptions of the company. Good reports provide the basic information but also discuss areas such as new product development, market share, the workforce, and prospects for the future. They discuss the performance of the company's business units, providing analysis of the key issues facing the company. Operational and financial goals linked to the company's mission and strategic plan are included. Good reports provide an overview of actual performance compared to the company's stated goals and strategic initiatives.

IN PRACTICE

And the Winner is . . .

In Canada, there are about 2,100 companies with shares listed on one of the two Canadian stock exchanges: The Toronto Stock Exchange (TSX) and the TSX Venture Exchange. Each of these companies must produce an annual report to shareholders. Aside from providing the four principal financial statements, all annual reports must provide insight into the company's operation, management procedures, and industry position. Many of today's reports are packed with concise information, attention-grabbing graphics and colours, and interactive CD-ROMs, which are a welcome depar-

ture from the blandness of reports of the past. But even with all the jazz, the reports shouldn't deviate from their main purpose: to communicate to shareholders clear, understandable, and useful company information. What separates an excellent, eye-opening annual report from one that simply provides basic information in an uninspired manner?

The *National Post* and the Canadian Institute of Chartered Accountants (CICA) sponsor a competition that picks winning annual reports in 20 categories. The Annual Report Awards program has been operating for ▶

IN PRACTICE

(Continued)

over 50 years. The purpose is to highlight the leaders across all industries in corporate reporting in Canada, to recognize the best reporting models in Canada, and to strengthen corporate reporting in general. All reports are reviewed by three judges who consider the highlights or overview section, the letter to shareholders, financial statement information, and management's discussion and analysis (MD&A) of performance.

In total, 20 gold awards of excellence are presented. In addition, 17 silver and bronze awards are also presented. The 2001 annual report awards were announced in December 2001. These awards were for annual reports for the 2000 fiscal year. The winner of the Overall Award of Excellence for the best annual report in Canada was the Bank of Nova Scotia. Other winners were Mark's Work Wearhouse Ltd. and TransCanada Pipelines Limited for excellence in corporate governance, TransAlta Corporation and Shell Canada for excellence in environmental and sustainability reporting, CN for the Domtar Award of Excellence in Design, and Barrick Gold Corporation, the inaugural winner of the TSE Award of Excellence in Electronic Disclosure.

Numerous factors influence the awards. The following comments from judges provide some insight into what is deemed important:

- The annual report is sophisticated, professional, yet friendly and straightforward in delivering an understanding of the company and industry.

- The report exudes honesty and grabs the reader's attention in a crafty opening section.
- The Letter to the Shareholders is precise, without an overload of distracting details.
- The report flows well and contains all the necessary information that investors need.
- The design is appealing, with easy-to-find-and-recognize sections.
- The logical layout of MD&A—complemented by colour-highlighted callouts, maps, and charts—adds to the flow and understanding.
- The financial statements, 11-year statistical review, and information on operations and products are well presented.
- This annual report is deemed superior to other companies' reports because of its excellence in readability and the focused message.

More details concerning the awards and an updated list of winners for the most recent year are available at the following Web site: **www.cica.ca**. Click on site search link at the bottom of the page and type "annual report awards" in the dialog box.

REFERENCES: Canadian Institute of Chartered Accountants of Canada and the *National Post*, "2001 Annual Report Awards," December 2001; "Scotiabank receives the Award of Excellence at the 50th Annual Report Awards," December 6, 2001; see: **www.newswire.ca/releases/December2001/ 06/c4666.html**.

? Review Questions

2–18   What are generally accepted accounting principles (GAAP), and who authorizes them? What role do regulators play in the financial reporting of Canadian companies?

2–19   List and describe the contents of a typical annual report for a publicly traded corporation.

2–20   What is the purpose of Management's Discussion and Analysis (MD&A) in an annual report? Why would regulators require companies include MD&A in the annual report?

2–21   What does the term "publicly traded corporation" mean?

2.5 Key Financial Concepts: The Language of Finance

For many introductory courses in functional areas like finance, marketing, or operations management, learning the language of the discipline is a vital step to understanding the topics discussed. Imagine a mathematics student not understanding words and concepts like model, probability, factors, functions, matrices, calculus, or logarithms. Without knowledge of some of the basic concepts of a subject, it would be impossible to understand applications of the concepts or advanced material based on the concepts. A foundation level of understanding in a discipline must be formed that can then be built upon. This section of the chapter provides a brief overview of some key financial concepts and introduces some key words in the language of finance. These concepts are covered in much greater detail later in the book.

Basic Accounting

A complete understanding of basic accounting and the four key financial statements is vital in order to become comfortable with managerial finance. Students should know the characteristics of each statement and all of the major items that appear on the statement, understand the relationships between the statements, and be able to work with the statements to determine missing data. At this point in the chapter, all readers should have this level of understanding.

Financial Forecasting

financial forecasting
The process used to estimate a company's requirement for financing for a future time period.

Financial forecasting is the process used to estimate a company's requirement for financing for a future time period. Financing is required to invest in assets. Assets are necessary to support increases in sales and profits. Generally, financial forecasting is associated with expected sales growth. A key part of the process is to forecast the company's financial statements. The future time period may be short term, for example, the next quarter or next year, or long term, forecasts for the next five to ten years. The key outputs of the financial forecasting process are the amount of funds the company will require to operate over the forecast period and the forecasted financial statements.

Financial Markets

Financial markets provide a forum where *savers of funds* and *users of funds* can transact business. These two groups must be able to make an exchange that is expected to be beneficial to both parties. Individuals, governments, and business organizations are all involved in the financial markets. In the financial markets, cash moves from savers to users, and users provide a financial security in return.

The financial security indicates the compensation the saver will receive in return for providing the funds. The compensation may be a rate of return on the funds, a promise to repay the funds at some point in the future, and/or a right of ownership. For financial markets to work, financial institutions, intermediaries that allow for the efficient and low cost transfer of the savings of individuals, governments, and business for financial securities, are necessary. These intermediaries include institutions like banks and investment dealers.

There are two distinct financial markets: the money market and the capital market. Debt securities that will mature within one year are traded in the **money market**. The principal money market security is Government of Canada treasury bills, or t-bills as they are more commonly known. In the **capital market**, long-term debt securities, like bonds and debentures, and preferred and common shares are traded. The term "market" may be misleading to describe this trading. There is no physical market for much of the trading of financial securities that occur in the financial markets. The "market" for all debt securities is the communication system that exists between the traders of these financial securities. All trading of these securities occurs in cyberspace, the networks that connect computers.

A second way to subdivide financial markets is by the nature of the transaction. A financial security must be "created," and this occurs in the primary market. The **primary market** is the market where a financial security is initially issued and where the issuer (the organization selling the financial security) receives the proceeds from the sale of the security to savers (investors). Again, there is no physical location for the primary market; the market exists in cyberspace. Once the security is created, a second market must exist to allow the initial purchaser of the security an opportunity to trade this and other securities.

This is the secondary market. The **secondary market** allows the owner of a previously created financial security to sell the security, to buy more of this or other securities, or for a buyer to express an interest in acquiring a financial security. This interaction between interested buyers and sellers in the secondary market sets the price of financial securities. As demand for a particular financial security increases, so too will the price. As more holders of a particular financial security wish to sell, prices will decline. The secondary market for all debt securities is in cyberspace.

For preferred and common shares, however, there is an actual, physical market. This is the stock market, which is also referred to as a stock exchange. A **stock exchange** allows investors to buy and sell preferred and common shares. The largest stock exchange in Canada is the Toronto Stock Exchange (TSX). The various stock exchanges in a country constitute the stock market. Millions of shares are traded each day on the various stock exchanges around the world. The company whose shares are being traded is not involved. All of these trades are between investors.

Risk/Return Trade-off

Most financial decisions entail a **risk/return trade-off**; that is, the return expected depends on the amount of risk taken. To receive a high rate of return, a high degree of risk must be taken. Those wishing to take less risk must be satisfied with a lower return. Individuals are assumed to be **risk-averse**. To be encouraged

money market
The market where debt securities that will mature within one year are traded.

capital market
The market that trades long-term debt securities and common and preferred equity securities.

primary market
Market in which financial securities are initially issued and where the issuer receives the proceeds from the sale of the financial security.

secondary market
The market that allows the owner of a previously created financial security to sell this security, to buy more of this or other securities, or for a buyer to express an interest in acquiring a financial security.

stock exchange
An actual, physical secondary market that allows investors to buy and sell preferred and common shares.

risk/return trade-off
The return expected depends on the amount of risk taken.

risk-averse
The attitude toward risk in which a higher return would be expected if risk increased.

to take more risk, a higher return must be offered or expected. A risk/return trade-off is associated with all financial decisions a company must make. For example, decisions regarding a company's production capacity, the level of investment in assets, and the mix of short-term debt, long-term debt, and equity financing used in the business all involve a risk/return trade-off. The **required rate of return** on an investment is based on a minimum acceptable return plus a premium for the level of risk taken. The greater the risk of loss, the greater the required risk premium and thus return.

Interest is the return paid on debt financing. The **interest rate** is the cost of money. Investors lending money to the Canadian government in the form of short-term debt (treasury bills) or long-term debt (bonds) will expect to receive a lower rate of interest (lower return) than if they lent their money to a corporation regardless of its size or perceived level of safety. A corporation is always more risky than the federal government. Therefore, the expected return is always higher. The greater the risk, the higher the expected return.

Cost of Capital

A company raises financing using a certain mix of debt and common equity financing. This is the company's capital structure. Investors providing the financing require a specific rate of return that compensates for the risk of the financial security. When lending money, various conditions are stated, one of which is the cost of the money: the interest rate on the loan. The providers of debt financing must be paid the stated rate of interest or they are entitled to force the firm into bankruptcy. This right reduces the risk of debt for the lender and thus the return required. On the other hand, the return expected on common equity is based on net income after tax. Common shareholders are entitled to receive the residual income of the company. Since there is no guarantee that a company will generate a profit, the risk of common equity is much higher than debt and so too is the return required.

Therefore, a company will be financed with a certain mix of lower cost debt and higher cost common equity. The percentage of debt multiplied by its cost is added to the percentage of equity multiplied by its cost to determine the company's overall cost of financing. This is the **cost of capital**, the cost to the company of raising additional financing in the percentages that are considered best for it.

Capital Budgeting

Companies raise financing from both internal and external sources. Internal sources include reinvested profits and amortization. This was considered in the discussion of the statement of cash flows. External sources are debt, both short- and long-term, preferred share, and common share financing. With the combined financing, the company will invest in assets. **Capital budgeting** is the process of analyzing the investment in assets with an expected life greater than one year. These assets may be a new piece of equipment, a new manufacturing facility, or a new product. These assets must be expected to provide a return that compensates for the cost of the financing that was used to acquire them. This is the basis of capital budgeting, ensuring that the return expected from the acquisition of an asset compensates for the cost of the funds invested in the asset. The cost of the funds, of course, is based on the risk of the financial security.

---

required rate of return
The minimum return required given the risk of an investment; the greater the risk of loss, the greater the required return.

interest
The return paid on debt financing.

interest rate
The cost of money. The greater the risk of the debt security, the higher the interest rate.

cost of capital
The overall cost to a company of a mix of debt and common equity financing.

capital budgeting
The process of analyzing the investment in assets with an expected life greater than one year.

? Review Questions

2–22 Define each of the following key financial concepts:
a. financial forecasting.
b. financial markets including their main function and types.
c. stock exchange.
d. risk/return trade-off.
e. required rate of return.
f. interest rates.
g. cost of capital.
h. cost of debt and equity financing.
i. capital budgeting.

SUMMARY

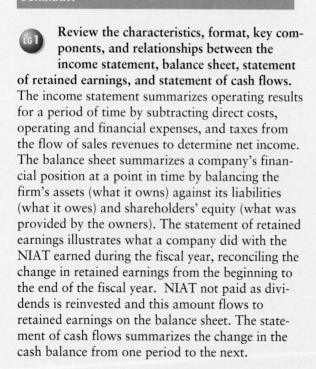

LG1 **Review the characteristics, format, key components, and relationships between the income statement, balance sheet, statement of retained earnings, and statement of cash flows.** The income statement summarizes operating results for a period of time by subtracting direct costs, operating and financial expenses, and taxes from the flow of sales revenues to determine net income. The balance sheet summarizes a company's financial position at a point in time by balancing the firm's assets (what it owns) against its liabilities (what it owes) and shareholders' equity (what was provided by the owners). The statement of retained earnings illustrates what a company did with the NIAT earned during the fiscal year, reconciling the change in retained earnings from the beginning to the end of the fiscal year. NIAT not paid as dividends is reinvested and this amount flows to retained earnings on the balance sheet. The statement of cash flows summarizes the change in the cash balance from one period to the next.

LG2 **Analyze a company's cash flows and develop and interpret the statement of cash flows.** The SCF provides a summary of inflows and outflows of cash over the same time period as the balance sheet, typically the fiscal year. The statement is divided into operating, investment, and financing cash flows. The statement of cash flows can be developed by following a six-step process. The first step is to note the correct answer: the change in cash (and marketable securities) from the previous year's to the current year's balance sheet. The next five steps determine the cash flows from the three categories—operating, investment, and financing—and the net overall change in cash.

LG3 **Introduce the basics of corporate taxation in Canada.** A corporation's earnings are subject to tax. Businesses can deduct all direct, operating, and financial expenses from sales to arrive at earnings before taxes. For corporate tax purposes in Canada, there are two distinct types of corporations: non-manufacturing (general) companies and companies engaged in manufacturing and processing. In addition, a company can be a Canadian-controlled private corporation (CCPC). Corporate tax rates vary by type of corporation and province of operation, but for the 2001 calendar year, rates range from 17 percent to 45 percent. (For many examples in this book, tax rates of between 20 percent and 40 percent are assumed.) Dividends received from investments in taxable Canadian corporation are tax-exempt while only one-half of capital gains are subject to tax.

LG4 **Understand how the tax deductibility of expenses reduce their actual, after-tax cost to a profitable company.** An expense of $100,000 for a company with a 30 percent tax rate has an actual cost of only $70,000. This is the case since the expense is deductible from income; therefore, the tax system reduces the actual, after-tax cost by the amount of the expense multiplied by the tax rate, in this example, $30,000.

 Discuss and illustrate the tax version of amortization, capital cost allowance (CCA), and how CCA increases a company's cash flows. Amortization, or the allocation of the cost of an asset over its useful life, is the most common type of non-cash expense. For tax purposes, however, companies are required to use capital cost allowance (CCA). CCA is simply the tax version of amortization. Since amortization (or CCA) is a non-cash expense, the effect is to increase a company's cash flows. Amortization, and other non-cash expenses, are added back to the company's net income after tax to determine cash flows from operations. Since non-cash expenses reduce taxable income without an actual cash outflow, they are a source of cash to the company.

 Review the information provided in a publicly traded company's annual report to shareholders. Companies must provide a report to shareholders each year that summarizes and documents for shareholders the company's financial activities during the year. This official report is known as the annual report. Annual reports for many large Canadian companies are lengthy documents providing a large quantity of information. A typical annual report provides valuable information to shareholders including: a summary of financial results, the letter to shareholders, management's discussion and analysis (MD&A) of financial performance, and the four key financial statements: income statement, balance sheet, statement of retained earnings, and statement of cash flows. Following the statements are notes that are an integral part of and provide more details regarding the financial statements.

 Discuss key concepts in finance and review the language of finance. For many introductory courses in functional areas like finance, learning the language of the discipline is vital in order to understand the topics discussed. Without knowledge of some of the basic concepts in a subject, it is very difficult to understand applications of the concepts or advanced material based on the concepts. A foundation level of understanding in a discipline must be formed that can then be built upon. Some of the key financial concepts and words in the language of finance to know include: basic accounting and the four key financial statements, financial forecasting, financial markets, risk/return trade-off, cost of capital, and capital budgeting.

SELF-TEST PROBLEMS   **(Solutions in Appendix B)**

 ST 2–1   Reviewing the balance sheet   For the 2002 fiscal year Alpha Company had current assets of $200,000, fixed assets of $525,000, intangible assets of $65,000, long-term debt of $250,000, and $175,000 of total common equity.
a. What balance sheet account is missing from Alpha Company's balance sheet? What is the missing amount?
b. During the 2003 fiscal year, Alpha Company sold 5,000 common shares for $8 each, earned NIAT of $105,000, and paid common share dividends of $22,500. What changes would this make to the balance sheet?
c. If Alpha Company also repaid $25,000 of long-term debt during 2003, what change would this make to the balance sheet?
d. Given the changes in parts b and c, what other changes would have to occur to the balance sheet for the 2003 fiscal year?

 ST 2–2   Corporate taxes   Montgomery Enterprises, a Canadian-controlled private corporation (CCPC) located in Quebec, manufactures ribblots. For the December 31, 2001 fiscal year, Montgomery Enterprises had earnings before interest and

taxes (EBIT) of $180,000. The company's interest expense was $42,400. During the year the company sold common shares that it held in another company for $260,000. The original cost of the shares was $112,500. Expenses incurred in selling the shares totalled $6,200. The impact of the sale of shares is not included in the EBIT.

a. Did Montgomery Enterprises realize a capital gain during the year? If so, what was the amount? What is the amount of the taxable capital gain?
b. What was Montgomery Enterprises' total taxable income for the year?
c. Using Table 2.6, calculate the company's total taxes payable and NIAT for 2001.
d. If Montgomery Enterprises was not a CCPC, what would be the total taxes payable and NIAT for 2001?
e. For part **d**, what is the after-tax cost of the interest payments Montgomery Enterprises made in 2001?

PROBLEMS

WARM-UP   **2–1**   **Reviewing basic financial statements**   The income statement for the year ended December 31, 2002, the balance sheets for December 31, 2001 and 2002, and the statement of retained earnings for the year ended December 31, 2002, for Technica, Inc., are given on this and the following page. Briefly discuss the form and informational content of each of these statements.

Income Statement
Technica, Inc.
for the year ended December 31, 2002

Sales revenue		$600,000
Less: Cost of goods sold		460,000
Gross margin		$140,000
Less: Operating expenses		
General and administrative expense	$30,000	
Amortization expense	30,000	
Total operating expenses		60,000
Operating earnings (EBIT)		$ 80,000
Less: Interest expense		10,000
Earnings before taxes		$ 70,000
Less: Taxes		27,100
Earnings available for common shareholders (EAC)		$ 42,900
Earnings per share (EPS)		$2.15

Balance Sheets
Technica, Inc.

	December 31	
Assets	2001	2002
Cash	$ 16,000	$ 15,000
Marketable securities	8,000	7,200
Accounts receivable	42,200	34,100
Inventories	50,000	82,000
Total current assets	$116,200	$138,300
Land and buildings	$150,000	$150,000
Machinery and equipment	190,000	200,000
Furniture and fixtures	50,000	54,000
Other	10,000	11,000
Total gross fixed assets	$400,000	$415,000
Less: Accumulated amortization	115,000	145,000
Net fixed assets	$285,000	$270,000
Total assets	$401,200	$408,300
Liabilities and shareholders' equity		
Accounts payable	$ 49,000	$ 57,000
Line of credit	16,000	13,000
Accruals	6,000	5,000
Total current liabilities	$ 71,000	$ 75,000
Long-term debt	$160,000	$150,000
Shareholders' equity		
Common shares (20,000 shares outstanding in 2001, 19,500 in 2002)	$120,000	$110,200
Retained earnings	50,200	73,100
Total shareholders' equity	$170,200	$183,300
Total liabilities and shareholders' equity	$401,200	$408,300

Statement of Retained Earnings
Technica, Inc.
for the year ended December 31, 2002

Retained earnings balance (January 1, 2002)	$50,200
Plus: Net income after taxes (for 2002)	42,900
Less: Cash dividends (paid during 2002)	(20,000)
Retained earnings balance (December 31, 2002)	$73,100

WARM-UP 2–2   **Financial statement account identification**   Mark each of the accounts listed in the following table as follows:

a.   In column (1), indicate in which statement—income statement (IS) or balance sheet (BS)—the account belongs.

b.   In column (2), indicate whether the account is a current asset (CA), current liability (CL), expense (E), fixed asset (FA), long-term debt (LTD), revenue (R), or shareholders' equity (SE).

Account name	(1) Statement	(2) Type of account
Accounts payable	_____	_____
Accounts receivable	_____	_____
Accruals	_____	_____
Accumulated amortization	_____	_____
Administrative expense	_____	_____
Buildings	_____	_____
Cash	_____	_____
Common shares	_____	_____
Cost of goods sold	_____	_____
Amortization	_____	_____
Equipment	_____	_____
General expense	_____	_____
Interest expense	_____	_____
Inventories	_____	_____
Land	_____	_____
Long-term debts	_____	_____
Machinery	_____	_____
Marketable securities	_____	_____
Line of credit	_____	_____
Operating expense	_____	_____
Preferred shares	_____	_____
Preferred share dividends	_____	_____
Retained earnings	_____	_____
Sales revenue	_____	_____
Selling expense	_____	_____
Taxes	_____	_____
Vehicles	_____	_____

INTERMEDIATE 2–3   **Income statement preparation**   Use the *appropriate items* from the following list to prepare in good form Perry Corporation's income statement for the year ended July 31, 2003.

Item	Values ($000) at or for year ended July 31, 2003
Accounts receivable	$350
Accumulated amortization	205
Cost of goods sold	285
Amortization expense	55
General and administrative expense	60
Interest expense	25
Preferred share dividends	10
Sales revenue	525
Selling expense	35
Common shares	265
Retained earnings	325
Taxes	rate = 40%

INTERMEDIATE

2–4   **Income statement preparation**   On December 31, 2002, Cathy Chen, a self-employed chartered accountant (CA), completed her first full year in business. During the year, she billed $180,000 for her accounting services. She had two employees: a bookkeeper and a clerical assistant. In addition to her *monthly* salary of $4,000, Ms. Chen paid *annual* salaries of $24,000 and $18,000 to the bookkeeper and the clerical assistant, respectively. Income taxes and other deductions for Ms. Chen and her employees totalled $17,300 for the year. Expenses for office supplies, including postage, totalled $5,200 for the year. In addition, Ms. Chen spent $8,500 during the year on tax-deductible travel and entertainment associated with client visits and new business development. Lease payments for the office space rented (a tax-deductible expense) were $1,350 *per month*. Amortization expense on the office furniture and fixtures was $7,800 for the year. During the year, Ms. Chen paid interest of $7,500 on the $60,000 borrowed to start the business. The tax rate for her business is 30 percent.

   a. Prepare an income statement for Cathy Chen, CA, for the year ended December 31, 2002.
   b. How much *cash flow from operations* did Cathy realize during 2002?
   c. Evaluate her 2002 financial performance.

INTERMEDIATE   2–5   **Calculation of EPS and retained earnings**   Philagem, Inc., ended 2002 with earnings *before* taxes of $218,000. The company is subject to a 40 percent tax rate and must pay $32,000 in preferred share dividends before distributing any earnings on the 85,000 common shares currently outstanding.

   a. Calculate Philagem's 2002 earnings per share (EPS).
   b. If the firm paid common share dividends of $0.80 per share, how many dollars would go to retained earnings?

INTERMEDIATE   2–6   **Balance sheet preparation**   Use the *appropriate items* from the following list to prepare in good form Owen Davis Company's balance sheet at July 31, 2003.

Item	Value ($000) at July 31, 2003
Accounts payable	$ 220
Accounts receivable	450
Accruals	55
Accumulated amortization	265
Buildings	225
Cash	215
Common shares	290
Cost of goods sold	2,500
Amortization expense	45
Equipment	140
Furniture and fixtures	170
General expense	320
Inventories	375
Land	100
Long-term debt	420
Machinery	420
Marketable securities	75
Line of credit	475
Preferred shares	100
Retained earnings	370
Sales revenue	3,600
Vehicles	25

WARM-UP **2–7** **Impact of net income on a firm's balance sheet** Conrad Air, Inc., reported net income *after tax* of $1,365,000 for the year ended August 31, 2003. Show the effect of these funds on the firm's balance sheet (given below for the previous year) in each of the following scenarios.

Balance Sheet
Conrad Air, Inc.
as of August 31, 2002

Assets		Liabilities and shareholders' equity	
Cash	$ 120,000	Accounts payable	$ 70,000
Marketable securities	35,000	Line of credit	55,000
Accounts receivable	45,000	Current liabilities	$ 125,000
Inventories	130,000	Long-term debt	2,700,000
Current assets	$ 330,000	Total liabilities	$2,825,000
Net equipment	$2,970,000	Common shares	$ 500,000
Net buildings	1,600,000	Retained earnings	1,575,000
Fixed assets	$4,570,000	Shareholders' equity	$2,075,000
Total assets	$4,900,000	Total liabilities and equity	$4,900,000

a. Conrad paid no dividends during the 2003 fiscal year and invested all profits in marketable securities.
b. Conrad paid dividends totalling $500,000 during the 2003 fiscal year and used the balance of the net income to retire (pay off) long-term debt.
c. Conrad paid dividends totalling $500,000 during the 2003 fiscal year and invested the balance of the net income in building a new hangar.
d. Conrad paid out all $1,365,000 as dividends to its shareholders during the 2003 fiscal year.

WARM-UP **2–8   Initial sale price of common shares**   Beck Corporation issued 6,250 preferred shares and only sold common shares to investors once. Given Beck's shareholders' equity account that follows, determine the original price per share at which the firm sold the preferred and common shares.

Shareholders' equity ($000)	
Preferred shares	$ 125
Common shares (300,000 shares outstanding)	2,850
Retained earnings	900
Total shareholders' equity	$3,875

CHALLENGE **2–9   Financial statement preparation**   The balance sheet for Rogers Industries for March 31, 2002, appears below. Information relevant to Rogers Industries' operations for the 2003 fiscal year is given following the balance sheet. Using the data presented:
a. Prepare in good form an income statement for Rogers Industries for the year ended March 31, 2003. Be sure to show earnings per share (EPS).
b. Prepare in good form a balance sheet for Rogers Industries for March 31, 2003.

Balance Sheet ($000)
Rogers Industries
March 31, 2002

Assets		Liabilities and shareholders' equity	
Cash	$ 40	Accounts payable	$ 50
Marketable securities	10	Line of credit	80
Accounts receivable	80	Accruals	10
Inventories	100	Total current liabilities	$140
Total current assets	$230	Long-term debt	$270
Gross fixed assets	$890	Preferred shares	$ 40
Less: Accumulated amortization	240	Common shares	320
Net fixed assets	$650	Retained earnings	110
Total assets	$880	Total shareholders' equity	$470
		Total liabilities and shareholders' equity	$880

Rogers Industries
Relevant information for the 2003 fiscal year

1. Sales were $1,200,000.
2. Cost of goods sold equals 60 percent of sales.
3. Operating expenses equal 15 percent of sales.
4. Interest expense is 10 percent of the total beginning balance of the line of credit and long-term debt.
5. The firm pays 40 percent taxes on taxable income.
6. Preferred share dividends of $4,000 were paid.
7. Cash and marketable securities are unchanged.
8. Accounts receivable equal 8 percent of sales.
9. Inventory equals 10 percent of sales.
10. The firm acquired $30,000 of additional fixed assets in 2003.
11. Amortization expense was $20,000.
12. Accounts payable equal 5 percent of sales.
13. Line of credit, long-term debt, preferred shares, and common shares remain unchanged.
14. Accruals are unchanged.
15. Cash dividends of $119,000 were paid to common shareholders.

INTERMEDIATE **2–10** **Statement of retained earnings** Hayes Enterprises began 2002 with a retained earnings balance of $928,000. During 2002, the firm earned $377,000 after taxes. From this amount, preferred shareholders were paid $47,000 in dividends. At year-end 2002, the firm's retained earnings totalled $1,048,000. The firm had 140,000 common shares outstanding during 2002.

    a. Prepare a statement of retained earnings for the year ended December 31, 2002, for Hayes Enterprises. (*Note:* Be sure to calculate and include the amount of cash dividends paid in 2002.)

    b. Calculate the firm's 2002 earnings per share (EPS).

    c. How large a per-share cash dividend did the firm pay to common shareholders during 2002?

CHALLENGE **2–11** **Understanding financial statements** The financial statements for Barrie Corporation for the fiscal years ended August 31, 2002 and 2003 are provided below. In fiscal 2002, Barrie's NIAT was $162,500 and the company paid preferred share dividends of $10,000 and common share dividends of $22,250. In 2003, Barrie paid $12,500 in preferred share dividends. The number of common shares outstanding was 20,000 in 2002 and 21,000 in 2003. No new common shares were issued in 2001 or 2002.

Barrie Corporation
Income Statement
for the year ended August 31, 2003

Sales	$4,135,000
Cost of goods sold	3,308,000
Gross margin	$ 827,000
General administrative and selling expense	318,000
Amortization	117,000
Miscellaneous	54,000
Earnings before taxes	$ 338,000
Taxes (40 percent)	135,200
Net income after taxes	$ 202,800

Barrie Corporation
Balance Sheets
as of August 31

	2002	2003
Cash	$ 65,000	$ 76,250
Accounts receivable	284,000	401,600
Inventory	306,000	493,000
Total current assets	655,000	970,850
Land and building	95,000	126,150
Machinery	128,000	169,000
Other fixed assets	57,000	74,600
Total assets	$935,000	$1,340,600
Accounts payable	$160,000	$ 152,700
Accruals	78,000	78,500
Total current liabilities	$238,000	$ 231,200
Long-term debt	126,000	???,???
Preferred equity	100,000	125,000
Common shares	410,000	500,000
Retained earnings	61,000	230,150
Total liabilities and equity	$935,000	$1,340,600

Determine the following for Barrie Corporation:
a. The amount of long-term debt outstanding in 2003.
b. The total dollar investment in assets made during 2003 and the sources of the funds invested.
c. Barrie's earnings per share (EPS) in 2002 and 2003.
d. The total dividends paid in 2003 and DPS in 2002 and 2003.
e. The average amount Barrie received from the sale of all of the common shares outstanding at the end of 2002 and those sold in 2003.

    f. Retained earnings as of the beginning of the 2002 fiscal year.

    g. Barrie's book value and book value per share at the end of fiscal 2001, 2002, and 2003.

INTERMEDIATE 2–12   **Understanding financial statements**   Montague Corporation's financial statements are provided below. Use these statements to determine the following:

    a. The total investment in assets made during 2002.

    b. The sources of the funds invested.

    c. Total investment in *fixed assets* during 2002.

    d. The total dividends paid in 2002.

    e. The average issue price per common share during 2002.

    f. The book value per common share in 2001 and 2002.

Montague Corporation
Income Statement
for the year ended December 31, 2002

Sales	$8,750,000
Cost of goods sold	6,200,000
Gross margin	2,550,000
General and administrative expense	830,000
Amortization	550,000
EBIT	1,170,000
Interest	300,000
Earnings before taxes	870,000
Taxes	304,500
Net income after taxes	$565,500

Montague Corporation
Balance Sheet
as at December 31, 2002

	2001	2002
Cash	$ 300,000	$ 350,000
Accounts receivable	690,000	560,000
Inventory	1,020,000	1,400,000
Total current assets	2,010,000	2,310,000
Net fixed assets	5,600,000	6,200,000
Total assets	$7,610,000	$8,510,000
Accounts payable	500,000	450,000
Accruals	130,000	175,000
Total current liabilities	630,000	625,000
Long-term debt	4,600,000	5,100,000
Preferred equity	550,000	575,000
Common shares*	1,400,000	1,450,000
Retained earnings	430,000	760,000
Total liabilities and shareholders' equity	$7,610,000	$8,510,000

*There were 40,000 shares outstanding at the end of 2001 and 41,250 outstanding at the end of 2002.

INTERMEDIATE 2–13 **Changes in shareholders' equity**   Listed are the equity sections of balance sheets for the 2002 and 2003 fiscal years as reported by Mountain Air Ski Resorts, Inc. The overall value of shareholders' equity has risen from $2,000,000 to $7,500,000. Use the statements to discover how and why this happened.

	Mountain Air Ski Resorts, Inc.	
	2002	**2003**
Shareholders' equity		
Common shares		
Authorized—5,000,000 shares		
Outstanding— 500,000 shares 2002		
—1,500,000 shares 2003	$1,000,000	$6,000,000
Retained earnings	1,000,000	1,500,000
Total shareholders' equity	$2,000,000	$7,500,000

The company paid total dividends of $200,000 during fiscal 2003.
  a. What was Mountain Air's net income for fiscal 2003?
  b. How many new common shares did the corporation issue and sell during the year?
  c. For the new common shares sold during 2003, what was the average price per share?
  d. At what price per share did Mountain Air's original 500,000 shares sell?

WARM-UP 2–14 **Classifying inflows and outflows**   Classify each of the following items as a cash inflow (I), a cash outflow (O), or as neither (N).

Item	Change ($)	Item	Change ($)
Cash	+100	Accounts receivable	−700
Accounts payable	−1,000	NIAT	+600
Line of credit	+500	Amortization	+100
Long-term debt	−2,000	Repurchase of common shares	+600
Inventory	+200	Cash dividends	+800
Fixed assets	+400	Sale of common shares	+1,000

  2–15 **Finding dividends paid**   Colonial Paint's net income after taxes in 2002 totalled $186,000. The firm's year-end 2001 and 2002 retained earnings on its balance sheet totalled $736,000 and $812,000, respectively. Did Colonial pay dividends in 2002 and, if so, how much was paid?

WARM-UP

INTERMEDIATE 2–16 **Preparing a statement of cash flows**   Given the balance sheets and selected data from the income statement of Keith Corporation that follow:
  a. Prepare the firm's statement of cash flows for the year ended December 31, 2002.

b. Reconcile the resulting "net increase (decrease) in cash and marketable securities" with the actual change in cash and marketable securities for the year.

c. Interpret the statement prepared in **a.**

Balance Sheets Keith Corporation (in $000)		
	December 31	
Assets	2001	2002
Cash	$ 1,000	$ 1,500
Marketable securities	1,200	1,800
Accounts receivable	1,800	2,000
Inventories	2,800	2,900
Total current assets	$ 6,800	$ 8,200
Gross fixed assets	$28,100	$29,500
Less: Accumulated amortization	13,100	14,700
Net fixed assets	$15,000	$14,800
Total assets	$21,800	$23,000
Liabilities and shareholders' equity		
Accounts payable	$ 1,500	$ 1,600
Line of credit	2,200	2,800
Accruals	300	200
Total current liabilities	$ 4,000	$ 4,600
Long-term debt	$ 5,000	$ 5,000
Common shares	$10,000	$10,000
Retained earnings	2,800	3,400
Total shareholders' equity	$12,800	$13,400
Total liabilities and shareholders' equity	$21,800	$23,000
Income statement data (2002)		
Total sales		$26,340
Net income before tax		2,110
Amortization expense		1,600
Net income after taxes		1,400

INTERMEDIATE   **2–17 Preparing a statement of cash flows** Using the 2002 income statement and the 2001 and 2002 balance sheets for Technica, Inc., given in Problem 2–1, do the following:

a. Prepare the firm's statement of cash flows for the year ended December 31, 2002.

b. Reconcile the resulting "net increase (decrease) in cash and marketable securities" with the actual change in cash and marketable securities for the year.

c. Interpret the statement prepared in **a.**

WARM-UP **2–18**   **Corporate taxes**   Tantor Supply, Inc., is a small Canadian-controlled corporation based in Nova Scotia acting as the exclusive distributor of a major line of sporting goods. During 2002 the firm earned $92,500 before taxes.
  a. Calculate the firm's tax liability using the corporate tax rate schedule given in Table 2.6.
  b. How much is Tantor Supply's 2002 after-tax income?

WARM-UP **2–19**   **Corporate taxes**   Using the corporate tax rate schedule given in Table 2.6, calculate the total taxes and after-tax earnings for the following levels of corporate earnings before taxes: $10,000; $80,000; $300,000; $500,000; $1.5 million; $10 million; and $15 million. Assume the company is a CCPC based in Ontario.

WARM-UP **2–20**   **Capital gains taxes**   Perkins Manufacturing is considering the sale of two noncapital assets, X and Y, that are not amortized. Asset X was purchased for $2,000 and will be sold today for $2,250. Asset Y was purchased for $30,000 and will be sold today for $35,000. The firm's tax rate is 20.6 percent.
  a. Calculate the amount of capital gain, if any, realized on each of the assets.
  b. Calculate the tax on the sale of each asset.

WARM-UP **2–21**   **Capital gains taxes**   The following table contains purchase and sale prices and costs incurred in selling the assets for the nonamortizable capital assets of a major corporation. The firm's tax rate is 26.1 percent.

Asset	Purchase price	Sale price	Costs incurred
A	$ 3,000	$ 3,800	$ 400
B	12,000	12,360	360
C	62,000	81,000	1,000
D	41,000	45,460	460
E	16,500	18,125	125

  a. Determine the amount of capital gain realized on each of the five assets.
  b. Calculate the amount of tax paid on each of the assets.

WARM-UP **2–22**   **Calculating taxes**   For the year ended December 31, 2002, Cavendish Enterprises had taxable income of $265,000. The company is a Canadian-controlled private corporation. Calculate the taxes payable and NIAT under each of the following scenarios:
  a. The company manufactures windows and is based in British Columbia.
  b. The company is a tourism operator in Prince Edward Island.

WARM-UP **2–23**   **Calculating taxes**   For the year ended August 31, 2003, Collins Corporation had taxable income of $1,238,000. The company is a publicly traded corporation. Calculate the taxes payable and NIAT under each of the following scenarios:
  a. The company is an oil and gas producer in Saskatchewan.
  b. The company is a dry goods wholesaler in New Brunswick.

INTERMEDIATE **2–24 Calculating taxes** The bookkeeper for Wabush Inc., a Canadian-controlled private corporation, compiled the following information for the 2001 fiscal year. Sales were $3,200,000, while expenses totalled $2,500,000. Wabush received $120,000 in dividends from taxable Canadian corporations. The company also earned a capital gain on investments in the common shares of other companies of $148,600. Using this information and the tax rates provided in Table 2.6, calculate Wabush Inc.'s total taxes payable, NIAT, and average tax rate under the following conditions.
a. The company is a manufacturing corporation in Ontario.
b. The company is a non-manufacturing corporation in Newfoundland.
c. The company is not a CCPC in both parts a and b.

INTERMEDIATE **2–25 Interest versus dividend expense** Michaels Corporation expects earnings before interest and taxes to be $40,000 for this period. Assuming a tax rate of 19 percent, compute the firm's earnings after taxes and earnings available for common shareholders under the following conditions:
a. The firm pays $10,000 in interest.
b. The firm pays $10,000 in preferred shares dividends.

  2–26 Cash flow A firm had net income after taxes of $50,000 in 2002. Amortization expenses of $30,000 were incurred. What was the firm's net *cash flow from operations* during 2002?

WARM-UP

WARM-UP **2–27 Tax deductibility of expenses** AX Company's salary expense for the 2003 fiscal year was $475,000. AX's tax rate is 44.1 percent. What was the actual, after-tax cost of the salary expense to AX Company for the 2003 fiscal year?

INTERMEDIATE **2–28 Tax deductibility of expenses** Laytin Lumber recently finished replanting 5,000 acres of forest land at a cost of $3,675,000. Laytin's tax rate is 38.6 percent.
a. Of the total cost, what percentage and dollar amount is actually paid through the tax system?
b. What was the actual, after-tax cost of the replanting to Laytin?

 2–29 Amortization and cash flow A firm is in the third year of amortizing its only asset, originally costing $180,000 and having a 10-year life for straight-line amortization purposes. The following data is relative to the current year's operations.

INTERMEDIATE

Accruals	$ 15,000
Current assets	120,000
Interest expense	15,000
Sales revenue	400,000
Inventory	70,000
Total costs before amortization, interest, and taxes	290,000
Tax rate	18.1%

a. Use the *relevant data* to determine the *cash flow from operations* for the current year.

b. Explain the impact that amortization, as well as any other non-cash charges, has on a firm's cash flows.

CASE   CHAPTER 2   **Analyzing Cline Custom Bicycles' Cash Flows**

Darin Cline, formerly an internationally renowned professional bicycle racer, owns and operates Cline Custom Bicycles—a firm that builds and markets custom bicycles to shops throughout Canada and the western United States. Darin has just received his firm's 2003 income statement and balance sheet. These statements are provided below. Also included is the balance sheet for the 2002 fiscal year. Although he is quite pleased to have achieved record earnings of $106,000 in 2003, Darin is concerned about the firm's cash flows. Specifically, he is finding it more and more difficult to pay the firm's bills in a timely manner. To gain insight into the firm's cash flow problems, Darin is planning to have the firm's 2003 statement of cash flows prepared and evaluated.

Income Statement
Cline Custom Bicycles
for the year ended March 31, 2003 (in $000)

Sales revenue		$2,200
Less: Cost of goods sold		1,420
Gross margin		$ 780
Less: Operating expenses		
Selling expense	$300	
General and administrative expense	270	
Amortization expenses	30	
Total operating expense		600
Operating earnings (EBIT)		$ 180
Less: Interest expense		29
Earnings before taxes		$ 151
Less: Taxes (30%)		45
Net income after taxes		$ 106

Balance Sheets
Cline Custom Bicycles (in $000)

Assets	March 31 2002	2003
Current assets		
Cash	$ 50	$ 30
Marketable securities	20	10
Accounts receivable	350	320
Inventories	320	460
Total current assets	$ 740	$ 820
Gross fixed assets	$ 520	$ 560
Less: Accumulated amortization	150	180
Net fixed assets	$ 370	$ 380
Total assets	$1,110	$1,200

Liabilities and shareholders' equity		
Current liabilities		
Accounts payable	$ 320	$ 390
Line of credit	90	110
Accruals	20	20
Total current liabilities	$ 430	$ 520
Long-term debt	$ 350	$ 320
Total liabilities	$ 780	$ 840
Shareholders' equity		
Common shares	$ 250	$ 250
Retained earnings	80	110
Total shareholders' equity	$ 330	$ 360
Total liabilities and shareholders' equity	$1,110	$1,200

Required

a. Use the financial data presented to prepare Cline's statement of retained earnings for the fiscal year ended March 31, 2003.

b. Use the financial data presented to prepare Cline Custom Bicycles' statement of cash flows for the fiscal year ended March 31, 2003.

c. Evaluate the statement prepared in b in light of Cline's current cash flow difficulties.

d. On the basis of your evaluation in c, what recommendations might you offer Darin Cline?

WEB EXERCISE   LINKS TO PRACTISE

Visit the following Web sites and complete the suggested exercises. These exercises will allow you to review practical applications of the chapter topics as well as explore the wealth of information regarding managerial finance that is available on the Internet.

www.profs.management.mcgill.ca/johnson/default.html
Visit the site, Demystifying Financial Statements. This multimedia Web site gives you an overall understanding of how financial statements work and how you can learn to analyze the information provided. You can view the complete multimedia presentation or only the topics that are of interest at the time. Ian McLaughlin, a former business professor at McGill University, reviews the characteristics of financial statements and then moves on to ratios and examines their use as analytical tools. Along the way, successful businesspeople explain what they look for and why.

www.nationalpost.com
Click on the News link and then use some of the key terms from this chapter in the search feature to search for practical examples of the topic. Try the following terms in quotes: balance sheet, cash flow, amortization, GAAP, goodwill, book value, financial forecasting, capital market, treasury bills, capital structure, capital budgeting, capital spending, or stock exchange. Print the article and discuss how the financial term is used in the article.

www.cica.ca
Use the search facility to search for additional information on the Annual Report Award program. What are some other characteristics of an award-winning annual report? Search for additional detail on the Management Discussion and Analysis section of the annual report, on the use of GAAP, on accounting standards, or on any other topic relating to accounting.

www.sedar.com
Search the SEDAR database for the filings made by publicly traded companies. SEDAR is the System for Electronic Document Analysis and Retrieval, the electronic filing system for the disclosure documents of public companies across Canada. All Canadian public companies are required to file their documents in the SEDAR system. Search for the public filings for some of the companies discussed in this chapter or for some of the companies that won annual report awards.

www.globeinvestor.com
Use the filter feature to determine how many public companies are listed on the two Canadian stock exchanges. Select one of the companies from the list and visit their home page to determine the type of financial documents available.

PART

2

Financial Analysis and Planning

3

Financial Statement Analysis

LEARNING GOALS

LG1 Introduce the parties interested in completing a financial ratio analysis, the three types of ratio comparisons, and the four categories of ratios.

LG2 Analyze a company's liquidity and the company's effectiveness at managing inventory, accounts receivable, accounts payable, and fixed and total assets.

LG3 Discuss financial leverage and the ratios used to assess how the firm has financed assets, and the company's ability to cover the financing charges associated with the financing used.

LG4 Evaluate a company's profitability using common-size analysis and relative to the company's sales, total assets, common equity, and common share price.

LG5 Explore the link between the various categories of ratios, in particular between liquidity and activity and between leverage and profitability.

LG6 Use the DuPont system and a summary of financial ratios to perform a complete ratio analysis of a firm, and consider some cautions concerning ratio analysis.

3.1 Using Financial Ratios

In the preceding chapter, we reviewed the firm's four basic financial statements. The information contained in these statements is of major significance to various interested parties who regularly need to have relative measures of the company's operating efficiency. *Relative* is the key word here, because the analysis of financial statements is based on the knowledge and use of *ratios* or *relative values*.

ratio analysis
Involves the methods of calculating and interpreting financial ratios to assess the firm's performance.

Ratio analysis involves methods of calculating and interpreting financial ratios to assess the firm's performance. A ratio is simply a numerator divided by a denominator, with the resulting calculation being a ratio of one of three types:

Apples, Oranges, and Grapefruit!

You've been told many times that you can't compare apples and oranges. Does that adage mean you can't compare the financial performance of different companies? The answer depends on how you define apples and oranges. Look at the financial statements of two companies. The differences in figures can be staggering—one is an apple, one is an orange. Comparisons at this level are very difficult, if not impossible. To compare two companies, you must convert the raw numbers from the financial statements into comparable data—make the orange and apple a grapefruit! You can compare individual financial items for two companies, say the amount of debt, even though the two amounts are vastly different. The way to do it is to convert the apple and orange into a grapefruit by dividing each company's total debt by the total assets. This chapter will show you how to transform apples and oranges into grapefruit: how to use financial ratios to compare the financial performance of different firms at a point in time, and over time.

(1) a percent (e.g., 19.6%); (2) a times (e.g., 1.96 ×); or (3) a number of days (e.g., 19.6 days). You must understand the ratio to know the unit of the answer. You do not want to calculate a ratio of 0.8573 and convert it to a percent when it is supposed to be a times. The basic inputs to ratio analysis are the firm's income statement and balance sheet. The statement of cash flows is not used in a ratio analysis, since it is an analytical statement based on the balance sheet and income statement. Before we look at those inputs, though, we need to consider why a ratio analysis is completed, describe the parties interested in financial ratios, explain the general types of ratio comparisons, and introduce the four categories of ratios.

Why Complete a Ratio Analysis?

There are three reasons for completing a ratio analysis. First, as was discussed in Chapter 1, one of the tasks of financial managers is planning. To plan, you must be familiar with the company's current financial position, know the company's strengths and weaknesses. A ratio analysis provides this detail. Second, the financial statement provides raw data that is difficult to analyze. A ratio analysis puts the raw numbers in perspective. It is easier to look at a sequence of ratios by category than to look at all of the numbers on the underlying financial statements. When analyzing the ratios, however, it is often useful to refer to individual accounts on the statements. Third, from management's perspective, a ratio analysis is important in order to be able to anticipate the reaction of potential creditors and investors to a request for funds. Management must be able to anticipate the reaction of both creditors and shareholders to the most recent financial results and be able to explain the company's performance. A ratio analysis can provide the answers.

Interested Parties

Hint
Management should be the most interested party of this group. They not only have to worry about the financial situation of the firm, but they are also critically interested in what these other interest groups think about the firm.

Ratio analysis of a firm's financial statements is of interest to shareholders, creditors, and the firm's own management. Both present and prospective shareholders are interested in the firm's current and future level of risk and return, which directly affect share price. The firm's current and prospective creditors are primarily interested in the liquidity of the company, the current amount of debt, and the firm's ability to make interest and principal payments. A secondary concern of creditors is the firm's profitability; they want assurance that the business is healthy and will continue to be successful.

Management, like shareholders, is concerned with all aspects of the firm's financial situation. Thus, it attempts to produce financial results that will be considered favourable by both owners and creditors. In addition, management uses ratios to monitor the firm's performance from period to period. Any unexpected changes are examined, to isolate developing problems. Note, however, that the ratio analyses completed in this book are not for real companies. The book provides very little information about the sample companies. In reality, much more will be known about the situation than the information provided in even detailed textbook problems. The more that is known about the company, the more detailed and useful the ratio analysis.

Types of Ratio Comparisons

Ratio analysis is not merely the application of a formula to financial data to calculate a given ratio. More important is the *interpretation* of the ratio value. To answer such questions as, Is it too high or too low? Is it good or bad?, a meaningful basis for comparison is needed. Two types of ratio comparisons can be made: cross-sectional and time-series.

Cross-Sectional Analysis

cross-sectional analysis
Comparison of different firms' financial ratios at the same point in time; involves comparing the firm's ratios to those of other firms in its industry or to industry averages.

Cross-sectional analysis involves the comparison of different firms' financial ratios at the same time (i.e. same year or quarter). The typical business is interested in how well it has performed in relation to other firms in its industry. Often, the reported financial statements of competing firms will be available for analysis.[1] Frequently, a firm will compare its ratio values to those of a key competitor or group of competitors that it wishes to emulate. This type of cross-sectional analysis, called **benchmarking**, has become very popular. By comparing the firm's ratios to those of the *benchmark company* (or *companies*), it can identify areas in which it excels and, more importantly, areas for improvement.

benchmarking
A type of *cross-sectional analysis* in which the firm's ratio values are compared to those of a key competitor or group of competitors, primarily to identify areas for improvement.

Another popular type of comparison is to industry averages. These figures can be found in D&B's (formerly Dun & Bradstreet) *Industry Norms and Key Business Ratios*, the *Canada Company Handbook* published by Report on Business, Statistics Canada's *Financial Performance Indicators for Canadian Business*, and *The Canadian Corporate Financial Performance Survey* and *The Canadian Small Business Financial Performance Survey*, both published by the Canadian Institute of Chartered Accountants. Ratios in computerized databases are also available from companies such as Stock Guide, Info Globe, and Financial Post. Ratios are also on the Web at sites such as **www.marketguide.com** for publicly traded companies in the United States, **www.globeinvestor.com** for publicly traded companies in Canada, and **www.bizstat.com** for a wide range of U.S. industries and for U.S. corporations (small, medium, and large) as well as sole proprietorships and partnerships. A sample from one available source of industry averages is given in Table 3.1. A sample of the type of industry ratio data available is provided in Table 3.1 and Table 3.2 on the next page. This data is from D&B Canada. Table 3.1 provides 9 important ratios for four industries for three years: 1999–2001. The range of values across industries and across years for each industry should be noted. Table 3.2 provides the median and range of ratios for grocery stores in Canada for the years 1999 to 2001. D&B Canada and other similar organizations provide a broad range of ratio data for money industries.

Comparing a particular ratio to the standard should uncover any *deviations from the norm.* Many people mistakenly believe that as long as the firm being analyzed has a value "better than" the industry average, it can be viewed favourably. However, this "better than average" viewpoint can be misleading. Quite often a ratio value that is far better than the norm can indicate problems. These may, on more careful analysis, be more severe than had the ratio been worse than the industry average. It is therefore important to investigate *significant deviations to either side* of the industry standard. There may be "bad" reasons for what appears to be a positive ratio and "good" reasons for what appears to be a negative ratio.

Hint
Industry averages are not particularly useful when analyzing firms with multiproduct lines. In the case of multiproduct firms, it is difficult to select the appropriate benchmark industry.

The analyst must also recognize that ratios with large deviations from the norm are only the *symptoms* of a problem. Further analysis is typically required to isolate the *causes* of the problem. Once the reason for the problem is known, management must develop prescriptive actions for eliminating it. The fundamental point is this: *Ratio analysis merely directs attention to potential areas of concern; it does not provide conclusive evidence as to the existence of a problem.*

Example ▼ In August 2003, Mary Boyle, the chief financial analyst at Caldwell Manufacturing, a producer of heat exchangers, gathered data on the firm's financial performance for the fiscal year ended June 30, 2003. She calculated a variety of ratios and

---

1. Cross-sectional comparisons of firms operating in several lines of business are difficult to perform. The use of weighted-average industry ratios based on the firm's product-line mix or, if data are available, analysis of the firm on a product-line basis can be performed to evaluate a multiproduct firm.

TABLE 3.1   Industry Average Ratios (1999–2001) for Selected Lines of Business[a]

RATIOS

Industry (SIC code)[b]	Year	Current ratio (X)	Quick ratio (X)	Sales to inventory (X)	Collection period (days)	Assets to sales (%)	Total liabilities to net worth (%)	Return on sales (%)	Return on assets (%)	Return on net worth (%)
Department stores	2001	1.9	0.2	5.0	6.6	37.5	88.8	1.5	2.9	5.9
(5311)	2000	1.5	0.4	5.5	9.4	51.0	103.8	1.3	2.2	4.6
	1999	1.6	0.2	4.9	8.5	43.5	137.1	1.2	3.1	8.6
Manufactures	2001	1.4	0.8	11.2	22.0	24.7	95.8	0.1	0.2	5.2
personal computers	2000	1.3	0.8	10.9	47.2	30.3	134.3	1.2	3.6	14.4
(3575)	1999	1.3	0.7	8.6	34.5	41.2	81.4	1.1	4.2	24.3
Manufactures	2001	1.7	0.8	5.2	30.1	40.2	116.4	2.1	5.6	17.1
motor vehicles and	2000	1.4	0.7	4.7	58.1	55.1	172.2	1.8	2.4	6.8
passenger car bodies (3711)	1999	1.7	0.0	0.0	0.0	51.8	167.7	0.0	2.5	5.2
Retails—groceries	2001	2.1	0.7	10.7	11.6	46.9	30.8	1.4	3.9	6.4
(5411)	2000	1.9	0.5	13.1	8.6	41.4	41.4	1.5	6.2	11.2
	1999	1.6	0.6	10.9	9.8	42.6	36.8	2.1	5.6	12.0

[a]This is the median ratio for the industry. D&B also provides the upper and lower quartile for each of the ratios. An example of this information is provided in Table 3.2.

[b]The ratios provided are for companies in the industry with total assets of $1 million or more.

SOURCE: "Industry Norms and Key Business Ratios," D&B Canada, 2002. Reprinted with permission.

TABLE 3.2   Distribution of Ratios for Grocery Stores, 1999–2001

Industry quartiles	2001 Statement Sampling: 121[a]			2000 Statement Sampling: 144[a]			1999 Statement Sampling: 120[a]		
	Upper	Median[b]	Lower	Upper	Median[b]	Lower	Upper	Median[b]	Lower
Current ratio	3.6	2.1	1.1	3.8	1.9	1.1	3.5	1.6	1.0
Quick ratio	1.4	0.7	0.3	1.5	0.5	0.3	1.4	0.6	0.3
Sales/Inventory	17.7	10.7	7.9	21.0	13.1	7.9	19.6	10.9	7.5
Collection period	4.6	11.6	17.5	2.7	8.6	17.4	2.7	9.8	18.1
Assets/Sales	30.6%	46.9%	54.6%	27.0%	41.4%	51.6%	27.1%	42.6%	56.5%
Total liabilities/Net worth	14.1%	30.8%	110.9%	15.6%	41.4%	117.5%	11.5%	36.8%	138.9%
Return on sales	3.4%	1.4%	0.7%	3.7%	1.5%	0.9%	4.6%	2.1%	0.8%
Return on assets	7.9%	3.9%	1.6%	9.8%	6.2%	2.1%	10.6%	5.6%	1.7%
Return on net worth	14.5%	6.4%	2.6%	19.1%	11.2%	3.2%	17.7%	12.0%	4.1%

[a]Statement sampling indicates the number of companies on which the data is based

[b]The median is the middle value for a ratio listed from lowest to highest. The upper quartile is the median of the upper half of the list of ratios while the lower quartile is the median of the lower half.

SOURCE: "Industry Norms and Key Business Ratios," D&B Canada, 2002. Reprinted with permission.

obtained industry averages. She was especially interested in average age of inventory, which reflects the speed with which the firm moves its inventory from raw materials through production into finished goods and to the customer as a completed sale. Generally, lower values of this ratio are preferred, because they indicate a quicker sale of inventory. The average age of inventory for Caldwell Manufacturing and for the industry for June 30, 2003 are provided below.

	Average age of inventory, 2003
Caldwell Manufacturing	24.7 days
Industry average	43.4 days

Mary's initial reaction to these data was that the firm had managed its inventory significantly *better than* the average firm in the industry. The average age was almost 19 days faster than the industry average. Upon reflection, however, she realized that a very low average age of inventory could also mean very low levels of inventory. The consequence of low inventory could be excessive stockouts (insufficient inventory). Discussions with people in the manufacturing and marketing departments did in fact uncover such a problem: inventories during the year were extremely low, the result of numerous production delays that hindered the firm's ability to meet demand and resulted in lost sales. What had initially appeared to reflect extremely efficient inventory management was actually the symptom of a major problem. There were, in fact, "bad" reasons for what appeared to be a positive ratio.

Time-Series Analysis

time-series analysis
Evaluation of the firm's financial performance over time using financial ratio analysis.

Time-series analysis evaluates performance over time. Comparison of current to past performance, using ratios, allows the firm to determine whether it is progressing as planned. Developing trends can be seen by using multiyear comparisons, and knowledge of these trends can assist the firm in planning future operations. As in cross-sectional analysis, any significant year-to-year changes should be evaluated to assess whether they are symptomatic of a major problem. Additionally, time-series analysis is often helpful in checking the reasonableness of a firm's projected (pro forma) financial statements. Financial forecasting is covered in the following chapter. A comparison of *current* and *past* ratios to those resulting from an analysis of *projected* statements may reveal discrepancies or overoptimism.

Combined Analysis

The most informative approach to ratio analysis is one that combines cross-sectional and time-series analyses. A combined view permits assessment of the trend in the behaviour of the ratio in relation to the trend for the industry. Figure 3.1 depicts this type of approach using the average collection period ratio over the years 2000–2003 for Compton's Drinks, a bottler of specialty soft drinks. This ratio reflects the average amount of time it takes the firm to collect credit sales. Lower values of this ratio generally are preferred. The figure quickly discloses

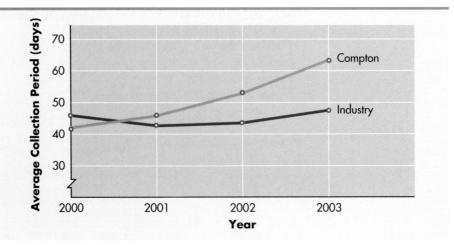

FIGURE 3.1

Combined Analysis
Combined cross-sectional and time-series view of Compton Drinks' average collection period, 2000–2003

that Compton's average collection period: (1) is now much higher than the industry's, (2) has gone from being better than the industry's to much worse, and (3) has consistently increased over the four years, while the industry's has

TABLE 3.3   **Bartlett Company Income Statements ($000)**

	For the years ended December 31	
	2001	2002
Sales revenue	$2,567	$3,074
Less: Cost of goods sold	1,711	2,088
Gross margin	$ 856	$ 986
Less: Operating expenses		
Selling expense	$ 108	$ 100
General and administrative expenses	187	194
Lease expense[a]	35	35
Amortization expense	223	239
Total operating expense	$ 553	$ 568
Operating earnings (EBIT)	$ 303	$ 418
Less: Interest expense	91	93
Earnings before taxes (EBIT)	$ 212	$ 325
Less: Taxes	64	94
Net income after taxes (NIAT)	$ 148	$ 231
Less: Preferred share dividends	10	10
Earnings available for common shareholders	$ 138	$ 221
Earnings per share (EPS)[b]	$ 1.81	$ 2.90

[a]Lease expense is shown here as a separate item rather than being grouped with other expenses such as interest expense and amortization.

[b]Calculated by dividing the earnings available for common shareholders by the number of shares of common shares outstanding—76,244 in 2001 and 76,262 in 2002.

remained relatively constant. Clearly, Compton's Drinks must become more effective in collecting accounts receivable.

TABLE 3.4	Bartlett Company Balance Sheets ($000)	

| | December 31 | |
Assets	2001	2002
Current assets		
Cash	$ 288	$ 363
Marketable securities	51	68
Accounts receivable	365	503
Inventories	300	289
Total current assets	$1,004	$1,223
Gross fixed assets (at cost) [a]		
Land and buildings	$1,903	$2,072
Machinery and equipment	1,693	1,866
Furniture and fixtures	316	358
Vehicles	314	275
Other (includes financial leases)	96	98
Total gross fixed assets (at cost)	$4,322	$4,669
Less: Accumulated amortization	2,056	2,295
Net fixed assets	$2,266	$2,374
Total assets	$3,270	$3,597
Liabilities and shareholders' equity		
Current liabilities		
Accounts payable	$ 270	$ 382
Line of credit	99	79
Accruals	114	159
Total current liabilities	$ 483	$ 620
Long-term debt (includes financial leases) [b]	$ 967	$1,023
Total liabilities	$1,450	$1,643
Shareholders' equity		
Preferred shares—cumulative 5%, $100 par, 2,000 shares authorized and issued [c]	$ 200	$ 200
Common shares—100,000 shares authorized, shares issued and outstanding in 2001: 76,244; in 2002: 76,262	608	619
Retained earnings	1,012	1,135
Total shareholders' equity	$1,820	$1,954
Total liabilities and shareholders' equity	$3,270	$3,597

[a]In 2002, the firm has a 6-year financial lease requiring annual beginning-of-year payments of $35,000. Four years of the lease have yet to run.

[b]Annual principal repayments on a portion of the firm's total outstanding debt amount to $71,000.

[c]The annual preferred share dividend would be $5 per share (5% × $100 par), or a total of $10,000 annually ($5 per share × 2,000 shares).

Categories of Financial Ratios

Financial ratios are grouped into four basic categories: liquidity ratios, activity ratios, leverage ratios, and profitability ratios. Liquidity, activity, and leverage ratios primarily measure risk; profitability ratios measure return. Both the short- and long-term survival of the firm are dependent on all four categories of ratios. One or two of the categories of ratios can be poorer than industry averages for a short period of time, but for the company to survive and prosper and for the company to meet the goal of maximizing shareholder wealth, none of the categories can consistently be below average.

As a rule, the necessary inputs to an effective financial analysis include, at minimum, the income statement and the balance sheet. We will use these statements for Bartlett Company for the fiscal years ended December 31, 2001 and 2002 to illustrate ratio analysis. Bartlett is a manufacturer of patio furniture located in the Ottawa area. The company sells their products throughout Canada. The income statements and balance sheets are provided in Tables 3.3 and 3.4. The ratios presented in the remainder of this chapter can be applied to nearly any company. Of course, many companies in different industries use ratios that are particularly focused on aspects peculiar to their industry.

❓ Review Questions

3–1 Why should a ratio analysis be completed? For a ratio analysis of a firm, how do the viewpoints held by the firm's present and prospective shareholders, creditors, and management differ? How can these viewpoints be related to the firm's fund-raising ability?

3–2 How can ratio analysis be used for *cross-sectional* and *time-series* comparisons? What is *benchmarking?* Which type of ratio comparison would be more common for internal analysis?

3–3 To what types of deviations from the norm should the analyst devote primary attention when performing cross-sectional ratio analysis? Why?

3.2 Analyzing Liquidity

liquidity
A firm's ability to satisfy its short-term obligations *as they come due.*

The **liquidity** of a business firm is measured by its ability to satisfy its short-term obligations *as they come due*. Liquidity refers to the solvency of the firm's *overall* financial position—the ease with which it can pay its bills. Note that at the end of the 2002 fiscal year, Bartlett has current liabilities of $620,000 (see Table 3.4). The firm must repay this amount over the upcoming two months or, in the case of the line of credit, on demand. Liquidity ratios consider the firm's ability to repay this amount with current assets. The three basic measures of liquidity are (1) net working capital, (2) the current ratio, and (3) the quick (acid-test) ratio.

Net Working Capital

net working capital
A measure of liquidity calculated by subtracting current liabilities from current assets.

Net working capital, although not actually a ratio, is a common measure of a firm's overall liquidity. It is calculated as follows:

$$\text{Net working capital} = \text{current assets} - \text{current liabilities}$$

The net working capital for Bartlett Company in 2002 is:

$$\text{Net working capital} = \$1,223,000 - \$620,000 = \$603,000$$

This figure is *not* useful for comparing the performance of different firms, but it is quite useful for internal control.[2] Often the contract under which a long-term debt is incurred specifically states a minimum level of net working capital that the firm must maintain. This requirement protects creditors by forcing the firm to maintain sufficient operating liquidity. A time-series comparison of the firm's net working capital is often helpful in evaluating its operations.

Current Ratio

current ratio
A measure of liquidity calculated by dividing the firm's current assets by its current liabilities.

The **current ratio,** one of the most commonly cited financial ratios, measures the firm's ability to meet its short-term obligations. It is expressed as follows:

$$\text{Current ratio} = \frac{\text{current assets}}{\text{current liabilities}}$$

The current ratio for Bartlett Company in 2002 is:[3]

$$\frac{\$1,223,000}{\$620,000} = 1.97$$

The current ratio indicates the dollar amount of current assets the firm has for every dollar of current liabilities. The rule of thumb is 2. This means that for every dollar of current liabilities, the firm has $2 of current assets. Bartlett's current ratio meets the rule of thumb almost exactly. The evaluation of a ratio, however, depends on the industry in which the firm operates. For example, a current ratio of 1.0 would be considered acceptable for a utility but might be unacceptable for a manufacturing firm. The more predictable a firm's cash flows, the lower the acceptable current ratio. If Bartlett Company had a relatively predictable annual cash flow, its current ratio of 1.97 would be quite acceptable.

If the firm's current ratio is divided into 1.0 and the resulting quotient is subtracted from 1.0, the difference multiplied by 100 represents the percentage by which the firm's current assets could shrink with the firm still being able to repay its current liabilities.[4] For example, a current ratio of 1.85 means that the firm can still cover its current liabilities even if its current assets shrink by 45.9 percent ($[1.0 - (1.0 \div 1.85)] \times 100$).

---

2. To make cross-sectional as well as better time-series comparisons, *net working capital as a percent of sales* can be calculated. For Bartlett Company in 2002, this ratio would be 19.6 percent ($603,000 ÷ $3,074,000). In general, the larger this value, the greater the firm's liquidity, and the smaller this value, the lesser the firm's liquidity. Because of the relative nature of this measure, it is often used to make liquidity comparisons.

3. For the calculation of ratios, we will be using financial data as of the end of the fiscal year. In practice, average data are sometimes used. The average is calculated by dividing the sum of the beginning-of-year and end-of-year account balances by 2. Users of this approach feel that the resulting average ratio better reflects the firm's financial position.

4. This transformation actually results in the ratio of *net working capital to current assets*. Clearly, current assets can shrink by the amount of net working capital (i.e., their excess over current liabilities) while still retaining adequate current assets to just meet current liabilities.

It is useful to note that whenever a firm's current ratio is 1.0, net working capital is zero. If a firm has a current ratio of less than 1.0, it will have negative net working capital. Net working capital is useful only in comparing the liquidity of the same firm over time. It should not be used to compare the liquidity of different firms; the current ratio should be used instead.

Quick (Acid-Test) Ratio

quick (acid-test) ratio
A measure of liquidity calculated by dividing the firm's current assets minus inventory by current liabilities.

The **quick (acid-test) ratio** is similar to the current ratio except that it includes only the most liquid current assets: cash, marketable securities, and accounts receivable. Illiquid current assets such as inventory, prepaid expenses, and others are excluded. The generally low liquidity of inventory results from two primary factors: (1) many types of inventory cannot be easily sold because they are partially completed items, special-purpose items, and the like; and (2) inventory is typically sold on credit, which means that it becomes an account receivable before being converted into cash. The quick ratio acknowledges that the cash required to repay current liabilities will come from the most liquid current assets. The quick ratio considers whether Bartlett can repay the $620,000 of current liabilities over the upcoming two months with the most liquid current assets. The quick ratio is calculated as follows:[5]

$$\text{Quick ratio} = \frac{\text{cash + marketable securities + accounts receivable}}{\text{current liabilities}}$$

The quick ratio for Bartlett Company in 2002 is:

$$\frac{\$363,000 \ 1 \ \$68,000 \ 1 \ \$503,000}{\$620,000} = \frac{\$934,000}{\$620,000} = 1.51$$

The rule of thumb for the quick ratio is 1, meaning that for every dollar of current liabilities, the firm has $1 of the most liquid current assets. But, as with the current ratio, an acceptable value depends largely on the industry. The quick ratio provides a better measure of overall liquidity only when a firm's inventory cannot be easily converted into cash. If inventory is liquid, the current ratio is a preferred measure of overall liquidity. The inventory for a food retailer like, for example, Tim Hortons would be very liquid. For such companies, the current and quick ratios would give almost identical results.

Note that for all three liquidity measures—net working capital, current ratio, and quick (acid-test) ratio—the higher their value, the more liquid the firm is typically considered to be. As will be explained in Chapter 14, excessive liquidity reduces and increases the ability of a firm's risk to satisfy its short-term obligations *as they come due* but sacrifices profitability because (1) current assets are less profitable than fixed assets and (2) current liabilities are a less expensive financing source than long-term funds. For now, suffice it to say that there is a cost of increased liquidity—a trade-off exists between profitability and liquidity (risk).

---

5. Sometimes the quick ratio is defined as (current assets − inventory) ÷ current liabilities. If a firm were to show as current assets items other than cash, marketable securities, accounts receivable, and inventories, its quick ratio would vary, depending on the method of calculation.

3–4   What do liquidity ratios measure? Define the three liquidity ratios. What are their formulas? In what units are the output of the calculation? What do the answers mean?

3–5   Why is net working capital useful only in time-series comparisons of overall liquidity, whereas the current and quick ratios can be used for both cross-sectional and time-series analysis?

3.3 Analyzing Activity

activity ratios
Measure the company's effectiveness at managing accounts receivable, inventory, accounts payable, fixed assets, and total assets.

Activity ratios measure the company's effectiveness at managing accounts receivable, inventory, accounts payable, fixed assets, and total assets. With regard to current accounts, measures of liquidity are generally inadequate, because differences in the *composition* of a firm's current accounts can significantly affect its "true" liquidity. Activity ratios should be considered as a way to further analyze a company's liquidity. A company may have what is considered to be a good current ratio, which may suggest adequate liquidity. But there may be major problems with individual current assets or liabilities that will not be obvious when liquidity ratios are considered in isolation. Activity ratios are a way to uncover problems with individual current accounts. For example, consider the current assets and liabilities on the balance sheets for Firms A and B below:

Firm A			
Cash	$ 0	Accounts payable	$ 0
Marketable securities	0	Line of credit	10,000
Accounts receivable	0	Accruals	0
Inventories	20,000	Total current liabilities	$10,000
Total current assets	$20,000		

Firm B			
Cash	$ 5,000	Accounts payable	$ 5,000
Marketable securities	5,000	Line of credit	3,000
Accounts receivable	5,000	Accruals	2,000
Inventories	5,000	Total current liabilities	$10,000
Total current assets	$20,000		

The firms appear to be equally liquid, because their current ratios are both 2.0 ($20,000 ÷ $10,000). However, a closer look at the differences in the composition of current assets and liabilities suggests that *Firm B is more liquid than Firm A.* This is true for two reasons: (1) Firm B has more liquid assets in the form of cash and marketable securities than Firm A, which has only a single, relatively illiquid asset in the form of inventories, and (2) Firm B's current liabilities are in general more flexible than the single current liability—line of credit—of Firm A. The quick ratio confirms this. The quick ratio for Firm A is zero, but 1.5 for Firm B. This analysis, though, is still not adequate to uncover problems with individual current accounts.

It is important to look beyond measures of overall liquidity to assess the effectiveness of the management of specific current accounts. A number of ratios are available for measuring the activity of the most important current accounts, which include inventory, accounts receivable, and accounts payable.[6] The activity (efficiency of utilization) of both fixed and total assets should also be assessed.

Average Age of Inventory

average age of inventory
Measures the effectiveness of the company's management of inventory; it is the average length of time inventory is held by the company.

Average age of inventory measures the effectiveness of the company's management of inventory. It is the average length of time inventory is held by the company. The ratio is calculated as follows:

$$\text{Average age of inventory} = \frac{\text{inventory}}{\text{daily COGS}}$$

$$= \frac{\text{inventory}}{\frac{\text{COGS}}{365}}$$

The average age of inventory for Bartlett for the 2002 fiscal year is:[7]

$$\text{Average age of inventory} = \frac{\$289,900}{\frac{\$2,088,000}{365}} = \frac{\$289,900}{\$5,721} = 50.7 \text{ days}$$

Bartlett manufactures the patio furniture and it flows to inventory. In 2002, it took Bartlett 50.7 days to sell an average item of inventory. To analyze this answer, it must be compared to that of other firms in the same industry and to Bartlett's past average age of inventory. It would be inappropriate to compare Bartlett's result to the average age of inventory for grocery stores or airline manufacturers. An average age of inventory of 18 days would be usual for a grocery store, whereas for an airline manufacturer, the average age might be 143 days.

Average Collection Period

average collection period
The average amount of time needed to collect accounts receivable.

The **average collection period,** or average age of accounts receivable, is useful in evaluating credit and collection policies. It is arrived at by dividing the average daily sales into the accounts receivable balance:

---

6. Internal users of ratios may calculate the three current account ratios monthly. The management of net working capital is vital for all businesses, but particularly small businesses and businesses involved in the service sector and retailers. Timely analysis of the company's effectiveness at managing these three current accounts is vital.

7. Sometimes, inventory turnover rather than average age of inventory is used to analyze inventory. Inventory turnover is cost of goods sold ÷ inventory. Both ratios measure the effectiveness of inventory management; however, the days-based ratio is an easier concept to understand. It is also consistent with the other two current-account-based activity ratios. An alternative method to calculate average age of inventory is: 365 ÷ inventory turnover.

$$\text{Average collection period} = \frac{\text{accounts receivable}}{\text{average sales per day}}$$

$$= \frac{\text{accounts receivable}}{\dfrac{\text{annual sales}}{365}}$$

The average collection period for Bartlett Company in 2002 is:[8]

$$\frac{\$503,000}{\dfrac{\$3,074,000}{365}} = \frac{\$503,000}{\$8,422} = 59.7 \text{ days}$$

On the average it takes the firm 59.7 days to collect an account receivable.

The average collection period is meaningful only in relation to the firm's credit terms, industry averages, and past experience. If Bartlett Company extends 30-day credit terms to customers, an average collection period of 59.7 days may indicate a poorly managed credit or collection department, or both. Or, the lengthened collection period could be the result of an intentional relaxation of credit-term enforcement in response to competitive pressures. If the firm had extended 60-day credit terms, the 59.7-day average collection period would be quite acceptable. If the company's past experience was like that for Compton's Drinks depicted in Figure 3.1, then, again, a problem is indicated. Clearly, additional information would be required to draw definitive conclusions about the effectiveness of the firm's credit and collection policies.

It is worthwhile noting that in most industries where credit is granted to customers, the usual credit terms are net 30. That is, the seller grants the buyer a 30-day period in which to pay for the purchase. The seller expects to receive payment 30 days (or less) following the sale. It is common, however, for purchasers to "stretch" the payment period past the allowed credit period. Therefore, for a company which grants credit terms of net 30, it is not unusual to observe an average collection period of 40 or more days.

Average Payment Period

average payment period
The average amount of time needed to pay accounts payable.

The **average payment period,** or average age of accounts payable, is calculated in the same manner as the previous two activity ratios:

$$\text{Average payment period} = \frac{\text{accounts payable}}{\text{average purchases per day}}$$

$$= \frac{\text{accounts payable}}{\dfrac{\text{annual purchases}}{365}}$$

The difficulty in calculating this ratio stems from the need to find annual purchases[9]—a value not available in published financial statements. If information

---

8. The average collection period is sometimes called the *days' sales outstanding (DSO)*. A discussion of the evaluation and establishment of credit and collection policies is presented in Chapter 14. The formula as presented assumes, for simplicity, that all sales are made on a credit basis. If such is not the case, *average credit sales per day* should be substituted for average sales per day.

9. Technically, annual *credit* purchases—rather than annual purchases—should be used in calculating this ratio. For simplicity, this refinement is ignored here.

regarding purchases is not provided, then cost of goods sold is used instead. If we assume that Bartlett Company's purchases equalled 70 percent of its cost of goods sold in 2002, its average payment period is:

$$\frac{\$382,000}{\dfrac{0.70 \times \$2,088,000}{365}} = \frac{\$382,000}{\$4,004} = 95.4 \text{ days}$$

Again, this figure is meaningful only in relation to the average credit terms extended to the firm, industry averages, and past experience. If Bartlett Company's suppliers, on the average, have extended 30-day credit terms, an analyst would give it a low credit rating. If the firm has been generally extended 90-day credit terms, its credit would be acceptable. Prospective lenders and suppliers of trade credit are especially interested in the average payment period, because it provides them with a sense of the bill-paying patterns of the firm. Again, it is not unusual to observe average payment periods that are longer than the credit terms granted by the company to customers. Companies will "stretch" their payables trying to match their average collection period and avoid the need to finance their accounts receivable. This issue is discussed in detail in the following chapter.

Fixed and Total Asset Turnover

fixed asset turnover
Indicates the efficiency with which the firm uses its net fixed assets to generate sales.

The **fixed asset turnover** indicates the efficiency with which the firm uses its net fixed assets to generate sales. Generally, the higher a firm's fixed asset turnover, the more efficiently its fixed assets have been used. This ratio is of greatest interest to companies with a large investment in fixed assets. For retailers and service providers, the fixed asset turnover is less important since, in most cases, the investment in fixed assets is quite modest. Fixed asset turnover is calculated as follows:

$$\text{Fixed asset turnover} = \frac{\text{sales}}{\text{net fixed assets}}$$

Bartlett's fixed asset turnover for 2002 is:

$$\frac{\$3,074,000}{\$2,374,000} = 1.29$$

The fixed asset turnover indicates the dollar amount of sales generated by each dollar of net fixed assets. Bartlett generates $1.29 of sales for every dollar of net fixed assets. Note that for this ratio, only productive fixed assets are considered. Items like intangibles are ignored.

total asset turnover
Indicates the efficiency with which the firm uses its assets to generate sales.

The **total asset turnover** indicates the efficiency with which the firm uses its total assets to generate sales. It is calculated as follows:

$$\text{Total asset turnover} = \frac{\text{sales}}{\text{total assets}}$$

Bartlett Company's total asset turnover in 2002 is:

$$\frac{\$3,074,000}{\$3,597,000} = 0.85$$

Therefore, Bartlett generates $0.85 of sales with every dollar of total assets. The total asset turnover measures whether the company has been efficient at generating sales and profits on behalf of the suppliers of funds to the company. As with other ratios, the fixed and total asset turnovers are only meaningful when compared to previous values for the company or to an industry average. Generally, higher values are preferable to lower values, but it is also possible for these ratios to be too high. Very high turnovers, together with declining assets, may suggest a company is not reinvesting in (overextending) their assets. In addition, these ratios can indicate the type of company being analyzed.

A company with a very high fixed asset turnover and low total asset turnover has a low level of fixed assets in relation to current assets. Retailers and service-oriented companies display this pattern. For such companies, the management of current assets is vital. For industrial and resource companies (e.g., steel, oil and gas, aircraft, automotive, utility, telephone, durable goods, and mining), a much larger percentage of assets are fixed and therefore the fixed and total asset turnover ratios will likely be low and in a similar range. Bartlett manufactures patio furniture. A glance at the company's 2002 balance sheet indicates that a large percentage of the company's assets are fixed. Bartlett's fixed and total asset turnovers are low and in a similar range.

One caution with respect to use of these ratios: they use the *historical costs* of assets. Because some firms have significantly newer or older assets than others, comparing asset turnovers of those firms can be misleading. Because of inflation and the use of historical costs, firms with newer assets will tend to have lower turnovers than those with older assets. The differences in these turnovers could therefore result from more costly assets rather than from differing operating efficiencies. The financial manager should be cautious when using this ratio for cross-sectional comparisons.

! Hint

The higher the cost of the new assets, the larger the denominator and therefore the smaller the ratio.

? Review Question

3–6   What do activity ratios measure? Define the five activity ratios. What are their formulas and in what units are their output? What do the answers mean?

3–7   To assess the reasonableness of the firm's average collection period and average payment period ratios, what additional information is needed? Explain.

3–8   A company has a fixed asset turnover of 8.37 and a total asset turnover of 1.53. What does this data suggest? Develop a simple example displaying this concept.

LG3   LG5

3.4   Analyzing Leverage

Leverage indicates the amount of borrowed money (debt) being used in an attempt to maximize shareholder wealth. In general, the financial analyst is most concerned with long-term debt, since it commits the firm to paying interest, and eventually the principal, over the long run. Because creditors' claims must be satisfied before earnings can be distributed to shareholders, present and prospective

capitalization ratios
Show how a firm has financed the investment in assets. There are three alternatives: debt, preferred equity, and common equity.

coverage ratios
Measure the firm's ability to service the sources of financing.

shareholders pay close attention to the amount of leverage used by the company and the company's ability to make payments on the debt. Current and prospective creditors are also concerned about the firm's indebtedness, because the more indebted the firm, the more likely it will be unable to satisfy the creditors' claims. Management obviously must be concerned with leverage.

There are two types of leverage ratios: capitalization and coverage. **Capitalization ratios** show how a firm has financed the investment in assets. Recall that there are three alternatives: debt, preferred equity, and common equity. The greater the use of debt as a percent of total assets, the greater the financial leverage. Later in this chapter, financial leverage is discussed in greater detail. **Coverage ratios** assess the firm's ability to service the sources of financing. This includes making the contractual interest payments and principal repayments on debt, lease payments on financial leases, and dividend payments on preferred shares. These required payments are referred to as fixed financial charges. Typically, higher coverage ratios are preferred, but too high a ratio (above industry norms) may indicate unnecessarily low risk and returns. Alternatively, the lower the firm's coverage ratios, the more risky the firm is considered to be. "Riskiness" here refers to the firm's ability to pay fixed obligations. If a firm is unable to pay these obligations, it will be in default, and its creditors may seek immediate repayment. In most instances this would force a firm into bankruptcy. Two coverage ratios—the times interest earned ratio and the fixed-charge coverage ratio—are discussed in this section.

Debt Ratio

debt ratio
Measures the proportion of total assets financed by the firm's creditors.

The **debt ratio** measures the proportion of total assets financed by the firm's creditors. The higher this ratio, the greater the amount of other people's money being used in an attempt to generate profits. The ratio is calculated as follows:

$$\text{Debt ratio} = \frac{\text{total liabilities}}{\text{total assets}}$$

The debt ratio for Bartlett Company in 2002 is

$$\frac{\$1,643,000}{\$3,597,000} = 0.457 = 45.7\%$$

preferred equity ratio
Measures the proportion of total assets financed by preferred shareholders.

common equity ratio
Measures the proportion of total assets financed by common shareholders.

Higher ratios indicate greater reliance on debt financing, meaning higher risk and more financial leverage. For Bartlett, 45.7 percent of the assets have been financed by debt. By reviewing the 2002 balance sheet, the sources of the remaining financing can also be observed. Bartlett has preferred equity and common equity financing. The **preferred equity ratio** shows the proportion of total assets financed by preferred shareholders. For Bartlett for 2002, this ratio is 5.6 percent ($200,000 ÷ $3,597,000). The **common equity ratio** shows the percentage of assets financed by common shareholders. The total investment made by common shareholders includes the direct investment made when purchasing the common shares and the indirect investment made by reinvesting profits. For Bartlett for 2002, this totals $1,754,000. Therefore, the common equity ratio is 48.8 percent ($1,754,000 ÷ $3,597,000). These three ratios display the capital structure of Bartlett and must, by definition, sum to 100 percent (excluding rounding).

Companies must carefully monitor their capital structure (capitalization). Too much debt can lead to major financial problems. There are literally thousands of companies that have gone bankrupt because they used too much debt financing.

Debt/Equity Ratio

debt/equity ratio
Measures the proportion of long-term debt to common equity.

The **debt/equity ratio** measures the proportion of long-term debt to common equity. This ratio focuses on the long-term sources of financing to evaluate the relative amount of debt financing used. Since the debt ratio considers all debt, the result can be affected by large amounts of current liabilities like accounts payable and accruals. Since these forms of debt have no direct cost, the debt ratio can provide a misleading picture of the true debt situation. Since long-term debt requires long-term payment of both interest and principal, it may be a better measure of the use of debt financing. The debt/equity ratio is calculated as follows:

$$\text{Debt/equity ratio} = \frac{\text{long-term debt}}{\text{common equity}}$$

The debt/equity ratio for Bartlett Company in 2002 is:

$$\frac{\$1,023,000}{\$1,754,000} = 0.583 = 58.3\%$$

For every dollar of common equity financing, Bartlett is using $0.583 of long-term debt. A suggested maximum for the debt/equity ratio is 100 percent, meaning for $1 of common equity financing, the company has $1 of long-term debt. Bartlett is well below this level. But, as with all of the ratios, the result should be compared to the previous years' ratios and to an industry average. How a company chooses to finance assets (capitalization decisions) can differ significantly across the companies in an industry. Some firms use conservative strategies, others aggressive. The key question regarding the financing used is "Can the firm meet their required financial payments?" This is considered by the two coverage ratios. The coverage ratios link the leverage ratios to the profitability ratios. An analysis of the coverage ratios provide hints regarding the profitability of the company.

Times Interest Earned Ratio

times interest earned ratio
Sometimes called the *interest coverage ratio*, it measures the firm's ability to make contractual interest payments.

The **times interest earned ratio,** sometimes called the *interest coverage ratio,* measures the firm's ability to make contractual interest payments. The higher the value of this ratio, the better able the firm is to fulfill its interest obligations. The times interest earned ratio is calculated as follows:

$$\text{Times interest earned} = \frac{\text{earnings before interest and taxes (EBIT)}}{\text{interest}}$$

Applying this ratio to Bartlett Company yields the following 2002 value:

$$\text{Times interest earned} = \frac{\$418,000}{\$93,000} = 4.49$$

Earnings before interest and taxes is the same as *operating earnings*. The times interest earned ratio indicates the dollar amount of earnings available to make interest payments, for every dollar of interest. Bartlett, for 2002, has $4.49 of earnings for every dollar of interest. The firm's times interest earned ratio seems acceptable. As a rule, a value of at least 3.0—and preferably closer to 5.0—is suggested. If the firm's earnings before interest and taxes were to shrink by 78 percent [(4.49 − 1.0) ÷ 4.49], the firm would still be able to pay the $93,000 in interest it owes. Thus, it has a good margin of safety. The lowest acceptable times interest earned ratio is 1. A value of 1 indicates the company would have just enough EBIT to cover the required interest payments. The company's earnings before taxes would be zero. A times interest earned ratio less than 1 indicates the company is losing money (has negative earnings before taxes) and must raise financing to cover the interest payments.

Higher coverage ratios (above the industry average) are preferred since this indicates that the company's profitability is higher than the industry's. Too high a ratio (well above the industry norms) may indicate the company has very little debt and little risk, but lower returns since the company is not benefiting from financial leverage. If the company's debt ratio is comparable to the industry, but the coverage ratios are higher, then the company's profitability is well above industry averages. A low times interest earned ratio implies high risk and a questionable ability to service the required payments on debt. If a company is unable to pay these obligations, bankruptcy is a real possibility.

Fixed-Charge Coverage Ratio

fixed-charge coverage ratio
Measures the firm's ability to meet all fixed-payment obligations.

The **fixed-charge coverage ratio** measures the firm's ability to meet all fixed financial payments. Like the times interest earned ratio, the higher this value, the better. There are four fixed financial payments: interest on debt, principal repayments on debt, lease payments, and preferred share dividends.[10] The formula for the fixed-charge coverage ratio is as follows:

$$\frac{\text{earnings before interest and taxes} + \text{lease payments}}{\text{interest} + \text{lease payments} + \dfrac{\text{principal payments}}{1 - T} + \dfrac{\text{preferred share dividends}}{1 - T}}$$

where *T* is the corporate tax rate applicable to the firm's income. Principal payments and preferred share dividends must be divided by (1 − T) to adjust for the fact that these payments are made out of after-tax income. Interest and lease payments are deductible for tax purposes, so no adjustment is necessary. To put principal repayments and preferred dividends on a before-tax basis, divide them by (1 − T).

Example ▼ J & K Inc. must repay $140,000 of principal on their long-term debt and pay $70,000 of preferred share dividends this year. How much earnings before tax does J & K Inc. require to make these payments? J & K's tax rate is 30 percent. Since the required payments are made out of after-tax income, J & K needs sub-

---

10. Although preferred share dividends, which are stated at the time of issue, can be "passed" (not paid) at the option of the firm's directors, it is generally believed that the payment of such dividends is necessary. *This text therefore treats preferred share dividends as a contractual obligation, to be paid as a fixed amount, as scheduled.*

stantially more before-tax income to make the required payments. The amount of before-tax income for the principal requirement is:

$$\frac{\$140,000}{1-0.30} = \frac{\$140,000}{0.70} = \$200,000$$

With $200,000 of earnings before taxes, J & K will pay $60,000 of taxes ($200,000 × 0.30) and will have the necessary $140,000 of after-tax income to make the principal repayment. For the preferred share dividends, J & K requires $100,000 of before-tax income ($70,000 ÷ 0.70).

Applying the formula to Bartlett Company's 2002 data yields the following fixed-charge coverage ratio:

$$\frac{\$418,000 + \$35,000}{\$93,000 + \$35,000 + \dfrac{\$71,000}{1-0.29} + \dfrac{\$10,000}{1-0.29}}$$

$$= \frac{\$453,000}{\$93,000 + \$35,000 + \$100,000 + \$14,085} = \frac{\$453,000}{\$242,085} = 1.87$$

This indicates that for every dollar of fixed financial charges, Bartlett has $1.87 of earnings available to make the payments. Thus, the firm appears able to safely meet its fixed payments.

Like the times interest earned ratio, the fixed-charge coverage ratio measures the risk of the firm being unable to meet scheduled fixed payments and thus be driven into bankruptcy. The lower the ratio, the greater the risk to both lenders and owners, and the greater the ratio, the lower the risk. Higher ratios also imply the company may be more profitable than the industry, on average. This ratio therefore allows owners, creditors, and managers to assess the firm's ability to handle fixed financial obligations.

? Review Question

3–9   What do leverage ratios measure? What are the two types of leverage ratios? What are the formulas for the various leverage ratios? In what units are the output? What do the answers mean?

3–10 A company has a times interest earned ratio of 28.63, while the industry average is 12.31. Why might the company's ratio be so much higher than the industry average?

3.5 Analyzing Profitability

There are many measures of profitability. As a group, these measures evaluate the firm's earnings with respect to a given level of sales, a certain level of assets, the owners' investment, or share value. Without profits, a firm could not attract outside capital. Moreover, present owners and creditors would become concerned about the company's future and attempt to recover their funds. Owners, creditors, and management pay close attention to boosting profits due to the great importance placed on earnings in the marketplace.

Common-Size Income Statements

common-size income statement
An income statement in which each item is expressed as a percentage of sales.

A popular tool for evaluating profitability in relation to sales is the **common-size income statement.**[11] On this statement, each item is expressed as a percentage of sales, thus highlighting the relationship between sales and specific costs, expenses, and forms of income. Common-size income statements are especially useful in comparing performance across years. Three frequently cited ratios of profitability that can be read directly from the common-size income statement are (1) the gross margin, (2) the operating margin, and (3) the profit margin.

Common-size income statements for 2001 and 2002 for Bartlett Company are presented and evaluated in Table 3.5. The statements reveal that the firm's cost of goods sold increased from 66.7 percent of sales in 2001 to 67.9 percent in 2002, resulting in the gross margin declining. The **gross margin** measures the percent of each sales dollar remaining after the company has paid the direct costs of the products sold (the COGS). The higher the gross margin, the better. The lower the gross margin, the higher the relative cost of the products sold. See Table 3.7 for the formula.

gross margin
Measures the percentage of each sales dollar remaining after the firm has paid the direct costs of the products sold (COGS).

⚠ Hint
This is a very significant ratio for manufacturers and retailers, especially during times of high inflation. If a company does not raise prices when the cost of the goods sold is rising, the gross margin will decline.

Table 3.5 reveals that, as a percent of sales, all four operating expenses decline. Overall, operating expenses decline by 3 percent of sales, a very positive trend that more than offsets the increasing COGS as a percent of sales. As a result, the operating margin (EBIT) as a percent of sales increases 1.8 percent, to 13.6 percent. The **operating margin** measures the percent of each sales dollar remaining after all expenses associated with producing and selling the product and operating the company are deducted. See Table 3.7 for the formula. Obviously, the higher the operating margin, the better.

operating margin
Measures the percent of each sales dollar remaining after all expenses associated with producing and selling the product and operating the company are deducted.

The **profit margin** measures the percentage of each sales dollar remaining after all expenses, including financing expenses and taxes, have been deducted. For Bartlett for 2002, interest expenses as a percent of sales declined by 0.5 percent even though the dollar amount of total debt and interest expense increased. Sales increased faster than the interest expense, meaning interest expense as a percent of sales declined. Taxes as a percent of sales increased significantly even though the tax rate itself declined by about 1 percent. Bartlett's earnings before taxes were much higher in 2002 than in 2001, accounting for much higher taxes. On a bottom-line basis, the profit margin as a percent of sales increased 1.7 percent to 7.5 percent, a positive trend. "Good" profit margins vary across industries. For a grocery store, a profit margin of 3 percent would be considered normal (grocery stores make money on volume) while for a jewellery store a profit margin of 12 percent would be low (jewellery stores make money one item at a time).

profit margin
Measures the percentage of each sales dollar remaining after all expenses, including financing expenses and taxes, have been deducted.

To complete the analysis of profitability, four other measures should also be calculated and added to the end of the common-size income statement. Table 3.5 provides these four measures; the sections below provide details regarding each.

---

11. This statement is sometimes called a *percent income statement* or a *vertical analysis*. The same treatment is often applied to the firm's balance sheet to make it easier to evaluate changes in the asset and financial structures of the firm. In addition to measuring profitability, these statements in effect can be used as an alternative or supplement to liquidity, activity, and debt-ratio analysis.

TABLE 3.5	Bartlett Company Common-Size Income Statements		
	For the years ended December 31		Evaluation[a]
	2001	**2002**	**1999–2000**
Sales revenue	100.0%	100.0%	same
Less: Cost of goods sold	66.7	67.9	worse
(1) Gross margin	33.3%	32.1%	worse
Less: Operating expenses			
Selling expense	4.2%	3.3%	better
General and administrative expenses	7.3	6.3	better
Lease expense	1.3	1.1	better
Amortization expense	8.7	7.8	better
Total operating expense	21.5%	18.5%	better
(2) Operating margin (EBIT)	11.8%	13.6%	better
Less: Interest expense	3.5	3.0	better
Earnings before taxes	8.3%	10.6%	better
Less: Taxes	2.5	3.1	worse[b]
(3) Profit margin (NIAT)	5.8%	7.5%	better
(4) Return on assets (ROA)	4.5%	6.4%	better
(5) Return on equity (ROE)	8.5%	12.6%	better
(6) Earnings per share (EPS)	$1.81	$2.90	better
(7) Price/earnings ratio (P/E)	10.0	11.1	better

[a]Subjective assessments based on data provided.

[b]Taxes as a percent of sales increased noticeably between 2001 and 2002 due to differing costs and expenses, whereas the average tax rates (taxes ÷ earnings before taxes) for 2001 and 2002 remained about the same—30% and 29%, respectively.

Return on Total Assets (ROA)

return on total assets (ROA) Measures the firm's overall effectiveness in generating profits with its available assets; also called the *return on investment (ROI)*.

The **return on total assets (ROA)**, also called the *return on investment (ROI)*, measures the firm's overall effectiveness in generating profits with its available assets. The higher the firm's return on total assets, the better. The return on total assets is calculated as follows:

$$\text{Return on total assets} = \frac{\text{net income after taxes}}{\text{total assets}}$$

Bartlett Company's return on total assets in 2002 is

$$\frac{\$231,000}{\$3,597,000} = 6.4\%$$

For every $100 of assets, Bartlett generates a return of $6.42. To assess Bartlett's 6.4 percent return on total assets, appropriate cross-sectional and time-series data would be needed.

Return on Equity (ROE)

return on equity (ROE)
Measures the return earned on the owners' investment in the firm.

The **return on equity (ROE)** measures the return earned on the owners' investment in the firm. Generally, the higher this return, the better off are the owners. Return on equity is calculated as follows:

$$\text{Return on equity} = \frac{\text{earnings available for common shareholders}}{\text{common equity}}$$

This ratio for Bartlett Company in 2002 is:

$$\frac{\$221,000}{\$1,754,000} = 12.6\%$$

For every $100 of common equity financing, Bartlett generates a return of $12.60. To evaluate Bartlett's 12.6 percent return on equity, appropriate cross-sectional and time-series data would be needed. Note, though, that ROE is always higher than ROA (assuming EAC is positive). This is due to financial leverage.

Earnings per Share (EPS)

Hint
EPS represents the dollar amount earned *on behalf of* each share — not the amount of earnings *actually distributed* to shareholders.

The firm's *earnings per share (EPS)* are generally of interest to present or prospective shareholders and to management. The earnings per share represent the number of dollars earned on behalf of each outstanding share of common share. Earnings per share are calculated as follows:

$$\text{Earnings per share} = \frac{\text{earnings available for common shareholders}}{\text{number of common shares outstanding}}$$

The value of Bartlett Company's earnings per share in 2002 is:

$$\frac{\$221,000}{76,262} = \$2.90$$

The earnings generated for the owners are $2.90 per share.

This measure is closely watched by the investing public and is considered an important indicator of corporate success.

Price/Earnings (P/E) Ratio

price/earnings (P/E) ratio
Measures the amount investors are willing to pay for each dollar of the firm's earnings; the higher the P/E ratio, the greater the investor confidence.

Though not a true measure of profitability, the **price/earnings (P/E) ratio** is commonly used to assess the owners' appraisal of share value.[12] The P/E ratio measures the amount investors are willing to pay for each dollar of the firm's earnings. This ratio indicates the degree of confidence that investors have in the firm's future performance. The higher the P/E ratio, the greater the investor confidence.[13] The P/E ratio is calculated as follows:

---

12. Use of the price/earnings ratio to estimate the value of the firm is part of the discussion of "Other approaches to common shares valuation" in Chapter 8.

13. Another popular measure of investor confidence is the *market/book (M/B) ratio,* calculated by dividing the current common shares price per share by the per share book (accounting) value of shareholders' equity. The M/B ratio reflects the level of return on equity and the degree of investor confidence. Typically, relatively high M/B ratios are associated with good equity returns and investor optimism. Relatively low M/B ratios are associated with generally poor equity returns and investor pessimism. This ratio is of greatest interest to investors.

$$\text{Price/earnings (P/E) ratio} = \frac{\text{market price per common share}}{\text{earnings per share}}$$

If Bartlett Company's common shares at the end of 2002 was selling for $32.25, using the *earnings per share (EPS)* of $2.90 from Table 3.4, the P/E ratio at year-end 2002 is:

$$\frac{\$32.25}{\$2.90} = 11.12$$

leverage
The advantage gained by using a lever.

financial leverage
The use of debt financing to acquire assets.

Thus, investors were paying $11.12 for each $1 of earnings.

Financial Leverage and Measures of Profitability

⚠ Hint
Financial leverage is used to reduce the amount of funds the owners must invest and to magnify the returns generated by the business on behalf of the owners. Financial leverage is a method used to maximize shareholder returns and wealth, but, with leverage, the risk of the company also increases.

Leverage is the advantage gained by using a lever. For example, to move a large boulder, the lever might be a smaller rock and a long piece of wood. By leveraging the piece of wood between the small rock and large boulder, the boulder can be moved. Applying this to finance, the boulder is the maximization of the return to shareholders. The lever is debt financing. As discussed in Section 3.4, **financial leverage** is the use of debt financing to acquire assets. A company uses financial leverage to reduce the amount of funds the owners must invest and to maximize shareholder returns and wealth.

Example ▼

Rose Fitzpatrick is heading a group of investors that plan to start a new high tech business. To begin the business, a total investment of $1,000,000 is required. To finance the business, Rose has developed two plans that she will present to the investors. Plan 1 requires the group to invest $800,000 of equity and the company borrow the remaining $200,000 at a 10 percent interest rate. Plan 2 is to invest $200,000 of equity and borrow the remaining $800,000 at a 14 percent interest rate. Regardless of the choice, sales are expected to average $1,700,000, expenses total $1,380,000, and the company's tax rate will be 22 percent. Rose wonders which alternative she should recommend to her group of investors. The partial financial statements for the two alternatives are presented in Table 3.6. While both plans use financial leverage, Plan B uses a much greater level of leverage. One of the benefits of leverage is that the owners fully control the company regardless of the dollar amount of their investment. Therefore, under Plan B, the owners fully control the company, but they have only contributed 20 percent of the required financing. A partial disadvantage to this is that the potential creditors have recognized this fact and have charged a higher interest rate than in Plan A. To illustrate the second advantage of leverage, ratios must be calculated. At the bottom of Table 3.6, two profitability ratios are provided: ROA and ROE.

The return on assets suggests that Plan A is superior to Plan B. The respective ROAs are 23.4 percent versus 16.22 percent. Should Rose recommend Plan A? No. ROA considers the return on the total funds invested in the company. The owners are not concerned with the return provided on all of the funds invested in the company, only the funds they invest. Return on equity focuses on the return to the common shareholders. For Plan A, the owners are entitled to the $234,000 of profits on a total investment of $800,000, a ROE of 29.25 percent, a very attractive return. For Plan B, the owners are entitled to $162,240 on an investment of $200,000; the ROE is an impressive 81.12 percent. Obviously, if the estimates for sales and expenses are accurate, Rose should recommend Plan B to

TABLE 3.6   Rose Fitzpatrick is Financing Plans for the New Business (in $000)

	Plan A	Plan
Financial structure		
Debt (cost: 10% for A, 14% for B)	$200	$800
Equity	800	200
Total assets	$1,000	$1,000
Simplified income statement		
Sales	$1,700	$1,700
Expenses	1,380	1,380
EBIT	320	320
Interest expense	20	112
EBT	300	208
Taxes (22%)	66	45.76
NIAT	$234	$162.24
ROA	23.4%	16.22%
ROE	29.25%	81.12%

her investors. The investors contribute only 20 percent of the funds required to start the company, yet fully control the company and receive a return of 81 percent on the funds invested. The use of leverage has magnified the return on the invested capital. ▲

The above example focused on the advantages of financial leverage. As discussed in Chapter 2, all financial decisions entail a risk/return trade-off. The return associated with the use of leverage has been considered but if there were only advantages, all companies would have leverage ratios of 90 percent or above. This is not the case, there are major risks associated with financial leverage. Consider that if sales decline and costs increase, EBIT is squeezed. If, in the above example, EBIT falls to $110,000, Plan A still generates NIAT of $70,200. For Plan B, however, the company will lose money. The danger of financial leverage is associated with the company's ability to service the debt. If the company is unable to make the required payments, bankruptcy will occur. More discussion concerning leverage and the capital structure decisions of companies is provided in Chapter 10.

❓ Review Questions

3–11 What is a *common-size income statement?* What three key profitability ratios are found on this statement?

3–12 What would explain a firm's having a high gross margin and a low profit margin?

IN PRACTICE

Stock Options = Vanishing Profits?

Almost all publicly traded companies grant stock options to management. This is done for two reasons. First, granting options is a way to deal with the agency problem discussed in Chapter 1. Managers act as agents for the owners. Options are a way to align management's interests with those of shareholders; that is, to maximize the value of the company's common shares. Second, options are a way to attract and retain key employees. The technology industry is known for fierce competition for knowledgeable employees and so use of options is widespread. JDS Uniphase Corporation, a Canadian telecommunications equipment maker, has been one such company that has used options extensively.

For the 2001 fiscal year, Jozef Straus, CEO of JDS Uniphase, made US$150 million on stock options. In addition, three other managers made about US$124 million on stock options. This was at a time when the company reported the largest loss in history, US$56.1 billion, and the stock priced declined from a high of $165 to a low of about $16 on the TSX. This example illustrates the agency issue. It also highlights an important issue regarding how profits are calculated.

Under current accounting regulations, companies are not required to record options as an expense yet they are allowed to deduct them for tax purposes. Naturally, this inflates the profits reported by companies that use stock options to compensate management. While companies do not recognize the cost of this form of compensation, shareholders pay since the larger number of shares dilute EPS. Generous stock option plans mislead investors, by overstating NIAT, and transfer wealth from shareholders to senior management.

A financial analyst described options as "a ticking time bomb for many companies, an amazing stock option bubble that has been caused by company management using stock options to overstate profits." Another analyst states: "I think shareholders have to wake up and smell the coffee. They have to take more interest as owners of corporations. Stock options are a huge cost that just aren't being reflected in the earnings of many companies."

Merrill Lynch, a large investment dealer, reports that for 2001, the company where stock options had the biggest effect on profits was Yahoo! Inc., operator of the busiest site on the Internet. Yahoo's US$1.3 billion in option costs would have blown away its reported US$71 million net income, resulting in a US$1.2 billion loss. This large expense never appeared on any income statement.

The Canadian Institute of Chartered Accountants supports new rules that would require that Canadian companies treat options as an expense and disclose the cost of stock option plans in the financial statements. But standard-setting is a slow process, and so, in the meantime, users of financial statements must be wary.

REFERENCES: Sinclair Stewart, "Option Value Payouts Keep Soaring," *National Post*, May 20, 2002; John Gray, "Optional Illusion," *Canadian Business*, March 4, 2002; Steve Maich, "Tech Profits Overstated: Accounting Shenanigans," *National Post*, June 20, 2001; Jill Vardy, "JDS Uniphase Boss Makes More than US$150M on Options," *National Post*, October 6, 2001.

3–13   Define and differentiate between return on total assets (ROA), return on equity (ROE), and earnings per share (EPS). Which measure is probably of greatest interest to owners? Why?

3–14   What is the *price/earnings (P/E) ratio*? How does it relate to investor confidence in the firm's future? Is the P/E ratio a true measure of profitability?

3–15   What is financial leverage? What are the advantages and disadvantages of financial leverage? What are the potential advantages and disadvantages if a company has: (**a**) a 5 percent debt ratio; (**b**) a 90 percent debt ratio?

3.6 A Complete Ratio Analysis

Analysts frequently wish to take a global look at a firm's financial performance. As noted earlier, no single ratio is adequate for assessing all aspects of a firm's financial condition. Here we consider two popular approaches to a complete ratio analysis: (1) the DuPont system of analysis, and (2) the summary analysis of a large number of ratios. Each of these approaches has merit. The DuPont system acts as a *diagnostic tool* with which to assess the key areas responsible for the firm's financial condition. The summary analysis approach tends to view *all aspects* of the firm's financial activities to isolate key areas of responsibility.

DuPont System of Analysis

DuPont system of analysis
System used by management to dissect the firm's financial statements and to assess its financial condition.

The **DuPont system of analysis** is named for the DuPont Corporation, which originally popularized its use. It is used by financial managers to dissect the firm's financial statements and to assess its financial condition. The DuPont system merges the income statement and balance sheet into two summary measures of profitability: return on total assets (ROA) and return on equity (ROE). Figure 3.2 depicts the basic DuPont system with Bartlett Company's 2002 monetary and ratio values. The upper portion of the chart summarizes the income statement activities; the lower portion summarizes the balance sheet activities.

The DuPont system links the *profit margin* (which measures the firm's profitability on sales) with its *total asset turnover* (which indicates how efficiently the firm has used its assets to generate sales). The **DuPont formula** then multiplies these two ratios to find the firm's *return on total assets (ROA):*

DuPont formula
Multiplies the firm's *profit margin* by its *total asset turnover* to calculate the firm's *return on total assets (ROA).*

$$\text{ROA} = \text{profit margin} \times \text{total asset turnover}$$

Substituting the appropriate formulas into the equation and simplifying produces the formula given earlier:

$$\text{ROA} = \frac{\text{net income after taxes}}{\text{sales}} \times \frac{\text{sales}}{\text{total assets}} = \frac{\text{net income after taxes}}{\text{total assets}}$$

If the 2002 values of the profit margin and total asset turnover for Bartlett Company, calculated earlier, are substituted into the DuPont formula, the result is

$$\text{ROA} = 7.2\% \times 0.85 = 6.1\%$$

As expected, this value is the same as that calculated directly in an earlier section. The DuPont formula allows the firm to break down its return on total assets into a profit-on-sales and an efficiency-of-asset-use component. Typically, a firm with a low profit margin has a high total asset turnover, which results in a reasonably good return on total assets. Often, the opposite situation exists.

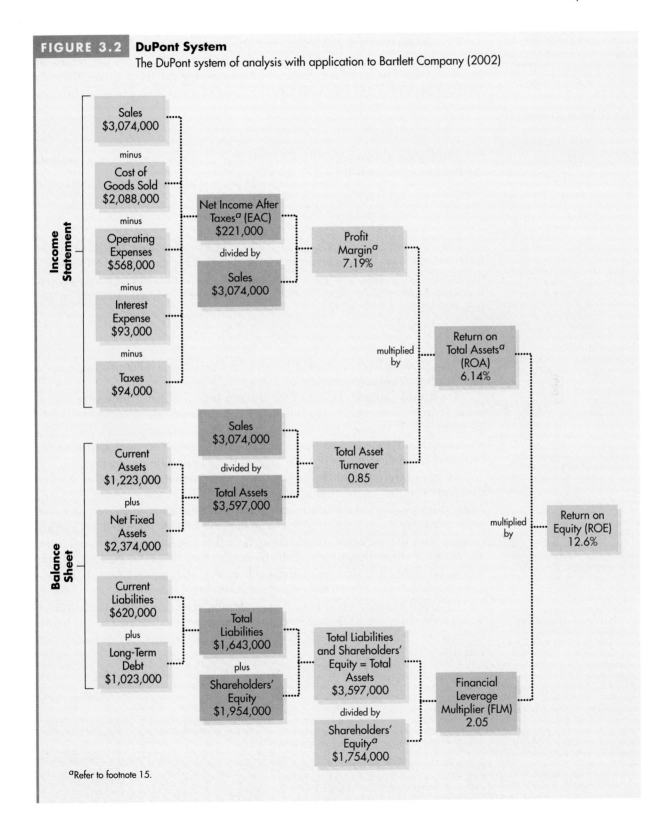

FIGURE 3.2   DuPont System
The DuPont system of analysis with application to Bartlett Company (2002)

*a*Refer to footnote 15.

modified DuPont formula
Relates the firm's return on total assets (ROA) to its return on equity (ROE) using the *financial leverage multiplier (FLM)*.

financial leverage multiplier (FLM)
The ratio of the firm's total assets to shareholders' equity.

The second step in the DuPont system employs the **modified DuPont formula.** This formula relates the firm's return on total assets (ROA) to the return on equity (ROE). The latter is calculated by multiplying the ROA by the **financial leverage multiplier (FLM)**, which is the ratio of total assets to shareholders' equity:[14]

$$ROE = ROA \times FLM$$

Substituting the appropriate formulas into the equation and simplifying produces the formula given earlier:[15]

$$ROE = \frac{\text{net income after taxes}}{\text{total assets}} \times \frac{\text{total assets}}{\text{shareholders' equity}} = \frac{\text{net income after taxes}}{\text{shareholders' equity}}$$

Use of the financial leverage multiplier (FLM) to convert the ROA to the ROE reflects the impact of leverage (use of debt) on owners' return. Substituting the values for Bartlett Company's ROA of 6.14 percent, calculated earlier, and Bartlett's FLM of 2.05 ($3,597,000 total assets ÷ $1,754,000 common equity) into the modified DuPont formula yields

$$ROE = 6.14\% \times 2.05 = 12.6\%$$

The 12.6 percent ROE calculated by using the modified DuPont formula is the same as that calculated directly.

The considerable advantage of the DuPont system is that it allows the firm to break its return on equity into three parts: a profit-on-sales component (profit margin), an efficiency-of-asset-use component (total asset turnover), and a use-of-leverage component (financial leverage multiplier). The total return to the owners therefore can be analyzed in light of these important dimensions.

As an illustration, look at the ratio values summarized in Table 3.6. Bartlett Company's profit margin and total asset turnover increased between 2001 and 2002 to levels above the industry average. In combination, improved profit on sales and better use of assets resulted in an improved ROA. Increased asset return coupled with the increased use of debt reflected in the increased financial leverage multiplier (not shown) caused the owners' return (ROE) to increase. Simply stated, the DuPont system of analysis shows that the improvement in Bartlett Company's 2002 ROE resulted from greater profit on sales, better use of assets, and increased leverage. Of course, it is important to recognize that the increased return reflected in the ROE may be due to the increased risk caused by the higher leverage. In other words, the use of more financial leverage increases *both* return and risk.

---

14. The financial leverage multiplier is equivalent to 1/(1 − debt ratio) and represents 1 divided by the percentage of total financing raised with equity. For computational convenience, the financial leverage multiplier is utilized here rather than the seemingly more descriptive debt ratio.

15. For companies with preferred equity outstanding, the DuPont analysis becomes somewhat complicated. Rather than NIAT, earnings available for common shareholders is used to calculate profit margin. This changes the previously calculated profit margin and ROA. To calculate the FLM, common equity, not total shareholders' equity, is used as the denominator. These changes are necessary, since the ultimate outcome of the DuPont analysis is to calculate ROE and this ratio is based on common equity: the earnings available for common shareholders and the total investment made by the common shareholders. For companies that have not issued preferred equity, no adjustments are required.

IN PRACTICE

DuPont Analysis: Still Useful After All These Years

Since 1919, when first developed by the DuPont Company, financial managers and those who analyze the financial performance of companies have used the DuPont system to evaluate return on equity. Heavy equipment manufacturer Caterpillar Inc. and Nucor, a steel manufacturer, both use the DuPont analysis to improve financial performance. The budget and forecasts manager at Caterpillar states that, "DuPont is a good tool for getting people started in understanding how they can have an impact on results." Nucor's CFO says, "It's simple. All of our people understand it. It has worked for us."

To illustrate the DuPont system of analysis, consider the financial results for the following three Canadian companies for the 2001 fiscal year. Liquidation World, based in Calgary, retails merchandise from distress situations, such as bankruptcies, close-outs, inventory overruns, and insurance claims.The company has 93 retail outlets in both Canada and the United States. Onex Corporation is a diversified, Canadian-controlled company with operations in a variety of industries, including electronics manufacturing services, customer management services, automotive products, engineered building products, sugar refining, communications infrastructure, and feature film exhibition. Talisman Energy is a large, diversified oil and gas producer with operations in Canada, the United States, and internationally.

Company	Sales	NIAT	Total assets	Common equity
Liquidation World (in $000s)	$185,459	$6,981	$57,985	$52,355
Onex Corporation (in $millions)	$ 23,803	$ 798	$20,870	$ 2,219
Talisman Energy (in $millions)	$ 4,058	$ 762	$10,906	$ 3,798

What does a DuPont analysis reveal about the three companies? The components of the DuPont analysis for the three companies are provided in the following table. The formulas used to calculate the numbers are shown in Figure 3.2.

Company	Profit margin	×	Total asset turnover	=	ROA	×	FLM	=	ROE
Liquidation World	3.76%	×	3.20	=	12.03%	×	1.11	=	13.35%
Onex Corporation	3.35%	×	1.14	=	3.82%	×	9.41	=	35.95%
Talisman Energy	18.78%	×	0.37	=	6.95%	×	2.87	=	19.95%

The results are very different for the three companies. Liquidation World's ROE, at 13.33 percent, is the lowest of the three. Driving the result is the very rapid total asset turnover. Given that Liquidation World relies on rapid sales of inventory, no accounts receivables, and low investment in fixed assets, low profit margin and high total asset turnover are not surpring. Liquidation World uses very little financial leverage. The financial earnings multiplier is close to 1. Onex, on the other hand, relies on leverage for the very high ROE of almost 36 percent. ROA is quite low due to a low profit margin and total asset turnover. Onex has used very little common equity financing, however, so the financial leverage multiplier is over 9, which magnifies the ROE. Talisman's acceptable ROE of 20 percent is due to the very high profit margin of 18.8 percent. Total asset turnover is very low due to the large investment that an oil and gas company must make in properties and operations. While Talisman's ROA is 7 percent, the significant use of financial leverage magnifies the ROE to over 20 percent.

The DuPont system is a powerful way for management, creditors, shareholders, and other interested parties to examine overall company performance and risk as measured by ROA and ROE. It is a relatively simple tool that can be used to track down reasons for poor returns and lead to major insights concerning a company's operations.

▶

IN PRACTICE

(Continued)

REFERENCES: Robbin Goldwyn Blumenthal, "'T is the Gift to Be Simple," *CFO*, January 1998, downloaded from **www.cfonet.com**; Peter C. Eisemann, "Return on Equity and Systematic Ratio Analysis," *Commercial Lending Review*, July 1,

1997. 2001 Annual Reports of Liquidation World, Onex Corporation, and Talisman Energy. These reports are available at **www.sedar.com**.

Summarizing All Ratios

Ratio values calculated for 2000 through 2002 for Bartlett Company, along with the industry average ratios for 2002, are summarized in Table 3.7. The table shows the formula for each ratio. Using these data, we can discuss the four key aspects of Bartlett's performance—(1) liquidity, (2) activity, (3) leverage, and (4) profitability—on a cross-sectional and time-series basis.

Liquidity

The overall liquidity of the firm seems to exhibit a reasonably stable trend, having been maintained at a level that is relatively consistent with the industry average in 2002. While the current ratio declined between 2001 and 2002 and is lower than the industry average in 2002, the quick ratio increased and is higher than the industry average. This implies that a greater portion of Bartlett's current assets are liquid, a positive sign. The quick ratio also suggests that the firm has very good control of inventory. A review of the appropriate accounts on the balance sheet (see Table 3.4) reveal that in 2002 the three liquid current assets increased by 32.7% [(934,000 ÷ 704,000) − 1] × 100, inventory declined by 3.7% [($289,000 ÷ $300,000) − 1] × 100, while current liabilities increased by 28.4% [($620,000 ÷ $483,000) − 1] × 100. The net impact of these changes for 2002 is that the current ratio will decline but the quick ratio will increase. The very large increase in accounts receivable and accounts payable should also be noted. These accounts increased 37.8 percent and 41.5 percent, respectively. Since the increase in sales was less, 19.8 percent, the implication is that the activity ratios for these two accounts will deteriorate. Overall, the firm's liquidity seems to be good.

Activity

The trends discussed above are reflected in the activity ratios. Bartlett's average age of inventory declined by almost 21 days over the three years and is now almost 5 days lower than the industry average. This is a very positive sign. Inventory management has improved as suggested by the liquidity ratios. Unfortunately, the average collection period, as anticipated, has increased by 15 days and is now about 15 days higher than the industry average. Assuming Bartlett's credit terms are net 30, their receivables are, on average, 30 days overdue. Bartlett's must improve their collection procedures, as carrying excessive receivables is costly and can lead to bad debts.

Bartlett also appears to be slow in paying its bills—nearly 30 days later than the industry average. Payment procedures should be examined to ensure that the company's credit standing is not adversely affected. It appears Bartlett is stretching their payables to finance the increasing investment in accounts receivable. Bartlett's suppliers may soon refuse to ship on credit. Bartlett's fixed and total asset turnover are similar, with both increasing above the industry average after declining in 2001. It appears the company made a large investment in assets in 2001 that resulted in these ratios declining. The increase in the turnovers in 2002 is positive. As is clear from the DuPont system, higher asset turnovers impact favourably on ROE. Overall, the activity ratios are acceptable; however, Bartlett must improve both their average collection period and the average payment period.

Leverage

Bartlett's capital structure has significantly changed over the three years and is now quite different from the industry average. Debt and preferred equity financing both require fixed payments. The combination of these two sources is 51.3 percent, over 11 percent higher than the industry average. Common equity is a comparable amount below the industry average. Bartlett is using a great deal of financial leverage. The debt-equity ratio confirms this, but the ratio is well below the accepted maximum of 100 percent and actually declined in 2002. Bartlett's common equity grew at a faster rate than long-term debt. The growth in equity came from selling common shares plus reinvesting profits. Of the $221,000 of earnings available for common shareholders, Bartlett reinvested $123,000 in 2002. The company paid $98,000 in common dividends (see the change in retained earnings). Bartlett's capital structure could be positive or negative depending on the company's ability to meet the required payments on the financing. The coverage ratios increased in 2002 after a significant decline in 2001. Increasing debt in 2001, to finance the increasing assets, caused a deterioration in Bartlett's ability to service their financial obligations. The coverage ratios improved in 2002 and suggest that Bartlett's profitability in 2002 is better than the industry's. So, while Bartlett uses more financial leverage than the average firm in the industry, the company is able to service their obligations.

Profitability

As discussed earlier, Bartlett's gross margin as a percent of sales declined in 2002 but, even so, it is 2 percent better than the industry average. As displayed in Table 3.5, Bartlett's operating expenses as a percent of sales declined by 3 percent to 18.5 percent. This ability to control costs resulted in Bartlett reducing operating costs as a percent of sales to a level slightly better than the industry average of 19 percent (the difference between the industry values for gross margin and operating margin). As a result, Bartlett's operating margin, as a percent of sales, is 2.6 percent better than the industry's. Since Bartlett uses much more financial leverage, however, Bartlett's profit margin is only 1.1 percent higher than the industry. Bartlett pays a full 1.5 percent of sales more in interest than the average company in the industry. Bartlett's objective should be to return to the level of profitability enjoyed in 2000.

⚷ Career Key

Accounting personnel have the major responsibility in informing the analyst of the areas where differing accounting treatment exists within the firm. When possible, they should inform the analyst of differences between the firm and its benchmark.

The firm's ROA, ROE, and EPS behaved similar to its profit margin over the 2000–2002 period. Bartlett appears to have experienced a rapid expansion in assets between 2000 and 2001. The owners' return, as evidenced by the high 2002 ROE, suggests that the firm is performing well. Of course, as noted in the DuPont system of analysis of Bartlett's 2002 results, the increased ROE actually resulted from increased returns and increased risk. This can be seen in the firm's increased leverage ratios and financial leverage multiplier (FLM). In addition, although the price/earnings (P/E) ratio is below that of the industry, some improvement occurred between 2000 and 2002. The firm's above-average returns—profit margin, ROA, ROE, and EPS—may be due to its above-average risk, as reflected in its below-industry-average P/E ratio.

In summary, the firm appears to be growing and has recently expanded its assets, primarily through the use of debt. The 2000–2002 period seems to reflect a phase of adjustment and recovery from the rapid growth in assets. Bartlett's sales, profits, and other performance factors seem to be growing with the increase in the size of the operation. The main problem areas are with the management of receivables and payables. High levels of receivables seem to be squeezing the firm's ability to pay their accounts payables in a timely manner. The company must also refrain from using more debt financing and perhaps should try to reduce the level of debt. Bartlett's common shareholders will want the P/E ratio to improve. A company with higher profitability than the industry average should also have a P/E ratio that is higher. This should occur as the company continues to adjust to the rapid growth that occurred in 2001. In short, the firm appears to have done quite well in 2002.

Cautions about Ratio Analysis

To conclude the discussion of ratios, we should consider the following cautions:

1. A single ratio does not generally provide sufficient information from which to judge the *overall* performance of the firm. Only when a group of ratios is used can reasonable judgments be made. However, if an analysis is concerned only with certain *specific* aspects of a firm's financial position, one or two ratios may be sufficient. Remember, when analyzing ratios, it is useful to refer to the appropriate accounts on the financial statements. The combination of considering both the ratio and the underlying numbers on the financial statements will allow for a more complete analysis.

2. The financial statements being compared should be dated at the same point in time during the year. If they are not, the effects of *seasonality* may produce erroneous conclusions and decisions. For example, comparison of the average age of inventory of a toy manufacturer at the end of June with its end-of-December value can be misleading. Clearly the seasonal impact of the December holiday selling season would skew any conclusions about the firm's inventory management drawn from such a comparison. Erroneous conclusions can be avoided by comparing results for June of the current year to June of the prior year, December to December, and so forth, to eliminate the effects of seasonality.

3. It is preferable to use audited financial statements for ratio analysis. If the statements have not been audited, the data contained in them may not reflect

the firm's true financial condition. For smaller, private companies a review engagement often takes the place of an audit.

4. The financial data being compared should have been developed in the same way. The use of differing accounting treatments—especially relative to inventory, profitability, and amortization—can distort the results of ratio analysis, regardless of whether cross-sectional or time-series analysis is used.

5. When the ratios of one firm are compared with those of another or with those of the firm itself over time, results can be distorted due to inflation. Inflation can cause the book values of inventory and depreciable assets to differ greatly from their true (replacement) values. Additionally, inventory costs and amortization of fixed assets can differ from their true values, thereby distorting profits. These inflationary effects typically have greater impact the larger the differences in the ages of the assets of the firms being compared. Without adjustment, inflation tends to cause older firms (older assets) to appear more efficient and profitable than newer firms (newer assets). Clearly, care must be taken in comparing ratios of older to newer firms or a firm to itself over a long period of time.

6. It is sometimes very difficult to define what is a good and bad ratio. This can be the case due to the type of industry or due to specific company policies. A current ratio of 2 meets the rule of thumb and is generally considered satisfactory. If the company carries little inventory and all sales are for cash, the implication is that current assets are primarily cash and marketable securities. While carrying such a large amount of cash provides safety, cash is an unproductive asset—the rate of return on cash is very low. Therefore is the current ratio of 2 good or bad? It depends on the company's plans for the cash and their tolerance for risk. The industry average is really a secondary consideration. Without knowing more details, it is almost impossible to say the ratio is good or bad. It is important, however, for the analyst to note the very high levels of cash. Many ratios are subject to these kinds of interpretation complexities. This is particularly the case for ratios such as fixed and total asset turnover, debt/equity ratio, average payment period, fixed-charge coverage, and the price/earnings ratio. Numerous factors influence these ratios and it is not a simple task to conclude that a particular value is good or bad. Calculating ratios is straightforward; analyzing ratios can be quite complex.

? Review Questions

3–16 Financial ratio analysis is often divided into four areas: *liquidity, activity, leverage,* and *profitability* ratios. Differentiate each of these areas of analysis from the others. Which is of the greatest relative concern to creditors?

3–17 What three areas of analysis are combined in using the *modified DuPont formula*? How are they combined to explain the firm's return on equity (ROE)? How is risk from financial leverage captured in this system?

3–18 Describe how you would approach a complete ratio analysis of the firm by summarizing a large number of ratios.

3–19 Why is it preferable to compare financial statements that are dated at the same point in time during the year?

TABLE 3.7   Summary of Bartlett Company Ratios (2000–2002, including 2002 industry averages)

Ratio	Formula	Year 2000[a]	Year 2001[b]	Year 2002[b]	Industry average 2002[c]	Evaluation[d] Cross-sectional 2002	Evaluation[d] Time-series 2000–2002	Evaluation[d] Overall
Liquidity								
Net working capital	current assets − current liabilities	$583,000	$521,000	$603,000	$427,000	good	good	good
Current ratio	$\dfrac{\text{current assets}}{\text{current liabilities}}$	2.04	2.08	1.97	2.05	OK	OK	OK
Quick (acid-test) ratio	$\dfrac{\text{cash + marketable securities + accounts receivable}}{\text{current liabilities}}$	1.32	1.46	1.51	1.43	good	excellent	good
Activity								
Average age of inventory	$\dfrac{\text{inventory}}{\text{average COGS per day}}$	71.6 days	64 days	50.7 days	55.3 days	excellent	excellent	excellent
Average collection period	$\dfrac{\text{accounts receivable}}{\text{average sales per day}}$	44.5 days	51.9 days	59.7 days	44.9 days	very poor	very poor	very poor
Average payment period	$\dfrac{\text{accounts payable}}{\text{average purchases per day}}$	76.9 days	82.3 days	95.4 days	67.4 days	very poor	very poor	very poor
Fixed asset turnover	$\dfrac{\text{sales}}{\text{net fixed assets}}$	1.38	1.13	1.29	1.15	good	OK	good
Total asset turnover	$\dfrac{\text{sales}}{\text{total assets}}$	0.94	0.79	0.85	0.75	good	OK	good
Leverage								
Capitalization:								
Debt ratio	$\dfrac{\text{total liabilities}}{\text{total assets}}$	36.8%	44.3%	45.7%	40.0%	higher	increasing	questionable
Preferred equity ratio	$\dfrac{\text{preferred equity}}{\text{total assets}}$	6.8%	6.1%	5.6%	0%	OK	OK	OK
Common equity ratio	$\dfrac{\text{common equity}}{\text{total assets}}$	56.4%	49.5%	48.8%	60%	lower	decreasing	questionable
Debt/equity ratio	$\dfrac{\text{long-term debt}}{\text{common equity}}$	43.5%	59.7%	58.3%	47.4%	higher	slight decrease	questionable

Ratio	Formula	2000[a]	2001[b]	2002[b]	Industry average 2002[c]	Cross-sectional 2002	Time series 2000–2002	Overall
Leverage (continued)								
Coverage:								
Times interest earned ratio	$\dfrac{\text{earnings before interest and taxes}}{\text{interest}}$	5.6	3.3	4.5	4.3	good	OK	OK
Fixed-charge coverage ratio	$\dfrac{\text{earnings before interest and taxes + lease payments}}{\text{int. + lease pay.} + \frac{\text{prin.}}{1-T} + \frac{\text{pref. div.}}{1-T}}$	2.4	1.4	1.9	1.5	good	OK	good
Profitability[e]								
Gross margin	$\dfrac{\text{gross margin}}{\text{sales}}$	31.4%	33.3%	32.1%	30.0%	very good	OK	good
Operating margin	$\dfrac{\text{operating earnings}}{\text{sales}}$	14.6%	11.8%	13.6%	11.0%	very good	OK	good
Profit margin	$\dfrac{\text{net income after taxes}}{\text{sales}}$	8.8%	5.8%	7.5%	6.4%	very good	OK	good
Return on total assets (ROA)	$\dfrac{\text{net income after taxes}}{\text{total assets}}$	8.3%	4.5%	6.4%	4.8%	very good	OK	good
Return on equity (ROE)	$\dfrac{\text{earnings available for common shareholders}}{\text{common equity}}$	14.1%	8.5%	12.6%	8.0%	excellent	OK	good
Earnings per share (EPS)	$\dfrac{\text{earnings available for common shareholders}}{\text{number of common shares outstanding}}$	$3.26	$1.81	$2.90	$2.26	N/A	OK	N/A
Price/earnings (P/E) ratio	$\dfrac{\text{market price per common share}}{\text{earnings per share}}$	10.5	10.0	11.1	12.5	Poor	OK	OK

[a]Calculated from data not included in the chapter.
[b]Calculated by using the financial statements presented in Tables 3.3 and 3.4.
[c]Obtained from sources not included in this chapter.
[d]Subjective assessments based on data provided.
[e]Due to space limitations, the common-size analysis is not provided. The common-size analysis as depicted in Table 3.5 should always be used to analyze profitability.

SUMMARY

LG1 **Introduce the parties interested in completing a financial ratio analysis, the three types of ratio comparisons, and the four categories of ratios.** Ratio analysis allows present and prospective shareholders and lenders and the firm's management to evaluate the firm's financial performance. It can be performed on a cross-sectional or a time-series basis. Benchmarking is a popular type of cross-sectional analysis. There are four categories of ratios: liquidity, activity, leverage, and profitability.

LG2 **Analyze a company's liquidity and the company's effectiveness at managing inventory, accounts receivable, accounts payable, and fixed and total assets.** The liquidity, or ability of the firm to pay its bills as they come due, can be measured by net working capital, the current ratio, or the quick (acid-test) ratio. Activity ratios measure a company's effectiveness at managing current accounts and fixed and total assets. Inventory activity is measured by average age of inventory, accounts receivable by the average collection period, and accounts payable by the average payment period. Fixed and total asset turnovers measure the efficiency with which the firm uses its assets to generate sales. Formulas for these liquidity and activity ratios are summarized in Table 3.7.

LG3 **Discuss financial leverage and the ratios used to assess how the firm has financed assets and the company's ability to cover the financing charges associated with the financing used.** The more debt a firm uses, the greater its financial leverage, which magnifies both risk and return. Leverage ratios measure both the capitalization of the company and the ability to service debts. A common measure of leverage is the debt ratio. The ability to pay fixed charges can be measured by times interest earned and fixed-charge coverage ratios. Formulas for these leverage ratios are summarized in Table 3.7.

LG4 **Evaluate a company's profitability using common-size analysis and relative to the** company's sales, total assets, common equity, and common share price. The common-size income statement, which shows all items as a percentage of sales, can be used to determine gross margin, operating margin, and profit margin. Other measures of profitability include return on total assets, return on equity, earnings per share, and the price/earnings ratio. Formulas for these profitability ratios are summarized in Table 3.7.

LG5 **Explore the link between the various categories of ratios, in particular between liquidity and activity and between leverage and profitability.** The activity ratios depict the three major current accounts on which liquidity is based. The liquidity ratios should provide hints regarding the levels of the activity ratios. Total asset turnover is an important part of return on equity (ROE). Coverage ratios provide an indication of the profitability of the company. Financial leverage directly impacts on ROE.

LG6 **Use the DuPont system and a summary of financial ratios to perform a complete ratio analysis of a firm, and consider some cautions concerning ratio analysis.** The DuPont system of analysis is a diagnostic tool used to find the key areas responsible for the firm's financial performance. It allows the firm to break the return on equity into three components: profit on sales, efficiency of asset use, and use of leverage. The DuPont system of analysis, summarized in Figure 3.2, makes it possible to assess all aspects of the firm's activities in order to isolate key areas of responsibility. Some cautions: (1) A single ratio does not generally provide sufficient information. (2) Financial statements being compared should be dated at the same point in time during the year. (3) Audited financial statements should be used. (4) Data should be checked for consistency of accounting treatment. (5) Inflation and different asset ages can distort ratio comparisons. (6) It is difficult to define a "good" and a "bad" ratio.

ST 3–1   Ratio formulas and interpretations   Without referring to the text, indicate for each of the following ratios the formula for its calculation and the kinds of problems, if any, the firm is likely to have if these ratios are too high relative to the industry average. What if they are too low relative to the industry? Create a table similar to the one that follows and fill in the empty blocks.

Ratio	Too high	Too low
Current ratio =		
Average age of inventory =		
Times interest earned =		
Gross margin =		
Return on total assets =		

ST 3–2   Balance sheet completion using ratios   Complete the 2002 balance sheet for O'Keefe Industries using the information that follows it.

Balance Sheet
O'Keefe Industries
December 31, 2002

Cash	$ 30,000	Accounts payable	$120,000
Marketable securities	25,000	Line of credit	
Accounts receivable	_____	Accruals	20,000
Inventories	_____	Total current liabilities	_____
Total current assets	_____	Long-term debt	_____
Net fixed assets	_____	Shareholders' equity	_____
Total assets	══════	Total liabilities and shareholders' equity	══════

The following financial data for 2002 are also available:
(1) Sales totalled $1,825,000.
(2) The gross margin was 25 percent.
(3) Average age of inventory was 60 days.
(4) The average collection period was 40 days.
(5) The current ratio was 1.60.
(6) The total asset turnover ratio was 1.25.
(7) The debt ratio was 60 percent.

PROBLEMS

WARM-UP

3–1   Ratio comparisons   Robert Arias recently inherited a stock portfolio from his uncle. Wishing to learn more about the companies that he is now invested in, Robert performs a ratio analysis on each one and decides to compare them to each other. Some of his ratios are listed.

	Island Electric Utility	Burger Heaven	Fink Software	Roland Motors
Current ratio	1.10	1.3	6.8	4.5
Quick ratio	.90	.82	5.2	3.7
Debt ratio	68.2%	46.1%	0%	34.9%
Profit margin	6.2%	14.3%	28.5%	8.4%

Assuming that his uncle was a wise investor who assembled the portfolio with care, Robert finds the wide differences in these ratios confusing. Help him out.

a. What problems might Robert encounter in comparing these companies to one another on the basis of their ratios?

b. Why might the current and quick ratios for the electric utility and the fast-food stock be so much lower than the same ratios for the other companies?

c. Why might it be all right for the electric utility to carry a large amount of debt, but the same is not true for the software company?

d. Why wouldn't investors invest all of their money in software companies instead of less profitable companies? (Focus on risk and reward.)

WARM-UP

3–2   Liquidity management   Bauman Company's total current assets, net working capital, and inventory for each of the past 4 years follow:

Item	2000	2001	2002	2003
Total current assets	$16,950	$21,900	$22,500	$27,000
Net working capital	7,950	9,300	9,900	9,600
Inventory	6,000	6,900	6,900	7,200

a. Calculate the firm's current and quick ratios for each year. Compare the resulting time series of each measure of liquidity (i.e., net working capital, the current ratio, and the quick ratio).

b. Comment on the firm's liquidity over the 2002–2003 period.

c. If you were told that Bauman Company's average age of inventory for each year in the 2000–2003 period and the industry averages were as follows, would this support or conflict with your evaluation in **b**? Why?

Average age of inventory (in days)	2000	2001	2002	2003
Bauman Company	57.9	53.7	52.1	57.0
Industry average	34.4	32.6	33.8	33.2

WARM-UP **3–3** **Inventory management**   Wilkins Manufacturing has sales of $4 million and a gross margin of 40 percent. Its *end-of-quarter inventories* are as follows:

Quarter	Inventory
1	$ 400,000
2	800,000
3	1,200,000
4	200,000

a. Find the average quarterly inventory and use it to calculate the firm's average age of inventory.
b. Assuming that the company is in an industry with an average age of inventory of 2.0, how would you evaluate the activity of Wilkins' inventory?

WARM-UP **3–4** **Accounts receivable management**   An evaluation of the books of Blair Supply, shown in the following table, gives the end-of-year accounts receivable balance, which is believed to consist of amounts originating in the months indicated. The company had annual sales of $2.4 million. The firm extends 30-day credit terms.

Month of origin	Amounts receivable
July	$ 3,875
August	2,000
September	34,025
October	15,100
November	52,000
December	193,000
Year-end accounts receivable	$300,000

a. Use the year-end total to evaluate the firm's collection system.
b. If 70 percent of the firm's sales occur between July and December, would this affect the validity of your conclusion in **a**? Explain.

  3–5 **Interpreting liquidity and activity ratios**   The new owners of Bluegrass Natural Foods, Inc., have hired you to help them diagnose and cure problems that the company has had in maintaining enough working capital. As a first step, you perform a liquidity analysis. You then do an analysis of the company's short-term activity ratios. Your calculations and appropriate industry norms are listed.

INTERMEDIATE

	Bluegrass	Industry norm
Current ratio	4.5	4.0
Quick ratio	2.0	3.1
Average age of inventory	60.8 days	35.1 days
Average collection period	73 days	52 days
Average payment period	31 days	40 days

a. What recommendations relative to the amount and the handling of inventory could you make to the new owners?

b. What recommendations relative to amount and handling of accounts receivable could you make to the new owners?

c. What recommendations relative to amount and handling of accounts payable could you make to the new owners?

d. What results, overall, would you hope your recommendations would achieve? Why might your recommendations not be effective?

WARM-UP

3–6   Debt analysis   Springfield Bank is evaluating Creek Enterprises, which has requested a $4,000,000 loan, to assess the firm's financial leverage and financial risk. On the basis of the leverage ratios for Creek, along with the industry averages and Creek's recent financial statements (which follow), evaluate and recommend appropriate action on the loan request.

Income Statement Creek Enterprises for the year ended August 31, 2003		
Sales revenue		$30,000,000
Less: Cost of goods sold		21,000,000
Gross margin		$ 9,000,000
Less: Operating expenses		
Selling expense	$3,000,000	
General and administrative expenses	1,800,000	
Lease expense	200,000	
Amortization expense	1,000,000	
Total operating expense		6,000,000
Operating earnings		$ 3,000,000
Less: Interest expense		1,000,000
Earnings before taxes		$ 2,000,000
Less: Taxes (rate = 40%)		800,000
Net income after taxes		$ 1,200,000

Balance Sheet
Creek Enterprises
August 31, 2003

Assets		Liabilities and shareholders' equity	
Current assets		Current liabilities	
Cash	$ 1,000,000	Accounts payable	$ 8,000,000
Marketable securities	3,000,000	Line of credit	8,000,000
Accounts receivable	12,000,000	Accruals	500,000
Inventories	7,500,000	Total current liabilities	$16,500,000
Total current assets	$23,500,000	Long-term debt (includes financial leases)[b]	$20,000,000
Gross fixed assets (at cost)[a]		Shareholders' equity	
Land and buildings	$11,000,000	Preferred shares (25,000 shares,	
Machinery and equipment	20,500,000	$4 dividend)	$ 2,500,000
Furniture and fixtures	8,000,000	Common shares (1 million shares)	9,000,000
Gross fixed assets	$39,500,000	Retained earnings	2,000,000
Less: Accumulated amortization	13,000,000	Total shareholders' equity	$13,500,000
	$26,500,000	Total liabilities and shareholder' equity	$50,000,000
Total assets	$50,000,000		

[a]The firm has a 4-year financial lease requiring annual beginning-of-year payments of $200,000. Three years of the lease have yet to run.
[b]Required annual principal payments are $800,000.

Industry averages	
Debt ratio	51%
Debt/equity ratio	92%
Times interest earned ratio	7.30
Fixed-charge coverage ratio	1.85

CHALLENGE

3–7 The relationship between financial leverage and profitability   Pelican Paper, Inc., and Timberland Forest, Inc., are rivals in the manufacture of craft papers. Some financial statement values for each company are listed. Use them in a ratio analysis that compares their financial leverage and profitability.

	Pelican Paper, Inc.	Timberland Forest, Inc.
Total assets	$10,000,000	$10,000,000
Total equity	9,000,000	5,000,000
Total debt	1,000,000	5,000,000
Annual interest	100,000	500,000
Total sales	$25,000,000	$25,000,000
EBIT	6,250,000	6,250,000
Net income	3,690,000	3,450,000

a. Calculate the following leverage and coverage ratios for the two companies. Discuss their financial risk and ability to cover the costs in relation to each other.
   (1) Debt ratio.
   (2) Times interest earned.
b. Calculate the following profitability ratios for the two companies. Discuss their profitability relative to each other.
   (1) Operating margin.
   (2) Profit margin.
   (3) Return on assets.
   (4) Return on equity.
c. In what way has the larger debt of Timberland Forest made it more profitable than Pelican Paper? What are the risks that Timberland's investors undertake when they choose to purchase its stock instead of Pelican's?

  3–8 **Common-size statement analysis** A common-size income statement for Creek Enterprises' 2002 operations follows. Using the firm's 2003 income statement presented in Problem 3–6, develop the 2003 common-size income statement and compare it to the 2002 statement. Which areas require further analysis and investigation?

INTERMEDIATE

Common-size Income Statement Creek Enterprises for the year ended August, 2002		
Sales revenue ($35,000,000)		100.0%
Less: Cost of goods sold		65.9
Gross margin		34.1%
Less: Operating expenses		
Selling expense	12.7%	
General and administrative expenses	6.3	
Lease expense	.6	
Amortization expense	3.6	
Total operating expense		23.2
Operating earnings		10.9%
Less: Interest expense		1.5
Earnings before taxes		9.4%
Less: Taxes (rate = 40%)		3.8
Net income after taxes		5.6%

  3–9 **Ratio proficiency** MacDougal Printing, Inc., had sales totalling $40,000,000 in fiscal year 2003. Some ratios for the company are listed. Use this information to determine the dollar values of various income statement and balance sheet accounts as requested.

WARM-UP

MacDougal Printing, Inc. year ended June 30, 2003	
Sales	$40,000,000
Gross margin	80%
Operating margin	35%
Profit margin	8%
Return on total assets	16%
Annual purchases	72% of cost of goods sold
Return on equity	20%
Total asset turnover	2
Average collection period	62.2 days
Average payment period	43.4 days

Calculate values for the following:
a. Gross margin.
b. Cost of goods sold.
c. Operating earnings.
d. Operating expenses.
e. Net income after taxes.
f. Total assets.
g. Total equity.
h. Accounts receivable.
i. Accounts payable.

INTERMEDIATE 3–10 **DuPont system of analysis**   Use the following ratio information for Johnson International and the industry averages for Johnson's line of business:
a. To construct the DuPont system of analysis for both Johnson and the industry.
b. To evaluate Johnson (and the industry) over the 3-year period.
c. In which areas does Johnson require further analysis? Why?

Johnson	1998	1999	2000
Financial leverage multiplier	1.75	1.75	1.85
Profit margin	5.9%	5.8%	4.9%
Total asset turnover	2.11	2.18	2.34
Industry averages			
Financial leverage multiplier	1.67	1.69	1.64
Profit margin	5.4%	4.7%	4.1%
Total asset turnover	2.05	2.13	2.15

INTERMEDIATE **3–11**   **Cross-sectional ratio analysis**   Use the following financial statements for Fox
Manufacturing Company for the year ended March 31, 2003, along with the
industry average ratios also given in what follows, to:
a. Prepare and interpret a ratio analysis of the firm's 2003 operations.
b. Summarize your findings and make recommendations.

Income Statement
Fox Manufacturing Company
for the year ended March 31, 2003

Sales revenue		$600,000
Less: Cost of goods sold		460,000
Gross margin		$140,000
Less: Operating expenses		
General and administrative expenses	$30,000	
Amortization expense	30,000	
Total operating expense		60,000
Operating earnings		$ 80,000
Less: Interest expense		10,000
Earnings before taxes		$ 70,000
Less: Taxes		27,100
Net income after taxes (earnings available for common shareholders)		$ 42,900
Earnings per share (EPS)		$ 2.15

Balance Sheet
Fox Manufacturing Company
March 31, 2003

Assets	
Cash	$ 15,000
Marketable securities	7,200
Accounts receivable	34,100
Inventories	82,000
Total current assets	$138,300
Net fixed assets	$270,000
Total assets	$408,300

Liabilities and shareholders' equity	
Accounts payable	$ 57,000
Line of credit	13,000
Accruals	5,000
Total current liabilities	$ 75,000
Long-term debt	$150,000
Shareholders' equity	
Common shares (20,000 shares outstanding)	$110,200
Retained earnings	73,100
Total shareholders' equity	$183,300
Total liabilities and shareholders' equity	$408,300

Ratio	Industry average, 2003
Net working capital	$125,000
Current ratio	2.35
Quick ratio	.87
Average age of inventory[a]	80.2 days
Average collection period[a]	35.3 days
Fixed asset turnover	1.59
Total asset turnover	1.09
Debt ratio	30.0%
Debt/equity ratio	46.1%
Times interest earned ratio	12.3
Gross margin	20.2%
Operating margin	13.5%
Profit margin	9.1%
Return on total assets (ROA)	9.9%
Return on equity (ROE)	16.7%
Earnings per share (EPS)	$3.10

[a]Based on end-of-year figures.

INTERMEDIATE 3–12 **Financial statement analysis**   The financial statements of Zach Industries for the year ended December 31, 2002, follow.

Income Statement
Zach Industries
for the year ended December 31, 2002

Sales revenue	$160,000
Less: Cost of goods sold	106,000
Gross margin	$ 54,000
Less: Operating expenses	
Selling expense	$ 16,000
General and administrative expenses	10,000
Lease expense	1,000
Amortization expense	10,000
Total operating expense	$ 37,000
Operating earnings	$ 17,000
Less: Interest expense	6,100
Earnings before taxes	$ 10,900
Less: Taxes	4,360
Net income after taxes	$ 6,540

Balance Sheet
Zach Industries
December 31, 2002

Assets

Cash	$ 500
Marketable securities	1,000
Accounts receivable	25,000
Inventories	45,500
Total current assets	$ 72,000
Land	$ 26,000
Buildings and equipment	90,000
Less: Accumulated amortization	38,000
Net fixed assets	$ 78,000
Total assets	$150,000

Liabilities and shareholders' equity

Accounts payable	$ 22,000
Line of credit	47,000
Total current liabilities	$ 69,000
Long-term debt	$ 22,950
Common shares	$ 31,500
Retained earnings	$ 26,550
Total liabilities and shareholders' equity	$150,000

a. Use the preceding financial statements to complete the following table. Assume that the industry averages given in the table are applicable for both 2001 and 2002.

b. Analyze Zach Industries' financial condition as it relates to (1) liquidity, (2) activity, (3) leverage, and (4) profitability. Summarize the company's overall financial condition.

Ratio	Industry average	Actual 2001	Actual 2002
Current ratio	1.80	1.84	_____
Quick ratio	.70	.78	_____
Average age of inventory[a]	146 days	140.9 days	_____
Average collection period[a]	37 days	36 days	_____
Average payment period	62 days	63.8 days	_____
Debt ratio	65%	67%	_____
Times interest earned ratio	3.8	4.0	_____
Gross margin	38%	40%	_____
Profit margin	3.5%	3.6%	_____
Return on total assets	4.0%	4.0%	_____
Return on equity	9.5%	8.0%	_____

[a]Based on end-of-year figures.

CHALLENGE **3–13** **Integrative—Complete ratio analysis**   Given the following financial statements, historical ratios, and industry averages, calculate the Sterling Company's financial ratios for the most recent year. Analyze its overall financial situation from both a cross-sectional and a time-series viewpoint. Break your analysis into an evaluation of the firm's liquidity, activity, leverage, and profitability. Use a common-size analysis for profitability. Use the DuPont system to analyze ROE.

Income Statement Sterling Company for the year ended December 31, 2002		
Sales revenue		$10,000,000
Less: Cost of goods sold		7,500,000
Gross margin		$ 2,500,000
Less: Operating expenses		
Selling expense	$300,000	
General and administrative expenses	650,000	
Lease expense	50,000	
Amortization expense	200,000	
Total operating expense		1,200,000
Operating earnings (EBIT)		$ 1,300,000
Less: Interest expense		200,000
Earnings before taxes		$ 1,100,000
Less: Taxes (rate = 40%)		440,000
Net income after taxes		$ 660,000
Less: Preferred share dividends		50,000
Earnings available for common shareholders		$ 610,000
Earnings per share (EPS)		$3.05

Balance Sheet Sterling Company December 31, 2002					
Assets			**Liabilities and shareholders' equity**		
Current assets			Current liabilities		
Cash		$ 200,000	Accounts payable[b]		$ 900,000
Marketable securities		50,000	Line of credit		200,000
Accounts receivable		800,000	Accruals		100,000
Inventories		950,000	Total current liabilities		$ 1,200,000
Total current assets		$ 2,000,000	Long-term debt (includes financial leases)[c]		$ 3,000,000
Gross fixed assets (at cost)[a]	$12,000,000		Shareholders' equity		
Less: Accumulated amortization	3,000,000		Preferred shares (25,000 shares, $2 dividend)		$ 1,000,000
Net fixed assets		$ 9,000,000	Common shares (200,000 shares)[d]		5,800,000
Other assets		$ 1,000,000	Retained earnings		1,000,000
Total assets		$12,000,000	Total shareholders' equity		$ 7,800,000
			Total liabilities and shareholders' equity		$12,000,000

[a]The firm has an 8-year financial lease requiring annual beginning-of-year payments of $50,000. Five years of the lease have yet to run.

[b]Annual credit purchases of $6,200,000 were made during the year.

[c]The annual principal payment on the long-term debt is $100,000.

[d]On December 31, 2002, the firm's common shares closed at $27.50).

Historical and Industry Average Ratios for Sterling Company

Ratio	Actual 2000	Actual 2001	Industry average, 2002
Net working capital	$760,000	$720,000	$1,600,000
Current ratio	1.40	1.55	1.85
Quick ratio	1.00	.92	1.05
Average age of inventory	38.3 days	39.6 days	42.4 days
Average collection period	45.0 days	36.4 days	35.0 days
Average payment period	58.5 days	60.8 days	45.8 days
Total asset turnover	0.74	0.80	0.74
Debt ratio	20%	20%	30%
Debt/equity ratio	24.8%	25.2%	36.9%
Times interest earned ratio	8.2	7.3	8.0
Fixed-charge coverage ratio	4.5	4.2	4.2
Gross margin	30%	27%	25%
Operating margin	12%	12%	10%
Profit margin	6.7%	6.7%	5.8%
Return on total assets (ROA)	4.9%	5.4%	4.3%
Return on equity (ROE)	6.7%	7.5%	7.4%
Earnings per share (EPS)	$1.75	$2.20	$1.50
Price/earnings (P/E) ratio	12.0	10.5	11.2

INTERMEDIATE   3–14 **Complete ratio analysis, recognizing significant differences**   Home Health, Inc., has come to Jane Ross for a yearly financial checkup. As a first step, Jane has prepared a complete set of ratios for fiscal years 2002 and 2003. She will use them to look for significant changes in the company's situation from one year to the next.

Home Health, Inc.

	2002	2003
Net working capital	$55,000	$58,000
Current ratio	3.25	3.00
Quick ratio	2.50	2.20
Average age of inventory	28.5 days	35.4 days
Average collection period	42 days	31 days
Total asset turnover	1.40	2.00
Debt ratio	45.3%	62.5%
Times interest earned	4.00	3.85
Gross margin	68%	65%
Operating margin	14%	16%
Profit margin	8.3%	8.1%
Return on total assets	11.6%	16.2%
Return on equity	21.1%	42.6%

a. In order to focus on the degree of change, calculate the year-to-year proportional change by dividing the 2003 ratio by the 2002 ratio, subtracting 1, and multiplying the result by 100. Preserve the positive or negative sign. The result is the percentage change in the ratio from 2002 to 2003. Calculate the proportional change for the ratios shown here.

b. For any ratio that shows a year-to-year difference of 10 percent or more, state whether the difference is in the company's favour or not.

CHALLENGE

c. For the most significant changes (25 percent or more), look at the other ratios and name at least one other change that may have contributed to the change in the ratio that you are discussing.

CASE   CHAPTER 3   Assessing Martin Manufacturing's Current Financial Position

Terri Spiro, an experienced budget analyst at Martin Manufacturing Company, has been charged with assessing the firm's financial performance during 2002 and its financial position at year-end 2002. To complete this assignment, she gathered the firm's 2002 financial statements, shown below. In addition, Terri obtained the firm's ratio values for 2000 and 2001, along with the 2002 industry average ratios (also applicable to 2000 and 2001). These are presented in the "Historical ratios" table on the next page.

Income Statement
Martin Manufacturing Company
for the year ended December 31, 2002

Sales revenue		$5,075,000
Less: Cost of goods sold		3,704,000
Gross margin		$1,371,000
Less: Operating expenses		
Selling expense	$650,000	
General and administrative expenses	416,000	
Amortization expense	152,000	
Total operating expense		1,218,000
Operating earnings (EBIT)		$ 153,000
Less: Interest expense		93,000
Earnings before taxes		$ 60,000
Less: Taxes (rate = 40%)		24,000
Net income after taxes		$ 36,000

Required

a. Calculate the firm's 2002 financial ratios, and then complete the ratio table.

b. Analyze the firm's current financial position from both a cross-sectional and a time-series viewpoint. Break your analysis into an evaluation of the firm's liquidity, activity, leverage, and profitability. Use a common-size analysis for profitability. Use the DuPont system to analyze ROE.

c. Summarize the firm's overall financial position based on your findings in b.

Balance Sheets
Martin Manufacturing Company

Assets	December 31	
	2001	2002
Current assets		
Cash	$ 24,100	$ 25,000
Accounts receivable	763,900	805,556
Inventories	763,445	700,625
Total current assets	$1,551,445	$1,531,181
Gross fixed assets (at cost)	$1,691,707	$2,093,819
Less: Accumulated amortization	348,000	500,000
Net fixed assets	$1,343,707	$1,593,819
Total assets	$2,895,152	$3,125,000

Liabilities and shareholders' equity		
Current liabilities		
Accounts payable	$ 400,500	$ 230,000
Line of credit	370,000	311,000
Accruals	100,902	75,000
Total current liabilities	$ 871,402	$ 616,000
Long-term debt	$ 700,000	$1,165,250
Total liabilities	$1,571,402	$1,781,250
Shareholders' equity		
Preferred shares	$ 50,000	$ 50,000
Common shares	293,750	293,750
Retained earnings	980,000	1,000,000
Total shareholders' equity	$1,323,750	$1,343,750
Total liabilities and shareholders' equity	$2,895,152	$3,125,000

Historical ratios
Martin Manufacturing Company

Ratio	Actual 2000	Actual 2001	Actual 2002	Industry average 2002
Current ratio	1.7	1.8	_____	1.5
Quick ratio	1.0	.9	_____	1.2
Average age of inventory	70.2 days	73 days	_____	35.8 days
Average collection period	50 days	55 days	_____	46 days
Total asset turnover (times)	1.5	1.5	_____	2.0
Debt ratio	45.8%	54.3%	_____	24.5%
Times interest earned ratio	2.2	1.9	_____	2.5
Gross margin	27.5%	28.0%	_____	26.0%
Profit margin	1.1%	1.0%	_____	1.2%
Return on total assets (ROA)	1.7%	1.5%	_____	2.4%
Return on equity (ROE)	3.1%	3.3%	_____	3.2%

WEB EXERCISES   LINKS TO PRACTISE

Visit the following Web sites and complete the suggested exercises. These exercises will allow you to review practical applications of the chapter topics as well as explore the wealth of information regarding managerial finance that is available on the Internet.

www.dnbdirect.ca
Complete a search for a company located in your community. What D&B reports are available for this company? Review the reports by clicking on the Description and Sample links. What kind of information is provided in these reports? If you were completing a ratio analysis of the company, which of the reports would you find most useful, and why?

www.sedar.com/homepage_en.htm
Search for the most recent annual report for Canadian National Railway (CN) and Empire Company or Barrick Gold and Hudson's Bay Company. Describe the companies. What do they do? Review the financial statements for both companies and answer the following questions:

1. Comment on the liquidity of the companies. For which company is liquidity more important? Why?
2. For which company is the management of current assets and current liabilities most important? Why? Which company has the largest investment in fixed assets? For both companies, what percentage of total assets are current and fixed? What is the implication of this analysis regarding the management of assets for the two companies?
3. How have the two companies financed the investment in assets? Are both companies able to cover their financing costs? What does this analysis imply about the profitability of the two companies?
4. How profitable are the two companies relative to total sales, assets, common equity, and share price? What do the price/earnings multiples for the two companies suggest about investors' attitudes toward the companies?
5. What does a DuPont analysis suggest about the companies?

www.pimsonline.com
Describe the PIMS (Profit Impact of Market Strategy) program. Now, click on the Tutorial link and then the pimsonline.com criteria link about halfway down the page.

What factors does PIMS believe influence a company's ROA? What business functional areas are these factors related to? Select four of the factors and fully describe them. Illustrate how each of the four factors would influence a company's ROA.

Financial Planning and Forecasting

LEARNING GOALS

LG 1 Understand the financial planning process, including long-term (strategic) financial plans and short-term (operating) plans.

LG 2 Discuss the cash budget, the importance of sales forecasts, procedures for preparing a cash budget, and how to cope with uncertainty when preparing a cash budget.

LG 3 Discuss the fundamentals associated with preparing the pro forma income statement and balance sheet.

LG 4 Discuss and illustrate three approaches to preparing a pro forma income statement.

LG 5 Discuss and illustrate the judgmental approach to preparing a pro forma balance sheet and determine the amount of external financing required for a company to operate during the forecast year.

4.1 The Financial Planning Process

Financial planning is an important aspect of the firm's operations because it provides road maps for guiding, coordinating, and controlling the firm's actions to achieve its objectives. Three key aspects of the financial planning process are *cash planning (forecasting the need for cash), forecasting future profitability,* and *forecasting the need for financing.* Cash forecasting involves the preparation of the firm's cash budget. Profits are forecast by developing a pro forma or projected income statement; financing needs are forecasted through the preparation of

"If Only I'd Known…"

If you knew or could accurately predict what was in your future, you could make decisions today that would help bring about the results you want. Some outcomes are pretty much within your control (your grades, for example). For other outcomes, you can't do much more than make plans based on what you currently know, and hope for the best. (A good sense of humour—the ability to laugh at absurdity—will help you deal with whatever comes along.) Companies are pretty much in the same position. Because there is much in the business environment that is beyond their control, they try to control their future by careful and extensive planning and then forecasting, for both the long term and the short term. This chapter outlines the financial planning process, with particular attention to planning focused on the firm's cash and its future financial position as depicted in a forecasted income statement and balance sheet.

pro forma statements
Projected, or forecasted, financial statements: the income statement and the balance sheet.

financial planning process
Planning that begins with long-term (strategic) financial plans that in turn guide the formulation of short-term (operating) plans and budgets.

both **pro forma statements**: the projected, or forecasted, income statement and the balance sheet. These statements not only are useful for internal financial planning, but also are routinely required by existing and prospective lenders.

The **financial planning process** begins with long-term, or strategic, financial plans that in turn guide the formulation of short-term, or operating, plans and budgets. Generally, the short-term plans and budgets implement the firm's long-term strategic objectives. The major emphasis in this chapter is on short-term financial plans and budgets, though a few comments on long-term financial plans are provided below.

Long-Term (Strategic) Financial Plans

long-term (strategic)
financial plans
Planned financial actions and the
anticipated financial impact of those
actions over periods ranging from 2 to
10 years.

Long-term (strategic) financial plans lay out a company's planned financial actions and the anticipated financial impact of those actions over periods ranging from 2 to 10 years. The use of 5-year strategic plans, which are revised as significant new information becomes available, is common. Generally, firms that are subject to relatively short production cycles tend to use shorter planning horizons.

Long-term financial plans are part of an integrated strategy that, along with production and marketing plans, guides the firm toward achievement of its strategic goals. Those long-term plans consider proposed fixed asset outlays, research and development activities, marketing and product development actions, capital structure, and major sources of financing. Also included would be termination of existing projects, product lines, or lines of business; repayment or retirement of outstanding debts; and any planned acquisitions. Such plans tend to be supported by a series of annual budgets and profit plans. Given the long-term nature of strategic plans, they are subject to regular revision. As the operating environment and the firm's own circumstances change, so too should the plans.

Short-Term (Operating) Financial Plans

short-term (operating)
financial plans
Planned short-term financial actions
and the anticipated impact of those
actions.

Short-term (operating) financial plans specify short-term financial actions and the anticipated impact of those actions. These plans most often cover a 1- to 2-year period. Key inputs include the sales forecast and various forms of operating and financial data. Key outputs include a number of operating budgets, the cash budget, and pro forma financial statements. The entire short-term financial planning process is outlined in the flow diagram of Figure 4.1.

Short-term financial planning begins with the sales forecast. From it production plans are developed that take into account lead (preparation) times and include estimates of the required types and quantities of raw materials. Using the production plans, the firm can estimate direct labour requirements, factory overhead outlays, and operating expenses. Once these estimates have been made, the firm's pro forma income statement and cash budget can be prepared. With the basic inputs—pro forma income statement, cash budget, fixed asset outlay plan, long-term financing plan, and current-period balance sheet—the pro forma balance sheet can finally be developed. Throughout the remainder of this chapter, we will concentrate on the key outputs of the short-term financial planning process: the cash budget, the pro forma income statement, and the pro forma balance sheet.

! **Hint**
Electronic spreadsheets such as Excel
and QuattroPro are widely used to
streamline the process of preparing and
evaluating these short-term financial
planning statements.

? Review Questions

4–1   What is the *financial planning process?* Define and contrast *long-term (strategic) financial plans* and *short-term (operating) financial plans.*

4–2   Which three statements result as part of the short-term (operating) financial planning process? Describe the flow of information from the sales forecast through the preparation of these statements.

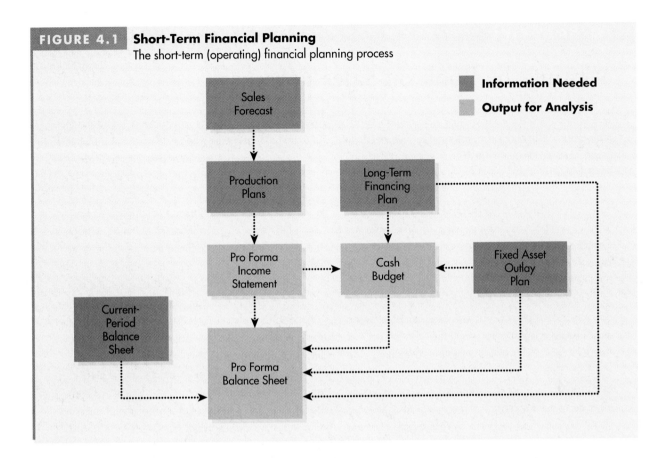

FIGURE 4.1 **Short-Term Financial Planning**
The short-term (operating) financial planning process

4.2 Cash Planning: The Cash Budget

cash budget (cash forecast)
A statement of the firm's planned inflows and outflows of cash that is used to estimate its short-term cash requirements.

The **cash budget,** or **cash forecast,** is a statement of the firm's planned inflows and outflows of cash. It is used by the firm to estimate its short-term cash requirements, with particular attention to planning for surplus cash and for cash shortages. A firm expecting a cash surplus can plan short-term investments (marketable securities), whereas a firm expecting shortages in cash must arrange for short-term financing (line of credit). The cash budget gives the financial manager a clear view of the timing of the firm's expected cash inflows and outflows over a given period.

Typically, the cash budget is designed to cover a 6-month or 1-year period, divided into shorter time intervals. The number and type of intervals depend on the nature of the business. The more seasonal and uncertain a firm's cash flows, the greater the number of intervals. Because many firms are confronted with a seasonal cash flow pattern, the cash budget is quite often presented on a monthly basis. Given the widespread use of computer spreadsheets, many companies, particularly those in the retail or service sectors, develop one-month cash budgets divided into days or weeks. For companies in those sectors, cash management is vital and a constant concern.

IN PRACTICE

Writing the Book on Sales Forecasts

Sales forecasts are the basis on which companies estimate their cash budgets, profitability, investment in assets, and the amount of financing required to support the forecasted level of sales. Because the financial planning process is dependent on the sales forecast, accuracy is crucial. Unsound financial planning is disastrous for any company. Chapters, who at one time was Canada's leading book retailer, was a casualty of erroneous financial planning and, as a result, was acquired by and merged with Indigo.

During the early 1990s when the tech/dot-com boom was at its peak, Chapters' CEO Larry Stevenson envisioned a company that would follow in the steps of Amazon.com and become a giant in e-retailing. The strategic goal was to get as big as possible, as fast as possible. This goal was depicted in a line company managers would quote from the movie *Field of Dreams*: "If you build it, they will come." While a great line in a movie, the slogan fails to consider the basics of financial planning—in order to know how much financing to raise, accurate sales forecasts are key.

Chapters gravely miscalculated. While the company built, customers did not come and buy. Millions were lost on Chapters' vast and costly Web site, its over-ambitious distribution centre, and the abundance of marginal superstores. The over-hyped business model resulted in inflated sales forecasts and too large an investment in assets. Bigger did not mean better. Bigger resulted in over-investment, very low productivity, too much costly financing, and large losses.

After years of poor financial planning, Chapters merged with rival Indigo. Since then the goals of management have been to reduce the chain from its over-inflated size to one more appropriate given the size of the book market in Canada, and to become profitable. With aggressive sales forecasts, a company can grow too quickly and collapse under its own weight. Now, Indigo Chapters is getting back to business basics: making reasonable sales forecasts, managing cash and inventory, paying suppliers on time, providing better customer service and sharper merchandising, and investing appropriately in assets. The financial planning process includes all of these tasks.

REFERENCES: Ian Portsmouth, "The Aftermath Economy," *Profit: The Magazine for Canadian Entrepreneurs*, v. 20 (7), November 2001, pp. 48–56; John Lorinc, "Troubleshooting: To Revitalize an Overextended Chain, Chapters' New Executive Team Must Get Back to Bookselling Basics," *Quill & Quire*, v. 67 (9), September 2001, pp. 17–19.

The Sales Forecast

sales forecast
The prediction of the firm's sales over a given period, based on external and internal data, and used as the key input to the financial planning process.

🔑 Career Key
The *marketing* department will provide key input into the sales forecast. Marketing personnel will need to inform the financial planners of new-product introductions and the significant changes in promotion that will occur.

The key input to the financial planning process, and therefore the three forecasted statements displayed in Figure 4.1—the cash budget, pro forma income statement, and pro forma balance sheet—is the firm's **sales forecast.** This is the prediction of the firm's sales over a given period and is ordinarily furnished to the financial manager by the marketing department. On the basis of this forecast, the financial manager estimates the monthly cash flows that will result from projected sales receipts and from outlays related to production, inventory, and sales. The manager also determines the level of fixed assets required and the amount of financing, if any, needed to support the forecast level of production and sales. In practice, obtaining good data is the most difficult aspect of forecasting.[1] The sales forecast is normally based on an analysis of external and internal data.

---

1. A discussion of the calculation of the various forecasting techniques, such as regression, moving averages, and exponential smoothing, is not included in this text. For a description of the technical side of forecasting, refer to a basic statistics, econometrics, or management science text.

external forecast
A sales forecast based on the relationships observed between the firm's sales and certain key external economic indicators.

An **external forecast** is based on the relationships observed between the firm's sales and certain key external economic indicators such as the gross domestic product (GDP), disposable personal income, and/or monetary indicators such as interest rates and growth in the money supply. Forecasts containing these indicators are readily available. The rationale for this approach is that because the firm's sales are often closely related to some aspect of overall national economic activity, a forecast of economic activity should provide insight into future sales.

internal forecast
A sales forecast based on a buildup, or consensus, of forecasts through the firm's own sales channels.

Internal forecasts are based on a buildup, or consensus, of sales forecasts through the firm's own sales channels. Typically, the firm's salespeople in the field are asked to estimate the number of units of each type of product that they expect to sell in the coming year. These forecasts are collected and totalled by the sales manager, who may adjust the figures using knowledge of specific markets or of the salesperson's forecasting ability. Finally, adjustments may be made for additional internal factors, such as production capabilities.

🔲 Hint
The firm needs to spend a great deal of time and effort to make the sales forecast as precise as possible. An "after-the-fact" analysis of the prior year's forecast will help the firm determine which approach or combination of approaches will give it the most accurate forecasts.

Firms generally use a combination of external and internal forecast data to make the final sales forecast. The internal data provide insight into sales expectations, and the external data provide a means of adjusting these expectations to take into account general economic factors. The nature of the firm's product also often affects the mix and types of forecasting methods used.

Preparing the Cash Budget

The general format of the cash budget is presented in Table 4.1. We will discuss each of its components individually.

Cash Receipts

cash receipts
All of a firm's inflows of cash in a given financial period.

Cash receipts include all of a firm's inflows of cash in a given financial period. The most common components of cash receipts are cash sales, collections of accounts receivable, and other cash receipts.

Example ▼ Coulson Industries, a defence contractor, is developing a cash budget for October, November, and December. Coulson's sales in August and September were $100,000 and $200,000, respectively. Sales of $400,000, $300,000, and $200,000

| TABLE 4.1 | The General Format of the Cash Budget |

	Jan.	Feb.	. . .	Nov.	Dec.
Cash receipts	$XXX	$XXG		$XXM	$XXT
Less: Cash disbursements	XXA	XXH	. . .	XXN	XXU
Net cash flow	XXB	XXI		XXO	XXV
Add: Beginning cash	XXC	XXD	XXJ	XXP	XXQ
Ending cash	XXD	XXJ		XXQ	XXW
Less: Minimum cash balance	XXE	XXK	. . .	XXR	XXY
Required total financing	$XXX	$XXL		$XXS	$XXX
Excess cash balance	$XXF				$XXZ

have been forecast for October, November, and December, respectively. Historically, 20 percent of the firm's sales have been for cash, 50 percent have generated accounts receivable collected after 1 month, and the remaining 30 percent have generated accounts receivable collected after 2 months. Bad debt expenses (uncollectible accounts) have been negligible.[2] In December, the firm will receive a $30,000 dividend from common shares held in a subsidiary. The schedule of expected cash receipts for the company is presented in Table 4.2. It contains the following items:

Forecast sales   Sales forecasts are the beginning point for any financial forecasting exercise. Sales forecasts are needed to develop the cash budget and pro forma income statement and balance sheet. For the cash budget, collections of cash are based on sales forecasts. As well, purchases are often based on projected sales. Sales forecasts can be on a daily, weekly, or monthly basis.

Cash sales   The cash sales shown for each month represent 20 percent of the total sales forecast for that month.

Collections of A/R   These entries represent the collection of accounts receivable (A/R) resulting from sales in earlier months.

   Lagged 1 month   These figures represent sales made in the preceding month that generated accounts receivable collected in the current month. Because 50 percent of the current month's sales are collected 1 month later, the collections of A/R with a 1-month lag shown for September represent 50 percent of the sales in August, collections for October represent 50 percent of September sales, and so on.

   Lagged 2 months   These figures represent sales made 2 months earlier that generated accounts receivable collected in the current month. Because 30 percent of sales are collected 2 months later, the collections with a 2-month lag shown for October represent 30 percent of the sales in August, and so on.

TABLE 4.2   A Schedule of Projected Cash Receipts for Coulson Industries ($000)

	Aug.	Sept.	Oct.	Nov.	Dec.
Forecast sales	$100	$200	$400	$300	$200
Cash sales (20%)	$ 20	$ 40	$ 80	$ 60	$ 40
Collections of A/R:					
Lagged 1 month (50%)		50	100	200	150
Lagged 2 months (30%)			30	60	120
Other cash receipts					30
Total cash receipts			$210	$320	$340

2. Normally, it would be expected that the collection percentages would total slightly less than 100 percent, because some of the accounts receivable would be uncollectible. In this example, the sum of the collection percentages is 100 percent (20% + 50% + 30%), which reflects the fact that all sales are assumed to be collected.

Other cash receipts   These are cash receipts expected from sources other than sales. Interest received, dividends received, proceeds from the sale of equipment, stock and bond sale proceeds, and lease receipts may show up here. For Coulson Industries, the only other cash receipt is the $30,000 dividend due in December.

Total cash receipts   This figure represents the total of all the cash receipts listed for each month. For Coulson Industries, we are concerned only with October, November, and December, as shown in Table 4.2.

Cash Disbursements

cash disbursements
All outlays of cash by the firm during a given financial period.

Cash disbursements include all outlays of cash by the firm during a given financial period. The most common cash disbursements are

Cash purchases	Fixed asset outlays
Payments of accounts payable	Interest payments
Rent (and lease) payments	Cash dividend payments
Wages and salaries	Principal payments (loans)
Tax payments	Repurchases or retirements of common shares

It is important to recognize that *amortization and other non-cash charges are NOT included in the cash budget*, because they merely represent a scheduled write-off of an earlier cash outflow. The impact of amortization, as noted in Chapter 2, is reflected in the cash outflow for the tax payments.

Example ▼ Coulson Industries has gathered the following data needed for the preparation of a cash disbursements schedule for October, November, and December.

Purchases   The firm's purchases represent 70 percent of sales. Of this amount, 10 percent is paid in cash, with the remainder becoming accounts payable. Of the 90 percent of purchases which become accounts payable, 70 percent are paid in the month immediately following the month of purchase, and the remaining 20 percent are paid 2 months following the month of purchase.[3]

Rent payments   Rent of $5,000 will be paid each month.

Wages and salaries   The firm's wages and salaries are estimated by adding 10 percent of its monthly sales to the $8,000 fixed cost figure.

Tax payments   Taxes of $25,000 must be paid in December.

Fixed asset outlays   New machinery costing $130,000 will be purchased in September and paid for in November.

Interest payments   An interest payment of $10,000 is due in December.

---

3. Unlike the collection percentages for sales, the total of the payment percentages should equal 100 percent, because it is expected that the firm will pay off all of its accounts payable.

Cash dividend payments   Cash dividends of $20,000 will be paid in October.

Principal payments (loans)   A $20,000 principal payment is due in December.

Repurchases or retirements of common shares   No repurchase or retirement of common shares is expected during the October–December period.

The firm's cash disbursements schedule is presented in Table 4.3. Some items in the table are explained in greater detail below.

Purchases   Purchases are 70 percent of the forecast sales for each month. Purchases are included to facilitate the calculation of the cash purchases and related payments.

Cash purchases   The cash purchases represent 10 percent of each month's purchases.

Payments of A/P   These entries represent the payment of accounts payable (A/P) resulting from purchases in earlier months.

Lagged 1 month   These figures represent purchases made in the preceding month that are paid for in the current month. Because 70 percent of the firm's purchases are paid for 1 month later, the payments with a 1-month lag shown for September represent 70 percent of the August purchases, payments for October represent 70 percent of September purchases, and so on.

Lagged 2 months   These figures represent purchases made 2 months earlier that are paid for in the current month. Because 20 percent of the firm's purchases are paid for 2 months later, the payments with a 2-month lag for October represent 20 percent of the August purchases, and so on.

TABLE 4.3   A Schedule of Projected Cash Disbursements for Coulson Industries ($000)

	Aug.	Sept.	Oct.	Nov.	Dec.
Purchases (70% × sales)	$70	$140	$280	$210	$140
Cash purchases (10%)	$ 7	$ 14	$ 28	$ 21	$ 14
Payments of A/P:					
Lagged 1 month (70%)		49	98	196	147
Lagged 2 months (20%)			14	28	56
Rent payments			5	5	5
Wages and salaries			48	38	28
Tax payments					25
Fixed asset outlays				130	
Interest payments					10
Cash dividend payments			20		
Principal payments					20
Total cash disbursements			$213	$418	$305

net cash flow
The mathematical difference between the firm's cash receipts and its cash disbursements in each period.

ending cash
The sum of the firm's beginning cash and its net cash flow for the period.

required total financing
Amount of funds needed by the firm if the ending cash for the period is less than the desired minimum cash balance; typically represented by a line of credit.

excess cash balance
The (excess) amount available for investment by the firm if the period's ending cash is greater than the desired minimum cash balance; assumed to be invested in marketable securities.

Wages and salaries   These amounts were obtained by adding $8,000 to 10 percent of the *sales* in each month. The $8,000 represents the salary component; the rest represents wages.

▲ The remaining items on the cash disbursements schedule are self-explanatory.

Net Cash Flow, Ending Cash, Financing, and Excess Cash

Now look back at the general-format cash budget in Table 4.1. We have inputs for the first two entries and now continue calculating the firm's cash needs. The firm's **net cash flow** is found by subtracting the cash disbursements from cash receipts in each period. Then, by adding beginning cash to the firm's net cash flow, the **ending cash** for each period can be found. Finally, subtracting the desired minimum cash balance from ending cash yields the **required total financing** or the **excess cash balance**. If the ending cash is less than the minimum cash balance, *financing* is required. Such financing is typically viewed as short-term and therefore represented by a line of credit. If the ending cash is greater than the minimum cash balance, *excess cash* exists. Any excess cash is assumed to be invested in a liquid, short-term, interest-paying vehicle—that is, in marketable securities.

Example ▼ Table 4.4 presents Coulson Industries' cash budget, based on the cash receipt and cash disbursement data already developed. At the end of September, Coulson's cash balance was $50,000 and its line of credit and marketable securities equalled $0.[4] The company wishes to maintain as a reserve for unexpected needs a minimum cash balance of $25,000.

For Coulson Industries to maintain its required $25,000 ending cash balance, it will need to have borrowed $76,000 in November and $41,000 in December. In October, the firm will have an excess cash balance of $22,000, which can be held in an interest-earning marketable security. The required total financing figures in the cash budget refer to *how much will be owed at the end of the month*; they do *not* represent the monthly changes in borrowing.

The monthly changes in borrowing and in excess cash can be found by further analyzing the cash budget. In October, the $50,000 beginning cash, which becomes $47,000 after the $3,000 net cash outflow, results in a $22,000 excess cash balance once the $25,000 minimum cash is deducted. In November, the $76,000 of required total financing resulted from the $98,000 net cash outflow less the $22,000 of excess cash from October. The $41,000 of required total financing in December resulted from reducing November's $76,000 of required total financing by the $35,000 of net cash inflow during December. Summarizing, the financial actions for each month would be as follows:

October: Invest $22,000 of excess cash.
November: Liquidate $22,000 of excess cash and borrow $76,000.
▲   December: Repay $35,000 of amount borrowed.

---

4. If Coulson had either an outstanding line of credit or held marketable securities at the end of September, its "beginning cash" value would be misleading. It could be either overstated or understated, depending on whether the firm had a line of credit or marketable securities, respectively, on its books at that time. For simplicity, the cash budget discussions and problems presented in this chapter assume that the firm's line of credit and marketable securities equal $0 at the beginning of the period of concern.

TABLE 4.4	**A Cash Budget for Coulson Industries ($000)**		
	Oct.	Nov.	Dec.
Total cash receipts[a]	$210	$320	$340
Less: Total cash disbursements[b]	213	418	305
Net cash flow	$ (3)	$ (98)	$ 35
Add: Beginning cash	50	47	(51)
Ending cash	$ 47	$ (51)	$ (16)
Less: Minimum cash balance	25	25	25
Required total financing (line of credit)[c]	—	$ 76	$ 41
Excess cash balance (marketable securities)[d]	$ 22	—	—

[a]From Table 4.2.

[b]From Table 4.3.

[c]Values are placed in this line when the ending cash is less than the desired minimum cash balance. These amounts are typically financed short-term and therefore are represented by a line of credit.

[d]Values are placed in this line when the ending cash is greater than the desired minimum cash balance. These amounts are typically assumed to be invested short-term and therefore are represented by marketable securities.

Evaluating the Cash Budget

The cash budget provides the firm with figures indicating whether a cash shortage or surplus is expected to result in each of the months covered by the forecast. Each month's figure is based on the internally imposed requirement of a minimum cash balance and *represents the total balance at the end of the month*.

At the end of each of the 3 months, Coulson expects the following balances in cash, marketable securities, and notes payable:

	End-of-month balance ($000)		
Account	Oct.	Nov.	Dec.
Cash	$25	$25	$25
Marketable securities	22	0	0
Line of credit	0	76	41

Note that the firm is assumed to first liquidate its marketable securities to meet deficits and then borrow using a line of credit if additional financing is needed. As a result, a firm will not have marketable securities and a line of credit outstanding on its cash budget at the same time. Note, though, that it is possible for both items to appear on the balance sheet. A company may hold marketable securities and have a line of credit outstanding as at a point in time. The expectation is that this situation would not be in effect for a long period of time.

Because it may be necessary for the firm to borrow up to $76,000 for the 3-month period, the financial manager should be sure that a line of credit is established or some other arrangement made to ensure the availability of these funds.

Coping with Uncertainty in the Cash Budget

Aside from careful estimating of the inputs to the cash budget, there are two ways of coping with the uncertainty of the cash budget.[5] One is to prepare several cash budgets—based on pessimistic, most likely, and optimistic forecasts. From this range of cash flows, the financial manager can determine the amount of financing needed to cover the most adverse situation. The use of several cash budgets based on differing assumptions also should give the financial manager a sense of the riskiness of alternatives so that he or she can make more intelligent short-term financial decisions. This sensitivity analysis, or "what if" approach, is often used to analyze cash flows under a variety of possible circumstances. Computers and electronic spreadsheets are commonly used to simplify the process of sensitivity analysis.

Example ▼ Table 4.5 presents the summary of Coulson Industries' cash budget prepared for each month of concern using pessimistic, most likely, and optimistic estimates of cash receipts and disbursements. The most likely estimate is based on the expected outcomes presented earlier in Tables 4.2 through 4.4.

During the month of October, Coulson will at worst need a maximum of $15,000 of financing, and at best it will have a $62,000 excess cash balance available for short-term investment. During November, its financing requirement will be between $0 and $185,000, or it could experience an excess cash balance of $5,000 during November. The December projections show maximum borrowing of $190,000 with a possible excess cash balance of $107,000. By considering

| TABLE 4.5 | A Sensitivity Analysis of Coulson Industries' Cash Budget ($000) | | | | | | | | |

| | October | | | November | | | December | | |
	Pessi-mistic	Most likely	Opti-mistic	Pessi-mistic	Most likely	Opti-mistic	Pessi-mistic	Most likely	Opti-mistic
Total cash receipts	$160	$210	$285	$ 210	$320	$ 410	$ 275	$340	$422
Less: Total cash disbursements	200	213	248	380	418	467	280	305	320
Net cash flow	$(40)	$ (3)	$ 37	$(170)	$ (98)	$ (57)	$ (5)	$ 35	$102
Add: Beginning cash	50	50	50	10	47	87	(160)	(51)	30
Ending cash	$ 10	$ 47	$ 87	$(160)	$ (51)	$ 30	$(165)	$(16)	$132
Less: Minimum cash balance	25	25	25	25	25	25	25	25	25
Required total financing	$ 15	—	—	$ 185	$ 76	—	$ 190	$ 41	—
Excess cash balance	—	$ 22	$ 62	—	—	$ 5	—	—	$107

---

5. The term *uncertainty* is used here to refer to the variability of the cash flow outcomes that may actually occur.

the extreme values reflected in the pessimistic and optimistic outcomes, Coulson Industries should be better able to plan cash requirements. For the 3-month period, the peak borrowing requirement under the worst circumstances would be $190,000, which is considerably greater than the most likely estimate of $76,000 ▲ for this period.

Career Key

Information systems analysts will design financial planning and budgeting modules within the financial information system. They will also help design forecasting systems and will assist in sensitivity analysis.

A second and much more sophisticated way of coping with uncertainty in the cash budget is *simulation*.[6] By simulating the occurrence of sales and other uncertain events, the firm can develop a probability distribution of its ending cash flows for each month. The financial decision maker can then use the probability distribution to determine the amount of financing necessary to provide a desired degree of protection against a cash shortage.

Cash Flow Within the Month

Because the cash budget shows cash flows only on a total monthly basis, the information provided by the cash budget is not necessarily adequate for ensuring solvency. A firm must look more closely at its pattern of daily cash receipts and cash disbursements to ensure that adequate cash is available for paying bills as they come due. For an example related to this topic, see the book's Web site at **www.pearsoned.ca/gitman**.

The synchronization of cash flows in the cash budget at month-end does not ensure that the firm will be able to meet daily cash requirements. Because a firm's cash flows are generally quite variable when viewed on a daily basis, effective cash planning requires a look *beyond* the cash budget. The financial manager must therefore plan and monitor cash flow more frequently than on a monthly basis. The greater the variability of cash flows from day to day, the greater the attention required.

? Review Questions

4–3 What is the purpose of the *cash budget?* The key input to the cash budget is the sales forecast. What is the difference between *external* and *internal* forecast data?

4–4 Briefly describe the basic format of the cash budget, beginning with forecast sales and ending with *required total financing* or *excess cash balance.*

4–5 How can the two "bottom lines" of the cash budget be used to determine the firm's short-term borrowing and investment requirements?

4–6 What is the cause of uncertainty in the cash budget? What two techniques can be used to cope with this uncertainty?

4–7 What actions or analysis beyond preparation of the cash budget should the financial manager undertake to ensure that cash is available when needed? Why?

6. A more detailed discussion of the use of simulation is included among the approaches for dealing with risk in capital budgeting in Chapter 13.

4.3 Fundamentals of Preparing the Pro Forma Financial Statements

The cash budget focuses on forecasting the flow of cash to ensure the firm has access to sufficient cash to operate and remain solvent. The cash may be generated by operations, by liquidating marketable securities, or from utilizing a line of credit or another source of financing. A cash budget is not the only statement that must be forecasted. Figure 4.1 indicates that a company must also forecast profitability by preparing a pro forma income statement and determine their future financial position and need for financing by preparing a pro forma balance sheet. *Pro forma statements* are vital for management to evaluate the future expected financial position and for current and prospective investors (shareholders) and creditors to evaluate the firm's ability to provide a return on the funds invested. The preparation of these statements requires a careful blending of a number of procedures to account for the revenues, expenses, assets, liabilities, and equity resulting from the firm's anticipated level of operations. The basic steps in this process were shown in the flow diagram of Figure 4.1.

The financial forecasting process considers expected profitability and estimates the amount of financing the firm requires to operate over the forecast period. There are three key outputs of the financial forecasting process: (1) a pro forma income statement; (2) a pro forma balance sheet; and (3) a statement of external financing required. Financing is required to invest in assets. Assets are required to support increasing sales and profits. Therefore, financial forecasting is associated with increasing sales. As stated earlier in the chapter, an accurate sales forecast is the starting point for financial planning and forecasting.

Example ▼ For the 2002 fiscal year, Franklin Inc.'s sales were $800,000 and the company's total assets were $510,000. Obviously, Franklin must also have $510,000 of liabilities and shareholders' equity, which indicates the financing the firm used to acquire the assets. For 2003, Franklin expects sales will increase by 25 percent or by $200,000 to $1,000,000. Franklin estimates that in order to generate and support the increased sales, assets must increase by $130,000. Therefore, total assets will increase to $640,000. The implication is that Franklin must raise $130,000 of financing as debt, equity, or a combination of the two. Note that a portion of the $130,000 may come from profits, so some of the financing may be generated internally. The expected amount of reinvested profits is based on the ▲ pro forma income statement.

Items Required for Forecasting the Pro Forma Statements

To prepare a pro forma statement, three inputs are required: (1) financial statements for the previous year, (2) sales forecast for the forecast year, and (3) forecasts for all other financial statement accounts. When forecasting, a large number of assumptions (forecasts) must be made. An important point to note is that financial forecasting simply reflects a set of assumptions regarding a company's financial situation for the forecast period. The first assumption (or forecast) is expected sales. Other assumptions are then made and these are reflected in the pro forma financial statements.

? Review Questions

4–8   What is the purpose of preparing pro forma statements? What inputs are required?

4–9   What are the outputs of the financial forecasting process? What is reflected in these outputs?

4.4 Preparing the Pro Forma Income Statement

> **! Hint**
> A key point in understanding pro forma statements is that these are the goals and objectives of the firm for the planning period. In order for these goals and objectives to be achieved, operational plans will have to be developed. Financial plans can be realized only if the correct actions are implemented.

To illustrate financial forecasting, consider Vectra Manufacturing, which manufactures and sells one product. It has two basic models—model X and model Y—which are produced by the same process but require different amounts of raw material and labour. The income statement for the firm's 2002 operations is given in Table 4.6. It indicates that Vectra had sales of $100,000, total cost of goods sold of $80,000, earnings before taxes of $9,000, and net income after taxes of $7,650. The firm paid $4,000 in cash dividends, leaving $3,650 to be invested and transferred to retained earnings. The firm's balance sheet for 2002 is given in Table 4.7.

Like the cash budget, the key input for the development of pro forma statements is the sales forecast. The sales forecast for the 2003 forecast year for Vectra Manufacturing is given in Table 4.8. This forecast is based on both external and internal data. The unit sale prices of the products reflect an increase from

TABLE 4.6	Income Statement for Vectra Manufacturing for the Year Ended December 31, 2002

Sales revenue		
Model X (1,000 units at $20/unit)	$20,000	
Model Y (2,000 units at $40/unit)	80,000	
Total sales		$100,000
Less: Cost of goods sold		
Labour	$28,500	
Material A	8,000	
Material B	5,500	
Overhead	38,000	
Total cost of goods sold		80,000
Gross margin		$ 20,000
Less: Operating expenses		10,000
Operating earnings		$ 10,000
Less: Interest expense		1,000
Earnings before taxes		$ 9,000
Less: Taxes (15%)		1,350
Net income after taxes		$ 7,650
Less: Common share dividends		4,000
Reinvested profits (to retained earnings)		$ 3,650

TABLE 4.7	Balance Sheet for Vectra Manufacturing (December 31, 2002)

Assets		Liabilities and equities	
Cash	$ 6,000	Accounts payable	$ 7,000
Marketable securities	4,000	Taxes payable	300
Accounts receivable	13,000	Line of credit	8,300
Inventories	16,000	Other current liabilities	3,400
Total current assets	$39,000	Total current liabilities	$19,000
Net fixed assets	$51,000	Long-term debt	$18,000
Total assets	$90,000	Shareholders' equity	
		Common shares	$30,000
		Retained earnings	$23,000
		Total liabilities and shareholders' equity	$90,000

$20 to $25 for model X and from $40 to $50 for model Y. These increases are required to cover anticipated increases in the costs of labour, material, overhead, and operating expenses.

Tables 4.6, 4.7, and 4.8 provide the first two inputs for Vectra. To prepare the pro forma income statement, assumptions regarding the various expenses are required. An assumption that can be made to simplify the process is that all expenses remain the same percent of sales in the forecast year as they were in the most recent fiscal year. This approach to financial forecasting is the **percent-of-sales method**. For Vectra, the expenses as a percent of sales for the 2002 fiscal year were:

percent-of-sales method
A method of developing the pro forma income statement that assumes all expenses remain the same percent of sales in the forecast year as they were in the most recent fiscal year.

$$\frac{\text{cost of goods sold}}{\text{sales}} = \frac{\$80,000}{\$100,000} = 80.0\%$$

$$\frac{\text{operating expenses}}{\text{sales}} = \frac{\$10,000}{\$100,000} = 10.0\%$$

$$\frac{\text{interest expense}}{\text{sales}} = \frac{\$1,000}{\$100,000} = 1.0\%$$

$$\frac{\text{taxes}}{\text{sales}} = \frac{\$1,350}{\$100,000} = 1.35\%$$

TABLE 4.8	2003 Sales Forecast for Vectra Manufacturing

Unit sales	
Model X	1,700
Model Y	1,950
Dollar sales	
Model X ($25/unit)	$ 42,500
Model Y ($50/unit)	97,500
Total	$140,000

TABLE 4.9	Pro Forma Income Statement, Using the Percent-of-Sales Method, for Vectra Manufacturing for the Year Ended December 31, 2003

Sales revenue	$140,000
Less: Cost of goods sold (80%)	112,000
Gross margin	$ 28,000
Less: Operating expenses (10%)	14,000
Operating earnings	$ 14,000
Less: Interest expense (1%)	1,400
Earnings before taxes	$ 12,600
Less: Taxes (15% or 1.35% of sales)	1,890
Net income after taxes	$ 10,710
Less: Common share dividends	4,000
Reinvested profits (to retained earnings)	$ 6,710

Note that the dollar amounts used in the above calculations are taken from the 2002 income statement (Table 4.6). The percent-of-sales approach assumes these percentages for the 2002 fiscal year will also apply for the 2003 forecast year. Reflect this assumption in the pro forma income statement. Vectra's sales for 2003 are forecasted to be $140,000 (see Table 4.8) and applying the percent-of-sales assumption results in the pro forma income statement provided in Table 4.9. Note that for Table 4.9, it is assumed that common share dividends remain at $4,000. This, of course, is an assumption and a different assumption could be made.

With the percent-of-sales approach, all costs increase with sales. So, with sales increasing 40 percent, so too will cost of goods sold, all operating expenses, interest expense, and taxes. The net effect is that net income after tax (NIAT) will also increase 40 percent. This is exactly what occurs. Note in 2002 that NIAT was $7,650. The forecast for NIAT for 2003 is $10,710. This is a 40 percent increase. (See the highlighted number on Tables 4.6 and 4.9.)

Weaknesses of the Percent-of-Sales Approach

There are three weaknesses of the percent-of-sales approach to financial forecasting. First, it is unrealistic to assume that all expenses will remain exactly the same percent of sales from one fiscal year to the next. This will never occur in reality and therefore it is illogical to assume it will when preparing a pro forma income statement. Second, with the percent-of-sales method, a company is essentially locked into a given profit margin. Note that for the 2002 actual and 2003 pro forma income statements, the profit margin is 7.65 percent. The percent-of-sales approach precludes the idea that a company may reduce costs and therefore increase profit margins. An alternative method of forecasting is the judgmental approach, where values of individual accounts are estimated based on an analysis of the current situation.

Example ▼ Vectra Manufacturing's actual income statement for the fiscal year ended December 31, 2002 is provided in Table 4.10. As discussed earlier for 2002, cost of goods sold is very high at 80 percent of sales. The profit margin is low at 7.65 percent. Assume that a ratio analysis revealed that the industry average was 28 percent for gross margin and 12.6 percent for profit margin. With these comparative figures, perhaps Vectra would want to attempt to gain better control of costs and increase profits. For the 2003 forecast year, Vectra plans to reduce cost of goods sold to 76 percent of sales as a first step in trying to achieve the industry standard for profitability. In addition, operating expenses are expected to increase slightly to 11 percent of sales while interest expense will increase to $1,100. Vectra's tax rate is expected to remain at 15 percent of earnings before taxes. The company plans to reduce common share dividends to $1,000 in order to increase the amount of reinvested profits (increase internal sources of financing). These assumptions are reflected in the pro forma income statement provided in the second column of Table 4.10. Note, the assumption used to generate the forecast is shown to the right of the number. Using these assumptions, all of the expense figures are a different percent of sales from 2002. As well, the profit margin increases to 10.38 percent, which now approaches the industry average. ▲ The judgmental approach is a more realistic approach to financial forecasting.

The third weakness of the percent-of-sales approach is that it assumes that all of the firm's costs are variable. If a firm has no fixed costs, it will not receive the benefits that often result from them.[7] Therefore, the use of past cost and expense ratios generally *tends to understate profits when sales are increasing and overstate profits when sales are decreasing.* Clearly, if a firm has fixed costs and these costs do not change when sales increase, the result is increased profits. By remaining unchanged when sales decline, these costs tend to lower profits. The

| TABLE 4.10 | Vectra Manufacturing: Actual Income Statements for 2002 and Pro Forma for 2003 Prepared Using the Judgmental Approach |

	2002 Actual	2003 Pro forma	
Sales revenue	$100,000	$140,000	
Less: Cost of goods sold	80,000	106,400	(76% of sales)
Gross margin	$ 20,000	33,600	
Less: Operating expenses	10,000	15,400	(11% of sales)
Operating earnings	$ 10,000	18,200	
Less: Interest expenses	1,000	1,100	(stated dollar amount)
Earnings before taxes	$ 9,000	17,100	
Less: Taxes (15%)	1,350	2,565	(15% of EBT)
Net income after tax	$ 7,650	14,535	
Less: Common share dividends	4,000	1,000	(stated dollar amount)
Reinvested profits (to retained earnings)	$ 3,650	$ 13,535	

7. The potential returns as well as risks resulting from use of fixed (operating and financial) costs to create "leverage" are discussed in Chapter 10. The key point to recognize here is that when the firm's revenue is *increasing,* fixed costs can magnify returns.

best way to adjust for the presence of fixed costs in pro forma income statement preparation is to break the firm's historical costs and expenses into *fixed* and *variable components*.[8]

Example ▼ Vectra Manufacturing's 2002 actual and 2003 pro forma income statements, broken into fixed and variable cost components, are provided in Table 4.11.

Breaking Vectra's expenses into fixed and variable components may provide a more accurate projection of its pro forma profit. Had the firm treated all costs as variable, its pro forma NIAT would equal 7.65% of sales, just as was the case in 2002 ($7,650 NIAT ÷ $100,000 sales). As shown in Table 4.9, by assuming that *all* costs are variable, the NIAT would have been $10,710 (7.65% × $140,000 projected sales) instead of the $26,350 of NIAT obtained above by using the firm's fixed cost–variable cost breakdown.

This example should make it clear that ignoring fixed costs in the pro forma income statement preparation process may result in the misstatement of the firm's forecast profit. Therefore, when preparing the pro forma income statement, break expenses down into their fixed and variable components if the infor-
▲ mation is available.

TABLE 4.11	**Vectra Manufacturing: Actual Income Statements for 2002 and Pro Forma for 2003 Prepared Assuming Some Costs Are Fixed**

Assuming prepaid fixed costs	2002 Actual	2003 Pro forma
Sales revenue	$100,000	$140,000
Less: Cost of goods sold		
Fixed cost	40,000	40,000
Variable cost (40% × sales)	40,000	56,000
Gross margin	$ 20,000	$ 44,000
Less: Operating expenses		
Fixed expense	5,000	5,000
Variable expense (5% × sales)	5,000	7,000
Operating earnings	$ 10,000	$ 32,000
Less: Interest expense (all fixed)	1,000	1,000
Earnings before taxes	$ 9,000	$ 31,000
Less: Taxes (15%)	1,350	4,650
Net income after taxes	$ 7,650	$ 26,350

---

8. The application of *regression analysis*—a statistically based technique for measuring the relationship between variables—to past cost data as they relate to past sales could be used to develop equations that recognize the fixed and variable nature of each cost. Such equations could be employed when preparing the pro forma income statement from the sales forecast. The use of the regression approach in pro forma income statement preparation is widespread, and many computer software packages for use in pro forma preparation rely on this technique. Expanded discussions of the application of this technique can be found in most second-level managerial finance texts.

? Review Questions

4–10   Briefly describe the pro forma income statement preparation process using the *percent-of-sales method*. What are the strengths of this simplified approach? What are the weaknesses?

4–11   Instead of the percent-of-sales approach, what other methods can be used to develop the pro forma income statement? What are the advantages of these other methods in comparison to the percent-of-sales approach?

4–12   Comment on the following statement: "Because nearly all firms have fixed costs, ignoring them in the pro forma income statement preparation process typically results in misstatement of the firm's forecast profit." How can such a "misstatement" be avoided?

4.5   Preparing the Pro Forma Balance Sheet

judgmental approach
A method for developing the pro forma balance sheet in which the values of certain balance sheet accounts are estimated, and others are calculated, based on a ratio analysis.

A number of approaches are available for preparing the pro forma balance sheet. Probably the best and most popular is the judgmental approach.[9] Under the **judgmental approach,** stated assumptions for the balance sheet accounts are reflected in the pro forma balance sheet. These assumptions may be a value or may be a stated objective based on a ratio analysis. For example, a ratio analysis may reveal that a company's average collection period is 73.2 days. If the industry average were 42.6 days, the firm's objective may be to reduce the average collection period to the industry average over a three-year period. For the upcoming year, the firm's goal may be to reduce the average collection period to 63 days. This target is used to forecast the firm's accounts receivable for the forecast year. A similar procedure can be used for inventory and accounts payable.

total financing required
The change in total assets from the latest fiscal year to the forecast year.

Reflecting each of the stated assumptions in the pro forma balance sheet generates values for each account. The change in assets from the latest fiscal year (i.e., 2002) to the forecast year (i.e., 2003) determines the **total financing required** (TFR). The firm's total assets will change. An increase in total assets reflects the need for financing. A portion of the TFR may be generated internally. The most obvious source of internal financing is reinvested profits, as discussed earlier. Reinvested profits will provide a portion, in some case, all of the TFR. A second source of reinvested profits is accounts payable and accruals such as taxes payable or wage payables. Accounts payable and accruals are amounts a company owes but for which there is no obvious direct financing cost. For example, taxes payable is an amount owed by the firm but as long as the company pays the amount owed by the due date, there is no financing cost. These types of current liabilities can provide a source of financing.

spontaneous sources of financing
Changes in accounts payable and accruals.

Recall from Chapter 2, for the statement of cash flows, that if a current liability increases, this is a source of cash. For financial forecasting, increases in accounts payable and accruals are termed **spontaneous sources of financing**. The term "spontaneous" is used since these accounts will increase as sales increase.

---

9. The judgmental approach represents an improved version of the *percent-of-sales approach* to pro forma balance sheet preparation. Because the judgmental approach requires only slightly more information and should yield better estimates than the naive percent-of-sales approach, it is presented here.

As sales increase, the firm will purchase more from their suppliers; therefore, they will incur more payables and higher levels of accruals. An increase in a current liability is a source of financing, an internal source of financing for financial forecasting purposes. Therefore, the difference between TFR and two internal sources of financing is the amount of external financing the firm requires to operate during the forecast year. The **external financing required** (EFR) is the figure that makes the balance sheet balance.

external financing required
The difference between total financing required and two internal sources of financing.

To apply the judgmental approach to prepare Vectra Manufacturing's 2003 pro forma balance sheet, a number of assumptions must be made:

1. A minimum cash balance of $8,000 is desired.
2. Marketable securities are assumed to remain unchanged from their current level of $4,000.
3. For the 2002 fiscal year, the average collection period was 47.45 days ($13,000/($100,000 ÷ 365)). Assuming that this is 10 days higher than the industry average, Vectra plans to target a 41-day average collection period for 2003. Therefore, accounts receivable for 2003 is $15,726 (($140,000 ÷ 365) × 41 days), where the $140,000 is the sales forecast for the 2003 forecast year.
4. For the 2002 fiscal year, days in inventory was 73 days ($16,000/($80,000 ÷ 365)). Assuming that this is comparable to the industry average, Vectra is planning to target the same number of days for the 2003 forecast year. To complete the pro forma balance sheet, the pro forma income statement developed in Table 4.10 will be used. Therefore, the forecast for inventory for 2003 is $21,280 (($106,400 ÷ 365) × 73 days).
5. In 2003, Vectra plans to acquire a new machine costing $35,000. Total amortization in 2003 will be $7,000. (Note that the increase in operating expenses to 11 percent of sales in Table 4.10 reflects the increased amortization.) Adding the $35,000 to net fixed assets of $51,000 and subtracting the amortization of $7,000 results in net fixed assets of $79,000 in 2003.
6. Purchases are 45 percent of cost of goods sold. Vectra's average payment period in 2002 was 71 days [$7,000/(($80,000 × 45%) ÷ 365)]. Vectra's suppliers have been requesting more rapid payment so the company plans to reduce the average payment period to 62 days in 2003. Therefore, accounts payable in 2003 is $8,133 [(($106,400 × 45%) ÷ 365) × 62 days].
7. Taxes payable are expected to be 25 percent of the forecasted amount of taxes payable; in this case, $641 ($2,565 × 25%).
8. The line of credit is assumed to remain unchanged from the current level of $8,300. This is the usual assumption for any liability or equity account with an obvious cost of financing (e.g., line of credit, long-term debt, preferred equity, and common shares). This assumption is usually made since the objective of preparing the pro forma balance sheet is to determine the amount of financing the company requires for the forecast year. So, unless different information is provided, always assume that items with an obvious cost of financing remain unchanged.
9. No change in other current liabilities is expected. They remain at the level of the previous year: $3,400.
10. The firm's long-term debt and its common shares are expected to remain unchanged at $18,000 and $30,000, respectively; no issues, retirements, or repurchases of bonds or stocks are planned. Again, this is the usual assumption.

11. Retained earnings will increase from the beginning level of $23,000 (from the balance sheet dated December 31, 2002, in Table 4.7) to $36,535. The increase of $13,535 represents the amount of reinvested profits calculated in the 2003 pro forma income statement in Table 4.10.

The 2003 pro forma balance sheet for Vectra Manufacturing, presented in Table 4.12, reflects the 11 assumptions above. Note that the external financing required is the figure that makes the balance sheet balance. In this case, Vectra must raise about $23,000 of external financing to be able to acquire the assets required to support sales increasing 40 percent to $140,000.[10]

To reinforce financial forecasting concepts and to ensure that your calculations in the pro forma balance sheet are correct, it is useful to determine EFR by calculating total financing required and then subtracting the internal sources of

---

TABLE 4.12   **Vectra Manufacturing Balance Sheets as of December 31**

	2002 Actual	2003 Pro forma
Assets		
Cash	$ 6,000	$ 8,000
Marketable securities	4,000	4,000
Accounts receivable	13,000	15,726
Inventory	16,000	21,280
Total current assets	$39,000	$ 49,006
Net fixed assets	51,000	79,000
Total assets	$90,000	$128,006
Liabilities and equity		
Accounts payable	$ 7,000	$ 8,133
Taxes payable	300	641
Line of credit	8,300	8,300
Other current liabilities	3,400	3,400
Total current liabilities	$19,000	$ 20,474
Long-term debt	$18,000	$ 18,000
Shareholders' equity		
Common shares	$30,000	$ 30,000
Retained earnings	23,000	36,535
Total liabilities and equity	$90,000	$105,009
External financing required		22,997
Adjusted total liabilities and equity		$128,006

---

10. Note that on the 2003 balance sheet, marketable securities of $4,000 are included. Generally, marketable securities provide a much lower rate of return than the cost of financing to a company. It makes no sense for Vectra to raise $23,000 of financing when they hold $4,000 of low return marketable securities. Therefore, prior to raising financing, the expectation is that Vectra will liquidate the marketable securities, thereby reducing EFR by $4,000. The revised amount of $19,000 will appear on the balance sheet as debt and/or equity financing.

TABLE 4.13	Vectra Manufacturing Calculation of External Financing Required (EFR) for the Forecast Year Ended December 31, 2003

Total financing required (TFR) (Change in total assets)		$38,006
Less: Internal sources		
Increase in payables	$ 1,133	
Increase in taxes payable	341	
Reinvested profits	13,535	
Total internal sources		15,009
External financing required		$22,997

financing. This analysis is provided for Vectra for the 2003 forecast year in Table 4.13.

A *positive* value for "external financing required," like that shown in Tables 4.12 and 4.13, means that to support the forecast level of operation, the firm must raise funds externally using debt and/or equity financing. Once the form of financing is determined, the pro forma balance sheet is modified to replace "external financing required" with the planned increases in the debt and/or equity accounts.

A *negative* value for external financing required indicates that the firm's forecast financing is in excess of its needs. In this case, funds would be available for use in repaying debt, repurchasing common shares, increasing dividends, or investing in assets. Once the specific actions are determined, "external financing required" is replaced in the pro forma balance sheet with the planned reductions in the debt and/or equity accounts, or increases in assets.

Using Pro Forma Statements

In addition to estimating the amount of external financing that is required to support a given level of sales, pro forma statements also provide a basis for analyzing in advance the level of profitability and overall financial performance of the firm in the coming year. Using pro forma statements, both financial managers and lenders can analyze the firm's expected financial performance. Sources and uses of cash can be evaluated by preparing a pro forma statement of cash flows. Various ratios can be calculated from the pro forma income statement and balance sheet to evaluate performance.

After analyzing the pro forma statements, the financial manager can take steps to adjust planned operations to achieve short-term financial goals. For example, if profits on the pro forma income statement are too low, a variety of pricing or cost-cutting actions, or both, might be initiated. If the projected level of accounts receivable on the pro forma balance sheet is too high, changes in credit or collection policy may be called for. Pro forma statements are therefore of key importance in solidifying the firm's financial plans for the coming year.

IN PRACTICE

Financial Planning for Nickel

Most business decisions involve financial planning and forecasting. Before deciding to invest $1,000, $100,000, $1 million, or $1 billion in a project, a company must forecast future cash flow, profitability, and the requirement for financing. In June 2002, Inco, a Canadian company that is the dominant nickel producer in the world, reached a formal agreement with the government of Newfoundland and Labrador to develop the giant Voisey's Bay nickel mine located in Labrador.

Like many great discoveries, the Voisey's Bay deposit was found by accident in 1993. In 1996, after a protracted bidding war with Falconbridge, another large Canadian mining company, Inco acquired the rights to the Voisey's Bay deposit, paying a total of $4.7 billion. The deposit then sat untouched due to the declining price of nickel and an inability to negotiate a deal with the Newfoundland government over where the ore would be processed. By 2002, with further work completed on determining the size and grade of the deposit and with the price of nickel recovering, Inco was able to reach a development agreement with the province.

Voisey's Bay holds about 31 million tonnes of nickel. In order to access the nickel, Inco will invest $2.9 billion over 30 years in developing the mine and building a processing facility. While the mine will be ready for production in 2006, a plant to process the ore will not be ready until 2011. In between, Inco will ship the ore to other processing facilities in Canada. Scott Hand, Inco's CEO, states: "Inco is well positioned to handle a phased project that responsibly develops our assets. The willingness of the province to allow us to loan our other Canadian operations ore during the first phase of development will produce the kind of cash flows required to help finance the second phase of the project." Mr. Hand added: "I have no interest or desire to issue equity. Inco plans to finance the project with cash flow and profits [internal financing] and debt [external financing]."

And, the project will generate substantial cash flows and profits. The Voisey's Bay mine will produce about 110 million pounds of nickel annually at a cash cost of $1.50 per pound, one of the lowest cost mines in the world. In June, as the development deal was being finalized, nickel was trading for $4.95 per pound. Scott Hand's view of the project is suggestive of the type of forecasting completed: "The mine will deliver attractive returns to our shareholders."

REFERENCES: "Inco Limited Agrees on Statement of Principles with Province of Newfoundland and Labrador for Development of Voisey's Bay Deposits," Inco Press Release, June 11, 2002; Allan, Robinson, "Agreement Calls for Processing Complex by 2011," *The Globe and Mail*, June 12, 2002; Allan, Robinson, "Megaprojects Seen Aiding Inco Status," *The Globe and Mail*, June 12, 2002.

? Review Questions

4–13   Describe the *judgmental approach* for simplified preparation of the pro forma balance sheet. Contrast this with the more detailed approach shown in Figure 4.1.

4–14   Discuss the process used to calculate *external financing required*. Differentiate between the interpretation and strategy associated with positive and negative values for *external financing required*.

4–15   What is the financial manager's objective in evaluating pro forma statements?

SUMMARY

 Understand the financial planning process, including long-term (strategic) financial plans and short-term (operating) plans. The three key aspects of the financial planning process are cash planning, forecasting future profitability, and forecasting the need for financing. To forecast cash requirements, a cash budget must be prepared. Forecasting profitability requires a pro forma income statement, while both an income statement and balance sheet must be forecast to estimate the amount of financing required. Long-term (strategic) financial plans act as a guide for preparing short-term (operating) financial plans. Long-term plans tend to cover periods ranging from 2 to 10 years and are updated regularly. Short-term plans most often cover a 1- to 2-year period.

 Discuss the cash budget, the importance of sales forecasts, procedures for preparing a cash budget, and how to cope with uncertainty when preparing a cash budget. The cash planning process uses the cash budget, based on a sales forecast, to estimate short-term cash surpluses and shortages. The sales forecast is based on external and internal data. The cash budget is typically prepared for a 1-year period divided into months. It nets cash receipts and disbursements for each period to calculate net cash flow. Ending cash is estimated by adding beginning cash to the net cash flow. By subtracting the desired minimum cash balance from the ending cash, the financial manager can determine required total financing (typically a line of credit) or the excess cash balance (typically held as marketable securities). To cope with uncertainty in the cash budget, sensitivity analysis (preparation of several cash budgets) or computer simulation can be used.

 Discuss the fundamentals associated with preparing the pro forma income statement and balance sheet. There are three required inputs for financial forecasting: the previous year's financial statements, sales forecasts, and forecasts for all other financial statement accounts. There are three outputs: a pro forma income statement, pro forma balance sheet, and a statement of external financing required (EFR). Financial forecasting simply reflects a set of assumptions regarding a company's financial position for a forecast period.

 Discuss and illustrate three approaches to preparing a pro forma income statement. There are three approaches to preparing the pro forma income statement. The percent-of-sales method assumes that all income statement items remain the same percent of sales for the forecast year as for the previous fiscal year. This method has three weaknesses: it is unrealistic, it locks a company into a given level of profitability, and it assumes that all costs are variable. The second method is the judgmental approach, where values of individual accounts are estimated based on an analysis of the current situation. The third approach is to break historical expenses into fixed and variable components. The latter two methods are superior approaches to preparing the pro forma income statement.

 Discuss and illustrate the judgmental approach to preparing a pro forma balance sheet and determine the amount of external financing required for a company to operate during the forecast year. With the judgmental approach, stated assumptions for the balance sheet accounts are reflected in the pro forma balance sheet. These assumptions may be a value or a stated objective based on a ratio analysis. External financing required is the difference between total financing required, which is based on the change in total assets from the previous fiscal year to the forecast year, and internal sources, the combination of reinvested profits and the change in spontaneous liabilities between years. A positive value for external financing required means that the firm must raise funds externally; a negative value indicates that funds are available for use in repaying debt, repurchasing stock, increasing dividends, or acquiring assets. Pro forma statements are commonly used to analyze the firm's level of profitability and overall financial performance so that adjustments can be made to planned operations to achieve short-term financial goals.

(Solutions in Appendix B)

  ST 4–1 **Cash budget and pro forma balance sheet inputs**   Jane McDonald, a financial analyst for Carroll Company, has prepared the following sales and cash disbursement estimates for the period February–June of the current year.

Month	Sales	Cash disbursements
February	$500	$400
March	600	300
April	400	600
May	200	500
June	200	200

Ms. McDonald notes that historically, 30 percent of sales have been for cash. Of *credit sales,* 70 percent are collected 1 month after the sale, and the remaining 30 percent are collected 2 months after the sale. The firm wishes to maintain a minimum ending balance in its cash account of $25. Balances above this amount would be invested in short-term government securities (marketable securities), whereas any deficits would be financed through short-term bank borrowing (line of credit). The beginning cash balance at April 1 is $115.

a. Prepare a cash budget for April, May, and June.

b. How much financing, if any, at a maximum would Carroll Company need to meet its obligations during this 3-month period?

c. If a pro forma balance sheet dated at the end of June were prepared from the information presented, give the size of each of the following: cash, line of credit, marketable securities, and accounts receivable.

 ST 4–2 **Pro forma income statement**   Euro Designs, Inc., expects sales during 2003 to rise from the 2002 level of $3.5 million to $3.9 million. Due to a scheduled large loan payment, the interest expense in 2003 is expected to drop to $325,000. The firm plans to increase its cash dividend payments during 2003 to $320,000. The company's year-end 2002 income statement follows.

Income Statement Euro Designs, Inc. for the year ended December 31, 2002	
Sales revenue	$3,500,000
Less: Cost of goods sold	1,925,000
Gross margin	$1,575,000
Less: Operating expenses	420,000
Operating earnings	$1,155,000
Less: Interest expense	400,000
Earnings before taxes	$ 755,000
Less: Taxes (40%)	302,000
Net income after taxes	$ 453,000
Less: Cash dividends	250,000
To retained earnings	$ 203,000

a. Use the *percent-of-sales method* to prepare a 2003 pro forma income statement for Euro Designs, Inc.

b. Explain why the statement may underestimate the company's actual 2003 pro forma income.

PROBLEMS

  4–1   Cash receipts   A firm has actual sales of $65,000 in April and $60,000 in May. It expects sales of $70,000 in June and $100,000 in July and in August. Assuming that sales are the only source of cash inflows and that half of these are for cash and the remainder are collected evenly over the following 2 months, what are the firm's expected cash receipts for June, July, and August?

  4–2   Cash disbursements schedule   Maris Brothers, Inc., needs a cash disbursements schedule for the months of April, May, and June. Use the format of Table 4.3 and the following information in its preparation.

Sales: February = $500,000; March = $500,000; April = $560,000; May = $610,000; June = $650,000; July = $650,000

Purchases: Purchases are calculated as 60 percent of the next month's sales, 10 percent of purchases are made in cash, 50 percent of purchases are paid for 1 month after purchase, and the remaining 40 percent of purchases are paid for 2 months after purchase.

Rent: The firm pays rent of $8,000 per month.

Wages and salaries: Base wage and salary costs are fixed at $6,000 per month plus a variable cost of 7 percent of the current month's sales.

Taxes: A tax payment of $54,500 is due in June.

Fixed asset outlays: New equipment costing $75,000 will be bought and paid for in April.

Interest payments: An interest payment of $30,000 is due in June.

Cash dividends: Dividends of $12,500 will be paid in April.

Principal repayments and retirements: No principal repayments or retirements are due during these months.

 4–3   Cash budget—Basic   Grenoble Enterprises had sales of $50,000 in March and $60,000 in April. Forecast sales for May, June, and July are $70,000, $80,000, and $100,000, respectively. The firm has a cash balance of $5,000 on May 1 and wishes to maintain a minimum cash balance of $5,000. Given the following data, prepare and interpret a cash budget for the months of May, June, and July.

(1) The firm makes 20 percent of sales for cash, 60 percent are collected in the next month, and the remaining 20 percent are collected in the second month following sale.

(2) The firm receives other income of $2,000 per month.

(3) The firm's actual or expected purchases, all made for cash, are $50,000, $70,000, and $80,000 for the months of May through July, respectively.

(4) Rent is $3,000 per month.

(5) Wages and salaries are 10 percent of the previous month's sales.

(6) Cash dividends of $3,000 will be paid in June.

(7) Payment of principal and interest of $4,000 is due in June.

(8) A cash purchase of equipment costing $6,000 is scheduled in July.

(9) Taxes of $6,000 are due in June.

CHALLENGE   4–4   **Cash budget—Advanced**   The actual sales and purchases for Xenocore, Inc., for September and October 2003, along with its forecast sales and purchases for the period November 2003 through April 2004, follow.

Year	Month	Sales	Purchases
2003	September	$210,000	$120,000
2003	October	250,000	150,000
2003	November	170,000	140,000
2003	December	160,000	100,000
2004	January	140,000	80,000
2004	February	180,000	110,000
2004	March	200,000	100,000
2004	April	250,000	90,000

The firm makes 20 percent of all sales for cash and collects on 40 percent of its sales in each of the 2 months following the sale. Other cash inflows are expected to be $12,000 in September and April, $15,000 in January and March, and $27,000 in February. The firm pays cash for 10 percent of its purchases. It pays for 50 percent of its purchases in the following month and for 40 percent of its purchases 2 months later.

Wages and salaries amount to 20 percent of the preceding month's sales. Rent of $20,000 per month must be paid. Interest payments of $10,000 are due in January and April. A principal payment of $30,000 is also due in April. The firm expects to pay cash dividends of $20,000 in January and April. Taxes of $80,000 are due in April. The firm also intends to make a $25,000 cash purchase of fixed assets in December.

a. Assuming that the firm has a cash balance of $22,000 at the beginning of November, determine the end-of-month cash balances for each month, November through April.

b. Assuming that the firm wishes to maintain a $15,000 minimum cash balance, determine the required total financing or excess cash balance for each month, November through April.

c. If the firm were requesting a line of credit to cover needed financing for the period November to April, how large would this line have to be? Explain your answer.

WARM-UP   4–5   **Cash flow concepts**   The following represent financial transactions that Johnsfield & Co. will be undertaking in the next planning period. For each transaction, check the statement or statements that will be affected immediately.

	Statement		
Transaction	Cash budget	Pro forma income statement	Pro forma balance sheet
Cash sale			
Credit sale			
Accounts receivable are collected			
Asset with 5-year life is purchased			
Amortization is taken			
Amortization of goodwill is taken			
Sale of common shares			
Retirement of outstanding bonds			
Fire insurance premium is paid for the next 3 years			

INTERMEDIATE **4–6   Cash budget—Sensitivity analysis**   Trotter Enterprises, Inc., has gathered the following data in order to plan for its cash requirements and short-term investment opportunities for October, November, and December. All amounts are shown in thousands of dollars.

	October			November			December		
	Pessi-mistic	Most likely	Opti-mistic	Pessi-mistic	Most likely	Opti-mistic	Pessi-mistic	Most likely	Opti-mistic
Total cash receipts	$260	$342	$462	$200	$287	$366	$191	$294	$353
Total cash disbursements	285	326	421	203	261	313	287	332	315

a. Prepare a sensitivity analysis of Trotter's cash budget using −$20,000 as the beginning cash balance for October and a minimum required cash balance of $18,000.

b. Use the analysis prepared in part **a** to predict Trotter's financing needs and investment opportunities over the months of October, November, and December. Discuss how the knowledge of the timing and amounts involved can aid the planning process.

INTERMEDIATE **4–7   Multiple cash budgets—Sensitivity analysis**   Brownstein, Inc., expects sales of $100,000 during each of the next 3 months. It will make monthly purchases of $60,000 during this time. Wages and salaries are $10,000 per month plus 5 percent of sales. Brownstein expects to make a tax payment of $20,000 in the next month and a $15,000 purchase of fixed assets in the second month and to receive $8,000 in cash from the sale of an asset in the third month. All sales and purchases are for cash. Beginning cash and the minimum cash balance are assumed to be zero.

a. Construct a cash budget for the next 3 months.

b. Brownstein is unsure of the sales levels, but all other figures are certain. If the most pessimistic sales figure is $80,000 per month and the most optimistic is $120,000 per month, what are the monthly minimum and maximum ending cash balances that the firm can expect for each of the 1-month periods?

c. Briefly discuss how the financial manager can use the data in **a** and **b** to plan for financing needs.

INTERMEDIATE

4–8   **Pro forma income statement**   The marketing department of Metroline Manufacturing estimates that its sales in 2003 will be $1.5 million. Interest expense is expected to remain unchanged at $35,000, and the firm plans to pay $70,000 in cash dividends during 2003. Metroline Manufacturing's income statement for the year ended December 31, 2002, is given below, followed by a breakdown of the firm's cost of goods sold and operating expenses into their fixed and variable cost components.

Income Statement
Metroline Manufacturing
for the year ended December 31, 2002

Sales revenue	$1,400,000
Less: Cost of goods sold	910,000
Gross margin	$ 490,000
Less: Operating expenses	120,000
Operating earnings	$ 370,000
Less: Interest expense	35,000
Earnings before taxes	$ 335,000
Less: Taxes (40%)	134,000
Net income after taxes	$ 201,000
Less: Cash dividends	66,000
To retained earnings	$ 135,000

Fixed and Variable Cost Breakdown
Metroline Manufacturing
for the year ended December 31, 2002

Cost of goods sold	
Fixed cost	$210,000
Variable cost	700,000
Total cost	$910,000
Operating expenses	
Fixed expenses	$ 36,000
Variable expenses	84,000
Total expenses	$120,000

a. Use the *percent-of-sales method* to prepare a pro forma income statement for the year ended December 31, 2003.
b. Use *fixed and variable cost data* to develop a pro forma income statement for the year ended December 31, 2003.
c. Compare and contrast the statements developed in **a** and **b**. Which statement will likely provide the better estimates of 2003 income? Explain why.

CHALLENGE

4–9   **Pro forma income statement—Sensitivity analysis**   Allen Products, Inc., wants to do a sensitivity analysis for the coming year. The pessimistic prediction for sales is $900,000; the most likely amount of sales is $1,125,000; and the optimistic prediction is $1,280,000. Allen's income statement for the most recent year is as follows.

Income Statement	
Allen Products, Inc.	
for the year ended July 31, 2003	
Sales revenue	$937,500
Less: Cost of goods sold	421,875
Gross margin	$515,625
Less: Operating expenses	234,375
Operating earnings	$281,250
Less: Interest expense	30,000
Earnings before taxes	$251,250
Less: Taxes (25%)	62,813
Net income after taxes	$188,437

a. Use the *percent-of-sales method,* the income statement for July 31, 2003, and the sales revenue estimates to develop pessimistic, most likely, and optimistic pro forma income statements for the coming year.
b. Explain how the percent-of-sales method could result in an overstatement of profits for the pessimistic case and an understatement of profits for the most likely and optimistic cases.
c. Restate the pro forma income statements prepared in part **a** to incorporate the following assumptions about costs:
   $250,000 of the cost of goods sold is fixed; the rest is variable.
   $180,000 of the operating expenses is fixed; the rest is variable.
   All of the interest expense is fixed.
d. Compare your findings in part **c** to your findings in part **a**. Do your observations confirm your explanation in part **b**?

INTERMEDIATE

4–10   **Pro forma balance sheet—Basic**   Leonard Industries wishes to prepare a pro forma balance sheet for December 31, 2003. The firm expects 2003 sales to total $3,000,000. The following information has been gathered.
(1) A minimum cash balance of $50,000 is desired.
(2) Marketable securities are expected to remain unchanged.
(3) Accounts receivable represent 10% of sales.

(4) Inventories represent 12% of sales.

(5) A new machine costing $90,000 will be acquired during 2003. Total amortization for the year will be $32,000.

(6) Accounts payable represent 14% of sales.

(7) Accruals, other current liabilities, long-term debt, and common shares are expected to remain unchanged.

(8) The firm's profit margin is 4%, and it expects to pay out $70,000 in cash dividends during 2003.

(9) The December 31, 2002, balance sheet follows.

Balance Sheet			
Leonard Industries			
December 31, 2002			
Assets		**Liabilities and equities**	
Cash	$ 45,000	Accounts payable	$ 395,000
Marketable securities	15,000	Accruals	60,000
Accounts receivable	255,000	Other current liabilities	30,000
Inventories	340,000	Total current liabilities	$ 485,000
Total current assets	$ 655,000	Long-term debt	$ 350,000
Net fixed assets	$ 600,000	Common shares	$ 200,000
Total assets	$1,255,000	Retained earnings	$ 220,000
		Total liabilities and shareholders' equity	$1,255,000

a. Use the *judgmental approach* to prepare a pro forma balance sheet dated December 31, 2003, for Leonard Industries.

b. How much, if any, external financing will Leonard Industries require in 2003? Discuss. Develop a statement of EFR.

c. Could Leonard Industries adjust its planned 2003 dividend to avoid the situation described in **b**? Explain how.

  4–11 **Pro forma balance sheet**   Peabody & Peabody has 2002 sales of $10 million. It wishes to analyze expected performance and financing needs for 2004—2 years ahead. Given the following information, answer questions **a** and **b**.

INTERMEDIATE

(1) The percent of sales for items that vary directly with sales are as follows:

  Accounts receivable, 12%

  Inventory, 18%

  Accounts payable, 14%

  Profit margin, 3%

(2) Marketable securities and other current liabilities are expected to remain unchanged.

(3) A minimum cash balance of $480,000 is desired.

(4) A new machine costing $650,000 will be acquired in 2003, and equipment costing $850,000 will be purchased in 2004. Total amortization in 2003 is forecast as $290,000, and in 2004 $390,000 of amortization will be taken.

(5) Accruals are expected to rise to $500,000 by the end of 2004.

(6) No sale or retirement of long-term debt is expected.
(7) No sale or repurchase of common shares is expected.
(8) The dividend payout of 50 percent of net profits is expected to continue.
(9) Sales are expected to be $11 million in 2003 and $12 million in 2004.
(10) The December 31, 2002, balance sheet follows.

Balance Sheet
Peabody & Peabody
December 31, 2002
($000)

Assets		Liabilities and equities	
Cash	$ 400	Accounts payable	$1,400
Marketable securities	200	Accruals	400
Accounts receivable	1,200	Other current liabilities	80
Inventories	1,800	Total current liabilities	$1,880
Total current assets	$3,600	Long-term debt	$2,000
Net fixed assets	$4,000	Common equity	$3,720
Total assets	$7,600	Total liabilities and shareholders' equity	$7,600

a. Prepare a pro forma balance sheet dated December 31, 2004.
b. Discuss the financing changes suggested by the statement prepared in a.

   4–12   Integrative—Pro forma statements   Red Queen Restaurants wishes to prepare financial plans. Use the financial statements and the other information provided below to prepare the financial plans.

CHALLENGE

Income Statement
Red Queen Restaurants
for the year ended December 31, 2002

Sales revenue	$800,000
Less: Cost of goods sold	600,000
Gross margin	$200,000
Less: Operating expenses	100,000
Earnings before taxes	$100,000
Less: Taxes (40%)	40,000
Net income after taxes	$ 60,000
Less: Cash dividends	20,000
Reinvested profits (to retained earnings)	$ 40,000

Balance Sheet
Red Queen Restaurants
December 31, 2002

Assets		Liabilities and equities	
Cash	$ 32,000	Accounts payable	$100,000
Marketable securities	18,000	Taxes payable	20,000
Accounts receivable	150,000	Other current liabilities	5,000
Inventories	100,000	Total current liabilities	$125,000
Total current assets	$300,000	Long-term debt	$200,000
Net fixed assets	$350,000	Common shares	$150,000
Total assets	$650,000	Retained earnings	$175,000
		Total liabilities and shareholders' equity	$650,000

The following financial data are also available:
(1) The firm has estimated that its sales for 2003 will be $900,000.
(2) The firm expects to pay $35,000 in cash dividends in 2003.
(3) The firm wishes to maintain a minimum cash balance of $30,000.
(4) Accounts receivable represent approximately 18 percent of annual sales.
(5) The firm's ending inventory will change directly with changes in sales in 2003.
(6) A new machine costing $42,000 will be purchased in 2003. Total amortization for 2003 will be $17,000.
(7) Accounts payable will change directly in response to changes in sales in 2003.
(8) Taxes payable will equal 25 percent of the tax liability on the pro forma income statement.
(9) Marketable securities, other current liabilities, long-term debt, and common shares will remain unchanged.

a. Prepare a pro forma income statement for the year ended December 31, 2003, using the *percent-of-sales method*.
b. Prepare a pro forma balance sheet dated December 31, 2003, using the *judgmental approach*.
c. Analyze these statements, and discuss the resulting *external financing required*. Prepare a statement of EFR.

CHALLENGE

4–13   Integrative—Pro forma statements   Provincial Imports, Inc., has assembled statements and information to prepare financial plans for the coming year.

Income Statement
Provincial Imports, Inc.
for the year ended December 31, 2002

Sales revenue	$5,000,000
Less: Cost of goods sold	2,750,000
Gross margin	$2,250,000
Less: Operating expenses	862,000
Less: Amortization	88,000
Operating earnings	$1,300,000
Less: Interest expense	100,000
Earnings before taxes	$1,200,000
Less: Taxes (40%)	480,000
Net income after taxes	$ 720,000
Less: Cash dividends	288,000
Reinvested profits (to retained earnings)	$ 432,000

Balance Sheet
Provincial Imports, Inc.
December 31, 2002

Assets		Liabilities and equities	
Cash	$ 200,000	Accounts payable	$ 700,000
Marketable securities	275,000	Taxes payable	95,000
Accounts receivable	625,000	Line of credit	200,000
Inventories	500,000	Other current liabilities	5,000
Total current assets	$1,600,000	Total current liabilities	$1,000,000
Net fixed assets	$1,400,000	Long-term debt	$ 550,000
Total assets	$3,000,000	Common shares	$ 75,000
		Retained earnings	$1,375,000
		Total liabilities and equity	$3,000,000

Information related to financial projections for the year 2003 is provided below:

(1) Sales are projected to increase by 20 percent.

(2) The industry average for gross margin is 46.5 percent and the company plans to attain that level in 2003.

(3) The industry average for operating expenses is 18.2 percent of sales. This includes amortization. Excluding amortization, Provincial Imports expects operating expenses to be 17.1 percent of sales in 2003. Amortization expense for 2003 will be $110,000. The increase in amortization is due to a new computer system costing $486,000 that will be purchased in 2003.

(4) Interest expense is based on the amount of debt outstanding. The interest rate on the long-term debt is 12 percent and the amount of long-term debt outstanding did not change during the 2002 fiscal year. The interest rate on the line of credit averaged 13.6 percent in 2002 and the average amount of line of credit outstanding was $250,000. The company expects the interest rate on the line of credit will average 13 percent in 2003. Total interest expense is expected to be $92,000 in 2003.

(5) Due to changes in tax legislation, the company expects the tax rate will fall to 36 percent. Provincial's goal is to pay 40 percent of NIAT as dividends to the common shareholders.

(6) Cash, marketable securities, and other current liabilities will remain unchanged for 2003.

(7) For the 2003 forecast year, the company is planning for an average collection period of 44 days, an average age of inventory of 65 days, and average payment period, based on COGS, of 85 days.

(8) Taxes payable will be 30 percent of the taxes owed for 2003.

(9) If the company requires external financing, they will first sell their marketable securities. Any remaining financing will be raised by using the line of credit. If surplus financing is generated internally, Provincial Imports will repay the line of credit.

a. Prepare a pro forma income statement and balance sheet and a statement of EFR for Provincial Imports, Inc., for the 2003 fiscal year. Which approach to financial forecasting will you use?

b. Reconsider the forecasted statements. Based on the information available, which estimates, if any, do you believe are incorrect? Explain.

c. Calculate Provincial Imports' current ratio, total asset turnover, debt ratio, times interest earned, profit margin, and return on equity ratios for 2002 and 2003. Comment on the trends.

CASE   CHAPTER 4   **Preparing Martin Manufacturing's 2003 Pro Forma Financial Statements**[11]

To improve its competitive position, Martin Manufacturing is planning to implement a major plant-modernization program. Included will be construction of a state-of-the-art manufacturing facility that will cost $400 million in 2003 and is expected to lower the variable cost per tonne of steel. Terri Spiro, an experienced budget analyst, has been charged with preparing a forecast of the firm's 2003 financial position assuming construction of the proposed new facility. She plans to use the 2002 financial statements presented in the Case for Chapter 3, along with the forecasts for other financial accounts provided in the following table.

---

11. This is a continuation of the case from Chapter 3.

Key Projected Financial Data (2003)
Martin Manufacturing Company
($000)

Data item	Value
Sales	Increase to $6,500,000
Cost of goods sold	Remain the same percent of sales
Selling expense	Increase by 22%
General and administrative expense	Increase by 37.5%
Amortization expense	Increase to $185,000
Interest expense	Increase to $97,000
Tax rate	40%
Dividend payments	$20,000
Average ages of inventory	56 days
Average collection period	52 days
Average ages of payables	26 days
Accruals	Increase to $96,000
Line of credit, long-term debt, preferred shares, and common shares	Remain the same

Required

a. Use the historic and projected financial data provided to prepare a pro forma income statement and balance sheet for the year ended December 31, 2003.

b. Will Martin Manufacturing Company need to obtain *external financing* to fund construction of the proposed facility? Explain. Prepare a statement of EFR.

c. How would you recommend Martin raise the required financing?

 WEB EXERCISE   LINKS TO PRACTISE

Visit the following Web site and complete the suggested exercises. These exercises will allow you to review practical applications of the chapter topics, as well as explore the wealth of information regarding managerial finance that is available on the Internet.

www.strategis.ic.gc.ca/sc_mangb/stepstogrowth/engdoc/newtech/nt-0-1.php
Read about New Tech Distributors Corp. (New Tech), a company that assembles and distributes computer components from their facilities in Burnaby, British Columbia, at the above Web site.

Describe, in more detail, what the company does. What are their current sales? Who are New Tech's customers? What are the company's plans for growth and the challenges these plans present to the company? How might these plans impact on New Tech's need for financing? Assume you are Grant Argent, New Tech's financial advisor. What is the first step you will complete?

Click on Next at the bottom of the page.

What is the main challenge for New Tech and Grant Argent? How will New Tech determine its financing needs? What are the key assumptions New Tech used to develop its financial projections?

Click on Financial Projections in the margin on the left side of the page. Click on Income Statement. (A page will open in a new window.) What are the main conclusions you can reach regarding New Tech's expected level of profitability over the two forecast years?

Go back to the original window and click on Balance Sheet. (A page will open in a new window.) What are the main conclusions you can reach regarding the increased investment in assets New Tech must make to support increasing sales over the two forecast years? What are the sources of the financing required to fund the increase in assets over the two forecast years?

Go back to the original window and click on Statement of Retained Earnings. (A page will open in a new window.) What does the company plan on doing with net income after tax? Does this seem reasonable? Comment.

Go back to the original window and click on Have a Look at New Tech's Projected Financial Statements and Other Forecasts on the top right part of the page. (A page will open in a new window.) Click on Monthly Cash Budget. For which month is the maximum financing required, and what is the total amount of the financing? What is the anticipated source of this financing? For the year, does New Tech run a deficit or surplus? What is the amount and what source of financing does the company plan on using over the year? Examining New Tech's Statements of Changes in Financial Position may help with this analysis.

Go back to the original window and click on Have a Look at New Tech's Projected Financial Statements and Other Forecasts on the top right part of the page. (A page will open in a new window.) Click on Financial Needs and Financing Requirements. Modify this statement so that it is similar to the Statement of EFR. What is New Tech's TFR, internal sources of financing, total EFR, and sources of the EFR?

Go back to the original window and click on Sensitivity Analysis. How sensitive is New Tech's profitability to changes in sales? What impact would these changes have on the company's need for financing?

Go back to the original window and click on Financial Ratios. Discuss the company's current and projected financial position. What are the company's major financial strengths and weaknesses?

After completing this analysis, would you, as a potential creditor, lend money to New Tech? After completing this analysis, would you, as a potential investor, provide equity financing to New Tech? Comment.

TRACK SOFTWARE, INC.

Seven years ago, after 15 years in public accounting, Stanley Booker, CA, resigned his position as Manager with a national accounting firm and started Track Software, Inc. In the 2 years preceding his resignation, Stanley had spent nights and weekends developing a sophisticated cost accounting software program that became Track's initial product offering. As the firm grew, Stanley planned to develop and expand the software product offerings—all of which would be related to streamlining the accounting processes of medium- to large-sized manufacturers.

Although Track experienced losses during its first 2 years of operation—1996 and 1997—its profit has increased steadily from 1998 to the present (2002). The firm's profit history, including dividend payments, is summarized in Table 1.

Stanley started the firm with a $100,000 investment—his savings of $50,000 as equity and a $50,000 long-term loan from the bank. He had hoped to maintain his initial 100 percent ownership in the corporation, but after experiencing a $50,000 loss during the first year of operation (1996), he sold 60 percent of the business to a group of investors to obtain needed funds. Since then, no other common share transactions have taken place. Although he owns only 40 percent of the firm, Stanley actively manages all aspects of its activities; the other shareholders are not active in management of the firm.

Stanley has just prepared the firm's 2002 income statement and balance sheet, shown in Tables 2 and 3. The 2001 income statement and balance sheet are also provided. In addition, he has collected 2002 industry average ratio values, which are applicable to both 2001 and 2002 and summarized in

TABLE 1

	Profits and dividends, 1996–2002 Track Software, Inc.	
Year	Net income after taxes	Dividends paid
1996	($50,000)	$ 0
1997	(20,000)	0
1998	15,000	0
1999	35,000	0
2000	40,000	1,000
2001	43,000	3,000
2002	48,000	5,000

Table 4. He is quite pleased to have achieved record earnings of $48,000 in 2002, but he is concerned about the firm's cash flows. He plans to complete a ratio analysis to evaluate the company's financial position. Specifically, he is finding it more and more difficult to pay the firm's bills in a timely manner. To gain insight into these cash flow problems, Stanley is planning to prepare the firm's 2002 statement of cash flows.

Stanley is further frustrated by the firm's inability to afford to hire a software developer to complete development of a cost estimation package that is believed to have "blockbuster" sales potential. Stanley began development of this package 2 years ago, but the firm's growing complexity has forced him to devote more of his time to administrative duties, thereby halting the development of this product. Stanley's reluctance to fill this position stems from his concern that the added $80,000 per year in salary and benefits for the position would lower the firm's earnings per share (EPS) over the next couple of years. Although the project's success is in no way guaranteed, Stanley believes that if the money were spent to hire the software developer, the firm's sales and earnings would significantly rise once the 2- to 3-year development, production, and marketing process was completed.

Another of Stanley's concerns is the firm's rising interest expense. Because the firm relies heavily on short-term borrowing to maintain financial flexibility, recent rises in interest rates have resulted in rapid rises in Track's interest expense. In an attempt to get a feel for interest rates, Stanley researched the rates of interest on loans of varying maturities. These are shown in Table 5.

Table 2

Income Statement ($000) Track Software, Inc. for the year ended December 31		
	2001	2002
Sales revenue	$1,434	$1,550
Less: Cost of goods sold	974	1,030
Gross margin	$ 460	$ 520
Less: Operating expenses		
Selling expense	$ 129	$ 150
General and administrative expense	242	270
Amortization expense	10	11
Total operating expense	381	431
Operating earnings	$ 79	$ 89
Less: Interest expense	26	29
Earnings before taxes	$ 53	$ 60
Less: Taxes (20%)	10	12
Net income after taxes	$ 43	$ 48

Table 3

Balance Sheets ($000) Track Software, Inc.		
	December 31	
Assets	2001	2002
Current assets		
Cash	$ 31	$ 12
Marketable securities	82	66
Accounts receivable	104	152
Inventories	145	191
Total current assets	$362	$421
Gross fixed assets	$180	$195
Less: Accumulated amortization	52	63
Net fixed assets	$128	$132
Total assets	$490	$553
Liabilities and shareholders' equity		
Current liabilities		
Accounts payable	$126	$136
Line of credit	190	200
Accruals	25	27
Total current liabilities	$341	$363
Long-term debt	$ 40	$ 38
Total liabilities	$381	$401
Shareholders' equity		
Common shares (100,000 shares outstanding)	$ 50	$ 50
Retained earnings	59	102
Total shareholders' equity	$109	$152
Total liabilities and shareholders' equity	$490	$553

Table 4

Ratio	Industry average 2002
Net working capital	$96,000
Current ratio	1.82
Quick ratio	1.10
Average age of inventory	47.4 days
Average collection period	20.5 days
Average payment period	38.1 days
Fixed asset turnover	14.1
Total asset turnover	3.92
Debt ratio	55.1%
Debt/equity ratio	51.6%
Times interest earned ratio	5.6
Common size analysis	
Sales	100.0%
COGS	57.7%
Gross margin	42.3%
Operating expenses	29.9%
Operating earnings	12.4%
Interest expenses	2.2%
EBT	10.2%
Taxes	2.0%
NIAT	8.2%
Return on total assets	15.6%
Return on equity	34.7%

With all of these concerns in mind, Stanley set out to review the various data to develop strategies that would help to ensure a bright future for Track Software. As part of this process, Stanley believed that a thorough ratio analysis of the firm's 2001 and 2002 results would provide important additional insights. Stanley also wanted to prepare pro forma financial statements for 2003. Table 6 provides the assumptions Stanley feels are appropriate for the 2003 forecast year. Stanley also feels he should complete a ratio analysis once he has finalized the 2003 pro forma statements.

TABLE 5 Interest Rates for Various Loan Maturities

Loan maturity	Interest rate
3 months	12.0%
6 months	11.7
1 year	11.5
3 years	11.0
5 years	10.4
10 years	9.9
20 years	9.5

TABLE 6 Projections for the 2003 Forecast Year

(1) Sales are expected to increase by 22 percemt.

(2) Stanley wishes to reduce COGS to 64 percent of sales. The company will hold the increase in selling and general and administrative expenses to 10 percent from the 2002 amounts. In addition, Stanley plans to recommend to Track Software's Board of Directors that the company hire the new software developer at a salary of $80,000. This amount will be added to the general and administrative expense.

(3) Given that Track plans to hire the new software developer, Stanley would like to keep fixed asset acquisitions to a minimum. However, the company has delayed acquiring certain fixed assets in the past and must now invest $145,000 in fixed assets in 2003. In 2003, amortization will be $22,000.

(4) The interest expense is dependent on the amount of debt Track will have outstanding in 2003 and the maturity of the loan. Stanley must determine the total amount of costly debt Track must secure in 2003 and use Table 5 to determine the cost of the debt. The long-term debt of $38,000 currently outstanding can be renegotiated.

(5) Track's tax rate will remain unchanged for 2003. Stanley will recommend to Track's board that no dividends be paid in 2003.

(6) Stanley feels the liquidity of the company must be improved. He plans to increase cash to $35,000 and maintain the current level of marketable securities unless external financing is required in which case they will be sold. Stanley has recognized the problem with the activity ratios and for 2003, he wants to reduce Track's ACP to 32 days, average age of inventory to 56 days, and average payment period, based on COGS, to 43 days.

(7) Accruals will increase with sales. No changes are anticipated with long-term debt and common shares. Once the need for financing is determined, a decision will be made regarding the form of financing.

REQUIRED

a. (1) Upon what financial goal does Stanley seem to be focusing? Is it the correct goal? Why or why not?

   (2) Could a potential agency problem exist in this firm? Explain.

b. Calculate the firm's earnings per share (EPS) for each year, recognizing that the number of common shares outstanding has remained *unchanged* since 1997. Comment on the EPS performance in view of your response in **a**.

c. Use the financial data presented to prepare a statement of cash flows for the year ended December 31, 2002. Evaluate the statement in light of Track's current cash flow difficulties.

d. Analyze the firm's financial condition in 2001 and 2002 as it relates to (1) liquidity, (2) activity, (3) leverage, and (4) profitability using the financial statements provided in Tables 2 and 3 and the ratio data included in Table 4. Be sure to *evaluate* the firm on both a cross-sectional and a time-series basis.

e. Using the forecasts provided in Table 6, prepare a pro forma income statement and balance sheet and a Statement of EFR for Track Software for the 2003 forecast year. In view of your ratio analysis and the data provided in Table 5, what financing strategy would you recommend for Track? Hint: In order to complete the pro forma income statement, you must decide on the amount and type of debt Track should use for the 2003 forecast year.

f. Based on the pro forma financial statements prepared above, complete a ratio analysis for 2003 and add it to the ratios calculated in part **d**. Comment on the company's financial position in 2003. What improvements have occurred? Have any ratios deteriorated? Comment.

PART

3

Important Financial Concepts

Time Value of Money

LEARNING GOALS

LG1 Discuss the role of time value of money in finance and the use of computational aids to simplify its application.

LG2 Understand the concept of future value, its calculation for a single amount, and the effects of compounding interest more frequently than annually.

LG3 Find the future value of an ordinary annuity and an annuity due and compare these two types of annuities.

LG4 Understand the concept of present value, its calculation for a single amount, and the relationship of present to future value.

LG5 Calculate the present value of a mixed stream of cash flows, an annuity, a mixed stream with an embedded annuity, and a perpetuity.

LG6 Describe the procedures involved in (1) determining the periodic investments required to accumulate a future sum, (2) loan amortization, and (3) determining growth and interest rates.

LG1

5.1 The Role of Time Value in Finance

Hint
The time value of money is one of the most important concepts in finance. Money that the firm has in its possession today is more valuable than future payments because the money it now has can be invested and earn positive returns.

Firms are regularly presented with opportunities to earn positive rates of return on their funds, either through investment in real assets or in financial securities such as treasury bills, bonds, preferred shares, or common shares or deposits in a bank. Therefore, the timing of cash flows—both outflows and inflows—has important economic consequences, which financial managers explicitly recognize as the *time value of money*. Time value is based on the belief that a dollar today is worth more than a dollar that will be received tomorrow or at some future date. We begin our study of time value in finance by considering two

Money Time

Time and money are inextricably related. We regularly pay for time, from parking meters, to video rentals, to overnight package delivery services. One of the principal ideas in finance is the relationship between time and money. Called the *time value of money,* this economic principle recognizes that the passage of time affects the value of money. It advises you that if offered a dollar either today or next

month, you'd be better off to take the dollar today. You'll have the use of the dollar now, which you can put to some productive use for the whole month. (Also, you're more likely to *get* the dollar today; the person making the offer may not actually come through with the payment next month!) This chapter explores the concept and various applications of the time value of money.

views of time value—future value and present value—and the computational aids used to streamline time value calculations.

Future Versus Present Value

Financial values and decisions can be assessed by using either future value or present value techniques. Although these techniques will result in the same decisions, they view the decision differently. Future values are cash flows that occur at some point in the future: next week, month, year, or each year over the next 25 years. As well, cash flows that occur earlier in time can be deemed to occur at

FIGURE 5.1

Time Line

Time line depicting an investment's cash flows

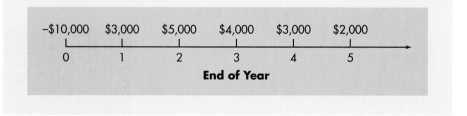

time line

A horizontal line on which time zero appears at the leftmost end and future periods are marked from left to right; can be used to depict investment cash flows.

a single point in time in the future, and converted to future values. Present values convert cash flows that will occur in the future to their equivalent value today, in the present. For time value, today or the present is referred to as time zero (0). *Future value* is cash you will receive at a given future date, and present value is just like cash in hand today.

A **time line** can be used to depict the cash flows associated with a given investment. It is a horizontal line on which time zero appears at the leftmost end and future periods are marked from left to right. A time line covering five periods (in this case, years) is given in Figure 5.1. The cash flow occurring at time zero and at the end of each year is shown above the line; the negative values represent *cash outflows* ($10,000 at time zero) and the positive values represent *cash inflows* ($3,000 inflow at the end of year 1, $5,000 inflow at the end of year 2, and so on). Time lines allow the analyst to fully understand the cash flows associated with a given investment.

Because money has a time value, all of the cash flows associated with an investment, such as those in Figure 5.1, must be measured at the same point in time. Typically, that point is either the end or the beginning of the investment's life. The future value technique uses *compounding* to find the future value of each cash flow at the end of the investment's life and then sums those values to find the investment's future value. This approach is depicted above the time line in Figure 5.2, which shows that the future value of each cash flow is measured at

FIGURE 5.2

Compounding and Discounting

Time line showing compounding to find future value and discounting to find present value

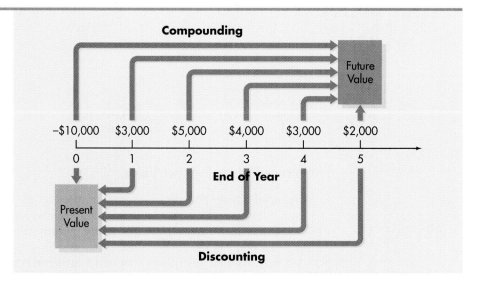

the end of the investment's 5-year life. Alternatively, the present value technique uses *discounting* to find the present value of each cash flow at time zero and then sums these values to find the investment's value today. Application of this approach is depicted below the time line in Figure 5.2.

Career Key
The time value of money is of great concern to *management*. They plan the firm's cash collections and disbursements so that the firm will get maximum benefit from its money.

The meaning and mechanics of both compounding to find future value and discounting to find present value are covered later in this chapter. Although future value and present value result in the same decisions, *financial managers—because they make decisions at time zero—tend to rely primarily on present value techniques.*

Computational Aids

Time-consuming calculations are often involved in finding future and present values. Although you should understand the concepts and mathematics underlying these calculations, the practical application of these important time value techniques can be streamlined. Here we focus on the use of financial tables and hand-held financial calculators as computational aids. Various computer software packages can also be used to simplify time value calculations.

Financial Tables

Financial tables, easily developed from formulas, include various future and present value interest factors that simplify time value calculations. Although the degree of decimal precision (rounding) varies, the tables are typically indexed by the interest or discount rate (in columns) and the number of periods (in rows). Figure 5.3 shows this general layout. If we wished to find the time value factor at a 20 percent interest rate for 10 years, its value would be found at the intersection of the 20 percent column and the 10-year row as shown by the dark blue box. A full set of the four basic financial tables is included in Appendix A, at the end of the book. These tables are described more fully later in the chapter and are used to demonstrate the application of time value techniques.

FIGURE 5.3
Financial Tables
Layout and use of a financial table

	Interest or Discount Rate ↓							
Period	1%	2%	...	10%	...	**20%**	...	50%
1			...		...	⋮	...	
2			...		...	⋮	...	
3			...		...	⋮	...	
⋮	⋮	⋮	...	⋮	...	⋮	...	⋮
→ 10	...	...	...	...	...	**X.XXX**	...	...
⋮	⋮	⋮	...	⋮	...	⋮	...	⋮
20			...		...		...	
⋮	⋮	⋮	...	⋮	...	⋮	...	⋮
50			...		...		...	

FIGURE 5.4
Calculator Keys
Important financial keys
on the typical financial
calculator

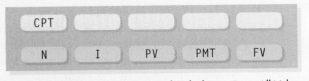

CPT — Compute Key Used to Initiate Financial Calculation Once All Values Are Input
N — Number of Periods
I — Interest or Discount Rate per Period
PV — Present Value
PMT — Amount of Payment; Used Only for Annuities
FV — Future Value

Financial Calculators

During the past 15 years, the power of the financial calculator has improved dramatically, and its cost has declined. Today, a powerful financial calculator can be purchased for $20 to $30. Generally, *financial calculators* include numerous pre-programmed, often menu-driven financial routines. This chapter and those that follow show the keystrokes for calculating interest factors and making other financial computations. For convenience, we use the important financial keys, labelled in a fashion consistent with most major financial calculators.

We focus primary attention on the keys pictured and defined in Figure 5.4. We typically use the compute (**CPT**) key and four of the five keys in the second row, with one of the four keys representing the unknown value being calculated. (Occasionally, all five of the keys, with one representing the unknown value, are used.) The keystrokes on some of the more sophisticated calculators are menu-driven, so that after you select the appropriate routine, the calculator prompts you to input each value; on these calculators, a compute key is not needed to obtain a solution. Regardless, any calculator with the basic future and present value functions can be used in lieu of financial tables. The keystrokes of other financial calculators are explained in the reference guides that accompany them.

Although this text demonstrates the use of both financial tables and financial calculators, you are strongly urged to use a calculator to streamline routine financial calculations *once you understand the basic underlying concepts*. With a little practice, both the speed and accuracy of financial computations using a calculator can be greatly enhanced. Note that because of a calculator's greater precision, slight differences are likely to exist between values calculated by using financial tables and those found with a financial calculator. Remember, conceptual understanding of the material is the objective. An ability to solve problems with the aid of a calculator does not necessarily reflect such an understanding, so don't settle just for answers. Work with the material until you are sure you also understand the concepts.

🖊 Hint
Anyone familiar with electronic spreadsheets, such as Lotus, Excel, and Quattro Pro, realizes that most of the time value of money calculations can be done expeditiously by using the special functions contained in the spreadsheet.

? Review Questions

5–1   Why does the timing of cash flows have economic consequences? What is a *time line*, and how does it depict cash flows?

5–2   What is the difference between *future value* and *present value?* Which approach is preferred by financial managers? Why?

5–3   How are financial tables laid out and accessed? Does an ability to solve problems on a financial calculator reflect conceptual understanding?

5.2 Future Value of a Single Amount

Imagine that at age 25 you begin making annual cash deposits of $2,000 into a savings plan that provides a 5 percent annual rate of return. At the end of 40 years, at age 65, you would have made deposits totalling $80,000 (40 years × $2,000 per year). Assuming that you have made no withdrawals, what do you think your account balance would be? $100,000? $150,000? $200,000? No, your $80,000 would have grown to $242,000! Why? Because the time value of money allowed the deposits to earn interest, and interest on interest, over the 40 years.

compound interest
Interest earned on a given deposit that has become part of the principal at the end of a specified period.

principal
The amount of money on which interest is paid.

future value
The value of a present amount at a future date found by applying *compound interest* over a specified period of time.

The Concept of Future Value

We speak of **compound interest** to indicate that the amount of interest earned on a given deposit has become part of the principal at the end of a specified period. The term **principal** refers to the amount of money on which the interest is paid. Annual compounding is the most common type although for savings accounts at all financial institutions in Canada, daily compounding of balances is the norm. The impact that different compounding periods have on future values is discussed in a few pages. The **future value** of a present amount is found by applying *compound interest* over a specified period of time. The concept of future value with annual compounding can be illustrated by a simple example.

Example ▼ If Fred Moreno places $100 in a savings account paying 8 percent interest compounded annually, at the end of 1 year he will have $108 in the account—the initial principal of $100 plus 8 percent ($8) in interest. The future value at the end of the first year is calculated by using Equation 5.1:

$$\text{Future value at end of year 1} = \$100 \times (1 + 0.08) = \$108 \tag{5.1}$$

If Fred were to leave this money in the account for another year, he would be paid interest at the rate of 8 percent on the new principal of $108. At the end of this second year there would be $116.64 in the account—the principal at the beginning of year 2 ($108) plus 8 percent of the $108 ($8.64) in interest. The future value at the end of the second year is calculated by using Equation 5.2:

$$\text{Future value at end of year 2} = \$108 \times (1 + 0.08) \tag{5.2}$$
$$= \$116.64$$

Substituting the expression between the equal signs in Equation 5.1 for the $108 figure in Equation 5.2 gives us Equation 5.3:

$$\text{Future value at end of year 2} = \$100 \times (1 + 0.08) \times (1 + 0.08) \tag{5.3}$$
$$= \$100 \times (1 + 0.08)^2$$
$$= \$116.64$$

▲ This equation leads to a more general formula for calculating future value.

The Equation for Future Value

The basic relationship in Equation 5.3 can be generalized to find the future value after any number of periods. Let

FV_n = future value at the end of period n
PV = initial principal, or present value
k = annual rate of return (*Note:* On financial calculators, **I** or **i**% is typically used to represent this rate.)
n = number of periods—typically years—the money is left on deposit

By using this notation, a general equation for the future value at the end of period n can be formulated:

$$FV_n = PV \times (1 + k)^n \tag{5.4}$$

The application of Equation 5.4 can be illustrated by a simple example.

Example ▼ Jane Farber placed $800 in a savings account paying 6 percent interest compounded annually and wonders how much money will be in the account at the end of 5 years. Substituting $PV = \$800$, $k = 0.06$, and $n = 5$ into Equation 5.4 gives the amount at the end of year 5:

$$FV_5 = \$800 \times (1 + 0.06)^5 = \$800 \times (1.3382256) = \$1,070.58$$

Jane will have $1,070.58 in the account at the end of the fifth year. Note, to raise 1.06 to the fifth power, key 1.06 in your calculator, press the y^x key, key in 5 for the power, and press the equal sign. This calculation provides the time value factor. Then multiply this time value factor by the initial investment.

Time-Line Use This analysis can be depicted on a time line as shown:

Time line for future value of a single amount ($800 initial principal, earning 6%, at the end of 5 years)

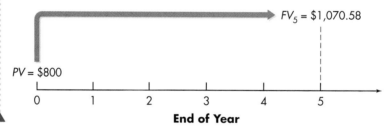

Using Tables and Calculators to Find Future Value

Solving the equation in the preceding example is very straightforward and the equation can be easily used by students. Students can also use financial tables or a financial calculator to solve the problem however. A table that provides values for $(1 + k)^n$ in Equation 5.4 is included in Appendix A, Table A-1.[1] The value in each cell of the table is called the **future value interest factor**. This factor is the

future value interest factor
The multiplier used to calculate at a specified interest rate the future value of a present amount as of a given time.

---

1. This table is commonly referred to as a "compound interest table" or a "table of the future value of one dollar." As long as you understand the source of the table values, the various names attached to it should not create confusion; you can always make a trial calculation of a value for one factor, as a check.

multiplier used to calculate at a specified interest rate the future value of a present amount as of a given time. The future value interest factor for an initial principal of $1 compounded at k percent for n periods is referred to as $FVIF_{k,n}$:

$$\text{Future value interest factor} = FVIF_{k,n} = (1 + k)^n \qquad (5.5)$$

By finding the intersection of the annual interest rate, k, and the appropriate periods, n, you will find the future value interest factor relevant to a particular problem.[2] By letting $FVIF_{k,n}$ represent the appropriate factor, we can rewrite Equation 5.4 as follows:

$$FV_n = PV \times (FVIF_{k,n}) \qquad (5.6)$$

That expression indicates that to find the future value at the end of period n of an initial deposit, we have merely to multiply the initial deposit, PV, by the appropriate future value interest factor.[3]

Example ▼ In the preceding example, Jane Farber placed $800 in her savings account at 6 percent interest compounded annually and wishes to find out how much will be in the account at the end of 5 years.

Table Use The future value interest factor for an initial principal of $1 on deposit for 5 years at 6 percent interest compounded annually, $FVIF_{6\%,5yrs}$, found in Table A-1, is 1.338. Multiplying the initial principal of $800 by this factor results in a future value at the end of year 5 of $1,070.40.

Calculator Use[4] The preprogrammed financial functions in the financial calculator can be used to calculate the future value directly. First, key in $800 and press **PV**; next, key in 5 and press **N**; then, key in 6 and press **I** (or **i%**) (which is equivalent to "k" in our notation)[5]; finally, to calculate the future value, press **CPT** and then **FV**.[6] The future value of $1,070.58 should appear on the calculator display. On many calculators, this value will be preceded by a minus sign (i.e.,

---

2. Although we commonly deal with years rather than periods, financial tables are frequently presented in terms of periods to provide maximum flexibility.

3. Occasionally, you may want to roughly estimate how long a given sum must earn at a given annual rate to double the amount. The *Rule of 72* is used to make this estimate; dividing the annual rate of interest into 72 results in the approximate number of periods it will take to double one's money at the given rate. For example, to double one's money at a 10 percent annual rate of interest will take about 7.2 years (72 ÷ 10 = 7.2). Looking at Table A-1, we can see that the future value interest factor for 10 percent and 7 years is slightly below 2 (1.949); this approximation therefore appears to be reasonably accurate.

4. Many calculators allow the user to set the number of payments per year. Most of these calculators are preset for monthly payments—12 payments per year. Because we work primarily with annual payments—one payment per year—it is important to *make sure that your calculator is set for one payment per year*. Although most calculators are preset to recognize that all payments occur at the end of the period, it is also important to *make sure that your calculator is correctly set on the* END *mode*. Consult the reference guide that accompanies your calculator for instructions for setting this value.

5. The known values *can be keyed into the calculator in any order;* the order specified in this as well as other calculator use demonstrations included in this text results merely from convenience and personal preference.

6. Note that the PMT function is not used in this example. If a value was inputted into this function the last time the calculator was used, the value is still in the calculator and will be used in this calculation. Therefore, to avoid calculating incorrect answers, follow *one* of the following two procedures when using financial functions. First, key in zero (0) and press the function that is not being used, in this example PMT. This clears any previous value in the function, meaning the function will not be used. *Or*, clear the financial function register *before* inputting values and making computations. The first method is easier and is the preferred approach to dealing with this potential problem. Users of financial calculators *must* get into the habit of using one of the above procedures or else incorrect answers will result.

−1,070.58). *If a minus sign appears on your calculator, ignore it here, as well as in all other "Calculator Use" illustrations in this text.*[7]

Inputs: 800 5 6

Functions: PV N I CPT FV

Outputs: 1070.58

Because the calculator is more accurate than the future value of factors, which have been rounded to the nearest 0.001, a slight difference—in this case, $0.18—will frequently exist between the values found by using the tables and the financial calculator. Clearly, the improved accuracy and ease of calculation tend to favour the use of the calculator. *Note: In future examples of calculator use, we will use only a display similar to that shown above. If you need a reminder of the procedures involved, go back and review the paragraph just before the display.*

A Graphic View of Future Value

Remember that we measure future value at the *end* of the given period. The relationship between various interest or discount rates, the number of periods, and the future value of one dollar is illustrated in Figure 5.5. It clearly shows that (1) the higher the interest rate, the higher the future value and (2) the longer the period of time, the higher the future value. Note that for an interest rate of 0 percent, the future value always equals the present value ($1). But for any interest rate greater than zero, the future value is greater than the present value of $1.

FIGURE 5.5

Future Value Relationship
Interest rates, time periods, and future value of one dollar

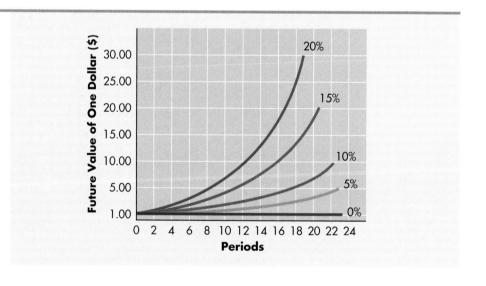

---

7. The calculator differentiates inflows from the outflows by preceding outflows with a negative sign. For example, in the problem just demonstrated, the $800 present value (PV), because it was keyed as a positive number (i.e., 800) is considered an inflow or deposit. Therefore, the calculated future value (FV) of −1070.58 is preceded by a minus sign to show that it is the resulting outflow or withdrawal. Had the $800 present value been keyed in as a negative number (i.e., −800), the future value of $1,070.58 would be displayed as a positive number (i.e., 1070.58). Simply stated, *the cash flows—present value (PV) and future value (FV)—will have opposite signs.*

Compounding More Frequently Than Annually

Rates of return are often compounded more frequently than once a year. Savings can be compounded semiannually, quarterly, monthly, weekly, daily, or even continuously. This section discusses various issues and techniques related to compounding more frequently than annually.

Semiannual Compounding

semiannual compounding
Compounding of interest over two periods within the year.

Semiannual compounding of interest involves two compounding periods within the year. Instead of the stated interest rate being paid once a year, one-half of the stated interest rate is paid twice a year.

E x a m p l e ▼ Fred Moreno has decided to invest $100 in a savings account paying 8 percent interest *compounded semiannually*. If he leaves his money in the account for 2 years, he will be paid 4 percent interest compounded over four periods, each of which is 6 months long. Table 5.1 uses interest factors to show that at the end of 1 year, with 8 percent semiannual compounding, Fred will have $108.16; at the **▲** end of 2 years, he will have $116.99.

Quarterly Compounding

quarterly compounding
Compounding of interest over four periods within the year.

Quarterly compounding of interest involves four compounding periods within the year. One-fourth of the stated interest rate is paid four times a year.

E x a m p l e ▼ Fred Moreno has found an institution that will pay him 8 percent interest *compounded quarterly*. If he leaves his money in this account for 2 years, he will be paid 2 percent interest compounded over eight periods, each of which is 3 months long. Table 5.2 uses interest factors to show the amount Fred will have at the end of 2 years. At the end of 1 year, with 8 percent quarterly compound-**▲** ing, Fred will have $108.24; at the end of 2 years, he will have $117.17.

Table 5.3 compares values for Fred Moreno's $100 at the end of years 1 and 2 given annual, semiannual, and quarterly compounding at the 8 percent rate. As shown, *the more frequently interest is compounded, the greater the amount of money accumulated*. This is true for any interest rate for any period of time.

TABLE 5.1   The Future Value from Investing $100 at 8% Interest Compounded Semiannually Over 2 Years

Period	Beginning principal (1)	Future value interest factor (2)	Future value at end of period [(1) × (2)] (3)
6 months	$100.00	1.04	$104.00
1 year	104.00	1.04	108.16
18 months	108.16	1.04	112.49
2 years	112.49	1.04	116.99

TABLE 5.2	The Future Value from Investing $100 at 8% Interest Compounded Quarterly Over 2 Years		
Period	Beginning principal (1)	Future value interest factor (2)	Future value at end of period [(1) × (2)] (3)
3 months	$100.00	1.02	$102.00
6 months	102.00	1.02	104.04
9 months	104.04	1.02	106.12
1 year	106.12	1.02	108.24
15 months	108.24	1.02	110.41
18 months	110.41	1.02	112.62
21 months	112.62	1.02	114.87
2 years	114.87	1.02	117.17

A General Equation for Compounding More Frequently Than Annually

It should be clear from the preceding examples that if m equals the number of times per year interest is compounded, Equation 5.4 (our formula for annual compounding) can be rewritten as

Hint
If $m = 1$, Equation 5.7 reduces to Equation 5.4. Thus, if interest is compounded annually, Equation 5.7 will provide the same result as Equation 5.4.

$$FV_n = PV \times \left(1 + \frac{k}{m}\right)^{m \times n} \tag{5.7}$$

The general use of Equation 5.7 can be illustrated with a simple example.

Example ▼ The preceding examples calculated the amount that Fred Moreno would have at the end of 2 years if he deposited $100 at 8 percent interest compounded semiannually and quarterly. For semiannual compounding, m would equal 2 in Equation 5.7; for quarterly compounding, m would equal 4. Substituting the appropriate values for semiannual and quarterly compounding into Equation 5.7:

1. *For semiannual compounding:*

$$FV_2 = \$100 \times \left(1 + \frac{0.08}{2}\right)^{2 \times 2} = \$100 \times (1 + 0.04)^4 = \$116.99$$

TABLE 5.3	The Future Value from Investing $100 at 8% Interest for Years 1 and 2 Given Various Compounding Periods		
		Compounding period	
End of year	Annual	Semiannual	Quarterly
1	$108.00	$108.16	$108.24
2	116.64	116.99	117.17

2. *For quarterly compounding:*

$$FV_2 = \$100 \times \left(1 + \frac{0.08}{4}\right)^{4 \times 2} = \$100 \times (1 + 0.02)^8 = \$117.17$$

Remember, to raise a number by a power greater than 2, use the y^x key, where y is the number you wish to raise and x is the power. These results agree with the values for FV_2 in Tables 5.1 and 5.2.

If the interest were compounded monthly, weekly, or daily, m would equal 12, 52, or 365, respectively. The resulting answers are $117.29, 117.34, and 117.35.

Using Tables and Calculators

We can use the future value interest factors for one dollar, given in Table A-1, when interest is compounded m times each year. Instead of indexing the table for k percent and n years, as we do when interest is compounded annually, we index it for $(k \div m)$ percent and $(m \times n)$ periods. However, the table is less useful, because it includes only selected rates for a limited number of periods. Instead, a financial calculator or computer software package is typically required.

E x a m p l e ▼ Fred Moreno wished to find the future value of $100 invested at 8 percent compounded both semiannually and quarterly for 2 years. The number of compounding periods, m, the interest rate, and number of periods used in each case, along with the future value interest factor, are:

Compounding period	m	Interest rate $(k = m)$	Periods $(m \times n)$	Future value interest factor from Table A-1
Semiannual	2	8% ÷ 2 = 4%	2 × 2 = 4	1.170
Quarterly	4	8% ÷ 4 = 2%	4 × 2 = 8	1.172

Table Use   Multiplying each of the factors by the initial $100 deposit results in a value of $117 (1.170 × $100) for semiannual compounding and a value of $117.20 (1.172 × $100) for quarterly compounding.

Calculator Use   If the calculator were used for the semiannual compounding calculation, the number of periods would be 4 and the interest rate would be 4 percent. The future value of $116.99 should appear on the calculator display.

Inputs: [100]   [4]   [4]

Functions: [PV]   [N]   [I]   [CPT]   [FV]

Outputs: [116.99]

For the quarterly compounding case, the number of periods would be 8 and the interest rate would be 2 percent. The future value of $117.17 should appear on the calculator display.

Inputs: 100   8   2

Functions: PV   N   I   CPT   FV

Outputs: 117.17

Comparing the calculator and table values, we can see that the calculator values generally agree with those values given in Table 5.3, but are more precise ▲ because the table factors have been rounded.

Continuous Compounding

continuous compounding
Compounding of interest an infinite number of times per year at intervals of microseconds.

In the extreme case, interest can be compounded continuously. **Continuous compounding** involves compounding over every microsecond—the smallest time period imaginable. In this case, m in Equation 5.7 would approach infinity, and through the use of calculus, the equation would become:

$$FV_n \text{ (continuous compounding)} = PV \times (e^{k \times n}) \quad (5.8)$$

where e is the exponential function, which has a value of 2.7183.[8] The future value interest factor for continuous compounding is therefore

$$FVIF_{k,n} \text{ (continuous compounding)} = e^{k \times n} \quad (5.9)$$

Example ▼ To find the value at the end of 2 years ($n = 2$) of Fred Moreno's $100 deposit ($PV = \$100$) in an account paying 8 percent annual interest ($k = 0.08$), compounded continuously, we can substitute into Equation 5.8:

$$FV_2 \text{ (continuous compounding)} = \$100 \times e^{.08 \times 2} = \$100 \times 2.7183^{.16}$$
$$= \$100 \times 1.1735 = \$117.35$$

Calculator Use   To find this value using the calculator, first, find the value of $e^{.16}$ by punching in .16 and then pressing **2nd** and then e^x to get 1.1735. Next multiply this value by $100 to get the future value of $117.35. (*Note:* On some calculators, **2nd** may not have to be pressed before pressing e^x.)

Inputs: .16   100

Functions: 2nd e^x X   =

Outputs: 1.1735   117.35

The future value with continuous compounding therefore equals $117.35, which, as expected, is larger than the future value of interest compounded semi-

---

8. Most calculators have the exponential function, typically noted by e^x, built into them. The use of this key is especially helpful in calculating future value when interest is compounded continuously.

annually ($116.99) or quarterly ($117.17). As was noted earlier, $117.35 is the largest amount that would result from compounding the 8 percent interest more frequently than annually, given an initial deposit of $100 and a 2-year time horizon. But, unless the amount invested is very large, the differences between monthly, weekly, daily, or continuous compounding is slight. Note that for Fred Moreno, the difference between weekly, daily, and continuous compounding is just one penny! ▲

Nominal and Effective Annual Rates of Interest

nominal (stated) annual rate
Contractual annual rate of interest charged by a lender or promised by a borrower.

effective (true) annual rate (EAR)
The annual rate of interest actually paid or earned.

Both consumers and businesses need to make objective comparisons of loan costs or investment returns over different compounding periods. In order to put interest rates on a common basis, to allow comparison, we distinguish between nominal and effective annual rates. The **nominal,** or **stated, annual rate** is the contractual annual rate charged by a lender or promised by a borrower. The **effective,** or **true, annual rate (EAR)** is the annual rate of interest actually paid or earned.

The effective annual rate reflects the impact of compounding frequency, whereas the nominal annual rate does not. In terms of interest earnings, the EAR is probably best viewed as the *annual* interest rate that would result in the same future value as that resulting from application of the nominal annual rate using the stated compounding frequency. It increases with increased compounding frequency.

Using the notation introduced earlier, we can calculate the effective annual rate, EAR, by substituting values for the nominal annual rate, k, and the compounding frequency, m, into Equation 5.10.

$$EAR = \left(1 + \frac{k}{m}\right)^m - 1 \tag{5.10}$$

We can apply this equation using data from preceding examples.

Example ▼ Fred Moreno wishes to find the effective annual rate associated with an 8 percent nominal annual rate ($k = .08$) when interest is compounded (1) annually ($m = 1$); (2) semiannually ($m = 2$); and (3) quarterly ($m = 4$). Substituting these values into Equation 5.10, we get the following:

1. *For annual compounding:*

$$EAR = \left(1 + \frac{0.08}{1}\right)^1 - 1 = (1 + 0.08)^1 - 1 = 1 + 0.08 - 1 = 0.08 = 8\%$$

2. *For semiannual compounding:*

$$EAR = \left(1 + \frac{0.08}{2}\right)^2 - 1 = (1 + 0.04)^2 - 1 = 1.0816 - 1 = 0.0816 = 8.16\%$$

3. *For quarterly compounding:*

$$EAR = \left(1 + \frac{0.08}{4}\right)^4 - 1 = (1 + 0.02)^4 - 1 = 1.082432158 - 1 = 0.0824322 = 8.24322\%$$

These values demonstrate two important points: (1) The nominal and effective rates are equivalent for annual compounding, and (2) the effective annual rate increases with increasing compounding frequency.[9]

When dealing with interest rates, consumers should be aware of the effect compounding has on the effective annual rate. For example, the interest rate on credit cards is often quoted on a monthly basis. The **annual percentage rate (APR)** is the *nominal annual rate* found by multiplying the periodic rate by the number of periods in 1 year. For example, a bank credit card that charges $1\frac{1}{2}$ percent per month would have an APR of 18 percent (1.5% per month $\times$ 12 months per year). The effective interest rate, however, is a much higher 19.56 percent $[(1.015)^{12} - 1]$. This is the effective rate paid when a consumer carries credit card balances from one month to the next.

annual percentage rate (APR)
The *nominal annual rate* of interest, found by multiplying the periodic rate by the number of periods in 1 year.

? Review Questions

5–4   How is the *compounding process* related to the payment of interest on savings? What is the general equation for the future value, FV_n, in period n if PV dollars are deposited in an account paying k percent annual interest?

5–5   What effect would (**a**) a *decrease* in the interest rate or (**b**) an *increase* in the holding period of a deposit have on its future value? Why?

5–6   What effect does compounding interest more frequently than annually have on (**a**) the future value generated by a beginning principal and (**b**) the *effective annual rate (EAR)?* Why?

5–7   What is *continuous compounding?* How does the magnitude of the future value of a given deposit at a given rate of interest obtained by using continuous compounding compare to the value obtained by using annual or any other compounding period?

5–8   Differentiate between a *nominal annual rate* and an *effective annual rate (EAR).* Define *annual percentage rate* (APR). Under what compounding period are the APR and the EAR equivalent?

5.3 Future Value of an Annuity

annuity
A stream of equal annual cash flows. These cash flows can be *inflows* of returns earned on investments or *outflows* of funds invested to earn future returns.

An **annuity** is a stream of equal annual cash flows. These cash flows can be *inflows* of returns earned on investments or *outflows* of funds invested to earn future returns. Before looking at how to calculate the future value of annuities, we should distinguish between the two basic types of annuities.

---

9. The *maximum* effective annual rate for a given nominal annual rate occurs when interest is compounded *continuously.* The effective annual rate for this extreme case can be found by using the following equation:

$$EAR \text{ (continuous compounding)} = e^k - 1 \qquad (5.10a)$$

For the 8 percent nominal annual rate ($k = 0.08$), substitution into Equation 5.10a results in an effective annual rate of

$$e^{.08} - 1 = 1.083287065 - 1 = 0.0832871 = 8.32871\%$$

in the case of continuous compounding. This is the highest effective annual rate attainable with an 8 percent nominal rate.

ordinary annuity
An annuity for which the cash flow occurs at the *end* of each period.

annuity due
An annuity for which the cash flow occurs at the *beginning* of each period.

Types of Annuities

The two basic types of annuities are the *ordinary annuity* and the *annuity due*. For an **ordinary annuity**, the *cash flow occurs at the end of each period*. For an **annuity due**, the *cash flow occurs at the beginning of each period*.

Example ▼ Fran Abrams is trying to choose between two annuities: A and B. Both are 5-year, $1,000 annuities; annuity A is an ordinary annuity, and annuity B is an annuity due. To better understand the difference between these annuities, she has listed their cash flows in Table 5.4. Note that the amount of each annuity totals $5,000, but the two annuities differ in the timing of their cash flows: the cash flows are received sooner with the annuity due than with the ordinary annuity. ▲

■ Hint
The most common occurrences of annuities in business are fixed loan payments, the interest on corporate bonds, and the dividends paid to preferred stockholders. In all three of these examples, the amount of payment at the end of each time period is the same.

Although the cash flows of both annuities in Table 5.4 total $5,000, the annuity due would have a higher future value than the ordinary annuity because each of its five annual cash flows can earn a return for one year more than each of the ordinary annuity's cash flows. In general, as is demonstrated below, *the future value of an annuity due is always greater than the future value of an otherwise identical ordinary annuity.*

Because ordinary annuities are more frequently used in finance, *unless otherwise specified, the term "annuity" is used throughout this book to refer to ordinary annuities.*

Finding the Future Value of an Ordinary Annuity

The calculations required to find the future value of an ordinary annuity can be illustrated by the following example.

Example ▼ Fran Abrams wishes to determine how much money she will have at the end of 5 years if she deposits $1,000 annually at the *end of each* of the next 5 years into

---

TABLE 5.4	Comparison of Ordinary Annuity and Annuity Due Cash Flows ($1,000, 5 Years)

	Annual cash flows	
End of year[a]	Annuity A (*ordinary*)	Annuity B (*annuity due*)
0	$ 0	$1,000
1	1,000	1,000
2	1,000	1,000
3	1,000	1,000
4	1,000	1,000
5	1,000	0
Totals	$5,000	$5,000

[a]The ends of years 0, 1, 2, 3, 4, and 5 are equivalent to the beginnings of years 1, 2, 3, 4, 5, and 6, respectively.

an investment account with a 7 percent annual return. (Her cash flows are represented by annuity A—the ordinary annuity—in Table 5.4.) Table 5.5 presents the calculations required to find the future value of this annuity at the end of year 5.

Time-Line Use   This situation is depicted on the following time line:

Time line for future value of an ordinary annuity ($1,000 end-of-year deposit, earning 7%, at the end of 5 years)

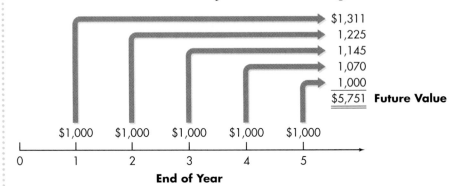

As the table and figure show, at the end of year 5, Fran will have $5,751 in her account. Column 2 of the table indicates that because the deposits are made at the end of the year, the first deposit will earn interest for 4 years, the second for 3 years, and so on. The future value interest factors in column 3 correspond to these interest-earning periods and the 7 percent rate of interest.

Simplifying the Future Value of an Annuity Calculation

Hint

This is true only in the case of an annuity, because only with an annuity are the payments equal.

The calculations in the preceding example can be simplified somewhat, because each of the factors is multiplied by the same dollar amount. The calculations can be expressed as follows:

$$\text{Future value of annuity at end of year 5} = [\$1,000 \times (1.311)] \quad (5.11)$$
$$+ [\$1,000 \times (1.225)]$$
$$+ [\$1,000 \times (1.145)]$$
$$+ [\$1,000 \times (1.070)]$$
$$+ [\$1,000 \times (1.000)]$$
$$= \$5,751$$

TABLE 5.5   The Future Value of a $1,000 5-Year Ordinary Annuity Compounded at 7%

End of year	Amount deposited (1)	Number of years compounded (2)	Future value interest factors from Table A-1 (3)	Future value at end of year [(1) × (3)] (4)
1	$1,000	4	1.311	$1,311
2	1,000	3	1.225	1,225
3	1,000	2	1.145	1,145
4	1,000	1	1.070	1,070
5	1,000	0	1.000	1,000
			Future value of ordinary annuity at end of year 5	$5,751

Factoring out the $1,000, we can rewrite Equation 5.11 as:

$$\text{Future value of annuity at end of year 5} = \$1,000 \times (1.311 + 1.225 \tag{5.12}$$
$$+ 1.145 + 1.070$$
$$+ 1.000) = \$5,751$$

Equation 5.12 indicates that to find the future value of the annuity, the annual cash flow must be multiplied by the sum of the appropriate future value interest factors. This equation leads to a more general formula presented below.

Using Tables and Calculators to Find Future Value of an Annuity

Annuity calculations can be simplified by using an interest table or a financial calculator. A table for the future value of a $1 *ordinary annuity* is given in Appendix Table A-2. The factors in the table are derived by summing the future value interest factors for the appropriate number of years. In the case of Equation 5.12, summing these factors (the terms in parentheses) results in Equation 5.13:

$$\text{Future value of annuity at end of year 5} = \$1,000 \times (5.751) \tag{5.13}$$
$$= \$5,751$$

future value interest factor for an annuity
The multiplier used to calculate the future value of an *ordinary annuity* at a specified interest rate over a given period of time.

The formula for the **future value interest factor for an annuity** when interest is compounded annually at k percent for n periods, $FVIFA_{k,n}$, is

$$FVIFA_{k,n} = \sum_{t=1}^{n}(1+k)^{t-1} \tag{5.14}$$

This factor is the multiplier used to calculate the future value of an *ordinary annuity* at a specified interest rate over a given period of time. The formula merely states that the future value interest factor for an n-year ordinary annuity is found by adding the sum of the first $(n-1)$ future value interest factors to 1.000 (i.e., $FVIFA_{k,n} = 1.000 + \sum_{t=1}^{n-1} FVIF_{k,t}$). This relationship can be easily verified by reviewing the terms in Equation 5.12.[10]

Now that we know how $FVIFA_{k,n}$ is calculated, let's put it to use to find the future value of an annuity. Using FVA_n for the future value of an n-year annuity, PMT for the amount to be deposited annually at the end of each year, and $FVIFA_{k,n}$ for the appropriate *future value interest factor for a one-dollar annuity compounded at k percent for n years*, the relationship among these variables can be expressed as follows:

$$FVA_n = PMT \times (FVIFA_{k,n}) \tag{5.15}$$

An example will illustrate this calculation for both a table and a financial calculator.

---

10. A mathematical expression that can be applied to calculate the future value interest factor for an ordinary annuity more efficiently is:

$$FVIFA_{k,n} = \left[\frac{(1+k)^n - 1}{k}\right] \tag{5.14a}$$

This expression is especially useful in the absence of the appropriate financial tables or a financial calculator or personal computer.

Example ▼ As noted earlier, Fran Abrams wishes to find the future value (FVA_n) at the end of 5 years (n) of an annual *end-of-year deposit* of $1,000 *(PMT)* into an account providing a 7 percent annual return (k) during the next 5 years.

Table Use The appropriate future value interest factor for an ordinary 5-year annuity at 7 percent $(FVIFA_{7\%,5yrs})$ found in Table A-2, is 5.751. Using Equation 5.15, the $1,000 deposit $\times$ 5.751 results in a future value for the annuity of $5,751.

Calculator Use Using the calculator inputs shown, you should find the future value of the ordinary annuity to be $5,750.74—a more precise answer than that found using the table.

Inputs: 1000   5   7

Functions: PMT   N   I   CPT   FV

▲ **Outputs:**   5750.74

Finding the Future Value of an Annuity Due

The calculations to find the future value of the less common form of an annuity—an annuity due—can be demonstrated by the following example.

Example ▼ Fran Abrams wishes to find out how much money she would have at the end of 5 years if she deposits $1,000 annually at the *beginning of each* of the next 5 years into a savings account providing a 7 percent annual return. Her cash flows in this case are represented by annuity B—the annuity due—in Table 5.4. Table 5.6 demonstrates the calculations required.

Time line for future value of an annuity due ($1,000 beginning-of-year deposit, earning 7%, at the end of 5 years)

TABLE 5.6 **The Future Value of a $1,000 5-Year Annuity Due Compounded at 7%**

End of year[a]	Amount deposited (1)	Number of years compounded (2)	Future value interest factors from Table A-1 (3)	Future value at end of year [(1) × (3)] (4)
0	$1,000	5	1.403	$1,403
1	1,000	4	1.311	1,311
2	1,000	3	1.225	1,225
3	1,000	2	1.145	1,145
4	1,000	1	1.070	1,070
		Future value of annuity due at end of year		$6,154

[a]The ends of years 0, 1, 2, 3, and 4 are equivalent to the beginnings of years 1, 2, 3, 4, and 5, respectively.

Time-Line Use   This situation is depicted on the following time line:

Time line for future value of an annuity due ($1,000 beginning-of-year deposit, earning 7%, at the end of 5 years)

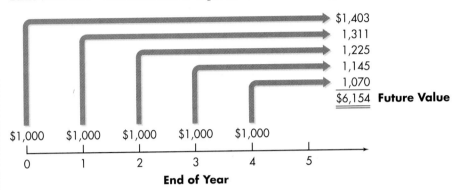

As the table and figure show, at the end of year 5, Fran will have $6,154 in her account. Column 2 of the table indicates that because the deposits are made at the beginning of each year, the first deposit earns interest for 5 years, the second for 4 years, and so on. The future value interest factors in column 3 correspond to those interest-earning periods and the 7 percent rate of interest.

Using Tables and Calculators to Find Future Value of an Annuity Due

A simple conversion can be applied to use the future value interest factors for an ordinary annuity in Table A-2 with annuities due. Equation 5.16 presents this conversion:

$$FVIFA_{k,n} \text{ (annuity due)} = FVIFA_{k,n} \times (1 + k) \qquad (5.16)$$

This equation says that the future value interest factor for an n-year annuity due at k percent can be found merely by multiplying the future value interest factor for an ordinary annuity at k percent for n years by $(1 + k)$. Why is this adjustment necessary? Because each cash flow of an annuity due earns interest for 1 year more than an ordinary annuity (from the start to the end of the year). Multiplying $FVIFA_{k,n}$ by $(1 + k)$ simply adds an additional year's return to *each* annuity cash flow. An example will demonstrate how to use Equation 5.16 and a financial calculator to find the future value of an annuity due.

Example ▼ As noted, Fran Abrams wishes to find the future value (FVA_n) at the end of 5 years (n) of an annual *beginning-of-year deposit* of $1,000 *(PMT)* into an account providing a 7 percent annual return (k) during the next 5 years.

Table Use   Substituting $k = 7\%$ and $n = 5$ years into Equation 5.16, with the aid of the appropriate interest factor from Table A-2, we get:

$$FVIFA_{7\%,5yrs} \text{ (annuity due)} = FVIFA_{7\%,5yrs} \times (1 + 0.07) = 5.751 \times 1.07 = 6.154$$

Then, substituting $PMT = \$1,000$ and $FVIFA_{7\%,5yrs}$ (annuity due) $= 6.154$ into Equation 5.15, we get a future value for the annuity due:

$$FVA_5 = \$1,000 \times 6.154 = \$6,154$$

Calculator Use   Before using your calculator to find the future value of an annuity due, depending upon the specific calculator, you must either switch it to

BEGIN mode or use the DUE key. Then, using the inputs shown, you should find the future value of the annuity due to be $6,153.29.

   Note: Switch calculator to BEGIN mode.

Inputs: 1000   5   7

Functions: PMT   N   I   CPT   FV

Outputs: 6153.29

   Note: Because we almost always assume end of period cash flows, *be sure to switch your calculator back to* END *mode when you have completed your annuity* ▲ *due calculations.*

Comparison with an Ordinary Annuity

As noted earlier, the future value of an annuity due is always greater than the future value of an otherwise identical ordinary annuity. We saw this in comparing the future values at the end of year 5 of Fran Abrams's two annuities:

   Ordinary annuity $5,751 (from Table 5.5)
   Annuity due $6,154 (from Table 5.6)

Because the annuity due's cash flow occurs at the beginning of the period rather than at the end, its future value is greater. In the example, Fran would earn $403 more with the annuity due.

   In spite of their superior earning power, annuities due are much less frequently encountered. Throughout the remainder of this text we therefore emphasize ordinary annuities. To reiterate, *unless otherwise specified, the term "annuity" refers to ordinary annuities, to which the* FVIFA *factors in Table A-2 directly apply and which financial calculators view as standard.*

? Review Questions

5–9   Differentiate between (a) an *ordinary annuity* and (b) an *annuity due.* Which always has greater future value for otherwise identical annuities and interest rates? Why? Which form is more common?

5–10   Explain how to conveniently determine the future value of an ordinary annuity. How can the future value interest factors for an ordinary annuity be conveniently modified to find the future value of an annuity due?

5.4 Present Value of a Single Amount

present value
The current dollar value of a future amount; the amount of money that would have to be invested today at a given rate of return over a specified period to equal the future amount.

It is often useful to determine the value today of a future amount of money. **Present value** is the current dollar value of a future amount—the amount of money that would have to be invested today at a given rate of return over a specified period to equal the future amount. Present value depends largely on the investment opportunities of the recipient and the point in time at which the amount is to be received. This section explores the present value of a single amount.

The Concept of Present Value

discounting cash flows
The process of finding present values; the inverse of compounding interest.

The process of finding present values is often referred to as **discounting cash flows.** It is concerned with answering the question: "If I can earn k percent on my money, what is the most I would be willing to pay now for an opportunity to receive FV_n dollars n periods from today?" This process is actually the inverse of compounding interest. Instead of finding the future value of present dollars invested at a given rate discounting determines the present value of a future amount, assuming the opportunity to earn a certain return, k, on the money. This annual rate of return is variously referred to as the *discount rate, required return, cost of capital,* or *opportunity cost.*[11] These terms will be used interchangeably in this text.

Career Key
Present value is an area of particular interest to the *marketing* department, which will need to justify funding for new programs and products by using *PV* techniques. *Accounting* personnel will also frequently use such techniques in calculating loan amortization schedules and bond discount and premium values.

Example ▼ Paul Shorter has an opportunity to receive $300 one year from now. If he can earn 6 percent on his investments in the normal course of events, what is the most he should pay now for this opportunity? To answer this question, he must determine how many dollars would have to be invested at 6 percent today to have $300 one year from now. By letting PV equal this unknown amount and using the same notation as in the future value discussion:

$$PV \times (1 + 0.06) = \$300 \qquad (5.17)$$

Solving Equation 5.17 for PV gives us Equation 5.18:

$$PV = \frac{\$300}{(1 + 0.06)} \qquad (5.18)$$
$$= \$283.02$$

The "present value" of $300 received one year from today, given an opportunity cost of 6 percent, is $283.02. That is the investment of $283.02 today at a 6 percent rate of return would result in $300 at the end of one year. ▲

The Equation for Present Value

The present value of a future amount can be found mathematically by solving Equation 5.4 for PV. In other words, the present value, PV, of some future amount, FV_n, to be received n periods from now, assuming an opportunity cost of k, is calculated as:

$$PV = \frac{FV_n}{(1 + k)^n} = FV_n \times \left[\frac{1}{(1 + k)^n} \right] \qquad (5.19)$$

Note the similarity between this general equation for present value and the equation in the preceding example (Equation 5.18). The use of this equation can be illustrated by a simple example.

---

11. The theoretical underpinning of this "required return" is introduced in Chapter 7 and further refined in subsequent chapters.

E x a m p l e ▼ Pam Valenti wishes to find the present value of $1,700 that will be received 8 years from now. Pam's opportunity cost is 8%. Substituting $FV_8 = \$1,700$, $n = 8$, and $k = 0.08$ into Equation 5.19 yields:

$$PV = \frac{\$1,700}{(1 + .08)^8} = \frac{\$1,700}{1.851} = \$918.42 \qquad (5.20)$$

Time-Line Use   This analysis can be depicted on the following time line:

Time line for present value of a single amount ($1,700 future amount, discounted at 8%, from the end of 8 years)

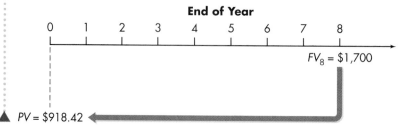

E x a m p l e ▼

Using Tables and Calculators to Find Present Value

present value interest factor
The multiplier used to calculate at a specified discount rate the present value of an amount to be received in a future period.

The present value calculation can be simplified by using a **present value interest factor.** This factor is the multiplier used to calculate at a specified discount rate the present value of an amount to be received in a future period. The present value interest factor for the present value of $1 discounted at k percent for n periods is referred to as $PVIF_{k,n}$:

$$\text{Present value interest factor} = PVIF_{k,n} = \frac{1}{(1 + k)^n} \qquad (5.21)$$

Appendix Table A-3 presents present value interest factors for $1. By letting $PVIF_{k,n}$ represent the appropriate factor, we can rewrite Equation 5.19:

$$PV = FV_n \times (PVIF_{k,n}) \qquad (5.22)$$

This expression indicates that to find the present value of an amount to be received in a future period, n, we have merely to multiply the future amount, FV_n, by the appropriate present value interest factor.

E x a m p l e ▼ As noted, Pam Valenti wishes to find the present value of $1,700 to be received 8 years from now, assuming an 8 percent rate of return.

Table Use   The present value interest factor for 8 percent and 8 years, $PVIF_{8\%,8yrs}$, found in Table A-3, is 0.540. Multiplying the $1,700 future value by this factor results in a present value of $918.

Calculator Use   Using the calculator's financial functions and the inputs shown below, you should find the present value to be $918.46.

The value obtained with the calculator—$918.46—is more accurate than the values found using the equation or the table, although for purposes of this text, ▲ these differences are insignificant.

A Graphic View of Present Value

Remember that present value calculations assume that the future values are measured at the *end* of the given period. The relationship among various discount rates, time periods, and the present value of one dollar is illustrated in Figure 5.6. Everything else being equal, the figure clearly shows that: (1) the higher the discount rate, the lower the present value, and (2) the longer the period of time, the lower the present value. Also note that given a discount rate of 0 percent, the present value always equals the future value ($1). But for any discount rate greater than zero, the present value is less than the future value of $1.

Comparing Present Value and Future Value

We will close this section with a couple of important observations about present values. One is that the expression for the present value interest factor for k percent and n periods, $1/(1 + k)^n$, is the inverse of the future value interest factor for k percent and n periods, $(1 + k)^n$. This fact can be confirmed by dividing a present value interest factor for k percent and n periods, $PVIF_{k,n}$, into 1.0 and comparing the resulting value to the future value interest factor given in Table A-1 for k percent and n periods, $FVIF_{k,n}$. The two values should be equivalent.

Second, because of the relationship between present value interest factors and future value interest factors, we can find the present value interest factors given a table of future value interest factors, and vice versa. For example, the future value interest factor from Table A-1 for 10 percent and 5 periods is 1.611. Dividing this value into 1.0 yields 0.621, which is the present value interest factor given in Table A-3 for 10 percent and 5 periods.

FIGURE 5.6

Present Value Relationship
Discount rates, time periods, and present value of one dollar

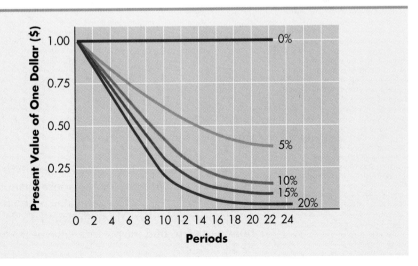

5–11   What is meant by "the present value of a future amount"? What is the equation for the present value, PV, of a future amount, FV_n, to be received in period n, assuming that the firm requires a minimum return of k percent? How are present value and future value calculations related?

5–12   What effect does *increasing* (**a**) the required return and (**b**) the time period have on the present value of a future amount? Why?

5.5 Present Value of Cash Flow Streams

Quite often in finance there is a need to find the present value of a *stream* of cash flows that will be received in various future periods. Two basic types of cash flow streams are possible: the mixed stream and the annuity. A **mixed stream** is cash flows of different amounts. An *annuity*, as stated earlier, is a stream of cash flows of the same amount. Because certain shortcuts are possible in finding the present value of an annuity, we will discuss mixed streams and annuities separately. In addition, the present value of mixed streams with embedded annuities and perpetuities are considered in this section.

mixed stream
A stream of cash flows of different amounts.

Present Value of a Mixed Stream

To find the present value of a mixed stream of cash flows, we determine the present value of each future amount, as described in the preceding section, and then add together all the individual present values.

Example ▼   Frey Company, a shoe manufacturer, has the opportunity to receive the following mixed stream of cash flows over the next 5 years:

Year	Cash flow
1	$400
2	800
3	500
4	400
5	300

If the firm must earn at least 9 percent on its investments, what is the most it should pay for this opportunity?

Table Use   To solve this problem, determine the present value of each cash flow discounted at 9 percent for the appropriate number of years. The sum of these individual values is the present value of the total stream. The present value interest factors required are those shown in Table A–3. Table 5.7 presents the calculations needed to find the present value of the cash flow stream, which turns out to be $1,904.60.

TABLE 5.7	The Present Value of a Mixed Stream of Cash Flows		
Year (n)	Cash flow (1)	$PVIF_{9\%,n}$ [a] (2)	Present value [(1) × (2)] (3)
1	$400	0.917	$ 366.80
2	800	0.842	673.60
3	500	0.772	386.00
4	400	0.708	283.20
5	300	0.650	195.00
		Present value of mixed stream	$1,904.60

[a]Present value interest factors at 9% are from Table A-3.

Calculator Use   You can use a calculator to find the present value of each individual cash flow, as demonstrated earlier; then add the present values, to get the present value of the stream. However, most financial calculators have a function that allows you to punch in *all cash flows*, specify the discount rate, and then directly calculate the present value of the entire cash flow stream. Because calculators provide more precise solutions than those based on rounded table factors, the present value of Frey Company's cash flow stream found using a calculator is $1,904.76, close, but not precisely equal, to the $1,904.60 value calculated before.

Paying $1,904.76 would provide exactly a 9 percent return. Frey should not pay more than that amount for the opportunity to receive these cash flows.

Time-Line Use   This situation is depicted on the following time line:

Time line for present value of a mixed stream (end-of-year cash flows, discounted at 9%, over the corresponding number of years)

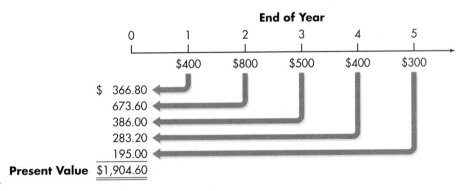

Present Value of an Annuity[12]

The method for finding the present value of an annuity is similar to that used for a mixed stream, but can be simplified somewhat.

---

12. Consistent with the discussions of future value, our concern here is only with *ordinary annuities*—those with cash flows occurring at the *end* of each period.

Example ▼ Braden Company, a small producer of plastic toys, wants to determine the value of annuity that provides cash flows of $700 per year for 5 years. The firm requires a minimum return of 8 percent on all investments. Table 5.8 shows the long method for finding the present value of the annuity—which is the same as the method used for the mixed stream. This procedure yields a present value of $2,795.10.

Time-Line Use Similarly, this situation is depicted on the following time line:

Time line for present value of an annuity ($700 end-of-year cash flows, discounted at 8%, over 5 years)

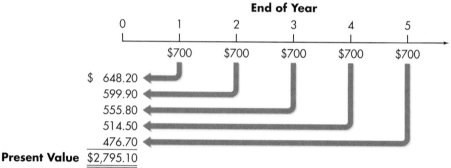

Simplifying the Present Value of an Annuity Calculation

The calculations in the preceding example can be simplified by recognizing that each of the five present value interest factors was multiplied by the same annual amount ($700). This calculation can be expressed as follows:

$$\text{Present value of annuity} = [\$700 \times (0.926)] + [\$700 \times (0.857)] \qquad (5.23)$$
$$+ [\$700 \times (0.794)] + [\$700 \times (0.735)]$$
$$+ [\$700 \times (0.681)] = \$2,795.10$$

Hint
The simplification in the present value of an annuity calculation here is similar to that made in Equation 5.12 for the future value of an annuity.

Simplifying Equation 5.23 by factoring out the $700 yields Equation 5.24:

$$\text{Present value of annuity} = \$700 \times (0.926 + 0.857 + 0.794 + 0.735 + 0.681) \qquad (5.24)$$
$$= \$2,795.10$$

Thus, the present value of an annuity can be found by multiplying the annual cash flow by the sum of the appropriate present value interest factors. This equation leads to a more general formula introduced below.

Using Tables and Calculators to Find Present Value of an Annuity

Annuity calculations can be simplified by using an interest table for the present value of an annuity or a financial calculator. The values for the present value of a $1 annuity are given in Appendix Table A-4. The factors in the table are derived by summing the present value interest factors for the appropriate number of years. In the case of Equation 5.24, summing these factors results in Equation 5.25:

$$\text{Present value of annuity} = \$700 \times (3.993) = \$2,795.10 \qquad (5.25)$$

The interest factors in Table A-4 actually represent the sum of the first n present value interest factors in Table A-3 for a given discount rate. The formula

TABLE 5.8	The Long Method for Finding the Present Value of an Annuity		

Year (n)	Cash flow (1)	$PVIF_{8\%,n}{}^{a}$ (2)	Present value [(1) × (2)] (3)
1	$700	0.926	$ 648.20
2	700	0.857	599.90
3	700	0.794	555.80
4	700	0.735	514.50
5	700	0.681	476.70
		Present value of annuity	$2,795.10

[a]Present value interest factors at 8% are from Table A-3.

present value interest factor for an annuity
The multiplier used to calculate the present value of an annuity at a specified discount rate over a given period of time.

for the **present value interest factor for an annuity** with end-of-year cash flows that are discounted at k percent for n periods, $PVIFA_{k,n}$, is:[13]

$$PVIFA_{k,n} = \sum_{t=1}^{n} \frac{1}{(1 + k)^{t}} \qquad (5.26)$$

This factor is the multiplier used to calculate the present value of an annuity at a specified discount rate over a given period of time. The formula merely states that the present value interest factor for an n-year annuity is found by summing the first n present value interest factors at the given rate (i.e., $PVIFA_{k,n} = \sum_{t=1}^{n} PVIF_{k,t}$). This relationship can be verified by reviewing the terms in Equation 5.24.[14]

By letting PVA_n equal the present value of an n-year annuity, PMT equal the amount to be received annually at the end of each year, and $PVIFA_{k,n}$ represent the appropriate value for the *present value interest factor for a one-dollar annuity discounted at* k *percent for* n *years*, the relationship among these variables can be expressed as follows:

$$PVA_n = PMT \times (PVIFA_{k,n}) \qquad (5.27)$$

An example will illustrate this calculation for both a table and a financial calculator.

13. The formula for the present value interest factor for an *annuity due* is $\sum_{t=1}^{n} 1/(1 + k)^{t-1}$, because in this case, all cash flows occur at the beginning of each period. The factor therefore merely represents 1.0 plus the sum of the first $(n - 1)$ present value interest factors. The present value interest factor for an annuity due can be found by multiplying the present value interest factor for an ordinary annuity, $PVIFA_{k,n}$, by $(1 + k)$.

14. A mathematical expression that can be applied to calculate the present value interest factor for an ordinary annuity more efficiently is:

$$PVIFA_{k,n} = \left[\frac{1 - \dfrac{1}{(1 + k)^{n}}}{k} \right] \qquad (5.26a)$$

This expression is especially useful in the absence of the appropriate financial tables or a financial calculator or personal computer.

E x a m p l e ▼ Braden Company, as noted, wants to find the present value of a 5-year annuity of $700 assuming an 8 percent opportunity cost.

Table Use   The present value interest factor for an annuity at 8 percent for 5 years ($PVIFA_{8\%, 5yrs}$) found in Table A-4, is 3.993. Using Equation 5.27, $700 × 3.993 results in a present value of $2,795.10.

Calculator Use Using the calculator's financial functions and the inputs shown below, you should find the present value of the annuity to be $2,794.90.

Inputs:	700	5	8		
Functions:	PMT	N	I	CPT	PV
Outputs:					2794.90

The value obtained with the calculator—$2,794.90—is more accurate than those found using the equation or the table, although for purposes of this text ▲ these differences are insignificant.

Present Value of a Mixed Stream with an Embedded Annuity

Occasionally, a mixed stream of cash flows will have an annuity embedded within it. In such a case, the computations can be streamlined by the following three-step procedure:

Step 1   Find the present value of the annuity at the specified discount rate using the regular procedure. (*Note:* The resulting present value is measured at the beginning of the annuity, which is equivalent to the end of the period immediately preceding the start of the annuity.)

Step 2   Add the present value calculated in Step 1 to any other cash flow occurring in the period just before the start of that annuity, and eliminate the individual annuity cash flows, to determine the revised cash flows.

Step 3   Discount the revised cash flows found in Step 2 back to time zero in the normal fashion at the specified discount rate.

An example will illustrate this three-step procedure.

E x a m p l e ▼ Powell Products expects an investment to generate the cash flows shown in column 1 of Table 5.9. If the firm must earn 9 percent on its investments, what is the present value of the expected cash flow stream?

Table Use   The three-step procedure is applied to Powell's cash flows in Table 5.9, because it has a 4-year $7,000 annuity embedded in its cash flows.

Step 1   As noted in column 2 of Table 5.9, the present value of the embedded $7,000 annuity is calculated by multiplying the $7,000 by the present value of an annuity interest factor at 9 percent for 4 years ($PVIFA_{9\%, 4yrs}$). Its present value at the beginning of year 3 (i.e., the end of year 2) is $22,680.

TABLE 5.9	**The Present Value of a Mixed Stream with an Embedded Annuity**				
		Step 1	Step 2		Step 3
Year (n)	Cash flow (1)	Present value of annuity (2)	Revised cash flow [(1) + (2)] (3)	$PVIF_{9\%,n}$ (4)	Present value [(3) × (4)] (5)
1	$5,000		$ 5,000	0.917	$ 4,585.00
2	6,000	22,680	28,680	0.842	24,148.56
3	7,000	↑	0	0.772	0
4	7,000	$PVIFA_{9\%,4yrs}$	0	0.708	0
5	7,000	× 3.240	0	0.650	0
6	7,000		0	0.596	0
7	8,000		8,000	0.547	4,376.00
8	9,000		9,000	0.502	4,518.00
			Present value of mixed stream		$37,627.56

Step 2   The end-of-year-2 value of the annuity, from Step 1, is added to the end-of-year-2 cash flow of $6,000 to determine the revised cash flow noted in column 3 of Table 5.9. This results in total cash flow of $28,680 in year 2 and the elimination of the annuity cash flow for years 3 through 6.

Step 3   Multiplying the revised cash flows in column 3 of Table 5.9 by the appropriate present value interest factors at 9 percent in column 4 results in the present values shown in column 5 of the table. The present value of this mixed stream, found by summing column 5, is $37,627.56.

The present value calculation has been simplified by first finding the present value of the embedded $7,000 annuity.

Calculator Use   A similar procedure to that just demonstrated would be applied in using a calculator. The resulting answer would be $37,617.96, which is close to, but more precise than, the value calculated in Table 5.9.[15]

Time-Line Use   The computation used in this situation is presented on the following time line:

Time line for present value of a mixed stream with an embedded annuity (end-of-year cash flows, discounted at 9%, over the corresponding number of years)

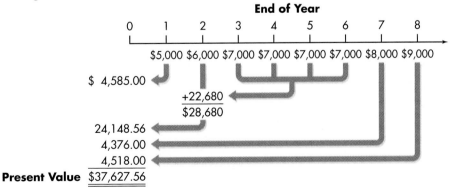

15. Most financial calculators have a frequency function that allows easy input of cash flow streams that have annuities embedded in them. The use of this feature, if it is available, is explained in the calculator's reference guide.

Present Value of a Perpetuity

perpetuity
An annuity with an infinite life, providing continual annual cash flow.

A **perpetuity** is an annuity with an infinite life—in other words, an annuity that never stops providing its holder with a cash flow at the end of each year. It is sometimes necessary to find the present value of a perpetuity. The present value interest factor for a perpetuity discounted at the rate k is

$$PVIFA_{k,\infty} = \frac{1}{k} \tag{5.28}$$

As the equation shows, the appropriate factor, $PVIFA_{k,\infty}$, is found merely by dividing the discount rate, k (stated as a decimal), into 1. The validity of this

IN PRACTICE

It All Starts with Time Value

How much will an investment earn over its life? What's the monthly payment on a loan to buy equipment, and will this machinery result in sufficient cost savings to warrant the investment? How does the compound growth rate of our company's earnings per share compare to those of competitors? Time value of money calculations make it possible to answer questions like these.

Financial managers are using traditional time value techniques in new ways. Lexus and credit card issuer MBNA determine the value of a new customer or an existing one by calculating the present value of profits generated by customers in the future. With this information, companies can decide whether to spend to acquire new customers or increase repeat purchases and to target groups that warrant larger investments. Research shows that increasing customer retention by 5 percent raised the value of the average customer by 25 to 95 percent, depending on the industry.

Interbrand Corp. applies similar techniques to brand valuation. Interbrand, a pioneer in brand valuation, claims that: "brands are assets with significant quantifiable economic value, as much as 70% of total corporate worth. Brand valuation quantifies the economic value of a brand." The value of a brand is assessed using a brand valuation model. Interbrand's model calculates brand value as the present value of the earnings the brand is expected to generate in the future. To complete the analysis, financial forecasts for

a brand are prepared. The forecasts consider all sales revenues the brand is expected to generate in the future. From this, all operating costs, taxes, and a charge for the capital employed are deducted from sales revenue. The difference is termed net brand earnings.

Next, a discount rate is determined by assessing the strength of the brand. The value of a brand is the present value of the projected brand earnings. Stronger brands have lower discount rates and, therefore, higher values. The value of the brand depends on both a good financial performance and a strong marketing position. If short-term earnings performance is weakened, investment in the brand can produce better long-term results, a stronger brand, and, consequently, a higher brand value. For 2002, the most valuable brand in the world, according to Interbrand, was Coca-Cola with a value of $69.6 billion. A listing of the world's 100 most valuable brands in 2002, as calculated by Interbrand using the present value methodology, is provided at the following Web site: www.finfacts.com/brands2001htm.

REFERENCES: Khermouch, G., "The Best Global Brands," *BusinessWeek* magazine, August 5, 2002. Available at: www.businessweek.com/magazine/content/02_31/b37994032.htm; "2002 Methodology for the World's Most Valuable Brands as Ranked by Interbrand." Available at: www.brandchannel.com/interbrand/test/html/events/ext_sur.html.

method can be seen by looking at the factors in Table A-4 for 8, 10, 20, and 40 percent: as the number of periods (typically years) approaches 50, the values of these factors approach 12.500 (1 ÷ 0.08), 10.000 (1 ÷ 0.10), 5.000 (1 ÷ 0.20), and 2.500 (1 ÷ 0.40), respectively.

Example ▼ Ross Clark wishes to determine the present value of a $1,000 perpetuity discounted at 10 percent. The appropriate present value interest factor can be found by dividing 1 by 0.10, as noted in Equation 5.28. Substituting the resulting factor, 10, and the amount of the perpetuity, $PMT = \$1,000$, into Equation 5.27 results in a present value of $10,000 for the perpetuity. In other words, the receipt of $1,000 every year for an indefinite period is worth only $10,000 today if Ross can earn 10 percent on his investments. If he had $10,000 and earned 10 percent interest on it each year, $1,000 a year could be withdrawn indefinitely without
▲ touching the initial $10,000, which would never be drawn upon.

❓ Review Questions

5–13   How is the present value of a mixed stream of cash flows calculated? How can the calculations required to find the present value of an annuity be simplified? How can the calculation of the present value of a mixed stream with an embedded annuity be streamlined?

5–14   What is a *perpetuity*? How might the present value interest factor for such a stream of cash flows be determined?

5.6 Special Applications of Time Value

Future value and present value techniques have a number of important applications. We'll study three of them in this section: (1) the calculation of the periodic investments required to accumulate a future sum, (2) the calculation of amortization on loans, and (3) the determination of growth rates.

Investments Required to Accumulate a Future Sum

Suppose you want to buy a house 5 years from now and estimate that an initial down payment of $20,000 will be required at that time. You wish to make equal annual end-of-year investments in an account providing an annual return of 6 percent, so you must determine the annuity that will result in a lump sum equal to $20,000 at the end of year 5. The solution to this problem is closely related to the process of finding the future value of an annuity.

Earlier in the chapter, we found the future value of an *n*-year annuity, FVA_n, by multiplying the annual deposit, PMT, by the appropriate interest factor, $FVIFA_{k,n}$. The relationship of the three variables has been defined by Equation 5.15, which is rewritten here as Equation 5.29:

$$FVA_n = PMT \times (FVIFA_{k,n})$$

(5.29)

We can find the annual deposit required to accumulate FVA_n dollars, given a specified interest rate, k, and a certain number of years, n, by solving Equation 5.29 for PMT. Isolating PMT on the left side of the equation gives us

$$PMT = \frac{FVA_n}{FVIFA_{k,n}} \tag{5.30}$$

Once this is done, we have only to substitute the known values of FVA_n and $FVIFA_{k,n}$ into the right side of the equation to find the annual deposit required.

Example ▼ As just stated, you want to determine the equal annual end-of-year deposits required to accumulate $20,000 at the end of 5 years given a rate of return of 6 percent.

Table Use Table A-2 indicates that the future value interest factor for an annuity at 6 percent for 5 years ($FVIFA_{6\%,5yrs}$) is 5.637. Substituting $FVA_5 = \$20,000$ and $FVIFA_{6\%,5yrs} = 5.637$ into Equation 5.30 yields an annual required deposit, PMT, of $3,547.99. Thus, if that amount is deposited at the end of each year for 5 years, at 6 percent interest, there will be $20,000 in the account at the end of the 5 years.

Calculator Use Using the calculator inputs shown, you should find the annual deposit amount to be $3,547.93. Note that this value, except for a slight rounding difference, agrees with the value found by using Table A-2.

Inputs: 20000 | 5 | 6

Functions: FV | N | I | CPT | PMT

▲ **Outputs:** 3547.93

Loan Amortization

loan amortization
The determination of the equal annual loan payments necessary to provide a lender with a specified interest return and to repay the loan principal over a specified period.

loan amortization schedule
A schedule of equal payments to repay a loan. It shows the allocation of each loan payment to interest and principal.

The term **loan amortization** refers to the determination of the equal annual loan payments necessary to provide a lender with a specified interest return and repay the loan principal over a specified period. The loan amortization process involves finding the future payments (over the term of the loan) whose present value at the loan interest rate equals the amount of initial principal borrowed. Lenders use a **loan amortization schedule** to determine these payment amounts and the allocation of each payment to interest and principal. In the case of home mortgages, these tables are used to find the equal *monthly* payments necessary to *amortize*, or pay off, the mortgage at a specified interest rate over a 15- to 30-year period.

Amortizing a loan actually involves creating an annuity out of a present amount. For example, say you borrow $6,000 at 10 percent and agree to make equal annual end-of-year payments over 4 years. To find the size of the payments, the lender determines the amount of a 4-year annuity discounted at 10 percent that has a present value of $6,000. This process is actually the inverse of finding the present value of an annuity.

Earlier in this chapter, we found the present value, PVA_n, of an n-year annuity by multiplying the annual amount, PMT, by the present value interest factor for an annuity, $PVIFA_{k,n}$. This relationship, which was originally expressed as Equation 5.27, is rewritten here as Equation 5.31:

$$PVA_n = PMT \times (PVIFA_{k,n}) \qquad (5.31)$$

To find the equal annual payment required to amortize the loan, PVA_n, over a certain number of years at a specified interest rate, we need to solve Equation 5.31 for PMT. Isolating PMT on the left side of the equation gives

$$PMT = \frac{PVA_n}{PVIFA_{k,n}} \qquad (5.32)$$

Once this is done, we have only to substitute the known values into the right side of the equation to find the annual payment required.

Example ▼ As just stated, you want to determine the equal annual end-of-year payments necessary to amortize fully a $6,000, 10 percent loan over 4 years.

Table Use   Table A-4 indicates that the present value interest factor for an annuity corresponding to 10 percent and 4 years ($PVIFA_{10\%,4yrs}$) is 3.170. Substituting $PVA_4 = \$6,000$ and $PVIFA_{10\%,4yrs} = 3.170$ into Equation 5.32 and solving for PMT yields an annual loan payment of $1,892.74. Thus, to repay the interest and principal on a $6,000, 10 percent, 4-year loan, equal annual end-of-year payments of $1,892.74 are necessary.

Calculator Use   Using the calculator inputs shown, you should find the annual payment amount to be $1,892.82. Except for a slight rounding difference, this value agrees with the one found using Table A-4.

Inputs: 6000   4   10

Functions: PV   N   I   CPT   PMT

Outputs: 1892.82

The allocation of each loan payment to interest and principal can be seen in columns 3 and 4 of the *loan amortization schedule* in Table 5.10. The portion of each payment representing interest (column 3) declines over the repayment period, and the portion going to principal repayment (column 4) increases. This pattern is typical of amortized loans; with level payments, as the principal is reduced, the interest component declines, leaving a larger portion of each subsequent payment to repay principal.[16]

---

16. Most financial calculators have a function that allows the user to determine the breakdown of principal and interest for every loan payment made over the amortization period.

TABLE 5.10	Loan Amortization Schedule ($6,000 Principal, 10% Interest, 4-Year Repayment Period)

| End of year | Loan payment (1) | Beginning-of-year principal (2) | Payments | | End-of-year principal [(2) − (4)] (5) |
			Interest [0.10 × (2)] (3)	Principal [(1) − (3)] (4)	
1	$1,892.74	$6,000.00	$600.00	$1,292.74	$4,707.26
2	1,892.74	4,707.26	470.73	1,422.01	3,285.25
3	1,892.74	3,285.25	328.53	1,564.21	1,721.04
4	1,892.74	1,721.04	172.10	1,720.64	—[a]

[a]Due to rounding, a slight difference ($0.40) exists between the beginning-of-year-4 principal (in column 2) and the year-4 principal payment (in column 4).

Growth or Interest Rates

It is often necessary to calculate the compound annual *growth rate* (i.e., annual rate of change in values) of a series of cash flows. In doing this, either future value or present value interest factors can be used. The approach using present value interest factors is described in this section. The simplest situation is where you wish to find the rate of growth in a *series of cash flows*.

Example ▼ Ray Noble wishes to find the rate of growth in the following series of cash flows:

Year	Cash flow	
1998	1,250	1
1999	1,300	2
2000	1,370	3
2001	1,440	4
2002	$1,520	

By using the first year (1998) as a base year, we see that the cash flows have had four opportunities to grow. There are 5 years but four growth periods.

Table Use   The first step in finding the growth rate is to divide the amount received in the earliest year by the amount received in the latest year. This gives the present value interest factor for a *single amount* for 4 years, $PVIF_{k,4yrs}$, which is 0.822 ($1,250 ÷ $1,520). The interest rate in Table A-3 associated with the factor closest to 0.822 for 4 years is the growth rate of Ray's cash flows. In the row for year 4 in Table A-3, the factor for 5 percent is 0.823—almost exactly the 0.822 value. Therefore, the growth rate of the given cash flows is approximately (to the nearest whole percent) 5 percent.[17]

17. To obtain more precise estimates of growth rates, *interpolation*—a mathematical technique for estimating unknown intermediate values—can be applied. For information on how to interpolate a more precise answer in this example, see the book's home page at **www.pearsoned.ca/gitman**.

Calculator Use   Using the calculator, we treat the earliest value as a present value, *PV*, and the latest value as a future value, FV_n. (*Note:* Most calculators require *either* the *PV* or *FV* value to be inputted as a negative number in order to calculate an unknown growth rate. Experiment with your calculator to determine which process you should follow. Using the inputs shown below, you should find the growth rate to be 5.01 percent, which is consistent with, but more precise than, the value found using Table A-3.

Inputs: | 1250 | -1520 | 4 |

Functions: | PV | FV | N | CPT | I |

Outputs: | 5.01 |

Another type of problem involves finding the interest rate associated with an *annuity*, or equal-payment loan.

Example ▼ Jan Jacobs can borrow $2,000 to be repaid in equal annual end-of-year amounts of $514.14 for the next 5 years. She wants to find the interest rate on this loan.

Table Use   Substituting $PVA_5 = \$2,000$ and $PMT = \$514.14$ into Equation 5.31 and rearranging the equation to solve for $PVIFA_{k,5\text{yrs}}$, we get

$$PVIFA_{k,5\text{yrs}} = \frac{PVA_5}{PMT} = \frac{\$2,000}{\$514.14} = 3.890 \tag{5.33}$$

The interest rate for 5 years associated with the annuity factor closest to 3.890 in Table A-4 is 9 percent. Therefore, the interest rate on the loan is approximately (to the nearest whole percent) 9 percent.

Calculator Use   (*Note:* Most calculators require *either* the *PMT* or *PV* value to be input as a negative number in order to calculate an unknown interest rate on an equal-payment loan. Experiment with your calculator to determine which process you should follow.) Using the inputs shown, you should find the interest rate to be 9 percent, which is consistent with, but more precise than, the approximate value found using Table A-4.

Inputs: | 514.14 | -2000 | 5 |

Functions: | PMT | PV | N | CPT | I |

Outputs: | 9.00 |

A final type of interest-rate problem involves finding the interest rate associated with a mixed stream of payments expected to result from a given initial investment. For example, assume that in exchange for an initial $1,000 investment, you will receive annual cash flows over years 1 through 5 of $200, $400, $300, $500, and $200, respectively. What interest rate would you earn on this investment? This rate is called the *internal rate of return (IRR)*. Because of the relatively

IN PRACTICE   Personal Finance

Really, Time Is on Your Side

For those saving money, to paraphrase Mick Jagger, "time is on your side." Those in debt, to quote W. B. Yeats, "have no enemy but time." To illustrate the ideas associated with these quotes, consider the following examples.

Upon graduation from university, 24-year-old Early Emily Edenhurst starts work and decides to start investing $150 per month in a retirement account (an RRSP) that is expected to generate a 12 percent return per year. Early Emily sets up an automatic withdrawal plan for the $150 monthly contribution and immediately forgets about the plan. She then works 36 years, retiring at age 60. At this point in time, Early Emily receives a letter from the investment company indicating the amount of money that is in the RRSP. How much is there? Way back 36 years ago, Emily set up an annuity of $150 per month, that provided a return of 1 percent (12%/12 months) per month. Over the 432 months (36 years × 12) the plan was set up, Emily invested a total of $64,800. The future value of this annuity, however, is $1,088,887. Emily can begin to enjoy her retirement!

On the other hand, Late Larry Linton, who graduated with Early Emily, delayed planning for retirement. Larry only thought about retirement when he turned 50. Larry also wants to retire when he turns 60 and he wants the same amount of money as Emily. If his investment also earns 12 percent per year, how much must Larry save each month between now and retirement? Larry wants a future value of $1,088,887 in 120

months, and he expects a return of 1 percent per month. Larry must save $4,733.50 per month or $568,020 in total to have the same amount of money as Emily. Mick Jagger didn't lie. Time really is on your side.

A common type of debt most individuals have at some point in their lives is a car loan. Assume you buy a car that has a sticker price of $24,500. After all other charges and taxes, the cost of the car is $28,890. You need to borrow the total amount so you visit your financial institution and negotiate a loan. The loans officer indicates that the borrowing rate is 10 percent, with monthly payments required, and she suggests an amortization period of 12 years. What are the monthly payments on the loan? The present value is the amount borrowed or $28,890, there are 144 periods, and the monthly borrowing rate is 0.833 percent (10%/12 months). Compute PMT. The monthly payment is $345.26.

Over the 12 years the loan is outstanding, the total interest paid on the loan is $20,827, or 72.1 percent of the amount borrowed. If instead of 12 years, you choose a 6-year amortization period, what is the impact? The monthly payment increases to $535.21. *But* the amount of interest paid falls to $9,645, about one-third of the amount borrowed. For those in debt, time is an enemy, since it increases the cost of debt.

Time value teaches us that the longer the period of time you save and the shorter the period of time you borrow, the better.

complex nature of this computation, which can be greatly simplified using a financial calculator, we will defer discussion of it until it is applied in Chapter 12.

? Review Questions

5–15 How can you determine the size of the equal annual end-of-year deposits necessary to accumulate a certain future sum in a specified future period?

5–16 Describe the procedure used to amortize a loan into a series of equal annual payments. What is a *loan amortization schedule*?

5–17 Which present value interest factors would be used to find (**a**) the growth rate associated with a series of cash flows and (**b**) the interest rate associated with an equal-payment loan?

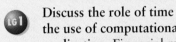

 Discuss the role of time value in finance and the use of computational aids to simplify its application. Financial managers use time value of money techniques when assessing the value of the expected cash flow streams associated with decision alternatives. Alternatives can be assessed by either compounding to find future value or discounting to find present value. Because they are at time zero when making decisions, financial managers rely primarily on present value techniques. Both financial tables and financial calculators can streamline the application of time value techniques.

 Understand the concept of future value, its calculation for a single amount, and the effects of compounding interest more frequently than annually. Future value relies on compound interest to measure future amounts: The initial principal or deposit in one period, along with the interest earned on it, becomes the beginning principal of the following period. Interest can be compounded at intervals ranging from annually to daily, and even continuously. The more frequently interest is compounded, the larger the future amount that will be accumulated and the higher the effective annual rate (EAR). The annual percentage rate (APR)—a nominal annual rate—is quoted on credit cards and loans. The interest factor formulas and basic equation for the future value of a single amount are given in Table 5.11.

Find the future value of an ordinary annuity and an annuity due and compare these two types of annuities. An annuity is a pattern of equal annual cash flows. For an ordinary annuity, cash flows occur at the end of the period. For an annuity due, cash flows occur at the beginning of the period. The future value of an ordinary annuity can be found by using the future value interest factor for an annuity; an adjustment is required to find the future value of an annuity due. The interest factor formulas and basic equation for the future value of an annuity are given in Table 5.11.

 Understand the concept of present value, its calculation for a single amount, and the relationship of present to future value. Present value is the inverse of future value. The present value of a future amount is the amount of money today that is equivalent to the given future amount, considering the return that can be earned on the current money. The interest factor formula and basic equation for the present value of a single amount are given in Table 5.11.

 Calculate the present value of a mixed stream of cash flows, an annuity, a mixed stream with an embedded annuity, and a perpetuity. The present value of a mixed stream of cash flows is the sum of the present values of each individual cash flow in the stream. The present value of an annuity can be found by using the present value interest factor for an annuity. For a mixed stream with an embedded annuity, the present value of the annuity is found, then used to replace the annuity flows, and the new mixed stream's present value is calculated. The present value of a perpetuity—an infinite-lived annuity—is found using 1 divided by the discount rate to represent the present value interest factor. The interest factor formulas and basic equation for the present value of an annuity are given in Table 5.11.

 Describe the procedures involved in (1) determining the periodic deposits required to accumulate a future sum, (2) loan amortization, and (3) finding growth or interest rates. The annual deposit to accumulate a given future sum can be found by solving the equation for the future value of an annuity for the annual payment. A loan can be amortized into equal annual payments by solving the equation for the present value of an annuity for the annual payment. Growth or interest rates can be estimated by finding the unknown rate in the equation for the present value of a single amount, an annuity, or a mixed stream.

TABLE 5.11   Summary of Key Definitions, Formulas, and Equations for Time Value of Money

Variable definitions

e = exponential function = 2.7183
EAR = effective annual rate
FV_n = future value or amount at the end of period n
FVA_n = future value of an n-year annuity
k = annual rate of interest
m = number of times per year interest is compounded
n = number of periods—typically, years—over which money earns a return
PMT = amount deposited or received annually at the end of each year
PV = initial principal or present value
PVA_n = present value of an n-year annuity
t = period number index

Interest factor formulas

Future value of a single amount:

$$FVIF_{k,n} = \left(1 + \frac{k}{m}\right)^{m \times n}$$ [Eq. 5.7]

for annual compounding, $m = 1$,

$$FVIF_{k,n} = (1 + k)^n$$ [Eq. 5.5; factors in Table A–1]

for continuous compounding, $m = \infty$,

$$FVIF_{k,n} = e^{k \times n}$$ [Eq. 5.9]

to find the effective annual rate,

$$EAR = \left(1 + \frac{k}{m}\right)^m - 1$$ [Eq. 5.10]

Future value of an (ordinary) annuity:

$$FVIFA_{k,n} = \sum_{t=1}^{n} (1 + k)^{t-1}$$ [Eq. 5.14; factors in Table A–2]

$$FVIFA_{k,n} = \left[\frac{(1 + k)^n - 1}{k}\right]$$ [Eq. 5.14a]

Future value of an annuity due:

$$FVIFA_{k,n} \text{ (annuity due)} = FVIFA_{k,n} \times (1 + k)$$ [Eq. 5.16]

Present value of a single amount:

$$PVIF_{k,n} = \frac{1}{(1 + k)^n}$$ [Eq. 5.21; factors in Table A–3]

Present value of an annuity:

$$PVIFA_{k,n} = \sum_{t=1}^{n} \frac{1}{(1 + k)^t}$$ [Eq. 5.26; factors in Table A–4]

$$PVIFA_{k,n} = \left[1 - \frac{1}{(1 + k)^n}\right]$$ [Eq. 5.26a]

Present value of a perpetuity:

$$PVIFA_{k,\infty} = \frac{1}{k}$$ [Eq. 5.28]

Basic equations

Future value (single amount):	$FV_n = PV \times (FVIF_{k,n})$	[Eq. 5.6]
Future value (annuity):	$FVA_n = PMT \times (FVIFA_{k,n})$	[Eq. 5.15]
Present value (single amount):	$PV = FV_n \times (PVIF_{k,n})$	[Eq. 5.22]
Present value (annuity):	$PVA_n = PMT \times (PVIFA_{k,n})$	[Eq. 5.27]

(Solutions in Appendix B)

 ST 5–1 **Future values**   Delia Martin has $10,000 that she can deposit in any of three savings accounts for a 3-year period. Bank A compounds interest on an annual basis, bank B compounds interest twice each year, and bank C compounds interest each quarter. All three banks have a stated annual interest rate of 4%.
   a. What amount would Ms. Martin have at the end of the third year, leaving all interest paid on deposit, in each bank?
   b. What effective annual rate (EAR) would she earn in each of the banks?
   c. On the basis of your findings in **a** and **b,** which bank should Ms. Martin deal with? Why?
   d. If a fourth bank—Bank D, also with a 4 percent stated interest rate—compounds interest continuously, how much would Ms. Martin have at the end of the third year? Does this alternative change your recommendation in **c?** Explain why or why not.

 ST 5–2 **Future values of annuities**   Ramesh Abdul wishes to choose the better of two equally costly cash flow streams—annuity X and annuity Y. X is an *annuity due* with a cash inflow of $9,000 for each of 6 years. Y is an *ordinary annuity* with a cash inflow of $10,000 for each of 6 years. Assume that Ramesh can earn 15 percent on his investments.
   a. On a purely intuitive basis, which annuity do you think is more attractive? Why?
   b. Find the future value at the end of year 6, FVA_6, for both annuities—X and Y.
   c. Use your finding in **b** to indicate which annuity is more attractive. Why? Compare your finding to your intuitive response in **a.**

  ST 5–3 **Present values**   You have a choice of accepting either of two 5-year cash flow streams or lump-sum amounts. One cash flow stream is an annuity, and the other is a mixed stream. You may accept alternative A or B—either as a cash flow stream or as a lump sum. Given the cash flow stream and lump-sum amounts associated with each, and assuming a 9 percent opportunity cost, which alternative (A or B) and in which form (cash flow stream or lump-sum amount) would you prefer?

	Cash flow stream	
End of year	Alternative A	Alternative B
1	$700	$1,100
2	700	900
3	700	700
4	700	500
5	700	300
	Lump-sum amount	
At time zero	$2,825	$2,800

ST 5–4   **Investments required to accumulate a future sum**   Judi Jordan wishes to accumulate $8,000 by the end of 5 years by making equal annual end-of-year deposits over the next 5 years. If Judi can earn 7 percent on her investments, how much must she deposit at the *end of each year* to meet this goal?

PROBLEMS

WARM-UP   5–1   **Using a time line**   The financial manager at Starbuck Industries is considering an investment that requires an initial outlay of $25,000 and is expected to result in cash inflows of $3,000 at the end of year 1, $6,000 at the end of years 2 and 3, $10,000 at the end of year 4, $8,000 at the end of year 5, and $7,000 at the end of year 6.
a. Draw and label a time line depicting the cash flows associated with Starbuck Industries' proposed investment.
b. Use arrows to demonstrate, on the time line in **a,** how compounding to find future value can be used to measure all cash flows at the end of year 6.
c. Use arrows to demonstrate, on the time line in **b,** how discounting to find present value can be used to measure all cash flows at time zero.
d. Which of the approaches—future value or present value—is most often relied on by the financial manager for decision-making purposes? Why?

WARM-UP   5–2   **Future value calculation**   *Without referring to tables or the preprogrammed function on your financial calculator,* use the basic formula for future value along with the given interest rate, k, and number of periods, n, to calculate the future value interest factor in each of the cases shown in the following table. Compare the calculated value to the table value in Appendix Table A-1.

Case	Interest rate, k	Number of periods, n
A	12%	2
B	6	3
C	9	2
D	3	4

WARM-UP   5–3   **Future value tables**   Use the future value interest factors in Appendix Table A-1 in each of the cases shown in the following table to estimate, to the nearest year, how long it would take an initial deposit, assuming no withdrawals,
a. To double.
b. To quadruple.

Case	Interest rate
A	7%
B	40
C	20
D	10

INTERMEDIATE   **5–4   Future values**   For each of the cases shown in the table below, calculate the future value of the single cash flow deposited today that will be available at the end of the deposit period if the interest is compounded annually at the rate specified over the given period.

Case	Single cash flow	Interest rate	Deposit period (years)
A	$ 200	5%	20
B	4,500	8	7
C	10,000	9	10
D	25,000	10	12
E	37,000	11	5
F	40,000	12	9

INTERMEDIATE **5–5   Future value**   You have $1,500 to invest today at 7 percent interest compounded annually.
   a. How much will you have accumulated in the account at the end of
     (1) 3 years?
     (2) 6 years?
     (3) 9 years?
   b. Use your findings in **a** to calculate the amount of interest earned in
     (1) the first 3 years (years 1 to 3).
     (2) the second 3 years (years 4 to 6).
     (3) the third 3 years (years 7 to 9).
   c. Compare and contrast your findings in **b.** Explain why the amount of interest earned increases in each succeeding 3-year period.

CHALLENGE **5–6   Inflation and future value**   As part of your financial planning you wish to purchase a new car exactly 5 years from today. The car you wish to purchase costs $14,000 today, and your research indicates that its price will increase by 2 percent to 4 percent per year over the next 5 years.
   a. Estimate the price of the car at the end of 5 years if inflation is
     (1) 2 percent per year.
     (2) 4 percent per year.
   b. How much more expensive will the car be if the rate of inflation is 4 percent rather than 2 percent?

CHALLENGE **5–7   Future value and time**   You can invest $10,000 in a company's common shares that are expected to provide a 9 percent annual rate of return either today or exactly 10 years from today. How much better off will you be at the end of 40 years if you decide to make the investment today rather than 10 years from today?

CHALLENGE **5–8   Future value calculation**   Misty needs to have $15,000 at the end of 5 years in order to fulfill her goal of purchasing a small sailboat. She is willing to invest the funds as a single amount today but wonders what sort of investment return she will need to earn. Use your calculator or the time value tables to figure out the approximate annually compounded rate of return needed in each of these cases:

a. Misty can invest $10,200 today.
b. Misty can invest $8,150 today.
c. Misty can invest $7,150 today.

 5–9   Single-payment loan repayment   A person borrows $200 to be repaid in 8 years
with 14 percent annually compounded interest. The loan may be repaid at the
end of any earlier year with no prepayment penalty.
a. What amount would be due if the loan is repaid at the end of year 1?
b. What is the repayment at the end of year 4?
c. What amount is due at the end of the eighth year?

 5–10   Changing compounding frequency   Using annual, semiannual, and quarterly
compounding periods, for each of the following: (1) calculate the future value if
$5,000 is initially deposited, and (2) determine the effective annual rate (EAR):
a. At 12 percent annual interest for 5 years.
b. At 16 percent annual interest for 6 years.
c. At 20 percent annual interest for 10 years.

 **5–11   Compounding frequency, future value, and effective annual rates**   For each of
the following cases:

Case	Amount of initial deposit	Nominal annual rate, k	Compounding frequency, m (times/year)	Deposit period (years)
A	$ 2,500	6%	2	5
B	50,000	12	6	3
C	1,000	5	1	10
D	20,000	16	4	6

a. Calculate the future value at the end of the specified deposit period.
b. Determine the effective annual rate, EAR.
c. Compare the nominal annual rate, k, to the effective annual rate, EAR. What
relationship exists between compounding frequency and the nominal and
effective annual rates?

 5–12   Continuous compounding   For each of the following cases, find the future
value at the end of the deposit period, assuming that interest is compounded
continuously at the given nominal annual rate.

Case	Amount of initial deposit	Nominal annual rate, k	Deposit period (years)
A	$1,000	9%	2
B	600	10	10
C	4,000	8	7
D	2,500	12	4

CHALLENGE 5–13 **Compounding frequency and future value**   You plan to invest $2,000 in an investment account today and you expect a *nominal annual rate of return* of 8 percent, which is expected to apply to all future years.

a. How much will you have in the account at the end of 10 years if interest is compounded
   (1) annually?
   (2) semiannually?
   (3) daily?
   (4) continuously?
b. What is the *effective annual rate, EAR,* for each compounding period in **a**?
c. How much greater will your account balance be at the end of 10 years if interest is compounded continuously rather than annually?
d. How does the compounding frequency affect the future value and effective annual rate for a given deposit? Explain in terms of your findings in **a** through **c**.

CHALLENGE 5–14 **Comparing compounding periods**   René Levin wishes to determine the future value at the end of 2 years of a $15,000 investment made today into an account providing an annual rate of return of 12 percent.

a. Find the future value of René's investment assuming that interest is compounded
   (1) annually.
   (2) quarterly.
   (3) monthly.
   (4) continuously.
b. Compare your findings in **a,** and use them to demonstrate the relationship between compounding frequency and future value.
c. What is the maximum future value obtainable given the $15,000 investment, 2-year time period, and 12 percent nominal annual rate?

INTERMEDIATE 5–15 **Future value of an annuity**   For each of the following cases:

Case	Amount of annuity	Rate of return	Deposit period (years)
A	$ 2,500	8%	10
B	500	12	6
C	30,000	20	5
D	11,500	9	8
E	6,000	14	30

a. Calculate the future value of the annuity assuming that it is an
   (1) ordinary annuity.
   (2) annuity due.
b. Compare your findings in **a**(1) and **a**(2). All else being identical, which type of annuity—ordinary or annuity due—is preferable? Explain why.

CHALLENGE 5–16 **Ordinary annuity versus annuity due** Marian Kirk wishes to select the better of two 10-year annuities—C and D—as described.

> **Annuity C** An ordinary annuity of $2,500 per year for 10 years.
>
> **Annuity D** An annuity due of $2,200 per year for 10 years.

a. Find the future value of both annuities at the end of year 10 assuming that Marian can earn
   (1) 10 percent annual interest.
   (2) 20 percent annual interest.
b. Use your findings in **a** to indicate which annuity has the greater future value at the end of year 10 for both the (1) 10 percent and (2) 20 percent interest rates.
c. Briefly compare, contrast, and explain any differences between your findings using the 10 percent and 20 percent interest rates in **b**.

CHALLENGE 5–17 **Future value of a retirement annuity** Cal Thomas, a 25-year-old college graduate, wishes to retire at age 65. To supplement other sources of retirement income, he plans to deposit $2,000 each year into a tax-deferred registered retirement savings plan (RRSP). The RRSP will be invested to earn an annual return of 10 percent over the next 40 years.

a. If Cal makes annual end-of-year $2,000 deposits into the RRSP, how much would he have accumulated by the end of his 65th year?
b. If Cal decides to wait until age 35 to begin making annual end-of-year $2,000 deposits into the RRSP, how much would he have accumulated by the end of his 65th year?
c. Using your findings in **a** and **b**, discuss the impact of delaying making deposits into the RRSP for 10 years (age 25 to age 35) on the amount accumulated by the end of Cal's 65th year.
d. Rework parts **a, b,** and **c** assuming that Cal makes all deposits at the beginning rather than at the end of each year. Discuss the effect of beginning-of-year deposits on the future value accumulated by the end of Cal's 65th year.

INTERMEDIATE 5–18 **Annuities and compounding** Janet Boyle intends to deposit $300 per year in an account at a credit union for the next 10 years. The credit union pays an annual interest rate of 8 percent.

a. Determine the future value that Janet will have at the end of 10 years given that end-of-period deposits are made and no interest is withdrawn if
   (1) $300 is deposited annually and the credit union pays interest annually.
   (2) $150 is deposited semiannually and the credit union pays interest semiannually.
   (3) $75 is deposited quarterly and the credit union pays interest quarterly.
b. Use your finding in **a** to discuss the effect of more frequent deposits and compounding of interest on the future value of an annuity.

CHALLENGE 5–19 **Future value of a mixed stream** For each of the mixed streams of cash flows shown in the following table, determine the future value at the end of the final year if deposits are made at the *beginning of each year* into an account providing an annual return of 12 percent, assuming that no withdrawals are made during the period.

| | Cash flow stream | | |
Year	A	B	C
1	$ 900	$30,000	$1,200
2	1,000	25,000	1,200
3	1,200	20,000	1,000
4		10,000	1,900
5		5,000	

INTERMEDIATE 5–20 **Future value of lump sum versus a mixed stream**   Gina Trembly has just contracted to sell a small parcel of land that she inherited a few years ago. The buyer is willing to pay $24,000 at closing of the transaction or will pay the amounts shown in the following table at the *beginning* of each of the next 5 years. Gina doesn't really need the money today, so she plans to let it accumulate in an account that earns 7 percent annual interest.

Mixed stream	
Beginning of year	Cash flow
1	$ 2,000
2	4,000
3	6,000
4	8,000
5	10,000

a. What is the future value of the lump sum at the end of year 5?
b. What is the future value of the mixed stream at the end of year 5?
c. Based on your findings in a and b, which alternative should Gina take?
d. If Gina could earn 10 percent rather than 7 percent on the funds, would your recommendation in c change? Explain.

WARM-UP 5–21 **Present value calculation**   *Without referring to tables or the preprogrammed function on your financial calculator,* use the basic formula for present value along with the given opportunity cost, *k*, and number of periods, *n*, to calculate the present value interest factor in each of the cases shown in the following table. Compare the calculated value to the table value.

Case	Opportunity cost, k	Number of periods, n
A	2%	4
B	10	2
C	5	3
D	13	2

WARM-UP 5–22   **Present values**   For each of the cases shown in the following table, calculate the present value of the cash flow, discounting at the rate given and assuming that the cash flow is received at the end of the period noted.

Case	Single cash flow	Discount rate	End of period (years)
A	$ 7,000	12%	4
B	28,000	8	20
C	10,000	14	12
D	150,000	11	6
E	45,000	20	8

INTERMEDIATE 5–23   **Present value concept**   Answer each of the following questions.
  a. What single investment, made today, earning a 12 percent annual return, will be worth $6,000 at the end of 6 years?
  b. What is the present value of $6,000 to be received at the end of 6 years if the discount rate is 12 percent?
  c. What is the most you would pay today for a promise to repay you $6,000 at the end of 6 years if your opportunity cost is 12 percent?
  d. Compare, contrast, and discuss your findings in **a** through **c.**

WARM-UP 5–24   **Present value**   Jim Nance has been offered a future payment of $500 three years from today. If his opportunity cost is 7 percent compounded annually, what value should he place on this opportunity today? What is the most he should pay to purchase this payment today?

INTERMEDIATE 5–25   **Present value**   An Ontario savings bond can be converted to $100 at maturity 6 years from purchase. If the Ontario bonds are to be competitive with Government of Canada bonds, which pay 8 percent annual interest, at what price must the province sell its bonds? Assume no cash payments on bonds prior to redemption.

INTERMEDIATE 5–26   **Present value and discount rates**   You just won a lottery that promises to pay you $1,000,000 exactly 10 years from today. Because the $1,000,000 payment is guaranteed by the government, opportunities exist to sell the claim today for an immediate lump-sum cash payment.
  a. What is the least you will sell your claim for if you could earn the following rates of return during the 10-year period?
     (1) 6 percent
     (2) 9 percent
     (3) 12 percent
  b. Rework **a** under the assumption that the $1,000,000 payment will be received in 15 rather than 10 years.
  c. Based on your findings in **a** and **b,** discuss the effect of both the size of the rate of return and the time until receipt of payment on the present value of a future sum.

INTERMEDIATE 5-27   **Present value comparisons of lump sums**   In exchange for a $20,000 payment today, a well-known company will allow you to choose *one* of the alternatives shown in the following table. Your opportunity cost is 11 percent.

Alternative	Lump-sum amount
A	$28,500 at end of 3 years
B	$54,000 at end of 9 years
C	$160,000 at end of 20 years

    a. Find the value today of each alternative.
    b. Are all the alternatives acceptable, i.e., worth $20,000 today?
    c. Which alternative, if any, would you take?

INTERMEDIATE 5-28   **Cash flow investment decision**   Tom Alexander has an opportunity to purchase any of the investments shown in the following table. The purchase price, the amount of the single cash inflow, and its year of receipt are given for each investment. Which purchase recommendations would you make, assuming that Tom can earn 10 percent on his investments?

Investment	Price	Single cash inflow	Year of receipt
A	$18,000	$30,000	5
B	600	3,000	20
C	3,500	10,000	10
D	1,000	15,000	40

  5-29   **Relationship between future value and present value**   Using *only* the information in the following table:

INTERMEDIATE

Year (t)	Cash flow	Future value interest factor at 5% ($FVIF_{5\%,t}$)
1	$ 800	1.050
2	900	1.103
3	1,000	1.158
4	1,500	1.216
5	2,000	1.276

    a. Determine the *present value* of the mixed stream of cash flows using a 5 percent discount rate.
    b. How much would you be willing to pay for an opportunity to buy this stream, assuming that you can at best earn 5 percent on your investments?
    c. What effect, if any, would a 7 percent rather than a 5 percent opportunity cost have on your analysis? Would you pay more, less, or the same for this cash flow stream? Explain.

INTERMEDIATE 5–30   **Present value of an annuity**   Anna Doyle was seriously injured in an industrial accident. She sued the responsible parties and was awarded a judgment of $2,000,000. Today, she and her lawyer are attending a settlement conference with the defendants. The defendants have made an initial offer of $156,000 per year for 25 years. Anna plans to counteroffer at $255,000 per year for 25 years. Both offer and counteroffer have a present value of $2,000,000, the amount of the judgment. Both assume payments at the end of each year.

a. What interest rate assumption have the defendants used in their offer?
b. What interest rate assumption have Anna and her lawyer used in their counteroffer?
c. Anna is willing to settle for an annuity that carries an interest rate assumption of 9 percent. What annual payment would be acceptable to her?

CHALLENGE 5–31   **Present value of an annuity**   Tim Smith is shopping for a used car. He has found one priced at $4,500. The dealer has told Tim that if he can come up with a down payment of $500, the dealer will finance the balance of the car's cost at an interest rate of 12 percent over the 2 years.

a. Assuming that Tim accepts the dealer's offer, what will his *monthly* (end-of-month) payments be? Use a financial calculator or Equation 5.26a, found in footnote 14.
b. What would Tim's *monthly* payment be if the dealer was willing to finance the balance of the car's cost at a 9 percent interest rate?

WARM-UP 5–32   **Present value—Mixed streams**   Find the present value of the streams of cash flows shown in the following table. Assume that the firm's opportunity cost is 12%.

A		B		C	
Year	Cash flow	Year	Cash flow	Year	Cash flow
1	−$2,000	1	$10,000	1–5	$10,000/yr
2	3,000	2–5	5,000/yr	6–10	8,000/yr
3	4,000	6	7,000		
4	6,000				
5	8,000				

INTERMEDIATE 5–33   **Present value—Mixed streams**   Given the mixed streams of cash flows shown in the following table:

	Cash flow stream	
Year	A	B
1	$ 50,000	$ 10,000
2	40,000	20,000
3	30,000	30,000
4	20,000	40,000
5	10,000	50,000
Totals	$150,000	$150,000

a. Find the present value of each stream using a 15 percent discount rate.
b. Compare the calculated present values and discuss them in light of the fact that the undiscounted total cash flows total $150,000 in each case.

5–34 **Present value of a mixed stream**   Harte Systems, Inc., a maker of electronic surveillance equipment, is considering selling to a well-known hardware chain the rights to market its home security system. The proposed deal calls for Harte to receive payments of $30,000 and $25,000 at the end of years 1 and 2 and annual year-end payments of $15,000 in years 3 through 9. A final payment of $10,000 would be due at the end of year 10.

INTERMEDIATE

a. Lay out the cash flows involved in the offer on a time line.
b. If Harte applies a required rate of return of 12 percent to them, what is the present value of this series of payments?
c. A second company has offered Harte a one-time payment of $100,000 for the rights to market the home security system. Which offer should Harte accept?

INTERMEDIATE **5–35** **Funding budget shortfalls**   As part of your personal budgeting process, you have determined that in each of the next 5 years you will have budget shortfalls. In other words, you will need the amounts shown in the following table at the end of the given year to balance your budget, that is, inflows = outflows. You expect to be able to earn 8 percent on your investments during the next 5 years and wish to fund the budget shortfalls over the next 5 years with a single lump sum.

End of year	Budget shortfall
1	$ 5,000
2	4,000
3	6,000
4	10,000
5	3,000

a. How large must be the lump-sum deposit today into an account paying 8 percent annual interest to provide for full coverage of the anticipated budget shortfalls?
b. What effect would an increase in your earnings rate have on the amount calculated in **a**? Explain.

WARM-UP **5–36** **Present value of an annuity**   For each of the cases shown in the following table, calculate the present value of the annuity, assuming that the annuity cash flows occur at the end of each year.

Case	Amount of annuity	Interest rate	Period (years)
A	$ 12,000	7%	3
B	55,000	12	15
C	700	20	9
D	140,000	5	7
E	22,500	10	5

INTERMEDIATE 5–37   **Present value of a retirement annuity**   An insurance agent is trying to sell you a retirement annuity, which for a lump-sum amount paid today, the annuity will provide you with $12,000 per year for the next 25 years. You currently earn 9 percent on investments comparable to the retirement annuity. Ignoring taxes, what is the most you would pay for this annuity?

CHALLENGE 5–38   **Funding your retirement**   You plan to retire in exactly 20 years. Your goal is to create a fund that will allow you to receive $20,000 per year for the 30 years between retirement and death (a psychic told you would die after 30 years). You know that you will be able to earn 11 percent per year during the 30-year retirement period.

a. How large a fund will you need *when you retire* in 20 years to provide the 30-year, $20,000 retirement annuity?

b. How much would you need *today* as a lump sum to provide the amount calculated in **a** if you earn only 9 percent per year during the 20 years preceding retirement?

c. What effect would an increase in the rate you can earn both during and prior to retirement have on the values found in **a** and **b**? Explain.

INTERMEDIATE 5–39   **Present value of an annuity versus a lump sum**   Assume that you just won the lottery. Your prize can be taken either in the form of $40,000 at the end of each of the next 25 years (i.e., $1,000,000 over 25 years) or as a lump sum of $500,000 paid immediately.

a. If you expect to be able to earn 5 percent annually on your investments over the next 25 years, ignoring taxes and other considerations, which alternative should you take? Why?

b. Would your decision in **a** be altered if you could earn 7 percent rather than 5 percent on your investments over the next 25 years? Why?

c. On a strict economic basis, at what rate of return would you be indifferent in choosing between the two plans?

INTERMEDIATE 5–40   **Present value of a mixed stream with an embedded annuity**   In each of the cases shown in the following table, the mixed cash flow stream has an annuity embedded within it. Use the three-step procedure presented in the text to streamline the calculation of the present value of each of these streams, assuming a 12 percent discount rate in each case.

A		B		C	
Year	Cash flow	Year	Cash flow	Year	Cash flow
1	$12,000	1	$15,000	1–5	$ 1,000/yr
2	10,000	2–10	20,000/yr	6	6,000
3	8,000	11–30	25,000/yr	7	7,000
4	8,000			8	8,000
5	8,000			9–15	10,000/yr
6	8,000				
7	8,000				
8	5,000				

WARM-UP LG5 5–41 **Perpetuities** Given the data in the following table, determine for each of the perpetuities:

Perpetuity	Annual amount	Discount rate
A	$ 20,000	8%
B	100,000	10
C	3,000	6
D	60,000	5

a. The appropriate present value interest factor. Use your calculator.
b. The present value.

INTERMEDIATE LG5 5–42 **Creating an endowment** On completion of her introductory finance course, Kieran was so pleased with the amount of useful and interesting knowledge she gained that she convinced her parents, who were wealthy alums of the university she was attending, to create an endowment. The endowment would allow three needy students to take the introductory finance course each year into perpetuity. The guaranteed annual cost of tuition and books for the course was $600 per student. The endowment would be created by making a lump-sum payment to the university. The university expected to earn exactly 6 percent per year on these funds.
a. How large an initial lump-sum payment must Kieran's parents make to the university to fund the endowment?
b. What amount would be needed to fund the endowment if the university could earn 9 percent rather than 6 percent per year on the funds?

WARM-UP LG6 5–43 **Investments to accumulate future sums** For each of the cases shown in the following table, determine the amount of the equal annual end-of-year investment required to accumulate the given sum at the end of the specified period, assuming the stated annual rate of return.

Case	Sum to be accumulated	Accumulation period (years)	Rate of return
A	$ 5,000	3	12%
B	100,000	20	7
C	30,000	8	10
D	15,000	12	8

INTERMEDIATE LG6 5–44 **Creating a retirement fund** To supplement your planned retirement in exactly 42 years, you estimate that you need to accumulate $220,000 by the end of 42 years from today. You plan to make equal annual end-of-year investments into an account providing an 8 percent annual rate of return.
a. How large must the annual investments be to create the $220,000 fund by the end of 42 years?
b. If you can afford to deposit only $600 per year into the account, how much will you have accumulated by the end of the 42nd year?

5–45 **Accumulating a growing future sum**   A retirement home at Deer Trail Estates now costs $85,000. Inflation is expected to cause this price to increase at 6 percent per year over the 20 years before C. L. Donovan retires. How much must Donovan invest each year to have the cash required to purchase a home at retirement if he can earn a 10 percent return?

INTERMEDIATE

  5–46 **Deposits to create a perpetuity**   You have decided to endow your favorite university with a scholarship. It is expected to cost $6,000 per year to attend the university into perpetuity. You expect to give the university the endowment in 10 years and will accumulate it by making annual (end-of-year) deposits into an account. The rate of return is expected to be 10 percent for all future time periods.
   a. How large must the endowment be?
   b. How much must you deposit at the end of each of the next 10 years to accumulate the required amount?

INTERMEDIATE

  5–47 **Inflation, future value, and annual deposits**   While vacationing in Florida, John Kelley saw the vacation home of his dreams. It was listed with a sale price of $200,000. The only catch is that John is 40 years old and plans to continue working until he is 65. John believes that he can earn 9 percent annually after taxes on his investments. He is willing to invest a fixed amount at the end of each of the next 25 years to fund the cash purchase of such a house when he retires.
   a. The house price is expected to increase 5 percent a year for the next 25 years. What will John's dream house cost when he retires?
   b. How much must John invest at the end of each of the next 25 years in order to have the cash purchase price of the house when he retires?
   c. If John invests at the beginning instead of at the end of each of the next 25 years, how much must he invest each year?

CHALLENGE

 5–48 **Loan amortization**   Determine the equal annual end-of-year payment required each year over the life of the loans shown in the following table to repay them fully during the stated term of the loan.

WARM-UP

Loan	Principal	Interest rate	Term of loan (years)
A	$12,000	8%	3
B	60,000	12	10
C	75,000	10	30
D	4,000	15	5

 5–49 **Loan amortization schedule**   Joan Messineo borrowed $15,000 at a 14 percent annual rate of interest to be repaid over 3 years. The loan is amortized into three equal annual end-of-year payments.
   a. Calculate the annual end-of-year loan payment.
   b. Prepare a loan amortization schedule showing the interest and principal breakdown of each of the three loan payments.
   c. Explain why the interest portion of each payment declines with the passage of time.

INTERMEDIATE

5–50   **Loan interest deductions**   Liz Rogers just closed a $10,000 business loan that is to be repaid in three equal annual end-of-year payments. The interest rate on the loan is 13 percent. As part of her firm's detailed financial planning, Liz wishes to determine the annual interest deduction attributable to the loan. (Because it is a business loan, the interest portion of each loan payment is tax-deductible to the business.)

a.   Determine the firm's annual loan payment.

b.   Prepare an amortization schedule for the loan.

c.   How much interest expense will Liz's firm have in *each* of the next 3 years as a result of this loan?

d.   If the company's tax rate is 30 percent, what is the actual, after-tax amount of interest the company pays each year?

  5–51   **Growth rates**   You are given the series of cash flows shown in the following table:

	Cash flows		
Year	A	B	C
1	$500	$1,500	$2,500
2	560	1,550	2,600
3	640	1,610	2,650
4	720	1,680	2,650
5	800	1,760	2,800
6		1,850	2,850
7		1,950	2,900
8		2,060	
9		2,170	
10		2,280	

a.   Calculate the compound annual growth rate associated with each cash flow stream.

b.   If year 1 values represent initial deposits in a savings account paying annual interest, what is the annual rate of interest earned on each account?

c.   Compare and discuss the growth rate and interest rate found in **a** and **b**, respectively.

  5–52   **Rate of return**   Rishi Singh has $1,500 to invest. His investment counsellor suggests an investment that pays no stated interest but will return $2,000 at the end of 3 years.

a.   What annual rate of return will Mr. Singh earn with this investment?

b.   Mr. Singh is considering another investment, of equal risk, which earns an annual return of 8 percent. Which investment should he take, and why?

  5–53   **Rate of return and investment choice**   Clare Jaccard has $5,000 to invest. Because she is only 25 years old, she is not concerned about the length of the investment's life. What she is sensitive to is the rate of return she will earn on the investment. With the help of her financial advisor Clare has isolated the four equally risky investments, each providing a lump-sum return, shown in the following table. All of the investments require an initial $5,000 payment.

Investment	Lump-sum return	Investment life (years)
A	$ 8,400	6
B	15,900	15
C	7,600	4
D	13,000	10

a. Calculate the rate of return on each of the four investments available to Clare.
b. Which investment would you recommend to Clare given her goal of maximizing the rate of return?

INTERMEDIATE 5–54 **Rate of return—Annuity** What is the rate of return on an investment of $10,606 if the company expects to receive $2,000 each year for the next 10 years?

INTERMEDIATE 5–55 **Choosing the best annuity** Raina Rashad wishes to choose the best of four immediate retirement annuities available to her. In each case, in exchange for paying a single premium today, she will receive equal annual end-of-year cash benefits for a specified number of years. She considers the annuities to be equally risky and is not concerned about their differing lives. Her decision will be based solely on the rate of return she will earn on each annuity. The key terms of each of the four annuities are shown in the following table.

Annuity	Premium paid today	Annual benefit	Life (years)
A	$30,000	$3,100	20
B	25,000	3,900	10
C	40,000	4,200	15
D	35,000	4,000	12

a. Calculate the rate of return on each of the four annuities being considered by Raina.
b. Given Raina's stated decision criterion, which annuity would you recommend?

INTERMEDIATE 5–56 **Loan rates of interest** John Fleming has been shopping for a loan to finance the purchase of a used car. He has found three possibilities that seem attractive and wishes to select the one having the lowest interest rate. The information available with respect to each of the three $5,000 loans is shown in the following table:

Loan	Principal	Annual payment	Term (years)
A	$5,000	$1,352.81	5
B	5,000	1,543.21	4
C	5,000	2,010.45	3

a. Determine the interest rate associated with each of the loans.
b. Which loan should Mr. Fleming take?

CASE   CHAPTER 5   **Finding Jill Moran's Retirement Annuity**

Sunrise Industries wishes to accumulate funds to provide a retirement annuity for its vice president of research, Jill Moran. Ms. Moran by contract will retire in exactly 12 years' time. Upon retirement, she is entitled to receive an annual end-of-year payment of $42,000 for 20 years. If she dies prior to the end of the 20-year period, the annual payments will pass to her heirs. During the 12-year "accumulation period" Sunrise wishes to fund the annuity by making equal annual end-of-year deposits into an account earning a 9 percent return. Once the 20-year "payment period" begins, Sunrise plans to move the accumulated monies into a safer account earning a guaranteed 7 percent per year. At the end of the 20-year payment period, the account balance will equal zero. Note that the first deposit will be made at the end of year 1 and the first distribution payment will be received at the end of year 13.

Required

a. Draw a time line depicting all of the cash flows associated with Sunrise's view of the retirement annuity.
b. How large a sum must Sunrise accumulate by the end of year 12 to provide the 20-year, $42,000 annuity?
c. How large must Sunrise's equal annual end-of-year investments into the account be over the 12-year accumulation period to fund fully Ms. Moran's retirement annuity?
d. How much would Sunrise have to deposit annually during the accumulation period if it could earn 10 percent rather than 9 percent during the accumulation period?
e. How much would Sunrise have to invest annually during the accumulation period if Ms. Moran's retirement annuity was a perpetuity and all other terms were the same as initially described?

WEB EXERCISE   LINKS TO PRACTISE

Visit the following Web sites and complete the suggested exercises. These exercises will allow you to review practical applications of the chapter topics as well as explore the wealth of information regarding managerial finance that is available on the Internet.

www.bus.utk.edu/finance/D.%20Murphy/510_fall01/fin510fall2001.htm
Visit the above site and click on Time Value Concepts. You will be prompted to download a PowerPoint Presentation file. Either open the file or save the file to the hard drive, floppy drive, or CD drive of your computer. Press F5 to play the slide show and answer the following questions.

1. The slide show covers eight topics. What are they?
2. Why is "time" an important concept for time value? What is "opportunity cost"?
3. How can you compare cash flows from different time periods?
4. What is compound interest? Why is this an important concept for time value?
5. Can you calculate future values and present values without using the financial functions on your calculator? What are the calculator key strokes to compute future values and present values?
6. Define the term "present value."
7. What is the general formula for finding the number of periods or the rate of return for present and future values?
8. Define the term "annuity" and provide some examples of annuities.
9. What process would you follow to determine the present value of a series of five cash flows, each a different amount, received over the next five years? Is there a way you can input the five values in your calculator to determine the present value?
10. Describe bond valuation in terms of a time value problem.
11. Go to slide 35. Click on Problem 1. Answer the problem.
12. Go back to slide 35. Click on Problem 2. Answer the problem.
13. Go back to slide 35. Click on Problem 3. Answer the problem.
14. What did you learn from this slide show?

www.studyfinance.com/lessons/timevalue/index.html
www.studyfinance.com/lectures/timevalue/index.html
www.studyfinance.com/lectures/fincalc/index.html
The first link provides 12 slides on time value, a problem set, and an Excel spreadsheet that provides Excel formulas for time value problems. The second link is a lecture on time value. The third link is a lecture on the use of financial calculators for time value problems. To listen to the lectures, click on Begin the Lecture. You will require the free Real Player plug-in to listen to the lectures. There are no specific questions for this exercise but students may wish to view the complete slide show and listen to all or a portion of the lectures to reinforce their understanding of time value and the use of financial calculators.

www.busadm.mu.edu/mandell/dq.html#DQ
www.busadm.mu.edu/mandell/prob.html#PROB
The first link provides six discussion questions on time value. The second provides 22 time value problems. Complete the exercise your instructor assigns from these two links.

www-ec.njit.edu/~mathis/interactive/TVMCalcIntro.html
www-ec.njit.edu/~mathis/interactive/FCBase3.html
The first site provides an introduction to the use of a free time value calculator. The link to the actual calculator is on the bottom of the page. Complete the self-test problems from the book using this calculator. The second link provides numerous problems that can be used with the calculator. Complete as many problems as you like to reinforce time value concepts.

Financial Markets, Institutions, and Securities

LEARNING GOALS

LG 1 Introduce the types of financial markets and how the markets operate, the important role played by financial institutions, the major types of financial securities, and the importance of trust to the operation of the financial markets.

LG 2 Describe the money market and the major instruments traded in the market, particularly treasury bills.

LG 3 Describe the key characteristics of long-term debt, one of the major capital market securities.

LG 4 Describe the key characteristics of common and preferred shares, two additional capital market securities.

LG 5 Differentiate between debt, preferred equity, and common equity capital.

LG 6 Review the process of how financial securities are created and issued, and the important role played by the investment banker.

6.1 Financial Markets and Institutions

For an economy to develop and economic wealth to be created, a country needs efficient and well-developed financial markets. Unfortunately, for much of the world's population, effective and organized financial markets are only found in a handful of countries. Generally, only countries that are democratic and follow the capitalistic economic model have well functioning financial markets. The benefits of financial markets to a country include consistent economic growth, industrialization, increasing living standards, better jobs, higher incomes, and increased access to quality education and health care.

Financial Fabric

The financial environment is like a fabric woven from many different threads—savers (suppliers) and users (demanders) of funds, financial institutions like banks, financial markets such as the money market and stock exchanges, and the federal government and its regulatory agencies. The common thread running through the entire fabric is money. Those who have excess money are willing to put it to use in ways that make it possible for those who need money to obtain it, for a cost. This chapter will describe the prominent threads in the fabric of the financial environment: the participants, the institutions and markets that channel money from savers to users, and the types of debt and equity securities created when the transaction occurs. For a financial market to exist, the participants must have a great deal of trust in the strength of the fabric.

As a country's financial markets develop, a middle class evolves and flourishes. As the middle class becomes the largest percentage of the population, the economy expands, leading to increased opportunities for all members of society. For non- or under-developed countries, democracy and capitalism are often missing meaning that financial markets are either non-existent or inefficient. As a consequence, the nation's wealth is usually in the hands of a small number of the country's political and military leaders. The vast majority of the population lives in poverty. For a country to develop economically, financial markets are a necessity.

An Overview of Financial Markets

Financial markets provide a forum where suppliers of funds (savers) and demanders of funds (users) can transact business. Financial markets exist to facilitate the transfer of funds between savers and users of funds. Savers and users of funds must be able to interact and to make an exchange that is beneficial to both parties. Financial markets exist for one purpose: to bring savers and users of funds together to make a fair exchange, one that provides value to both parties.

In the financial markets, cash moves from savers to users, and users provide a financial security in return. The financial security indicates the compensation the saver will receive in return for providing the funds. The compensation may be a rate of return on the funds, a promise to repay the funds at some point in the future, and/or a right of ownership. For financial markets to function efficiently, financial institutions, intermediaries that allow for the efficient and low-cost transfer of the savings of individuals, governments, and business for financial securities, are necessary.

There are many types of financial intermediaries, institutions like banks and investment dealers, but they all serve the same purpose: to channel funds from those who wish to save to those who wish to spend or invest. Economic markets match the demand and supply of valuable items. Financial markets perform the same function, with money, but they are special in one critical way: They link the present and the future. Financial markets allow savers to convert current cash into future spending, and users to convert future cash into current spending. By acting as a channel through which savings can finance investment, the financial system helps drive growth.

Participants in the Financial Markets

Savers and users of funds in the financial markets include individuals, business organizations, and the various levels of government: federal, provincial, and municipal. In an advanced economy like Canada's, almost everyone is part of the financial markets, whether they know it or not. Individuals regularly save and invest money and, in so doing, use the financial markets. Individuals also purchase high-cost items like cars, houses, appliances, and travel, for which they may not have the available cash. To make these purchases, individuals must access the financial markets. As we saw in Chapter 4, companies require cash from external sources to support increasing assets and sales. Governments regularly raise cash in the financial markets when expenditures are not matched by tax revenues and other sources of income.

Individuals are large net suppliers of funds while businesses and governments have historically been large net demanders of funds. While some businesses can be savers, with large cash balances invested in financial securities, overall the business sector is a net demander of funds. At best, the government sector is in balance, neither a net demander or supplier of funds. Since the mid-1970s, however, the government sector in Canada has been a large net demander of funds. While the various levels of government in Canada, particularly the federal government, have eliminated operating deficits in the last few years, when all government expenditures are considered, the government sector in Canada is a net demander of funds.

Since the early 1990s, a growing trend is the internationalization of financial markets. In Canada, it is relatively easy for individuals to purchase financial securities in most developed countries throughout the world. Businesses and governments regularly raise cash in foreign markets. For example, it is not unusual for a Canadian company to raise cash in the European financial markets or for the federal government of Canada to borrow money in the American financial markets. There are domestic and international participants in the financial markets of all developed economies. The international sector can be a net supplier or demander of funds in a particular country. In Canada, for example, the international sector is a net demander of funds. More money flows out of the Canadian economy to international participants than flows in from international participants.

Classifying Financial Markets

There are two distinct financial markets: the *money market* and the *capital market*. Debt securities that will mature within one year are traded in the money market. The principal money market security is Government of Canada treasury bills, or t-bills, as they are more commonly known. The capital market involves the trading of long-term debt securities, like bonds and debentures, and preferred and common shares.

A second way to classify financial markets is by the nature of the transaction. A financial security must be "created" and this occurs in the *primary market*. With the security created, a *secondary market* must exist that allows the owner of a previously created financial security to sell the security, to buy more of this or other securities, or for a buyer to acquire a financial security. Both the money and capital markets have a primary and secondary market. The primary market creates and places an initial value on financial securities. Savers now own financial securities that they may, at some point, want to sell for cash. This is the function of the secondary market: It allows for the subsequent trading of previously created financial securities.

Figure 6.1 presents this classification of financial markets. Note that the life of the security created is a distinguishing feature of the money and capital markets. While long-term debt may be outstanding for 25 or more years and common shares for 50 or more years, money market securities may exist for only 90 days.

Flow of Funds in the Financial Markets

Figure 6.2 depicts the financial markets as they exist in most developed countries. There are three distinct flow of funds channels shown. For the first channel,

FIGURE 6.1

Classification of Financial Markets

Money market	**Capital market**
Trades debt securities that will mature within one year.	Trades long-term debt securities, like bonds and debentures, and preferred and common shares.

Both markets have a primary market that creates and places an initial value on financial securities and a secondary market that allows for the subsequent trading of previously created financial securities.

labelled ①, cash flows from savers through financial intermediaries to users. For example, consider a simple transaction like depositing $500 in a bank account. This creates a simple financial security, a "loan" to the bank. You have agreed to lend the bank your $500 and by accepting the deposit, the bank agrees to give you access to your money at any time and pay you a modest rate of interest while the funds remain deposited. The bank then pools your $500 with other deposits and lends them out to users in the form of loans and mortgages. Each of these transactions creates additional financial securities.

For the second channel, labelled ② in Figure 6.2, cash flows from savers to financial intermediaries, who then provide funds to users via the money or capital markets. These are primary market transactions. For example, assume a company needs to build a new production plant costing $500 million. To raise the required financing, the company decides to sell common shares. The company creates the common shares, uses a financial intermediary (an investment dealer) to sell the shares, and savers pay cash. The transaction occurs in the primary market within the capital market. In the primary market, financial securities are created and demanders of funds receive cash from savers.

For the third channel, labelled ③ in Figure 6.2, cash flows from savers to financial intermediaries who buy and sell financial securities on behalf of savers in the money or capital markets. These are secondary market transactions. As an example, consider the primary market sale of common shares discussed above. With this transaction complete, the primary market has "done its job." Savers now own the common shares. Assuming the savers wish to sell the shares at some point, a secondary market must exist that allows for the subsequent trading of financial securities. Note that for this third channel, the company whose securities are being traded is not involved. All of these trades are between investors. In this case, the buyer of the shares is the saver of funds, and the seller is the user.

FIGURE 6.2

Flow of Funds in the Financial Markets

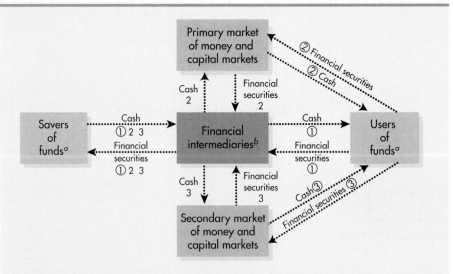

[a]Both savers and users of funds are individuals, business organizations, and governments.

[b]The financial intermediaries are: deposit-taking, loan-making institutions; investment dealers; mutual funds; pension funds; insurance companies; and the Bank of Canada.

For both the second and third channels described above, the financial intermediary may hold the security on behalf of the savers or the savers may directly receive the security. Also, for these two channels, the term "market" may be misleading. Many think of markets as physical locations where buyers and sellers meet. The only physical market where financial securities are traded is the secondary market for preferred and common shares—the stock market or stock exchange. All primary market transactions and the secondary market trading of debt securities (in both the money and capital markets) occurs in the computer networks between financial intermediaries.

The Financial Markets in Operation

Financial markets allow for the transfer of cash for financial securities. How does this transfer occur? Assume you wish to buy a car costing $25,000. You don't have the required cash, but you are working full time and would be able to buy the car after saving money for three years. Obviously, this alternative would not be ideal for you. You want the car now! What can you do? You could approach family and friends to try to raise the money but this can lead to strained relations, broken friendships, and the word "no" being used more often than you would like. As an alternative, you could advertise in your local newspaper looking for people who would like to lend you money that you will repay over the next three years. Would you do this? Likely not. First, it will take a long time to try to raise the money. And second, you may end up with 25 different agreements in place with the various people who lent you money. In short, this type of financial transaction is not timely, effective, or efficient. What could you do instead?

An obvious alternative is to go to your local bank (or trust company, credit union or—in Quebec—caisse populaire) to arrange for a $25,000 loan that will be repaid over three years. By doing this, you are using the financial markets. Review Figure 6.2. You, the car buyer, are a demander of funds. You will use a financial intermediary (a bank) to acquire the money needed to buy the car. The cash the bank lends you was obtained from savers, the suppliers of funds. The savers may be your friends, family, or the people who may have responded to your newspaper ad seeking money: in short, people who have "lent" the financial institution money through a savings (or chequing) account or another type of financial security.

You, the car buyer, may end up receiving the money from the very people you originally thought of approaching. Instead of directly receiving the money, however, you have used a financial intermediary and created a financial security, a car loan. This type of transaction happens thousands of times a day in the Canadian financial market and takes 30 minutes or less. It is an organized and efficient way to having money move from savers to users.

If we didn't have financial markets in Canada, think of the alternative scenario of raising money. Would you buy a car, or house, or big-screen television if you had to approach family and friends or strangers every time you wished to buy a product or service for which you didn't have the required amount of cash? Would these people lend you money, *if* they had money? Think of the impact this would have on the Canadian economy. Very few high-cost items would be sold and the economy would become subsistence based. Items that allowed for basic living would be available, but little else. The importance of the financial markets and financial intermediaries to an advanced economy cannot be overstated; they are key factors enabling an economy to operate and grow. The various types of financial intermediaries are discussed in the following section.

Financial Intermediaries

There are six principal financial intermediaries in Canada: (1) deposit-taking, loan-making institutions; (2) investment dealers; (3) mutual funds; (4) pension funds; (5) life insurance companies; and (6) the Bank of Canada. Table 6.1 details the total assets managed by these financial intermediaries in 1991, 1996, and 2001. Two items should be noted from a review of this table. First, the scale of the numbers is immense and difficult to fathom. In 2001, the total assets of the six intermediaries totalled $3.3 trillion. Every dollar of this was provided by savers and flowed through the financial markets to demanders of funds. The financial intermediaries handle tremendous volumes of cash. Second, the flow of cash in the Canadian financial system has grown by 142.7 percent over the 11 years. This is an average yearly growth rate of 9.3 percent and is much higher than growth in the overall economy.

The largest and most visible financial intermediaries in any economy are deposit-taking, loan-making institutions. These institutions account for almost 52 percent of the total assets managed by the financial intermediaries in 2001. Almost every individual in Canada, from the very young to the old, deal with at least one of these institutions. These include the big six Canadian chartered

TABLE 6.1	Total Assets of the Major Financial Intermediaries in Canada for Three Years: 1991, 1996, and 2001 (in millions)		
Financial intermediary	1991	1996	2001
Deposit-taking, loan-making			
Chartered banks	$ 634,340	$1,104,828	1,710,432
Trust and mortgage loan	135,055	72,301	9,701
Credit unions and caisses populaires	79,858	104,441	134,955
Other	41,866	51,763	85,933
Total	$ 891,119	$1,333,333	$1,941,021
Life insurance companies	$ 156,046	$ 208,098	$282,414
Mutual funds	53,700	216,745	438,179
Pension funds	225,762	419,665	576,933
Investment dealers[a]	2,898	7,158	12,454
Bank of Canada	27,045	30,584	41,804
Total assets of all financial intermediaries	$1,356,570	$2,215,583	$3,292,805

[a]For investment dealers, the amount shown is regulatory capital.

SOURCES: *Bank of Canada Banking and Financial Statistics*, June 2002, Tables C3 and D1–D5; *Quarterly Estimates of Trusteed Pension Funds*, Statistics Canada, Catalogue No. 74-001; and *Annual Securities Industry Statistics*, Investment Dealers Association of Canada, 1990–2001.

banks (and eight other domestic banks), trust companies, credit unions (caisses populaires in Quebec), finance companies, and sales finance companies. The first three institutions provide most of the financial services required by individuals. Savings and chequing accounts, all types of loans, and even access to financial securities like common shares, preferred shares, and bonds and debentures are available at these institutions.

Finance companies raise funds in the money market that they then lend to individuals at very high interest rates. Finance companies in Canada include Household Finance, Trans Canada Credit, and Associate Financial Services. Sales finance companies also raise funds in the money market for subsequent loan to consumers for the purchase of goods. Canadian Tire, Sears, major car manufacturers, and major retailers all either have their own sales finance companies or use the services of one.

The second financial intermediary, investment dealers, perform two basic functions that ensure the smooth operation of the money and capital markets. First, they act as agents for financial security transactions completed by both individual and institutional investors in the secondary markets of the money and capital markets. The current owner of a financial security may wish to sell a security, while another individual may wish to buy. Investors must use an investment dealer, acting as an agent, to buy or sell financial securities. The investment dealer receives a fee, termed a commission, for providing this service. The second function performed by investment dealers is the underwriting or investment banking function. This is discussed in more detail in Section 6.6.

Example ▼ Tom Driscoll wishes to sell the 500 common shares of Dire Corp. that he owns. Tom approaches an investment dealer and places the order to sell. The investment dealer, acting as Tom's agent, sends the order to the Toronto Stock Exchange (TSX). Another investment dealer has an order to buy 500 shares of Dire Corp. The two orders are crossed on the TSX and a financial market transaction occurs. The investment dealer, as the financial intermediary, used the capital market to raise cash for Tom, the user of funds. A saver of funds provided the cash and received Tom's 500 common shares. This is an example of a secondary market transaction in the capital market. Thousands of these transactions, involving millions of common shares, happen each trading day on the TSX.

The next three financial intermediaries all perform the same basic function: They invest money for the future benefit of savers (primarily individuals) and are large holders of financial securities. These three intermediaries—mutual funds, pension funds, and life insurance companies—are termed **institutional investors.** **Mutual funds** are investment companies that receive cash from individuals for investment in both money and capital market securities. The individuals providing the funds are the owners of the mutual fund. The money is managed by professionals to achieve a specific investment objective such as safety, growth, income, high risk, liquidity, or some combination of objectives. The money could be invested in Canada, the United States, or any international market. Thousands of mutual funds, with a wide variety of investment objectives and mandates, are available to individuals in Canada. The returns earned on the securities purchased by the fund managers flow back to the owners. A mutual fund is similar in nature to a corporation. Professional managers act on behalf of owners to

institutional investors
Financial intermediaries such as mutual funds, pension funds, and life insurance companies.

mutual funds
Investment companies that receive cash from individuals for investment in both money and capital market securities.

pension funds
Investment entities established by employers to provide a pension to employees during retirement.

life insurance companies
Invest premiums from life insurance policyholders to ensure sufficient funds are available to pay out the stated value of the life insurance policy upon the death of the policyholder.

Bank of Canada
The central bank in Canada whose main function is to manage monetary policy.

generate a return on the money invested by the owners. Note the tremendous rate of growth in mutual fund assets in Table 6.1.

Pension funds are investment entities established by employers to provide a pension to employees during retirement. Each pay period a certain dollar amount is withheld from each employee's pay. Employers often match this contribution. The total contributions are then forwarded to the pension fund for investment in money and capital market securities. The funds are invested to ensure sufficient funds are available to pay retired employees their pensions. **Life insurance companies** receive premiums from life insurance policyholders. The premiums are invested to ensure sufficient funds are available to pay out the stated value of the life insurance policy upon the death of the policyholder.

The sixth financial intermediary is a country's central bank. In Canada, this institution is the **Bank of Canada**. The main function of the central bank is to manage monetary policy. Monetary policy consists of two components: the level of short-term interest rates and the exchange rate for the Canadian dollar. The combined effect of these two variables is termed *monetary conditions*. The goal of the bank is keep inflation low, which keeps interest rates low. Low inflation results in productive long-term investment leading to long-lasting economic growth and job creation.

A second function of the Bank of Canada is to raise funds on behalf of the federal government. The Bank of Canada may sell treasury bills or bonds of various maturities. The choice made will depend on the planned use and cost of the money in the market. This function is similar to that performed by the finance department for a company. Essentially the Bank of Canada is the fiscal and monetary agent for the government of Canada.

Table 6.2 provides a balance sheet for all of the Canadian chartered banks. Note that loans are a major asset for the banks while the deposits of customers are a major liability. From the table, it is clear that the banks are major partici-

TABLE 6.2   Assets and Liabilities of the Chartered Banks as of December 31, 2001 (in millions)

Assets		Liabilities and equity	
Cash	$ 6,070	Individual savings accounts	$ 352,499
T-bills	20,831	Business savings accounts	176,608
Government of Canada bonds	79,328	Chequing accounts	92,779
Loans to		Government deposits	4,124
Individuals	131,376	Bankers' acceptances	44,288
Businesses	195,119	Non-deposit liabilities	177,823
Governments	2,446	Subordinated debentures	19,106
International loans and investments	729,626	Preferred shares	8,159
Mortgages	311,239	Common shares	25,758
Provincial and municipal securities	15,137	Retained earnings	45,290
Business securities	89,024	International liabilities	763,998
Other Canadian assets	130,236	Total liabilities and equity	$1,710,432
Total assets	$1,710,432		

SOURCE: *Bank of Canada Banking and Financial Statistics*, June 2002, Tables C3–C4.

pants in the international financial markets. Also note the low amount of equity on the balance sheet. Banks operate with very little equity and make money on the difference in the interest they pay on their liabilities (deposits) and charge on their assets (loans).

To put these numbers for the Canadian chartered banks in context consider Table 6.3, that lists the 10 largest banks in the world by country of origin and by total assets. This table also indicates where the Big 5 Canadian banks rank. The relatively low ranking of the Canadian banks may be surprising. In comparison to the top 10 world banks, the "big" 5 Canadian banks are small players in the world's financial markets. The largest Canadian bank, the Royal Bank, is only the 39th largest bank in the world. The combined assets of the Big 5, US$915,998, is less than each of the top 3 world banks. While the numbers for the Canadian banks and for the Canadian financial markets are large, Table 6.3 makes it clear that the financial institutions and markets in other developed countries are gargantuan.

Table 6.1 also indicates that the three institutional investors managed a total of $1.3 trillion on behalf of individuals in 2001. Obviously, based on these numbers, the level of individual savings in Canada is substantial. In comparison, the remaining two financial intermediaries appear to be very minor players in the Canadian financial markets. The assets of investment dealers and the Bank of Canada are very modest, a very small fraction of the other intermediaries. The importance of these two intermediaries is measured, not in terms of assets, but in

TABLE 6.3   World's Top Banking Companies by Assets as of Dec. 31, 2001 (in millions of US dollars)

Rank	Name of bank	Country	Total assets
1	Mizuho Holdings[a]	Japan	$1,281,389
2	Citigroup Inc.	U.S.	1,051,450
3	Sumitomo Mitsui Banking Corp.	Japan	924,146
4	Mitsubishi Tokyo Financial Group	Japan	854,749
5	Deutsche Bank	Germany	815,126
6	Allianz AG	Germany	805,433
7	UBS AG	Switzerland	753,833
8	BNP Paribas	France	734,833
9	HSBC Holdings PLC	U.K.	694,590
10	J.P. Morgan & Chase Co.	U.S.	693,575
	Canadian banks		
39	Royal Bank		$225,403
46	TD-Canada Trust (T-D)		181,145
47	Canadian Imperial Bank of Commerce (CIBC)		180,550
49	Bank of Nova Scotia		178,479
56	Bank of Montreal		150,421

[a]Created by merger of the Dai-Ichi Kangyo Bank, Fuji Bank, and Industrial Bank of Japan.
SOURCE: "World's Top Banking Companies by Assets," *American Banker*, July 12, 2002.

terms of the key functions performed. Without investment dealers or the Bank of Canada, the financial markets would not operate efficiently. For example, investment dealers handle every dollar invested by the three large institutional investors. The Bank of Canada manages monetary policy, which determines the cost of money.

Trust and Financial Markets

A key but often overlooked concept associated with financial markets is "trust." In order for financial markets to function efficiently, the participants in the market must have trust in the system. When individuals deposit money in a bank, invest in the debt securities of a company or government, or buy common or preferred shares, they are displaying trust in the system. They believe their money will be available when they require it. For example consider Maureen, who deposits $5,000 in a savings account. She is giving up possession of the money. Maureen would do this only if she believed she would receive an appropriate rate of return on the deposited funds, and have instant access to the money. If she lacked trust in the system, if she did not believe that both of these conditions would be met, then she would not deposit the money. If individuals do not deposit their money, then financial markets will not exist. The same concept applies to investments in all other financial securities.

In non-democratic, non-capitalistic countries, there is no trust in the financial markets. This is the case since the country's currency is often worthless and the financial system is often corrupt. In these cases, another medium of exchange is used. Sometimes real assets like gold or diamonds might be used, but most often a hard currency like the U.S. dollar becomes the medium of exchange. In these economies there is no trust in the country's currency, so a substitute is used. Residents keep their wealth in paper form: the currency of another country.

Countries in this situation will remain underdeveloped, since substantive financial markets do not exist or are underdeveloped. Trust in the country's financial system is lacking, so money is never provided to financial intermediaries. The exchange between savers and users never occurs. The black market in U.S. dollars becomes the country's *de facto* financial market. There is no faith that the country's currency will retain its value, or that a deposit to a bank will be returned. So even very modest individual wealth is kept close at hand, and financial markets do not develop.

? Review Questions

6–1   Why are financial markets important?

6–2   What basic function do the financial markets perform?

6–3   Who are the main participants in the financial markets? Are they net suppliers or demanders of funds?

6–4   How can financial markets be classified?

6–5   Discuss the three flow of funds channels that exist in the financial markets.

6–6   List and briefly discuss the key function performed by the various financial intermediaries in the Canadian financial markets.

6–7   Why is trust an important concept when dealing with financial markets?

6.2 The Money Market

The money market involves the trading of debt securities that will mature within one year. Note, though, that Government of Canada bonds with up to three years to run until maturity are also considered money market instruments because of their very high level of safety and liquidity. There is no physical location for the money market. It is an artificial market—the computer networks between investment dealers. In Canada, the money market came into existence in March 1935 when the federal government established the Bank of Canada. The money market developed as an important part of the financial markets during 1953–1954 when a number of changes were made to the operation of the Bank of Canada. These changes led to and encouraged the trading of money market instruments between financial institutions. Since that period, the money market has substantially increased in size and the Bank of Canada has maintained its position as the central and most prominent financial institution within the market.

Money Market Instruments

The principal money market security is Government of Canada treasury bills (t-bills). As of July 2002, there were approximately $100 billion of t-bills outstanding. Other types of money market instruments traded are short-term government bonds, commercial paper, bankers' acceptances, and finance company paper. As of May 2002, there were approximately $166 billion of corporate money market securities outstanding. Statistics regarding the value of money market securities outstanding are available at: **www.collection.nlc-bnc.ca/ 100/201/301/weekly_fin_stat/**. These money market securities are discussed individually in the following section.

Treasury Bills

Due to the large quantity of treasury bills outstanding, they occupy a key position in the money market. Treasury bills were originally issued in March 1934, but were rarely traded. As the market evolved and the federal government's need for financing increased, t-bills were issued every week and huge volumes traded in the secondary market. Now, t-bills are auctioned every second Tuesday and previously issued t-bills mature. T-bills are sold by the Bank of Canada, who acts as the federal government's banker. Sales are made to the distributors of Government of Canada securities. The government securities distributors are specified chartered banks, investment dealers, and the Bank of Canada. For a current list of government securities distributors, see the following Web site: **www.bankofcanada.ca/en/auct.htm#rules**.

These distributors purchase the bills through a competitive bidding process. A week before each tender, the Bank of Canada announces the amounts and maturities of the bills to be offered. The value of t-bills auctioned varies by week, but is usually in the $1 to $9 billion range. The maturities offered are those that best meet the federal government's requirement for financing. For a tender announcement, see: **www.bankofcanada.ca/en/cars.htm**.

The distributors submit their bids to the Bank of Canada by computer. The highest bidder receives all of the bills for the maturity for which they bid (subject to limits). Succeeding high bids are then allocated bills. If there are a number of bids at the lowest successful price, then the remainder of the bills are allotted on a *pro rata* basis. The bills are dated the Thursday of the week of the auction and will mature on a Thursday a number of weeks in the future.

An average, high, and low bid are announced together with the corresponding yields. It is usual for bidders to submit several bids at varying prices and amounts in order that at least one bid will be successful. The Bank of Canada usually submits two bids: one for the bills it seeks for its own portfolio and another as a reserve bid to acquire the entire issue. This latter bid has two objectives. First, it will guarantee that the entire issue will be sold, avoiding any embarrassment to the government. Second, it prevents collusion on the part of other bidders to artificially lower the price of the minimum successful bid. The Bank also has the right to refuse all bids and leave the issue of t-bills unsold.

The results of the information released from a t-bill auction is provided at the following Web site: **www.bankofcanada.ca/en/cars.htm**. After the t-bill auction, the government securities distributors begin to sell t-bills to other financial institutions, business organizations, and individuals. The regularity of issue process means that t-bills with maturities ranging from one day to 364 will be outstanding and available to the market. Thus, investors may choose the particular maturity that best coincides with the period of time they wish to invest funds. The yield on the bills sold in the secondary market is less than that received by the distributors. The difference is the return the distributor earns on the t-bill transaction. While t-bill transactions for amounts as low as $5,000 of par value can occur, most secondary market transactions are usually in multiples of $1,000,000.

T-bills are sold on a discount basis at both the auction and the subsequent trading in the secondary market. This means that the price paid for the bill is less than its par value. The yield is the difference between the two amounts. For example, assume a $1,000 par value, 91-day t-bill was purchased for $978. When the t-bill matures (in 91 days), the investor will receive the par value of $1,000. In this case, the return is $22 over the 91 days. In order to determine the percentage return, on a yearly basis, the following formula can be used:

$$V = P \times \left[1 + \frac{i \times n}{365} \right]$$

where:

v = par value of the t-bill which is always assumed to be $1,000
P = price paid
i = yield on t-bills
n = number of days to maturity

For the previous example, the following calculation applies:

$$\$1,000 = \$978 \times \left[1 + \frac{i \times 91}{365} \right]$$

In order to solve this problem, the first step is to multiply the discounted price paid by the figures in the brackets. Doing this, the following result is obtained:

$$\$1,000 = \$978 + \left[\frac{\$978 \times 91 \times i}{365} \right]$$

$$i = 9.02\%$$

Therefore by purchasing and holding this t-bill for the 91 days to maturity, an investor would receive a return of 9.02 percent on a yearly basis.

Rather than the price, the yield may be provided and you must calculate the price to be paid. For example, how much should be paid for a t-bill with 81 days to run to maturity, providing a yield of 8.76 percent? In order to solve this problem, the same formula provided above will be used. In this case P, the amount an investor would pay for this t-bill, would be $983.93.

$$\$1{,}000 = \$P \times \left[1 + \frac{0.0876 \times 81}{365} \right]$$

$$P = \$980.93$$

The auction of t-bills has two purposes. First, the funds raised will be used to repay holders of the maturing series of t-bills. Second, if the dollar amount of t-bills offered is greater than the amount maturing, the funds raised will be used by federal government operations. From March 1980 to February 1996, the weekly t-bill auction also was used to set the **bank rate**, the interest rate the Bank of Canada charges on one-day loans to financial institutions (chartered banks and investment dealers) as the lender of last resort. The procedure used to set the bank rate has significantly changed since 1996.

Now the Bank Rate is based on the **overnight rate**, the average interest rate the Bank of Canada wants financial institutions to use when they lend each other money for one day, or "overnight." The overnight rate is the main tool used by the Bank of Canada to conduct monetary policy. The overnight rate is also the foundation for other interest rates in the economy. When the overnight rate changes, all financial institutions adjust their interest rate for both savings and lending.

The Bank of Canada operates the system to make sure trading in the overnight market stays within its **operating band**. This band, which is one-half of a percentage point wide, always has the overnight rate target at its centre. For example, if the operating band is 4.25 percent to 4.75 percent, the overnight rate target is 4.50 percent. Since financial institutions know that the Bank of Canada will always lend money at the bank rate, which is the rate at the top of the band, and pay interest on deposits at the bottom, it makes no sense for the institutions to trade overnight funds at rates outside the band. The Bank of Canada can also intervene in the overnight market, if the market rate is moving away from the target rate. Through this system, the Bank of Canada controls the level of interest rates prevalent in the economy. Visit the following Web site for further discussion of how the Bank of Canada influences interest rates in Canada: **www.bankofcanada.ca/en/backgrounders/bg-p2.htm**.

Short-Term and Short-Dated Government Bonds

Long-term government bonds that are approaching maturity, known as **short-dated bonds**, are also traded in the money market. Generally, the one- to three-year bonds will have higher yields than treasury bills because of the longer period of time to maturity and thus the greater risk of price fluctuations if interest rates change. There has been a large increase in the use of short-term bonds by the federal government since 1980.

bank rate
The interest rate the Bank of Canada charges on one-day loans to financial institutions (chartered banks and investment dealers) as the lender of last resort.

overnight rate
The average interest rate the Bank of Canada wants financial institutions to use when they lend each other money for one day, or "overnight."

operating band
A band, one-half of a percentage point wide, with the overnight rate at the centre and the bank rate at the top.

short-dated bonds
Long-term government bonds that are approaching maturity.

Commercial Paper

commercial paper
Short-term, unsecured promissory notes issued by corporations; sometimes referred to as corporate paper.

Commercial paper, sometimes referred to as corporate paper, this instrument is short-term, unsecured promissory notes issued primarily by financial and industrial corporations with excellent credit reputations. Corporate paper is usually supported by a stand-by line of credit from a bank or a guarantee from a parent or affiliate company. The paper is sold at a discount to provide a yield at maturity when it is redeemed for its face value. Issued in large denominations, normally not less than $500,000, the maturities can vary from 1 day to 365 days. Most common, however, are maturities of 30, 60, or 90 days.

Finance Company Paper

finance company paper
Short-term secured promissory notes issued by sales finance companies.

Short-term secured promissory notes issued by sales finance companies are known as **finance company paper**. These notes are usually secured by a pledge of installment obligations due to the company in amounts providing a reasonable margin or cushion of protection to the lender. Minimum amounts offered are $50,000 with maturities ranging from 30 to 365 days. To issue finance company paper, the sales finance company purchases installment debt (conditional sales contracts) from retail organizations that deal in consumer durables (e.g., furniture stores). The contracts have been signed by purchasers of these durables. The contracts are then packaged according to maturity. The "packages" are used as collateral for promissory notes issued by the finance companies and sold to financial institutions. These notes are called finance company or "acceptance paper."

Bankers' Acceptances

bankers' acceptances
Created when a chartered bank adds its guarantee of payment to the promissory note of a corporate borrower.

Bankers' acceptances are corporate paper with an additional guarantee. A bankers' acceptance is created when a chartered bank adds its guarantee of payment to the promissory note of a corporate borrower. The borrowing company receives the money from the bank. The bank then sells the bankers' acceptances, through an investment dealer, in the money market. As with most other money market securities, bankers' acceptances are traded on a discount basis to yield the par value. Bankers' acceptances usually trade to yield a rate slightly lower than corporate paper, given the greater security offered by the bank's guarantee. Bankers' acceptances are issued in multiples of $100,000 and have a term of 180 days or less. The usual terms are 30, 60, or 90 days. At maturity, the banker repays the holder the face value and the borrowing company repays the bank.

Bankers' acceptances were introduced in 1962 but were very slow to develop as a method for raising funds. The principal reason was the high "stamping fee" the banks charged in order to add their guarantee to the paper. Beginning in the late 1970s, competition between banks resulted in the stamping fee being reduced to between 0.35 percent and 1.5 percent of the face value of the bankers' acceptance. This resulted in a dramatic increase in the use of this form of short-term financing.

Day Loans

day loans
Made by chartered banks to investment dealers who are major holders of treasury bills.

Day loans are made by chartered banks to investment dealers who are major holders of treasury bills. These loans are not made for any fixed period, but the banks can demand repayment at any time. If the demand is made before noon, repayment must be made by 3:00 p.m. the same day. The dealers pledge their inventories of securities as collateral for the loan. The immediate repayment provision makes these loans the most liquid asset next to cash itself, held by the banks. Therefore, the banks are willing to make day-to-day loans at much lower interest rates than ordinary commercial loans. The day-to-day loan rate is marginally less than the current yield on treasury bills and, hence, the dealers can earn a small profit on the securities they have pledged as collateral. The rate can be adjusted daily.

For this system to work, the investment dealers must be able to pay, within hours, loans totalling millions of dollars. This works because the Bank of Canada has extended special purchase and resale agreements (repos) to these investment dealers. The Bank stands ready to buy treasury bills and short-term government bonds from the dealers, subject to an agreement whereby the dealers must repurchase these securities within a certain period at a price to net the Bank a return equal to the bank rate. While day-to-day loans and repos are not large in terms of amounts outstanding, they are fundamental to the effective operation of the overnight money market. Without these two instruments, the money market would not operate as effectively as it does.

The Eurocurrency Market

Eurocurrency market
The market for short-term bank deposits denominated in U.S. dollars or other easily convertible currencies.

The international equivalent of the domestic money market is called the **Eurocurrency market**. This is a market for short-term loans and deposits denominated in U.S. dollars or other easily convertible currencies. Historically, the Eurocurrency market has been centred in London, but it has evolved into a large, global market. A Eurocurrency deposit arises when funds are deposited in a bank in a currency other than the local currency of the country where the bank is located. For example, if a Canadian corporation deposited Canadian dollars in a London bank, this would create a Eurodollar deposit (a dollar deposit at a bank in Europe). Almost all Eurodeposits are *time deposits*, meaning that the bank promises to repay the deposit, with interest, at a fixed date in the future—say, 6 months.

London Interbank Offered Rate (LIBOR)
The base interest rate on all Eurocurrency loans.

The bank then loans these deposits to creditworthy corporate or government borrowers. The Eurodollar loans are usually unsecured, made in multiples of $1 million, and for between 30 days and one year. The interest rate on Eurocurrency loans is the **London Interbank Offered Rate (LIBOR)**, plus a premium for the risk of the borrower. For example, the borrowing rate may be quoted as LIBOR plus 100. The 100 refers to basis points of interest where 1 basis point is 1/100th of a percent. Therefore, 100 basis points is 1 percent. The LIBOR is the rate on Eurocurrency loans made between banks. This is a floating rate that changes daily. For the current and historic LIBORs see: **www.bba.org.uk/public/libor**.

The Eurocurrency market has grown rapidly, primarily because it is an unregulated, wholesale, and a truly global market that fills the needs of both borrowers and lenders. Those with excess cash are able to make large, short-term, and safe deposits at attractive interest rates. Borrowers are able to arrange large loans quickly, confidentially, and at attractive interest rates.

There are a number of other types of instruments issued in the money market. These include certificates of deposit, foreign exchange swaps, interbank deposits, swapped deposits, bearer deposit notes, provincial and municipal paper, and foreign short-term securities. The money market continually changes and develops, and new instruments appear to fill perceived needs of the market. The items discussed here are those of major importance. They provide an adequate cross-section of money market instruments. An understanding of their features and diversity will go far towards explaining what contributes to the myriad of interest rates in evidence in the Canadian economy.

? Review Questions

6–8   What is the money market, and what is the principal security traded?

6–9   What are treasury bills? Who issues them and why, and how are they issued?

6–10   Money market securities are said to be "sold at a discount." What does this mean? What is the general equation used to determine the price or yield on money market securities?

6–11   What is the bank rate? Overnight rate? Operating band?

6–12   List and briefly discuss the other principal money market securities that trade in Canada.

6–13   What is the Eurocurrency market? What is the London Interbank Offered Rate (LIBOR), and how is it used in the Eurocurrency market?

6.3 Capital Market Securities: Long-Term Debt

There are three major capital market securities: (1) debt with a maturity greater than one year (long-term debt), (2) common shares, and (3) preferred shares. When most people think of financial securities, these are the ones that are top-of-mind. This is the case since these securities, particularly common shares, are very visible. First, they are the subject of a great deal of media attention. Both television and newspapers provide details on a daily basis regarding stock market trading and information on how the common shares of major companies have fared in the day's trading. Second, the majority of adult Canadians are owners of common shares, either directly through purchases on the stock market, or indirectly through pension plans or mutual funds. Events in the capital market have a pronounced impact on many Canadians. The first capital market security, long-term debt, is discussed in this section.

Basic Characteristics of Long-Term Debt

term loan
A borrowing arrangement, usually with a bank, for a certain amount at a stated interest rate for a specific time period.

There are two major types of long-term debt. The first is bank-supplied financing like a term loan. With a **term loan**, a certain amount is borrowed at a stated interest rate for a specific time period. It is similar in nature to a long-term loan made by an individual when purchasing a high-cost item like a car or house. A term loan is usually secured by a fixed asset and is generally not callable by the bank, assuming the borrower makes the regular payment. The interest rate may float with the prime rate or it may be fixed for a stated number of years.

Payments are usually on a monthly basis and consist of both principal and interest. These payments will retire the loan over the amortization period. The remainder of the discussion on long-term debt in this section is on debt securities issued by borrowers, not on term loans from financial institutions like banks.

The second type of long-term debt is that raised in the capital market by both governments and corporations. There are two general categories: bonds and debentures. The major distinction is that a **bond** is secured by a specific asset or assets pledged as collateral. A mortgage on a property is a concept equivalent to a bond. The property is the collateral for the mortgage. A **debenture** is an unsecured loan. The general earnings potential of the issuer is the only backing for the issue. The term bond is often used as the general descriptor for long-term debt. For example, government debt is referred to as bonds. Note though, that governments do not pledge collateral for long-term debt financing so this description is incorrect. Governments issue debentures.

Long-term debt is a contractual liability between the two parties: the borrower (issuer) and the lender (saver). The agreement specifies that the issuer has borrowed a stated amount of money, termed the par value, and promises to repay it in the future under clearly defined terms. Also, while the debt is outstanding, the issuer will pay the investor a stated rate of interest. Long-term debt is usually issued for between 10 and 30 years. The basic par value denomination used is $1,000. For long-term debt, the interest rate is termed the **coupon rate** and it is set at the time of the issue and is constant for the full term of the issue. The coupon rate is quoted on a yearly basis, but is paid semi-annually, or every six months.

bond
A long-term debt security that has a specific asset or assets pledged as collateral.

debenture
An unsecured long-term debt security that is backed by the general earnings potential of the corporation.

long-term debt
A contractual liability between the two parties, the borrower (issuer) and the lender (saver).

coupon rate
The interest rate on a long-term debt issue which is set at the time of the issue and is constant for the full term of the issue.

Example ▼ Today, the federal government issued $850 million of long-term debt with a coupon rate of 7.5 percent and a term of 20 years. This is a debenture that will mature 20 years from today, when the government will repay the holders of the debenture the $850 million. In the meantime, the government will pay the debenture holders interest of 7.5 percent per year. So, for a single $1,000 denomination of debentures, the government will pay $75 of interest each year. Since interest is paid twice a year, not monthly or yearly, investors will receive $37.50 every six months. Six months from today, the first coupon payment will be made. Six months later, on the anniversary of the issue, the second $37.50 is paid. In total, 40 coupon payments will be made. A key fact to remember about long-term debt is that the par value and the coupon rate remain constant for the life of the issue. The par value is always $1,000, and the coupon rate is fixed and ▲ does not change. In this case it will be 7.5 percent for the full 20 years.

Types of Bonds and Debentures

Table 6.4 lists and discusses the characteristics of the various types of long-term debt securities that may be issued by borrowers in Canada. There are two categories of debt securities discussed in the table: traditional and contemporary. Traditional securities include *mortgage bonds, debentures,* and *subordinated debentures.* Contemporary securities include *income bonds, zero-coupon bonds, junk bonds, floating-rate bonds, extendible notes, retractable bonds, convertible bonds,* and *real return bonds.* Note that these are all referred to as bonds, but in many cases they are really debentures since they are unsecured.

TABLE 6.4   Major Types and Characteristics of Long-Term Debt Securities

Type of debt security	Characteristics
Traditional Debt Securities	
Mortgage bonds	Long-term debt financing secured by real estate, buildings, manufacturing facilities, or other fixed assets. Lenders have claim on the proceeds from the sale of mortgaged assets. If the claim is not fully satisfied, the lender becomes a general creditor. The *first-mortgage* claim must be fully satisfied before distribution of proceeds to *second-mortgage* holders, and so on. A number of mortgages can be issued against the same collateral. In the event of bankruptcy, secured debtholders normally receive most of the financing they provided.
Debentures	Unsecured bonds that only creditworthy firms can issue. The lenders' claims are the same as those of any general creditor. May have other unsecured bonds subordinated to them.
Subordinated debentures	Claims are not satisfied until those of the creditors holding senior debts have been fully satisfied. The lender's claim is that of a general creditor but not as good as a senior debt claim.
Contemporary Debt Securities	
Income bonds	Payment of interest is required only when earnings are available. Commonly issued in the reorganization of a failing firm. The lenders claim is that of a general creditor. The "bonds" are not in default when interest payments are missed, because they are contingent only on earnings being available.
Zero (or low) coupon bonds	Issued with no (zero) or a very low coupon rate and sold at a large discount from par. A significant portion (or all) of the investor's return comes from gain in value (i.e., par value minus purchase price).
Junk bonds	Debt rated below investment grade by one of the major debt rating agencies either in Canada or the United States Investment grade debt is BBB or above. Since the 1980s, junk bonds have been regularly used by rapidly growing firms to obtain growth capital or as a way to finance mergers and takeovers. These are high-risk bonds with high yields—typically yielding between 3 percent and 8 percent more than the best-quality corporate debt.
Floating-rate bonds	Stated interest rate is adjusted periodically within stated limits in response to changes in specified money or capital market rates. Popular when future inflation and interest rates are uncertain. Tend to sell at close to par due to the automatic adjustment to changing market conditions. Some issues provide for annual redemption at par at the option of the bondholder.
Extendible bonds (notes)	Short maturities, typically 1 to 5 years, that can be renewed for a similar period at the option of holders. An issue might be a series of 3-year renewable notes over a period of 15 years. Every 3 years, the holders could extend the notes for another 3 years, at a new rate competitive with market interest rates at the time of renewal.
Retractable bonds	Gives the bondholder the option to sell the bond back to the company at par ($1,000) either on a specific date, and every 1 to 5 years thereafter, or if the firm is acquired, acquires another company, or issues a large amount of additional debt. In return for the retraction privilege, the bond's yield is lower than that of a non-retractable bond.
Real return bonds (RRB)	Bonds that adjust the semi-annual coupon payments and the par value for inflation. This feature ensures that investors' purchasing power is maintained regardless of the future rate of inflation. The coupon payment on RRB is based on the inflation-adjusted principal and, at maturity, the principal is repaid in inflation-adjusted dollars. Real return bonds are primarily issued by governments but were used to finance the construction of two major mega-projects: the 108 kilometre 407 Express Toll Route which connects major centres in the greater Toronto area, and the 12.9 kilometre Confederation Bridge between New Brunswick and Prince Edward Island.
Convertible bonds	A bond that at the option of the holder can be converted into a predetermined number of common shares of the issuer on a specified date. There may be multiple opportunities to convert. Convertible bonds are termed a hybrid security since the holder receives guaranteed coupon payments but also benefits if the company's share price increases. The coupon rate on convertibles is lower than on regular bonds but offers the opportunity of a large gain if the company's common share price increases.

In recent years, changing market conditions and investor preferences have spurred innovations in debt financing. Designing new financial securities or processes is referred to as **financial engineering**. Investment dealers, who underwrite the risks of financing for issuers, are usually responsible for these innovations. Successful financial engineering reduces the costs of financing and minimizes taxes, while meeting market needs and all regulatory requirements. Financial engineering in the long-term debt market will likely continue into the future.

financial engineering
Designing new financial securities or processes due to changing market conditions and investor preferences.

Trust Indenture

trust indenture
The legal document that details the contractual relationship between the borrower and lender.

trustee
A third party who acts on behalf of the purchasers of the debt securities.

The **trust indenture** or deed is the legal document that details the contractual relationship between the borrower and lender. It is a very long and complex document. The indenture specifies a **trustee** who acts as a third party on behalf of the purchasers of the debt securities. The trustee is usually a commercial trust company, with most of these companies now being divisions of the chartered banks. The trustee is paid to act as a watchdog on behalf of the debtholders and is empowered to take action if the terms of the indenture are violated.

The trustee ensures that the issuer does not default on its contractual obligations to the debtholders. The indenture specifies the rights of the debtholders and the duties of the issuer. Included in the indenture are all financial information regarding the issue and the issuer, a description of any collateral pledged, restrictive covenants on the operation of the company, call provision (redemption clause), and, possibly, a sinking fund provision.

Financial Information

Obviously, all financial information regarding the issue such as the amount of funding raised, the coupon rate, the maturity date, and the firm's plans for the money would be included in the information provided to investors. In addition, all financial statements and certain key ratios of the issuer would be included in the document.

Collateral

The indenture will include a detailed description of the collateral pledged for a bond issue. For example, if a manufacturing plant was used as collateral, all details of the plant, its location, and the equipment and materials inside that plant will be provided. If the company defaulted on the loan, the lenders of the funds would know exactly what the collateral was and where it was located. Usually, the disposition of the collateral in various circumstances is specified.

Restrictive Covenants

restrictive covenants
Contractual clauses that place operating and financial constraints on the borrower.

Trust indentures normally include certain **restrictive covenants**—contractual clauses that place operating and financial constraints on the borrower. Restrictive covenants, coupled with standard debt provisions, help protect bondholders against increases in borrower risk. Without these provisions, the borrower could increase the firm's risk but not have to pay an increased return (interest). The most common restrictive covenants are:

1. Require that the borrower *maintain minimum ratio positions*, particularly regarding liquidity, leverage, and profitability. These requirements ensure against loan default and the ultimate failure of the company.
2. *Prohibit borrowers from selling accounts receivable* to generate cash. Doing so could cause a long-run cash shortage if proceeds are used to meet current obligations.
3. Impose *restrictions on the purchase and sale of fixed assets* by the borrower. The sale of fixed assets could damage the firm's ability to repay the bonds. The purchase of fixed assets may lead to excess levels of unproductive assets or of capital.
4. *Constrain subsequent borrowing.* Additional long-term debt may be prohibited, or additional borrowing may be subordinated to the original loan. **Subordination** means that subsequent creditors agree to wait until all claims of the *senior debt* are satisfied.
5. *Limit the firm's annual cash dividend payments* to a specified percentage or amount or restrict payment if the firm does not meet a certain profit level.
6. *Protect against a reduction in value of collateral pledged* against the debt issue. The protection of bond collateral is crucial to increase the safety of a bond issue.

subordination
A stipulation that subsequent creditors agree to wait until all claims of the *senior debt* are satisfied.

Other restrictive covenants may sometimes be included in bond indentures. All restrictive covenants are intended to protect bondholders' funds against increased risk. The violation of any provision by the borrower gives the bondholders the right to demand immediate repayment of the debt. Generally, the trustee, acting for the bondholders, will evaluate any violation to determine whether it is serious enough to jeopardize the loan. The bondholders may then decide to demand immediate repayment, continue the loan, or alter the terms of the bond indenture.

Call Feature

call price (bond)
The stated price at which bonds may be repurchased prior to maturity by using the call feature.

call premium
The amount by which the call price exceeds the bond's par value.

This provision is included in almost all long-term debt issues. It gives the issuer the opportunity to repurchase bonds prior to maturity. The **call price** is the stated price at which bonds may be repurchased prior to maturity. Sometimes the call feature can be exercised only during a certain period. The call price is always par plus a **call premium**, the amount by which the call price exceeds the bond's par value, that is quoted as a percent of par. For example, if the call premium were 4 percent, the call price would be $1,040 ($1,000 + 4% × $1,000). The premium compensates bondholders for having the bond called away from them, and it is the cost to the issuer of calling the bonds.

The call feature enables the issuer to retire outstanding debt prior to maturity. Thus, when interest rates fall, an issuer can call an outstanding bond and reissue a new bond at a lower interest rate. When interest rates rise, the call privilege will not be exercised—it would not make financial sense. Of course, to sell a callable bond, the issuer must pay a higher interest rate than on non-callable bonds of equal risk to compensate bondholders for the risk of having the bonds called away from them.

Sinking-Fund Requirements

sinking-fund requirement
A provision providing for the systematic retirement of long-term debt prior to maturity.

An additional restrictive provision often included in a bond indenture is a **sinking-fund requirement**. Its objective is to provide for the systematic retirement of long-term debt prior to maturity. To carry out this requirement, the corporation makes semi-annual or annual payments to a *trustee*, who uses these funds to purchase and retire bonds. For a sinking fund, the company only has to pay a maximum of the par value of the bonds purchased.

The sinking fund is exercised in one of two ways: either in the open market or called through a lottery process. The company purchases in the open market when the market price of the debt is less than the par value at the time that the sinking fund must be exercised. The bonds would be repurchased using the lottery system when the market price is higher than the par of $1,000.

Bond Ratings

A bond rating is an independent and objective assessment of the investment quality of a long-term debt issue. A rating is a basic measure of the default risk of the issuer and the issue. Rating agencies judge the default risk of the borrower. There is one major debt rating agency in Canada, the Dominion Bond Rating Service (DBRS), and three in the United States: Standard & Poor's (S&P), Moody's, and Fitch Ratings. The issuer, either a government or corporate borrower, pays one or more of the bond rating services to provide a rating for their debt issue. The debt rating agency rates the issue and provides on-going coverage for the complete term of the issue. Debt issuers pay the agencies for a bond rating in order to send a message to the market of the quality of their issue.

The rating assigned to an issue is based on both quantitative and qualitative factors. For quantitative factors, a comprehensive financial profile of the company is completed. Financial ratio and cash flow analyses are used to assess the likely payment of interest and principal. For long-tem debt, all categories of ratios are important; but, the leverage and profitability ratios may be the most important categories. Qualitative factors include items such as the record and quality of management, future developments in the industry, market potential, nature and diversification of product lines, changes in the government regulations, social changes, and the company's market share, expansion record, accounting policies, and level of development in comparison to competitors. Quantitative factors may be at least as important as quantitative analysis in rating a debt security. Table 6.5 provides the rating system used by DBRS.

For DBRS, the top rating is AAA and the ratings decline to C. There are 16 possible ratings. In the AA, A, and BBB categories there are three ratings. For example, a bond could be rated AA (high), AA, which implies average, and AA (low). There are no qualifiers associated with the top rating, AAA, so the total number of ratings in these four categories is 10. The remaining categories add 5 more ratings. The default rating makes a total of 16 ratings.

The higher the rating, the lower the risk; the lower the risk, the lower the required yield. So at the time of issue, a AAA-rated bond, of a given maturity, would have the lowest coupon rate, and the bond would trade in the market at the lowest yields. This is the basic risk–return tradeoff. The lower the risk the investor takes as measured by a bond rating, the lower the expected return. In all developed countries the federal government is the least risky borrower.

TABLE 6.5	The Long-Term Debt Rating Scale Used by the Dominion Bond Rating Service[a]

Rating	Brief description[b]
AAA	Highest credit quality
AA	Superior credit quality
A	Satisfactory credit quality
BBB	Adequate credit quality
BB	Speculative
B	Highly speculative
CCC	Very highly speculative
CC	Very highly speculative
C	Very highly speculative
D	Bonds in default of either interest or principal

[a]Note that "high" and "low" qualifiers are used to indicate the relative standing of a credit within a particular rating category. The lack of one of these designations indicates a rating which is essentially in the middle of the category. The high and low qualifiers are not used for the AAA category or for ratings under BBB.

[b]For a more detailed description, see DBRS's Web site at the address provided below.

SOURCE: Dominion Bond Rating Service Limited; and Web site, **www.dbrs.com/web/jsp/pub_ratingscale_bond.jsp.**

Therefore, the federal government will pay the lowest coupon rate on a new debt issue and federal government debt will trade at the lowest yields. All other borrowers (both government and corporate) pay some premium over the federal government rate. The premium is measured in a certain number of basis points. A basis point is 1/100 of a percent, so 50 basis points is 0.50 percent.

Maintaining a rating of BBB or above is vital for issuers of long-term debt. This is the case since institutional investors, particularly life insurance companies and pension plans, are restricted, by law, from investing in debt with less than a BBB rating. So a bond or debenture rated BBB (low) could be purchased by a pension plan or life insurance company, but if it were rated BB (high) it could not. Most mutual funds also adhere to this rule. A debt security with a rating less than BBB is referred to as a junk bond. A junk bond is a long-term debt security of low quality expected to provide a high rate of return. Based on the risk–return tradeoff, however, the higher the return, the greater the default risk.

Bond rating agencies continually review the companies which they rate and ratings of outstanding issues are often either downgraded or upgraded. The change in rating can be quite large or quite small, but most often it is one or two rating notches. For example, a downgrade from AA (high) to AA is a one rating notch downgrade. A change in rating from AA (high) to AA (low) is a two rating notch downgrade. If a rating is downgraded, it is because the risk of the issue has increased and the price of the debt issue will decline. Downgrades lead to decreasing prices for the long-term debt issue, while the reverse is true for upgrades.

Note, however, that immediately after a change in ratings, the organization issuing the debt is unaffected. Investors are affected since the price of all of the organization's outstanding financial securities will change. The organization is only affected when they issue new debt securities. A downgrade will result in higher interest rates being required on new loans, while an upgrade will result in lower interest rates on new issues of debt securities.

Setting Coupon Rates

As discussed earlier, the coupon rate on a long-term debt issue is set at the time of the issue and is constant for the term of the issue. The coupon rate is based on two factors. The first is the floor rate. The **floor rate** for debt of any maturity is the yield provided on federal government debt. The federal government is the least risky issuer of long-term debt securities in any developed economy. At any point in time, the federal government will have debt outstanding for very short to very long maturities. To set the coupon rate on a 20-year debenture issue, for example, the beginning point is to determine the yield on 20-year government of Canada debt. Bond prices and yields are available from newspapers, financial intermediaries, such as investment dealers, and on the Internet.

> **floor rate**
> The yield on federal government debt for any maturity.

Figure 6.3 is an excerpt from the July 13, 2002 issue of the *National Post* providing bond quotations for a variety of issuers. The first column is the issuer, the second the coupon rate on the issue, the third the maturity date by month, day, and year, the fourth is the price as a percent of par, and the last is the yield based on the previous items. (The process used to calculate yield is covered in Chapter 8.) Consider the second highlighted issue for the federal government. The issue carries a coupon rate of 9.25 percent, matures in about 20 years from the date of the quote, is trading for 141.98 percent of par, or $1,419.80 per $1,000 of par, and provides a yield of 5.69 percent. On July 12, 2002 in Canada, this was the floor rate for 20-year debt, the rate acceptable to savers. This type of information can also be seen at the following two Web sites: **www.bloomberg.com/markets/canada.html** or **www.bankofcanada.ca/en/bonds.htm**.

For any issuer other than the federal government, the coupon rate on a 20-year debt issue will be more than 5.69 percent. The additional return is based on the second factor determining coupon rates: the risk premium. The **risk premium** is the additional coupon investors will demand based on the risk of the issuer and of the debt issue. Issuer risk is based on a bond rating while issue risk is based on the specifics of the debt issue. The market will rationally evaluate both aspects and demand an appropriate premium. As an example, consider the highlighted bond issues for the Province of British Columbia and of Nova Scotia in Figure 6.3. Both of these mature in about 20 years from the date of the quote. The respective yields on 20-year debt are 6.11 percent and 6.25 percent. Since the features of all government debt issues are essentially identical, the different yields are based on debt ratings.

> **risk premium**
> The additional coupon investors will demand based on the risk of the issuer and of the debt issue.

The floor rate for 20-year debt is 5.69 percent. The Province of B.C. is rated AA by DBRS so the risk is slightly higher than for the federal government. The risk premium is 0.42 percent, or 42 basis points. Nova Scotia is rated BBB, meaning higher risk. The risk premium is 56 basis points. The coupon for corporate issuers will be greater. This is clear from looking at the difference in yields between the first highlighted federal government issue, the one that matures on June 1, 2011, and the highlighted issues for Bell Canada, Royal Bank, and Thomson Corp. All four issues mature in about nine years from the date of the quote; however, the yields are very different. The risk premiums are 165, 117, and

Selected Bond Quotations for July 12, 2002

Federal	Coupon	Mat. date	Bid	Yld %
Canada	9.500	Oct. 01/03	107.31	3.28
Canada	10.250	Feb. 01/04	110.17	3.43
Canada	10.500	Oct. 01/04	114.11	3.78
Canada	12.000	Mar. 01/05	119.17	4.02
Canada	12.250	Sept. 01/05	123.35	4.20
Canada	14.000	Oct. 01/06	135.85	4.54
Canada	4.500	Sept. 01/07	98.96	4.73
Canada	11.750	Oct. 01/08	135.84	4.97
Canada	10.750	Oct. 01/09	133.52	5.13
Canada	8.750	Oct. 01/10	123.26	5.23
Canada	6.000	June 01/11	105.07	5.28
Canada	11.250	June 01/15	153.93	5.39
Canada	9.250	June 01/22	141.98	5.69
Canada	9.000	June 01/25	140.62	5.78
Provincial				
BC	8.000	Aug. 23/05	110.64	4.30
BC	5.250	Dec. 01/06	102.14	4.70
BC	8.750	Aug. 19/22	130.32	6.11
Nova Scotia	7.250	Oct. 11/06	109.75	4.68
Nova Scotia	6.400	Sept. 01/10	105.44	5.56
Nova Scotia	9.600	Jan. 30/22	137.51	6.25
Ontario	9.000	Sept. 15/04	110.62	3.83
Ontario	6.125	Sept. 12/07	105.56	4.89
Ontario	9.500	Jul. 13/22	139.86	6.04
Corporate				
Air Canada	6.750	Feb. 02/04	89.00	14.98
Bell	6.900	Dec. 15/11	99.81	6.93
Bombardier	6.600	Nov. 29/04	103.32	5.09
CIBC	7.000	Oct. 23/06	107.40	5.05
Ford Can	6.000	Mar. 08/04	101.50	5.03
IBM Can	5.810	Aug. 07/03	102.07	3.79
Loblaw	7.100	May 11/10	108.16	5.79
Rogers	8.750	Jul. 15/07	88.00	12.01
Royal Bank	7.183	Jun. 30/11	104.95	6.45
Shaw Cable	7.400	Oct. 17/07	93.69	8.93
Suncor	6.700	Aug. 22/11	102.90	6.28
TD Bank	6.550	Jul. 31/07	105.57	5.28
Thomson	6.850	Jun. 01/11	103.64	6.31

SOURCE: *The Financial Post*, July 13, 2002.

103 basis points, respectively. Obviously, the debt issues of even large, very secure corporations carry much higher levels of default risk than the federal government.

International Bond Issues

Companies and governments borrow internationally using Eurobonds and foreign bonds. Both of these provide creditworthy borrowers the opportunity to obtain large amounts of long-term debt financing quickly, in their choice of currency, with flexible repayment terms, and with less regulation. A **Eurobond** is issued by an international borrower in a currency other than that of the country in which it is sold. For example, a Canadian company could sell a Eurobond denominated in Japanese yen in Germany. From the founding of the Eurobond

Eurobond
Long-term debt issued by an international borrower in a currency other than that of the country in which it is sold.

market in the 1960s until the mid-1980s, "blue chip" U.S. corporations were the largest single class of Eurobond issuers. Many of these companies were able to borrow in this market at interest rates below those paid by the U.S. government.

As the market matured, issuers were able to choose the currency in which they borrowed, and European, Canadian, and Japanese borrowers became major participants. In recent years, the Eurobond market has become much more balanced in terms of the mix of borrowers, total issue volume, and currency of denomination. Only large, internationally known, very secure companies can issue Eurobonds. For such companies the use of Eurobonds can result in significantly lower debt costs. The Canadian dollar segment of the Eurobond market is relatively small.

foreign bond
Long-term debt issued in a country's financial market, in that country's currency, by a foreign borrower.

A **foreign bond** is issued in a country's financial market, in that country's currency, by a foreign borrower. A yen-denominated bond issued in Japan by a Canadian company is an example of a foreign bond. The largest foreign bond market is in the United States. Most foreign bonds issued by Canadian companies are issued in U.S. dollars in the United States. The federal and provincial governments and corporations with high sales in the United States are major issuers of U.S. foreign bonds.

? Review Questions

6–14   What is the difference between a term loan and long-term debt? What is the difference between a bond and debenture?

6–15   What are the basic characteristics of long-term debt financing?

6–16   List and briefly describe the various types of bonds and debentures.

6–17   What is the trust indenture, and what provisions are usually included in the document? What role does the trustee play for a long-term debt issue?

6–18   What is a bond rating and what role does it have for a debt issue? Who are the major bond rating agencies in North America?

6–19   What is a high rating, and what is the benefit of having a high rating for an issuer? What happens when a organization's debt is downgraded?

6–20   How are coupon rates set on new debt issues? Why is the floor rate an important concept in this process?

6–21   What are the basic characteristics of and differences between Eurobonds and foreign bonds?

6.4 Capital Market Securities: Common and Preferred Shares

The previous section examined the first capital market security: long-term debt. This section discusses the two remaining capital market securities: common shares and preferred shares. Common shares signify ownership of the company. All corporations must issue common shares and be owned by shareholders. The sale also raises equity capital. Some firms may later issue a second class of equity, preferred shares, to raise additional equity capital. Although both common and preferred shares are forms of equity capital, the characteristics of preferred shares make them more similar to debt than common equity. Here we consider the key features and behaviours of both common and preferred shares.

Common Shares

Common shareholders, the owners of corporations, are sometimes referred to as residual owners. They have no guarantee of receiving any cash inflows, but receive what is left—the residual—after all other claims on the firm's income and assets have been satisfied. They are assured of only one thing: that they cannot lose any more than they have invested in the firm. This important feature of common equity is referred to as **limited liability**. As a result of their generally uncertain position, common shareholders expect to be compensated with adequate dividends and, ultimately, capital gains. The fundamental characteristics of common shares are discussed below.

Ownership

The common shares of a firm can be **privately owned** by a single individual, **closely owned** by a small group of investors (such as a family), or **publicly owned** by a broad group of unrelated individual or institutional investors. Typically, small corporations are privately owned, and if their shares are traded, this occurs infrequently and in small amounts. Large corporations, which are emphasized in the following discussions, are publicly owned, and their shares are generally actively traded on a stock exchange.

Preemptive Rights

The **preemptive right** allows common shareholders to maintain their proportionate ownership in the corporation when new shares are issued. The preemptive right allows existing shareholders to maintain the same percentage of the vote and protect against the dilution of their ownership. **Dilution of ownership** usually results in the dilution of earnings, because each present shareholder has a claim on a *smaller* part of the firm's earnings than previously.

Example ▼ Johnson's Electronics' earnings available for common shareholders (EAC) for the fiscal year ended July 31, 2003 was $35,250,000. The company has 14.1 million common shares outstanding. Therefore, the company's EPS was $2.50. If on July 2, 2003, Johnson's sold an additional 3 million shares for $34.50 each, does a dilution of earnings occur? With the sale of shares, Johnson's would have 17.1 million common shares outstanding as of July 31, 2003, rather than 14.1 million. Now EPS would be $2.06, resulting in earnings dilution of $0.44 per share. ▲

With a *rights offering*, the firm grants **rights** to its shareholders. These financial instruments permit shareholders to purchase additional shares at a stated price, below the market price, in direct proportion to their number of owned shares. Rights are primarily used by smaller corporations whose shares are either *closely owned* or *publicly owned* and not actively traded. In these situations, rights are an important financing tool without which shareholders would run the risk of losing their proportionate control of the corporation and share of the profits. Rights are tradeable in the same market that trades the underlying common shares but are very short-term in nature, usually outstanding for less than 30 days. From the firm's viewpoint, the use of rights offerings to raise new

limited liability
A feature of common equity meaning that investors cannot lose more than they have invested in the firm.

privately owned (company)
All common shares of a firm are owned by a single individual.

closely owned (company)
All common shares of a firm are owned by a small group of investors (such as a family).

publicly owned (company)
Common shares of a firm are owned by a broad group of unrelated individual or institutional investors.

preemptive right
Allows common shareholders to maintain their proportionate ownership in the corporation when new shares are issued.

dilution of ownership
Occurs when a new share issue results in each present shareholder having a claim on a smaller part of the firm's earnings than previously.

rights
Financial instruments that permit shareholders to purchase additional shares at a price below the market price, in direct proportion to their number of owned shares.

equity capital may be less costly and generate more interest than a public offering of shares.

Authorized, Outstanding, and Issued Shares

A company's *articles of incorporation* define the type and number of common shares it may issue. Most large companies and all publicly traded companies in Canada are incorporated under the *Canada Business Corporation Act*. Under the Act, companies must issue common shares *without* a par value. In the *articles of incorporation*, a company may be authorized to issue a certain number of common shares and/or a certain value of common share. Or, the company could be authorized to issue an unlimited number of common shares. If a limited number or value of shares is authorized, and the company later realizes that more shares must be issued, the company must obtain approval from shareholders to amend the articles of incorporation. On the balance sheet, common shares are valued at the price sold. For example, if a company sold 240,000 common shares to investors for $10 per share, the common share account on the balance sheet would increase by $2,400,000 (240,000 common shares × $10).

Authorized shares become issued and outstanding when they are sold to investors. If the firm repurchases any of their outstanding shares, these shares are deducted from shareholders' equity on the balance sheet. A company repurchases common shares from investors when they feel their common shares are undervalued in the market. The company must obtain approval from the stock exchange that lists the shares (the TSX, in Canada) for the repurchase. When the shares are repurchased, they are cancelled by the company and the number of issued and outstanding shares fall. The amount paid by the company when repurchasing is first deducted from the value of common shares, but if the amount paid is more than the proceeds received when the shares were originally sold, the excess is deducted from retained earnings.

Example ▼ Golden Enterprise, a producer of medical pumps, is authorized to issue 35 million common shares. The company sold 15 million shares in 1991 for $8.50 per share. On October 29, 2002, Golden repurchased 1 million common shares on the TSX, paying $19.25 per share, and then cancelled the shares. What impact will the repurchase have on the company's shareholders' equity accounts? On June 29, 2002, how many shares of additional common shares can Golden sell without gaining approval from its shareholders?

The firm has 35 million authorized shares, 15 million issued shares, and 1 million repurchased and cancelled shares. Thus, 14 million shares are outstanding (15 million issued shares – 1 million repurchased shares), and Golden can issue 21 million additional shares (35 million authorized shares – 14 million outstanding shares) without seeking shareholder approval. This total includes the repurchased shares since these were cancelled.

For the dollar impact of the repurchase, consider that the repurchased shares were originally sold for $8,500,000 (1 million shares × $8.50) and the shares were repurchased for $19,250,000 (1 million shares × $19.25). Of this amount, $8,500,000 would be deducted from the value of the common shares while the difference, $10,750,000, would be deducted from retained earnings on Golden's balance sheet. But if the company was correct and the share subsequently increased in price to $30 per share, Golden can reissue 1 million shares and essentially make money on the transaction.

Voting Rights

Generally, each common share entitles the holder to one vote at the company's annual meeting of shareholders, where the board of directors is elected and other matters voted upon, and on special issues like a takeover offer. In recent years, many firms have issued another class of common shares with different voting rights. The issuance of different classes of shares has been frequently used when the individuals who founded the corporation wish to raise capital through the sale of common shares but do not want to give up control.

non-voting common shares
Common shares that carry no right to vote on issues affecting the company.

subordinate voting common shares
Common shares that carry a right to vote on issues affecting the company but the vote is inferior to the votes of other shares.

superior voting shares
Common shares that carry superior voting privileges to other common shares.

The original owners could issue either **non-voting common shares** or **subordinate voting common shares** while they hold a much smaller number of **superior voting shares**. In this way, the original owners of the corporation may own a minority of the total number of common shares outstanding and have provided a small fraction of the total funds provided from the sale of common shares, *but* they fully control the affairs of the company through the superior voting privileges. When different classes of common shares are issued on the basis of unequal voting rights, there is no general convention regarding the designation of the voting and non-voting or restricted voting common shares. In some cases, the shares are designated as class A or B, with either being the superior voting shares. In other cases, a designation is not used. But in all cases, a bit of background reading will make it clear which class carries the superior voting privileges.

coattail provision
In the event of a takeover offer for the company, this provision allows the holders of the non-voting or restricted voting shares the right to convert their shares into an equal number of the superior voting shares.

In most cases, the superiority of the voting shares is limited to the vote. Both classes of shares are entitled to receive the same dividend (in some cases the subordinate shares may receive a higher dividend) and share on a *pro rata* basis in the event of the company's liquidation. As well, in the event of a takeover offer for the company, the **coattail provision** gives the holders of the non-voting or restricted voting shares the right to convert their shares into an equal number of the superior voting shares. The coattail provision is vital to protect the interests of the subordinate voting shares in the event of a takeover offer for the company. Since in a takeover the number of votes decides the outcome, the possibility exists that a small number of superior voting shares could be acquired by the bidder at a large premium to their current value. This would allow the bidder to acquire the majority of the votes in the company while ignoring the interests of the large majority of the common shareholders. Such an event would not be fair, so in all cases where two classes of shares are outstanding a coattail provision exists.[1]

proxy statement
A statement giving the votes of a shareholder to another party.

Because most small shareholders do not attend the annual meeting to vote, they may sign a **proxy statement** giving their votes to another party. The solicitation of the proxies from shareholders is closely controlled by regulatory bodies to protect against proxies being solicited on the basis of misleading information. Existing management generally receives the shareholders' proxies, because it is able to solicit them at company expense. Occasionally, when the firm is widely

---

1. The dual-class common share structure is widespread among Canadian publicly traded corporations and is a complicating issue for corporate governance and valuation issues. See the following papers for discussion: C. Robinson, J. Rumsey, and A. White (1996), "Market Efficiently in the Valuation of Corporate Control: Evidence from Dual Class Equity," *Canadian Journal of Administrative Sciences*, 13, 251–263, and B. Smith and B. Amoako-Adu (1995), "Relative Prices of Dual Class Shares," *Journal of Financial and Quantitative Analysis*, 30, 223–239.

IN PRACTICE

Benefits of Two Classes

One of the key characteristics of common shares is that one share equals one vote. Therefore, a shareholder owning 50,000 common shares of a company where 1 million common shares are outstanding owns 5 percent of the company and is entitled to 5 percent of the votes. (This shareholder is also entitled to 5 percent of the earnings available for common shareholders.) In Canada, however, there are a large number of companies with two classes of common shares: one class with superior voting privileges, one with subordinate. For the company's founders, this situation is highly attractive. By selling subordinate voting shares, the founders enjoy the advantage of raising financing using common shares without the disadvantage of losing control.

For example, Bombardier, a company based in Montreal with operations around the world, is a leading manufacturer of aircraft, rail transportation equipment, and motorized recreational products. For the fiscal year ended January 31, 2002, the company had sales of over $21.6 billion and assets of $27.8 billion. The company has two classes of common shares. As of January 31, 2002, there were 342.4 million Class A shares and over 1 billion class B shares outstanding. The total capital provided by the class A shareholders was $47.4 million; the B provided $849

million. The A shares have 10 votes each; the B, one. For the common shares in total, there was a total of 4,453,234,222 votes. The Bombardier family, the offspring of Armand Bombardier, the company's founder, owned 81.9 percent or 280.4 million class A shares. Therefore, the Bombardiers owned 20.4 percent of total number of shares but had 63% of the votes, while only providing 4.3% of the common share financing.

The opportunity to be able to sell subordinate voting shares has greatly benefited the Bombardier family. They have been able to retain majority control of the company while providing a minority of the common equity financing. The Bombardier family members, however, have not been the only ones to benefit from this arrangement—the subordinate shareholders have also profited. Consider that on January 31, 1993, the subordinate shares were trading on the TSX for $1.45 per share. During the 2002 fiscal year, the shares traded as high as $24.65 (implying an annual gain of 37 percent) and closed the fiscal year at $14.70 (an annualized gain of 29.4 percent). Obviously, allowing the founding owners control can benefit all shareholders.

REFERENCES: Bombardier, Inc., *2002 Annual Report and Management Proxy Circular*, May 3, 2002.

---

proxy battle
The attempt by a non-management group to gain control of the management of a firm by soliciting a sufficient number of proxy votes.

owned, outsiders may wage a **proxy battle** to unseat the existing management and gain control. To win a corporate election, a simple majority of the shares voted, 50 percent plus 1, is all that is required. However, the odds of a non-management group winning a proxy battle are generally slim.

Dividends

The payment of dividends is at the discretion of the board of directors, and the large majority of companies listed on the TSX do not pay dividends on common shares. Those that do, normally pay dividends quarterly. For example, on July 23, 2002, the board of the Bank of Montreal declared a quarterly dividend of $0.30 on their common shares payable on August 29. This dividend indicated that the annual dividend paid by the Bank was $1.20 per share. Once the dividend is declared by the board, the company is legally obliged to pay it. Dividends may be paid in cash or additional common shares. Cash dividends are the most common.

Common shareholders are not promised a dividend, but once a company starts to pay dividends, shareholders come to expect certain payments based on the historical payment pattern. The board, however, can increase, decrease, or completely eliminate the dividend at any time. Before dividends are paid to common shareholders, the claims of the government, all creditors, and preferred shareholders must be satisfied. Because of the importance of the dividend decision to the growth and valuation of the firm, detailed discussion of the dividends is included in Chapter 11.

International Share Issues

international equity market
A vibrant equity market that emerged in the past 20 years to allow corporations to sell blocks of shares in several different countries simultaneously.

Although the international market for common shares is not as large as the international market for debt securities, a vibrant **international equity market** has emerged in the past 20 years. Much of this increase is due to a growing desire on the part of investors to diversify their investment portfolios internationally. Many corporations have discovered that they can sell blocks of shares to investors in a number of different countries simultaneously.

For example, many large Canadian multinational companies have listed their shares on multiple stock markets. The New York, Nasdaq, London, Frankfurt, and Tokyo markets are the most popular. Some of the better known Canadian companies that have done this include BCE, Alcan, the Big 5 banks, Canadian Natural Resources, Research in Motion, Barrick Gold, Celestica, Petro-Canada, Magna International, Quebecor World, ATI Technologies, and Fairmont Hotels & Resorts.

Issuing shares internationally broadens the ownership base and helps a company integrate itself into the local business scene. It also enables corporations to raise far larger amounts of capital than they could have raised in any single national market. A listing on a foreign stock exchange both increases local business press coverage and serves as effective corporate advertising. Having locally traded shares can also facilitate corporate acquisitions because shares can be used as an acceptable method of payment. International equity sales have also proven to be indispensable to governments that have sold state-owned companies to private investors in recent years.

American Depository Receipts (ADRs)
Claims issued by U.S. banks that represent ownership of a foreign company's common shares held by the bank in the foreign market.

American Depository Receipts (ADRs) have become a popular way for foreign companies to tap the North American capital market. ADRs are issued by U.S. banks and represent ownership of a foreign company's common shares held by the bank in the foreign market. Because ADRs are issued in U.S. dollars, they often trade at prices very different from what the common shares of the underlying company trade for in the home market. ADRs give investors the opportunity to diversify their portfolios internationally. Additional information regarding ADRs is provided at the following Web site: **invest-faq.com/articles/stock-adrs.html**. A complete listing of all ADRs available for companies around the world is available at the following Web site: **www.site-by-site.com/adr/toc.htm**.

preferred equity
The third major source of long-term financing for corporations that broadens the firm's capital structure, raising financing without giving up ownership or incurring obligations.

Preferred Shares

Preferred equity is the third major source of long-term financing for corporations. In general, preferred equity broadens the firm's capital structure, raising financing without giving up ownership (like common stock) or incurring obligations (like debt), thus reducing the risk of the company. Preferred equity is a second class of equity that is preferred in terms of the payment of dividends and at the dissolution of the corporation. The firm must pay preferred dividends prior to common, and preferred shareholders receive payments prior to common shareholders at liquidation. Each preferred share issue is unique and creates a new preferred share series. Some companies who rely on preferred share financing have 10 or more different series of preferred shares outstanding. For example, the Canadian Imperial Bank of Commerce (CIBC) lists 14 different preferred share issues on their Web site: **www.cibc.com/solution/service/pers/about_cibc/investor_relations_main.jsp**. The fundamental characteristics of preferred shares are discussed below.

Stated Values and Dividends

stated value
The value of the preferred share on the issue date.

Preferred shares are issued with a **stated value**, which is the value of the preferred share on the issue date. The usual stated values are $10, $20, $25, $50, or $100, with $25 being the most common. Preferred shareholders receive a dividend that is based on the stated value and is constant for as long as the preferred share issue is outstanding. For example, CIBC has a Series 17 preferred share outstanding with a stated value of $25 paying a dividend of $1.3625. If the dividend in dollars is known, the dividend in percent can be calculated. The dividend in percent is equal to the dollar dividend divided by the stated value, in this case $1.3625 divided by $25. The dividend percentage is 5.45 percent. Dividends are quoted yearly but paid quarterly. For the CIBC example, the yearly dividend is $1.3625 and this is paid quarterly, so the holder of the preferred share would receive $0.340625 per share every three months.

There is no guarantee the investor will receive preferred share dividends. As with common shares, the payment of dividends is at the discretion of the board. If a company fails to pay the dividends, preferred shareholders do not have the ability to put the firm into bankruptcy. Alleviating that problem is the **cumulative feature** associated with preferred shares. If a company misses a dividend payment, dividends are said to be in arrears. In this case, the dividends accumulate; the company would owe two dividend payments the following quarter. Referring to the CIBC example, if CIBC failed to pay the dividend one quarter, then on the next quarterly dividend date, they would be required to make a dividend payment of $0.68125. This payment would have to be made before the company could pay common share dividends.

cumulative feature
Missed dividend payments on preferred shares accumulate, meaning that dividends in arrears must be paid with the current dividend prior to the payment of dividends to common shareholders.

In theory this seems to be a positive aspect that minimizes the non-guarantee of dividend payments for preferred shareholders. In reality, however, if a company misses a preferred dividend payment the message being sent to the market is that the firm is having major financial problems. The likelihood is that the firm will end up restructuring its finances and preferred shareholders will lose a major portion of their invested capital.

Preferred Share Ratings

Given the danger associated with missed dividend payments, it makes sense for potential investors to evaluate the risk of this happening. As with long-term debt, the same rating agencies rate the default risk of preferred shares. Table 6.6

TABLE 6.6	The Preferred Share Rating Scale Used by the Dominion Bond Rating Service[a]

Rating	Brief description[b]
Pfd-1	Superior credit quality
Pfd-2	Satisfactory credit quality
Pfd-3	Adequate credit quality
Pfd-4	Speculative
Pfd-5	Highly speculative

[a]Note that "high" and "low" qualifiers are used to indicate the relative standing of an issuer within a particular rating category. The lack of one of these designations indicates a rating which is essentially in the middle of the category. The high and low qualifiers are used for all categories.

[b]For a more detailed description, see DBRS's Web site at the address provided below.

SOURCES: Dominion Bond Rating Service Limited; and Web site: **www.dbrs.com/web/jsp/pub_ratingscale_preferred.jsp**.

provides the preferred share rating used by DBRS. The preferred share ratings are meant to give an indication of the risk that the borrower will not make the dividend payments. The ratings do not take factors such as pricing or market risk into consideration. The ratings are based on quantitative and qualitative considerations that are relevant for the company.

As with debt, the higher the rating, the lower the risk, and, therefore, the lower the required dividend payment on a new issue of preferreds. The rating can be downgraded or upgraded with similar repercussions for both the investor and issuer as discussed under long-term debt.

Call Feature

call price (preferred)
The repurchase price for a preferred share issue generally the stated value plus a call premium.

This provision is included in almost all preferred share issues and is often referred to as the redemption provision. This provision gives the company the option to purchase and retire the total preferred share issue on a specific date. For many issues, there are multiple call dates. The repurchase price is termed the **call price** and is generally the stated value plus a call premium. The call premium is often quoted as a percent that is based on the stated value, but on some issues just the call price is provided. For example, on the nine issues that Telus Corporation, the major telephone utility in western Canada, has outstanding, the call premiums range from a low of 4 percent to a high of 10 percent. On other issues, the call price is stated and the call premium is the difference between the call price and stated value.

If a company were redeeming a preferred share with a $100 stated value and a call premium of 4 percent, then the company would pay investors $104, $100 for the stated value and $4 for the call premium. For issues with multiple call dates, it is normal for the call premium to decline if the issue is not called. This may happen over three to four call dates and the premium is gradually reduced to zero. For example, CIBC has a Series 15 preferred share issue where the first redemption date is July 31, 2004. The call price is $26, implying a call premium of $1. If the company does not call the issue, the next call date is July 31, 2005 and the call price is $25.50. The final call date is July 31, 2006 and the call price is the stated value: $25.

A company will exercise the redemption feature when the required dividend rate on a new preferred share issue is lower than the dividend on the current issue. For example, if a company had a preferred share outstanding with an 8 percent dividend but companies with similar risk ratings were issuing new preferreds with a 6 percent dividend, then it makes sense for the company to redeem the 8 percent issue. The implication is that the company can then reissue preferred shares with a 6 percent dividend rate. The company could save 2 percent dividend on the stated value. When dividend rates decline between the original date of the preferred share issue and the time the redemption feature is exercisable, then the company will redeem the issue.

Types of Preferred Shares

One area where financial engineering has had a tremendous impact in Canada is with preferred shares. There are numerous varieties of preferred shares in Canada. Arguably, Canada has the most developed market for preferred shares in the world. There are two reasons for this. First, as discussed in Chapter 2, for corporations, dividends received from a taxable Canadian company are exempt from taxes. This is an attractive opportunity for corporations to earn a tax-free, low risk return (based on the rating) on excess cash balances. Second, as will be discussed in Chapter 8, for individuals, the taxes paid on dividend income are much lower than on interest income. This tax advantage reduces the attraction of debt securities and encourages individuals to invest in preferred shares, thus broadening the market for potential issuers. In this section, four types of preferred shares are discussed. This is an introductory discussion meant to give the reader a taste of the topic, not provide a full-course meal.

retractable preferreds
The holder has the right to force the issuer to repurchase the preferred share at the stated value.

Retractable preferred shares: These are similar to retractable bonds—the redemption provision in reverse. With **retractable preferreds**, the holder has the right to request that the issuer repurchase the preferred shares. The retraction price is always the stated value and there may be multiple retraction dates. The retraction provision will be exercised by investors if dividend rates increased between the time of issue and the time the retraction provision is exercisable. For example, if a company had a preferred share outstanding with an 8 percent dividend but companies with similar risk ratings were issuing new preferreds with a 10 percent dividend, then it makes sense for investors to retract the issue. Investors could then go to the market and purchase preferred shares with a 10 percent dividend rate.

floating rate preferreds
The quarterly dividend paid is based on interest rates in the market and will float with these rates.

Floating rate preferred shares: For most preferred share issues, the dividend is fixed at the time of issue. Each quarter, the same dollar amount of dividend is paid. **Floating rate preferreds** are structured differently: the dividend rate floats along with interest rates in the market. The dividend rate is most often based on the prime rate at chartered banks. For floating rate preferreds, as interest rates fluctuate in the market, the quarterly dividend paid changes as well. Since the dividend rate changes, the market price will remain very close to the stated value of the preferred share.

convertible preferreds
Holders have the option of converting the preferred share into a predetermined number of common shares on a specific date.

Convertible preferred shares: With **convertible preferreds**, the holder has the option of converting the preferred share into a predetermined number of common shares on a specific date. With convertible preferreds the market price is based partially on the dividend rate, but also on the changing price of the common shares. This is a hybrid security, since the holder receives dividend payments but also benefits if the company's common share price increases. The dividend rate on convertibles is lower than on regular preferreds but offers the opportunity of a large gain if the company's common share price increases.

Dutch Auction preferred shares
Similar to money market securities with no stated maturity; the dividend rate is reset on a regular basis through a Dutch auction process.

Dutch Auction preferred shares: Similar to money market securities, **Dutch Auction preferred shares** have no stated maturity and can be viewed as a perpetuity. The dividend rate is reset on a regular basis through a Dutch auction process. These auctions can occur weekly, quarterly, or at some point in between. Institutional investors are the principal participants in the bidding, with highest bid winning the portion of the offering sought. Succeeding bids are then allotted shares. The frequent repricing provides a mechanism for the shares to accurately reflect prevailing rates, and therefore they trade at the stated value. The yields are comparable to commercial paper.

When reviewing the characteristics of preferred shares, it is clear that even though they are termed an equity, they share more similarities with long-term debt than with common equity. This will be an important point when it comes time to value these shares in Chapter 8.

Trading Preferred and Common Shares

When financial securities are created in the primary market transaction, a secondary marketplace must exist that allows for the subsequent trading of these financial securities. These marketplaces are the **securities exchanges**. There are two types: physical, tangible exchanges and artificial exchanges. The trading of many equity securities occurs on a physical exchange, which is often referred to as the stock market. The largest and most important stock market in Canada is the Toronto Stock Exchange (TSX). Artificial exchanges trade all debt securities and some equities. There is no physical location for the trading of these securities; rather, the trading takes place in the communication system that exists between financial intermediaries. The market is, in essence, cyberspace, the computer networks between investment dealers.

securities exchanges
The secondary marketplace that allows for the subsequent trading of financial securities created in the primary market.

The Role of Securities Exchanges

efficient market
A market that allocates funds to their most productive uses due to competition among wealth-maximizing investors; it determines and publicizes prices that are believed to be close to their true value.

Securities exchanges create continuous liquid markets where trading can occur efficiently. **Efficient markets** allocate funds to their most productive uses. This is especially true for securities that are actively traded on major exchanges where competition among wealth-maximizing investors determines and publicizes prices that are believed to be close to their true value. The price of the individual security is determined by the demand for and supply of the security. Figure 6.4 depicts the interaction of forces of demand (represented by line D_0) and supply (represented by line S) for a given security currently selling at an equilibrium price P_0. At that price, Q_0 shares of the stock are traded.

FIGURE 6.4

Supply and Demand
Supply and demand for a security

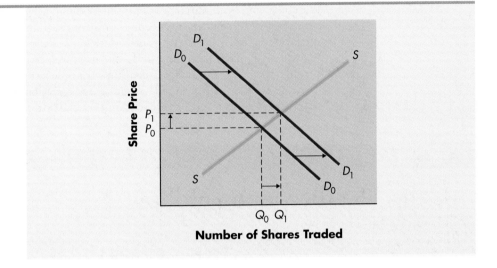

The competitive market created by the major securities exchanges provides a forum in which share price is continuously adjusted to changing demand and supply.

Changing evaluations of a firm's prospects will change the demand for and supply of a security and ultimately result in a new price for the securities. Suppose, for example, that a favourable discovery by the firm shown in Figure 6.4 is announced and investors in the marketplace increase the demand for the shares from D_0 to D_1. The changing evaluation results in a higher quantity of shares traded, Q_1, at a higher equilibrium price, P_1. The competitive market created by the major securities exchanges provides a forum in which share price is continuously adjusted to changing demand and supply.

The Toronto Stock Exchange

The Toronto Stock Exchange (TSX) is one of only two stock markets in Canada. The other is the TSX Venture Exchange, which trades the common shares of early-stage, smaller companies. The TSX is where the common shares of most large Canadian companies trade. Companies like Alcan, Loblaws, BCE, Canadian Tire, Barrick Gold, the Big 5 banks, and numerous others that are household names have their shares listed on the TSX. Note, though, that other large Canadian companies are still privately owned and their common shares are not listed on an exchange. Companies like Irvings, McCain Foods, the Jim Pattison Group, AIC Mutual Funds, and Roots are still owned by the founding families.

Both the TSX and Venture Exchange operate as automated, continuous auction markets where buy and sell orders of the listed securities are queued and matched in price-time priority sequence. To make transactions on the "floor" of the TSX, a firm must be a "participating organization" of the exchange. There are over 100 participating organizations, with the major Canadian investment dealers being the largest. These include BMO Nesbitt Burns, CIBC Wood Gundy, National Bank Financial, RBC Dominion Securities, Scotia MacLeod, and TD Waterhouse. The broker-dealers who are participating organizations employ approved traders to enter orders into the system by computer in their brokerage offices.

The goal of trading is to fill buy orders (orders to purchase securities) at the lowest price and to fill sell orders (orders to sell securities) at the highest price, thereby giving both purchasers and sellers the best possible deal. Once placed, an order to buy or sell can be executed in seconds, thanks to the sophisticated trading system used. New Internet-based brokerage systems enable individual investors to place their buy and sell orders electronically. These orders flow through the participating organization's trading system and on to the floor of the TSX, where they are executed. An individual can place a buy order at the current market price and receive confirmation that the order was filled in seconds.

IN PRACTICE

Is the TSX Becoming Hollow?

The trend towards globalization is seen in many different areas. One of these is the financial markets. Large corporations and major governments use the global financial markets on a regular basis. Does this trend mean the Canadian capital market is at risk of becoming obsolete? Likely not for the debt market, but there is some suggestion this may be occurring in the equity portion of the capital market. This is the result of a trend termed the *hollowing out* of corporate Canada.

The performance of a stock market is usually measured by an index that tracks the prices of the common shares of the major companies that trade on an exchange. On the TSX, the S&P/TSX Composite Index (formerly the TSE 300 Index) is the main index. Over the past 10 years, a dramatic shift has occurred with the companies on the Index. Many of the large, internationally known companies that had major weights in the TSX Index have been taken over by foreign companies and have disappeared from the TSX. Much smaller companies with no national, let alone international, presence have taken their places on the Index. As a result, the large companies that still trade on the TSX have taken dominant positions on the Index.

For example, in September 2002, of the 247 companies included on the S&P/TSX Composite Index (this reduction from the original 300 is also seen as a sign of the hollowing out effect), just 20 accounted for 52.4 percent of the value of the Index. The average share on the Index is small and has very little impact on the overall market. In addition, most of the large

stocks on the Index are regulated companies that are required to be Canadian-controlled or have controlling shareholders who are less likely to sell. These include the chartered banks, telephone, cable, electrical, and gas utilities, and companies such as Onex, Bombardier, Brascan, and Celestica. Some companies that have disappeared from the TSX include Seagrams, Gulf Canada, John Labatt, Franco-Nevada Mining, Newbridge Networks, Bio-Chem Pharma, Trimark Financial, and MacMillan Bloedel. All of these were internationally known, multibillion-dollar companies, and, in many cases, household names.

Between December 2000 and May 2002, an 18-month period, companies with a market capitalization of $77 billion were replaced on the S&P/TSX Index by companies with a $3.4 billion market capitalization. Commenting on this situation, a pension fund manager says: "We've got a lot fewer quality, large names than we had before. And as you are confronted with fewer quality names, you have to go up the risk scale. My first and most important tactic [to deal with this problem] is to get the money out of Canada." Is the TSX a big enough stock exchange to handle the growing amounts of investable assets in Canada? This is a key question for investors to consider looking into the future.

REFERENCES: Sandra Rubin, "Bay Street Worries as Takeovers Accelerate," *National Post*, May 22, 2002; Andrea Mandel-Campbell, "Protection or Costly Fairytale?" *National Post*, May 23, 2002; and Components of the S&P/TSX Composite Index, *The TSX Review*, 2002.

The Over-the-Counter Exchange

over-the-counter exchange
An intangible market for the purchase and sale of securities not listed on organized exchanges.

Nasdaq
The National Association of Securities Dealers Automated Quotation System, the best known OTC market in the world, that rivals the New York Stock Exchange in trading volumes.

The **over-the-counter (OTC) exchange** is an intangible market for the trading of common and preferred shares not listed on an organized exchange. OTC traders, known as dealers, are linked through a networked trading system. In the United States, the major OTC exchange is the National Association of Securities Dealers Automated Quotation (Nasdaq) System. **Nasdaq** is the best known OTC market in the world and rivals the New York Stock Exchange in trading volumes. Some of the best known technology companies in the world trade on Nasdaq including Microsoft, Intel, Dell, Cisco, Yahoo, and Oracle. This sophisticated communications network provides current bid and ask prices on thousands of actively traded OTC securities. The bid price is the highest price offered by the dealer to purchase a given security, and the ask price is the lowest price at which the dealer is willing to sell the security. The dealer in effect adds securities to his or her inventory by purchasing them at a bid price and sells securities from the inventory at the ask price, hoping to profit from the spread between the bid and ask price.

In Canada, the major OTC market for equities was the Canadian Dealing Network. In October 2000, this network ceased operations and all quoted securities were moved to Tier 3 of the TSX Venture Exchange. A new OTC market was created, the Canadian Unlisted Board (CUB), but listings are few and trading light. In November 2000, Nasdaq established an OTC operation in Canada, but the exchange has been slow to attract new listings. In June 2001, the Canadian Trading and Quotation System (CNQ) applied to launch an electronic OTC market in Canada. At the time of writing, the Ontario Securities Commission (OSC), the regulator of trading, was still reviewing the application. The CNQ was looking to become a trading base for about 1,000 reporting issuers in Canada that are not currently listed on an exchange.

Stock Price Quotations

The financial manager needs to stay abreast of the market values of the firm's outstanding securities, particularly the common shares, whether they are traded on an organized exchange, over the counter, or in international markets. Similarly, existing shareholders need to monitor the prices of the securities they own. Information on shares and other securities is provided in quotations, which include price data along with other statistics on recent price behaviour and is widely published in news media. Security price quotations are readily available for actively traded securities.

A summary of the previous day's trading, including price and volume statistics is reported in various media, including major newspapers like *The Globe and Mail* and *National Post* and the business sections of daily general newspapers. Trading information is also available on numerous Web sites including **www.globeinvestor.com, www.tse.com**, or **ca.finance.yahoo.com**.

The most timely stock quotes are available directly from investment dealers (often referred to as stockbrokers for the trading function they perform for investors) or over the Internet at the sites mentioned above, but also at many others. On these sites, quotes are often delayed by 15 to 20 minutes. For real-time quotes over the Internet, investors must pay a fee or have an investment account with an investment dealer.

Figure 6.5 is an excerpt from the *National Post*, providing summary trading statistics reported on July 26, 2002 for transactions that occurred on July 25, 2002. We'll look at both the common share and preferred share quotations for CIBC, highlighted in Figure 6.5. The quotations show that most share prices are quoted in multiples of 1 cent. If shares trade for under $1, they can be traded in multiples of one-half cent.

The first two columns, labelled "52W High" and "52W Low," are the highest and lowest price at which the shares sold during the preceding 52 weeks. CIBC's common share traded between $38.75 and $58.04 during the 52-week period ending July 25, 2002. Next is the company's abbreviated name followed by the share's ticker symbol, CM for CIBC. Systems that provide share quotes are based on ticker symbols and these must be used in order to obtain current price data.

To the right of the symbol, under "Div," is the indicated annual cash dividend. This is based on the most recently paid quarterly dividend on each common share. The indicated dividend for CIBC is $1.64 per share, so CIBC's most recent quarterly dividend was $0.41 per common share. The next item, labelled "Yield %," is the dividend yield, which is found by dividing the indicated dividend by the closing share price. The dividend yield for CIBC is 4 percent ($1.64 /$41.25 = 0.0398 ≃ 4%).

FIGURE 6.5

Select Common and Preferred Share Quotations for July 25, 2002

52W High	52W Low	Stock	Ticker	Div.	Yield %	P/E	Vol 00s	High	Low	Close	Net Chg
26.50	13.50	CdaBread	CBY	0.24	1.1	15.6	465	22.80	21.49	22.00	+1.00
47.91	32.16	CdaLifFin	CL	0.60	1.8	14.7	2265	33.25	32.25	33.25	+0.23
27.00	25.00	CdaLifeBpf		1.56	5.9	—	11	26.65	26.60	26.65	+0.17
2.85	1.08	CdnBkNote	CBK	—	—	23.3	40	2.10	2.10	2.10	—
3.31	1.63	Cdn88En	EEE	—	—	—	6338	2.35	2.20	2.20	+0.03
36.51	25.11	CdnFinNT	CFX	0.16	0.6	—	20	28.00	26.98	26.98	+0.85
10.25	7.56	CdnGenInv	CGI	0.49	5.5	—	17	8.90	8.88	8.88	+0.03
26.50	24.80	CdnGen pf		1.35	5.2	—	25	25.75	25.55	25.75	—
2.78	1.80	CdnHydro	KHD	—	—	21.0	77	2.18	2.10	2.10	−0.05
58.04	38.75	CIBC	CM	1.64	4.0	13.1	22272	43.68	40.30	41.25	−1.10
26.95	25.01	CIBC23pf		1.32	5.1	—	85	26.15	25.81	25.81	−0.30
26.35	24.90	CIBC24pf		1.50	5.9	—	276	25.45	25.37	25.45	+0.05
25.73	24.75	CIBC25pf		1.50	5.9	—	70	25.45	25.16	25.39	+0.24
27.65	25.70	CIBC14pf		1.48	5.6	—	8	26.62	26.62	26.62	+0.01
27.35	25.40	CIBC15pf		1.41	5.3	—	8	26.80	26.80	26.80	+0.04
27.00	25.10	CIBC17pf		1.36	5.2	—	25	26.35	26.30	26.30	−0.10
26.00	23.44	CIBC18pf		1.37	5.6	—	82	24.75	24.39	24.65	+0.15
26.25	24.40	CIBC19pf		1.23	4.8	—	38	25.90	25.50	25.90	+0.01
28.40	26.10	CIBC21pf		1.50	5.5	—	20	27.07	27.05	27.07	−0.23
34.10	17.36	CndMedLab	CLC	—	—	13.9	141	30.40	29.40	29.50	−0.65
85.53	51.00	CN Rail	CNR	0.86	1.2	21.4	4468	72.85	70.05	72.85	+1.56
54.54	35.90	CdnNatRes	CNQ	0.50	1.0	10.1	6240	49.10	47.25	48.15	−0.45
n37.98	20.00	CdnPacRail	CP	0.51	1.5	9.7	4727	34.55	32.64	33.77	+0.77
3.41	1.17	CdnSupEn	SNG	—	—	15.0	966	2.68	2.51	2.55	−0.10
33.15	18.50	CdnTireA	CTR	0.40	1.4	12.7	2271	29.85	28.60	28.75	−0.90
60.10	47.31	CdnUtil A	CU	1.96	3.6	11.5	265	55.00	53.25	54.99	+1.24
60.50	47.25	CdnUtil B		1.96	3.7	11.1	z25	55.00	55.00	55.00	—
29.75	22.75	CdnWstBk	CWB	0.40	1.7	9.8	681	24.10	23.50	23.75	−0.25
0.32	0.12	CdnZinc	CZN	—	—	—	115	0.23	0.21	0.22	—
10.00	7.05	CanManA	CAM	0.16	2.0	14.9	104	8.34	8.15	8.17	+0.07

SOURCE: *National Post*, July 26, 2002.

The price/earnings (P/E) ratio is next. It is calculated by dividing the closing market price by the firm's most recent annual earnings per share (EPS). The **price/earnings (P/E) ratio** measures the amount investors are willing to pay for each dollar of the firm's earnings. CIBC's P/E ratio was 13.1: the share was trading at 13.1 times its earnings. The P/E ratio is believed to reflect investor expectations concerning the firm's future prospects. Higher P/E ratios reflect investor optimism and confidence; lower P/E ratios reflect investor pessimism and concern.

Next is the daily volume, labelled "Vol 00s." Most shares trade in broad lots of 100 shares, so the day's trading is quoted in lots of 100 shares. The value 22272 for CIBC indicates that 2,227,200 common shares were traded on July 25, 2002. The High, Low, and Close columns contain the highest, lowest, and closing (last) price, respectively, at which the share sold on the given day. These values for CIBC were a high of $43.68, a low of $40.30, and a closing price of $41.25. The final column, "Net Chg.," indicates the change in the closing price from that of the previous trading day. CIBC closed down $1.10 from July 24, which means the closing price on that day was $42.35.

Note that preferred shares are listed below common shares. For example, following CIBC's common share in Figure 6.5 are a number of different issues of preferred share. These are identified first by the series and then by the letters "pf." Note that the Series 17 preferred share for the CIBC is the issue discussed on page 271 for dividends. The quotation for preferred share is nearly identical to that of common share except that no ticker symbol is provided and the value for the P/E ratio is left blank because it is irrelevant in the case of preferred shares. For preferred shares, the dividend yield is an important figure since investors buy preferred shares primarily for the dividend. It should also be noted that when a share is not traded on a given day, it generally is not quoted in the trading report.

Value of Trading in the Money and Capital Markets

Table 6.7 provides the dollar value of trading that occurred in the money and capital markets in three years: 1991, 1996, and 2001. Surprising to most people, the value of the securities traded on the stock market is a fraction of the value of trading in the money and bond markets. The money market is a very large and important component of the Canadian financial system but is "hidden" to most

price/earnings (P/E) ratio
Measures the amount common share investors are willing to pay for each dollar of the firm's earnings.

TABLE 6.7   Annual Dollar Value of Trading in the Canadian Financial Markets: 1991, 1996, and 2001 (in billions of dollars)

	1991	1996	2001
Money market	$1,339.7	$1,548.2	$1,490.9
Bond market	942.0	1,138.0	997.9
Stock market	90.1	331.3	712.5
Total value of trading	$2,371.8	$3,017.5	$3,201.3

SOURCES: *Toronto Stock Exchange Review*, various issues, "*Historical Record of Trading*," and *Bank of Canada Banking and Financial Statistics*, various issues, Tables F11, F12.

observers; the stock market gets all the press. Note, though, that while the value of the securities traded in the money and bond markets remained relatively flat over the 11 years, the value of stock market trading has grown at an average annual rate of 23 percent. The value of stock market trading is about 70 percent of bond market trading, but still less than half of the value of money market trading.

The reason money market securities have such high trading volumes is that a single money market security may trade seven, eight, or ten times in its very short-term life. For example, for an issue of 98-day federal government treasury bills, the first purchaser of the treasury bill in the secondary market may only hold the t-bill for 34 days. After 34 days, the holder will sell it. The next buyer may only want to hold the t-bill for 15 days, while the next buyer may want to hold it for 8 days, etc. Therefore, a 98-day t-bill may trade many times during its relatively short life. This type of trading inflates the trading statistics for money market securities.

Bond market trading has increased significantly since the mid-1970s. Trading of bonds has greatly expanded over the last 25 years, as both the federal and provincial governments began to run large budget deficits and used very long-term debt to help finance the shortfall. The amount of government debt greatly expanded, and this strongly affected bond trading. With the return to balanced budgets and even surpluses, the dollar amount of government debt outstanding has declined. This has already affected the value of bonds traded and will continue to do so in the future.

? Review Questions

6–22 Why are common shareholders referred to as residual owners? What is meant by the term *limited liability*?

6–23 What is *dilution of ownership*? Provide an example. How can dilution of ownership be prevented?

6–24 Distinguish between *authorized*, *issued*, and *outstanding* common shares. Is *par value* a useful term when referring to common shares?

6–25 What is the benefit to the original owners of issuing subordinate voting shares? What is the *coattail provision* and why is it important?

6–26 Are common share dividends guaranteed? Discuss.

6–27 Discuss the characteristics of preferred shares in terms of risk for the issuing company and the investor, stated values, dividends, ratings, and call features. What various types of preferred shares can be issued?

6–28 What is the purpose of a securities exchange? What is the difference between a physical and an artificial securities exchange?

6–29 What is meant by the term *efficient markets*?

6–30 What information is provided in the stock trading reports provided in newspapers? Are there other sources of more timely stock price data? Where?

6–31 What does the price/earnings (P/E) ratio indicate?

6–32 How are preferred share quotes different from those of common shares?

6–33 Why are the trading volumes of money and bond market securities so much higher than stock market securities?

6.5 Differences between Debt and Equity Capital

The term *capital* denotes the long-term funds of the firm. All items on the right-hand side of the firm's balance sheet *with an obvious financing cost* (this excludes current liabilities like payables and accruals) are sources of capital. *Debt* capital includes all loans made by the firm, both short- and long-term. *Equity* capital consists of long-term funds provided by preferred and common shareholders. *Preferred* equity capital is raised by selling preferred shares. *Common* equity capital are funds provided by the firm's owners and can be raised *internally*, through reinvested profits, or externally, by selling common shares. The key differences between debt, preferred, and common equity are summarized in Table 6.8. These differences relate to voice in management, claims on the firm's income and assets, maturity, and tax treatment.

Voice in Management

Unlike creditors (lenders), the common shareholders are the owners of the firm. Holders of common shares have voting rights that permit them to select the firm's board of directors and to vote at the company's annual meeting of shareholders and on special issues. Debtholders and preferred shareholders may receive voting privileges only when the firm has violated its stated contractual obligations to them. The power of debtholders is to put the firm into bankruptcy if the company fails to meet the conditions of the loan. Arguably, this provides creditors with greater power than common shareholders.

Claims on Income and Assets

With income, the company must pay interest owed to creditors or face the risk of bankruptcy. The creditors are entitled to the interest owed and the principal

---

TABLE 6.8 Key Differences among Debt, Preferred, and Common Equity Capital

	Type of capital		
Characteristic	Debt	Preferred	Common
Voice in management[a]	No, but power to bankrupt company	No and no bankruptcy power	Yes, through the board of of directors
Claims on income	Senior to equity and less risky, but limited to interest	Subordinate to debt, preference over common equity	Subordinate to debt and preferred, but unlimited with increasing profits
Claims on assets	First claim, secured then unsecured	Second claim preference over common equity	Residual claim
Maturity	Stated with a finite life	None, but callable	None, but can be repurchased
Tax treatment	Interest deducted from income	No deduction; dividends paid from after-tax income	No deduction; dividends paid from after-tax income

[a]In the event the issuer violates its stated contractual obligations, debtholders and preferred shareholders *may* receive a voice in management; otherwise, only common shareholders have voting rights.

repaid at the maturity of the loan. Regardless of how profitable the firm becomes, this is all creditors are entitled to receive. Preferred shareholders are entitled to receive dividends. If the firm fails to pay dividends, they accumulate. Common shareholders have claim on all residual income after the two previous payments are made. Their claim on income is unlimited given increasing profits, but the risk of receiving a benefit is greater given that the company's profits may decline or turn negative. Common shareholders receive the benefit of increasing profits through the payment of dividends, which is at the discretion of the board of directors, and through increasing share prices, the ultimate goal of the firm.

The equity holders' *claims on assets* of the firm also are secondary to the claims of creditors. If the firm fails, assets are sold, and the proceeds are distributed in this order: the government, employees, customers, secured creditors, unsecured creditors, preferred shareholders, and finally common shareholders. Because equity holders are the last to receive any distribution of assets in the event of bankruptcy, they expect greater returns from dividends and/or increases in share price. As is explained in Chapter 8, the cost to the firm of the various forms of equity financing are generally higher than debt. This is the case since the suppliers of equity capital take more risk because of their subordinate claims on income and assets. Despite being more costly, equity capital is necessary for the firm to grow. All firms must initially be financed with common equity and this financing continues, assuming the firm is profitable.

Maturity

Unlike debt, both preferred and common equity are *permanent forms* of financing. Equity does not mature and therefore repayment is not required. Although a ready market may exist for the firm's preferred and common shareholders, the price that can be realized may fluctuate. This potential fluctuation of the market price of equity makes the overall returns more risky. Note that although preferred and common shares do not mature, preferred shares can be redeemed by the firm in certain circumstances. Common shares may be repurchased and cancelled by the company. This is regularly done by companies in Canada for various reasons, but often because the firm's management believes the shares are undervalued in the market.

Tax Treatment

Interest payments to debtholders are treated as tax-deductible expenses on the firm's income statement, whereas dividend payments to common and preferred shareholders are not tax deductible. The tax deductibility of interest lowers the cost of debt financing, thereby further causing the cost of debt financing to be lower than the cost of equity financing.

? Review Questions

6–34 What are debt and equity capital? What are the key differences between them with respect to voice in management, claims on income and assets, maturity, and tax treatment?

6–35   Debtholders are only entitled to receive the promised coupon payment. How is this a benefit? How is this a potential "cost" to debtholders?

6.6 How Financial Securities Are Created and Issued

underwriting
The means by which new financial securities are created in the primary market, the basic financial market transaction.

Underwriting is the means by which new financial securities are created in the primary market. This is the basic financial market transaction. The user raises cash, the saver receives a financial security: long-term debt, preferred shares, or common shares. Money market securities are also created in a similar manner; however, the focus of this discussion is on long-term securities. The issuer could be a government or corporation. The underwriter is the financial intermediary, who acts as the agent for the organization raising the funds. Investment dealers perform this function, and in this role are often referred to as **investment bankers**.

investment banker
A term for investment dealers when performing the underwriting function.

Types of Underwriting Transactions

private placements
The sale of the security directly to a group of investors or an institutional investor; these securities will not trade on financial markets after issue.

public offerings
The sale of securities that will be traded on secondary financial markets.

initial public offering (IPO)
Referred to as *going public*, the process of offering common shares of a privately owned company to the general public for the first time.

new issue
An issue of long-term debt, preferred share, or common share issues where the funds raised flow to the company.

seasoned issue
A new issue of common shares; the shares sold add to the existing pool of common shares.

secondary offering
The sale to the public of a large block of common shares held by the founding owners or a controlling company.

There are two types of primary market transactions: private placements and public financing. **Private placements** are the sale of a security directly to a group of investors or an institutional investor. These securities will not be traded on secondary financial markets, but the original investor may be able to arrange for a sale to another investor. **Public offerings** are the sale of securities that will be traded on secondary financial markets, the bond and stock markets, after issue. This discussion will focus on public financing.

Offering of securities can also be classified by title. Securities could be a new issue, a secondary offering, or the initial public offering. The **initial public offering (IPO)** title only applies to common shares and is referred to as *going public*. Going public is the process of offering common shares of a privately owned company to the general public for the first time. A **new issue** refers to long-term debt, preferred share, or common share issue. As discussed earlier, each issue of long-term debt and preferred shares is unique and does not add to the existing pool of securities. Each issue creates a new series of securities. A new issue of common shares is referred to as a **seasoned issue,** with these shares adding to the existing pool of common shares. New issues of common shares are sold by the company. A **secondary offering** occurs when a large block of previously unissued common shares held by the founding owners or a controlling company is sold to the public. The funds raised go to the sellers, not to the company whose shares are sold. These types of offering are very common in Canada.

Steps in the Underwriting Process

The underwriting process is a seven step procedure as described below.

Step 1   The organization decides to raise long-term financing. The process by which the organization would have realized funds were required was covered in Chapter 4. This financing would be needed to invest in assets, either current or fixed.

Step 2   Select a lead underwriter and hold discussions (the pre-underwriting conference). The organization chooses the lead underwriter, the investment dealer ultimately responsible for selling the issue and receiving the largest percentage of the fees paid. Often organizations (both governments and companies) will deal with the same investment dealer for many years. For companies, it may be the underwriter who was associated with the companies' initial public offering (IPO) of shares.

The first item considered in the discussions is whether the firm really needs to raise additional external financing. If so, then a broad range of topics is discussed, including the firm's current financial position; current and projected economic and financial market conditions; the future outlook for industry and company; the amount, purpose, and type of the financing; coupon or dividend rate (if applicable); tax consequences of the issue; the timing of issue; and the area of distribution. Preliminary decisions will be made concerning each of these issues and the underwriting process will continue.

Step 3   Decide on the details of the issue and prepare and issue the preliminary prospectus. At this point, the economic, financial market, and organization-specific factors have been analyzed and the organization and underwriter have decided to proceed with the issue. Decisions regarding all aspects of the issue will have been made, but not finalized. The **preliminary prospectus** is the document that provides all the information investors require to make a decision regarding the investment merits of the security issue.

preliminary prospectus
The document that provides all information investors require to make a decision regarding the investment merits of the security issue.

The prospectus is required for all national issues of securities and must be filed with the appropriate securities commissions for approval.[2] In Canada, each province has its own securities commission that must approve the sale of all securities in the province. The preliminary prospectus is often referred to as the **red herring** because on the first page, a statement in red ink appears stating that the securities have not been approved for sale by the provincial securities commission and sale must await the approval of the final prospectus. The preliminary prospectus will include the following types of information:

red herring
Another term for the preliminary prospectus, so called due to the statement on the first page printed in red ink stating that the securities have not been approved for sale.

1. A one- to four-page summary of the information provided.
2. Legal opinions as to the eligibility of the security for investment purposes. (For example, in RRSPs, for pension plans, mutual funds, and so on.)
3. History of the company and industry and full description of the business of the company, including any significant changes over the previous 2 to 5 years.
4. Audited financial statements for the company for the past three to five years and management's discussion and analysis (MD&A) of the financial and operational results.
5. Description of how the proceeds of issue will be used by the organization.
6. Management's projections of future financial results.
7. Financial statement after giving effect to the offering.

---

2. A number of provinces, including Ontario, require a preliminary prospectus. Since most organizations issuing securities in Canada wish to sell their securities in Ontario, most issues have a preliminary prospectus.

8. Full disclosure of all risks associated with the issue. This clause is important in order to limit the liability of all involved in the process: the organization, underwriters, and law firms. This clause is the result of **due diligence**, the process completed by the underwriter to ensure there are no misrepresentations and that the prospectus contains full and true disclosure.

9. Discussion of tax considerations for the investor.

10. The area the issue will be sold: regional, national, and/or international.

11. Compensation of executive officers.

12. Conditions or covenants associated with the issue, especially for a long-term debt issue.

due diligence
The process completed by the underwriter to ensure there is no misrepresentation and that the prospectus contains full and true disclosure.

The preliminary prospectus is rigorously reviewed for compliance by all provincial securities commissions to which it is submitted. The review process can take up to 4 weeks, at which time the commissions will issue a *comment letter* that indicates required changes, seeks clarification, requests other information, and asks questions. While some issuers have decided not to proceed with an offering of securities once the process has reached this stage, it is highly unusual for the issue not to proceed.

Some important information is missing from the preliminary prospectus. The price of the issue, the number of securities to be issued, the dollar amount of the issue, the interest rate or dividend on the issue, and the underwriting fees are not included. These items are omitted since one of the purposes of the preliminary prospectus is for the underwriter to identify the extent of public interest in the issue. Once the underwriter has a better read on the market's response to the issue, these details are finalized. This occurs in the final days of the offering period and are included in the final prospectus. At this point, a range (low to high) in issue size will be suggested.

underwriting syndicate
The group of investment dealers who buy the security issue from the company and then resell it to investors (savers).

banking group
Includes the lead underwriter and, in most larger deals, a number of other large investment dealers.

selling group
Smaller, regional investment dealers who do not assume any of the risks of underwriting, but only attempt to sell a certain portion of the issue.

Step 4 Assemble the underwriting syndicate. The **underwriting syndicate** is the group of investment dealers who buy the security issue from the company and then resell it to investors (savers). There are two groups in the syndicate: the banking group and the selling group. The **banking group** includes the lead underwriter and, in most larger deals, a number of other large investment dealers. The **selling group** is made up of other investment dealers (usually regional) who do not assume any of the risks of underwriting, but only attempt to sell a certain portion of the issue on a commission basis. For very large issues, there may be up to five investment dealers in the banking group, with many of the remaining investment dealers operating in Canada in the selling group.

firm agreement
An underwriting agreement where the syndicate agrees to buy all of the securities at the stated price, guaranteeing the organization receives the amount of money.

best efforts agreement
An underwriting agreement where the syndicate agrees to *try* to sell the issue, but the sale is not guaranteed.

There are two types of underwriting agreements: firm and best efforts. With a **firm agreement**, the syndicate agrees to buy all of the securities at the stated price, guaranteeing the organization receives the implied amount of money. With a **best efforts agreement**, the syndicate agrees to *try* to sell the issue, but the sale is not guaranteed. Most underwriting agreements in Canada are firm. The risks of underwriting are associated with firm offering. The banking group purchases the security from the issuer at the stated price, less fees. The syndicate then attempts to sell the security at the issue price. If the lead underwriter's read of the market was incorrect and the issue does not sell or not sell at the specified price, the banking group could lose money on the deal. The possibility of less money being raised than given to the organization is the risk associated with underwriting. The banking group underwrites price risk for the organization, thus providing an insurance function.

escape clauses
Provisions in the underwriting agreement that allow the syndicate to not buy the issue from the organization if specific conditions exist.

To protect the syndicate, many agreements include **escape clauses**. These allow the syndicate to opt out of the deal and not buy the issue from the organization if specific conditions exist. Examples include an order that restricts the trading of the organization's securities, incorrect statements in the prospectus, or events that have a significant impact on the company or the financial markets. For example, the stock market declining by a large percentage in a very short time period would likely trigger this clause for an issue of common shares.

road show
Presentations, by the company and lead underwriter, regarding the issue made to financial analysts and institutional investors across Canada.

green sheet
A document prepared by the underwriter that summarizes key information in the prospectus.

Step 5   Market the issue. Once the company addresses the concerns the securities commissions have regarding the preliminary prospectus, the company can market the issue. This is usually done by having people from the company and lead underwriter make presentations to financial analysts and institutional investors across Canada. This is referred to as the **road show**, and it may take up to two weeks. The presentations revolve around the information provided in the preliminary prospectus and the **green sheet**, a document prepared by the underwriter that summarizes key information in the prospectus. The greater the interest in the offering, the higher the proceeds to the organization.

Step 6   Prepare and distribute the final prospectus. The final prospectus contains all the information that was in the preliminary prospectus, but also includes the missing pricing information on both a total and per share basis. Decisions regarding these variables will be made based on the market response to the issue and the final prospectus submitted to the securities commission in each province in which the issue is to be sold.

blue skying
An investment industry term referring to the approval of the final prospectus by provincial securities commissions.

Note that for a firm underwriting agreement, the banking group does not commit to the offering and is not obliged to purchase the security issue from the organization until the final prospectus is submitted for approval. The syndicate only underwrites known risk; that is, when the dollar amount of the offering is finalized. Approval of the final prospectus, referred to as **blue skying** it, normally only takes 1 to 2 days, at which time the sale of the issue can proceed.

At this point, the issue may be advertised in the financial press. The advertising format used is referred to as a tombstone, due to the rectangular shape of the notice. The tombstone will provide the name of the company, the type of issue, the size, price, and date of the issue, and the investment dealers in both the banking and selling groups. The tombstone appears twice—once when the new issue is approved and again after it is sold. The only change in the two printings is the fine print at the top of the advertisement. The initial tombstone states that the securities are offered by means of a prospectus which is available from one of the investment dealers named on the tombstone. The second printing states that the securities have been sold.

While in theory the issue cannot be sold until the final prospectus is approved, in practice the underwriting syndicate began selling the issue when the decision to proceed was made by the company. These sales would have been made on the condition that the company proceed with the issue, and pending

approval of the final prospectus by the securities commissions. A sale is not finalized until an investor receives the final prospectus and 48 hours elapse. In this
period the investor can opt out of the purchase. Examples of both a preliminary
and a final prospectuses are available at the following Web site: **www.sedar.com**.

Step 7   Close. The closing of the deal will normally occur 2 to 3 weeks after the
initial offering date. On this date, the investors who purchased the issue
will be required to pay for the securities purchased. The lead underwriter, representing the banking group, will present the company issuing
the securities a cheque for the issue amount less the underwriting commission. Also, the investors will receive a certificate for the amount of
the issue purchased. (For example, this certificate could be for 100
shares of a preferred or common share issue.)

At this point the formal underwriting process has been finalized. The primary market transaction has been completed. Cash was transferred from savers to
users with a security outlining a financial position in the company flowing in the
opposite direction. An intermediary (underwriting syndicate) was used to allow
the transaction to be completed in the most efficient manner possible.

Time Required to Issue Securities

The seven-step underwriting process described above can take a great deal of
time. A large amount of data must be brought together and presented in a logical
and direct manner. For a new issue or secondary offering, the process could take
10 to 11 weeks. To complete an IPO, the average time required is about 100
days, although it often takes longer. Regardless, time is of the essence as the
prospectus is prepared, approval sought from securities regulators, and interest
generated from potential investors.

The POP System

For large, established companies, waiting 70 days to raise financing is an unnec-
essary impediment to growth. For companies like BCE, the big banks, Stelco, or
Magna, all information concerning their operations is freely available and easily
accessible by investors. Consequently, it seems pointless to make issuers like
these wait 70 days before they can raise capital. As recognition of this fact, most
provincial securities commissions allow issuers to use the **prompt offering
prospectus (POP) system**. Firms that meet certain size and reporting requirements can simply file a **short-form prospectus** as an addendum to current filing
with the securities commissions. Much of the information that is in a "regular"
prospectus can be omitted. This is allowed since all of this information is widely
available in reports the company must file. The short-form prospectus is usually
approved within a week.

The POP, short-form prospectus system has reduced costs for issuers and
increased flexibility to respond to market opportunities for security issues. It is
not unusual for companies regularly to file short-term prospectuses in anticipation of an opportunity to raise capital in the most opportune environment. By
allowing for increased flexibility, securities commissions have recognized the
changing nature of financial markets and the requirement that companies be able

**prompt offering prospectus
(POP) system**
A filing process for firms meeting certain
requirements that allows companies to
raise financing within five days of filing.

short-form prospectus
The document filed for the POP system
that omits much of the information that
is in a "regular" prospectus.

to act quickly to changing conditions. In Canada, the large majority of the financing raised in the capital markets is done through the POP system.

Issue Costs

For most organizations, the cost of issuing securities is reasonable. For high-risk organizations or for small issues, however, the costs can be substantial. The main cost is the commission paid to the underwriting syndicate. It is normal for commissions to be stated as a percent of the gross proceeds raised through the underwriting process. The second cost is fees and expenses such as accounting, legal, travel (particularly for the road show), printing, and regulatory fees.

The commission paid will vary depending on the type of security, the size of the issue, and the main purchasers of the issue. Long-term debt securities have the lowest commission, followed by preferred shares, and then common shares. The larger the issue, the lower the percentage commission. If the securities are sold primarily to institutional investors, the commission will be lower than if the primary purchasers are individual investors.

Commissions can be less than 1 percent or greater than 10 percent. The lower end applies to large issues of long-term debt and preferred shares sold to institutional investors; the high end to a small issue of common shares sold primarily to individual investors. The commission is split three ways—among the lead underwriter, the other members of the banking group, and the members of the selling group—with the allocation based on the functions performed. Consider the following example.

Example ▼ Raynor Plastics recently issued 10 million common shares at a price of $22 per share, raising $220 million. The commission on the issue was 6 percent while fees and expenses totalled $1.2 million. Therefore, while investors paid $22 per share, the commission consumed 6 percent or $1.32 per share of this, netting Raynor $20.68. On a total dollar basis, Raynor received $206.8 million, less the $1.2 million of fees and expenses or $205.6 million from the issue. Total issue costs were $14.4 million, or 6.55 percent of the gross proceeds. The underwriting syndicate splits the $1.32 per share, a total of $13.2 million. How is the commission split? Assume the deal between the members of the underwriting syndicate was as follows:

	Per share	Commission Per share	Commission Cumulative	Commission Percent	Commission Cumulative
Lead underwriter purchases common shares from Raynor: Pays	$20.68				
		$0.33	$0.33	1.5%	1.5%
Sells common shares to banking group	$21.01				
		$0.55	$0.88	2.5%	4%
Sells common shares to selling group	$21.56				
		$0.44	$1.32	2%	6%
Sell common shares to client	$22.00				

The lead underwriter makes money on every common share purchased, in this case a minimum of $0.33 per share or 1.5 percent of the total 6 percent commission. If the lead underwriter sold all 10 million shares to the other members of the banking group, the lead would make $3.3 million in total (10 million shares × $0.33). Assuming the lead sells 5 million shares to the banking group, 3 million shares to the selling group, and 2 million shares to their own clients, they would make $6.93 million (5 million × $0.33 + 3 million × $0.88 + 2 million × $1.32), or 52.5 percent of the total commission. If the members of the banking group sold 3 million of these shares to their own customers and 2 million shares to the selling group, their commission would be $4.07 million (3 million × $0.99 + 2 million × $0.55), or 30.83 percent of the total commission.

The selling group sells 5 million shares to their clients, making $0.44 per share, a total of $2.2 million or 16.67 percent of the total commission. The lead underwriter and the other members of the banking group are guaranteed to make money by selling shares to the members of the selling group. They can maximize their commissions by selling shares to their own clients. A member of the syndicate is said to be "flat" when they have sold all of their allotted shares. Based on this example, it is clear that underwriting is a very profitable activity for investment dealers.

Commissions account for the large majority of the total issue costs of new financial securities; however, fees and expenses are also a significant cost. Depending on issue size, fees can range from $100,000 to over $1,500,000. Total issue costs can range from less than 1 percent to 20 percent, depending on the particulars of the issue and issuer. For common share issues for many companies, total issue costs are in the 4 percent to 6 percent range.

For example, in July 2002 Optipress, a publishing and printing company, had their IPO. They issued 7 million common shares at $8.50 per share. The commission of the issue was 5 percent, while fees and expenses were $1.5 million. The IPO raised $59.5 million, but total issue costs were $4,475,000, or 7.52 percent of the gross proceeds. Also in July, Brascan Corporation issued 2,940,000 series 11 preferred shares, with a $25 stated value. The commission on the issue was 1 percent for shares sold to institutional investors and 3 percent for shares sold to others. Fees and expenses were $295,000. Therefore, gross proceeds of the issue were $73.5 million and Brascan netted $72,470,000 (assuming all shares were sold to institutions). Total issue costs were $1,030,000 or 1.4 percent of the gross proceeds. In May 2002, Imperial Oil issued $500 million of extendible notes. The commission was 0.2 percent, with no stated expenses. Imperial received net proceeds of $499 million.

 Visit the SEDAR Web site at **www.sedar.com/homepage_en.htm** and read the first page of a number of final prospectuses to determine the issue cost associated with some recent financing.

Bought Deals

bought deal
The lead underwriter(s) purchases the total amount of a new security issue from the issuing company with the intention of quickly selling the issue to investors.

A recent development affecting the underwriting process is the **bought deal**. The bought deal originated in Canada in early 1983 with Gordon Capital Corp., a maverick investment dealer whose actions helped reform the investment industry in Canada in the early 1980s. With a bought deal the lead underwriter(s) purchases the total amount of a new security issue from the issuing company. They

TABLE 6.9	Type and Dollar Amount of Equity Underwriting on the Toronto Stock Exchange (TSX) for the Five Years 1997–2001 (in millions $)				
Type of offering	1997	1998	1999	2000	2001
Initial public offerings (IPOs)	$13,742.6	$5,384.4	$6,110.4	$8,646.3	$9,260.1
Public offerings	6,799.4	6,934.2	10,304.0	10,125.4	10,132.7
Private placements	5,346.0	3,166.6	2,824.3	4,335.0	1,698.4
Total value of equity offerings	$25,888.0	$15,485.2	$19,238.7	$23,106.7	$21,091.2

SOURCES: The Toronto Stock Exchange *Review, Summary of New Equiry Financing.*

then attempt to quickly sell the issue at its face value to institutional and, in some cases, individual investors. The POP system has allowed bought deals to flourish in Canada and it is now a very common way for companies to issue securities.

This is the case since the underwriting commissions are lower than a public offering, usually a flat 4 percent for common shares. Also, the issuer receives their funds much quicker and there are no escape clauses: The underwriter assumes completely the risk of the issue not selling. If the price of the security declines between the time of the agreement but before the new issue is sold, then the underwriter can incur a loss on the issue. This is not likely to occur, however, given the short time frame between the decision to proceed with the issue and the actual sale of the issue. In fact, most bought deals are sold to institutional investors well before the underwriter agrees to the deal.

Underwriting Values

Table 6.9 provides a summary of the value of equity underwriting that occurred on the Toronto Stock Exchange (TSX) for the five years 1997 to 2001. The table also details the amount raised by the type of offering: IPOs, public offering, and private placements. As is clear from the table, there is no pattern to the amount or the type of offering used to raise equity financing over these five years. Equity offerings are very dependent on market conditions. The average amount of equity financing raised over the five years on the TSX was almost $21 billion per year, indicating that a sizeable equity market exists for Canadian corporations and underwriters.

? Review Questions

6–36 What is meant by *underwriting*? What is being underwritten?

6–37 What are the various types of underwriting transactions? What titles are used for underwriting offerings?

6–38 What are the major steps in the underwriting process? List and discuss each of the steps.

6–39   Discuss the following terms associated with underwriting: preliminary prospectus, red herring, due diligence, comment letter, underwriting syndicate, types of underwriting agreements, green sheet, blue skying, the closing.

6–40   What is the POP system, and why is it important for issuers of securities?

6–41   What issue costs are incurred when securities are offered? Are these a large cost item for issuers of securities?

6–42   What is a bought deal, and how does it differ from a public offering of securities?

SUMMARY

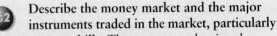 Introduce the types of financial markets and how the markets operate, the important role played by financial institutions, the major types of financial securities, and the importance of trust to the operation of the financial markets. For an economy to develop and economic wealth created, a country needs efficient and well developed financial markets. Financial markets provide a forum where suppliers of funds (savers) and demanders of funds (users) can transact business. They bring savers and users of funds together to make a fair exchange, one that provides value to both parties. Savers and users of funds include individuals, business organizations, and the various levels of government. There are two distinct financial markets: the money market and the capital market. Both of these markets have primary and secondary markets. There are six principal financial intermediaries in Canada: (1) deposit-taking, loan-making institutions; (2) investment dealers; (3) mutual funds; (4) pension funds; (5) life insurance companies; and (6) the Bank of Canada. These institutions facilitate the transfer of funds from savers to users. There are three distinct flow of fund channels shown in Figure 6.2. For the first channel, cash flows from savers through financial intermediaries to users. In the second channel, cash flows from savers to financial intermediaries, who then provide funds to users via the money or capital markets. In the third channel, cash flows from savers to financial intermediaries who buy and sell financial securities on behalf of savers in the money or capital markets. In order for financial markets to function efficiently, the participants in the market must trust in the system.

Describe the money market and the major instruments traded in the market, particularly treasury bills. The money market involves the trading of debt securities that will mature within one year. There is no physical location for the money market: It is an artificial market, the computer networks between investment dealers. The principal money market security is Government of Canada treasury bills, or t-bills as they are more commonly known. T-bills are auctioned every second Tuesday by the Bank of Canada through a competitive bidding process. The Bank of Canada uses the overnight rate as the main tool to conduct monetary policy. Other money market securities include short-dated government bonds, commercial paper, finance company paper, bankers' acceptances, and day loans. All money market securities are sold on a discount basis in both the primary and secondary markets. This means that the price paid for the bill is less than its par value. The yield is the difference between the two amounts. The international equivalent of the domestic money market is called the Eurocurrency market.

Describe the key characteristics of long-term debt, one of the major capital market securities. Long-term debt is a contractual liability between the two parties: the borrower (issuer) and the lender (saver). The agreement specifies that the issuer has borrowed a stated amount of money, termed the par value, and promises to repay it in the future under clearly defined terms. Also, while the debt is outstanding, the issuer will pay the investor a stated rate of interest, the coupon rate. There are various types of long-term debt, but the two general categories are bonds and debentures. The trust indenture is the legal document that details the contractual relationship between the borrower and lender. It specifies a trustee who acts as a watchdog on behalf of the debtholders. The default risk of long-term debt is measured by means of a bond rating, an independent and objective assessment of the investment quality of a long-term debt issue. Ratings are used to help determine the coupon rates on debt issues. Companies and governments borrow internationally using Eurobonds and foreign bonds.

 Describe the key characteristics of common and preferred stock, two additional capital market securities. Common shares signify ownership of the company. All corporations must issue common shares and be owned by shareholders. The sale also raises equity capital. Generally, each common share entitles the holder to one vote on issues affecting the company; but, many companies in Canada have issued another class of common shares with restricted voting rights. Common shareholders may receive a dividend, but this payment is at the discretion of the board of directors and the large majority of companies listed on the Toronto Stock Exchange (TSX) do not pay dividends on common shares. Some firms issue a second class of equity, preferred shares, to raise additional equity capital. Preferred equity broadens the firm's capital structure, raising financing without giving up ownership (like common stock) or incurring obligations (like debt), thus reducing the risk of the company. Preferred shares are issued with a stated value and pay dividends which accumulate if the firm misses a payment. Preferred shares are rated also for the risk of default and there are many different varieties of preferreds in Canada. Although both common and preferred shares are forms of equity capital, the characteristics of preferred shares make them more similar to debt than common equity. Secondary markets exist that allow for the trading of financial securities. These marketplaces are the securities exchanges. There are two types: physical, tangible exchanges and artificial exchanges. Securities exchanges create continuous liquid markets where trading can occur efficiently. The common and preferred shares of most large Canadian companies trade on the TSX. A summary of daily trading appears in many publications and on the Internet.

 Differentiate between debt, preferred equity, and common equity capital. The key differences between debt, preferred, and common equity relate to voice in management, claims on the firm's income and assets, maturity, and tax treatment. Typically, only common shareholders have voting rights. Equity holders have claims on income and assets that are secondary to the claims of creditors. There is no maturity date associated with most common and preferred shares, while all long-term debt is repaid at some point in the future. For a company, interest payments are a tax-deductible expense whereas dividend payments are paid out of after-tax income.

 Review the process of how financial securities are created and issued, and the important role played by the investment banker. Underwriting is the means by which new financial securities are created in the primary market. The underwriter is the financial intermediary who acts as the agent for the organization raising the funds. Investment dealers perform this function, and are often referred to collectively as an investment banker. Underwriting is a seven-step process: the organization (1) decides to raise long-term financing; (2) selects a lead underwriter and holds discussions; (3) decides on the details of the issue and prepares and issues the preliminary prospectus; (4) assembles the underwriting syndicate; (5) markets the issue; (6) prepares and distributes the final prospectus; and (7) closes the deal. While the time to complete an underwriting deal can be quite lengthy, the prompt offering prospectus (POP) system has greatly decreased the time needed to raise cash. For most organizations, the cost of issuing securities is reasonable. The main cost is the commission paid to the underwriting syndicate; the second cost is fees and expenses. Bought deals reduce costs and increase the flexibility of issuers.

SELF-TEST PROBLEMS

(Solutions in Appendix B)

 ST 6–1   **Valuing t-bills**   A $1,000 par value Government of Canada Treasury Bill is trading for $985.84. It will mature in 126 days. What percentage rate of return (yield) would an investor buying this t-bill receive?

 ST 6–2   **Valuing commercial paper**   Ferris Chemicals has surplus cash that they wish to invest for 21 days. Their investment dealer indicates that a $75 million par value issue of commercial paper is available that would provide a yield of 2.94 percent over the 21 days. How much would Ferris have to pay for the issue, and what would be their dollar return on the investment?

PROBLEMS

WARM-UP **6–1**   **Valuing t-bills**   A treasury bill issued by the Canadian government with 86 days to maturity is trading to yield 3.69 percent. For $1,000 of par value, what is the maximum amount you should pay for the t-bill? Why?

INTERMEDIATE **6–2**   **Valuing t-bills**   A major investment dealer just purchased $300 million of 364 day treasury bills from the Bank of Canada. The investment dealer paid $287,631,317.50 for the bills.
   a. What is the yield on these t-bills?
   b. If the investment dealer can sell these t-bills to other investors in the secondary market at an average yield of 4.11 percent, how much money will the investment dealer make on their purchase of $300 million of t-bills from the Bank of Canada?

INTERMEDIATE **6–3**   **Valuing t-bills**   The Bank of Canada recently issued $1.3 billion of 98-day treasury bills on behalf of the federal government. The average bid received for the auction implied a yield of 3.114 percent.
   a. How much money was raised for the federal government?
   b. The high bid received implied a yield of 2.919 percent. If this were the average bid, how much *more* money would the Bank of Canada have raised?
   c. The low bid received implied a yield of 3.254 percent. If this were the average bid, how much *less* money would the Bank of Canada have raised?
   d. Based on the above analysis, what is the direct impact on the federal government when the Bank of Canada changes the overnight rate?

WARM-UP **6–4**   **Invest surplus cash**   Garrett Machinery must make a $42 million dividend payment in 9 days. The company currently has the cash available. Assuming they could invest the full amount in a certificate of deposit yielding 3.02 percent, would it make sense for them to make the investment? How much money would they make?

WARM-UP **6–5**   **Valuing bankers' acceptances**   AIX, a mutual fund company, plans to buy a bankers' acceptance issue that is about to be sold by NoTel, a large high tech company. The par value of the issue is $100 million and AIX's investment dealer indicates AIX would have to pay $99,062,031.83 for the issue. If the issue matures in 90 days, what rate of return would AIX receive on the issue?

CHALLENGE 6–6 **Valuing bankers' acceptances** For the above problem, assume AIX purchased the bankers' acceptance issue. After 24 days, AIX realizes they require money to meet redemption requests from the holders of the mutual funds. AIX approaches their investment dealers, who indicate to them that yields on bankers' acceptances in the secondary market have increased to 4.025 percent.

a. How much would AIX receive if they sold the full issue of bankers' acceptances? How much did they make on the original purchase of the paper?

b. How much would AIX have made if yields did not change between the date of purchase and sale?

c. How much would AIX have made if yields declined to 3.61 percent between the date of purchase and sale?

d. Based on the above, discuss the possible risks and rewards of trading money market securities in the secondary market.

e. What would cause yields on money market securities to change?

INTERMEDIATE 6–7 **Eurocurrency market** To develop a property in Malaysia, Zane Oil and Gas, based in Calgary, requires US$35 million. Zane is considering using the Eurocurrency market to raise the funds. Zane requires the money for 11 months, and they have been quoted an interest rate of LIBOR + 178.

a. What is the Eurocurrency market and how could a company based in Calgary access this market?

b. What does LIBOR + 178 mean?

c. If LIBOR was 2.73 percent, what would Zane's borrowing rate be?

d. If Zane went ahead with the loan, how much would they owe the lender in 11 months?

  6–8 **Bond interest payments before and after taxes** Zylex Corp. has issued 2,500 bonds with a total principal value of $2,500,000. The bonds have a coupon rate of 9.25 percent.

WARM-UP

a. What dollar amount of interest per bond can an investor expect to receive each year from Zylex Corp.?

b. What is Zylex's total interest expense per year associated with this bond issue?

c. Assuming that Zylex is in a 35 percent corporate tax bracket, what is the company's net after-tax interest cost associated with this bond issue?

  6–9 **Characteristics of long-term debt** On August 31, 2003, Charter Corp. issued 25,000 debentures with a total principal value of $25 million. The term of the issue was 25 years and the coupon rate was 7 percent.

INTERMEDIATE

a. What was the par value of each debenture?

b. When will the debentures mature?

c. When will Charter make the first coupon payment? How much will it be per debenture certificate and in total?

d. When will Charter make the second coupon payment?

e. When will Charter make the final coupon payment? How many coupon payments will be made in total?

f. If Charter's tax rate in 2004 is 30 percent, what is the after-tax interest cost associated with this debenture issue? What is the implication of this calculation?

g. What is the effective after-tax interest rate on this issue?

INTERMEDIATE 6–10 **Sinking fund**   Refer to Problem 6.8. Charter's debenture issue has a sinking-fund requirement that becomes exercisable on the 16th anniversary of the issue. The sinking fund will then retire the issue over the remaining time to maturity.

a. What is the maximum amount Charter will contribute to the sinking fund each year once it becomes exercisable?

b. Under what circumstance will Charter exercise the sinking-fund: (i) in the open market; (ii) using the lottery process? Provide examples.

c. At the beginning of the 20th year of the term of the debenture, how much of the issue is still outstanding? During the 20th year, what will Charter's total coupon payments be?

INTERMEDIATE 6–11 **Call feature**   Rockaway Entertainment has a $300 million bond issue outstanding with a coupon rate of 6.75 percent. The bond issue has a call feature that can be exercised in six months time. The call price is par + 5.6 percent.

a. In what circumstances would Rockaway exercise the call feature?

b. If the company does exercise the call feature, how much would they have to pay bondholders per $1,000 certificate and in total?

INTERMEDIATE 6–12 **Bond ratings**   The yield on corporate long-term debt securities with different bond ratings but all with the same features, maturing in 15 years, is provided below.

Rating	Yield	Rating	Yield
AAA	6%	BBB	7.08%
AA (H)	6.12%	BBB (L)	7.26%
AA	6.23%	BB	8.05%
AA (L)	6.38%	B	8.92%
A (H)	6.51%	CCC	9.81%
A	6.63%	CC	10.23%
A (L)	6.71%	C	11.65%
BBB (H)	6.90%		

a. Where do the biggest differences in yields for the different bond ratings begin? Why is this the case?

b. The yields provided are for corporate debt issues that mature in 15 years. In what range would be the yield on federal government debt that matures in 15 years? Why?

c. What is the premium in yield and as a percentage difference: (i) between AAA and A; (ii) between AAA and BBB; (L); (iii) between AAA and CCC; (iv) between AAA and C? What does this analysis suggest?

WARM-UP 6–13 **Zero-coupon bond**   A zero-coupon bond matures for $1,000 in exactly 12 years time. If you paid $385.63 today for the bond, what average yearly rate of return will you earn?

INTERMEDIATE **6–14** **Zero-coupon bond**   Assume you bought the bond in the problem above. Four years go by and you wish to sell the bond in the secondary market. If yields in the market for bonds of this risk level are 6.2 percent, how much money will you receive when you sell the bond? If yields were 10.8 percent, how much would you receive?

WARM-UP **6–15** **Bond quotation**   Assume that the following quote for the Financial Management Corporation's $1,000-par-value bond was found in the Wednesday, November 8, issue of the *National Post*. Using the quote, answer the questions.

Fin Mgmt	8.75	June 05	14	102.46	8.42

a. On what day did the trading occur?
b. When does the bond mature?
c. What is the bond's coupon rate?
d. When will you receive the first coupon payment?
e. What is the bond's *current yield*?
f. If you wished to buy $20,000 of par value of this bond, how much would it cost?
g. Why is the yield different than the coupon rate?

WARM-UP **6–16** **Authorized and available shares**   Aspin Corporation's charter authorizes issuance of 2,000,000 shares of common stock. Currently, 1,400,000 shares are outstanding and 100,000 shares are being held as treasury stock. The firm wishes to raise $48,000,000 for a plant expansion. The sale of new common stock will net the firm $60 per share.

a. What is the maximum number of new shares of common stock the firm can sell without receiving further authorization from shareholders?
b. Based on the data given and your finding in **a**, will the firm be able to raise the needed funds without receiving further authorization?
c. What must the firm do to obtain authorization to issue more than the number of shares found in **a**?

INTERMEDIATE **6–17** **Restricted voting shares**   In 1962, Frank Hughes established Hughes Machine Parts in rural Ontario. In 1975, Frank decided to go public and held an IPO. But, for the IPO Frank decided to issue subordinate voting shares, the B share. The B shares were entitled to one vote each. Frank and his family would hold the A shares which were entitled to 200 votes per share. After a number of secondary issues of shares, there were a total of 32,463,412 common shares outstanding; 265,000 of these were Class A shares.

a. Of the total shares issued, what percent are Class B shares?
b. What percent of the votes do the Class B shares hold?
c. What type of share is the Class A? The Class B?
d. Based on the above analysis, what possible danger exists for the Class B shareholders? Is there a protection for these shareholders?

CHALLENGE **6–18** **Preemptive rights and the issuance of new common shares**   Scarloti Pizza, Inc., has 10,000,000 authorized shares. The firm currently has 5,000,000 shares issued and outstanding. Anna Scarloti owns 500,000 shares. The firm's board of directors wishes to raise additional capital by selling 1,000,000 new shares. Anna is concerned that her ownership interest is going to be diluted by the proposed sale. Her uncle, Frank Scarloti, chairperson of the board, explains to her that she is protected by preemptive rights.

a. If the firm issues one right per share, how many rights will Anna receive?

b. How many rights will be required to purchase one of the new shares?

c. How many shares must Anna purchase to maintain her percentage of the firm's ownership?

d. If each new share is sold for $10, how much must Anna spend to maintain her percentage of the firm's ownership?

 INTERMEDIATE **6–19**   **Dilution of earnings**   Goodwood Golfing earnings available for common shareholders (EAC) for this fiscal year is $6.5 million. Goodwood has 5 million common shares outstanding. The current share price is $24.00. Goodwood is considering issuing 500,000 common shares that will net the company 95 percent of the current share price when all issue costs are considered.

a. Prior to the share issue, what is Goodwood's earnings per share (EPS)?

b. Assuming Goodwood issues the share this fiscal year, what is the immediate dilution of the new share issue?

c. Assume that the proceeds from the share issue are invested and provide a 12 percent return that flows to EAC. Is there a dilutive effect of the new share issue?

 INTERMEDIATE **6–20**   **Dividends in arrears**   QTL Tech has an issue of preferred shares outstanding with a $50 stated value that pays a dividend of 7.5 percent. There are 325,000 shares outstanding. QTL has not paid preferred share dividends for 3.5 years. The company's CEO wishes to retire the preferred share issue by paying the preferred shareholders 50 percent of the dividends in arrears plus 10 percent of the stated value of the preferred.

a. What would be the total payment QTL Tech would have to make to the preferred shareholders?

b. QTL Tech common shares are trading for $1.22 on the market. If the CEO offered to convert each preferred share into 5 common shares, would this be a better deal for the preferred shareholders?

CHALLENGE **6–21**   **Convertible preferred stock**   Valerian Corp. convertible preferred stocks has a fixed conversion ratio of 5 common shares per 1 share of preferred stock. The preferred stock pays a dividend of $10 per share per year. The common stock currently sells for $20 per share and pays a dividend of $1 per share per year.

a. Based on the conversion ratio and the price of the common shares, what is the current conversion value of each preferred share?

b. If the preferred shares are selling at $96 each, should an investor convert the preferred shares to common shares?

c. What factors might cause an investor not to convert from preferred to common?

 WARM-UP **6–22**   **Common share**   Assume that the following quote for the Advanced Business Machines stock (traded on the TSX) was found in the Thursday, December 14, issue of the *National Post*. Using the quote, answer the questions.

| 84.12 | 51.25 | AdvBusMach | 0.92 | 2.9 | 23 | 6432 | 31.76 | 30.12 | 31.75 | +1.62 |

    a. On what day did the trading activity occur?

    b. What are the highest and lowest prices at which the stock sold on the day quoted?

    c. What is the firm's price/earnings ratio? What does it indicate? What were ABM's most recent EPS?

    d. What is the last price at which the stock traded on the day quoted?

    e. What was the most recent quarterly dividend? What is the indicated dividend for ABM?

    f. What is the highest and lowest price at which the stock traded during the latest 52-week period?

    g. How many board lots of common shares and how many shares in total were traded on the day quoted?

    h. Did the common share price change from the previous trading day? If so, by how much? What did the share close at on the previous trading day?

WARM-UP **6–23** **Issue costs**   Blaine Lumber requires $25 million of financing and is considering a bond issue. The commission on the issue is expected to be 1.25 percent while issue costs are $325,000. What are the total issue costs on the bond issue in dollars and on a percentage basis? How much money will Blaine Lumber receive?

INTERMEDIATE **6–24** **Issue costs**   RDC Imperial Securities is the lead underwriter of the IPO for a major company that is about to go public. There will be 30 million common shares sold to the public for $44.00 per share. The underwriter's commission on the issue will be 4.5 percent with RDC getting a flat 1 percent for being the lead. Fees and expenses are expected to total $1.75 million.

    a. What is the total commission the company will pay on the IPO?

    b. What are the total issue costs on a total dollar and percentage basis? What is the net amount the company will receive?

    c. If RDC sells 25 million shares to the members of the banking group and the remaining 5 million shares to investors, what dollar amount of commission will RDC Imperial Securities make on the IPO? What percentage of the total commission will the lead underwriter make?

CASE   CHAPTER 6

Financing Lobo Enterprises' Expansion Program

Lobo Enterprises, based in Edmonton, began as a small radio station. In 1985, it used a sizable loan to purchase a much larger company involved in the exterminating business and has acquired other businesses since then. Net earnings have risen continuously through 2003, 12 years since Lobo Enterprises first went public. Currently, the firm's equity base is quite small in comparison to the amount of debt financing on its books.

    The company is doing well in its media, wallcovering, and burglary and fire protection systems businesses, but the exterminating business—benefiting from wider markets, new customers, and higher fees—is performing magnificently.

In the fiscal year ended June 30, 2003, gross income at Lobo Enterprises rose 17 percent; profits were held down somewhat by startup costs in several new businesses. Lobo's capital outlays have been about $11 million in each of the past two fiscal years, but higher expansion levels are likely in the near future and are expected to require an additional $23 million of financing.

A few years ago, Lobo's long-term debt was 85 percent of total assets, but debt has since been reduced to 70 percent of total assets. The debt carries an average interest rate of 11.7 percent before taxes. The debt reduction was partially financed by issuing $7.7 million of preferred shares with a $20 stated value and a 10 percent dividend rate.

Currently, the directors must decide on a method of financing the $23 million expansion. They are primarily interested in an equity financing plan using preferred or common shares because funds could be obtained without incurring added mandatory interest payments that would result in greater risk. Additional equity would allow Lobo Enterprises to avoid restrictive covenants that are often tied to long-term debt financing and would provide a more flexible foundation from which debt could be issued when interest rates fall. The decision, however, could result in the dilution of the current shareholders' interests in the company. Rebecca Marks, the chief financial officer, has been charged with advising Lobo's board with regard to common and preferred stock financing alternatives.

Required

a. Discuss the overall advantages of equity financing for Lobo Enterprises at this time.

b. Discuss the advantages and disadvantages of selling common shares. Compare and contrast its use to the use of debt financing.

c. Discuss the advantages and disadvantages of selling preferred shares. Compare and contrast its use to the use of common share financing.

d. In the event Lobo Enterprises decides to use common share financing, discuss the advantages and disadvantages of using a rights offering rather than the public sale of new common shares.

e. Provide an example illustrating how issuing common shares could result is the dilution of the current shareholders' interests in the company, focusing on both earnings per share (EPS) and voting control.

f. Based solely on the nonquantitative factors discussed in **a** through **d**, what recommendation should Rebecca Marks make to Lobo's board about how to finance the firm's $23 million need? Justify your recommendation in light of the alternatives.

WEB EXERCISE   LINKS TO PRACTISE

Visit the following Web sites and complete the suggested exercises. These exercises will allow you to review practical applications of the chapter topics as well as explore the wealth of information regarding managerial finance that is available on the Internet.

www.cba.ca/eng/Statistics/statistics_index.htm
Click on the Fast Stats—pdf link. On what date was the Fast Stats updated?

1. How many domestic banks are there in Canada? Name them. Which are the six largest domestic banks? Do you deal with a deposit-taking, loan-making institution? Which one do you deal with and why?

2. Besides banks, how many other financial institutions are there in Canada? Which is the largest in terms of numbers?

3. How many credit cards are in circulation in Canada, and what was the total amount charged on these credit cards during the most recent fiscal year?

4. How many Interac direct payment transactions were there in Canada during the most recent fiscal year? What was the rate of growth in Interac transactions during the period for which statistics are provided?

5. Click through to **www.interac.org**. Click on the link for Statistics. Click on IDP Stats. What does IDP stand for? What was the value of the number of transactions determined above? How many IDP users, merchants, and terminals are there in Canada? How many IDP users are there in your province? Do you use a credit card or IDP card? Why?

6. What other interesting statistics are provided on the Interac.org site?

7. Discuss how credit cards and IDP cards are part of the financial markets.

www.tse.com/en/productsAndServices/listings/index.html
Click on Listing on the Toronto Stock Exchange. What are the benefits to a company of listing on the Toronto Stock Exchange (TSX)? What are the requirements for a company to list their common shares on the TSX? Return to the above page. Click on Listing on TSX Venture Exchange. What type of companies would list their shares on the TSX Venture Exchange? Discuss the three ways a company could list on the TSX Venture Exchange. What are the costs of going public?

www.bankofcanada.ca/en/backgrounders.htm
The above Web site provides a brief reading describing the Bank of Canada's main functions. Click on Interest Rates. What is an interest rate? What is the difference between a nominal and real interest rate? Why are short-term and longer term interest rates different? What interest rate does the Bank of Canada have influence over, and how?

Go back to the main Web page. Click on What is Money. Why does the money you have in your wallet or purse have value? What are the principal roles of money? How does the Bank of Canada ensure Canadian money retains its value?

Go back to the main Web page. Click on Bank Rate. What is the Large Value Transfer System (LVTS), and why is it important to the Bank of Canada's control over interest rates?

Go back to the main Web page. Click on Target for the Overnight Rate. What objectives does the Bank of Canada have when it sets the overnight rate? The Bank of Canada's official rate (or key policy rate) is the overnight rate. How does this rate compare to those of other countries?

Visit the following site: **www.bankofcanada.ca/en/target.htm**. Discuss the system of eight "fixed" or pre-specified dates each year for announcing changes to the official rate that the Bank of Canada introduced in December 2000. Read one of the announcements provided on the right-hand side of the Web page.

Beginning in November 2000, the Bank of Canada introduced a new system of eight "fixed" or pre-specified dates each year for announcing any changes to the official interest rate it uses to implement monetary policy. The Bank concluded that a fixed-date approach leads to more effective monetary policy for Canada. Fixed announcement dates replaced the old approach of announcing monetary policy actions under which the Bank could, in principle, adjust interest rates on any business day. With the new approach, the Bank of Canada joined many other central banks in the industrialized countries, including the U.S. Federal Reserve System, the Bank of England, the European Central Bank, and the Bank of Japan, all of which have pre-set dates for announcing interest rate changes. Visit the following Web site for further discussion of how the Bank of Canada influences interest rates in Canada: **www.bankofcanada.ca/fixed-dates**.

www.dbrs.com

Link to the above Web site. In the upper right-hand corner there is a "Quick Search" box allowing the user to search for the ratings on all of the available financial securities for a particular company. Find and report the rating for two different types of financial securities for three different companies. Comment on the risks to an investor of buying the company's financial securities. Were there any recent events for the company and, if so, what were they? Provide your report in the following format:

Company	Financial security	Rating action	Rating	Trend
BCE Inc.	Commercial paper	Confirmed	R-1 (middle)	Stb
BCE Inc.	Unsecured debentures	Confirmed	A (high)	Stb
BCE Inc.	All classes preferred shares	Confirmed	Pfd-2 (high)	Stb

Comments and discussion of recent events:

CHAPTER

7

Risk and Return

LEARNING GOALS

LG1 Understand the meaning and fundamentals of risk, return, and risk preferences.

LG2 Describe procedures for measuring the risk of a single asset.

LG3 Discuss the measurement of return and standard deviation for a portfolio and the various types of correlation that can exist between series of numbers.

LG4 Understand the risk and return characteristics of a portfolio in terms of correlation and diversification, and the impact of international assets on a portfolio.

LG5 Review the two types of risk and the derivation and role of beta in measuring the relevant risk of both an individual security and a portfolio.

LG6 Explain the capital asset pricing model (CAPM), its relationship to the security market line (SML), and shifts in the SML caused by changes in inflationary expectations and risk aversion.

7.1 Risk and Return Fundamentals

To maximize share price, the financial manager must learn to assess two key determinants: risk and return.[1] Each financial decision presents certain risk and return characteristics, and the unique combination of these characteristics has an impact on share price. Risk can be viewed as it relates either to a single asset or

---

1. Two important points should be recognized here: (1) Although for convenience the publicly traded corporation is being discussed, the risk and return concepts presented apply equally well to all firms; and (2) concern centres only on the wealth of common shareholders, because they are the "residual owners" whose returns are in no way specified in advance.

"Not for a Million Bucks!"

Expressions like this one and "Make it worth my while" touch on one of the key concepts of finance—that risk and return are linked. The idea that return should increase if risk increases is fundamental in finance. Of course, people, as well as firms, have different views of risk, depending on who they are and what they know how to do. Also, some people and some firms are simply more willing to take risks than are others—and for some, the mere thrill of risk is almost enough return in itself. Generally, though, most financial managers, like most people, shy away from undue risk and so must be compensated for taking on risk. As this chapter will show, firms can quantify and assess the risk and return for individual assets and for groups of assets, using various tools and techniques.

portfolio
A collection, or group, of assets.

to a **portfolio**—a collection, or group, of assets. We will look at both, beginning with the risk of a single asset. First, though, it is important to introduce some fundamental concepts about risk, return, and risk preferences.

Risk Defined

risk
The chance of financial loss or, more formally, the variability of returns associated with a given asset.

In the most basic sense, **risk** is the chance of financial loss. Assets having greater chances of loss are viewed as more risky than those with lesser chances of loss. More formally, the term *risk* is used interchangeably with *uncertainty* to refer to the *variability of returns associated with a given asset*. A government bond that guarantees its holder $100 interest after 30 days has no risk, because there is no variability associated with the return. A $100 investment in a firm's common stock, which over the same period may earn anywhere from –$50 to $100, is very risky due to the high variability of return. The more certain the return from an asset, the less variability and therefore the less risk.

Return Defined

return
The total gain or loss experienced on an investment over a given period of time; calculated by dividing the asset's change in value plus any cash distributions during the period by its beginning-of-period investment value.

Obviously, if we are going to assess risk based on variability of return, we need to be certain we know what *return* is, and how to measure it. The **return** is the total gain or loss experienced on an investment over a given period of time. It is commonly measured as the change in value plus any cash distributions during the period, expressed as a percentage of the beginning-of-period investment value. The expression for calculating the rate of return earned on any asset over period t, k_t, is commonly defined as:

$$k_t = \frac{P_t - P_{t-1} + C_t}{P_{t-1}} \tag{7.1}$$

where

k_t = actual, expected, or required rate of return[2] during period $t - 1$ to t
P_t = price (value) of asset at time t
P_{t-1} = price (value) of asset at time $t - 1$
C_t = cash (flow) received from the asset investment in the time period $t - 1$ to $t - 1$ to t

The return, k_t, reflects the combined effect of changes in value, $P_t - P_{t-1}$, and cash flow, C_t, over period $t - 1$ to t.[3]

Equation 7.1 is used to determine the rate of return over a time period as short as 1 day or as long as 10 years or more. However, in most cases, t is 1 year, and k therefore represents an annual rate of return.

E x a m p l e ▼ Robin's Gameroom, a high-traffic video arcade, wishes to determine the return on two of its video machines, Conqueror and Demolition. Conqueror was purchased 1 year ago for $20,000 and currently has a market value of $21,500. During the year, it generated $800 of after-tax cash receipts. Demolition was purchased 4 years ago; its value in the year just completed declined from $12,000 to $11,800. During the year, it generated $1,700 of after-tax cash receipts. Substituting into Equation 7.1, we can calculate the annual rate of return, k, for each video machine:

Conqueror (C):

$$k_C = \frac{\$21,500 - \$20,000 + \$800}{\$20,000} = \frac{\$2,300}{\$20,000} = \underline{\underline{11.5\%}}$$

---

2. The terms *expected return* and *required return* are used interchangeably throughout this text, because in an efficient market (discussed later) they would be expected to be equal. The actual return is an *ex post* value, whereas expected and required returns are *ex ante* values. Therefore, the actual return may be greater than, equal to, or less than the expected/required return.

3. The beginning-of-period value, P_{t-1}, and the end-of-period value, P_t, are not necessarily *realized values*. They are often *unrealized*, which means that although the asset was *not* actually purchased at time $t - 1$ and sold at time t, values P_{t-1} and P_t *could* have been realized had those transactions been made.

Demolition (D):

$$k_D = \frac{\$11,800 - \$12,000 + \$1,700}{\$12,000} = \frac{\$1,500}{\$12,000} = \underline{\underline{12.5\%}}$$

Although the market value of Demolition declined during the year, its cash flow caused it to earn a higher rate of return than that earned by Conqueror during the same period. Clearly, the combined impact of changes in value and cash flow ▲ measured by the rate of return is important.

Risk Preferences

Feelings about risk differ among managers (and firms).[4] Thus, it is important to specify a generally acceptable level of risk. The three basic risk preference behaviours—risk-averse, risk-indifferent, and risk-seeking—are depicted graphically in Figure 7.1.

risk-indifferent
The attitude toward risk in which no change in return would be required for an increase in risk.

risk-averse
The attitude toward risk in which an increased return would be required for an increase in risk.

risk-seeking
The attitude toward risk in which a decreased return would be accepted for an increase in risk.

- For the **risk-indifferent** manager, the required return does not change as risk goes from x_1 to x_2. In essence, no change in return would be required for the increase in risk. Clearly, this attitude is nonsensical in almost any business context.
- For the **risk-averse** manager, the required return increases for an increase in risk. Because they shy away from risk, these managers require higher expected returns to compensate them for taking greater risk.
- For the **risk-seeking** manager, the required return decreases for an increase in risk. Theoretically, because they enjoy risk, these managers are willing to give up some return to take more risk. Such behaviour would be considered irrational and would likely negatively affect the firm and the manager.

FIGURE 7.1

Risk Preferences
Risk preference behaviours

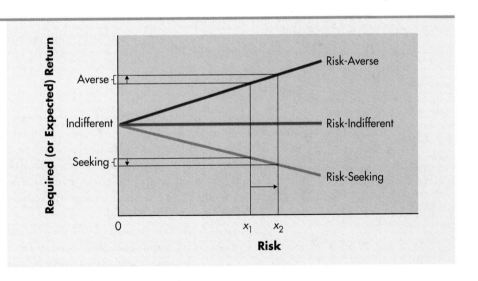

4. The risk preferences of the managers in theory should be consistent with the risk preferences of the firm. Although the *agency problem* suggests that in practice managers may not behave in a manner consistent with the firm's risk preferences, it is assumed here that they do. Therefore, the managers' risk preferences and those of the firm are assumed to be identical.

It is generally assumed that people are risk-averse; for a given increase in risk, they require an increase in return. They generally tend to be conservative rather than aggressive when accepting risk for their firm. Accordingly, a *risk-averse financial manager requiring higher returns for greater risk is assumed throughout this text.*

? Review Questions

7–1   Define *risk* as it relates to financial decision making. Do any assets have perfectly certain returns?

7–2   Define *return*. Describe the basic calculation involved in finding the return on an investment.

7–3   Compare the following risk preferences: (**a**) risk-averse, (**b**) risk-indifferent, and (**c**) risk-seeking. Which is most common among financial managers?

7.2 Risk of a Single Asset

The concept of risk is best developed by first considering a single asset held in isolation. Although you will later see that the risk of a portfolio of assets is measured in much the same way as the risk of a single asset, certain benefits accrue to holders of portfolios. For both single assets and for portfolios, we can assess risk by looking at the expected return behaviour of assets, and we can measure the risk using statistics.

Risk Assessment

Risk can be assessed using sensitivity analysis and probability distributions, which provide a feel for the level of risk embodied in a given asset.

sensitivity analysis
An approach for assessing risk that uses a number of possible return estimates to obtain a sense of the variability among outcomes.

range
A measure of an asset's risk, which is found by subtracting the pessimistic (worst) outcome from the optimistic (best) outcome.

Sensitivity Analysis

Sensitivity analysis uses a number of possible return estimates to obtain a sense of the variability among outcomes.[5] One common method involves estimating the pessimistic (worst), the most likely (expected), and the optimistic (best) returns associated with a given asset. In this case, the asset's risk can be measured by the **range,** which is found by subtracting the pessimistic outcome from the optimistic outcome. The greater the range for a given asset, the more variability, or risk, it is said to have.

Example ▼ Norman Company, a custom golf equipment manufacturer, wants to choose the better of two investments, A and B. Each requires an initial outlay of $10,000 and each has a *most likely* annual rate of return of 15 percent. Management has also made *pessimistic* and *optimistic* estimates of the returns associated with

5. The term "sensitivity analysis" is intentionally used in a general rather than technically correct fashion here to simplify this discussion. A more technical and precise definition and discussion of this technique and "scenario analysis" is presented in Chapter 13.

TABLE 7.1	Assets A and B	
	Asset A	Asset B
Initial investment	$10,000	$10,000
Annual rate of return		
Pessimistic	13%	7%
Most likely	15%	15%
Optimistic	17%	23%
Range	4%	16%

each. The three estimates for each asset, along with its range, are given in Table 7.1. Asset A appears to be less risky than asset B; its range of 4 percent (17% − 13%) is less than the range of 16 percent (23% − 7%) for asset B. The risk-averse decision maker would prefer asset A over asset B, because A offers the same most likely return as B (15%) but with lower risk (smaller range).

Although the use of sensitivity analysis and the range is rather crude, it does provide the decision maker with a feel for the behaviour of returns that can be used to assess roughly the risk involved.

Probability Distributions

Probability distributions provide a more quantitative insight into an asset's risk. The **probability** of a given outcome is its *chance* of occurring. If an outcome has an 80 percent probability of occurrence, the given outcome would be expected to occur 8 out of 10 times. If an outcome has a probability of 100 percent, it is certain to occur. Outcomes having a probability of zero will never occur.

probability
The *chance* that a given outcome will occur.

Example ▼ Norman Company's past estimates indicate that the probabilities of the pessimistic, most likely, and optimistic outcomes are 25 percent, 50 percent, and 25 percent, respectively. The sum of these probabilities must equal 100 percent; ▲ that is, they must be based on all the alternatives considered.

probability distribution
A model that relates probabilities to the associated outcomes.

bar chart
The simplest type of probability distribution; shows only a limited number of outcomes and associated probabilities for a given event.

continuous probability distribution
A probability distribution showing all the possible outcomes and associated probabilities for a given event.

A **probability distribution** is a model that relates probabilities to the associated outcomes. The simplest type of probability distribution is the **bar chart,** which shows only a limited number of outcome–probability coordinates. The bar charts for Norman Company's assets A and B are shown in Figure 7.2. Although both assets have the same most likely return, the range of return is much more dispersed for asset B than for asset A—16 versus 4 percent.

If we knew all the possible outcomes and associated probabilities, we could develop a **continuous probability distribution.** This type of distribution can be thought of as a bar chart for a very large number of outcomes.[6] Figure 7.3 presents

6. To develop a continuous probability distribution, one must have data on a large number of historical occurrences for a given event. Then, by developing a frequency distribution indicating how many times each outcome has occurred over the given time horizon, one can convert these data into a probability distribution. Probability distributions for risky events can also be developed by using *simulation*—a process discussed briefly in Chapter 13.

FIGURE 7.2

Bar Charts

Bar charts for asset A's and asset B's returns

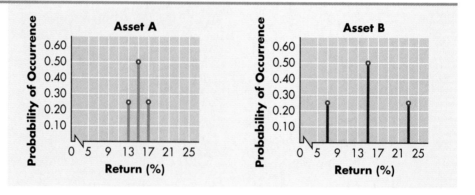

continuous probability distributions for assets A and B.[7] Note in Figure 7.3 that although A and B have the same most likely return (15 percent), the distribution of returns for asset B has much greater *dispersion* than the distribution for asset A. Clearly, asset B is more risky than asset A.

Risk Measurement

In addition to its *range,* the risk of an asset can be measured quantitatively using statistics. Here we consider two statistics—the standard deviation and the coefficient of variation—that can be used to measure the variability of asset returns.

standard deviation (σ_k)
The most common statistical indicator of an asset's risk; it measures the dispersion around the *expected value.*

Standard Deviation

The most common statistical indicator of an asset's risk is the **standard deviation,** σ_k, which measures the dispersion around the *expected value.*[8] The **expected**

FIGURE 7.3

Continuous Probability Distributions

Continuous probability distributions for asset A's and asset B's returns

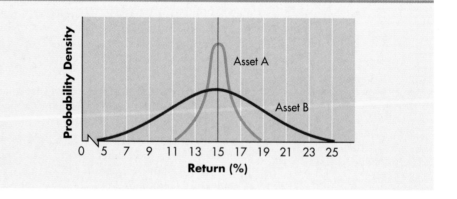

7. The continuous distribution's probabilities change due to the large number of additional outcomes considered. The area under each of the curves is equal to 1, which means that 100 percent of the outcomes, or all the possible outcomes, are considered.

8. Although risk is typically viewed as determined by the dispersion of outcomes around an expected value, many people believe that risk exists only when outcomes are below the expected value, because only returns below the expected value are considered bad. Nevertheless, the common approach is to view risk as determined by the variability on either side of the expected value, because the greater this variability, the less confident one can be of the outcomes associated with an investment.

expected value of a return ($\bar{k}$)
The most likely return on a given asset.

value of a return, $\bar{k}$, is the most likely return on an asset, which is calculated as:[9]

$$\bar{k} = \sum_{i=1}^{n} k_i \times Pr_i \tag{7.2}$$

where

$$k_i = \text{return for the } i\text{th outcome}$$
$$Pr_i = \text{probability of occurrence of the } i\text{th outcome}$$
$$n = \text{number of outcomes considered}$$

E x a m p l e ▼ The expected values for Norman Company's assets A and B are presented in Table 7.2. Column 1 gives the Pr_i's and column 2 gives the k_i's. In each case n equals 3. The expected value for each asset's return is 15 percent. **▲**

The expression for the *standard deviation of returns*, σ_k, is:[10]

$$\sigma_k = \sqrt{\sum_{i=1}^{n} (k_i - \bar{k})^2 \times Pr_i} \tag{7.3}$$

In general, the higher the standard deviation, the greater the risk.

E x a m p l e ▼ Table 7.3 presents the standard deviations for Norman Company's assets A and B, based on the earlier data. The standard deviation for asset A is 1.41 percent, and the standard deviation for asset B is 5.66 percent. The higher risk of asset B is clearly reflected in its higher standard deviation. **▲**

normal probability distribution
A symmetrical probability distribution whose shape resembles a "bell-shaped" curve.

A **normal probability distribution**, depicted in Figure 7.4, always resembles a "bell-shaped" curve. It is symmetrical: From the peak of the graph, the curve's extensions are mirror images (reflections) of each other. The symmetry of the curve means that half the probability is associated with the values to the left of the peak and half with values to the right. As noted on the figure, for normal probability distributions, 68 percent of the possible outcomes will lie between ±1 standard deviation from the expected value, 95 percent of all outcomes will lie between ±2 standard deviations from the expected value, and 99 percent of all outcomes will lie between ±3 standard deviations from the expected value.[11]

---

9. The formula for finding the expected value of return, $\bar{k}$, when all of the outcomes, k_i, are known *and* their related probabilities are assumed to be equal, is a simple arithmetic average:

$$k = \frac{\sum_{i=1}^{n} k_i}{n} \tag{7.2a}$$

where n is the number of observations. Equation 7.2 is emphasized in this chapter because returns and related probabilities are often available.

10. The formula that is commonly used to find the standard deviation of returns, σ_k, in a situation in which *all* outcomes are known *and* their related probabilities are assumed equal, is

$$\sigma_k = \sqrt{\frac{\sum_{i=1}^{n} (k_i - k)^2}{n - 1}} \tag{7.3a}$$

where n is the number of observations. Equation 7.3 is emphasized in this chapter because returns and related probabilities are often available.

11. Tables of values indicating the probabilities associated with various deviations from the expected value of a normal distribution can be found in any basic statistics text. These values can be used to establish confidence limits and make inferences about possible outcomes. Such applications may be found in most basic statistics and upper-level managerial finance textbooks.

TABLE 7.2   Expected Values of Returns for Assets A and B

Possible outcomes	Probability (1)	Returns (2)	Weighted value [(1) × (2)] (3)
Asset A			
Pessimistic	0.25	13%	3.25%
Most likely	0.50	15	7.50
Optimistic	0.25	17	4.25
Total	1.00	Expected return	15.00%
Asset B			
Pessimistic	0.25	7%	1.75%
Most likely	0.50	15	7.50
Optimistic	0.25	23	5.75
Total	1.00	Expected return	15.00%

TABLE 7.3   The Calculation of the Standard Deviation of the Returns for Assets A and B[a]

Asset A

i	k_i	$\bar{k}$	$k_i - \bar{k}$	$(k_i - \bar{k})^2$	Pr_i	$(k_i - \bar{k})^2 \times Pr_i$
1	13%	15%	−2%	4%	0.25	1%
2	15	15	0	0	0.50	0
3	17	15	2	4	0.25	1

$$\sum_{i=1}^{3} (k_i - \bar{k})^2 \times Pr_i = 2\%$$

$$\sigma_{k_A} = \sqrt{\sum_{i=1}^{3} (k_i - \bar{k})^2 \times Pr_i} = \sqrt{2}\% = \underline{\underline{1.41\%}}$$

Asset B

i	k_i	$\bar{k}$	$k_i - \bar{k}$	$(k_i - \bar{k})^2$	Pr_i	$(k_i - \bar{k})^2 \times Pr_i$
1	7%	15%	−8%	64%	0.25	16%
2	15	15	0	0	0.50	0
3	23	15	8	64	0.25	16

$$\sum_{i=1}^{3} (k_i - \bar{k})^2 \times Pr_i = 32\%$$

$$\sigma_{k_B} = \sqrt{\sum_{i=1}^{3} (k_i - \bar{k})^2 \times Pr_i} = \sqrt{32}\% = \underline{\underline{5.66\%}}$$

[a]Calculations in this table are made in percentage form rather than decimal form—e.g., 13% rather than 0.13. As a result, some of the intermediate computations may appear to be inconsistent with those that would result from using decimal form. Regardless, the resulting standard deviations are correct and identical to those that would result from using decimal rather than percentage form.

Career Key
The *marketing* department considers standard deviation when deciding to add or delete product lines. The addition and/or deletion of product lines might produce an erratic earnings pattern that would increase the risk of the firm. And the standard deviation can be influenced by the *operations* department, which can help stabilize earnings by entering into long-term contracts with suppliers that will reduce the fluctuations in raw material prices and subsequently in earnings.

FIGURE 7.4

Bell-Shaped Curve
Normal probability distribution, with ranges

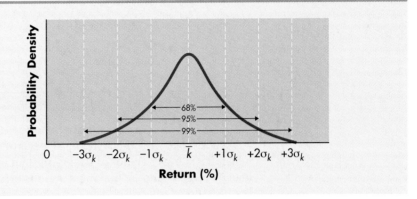

Example ▼ If we assume that the probability distribution of returns for the Norman Company is normal, 68 percent of the possible outcomes would have a return ranging between 13.59 and 16.41 percent for asset A and between 9.34 and 20.66 percent for asset B; 95 percent of the possible return outcomes would range between 12.18 and 17.82 percent for asset A and between 3.68 and 26.32 percent for asset B; and 99 percent of the possible return outcomes would range between 10.77 and 19.23 percent for asset A and between −1.98 and 31.98 percent for asset B. The greater risk of asset B is clearly reflected by its much wider range of
▲ possible returns for each level of confidence (68%, 95%, etc.).

Coefficient of Variation

coefficient of variation (CV)
A measure of relative dispersion that is useful in comparing the risk of assets with differing expected returns.

The **coefficient of variation, CV,** is a measure of relative dispersion that is useful in comparing the risk of assets with differing expected returns. Equation 7.4 gives the expression for the coefficient of variation:

$$CV = \frac{\sigma_k}{\bar{k}} \tag{7.4}$$

The higher the coefficient of variation, the greater the risk.

Example ▼ When the standard deviation (from Table 7.3) and the expected returns (from Table 7.2) for assets A and B are substituted into Equation 7.4, the coefficients of variation for A and B are 0.094 (1.41% ÷ 15%) and 0.377 (5.66% ÷ 15%), respectively. Asset B has the higher coefficient of variation and is therefore more risky than asset A—which we already know from the standard deviation. Because both assets have the same expected return, the coefficient of variation
▲ has not provided any new information.

The real utility of the coefficient of variation comes in comparing the risk of assets that have *different* expected returns.

Example ▼ A firm wants to select the less risky of two alternative assets—X and Y. The expected return, standard deviation, and coefficient of variation for each of these assets' returns are

Statistics	Asset X	Asset Y
(1) Expected return	12%	20%
(2) Standard deviation	9%[a]	10%
(3) Coefficient of variation [(2) ÷ (1)]	0.75	0.50[a]

[a]Preferred asset using the given risk measure.

Based solely on their standard deviations, the firm would prefer asset X, which has a lower standard deviation than asset Y (9% versus 10%). However, management would be making a serious error in choosing asset X over asset Y, because the relative dispersion—the risk—of the assets as reflected in the coefficient of variation is lower for Y than for X (0.50 versus 0.75). Clearly, the use of the coefficient of variation to compare asset risk is effective because it also considers the relative size, or expected return, of the assets.

? Review Questions

7–4   How can *sensitivity analysis* be used to assess asset risk? Define and describe the role of the *range* in sensitivity analysis.

7–5   What does a plot of the *probability distribution* of outcomes show a decision maker about an asset's risk? What is the difference between a *bar chart* and a *continuous probability distribution?*

7–6   What does the *standard deviation* of asset returns indicate? What relationship exists between the size of the standard deviation and the degree of asset risk?

7–7   What is the *coefficient of variation?* How is it calculated? When is it preferred over the standard deviation for comparing asset risk?

7.3 Risk of a Portfolio

efficient portfolio
A portfolio that maximizes return for a given level of risk or minimizes risk for a given level of return.

The risk of any single proposed asset investment should not be viewed independent of other assets. New investments must be considered in light of their impact on the risk and return of the *portfolio* of assets.[12] The financial manager's goal is to create an **efficient portfolio,** one that maximizes return for a given level of risk or minimizes risk for a given level of return. We therefore need a way to measure the return of a portfolio of assets. Once we can do that, we will look at the statistical concept of *correlation*, which underlies the process of diversification that is used to develop an efficient portfolio.

---

12. The portfolio of a firm, which would consist of its total assets, is not differentiated from the portfolio of an owner, which would likely contain a variety of different investment vehicles (i.e., assets). The differing characteristics of these two types of portfolios should become clear upon completion of Chapter 13.

Portfolio Return and Standard Deviation

The *return on a portfolio* is a weighted average of the returns on the individual assets from which it is formed. We can use Equation 7.5 to find the portfolio return, k_p:

$$k_p = (w_1 \times k_1) + (w_2 \times k_2) + \cdots + (w_n \times k_n) = \sum_{j=1}^{n} w_j \times k_j \qquad (7.5)$$

where

w_j = proportion of the portfolio's total dollar value represented by asset j
k_j = return on asset j

Of course, $\sum_{j=1}^{n} w_j = 1$, which means that 100 percent of the portfolio's assets must be included in this computation.

The *standard deviation of a portfolio's returns* is found by applying the formula for the standard deviation of a single asset. Specifically, Equation 7.3 would be used when the probabilities of the returns are known, and Equation 7.3a (from footnote 10) would be applied when the outcomes are known and their related probabilities of occurrence are assumed to be equal.

Example ▼ Assume that we wish to determine the expected value and standard deviation of returns for portfolio XY, created by combining equal portions (50%) of assets X and Y. The expected returns of assets X and Y for each of the next 5 years (2003–2007) are given in columns 1 and 2, respectively, in part A of Table 7.4. In column 3, the weights of 50 percent for both assets X and Y along with their respective returns from columns 1 and 2 are substituted into Equation 7.5. Column 4 shows the results of the calculation—an expected portfolio return of 12 percent for each year, 2003 to 2007.

Furthermore, as shown in part B of Table 7.4, the expected value of these portfolio returns over the 5-year period is also 12 percent (calculated by using Equation 7.2a, in footnote 9). In part C of Table 7.4, portfolio XY's standard deviation is calculated to be 0 percent (using Equation 7.3a, in footnote 10). This value should not be surprising because the expected return each year is the same—12 percent. No variability is exhibited in the expected returns from year
▲ to year.

correlation
A statistical measure of the relationship, if any, between series of numbers representing data of any kind.

positively correlated
Descriptive of two series that move in the same direction.

negatively correlated
Descriptive of two series that move in opposite directions.

Correlation

Correlation is a statistical measure of the relationship, if any, between series of numbers representing data of any kind, from returns to test scores. If two series move in the same direction, they are **positively correlated;** if the series move in opposite directions, they are **negatively correlated.**[13]

13. The general *long-term trend* of two series could be the same (both increasing or both decreasing) or different (one increasing, the other decreasing), and the correlation of their *short-term (point-to-point) movements* in both situations could be either positive or negative. In other words, the pattern of movement around the trends could be correlated independent of the actual relationship between the trends. Further clarification of this seemingly inconsistent behaviour can be found in most basic statistics texts.

TABLE 7.4	Expected Return, Expected Value, and Standard Deviation of Returns for Portfolio XY

A. Expected portfolio returns

	Expected return			Expected portfolio
	Asset X	Asset Y	Portfolio return calculation[a]	return, k_p
Year	(1)	(2)	(3)	(4)
2003	8%	16%	$(0.50 \times 8\%) + (0.50 \times 16\%) =$	12%
2004	10	14	$(0.50 \times 10\%) + (0.50 \times 14\%) =$	12
2005	12	12	$(0.50 \times 12\%) + (0.50 \times 12\%) =$	12
2006	14	10	$(0.50 \times 14\%) + (0.50 \times 10\%) =$	12
2007	16	8	$(0.50 \times 16\%) + (0.50 \times 8\%) =$	12

B. Expected value of portfolio returns, 2003–2007[b]

$$\bar{k}_p = \frac{12\% + 12\% + 12\% + 12\% + 12\%}{5} = \frac{60\%}{5} = \underline{\underline{12\%}}$$

C. Standard deviation of expected portfolio returns[c]

$$\sigma_{k_p} =$$

$$\sqrt{\frac{(12\% - 12\%)^2 + (12\% - 12\%)^2 + (12\% - 12\%)^2 + (12\% - 12\%)^2 + (12\% - 12\%)^2}{5-1}}$$

$$= \sqrt{\frac{0\% + 0\% + 0\% + 0\% + 0\%}{4}} = \sqrt{\frac{0}{4}}\% = \underline{\underline{0\%}}$$

[a]Using Equation 7.5.
[b]Using Equation 7.2a found in footnote 9.
[c]Using Equation 7.3a found in footnote 10.

correlation coefficient
A measure of the degree of correlation between two series.

perfectly positively correlated
Describes two *positively correlated* series that have a *correlation coefficient* of +1.

perfectly negatively correlated
Describes two *negatively correlated* series that have a *correlation coefficient* of −1.

The degree of correlation is measured by the **correlation coefficient,** which ranges from +1 for **perfectly positively correlated** series to −1 for **perfectly negatively correlated** series. These two extremes are depicted for series M and N in Figure 7.5. The perfectly positively correlated series move exactly together; the perfectly negatively correlated series move in exactly opposite directions.

Diversification

The concept of correlation is essential to developing an efficient portfolio. To reduce overall risk, it is best to combine or add to the portfolio assets that have a negative (or a low positive) correlation. Combining negatively correlated assets can reduce the overall variability of returns. Figure 7.6 shows that a portfolio containing the negatively correlated assets F and G, both having the same expected return, $\bar{k}$, also has the return $\bar{k}$ but has less risk (variability) than either of the

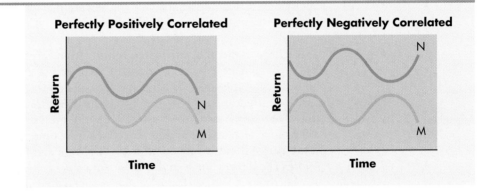

FIGURE 7.5

Correlations
The correlation between series M and N

individual assets. Even if assets are not negatively correlated, the lower the positive correlation between them, the lower the resulting risk.

Some assets are **uncorrelated**—that is, there is no interaction between their returns. Combining uncorrelated assets can reduce risk—not as effectively as combining negatively correlated assets, but more effectively than combining positively correlated assets. The correlation coefficient for uncorrelated assets is close to zero and acts as the midpoint between perfect positive and perfect negative correlation.

The creation of a portfolio by combining two assets with perfectly positively correlated returns *cannot* reduce the portfolio's overall risk below the risk of the least risky asset. Alternatively, a portfolio combining two assets with less than perfectly positive correlation *can* reduce total risk to a level below that of either of the components, which in certain situations may be zero. For example, assume that you manufacture machine tools. The business is very *cyclical*, with high sales when the economy is expanding and low sales during a recession. If you acquired another machine-tool company, with sales positively correlated with those of your firm, the combined sales would still be cyclical, and risk would remain the same. Alternatively, however, you could acquire a sewing-machine manufacturer, which is *countercyclical*. It typically has low sales during economic expansion and high sales during recession (when consumers are more likely to make their

uncorrelated
Describes two series that lack any interaction and therefore have a *correlation coefficient* close to zero.

🔑 **Career Key**
Management is concerned about the effect on its risk level of its product diversification decisions. Adding and/or deleting product groups will affect the firm's portfolio of products and the level of risk that is associated with it.

FIGURE 7.6

Diversification
Combining negatively correlated assets to diversify risk

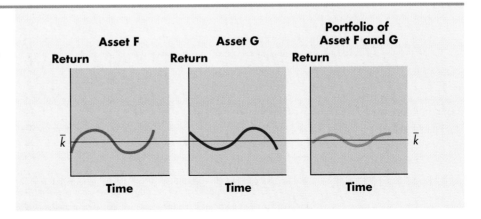

own clothes). Combination with the sewing-machine manufacturer, which has negatively correlated sales, should reduce risk.

Example ▼   Table 7.5 presents the anticipated returns from three different assets—X, Y, and Z—over the next 5 years, along with their expected values and standard deviations. Each of the assets has an expected value of return of 12 percent and a standard deviation of 3.16 percent. The assets therefore have equal return and equal risk. The return patterns of assets X and Y are perfectly negatively correlated. They move in exactly opposite directions over time. The returns of assets X and Z are perfectly positively correlated. They move in precisely the same direction. (*Note:* The returns for X and Z are identical.)[14]

Portfolio XY   Portfolio XY (shown in Table 7.5) is created by combining equal portions of assets X and Y—the perfectly negatively correlated assets.[15]

TABLE 7.5   Returns, Expected Values, and Standard Deviations for Assets X, Y, and Z and Portfolios XY and XZ

	Assets			Portfolios	
Year	X	Y	Z	XY[a] (50%X + 50%Y)	XZ[b] (50%X + 50%Z)
2003	8%	16%	8%	12%	8%
2004	10	14	10	12	10
2005	12	12	12	12	12
2006	14	10	14	12	14
2007	16	8	16	12	16
Statistics:[c]					
Expected value	12%	12%	12%	12%	12%
Standard deviation[d]	3.16%	3.16%	3.16%	0%	3.16%

[a]Portfolio XY, which consists of 50% of asset X and 50% of asset Y, illustrates *perfect negative correlation,* because these two return streams behave in completely opposite fashion over the 5-year period. The return values shown here were calculated in part A of Table 7.4.

[b]Portfolio XZ, which consists of 50% of asset X and 50% of asset Z, illustrates *perfect positive correlation,* because these two return streams behave identically over the 5-year period. These return values were calculated by using the same method demonstrated for portfolio XY in part A of Table 7.4.

[c]Because the probabilities associated with the returns are not given, the general equations, Equation 7.2a in footnote 9 and Equation 7.3a in footnote 10, were used to calculate expected values and standard deviations, respectively. Calculation of the expected value and standard deviation for portfolio XY is demonstrated in parts B and C, respectively, of Table 7.4.

[d]The portfolio standard deviations can be directly calculated from the standard deviations of the component assets using the following formula:

$$\sigma_{k_p} = \sqrt{w_1^2\sigma_1^2 + w_2^2\sigma_2^2 + 2w_1w_2r_{1,2}\sigma_1\sigma_2}$$

where w_1 and w_2 are the proportions of component assets 1 and 2, σ_1 and σ_2 are the standard deviations of component assets 1 and 2, and $r_{1,2}$ is the correlation coefficient between the returns of component assets 1 and 2.

14. Identical return streams are used in this example to permit clear illustration of the concepts, but it is *not* necessary for return streams to be identical for them to be perfectly positively correlated. Any return streams that move (i.e., vary) exactly together—regardless of the relative magnitude of the returns—are perfectly positively correlated.

15. For illustrative purposes it has been assumed that each of the assets—X, Y, and Z—can be divided up and combined with other assets to create portfolios. This assumption is made only to permit clear illustration of the concepts. The assets are not actually divisible.

(Calculation of portfolio XY's annual expected returns, their expected value, and the standard deviation of expected portfolio returns was demonstrated in Table 7.4.) The risk in this portfolio, as reflected by its standard deviation, is reduced to 0 percent, while the expected return remains at 12 percent. Thus, the combination results in the complete elimination of risk. Whenever assets are perfectly negatively correlated, an optimum combination (similar to the 50–50 mix in the case of assets X and Y) exists for which the resulting standard deviation will equal 0.

Portfolio XZ Portfolio XZ (shown in Table 7.5) is created by combining equal portions of assets X and Z—the perfectly positively correlated assets. The risk in this portfolio, as reflected by its standard deviation, is unaffected by this combination. Risk remains at 3.16 percent, and the expected return value remains at 12 percent. Whenever perfectly positively correlated assets such as X and Z are combined, the standard deviation of the resulting portfolio cannot be reduced *below that of the least risky asset;* the maximum portfolio standard deviation will be that of the riskiest asset. Because assets X and Z have the same standard deviation, the minimum and maximum standard deviations are the same (3.16%). This result can be attributed to the unlikely situation that X and Z are identical assets.

Correlation, Diversification, Risk, and Return

In general, the lower the correlation between asset returns, the greater the potential diversification of risk. (This should be clear from the behaviours illustrated in Table 7.5.) For each pair of assets, there is a combination that will result in the lowest risk (standard deviation) possible. How much risk can be reduced by this combination depends on the degree of correlation. Many potential combinations (assuming divisibility) could be made, but only one combination of the infinite number of possibilities will minimize risk.

Three possible correlations—perfect positive, uncorrelated, and perfect negative—illustrate the effect of correlation on the diversification of risk and return. Table 7.6 summarizes the impact of correlation on the range of return and risk for various two-asset portfolio combinations. The table shows that as we move

⚠ Hint

Remember, low correlation between two series of numbers is less positive and more negative—indicating greater dissimilarity of behaviour of the two series.

TABLE 7.6 Correlation, Return, and Risk for Various Two-Asset Portfolio Combinations

Correlation coefficient	Range of return	Range of risk
+1 (perfect positive)	Between returns of two assets held in isolation	Between risk of two assets held in isolation
0 (uncorrelated)	Between returns of two assets held in isolation	Between risk of most risky asset and an amount less than risk of least risky asset but greater than 0
−1 (perfect negative)	Between returns of two assets held in isolation	Between risk of most risky asset and 0

from perfect positive correlation to uncorrelated assets to perfect negative correlation, the ability to reduce risk is improved. Note that in no case will a portfolio of assets be riskier than the riskiest asset included in the portfolio.

Example ▼ A firm has calculated the expected return and the risk for each of two assets—R and S.

Asset	Expected return, $\bar{k}$	Risk (standard deviation), σ
R	6%	3%
S	8	8

Clearly, asset R is a lower return, lower risk asset than asset S.

To evaluate possible combinations, the firm considered three possible correlations—perfect positive, uncorrelated, and perfect negative. The results of the analysis are shown in Figure 7.7, using the ranges of return and risk noted above. In all cases, the return will range between the 6 percent return of R and the 8 percent return of S, depending on the percentage of the portfolio invested in assets R and S. The risk, on the other hand, ranges between the individual risks of R and S (from 3 to 8%) in the case of perfect positive correlation, from below 3 percent (the risk of R) and greater than 0 percent to 8 percent (the risk of S) in the uncorrelated case, and between 0 and 8 percent (the risk of S) in the perfectly negatively correlated case. Again, the actual level of portfolio risk is dependent on the percentage of the portfolio invested in assets R and S.

Note that *only in the case of perfect negative correlation can the risk be reduced to 0*. Also note that as the correlation becomes less positive and more negative (moving from the top of the figure down), the ability to reduce risk improves. The amount of risk reduction achieved depends on the proportions in which the assets are combined. Although determining the risk-minimizing combination is beyond the scope of this discussion, it is an important issue in developing portfolios of assets. ▲

FIGURE 7.7

Possible Correlations
Range of portfolio return ($\bar{k}_p$) and risk (σ_{k_p}) for combinations of assets R and S for various correlation coefficients

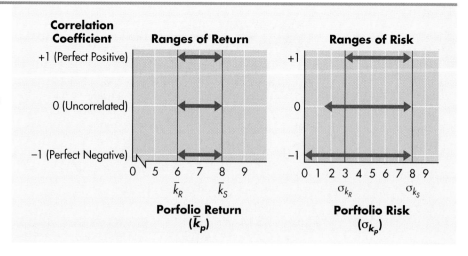

IN PRACTICE

Less Risk Through Diversification?

"Don't put all your eggs in one basket." That old saying is a good description of diversification. Don't put all your eggs in one basket because if the basket falls, all of your eggs break, not just a few. Does the adage also apply to companies? There are different views on the issue. In Canada, numerous companies have followed diversification strategies, some with great success, others with less.

In 1946, Atco, builders of the world's first portable industrial housing, started life in the Southern family garage. Atco's housing is now found around the world wherever there are construction or development projects. From oil developments in the far north to dam construction in Asia, Atco has provided housing from a single trailer to whole camps, really small towns, for projects in more than 100 countries.

By 1980, Atco was flourishing, driven by the boom in oil exploration. But the founder's son, Ron Southern, decided to take Atco in a different direction. Against all advice and perceived wisdom, he paid $350 million for controlling interest in a stodgy, regulated power utility in northern Alberta named Canadian Utilities. Explains Ron: "I wanted a non-cyclical business to build a stable future." He wanted to diversify Atco's cash flows from being totally dependent on construction and natural resource development. Today Atco

is a true diversified conglomerate. The company still builds housing and generates, transmits, and distributes electricity in Alberta (the two original businesses) but they also generate power in Europe and Australia, build and operate gas pipelines and gas storage facilities, are project managers for companies in five different industries, and run noise reduction, call centre, IT application, travel, wood preservative, and coal combustion companies. The family also owns the Spruce Meadows Equestrian Centre outside Calgary.

While some may consider Atco's business combinations "weird," the company spreads risk through diversification, looking for growth in one area to compensate for slower growth in others. Atco blends riskier companies, whose performance is directly tied to the economy, with ones that will perform consistently, regardless of economic conditions. Has the diversification strategy worked for Atco? For the fiscal year ended December 31, 2001, Atco had total assets of $5.8 billion, sales were almost $3.8 billion, while net income after tax was $259.5 million. In June 2002, Atco's market capitalization was $1.6 billion. Not bad for a company founded in the family garage.

SOURCES: Atco Group, *2001 Annual Report,* available at **www.atco.com**; Diane Francis, "The Making of an Energy Empire," *National Post,* June 15, 2002.

International Diversification

The ultimate example of portfolio diversification involves including foreign assets in a portfolio. The inclusion of assets from countries that are less sensitive to the Canadian business cycle (i.e., that are negatively correlated) reduces the portfolio's responsiveness to market movements and to foreign currency fluctuations.

Returns from International Diversification

Over long periods, returns from internationally diversified portfolios tend to be superior to those of purely domestic ones. This is particularly so if the Canadian economy is performing relatively poorly and the dollar is depreciating in value against most foreign currencies. At such times the dollar returns to Canadian investors on a portfolio of foreign assets can be very attractive indeed. However, over any single short or intermediate period, international diversification can yield subpar returns—particularly during periods when the dollar is appreciating in value relative to other currencies. When the Canadian currency gains in value, the dollar value of a foreign-currency-denominated portfolio of assets declines. Even if this portfolio yields a satisfactory return in local currency, the return to Canadian investors will be reduced when translated into dollars. Subpar local currency portfolio returns, coupled with an appreciating dollar, can yield truly dismal dollar returns to Canadian investors.

Overall, though, the logic of international portfolio diversification assumes that these fluctuations in currency values and relative performance will average out over long periods and that an internationally diversified portfolio will tend to yield a comparable return at a lower level of risk than will similar purely domestic portfolios.

Risks of International Diversification

political risk
Risk that arises from the possibility that a host government might take actions harmful to foreign investors or that political turmoil in a country might endanger investments made in that country by foreign nationals.

Canadian investors should, however, also be aware of the potential dangers of international investing. In addition to the risk induced by currency fluctuations, several other financial risks are unique to international investing. The most important of these fall in the category of political risk. **Political risk** arises from the possibility that a host government might take actions harmful to foreign investors or that political turmoil in a country might endanger investments made in that country by foreign nationals. Political risks are particularly acute in developing countries, where unstable or ideologically motivated governments may attempt to block return of profits by foreign investors or even seize (nationalize) their assets in the host country.

Even where governments do not impose exchange controls or seize assets, international investors may suffer if a shortage of hard currency prevents payment of dividends or interest to foreigners. When governments are forced to allocate scarce foreign exchange, they rarely give top priority to the interests of foreign investors. Instead, hard currency reserves are typically used to pay for necessary imports such as food and industrial materials and to pay interest on the government's own debts. Because most of the debt of developing countries is held by banks rather than individuals, foreign investors are often badly harmed when a country experiences political or economic problems. If a country does not have well developed financial markets, the possibility of political risk can be high.

? Review Questions

7–8   Why must assets be evaluated in a portfolio context? What is an *efficient portfolio*? How can the return and standard deviation of a portfolio be determined?

7–9   Why is the *correlation* between asset returns important? How does diversification allow risky assets to be combined so that the risk of the portfolio is less than the risk of the individual assets in it?

7–10   How does international diversification enhance risk reduction? When might international diversification result in subpar returns? What are *political risks,* and how do they affect international diversification?

  ## 7.4   Risk and Return: The Capital Asset Pricing Model (CAPM)

capital asset pricing model (CAPM)
The basic theory that links together risk and return for all assets.

The most important aspect of risk is the *overall risk* of the firm as viewed by investors in the marketplace. Overall risk significantly affects investment opportunities—and even more important, the owners' wealth. The basic theory that links together risk and return for all assets is the **capital asset pricing model (CAPM).**[16] We will use CAPM to understand the basic risk-return tradeoffs involved in all types of financial decisions.

Types of Risk

To understand the basic types of risk, consider what happens to the risk of a portfolio consisting of a single security (asset), to which we add securities randomly selected from, say, the population of all actively traded securities. Using the standard deviation of return, σ_{k_p}, to measure the total portfolio risk, Figure 7.8 depicts the behaviour of the total portfolio risk (*y* axis) as more securities are added (*x* axis). With the addition of securities, the total portfolio risk declines, due to the effects of diversification, and tends to approach a limit. Research has shown that, on average, most of the risk-reduction benefits of diversification can be gained by forming portfolios containing 15 to 20 randomly selected securities.

FIGURE 7.8

Risk Reduction
Portfolio risk and diversification

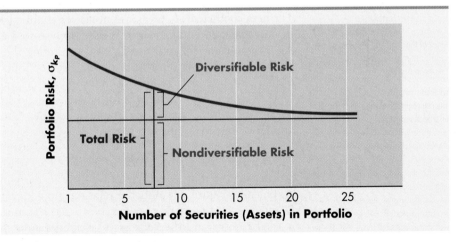

---

16. The initial development of this theory is generally attributed to William F. Sharpe, "Capital Asset Prices: A Theory of Market Equilibrium Under Conditions of Risk," *Journal of Finance* 19 (September 1964), pp. 425–442, and John Lintner, "The Valuation of Risk Assets and the Selection of Risky Investments in Stock Portfolios and Capital Budgets," *Review of Economics and Statistics* 47 (February 1965), pp. 13–37. A number of authors subsequently advanced, refined, and tested this now widely accepted theory.

total risk
The combination of a security's nondiversifiable and diversifiable risk.

The **total risk** of a security can be viewed as consisting of two parts:

$$\text{Total security risk} = \text{nondiversifiable risk} + \text{diversifiable risk} \tag{7.6}$$

diversifiable risk
The portion of an asset's risk that is attributable to firm-specific, random causes; can be eliminated through diversification.

nondiversifiable risk
The relevant portion of an asset's risk attributable to market factors that affect all firms; cannot be eliminated through diversification.

Diversifiable risk, sometimes called *unsystematic risk,* represents the portion of an asset's risk that is associated with random causes that can be eliminated through diversification. It is attributable to firm-specific events, such as strikes, lawsuits, regulatory actions, and loss of a key account. **Nondiversifiable risk,** also called *systematic risk,* is attributable to market factors that affect all firms; it cannot be eliminated through diversification. Factors such as war, inflation, international incidents, and political events account for nondiversifiable risk.

Because any investor can create a portfolio of assets that will eliminate virtually all diversifiable risk, *the only relevant risk is nondiversifiable risk.* Any investor or firm therefore must be concerned solely with nondiversifiable risk. The measurement of nondiversifiable risk is thus of primary importance in selecting assets with the most desired risk-return characteristics.

The Model: CAPM

The capital asset pricing model (CAPM) links together nondiversifiable risk and return for all assets. We will discuss the model in five sections. The first defines, derives, and describes the beta coefficient, which is a measure of nondiversifiable risk. The second section presents an equation of the model itself, and the third graphically describes the relationship between risk and return. The fourth section discusses the effects of changes in inflationary expectations and risk aversion on the relationship between risk and return. The final section offers some general comments on CAPM.

Beta Coefficient

beta coefficient (b)
A measure of nondiversifiable risk. An *index* of the degree of movement of an asset's return in response to a change in the *market return.*

market return
The return on the market portfolio of all traded securities.

The **beta coefficient,** b, measures nondiversifiable risk. It is an *index* of the degree of movement of an asset's return in response to a change in the *market return.* An asset's historical returns are used in finding the asset's beta coefficient. The **market return** is the return on the market portfolio of all traded securities. The *S&P/TSX Composite Index* or some similar stock index is commonly used as the market return. Although betas for actively traded stocks can be obtained from a variety of sources, you should understand how they are derived and interpreted and how they are applied to portfolios.

Deriving Beta from Return Data   The relationship between an asset's return and the market return and its use in deriving beta can be demonstrated graphically. Figure 7.9 plots the relationship between the returns of two assets— R and S—and the market return. Note that the horizontal (x) axis measures the market returns and the vertical (y) axis measures the individual asset's returns. The first step in deriving beta involves plotting the coordinates for the market return and asset returns from various points in time. Such annual market return–asset return coordinates are shown *for asset S only* for the years 1995 through 2002. For example, in 2002, asset S's return was 20 percent when the market return was 10 percent. By use of statistical techniques, the "characteristic line" that best explains the relationship between the asset return and the market

FIGURE 7.9

Beta Derivation[a]

Graphic derivation of beta for assets R and S

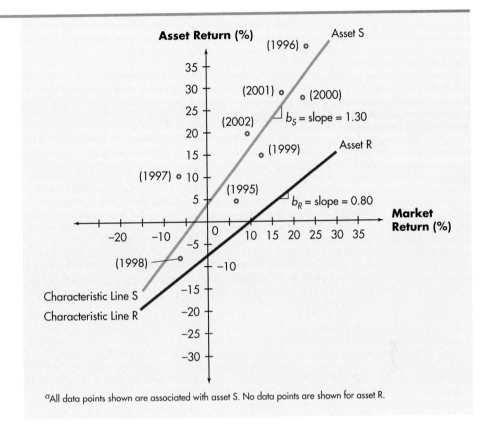

[a]All data points shown are associated with asset S. No data points are shown for asset R.

return coordinates is fit to the data points.[17] The slope of this line is beta. The beta for asset R is about 0.80 and that for asset S is about 1.30. Clearly, asset S's higher beta (steeper characteristic line slope) indicates that its return is more responsive to changing market returns. Therefore it is more risky than asset R.[18]

---

17. The empirical measurement of beta is approached by using *least-squares regression analysis* to find the regression coefficient (b_j) in the equation for the "characteristic line":

$$k_j = a_j + b_j k_m + e_j$$

where

k_j = return on asset j

a_j = intercept

b_j = beta coefficient, which equals $\dfrac{Cov\,(k_j,\,k_m)}{\sigma_m^2}$

k_m = required rate of return on the market portfolio of securities

e_j = random error term, which reflects the diversifiable, or unsystematic, risk of asset j

where

$Cov\,(k_j,\,k_m)$ = covariance of the return on asset j, k_j, and the market portfolio, k_m

σ_m^2 = variance of the return on the market portfolio

The calculations involved in finding betas are somewhat rigorous. If you want to know more about these calculations, consult an advanced managerial finance or investments text.

18. The values of beta also depend on the time interval used for return calculations and the number of returns used in the regression analysis. In other words, betas calculated using monthly returns would not necessarily be comparable to those calculated using daily returns over the same time period.

Interpreting Betas   The beta coefficient for the market is considered to be equal to 1.0; all other betas are viewed in relation to this value. Asset betas may take on values that are either positive or negative, but positive betas are the norm. The majority of beta coefficients fall between 0.5 and 2.0. The return of a stock that is half as responsive as the market ($b = 0.5$) is expected to change by 1/2 percent for each 1 percent change in the return of the market portfolio. A stock that is twice as responsive as the market ($b = 2.0$) is expected to experience a 2 percent change in its return for each 1 percent change in the return of the market portfolio. Table 7.7 provides some selected beta values and their interpretations. Beta coefficients for actively traded common shares can be obtained from investment dealers, in publications such as *Financial Post Corporate Reports* or *The Investment Reporter*, and on the Internet at sites such as **www.marketguide.com**. Betas for the common shares of selected companies are provided in Table 7.8.

Portfolio Betas   The beta of a portfolio can be easily estimated using the betas of the individual assets it includes. Letting w_j represent the proportion of the portfolio's total dollar value represented by asset j and b_j equal the beta of asset j, we can use Equation 7.7 to find the portfolio beta, b_p:

$$b_p = (w_1 \times b_1) + (w_2 \times b_2) + \ldots + (w_n \times b_n) = \sum_{j=1}^{n} w_j \times b_j \qquad (7.7)$$

Of course, $\sum_{j=1}^{n} w_j = 1$, which means that 100 percent of the portfolio's assets must be included in this computation.

Portfolio betas are interpreted in the same way as individual asset betas. They indicate the degree of responsiveness of the *portfolio's* return to changes in the market return. For example, when the market return increases by 10 percent, a portfolio with a beta of 0.75 will experience a 7.5 percent increase in its return ($0.75 \times 10\%$); a portfolio with a beta of 1.25 will experience a 12.5 percent increase in its return ($1.25 \times 10\%$). Clearly, a portfolio containing mostly low-beta assets will have a low beta, and one containing mostly high-beta assets will have a high beta.

E x a m p l e ▼ The Austin Fund, a large investment company, wishes to assess the risk of two portfolios—V and W. Both portfolios contain the common shares of five companies, with the proportions and betas shown in Table 7.9. The betas for the two

Hint

Remember that published and calculated betas are based on historical data. When investors use beta for decision making, they should recognize that past performance relative to the market average may not predict future performance.

Hint

Mutual fund managers are key users of the portfolio beta and return concepts. They are continually evaluating what would happen to the fund's beta and return if the securities of a particular firm are added or deleted from the fund's portfolio.

TABLE 7.7	Selected Beta Coefficients and Their Interpretations

Beta	Comment	Interpretation
2.0	Move in same direction as market	Twice as responsive, or risky, as the market
1.0		Same response or risk as the market (i.e., average risk)
0.5		Only half as responsive, or risky, as the market
0		Unaffected by market movement
−0.5	Move in opposite direction to market	Only half as responsive, or risky, as the market
−1.0		Same response or risk as the market (i.e., average risk)
−2.0		Twice as responsive, or risky, as the market

TABLE 7.8	Beta Coefficients for the Common Shares of Selected Companies (August 6, 2002)

Stock	Beta	Stock	Beta
Abitibi Consolidated	1.07	Magna International	1.20
Air Canada	2.58	Manulife Financial	1.02
Alcan	1.29	Maple Leaf Foods	0.80
Bank of Montreal	0.83	Molson Inc.	1.00
BCE Inc.	0.67	Onex Corp.	0.79
Bombardier	1.87	Pantheon Inc.	1.76
Canadian Natural Resources	0.77	Petro-Canada	0.67
Canadian National Railway	1.01	Potash Corp. of Saskatchewan	0.77
Canadian Tire	0.97	Rogers Communications	1.43
CIBC	1.16	Royal Bank	0.91
Falconbridge	1.03	Sears	1.79
Fortis Inc.	0.33	Sobeys	0.54
Forzani Group	1.51	Stelco Inc.	1.51
Imperial Oil	0.55	Thompson Corp.	0.98
Inco	1.39	Toronto-Dominion Bank	1.15
Intrawest Corp.	1.28	Van Houtte	0.53
Loblaw Companies	0.35	WestJet Airlines	1.07

SOURCE: TD Waterhouse, August 6, 2002.

portfolios, b_v and b_w, can be calculated by substituting data from the table into Equation 7.7:

$$b_v = (0.10 \times 1.65) + (0.30 \times 1.00) + (0.20 \times 1.30) + (0.20 \times 1.10) + (0.20 \times 1.25)$$
$$= 0.165 + 0.300 + 0.260 + 0.220 + 0.250 = 1.195 = \underline{\underline{1.20}}$$

$$b_w = (0.10 \times 0.80) + (0.10 \times 1.00) + (0.20 \times 0.65) + (0.10 \times 0.75) + (0.50 \times 1.05)$$
$$= 0.080 + 0.100 + 0.130 + 0.075 + 0.525 = \underline{\underline{0.91}}$$

TABLE 7.9	Austin Fund's Portfolios V and W

Common Share	Portfolio V Proportion	Portfolio V Beta	Portfolio W Proportion	Portfolio W Beta
1	0.10	1.65	0.10	0.80
2	0.30	1.00	0.10	1.00
3	0.20	1.30	0.20	0.65
4	0.20	1.10	0.10	0.75
5	0.20	1.25	0.50	1.05
Totals	1.00		1.00	

Portfolio V's beta is 1.20, and portfolio W's is 0.91. These values make sense, because portfolio V contains relatively high-beta assets and portfolio W contains relatively low-beta assets. Clearly, portfolio V's returns are more responsive to changes in market returns and are therefore more risky than portfolio W's.

The Equation

By using the beta coefficient to measure nondiversifiable risk, the *capital asset pricing model (CAPM)* is given in Equation 7.8:

$$k_j = R_F + [b_j \times (k_m - R_F)] \tag{7.8}$$

where

k_j = required return on asset j

R_F = risk-free rate of return, commonly measured by the return on short-term Government of Canada treasury bills

b_j = beta coefficient or index of nondiversifiable risk for asset j

k_m = market return; return on the market portfolio of assets

The required return on an asset, k_j, is an increasing function of beta, b_j, which measures nondiversifiable risk. In other words, *the higher the risk, the higher the required return, and the lower the risk, the lower the required return.*

The model can be divided into two parts: (1) the *risk-free rate,* and (2) the *risk premium.* These are, respectively, the two elements on either side of the addition sign in Equation 7.8. The $(k_m - R_F)$ portion of the risk premium is called the *market risk premium,* because it represents the premium the investor must receive for taking the average amount of risk associated with holding the market portfolio of assets.[19]

Example ▼ Benjamin Corporation, a growing computer-software developer, wishes to determine the required return on an asset Z, which has a beta of 1.5. The risk-free rate of return is estimated to be 7 percent; the return on the market portfolio of assets is 11 percent. Substituting $b_z = 1.5$, $R_F = 7\%$, and $k_m = 11\%$ into the capital asset pricing model given in Equation 7.8 yields a required return:

$$k_z = 7\% + [1.5 \times (11\% - 7\%)] = 7\% + 6\% = \underline{\underline{13\%}}$$

The market risk premium of 4 percent ($11\% - 7\%$), when adjusted for the asset's index of risk (beta) of 1.5, results in a risk premium of 6 percent ($1.5 \times 4\%$). That risk premium, when added to the 7 percent risk-free rate, results in a 13 percent required return. Other things being equal, the higher the beta, the higher the required return, and the lower the beta, the lower the required return. ▲

To use the CAPM in practice, information regarding the expected market return and risk-free rate is required. Rather than estimating the market return,

---

19. Although CAPM has been widely accepted, a broader theory, *arbitrage pricing theory (APT),* first described by Stephen A. Ross, "The Arbitrage Theory of Capital Asset Pricing," *Journal of Economic Theory* (December 1976), pp. 341–360, has in recent years received a great deal of attention in the financial literature. The theory suggests that the risk premium on securities may be better explained by a number of factors underlying and in place of the market return used in CAPM. The CAPM in effect can be viewed as being derived from APT. Although testing of APT theory confirms the importance of the market return, it has thus far failed to clearly identify other risk factors. As a result of this failure as well as APT's lack of practical acceptance and usage, we concentrate our attention here on CAPM.

however, an estimate for the market risk premium is often used. A reasonable way to estimate the market risk premium is to base it on the average market risk premium over a long period of time. In Canada, the average market return, as measured by the total return on the S&P/TSX Index (formerly the TSE 300 Index) from 1951 to 2000, was 12.08 percent. The average return on 3-month Government of Canada treasury bills over this same period was 6.65 percent.

Therefore, the market risk premium over this long period of time averaged 5.43 percent. Based on this data, a reasonable estimate of the premium investors would demand to invest in the risky market portfolio of common shares would be about 5.5 percent. Recognize, however, that this is just an estimate and is subject to change based on the expectations of the user of the CAPM. The risk-free rate used in the model is usually based on current expectations regarding the expected yield on Government of Canada treasury bills.

In their paper, "Long-Run Global Capital Market Returns and Risk Premia," Elroy Dimson, Paul Marsh, and Mike Staunton provide an excellent summary and discussion of the returns earned on common shares, bonds, and treasury bills, over the 101-year period from 1900 to 2000, in the U.S. and 15 other countries including Canada. This paper is available at: **papers.ssrn.com/abstract=217849** and is based on their book *Triumph of the Optimists: 101 Years of Global Investment Returns*, Princeton University Press, 2002.

The Graph: The Security Market Line (SML)

security market line (SML)
The depiction of the *capital asset pricing model (CAPM)* as a graph that reflects the required return in the marketplace for each level of nondiversifiable risk (beta).

When the capital asset pricing model (Equation 7.8) is depicted graphically, it is called the **security market line (SML)**. The SML will, in fact, be a straight line. It reflects the required return in the marketplace for each level of nondiversifiable risk (beta). In the graph, risk as measured by beta, b, is plotted on the x axis, and required returns, k, are plotted on the y axis. The risk-return tradeoff is clearly represented by the SML.

Example ▼ In the preceding example for Benjamin Corporation, the risk-free rate, R_F, was 7 percent, and the market return, k_m, was 11 percent. The SML can be plotted by using the two sets of coordinates for the betas associated with R_F and k_m, b_{R_F} and b_m (i.e., $b_{R_F} = 0$,[20] $R_F = 7\%$; and $b_m = 1.0$, $k_m = 11\%$). Figure 7.10 presents the resulting security market line. As traditionally shown, the security market line in Figure 7.10 presents the required return associated with all positive betas. The market risk premium of 4 percent (k_m of 11% − R_F of 7%) has been highlighted. For a beta for asset Z, b_z, of 1.5, its corresponding required return, k_z, is 13 percent. Also shown in the figure is asset Z's risk premium of 6 percent (k_z of 13% − R_F of 7%). It should be clear that for assets with betas greater than 1, the risk premium is greater than that for the market; for assets with betas less ▲ than 1, the risk premium is less than that for the market.

Shifts in the Security Market Line

The security market line is not stable over time, and shifts in the security market line can result in a change in required return. The position and slope of the SML

---

20. Because R_F is the rate of return on a risk-free asset, the beta associated with the risk-free asset, b_{R_F}, would equal 0. The 0 beta on the risk-free asset reflects not only its absence of risk but also that the asset's return is unaffected by movements in the market return.

FIGURE 7.10

Security Market Line
Security market line (SML)
with Benjamin Corporation's
asset Z data shown

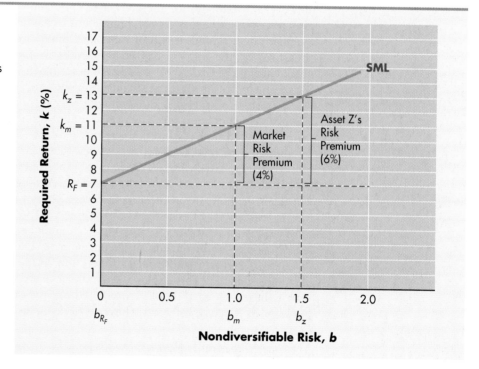

is affected by two major forces—inflationary expectations and risk aversion—which are separately analyzed next.[21]

Changes in Inflationary Expectations   Changes in inflationary expectations affect the risk-free rate of return, R_F. The equation for the risk-free rate of return is:

$$R_F = k^* + IP \tag{7.9}$$

This equation shows that assuming a constant real rate of interest, k^*, changes in inflationary expectations, reflected in an inflation premium, IP, will result in corresponding changes in the risk-free rate. Therefore, a change in inflationary expectations resulting from events such as international trade embargoes or major changes in Bank of Canada policies will result in a shift in the SML. Because the risk-free rate is a basic component of all rates of return, any change in R_F will be reflected in *all* required rates of return.

Changes in inflationary expectations result in parallel shifts in the SML in direct response to the magnitude and direction of the change. This effect can best be illustrated by an example.

Example ▼ In the preceding example, using CAPM, the required return for asset Z, k_Z, was found to be 13 percent. Assuming that the risk-free rate of 7 percent includes a 2 percent real rate of interest, k^*, and a 5 percent inflation premium, IP, then Equation 7.9 confirms that

$$R_F = 2\% + 5\% = 7\%$$

---

21. A firm's beta can change over time as a result of changes in the firm's asset mix, in its financing mix, or in external factors not within management's control, such as earthquakes, toxic spills, and so on. The impacts of changes in beta on value are discussed in Chapter 8.

Now assume that recent economic events have resulted in an *increase of 3 percent in inflationary expectations, raising the inflation premium* to 8 percent (IP_1). As a result, all returns would likewise rise by 3 percent. In this case, the new returns (noted by subscript 1) are

$$R_{F_1} = 10\% \text{ (rises from 7\% to 10\%)}$$
$$k_{m_1} = 14\% \text{ (rises from 11\% to 14\%)}$$

Substituting these values, along with asset Z's beta (b_Z) of 1.5, into the CAPM (Equation 7.8), we find that asset Z's new required return (k_{Z_1}) can be calculated:

$$k_{Z_1} = 10\% + [1.5 \times (14\% - 10\%)] = 10\% + 6\% = \underline{\underline{16\%}}$$

Comparing k_{Z_1} of 16 percent to k_Z of 13 percent, we see that the change of 3 percent in asset Z's required return exactly equals the change in the inflation premium. The same 3% increase would result for all assets.

Figure 7.11 depicts the situation just described. It shows that the 3 percent increase in inflationary expectations results in a parallel shift upward of 3 percent in the SML. Clearly, the required returns on all assets rise by 3 percent. Note that the rise in the inflation premium from 5 to 8 percent (IP to IP_1) causes the risk-free rate to rise from 7 to 10 percent (R_F to R_{F_1}) and the market return to increase from 11 to 14 percent (k_m to k_{m_1}). The security market line therefore shifts upward by 3 percent (SML to SML_1), causing the required return on all risky assets, such as asset Z, to rise by 3 percent. It should now be clear that *a given change in inflationary expectations will be fully reflected in a corresponding change in the returns of all assets, as reflected graphically in a parallel shift of the SML.*

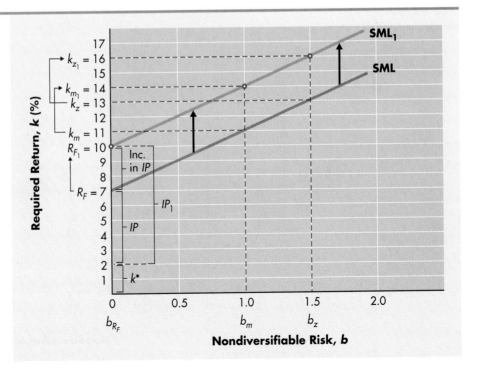

FIGURE 7.11

Inflation Shifts SML
Impact of increased inflationary expectations on the SML

Changes in Risk Aversion The slope of the security market line reflects the general risk preferences of investors in the marketplace. As discussed earlier and shown in Figure 7.1, most investors are risk-averse—they require increased returns for increased risk. This positive relationship between risk and return is graphically represented by the SML, which depicts the relationship between non-diversifiable risk as measured by beta (x axis), and the required return (y axis). The slope of the SML reflects the degree of risk aversion: *the steeper its slope, the greater the degree of risk aversion,* because a higher level of return would be required for each level of risk as measured by beta. In other words, *risk premiums increase with increasing risk avoidance.*

Changes in risk aversion, and therefore shifts in the SML, result from changing preferences of investors, which generally result from economic, political, and social events. Examples of events that *increase* risk aversion would be a stock market crash, political uncertainty, the outbreak of war, and so forth. In general, widely accepted expectations of hard times ahead tend to cause investors to become more risk-averse, requiring higher returns as compensation for accepting a given level of risk. The impact of increased risk aversion on the SML can best be demonstrated by an example.

E x a m p l e ▼ In the preceding examples, the SML in Figure 7.10 reflected a risk-free rate (R_F) of 7 percent, a market return (k_m) of 11 percent, a market risk premium ($k_m - R_F$) of 4 percent, and a required return on asset Z (k_Z) of 13 percent with a beta (b_Z) of 1.5. Assume that recent economic events have made investors more risk-

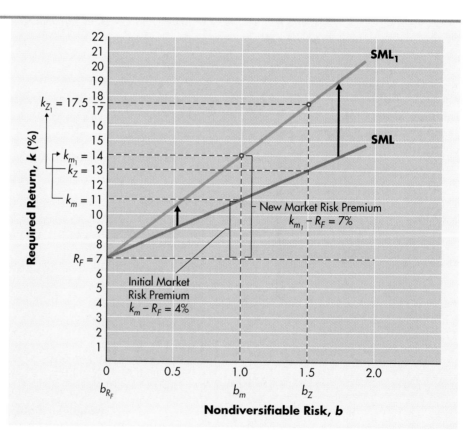

FIGURE 7.12

Risk Aversion Shifts SML

Impact of increased risk aversion on the SML

averse, causing a new higher market return (k_{m_1}) of 14 percent. Graphically, this change would cause the SML to shift upward as shown in Figure 7.12, causing a new market risk premium $(k_{m_1} - R_F)$ of 7 percent. As a result, the required return on all risky assets will increase. For asset Z, with a beta of 1.5, the new required return (k_{Z_1}) can be calculated by using CAPM (Equation 7.8):

$$k_{Z_1} = 7\% + [1.5 \times (14\% - 7\%)] = 7\% + 10.5\% = \underline{17.5\%}$$

This value can be seen on the new security market line (SML_1) in Figure 7.12. Note that although asset Z's risk, as measured by beta, did not change, its required return has increased due to the increased risk aversion reflected in the market risk premium. It should now be clear that *greater risk aversion results in higher required returns for each level of risk. Similarly, a reduction in risk aversion would cause the required return for each level of risk to decline.*

Some Comments on CAPM

The capital asset pricing model generally relies on historical data to estimate required returns. The betas, which are developed using data for the given asset as well as for the market, may or may not actually reflect the *future* variability of returns. Therefore the required returns specified by the model can be viewed only as rough approximations. Other users of betas commonly make subjective adjustments to reflect their expectations of the future when such expectations differ from the actual risk-return behaviours of the past.

The CAPM was actually developed to explain the behaviour of security prices and provide a mechanism whereby investors could assess the impact of a proposed security investment on their portfolio's overall risk and return. It is based on an assumed **efficient market**—a market in which there are many small investors, each having the same information and expectations with respect to securities; there are no restrictions on investment, no taxes, and no transaction costs; and all investors are rational, view securities similarly, and are risk-averse, preferring higher returns and lower risk.

efficient market
An assumed "perfect" market in which there are many small investors, each having the same information and expectations with respect to securities; there are no restrictions on investment, no taxes, and no transaction costs; and all investors are rational, view securities similarly, and are risk-averse, preferring higher returns and lower risk.

Although the perfect world of the efficient market appears to be unrealistic, empirical studies have provided some support for the existence of the expectational relationship described by CAPM in major markets such as the Toronto and New York Stock Exchanges.[22] In the case of real corporate assets, such as plant and equipment, research thus far has failed to prove the general applicability of CAPM because of indivisibility, relatively large size, limited number of transactions, and absence of an efficient market for such assets.

In spite of the fact that the risk-return tradeoff described by CAPM is not generally applicable to all assets, it provides a useful conceptual framework for evaluating and linking risk and return. An awareness of this tradeoff and an attempt to consider risk as well as return in financial decision making should aid the financial manager in achieving the goal of owner wealth maximization.

---

22. A large number of academic studies have raised serious questions regarding the validity of the CAPM in securities markets around the world. These studies fail to find a significant relationship between *historic* betas and *historic* returns on portfolios of large numbers of common shares over long periods of time. In other words, the *historic* beta and *historic* returns of common shares do not seem to be linked. Although these studies lead investors and researchers to question the validity of the CAPM, the theory has not been abandoned because of its logic and ease of understanding. As well, the theory's rejection as a *historical* model fails to reject its validity as an *expectational* model. Therefore, in spite of this challenge, CAPM continues to be viewed as a logical and useful framework—both conceptually and operationally—for linking *expected* nondiversifiable risk and return.

IN PRACTICE

What's at Risk? VAR Has the Answer

Financial managers, always on the lookout for new ways to manage risk, are adding value-at-risk (VAR) techniques to their repertoires. The VAR approach is attractive to managers since it reduces the analysis of risk to a single number that indicates how high a loss might be incurred if a series of "bad" events happened. VAR is usually measured in dollars and indicates the maximum loss that could occur within a stated time period and degree of certainty. Interest in VAR was stimulated after the Bank for International Settlements required that all commercial banks use the system to calculate the amount of capital needed to support their trading portfolios.

This measure is meant to protect the bank against "undue" market risk—the potential for loss from adverse changes in market factors. The trading portfolios VAR is meant to protect include money and capital market securities and also holdings of different currencies. VAR protects against changing interest and foreign exchange rates, and the prices of common shares and commodities. VAR has been modified by non-financial companies to predict the potential decrease in a company's book value if things go wrong. The company will calculate the financial risk of the future market value of a portfolio of assets, liabilities, and equity.

How does VAR work? A company takes a diverse portfolio of financial assets and calculates price swings by measuring performance on specific days in the past. Plotting the percentage gain or loss for hundreds of days would reveal the value at risk of that portfolio. If it was riskier than previously thought, traders could take corrective action—selling a particular type of security, for example—to reduce risk.

Like any quantitative model, VAR has its limitations. Perhaps its biggest drawback is the reliance on historical patterns that may not hold true in the future. However, VAR also can show companies whether they are properly diversified and whether they have sufficient capital. Among its other benefits: It tells managers if their actions are too aggressive or cautious, identifies potential risk trouble spots, and provides a way to compare business units that measure performance differently for internal reporting.

References: 2001 annual reports for Bank of Montreal and National Bank; and A. White, "What Is VAR? Value at Risk," *Canadian Investment Review*, Summer 1999.

? Review Questions

7–11   What is the relationship of total risk, nondiversifiable risk, and diversifiable risk? Why is nondiversifiable risk the *only relevant risk?*

7–12   What is *beta* and what does it measure? How are asset betas derived, and where can they be obtained? How can you find the beta of a portfolio?

7–13   What is the equation for the *capital asset pricing model (CAPM)?* Explain the meaning of each variable. Assuming a risk-free rate of 8 percent and a market return of 12 percent, draw the *security market line (SML).*

7–14   What impact would the following changes have on the security market line and therefore on the required return for a given level of risk? (a) An increase in inflationary expectations. (b) Investors become less risk-averse.

7–15   Why do financial managers have difficulty applying CAPM in decision making? Generally, what benefit does CAPM provide them?

SUMMARY

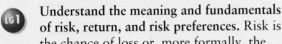 **Understand the meaning and fundamentals of risk, return, and risk preferences.** Risk is the chance of loss or, more formally, the variability of returns. Return is the change in value plus any cash distributions expressed as a percentage of the initial value. The variable definitions and equation for the rate of return are given in Table 7.10. The three basic risk preference behaviours are risk-averse, risk-indifferent, and risk-seeking. Most financial decision makers are risk-averse because they require higher expected returns as compensation for taking greater risk.

Describe procedures for measuring the risk of a single asset. The risk of a single asset is measured in much the same way as the risk of a portfolio, or collection, of assets. Sensitivity analysis and probability distributions can be used to assess risk. In addition to the range, the standard deviation and the coefficient of variation are statistics that can be used to measure risk quantitatively. The key variable definitions and equations for the expected value of a return, standard deviation of return, and the coefficient of variation are summarized in Table 7.10.

Discuss the measurement of return and standard deviation for a portfolio and the various types of correlation that can exist between series of numbers. The return of a portfolio is calculated as the weighted average of returns on the individual assets from which it is formed. The variable definitions and equation for portfolio return are given in Table 7.10. The portfolio standard deviation is found by using the formula for the standard deviation of a single asset. Correlation, the statistical relationship between series of numbers, can be positive (the series move in the same direction), negative (the series move in opposite directions), or uncorrelated (the series exhibit no discernible relationship). At the extremes, the series can be perfectly positively correlated (have a correlation coefficient of +1) or perfectly negatively correlated (have a correlation coefficient of −1).

Understand the risk and return characteristics of a portfolio in terms of correlation and diversification, and the impact of international assets on a portfolio. Diversification involves combining assets with low (less positive and more negative) correlation to reduce the risk of the portfolio. Although the return on a two-asset portfolio will lie between the returns of the two assets held in isolation, the range of risk depends on the correlation between the two assets. If they are perfectly positively correlated, the portfolio's risk will be between the individual asset's risks. If uncorrelated, the portfolio's risk will be between the risk of the most risky asset and an amount less than the risk of the least risky asset but greater than zero. If negatively correlated, the portfolio's risk will be between the risk of the most risky asset and zero. International diversification, which involves including foreign assets in a portfolio, can be used to further reduce a portfolio's risk.

Review the two types of risk and the derivation and role of beta in measuring the relevant risk of both an individual security and a portfolio. The total risk of a security consists of nondiversifiable and diversifiable risk. Nondiversifiable risk is the only relevant risk because diversifiable risk can be easily eliminated through diversification. Nondiversifiable risk can be measured by the beta coefficient, which reflects the relationship between an asset's return and the market return. Beta is derived by using statistical techniques to find the slope of the "characteristic line" that best explains the historic relationship between the asset's return and the market return. The beta of a portfolio is a weighted average of the betas of the individual assets that it includes.

 Explain the capital asset pricing model (CAPM), its relationship to the security market line (SML), and shifts in the SML caused by changes in inflationary expectations and risk aversion. The capital asset pricing model (CAPM) uses beta to relate an asset's risk relative to the market to the asset's required return. The variable definitions and equation for CAPM are given in Table 7.10. The graphic depiction of CAPM is the security market line (SML), which shifts over time in response to changing inflationary expectations

TABLE 7.10   Summary of Key Definitions and Formulas for Risk and Return

Variable definitions

b_j = beta coefficient or index of nondiversifiable risk for asset j

b_p = portfolio beta

C_t = cash received from the asset investment in the time period $t - 1$ to t

CV = coefficient of variation

$\bar{k}$ = expected value of a return

k_i = return for the ith outcome

k_j = required return on asset j

k_m = market return; the return on the market portfolio of assets

k_p = portfolio return

k_t = actual, expected, or required rate of return during period t

n = number of outcomes considered

P_t = price (value) of asset at time t

P_{t-1} = price (value) of asset at time $t - 1$

Pr_i = probability of occurrence of the ith outcome

R_F = risk-free rate of return

σ_k = standard deviation of returns

w_j = proportion of total portfolio dollar value represented by asset j

Risk and return formulas

Rate of return during period t:

$$k_t = \frac{P_t - P_{t-1} + C_t}{P_{t-1}} \qquad \text{[Eq. 7.1]}$$

Expected value of a return:
   for probabilistic data,

$$\bar{k} = \sum_{i=1}^{n} k_i \times Pr_i \qquad \text{[Eq. 7.2]}$$

general formula,

$$\bar{k} = \frac{\sum_{i=1}^{n} k_i}{n} \qquad \text{[Eq. 7.2a]}$$

Standard deviation of return:
   for probabilistic data,

$$\sigma_k = \sqrt{\sum_{i=1}^{n} (k_i - \bar{k})^2 \times Pr_i} \qquad \text{[Eq. 7.3]}$$

general formula,

$$\sigma_k = \sqrt{\frac{\sum_{i=1}^{n}(k_1 - \bar{k})^2}{n - 1}} \qquad \text{[Eq. 7.3a]}$$

Coefficient of variation:

$$CV = \frac{\sigma_k}{\bar{k}} \qquad \text{[Eq. 7.4]}$$

Portfolio return:

$$k_p = \sum_{j=1}^{n} w_j \times k_j \qquad \text{[Eq. 7.5]}$$

Total security risk = nondiversifiable
risk + diversifiable risk   [Eq. 7.6]

Portfolio beta:

$$b_p = \sum_{j=1}^{n} w_j \times b_j \qquad \text{[Eq. 7.7]}$$

Capital asset pricing model
(CAPM):

$$k_j = R_F + [b_j \times (k_m - R_F)] \qquad \text{[Eq. 7.8]}$$

and/or changes in investor risk aversion. Changes in inflationary expectations result in parallel shifts in the SML in direct response to the magnitude and direction of change. Increasing risk aversion results in a steepening in the slope of the SML, and decreasing risk aversion reduces the slope of the SML.

SELF-TEST PROBLEMS (Solutions in Appendix B)

ST 7–1 **Portfolio analysis** You have been asked for your advice in selecting a portfolio of assets and have been supplied with the following data:

| | Expected return | | |
Year	Asset A	Asset B	Asset C
2003	12%	16%	12%
2004	14	14	14
2005	16	12	16

No probabilities have been supplied. You have been told that you can create two portfolios—one consisting of assets A and B and the other consisting of assets A and C—by investing equal proportions (i.e., 50%) in each of the two component assets.

a. What is the expected return for each asset over the 3-year period?
b. What is the standard deviation for each asset's return?
c. What is the expected return for each of the two portfolios?
d. How would you characterize the correlations of returns of the two assets making up each of the two portfolios identified in c?
e. What is the standard deviation for each portfolio?
f. Which portfolio do you recommend? Why?

ST 7–2 **Beta and CAPM** A company's common shares have a beta, b, of 1.50. At this time, the risk-free rate of return, R_F, is 7 percent, and the return on the market portfolio of assets, k_m, is 10 percent. The common shares are actually *expected* to earn an annual rate of return of 11 percent.

a. If the return on the market portfolio were to increase by 10 percent, what would be expected to happen to the common shares' *required return*? What if the market return were to decline by 10 percent?
b. Use the capital asset pricing model (CAPM) to find the *required return* on the common shares.
c. On the basis of your calculation in **b**, would you recommend these common shares be purchased as an investment? Why or why not?
d. Assume that as a result of investors becoming less risk-averse, the market return drops by 1 percent to 9 percent. What impact would this change have on your responses in **b** and **c**?

PROBLEMS

WARM-UP **7–1 Rate of return** Douglas Keel, a financial analyst for Orange Industries, wishes to estimate the rate of return for two similar-risk investments—X and Y. Keel's research indicates that the immediate past returns will act as reasonable estimates of future returns. A year earlier, investment X had a market value of $20,000 and investment Y, of $55,000. During the year, investment X generated cash flow of $1,500 and investment Y generated cash flow of $6,800. The current market values of investments X and Y are $21,000 and $55,000, respectively.

a. What were the actual rates of return earned on investments X and Y during the most recent year?

b. What are the expected rates of return on investments X and Y for the upcoming year?

c. Assuming that the two investments are equally risky, which one should Keel recommend? Why?

WARM-UP **7–2 Return calculations** For each of the investments shown in the following table, calculate the rate of return earned over the unspecified time period.

Investment	Beginning-of-period value	End-of-period value	Cash flow during period
A	$ 800	$ 1,100	$ −100
B	120,000	118,000	15,000
C	45,000	48,000	7,000
D	600	500	80
E	12,500	12,400	1,500

INTERMEDIATE **7–3 Risk preferences** Sharon Smith, the financial manager for Barnett Corporation, wishes to evaluate three prospective investments—X, Y, and Z. Currently, the firm earns 12 percent on its investments, which have risk of 6 percent. The expected return and expected risk of the investments are as follows:

Investment	Expected return	Expected risk
X	14%	7%
Y	12	8
Z	10	9

a. If Sharon Smith were *risk-indifferent,* which investments would she select? Explain why.

b. If she were *risk-averse,* which investments would she select? Why?

c. If she were *risk-seeking,* which investments would she select? Why?

d. Given the traditional risk preference behaviour exhibited by financial managers, which investment would be preferred? Why?

INTERMEDIATE 7–4 **Risk analysis**   Solar Designs is considering two possible types of expansion to its product line. After investigating the possible outcomes, the company developed the estimates shown in the following table:

	Expansion A	Expansion B
Initial investment	$12,000	$12,000
Annual rate of return		
Pessimistic	16%	10%
Most likely	20%	20%
Optimistic	24%	30%

a. Determine the range of the rates of return for each of the two projects.
b. Which project is less risky? Why?
c. If you were making the investment decision, which one would you choose? Why? What does this imply about your feelings toward risk?
d. Assume that expansion B's most likely outcome is 21 percent per year and all other facts remain the same. Does this change your answer to part c? Why?

INTERMEDIATE 7–5 **Risk and probability**   Micro-Pub, Inc., is considering the purchase of one of two microfilm cameras—R or S. Both should provide benefits over a 10-year period, and each requires an initial investment of $4,000. Management has constructed the following table of estimates of probabilities and rates of return for pessimistic, most likely, and optimistic results:

	Camera R		Camera S	
	Amount	Probability	Amount	Probability
Initial investment	$4,000	1.00	$4,000	1.00
Annual rate of return				
Pessimistic	20%	0.25	15%	0.20
Most likely	25%	0.50	25%	0.55
Optimistic	30%	0.25	35%	0.25

a. Determine the range for the rate of return for each of the two cameras.
b. Determine the expected value of return for each camera.
c. Determine the standard deviation of returns for each camera.
d. Which camera is riskier? Why?

INTERMEDIATE 7–6 **Bar charts and risk**   Swan's Sportswear is considering bringing out a line of designer jeans. Currently, it is negotiating with two different well known designers. Because of the highly competitive nature of the industry, the two designs have been given code names. After market research, the firm has established the expectations shown in the following table about the annual rates of return:

Market acceptance	Probability	Annual rate of return	
		Line J	Line K
Very poor	0.05	0.0075	0.010
Poor	0.15	0.0125	0.025
Average	0.60	0.0850	0.080
Good	0.15	0.1475	0.135
Excellent	0.05	0.1625	0.150

Use the table to:
a. Construct a bar chart for each line's annual rate of return.
b. Calculate the expected value of return for each line.
c. Evaluate the relative riskiness for each jean line's rate of return using the bar charts.
d. Calculate the standard deviation of the returns for each line.

  7–7 Coefficient of variation   Metal Manufacturing has isolated four alternatives for meeting its need for increased production capacity. The data gathered relative to each of these alternatives is summarized in the following table.

Alternative	Expected return	Standard deviation of return
A	20%	7.0%
B	22	9.5
C	19	6.0
D	16	5.5

a. Calculate the coefficient of variation for each alternative.
b. If the firm wishes to minimize risk, which alternative do you recommend? Why?

  7–8 Standard deviation versus coefficient of variation as measures of risk
Greengage, Inc., a successful nursery, is considering several expansion opportunities. All of the alternatives promise to produce an acceptable return. The owners are extremely risk averse; therefore, they will choose the least risky of the alternatives. Data on four possible projects are as follows.

Project	Expected return	Range	Standard deviation
A	12.0%	0.040	0.029
B	12.5	0.050	0.032
C	13.0	0.060	0.035
D	12.8	0.045	0.030

a. Which alternative is least risky based on range?
b. Which alternative has the lowest standard deviation? Explain why standard deviation is not an appropriate measure of risk for purposes of this comparison.

c. Calculate the coefficient of variation for each alternative. What alternative will Greengage's owners choose? Explain why this may be the best measure of risk for comparing this set of opportunities.

CHALLENGE 7–9   **Assessing return and risk**   Swift Manufacturing must choose between two asset purchases. The annual rate of return and the related probabilities given in the following table summarize the firm's analysis to this point.

Project 257		Project 432	
Rate of return	Probability	Rate of return	Probability
−10%	0.01	10%	0.05
10	0.04	15	0.10
20	0.05	20	0.10
30	0.10	25	0.15
40	0.15	30	0.20
45	0.30	35	0.15
50	0.15	40	0.10
60	0.10	45	0.10
70	0.05	50	0.05
80	0.04		
100	0.01		

a. For each project, compute:
  (1) The range of possible rates of return.
  (2) The expected value of return.
  (3) The standard deviation of the returns.
  (4) The coefficient of variation.
b. Construct a bar chart of each distribution of rates of return.
c. Which project would you consider less risky? Why?

 7–10   **Integrative—Expected return, standard deviation, and coefficient of variation**   Three assets—F, G, and H—are currently being considered by Perth Industries. The probability distributions of expected returns for these assets are shown in the following table.

	Asset F		Asset G		Asset H	
i	Pr_i	Return, k_i	Pr_i	Return, k_i	Pr_i	Return, k_i
1	0.10	40%	0.40	35%	0.10	40%
2	0.20	10	0.30	10	0.20	20
3	0.40	0	0.30	−20	0.40	10
4	0.20	−5			0.20	0
5	0.10	−10			0.10	−20

a. Calculate the expected return, $\bar{k}$, for each of the three assets. Which provides the largest expected return?

b. Calculate the standard deviation, σ_k, for each of the three assets' returns. Which appears to have the greatest risk?

c. Calculate the coefficient of variation, CV, for each of the three assets. Which appears to have the largest *relative* risk?

CHALLENGE   **7–11   Normal probability distribution**   Assuming that the rates of return associated with a given asset investment are normally distributed and that the expected return, $\overline{k}$, is 18.9 percent and the coefficient of variation, CV, is 0.75, answer the following questions.

a. Find the standard deviation of returns, σ_k.

b. Calculate the range of expected return outcomes associated with the following probabilities of occurrence.

(1) 68 percent

(2) 95 percent

(3) 99 percent

c. Draw the probability distribution associated with your findings in **a** and **b**.

CHALLENGE   **7–12   Portfolio return and standard deviation**   Jamie Wong is considering investing in two assets, L and M. Asset L will represent 40 percent of the dollar value of the portfolio, and asset M will account for the other 60 percent. The expected returns over the next 6 years, 2004–2009, for each of these assets, are shown in the following table.

| | Expected return | |
Year	Asset L	Asset M
2004	14%	20%
2005	14	18
2006	16	16
2007	17	14
2008	17	12
2009	19	10

a. Calculate the expected portfolio return, k_p, for *each* of the 6 years.

b. Calculate the expected value of portfolio returns, $\overline{k}_p$, over the 6-year period.

c. Calculate the standard deviation of expected portfolio returns, σ_{k_p}, over the 6-year period.

d. How would you characterize the correlation of returns of the two assets L and M?

e. Discuss any benefits of diversification achieved through creation of the portfolio.

CHALLENGE   **7–13   Portfolio analysis**   You have been given the return data shown in the first table on three assets—F, G, and H—over the period 2004–2007.

	Expected return		
Year	Asset F	Asset G	Asset H
2004	16%	17%	14%
2005	17	16	15
2006	18	15	16
2007	19	14	17

Using these assets, you have isolated the three investment alternatives shown in the following table:

Alternative	Investment
1	100% of asset F
2	50% of asset F and 50% of asset G
3	50% of asset F and 50% of asset H

a. Calculate the expected return over the 4-year period for each of the three alternatives.
b. Calculate the standard deviation of returns over the 4-year period for each of the three alternatives.
c. Use your findings in **a** and **b** to calculate the coefficient of variation for each of the three alternatives.
d. On the basis of your findings, which of the three investment alternatives do you recommend? Why?

INTERMEDIATE   7–14   **Correlation, risk, and return**   Matt Peters wishes to evaluate the risk and return behaviours associated with various combinations of assets V and W under three assumed degrees of correlation—perfect positive, uncorrelated, and perfect negative. The expected return and risk values calculated for each of the assets are shown in the following table:

Asset	Expected return, $\bar{k}$	Risk (standard deviation), σ_k
V	8%	5%
W	13	10

a. If the returns of assets V and W are *perfectly positively correlated* (correlation coefficient = +1), describe the *range* of (1) expected return and (2) risk associated with all possible portfolio combinations.
b. If the returns of assets V and W are *uncorrelated* (correlation coefficient = 0), describe the *approximate range* of (1) expected return and (2) risk associated with all possible portfolio combinations.
c. If the returns of assets V and W are *perfectly negatively correlated* (correlation coefficient = −1), describe the *range* of (1) expected return and (2) risk associated with all possible portfolio combinations.

7–15 **International investment returns** Joe Martinez, a Canadian citizen living in

INTERMEDIATE

Toronto, invested in the common stock of Telmex, a Mexican corporation. He purchased 1,000 shares at 20.50 pesos per share. Twelve months later, he sold them at 24.75 pesos per share. He received no dividends during that time.

a. What was Joe's investment return (in total pesos and percentage terms) for the year, based on the peso value of the shares?

b. The exchange rate for pesos was 9.21 pesos per Can$1 at the time of the purchase. At the time of the sale, the exchange rate was 9.85 pesos per Can$1. Translate the purchase and sale prices into Canadian dollars.

c. Calculate Joe's investment return based on the Canadian dollar value of the shares.

d. Explain why the two returns are different. Which one is more important to Joe? Why?

INTERMEDIATE 7–16 **Total, nondiversifiable, and diversifiable risk** David Talbot randomly selected securities from all those listed on the Toronto Stock Exchange for his portfolio. He began with one security and added securities one by one until a total of 20 securities were held in the portfolio. After each security was added, David calculated the portfolio standard deviation, σ_{k_p}. The calculated values are shown in the following table:

Number of securities	Portfolio risk, σ_{k_p}	Number of securities	Portfolio risk, σ_{k_p}
1	14.50%	11	7.00%
2	13.30	12	6.80
3	12.20	13	6.70
4	11.20	14	6.65
5	10.30	15	6.60
6	9.50	16	6.56
7	8.80	17	6.52
8	8.20	18	6.50
9	7.70	19	6.48
10	7.30	20	6.47

a. On a graph, where the number of securities in the portfolio is the x axis and the portfolio risk is the y axis, plot what happens to portfolio risk as the number of securities increases.

b. Divide the total portfolio risk in the graph into its *nondiversifiable* and *diversifiable* risk components and label each of these on the graph.

c. Describe which of the two risk components is the *relevant risk,* and explain why it is relevant. How much of this risk exists in David Talbot's portfolio?

INTERMEDIATE 7–17 **Graphic derivation of beta** A firm wishes to graphically estimate the betas for two assets—A and B. It has gathered the following return data for the market portfolio and both assets over the ten years 1993–2002.

| | Actual return | | |
Year	Market portfolio	Asset A	Asset B
1993	6%	11%	16%
1994	2	8	11
1995	−13	−4	−10
1996	−4	3	3
1997	−8	0	−3
1998	16	19	30
1999	10	14	22
2000	15	18	29
2001	8	12	19
2002	13	17	26

a. On a graph, where the x axis is market return and the y axis is asset return, plot the data points and draw the characteristic lines for assets A and B. Use two graphs.
b. Use the characteristic lines from **a** to estimate the betas for assets A and B.
c. Use the betas found in **b** to comment on the relative risks of assets A and B.

 WARM-UP   **7–18**   **Interpreting beta**   A firm wishes to assess the impact of changes in the market return on an asset that has a beta of 1.20.
a. If the market return increased by 15 percent, what impact would this change be expected to have on the asset's return?
b. If the market return decreased by 8 percent, what impact would this change be expected to have on the asset's return?
c. If the market return did not change, what impact, if any, would be expected on the asset's return?
d. Would this asset be considered more or less risky than the market? Explain.

 WARM-UP   **7–19**   **Betas**   Answer the following questions for assets A to D shown in the table.

Asset	Beta
A	0.50
B	1.60
C	−0.20
D	0.90

a. What impact would a *10 percent increase* in the market return be expected to have on each asset's return?
b. What impact would a *10 percent decrease* in the market return be expected to have on each asset's return?
c. If you were certain that the market return would *increase* in the near future, which asset would you prefer? Why?
d. If you were certain that the market return would *decrease* in the near future, which asset would you prefer? Why?

7–20 **Betas and risk rankings** Stock A has a beta of 0.80, stock B has a beta of 1.40, and stock C has a beta of -0.30.

   a. Rank these stocks from the most risky to the least risky.

   b. If the return on the market portfolio increases by 12 percent, what change would you expect in the return for each of the stocks?

   c. If the return on the market portfolio declines by 5 percent, what change would you expect in the return for each of the stocks?

   d. If you felt that the stock market was just ready to experience a significant decline, which stock would you likely add to your portfolio? Why?

   e. If you anticipated a major stock market rally, which stock would you add to your portfolio? Why?

  7–21 **Portfolio betas** Rose Berry is attempting to evaluate two possible portfolios—both consisting of the same five assets, but held in different proportions. She is particularly interested in using beta to compare the risk of the portfolios and in this regard has gathered the data shown in the following table.

		Portfolio weights	
Asset	Asset beta	Portfolio A	Portfolio B
1	1.30	10%	30%
2	0.70	30	10
3	1.25	10	20
4	1.10	10	20
5	0.90	40	20
Totals		100%	100%

   a. Calculate the betas for portfolios A and B.

   b. Compare the risk of each portfolio to the market as well as to each other.

   c. Including the market portfolio, rank the three portfolios from lowest risk to highest risk.

  7–22 **Capital asset pricing model (CAPM)** For each of the cases shown in the following table, use the capital asset pricing model to find the required return.

Case	Risk-free rate, R_F	Market return, k_m	Beta, b
A	5%	8%	1.30
B	8	13	0.90
C	9	12	-0.20
D	10	15	1.00
E	6	10	0.60

  7–23 **Beta coefficients and the capital asset pricing model** Katherine Wilson is wondering how much risk she must undertake in order to generate an acceptable return on her portfolio. The risk-free return currently is 5 percent. The return on

the market portfolio is 16 percent. Use the CAPM to calculate the beta coefficient associated with each of the following portfolio returns.
a. 10 percent
b. 15 percent
c. 18 percent
d. 20 percent
e. Draw a security market line (SML) based on the above data. Katherine is
    risk-averse. What is the highest return she can expect if she is unwilling to
    take more than an average risk?

 INTERMEDIATE   **7–24 Manipulating CAPM** Use the basic equation for the capital asset pricing model
(CAPM) to work each of the following:
a. Find the *required return* for an asset with a beta of 0.90 when the risk-free
    rate and market return are 8 and 12 percent, respectively.
b. Find the *risk-free rate* for a firm with a required return of 15 percent and a
    beta of 1.25 when the market return is 14 percent.
c. Find the *market return* for an asset with a required return of 16 percent and
    a beta of 1.10 when the risk-free rate is 9 percent.
d. Find the *beta* for an asset with a required return of 15 percent when the risk-
    free rate and market return are 10 and 12.5 percent, respectively.

  7–25 Portfolio return and beta Jamie Peters invested $100,000 to set up the follow-
ing portfolio one year ago:

 CHALLENGE

Asset	Cost	Beta at purchase	Yearly income	Value today
A	$20,000	0.80	$1,600	$20,000
B	35,000	0.95	1,400	36,000
C	30,000	1.50	—	34,500
D	15,000	1.25	375	16,500

a. Calculate the portfolio beta based on the original cost figures.
b. Calculate the percentage return of each position in the portfolio for the year.
c. Calculate the percentage return of the portfolio based on original cost using
    income and gains during the year.
d. At the time Jamie made his investments, investors were estimating that the
    market return for the coming year would be 10 percent. The estimate of the
    risk-free rate of return averaged 4 percent for the coming year. Calculate an
    expected rate of return for each stock based on its beta and the expectations
    of market and risk-free returns.
e. Based on the actual results, explain how each stock in the portfolio per-
    formed relative to those CAPM-generated expectations of performance.
    What factors could explain these differences?

INTERMEDIATE   **7–26 Security market line, SML** Assume that the risk-free rate, R_F, is currently
9 percent and that the market return, k_m, is currently 13 percent.
a. Draw and label the security market line (SML).
b. Calculate and label the *market risk premium* on the axes in **a.**
c. Given the previous data, calculate the required return on asset A having a
    beta of 0.80 and asset B having a beta of 1.30.

d. Draw in the betas and required returns from **c** for assets A and B on the axes in **a**. Label the *risk premium* associated with each of these assets, and discuss them.

  7–27 **Shifts in the security market line** Assume that the risk-free rate, R_F, is currently 8 percent, the market return, k_m, is 12 percent, and asset A has a beta, b_A, of 1.10.

a. Draw and label the security market line (SML).

b. Use the CAPM to calculate the required return, k_A, on asset A, and depict asset A's beta and required return on the SML drawn in **a**.

c. Assume that as a result of recent economic events, inflationary expectations have declined by 2 percent, lowering R_F and k_m to 6 and 10 percent, respectively. Draw the new SML on the axes in **a**, and calculate and show the new required return for asset A.

d. Assume that as a result of recent events, investors have become more risk averse, causing the market return to rise by 1 percent to 13 percent. Ignoring the shift in part **c**, draw the new SML on the same set of axes as used before, and calculate and show the new required return for asset A.

e. From the previous changes, what conclusions can be drawn about the impact of (1) decreased inflationary expectations and (2) increased risk aversion on the required returns of risky assets?

  7–28 **Integrative—Risk, return, and CAPM** Wolff Enterprises must consider several investment projects, A through E, using the capital asset pricing model (CAPM) and its graphic representation, the security market line (SML). Relevant information is presented in the following table.

Item	Rate of return	Beta, b
Risk-free asset	9%	0
Market portfolio	14	1.00
Project A	—	1.50
Project B	—	0.75
Project C	—	2.00
Project D	—	0
Project E	—	−0.50

a. Calculate the required return and risk premium for each project, given its level of nondiversifiable risk.

b. Use your findings in **a** to draw the security market line.

c. Discuss the relative nondiversifiable risk of projects A through E.

d. Assume that recent economic events have caused investors to become less risk averse, causing the market return to decline by 2 percent, to 12 percent. Calculate the new required returns for assets A through E, and draw the new security market line on the same set of axes as used in **b**.

e. Compare your findings in **a** and **b** with those in **d**. What conclusion can you draw about the impact of a decline in investor risk aversion on the required returns of risky assets?

Analyzing Risk and Return on Wings Products' Investments

S teve Izerdam, a financial analyst for Wings Products, a manufacturer of sport products, must evaluate the risk and return of two assets—X and Y. The firm is considering adding these assets to its diversified portfolio of products. To assess the return and risk of each asset, Steve gathered data on the annual cash flow and beginning- and end-of-year values of each asset over the immediately preceding 10 years, 1994–2003. These data are summarized in the following table. Steve's investigation suggests that both assets, on average, will tend to perform in the future just as they have during the past 10 years. He therefore believes that the expected annual return can be estimated by finding the average annual return for each asset over the past 10 years.

Steve believes that each asset's risk can be assessed in two ways: in isolation and as part of the firm's diversified portfolio of assets. The risk of the assets in isolation can be found by using the standard deviation and coefficient of variation of returns over the past 10 years. The capital asset pricing model (CAPM) can be used to assess the asset's risk as part of the firm's portfolio of assets. Applying some sophisticated quantitative techniques, Steve estimates the betas of assets X and Y as 1.60 and 1.10, respectively. In addition, he found that the risk-free rate is currently 7 percent and the market return is 10 percent.

Return Data for Assets X and Y, 1994–2003

	Asset X			Asset Y		
		Value			Value	
Year	Cash flow	Beginning	Ending	Cash flow	Beginning	Ending
1994	$1,000	$20,000	$22,000	$1,500	$20,000	$20,000
1995	1,500	22,000	21,000	1,600	20,000	20,000
1996	1,400	21,000	24,000	1,700	20,000	21,000
1997	1,700	24,000	22,000	1,800	21,000	21,000
1998	1,900	22,000	23,000	1,900	21,000	22,000
1999	1,600	23,000	26,000	2,000	22,000	23,000
2000	1,700	26,000	25,000	2,100	23,000	23,000
2001	2,000	25,000	24,000	2,200	23,000	24,000
2002	2,100	24,000	27,000	2,300	24,000	25,000
2003	2,200	27,000	30,000	2,400	25,000	25,000

Required

a. Calculate the annual rate of return for each asset in *each* of the 10 preceding years, and use those values to find the average annual return for each asset over the 10-year period.

b. Use the returns calculated in **a** to find (1) the standard deviation and (2) the coefficient of variation of the returns for each asset over the 10-year period.

   c. Use your findings in **a** and **b** to evaluate and discuss the return and risk associated with each asset. Which asset appears to be preferable? Explain.

   d. Use the CAPM to find the required return for each asset. Compare this value with the average annual returns calculated in **a.**

   e. Compare and contrast your findings in **c** and **d.** What recommendations would you give Steve with regard to investing in either of the two assets? Explain to Steve why he is better off using beta rather than the standard deviation and coefficient of variation to assess the risk of each asset.

   f. Rework **d** and **e** under each of the following circumstances:

     (1) A rise of 1 percent in inflationary expectations causes the risk-free rate to rise to 8 percent and the market return to rise to 11 percent.

     (2) As a result of favourable political events, investors suddenly become less risk-averse, causing the market return to drop by 1 percent, to 9 percent.

WEB EXERCISES LINKS TO PRACTISE

Visit the following Web sites and complete the suggested exercises. These exercises will allow you to review practical applications of the chapter topics as well as explore the wealth of information regarding managerial finance that is available on the Internet.

news.morningstar.com/news/ms/Investing101/riskybus/riskybus1.html
This link provides three readings on risk. Click on the first reading, An Introduction to Investment Risks. What type of risks does this article discuss? Using your financial calculator, ensure the calculations shown on the bottom of the page are correct. Now, return to the top of the page and click on How Standard Deviation Works. Read the content and then answer the following questions.

1. What is the standard deviation?
2. How is the standard deviation calculated?
3. Is the standard deviation truly a measure of risk? Discuss.
4. What is one of the major strengths of standard deviation when dealing with financial securities? How should the standard deviation be used for financial securities?

Return to the top of the page and click on How to Use Beta. Read the content and then answer the following questions.

1. How does beta differ from the standard deviation?
2. How is beta calculated, and what information is required?
3. How can the concept of beta be compared to a swing set?
4. What are the drawbacks associated with beta as a risk measure?
5. What is the R-squared and why is it important when considering the beta of a common share?

www.ec.njit.edu/~mathis/interactive/ExpRetIntro.html
www.ec.njit.edu/~mathis/interactive/expreturn2.html
The first site provides an introduction to the use of a free expected return calcu-

lator. The link to the actual calculator is on the bottom of the page. Complete problems from the book using this calculator.

The second link provides a source of numerous problems that can be used with the calculator. Complete as many problems as you like to reinforce the concepts and calculation procedures for expected returns.

www.ec.njit.edu/~mathis/interactive/PortIntro.html
www.ec.njit.edu/~mathis/interactive/Portfolio.html
The first site provides an introduction to the use of a free two asset portfolio calculator that can be used to find the expected return and standard deviation for portfolios formed from two assets and to plot the reduction in risk associated with diversification. This calculator illustrates the principle of diversification. The link to the actual calculator is on the bottom of the page. Complete problems from the book using this calculator.

The second link provides a source of numerous problems that can be used with the calculator. Complete as many problems as you like to reinforce the concept of diversification and to ensure that you see the benefit associated with the concept.

www.ec.njit.edu/~mathis/interactive/CAPMCalcIntro.html
www.ec.njit.edu/~mathis/interactive/CAPMBase.html
The first site provides an introduction to the use of a free CAPM calculator that can be used to determine any of the four possible variables of the SML given the value of the other three variables. The link to the actual calculator is on the bottom of the page. Complete problems from the book using this calculator.

The second link provides a source of numerous problems that can be used with the calculator. Complete as many problems as you like to reinforce the concepts associated with the CAPM and the SML.

pages.stern.nyu.edu/~adamodar
Click on the Updated Data link in the left-hand margin and then scroll down the page to the Data Sets heading. Click on Historical Returns on Stocks, Bonds and Bills—United States and answer the following questions:
1. Compute the arithmetic average for the annual return for stocks, t-bills, and t-bonds for the last 10 years of data.
2. Compute the standard deviation for the averages calculated in Question 1.
3. Which has the highest arithmetic average—stocks, t-bills, or t-bonds?
4. Which has the largest standard deviation?
5. How much money would you have if you had invested $100 in stocks in 1926? If you had invested $100 in t-bills in 1926? If you had invested $100 in t-bonds in 1926?
6. Using the arithmetic average data given on this Web site, what is the risk premium of stocks versus t-bills for the shortest time period given in the charts?
7. Using the arithmetic average data given on this Web site, what is the risk premium of stocks versus t-bonds for the shortest time period given in the charts?
8. Explain the difference between your answer to Question 6 and your answer to Question 7.

8

Valuation of Financial Securities

LEARNING GOALS

LG1 Describe interest rate fundamentals and the factors that affect required rates of return.

LG2 Describe the key inputs and basic model used in the valuation process.

LG3 Apply the basic valuation model to long-term debt to determine value and yield to maturity (YTM) and describe the impact that changes in required rates of return and time to maturity have on bond values.

LG4 Understand the concept of market efficiency and four techniques used to determine the value of common shares: (1) the dividend valuation model (DVM), (2) book value, (3) liquidation value, and (4) the price/earnings (P/E) multiple.

LG5 Understand the relationships among financial decisions, return, risk, and the firm's value.

LG6 Discuss valuation concepts and the techniques used to determine the value and required returns on preferred shares.

8.1 Interest Rates and Required Returns

Chapter 6 detailed the role that financial markets and institutions play in ensuring that cash is transferred from savers of funds to users of funds. The level of funds that flow between suppliers and demanders can significantly affect economic growth. Growth results from the interaction of a variety of economic factors (such as the money supply, the exchange rate of the dollar, trade balances, and economic policies) that affect the cost of money—the interest rate or required return. The interest rate level acts as a regulating device that controls the flow of funds between suppliers and demanders. The Bank of Canada regu-

What's Baking?

With just three basic ingredients—flour, butter, and eggs—an experienced baker can create a variety of treats. The proportions used, plus the choice of other ingredients, give each creation its particular character. So, too, do three basic ingredients—returns, timing, and risk—determine the value of both real and financial assets. The choice of the other ingredients, and the market's taste for those other ingredients, determines the value of a firm's financial securities, the financial outcome of a firm's investments in real assets, and the value of a firm itself. Just as nutritionists have found ways to measure the nutritional value of food, so, too, have financial analysts devised ways, broadly called *valuation,* to measure the value of any asset. This chapter explains valuation and how the value of a firm's financial assets such as long-term debt and common and preferred shares is determined.

larly assesses economic conditions and, when necessary, initiates actions to raise or lower interest rates to control inflation, the exchange rate, and economic growth. Generally, the lower the interest rate, the greater the funds flow and therefore the greater the economic growth; the higher the interest rate, the lower the funds flow and economic growth.

Interest Rate Fundamentals

interest rate
The compensation paid by the borrower of funds to the lender; from the borrower's point of view, the cost of borrowing funds.

The interest rate or required return represents the cost of money. It is the compensation that a demander of funds must pay a supplier. When funds are lent, the cost of borrowing the funds is the **interest rate.** When funds are obtained by

required return
The cost of funds obtained by selling an ownership interest; it reflects the funds supplier's level of expected return.

liquidity preferences
General preferences of investors for shorter-term securities.

selling an ownership interest—as in the sale of common shares—the cost to the issuer (demander) is commonly called the **required return,** which reflects the funds supplier's level of expected return. In both cases the supplier is compensated for providing funds. Ignoring risk factors, the cost of funds results from the *real rate of interest* adjusted for inflationary expectations and **liquidity preferences—** general preferences of investors for shorter-term securities.

The Real Rate of Interest

real rate of interest
The rate that creates an equilibrium between the supply of savings and the demand for investment funds in a perfect world, without inflation, where funds suppliers and demanders have no liquidity preference and all outcomes are certain.

Assume a *perfect world* in which there is no inflation and in which funds suppliers and demanders are indifferent to the term of loans or investments because they have no liquidity preference and all outcomes are certain.[1] At any given point in time in that perfect world, there would be one cost of money—the **real rate of interest.** The real rate of interest creates an equilibrium between the supply of savings and the demand for investment funds. It represents the most basic cost of money. The real rate of interest in Canada is assumed to be stable and equal to around 2 percent. This supply–demand relationship is shown in Figure 8.1 by the supply function (labelled S_0) and the demand function (labelled D). An equilibrium between the supply of funds and the demand for funds ($S_0 = D$) occurs at a rate of interest k_0^*, the real rate of interest.

Clearly, the real rate of interest changes with changing economic conditions, tastes, and preferences. Actions taken by the Bank of Canada could result in an increased supply of funds, causing the supply function in Figure 8.1 to shift to, say, S_1. This could result in a lower real rate of interest, k_1^*, at equilibrium ($S_1 = D$). Likewise, a change in tax laws or other factors could affect the demand for funds, causing the real rate of interest to rise or fall to a new equilibrium level.

Nominal or Actual Rate of Interest (Return)

nominal rate of interest
The actual rate of interest charged by the supplier of funds and paid by the demander.

The **nominal rate of interest** is the actual rate of interest charged by the supplier of funds and paid by the demander. *Throughout this book, interest rates and*

FIGURE 8.1

Supply–Demand Relationship
Supply of savings and demand for investment funds

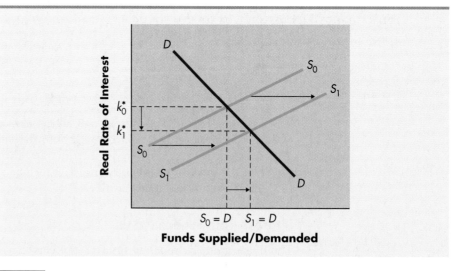

---

1. These assumptions are made to describe the most basic interest rate, the *real rate of interest.* Subsequent discussions relax these assumptions to develop the broader concept of the interest rate and required return.

required rates of return are nominal rates unless otherwise noted. The nominal rate of interest differs from the real rate of interest, k^*, as a result of two factors: (1) inflationary expectations reflected in an inflation premium (*IP*), and (2) issuer and issue characteristics, reflected in a risk premium (*RP*). The risk premium could be based on differing levels of default risk, on contractual provisions of the financial security, or on the type of financial security. Since the risk profile of long-term debt, preferred shares, and common shares is very different, so too will be the required rates of return. By using this notation, the nominal rate of interest for security *j*, k_j, is given in Equation 8.1:

$$k_j = \underbrace{k^* + IP}_{\substack{\text{risk-free} \\ \text{rate, } R_F}} + \underbrace{RP}_{\substack{\text{risk} \\ \text{premium}}} \tag{8.1}$$

As the horizontal braces below the equation indicate, the nominal rate, k_j, can be viewed as having two basic components: a risk-free rate of interest, R_F, and a risk premium, *RP*:

$$k_j = R_F + RP \tag{8.2}$$

To simplify the discussion, we will assume that the risk premium, RP_1, is equal to zero. By drawing from Equation 8.1,[2] the risk-free rate can be represented as:

$$R_F = k^* + IP \tag{8.3}$$

risk-free rate of interest, R_F
The required return on a risk-free asset, typically a 3-month government of Canada t-bill.

The **risk-free rate of interest, R_F**, is the required return on a risk-free asset. It embodies the real rate of interest plus the inflationary expectation. The yield on short-term government of Canada treasury bills, as discussed in Chapter 6, is commonly considered the yield on the risk-free asset. The usual maturity used is 91-day or 3-month t-bills. *The real rate of interest can be estimated by subtracting the inflation premium from the nominal rate of interest.* For the risk-free asset in Equation 8.3, the real rate of interest, k^*, would equal $R_F - IP$. A simple example can demonstrate the practical distinction between nominal and real rates of interest.

E x a m p l e ▼ Marilyn Carbo has $10 that she can spend on candy costing $0.25 per piece. She could therefore buy 40 pieces of candy ($10/$0.25) today. The nominal rate of interest on a 1-year deposit is currently 7 percent and the expected rate of inflation over the coming year is 4 percent. Instead of buying the 40 pieces of candy today, Marilyn can invest the $10 in a 1-year deposit account now. At the end of 1 year she would have $10.70 because she would have earned 7 percent interest—an additional $0.70 (0.07 × $10)—on her $10 deposit. The 4 percent inflation rate would over the 1-year period increase the cost of the candy by 4 percent—an additional $0.01 (0.04 × $0.25)—to $0.26 per piece. As a result, at the end of the 1-year period Marilyn would be able to buy about 41.2 pieces of candy ($10.70/$0.26), or roughly 3 percent more (41.2/40.0 = 1.03). The increase in the amount of money available to Marilyn at the end of 1 year is merely her nominal rate of return (7%), which must be reduced by the rate of inflation (4%) during the period to determine her real rate of return of 3 percent.

---

2. This equation is commonly called the *Fisher equation*, named for the renowned economist Irving Fisher, who first presented this approximate relationship between nominal interest and the rate of inflation. See Irving Fisher, *The Theory of Interest* (New York: Macmillan, 1930).

Marilyn's increased buying power therefore equals her 3 percent real rate of return.

The premium for *inflationary expectations* in Equation 8.3 represents the average rate of *inflation* expected over the life of a loan or investment. It is *not* the rate of inflation experienced over the immediate past; rather, it reflects the forecasted rate. Take, for example, the risk-free asset. During the week ended August 24, 2002, 3-month t-bills earned a 2.91 percent rate of return. Assuming an approximate 2 percent real rate of interest, funds suppliers were forecasting a 0.91 percent (annual) rate of inflation (2.91% − 2.00%) over the next 3 months. This expectation was in striking contrast to the expected rate of inflation 21 years earlier in 1981. At that time the 3-month t-bill rate averaged 19.1 percent, which meant an expected (annual) inflation rate of 17.1 percent (19.1% − 2.00%). The inflationary expectation premium changes over time in response to many factors, including recent rates, government policies, and international events.

Figure 8.2 illustrates the movement of the rate of inflation and the risk-free rate of interest during the period 1960–2001. During this period the two rates tended to move in a similar fashion. Beginning in 1972, inflation started to increase, and for 6 of the next 7 years exceeded the average yield on t-bills. From 1973 to 1982, the rate of inflation in Canada exceeded 7.5 percent, peaking at 12.4 percent in 1981. Beginning in 1983, inflation declined, and by 1992 returned to the level recorded in the early 1960s. The data clearly illustrate the significant impact of inflation on the nominal rate of interest for the risk-free asset and the major changes that took place in these two items over a relatively short time period.

FIGURE 8.2

Impact of Inflation
Relationship between annual rate of inflation and 3-month government of Canada t-bill average annual returns, 1960–2001

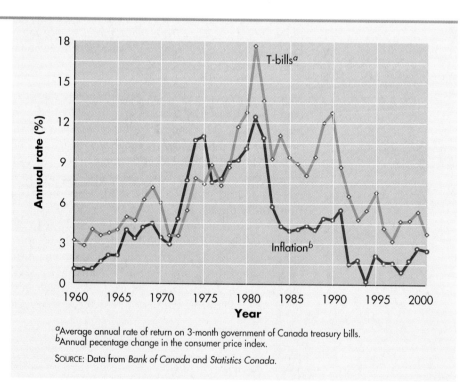

[a]Average annual rate of return on 3-month government of Canada treasury bills.
[b]Annual pecentage change in the consumer price index.
SOURCE: Data from *Bank of Canada* and *Statistics Conada.*

Term Structure of Interest Rates

For any class of similar-risk securities, the **term structure of interest rates** (TSIR) relates the interest rate or rate of return to the time to maturity. When constructing a TSIR, the norm is to use federal government securities as a class, but other classes could include securities that have similar overall quality or risk ratings, as determined by independent rating agencies like the Dominion Bond Rating Service (DBRS). Since federal government securities have no default risk, they provide a laboratory in which to develop the term structure.

Yield Curves

The annual rate of interest earned on a security purchased on a given day and held to maturity is its **yield to maturity.** At any point in time, the relationship between yield to maturity and the remaining time to maturity can be represented by a graph called the **yield curve.** The yield curve shows the pattern of interest rates on securities of equal quality and different maturity; it is a graphic depiction of the *term structure of interest rates.* Figure 8.3 shows three yield curves for government of Canada debt securities of various maturities, ranging from 1 month to 30 years: one at March 25, 1981; a second at March 6, 1991; and a third at May 15, 2002. Note that both the position and the shape of the yield curves change significantly over time. The March 25, 1981, curve indicates high short-term interest rates and lower longer-term rates. This curve is described as *downward-sloping,* reflecting generally cheaper long-term borrowing costs than short-term borrowing costs. Historically, the downward-sloping yield curve, which is often called an **inverted yield curve,** has been the exception. More frequently, yield curves similar to that of May 15, 2002, have existed. These *upward-sloping* or **normal yield curves** indicate that short-term borrowing costs are below long-term borrowing costs. Sometimes, a **flat yield curve,** similar to that of March 6, 1991, exists. It reflects relatively similar borrowing costs for both short- and longer term loans.

The shape of the yield curve has been an excellent predictor of future economic growth. In general, sharp upward-sloping curves signal a substantial rise in economic activity within a year, whereas inverted yield curves have preceded every recession since the 1950s. Most periods of flat or inverted yield curves occur when the Bank of Canada increases short-term rates, tightening monetary policy to control inflation or protect the value of the Canadian dollar. These higher rates curtail business growth and increase international demand for Canadian dollars.

Some inverted yield curves, however, result from falling long-term interest rates in the global economy. Financial turmoil can push investors toward high-quality, low-risk securities, reducing the demand for long-term bonds both in Canada and abroad. This reduced demand for longer-term debt securities will lead to lower yields that may result in an inverted yield curve.

The shape of the yield curve also affects the firm's financing decisions. A financial manager who faces a downward-sloping yield curve is likely to rely more heavily on cheaper, long-term financing; when the yield curve is upward-sloping, the manager is more likely to use cheaper, short-term financing. Although a variety of other factors also influence the choice of loan maturity, the shape of the yield curve provides useful insights into future interest-rate expectations.

FIGURE 8.3

Treasury Yield Curves
Yield curves for government of Canada securities: March 25, 1981; March 6, 1991; and May 15, 2002

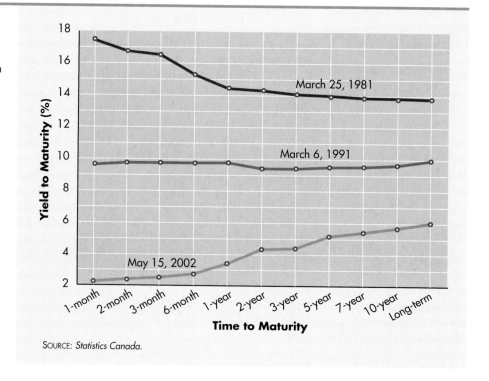

SOURCE: *Statistics Canada.*

Theories of Term Structure

The dominance of the upward-sloping yield curve can be simply explained: Short-term securities are less risky than long-term securities because near-term events are more certain than future events, and therefore they have lower returns. However, this explanation fails to explain why yield curves often take on different shapes, such as those shown in Figure 8.3. Three theories are frequently cited to better explain the general shape of the yield curve: the expectations hypothesis, liquidity preference theory, and market segmentation theory.

expectations hypothesis
Theory suggesting that the yield curve reflects investor expectations about future interest rates; an increasing inflation expectation results in an upward-sloping yield curve and a decreasing inflation expectation results in a downward-sloping yield curve.

Expectations Hypothesis   The **expectations hypothesis** suggests that the yield curve reflects investor expectations about future interest rates and inflation. Higher future rates of expected inflation will result in higher, long-term interest rates; the opposite occurs with lower future rates. This widely accepted explanation of the term structure can be applied to the securities of any issuer. For example, take the case of government of Canada securities. Thus far, we have concerned ourselves solely with the 3-month treasury bill. In fact, all federal government securities are *riskless* in terms of (1) the chance that the government will default on the issue and (2) the ease with which they can be liquidated for cash without losing value. Because it is believed to be easier to forecast inflation over shorter periods of time, the shorter-term 3-month treasury bill is considered the risk-free asset. Of course, differing inflation expectations associated with different maturities will cause nominal interest rates to vary. With the addition of a maturity subscript, t, Equation 8.3 can be rewritten as:

$$R_{F_t} = k^* + IP_t \qquad (8.4)$$

In other words, for government of Canada securities the nominal, or risk-free, rate for a given maturity varies with the inflation expectation over the term of the security.[3]

Example ▼ The nominal interest rate, R_F, for four maturities of government of Canada securities on August 23, 2002, is given in column 1 of the following table. Assuming that the real rate of interest is 2 percent, as noted in column 2, the inflation expectation for each maturity in column 3 is found by solving Equation 8.4 for IP_t. Although a 0.91 percent rate of inflation was expected over the 3-month period, beginning August 24, 2002, a 1.20 percent average rate of inflation was expected over the 1-year period, and so on. An analysis of the inflation expectations in column 3 for August 23, 2002, suggests that at that time a general expectation of slightly increasing inflation existed. Simply stated, the August 23, 2002, yield curve for government of Canada securities was upward-sloping as a result of the expectation that the rate of inflation would increase slightly in the future.

Maturity, t	Nominal interest rate, R_{F_t} (1)	Real interest rate, k^* (2)	Inflation expectation, IP_t [(1) − (2)] (3)
3 months	2.91%	2.00%	0.91%
1 year	3.20	2.00	1.20
5 years	4.52	2.00	2.52
30 years	5.56	2.00	3.56

Generally, under the expectations hypothesis, an increasing inflation expectation results in an upward-sloping yield curve; a decreasing inflation expectation results in a downward-sloping yield curve; and a stable inflation expectation results in a flat yield curve. Although, as we'll see, other theories exist, the observed strong relationship between inflation and interest rates (see Figure 8.2) supports this widely accepted theory.

Liquidity Preference Theory   The tendency for yield curves to be upward-sloping can be further explained by **liquidity preference theory**. This theory indicates that for a given issuer, long-term rates tend to be higher than short-term rates. This belief is based on two behavioural facts:

1. Investors perceive less risk in short-term securities than in longer-term securities and are therefore willing to accept lower yields on them. Debt securities with longer maturities are more sensitive to changing required returns (interest rates) in the market. For a given change in market rates, the price (value) of long-term debt securities will be more significantly changed (both up and down) than those with shorter maturities. This issue is discussed in more detail in Section 8.3.

liquidity preference theory
Theory suggesting that for any given issuer, long-term interest rates tend to be higher than short-term rates due to the lower liquidity and higher responsiveness to general interest rate movements of longer-term securities; causes the yield curve to be upward-sloping.

---

3. Although government of Canada securities have no risk of default or illiquidity, they do suffer from "maturity, or interest rate, risk"—the risk that interest rates will change in the future and thereby affect longer maturities more than shorter maturities. Therefore the longer the maturity of a federal government (or any other) security, the greater its interest rate risk. The impact of interest-rate changes on bond values is discussed later in the chapter.

2. Borrowers are generally willing to pay a higher rate for long-term than for short-term financing. By locking in funds for a longer period of time, they can eliminate the potential adverse consequences of having to roll over short-term debt at unknown costs to obtain long-term financing.

Investors (lenders) tend to require a premium for tying up funds for longer periods, whereas borrowers are generally willing to pay a premium to obtain longer-term financing. These preferences of lenders and borrowers cause the yield curve to tend to be upward-sloping. Simply stated, longer maturities tend to have higher interest rates than shorter maturities.

market segmentation theory
Theory suggesting that the market for loans is segmented on the basis of maturity and that the supply of and demand for loans within each segment determine its prevailing interest rate; the slope of the yield curve is determined by the general relationship between the prevailing rates in each segment.

Market Segmentation Theory   The **market segmentation theory** suggests that the market for loans is segmented on the basis of maturity and that the supply of and demand for loans within each segment determine its prevailing interest rate. In other words, the equilibrium between suppliers and demanders of short-term funds, such as seasonal business loans, would determine prevailing short-term interest rates, and the equilibrium between suppliers and demanders of long-term funds, such as bonds, would determine prevailing long-term interest rates. The slope of the yield curve would be determined by the general relationship between the prevailing rates in each market segment. Simply stated, low rates in the short-term segment and high rates in the long-term segment cause the yield curve to be upward-sloping. The opposite occurs for high short-term rates and low long-term rates.

⚠ Hint
An upward-sloping yield curve would result if the supply outstrips the demand for short-term loans, thereby resulting in relatively low short-term rates at a time when long-term rates are high because the demand for long-term loans is far above their supply.

All three theories of term structure have merit. From them we can conclude that at any time the slope of the yield curve is affected by (1) inflationary expectations, (2) liquidity preferences, and (3) the comparative equilibrium of supply and demand in the short- and long-term market segments. Upward-sloping yield curves result from higher future inflation expectations, lender preferences for shorter-maturity loans, and greater supply of short-term loans than of long-term loans relative to demand. The opposite behaviours would result in a downward-sloping yield curve. At any point in time, the interaction of these three forces will determine the prevailing slope of the yield curve.

Risk Premiums: Issuer and Issue Characteristics

So far we have considered only default-risk-free government of Canada securities. We now reintroduce the risk premium and assess it in view of risky non-federal government issues. Recall Equation 8.1, restated here:

$$k_j = \underbrace{k^* + IP}_{\substack{\text{risk-free} \\ \text{rate, } R_F}} + \underbrace{RP}_{\substack{\text{risk} \\ \text{premium}}}$$

In words, the nominal rate of interest for security j (k_j) is equal to the risk-free rate, consisting of the real rate of interest (k^*) plus the inflation expectation premium (IP), plus the risk premium (RP). The *risk premium* varies with specific issuer and issue characteristics[4]; it causes similar-maturity securities to have differing nominal rates of interest.

---

4. To provide for the same risk-free rate of interest, $k^* + IP$, it is necessary to assume equal maturities. By doing this the inflationary expectations premium, IP, and therefore R_F, will be held constant, and the issuer and issue characteristics premium, RP, becomes the key factor differentiating the nominal rates of interest on various securities.

Example ▼ On August 23, 2002, the nominal yields to maturity (YTM) on a number of classes of long-term debt securities with 10 years to maturity 2002 were as follows:

Issuer	DBRS rating	YTM	Risk premium
Government of Canada	AAA	5.16%	0
Province of New Brunswick	A	5.55	5.55% − 5.16% = 0.39%
Corporate bonds	AAA	6.06	6.06% − 5.16% = 0.90%
Corporate bonds	AA	6.31	6.31% − 5.16% = 1.15%
Corporate bonds	A	6.56	6.56% − 5.16% = 1.40%
Corporate bonds	BBB	8.88	8.88% − 5.16% = 3.72%

SOURCE: *National Post*, bond prices, August 24, 2002; and Dominion Bond Rating Service, bond ratings.

Because the government of Canada bond would represent the risk-free, long-term security (the floor rate), we can calculate the risk premium of the other securities by subtracting the risk-free rate, 5.16 percent, from the other YTM. The results are provided in the final column.

These risk premiums reflect differing levels of default risk. There is essentially no default risk on government of Canada debt securities. For the Province of New Brunswick, more default risk is present, but the risk premium is a relatively modest 39 basis points, or 0.39 percent. Corporate bonds carry more default risk than any government security and this is reflected in the risk premium. The risk premium for AAA corporates is almost 1 percent and the premium gradually increases for the AA and A rated corporate bonds. The risk premium explodes to 3.72 percent for the BBB rated bonds. In August 2002, the bond market was very wary of higher risk bonds and demanded a large premium for assuming the ▲ greater risk.

The risk premium consists of a number of issuer- and issue-related components including: default risk, maturity risk, liquidity risk, contractual provisions, and tax risk. Each of these components is briefly defined in Table 8.1. In general, the highest risk premiums, and therefore the highest returns, are to be found in securities issued by firms with a high risk of default and in long-term maturities that are not actively traded, have unfavourable contractual provisions, and have less security.

Risk and Return

The fact that a positive relationship exists between risk and the nominal or expected return should be evident. Investors tend to purchase those securities that are expected to provide a return commensurate with the perceived risk. The actual return earned on the security will affect whether investors sell, hold, or buy additional securities. In addition, most investors look to certain types of securities to provide a given range of risk-return behaviours.

risk-return tradeoff
The expectation that for accepting greater risk, investors must be compensated with greater returns.

As illustrated in Chapter 7, a **risk-return tradeoff** exists: Investors must be compensated for accepting greater risk with higher expected returns. This concept is illustrated in Figure 8.4. The various types of financial securities have very

TABLE 8.1	Issuer- and Issue-Related Risk Components
Component	**Description**
Default risk	The possibility that the issuer of debt will not pay the contractual interest or principal as scheduled. The greater the uncertainty as to the borrower's ability to meet these payments, the greater the risk premium. High bond ratings reflect low default risk, and low bond ratings reflect high default risk.
Maturity risk (also called *interest-rate risk*)	The fact that the longer the maturity, the more the value of a security will change in response to a given change in interest rates. If interest rates on otherwise similar-risk securities suddenly rise due to a change in the money supply, the prices of long-term bonds will decline by more than the prices of short-term bonds, and vice versa.[a]
Liquidity risk	The ease with which securities can be converted into cash without experiencing a loss in value. Generally, securities actively traded on major exchanges and over the counter have low liquidity risk, and less actively traded securities in a "thin market" have high liquidity risk.
Contractual provisions	Conditions that are often included in a debt agreement or a share issue. Some of these reduce risk, whereas others may increase risk. For example, a provision allowing a bond issuer to retire its bonds prior to their maturity under favourable terms would increase the bond's risk.
Tax risk	The chance that federal or provincial governments will make unfavourable changes in tax laws. The greater the potential impact of a tax law change on the return of a given security, the greater its tax risk. Generally, long-term securities are subject to greater tax risk than those that are closer to their maturity dates.

[a]A detailed discussion of the effects of interest rates on the price or value of bonds and other fixed-income securities is presented later in this chapter.

different risk profiles, and therefore very different required returns. Higher returns are required for securities with greater risk. The figure should look familiar to readers; it was shown a number of times in Chapter 7. The measure of risk could be the standard deviation or beta. When beta is used, the nondiversifiable risk of a security is measured and the line depicting the relationship between risk and return is the security market line (SML).

FIGURE 8.4

Risk-Return Tradeoff
Risk-return profile for popular securities

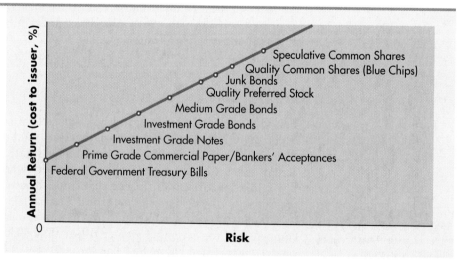

Career Key
The *marketing* department is particularly concerned about the risk-return relationship because it might be used by top management to reject new product proposals. Management might feel that if it accepted these proposals, the firm's risk would be too high.

Understanding the risk-return tradeoff is imperative not only for financial managers, but for all managers of a company. There are risks associated with the various financing alternatives available to a company, and also for investments in assets. All expenditures of company funds entail risk. So, in attempting to maximize share price, a company's management must always be aware of the impact of risk and return.

? Review Questions

8–1   What is the *real rate of interest?* Differentiate it from the *nominal rate of interest* for the risk-free asset, a 3-month government of Canada treasury bill. How can the real rate of interest be estimated?

8–2   What is the *term structure of interest rates*, and how does it relate to the *yield curve?* For a given class of similar-risk securities, what does each of the following yield curves reflect about interest rates: (**a**) downward-sloping; (**b**) upward-sloping; and (**c**) flat? Which form historically has been dominant?

8–3   Briefly describe the following theories of the general shape of the yield curve: (**a**) expectations hypothesis; (**b**) liquidity preference theory; and (**c**) market segmentation theory.

8–4   List and briefly describe the potential component risks that are embodied in the risk premium. What is meant by the *risk-return tradeoff?* How should this relationship affect the actions of financial managers?

8.2 Valuation Fundamentals

valuation
The process that links risk and return to determine the worth of an asset.

As was noted in Chapter 7, all major financial decisions must be viewed in terms of expected risk, expected return, and their combined impact on share price. **Valuation** is the process that links risk and return to determine the worth of an asset. It is a relatively simple process that can be applied to *expected* streams of benefits from real assets such as new manufacturing equipment or plants, new products or product line expansions, or new business development, and financial assets such as long-term debt and preferred and commom shares. To determine the worth of assets at a given point in time, the manager uses the time-value-of-money techniques presented in Chapter 5 and the concepts of risk and return developed in Chapter 7.

Key Inputs

The key inputs to the valuation process include cash flows (returns), timing, and the required return (risk). A description of each follows.

Cash Flows (Returns)

The value of any asset depends on the cash flow(s) it is *expected* to provide over the ownership period. To have value, an asset does not have to provide an annual cash flow; it can provide an intermittent cash flow or even a single cash flow over the period.

Example ▼ Celia Sargent, financial analyst for Groton Corporation, a diversified holding company, wishes to estimate the value of three of its assets—common shares in Michaels Enterprises, an interest in an oil well, and an original painting by a well known artist. Her cash flow estimates for each were as follows.

Shares of Michaels Enterprises *Expect* to receive cash dividends of $300 per year indefinitely.

Oil well *Expect* to receive cash flow of $2,000 at the end of 1 year, $4,000 at the end of 2 years, and $10,000 at the end of 4 years, when the well is to be sold.

Original painting *Expect* to be able to sell the painting in 5 years for $85,000.

With these cash flow estimates, Celia has taken the first step toward placing a ▲ value on each of these assets.

Timing

In addition to making cash flow estimates, we must know the timing of the cash flows. As is noted in Chapter 5, the point in time a cash flow is received is an important factor in determining the "true" value of the cash flow.[5] For example, Celia expected the cash flows of $2,000, $4,000, and $10,000 for the oil well to occur at the end of years 1, 2, and 4, respectively. In combination, the cash flow and its timing fully define the return expected from the asset.

Required Return (Risk)

As is clear from Section 8.1, the level of risk associated with a given cash flow can significantly affect its value. In general, the greater the risk of (or the less certain) a cash flow, the lower its value. Greater risk can be incorporated into an analysis by using a higher required return or discount rate. In the valuation process, just as in present value calculations, the required return incorporates risk into the analysis: the higher the risk, the greater the required return; the lower the risk, the less the required return.

Example ▼ Let's return to Celia Sargent's task of placing a value on Groton Corporation's original painting and consider two scenarios.

Scenario 1—Certainty A major art gallery has contracted to buy the painting for $85,000 at the end of 5 years. Because this is considered a certain situation, Celia views this asset as "money in the bank." She thus would use the prevailing risk-free rate, R_F, of 9 percent as the required return when calculating the value of the painting.

---

5. Although cash flows can occur at any time during a year, for computational convenience as well as custom, we will assume they occur at the end of the year unless otherwise noted.

IN PRACTICE   Small Business

Valuing a Dream

For many people, owning their own business represents the dream of a lifetime. But how much should this dream cost? To get an idea of how to value a small business, check out the Web site Value a Business—Sample Valuation Guidelines at www.businesstown.com. The site suggests that the amount to pay for a business ranges from 1 to 10 times current profits depending on: the length of time the business has been established, current market position, competitive pressures, volatility of earnings, value of assets, and level of dependency on management's skills for success.

An extremely well established and steady business with a rock-solid market position, whose continued earnings are not dependent upon a strong management team, may sell for a multiple of 8 to 10 times current earnings. A small personal service business where the new owner will be one of the only workers may sell for a multiple of 1 times current earnings. The Web site also lists a number of valuation techniques that could be used to value a business, including: a multiple of cash flow, book value, liquidation value, a discounted cash flow approach, common sense, and excess earnings methods. All experts agree that when it comes to buying a new business, the key is not to pay too much.

The Web site www.businessesforsale.com lists businesses for sale around the world. In September 2002, some of the offerings included a metal castings foundry in southern Ontario; a wine farm in Cape Town, South Africa; a public house (pub) in Manchester, England; a licensed Internet casino and sportsbetting business in Vanuatu in the South Pacific; a hardware wholesale distributor in Queensland, Australia; a log home manufacturer in southwestern British Columbia; and a credit reporting service in Orange, California.

For the credit reporting service business, the selling price was $1.7 million. The company's sales revenue for the most recent fiscal year was $1.3 million, and profits were $480,000. The company worked with banks and other lending institutions and consolidated credit reports into a single easy-to-read report. The company was in business for seven years, had between 8 and 12 employees depending on the season, and had "room to grow." When earnings are used to determine a value for a business, earnings before interest taxes, depreciation, and owner's compensation are often used. Given that the selling price was only a little over 3.5 times profits ($1,700,000/ $480,000), the selling price seemed quite reasonable. This view is reinforced upon learning that the selling price included $250,000 in accounts receivable and that one of the reasons the current owner was selling was that he was "set for life!"

SOURCES: Value a Business—Sample Valuation Guidelines at www.businesstown.com; Valuation Techniques, at www.businesstown.com; and www.businessesforsale.com.

Scenario 2—High Risk The value of original paintings by this artist has fluctuated widely over the past 10 years. Although Celia expects to be able to get $85,000 for the painting, she realizes that its sale price in 5 years could range between $30,000 and $140,000. Due to the high uncertainty surrounding the painting's value, Celia believes that a 15 percent required return is appropriate.

These two estimates of the appropriate required return illustrate how this rate captures risk. The often subjective nature of such estimates is also clear.

The Basic Valuation Model

Simply stated, the value of any asset is *the present value of all future cash flows it is expected to provide over the relevant time period.* The relevant time period is the useful life of the asset which could be as short as 1 year or as long as infinity. The value of an asset is therefore determined by discounting the expected cash flows back to their present value, using the required return that reflects the asset's risk. Utilizing the present value techniques presented in Chapter 5, we can express the value of any asset at time zero, V_0, as

$$V_0 = \frac{CF_1}{(1+k)^1} + \frac{CF_2}{(1+k)^2} + \cdots + \frac{CF_n}{(1+k)^n} \qquad (8.5)$$

where

$$
\begin{aligned}
V_0 &= \text{value of the asset at time zero} \\
CF_t &= \text{cash flow } \textit{expected} \text{ at the end of year } t \\
k &= \text{appropriate required rate of return (discount rate)} \\
n &= \text{relevant time period}
\end{aligned}
$$

Using the present value interest factor notation, $PVIF_{k,n}$ from Chapter 5, Equation 8.5 can be rewritten as

$$V_0 = [CF_1 \times (PVIF_{k,1})] + [CF_2 \times (PVIF_{k,2})] + \cdots + [CF_n \times (PVIF_{k,n})] \qquad (8.6)$$

Substituting the expected cash flows, CF_t, over the relevant time period, n, and the appropriate required return, k, into Equation 8.6, we can determine the value of any asset.

Example ▼ Celia Sargent, using appropriate required returns and Equation 8.6, calculated the value of each asset (using present value interest factors from Table A-3), as shown in Table 8.2. Michaels Enterprises stock has a value of $2,500, the oil well's value is $9,262, and the original painting has a value of $42,245. Had she instead used a calculator, the values of the oil well and original painting would have been $9,266.98 and $42,260.03, respectively. Note that regardless of the pattern of the expected cash flow from an asset, the basic valuation equation can
▲ be used to determine its value.

? Review Questions

8–5 Define *valuation* and explain why it is important for the financial manager to understand the valuation process.

8–6 Briefly describe the three key inputs to the valuation process. Does the valuation process apply only to assets providing an annual cash flow? Explain.

8–7 Define and specify the general equation for the value of any asset, V_0, in terms of its *expected* cash flow in each year and the appropriate required return.

TABLE 8.2	**Valuation of Groton Corporation's Assets by Celia Sargent**		

Asset	Cash flow, CF	Appropriate required return	Valuation
Michaels Enterprises stock[a]	$300/year indefinitely	12%	$V_0 = \$300 \times (PVIFA_{12\%,\infty})$ $= \$300 \times \dfrac{1}{0.12} = \underline{\underline{\$2,500}}$

Oil well[b]	Year (t)	CF_t	20%	
	1	$ 2,000		$V_0 = [\$2,000 \times (PVIF_{20\%,1})]$
	2	4,000		$\quad + [\$4,000 \times (PVIF_{20\%,2})]$
	3	0		$\quad + [\$0 \times (PVIF_{20\%,3})]$
	4	10,000		$\quad + [\$10,000 \times (PVIF_{20\%,4})]$
				$= [\$2,000 \times (0.833)]$
				$\quad + [\$4,000 \times (0.694)]$
				$\quad + [\$0 \times (0.579)]$
				$\quad + [\$10,000 \times (0.482)]$
				$= \$1,666 + \$2,776$
				$\quad + \$0 + \$4,820$
				$= \underline{\underline{\$9,262}}$

Original painting[c]	$85,000 at end of year 5	15%	$V_0 = \$85,000 \times (PVIF_{15\%,5})$ $= \$85,000 \times (0.497)$ $= \underline{\underline{\$42,245}}$

[a]This is a perpetuity (infinite-lived annuity), and therefore the present value interest factor given in Equation 5.28 is applied.

[b]This is a mixed stream of cash flows and therefore requires a number of *PVIF*s, as noted.

[c]This is a lump-sum cash flow and therefore requires a single *PVIF*.

8.3 Long-Term Debt Valuation

The basic valuation equation can be customized for use in valuing specific financial securities—long-term debt, preferred shares, and common shares. Long-term debt and preferred shares are similar, because they have stated contractual cash flows (interest and dividend). The dividends on common shares, on the other hand, are not known in advance. The principles associated with the valuation of long-term debt are discussed in this section, common shares in the following section, while preferred share valuation principles are covered in Section 8.6.

⚠ Hint

A bondholder receives two cash flows from a bond if held to maturity—interest and the bond's face value. For valuation purposes, the interest is an annuity and the face value is a single payment received at a specified future date.

Long-Term Debt Fundamentals

As discussed in Chapter 6, long-term debt is used by business and government to raise large sums of money, typically from a diverse group of lenders. Most long-term debt securities pay interest *semiannually* (every 6 months) at a stated *coupon rate*, have an initial *maturity* of 10 to 30 years, and have a *par*, or *face*, *value* of $1,000 that must be repaid at maturity.[6] An example will illustrate the terms of a corporate bond.

Example ▼ On January 1, 2001 Mills Company, a large defence contractor, issued a 10-year bond with a $1,000 par value and a 10 percent coupon rate that pays interest semiannually. Investors who buy this bond receive the contractual right to two cash flows: (1) $100 annual interest (10% coupon rate × $1,000 par value) with $50 (½ × $100) paid every 6 months and (2) the $1,000 par value at the end of **▲** the tenth year.

We will use data for Mills's bond issue to look at basic bond valuation.

Basic Bond Valuation

The value of a bond is the present value of the payments its issuer is contractually obligated to make, from the current time until it matures. The basic equation for the value, B_0, of a bond is given by Equation 8.7:

$$B_0 = I \times \left[\sum_{t=1}^{n} \frac{1}{(1 + k_d)^t} \right] + M \times \left[\frac{1}{(1 + k_d)^n} \right] \tag{8.7}$$

$$= I \times (PVIFA_{k_d,n}) + M \times (PVIF_{k_d,n}) \tag{8.7a}$$

where

$$B_0 = \text{value of the bond at time zero}$$
$$I = \textit{annual} \text{ interest paid in dollars[7]}$$
$$n = \text{number of years to maturity}$$
$$M = \text{par value in dollars}$$
$$k_d = \text{required rate of return on a bond}$$

We can calculate bond value using Equation 8.7a and the appropriate financial tables (A-3 and A-4) or by using a financial calculator.

Example ▼ *Assuming that interest on the Mills Company bond issue is paid annually and that the required return is equal to the bond's coupon rate, $I = \$100$, $k_d = 10\%$, $M = \$1,000$, and $n = 10$ years.*

Table Use   Substituting the values noted above into Equation 8.7a yields

$$B_0 = \$100 \times (PVIFA_{10\%,10yrs}) + \$1,000 \times (PVIF_{10\%,10yrs})$$
$$= \$100 \times (6.145) + \$1,000 \times (0.386)$$
$$= \$614.50 + \$386.00 = \underline{\$1,000.50}$$

The bond therefore has a value of approximately $1,000.[8]

---

6. As discussed in Chapter 6, long-term debt securities can be either bonds or debentures. The term *bond* is often used as a general descriptor of long-term debt, and this convention is used in the remainder of this chapter. Bonds often have features that allow them to be retired by the issuer prior to maturity; these call and conversion features were presented in Chapter 6. For the purpose of the current discussion, these features are ignored.

7. The payment of annual rather than semiannual coupons is assumed throughout the following discussion. This assumption simplifies the calculations involved while maintaining the conceptual accuracy of the valuation procedures presented.

8. Note that a slight rounding error ($0.50) results here due to the use of the table factors, which are rounded to the nearest thousandth.

Calculator Use   Using the Mills Company's inputs shown, you should find the bond value to be exactly $1,000.

Inputs: 10   10   100   1000

Functions: N   I   PMT   FV   CPT   PV

Outputs: 1000

Note that *the bond value calculated in the example is equal to its par value; this will always be the case when the required return is equal to the coupon rate.*[9]

Time-Line Use   The computations involved in finding the bond value are depicted graphically on the following time line.[10]

Graphic depiction of bond valuation (Mills Company's 10% coupon interest rate, 10-year maturity, $1,000 par, January 1, 2001, issue paying annual interest; required return = 10%)

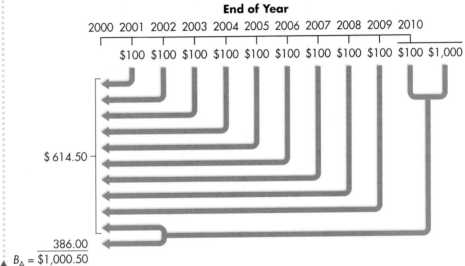

Bond Value Behaviour

In practice, the value of a bond in the marketplace is rarely equal to its par value. As was seen in the bond quotations in Figure 6.3, the closing prices of bonds differ from their par values of 100 (100% of par). Some are valued below par (quoted below 100%), and others are valued above par (quoted above 100%). A variety of forces in the economy as well as the passage of time tend to affect value. Because these external forces are in no way controlled by bond issuers or

9. Note that because bonds pay interest every 6 months, the prices at which they are quoted and traded reflect their value *plus* any accrued interest. For example, a $1,000 par value, 10 percent coupon bond paying interest semiannually and having a calculated value of $900 would pay interest of $50 at the end of each 6-month period. If it is now 3 months since the beginning of the interest period, three-sixths or one-half of the $50 interest, or $25 (i.e., 1/2 × $50), would be accrued. The bond would therefore be quoted at $925—its $900 value plus the $25 in accrued interest. For convenience, *throughout this book, bond values will always be assumed to be calculated at the beginning of the interest period*, thereby avoiding the need to consider accrued interest.

10. If the coupon payments on the Mills Company bond were semiannual, the coupon payments would be $50 and a payment would occur every six months. So, halfway between each year, a payment of $50 would appear and the payment at the end of the year would also be $50. On December 31, 2010, a payment of $50 and one of $1,000 would occur. In this example, the value of the bond is still $1,000.

investors, it is useful to understand the impact that required return and time to maturity have on bond value.

Required Returns and Bond Values

Recall from Chapter 6 that the coupon rate on a bond is set at the time of issue and does not change for the life of the bond. For many bonds, this could be for the term of 20 to 30 years. The coupon rate is based on the floor rate, the rate on government of Canada bonds with the same time to maturity, plus a premium for risk. The only time the coupon rate and the required rate of return for a bond might be equal, over the full life of the bond, may be the week the bond is issued.

Whenever the required return on a bond differs from the bond's coupon interest rate, the bond's value will differ from its par value. The required return on the bond is likely to differ from the coupon interest rate because either (1) economic conditions have changed, causing a shift in the basic cost of long-term funds, or (2) the firm's risk has changed. Increases in the basic cost of long-term funds or in risk will raise the required return; decreases in the cost of funds or in risk will lower the required return.

Regardless of the exact cause, what is important is the relationship between the required return and the coupon interest rate: When the required return is greater than the coupon interest rate, the bond value, B_0, will be less than its par value, M. In this case, the bond is said to sell at a **discount**, which will equal $M - B_0$. On the other hand, when the required return falls below the coupon interest rate, the bond value will be greater than par. In this situation the bond is said to sell at a **premium**, which will equal $B_0 - M$.

discount
The amount by which a bond sells at a value that is less than its par value.

premium
The amount by which a bond sells at a value that is greater than its par value.

E x a m p l e ▼ In the preceding example, we saw that when the required return equalled the coupon interest rate, the bond's value equalled its $1,000 par value. If for the same bond the required return were to rise to 12 percent, its value would be found as follows (using Equation 8.7a):

Table Use

$$B_0 = \$100 \times (PVIFA_{12\%,10yrs}) + \$1,000 \times (PVIF_{12\%,10yrs})$$
$$= \$100 \times (5.650) + \$1,000 \times (0.322) = \underline{\underline{\$887}}$$

Calculator Use   Using the inputs shown, you should find the value of the bond, with a 12 percent required return, to be $887.

Inputs: 10   12   100   1000

Functions: N   I   PMT   FV   CPT   PV

Outputs: 887.00

The bond would therefore sell at a *discount* of $113 ($1,000 par value − $887 value).

If, on the other hand, the required return fell to, say, 8 percent, the bond's value would be found as follows:

Table Use

$$B_0 = \$100 \times (PVIFA_{8\%,10\text{yrs}}) + \$1,000 \times (PVIF_{8\%,10\text{yrs}})$$
$$= \$100 \times (6.710) + \$1,000 \times (0.463) = \underline{\underline{\$1,134}}$$

Calculator Use   Using the inputs shown, you should find the value of the bond, with an 8 percent required return, to be \$1,134.20. Note that this value is more precise than the \$1,134 value calculated using the rounded financial table factors.

Inputs: 10   8   100   1000

Functions: N   I   PMT   FV   CPT   PV

Outputs: 1134.20

The bond would therefore sell for a *premium* of \$134.20 (\$1,134.20 value − \$1,000 par value). The results of this and earlier calculations for Mills Company's bond values are summarized in Table 8.3 and graphically depicted in Figure 8.5.

Time to Maturity and Bond Values

Whenever the required return is different from the coupon interest rate, the amount of time to maturity affects bond value. An additional factor is whether required returns are constant or changing over the life of the bond.

Constant Required Returns   When the required return is different from the coupon interest rate and is assumed to be *constant until maturity*, the value of the bond will approach its par value as the passage of time moves the bond's value closer to maturity. (Of course, when the required return *equals* the coupon interest rate, the bond's value will remain at par until it matures.)

Example ▼ Figure 8.6 depicts the behaviour of the bond values calculated earlier and presented in Table 8.3 for Mills Company's 10 percent coupon interest rate bond

TABLE 8.3	Bond Values for Various Required Returns (Mills Company's 10% Coupon Interest Rate, 10-Year Maturity, \$1,000 Par, January 1, 2001, Issue Paying Annual Interest)	
Required return, k_d	Bond value, B_0	Status
12%	\$ 887.00	Discount
10	1,000.00	Par value
8	1,134.20	Premium

FIGURE 8.5

Bond Values and Required Returns
Bond value and required returns (Mills Company's 10% coupon interest rate, 10-year maturity, $1,000 par, January 1, 2001, issue paying annual interest)

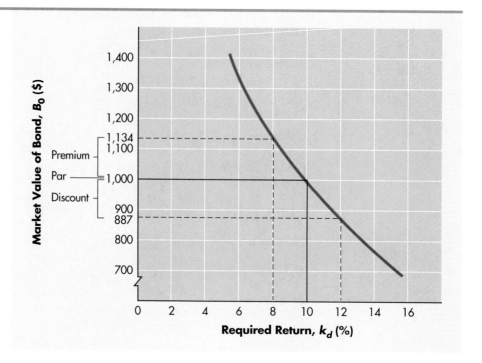

paying annual interest and having 10 years to maturity. Each of the three required returns—12, 10, and 8 percent—is assumed to remain constant over the 10 years to the bond's maturity. The bond's value in each case approaches and ultimately equals the bond's $1,000 par value at its maturity.

At the 12 percent required return, the bond's discount declines with the passage of time, as the bond's value increases from $887 to $1,000. When the 10 percent required return equals the bond's coupon interest rate, its value remains

FIGURE 8.6

Time to Maturity and Bond Values
Relationship between time to maturity, required returns, and bond values (Mills Company's 10% coupon interest rate, 10-year maturity, $1,000 par, January 1, 2001, issue paying annual interest)

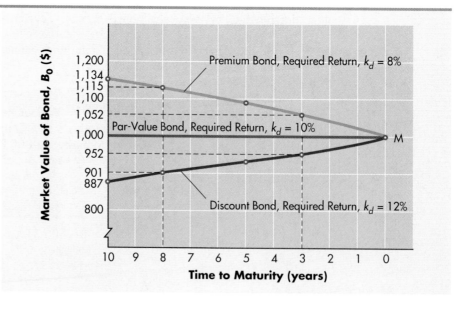

unchanged at $1,000 over its maturity. Finally, at the 8 percent required return, the bond's premium will decline as its value drops from $1,134.20 to $1,000 at maturity. With the required return assumed to be constant to maturity, the bond's value approaches its $1,000 par or maturity value as the time to maturity declines.

Changing Required Returns   The chance that interest rates will change and thereby change the required return and bond value is called **interest-rate risk.** Bondholders are typically more concerned with rising rates, which decrease bond value. The shorter the amount of time until a bond's maturity, the less responsive is its market value to a given change in the required return. In other words, short maturities have less interest-rate risk than do long maturities when all other features—coupon interest rate, par value, and interest-payment frequency—are the same.

interest-rate risk
The chance that interest rates will change and thereby change the required return and bond value. Rising rates, which result in decreasing bond values, are of greatest concern.

Example ▼ The effect of changing required returns on bonds of differing maturity can be illustrated by using Mills Company's bond and Figure 8.6. If, as denoted by the dashed line at 8 years to maturity, the required return rises from 10 percent to 12 percent, the bond's value decreases from $1,000 to $901—a 9.9 percent increase. If the same change in required return had occurred with only 3 years to maturity, as denoted by the dashed line, the bond's value would have dropped to just $952—only a 4.8 percent decrease. Similar types of responses can be seen in terms of the change in bond value associated with decreases in required returns. The shorter the time to maturity, the smaller the impact on bond value caused by ▲ a given change in the required return.

Yield to Maturity (YTM)

yield to maturity (YTM)
The rate of return investors earn if they buy a bond at a specific price and hold it until maturity. Assumes that issuer makes all scheduled interest and principal payments as promised.

When investors evaluate and trade bonds, they commonly consider **yield to maturity (YTM),** which is the rate of return investors earn if they buy the bond at a specific price and hold it until maturity. The measure assumes, of course, that the issuer makes all scheduled interest and principal payments as promised. The yield to maturity on a bond with a current price equal to its par value (i.e., $B_0 = M$) will always equal the coupon interest rate. When the bond value differs from par, the yield to maturity will differ from the coupon interest rate.

Assuming that interest is paid annually, the yield to maturity on a bond can be found by solving Equation 8.7 for k_d. In other words, the current value, B_0, the annual interest, I, the par value, M, and the years to maturity, n, are known, and the required return must be found. The required return is the bond's yield to maturity. The YTM can be found by trial and error or by use of a financial calculator. The calculator provides accurate YTM values with minimum effort. Finding YTM is demonstrated in the following example.

Example ▼ The Mills Company bond, which currently sells for $1,080, has a 10 percent coupon interest rate and $1,000 par value, pays interest annually, and has 10 years to maturity. Because $B_0 = \$1,080$, $I = \$100$ ($0.10 \times \$1,000$), $M = \$1,000$, and $n = 10$ years, substituting into Equation 8.7a, we get

$$\$1,080 = \$100 \times (PVIFA_{k_d,10\text{yrs}}) + \$1,000 \times (PVIF_{k_d,10\text{yrs}})$$

Our objective is to solve the equation for k_d—the YTM.

The Value of a Zero

The majority of long-term debt securities outstanding make coupon payments semiannually and repay the par value at maturity. For many investors, this is exactly what they require: a steady stream of known payments. So why would an investor buy a zero-coupon bond, one that makes no regular payments? One reason is their cost. Since zeros only pay the par value at maturity, they sell at a deep discount from the par value. For example, a $1,000 par value, 30-year government of Canada zero-coupon bond might cost $174.11. At maturity, the investor receives $1,000. The difference between the price paid now and the par value received at maturity is the return to the investor, in this case $825.89. What is the annual yield, in percent, that an investor would receive on the zero? Using your financial calculator results in an answer of 6 percent. Note that this answer represents compounding. Each year, over the term of the bond, it is assumed that the interest was paid and was then reinvested in the zero.

This is an important consideration for investors in Canada since the investor must claim the yearly gain in the value of the zero as interest income, even though no cash was actually received. To calculate the amount of interest that is deemed to be received, the zero's value must be calculated at the beginning and end of each year. To determine the values, the formula

$M/(1 + K_d)^n$ is used. For the formula, M is the par value, K_d is the required rate of return, and n is the time to maturity. Note that the values can be calculated using the formula, by using financial tables, or by using a financial calculator.

Assume that an investor buys a $1,000 par value zero-coupon bond with a yield of 6.5 percent and 5 years to maturity. Calculate the initial price of the bond. It is $729.88. The total return (interest) received on the bond over the 5 years is $270.12 ($1,000 − $729.88). A table can be easily developed indicating the zero's value at the beginning and end of each year, and the amount of interest that is deemed to be received. This is provided below. Given the high taxes on interest income, as discussed in Section 8.6, most individual investors should hold zero-coupon bonds in tax-sheltered accounts, like registered retirement savings plans (RRSPs).

Year	Beginning value	Ending value	Implicit interest expense
1	$729.88	$ 777.32	$ 47.44
2	777.32	827.85	50.53
3	827.85	881.66	53.81
4	881.66	938.97	57.31
5	938.97	1,000.00	61.03
Total			$270.12

Trial and Error   Because we know that a required return, k_d, of 10 percent (which equals the bond's 10% coupon interest rate) would result in a value of $1,000, the discount rate that would result in $1,080 must be less than 10 percent. (Remember that the lower the discount rate, the higher the present value, and the higher the discount rate, the lower the present value.) Trying 9 percent, we get

$$\$100 \times (PVIFA_{9\%,10yrs}) + \$1,000 \times (PVIF_{9\%,10yrs}) = \$100 \times (6.418) + \$1,000 \times (0.422)$$
$$= \$641.80 + \$422 = \$1,063.80$$

Because the 9 percent rate is not quite low enough to bring the value up to $1,080, we next try 8 percent and get

$$\$100 \times (PVIFA_{8\%,10yrs}) + \$1,000 \times (PVIF_{8\%,10yrs}) = \$100 \times (6.710) + \$1,000 \times (0.463)$$
$$= \$671 + \$463 = \$1,134$$

Because the value at the 8 percent rate is higher than $1,080 and the value at the 9 percent rate is lower than $1,080, the bond's yield to maturity must be between 8 and 9 percent. Because the $1,063.80 is closer to $1,080, the YTM to the nearest whole percent is 9 percent. (By using *interpolation*, we could eventually find the more precise YTM value to be 8.77%.)[11]

Calculator Use   [*Note:* Most calculators require *either* the present (B_0 in this case) or future (M in this case) values to be inputted as a negative number to calculate yield to maturity. Note that the PV is negative in this case.] Using the inputs shown, you should find the YTM to be 8.766 percent. Note that this number is more precise and easier to calculate than the YTM value found before by using the trial-and-error approach.

Inputs: | 10 | -1080 | 100 | 1000 |

Functions: | N | PV | PMT | FV | CPT | I |

▲ **Outputs:** | 8.766 |

Semiannual Coupon Payments and Bond Values

The procedure used to value bonds paying interest semiannually is similar to that shown in Chapter 5 for compounding interest more frequently than annually—except that here we need to find present value instead of future value. It involves

1. Converting annual interest, I, to semiannual interest by dividing I by 2.
2. Converting the number of years to maturity, n, to the number of 6-month periods to maturity by multiplying n by 2.
3. Converting the required stated (rather than effective)[12] return for similar-risk bonds that also pay semiannual interest from an annual rate, k_d, to a semiannual rate by dividing k_d by 2.

---

11. For information on how to interpolate a more precise answer, see the book's home page at **www.pearsoned.ca/gitman**.

12. As was noted in Chapter 5, the effective annual rate of interest, EAR, for stated interest rate k, when interest is paid semiannually ($m = 2$), can be found by using Equation 5.10:

$$EAR = \left(1 + \frac{k}{2}\right)^2 - 1$$

For example, a bond with a 12 percent required stated return, k_d, that pays semiannual interest would have an effective annual rate of

$$EAR = \left(1 + \frac{0.12}{2}\right)^2 - 1 = (1.06)^2 - 1 = 1.1236 - 1 = 0.1236 = \underline{12.36\%}$$

Because most bonds pay semiannual interest at semiannual rates equal to 50 percent of the stated annual rate, their effective annual rates are generally higher than their stated rates.

Substituting these three changes into Equation 8.7 yields

$$B_0 = \frac{I}{2} \times \left[\sum_{i=1}^{2n} \frac{1}{\left(1 + \frac{k_d}{2}\right)^t} \right] + M \times \left[\frac{1}{\left(1 + \frac{k_d}{2}\right)^{2n}} \right] \qquad (8.8)^{13}$$

$$= \frac{I}{2} \times \left(PVIFA_{\frac{k_d}{2}, 2n} \right) + M \times \left(PVIF_{\frac{k_d}{2}, 2n} \right) \qquad (8.8a)$$

An example will illustrate the application of this equation.

Example ▼ Assuming that the Mills Company bond pays interest semiannually and that the required stated return, k_d, is 12 percent for similar-risk bonds that also pay semiannual interest, substituting these values into Equation 8.8a yields

$$B_0 = \frac{\$100}{2} \times \left(PVIFA_{\frac{12\%}{2}, 2 \times 10\text{yrs}} \right) + \$1,000 \times \left(PVIF_{\frac{12\%}{2}, 2 \times 10\text{yrs}} \right)$$

Table Use

$$B_0 = \$50 \times (PVIFA_{6\%, 20 \text{ periods}}) + \$1,000 \times (PVIF_{6\%, 20 \text{ periods}})$$
$$= \$50 \times (11.470) + \$1,000 \times (0.312) = \underline{\$885.50}$$

Calculator Use Here, N is 20, I is 6, Pmt is 50, and FV is 1000. Using these inputs, you should find the bond value with semiannual interest to be $885.30. Note that this value is more precise than the value calculated using the rounded financial table factors.

Inputs: | 20 | | 6 | | 50 | | 1000 |

Functions: | N | | I | | PMT | | FV | | CPT | | PV |

Outputs: | 885.30 |

Comparing this result with the $887.00 value found earlier for annual compounding (see Table 8.3), we can see that the bond's value is lower when semiannual interest is paid. *This will always occur when the bond sells at a discount.* For bonds selling at a premium, the opposite will occur: the value with semiannual interest will be greater than with annual interest. For example, when the required return is 8 percent, the value of the Mills Company bond when coupons are paid annually was $1,134.20. With semiannual coupon payments, the value of the bond is $1,135.90.

❓ Review Questions

8–8   Describe the basic procedure used to value a bond that pays annual interest. What procedure is used to value bonds paying interest semiannually?

---

13. Although it may appear inappropriate to use the semiannual discounting procedure on the maturity value, M, this technique is necessary to find the correct bond value. One way to confirm the accuracy of this approach is to calculate the bond value for the case where the required stated return and coupon interest rate are equal; for B_0 to equal M, as would be expected in such a case, the maturity value must be discounted on a semiannual basis.

8–9   What relationship between the required return and coupon interest rate will cause a bond to sell (**a**) at a discount? (**b**) at a premium? and (**c**) at its par value? Explain.

8–10 If the required return on a bond differs from its coupon interest rate and is assumed to be constant until maturity, describe the behaviour of the bond value over the passage of time as the bond moves toward maturity.

8–11 As a risk-averse investor, to protect against the potential impact of rising interest rates on bond value, would you prefer bonds with short or long periods until maturity? Explain why.

8–12 What is meant by a bond's *yield to maturity (YTM)?* Briefly describe both the trial-and-error approach and the use of a financial calculator for finding YTM.

8.4 Valuation of Common Shares

Common shareholders expect to be rewarded through periodic cash dividends and an increasing—or at least nondeclining—share value. Like current owners, prospective owners and security analysts frequently estimate the firm's value. They purchase the stock when they believe that it is *undervalued*—that its true value is greater than its market price. They sell the stock when they feel that it is *overvalued*—that its market price is greater than its true value.

In this section, we will describe four specific stock valuation techniques. First, though, we will look at the concept of an efficient market, which questions whether the prices of actively traded stocks can differ from their true values.

Market Efficiency[14]

Economically rational buyers and sellers use their assessment of an asset's expected cash flows and its risk to determine its value. To a buyer, the asset's value represents the maximum price that he or she would pay to acquire it; a seller views the asset's value as a minimum sale price. In competitive markets with many active participants, such as the Toronto Stock Exchange, the interactions of many buyers and sellers result in an equilibrium price—the *market value*—for each security. This price reflects the collective actions of buyers and sellers based on all available information. Buyers and sellers are assumed to immediately digest new information as it becomes available, and through their purchase and sale activities to quickly create a new market equilibrium price.

! Hint
Be sure to clarify in your own mind the difference between the required return and the expected return. *Required return* is what an investor *has to have* to invest in a specific asset, and *expected return* is the return an investor *thinks she will get* if the asset is purchased.

Market Adjustment to New Information

The process of market adjustment to new information can be viewed in terms of rates of return. From Chapter 7, we know that for a given level of risk, investors require a specified periodic return—the *required return, k*—which can be esti-

14. A great deal of theoretical and empirical research has been performed in the area of market efficiency. For purposes of this discussion, generally accepted beliefs about market efficiency are described rather than the technical aspects of the various forms of market efficiency and their theoretical implications. For a good discussion of the theory and evidence relative to market efficiency, see W. Sean Cleary and Charles P. Jones, *Investments: Analysis and Management* (Toronto: John Wiley and Sons, 2000), Chapter 10.

mated by using beta and CAPM. Note that the equation of the CAPM is simply a different form of Equation 8.2, the basic required rate of return equation, shown earlier in the chapter. This is illustrated below:

$$K_j = R_F + RP \qquad \text{Required rate of return}$$
$$K_j = R_F + [b_j \times (k_m - R_F)] \qquad \text{CAPM}$$

The second component of the CAPM is simply the asset risk premium which is based on the market risk premium and the measure of nondiversifiable risk, beta.

expected return, $\hat{k}$
The return that is expected to be earned on a given asset each period over an infinite time horizon.

For common shares, investors regularly estimate the **expected return, $\hat{k}$**—the return that is expected to be earned on the shares each period over an infinite time horizon. The expected return can be estimated by using a simplified form of Equation 7.1:

$$\hat{k} = \frac{\text{expected benefit during upcoming period}}{\text{current price of the common shares}} \qquad (8.9)$$

Hint
This relationship between the expected return and the required return can be seen in Equation 8.9, where a decrease in the current share price will result in an increase in the expected return.

Whenever investors find that the expected return is not equal to the required return ($\hat{k} \neq k$), a market price adjustment will occur. If the expected return is less than the required return ($\hat{k} < k$), investors will sell the shares, because they do not expect it to earn a return commensurate with their risk. Such action would drive the price down, which (assuming no change in expected benefits) will cause the expected return to rise to the level of the required return. If the expected return were above the required return ($\hat{k} > k$), investors would buy the shares, driving their price up and the expected return down to the point where it equals the required return.

Example ▼ The common shares of Alton Industries (AI) are currently selling for $50 per share, and market participants expect them to generate benefits of $6.50 per share during each coming period. In addition, the risk-free rate, R_F, is currently 7 percent; the market return, k_m, is 12 percent; and the stock's beta, b_{AI}, 8.9 is 1.20. When these values are substituted into Equation 8.9, the firm's current expected return, $\hat{k}_0$, on the shares is

$$\hat{k}_0 = \frac{\$6.50}{\$50.00} = \underline{\underline{13\%}}$$

When the appropriate values are substituted into the CAPM (see above or Equation 7.8), the current required return, k_0, is

$$k_0 = 7\% + [1.20 \times (12\% - 7\%)] = 7\% + 6\% = \underline{\underline{13\%}}$$

Because $\hat{k}_0 = k_0$, the market is currently in equilibrium, and the stock is fairly priced at $50 per share.

Assume that a press release announces that a major product liability suit has been filed against Alton Industries. As a result, investors immediately adjust their risk assessment upward, raising the firm's beta from 1.20 to 1.40. The new required return, k_1, becomes

$$k_1 = 7\% + [1.40 \times (12\% - 7\%)] = 7\% + 7\% = \underline{\underline{14\%}}$$

Because the expected return of 13 percent is now below the required return of 14 percent, many investors would sell the stock—driving its price down to about $46.43—the price that would result in a 14 percent expected return, $\hat{k}_1$.

$$\hat{k}_1 = \frac{\$6.50}{\$46.43} = \underline{\underline{14\%}}$$

The new price of $46.43 brings the market back into equilibrium, because the expected return now equals the required return.

The Efficient Market Hypothesis

efficient market hypothesis (EMH)
Theory describing the behaviour of an assumed "perfect" market which states (1) securities are typically in equilibrium, (2) security prices fully reflect all public information available and react swiftly to new information, and, (3) because stocks are fairly priced, investors need not waste time looking for mispriced securities.

As noted in Chapters 6 and 7, active markets such as the Toronto Stock Exchange are believed to be both operationally and financially efficient. Millions of buy and sell orders on thousands of shares are quickly filled at the best possible price. The markets are made up of many rational investors who react quickly and objectively to new information. The **efficient market hypothesis (EMH)**, which is the basic theory describing the behaviour of such a "perfect" market, specifically states:

1. Securities are typically in equilibrium, meaning that they are fairly priced and their expected returns equal their required returns.
2. At any point in time, security prices fully reflect all public information available about the firm and its securities,[15] and these prices react swiftly to new information.
3. Because stocks are fully and fairly priced, investors need not waste their time trying to find and capitalize on mispriced (undervalued or overvalued) securities.

While most academic researchers believe in the EMH, most people who work in the investment industry (practitioners working for investment dealers) and many investors, both individual and institutional, do not believe in the EMH. Many feel that it is worthwhile to search for undervalued or overvalued securities and to trade them to profit from market inefficiencies. Others argue that it is mere luck that would allow market participants to correctly anticipate new information and as a result earn *excess returns*—that is, actual returns > required returns. They believe that it is unlikely that market participants can *over the long run* earn excess returns. Contrary to this belief, some well-known investors such as Warren Buffett of Berkshire Hathaway, Gerald Schwartz of Onex Corporation, and Irwin Michael, lead manager of the ABC Funds, a group of mutual funds *have,* over the long run, consistently earned excess returns on their portfolios. It is unclear whether their performance is the result of their superior ability to anticipate new information or some form of market inefficiency. For evidence of this consistent ability to "beat the market," see the following three Web sites: **www.berkshirehathaway.com/letters/2001.html, www.onex.com/tr/tr_menu/tr_menu.asp**, and **www.abcfunds.com/visitor**.

---

15. Those market participants who have nonpublic—*inside*—information may have an unfair advantage that permits them to earn an excess return. Since the mid-1980s with the disclosure of the insider-trading activities of a number of well known financiers and investors, major national attention has been focused on the "problem" of insider trading and its resolution. Clearly, those who trade securities based on inside information have an unfair and illegal advantage. Empirical research has confirmed that those with inside information do indeed have an opportunity to earn an excess return. Here we ignore this possibility, given its illegality and that enhanced surveillance and enforcement by the securities industry and the government have in recent years (it appears) significantly reduced insider trading. We, in effect, assume that all relevant information is public, and therefore the market is efficient.

In this section, it is assumed that the market is efficient. This means that the terms "expected return" and "required return" are used interchangeably, because they should be equal in an efficient market. This also means that share prices accurately reflect true value based on risk and return. In other words, we will operate under the assumption that the market price at any point in time is the best estimate of value. We're now ready to look closely at the mechanics of stock valuation.

The Basic Common Share Valuation Equation

Like bonds, the value of common shares is equal to the present value of all future benefits (dividends) it is expected to provide. In other words, *the value of common shares is equal to the present value of all future dividends the company is expected to pay over an infinite time horizon.*[16] Although a shareholder can earn capital gains by selling common shares at a price above that originally paid, what is really sold is the right to all future dividends. What about stocks that are not expected to pay dividends in the foreseeable future? Such stocks have a value attributable to a distant dividend expected to result from sale of the company or liquidation of its assets. Therefore, *from a valuation viewpoint, only dividends are relevant.* Redefining terms, the basic valuation model in Equation 8.5 can be specified for common shares as given in Equation 8.10:

$$P_0 = \frac{D_1}{(1+k_s)^1} + \frac{D_2}{(1+k_s)^2} + \cdots + \frac{D_\infty}{(1+k_s)^\infty} \tag{8.10}$$

where

P_0 = value of a company's common shares
D_t = per share dividend expected at the end of year t
k_s = required return on the company's common shares

dividend valuation model (DVM)
The value of common shares is dependent on the present value of the dividends received over an infinite time horizon.

This equation is referred to as the **dividend valuation model (DVM)**: the value of common shares is dependent on the present value of the dividends received. The equation can be simplified somewhat by redefining each year's dividend, D_t, in terms of anticipated growth. We will consider three cases here—zero growth, constant growth, and variable growth.

Zero Growth

zero-growth model
An approach to dividend valuation that assumes a constant, nongrowing dividend stream.

The simplest approach to dividend valuation, the **zero-growth model,** assumes a constant, nongrowing dividend stream. In terms of the notation already introduced,

$$D_1 = D_2 = \cdots = D_\infty$$

Letting D_1 represent the amount of the annual dividend, Equation 8.10 under zero growth would reduce to

$$P_0 = D_1 \times \sum_{t=1}^{\infty} \frac{1}{(1+k_s)^t} = D_1 \times (PVIFA_{k_s,\infty}) = D_1 \times \frac{1}{k_s} = \frac{D_1}{k_s} \tag{8.11}$$

16. The need to consider an infinite time horizon is not critical, because a sufficiently long period, say 50 years, will result in about the same present value as an infinite period for moderate-sized required returns. For example, at 15 percent, $1,000 to be received 50 years from now, $PVIF_{15\%,50yrs}$, is worth only about $0.92 today.

The equation shows that with zero growth, the value of a share would equal the present value of a perpetuity of D_1 dollars discounted at a rate k_s.

Example ▼ The dividend of Denham Company, an established textile producer, is expected to remain constant at $3 per share indefinitely. If the required return on its stock ▲ is 15 percent, the stock's value is $20 ($3 ÷ 0.15).

Constant Growth

constant-growth model
A widely cited dividend valuation approach that assumes that dividends will grow at a constant rate that is less than the required return.

The most widely cited dividend valuation approach, the **constant-growth model,** assumes that dividends will grow at a constant rate, g, that is less than the required return, k_s. The assumption that $k_s > g$ is a necessary mathematical condition for deriving this model.[17] By letting D_0 represent the most recent dividend, Equation 8.10 can be rewritten as follows:

$$P_0 = \frac{D_0 \times (1+g)^1}{(1+k_s)^1} + \frac{D_0 \times (1+g)^2}{(1+k_s)^2} + \cdots + \frac{D_0 \times (1+g)^\infty}{(1+k_s)^\infty} \qquad (8.12)$$

If we simplify Equation 8.10, it can be rewritten as follows:[18]

$$P_0 = \frac{D_1}{k_s - g} \qquad (8.13)$$

Gordon model
A common name for the *constant-growth model* that is widely cited in dividend valuation.

The constant-growth model in Equation 8.13 is commonly called the **Gordon model.** An example will show how it works.

Example ▼ From 1997 to 2002, Lamar Company, a small cosmetics company, paid the following per-share dividends:

---

17. Another assumption of the constant-growth model as presented is that earnings, dividends, and share price grow at the same rate. This assumption is true only in cases in which a firm pays out a fixed percentage of its earnings each year (has a fixed payout ratio) and over the very long term. In the case of a declining industry, a negative growth rate ($g < 0\%$) might exist. In such a case, the constant-growth model, as well as the variable-growth model presented in the next section, remains fully applicable to the valuation process.

18. For the interested reader, the calculations necessary to derive Equation 8.13 from Equation 8.12 follow. The first step is to multiply each side of Equation 8.12 by $(1 + k_s)/(1 + g)$ and subtract Equation 8.12 from the resulting expression. This yields

$$\frac{P_0 \times (1+k_s)}{1+g} - P_0 = D_0 - \frac{D_0 \times (1+g)^\infty}{(1+k_s)^\infty} \qquad (1)$$

Because k_s is assumed to be greater than g, the second term on the right side of Equation 1 should be zero. Thus,

$$P_0 \times \left(\frac{1+k_s}{1+g} - 1\right) = D_0 \qquad (2)$$

Equation 2 is simplified as follows:

$$P_0 \times \left[\frac{(1+k_s) - (1+g)}{1+g}\right] = D_0 \qquad (3)$$

$$P_0 \times (k_s - g) = D_0 \times (1+g) \qquad (4)$$

$$P_0 = \frac{D_1}{k_s - g} \qquad (5)$$

Equation 5 equals Equation 8.13.

Year	Dividend per share
1997	$1.00
1998	1.05
1999	1.12
2000	1.20
2001	1.29
2002	1.40

The annual growth rate of dividends is assumed to equal the expected constant rate of dividend growth, g. Using a financial calculator in conjunction with the technique described for finding growth rates in Chapter 5, we find that the annual growth rate of dividends equals 7 percent.[19] The company estimates that its dividend in 2003, D_1, will equal $1.50. The required return, k_s, is assumed to be 15 percent. By substituting these values into Equation 8.13, the value of the common shares is:

$$P_0 = \frac{\$1.50}{0.15 - 0.07} = \frac{\$1.50}{0.08} = \underline{\underline{\$18.75 \text{ per share}}}$$

▲ Assuming that the values of D_1, k_s, and g are accurately estimated, Lamar Company's common shares are worth $18.75 per share.

If it is assumed, as was done earlier in this section, that the market is efficient, then the true value of a company's common shares should be the current market price. This allows Equation 8.13 to be manipulated to solve for K_s, investors' required rate of return on common shares as follows:

$$K_s = \frac{D_1}{P_0} + g \tag{8.14}$$

This equation indicates that investors' required return is based on the expected dividend yield (D_1/P_0) plus the expected growth in earnings, dividends, and share price (g). Readers should note that this is an alternative method to the CAPM that can be used to calculate the required return on common shares.

Variable Growth

variable-growth model
A dividend valuation approach that allows for a change in the dividend growth rate.

The zero- and constant-growth common share models do not allow for any shift in expected growth rates. Because future growth rates might shift up or down due to changing expectations, it is useful to consider a **variable-growth model**

---

19. For a financial calculation, 1.00 is the PV, 1.40 is the FV, and N is 5. Although six dividends are shown, *they reflect only 5 years of growth*. The number of years of growth can alternatively be found by subtracting the earliest year from the most recent year, i.e., 2002 − 1997 = 5 *years of growth*.

(Most calculators require *either* the PV or FV value to be inputted as a negative number to calculate an unknown interest or growth rate. That approach is used here.) Using the inputs shown, you should find the growth rate to be 6.96 percent, which we round to 7 percent.

Inputs: 1.00 -1.40 5

Functions: PV FV N CPT I

Outputs: 6.96

that allows for a change in the dividend growth rate.[20] Letting g_1 equal the initial growth rate and g_2 equal the subsequent growth rate and assuming a single shift in growth rates occurs at the end of year N, we can use the following four-step procedure to determine the value of the common shares.

Step 1   Find the value of the cash dividends at the end of *each year*, D_t, during the initial growth period—years 1 through N. This step may require adjusting the most recent dividend, D_0, using the initial growth rate, g_1, to calculate the dividend amount for each year. Therefore, for the first N years:

$$D_t = D_0 \times (1 + g_1)^t = D_0 \times FVIF_{g_1,t}$$

Step 2   Find the present value of the dividends expected during the initial growth period. By using the notation presented earlier, this value can be given as

$$\sum_{t=1}^{N} \frac{D_0 \times (1+g_1)^t}{(1+k_s)^t} = \sum_{t=1}^{N} \frac{D_t}{(1+k_s)^t} = \sum_{t=1}^{N} (D_t \times PVIF_{k_s,t})$$

Step 3   Find the value of the shares *at the end of the initial growth period,* $P_N = (D_{N+1})/(k_s - g_2)$,   which is the present value of all dividends expected from year $N + 1$ to infinity—assuming a constant dividend growth rate, g_2. This value is found by applying the constant-growth model (presented as Equation 8.13 in the preceding section) to the dividends expected from year $N + 1$ to infinity. The present value of P_N would represent the value *today* of all dividends that are expected to be received from year $N + 1$ to infinity. This value can be represented by

$$\frac{1}{(1+k_s)^N} \times \frac{D_{N+1}}{k_s - g_2} = PVIF_{k_s,N} \times P_N$$

Step 4   Add the present value components found in Steps 2 and 3 to find the value of the shares, P_0, given in Equation 8.15:

$$P_0 = \sum_{t=1}^{N} \frac{D_0 \times (1+g_1)^t}{(1+k_s)^t} + \left[\frac{1}{(1+k_s)^N} \times \frac{D_{N+1}}{k_s - g_2} \right] \tag{8.15}$$

Present value   Present value of
of dividends   price of stock at
during initial   end of initial
growth period   growth period

The following example illustrates the application of these steps to a variable-growth situation with only one growth rate change.

Example ▼   The most recent (2002) annual dividend payment of Warren Industries, a rapidly growing boat manufacturer, was $1.50 per share. The firm's financial manager expects that these dividends will increase at a 10 percent annual rate, g_1, over the

---

20. Although more than one change in the growth rate can be incorporated in the model, to simplify the discussion we will consider only a single growth-rate change. The number of variable-growth valuation models is technically unlimited, but concern over all likely shifts in growth is unlikely to yield much more accuracy than a simpler model.

next 3 years (2003, 2004, and 2005) due to the introduction of a hot new boat. At the end of the 3 years (end of 2005), the firm's mature product line is expected to result in a slowing of the dividend growth rate to 5 percent per year for the foreseeable future (noted as g_2). The required return on the firm's common shares is 15 percent. To estimate the current (end of 2002 or beginning of 2003) value of Warren's common shares, $P_0 = P_{2002}$, the four-step procedure presented before must be applied to these data.

Step 1   The value of the cash dividends in each of the next 3 years is calculated in columns 1, 2, and 3 of Table 8.4. The 2003, 2004, and 2005 dividends are $1.65, $1.82, and $2, respectively.

Step 2   The present value of the three dividends expected during the 2003–2005 initial growth period is calculated in columns 3, 4, and 5 of Table 8.3. The sum of the present values of the three dividends is $4.14.

Step 3   The value of the shares at the end of the initial growth period ($N = 2005$) can be found by first calculating $D_{N+1} = D_{2006}$:

$$D_{2006} = D_{2005} \times (1 + 0.05) = \$2 \times (1.05) = \$2.10$$

By using $D_{2006} = \$2.10$, a 15 percent required return, and a 5 percent dividend growth rate, we can calculate the value of the shares at the end of 2005 as follows:

$$P_{2005} = \frac{D_{2006}}{k_s - g_2} = \frac{\$2.10}{0.15 - 0.05} = \frac{\$2.10}{0.10} = \$21$$

Finally, in Step 3, the share value of $21 at the end of 2005 must be converted into a present (end-of-2002) value. Using the 15% required return, we get

$$PVIF_{k_s,N} \times P_N = PVIF_{15\%,3} \times P_{2005} = 0.658 \times \$21 = \$13.82$$

Step 4   Adding the present value of the initial dividend stream (found in Step 2) to the present value of the shares at the end of the initial growth period

TABLE 8.4   **Calculation of Present Value of Warren Industries' Dividends (2003–2005)**

t	End of year	$D_0 = D_{2002}$ (1)	$FVIF_{10\%,t}$ (2)	D_t [(1) × (2)] (3)	$PVIF_{15\%,t}$ (4)	Present value of dividends [(3) × (4)] (5)
1	2003	$1.50	1.100	$1.65	0.870	$1.44
2	2004	1.50	1.210	1.82	0.756	1.38
3	2005	1.50	1.331	2.00	0.658	1.32

$$\text{Sum of present value of dividends} = \sum_{t=1}^{3} \frac{D_0 \times (1 + g_1)^t}{(1 + k_s)^t} = \$4.14$$

(found in Step 3) as specified in Equation 8.15, we get the current (end-of-2002) value of Warren Industries' common shares:

$$P_{2000} = \$4.14 + \$13.82 = \underline{\$17.96 \text{ per share}}$$

The shares are currently worth $17.96 per share.

Time-Line Use   The calculation of this value is summarized diagrammatically:

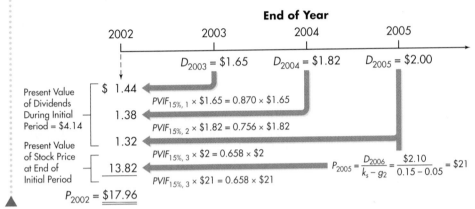

Finding Warren Industries' current (end-of-2002) value with variable growth

End of Year

It is important to recognize that the zero-, constant-, and variable-growth valuation models provide useful frameworks for estimating stock value. Clearly, the estimates produced cannot be very precise, given that the forecasts of future growth and discount rates are themselves necessarily approximate. Looked at another way, a great deal of rounding error can be introduced into the shares price estimate as a result of rounding growth and discount rate estimates to the nearest whole percent. When applying valuation models, it is therefore advisable to carefully estimate these rates and conservatively round them to the nearest tenth of a percent.

Other Approaches to Common Share Valuation

Many other approaches to common share valuation exist. The more popular approaches include book value, liquidation value, and some type of a price/earnings multiple.

Book Value

book value per share
The amount per share of common stock that would be received if all of the firm's assets were *sold for their exact book (accounting) value* and the proceeds remaining after paying all liabilities (and preferred shares) were divided among the common shareholders.

Book value per share is simply the amount per common share that would be received if all of the firm's assets were *sold for their exact book (accounting) value* and the proceeds remaining after paying all liabilities (and preferred shares) were divided among the common shareholders. This method lacks sophistication and can be criticized on the basis of its reliance on historical balance sheet data. It ignores the firm's expected earnings potential and generally lacks any true relationship to the firm's value in the marketplace. Let us look at an example.

Example ▼ At year-end 2002, Lamar Company's balance sheet shows total assets of $6 million, total liabilities and preferred shares of $4.5 million, and 100,000 common shares outstanding. Its book value per share therefore would be

$$\frac{\$6,000,000 - \$4,500,000}{100,000 \text{ shares}} = \underline{\$15 \text{ per share}}$$

⊙━ Career Key
This is an area that can be influenced by the *accounting* personnel. Their accounting practices will affect the book value of the firm and thus may change the investors' valuation of the firm. ▲

Because this value assumes that assets could be sold for their book value, it may not represent the minimum price at which shares are valued in the marketplace. As a matter of fact, although most shares sell above book value, it is not unusual to find shares selling below book value when investors believe either that assets are overvalued or the firm's liabilities are understated.

Liquidation Value

liquidation value per share
The *actual amount* per common share that would be received if all of the firm's assets were *sold for their market value*, liabilities (and preferred shares) are paid, and any remaining money were divided among the common shareholders.

Liquidation value per share is the *actual amount* per common share that would be received if all of the firm's assets were *sold for their market value*, liabilities (and preferred shares) were paid, and any remaining money were divided among the common shareholders.[21] This measure is more realistic than book value—because it is based on current market value of the firm's assets—but it still fails to consider the earning power of those assets. An example will illustrate.

Example ▼ Lamar Company found upon investigation that it could obtain only $5.25 million if it sold its assets today. The firm's liquidation value per common share therefore would be

$$\frac{\$5,250,000 - \$4,500,000}{100,000 \text{ shares}} = \underline{\$7.50 \text{ per share}}$$

▲ Ignoring liquidation expenses, this amount would be the firm's minimum value.

Price/Earnings (P/E) Multiples

The *price/earnings (P/E) ratio*, introduced in Chapter 3, reflects the amount investors are willing to pay for each dollar of earnings. The average P/E ratio for a company over a representative time period or the average P/E ratio for the firm's industry could be used to estimate the value of the company's common shares. This assumes that investors will continue to value the firm's earnings in the same way as they did in the past, or that the firm is like the average firm in the industry. The **price/earnings multiple approach** is a popular technique to estimate the firm's share value, by multiplying the firm's expected earnings per share (EPS) by an appropriate price/earnings (P/E) ratio.

price/earnings multiple approach
A technique to estimate the firm's share value; calculated by multiplying the firm's expected earnings per share (EPS) by an appropriate price/earnings (P/E) ratio.

The P/E multiple approach to valuing publicly traded companies is very straightforward given the ease of accessing data on both estimated earnings and historic price-earnings multiples. Such data is available from many sources, including Web sites such as **www.marketguide.com** or **www.globeinvestor.com**. The P/E multiple approach is also useful for valuing private companies. When used for privately owned or closely owned companies, a premium is added to the

---

21. In the event of liquidation, creditors' claims must be satisfied first, then those of the preferred shareholders. Anything left goes to common shareholders.

P/E multiple in order to account for the issue of control. A premium is necessary because the P/E ratio for publicly traded companies implicitly reflects a minority interest in the company. When buying a private company, a control stake is purchased and control stakes *always* trade at a premium.

In any case, the price/earnings multiple approach is considered superior to the use of book or liquidation values because it considers *expected* earnings.[22] An example will demonstrate the use of price/earnings multiples.

Example ▼ Lamar Company is expected to earn $2.60 per share in the next fiscal year (2003). This expectation is based on an analysis of the firm's historical earnings trend and expected economic and industry conditions. The average price/earnings (P/E) ratio for firms in the same industry is 7 and this is considered an appropriate P/E multiple to use to value Lamar. Multiplying Lamar's expected earnings per share (EPS) of $2.60 by 7 gives us a value for the firm's shares of $18.20. This analysis assumes that 7 is an appropriate P/E multiple to use for
▲ Lamar and that the $2.60 estimate for EPS is accurate.

⚠ Hint
From an investor's perspective, the stock in this situation would be an attractive investment only if it could be purchased at a price below its liquidation value—which in an efficient market could never occur.

So how much are Lamar Company's common shares really worth? We have calculated five different values in the above sections. That's a tricky question, because there's no one right answer. It is important to recognize that the answer depends on the assumptions made and the techniques used. Professional securities analysts typically use a variety of models and techniques to value shares. For example, an analyst might use the constant-growth model, liquidation value, and price/earnings (P/E) multiples to estimate the worth of a company's common shares. If the analyst feels comfortable with his or her estimates, the shares would be valued at no more than the largest estimate.

Of course, should the firm's estimated liquidation value per share exceed its "going concern" value per share, estimated by using one of the valuation models (zero-, constant-, or variable-growth) or the P/E multiple approach, the firm would be viewed as being "worth more dead than alive." In such an event, the firm would lack sufficient earning power to justify its existence and should probably be liquidated.

? Review Questions

8–13   In an *efficient market,* describe the events that occur in response to new information that causes the expected return on common shares to exceed the required return. What happens to the market value of the shares?

8–14   What does the *efficient market hypothesis* say about (**a**) securities prices, (**b**) their reaction to new information, and (**c**) investor opportunities to profit?

8–15   Describe, compare, and contrast the following common share valuation models: (**a**) zero-growth, (**b**) constant-growth, and (**c**) variable-growth.

---

22. The price/earnings multiple approach to valuation does have a theoretical explanation. If we view 1 divided by the price/earnings ratio, or the *earnings/price ratio,* as the rate at which investors discount the firm's earnings and if we assume that the projected earnings per share will be earned indefinitely (i.e., no growth in earnings per share), the price/earnings multiple approach can be looked on as a method of finding the present value of a perpetuity of projected earnings per share at a rate equal to the earnings/price ratio. This method is in effect a form of the zero-growth model presented in Equation 8.11.

8–16 Explain each of the three other approaches to common share valuation: (a) book value, (b) liquidation value, and (c) price/earnings (P/E) multiples. Which of these is considered the best?

8–17 When using the P/E multiple model to value common shares, why might an inaccurate estimate for value occur?

8.5 Decision Making and Common Share Value

Valuation equations measure the share value at a point in time based on expected return (D_1, g) and risk (k_s) data. Any decisions of the financial manager that affect these variables can cause the value of the firm, P_0, to change. Figure 8.7 depicts the relationship among financial decisions, return, risk, and share value.

Changes in Expected Returns

Career Key

The *marketing* department can greatly influence the value of a firm. Through product development, promotion, and sales strategies, marketing personnel can influence investors' expectations of cash flows, risks, and, consequently, value.

Assuming that economic conditions remain stable, any management action that would cause current and prospective common shareholders to raise their dividend expectations should increase the firm's value. In Equation 8.13,[23] we can see that P_0 will increase for any increase in D_1 or g. Any action of the financial manager that will increase the level of expected returns without changing risk (the required return) should be undertaken, because it will positively affect owners' wealth.

Example ▼ Using the constant-growth model, Lamar Company was found to have a share value of $18.75. On the following day, the firm announced a major technological breakthrough that would revolutionize its industry. Current and prospective shareholders would not be expected to adjust their required return of 15 percent as a result, but they would expect future dividends to increase. Specifically, they would feel that although the dividend next year, D_1, will remain at $1.50, the expected rate of growth thereafter will increase from 7 to 9 percent. If we substitute $D_1 = \$1.50$, $k_s = 0.15$, and $g = 0.09$ into Equation 8.13, the resulting value equals $25 [i.e., $1.50 ÷ (0.15 − 0.09)]. The increased value of the common

FIGURE 8.7

Decision Making and Common Share Value

Financial decisions, return, risk, and share value

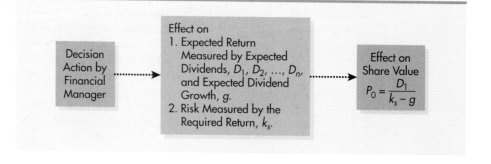

23. To convey the interrelationship among financial decisions, return, risk, and share value, the constant-growth dividend-valuation model is used. Other models—zero-growth or variable-growth—could be used, but the simplicity of exposition using the constant-growth model justifies its use here.

shares, therefore, resulted from the higher expected future dividends reflected in the increase in the growth rate.

Changes in Risk

Although k_s is defined as the required return it is (as pointed out in Chapter 7) directly related to the nondiversifiable risk, which can be measured by beta. The *capital asset pricing model (CAPM)* given in Equation 7.8 is restated as Equation 8.16:

$$k_s = R_F + [b \times (k_m - R_F)] \tag{8.16}$$

With the risk-free rate, R_F, and the market return, k_m, held constant, the required return, k_s, depends directly on beta. In other words, any action taken by the financial manager that increases risk will also increase the required return. In Equation 8.13, we can see that with all else constant, an increase in the required return, k_s, will reduce share value, P_0. Likewise, a decrease in the required return will increase share value. Thus, any action of the financial manager that increases risk contributes toward a reduction in value, and any action that decreases risk contributes toward an increase in value.

Example ▼ Assume that Lamar Company's 15 percent required return resulted from a risk-free rate of 9 percent, a market return of 13 percent, and a beta of 1.50. Substituting into the capital asset pricing model, Equation 8.16, we get a required return, k_s, of 15 percent:

$$k_s = 9\% + [1.50 \times (13\% - 9\%)] = \underline{\underline{15\%}}$$

With this return, the value of the firm was calculated to be $18.75 in the earlier example.

Now imagine that the financial manager makes a decision that, without changing expected dividends, increases the firm's beta to 1.75. Assuming that R_F and k_m remain at 9 and 13 percent, respectively, the required return will increase to 16 percent (i.e., $9\% + [1.75 \times (13\% - 9\%)]$) to compensate shareholders for the increased risk. Substituting $D_1 = \$1.50$, $k_s = 0.16$, and $g = 0.07$ into the valuation equation, Equation 8.13, results in a share value of $16.67 [i.e., $1.50 ÷ (0.16 - 0.07)]. As expected, raising the required return (without any corresponding increase in expected return) causes the firm's common share value to decline. Clearly, the financial manager's action was not in the owners' best interest. ▲

Combined Effect

A financial decision rarely affects return and risk independently; most decisions affect both factors. In terms of the measures presented, with an increase in risk (beta, b) one would expect an increase in return (D_1 or g, or both), assuming that R_F and k_m remain unchanged. The net effect on value depends on the size of the changes in these variables.

Example ▼ If we assume that the two changes illustrated for Lamar Company in the preceding examples occur simultaneously as a result of an action of the financial decision maker, key variable values would be $D_1 = \$1.50$, $k_s = 0.16$, and $g = 0.09$.

Substituting into the valuation model, we obtain a share price of $21.43 [$1.50 ÷ (0.16 − 0.09)]. The net result of the decision, which increased return (g from 7 to 9%) as well as risk (b from 1.50 to 1.75 and therefore k_s from 15 to 16%), is positive: The share price increased from $18.75 to $21.43. Assuming that the key variables are accurately measured, the decision appears to be in the best interest of the firm's owners, because it increases their wealth. ▲

? Review Questions

8–18   Explain the linkages among financial decisions, return, risk, and stock value. How do the *capital asset pricing model (CAPM)* and the *Gordon model* fit into this basic framework? Explain.

8–19   Assuming that all other variables remain unchanged, what impact would *each* of the following have on stock price? (a) The firm's beta increases. (b) The firm's required return decreases. (c) The dividend expected next year decreases. (d) The rate of growth in dividends is expected to increase. Explain your answers.

8.6 Valuation of Preferred Shares

As stated earlier, the value of any productive asset, real or financial, is the present value of the cash flows generated over the life of the asset. For preferred shares, there are two cash flows: dividends and the amount received when the preferred share is sold in the future. The discount rate used is the required return on preferred shares of comparable risk. To value preferred shares, the assumption made is that the preferred share is a perpetuity paying a constant dividend over an infinite period. For many preferred share issues, this is a reasonable assumption.

For example, assume a company issues a preferred share with a dividend rate of 4 percent. As years pass, yields in the market increase. If dividend yields on comparable risk preferred shares never drop below the dividend rate paid on an outstanding preferred share, then there is little reason for the company to redeem the preferred. Unless the share is retractable, preferred shareholders cannot force a company to redeem the shares. Therefore, if a preferred share is not redeemed, it will remain outstanding, essentially becoming a perpetuity. To value a perpetuity, Equation 8.11 is used; the slightly revised equation is provided below:

$$P_0 = \frac{D_1}{k_p} \tag{8.17}$$

where

P_0 = value of a company's preferred shares
D_1 = yearly dividend per preferred share
k_p = required return on the company's preferred shares

Example ▼ Telus Corporation has a preferred share issue outstanding with a stated value of $100 that pays a dividend of 4.375 percent. The preferred was issued in March

1965 and it is redeemable at a 4 percent premium. Telus's preferred shares are rated Pfd-3 (high), and required return on these preferred shares is 6.3 percent. This implies that if Telus issued new preferred shares, a 6.3 percent dividend rate would be required. Since the dividend rate on the preferred share outstanding is 4.375 percent, Telus will not redeem this issue and it would be considered a perpetuity. What is the value of the preferred share?

$$P_0 = \frac{\$4.375}{0.063} = \$69.44$$

The preferred share is trading well below its stated value, since required returns in the market have increased to a level above the dividend rate on the preferred share. Therefore, the preferred share will trade for an amount below its stated value and the company will not redeem the issue. The assumption that it will remain outstanding in perpetuity is valid.

Taxation Issues for Preferred Shares

As discussed in Chapter 6, preferred shares are similar in nature to long-term debt. However, preferred shares are riskier since, unlike debtholders, preferred shareholders do not have the power to put a company into bankruptcy. If preferred shares are riskier, the yield on preferred shares should be higher than on long-term debt. Is this the case?

Example ▼ Bank of Nova Scotia has a Series 12 preferred share issue outstanding with a stated value of $25 and an annual dividend of $1.3125 (or 5.25%). On August 23, 2002, the market price for this preferred was $24.60. Equation 8.17 is used to calculate the yield to perpetuity on preferred shares; the answer is 5.33 percent. On the same date, the yield on 20-year government of Canada debt was 5.55 percent. The yield ▲ on the preferred share *is less than* the yield on Canadian government debt.

While this result is based on actual data, it is an illogical outcome for two reasons. First, since preferred shares are riskier than long-term debt, the yield should be higher. Second, the issuer of the preferred share is riskier. The Bank of Nova Scotia is a very secure company and there is little chance of bankruptcy. But all corporations are riskier than the federal government. The federal government is the most secure issuer of financial securities in Canada, so therefore the yield on government of Canada debt should be lower than the yield on Bank of Nova Scotia preferred shares. The fact that it isn't seems to contradict the risk-return trade-off.

The explanation for this odd outcome, however, has nothing to so with risk; it is due to how the various types of investment income are taxed in Canada. Interest income is taxed at a much higher rate than income from equity securities (dividends and capital gains). Consider Table 8.5, where the taxation of the three types of investment income are considered. For the 2002 tax year for middle-income earners, the federal tax rate was 22 percent of taxable income and the provincial rate was 13 percent of taxable income. Other information used to calculate taxes are provided in the footnotes to the table. The net impact of the analysis is that interest income attracts $350 in taxes, providing an after-tax return of $650. Only $182 in taxes is paid on dividend income, providing an

TABLE 8.5 Taxation of Interest, Dividend, and Capital Gains Income for the 2002 Tax Year

	Interest	Dividend	Capital gains
Income received	$1,000	$ 1,000	$1,000
Tax adjustment	0	+250[a]	−500[b]
Taxable income	1,000	1,250	500
Federal tax (22%)[c]	220	275	110
Federal dividend tax credit[a]	—	166.67	—
Net federal tax payable	220	108.33	110
Provincial tax (13%)[d]	130	162.50	65
Provincial dividend tax credit[a]	—	89.00	—
Net provincial tax	130	73.50	65
Total taxes payable	350	181.83	175
After-tax return	$ 650	$818.17	$ 825

[a]For dividends received from taxable Canadian corporations, an individual must first gross-up (increase) the dividend by 25 percent. The taxable income is 1.25 times the actual amount received. But, to compensate for double-taxation issues, a dividend tax credit is allowed that reduces the effective amount of tax on the dividend. The federal dividend tax credit is 16 2/3 percent of the actual dividend received, while the average provincial dividend tax credit is 8.9 percent of the actual dividend received.

[b]Only 50 percent of capital gains are taxable, so 50 percent are excluded from income.

[c]For the 2002 tax year, the federal tax rate on taxable income of between $31,677 and $63,353 is 22 percent. Since this tax range is where most middle-income earners are taxed, this rate is used in the example.

[d]Provincial tax rates for middle-income earners for 2002 vary from a low of 9.15 percent in Ontario and British Columbia to a high of 16.16 percent in Newfoundland. The simple average of the provincial tax rates is 13 percent. This rate is used in the example.

after-tax return of $818, while the tax on capital gains is $175, providing an $825 after-tax return.

The focus of this analysis is on interest and dividends. Note that the difference in the after-tax returns is $168. This indicates that the raw *before-tax yields* on equity and long-term debt securities cannot be compared. A tax related adjustment termed the **interest equivalent factor** must be used to adjust the before-tax dividend yield on equity securities so it can be compared to the before-tax return on debt securities. The interest equivalent factor is calculated as follows:

interest equivalent factor
A tax-related adjustment that must be made that allows the before-tax dividend yield on equity securities to be compared to the before-tax yield on debt securities.

$$\text{Interest equivalent factor} = \frac{\text{after-tax dividend income}}{\text{after-tax interest income}} \tag{8.18}$$

For the above example, the interest equivalent factor is:

$$\text{Interest equivalent factor} = \frac{\$818}{\$650} = 1.2585$$

This factor means that to be in the same *after-tax* position, a middle-income investor receiving $1 of dividend income must receive $1.2585 of interest income. After taxes, both investors would have the same amount. An investor receiving $1,000 of dividend income will have $818 after tax. The same investor would have to receive $1,258.50 ($1,000 × 1.2585) of interest income to have $818 after-tax. The larger amount of interest income is required due to the differences in taxation.

Example ▼ The Bank of Nova Scotia example presented an illogical outcome. This was due to tax differences. Therefore, to complete the analysis, the 5.33 percent dividend yield on the Bank of Nova Scotia preferred shares cannot be compared to the 5.55 percent yield on 20-year government debt. These yields are in a different scale. The dividend yield must be adjusted for the differences in taxation by multiplying it by the interest equivalent factor. The interest equivalent yield is 6.71 percent (5.33% × 1.2585). The yield on the preferred share is now 116 basis points larger than the yield on the government of Canada debt. The risk-return ▲ tradeoff now applies.

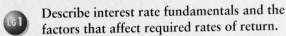 **Review Questions**

8–20 What assumption is made to value preferred shares and what is the equation to determine value? If you knew the amount of the yearly dividend and the current price of a preferred share, rewrite the equation to determine required return (yield).

8–21 What is the interest equivalent factor, why is it calculated, and how is it used?

SUMMARY

LG1 **Describe interest rate fundamentals and the factors that affect required rates of return.**
The flow of funds between savers (suppliers) and investors (demanders) is regulated by the interest rate or required return. In a perfect, inflation-free world there would be one cost of money: the real rate of interest. The nominal or actual interest rate is the sum of the risk-free rate, which is the sum of the real rate of interest and the inflationary expectation premium, and a risk premium reflecting issuer and issue characteristics. For any class of similar-risk securities, the term structure of interest rates reflects the relationship between the interest rate, or rate of return, and the time to maturity. Yield curves can be downward-sloping (inverted), upward-sloping (normal), or flat. Three theories— the expectations hypothesis, liquidity preference theory, and market segmentation theory—are cited to explain the general shape of the yield curve. Because investors must be compensated for taking risks, they expect higher returns for greater risk.

LG2 **Describe the key inputs and basic model used in the valuation process.** Key inputs to the valuation process include cash flows (returns), timing, and the required return (risk). The value, or worth, of any asset is equal to the present value of all future cash flows it is *expected* to provide over the relevant time period. The key variable definitions and the basic valuation formula for any asset are summarized in Table 8.6.

LG3 **Apply the basic valuation model to long-term debt to determine value and yield to maturity (YTM) and describe the impact changes in required rates of return and time to maturity have on bond values.** The value of a bond is the present value of its interest payments plus the present value of its par value. The key variable definitions and the basic valuation formula for a bond are summarized in Table 8.6. The discount rate used to determine bond value is the required return, which may differ from the bond's coupon interest rate. A bond can sell at a discount, at par, or at a premium, depending upon whether the required return is respectively greater than, equal to, or less than its coupon interest rate. The amount of time to maturity affects bond values even if required return remains constant. When required return is constant, the value of a bond will approach its par value as the passage of time moves the bond closer to maturity. The shorter the amount of time until a bond's

TABLE 8.6   Summary of Key Valuation Definitions and Formulas

Variable definitions

B_0 = bond value

CF_t = cash flow *expected* at the end of year t

D_0 = most recent per-share dividend

D_t = per-share dividend expected at the end of year t

g = constant rate of growth in dividends

g_1 = initial dividend growth rate (in variable growth model)

g_2 = subsequent dividend growth rate (in variable growth model)

I = interest on a bond (either annual or semiannual)

k = appropriate required return (discount rate)

k_d = required return on a bond

k_s = required return on common shares

k_p = required return on preferred shares

M = par, or face, value of a bond

n = relevant time period, or number of years to maturity

N = last year of initial growth period (in variable growth model)

P_0 = value of common or preferred shares

V_0 = value of the asset at time zero

Valuation formulas

Value of any asset:

$$V_0 = \frac{CF_1}{(1+k)^1} + \frac{CF_2}{(1+k)^2} + \cdots + \frac{CF_n}{(1+k)^n} \qquad \text{[Eq. 8.5]}$$

$$= [CF_1 \times (PVIF_{k,1}) + [CF_2 \times (PVIF_{k,2})] + \ldots + [CF_n \times (PVIF_{k,n})] \qquad \text{[Eq. 8.6]}$$

Bond value:

$$B_0 = I \times \left[\sum_{t=1}^{n} \frac{1}{(1+k_d)^t} \right] + M \times \left[\frac{1}{(1+k_d)^n} \right] \qquad \text{[Eq. 8.7]}$$

$$= I \times (PVIFA_{k_d,n}) + M \times (PVIF_{k_d,n}) \qquad \text{[Eq. 8.7a]}$$

Common share value:

Zero growth: $P_0 = \dfrac{D_1}{k_s}$ (also used to value preferred stock)   [Eq. 8.11]

Constant growth: $P_0 = \dfrac{D_1}{k_s - g}$ [Eq. 8.13]

Constant growth extension: $K_s = \dfrac{D_1}{P_0} + g$ [Eq. 8.14]

Variable growth: $P_0 = \displaystyle\sum_{t=1}^{N} \frac{D_0 \times (1+g_1)^t}{(1+k_s)^t} + \left[\frac{1}{(1+k_s)^N} \times \frac{D_{N+1}}{k_s - g_2} \right]$ [Eq. 8.15]

Preferred share value: $P_0 = \dfrac{D_1}{K_p}$ [Eq. 8.17]

maturity, the less responsive is its market value to a given change in the required return.

Yield to maturity (YTM) is the rate of return investors earn if they buy a bond at a specific price and hold it until maturity, assuming that the issuer makes all scheduled interest and principal payments as promised. YTM can be calculated by trial and error or financial calculator. Bonds that pay interest semiannually are valued by using the same procedure that is used to value bonds paying annual interest except that the interest payments are one-half of the annual interest payments, the number of periods is twice the number of years to maturity, and the required return used is one-half of the stated annual required return on similar-risk bonds.

LG4 Understand the concept of market efficiency and four techniques used to determine the value of common shares: the dividend valuation model (DVM), book value, liquidation value, and the price/earnings (P/E) multiple. Market efficiency suggests that there are many rational investors whose quick reactions to new information cause the market value of common shares to adjust upward or downward depending upon whether the expected return is above or below, respectively, the required return for the period. The efficient market hypothesis suggests that securities are fairly priced, they reflect fully all publicly available information, and investors should therefore not waste time trying to find and capitalize on mispriced securities. The value of a common share is the present value of all future dividends it is expected to provide over an infinite time horizon. Three cases of dividend growth—zero growth, constant growth, and variable growth—can be considered in common share valuation. The key variable definitions and the basic valuation formulas for each of these cases are summarized in Table 8.6. The most widely cited model is the constant-growth model.

Book value per share is the amount per common share that would be received if all of the firm's assets were *sold for their book (accounting) value* and the proceeds remaining after paying all liabilities and preferred shares were divided among the common shareholders.

Liquidation value per share is the *actual amount* per common share that would be received if all of the firm's assets were *sold for their market value*, liabilities and preferred shares were paid, and

the remaining money were divided among the common shareholders.

The price/earnings (P/E) multiples approach estimates share value by multiplying the firm's expected earnings per share (EPS) by an appropriate price/earnings (P/E) ratio. Of these approaches, P/E multiples are the most popular in practice because, unlike book and liquidation value, they view the firm as a going concern whose value lies in its earning power rather than its asset values.

LG5 Understand the relationships among financial decisions, return, risk, and the firm's value. In a stable economy, any action of the financial manager that increases the level of expected return without changing risk should increase share value, and any action that reduces the level of expected return without changing risk should reduce share value. Similarly, any action that increases risk (required return) will reduce share value, and any action that reduces risk will increase share value. In the constant-growth model, returns are measured by next year's dividend (D_1) and its growth rate (g), and risk is measured by the required return (k_s). Because most financial decisions affect both return and risk, an assessment of their combined effect on value must be part of the financial decision-making process.

LG6 Discuss valuation concepts and the techniques used to determine the value and required returns on preferred shares. To value preferred shares, the assumption made is that the preferred share is a perpetuity paying a constant dividend over an infinite period. For many preferred share issues, this is a reasonable assumption. The key variable definitions and basic valuation formulas are summarized in Table 8.6. Preferred shares are similar in nature to long-term debt. However, preferred shares are riskier since, unlike debtholders, preferred shareholders do not have the power to put a company into bankruptcy. Therefore, the yield on preferred shares should be higher than on long-term debt. This is not the case, however, when raw before-tax yields are considered. This is due to different taxation of interest and equity investment income. Since dividends are taxed more favourably than interest income, an interest equivalent factor must be used to adjust the dividend yield on equity securities so it can be compared to the before-tax return on debt securities.

SELF-TEST PROBLEMS

(Solutions in Appendix B)

 ST 8–1 **Bond valuation**   Lahey Industries has a $1,000 par value bond with an 8 percent coupon rate outstanding. The bond has 12 years remaining to its maturity date.

a. If interest is paid *annually,* what is the value of the bond when the required return is (1) 7 percent, (2) 8 percent, and (3) 10 percent?

b. Indicate for each case in **a** whether the bond is selling at a discount, at a premium, or at its par value.

c. Using a financial calculator, find the bond's value, in all three cases, when interest is paid *semiannually.*

 ST 8–2 **Yield to maturity**   Elliot Enterprises' bonds currently sell for $1,150, have an 11 percent coupon rate and a $1,000 par value, pay interest *annually,* and have 18 years to maturity.

a. Calculate the bonds' yield to maturity (YTM).

b. Compare the YTM calculated in **a** to the bonds' coupon interest rate, and use a comparison of the bonds' current price and their par value to explain this difference.

c. Using a financial calculator, calculate the bonds' YTM assuming the coupons are paid *semianually.*

 ST 8–3 **Common share valuation**   Perry Motors' common shares currently pay an annual dividend of $1.80 per share. The required return on the common shares is 12 percent. Estimate the value of the common shares under each of the following dividend-growth-rate assumptions.

a. Dividends are expected to grow at an annual rate of 0 percent to infinity.

b. Dividends are expected to grow at a constant annual rate of 5 percent to infinity.

c. Dividends are expected to grow at an annual rate of 5 percent for each of the next 3 years, followed by a constant annual growth rate of 4 percent in years 4 to infinity.

PROBLEMS

WARM-UP   **8–1** **Interest rate fundamentals: the real rate of return**   Carl Foster, a trainee at an investment banking firm, is trying to get an idea of what real rate of return investors are expecting in today's marketplace. He has looked up the rate paid on 3-month government of Canada t-bills and found it to be 5.5 percent. He has decided to use the rate of change in the Consumer Price Index as a proxy for the inflationary expectations of investors. That annualized rate now stands at 2 percent. Based on the information that Carl has collected, what estimate can he make of the real rate of return?

INTERMEDIATE   **8–2** **Real rate of interest**   To estimate the real rate of interest, the economics division of Atlantic Banks has gathered the data summarized in the following table. Because there is a high likelihood that new tax legislation will be passed in the near future, current data as well as data reflecting the likely impact of passage of the legislation on the demand for funds are also included in the table. (*Note:* The proposed legislation will not have any impact on the supply schedule of funds. Assume a perfect world in which inflation is expected to be zero, funds suppliers and demanders have no liquidity preference, and all outcomes are certain.)

| Amount of funds supplied/demanded ($ billion) | Currently | | With passage of tax legislation |
	Interest rate required by funds suppliers	Interest rate required by funds demanders	Interest rate required by funds demanders
$ 1	2%	7%	9%
5	3	6	8
10	4	4	7
20	6	3	6
50	7	2	4
100	9	1	3

a. Draw the supply curve and the demand curve for funds using the current data. (*Note:* Unlike Figure 8.1, the functions here will not appear as straight lines.)
b. Using your graph, label and note the real rate of interest using current data.
c. Add to the graph drawn in **a** the new demand curve expected in the event the proposed tax legislation becomes effective.
d. What is the new real rate of interest? Compare and analyze this finding in light of your analysis in **b**.

INTERMEDIATE   **LG1**   **8–3   Real and nominal rates interest**   Zane Perelli currently has $100 that he can spend today on polo shirts costing $25 each. Instead, he could invest the $100 in a risk-free government of Canada security that is expected to earn a 9 percent nominal rate of interest. The consensus forecast of leading economists is a 5 percent rate of inflation over the coming year.
a. How many polo shirts can Zane purchase today?
b. How much money would Zane have at the end of 1 year if he forgoes purchasing the polo shirts today?
c. How much would you expect the polo shirts to cost at the end of 1 year in light of the expected inflation?
d. Use your findings in **b** and **c** to determine how many polo shirts (fractions are OK) Zane could purchase at the end of 1 year. In percentage terms, how many more or fewer polo shirts can Zane buy at the end of 1 year?
e. What is Zane's real rate of return over the year? How does it relate to the percentage change in Zane's buying power found in **d**? Explain.

INTERMEDIATE   **LG1**   **8–4   Yield curve**   A firm wishing to evaluate interest rate behaviour has gathered yield data on five government of Canada debt securities, each having a different maturity and all measured at the same point in time. The summarized data follows:

Government of Canada security	Time to maturity	Yield
A	1 year	12.6%
B	10 years	11.2
C	6 months	13.0
D	20 years	11.0
E	5 years	11.4

a. Draw the yield curve associated with the data given.

b. Describe the resulting yield curve in **a,** and explain the general expectations embodied in it.

CHALLENGE **8–5** Nominal interest rates and yield curves   A recent study of inflationary expectations has disclosed that the consensus among economic forecasters yields the following average annual rates of inflation expected over the periods noted. (*Note:* Assume that the risk that future interest rate movements will affect longer maturities more than shorter maturities is zero; that is, there is no *maturity risk.*)

Period	Average annual rate of inflation
3 months	5%
1 year	6
5 years	8
10 years	8.5
20 years	9

a. If the real rate of interest is currently 2.5 percent, find the nominal interest rate on each of the following government of Canada debt issues: 20-year bond, 3-month bill, 1-year note, and 5-year bond.

b. If the real rate of interest suddenly drops to 2 percent without any change in inflationary expectations, what effect, if any, would this have on your answers in **a?** Explain.

c. Using your findings in **a,** draw a yield curve for government of Canada securities. Describe the general shape and expectations reflected by the curve.

d. What would a follower of the *liquidity preference theory* say about how the preferences of lenders and borrowers tend to affect the shape of the yield curve drawn in item **c?** Illustrate that effect by placing a dotted line on your graph that approximates the yield curve without the effect of liquidity preference.

e. What would a follower of the *market segmentation theory* say about the supply and demand for long-term loans versus the supply and demand for short-term loans given the yield curve constructed for part **c** of this problem?

CHALLENGE **8–6** Nominal and real rates and yield curves   A firm wishing to evaluate interest rate behaviour has gathered nominal rate of interest and inflationary expectation data on five government of Canada debt securities, each having a different maturity and each measured at a different point in time during the year just ended. (*Note:* Assume that the risk that future interest rate movements will affect longer maturities more than shorter maturities is zero; that is, there is no *maturity risk.*) These data are summarized in the following table.

Government of Canada security	Point in time	Maturity	Nominal rate of interest	Inflationary expectation
A	Jan. 7	1 year	12.6%	9.5%
B	Mar. 12	10 years	11.2	8.2
C	May 30	6 months	13.0	10.0
D	Aug. 15	20 years	11.0	8.1
E	Dec. 30	5 years	11.4	8.3

a. Using the preceding data, find the real rate of interest at each point in time.
b. Describe the behaviour of the real rate of interest over the year. What forces might be responsible for such behaviour?
c. Draw the yield curve associated with these data, assuming that the nominal rates were measured at the same point in time.
d. Describe the resulting yield curve in c, and explain the general expectations embodied in it.

INTERMEDIATE **8–7 Term structure of interest rates** The following yield data for a number of highest quality corporate bonds existed at each of the three points in time noted.

Time to maturity (years)	Yield		
	5 years ago	2 years ago	Today
1	9.1%	14.6%	9.3%
3	9.2	12.8	9.8
5	9.3	12.2	10.9
10	9.5	10.9	12.6
15	9.4	10.7	12.7
20	9.3	10.5	12.9
30	9.4	10.5	13.5

a. On the same set of axes, draw the yield curve at each of the three given times. Label the axes.
b. Label each curve in a as to its general shape (downward-sloping, upward-sloping, flat).
c. Describe the general inflationary and interest rate expectation existing at each of the three times.

WARM-UP **8–8 Risk-free rate and risk premiums** The real rate of interest is currently 3 percent; the inflation expectation and risk premiums for a number of securities follow:

Security	Inflation expectation premium	Risk premium
A	6%	3%
B	9	2
C	8	2
D	5	4
E	11	1

a. Find the risk-free rate of interest, R_F, that is applicable to each security.
b. Although not noted, what factor must be the cause of the differing risk-free rates found in **a**?
c. Find the nominal rate of interest for each security.

INTERMEDIATE **8–9** **Risk premiums**   Eleanor Burns is attempting to find the nominal rate of interest for two securities—A and B—issued by different firms at the same point in time. She has gathered the following data:

Characteristic	Security A	Security B
Time to maturity	3 years	15 years
Inflation expectation premium	9.0%	7.0%
Risk premium for:		
Default risk	1.0%	2.0%
Maturity risk	0.5%	1.5%
Liquidity risk	1.0%	1.0%
Other risk	0.5%	1.5%

a. If the real rate of interest is currently 2 percent, find the risk-free rate of interest applicable to each security.
b. Find the total risk premium attributable to each security's issuer and issue characteristics.
c. Calculate the nominal rate of interest for each security. Compare and discuss your findings.

WARM-UP **8–10** **Valuation fundamentals**   Imagine that you are trying to evaluate the economics of purchasing an automobile. You expect the car to provide annual after-tax cash benefits of $1,200 and that you can sell the car for after-tax proceeds of $5,000 at the end of the planned 5-year ownership period. All funds for purchasing the car will be drawn from your savings, which are currently earning 6 percent after taxes.
a. Identify the cash flows, their timing, and the required return applicable to valuing the car.
b. What is the maximum price you would be willing to pay to acquire the car? Explain.

WARM-UP **8–11** **Valuation of assets**   Using the information provided in the following table, find the value of each asset.

Asset	End of year	Cash flow Amount	Appropriate required return
A	1	$ 5,000	18%
	2	5,000	
	3	5,000	
B	1 through ∞	$ 300	15%
C	1	$ 0	16%
	2	0	
	3	0	
	4	0	
	5	35,000	
D	1 through 5	$ 1,500	12%
	6	8,500	
E	1	$ 2,000	14%
	2	3,000	
	3	5,000	
	4	7,000	
	5	4,000	
	6	1,000	

INTERMEDIATE   **8–12 Asset valuation and risk**   Laura Drake wishes to estimate the value of an asset expected to provide cash inflows of $3,000 per year at the end of years 1 through 4 and $15,000 at the end of year 5. Her research indicates that she must earn 10 percent on low-risk assets, 15 percent on average-risk assets, and 22 percent on high-risk assets.

  a. What is the most Laura should pay for the asset if it is classified as (1) low risk, (2) average risk, and (3) high risk?

  b. If Laura is unable to assess the risk of the asset and wants to be certain she's making a good deal, based on your findings in **a,** what is the most she should pay? Why?

  c. All else being the same, what effect does increasing risk have on the value of an asset? Explain in light of your findings in **a.**

INTERMEDIATE   **8–13 Basic bond valuation**   Complex Systems has an issue of $1,000-par-value bonds with a 12 percent coupon rate outstanding. The issue pays interest *annually* and has 16 years remaining to its maturity date.

  a. If bonds of similar risk are currently earning a 10 percent rate of return, how much should the Complex Systems bond sell for today?

  b. Describe the *two* possible reasons that similar-risk bonds are currently earning a return below the coupon interest rate on the Complex Systems bond.

  c. If the required return were at 12 percent instead of 10 percent, what would the current value of Complex Systems' bond be? Contrast this finding with your findings in **a** and discuss.

WARM-UP 8–14   **Bond valuation—Annual interest**   Calculate the value of each of the bonds shown in the following table, all of which pay interest *annually*.

Bond	Par value	Coupon rate	Years to maturity	Required return
A	$1,000	14%	20	12%
B	1,000	8	16	8
C	100	10	8	13
D	500	16	13	18
E	1,000	12	10	10

INTERMEDIATE 8–15   **Bond value and changing required returns**   Midland Utilities has outstanding a bond issue that will mature to its $1,000 par value in 12 years. The bond has a coupon rate of 11 percent and pays interest *semiannually*.

a. Find the value of the bond if the required return is (1) 11 percent, (2) 15 percent, and (3) 8 percent.

b. Plot your findings in **a** on a set of required return (*x* axis)–market value of bond (*y* axis) axes.

c. Use your findings in **a** and **b** to discuss the relationship between the coupon interest rate on a bond and the required return and the market value of the bond relative to its par value.

d. What two reasons cause the required return to differ from the coupon interest rate?

INTERMEDIATE 8–16   **Bond value and time—Constant required returns**   Pecos Manufacturing has just issued a 15-year, 12 percent coupon rate, $1,000-par bond that pays interest *annually*. The required return is currently 14 percent, and the company is certain it will remain at 14 percent until the bond matures in 15 years.

a. Assuming that the required return does remain at 14 percent until maturity, find the value of the bond with (1) 15 years, (2) 12 years, (3) 9 years, (4) 6 years, (5) 3 years, and (6) 1 year to maturity.

b. Plot your findings on a set of time to maturity (*x* axis)–market value of bond (*y* axis) axes constructed similarly to Figure 8.6.

c. All else remaining the same, when the required return differs from the coupon rate and is assumed to be constant to maturity, what happens to the bond value as time moves toward maturity? Explain in light of the graph in **b**.

CHALLENGE 8–17   **Bond value and time—Changing required returns**   Lynn Parsons is considering investing in either of two outstanding bonds. The bonds both have $1,000 par values and 11 percent coupon rates and pay *semiannual* interest. Bond A has exactly 5 years to maturity, and bond B has 15 years to maturity.

a. Calculate the value of bond A if the required return is (1) 8 percent, (2) 11 percent, and (3) 14 percent.

b. Calculate the value of bond B if the required return is (1) 8 percent, (2) 11 percent, and (3) 14 percent.

c. From your findings in **a** and **b**, complete the following table, and discuss the relationship between time to maturity and changing required returns.

Required return	Value of bond A	Value of bond B
8%	?	?
11	?	?
14	?	?

d. If Lynn wanted to minimize *interest-rate risk,* which bond should she purchase? Why?

  8–18 Yield to maturity   The relationship between a bond's yield to maturity and coupon rate can be used to predict its pricing level. For each of the bonds listed, state whether the price of the bond will be at a premium to par, at par, or at a discount to par.

Bond	Coupon rate	Yield to maturity	Price
A	6%	10%	
B	8	8	
C	9	7	
D	7	9	
E	12	10	

  8–19 Yield to maturity   The Salem Company bond currently sells for $955, has a 12 percent coupon rate and $1,000 par value, pays interest *annually,* and has 15 years to maturity.
a. Calculate the yield to maturity (YTM) on this bond.
b. Explain the relationship that exists between the coupon interest rate and yield to maturity and the par value and market value of a bond.

8–20 Yield to maturity   Each of the bonds shown in the following table pays interest *semiannually.*

Bond	Par value	Coupon rate	Years to maturity	Current value
A	$1,000	9%	8	$ 820
B	1,000	12	16	1,000
C	500	12	12	560
D	1,000	15	10	1,120
E	1,000	5	3	900

a. Calculate the yield to maturity (YTM) for each bond.
b. What relationship exists between the coupon interest rate and yield to maturity and the par value and market value of a bond? Explain.

  8–21 Bond valuation and yield to maturity   Mark Goldsmith's broker has shown him two bonds. Each has a maturity of 5 years, a par value of $1,000, and a yield to maturity of 12 percent. Bond A has a coupon rate of 6 percent paid annually. Bond B has a coupon rate of 14 percent paid annually.

a. Calculate the selling price for each of the bonds.

b. Mark has $20,000 to invest. Based on the price of the bonds, how many of either one could Mark purchase if he were to choose it over the other? (Mark cannot really purchase a fraction of a bond, but for purposes of this question, pretend that he can.)

c. Calculate the yearly interest income of each bond based on its coupon rate and the number of bonds that Mark could buy with his $20,000.

d. Assume that Mark will reinvest the interest payments as they are paid and that his rate of return on the reinvestment is only 10 percent. For each bond, calculate the value of the principal payment plus the value of Mark's reinvestment account at the end of the 5 years.

e. Why are the two values calculated in **d** different? If Mark were worried that he would earn less than the 12 percent yield to maturity rate on the reinvested interest payments, which of these two bonds would be a better choice?

INTERMEDIATE 8–22 **Bond valuation**   Find the value of a bond maturing in 6 years, with a $1,000 par value and a coupon rate of 10 percent, paid semiannually, if the required return on similar-risk bonds is 14 percent.

INTERMEDIATE 8–23 **Bond valuation**   Calculate the value of each of the bonds shown in the following table, all of which pay interest *semiannually*.

Bond	Par value	Coupon rate	Years to maturity	Required stated return
A	$1,000	10%	12%	8%
B	1,000	12	20	12
C	500	12	5	14
D	1,000	14	10	10
E	100	6	4	14

CHALLENGE 8–24 **Bond valuation—Quarterly interest**   Calculate the value of a $5,000-par-value bond paying quarterly interest at an annual coupon rate of 10 percent and having 10 years until maturity if the required return on similar-risk bonds is currently 12 percent.

WARM-UP 8–25 **Common share valuation—Zero growth**   Scotto Manufacturing is a mature firm in the machine-tool-component industry. The firm's most recent common stock dividend was $2.40 per share. Due to its maturity as well as stable sales and earnings, the firm's management feels that dividends will remain at the current level for the foreseeable future.

a. If the required return is 12 percent, what will be the value of Scotto's common stock?

b. If the firm's risk as perceived by market participants suddenly increases, causing the required return to rise to 20 percent, what will be the common stock value?

c. Based on your findings in **a** and **b**, what impact does risk have on value? Explain.

INTERMEDIATE 8–26 **Common share value—Zero growth** Kelsey Drums, Inc., is a well-established supplier of fine percussion instruments to orchestras all over Canada. The company's class A common shares have paid a dividend of $5 per share per year for the last 15 years. Management expects to continue to pay at that rate for the foreseeable future. Sally Talbot purchased 100 shares of Kelsey class A common 10 years ago, at a time when the required rate of return for the shares was 16 percent. She wants to sell her shares today. The current required rate of return for the shares is 12 percent. How much capital gain or loss will she have on her shares?

WARM-UP 8–27 **Common share value—Constant growth** Use the constant-growth model (Gordon model) to find the value of each of the firms shown in the following table.

Firm	Dividend expected next year	Dividend growth rate	Required return
A	$1.20	8%	13%
B	4.00	5	15
C	0.65	10	14
D	6.00	8	9
E	2.25	8	20

INTERMEDIATE 8–28 **Common share value—Constant growth** McCracken Roofing, Inc., common shares paid a dividend of $1.20 per share last year. The company expects earnings and dividends to grow at a rate of 5 percent per year for the foreseeable future.
a. What required rate of return would result in a price per share of $28 for these shares?
b. If McCracken had an earnings and dividend growth rate of 10 percent, what required rate of return would result in a price per share of $28?

 8–29 **Common share value—Constant growth** Elk County Telephone has paid the dividends shown in the following table over the past 6 years:

Year	Dividend per share
1998	$2.25
1999	2.37
2000	2.46
2001	2.60
2002	2.76
2003	2.87

The firm's dividend per share in 2004 is expected to be $3.02.
a. If you can earn 13 percent on similar-risk investments, what is the most you would pay for the common shares of this firm?

b. If you can earn only 10 percent on similar-risk investments, what is the most you would be willing to pay per share?

c. Compare and contrast your findings in **a** and **b,** and discuss the impact of changing risk on share value.

CHALLENGE 8–30   **Common share value—Variable growth**   Newman Manufacturing is considering a takeover of Grips Tool. During the year just completed, Grips earned $4.25 per share and paid cash dividends of $2.55 per share ($D_0 = \$2.55$). Grips' earnings and dividends are expected to grow at 25 percent per year for the next 3 years, after which they are expected to grow at 10 percent per year to infinity. What is the maximum price per common share Newman should pay for Grips if it has a required return of 15 percent on investments with risk characteristics similar to those of Grips?

CHALLENGE 8–31   **Common share value—Variable growth**   Home Place Hotels, Inc., is entering into a 3-year remodelling and expansion project. The construction will have a limiting effect on earnings during that time but should allow the company to enjoy much improved growth in earnings and dividends when it is complete. Last year, the company paid a dividend of $3.40. It expects zero growth in the next year. In years 2 and 3, 5 percent growth is expected, and in year 4, 15 percent growth. In year 5 and thereafter, growth should be a constant 10 percent per year. What is the maximum price that an investor who requires a return of 14 percent should pay for Home Place Hotels common shares?

CHALLENGE 8–32   **Common share value—Variable growth**   Lawrence Industries' most recent annual dividend was $1.80 per share ($D_0 = \$1.80$), and the firm's required return is 11 percent. Find the market value of Lawrence's shares when:

a. Dividends are expected to grow at 8 percent annually for 3 years followed by a 5 percent constant annual growth rate in years 4 to infinity.

b. Dividends are expected to grow at 8 percent annually for 3 years followed by 0 percent annual growth in years 4 to infinity.

c. Dividends are expected to grow at 8 percent annually for 3 years followed by a 10 percent constant annual growth rate in years 4 to infinity.

CHALLENGE 8–33   **Common share value—All growth models**   You are evaluating the potential purchase of a small business currently generating $42,500 of after-tax cash flow ($D_0 = \$42,500$). Based on a review of similar-risk investment opportunities, you must earn an 18 percent rate of return on the proposed purchase. Because you are relatively uncertain about future cash flows, you decide to estimate the firm's value using several possible cash flow, growth rate assumptions.

a. What is the firm's value if cash flows are expected to grow at an annual rate of 0 percent to infinity?

b. What is the firm's value if cash flows are expected to grow at a constant annual rate of 7 percent to infinity?

c. What is the firm's value if cash flows are expected to grow at an annual rate of 12 percent for the first 2 years followed by a constant annual rate of 7 percent in years 3 to infinity?

INTERMEDIATE 8–34   **Book and liquidation value**   The balance sheet for Gallinas Industries is as follows.

Balance Sheet
Gallinas Industries
December 31, 2002

Assets		Liabilities and shareholders' equity	
Cash	$ 40,000	Accounts payable	$ 100,000
Marketable securities	60,000	Line of credit	30,000
Accounts receivable	120,000	Accrued wages	30,000
Inventories	160,000	Total current liabilities	$160,000
Total current assets	$380,000	Long-term debt	$180,000
Land and buildings (net)	$150,000	Preferred shares	$ 80,000
Machinery and equipment	250,000	Common equity	360,000
Total fixed assets (net)	$400,000	Total liabilities and shareholders' equity	$780,000
Total assets	$780,000		

Additional information with respect to the firm is available:
(1) Preferred shares can be liquidated at book value.
(2) Accounts receivable and inventories can be liquidated at 90 percent of book value.
(3) The firm has 10,000 common shares outstanding.
(4) All interest and dividends are currently paid up.
(5) Land and buildings can be liquidated at 130 percent of book value.
(6) Machinery and equipment can be liquidated at 70 percent of book value.
(7) Cash and marketable securities can be liquidated at book value.

Given this information, answer the following:
a. What is Gallinas Industries' book value per share?
b. What is its liquidation value per share?
c. Compare, contrast, and discuss the values found in a and b.

WARM-UP 8–35 **Valuation with price/earnings multiples**   For each of the firms shown in the following table, use the data given to estimate their common share values employing price/earnings (P/E) multiples.

Firm	Expected EPS	Price/earnings multiple
A	$3.00	6.2
B	4.50	10.0
C	1.80	12.6
D	2.40	8.9
E	5.10	15.0

INTERMEDIATE 8–36 **Management action and stock value**   REH Corporation's most recent dividend was $3 per share, its expected annual rate of dividend growth is 5 percent, and the required return is now 15 percent. A variety of proposals are being considered by management to redirect the firm's activities. For each of the following proposed actions, determine the impact on share price and indicate the best alternative.
a. Do nothing, which will leave the key financial variables unchanged.
b. Invest in a new machine that will increase the dividend growth rate to 6 percent and lower the required return to 14 percent.

c. Eliminate an unprofitable product line, which will increase the dividend growth rate to 7 percent and raise the required return to 17 percent.
d. Merge with another firm, which will reduce the growth rate to 4 percent and raise the required return to 16 percent.
e. Acquire a subsidiary operation from another manufacturer. The acquisition should increase the dividend growth rate to 8 percent and increase the required return to 17 percent.

  8–37 Integrative—Valuation and CAPM formulas   Given the following information for the common shares of Foster Company, calculate its beta.

INTERMEDIATE

Current price per common share	$50
Expected dividend per share next year	$ 3
Constant annual dividend growth rate	9%
Risk-free rate of return	7%
Return on market portfolio	10%

  8–38 Integrative—Risk and valuation   Giant Enterprises has a beta of 1.20, the risk-free rate of return is currently 10 percent, and the market return is 14 percent. The company, which plans to pay a dividend of $2.60 per share in the coming year, anticipates that its future dividends will increase at an annual rate consistent with that experienced over the 1997–2003 period, when the following dividends were paid:

CHALLENGE

Year	Dividend per share
1997	$1.73
1998	1.80
1999	1.82
2000	1.95
2001	2.10
2002	2.28
2003	2.45

a. Use the capital asset pricing model (CAPM) to determine the required return on Giant Enterprises' common shares.
b. Using the constant-growth model and your finding in a, estimate the value of Giant Enterprises' common shares.
c. Explain what effect, if any, a decrease in beta would have on the value of Giant's common shares.

  8–39 Integrative—Valuation and CAPM   Hamlin Steel Company wishes to determine the value of Craft Foundry, a firm that it is considering acquiring. Hamlin wishes to use the capital asset pricing model (CAPM) to determine the applicable discount rate to use as an input to the constant-growth valuation model. Craft's stock is not publicly traded. After studying the betas of firms similar to Craft that are publicly traded, Hamlin believes that an appropriate beta for Craft's stock would be 1.25. The risk-free rate is currently 9 percent, and the market return is 13 percent. Craft's historic dividend per share for each of the past 6 years is shown in the following table. The expected growth is based on the historic growth in DPS.

Year	Dividend per share
1998	$2.45
1999	2.75
2000	2.90
2001	3.15
2002	3.28
2003	3.44

a. Determine the maximum amount Hamlin should pay for each common share of Craft.
b. Discuss the use of the CAPM for estimating the value of common shares, and describe the effect on the resulting value of Craft of:
   (1) A decrease in its dividend growth rate of 2 percent from that exhibited over the 1998–2003 period.
   (2) A decrease in its beta to 1.

INTERMEDIATE 8–40   **Preferred share valuation**   Jones Design wishes to estimate the value of its outstanding preferred share. The preferred issue has an $80 stated value and pays an annual dividend of $6.40 per share. Similar-risk preferred shares are currently earning a 9.3 percent annual rate of return.
a. What is the market value of the outstanding preferred shares?
b. If an investor purchases the preferred shares at the value calculated in **a**, how much does she gain or lose per share if she sells the shares when the required return on similar-risk preferreds has risen to 10.5 percent? Explain.

WARM-UP 8–41   **Preferred share valuation**   Henry Yachts Ltd. has two issues of $50 stated value preferred shares outstanding. The dividend on the first is $2.20, and $2.65 on the second. Southam is rated Pfd-2 and the required return on preferreds of this risk level is 5.2 percent. Calculate the maximum amount an investor should pay for these preferred shares.

WARM-UP 8–42   **Preferred share valuation**   Spenceley Enterprises have a Series C preferred share issue outstanding which is rated Pfd-2 (low). The stated value is $25 and the preferred share pays a dividend of 11 percent. The current price of the preferred is $27.25. Calculate the yield.

CHALLENGE 8–43   **Preferred share valuation**   Sandy Inc. has a $25 stated value preferred outstanding which pays a dividend of 8 percent. The current price of the preferred share is $24.10. The company can redeem the preferred in three years at the stated value plus a 2 percent call premium. Calculate the yield an investor would receive assuming:
a. The preferred share was not redeemed.
b. The preferred share was redeemed.

CHALLENGE **8–44**   **Interest equivalent factor**   Lori Stratton is considering investing in a bond that provides a yield of 8.35 percent or a preferred share with a yield of 7.09 percent. Lori lives in Ontario and at her level of taxable income, the federal tax rate is 29 percent and the provincial tax rate is 17.4 percent.

    a. What should Lori do to compare the yields earned on the two investments?

    b. What yields would Lori use to make the comparison? To answer this question, use the dividend tax credit rates provided in Table 8.5.

CASE   CHAPTER 8   **Assessing the Impact of Suarez Manufacturing's Proposed Risky Investment on Its Bond and Common Share Values**

Early in 2003, Inez Marcus, the chief financial officer for Suarez Manufacturing, was given the task of assessing the impact of a proposed risky investment on the firm's bond and common share values. To perform the necessary analysis, Inez gathered the following relevant data on the firm's bonds and common shares.

Bonds The firm has one bond issue currently outstanding. It has a $1,000 par value, a 9 percent coupon interest rate, and 18 years remaining to maturity. Interest on the bond is paid *semiannually,* and the bond's required return is currently 8 percent. After a great deal of research and consultation, Inez concluded that the proposed investment would not violate any of the bond's numerous provisions. Because the proposed investment will increase the overall risk of the firm, she expects that if it is undertaken, the required return on these bonds will increase to 10 percent.

Common Shares During the immediate past 5 years (1998–2002) the annual dividends paid on the firm's common shares were as follows:

Year	Dividend per share
1998	$1.30
1999	1.40
2000	1.55
2001	1.70
2002	1.90

The firm expects that without the proposed investment the dividend in 2003 would grow at the historic annual rate (rounded to the nearest whole percent) and this rate of growth would continue in the future. Currently, the required return on the common shares is 14 percent. Inez's research indicates that if the proposed investment is undertaken, the 2003 dividend will rise to $2.15 per share and the annual rate of dividend growth will increase to 13 percent. She feels that in the *best case,* the dividend would continue to grow at this rate each year into the future, and in the *worst case,* the 13 percent annual rate of growth in dividends would continue only through 2005, and then at the beginning of

2006, the rate of growth would return to the rate that was experienced between 1998 and 2002. As a result of the increased risk associated with the proposed risky investment, the required return on the common shares is expected to increase by 2 percent to an annual rate of 16 percent, regardless of which dividend-growth outcome occurs.

Armed with this information, Inez must now assess the impact of the proposed risky investment on the market value of Suarez's bonds and common shares. To simplify her calculations, she plans to round the historic growth rate in common share dividends to the nearest whole percent.

Required

a. Find the *current* value of $1,000 of par value of Suarez Manufacturing's bond.

b. Find the *current* value of Suarez Manufacturing's common shares.

c. Find the value of Suarez's bond in the event that it *undertakes the proposed risky investment.* Compare this value to that found in **a.** What effect would the proposed investment have on the firm's bondholders? Explain.

d. Find the value of Suarez's common shares in the event that it *undertakes the proposed risky investment* and assuming that the dividend growth rate stays at 13 percent forever. Compare this value to that found in **b.** What effect would the proposed investment have on the firm's common shareholders? Explain.

e. On the basis of your findings in **c** and **d**, who wins and who loses as a result of undertaking the proposed risky investment? Should the firm do it? Why?

f. Rework parts **d** and **e** assuming that at the beginning of 2006, the annual dividend growth rate returns to the rate experienced between 1998 and 2002.

 WEB EXERCISES   LINKS TO PRACTISE

Visit the following Web sites and complete the suggested exercises. These exercises will allow you to review practical applications of the chapter topics as well as explore the wealth of information regarding managerial finance that is available on the Internet.

 www.bloomberg.com/markets/canada.html
This site provides the latest information on the yields of government of Canada debt securities for maturities ranging from 3 months to 30 years. This information can be used to develop the current term structure of interest rates (TSIR) in Canada.

In general, what is the TSIR and what does it show? Develop a graph like the one shown in Figure 8.3 depicting the current TSIR in Canada. Describe the current TSIR in Canada. Based on the current TSIR, what is the current expectation for future interest rates in Canada?

www-ec.njit.edu/~mathis/interactive/TVMCalcIntro.html
www-ec.njit.edu/~mathis/interactive/FCBase4.html

The first site provides an introduction to a free bond calculator. This can be used to determine one of the four required variables for a bond validation problem. The link to the actual calculator is on the bottom of the page. Complete problems from the book using this calculator.

The second link provides a source of numerous problems that can be used with the calculator. Complete as many problems as you like to reinforce the concepts associated with the bond valuation and YTM.

www.smartmoney.com/onebond/index.cfm?story=bondcalculator
Read the instructions on how to use the bond calculator. Using the bond calculator:

1. Calculate the yield to maturity (YTM) for a bond whose coupon rate is 7.5 percent with a maturity date of July 2030, which you bought for 95.
2. What is the YTM of the above bond if you bought it for 105? For 100?
3. Change the Yield % box to 8.5. What would be the price of this bond?
4. Change the Yield % box to 9.5. What is this bond's price?
5. Change the maturity date to 2006 and reset Yield % to 6.5. What is the price of this bond?
6. Why is the price of the bond in Question 5 lower than the price of the bond in Question 4?

www.globeinvestor.com/static/hubs/quotes.html

To use the price/earnings multiples approach to valuation, you need to find a firm's projected earnings and determine an appropriate P/E multiple. The above Web site is a popular source to obtain this data for Canadian companies.

1. Enter bce-t in the Enter Symbol area and click on GO. What is the name of this company? Click on Company Snapshot. What does the company do and what is the company's trailing 12-month revenues, profit, and EPS? Go back to the previous page. What is the company's:
   (a) most recent closing price?
   (b) most recent EPS?
   (c) most recent dividends per share (DPS)?
   (d) current P/E multiple?
   (e) number of common shares outstanding?

   Click on Estimate Snapshot. What is the forecast for the EPS for the upcoming fiscal year? What were the EPS for the previous fiscal year? What is the expected change in EPS from the most recent to the forecast fiscal year in both dollars and percent? Using the forecast for EPS and the P/E ratio from 1(d) above, estimate the value of the company's common shares. What potential flaws are there when using these numbers to determine the value of the company's common shares?

2. Repeat the above for the following symbols: toc-t, bbd.b-t, l-t, ry-t.

INTEGRATIVE CASE 2

ENCORE INTERNATIONAL

In the world of trendsetting fashion, instinct and marketing savvy are prerequisites to success. Jordan Ellis had both. During 2002, his international casual-wear company, Encore, rocketed to $300 million in sales after 10 years in business. His fashion line covered a young woman from head to toe with hats, sweaters, dresses, blouses, skirts, pants, sweatshirts, socks, and shoes. In Montreal, Toronto, and Vancouver, there was an Encore shop every five or six blocks, each featuring a different colour. Some shops showed the entire line in mauve, and others featured it in canary yellow.

Encore had made it. The company's historical growth was so spectacular that no one could have predicted it. However, securities analysts speculated that Encore could not keep up the pace. They warned that competition is fierce in the fashion industry and that the firm might encounter little or no growth in the future. They estimated that common shareholders also should expect no growth in future dividends.

Contrary to the conservative security analysts, Jordan Ellis felt that the company could maintain a constant annual growth rate in dividends per share of 6 percent in the future, or possibly 8 percent for the next 2 years and 6 percent thereafter. Ellis based his estimates on an established long-term expansion plan into European and Latin American markets. By venturing into these markets the risk of the firm as measured by beta was expected to immediately increase from 1.10 to 1.25.

In preparing the long-term financial plan, Encore's chief financial officer has assigned a junior financial analyst, Marc Scott, to evaluate the firm's current stock price. He has asked Marc to consider the conservative predictions of the securities analysts and the aggressive predictions of the company founder, Jordan Ellis.

Marc has compiled these 2002 financial data to aid his analysis.

Data item	2002 value
Earnings per share (EPS)	$6.25
Price per common share	$40
Book value of common share equity	$60,000,000
Total common shares outstanding	2,500,000
Common share dividend per share	$4

REQUIRED

a. What is the firm's current book value per share?

b. What is the firm's current P/E ratio?

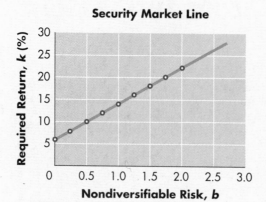

Security Market Line

Data Points	
b	**k**
0.00	6.00%
0.25	8.00
0.50	10.00
0.75	12.00
1.00	14.00
1.25	16.00
1.50	18.00
1.75	20.00
2.00	22.00

c. (1) What are the required return and risk premium for Encore stock using the capital asset pricing model, assuming a beta of 1.10? Use the security market line—with data points noted—given in the figure here to find the market return.

(2) What are the required return and risk premium for Encore's common shares using the capital asset pricing model, assuming a beta of 1.25?

(3) What is the effect on the required return if the beta rises as expected?

d. If the securities analysts are correct and there is no growth in future dividends, what is the value of the Encore's common shares? (*Note:* Beta = 1.25.)

e. (1) If Jordan Ellis's predictions are correct, what is the value of Encore's common shares if the firm maintains a constant annual 6 percent growth rate in future dividends? (*Note:* Beta = 1.25.)

(2) If Jordan Ellis's predictions are correct, what is the value per share of Encore's common shares if the firm maintains a constant annual 8 percent growth rate in dividends per share over the next 2 years and 6 percent thereafter? (*Note:* Beta = 1.25.)

f. Compare the current (2002) price of the common shares and the values found in **a, d,** and **e.** Discuss why these values may differ. Which valuation method do you believe most clearly represents the true value of Encore's common shares?

Long-Term Financial Decisions

The Cost of Capital

LEARNING GOALS

LG1 Understand the basic assumptions, concept, and specific sources of capital underlying the cost of capital.

LG2 Determine the cost of long-term debt and the cost of preferred equity.

LG3 Calculate the cost of common equity recognizing that there are two sources of common equity financing: reinvested profits and the sale of new common shares.

LG4 Find the weighted average cost of capital (WACC) and discuss the alternative weighting schemes.

LG5 Describe the rationale for and procedures used to determine break points and the marginal cost of capital (MCC).

LG6 Explain how the marginal cost of capital (MCC) can be used with the investment opportunities schedule (IOS) to make the firm's financing/investment decisions.

9.1 An Overview of the Cost of Capital

The cost of capital is an extremely important financial concept. It acts as a major link between the firm's long-term investment decisions (discussed in Part 5) and the wealth of the owners as determined by investors in the marketplace. It is in effect the "magic number" that is used to decide whether a proposed corporate investment will increase or decrease the firm's stock price. Clearly, only those investment projects whose expected returns are *greater than or equal to* the cost of the funds used to acquire the projects would be recommended. Such projects will result in a company's common shares increasing in value. Due to its key role

The Right Mix

If you and a friend each bought a pound of jelly beans, mixed from among your favourite flavours, would you each buy the same mix? Probably not. It's the same with two companies' choices of financing sources—each will choose proportions of debt and equity financing to suit its particular tastes. The success of any firm will depend in large part on the difference between the cost of the firm's funding from various sources and the return earned on investment projects. This chapter illustrates that a company's cost of capital is a function of the costs of the individual sources of financing—long-term debt, preferred equity, and common equity—and the percentage the individual sources of financing are in the company's *optimal* capital structure. The weighted average cost of capital is simply the sum of the individual costs multiplied by the individual weights. The right mix results in the lowest overall cost of capital and the highest value for the company's common shares.

in financial decision making, the importance of the cost of capital cannot be overemphasized.

cost of capital
The rate of return that a firm must earn on its investment projects to increase the market value of its common shares.

The **cost of capital** is the rate of return that a firm must earn on its investment projects to increase the market value of its common shares. It can also be thought of as the rate of return required by the market suppliers of capital to attract their funds to the firm. If risk is held constant, projects with a rate of return equal to or above the cost of capital will increase the value of the firm, and projects with a rate of return below the cost of capital will decrease the value of the firm. Since the objective of the firm is to maximize the value of the common shares, a key way to do this is to minimize the company's cost of capital. This concept is discussed in more detail in Chapter 10.

Basic Assumptions

The cost of capital is a dynamic concept affected by a variety of economic and firm factors. To isolate the basic structure of the cost of capital, we make some key assumptions relative to risk and taxes:

1. **Business risk**—the risk to the firm of being unable to cover operating costs—*is assumed to be unchanged.* This assumption means that the firm's acceptance of a given project does not affect its ability to meet operating costs.
2. **Financial risk**—the risk to the firm of being unable to cover required financial obligations (interest, lease payments, preferred share dividends)—*is assumed to be unchanged.* This assumption means that projects are financed in such a way that the firm's ability to meet required financing costs is unchanged.
3. After-tax costs are considered relevant. In other words, *the cost of capital is measured on an after-tax basis.* This assumption is consistent with the framework used to make decisions regarding investments in assets.

Risk and Financing Costs

Regardless of the type of financing employed, the following equation explains the general relationship between risk and financing costs:

$$k_l = r_l + bp + fp \tag{9.1}$$

where

$$k_l = \text{specific (or nominal) cost of the various types of} $$
$$\text{long-term financing, } l$$
$$r_l = \text{risk-free cost of the given type of financing, } l$$
$$bp = \text{business risk premium}$$
$$fp = \text{financial risk premium}$$

Equation 9.1 is merely another form of the nominal interest equation—Equation 8.2 presented in the last chapter—where r_l equals R_F and $bp + fp$ equals RP, the factor for issuer and issue characteristics. It indicates that the cost of each type of capital depends on the risk-free cost of that type of funds, the business risk of the firm, and the financial risk of the firm.[1] We can evaluate the equation in either of two ways:

1. *Time-series comparisons* are made by comparing the firm's cost of each type of financing *over time.* Here the differentiating factor is the risk-free cost of the given type of financing.
2. *Comparisons between firms* are made at a single point in time by comparing a firm's cost of each type of capital with its cost *to another firm.* In this case,

---

1. Although the relationship between r_l, bp, and fp is presented as linear in Equation 9.1, this is only for simplicity; the actual relationship is likely to be much more complex mathematically. The only definite conclusion that can be drawn is that the cost of a specific type of financing for a firm is somehow functionally related to the risk-free cost of that type of financing adjusted for the firm's business and financial risks [i.e., that $k_l = f(r_l, bp, fp)$].

the risk-free cost of the given type of financing would remain constant,[2] and the cost differences would be attributable to the differing business and financial risks of each firm.

Example ▼ Hobson Company, an Alberta-based meat packer, had a cost of long-term debt 2 years ago of 8 percent. This 8 percent represented a 4 percent risk-free cost of long-term debt, a 2 percent business risk premium, and a 2 percent financial risk premium. Currently, the risk-free cost of long-term debt is 6 percent. How much would you expect the company's cost of long-term debt to be today, assuming that its business and financial risk have remained unchanged? The previous business risk premium of 2 percent and financial risk premium of 2 percent will still prevail, because neither has changed. Adding that 4 percent total risk premium to the 6 percent risk-free cost of long-term debt results in a cost of long-term debt to Hobson Company of 10 percent. In this *time-series comparison,* in which business and financial risk are assumed to be constant, the cost of the long-term funds changes only in response to changes in the risk-free cost of the given type of funds.

Another company, Red Deer Meats, which has a 2 percent business risk premium and a 4 percent financial risk premium, can be used to demonstrate *comparisons between firms.* Although Red Deer and Hobson are both in the meat-packing business (and thus have the same business risk premium of 2%), the cost of long-term debt to Red Deer Meats is currently 12 percent (the 6% risk-free cost plus a 2% business risk premium plus a 4% financial risk premium). This is greater than the 10 percent cost of long-term debt for Hobson. The differ-
▲ ence is attributable to the greater financial risk associated with Red Deer.

The Basic Concept

The cost of capital is estimated at a given point in time. It reflects the expected average future cost of funds over the long run, based on the best information available. Although firms typically raise money in lumps, the cost of capital should reflect the interrelatedness of financing activities. For example, if a firm raises funds with debt (borrowing) today, it is likely that some form of equity, such as common shares, will have to be used next time. Most firms maintain a deliberate, optimal mix of debt and equity financing. This mix is commonly called a **target capital structure**—a topic that will be discussed in greater detail in Chapter 10. It is sufficient here to say that although firms raise money in lumps, they tend toward some desired *mix of financing.*

To capture the interrelatedness of financing assuming the presence of a target capital structure, we need to look at the *overall cost of capital* rather than the cost of the specific source of funds used to finance a given expenditure.

target capital structure
The desired optimal mix of debt and equity financing that most firms attempt to achieve and maintain.

⊙─┐ Career Key
Management will use the cost of capital when assessing the acceptability and relative ranking of capital expenditure projects. The firm's target capital structure policy will go a long way to determining what the firm's cost of capital will be.

---

2. The risk-free cost of each type of financing, r_l, may differ considerably. In other words, at a given point in time, the risk-free cost of long-term debt may be 6% while the risk-free cost of common shares may be 9%. The risk-free cost is expected to be different for each type of financing, *l*. The risk-free cost of different *maturities* of the same type of debt may differ, because, as discussed in Chapter 8, long-term issues are generally viewed as more risky than short-term issues.

E x a m p l e ▼ A firm is *currently* faced with an investment opportunity. Assume the following:

Best project available today

Cost = $100,000
Life = 20 years
Expected return = 7%

To finance the project, the firm could use the lowest-cost source of financing. This is debt with an after-tax cost of 6 percent. Since the company can earn a 7 percent return on the project, it seems to make sense for the company to invest in the project; the cost of the funds is less than the expected return.

Imagine that *1 week later* a new investment opportunity is presented with the same $100,000 cost, the same life of 20 years, *but* with an expected return of 12 percent. The lowest cost source of financing available is common equity with a cost of 14 percent. In this instance, the firm rejects the opportunity, because the 14 percent financing cost is greater than the 12 percent expected return.

Were the firm's actions in the best interests of its owners? No—it accepted a project yielding a 7 percent return and rejected one with a 12 percent return. Clearly, there should be a better way, and there is: The firm can use a combined cost, which over the long run would provide for better decisions. By weighting the cost of each source of financing by its target proportion in the firm's capital structure, the firm can obtain a *weighted average cost* that reflects the interrelationship of financing decisions. Assuming that a 50–50 mix of debt and equity is targeted, the weighted average cost above would be 10 percent [(0.50 × 6% debt) + (0.50 × 14% equity)].

With this cost, the first opportunity would be rejected, since the cost of financing the project (10%) is greater than the expected return of the project (7%). The second project would be accepted, since the expected return (14%) is greater than the cost of financing the project (10%). Such an outcome would ▲ clearly be more desirable.

The Cost of Specific Sources of Capital

This chapter focuses on finding the costs of specific sources of capital and combining them to determine and apply the weighted average cost of capital. Our concern is only with the *long-term* sources of funds available to a business firm, because these sources supply the permanent financing. Long-term financing supports the firm's fixed asset investments.[3] To determine which fixed asset investments should be selected, the cost of capital *must be known*. With the cost of capital, capital budgeting procedures are then used to determine which projects are selected. Capital budgeting is discussed in more detail in Part 5 of this book.

There are three basic sources of long-term funds for the business firm: long-term debt, preferred equity, and common equity. As discussed in Chapter 6, there are two sources of common equity financing. First, a company sells common shares to investors and the funds raised are obviously a source of financing. Second, an on-going source of financing is reinvested profits. Assuming a company is profitable and that all of the profits are not paid out as

---

3. The role of both long-term and short-term financing in supporting both fixed and current asset investments is addressed in Chapter 14. Suffice it to say that long-term funds are at minimum used to finance fixed assets.

dividends, the reinvested profits are a source of financing. The reinvested profits flow to the balance sheet and appear as retained earnings. The right-hand side of a balance sheet can be used to illustrate these sources:

Balance Sheet	
Current liabilities	
Long-term debt	⎫
Shareholders' equity Preferred shares Common equity Common shares Retained earnings	Sources of long-term funds

(Assets shown on the left-hand side of the balance sheet.)

Note that for the retained earnings account, the source of financing is the current year's contribution to retained earnings, reinvested profits, not the total of retained earnings shown on the balance sheet. Remember, retained earnings are simply the running total of reinvested profits. Retained earnings are used to determine the percentage of common equity in the optimal capital structure, but the current year's reinvested profits are a source of common equity financing.

Although not all firms will use each of these methods of financing, each firm is expected to have funds from some of these sources in its capital structure. The *specific cost* of each source of financing is the *after-tax* cost of obtaining the financing *today*, not the historically based cost reflected by the existing financing on the firm's books. Techniques for determining the specific cost of each source of long-term funds are presented on the following pages. Although these techniques tend to develop precisely calculated values, the resulting values are at best *rough approximations* because of the numerous assumptions and forecasts that underlie them. Although we round calculated costs to the nearest 0.1 percent throughout this chapter, it is not unusual for practicing financial managers to use costs rounded to the nearest 1 percent because the calculated values are merely estimates.

? Review Questions

9–1   What is the *cost of capital?* What role does it play in making long-term investment decisions? Why is use of a weighted average cost rather than the specific cost recommended?

9–2   Why are business and financial risk assumed to be unchanged when evaluating the cost of capital? Discuss the implications of these assumptions on the acceptance and financing of new projects.

9–3   Why is the cost of capital most appropriately measured on an after-tax basis?

9–4   You have just been told, "Because we are going to finance this project with debt, its required rate of return must exceed the cost of debt." Do you agree or disagree? Explain.

9.2 The Cost of Long-Term Debt

cost of long-term debt, k_i
The after-tax cost today of raising long-term funds through borrowing.

The **cost of long-term debt**, k_i, is the after-tax cost today of raising long-term funds through borrowing. The long-term borrowing could be raised by using either bonds or debentures; however, consistent with previous chapters, the term *bond* will be used to denote long-term debt. The coupon payments are assumed to be made *either* annually or semiannually.

Net Proceeds

net proceeds
Funds actually received from the sale of a security.

flotation costs
The total costs of issuing and selling a security.

discounts
Reductions in the price of the security that are required to sell this security to investors.

As discussed in Chapter 6, bonds are sold in the primary market of the capital market by using an underwriter (investment dealer). The **net proceeds** from the sale of a bond, or any security, are the funds that are actually received from the sale. There are two types of costs that can be incurred when selling financial securities. Both of these costs reduce the net proceeds from the sale of a security. The first is **flotation costs**—the total costs of issuing and selling a security—which reduce the net proceeds from the sale. These costs apply to all public offerings of securities—debt, preferred shares, and common shares. They include two components: (1) *underwriting costs*—compensation earned by investment bankers for selling the security—and (2) *administrative costs*—issuer expenses such as legal, accounting, printing, and other expenses.

The second cost is **discounts** to the price of the security that are required to sell the security to investors. Discounts from par value generally only apply to long-term debt. Discounts to the current share price apply to the sale of new common shares.

Example ▼ Duchess Corporation, a major hardware manufacturer, is contemplating selling $10 million worth of 20-year bonds with a 9 percent coupon rate (paid *annually*) and a par value of $1,000. Because similar-risk bonds earn returns slightly greater than 9 percent, the firm must discount the bonds by $20, selling them for $980 to compensate for the lower coupon rate. In addition, the flotation costs are 2 percent of the par value of the bond (2% × $1,000), or $20. The net pro-
▲ ceeds to the firm from the sale of each bond are therefore $960 ($980 − $20).

Before-Tax Cost of Debt

The before-tax cost of debt, k_d, for a bond can be obtained in one of three ways—quotation, calculation, or approximation.

! Hint
From the issuer's perspective, the IRR on a bond's cash flows is its *cost to maturity*; from the investor's perspective, the IRR on a bond's cash flows is its *yield to maturity (YTM)*, as explained in Chapter 8. These two measures are conceptually similar, although their point of view is different.

Using Cost Quotations

When the net proceeds from sale of a bond equal its par value, the before-tax cost would just equal the coupon rate. For example, a bond with a 10 percent coupon rate that sells for $1,000 would have a before-tax cost, k_d, of 10 percent.

A second quotation that is sometimes used is the *yield to maturity (YTM)* (see Chapter 8) on a similar-risk bond.[4] For example, if a similar-risk bond has a YTM of 9.7 percent, this value can be used as the before-tax cost of debt, k_d.

---

4. Generally, the yield to maturity of bonds with a similar "rating" is used. Bond ratings, which are published by independent agencies, were discussed in Chapter 6.

Calculating the Cost

This approach finds the before-tax cost of debt by calculating the *internal rate of return (IRR)* on the bond cash flows. From the issuer's point of view, this value can be referred to as the *cost to maturity* of the cash flows associated with the debt. The cost to maturity can be calculated by using either the trial-and-error techniques for finding IRR demonstrated in Chapter 12 or a financial calculator. It represents the annual before-tax percentage cost of the debt.

Example ▼ In the preceding example, the net proceeds for Duchess Corporation from the sale of the 20-year, $1,000-par-value bond with a 9 percent coupon rate paid annually was $960. The calculation of the annual cost is quite simple. The cash flow pattern is the opposite of the pattern from an investor's perspective. It consists of an initial inflow (the net proceeds) followed by a series of annual outlays (the interest payments). In the final year, when the debt is retired, an outlay representing the repayment of the principal also occurs. The cash flows associated with $1,000 of par value Duchess Corporation's bond are as follows:

End of year(s)	Cash flow
0	$ 960
1–20	−$ 90
20	−$1,000

The initial $960 inflow is followed by annual interest outflows of $90 (9% coupon interest rate × $1,000 par value) over the 20-year life of the bond. In year 20, an outflow of $1,000 (the repayment of the principal) occurs. The before-tax cost of debt can be determined by finding the IRR—the discount rate that equates the present value of the outflows with the initial inflow.

Trial and Error   We know from the discussions in Chapter 8 that discounting a bond's future cash flows at its coupon rate will result in its $1,000 par value. Therefore, the discount rate necessary to cause Duchess Corporation's bond value to equal $960 must be greater than its 9 percent coupon interest rate. (Remember that the higher the discount rate, the lower the present value, and the lower the discount rate, the higher the present value.) Applying a 10 percent discount rate to the bond's future cash flows, we get

$$B_0 = \$90 \times (PVIFA_{10\%,20yrs}) + \$1,000 \times (PVIF_{10\%,20yrs})$$
$$= \$90 \times (8.514) + \$1,000 \times (0.149)$$
$$= \$766.26 + \$149 = \$915.26$$

Because the bond's value of $1,000 at its 9 percent coupon interest rate is higher than $960 and the $915.26 value at the 10 percent discount rate is lower than $960, the bond's before-tax cost must be between 9 and 10 percent. Because the $1,000 value is closer to $960, the before-tax cost of the bond rounded to the nearest whole percent would be 9 percent. By using *interpolation* (as described on this book's homepage at **www.pearsoned.ca/gitman**), the more precise value for the bond's before-tax cost of 9.47 percent is obtained.

Calculator Use   [*Note:* Most calculators require either the present value (net proceeds) or future value (repayment of principal) to be inputted as a negative number to calculate cost to maturity. That approach is used here.] By using the calculator and the inputs shown, the before-tax cost (cost to maturity) of 9.452 percent should appear on the calculator display. Note that this number is the precise value of the bond's cost to maturity, which is closely approximated by the interpolated value of 9.47 percent found using the trial-and-error approach.

Inputs: 20   -960   90   1000

Functions: N   PV   PMT   FV   CPT   I

▲ **Outputs:**   9.452

Approximating the Cost

The before-tax cost of debt, k_d, for a bond with a $1,000 par value can be approximated by using the following equation:

$$k_d = \frac{I + \dfrac{\$1,000 - N_d}{n}}{\dfrac{N_d + \$1,000}{2}} \tag{9.2}$$

where

$$I = \text{annual interest in dollars}$$
$$N_d = \text{net proceeds from the sale of debt (bond)}$$
$$n = \text{number of years to the bond's maturity}$$

E x a m p l e ▼ Substituting the appropriate values from the Duchess Corporation example into the approximation formula given in Equation 9.2, we get:

$$k_d = \frac{\$90 + \dfrac{\$1,000 - \$960}{20}}{\dfrac{\$960 + \$1,000}{2}} = \frac{\$90 + \$2}{\$980}$$

$$= \frac{\$92}{\$980} = \underline{\underline{9.39\%}}$$

This approximate before-tax cost of debt does not differ greatly from the ▲ 9.452 percent value determined when using the calculator.

After-Tax Cost of Debt

As indicated earlier, the *specific cost* of financing must be stated on an after-tax basis. Because interest on debt is tax deductible, it reduces the firm's taxable income. The interest deduction therefore reduces taxes by an amount equal to the product of the deductible interest and the firm's tax rate. In light of this, the after-tax cost of debt, k_i, can be found by multiplying the before-tax cost, k_d, by 1 minus the tax rate, T, as stated in the following equation:

$$k_i = k_d \times (1 - T) \tag{9.3}$$

Example ▼ We can demonstrate the after-tax debt cost calculation using the 9.452 percent before-tax debt cost calculated for Duchess Corporation, the company's tax rate is 40 percent. Applying Equation 9.3 results in an after-tax cost of debt of 5.7 percent [$9.452\% \times (1 - 0.40)$]. The after-tax cost of long-term debt is less than the cost of any of the alternative forms of long-term financing, primarily because of the tax deductibility of interest. Since dividends are paid out of after-tax income, the cost of equity securities is after tax. Second, since long-term debt is the most secure source of financing, investors' required rate of return is the ▲ lowest. Therefore, the company cost is the lowest.

? Review Questions

9–5   What is meant by the *net proceeds* from the sale of a bond? What costs can be incurred when selling financial securities, and how do they affect a bond's net proceeds?

9–6   Describe the trial-and-error approach used to calculate the before-tax cost of debt. How does this calculation relate to a bond's *cost to maturity* and IRR? How can this value be found more efficiently and accurately?

9–7   What sort of general approximation can be used to find the before-tax cost of debt? How is the before-tax cost of debt converted into the after-tax cost? Why is the after-tax cost of debt used?

9.3 The Cost of Preferred Equity

Preferred equity represents a special type of ownership interest in the firm. It gives preferred shareholders the right to receive their *stated* dividends before any earnings can be distributed to common shareholders. Because preferred shares are a form of ownership, the proceeds from their sale are expected to be held for an infinite period of time. The key characteristics of preferred shares were described in Chapter 6.

Briefly, preferred shares are sold for their stated value. The main reason investors buy preferred shares is for the dividend. Dividends are stated either as a dollar amount, which is the amount paid each year, or as a percentage rate. If shown as a percent, the rate is a percent of the stated value. For instance, a preferred share with a $50 stated value and an 8 percent dividend would be expected to pay an annual dividend of $4 a share ($0.08 \times \$50$ stated value = $4). Before the cost of preferred stock is calculated, any dividends stated as percentages should be converted to annual dollar dividends.

cost of preferred equity, k_p
The relationship between the cost of the preferred equity and the amount of funds provided by the preferred share issue; found by dividing the annual dividend, D_p, by the net proceeds from the sale of the preferred share, N_p.

Calculating the Cost of Preferred Equity

The **cost of preferred equity, k_p,** is the ratio of the preferred share annual dividend to the net proceeds from the sale of the preferred shares—that is, the relationship between the annual dividend on the preferred shares, and the amount of funds provided by the preferred share issue. The net proceeds represent the amount of money to be received minus any flotation costs. Equation 9.4 gives the cost of preferred equity, k_p, in terms of the annual dollar dividend, D_p, and the net proceeds from the sale of the shares, N_p:

$$k_p = \frac{D_p}{N_p} \qquad\qquad (9.4)$$

Because preferred share dividends are paid out of the firm's *after-tax* income, a tax adjustment is not required.

Example ▼ Duchess Corporation is considering issuing a 10 percent (annual dividend) preferred share that is expected to sell for its $100 stated value. The cost of issuing and selling the shares is expected to be $5.60 per share. The first step in finding the cost of the stock is to calculate the dollar amount of the annual preferred dividend, which is $10 (0.10 × $100). The net proceeds from the proposed sale of stock can be found by subtracting the flotation costs from the sale price. This gives a value of $94.40 per share. Substituting the annual dividend, D_p, of $10 and the net proceeds, N_p, of $94.40 into Equation 9.4 gives the cost of preferred
▲ stock, 10.6 percent ($10 ÷ $94.40).

The cost of preferred stock (10.6%) is more expensive than the cost of long-term debt (5.7%). This difference is the result of the two reasons discussed earlier: interest is tax deductible and, from an investor's perspective, debt is less risky than preferred equity.

❓ Review Question

9–8   How is the cost of preferred equity calculated? Why do we concern ourselves with the net proceeds from the sale of the shares instead of its sale price (stated value)?

9.4 The Cost of Common Equity

The *cost of common equity* is the return required on a company's common equity by investors in the financial marketplace. There are two forms of common equity financing: (1) reinvested profits and (2) new issues of common shares. The cost of the two sources of common equity financing is based on the concepts associated with calculating the general cost of common equity. Therefore, consider the following general discussion concerning the cost of common equity.

Finding the Cost of Common Equity

cost of common equity, k_s
The expected return investors require to hold the common shares of a company.

The **cost of common equity, k_s,** is the expected return investors require to hold the common shares of a company. As discussed in Chapter 8, there are two techniques used to determine investors' required rate of return on common equity:

the constant-growth dividend valuation model (DVM) and the capital asset pricing model (CAPM).[5]

Using the Constant-Growth Dividend Valuation Model (DVM)

constant-growth dividend valuation (Gordon) model
Assumes that the value of a common share equals the present value of all future dividends (assumed to grow at a constant rate) that it is expected to provide over an infinite time horizon.

The **constant-growth dividend valuation model (DVM)**—the **Gordon model**—was presented in Chapter 8. It is based on the widely accepted premise that the value of a common share is equal to the present value of all future dividends (assumed to grow at a constant rate) over an infinite time horizon. The key expression derived in Chapter 8 and presented as Equation 8.13 is restated in Equation 9.5:

$$P_0 = \frac{D_1}{k_s - g}$$

(9.5)

where

P_0 = value of a common share
D_1 = per share dividend expected at the end of year 1
k_s = investors' required return on common equity
g = constant rate of growth in dividends

As shown in Chapter 8, solving Equation 9.5 for k_s results in the following expression for the *cost of common equity:*

$$k_s = \frac{D_1}{P_0} + g$$

(9.6)

Equation 9.6 indicates that the cost of common equity can be found by dividing the dividend expected at the end of year 1 by the current common share price and adding the expected growth rate. Remember, g represents the expected growth in DPS, EPS, and the price of the common shares. Because common share dividends are paid from *after-tax* income, no tax adjustment is required.

Example ▼ Duchess Corporation wishes to determine its cost of common equity, k_s. The market price, P_0, of its common stock is $50 per share. The dividends per share (DPS) paid on the common shares over the past 6 years (1997–2002) are provided below. The rate of growth in DPS over these past 6 years is expected to continue into the future.

Year	DPS
1997	$1.19
1998	1.30
1999	1.42
2000	1.55
2001	1.69
2002	1.83

---

5. Other more subjective techniques are available for estimating the cost of common equity. One popular technique is the *bond yield plus a premium;* it estimates the cost of common equity by adding a premium, typically between 3 and 5 percent, to the firm's current cost of long-term debt. Another even more subjective technique uses the firm's *expected return on equity (ROE)* as a measure of its cost of common equity. Here we focus only on the more theoretically based techniques.

Using the table for the present value interest factors, *PVIF* (Table A-3), or a financial calculator in conjunction with the technique described for finding growth rates in Chapter 5, we can calculate the annual growth rate of dividends, g. It turns out to be 9 percent (more precisely, it is 8.9885%). To calculate the cost of common equity we need D_1. The DPS expected in 2003 is based on the DPS actually paid in 2002 ($1.83) increased by the expected rate of growth (9%). Therefore, DPS in 2003 are expected to be:

$$D_1 = D_0 (1 + g)$$
$$= \$1.83 (1 + 0.09)$$
$$= \$1.83 (1.09)$$
$$= \$1.9947 \text{ (rounded up to \$2)}$$

Substituting $D_1 = \$2$, $P_0 = \$50$, and $g = 9\%$ into Equation 9.6 results in the cost of common equity for Duchess Corporation of:

$$k_s = \frac{\$2}{\$50} + 9\%$$
$$= 4\% + 9\% = 13.0\%$$

The 13.0 percent cost of common equity represents the return required by *existing* common shareholders. If Duchess achieves this return on the common equity in 2003, what happens? If the actual dividend paid in 2003 is $2 per share and investors' required return on common shares and rate of growth remain the same, what will happen to the value of the common shares by the end of 2003? For 2004, the expected dividend per share is $2.18 ($2 × 1.09). Submitting the known and assumed amounts into Equation 9.6 results in:

$$k_s = \frac{\$2.18}{P_0} + 9\% = 13\%$$
$$P_0 = \frac{\$2.18}{0.04} = \$54.50$$

The value (price) of Duchess's common shares will increase to $54.50 or by 9 percent, exactly what should happen given the assumptions of the constant-growth DVM.

Using the Capital Asset Pricing Model (CAPM)

capital asset pricing model (CAPM)
Illustrates the relationship between the required return, or cost of common equity, k_s, and the nondiversifiable risk of the firm as measured by the beta coefficient, b.

The **capital asset pricing model (CAPM)** was developed and discussed in Chapter 7. It illustrates the relationship between the required return, or cost of common stock equity, k_s, and the nondiversifiable risk of the firm as measured by the beta coefficient, b. The basic CAPM is given in Equation 9.7:

$$k_s = R_F + [b \times (k_m - R_F)] \tag{9.7}$$

where

$$R_F = \text{risk-free rate of return}$$
$$k_m = \text{market return; return on the market portfolio of assets}$$

By using CAPM, the cost of common equity is the return required by investors as compensation for assuming the firm's nondiversifiable risk, as measured by beta.

Example ▼ Duchess Corporation now wishes to calculate its cost of common equity, k_s, by using the capital asset pricing model. The firm's investment advisors and its own analyses indicate that the risk-free rate, R_F, equals 7 percent; the firm's beta, b, equals 1.5; and the market return, k_m, equals 11 percent. Substituting these values into Equation 9.7, the company estimates the cost of common stock equity, k_s, as follows:

$$k_s = 7.0\% + [1.5 \times (11.0\% - 7.0\%)] = 7.0\% + 6.0\% = \underline{\underline{13.0\%}}$$

The 13.0 percent cost of common stock equity, which is the same as that found by using the constant growth DVM, represents the required return of investors in ▲ Duchess Corporation common stock.[6]

Comparing the Constant-Growth DVM and CAPM Techniques

Use of CAPM differs from the constant-growth DVM in that it directly considers the firm's risk, as reflected by beta, in determining the *required* return or cost of common equity. The constant-growth DVM does not look at risk; it uses the market price, P_0, as a reflection of the *expected* risk-return preference of investors in the marketplace. The constant-growth DVM and CAPM techniques for finding k_s are, in a practical sense, theoretically equivalent. But it is difficult to demonstrate that equivalency, due to measurement problems associated with growth, beta, the risk-free rate (what is the expected rate), and the market return. The use of the constant-growth DVM is often preferred because the data required are more readily available.

Note though that the constant-growth DVM cannot be used for companies that do not pay dividends or for companies that do not have a history of stable dividend payments. The vast majority of companies that trade on the Toronto Stock Exchange fall into one of these two categories. Also, the CAPM has a stronger theoretical foundation than the DVM, though the computational appeal of the constant-growth DVM explains its widespread use. Therefore, those wishing to calculate the cost of common equity (or the equivalent concept of investors required rate of return) must know and be able to use both of the techniques described above.

The Cost of Reinvested Profits

Hint
Using reinvested profits as a major source of financing for capital expenditures does not give away control of the firm and does not dilute present earnings per share, as would occur if new common shares were issued. However, the firm must effectively manage reinvested profits, in order to produce returns that increase future earnings.

Reinvested profits are the amount of money remaining after a company pays common share dividends from the earnings available for common shareholders. Recall from Chapter 2 that all earnings remaining after the payment of preferred share dividends belong to the common shareholders. A company can pay all, or a portion, of these earnings to common shareholders who can then decide how to use the cash. Alternatively, the company could decide to retain all of these earnings for corporate purposes. By retaining the earnings, the company is using common shareholders' funds.

Common shareholders will not provide this money at zero cost. Common shareholders expect the company will invest their funds to earn the required rate of return. If the company invests the funds and earns, at minimum, the required

6. Note that, in reality, it is unusual for the cost of common equity calculated using the two techniques to be equal. The cost of common equity calculated using the DVM is usually different from the cost calculated using the CAPM.

return, the price of the common shares will increase. If the company invests the funds and earns less than the shareholders' required return, the common share price will decline. Reinvested profits are not free. These funds have a cost, which is common shareholders' required rate of return. This is the cost of common equity calculated above. Therefore, the **cost of reinvested profits, k_r,** is equal to the cost of common equity, k_s, as follows:

cost of reinvested profits, k_r
Since reinvested profits are common shareholders' money, these funds have a cost which is the cost of common equity, k_s.

$$k_r = k_s \tag{9.8}$$

It is not necessary to adjust the cost of reinvested profits for flotation costs, because by retaining earnings, the firm "raises" equity capital without incurring these costs.

Example ▼ The cost of reinvested profits for Duchess Corporation was actually calculated in the preceding examples: It is equal to the cost of common equity. Thus, k_r equals 13.0 percent. As we will show in the next section, the cost of reinvested profits is always lower than the cost of a new issue of common shares, due to the absence ▲ of flotation costs.

The Cost of New Issues of Common Shares

Our purpose in finding the firm's overall cost of capital is to determine the after-tax cost of *new* funds required for financing projects. Attention must therefore be given to the cost of a new issue of common shares, k_n. As will be explained later, this cost is important only when there are insufficient reinvested profits available to fund investment projects.

cost of a new issue of common shares, k_n
The cost of common shares, net of discounts and associated flotation costs.

discounted
Sold at a price below current market price, P_0.

The **cost of a new issue of common shares, k_n,** is determined by calculating the cost of common shares, net of discounts and associated flotation costs. Normally, to sell a new issue, it will have to be **discounted**—sold at a price below the current market price, P_0. Firms underprice new issues for a variety of reasons. First, when the market is in equilibrium (i.e., the demand for shares equals the supply of shares), additional demand for shares can be achieved only at a lower price. Second, when additional shares are issued, each share's percent of ownership in the firm is diluted, thereby justifying a lower share value. Third, many investors view the issuance of additional shares as a signal that management is selling additional common shares because it believes that the shares are currently overpriced. Recognizing this information, they will buy shares only at a price below the current market price. Clearly, these and other factors necessitate discounting new offerings of common shares. Flotation costs paid for issuing and selling the new issue will further reduce proceeds.

The cost of new issues can be calculated using the constant-growth DVM expression for the cost of existing common shares, k_s, as a starting point. If we let N_n represent the net proceeds from the sale of new common shares after subtracting the discount and flotation costs, the cost of the new issue, k_n, can be expressed as follows:[7]

$$k_n = \frac{D_1}{N_n} + g \tag{9.9}$$

---

7. An alternative, but computationally less straightforward, form of this equation is

$$k_n = \frac{D_1}{P_0 \times (1 - f)} + g \tag{9.9a}$$

where f represents the *percentage* reduction in current market price expected as a result of discounting and flotation costs. Simply stated, N_n in Equation 9.9 is equivalent to $P_0 \times (1 - f)$ in Equation 9.9a. For convenience, Equation 9.9 is used to define the cost of a new issue of common shares, k_n.

The CAPM can also be used to determine the cost of a new issue of common shares. Since the company will be receiving less than the full proceeds from the sale of new common shares, the company will have to generate a higher return on the net proceeds in order to meet investors' required rate of return. This requirement increases the risk associated with the financing raised through the sale of common shares. This increased risk will increase the cost of new common shares, k_n, expressed, for the CAPM, as follows:

$$k^n = R_F + \left[(k_m - R_F) \times b \times \frac{P_0}{N_n} \right] \tag{9.10}$$

The net proceeds from sale of new common shares, N_n, is always less than the current market price, P_0. Therefore, for both methods of calculating the cost of common equity, the cost of new issues, k_n, will always be greater than the cost of reinvested profits, k_r. *The cost of new common shares is greater than the cost of any other long-term source of financing.* Because common share dividends are paid from after-tax cash flows, no tax adjustment is required.

Example ▼ For Duchess Corporation, the cost of common equity, k_s, using both the constant-growth DVM and the CAPM was 13 percent. This is the cost of reinvested profits, k_r.

To determine its cost of *new* common shares, k_n, Duchess Corporation has estimated that new shares can be sold for $48.50. The $1.50 discount to the current price of $50 is necessary due to the dilution of earnings per share that will occur when new common shares are sold. Prospective purchasers of new common shares expect to pay less than the current market price for new common shares. A second cost associated with a new issue is flotation costs of $4 per share that would be paid to issue and sell the new issue. Therefore, the total of the discount and of flotation costs is expected to be $5.50 per share.

Subtracting the $5.50 per share from the current $50 share price, P_0, results in expected net proceeds, N_n, of $44.50 per share ($50 − $5.50). Substituting the appropriate amounts in Equation 9.9 results in a cost of new common shares using the constant-growth DVM as follows:

$$k_n = \frac{\$2}{\$44.50} + 9\%$$
$$= 4.5\% + 9\% = 13.5\%$$

Substituting the appropriate amounts into Equation 9.10 results in a cost of new common shares using the CAPM as follows:

$$k^r = 7\% + \left[(11\% - 7\%) \times 1.5 \times \frac{\$50}{\$44.50} \right]$$
$$= 7\% + 6.7\% = 13.7\%$$

The two techniques yield very similar results, so the average of the two, ▲ 13.6 percent, will be used to calculate Duchess Corporation's cost of capital.

? Review Questions

9–9   How can the cost of common equity be calculated? What are the equations used and what do each of the components of the equations represent?

9–10   Why do reinvested profits have a cost? Why shouldn't a company view reinvested profits as a free, internally generated source of funds?

9–11   Why do new issues of common shares have a different cost than reinvested profits? Is the cost higher or lower, and why?

9.5 The Weighted Average Cost of Capital (WACC)

weighted average cost of capital (WACC), k_a
Reflects the expected average future cost of funds for the upcoming year; found by weighting the cost of each specific type of capital by its proportion in the firm's capital structure.

Now that we have reviewed methods for calculating the cost of specific sources of financing, we can present techniques for determining the overall cost of capital. As noted earlier, the **weighted average cost of capital (WACC)**, k_a, reflects the expected average future cost of funds for the upcoming year. It is found by weighting the cost of each specific type of capital by its proportion in the firm's optimal capital structure.

Calculating the Weighted Average Cost of Capital (WACC)

The calculation of the weighted average cost of capital (WACC) is performed by multiplying the specific cost of each form of financing by its proportion in the firm's optimal capital structure and summing the weighted values. As an equation, the weighted average cost of capital, k_a, can be specified as follows:

$$k_a = (w_i \times k_i) + (w_p \times k_p) + (w_s \times k_{r\ or\ n}) \qquad (9.11)$$

Career Key
Accounting personnel will provide the data used to determine the firm's weighted average cost of capital. They will provide the book value and historic value data to measure the proportion of types of capital.

where

w_i = proportion of long-term debt in capital structure
w_p = proportion of preferred equity in capital structure
w_s = proportion of common equity in capital structure
$w_i + w_p + w_s = 1.0$

Three important points should be noted in Equation 9.11:

1. For computational convenience, it is best to convert the weights to decimal form and leave the specific costs in percentage terms.
2. *The sum of weights must equal 1.0.* Simply stated, all capital structure components must be accounted for.
3. The firm's common equity weight, w_s, is multiplied by either the cost of reinvested profits, k_r, or the cost of new common shares, k_n. Which cost is used depends on whether the firm's reinvested profits have been fully used for investment purposes.

Example ▼ In earlier examples, we found the costs of the various types of capital for Duchess Corporation to be as follows:

Cost of debt, k_i = 5.7%
Cost of preferred equity, k_p = 10.6%
Cost of reinvested profits, k_r = 13.0%
Cost of new common stock, k_n = 13.6%

The company's optimal capital structure (OCS) is:

Source of capital	OCS weight
Long-term debt	40%
Preferred equity	10
Common equity	50
Total	100%

Duchess has $300,000 of reinvested profits available, so in the initial calculation of cost of capital, the 13 percent cost is used as the cost of common equity. Since reinvested profits are generated internally and have a lower cost than a new issue of common shares, it is *always* assumed that reinvested profits will provide the first wave of common equity financing.

Duchess Corporation's weighted average cost of capital is calculated in Table 9.1. The resulting weighted average cost of capital for Duchess is 9.9 percent. Given the analysis to this point and assuming an unchanged risk level, the firm should accept all projects that will earn a return greater than or equal to 9.9 percent. This is the case, since the cost of the funds used to finance investment projects is 9.9 percent. A project *must* be expected to, at least, return its ▲ cost of financing.

Weighting Schemes

For the OCS, weights can be calculated based on *book value* or on *market value* and using *historic* or *target* proportions.

book value weights
Weights that use accounting values to measure the proportion of each type of capital in the firm's financial structure.

market value weights
Weights that use market values to measure the proportion of each type of capital in the firm's financial structure.

Book Value Versus Market Value

Book value weights use accounting values to measure the proportion of each type of capital in the firm's financial structure. **Market value weights** measure the proportion of each type of capital at its market value. Market value weights are appealing, because the market values of securities closely approximate the actual dollars to be received from their sale. Moreover, because the costs of the various

! Hint
For computational convenience, the financing proportion weights are listed in decimal form in column 1 and the specific costs are shown in percentage terms in column 2.

TABLE 9.1	Calculation of the Weighted Average Cost of Capital for Duchess Corporation

Source of capital	Weight (1)	Cost (2)	Weighted cost [(1) × (2)] (3)
Long-term debt	0.40	5.7%	2.3%
Preferred equity	0.10	10.6	1.1
Common equity	0.50	13.0	6.5
Totals	1.00		9.8%

Weighted average cost of capital = 9.9%

types of capital are calculated by using prevailing market prices, it seems reasonable to use market value weights. In addition, the long-term investment cash flows to which the cost of capital is applied are estimated in terms of current as well as future market values. *Market value weights are clearly preferred over book value weights.*

IN PRACTICE

Cost of Capital at Brascan Corporation

Brascan Corporation is a diversified conglomerate with holdings in three core businesses: real estate, financial services, and power generation. For the fiscal year ended December 31, 2001, Brascan had total sales of $4.7 billion, net income after tax of $311 million, and total assets of $21.9 billion. In their annual report, available at **www.sedar.com/homepage_en.htm**, Brascan provides their cost of capital, discusses, in detail, the factors affecting the cost of capital, and illustrates why it is important for the company to know and control the cost. The information provided in the annual report is summarized below.

Brascan is focused on increasing their return on equity by building cash flows and reducing the cost of capital. During 2001, the company's overall weighted average cost of capital (WACC) was reduced to 9.8 percent. This assumed a 20 percent return objective for common equity. In other words, Brascan assumed investors' required return on common equity was 20 percent. On a market value basis, Brascan's capital structure in 2001 consisted of 49.5 percent debt, 5.9 percent preferred shares, and 44.6 percent common equity.

For their capital structure, the company's objective is to maximize the use of low risk forms of non-participating capital to provide stable, low-cost financial leverage. The company also manages their finances to ensure adequate liquidity at all times. Brascan feels they have a lower WACC than other companies and that this creates a significant strategic and competitive advantage for the company.

The principal reasons the cost of capital was reduced in 2001 included: (1) access to a broad range of financing, including non-participating preferred equity issued over many years principally in the form of perpetual preferred shares; (2) the low-cost investment-grade financing that was supported by the high quality of their assets; and (3) solid investment-grade credit ratings. In addition, the diversity and strength of their assets and the cash flow generated by Brascan's operating businesses reduced financing costs below those of many peers, who operate in only one of their business sectors.

Driven by the objective of increasing returns on capital invested, Brascan raised financing from their real estate portfolio through fixed-rate mortgages on office properties. By locking in long-term debt costs of 7 percent, they lowered their risk and overall cost of capital employed in this business. In addition, in 2001, further progress was made in lowering the cost of capital when S&P and DBRS upgraded Brascan's credit ratings to A– and A (low), respectively. This broadened the company's access to financial markets, allowing them to prudently leverage common shareholders' equity.

Through the continuous monitoring of the balance between debt and equity financing, the company strives to reduce their WACC on a risk-averse basis, thereby improving common shareholder returns. This seemed to work in 2001. Investors recognized the strength of Brascan's cash flows and the fact that they were backed by long-term contracts. This led to a 31 percent increase in the company's common share price during the year.

REFERENCES: Adapted from information taken from 2001 *Annual Report* of Brascan Corporation.

Historic Versus Target

historic weights
Either book or market value weights based on *actual* capital structure proportions.

Historic weights can be either book or market value weights based on *actual* capital structure proportions. For example, past or current book value proportions would constitute a form of historic weighting, as would past or current market value proportions. Such a weighting scheme would therefore be based on real—rather than desired—proportions.

target weights
Either book or market value weights based on *desired* capital structure proportions.

Target weights, which can also be based on either book or market values, reflect the firm's *desired* capital structure proportions. Firms using target weights establish such proportions on the basis of the "optimal" capital structure they wish to achieve. (The development of these proportions and the optimal structure are discussed in detail in Chapter 10.)

⬤ᵣ Career Key
The *marketing* department will be concerned with the weighted average cost of capital because acceptance of its proposed projects will depend on whether its expected returns are greater than the WACC.

When one considers the somewhat approximate nature of the weighted average cost of capital calculation, the choice of weights may not be critical. However, from a strictly theoretical point of view, the *preferred weighting scheme is target market value proportions,* and these are assumed throughout this chapter.

❓ Review Question

9–12   What is the *weighted average cost of capital (WACC)*, and how is it calculated? Describe the logic underlying the use of *target capital structure weights*, and compare and contrast this approach with the use of *historic weights*.

9.6 The Marginal Cost and Investment Decisions

The firm's weighted average cost of capital is a key input to the investment decision-making process. As demonstrated earlier in the chapter, the firm should make only those investments for which the expected return is equal to or greater than the weighted average cost of capital. Of course, at any given time, the firm's financing costs and investment returns will be affected by the volume of financing and investment undertaken. The concepts of a *marginal cost of capital* and an *investment opportunities schedule* provide the mechanisms whereby financing and investment decisions can be made simultaneously.

The Marginal Cost of Capital (MCC)

marginal cost of capital (MCC)
The firm's average cost of capital associated with its *next dollar* of total new financing.

The weighted average cost of capital may vary at any time depending on the volume of financing the firm plans to raise. *As the volume of financing increases, the costs of the various types of financing will increase, raising the firm's weighted average cost of capital.* Therefore, it is useful to calculate the **marginal cost of capital** (MCC), which is simply the firm's weighted average cost of capital associated with its *next dollar* of total new financing. This marginal cost is relevant to decisions regarding investment projects.

Because the costs of the financing components—debt, preferred equity, and common equity—rise as larger amounts are raised, the MCC is an increasing function of the level of total new financing. Increases in the component financing costs occur because the larger the amount of new financing, the greater the risk to the funds supplier. Funds suppliers require greater returns in the form of interest, dividends, or growth as compensation for the increased risk introduced as larger volumes of *new* financing are undertaken.

Another factor that causes the weighted average cost of capital to increase is that once the amount of reinvested profits used to finance investment projects is exhausted, higher-cost new common share issues must be used to raise the assumed dollar amount of common equity financing. This will result in a higher MCC.

Finding Break Points

break point
The level of new financing at which the cost of one of the financing components rises, thereby causing an upward shift in the *marginal cost of capital (MCC)*.

To calculate the MCC, we must calculate the **break points,** which reflect the level of new financing at which the cost of one of the financing components rises. The following general equation can be used to find break points:

$$BP_j = \frac{AF_j}{w_j} \tag{9.12}$$

where

BP_j = break point for financing source j
AF_j = amount of funds available from financing source j at a given cost
w_j = capital structure weight (historic or target, stated in decimal form) for financing source j

A key assumption of Equation 9.12 is that a company will raise the financing used to fund investment projects in the optimal capital structure percentages. While this assumption is vital for calculating the weighted average cost of capital, it is not necessary for a company actually to do this.[8]

Example ▼ When Duchess Corporation exhausts its $300,000 of available reinvested profits with a cost of 13 percent ($k_r = 13.0\%$), it must use the more expensive new common share financing with a cost of 13.6 percent ($k_n = 13.6\%$) to meet its common equity needs. In addition, the firm expects that it can borrow only $400,000 of debt at the 5.6 percent cost; additional debt will have an after-tax cost (k_i) of 8.4 percent. Two break points therefore exist—(1) when the $300,000 of reinvested profits costing 13.0 percent is exhausted and (2) when the $400,000 of long-term debt costing 5.6 percent is exhausted.

The break points can be found by substituting these values and the corresponding capital structure weights given earlier into Equation 9.12. We get

$$BP_{\text{common equity}} = \frac{\$300,000}{0.50} = \$600,000$$

$$BP_{\text{long-term debt}} = \frac{\$400,000}{0.40} = \$1,000,000$$

▲

---

8. If the company raises all new financing in the OCS weights, then the OCS percentages will be retained. As will be shown in Chapter 10, however, the OCS is not at a specific percentage but within an acceptable range. Therefore, companies will usually not raise financing in the OCS weights but will use common equity in one instance, then perhaps debt, then preferred equity, and so on.

If Duchess raised $600,000 of financing, the assumption made is that it is raised in the optimal capital structure (OCS) weights. So, 40 percent or $240,000 is assumed to come from issuing long-term debt; 10 percent or $60,000 from selling preferred shares; and 50 percent or $300,000 from common equity. The $300,000 of common equity financing is reinvested profits. If Duchess raised one additional dollar of financing beyond $600,000, the assumption is that 40 percent will be long-term debt, 10 percent is preferred shares, and 50 percent is common equity. The 50 percent of common equity must be new common shares since once $600,000 of financing is raised, reinvested profits are exhausted.

At $1,000,000 of financing, the same assumption applies. So, 40 percent or $400,000 is long-term debt, 10 percent or $100,000 is preferred equity, and 50 percent or $500,000 is common equity. For common equity, the first $300,000 is reinvested profits; the other $200,000 is raised from selling new common shares. If Duchess raises one more dollar of financing beyond $1,000,000, then it is assumed that 40 percent comes from long-term debt, 10 percent from preferred shares, and 50 percent from common equity. The 40 percent of long-term debt will be the higher-cost debt, with an after-tax cost of 8.4 percent. The cost of the 10 percent preferred equity will remain the same, in this case 10.6 percent. The 50 percent of common equity must come from the sale of new shares with a cost of 13.6 percent. These assumptions are reflected when calculating the WACC and MCC.

Calculating the MCC

Once the break points have been determined, the next step is to calculate the weighted average cost of capital over the range of total new financing between break points. First, we find the WACC for a level of total new financing between zero and the first break point. Next, we find the MCC for a level of total new financing between the first and second break points, and so on. By definition, for each of the ranges of total new financing between break points, certain component capital costs will increase, causing the weighted average cost of capital to increase to a higher level than that over the preceding range.

Together, these data can be used to prepare the **marginal cost of capital (MCC) schedule,** which is a graph that relates the firm's weighted average cost of capital to the level of total new financing.

Example ▼ Table 9.2 summarizes the calculation of the WACC for Duchess Corporation over the three financing ranges created by the two break points—$600,000 and $1,000,000. Comparing the costs in column 3 of the table for each of the three ranges, we can see that the costs in the first range ($0 to $600,000) are those calculated in earlier examples and used in Table 9.1. The second range ($600,000 to $1,000,000) reflects the increase in the common equity cost to 13.6 percent. In the final range, the increase in the long-term debt cost to 8.4 percent is introduced.

The weighted average costs of capital (WACC) for the three ranges created by the two break points are summarized in the table shown at the bottom of Figure 9.1. These data describe the marginal cost of capital (MCC), which increases as levels of total new financing increase. Figure 9.1 presents the MCC schedule. Again, it is clear that the MCC is an increasing function of the amount ▲ of total new financing raised.

| TABLE 9.2 | Weighted Average Cost of Capital for Ranges of Total New Financing for Duchess Corporation | | | |

Range of total new financing	Source of capital (1)	Weight (2)	Cost (3)	Weighted cost [(2) × (3)] (4)
$0 to $600,000	Debt	0.40	5.7%	2.3%
	Preferred	0.10	10.6	1.1
	Common	0.50	13.0	6.5
	Weighted average cost of capital			9.9%
$600,000 to $1,000,000	Debt	0.40	5.7%	2.3%
	Preferred	0.10	10.6	1.1
	Common	0.50	13.6	6.8
	Weighted average cost of capital			10.2%
$1,000,000 and above	Debt	0.40	8.4%	3.4%
	Preferred	0.10	10.6	1.1
	Common	0.50	13.6	6.8
	Weighted average cost of capital			11.3%

The Investment Opportunities Schedule (IOS)

marginal cost of capital (MCC) schedule
Graph that relates the firm's weighted average cost of capital to the level of total new financing.

At any given time, a firm has certain investment opportunities available to it. These opportunities differ with respect to the size of investment and return.[9] The firm's **investment opportunities schedule (IOS)** is a ranking of investment possibilities from best (highest return) to worst (lowest return). As the cumulative amount of money invested in a firm's investment projects increases, the return (IRR) on the projects will decrease; generally, the first project selected will have the highest return, the next project the second highest, and so on. In other words, the return on investments will *decrease* as the firm accepts additional projects.

E x a m p l e ▼ Duchess Corporation's current investment opportunities schedule (IOS) lists the best (highest return) to the worst (lowest return) investment possibilities in column 1 of Table 9.3. Column 2 of the table shows the initial investment required by each project. Column 3 shows the cumulative total invested funds required to finance all projects better than and including the corresponding investment opportunity. Plotting the project returns against the cumulative investment (column 1 against column 3 in Table 9.3) and the MCC for the various financing ranges (as in Figure 9.1) results in the firm's investment opportunities schedule (IOS). A graph of the IOS for Duchess Corporation is given in Figure 9.2. Use of the IOS along with the MCC in decision making is discussed in ▲ the following section.

9. Because the calculated weighted average cost of capital does not apply to risk-changing investments, we assume that all opportunities have risk equal to that of the firm.

FIGURE 9.1

MCC Schedule
Marginal cost of capital (MCC) schedule for Duchess Corporation

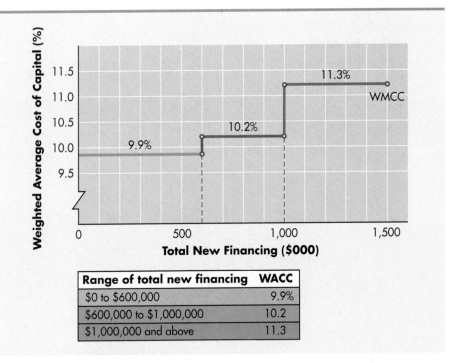

Range of total new financing	WACC
$0 to $600,000	9.9%
$600,000 to $1,000,000	10.2
$1,000,000 and above	11.3

Using the MCC and IOS to Make Financing/Investment Decisions

As long as a project's expected return (internal rate of return) is equal to or greater than the marginal cost of new financing, the firm should accept the project. The return will decrease with the acceptance of more projects, and the weighted marginal cost of capital will increase because greater amounts of financing will be required. The firm would therefore *accept projects up to the*

TABLE 9.3   Investment Opportunities Schedule (IOS) for Duchess Corporation

investment opportunities
schedule (IOS)
A ranking of investment possibilities from best (highest return) to worst (lowest return).

Investment opportunity	Internal rate of return (IRR) (1)	Initial investment (2)	Cumulative investment[a] (3)
A	15.0%	$100,000	$ 100,000
B	14.5	200,000	300,000
C	14.0	400,000	700,000
D	13.0	100,000	800,000
E	12.0	300,000	1,100,000
F	11.0	200,000	1,300,000
G	10.0	100,000	1,400,000

[a]The cumulative investment represents the total amount invested in projects with higher returns plus the investment required for the given investment opportunity.

FIGURE 9.2

IOS and MCC Schedules
Using the IOS and MCC to
select projects

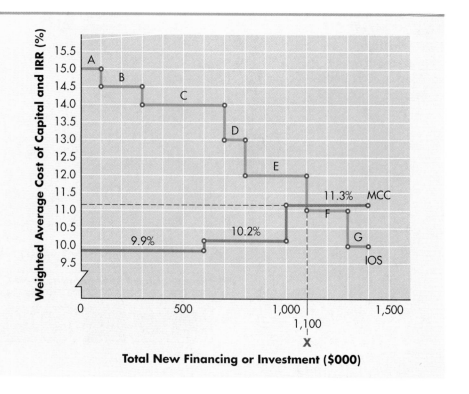

point at which the marginal return on its investment equals its marginal cost of capital. Beyond that point, its investment return will be less than its capital cost.

This approach is consistent with the maximization of shareholder wealth. The acceptance of investment projects beginning with those having the largest positive difference between expected return (IRR) and MCC declining to the point where the IRR of a project is equal to the MCC should result in the maximum total value for all investment projects accepted. Such an outcome is completely consistent with the firm's goal of owner wealth maximization. Returning to the Duchess Corporation example, we can demonstrate this procedure.

Example ▼ Figure 9.2 shows the Duchess Corporation's MCC schedule and IOS on the same set of axes. By using these two functions in combination, the firm's optimal capital budget ("X" in the figure) is determined. By raising $1.1 million of new financing and investing these funds in projects A, B, C, D, and E, the firm should maximize the wealth of its owners, because these projects result in the maximum total value. Note that the 12.0 percent return on the last dollar invested (in project E) *exceeds* its 11.3 percent weighted average cost; investment in project F is not feasible because its 11.0 percent return is *less than* the 11.3 percent cost of
▲ funds available for investment.

Note that at the point at which the IRR equals the weighted average cost of capital, k_a—the optimal capital budget of $1,100,000 at point X in Figure 9.2— the firm's size as well as its shareholder value will be optimized. In a sense, the size of the firm is determined by the market—the availability of and returns on investment opportunities, and the availability and cost of financing.

IN PRACTICE

Cost of Capital: Theory and Practice

Do public corporations practise what your finance professors teach? Two recent surveys of the cost of capital techniques used at companies in Canada and the United States showed that financial managers today pay more attention to the cost of capital and its role in capital budgeting and valuation of the firm than they did 15 years ago. A contributing factor is the growing popularity of performance evaluation models that use cost of capital in their formulas, such as economic value added (EVA®), discussed in Chapter 1.

The surveys, one of which updated an earlier study conducted in 1982, revealed that companies are becoming more sophisticated in their knowledge and use of financial techniques. The two studies, in total, provide the results of surveys of 201 American and 65 Canadian companies. The key findings of the two surveys are:

- Most firms calculate the cost of capital using long-term debt and equity, although some exclude capital leases and preferred equity.

- Most companies use multiple techniques to determine the cost of capital. For companies in both countries, the weighted average cost of capital (WACC) is the most popular technique, with one of the studies reporting that over 90 percent of the surveyed companies use this method.

- An interesting difference was that Canadian companies tended to use the WACC technique less than U.S. companies, but this was due primarily to the larger percentage of smaller companies in the Canadian sample. Smaller companies tended to rely on previous experience to calculate a discount rate that was then used to evaluate investment projects.

- Most firms use one cost of capital regardless of the total amount of financing they require. Nearly all use the cost of capital for new project decisions; over three-quarters use it to estimate the firm's value.

- Most companies base the calculation of the WACC on target or market capital structure weights rather than book value weights.

- The current capital structure of most respondents is consistent with their target capital structure. The average capital structure at the time of the survey was 34 percent debt, 5 percent preferred equity, and 61 percent common equity.

- Firms use more than one method to calculate cost of common equity. Most consider investors' required rate of return, calculated using the CAPM.

- Over 60 percent of firms differentiate project risk on an individual project basis and adjust the discount rate rather than cash flows.

- About half of the respondents recalculate their cost of capital when environmental conditions warrant (shifts in long-term rates); another 27 percent recompute it annually.

SOURCES: Janet D. Payne, Will Carrington Heath, and Lewis R. Gale, "Comparative Financial Practice in the U.S. and Canada: Capital Budgeting and Risk Assessment Techniques," *Financial Practice and Education* (Spring/Summer 1999), pp. 16–24; and Lawrence J. Gitman and Pieter A. Vandenberg, "Cost of Capital Techniques Used by Major U.S. Firms: 1997 vs. 1980," *Financial Practice and Education* (Fall/Winter 2000), pp. 53–68.

Of course, as will be discussed in Chapter 13, all companies will have a limited amount of funds to invest in projects. This situation is referred to as *capital rationing*. Management usually imposes an internal capital expenditure (and therefore financing) budget constraint that is below the optimum capital budget (where IRR $= k_a$). Suffice it to say that due to capital rationing, a gap frequently exists between the theoretically optimal capital budget and the firm's actual level of financing/investment.

? Review Questions

9–13   What is the *marginal cost of capital (MCC)?* What does the *MCC schedule* represent? Why does this schedule increase?

9–14   What is the *investment opportunities schedule (IOS)?* Is it typically depicted as an increasing or decreasing function of the level of investment at a given point in time? Why?

9–15   Use a graph to show how the MCC schedule and the IOS can be used to find the level of financing/investment that maximizes owner wealth. Why, on a practical basis, do many firms finance/invest at a level below this optimum?

SUMMARY

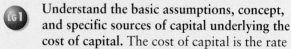 **Understand the basic assumptions, concept, and specific sources of capital underlying the cost of capital.** The cost of capital is the rate of return that a firm must earn on its investments to maintain its market value and attract needed funds. The specific costs of the basic sources of capital (long-term debt, preferred equity, and common equity) can be calculated individually. Only the cost of debt must be adjusted for taxes. The cost of each is affected by business and financial risks, which are assumed to be unchanged, and by the risk-free cost of the type of financing. To capture the interrelatedness of financing, a weighted average cost of capital should be used.

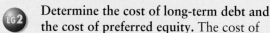 **Determine the cost of long-term debt and the cost of preferred equity.** The cost of long-term debt is the after-tax cost today of raising long-term funds through borrowing. Cost quotations, calculation using either trial-and-error techniques or a financial calculator, or an approximation can be used to find the before-tax cost of debt, which must then be tax-adjusted. The cost of preferred equity is the stated annual dividend expressed as a percentage of the net proceeds from the sale of preferred shares. The key variable definitions and formulas for the before- and after-tax cost of debt and the cost of preferred equity are given in Table 9.4.

 Calculate the cost of common equity, recognizing that there are two sources of common

equity financing: reinvested profits and the sale of new common shares. The cost of common equity can be calculated by using the constant-growth dividend valuation model (DVM) or the capital asset pricing model (CAPM). The cost of reinvested profits is equal to the cost of common equity. An adjustment in the cost of common equity to reflect discounting and flotation cost is required to find the cost of new issues of common shares. The key variable definitions and formulas for the cost of common equity, the cost of reinvested profits, and the cost of new issues of common shares are given in Table 9.4.

 Find the weighted average cost of capital (WACC) and discuss the alternative weighting schemes. The firm's WACC reflects the expected average future cost of funds for the upcoming year. It can be determined by combining the costs of specific types of capital after weighting each cost using historical book or market value weights, or target book or market value weights. The theoretically preferred approach uses target weights based on market values. The key variable definitions and formula for WACC are given in Table 9.4.

 Describe the rationale for and procedures used to determine break points and the marginal cost of capital (MCC). A firm's MCC reflects the fact that as the dollar amount of total new financing increases, the costs of the various

TABLE 9.4

Summary of Key Definitions and Formulas for Cost of Capital

Variable definitions

AF_j = amount of funds available from financing source j at a given cost

b = beta coefficient or measure of nondiversifiable risk

BP_j = break point for financing source j

D_1 = per share dividend expected at the end of year 1

D_p = annual preferred share dividend (in dollars)

g = constant rate of growth in dividends

I = annual interest in dollars

k_a = weighted average cost of capital

k_d = before-tax cost of debt

k_i = after-tax cost of debt

k_m = required return on the market portfolio

k_n = cost of a new issue of common shares

k_p = cost of preferred equity

k_r = cost of reinvested profits

k_s = required return on common equity

n = number of years to the bond's maturity

N_d = net proceeds from the sale of debt (bond)

N_n = net proceeds from the sale of new common shares

N_p = net proceeds from the sale of preferred shares

P_0 = value of common shares

R_F = risk-free rate of return

T = firm's tax rate

w_i = proportion of long-term debt in capital structure

w_j = capital structure proportion (historic or target, stated in decimal form) for financing source j

w_p = proportion of preferred equity in capital structure

w_s = proportion of common equity in capital structure

Cost of capital formulas

Before-tax cost of debt:

$$k_d = \frac{I + \dfrac{\$1{,}000 - N_d}{n}}{\dfrac{N_d + \$1{,}000}{2}}$$ [Eq. 9.2]

After-tax cost of debt:

$$k_i = k_d \times (1 - T)$$ [Eq. 9.3]

Cost of preferred equity:

$$k_p = \frac{D_p}{N_p}$$ [Eq. 9.4]

Cost of common equity:

Using constant-growth DVM:

$$k_s = \frac{D_1}{P_0} + g$$ [Eq. 9.6]

Using CAPM:

$$k_s = R_F + [b \times (k_m - R_F)]$$ [Eq. 9.7]

Cost of reinvested profits:

$$k_r = k_s$$ [Eq. 9.8]

Cost of new issue of common shares (DVM):

$$k_n = \frac{D_1}{N_n} + g$$ [Eq. 9.9]

Cost of new issue of common shares (CAPM):

$$k_n = R_F + \left[(k_m - R_F) \times b \times \frac{P_0}{N_n} \right]$$ [Eq. 9.10]

Weighted average cost of capital (WACC):

$$k_a = (w_i \times k_i) + (w_p \times k_p) + (w_s \times k_{r \text{ or } n})$$ [Eq. 9.11]

Break point:

$$BP_j = \frac{AF_j}{w_j}$$ [Eq. 9.12]

types of financing will increase, raising the firm's WACC. Break points, which are found by dividing the amount of funds available from a given financing source by its capital structure weight, represent the level of new financing at which the cost of one of the financing components rises, causing an upward shift in the MCC. The MCC is the firm's WACC associated with its next dollar of new financing. The MCC schedule relates the WACC to each level of total new financing.

 Explain how the marginal cost of capital (MCC) can be used with the investment opportunities schedule (IOS) to make the firm's financing/investment decisions. The IOS presents a ranking of currently available investments from those with the highest returns to those with the lowest returns. It is used in combination with the MCC to find the level of financing/investment that maximizes owners' wealth. With this approach, the firm accepts projects up to the point at which the marginal return on its investment equals its weighted marginal cost of capital.

SELF-TEST PROBLEM   (Solution in Appendix B)

ST 9–1   Specific costs, WACC, WMCC, and IOS   Humble Manufacturing is interested in measuring its overall cost of capital. Current investigation has gathered the following data. The firm's tax rate is 40 percent.

Debt   The firm can raise an unlimited amount of debt by selling $1,000 par value, 10 percent coupon rate, 10-year bonds on which *semiannual interest* payments will be made. To sell the issue, an average discount of $30 per bond must be given. The firm must also pay flotation costs of $20 per bond.

Preferred equity   The firm can sell $100 stated value preferred shares with an 11 percent dividend rate. The cost of issuing and selling the preferred shares is expected to be $4 per share. An unlimited amount of preferred shares can be sold under these terms.

Common equity   The firm expects to have $225,000 of reinvested profits available in the coming year. The firm's common shares currently sell for $80 per share. The most recent dividend paid by the firm on the common shares was $5.66 per share. The firm's dividends have been growing at an annual rate of 6 percent, and this rate is expected to continue in the future. The stock will have to be discounted by $2.50 per share, and flotation costs are expected to amount to $5.50 per share. The firm can sell an unlimited number of new common shares under these terms.

a. Calculate the specific cost of each source of financing. (Round to the nearest 0.1 percent.)
b. The firm uses the weights shown in the following table, which are based on target capital structure proportions, to calculate its weighted average cost of capital. (Round to the nearest 0.1 percent.)

Source of capital	Weight
Long-term debt	40%
Preferred equity	15
Common equity	45
Total	100%

(1) Calculate the single break point associated with the firm's financial situation. (*Hint:* This point results from the exhaustion of the firm's reinvested profits.)

(2) Calculate the weighted average cost of capital associated with new financing below the break point calculated in (1).

(3) Calculate the weighted average cost of capital associated with new financing above the break point calculated in (1).

c. Using the results of **b** along with the information shown in the following table on the available investment opportunities, draw the firm's marginal cost of capital (MCC) schedule and investment opportunities schedule (IOS).

Investment opportunity	Internal rate of return (IRR)	Initial investment
A	11.2%	$100,000
B	9.7	500,000
C	12.9	150,000
D	16.5	200,000
E	11.8	450,000
F	10.1	600,000
G	10.5	300,000

d. Which, if any, of the available investments do you recommend that the firm accept? Explain your answer. How much total new financing is required?

PROBLEMS

  9–1 **Cost of debt—Risk premiums**   Mulberry Printing's cost of long-term debt last year was 10 percent. This rate was attributable to a 7 percent risk-free cost of long-term debt, a 2 percent business risk premium, and a 1 percent financial risk premium. The firm currently wishes to obtain a long-term loan.

a. If the firm's business and financial risk are unchanged from the previous period and the risk-free cost of long-term debt is now 8 percent, at what rate would you expect the firm to obtain a long-term loan?

b. If, as a result of borrowing, the firm's financial risk will increase enough to raise the financial risk premium to 3 percent, how much would you expect the firm's borrowing cost to be?

c. One of the firm's competitors has a 1 percent business risk premium and a 2 percent financial risk premium. What is that firm's cost of long-term debt likely to be?

WARM-UP **9–2** **Concept of cost of capital**   Wren Manufacturing is in the process of analyzing its investment decision-making procedures. The two projects evaluated by the firm during the past month were projects 263 and 264. The basic variables for each project and the resulting decision actions are summarized in the following table.

Basic variables	Project 263	Project 264
Cost	$64,000	$58,000
Life	15 years	15 years
Expected return (IRR)	8%	15%
Least-cost financing		
Source	Debt	Equity
Cost (after-tax)	7%	16%
Decision		
Action	Accept	Reject
Reason	8% IRR > 7% cost	15% IRR < 16% cost

a. Evaluate the firm's decision-making procedures, and explain why the acceptance of project 263 and rejection of project 264 may not be in the owners' best interest.

b. If the firm maintains a capital structure containing 40 percent debt and 60 percent equity, find its weighted average cost using the data in the table.

c. Had the firm used the weighted average cost calculated in **b**, what actions would have been taken relative to projects 263 and 264?

d. Compare and contrast the firm's actions with your findings in **c.** Which decision method seems more appropriate? Explain why.

INTERMEDIATE **9–3** **Cost of debt using both methods**   Currently, Warren Industries can sell 15-year, $1,000 par-value bonds paying *annual interest* at a 12 percent coupon rate. As a result of current interest rates, the bonds can be sold for $1,010 each; flotation costs of $30 per bond will be incurred in this process. The firm is in the 40 percent tax bracket.

a. Find the net proceeds from sale of the bond, N_d.

b. Show the cash flows from the firm's point of view over the maturity of the bond.

c. Use the *IRR approach* with interpolation or a financial calculator to calculate the before-tax and after-tax cost of debt.

d. Use the *approximation formula* to estimate the before-tax and after-tax cost of debt.

e. Compare and contrast the cost of debt calculated in **c** and **d.** Which approach do you prefer? Why?

WARM-UP **9–4   Cost of debt using a financial calculator**   For each of the following $1,000 par-value bonds, assuming *semiannual interest* payment and a 40 percent tax rate, calculate the *after-tax* cost to maturity using a financial calculator.

Bond	Life	Underwriting fee	Discount (−) or premium (+)	Coupon rate
A	20 years	$25	−$20	9%
B	16	40	+ 10	10
C	15	30	− 15	12
D	25	15	Par	9
E	22	20	− 60	11

INTERMEDIATE **9–5   The cost of debt**   Gronseth Drywall Systems, Inc., is in discussions with its investment bankers regarding the issuance of new bonds. The investment banker has informed the firm that different maturities will carry different coupon rates and sell at different prices. The firm must choose among several alternatives. In each case, the bonds will have a $1,000 par value, the coupons will be paid semiannually, and flotation costs will be $30 per bond. The company is taxed at 40 percent. Calculate the after-tax cost of financing with each of the following alternatives.

Alternative	Coupon rate	Time to maturity	Premium or discount
A	9%	16 years	$250
B	7	5	50
C	6	7	par
D	5	10	−75

WARM-UP **9–6   Cost of preferred equity**   Taylor Systems has just issued preferred shares. The shares have a 12 percent annual dividend and a $100 stated value and were sold at $97.50 per share. In addition, flotation costs of $2.50 per share must be paid.
   a. Calculate the cost of the preferred shares.
   b. If the firm sells the preferred stock with a 10 percent annual dividend and nets $90 after flotation costs, what is its cost?

WARM-UP **9–7   Cost of preferred equity**   Determine the cost for each of the following preferred shares.

Preferred share	Stated value	Sale price	Flotation cost	Annual dividend
A	$100	$101	$9.00	11%
B	40	38	$3.50	8%
C	35	37	$4.00	$5.00
D	30	26	5% of par	$3.00
E	20	20	$2.50	9%

WARM-UP   **9–8** **Cost of common equity—CAPM** J&M Corporation common shares have a beta, b, of 1.2. The risk-free rate is 6 percent, and the market return is 11 percent.
a. Determine the market risk premium.
b. Determine the risk premium on J&M common stock.
c. Determine the required return that J&M common stock should provide.
d. Determine J&M's cost of common stock equity using the CAPM.

INTERMEDIATE   **9–9** **Cost of common equity** Ross Textiles wishes to measure its cost of common equity. The firm's common shares are currently selling for $57.50. The dividends per share paid for the past 5 years are shown in the following table.

Year	DPS
1998	$2.11
1999	2.30
2000	2.60
2001	2.92
2002	3.09

After discounting and flotation costs, the firm expects to net $52 per share on a new issue.
a. Determine the growth rate of dividends.
b. Determine the DPS the firm will pay in 2003.
c. Determine the net proceeds, N_n, that the firm actually receives.
d. Using the constant-growth DVM, determine the cost of reinvested profits, k_r.
e. Using the constant-growth DVM, determine the cost of new common shares, k_n.

INTERMEDIATE **9–10** **Cost of reinvested profits versus new common shares—DVM** Using the data for each firm shown in the following table, calculate the cost of reinvested profits and the cost of new common shares using the constant-growth DVM.

Firm	Current market price per share	Dividend growth rate	Projected dividend per share next year	Discount per share	Flotation cost per share
A	$50.00	8%	$2.25	$2.00	$1.00
B	20.00	4	1.00	0.50	1.50
C	42.50	6	2.00	1.00	2.00
D	19.00	2	2.10	1.30	1.70

INTERMEDIATE **9–11** **Cost of reinvested profits and new common shares—CAPM** Using the data for each firm shown in the following table, calculate the cost of reinvested profits and new common shares using the CAPM.

Firm	Beta	Current market price per share	Risk-free rate	Market-free premium	Total of discount and flotation costs
1	0.84	$15.40	3.2%	4.8%	$1.12
2	1.46	9.65	4.1	6.1	0.78
3	1.12	32.10	6.6	5.6	2.94
4	0.61	25.00	2.8	5.8	2.41

9–12 **The effect of tax rate on WACC**   Equity Lighting Corp. wishes to explore the effect the corporate tax rate has on its cost of capital. The firm wishes to maintain a capital structure of 30 percent debt, 10 percent preferred equity, and 60 percent common equity. The cost of financing with reinvested profits is 14 percent, the cost of preferred equity financing is 9 percent, and the before-tax cost of debt financing is 11 percent. Calculate the weighted average cost of capital (WACC) given the tax rate assumptions in parts **a** to **c**.

INTERMEDIATE

a. Tax rate = 40 percent
b. Tax rate = 35 percent
c. Tax rate = 25 percent
d. Describe the relationship between changes in the rate of taxation and the weighted average cost of capital. Explain the relationship.

WARM-UP

9–13 **WACC—Book weights**   Ridge Tool has on its books the amounts and specific (after-tax) costs shown in the following table for each source of capital.

Source of capital	Book value	Specific cost
Long-term debt	$700,000	5.3%
Preferred equity	50,000	12.0
Common equity	650,000	16.0

a. Calculate the firm's weighted average cost of capital using book value weights.
b. Explain how the firm can use this cost in the investment decision-making process.

INTERMEDIATE

9–14 **WACC—Book weights and market weights**   Webster Company has compiled the information shown in the following table.

Source of capital	Book value	Market value	After-tax cost
Long-term debt	$4,000,000	$3,840,000	6.0%
Preferred equity	40,000	60,000	13.0
Common equity	1,060,000	3,000,000	17.0
Total Value	$5,100,000	$6,900,000	

a. Calculate the weighted average cost of capital using book value weights.
b. Calculate the weighted average cost of capital using market value weights.
c. Compare the answers obtained in **a** and **b.** Explain the differences.

INTERMEDIATE  **9–15** **WACC and target weights** After careful analysis, Dexter Brothers has determined that its optimal capital structure is composed of the sources and target market value weights shown in the following table.

Source of capital	Target market value weight
Long-term debt	30%
Preferred equity	15
Common equity	55
Total	100%

The cost of debt is estimated to be 7.2 percent; the cost of preferred equity is estimated to be 13.5 percent; the cost of reinvested profits is estimated to be 16.0 percent; and the cost of new common shares is estimated to be 18.0 percent. All of these are after-tax rates. Currently, the company's debt represents 25 percent, preferred equity represents 10 percent, and common equity represents 65 percent of total capital based on the market values of the three components. The company expects to have a significant amount of reinvested profits available and does not expect to sell any new common shares.

a. Calculate the weighted average cost of capital based on historic market value weights.
b. Calculate the weighted average cost of capital based on target market value weights.
c. Explain the difference.

  9–16 **Cost of capital and break point** Edna Recording Studios, Inc., reported earnings available for common shareholders of $4,200,000 last year. From that, the company paid a dividend of $1.26 on each of its 1,000,000 common shares outstanding. The capital structure of the company includes 40 percent debt, 10 percent preferred equity, and 50 percent common equity. The company's tax rate is 40 percent.

CHALLENGE

a. If the market price of common stock is $40 and dividends are expected to grow at a rate of 6 percent a year for the foreseeable future, what is the company's cost of reinvested profits?
b. If flotation costs on new shares of common stock amount to $1 per share, what is the company's cost of financing with new common shares?
c. The company can issue preferred shares with a $25 par value and a $2 dividend. Flotation costs would amount to $3 per share. What is the cost of preferred equity financing?
d. The company can issue $1,000 par, 10 percent coupon, 5-year bonds paid semiannually that can be sold for $1,200 each. Flotation costs would amount to $25 per bond. Use your financial calculator to figure the cost of new debt financing.
e. What is the maximum investment that Edna Recording can make in new projects before it must issue new common shares?

f. What is the WACC for projects with a required investment of between zero and the amount calculated in part **e**?

g. What is the MCC for projects with a required investment above the amount calculated in part **e**? *Hint:* The only cost that changes is common equity.

 **9–17 Calculation of specific costs, WACC, and MCC**   Dillon Labs has asked its financial manager to measure the cost of each specific type of capital as well as the weighted average cost of capital. The weighted average cost is to be measured by using the following weights: 40 percent long-term debt, 10 percent preferred equity, and 50 percent common equity. The firm's tax rate is 40 percent.

CHALLENGE

Debt   The firm can sell for $980 a 10-year, $1,000-par-value bond paying *semiannual interest* at a 10 percent coupon rate. Flotation costs of 3 percent of the par value are required in addition to the discount of $20 per bond.

Preferred equity   Eight percent (annual dividend) preferred stock having a stated value of $100 can be sold for $65. An additional fee of $2 per share must be paid to the underwriters.

Common equity   The firm's common shares are currently selling for $50 per share. The dividend expected to be paid at the end of the coming year (2003) is $4. Its dividend payments, which have been approximately 60 percent of earnings per share in each of the past 5 years, are as shown in the following table.

Year	DPS
1998	$2.85
1999	3.15
2000	3.30
2001	3.50
2002	3.75

It is expected that, to sell, new common shares must be discounted at $5 per share and the firm must also pay $3 per share in flotation costs. Dividend payments are expected to continue at 60 percent of earnings.

a. Calculate the specific cost of each source of financing.

b. If earnings available for common shareholders are expected to be $7 million, what is the break point associated with reinvested profits?

c. Determine the weighted average cost of capital between zero and the break point calculated in **b**.

d. Determine the weighted average cost of capital for one dollar of additional financing just beyond the break point calculated in **b**.

 **9–18 Calculation of specific costs, WACC, and MCC**   Lang Enterprises is interested in measuring its overall cost of capital. Current investigation has gathered the following data. The firm's tax rate is 40 percent.

CHALLENGE

Debt   The firm can raise debt by selling $1,000-par-value, 8 percent coupon interest rate, 20-year bonds on which *semiannual interest* payments will be made. To sell the issue, an average discount of $30 per bond would have to be given. The firm also must pay flotation costs of $30 per bond.

Preferred equity   The firm can sell preferred shares with $95 stated value and an 8 percent dividend rate. The cost of issuing and selling the preferred shares is expected to be $5 per share. A sufficient amount of preferred shares can be sold under these terms to meet all financing needs.

Common equity   The firm's common shares are currently selling for $90 per share. The firm expects to pay cash dividends of $7 per share next year. The firm's dividends have been growing at an annual rate of 6 percent, and this is expected to continue into the future. The stock must be discounted by $7 per share, and flotation costs are expected to amount to $5 per share. The firm can sell a sufficient number of new common shares under these terms to meet all financing needs. Lang expects to have available $100,000 of reinvested profits in the coming year.

a. Calculate the specific cost of each source of financing. (Round answers to the nearest 0.1%.)
b. The firm's capital structure weights are shown below. Calculate Lang's weighted average cost of capital. (Round answer to the nearest 0.1%.)

Source of capital	Weight
Long-term debt	30%
Preferred equity	20
Common equity	50
Total	100%

c. Calculate the single break point associated with the firm's financial situation. To what financing range does the cost calculated in **b** apply?
d. Calculate the weighted average cost of capital associated with total new financing above the break point calculated in **c**.

     9–19   **Integrative—WACC, MCC, and IOS**   Cartwell Products has compiled the data shown in the following table for the current costs of its three sources of capital— long-term debt, preferred equity, and common equity—for various ranges of new financing.

CHALLENGE

Source of capital	Range of new financing	After-tax cost
Long-term debt	$0 to $320,000	6%
	$320,000 and above	8
Preferred equity	$0 and above	17%
Common equity	$0 to $200,000	20%
	$200,000 and above	24

The company's capital structure weights used in calculating its weighted average cost of capital are shown in the following table.

Source of capital	Weight
Long-term debt	40%
Preferred equity	20
Common equity	40
Total	100%

a. Determine the break points and ranges of new financing associated with each source of capital. At what financing levels will Cartwell's weighted average cost of capital change?
b. Calculate the weighted average cost of capital for each range of total new financing found in **a**. (*Hint:* There are three ranges.)
c. Using the results of **b** along with the following information on the available investment opportunities, draw the firm's marginal cost of capital (MCC) schedule and investment opportunities schedule (IOS).

Investment opportunity	Expected return (IRR)	Initial investment
A	19%	$200,000
B	15	300,000
C	22	100,000
D	14	600,000
E	23	200,000
F	13	100,000
G	21	300,000
H	17	100,000
I	16	400,000

d. Which, if any, of the available investments do you recommend that the firm accept? Explain your answer.

CHALLENGE

9–20 **Integrative—WACC, MCC, and IOS**   Grainger Corp., a supplier of fitness equipment, is trying to decide which proposed projects in its investment opportunities schedule (IOS) it should undertake. The firm's cost of capital schedule and investment opportunities schedule are presented as follows:

Cost of capital schedule

Range of new financing	Source	Weight	After-tax cost
0–$600,000	Debt	0.50	6.3%
	Preferred equity	0.10	12.5
	Common equity	0.40	15.3
$600,000–$1,000,000	Debt	0.50	6.3%
	Preferred equity	0.10	12.5
	Common equity	0.40	16.4
$1,000,000 and above	Debt	0.50	7.8%
	Preferred equity	0.10	12.5
	Common equity	0.40	16.4

Investment opportunities schedule

Investment opportunity	Internal rate of return	Cost
Project H	14.5%	$200,000
Project G	13.0	700,000
Project K	12.8	500,000
Project M	11.4	600,000

a. Complete the cost of capital schedule by calculating the WACC and MCC for the various ranges of new financing.

b. Identify those projects that you recommend Grainger Corp. undertake in the next year.

c. Illustrate your recommendations by drawing a graph of Grainger's costs and opportunities similar to Figure 9.2.

d. Explain why certain projects are recommended and other(s) are not.

9–21 Integrative—WACC and MCC   Henry Enterprises is planning to invest $7.5 million in new capital assets in the upcoming fiscal year. The company's VP of marketing knows the company has to determine the company's cost of capital, but is not sure how to do this. She approaches you, a junior finance executive in Henry Enterprises, to request your assistance in calculating the cost. She wants an answer in less than one hour.

Henry Enterprises has the following capital structure, which is viewed to be optimal:

Long-term debt (14% coupon, due in 15 years)	$25,000,000
Preferred shares (6% dividend, 25,000 shares outstanding)	2,500,000
Common shares (750,000 shares outstanding)	5,000,000
Retained earnings	7,500,000
Total capital	$40,000,000

Other information the marketing VP thought might be useful is provided below:
- The current bank prime rate is 8.0 percent.
- The yield on 3-month government of Canada t-bills is expected to be 7 percent.

- A new issue of long-term debt with a life of 25 years would require a coupon rate of 10 percent and would be sold at a discount of 1.5 percent of par. Flotation costs would be another 1.5 percent of par.
- The current issue of preferred shares has a stated value of $100. A new issue of preferred shares would require a dividend of 8 percent. Flotation costs would be 4 percent of the stated value.
- The rate of return on the market portfolio is expected to average 14 percent over the immediate future.
- Henry Enterprises' beta, whatever that is, is thought to be 1.3.
- Henry Enterprises' net income after tax was $2,025,000 and the company paid common share dividends of $1 per share.
- Henry's common shares are currently trading for $25 per share. A new share issue would be sold at a 2 percent discount to the current price and flotation costs would be $1 per share.
- The company's tax rate is 39 percent.

a. Calculate Henry Enterprises' cost of capital for the upcoming fiscal year. Explain to the VP of marketing what cost of capital is and how it would be used by the company.

b. Based on the above analysis, the VP of marketing is concerned that the company will reject launching a new product that was recently developed by the marketing department. Since Henry Enterprises can borrow at prime plus 50 basis points, she suggests that this rate be used to evaluate the proposed launch of the new product. Develop a detailed written response to the VP explaining your views on this suggestion.

| CASE CHAPTER 9 | Making Star Products' Financing/Investment Decision |

Star Products Company is a growing manufacturer of automobile accessories whose stock is actively traded on the Toronto Venture Exchange. During 2002, the Windsor, Ontario–based company experienced sharp increases in both sales and earnings. Because of this recent growth, Melissa Jen, the company's treasurer, wants to make sure that available funds are being used in the most efficient manner. Management policy is to maintain the current capital structure proportions of 30 percent long-term debt, 10 percent preferred equity, and 60 percent common equity for at least the next 3 years. The firm is in the 40 percent tax bracket.

Star's division and product managers have presented several competing investment opportunities to Ms. Jen. However, because funds are limited, choices of which projects to accept must be made. The investment opportunities schedule (IOS) is shown in the following table.

Investment Opportunities Schedule (IOS) for Star Products Company

Investment opportunity	Internal rate of return (IRR)	Initial investment
A	15%	$400,000
B	22	200,000
C	25	700,000
D	23	400,000
E	17	500,000
F	19	600,000
G	14	500,000

To estimate the firm's weighted average cost of capital (WACC), Ms. Jen contacted a leading investment banking firm, which provided the financing cost data shown in the following table.

Financing Cost Data Star Products Company

Long-term debt: The firm can raise $450,000 of additional debt by selling 15-year, $1,000-par-value, 9% coupon interest rate bonds that pay *semiannual interest*. It expects to net $960 per bond after flotation costs. Any debt in excess of $450,000 will have a before-tax cost, k_d, of 13%.

Preferred equity: Preferred shares can be issued with a $70 stated value, and pay a dividend of 14%. Star will net $65 per share after flotation costs.

Common equity: The firm expects dividends and earnings per share to be $0.96 and $3.20, respectively, in 2003 and to continue to grow at a constant rate of 11% per year. The firm's stock currently sells for $12 per share. Star expects to have $1,500,000 of reinvested profits available in the coming year. The firm can raise additional equity financing by selling new common shares, netting $9 per share after discounting and flotation costs.

Required

a. Calculate the cost of each source of financing, as specified:
   (1) Long-term debt, first $450,000.
   (2) Long-term debt, greater than $450,000.
   (3) Preferred equity.
   (4) Common equity, first $1,500,000.
   (5) Common equity, greater than $1,500,000.
b. Find the break points associated with each source of capital, and use them to specify each of the ranges of total new financing over which the firm's weighted average cost of capital (WACC) remains constant.
c. Calculate the weighted average cost of capital (WACC) over each of the ranges of total new financing specified in b.

d. Using your findings in **c** along with the investment opportunities schedule (IOS), draw the firm's marginal cost of capital (MCC) and IOS schedules on the same graph.

e. Which, if any, of the available investments would you recommend that the firm accept? Explain your answer.

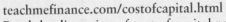

WEB EXERCISES   LINKS TO PRACTICE

Visit the following Web sites and complete the suggested exercises. These exercises will allow you to review practical applications of the chapter topics as well as explore the wealth of information regarding managerial finance that is available on the Internet.

teachmefinance.com/costofcapital.html
Read the discussion of cost of capital provided on this Web site and then answer the following questions.

1. Why do "retained earnings" (this should really read *reinvested profits*) have a cost? Why shouldn't a company consider reinvested profits as free money?
2. What methods can be used to calculate the cost of reinvested profits?
3. Summarize the remaining discussion of cost of capital provided on this site.

pages.stern.nyu.edu/~adamodar/New_Home_Page/datafile/wacc.htm
This Web site provides detailed information regarding the cost of capital for numerous industries in the United States and Canada. For the advertising, e-commerce, Canadian banking, average electric utility, and computer software and services industries, indicate the following:

1. The number of firms in the industry.
2. The risk of the industry as measured by beta.
3. The cost of equity and debt capital for the industry.
4. The average percentages of equity and debt in the capital structure of the industries.
5. The overall cost of capital for the industry.
6. What does this analysis indicate about the investment opportunities that the various industries could undertake?

www.bankofcanada.ca/pdf/annual_page44_page45.pdf
www.barra.com/research/canada_index/default.asp
The first Web site provides the prime business loan rate in Canada, by month, for the years 1935–2001. Consider the information and then answer the following questions.

1. What was the prime interest rate in January 1935?
2. Between January 1935 and December 1965, what was the range of the prime rate? What does this suggest to you?
3. What is the highest the prime interest rate has been? When was that?

4. What is the prime interest rate now? (You will need to explore the Web site further to find this data. Start by clicking the Back button on your browser.)
5. Over the past 10 years, what were the lowest and highest prime rates and in which month and year did these occur?

Click the Back button on your browser. Click on the All Corporates, long-term—B14048—Nov. 1997 link under the Other Bonds: Average Weighted Yield (Scotia Capital) heading.

6. Answer Questions 3 to 5 above, but replace prime rate with long-term corporate bond yields.

Now go to the second Web site listed above.

7. What was the annualized 10-year return (average annual return over 10 years) on common shares as measured by the Barra Canada Growth Index and Barra Canada Value Index? How do these returns compare to your answers in Questions 5 and 6?
8. What is the implication of the analysis completed above?

10 Leverage and Capital Structure

LEARNING GOALS

LG1 Discuss the role of breakeven analysis, how to determine the operating breakeven point, and the effect of changing costs on the breakeven point.

LG2 Understand operating, financial, and total leverage and the relationships among them.

LG3 Describe the basic types of capital, external assessment of capital structure, and capital structure theory.

LG4 Explain the optimal capital structure using a graphic view of the firm's debt, equity, and weighted average cost of capital functions, and a modified form of the zero-growth valuation model.

LG5 Discuss the graphic presentation, risk considerations, and basic shortcomings of using the EBIT–EPS approach to compare alternative capital structures.

LG6 Review the return and risk of alternative capital structures and their linkage to market value, and other important capital structure considerations.

10.1 Leverage

financial lever
The use of fixed assets in the company's operation and/or the use of debt financing in the capital structure.

Leverage is the advantage gained by using a lever. To move a large boulder, the lever might be a smaller rock and a long piece of wood. To lift a car, the lever is a jack. Applying this to finance, the boulder (or car) is the return to the company's owners which is measured by return on common equity (ROE) or earnings per share (EPS). The **financial lever** is the use of fixed assets in the company's operation and/or the use of debt financing in the capital structure. The benefit of leverage is that it can magnify returns to common shareholders, the owners of the company. The operating structure and capital structure

Jacking Up Owners' Wealth

Remember from your science class that a lever is a simple instrument that gives you more power. Although we think of levers being used principally to lift weights in various situations, the principle of leverage also is demonstrated in instruments such as scissors, nutcrackers, crowbars, and catapults. Leverage in finance involves the use of fixed costs and/or debt financing (the lever) to magnify returns to the company's owners. Leverage is desirable to common shareholders because it produces more earning power per common share.

However, the use of leverage in the firm's operating and capital structures has the potential also to increase the firm's risk. This chapter will show that leverage and capital structure are closely related concepts that can be used to minimize the firm's cost of capital and to maximize owners' wealth.

selected by a company significantly affect its value. Increases in leverage increase risk and expected return; decreases in leverage decrease risk and expected returns.

Unlike some causes of risk, management has almost complete control over the risk introduced through the use of leverage. Because of its effect on value, the financial manager must understand how to measure and evaluate leverage, particularly when making capital structure decisions.

The three basic types of leverage can best be defined with reference to the firm's income statement, as shown in the general income statement format in Table 10.1:

1. *Operating leverage* is concerned with the relationship between the firm's sales revenue and its earnings before interest and taxes, or EBIT. (EBIT is a descriptive label for *operating profits*.)
2. *Financial leverage* is concerned with the relationship between the firm's EBIT and its earnings per share (EPS).
3. *Total leverage* is concerned with the relationship between the firm's sales revenue and EPS.

We will examine the three types of leverage concepts in detail in sections that follow. First, though, we will look at breakeven analysis, which lays the foundation for leverage concepts by demonstrating the effects of fixed costs on the firm's operations.

Breakeven Analysis

breakeven analysis
Indicates the level of operations necessary to cover all operating costs and the profitability associated with various levels of sales.

operating breakeven point
The level of sales necessary to cover all *operating costs*; the point at which EBIT = $0.

🔑 **Career Key**
The *marketing* department uses breakeven analysis in pricing and new product decisions.

Breakeven analysis, sometimes called **cost-volume-profit analysis,** is used by the firm (1) to determine the level of operations necessary to cover all operating costs and (2) to evaluate the profitability associated with various levels of sales. The firm's **operating breakeven point** is the level of sales necessary to cover all *operating costs*. At that point, earnings before interest and taxes equals $0.[1]

The first step in finding the operating breakeven point is to separate all operating costs into two categories: fixed and variable operating costs. *Fixed costs* are a function of time, not sales volume, and are typically contractual; rent, for example, is a fixed cost. *Variable costs* vary directly with sales and are a function of volume, not time; shipping costs, for example, are a variable cost. Some costs are semi-variable; they are partly fixed and partly variable. Equipment maintenance is one example. Regardless of production volume, a certain amount of

---

TABLE 10.1 **General Income Statement Format and Types of Leverage**

Operating leverage {	Sales revenue
	Less: Cost of goods sold
	Gross margin
	Less: Operating expenses
	Earnings before interest and taxes (EBIT)
	Less: Interest
	Earnings before taxes
	Less: Taxes
Financial leverage {	Net income after taxes (NIAT)
	Less: Preferred share dividends
	Earnings available for common shareholders (EAC)
	Earnings per share (EPS)

Total leverage

---

1. Occasionally, the breakeven point is calculated so that it represents the point at which *all operating and financial costs* are covered. Our concern in this chapter is not with this method of calculating the breakeven point.

TABLE 10.2	Examples of Fixed, Variable, and Semivariable Expenses	
Fixed	Variable	Semi-variable
Rent	Raw materials	Maintenance
Amortization	Direct (factory) labour	Repairs
Management salaries	Direct factory overhead	Utilities
Property taxes	Sales commissions	
Marketing		
Research and development		

maintenance must be performed on production equipment (a fixed cost). At higher production volumes, more maintenance would have to be performed (a variable cost). In this chapter, it is assumed that all semi-variable costs are separated into their fixed and variable components. Table 10.2 provides examples of the three types of operating expenses.

The Algebraic Approach

Using the following variables, we can recast the operating portion of the firm's income statement given in Table 10.1 into the algebraic representation shown in Table 10.3.

$$P = \text{sale price per unit}$$
$$Q = \text{sales quantity in units}$$
$$FC = \text{fixed operating cost per period}$$
$$VC = \text{variable operating cost per unit}$$

Rewriting the algebraic calculations in Table 10.2 as a formula for earnings before interest and taxes yields Equation 10.1:

$$\text{EBIT} = (P \times Q) - (VC \times Q) - FC \qquad (10.1)$$

Simplifying Equation 10.1 yields

$$\text{EBIT} = Q \times (P - VC) - FC \qquad (10.2)$$

TABLE 10.3	Operating Leverage, Costs, and Breakeven Analysis	
	Item	Algebraic representation
Operating leverage	Sales revenue	$(P \times Q)$
	Less: Variable operating costs	$-(VC \times Q)$
	Less: Fixed operating costs	$- \quad FC$
	Earnings before interest and taxes	EBIT

As noted above, the operating breakeven point is the level of sales at which all fixed and variable *operating costs* are covered—the level at which EBIT equals $0. Setting EBIT equal to $0 and solving Equation 10.2 for Q yields:

$$Q = \frac{FC}{P - VC} \tag{10.3}$$

Since $P - VC$ is the gross margin per unit (GM/unit), Equation 10.3 can be further simplified as follows:

$$Q = \frac{FC}{GM/\text{unit}} \tag{10.4}$$

For Equations 10.3 and 10.4, Q is the company's operating breakeven point in *units*. This method of solving for the operating breakeven point implicitly assumes that the firm sells a single product, so Q is in number of units. Since many companies sell more than one product, the operating breakeven point is often found in terms of total sales revenue (S). In this case, rather than GM/unit, the gross margin percent ($GM\%$) is used as follows:

$$S = \frac{FC}{GM\%} \tag{10.5}$$

The $GM\%$ can be found on either a per unit or total dollar basis as follows:

Per unit	*Total dollar*
$P - VC = GM/\text{unit}$	$(P \times Q) - (VC \times Q) = Total\ GM$
$GM\% = \dfrac{GM/\text{unit}}{P}$	$GM\% = \dfrac{Total\ GM}{P \times Q}$

Therefore, the general formula for breakeven is $FC \div GM$. GM/unit is used to 1 point in total sales revenue (S).

Example ▼ Assume that Cheryl's Posters, a small poster retailer, has fixed operating costs of $2,500, its sale price per unit (poster) is $10, and its variable operating cost per unit is $5. Determine Cheryl's Posters' breakeven point in both units and total sales revenue. Applying Equations 10.4 and 10.5 yields:

$$Q = \frac{\$2,500}{\$10 - \$5} = \frac{\$2,500}{\$5} = 500 \text{ units}$$

$$S = \frac{\$2,500}{\dfrac{\$10 - \$5}{\$10}} = \frac{\$2,500}{\dfrac{\$5}{\$10}} = \frac{\$2,500}{0.50} = \$5,000$$

Note that once breakeven in units is calculated, an alternative to calculate breakeven in dollars is to multiply Q by P. For Cheryl's Posters, this would be $5,000 (500 units × $10) or $5,000 as calculated above.

At sales of 500 units ($5,000), the firm's EBIT should just equal $0. The firm will have positive EBIT for sales greater than 500 units ($5,000) and negative EBIT, or a loss, for sales less than 500 units ($5,000). We can confirm this by

FIGURE 10.1

Breakeven Analysis
Graphic operating
breakeven analysis

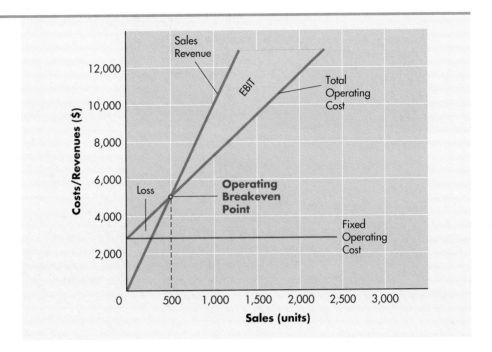

substituting values above and below 500 units, along with the other values given, into Equation 10.1.

The Graphic Approach

Figure 10.1 presents in graph form the breakeven analysis of the data in the preceding example. The firm's operating breakeven point is the point at which its *total operating cost*—the sum of its fixed and variable operating costs—equals sales revenue. At this point, EBIT equals $0. The figure shows that for sales *below* 500 units ($5,000), total operating cost exceeds sales revenue, and EBIT is less than $0 (a loss). For sales *above* the breakeven point of 500 units ($5,000), sales revenue exceeds total operating cost, and EBIT is greater than $0.

Changing Costs and the Operating Breakeven Point

A firm's operating breakeven point is sensitive to a number of variables: fixed operating cost (*FC*), the sale price per unit (*P*), and the variable operating cost per unit (*VC*). The effects of increases or decreases in these variables can be readily seen by referring to Equation 10.3. The sensitivity of the breakeven point to an *increase* in each of these variables is summarized in Table 10.4. As might be expected, an increase in cost (*FC* or *VC*) tends to increase the operating breakeven point, whereas an increase in the sale price per unit (*P*) will decrease the operating breakeven point.

Example ▼ Assume that Cheryl's Posters wishes to evaluate the impact of several options: (1) increasing fixed operating costs to $3,000, (2) increasing the sale price per unit to $12.50, (3) increasing the variable operating cost per unit to $7.50, and (4) simultaneously implementing all three of these changes. Substituting the appropriate data into Equation 10.4 yields the following results:

$$\text{(1) Operating breakeven point} = \frac{\$3,000}{\$10 - \$5} = 600 \text{ units}$$

$$\text{(2) Operating breakeven point} = \frac{\$2,500}{\$12.50 - \$5} = 333\frac{1}{3} \text{ units}$$

$$\text{(3) Operating breakeven point} = \frac{\$2,500}{\$10 - \$7.50} = 1,000 \text{ units}$$

$$\text{(4) Operating breakeven point} = \frac{\$3,000}{\$12.50 - \$7.50} = 600 \text{ units}$$

Comparing the resulting operating breakeven points to the initial value of 500 units, we can see that the cost increases (actions 1 and 3) raise the breakeven point, whereas the revenue increase (action 2) lowers the breakeven point. The combined effect of increasing all three variables (action 4) also results in an increased operating breakeven point. Note that in all four cases, the breakeven point in sales (S) is simply the breakeven point in units (Q) times the selling price per unit (P), $Q \times \$10$.

▲

We now turn our attention to the three types of leverage.

Operating Leverage

operating leverage
The use of *fixed operating costs* to magnify the effects of changes in sales on the firm's earnings before interest and taxes.

Operating leverage results from the existence of *fixed operating costs* in the firm's cost structure. Using the structure presented in Table 10.3, we can define **operating leverage** as the use of *fixed operating costs* to magnify the effects of changes in sales on the firm's earnings before interest and taxes.

E x a m p l e ▼ Using the data for Cheryl's Posters (sale price, $P = \$10$ per unit; variable operating cost, $VC = \$5$ per unit; fixed operating cost, $FC = \$2,500$), Figure 10.2 presents the operating breakeven graph originally shown in Figure 10.1. The additional notations on the graph indicate that as the firm's sales increase from 1,000 to 1,500 units (Q_1 to Q_2), its EBIT increases from $2,500 to $5,000 ($EBIT_1$ to $EBIT_2$). In other words, a 50 percent increase in sales (1,000 to 1,500 units) results in a 100 percent increase in EBIT. Table 10.5 includes the data for

TABLE 10.4	Sensitivity of Operating Breakeven Point to Increases in Key Breakeven Variables
Increase in variable	**Effect on operating breakeven point**
Fixed operating cost *(FC)*	Increase
Sale price per unit *(P)*	Decrease
Variable operating cost per unit *(VC)*	Increase

Note: Decreases in each of the variables shown would have the opposite effect from that indicated on the breakeven point.

FIGURE 10.2

Operating Leverage
Breakeven analysis and operating leverage

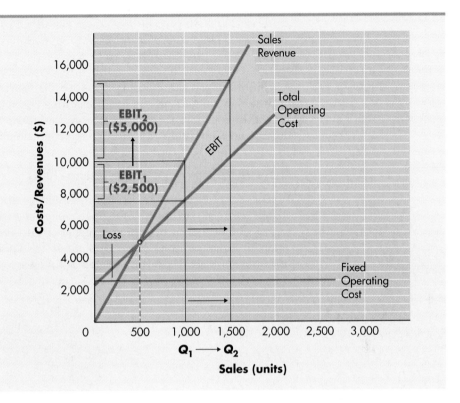

Career Key
The *operations* department will be concerned with the firm's operating leverage. The actions the firm takes and how it structures its operating costs will have a major impact on the firm's operating leverage.

Figure 10.2 as well as relevant data for a 500-unit sales level. We can illustrate two cases using the 1,000-unit sales level as a reference point:

Case 1   A 50 percent *increase* in sales (from 1,000 to 1,500 units) results in a 100 percent *increase* in earnings before interest and taxes (from $2,500 to $5,000).

TABLE 10.5   **The EBIT for Various Sales Levels**

		Case 2		Case 1
		−50%		+50%
Sales (in units)		500	1,000	1,500
Sales revenue[a]		$5,000	$10,000	$15,000
Less: Variable operating costs[b]		2,500	5,000	7,500
Less: Fixed operating costs		2,500	2,500	2,500
Earnings before interest and taxes (EBIT)		$ 0	$ 2,500	$ 5,000
		−100%		+100%

[a]Sales revenue = $10/unit × sales in units.
[b]Variable operating costs = $5/unit × sales in units.

Case 2   A 50 percent *decrease* in sales (from 1,000 to 500 units) results in a 100 percent *decrease* in earnings before interest and taxes (from $2,500 to $0).

From the preceding example, we see that operating leverage works in *both directions*. When a firm has fixed operating costs, operating leverage is present. An increase in sales results in a more-than-proportional increase in EBIT; a decrease in sales results in a more-than-proportional decrease in EBIT.

Measuring the Degree of Operating Leverage (DOL)

degree of operating leverage (DOL)
The numerical measure of the firm's operating leverage.

Whenever the percentage change in EBIT resulting from a given percentage change in sales is greater than the percentage change in sales, operating leverage exists. The **degree of operating leverage (DOL)** is the numerical measure of a company's operating leverage. As long as the DOL is greater than 1, there is operating leverage. DOL is calculated as follows:[2]

$$\text{DOL at base sales level } Q = \frac{(P \times Q) - (Q \times VC)}{(P \times Q) - (Q \times VC) - FC} \tag{10.6}$$

$$= \frac{TR - TVC}{TR - TVC - FC} \tag{10.6a}$$

$$= \frac{GM\$}{EBIT} \tag{10.6b}$$

Note that *TR* is total sales revenue and *TVC* is total variable costs, both at production volume of Q.[3]

Example ▼   Substituting $Q = 1,000$, $P = \$10$, $VC = \$5$, and $FC = \$2,500$ into Equation 10.6 yields the following result:

DOL at 1,000 units =

$$\frac{1,000 \times (\$10 - \$5)}{1,000 \times (\$10 - \$5) - \$2,500} = \frac{\$10,000 - \$5,000}{\$10,000 - \$5,000 - \$2,500} = \frac{\$5,000}{\$2,500} = 2.0$$

The use of the formula results in the same value for DOL (2.0) as that found by using Table 10.5. The DOL of 2 means that for every 1 percent change in sales (either up or down), EBIT will change by the DOL, in this case 2 percent (again either up or down). This was highlighted in Table 10.5.

For Case 1, if sales increase by 50 percent, EBIT is expected to increase by 100 percent (50% × 2). For Case 2, if sales decrease by 50 percent, EBIT is expected to decrease by 100 percent (−50% × 2). The higher the DOL, the greater the impact changes in sales have on EBIT. Higher levels of DOL imply greater operating risk. ▲

---

2. The degree of operating leverage also depends on the base level of sales used as a point of reference. The closer the base sales level used is to the operating breakeven point, the greater the operating leverage. *Comparison of the degree of operating leverage of two firms is valid only when the base level of sales used for each firm is the same.*

3. Because the concept of leverage is *linear*, positive and negative changes of equal magnitude will always result in equal degrees of leverage when the same base sales level is used as a point of reference. This relationship holds for all types of leverage discussed in this chapter.

Fixed Costs and Operating Leverage

Changes in fixed operating costs affect operating leverage significantly. Firms can sometimes incur fixed operating costs rather than variable operating costs and at other times may be able to substitute one type of cost for the other. For example, a firm could modernize its production facilities, replacing variable cost direct labour with fixed cost fixed assets. Technologically advanced equipment results in increased productivity, lower variable costs, and higher fixed costs. Or it could compensate sales representatives with a fixed salary and bonus rather than on a pure percent-of-sales commission basis. The effects of changes in operating costs on operating leverage can best be illustrated by continuing our example.

Example ▼ Assume that Cheryl's Posters exchanges a portion of its variable operating costs for fixed operating costs by eliminating sales commissions and increasing sales salaries. This exchange results in a reduction in the variable operating cost per unit from $5 to $4.50 and an increase in the fixed operating costs from $2,500 to $3,000. Table 10.6 presents an analysis like that in Table 10.5, but using new costs. Although the EBIT of $2,500 at the 1,000-unit sales level is the same as before the shift in operating cost structure, Table 10.6 shows that the firm has increased its operating leverage by shifting to greater fixed operating costs.

With the substitution of the appropriate values into Equation 10.6, the degree of operating leverage at the 1,000-unit base level of sales becomes

$$\text{DOL at 1,000 units} = \frac{1,000 \times (\$10 - \$4.50)}{1,000 \times (\$10 - \$4.50) - \$3,000} = \frac{\$5,500}{\$2,500} = 2.2$$

By comparing this value to the DOL of 2.0 before the shift to more fixed costs, it is clear that the higher the firm's fixed operating costs relative to variable operating costs, the greater the degree of operating leverage. Higher levels of DOL indicate both greater return and risk: greater return if sales increase, greater risk if
▲ sales decrease.

TABLE 10.6   **Operating Leverage and Increased Fixed Costs**

	Case 2		Case 1
	−50%		+50%
Sales (in units)	500	1,000	1,500
Sales revenue[a]	$5,000	$10,000	$15,000
Less: Variable operating costs[b]	2,250	4,500	6,750
Less: Fixed operating costs	3,000	3,000	3,000
Earnings before interest and taxes (EBIT)	−$ 250	$ 2,500	$ 5,250
	−110%		+110%

[a]Sales revenue was calculated as indicated in Table 10.5.
[b]Variable operating costs = $4.50/unit × sales in units.

IN PRACTICE

Simulating Operating Leverage

CAE is the world leader in the sale of full flight simulators used to train airline pilots, with a global market share exceeding 80 percent, and the second largest independent civil aviation training provider. The company is also the largest Canadian-based defence contractor. CAE has operations around the globe and, for the March 31, 2002 fiscal year, annual revenues of over $1.1 billion.

For the 2002 fiscal year, CAE achieved the goal of more profitable growth with net earnings from continuing operations increasing 42 percent from the previous year. This was driven by strong productivity improvements and significant growth from each of the core businesses: the civil and military simulation and training units, as well as marine. Net earnings more than doubled in two years. Future growth is underpinned by a record $2.7 billion backlog of orders. CAE views their business as a major provider of integrated training solutions for civilian and military customers engaged in flight, marine, and land-based activities.

Such an operation incurs the bulk of its costs up front, in the design and production of the product (the flight simulator) or in the establishment of the training programs. With CAE's sales coming from these two business lines, the potential for economies of scale to magnify returns is huge. In addition, in 2002, CAE was able to reduce production time by 22.2 percent, providing additional operational leverage. As a result, increases in sales lead to large increases in returns as measured by operating earnings (EBIT). The following results for CAE illustrate the benefit of operating leverage for the 2002 fiscal year:

	2001 fiscal year	2002 fiscal year	% change
Sales revenue (in millions)	$891.4	$1,126.5	26.37
EBIT (in millions)	$151.9	$242.3	59.51
DOL		2.26	

In this example, DOL was calculated by dividing the percentage change in EBIT by the percentage change in sales (59.51% ÷ 26.37%). This is an alternative method to calculate DOL when information for two separate periods (like two fiscal years) is provided. CAE's use of operating leverage magnified the increase in EBIT in 2002. Every 1 percent increase in sales resulted in a 2.26 percent increase in EBIT. Obviously, the owners of CAE (the common shareholders) would benefit from operating leverage through higher returns.

Over these two fiscal years (April 1, 2000 to March 31, 2002), the price of CAE's common shares on the Toronto Stock Exchange increased from $6.70 to $11.72, hitting a high of $15.45. CAE's use of operating leverage magnified returns to shareholders. (*Note:* It is important to remember that this example represents only two years of data and the CAE's DOL may change in the future).

REFERENCES: CAE, 2002 Annual Report.

Financial Leverage

financial leverage
The use of *fixed financial costs* to magnify the effects of changes in earnings before interest and taxes on the firm's earnings per share.

Financial leverage results from the presence of *fixed financial costs* in the firm's income stream. Using the framework in Table 10.1, we can define **financial leverage** as the use of *fixed financial costs* to magnify the effects of changes in earnings before interest and taxes on the firm's earnings per share.[4] The two

---

4. Rather than EPS, return on common equity (ROE) could be used to evaluate financial leverage. When EPS is used to examine financial leverage, the number of common shares must remain unchanged at different levels of EBIT.

fixed financial costs that may be found on the firm's income statement are (1) interest on debt and (2) preferred share dividends. These charges must be paid regardless of the amount of EBIT available to pay them.[5]

Example ▼ Chen Foods, a small Oriental food company, expects EBIT of $10,000 in the current year. It has a $20,000 bond with a 10 percent (annual) coupon rate and an issue of 600 shares of $4 (annual dividend per share) preferred shares outstanding. It also has 1,000 common shares outstanding. The annual interest on the bond issue is $2,000 (0.10 × $20,000). The annual dividends on the preferred shares are $2,400 ($4/share × 600 shares). Table 10.7 presents the EPS corresponding to levels of EBIT of $6,000, $10,000, and $14,000, assuming that the firm is in the 40 percent tax bracket. Two situations are shown:

Case 1   A 40% *increase* in EBIT (from $10,000 to $14,000) results in a 100% *increase* in earnings per share (from $2.40 to $4.80).

Case 2   A 40% *decrease* in EBIT (from $10,000 to $6,000) results in a 100% *decrease* in earnings per share (from $2.40 to $0).

The effect of financial leverage is such that an increase in the firm's EBIT results in a more-than-proportional increase in the firm's earnings per share, whereas a decrease in the firm's EBIT results in a more-than-proportional decrease in EPS.

TABLE 10.7   **The EPS for Various EBIT Levels**[a]

	Case 2		Case 1
	−40%		+40%
EBIT	$6,000	$10,000	$14,000
Less: Interest (*I*)	2,000	2,000	2,000
Earnings before taxes	$4,000	$ 8,000	$12,000
Less: Taxes (*T* = 0.40)	1,600	3,200	4,800
Net income after taxes (NIAT)	$2,400	$ 4,800	$ 7,200
Less: Preferred share dividends (*PD*)	2,400	2,400	2,400
Earnings available for common (EAC)	$ 0	$ 2,400	$ 4,800
Earnings per share (EPS)	$\frac{\$0}{1,000} = \$0$	$\frac{\$2,400}{1,000} = \$2.40$	$\frac{\$4,800}{1,000} = \$4.80$
	−100%		+100%

[a]As noted in Chapter 2, for accounting and tax purposes, interest is a *tax-deductible expense,* whereas dividends must be paid from after-tax cash flows.

5. As noted in Chapter 6, although preferred share dividends can be "passed" (not paid) at the option of the firm's directors, it is generally believed that payment of such dividends is necessary. *This text treats the preferred share dividend as a contractual obligation, not only to be paid as a fixed amount, but also to be paid as scheduled.* Although failure to pay preferred dividends cannot force the firm into bankruptcy, it increases the common shareholders' risk because they cannot be paid dividends until the claims of preferred shareholders are satisfied.

Measuring the Degree of Financial Leverage (DFL)

degree of financial leverage (DFL)
The numerical measure of the firm's financial leverage.

The **degree of financial leverage (DFL)** is the numerical measure of the firm's financial leverage. Whenever the percentage change in EPS resulting from a given percentage change in EBIT is greater than the percentage change in EBIT, financial leverage exists. This means that whenever DFL is greater than 1, there is financial leverage.

The DFL is calculated at a base level of EBIT. For Chen Foods in the previous example, the base level of EBIT is $10,000. The following equation is used to calculate DFL where the notation is taken from Table 10.7. Note that in the denominator, the term $(1 - T)$ converts the after-tax preferred share dividend to a before-tax amount for consistency with the other terms in the equation.

$$\text{DFL at base level EBIT} = \frac{\text{EBIT}}{\text{EBIT} - I - \left(\dfrac{PD}{1 - T}\right)} \tag{10.7}$$

Example ▼ Substituting EBIT = $10,000, I = $2,000, PD = $2,400, and the tax rate (T = 0.40) into Equation 10.7 yields the following result:

$$\text{DFL at \$10,000 EBIT} = \frac{\$10,000}{\$10,000 - \$2,000 - \left(\dfrac{\$2,400}{1 - 0.40}\right)}$$

$$= \frac{\$10,000}{\$4,000} = 2.5$$

Since the DFL at EBIT of $10,000 is greater than 1, Chen Foods is using financial leverage. The higher the value, the greater the DFL and the greater the impact changing levels of EBIT have on EPS. For Chen Foods, the DFL of 2.5 means that for every 1 percent change in EBIT, EPS will change by 2.5 percent.

For case 1, where EBIT increases by 40 percent, EPS is expected to increase by 100 percent (40% × 2.5). Based on the results provided in Table 10.7, this is exactly what happens. For case 2, where EBIT decreases by 40 percent, EPS is expected to decrease by 100 percent (–40% × 2.5). Again, this is what occurs in Table 10.7. As with DOL, DFL is a measure of risk and returns—returns when EBIT increases, risk when EBIT decreases. The higher the value of DFL, the greater the risk, but also the greater the potential return. ▲

Total Leverage

total leverage
The use of *fixed costs, both operating and financial,* to magnify the effect of changes in sales on the firm's earnings per share.

We also can assess the combined effect of operating and financial leverage on the firm's risk using a framework similar to that used to develop the individual concepts of leverage. This combined effect, or **total leverage,** can be defined as the use of *fixed costs, both operating and financial,* to magnify the effect of changes in sales on the firm's earnings per share. Total leverage can therefore be viewed as the *total impact of the fixed costs* in the firm's operating and financial structure.

Example ▼ Cables Inc., a computer cable manufacturer, expects sales of 20,000 units at $5 per unit in the coming year and must meet the following: variable operating costs of $2 per unit, fixed operating costs of $10,000, interest of $20,000, and preferred share dividends of $12,000. The firm is in the 40 percent tax bracket and

TABLE 10.8	The Total Leverage Effect

	+50%		
Sales (in units)	20,000	30,000	DOL =
Sales revenue[a]	$100,000	$150,000	
Less: Variable operating costs[b]	40,000	60,000	$\dfrac{\$108,000 - \$40,000}{\$60,000 - \$40,000} = 1.2$
Less: Fixed operating costs	10,000	10,000	
Earnings before interest and			
taxes (EBIT)	$ 50,000	$ 80,000	
	+60%		DTL = 1.2 × 5.0 = 6.0
Less: Interest	20,000	20,000	DFL =
Earnings before taxes	$ 30,000	$ 60,000	
Less: Taxes (T = 0.40)	12,000	24,000	$\dfrac{\$50,000}{\$30,000 - \dfrac{\$12,000}{1 - 0.40}} = 5.0$
Net income after taxes	$ 18,000	$ 36,000	
Less: Preferred share dividends	12,000	12,000	
Earnings available for common	$ 6,000	$ 24,000	
Earnings per share (EPS)	$\dfrac{\$6,000}{5,000} = \$1.20$	$\dfrac{\$24,000}{5,000} = \$4.80$	
	+300%		

[a]Sales revenue = $5/unit × sales in units.
[b]Variable operating costs = $2/unit × sales in units.

has 5,000 common shares outstanding. Table 10.8 presents the levels of earnings per share associated with the expected sales of 20,000 units and with sales of 30,000 units.

The table illustrates that as a result of a 50 percent increase in sales (from 20,000 to 30,000 units), the firm would experience a 300 percent increase in earnings per share (from $1.20 to $4.80). Although not shown in the table, a 50 percent decrease in sales would, conversely, result in a 300 percent decrease in earnings per share to –$2.40 per share. The linear nature of the leverage relationship accounts for the fact that sales changes of equal magnitude in opposite directions result in EPS changes of equal magnitude in the corresponding direction. At this point, it should be clear that whenever a firm has fixed costs—operating or financial—in its structure, total leverage will exist.

Measuring the Degree of Total Leverage (DTL)

degree of total leverage (DTL)
The numerical measure of the firm's total leverage.

The **degree of total leverage (DTL)** is the numerical measure of the firm's total leverage. Whenever the percentage change in EPS resulting from a given percentage change in sales is greater than the percentage change in sales, total leverage exists. This means that as long as the DTL is greater than 1, there is total leverage.

The DTL is calculated at a base level of sales. For Cables Inc., the base level is sales of $100,000. Total leverage reflects the *combined impact* of operating and financial leverage on the firm. High operating leverage and high financial leverage will cause total leverage to be high. The opposite will also be true. The relationship between operating leverage and financial leverage is *multiplicative* rather than *additive*. The relationship between the degree of total leverage (DTL) and the degrees of operating leverage (DOL) and financial leverage (DFL) is given by Equation 10.8.

$$DTL = DOL \times DFL \tag{10.8}$$

Example ▼ Substituting the values calculated for DOL and DFL, shown on the right-hand side of Table 10.8, into Equation 10.8 yields

$$DTL = 1.2 \times 5.0 = 6.0$$

The DTL indicates what is expected to happen to EPS given a change in sales. For Cables Inc., the DTL of 6 means that for a 1 percent change in sales, EPS is expected to change by 6 percent. This 6 percent change consists of a 1.2 percent change in EBIT, which leads to a 5 percent change in EPS. The total effect is multiplicative. For the example in Table 10.8, the 50 percent increase in sales leads to a 300 percent (50% × 6) increase in EPS. This total increase consists of two separate items. First, based on a 50 percent increase in sales, EBIT is expected to increase by 60 percent (50% × 1.2). Second, the 60 percent increase in EBIT leads to a 300 percent (60% × 5) increase in EPS.

What happens if sales decrease 20 percent? EPS is expected to decline by 120 percent (–20% × 6). This decrease consists of two separate components. First, EBIT is expected to decline 24 percent (–20% × 1.2), to $38,000. Based on the 24 percent decrease in EBIT, EPS is expected to decline 120 percent (–24% × 5), to −0.24 ($1.20 × [1 − 1.20)]. Obviously, the higher the DTL, the greater the potential return (if sales increase) and risk (if sales decrease). ▲

Another method to calculate the degree of total leverage at a given base level of sales, *Q*, is given by Equation 10.9, which uses the same notation presented earlier:

$$\text{DTL at base sales level } Q = \frac{Q \times (P - VC)}{Q \times (P - VC) - FC - I - \left(PD \times \dfrac{1}{1 - T} \right)} \tag{10.9}$$

$$= \frac{TR - TVC}{TR - TVC - FC - I - \dfrac{PD}{1 - T}} \tag{10.9a}$$

$$= \frac{GM\$}{EBT - \dfrac{PD}{1 - T}} \tag{10.9b}$$

Example ▼ Substituting the required variables from Table 10.8 into Equation 10.9 yields the following:

$$\text{DTL at \$100,000 sales} = \frac{\$100,000 - \$40,000}{\$100,000 - \$40,000 - \$10,000 - \$20,000 - \dfrac{\$12,000}{1 - 0.4}}$$

$$= \frac{\$60,000}{\$10,000} = 6$$

▲

Clearly, Equation 10.8 provides a much more direct and intuitive method for calculating the DTL.

? Review Questions

10–1   What is meant by the term *leverage?* How do operating leverage, financial leverage, and total leverage relate to the income statement?

10–2   What is the *operating breakeven point?* How do changes in fixed operating costs, the sale price per unit, and the variable operating cost per unit affect it?

10–3   What is *operating leverage?* What causes it? How is the *degree of operating leverage (DOL)* measured?

10–4   What is *financial leverage?* What causes it? How is the *degree of financial leverage (DFL)* measured?

10–5   What is the general relationship among operating leverage, financial leverage, and the total leverage of the firm? Do these types of leverage complement each other? Why or why not?

10.2 The Firm's Capital Structure

Capital structure is one of the most complex areas of financial decision making due to its interrelationship with other financial decision variables.[6] Poor capital structure decisions can result in a high cost of capital, thereby making more investment projects unacceptable. Effective decisions can lower the cost of capital, resulting in more acceptable projects, thereby increasing the value of the firm. This section links together the concepts presented in Chapters 5 through 9 and the discussion of leverage in this chapter.

Types of Capital

All of the items on the right-hand side of the firm's balance sheet, excluding current liabilities, are sources of capital. The following simplified balance sheet illustrates the basic breakdown of total capital into its two components—*debt capital* and *equity capital*.

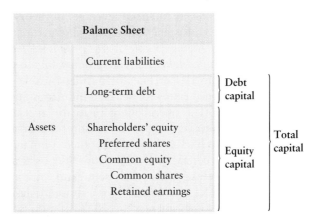

---

6. Of course, although capital structure is financially important, it, like many business decisions, is generally not as important as the firm's products or services. In a practical sense, a firm can probably more readily increase its value by improving quality and reducing costs rather than by fine-tuning its capital structure.

The various types and characteristics of *long-term debt*, a major source of *capital*, were discussed in detail in Chapter 6. In Chapter 9, the cost of debt was found to be less than the cost of other forms of financing. Lenders demand relatively lower returns because they take the least risk of any long-term contributors of capital. Consider: (1) they have a higher priority of claim against any earnings or assets available for payment, (2) they have a far stronger legal pressure against the company to make payment than do preferred or common shareholders, and (3) the tax deductibility of interest payments lowers the debt cost to the firm substantially.

Unlike borrowed funds that must be repaid at a specified future date, *equity capital* is expected to remain in the firm for an indefinite period of time. The two basic sources of equity capital are (1) preferred shares and (2) common equity, which includes common shares and retained earnings. As was demonstrated in Chapter 9, common shares are typically the most expensive form of equity, followed by reinvested profits and preferred shares, respectively. Our concern here is the relationship between debt and equity capital. Key differences between these two types of capital, relative to voice in management, claims on income and assets, maturity, and tax treatment, were summarized in Chapter 6, Table 6.8. Due to its secondary position relative to debt, suppliers of equity capital take greater risk and therefore must be compensated with higher expected returns than suppliers of debt capital.

Capital Structure of Canadian Companies

Earlier it was shown that *financial leverage* results from the use of fixed-payment financing, such as debt and preferred shares, to magnify return and risk. Leverage ratios, which measure the firm's degree of financial leverage, were presented in Chapter 3. A direct measure of the degree of indebtedness is the *debt ratio*. The higher this ratio, the greater the firm's financial leverage. Measures of the firm's ability to meet fixed payments associated with debt include the *times interest earned ratio* and the *fixed-payment coverage ratio*. These ratios provide indirect information on financial leverage. The smaller these ratios, the less able the firm is to meet payments as they come due. In general, low debt payment ratios are associated with high degrees of financial leverage. The more risk a firm takes, the greater its financial leverage. In theory, the firm should maintain financial leverage consistent with a capital structure that maximizes owners' wealth.

An acceptable degree of financial leverage for one industry or line of business can be highly risky in another, due to differing operating characteristics between industries or lines of business. Table 10.9 presents the debt and times interest earned ratios for selected industries and lines of business.

The overall debt ratio for all Canadian industries is 74.9 percent which seems very high. The reason for this very high ratio is because financial companies like banks and insurance companies are included. These types of companies have very high debt ratios (deposits are liabilities for banks) which artificially increases the overall debt ratio for companies in Canada. For non-finance companies, the debt ratio is a more modest, but still high, 62 percent. Also note that the times interest earned (TIE) ratio is essentially identical for both industry categories. At 2.70, the TIE indicates that both major industry sectors adequately cover the required interest payments on the debt.

TABLE 10.9   Debt Ratios and Times Interest Earned Ratios for Selected Industries for 1999

Industry	Debt ratio	Times interest earned ratio
Total for all industries	74.9%	2.70
Total finance and insurance industries	87.5	2.69
Total non-financial industries	62.0	2.70
Primary industries		
Agriculture, forestry, fishing, and hunting	61.4	1.67
Oil and gas extraction and coal mining	65.4	1.52
Mining	38.8	0.81
Utilities	71.9	1.54
Construction	73.0	2.35
Manufacturing industries		
Food manufacturing	58.9	3.73
Beverage and tobacco product manufacturing	42.4	3.58
Clothing, textile, and leather manufacturing	63.9	3.01
Wood and paper manufacturing	56.4	2.95
Printing and related support activities	51.6	3.55
Petroleum and coal products manufacturing	49.5	7.74
Chemicals, plastic, and rubber manufacturing	53.0	4.43
Non-metallic mineral product manufacturing	42.5	8.90
Primary metal manufacturing	48.3	3.26
Fabricated metal product manufacturing	59.9	5.50
Machinery manufacturing	53.6	5.25
Computer and electronic product manufacturing	42.7	7.20
Electrical equipment, appliance, and component manufacturing	59.0	10.11
Motor vehicles and parts manufacturing	63.3	11.82
Other transportation equipment manufacturing	57.6	6.34
Furniture and related product manufacturing	61.5	8.09
Miscellaneous manufacturing	62.4	3.84
Wholesaling industries		
Wholesale food, beverage, and tobacco	81.9	1.15
Petroleum product wholesaler-distributors	61.5	1.73
Motor vehicle and parts wholesaler-distributors	71.3	3.19
Building material and supplies wholesaler-distributors	58.0	3.25
Machinery, equipment, and supplies wholesaler-distributors	67.5	4.11
Other wholesale	68.7	3.62
Retailing industries		
Motor vehicle and parts dealers	80.1	1.94
Furniture and home furnishing stores and electronics	69.0	4.37
Building material and garden equipment and supplies	67.5	4.05
Food and beverage stores	64.7	10.69
Clothing and clothing accessories stores	65.4	2.87
General merchandise stores	58.7	2.75
Other retail	67.9	2.98
Service industries		
Transportation and warehousing	70.0	1.68
Telecommunications	60.0	1.56
Publishing and broadcasting	56.3	1.91
Real estate	68.0	1.25
Other rental companies	66.0	1.07
Professional, scientific, and technical services	56.5	4.54

(continued)

TABLE 10.9	Debt Ratios and Times Interest Earned Ratios for Selected Industries for 1999 *(continued)*		
Industry		Debt ratio	Times interest earned ratio
Computer systems design and related services		63.5	3.29
Administrative and support, waste management, and remediation services		65.0	3.11
Educational services		77.4	1.39
Health care and social assistance		60.0	3.90
Arts, entertainment, and recreation		68.2	15.08
Accommodation and food services		78.8	1.62
Other services (except public administration)		58.7	3.01
Management companies		28.2	3.77

SOURCE: "Debt Ratios and Times Interest Earned for Selected Industries for 1999," adapted from the Statistics Canada CANSIM II Database <cansim2.statscan.ca/cgi-win/CNSMCGI.EXE>, table 180-0003.

Table 10.9 also indicates that significant differences in both ratios exist across industries. For 1999, the debt ratio ranges from a low of 28.2 percent for management companies to a high of 81.9 percent for wholesale food, beverage, and tobacco companies. For TIE, the ratio ranges from a low of 0.81 for the mining industry, even though the debt ratio is only 38.8 percent, to a high of 15.08 for the arts, entertainment, and recreation industry with a debt ratio of 68.2 percent. The wide range of outcomes for these ratios indicates significant differences in operation and financial structures. Differences in these ratios are also likely to exist *within* an industry or line of business.

Capital Structures in Other Countries

In general, Canadian and U.S. companies have similar debt ratios, given the high degree of integration between the two countries. Also, companies in both countries have similar capital markets, creditors, and investors. It is not surprising, therefore, that creditors and investors in the two countries seek similar characteristics in the companies they lend to and invest in.

For non–North American companies, particularly in Europe and Japan, different capital market and corporate ownership structures result in different capital structures for corporations. Companies in these countries generally have higher debt ratios than similar companies in North America. This is the case since in these countries, banks are allowed to hold equity investments in corporations, a practice that is very rare in North America. Also, in these countries, corporate ownership is more tightly controlled among fewer large investors. Such a structure reduces agency problems and costs, thus allowing these companies to tolerate higher debt ratios.

Capital Structure Theory

Research suggests that there is an optimal capital structure range. However, *the understanding of capital structure at this point does not provide financial man-*

agers with a direct approach to use to determine a firm's optimal capital structure. Nevertheless, financial theory does provide help in understanding how a firm's chosen financing mix affects the firm's value.

In 1958, Franco Modigliani and Merton H. Miller[7] (commonly known as "M and M") demonstrated algebraically that, assuming perfect markets,[8] the capital structure that a firm chooses does not affect its value. Many researchers, including M and M, have examined the effects of less restrictive assumptions on the relationship between capital structure and the firm's value. The result is a theoretical *optimal* capital structure based on balancing the benefits and costs of debt financing. The major benefit of debt financing is the tax shield, which allows interest payments to be deducted in calculating taxable income. The cost of debt financing results from (1) the increased probability of bankruptcy caused by debt obligations, (2) the *agency costs* of the lender's monitoring the firm's actions, and (3) the costs associated with managers having more information about the firm's prospects than do investors.

Tax Benefits

Allowing firms to deduct interest payments on debt when calculating taxable income reduces the amount of the firm's earnings paid in taxes, thereby making more earnings available for bondholders and shareholders. The deductibility of interest means the cost of debt, k_i, to the firm is subsidized by taxpayers. Letting k_d equal the before-tax cost of debt and T equal the tax rate, from Chapter 9, we have $k_i = k_d \times (1 - T)$.

Probability of Bankruptcy

The chance that a firm will become bankrupt due to an inability to meet its obligations as they come due depends largely on its level of both business risk and financial risk.

Business Risk   In Chapter 9, we defined *business risk* as the risk to the firm of being unable to cover its operating costs. In general, the greater the firm's *operating leverage*—the use of fixed operating costs—the higher its business risk. Although operating leverage is an important factor affecting business risk, two other factors—revenue stability and cost stability—also affect it. *Revenue stability* refers to the relative variability of the firm's sales revenues. Firms with reasonably stable levels of demand and with products that have stable prices have stable revenues. The result is low levels of business risk. Firms with highly volatile product demand and prices have unstable revenues that result in high levels of business risk. *Cost stability* refers to the relative predictability of input prices such as those for labour and materials. The more predictable and stable these input prices are, the lower the business risk; the less predictable and stable they are, the higher the business risk.

---

7. Franco Modigliani and Merton H. Miller, "The Cost of Capital, Corporation Finance, and the Theory of Investment," *American Economic Review* (June 1958), pp. 261–297.

8. Perfect market assumptions include (1) no taxes, (2) no brokerage or flotation costs for securities, (3) symmetrical information—investors and managers have the same information about the firm's investment prospects, and (4) investors can borrow at the same rate as corporations.

Business risk varies among firms, regardless of their lines of business, and is not affected by capital structure decisions. The level of business risk must be taken as a "given." The higher a firm's business risk, the more cautious the firm must be in establishing its capital structure. Firms with high business risk therefore tend toward less highly leveraged capital structures, and firms with low business risk tend toward more highly leveraged capital structures.

For example, Table 10.9 indicates that the petroleum and coal manufacturing industry has a debt ratio of 49.5 percent. Given the uncertainty of revenues in this industry (since revenues are based on the world price of commodities), it makes sense for this industry to have a lower than average debt ratio. On the other hand, the wholesale food, beverage, and tobacco industry has very secure revenues, therefore the industry can tolerate a very high debt ratio. We will hold business risk constant throughout the discussions that follow.

Example ▼ Cooke Company, a soft drink manufacturer, is preparing to make a capital structure decision. It has obtained estimates of sales and the associated levels of earnings before interest and taxes (EBIT) from its forecasting group: There is a 25 percent chance that sales will total $400,000, a 50 percent chance that sales will total $600,000, and a 25 percent chance that sales will total $800,000. Fixed operating costs total $200,000, and variable operating costs equal 50 percent of sales. These data are summarized and the resulting EBIT calculated in Table 10.10.

The table shows that there is a 25 percent chance that the EBIT will be $0, a 50 percent chance that it will be $100,000, and a 25 percent chance that it will be $200,000. The financial manager must accept as given these levels of EBIT and their associated probabilities when developing the firm's capital structure. These EBIT data effectively reflect a certain level of business risk that captures the firm's operating leverage, sales revenue variability, and cost predictability. **▲**

⚠ Hint
The cash flows to investors from bonds are less risky than the dividends from preferred shares, which are less risky than dividends from common shares. Only with bonds is the issuer contractually obligated to pay the scheduled interest, and the amounts due to bondholders and preferred shareholders are usually fixed. Therefore, the required return for bonds is generally lower than for preferred shares, which is lower than for common shares.

Financial Risk   The firm's capital structure directly affects its *financial risk*, which is the risk to the firm of being unable to cover required financial obligations. The penalty for not meeting financial obligations is bankruptcy. The more fixed cost financing—debt (including financial leases) and preferred shares—a firm has in its capital structure, the greater its financial leverage and risk. Financial risk depends on the capital structure decision made by the management, and that decision is affected by the business risk the firm faces.

The *total risk* of a firm—business and financial risk combined—determines its probability of bankruptcy. Financial risk, its relationship to business risk, and their combined impact can be demonstrated by continuing the Cooke Company example.

TABLE 10.10	**Sales and Associated EBIT Calculations for Cooke Company ($000)**		
Probability of sales	0.25	0.50	0.25
Sales revenue	$400	$600	$800
Less: Fixed operating costs	200	200	200
Less: Variable operating costs (50% of sales)	200	300	400
Earnings before interest and taxes (EBIT)	$ 0	$100	$200

Example ▼ Cooke Company's current capital structure is as shown:

Current capital structure	
Long-term debt	$ 0
Common equity (25,000 shares at $20)	500,000
Total capital	$500,000

Hint
As you learned in Chapter 3, the debt ratio is equal to the amount of total debt divided by the total assets. The higher this ratio, the more financial leverage a firm is using.

Common equity is the combination of the proceeds from the sale of common shares and retained earnings. For the purposes of the example, we will assume that the book value of common equity is $20 per share and that at a 100 percent equity ratio (0% debt ratio), Cooke Company has 25,000 common shares outstanding. For the remainder of the Cooke Company example, we will assume the $20 book value per share figure does not change.

Let us assume that the firm is considering seven alternative capital structures. If we measure these structures using the debt ratio, they are associated with ratios of 0, 10, 20, 30, 40, 50, and 60 percent. Assuming (1) the firm has no current liabilities, (2) its capital structure currently contains all equity as shown, and (3) the total amount of capital remains constant at $500,000, the mix of debt and equity associated with the seven debt ratios are shown in Table 10.11. Also shown in the table is the number of common shares outstanding under each alternative.

Associated with each of the debt levels in column 3 of Table 10.11 would be an interest rate that would be expected to increase with increases in financial leverage. The level of debt, the associated interest rate (assumed to apply to *all* debt), and the dollar amount of annual interest associated with each of the alternative capital structures are summarized in Table 10.12. Because both the level

TABLE 10.11   Capital Structures Associated with Alternative Debt Ratios for Cooke Company

Debt ratio (1)	Total assets[a] (2)	Debt [(1) × (2)] (3)	Equity [(2) − (3)] (4)	Number of common shares outstanding [(4) ÷ $20][b] (5)
0%	$500	$ 0	$500	25,000
10	500	50	450	22,500
20	500	100	400	20,000
30	500	150	350	17,500
40	500	200	300	15,000
50	500	250	250	12,500
60	500	300	200	10,000

[a]Because the firm, for convenience, is assumed to have no current liabilities, its total assets equal its total capital of $500,000.
[b]The $20 value represents the book value per common share as noted earlier.

TABLE 10.12	Level of Debt, Interest Rate, and Dollar Amount of Annual Interest Associated with Cooke Company's Alternative Capital Structures		
Capital structure debt ratio	Debt ($000) (1)	Interest rate on *all* debt (2)	Interest ($000) [(1) × (2)] (3)
0%	$ 0	0.0%	$ 0.00
10	50	9.0	4.50
20	100	9.5	9.50
30	150	10.0	15.00
40	200	11.0	22.00
50	250	13.5	33.75
60	300	16.5	49.50

of debt and the interest rate increase with increasing financial leverage (debt ratios), the annual interest increases as well.

Table 10.13 uses the levels of EBIT and associated probabilities developed in Table 10.10, the number of common shares found in column 5 of Table 10.11, and the annual interest values calculated in column 3 of Table 10.12 to calculate the earnings per share (EPS) for debt ratios of 0, 30, and 60 percent. A 40 percent tax rate is assumed. Also shown are the resulting expected EPS, the standard deviation of EPS, and the coefficient of variation of EPS associated with each debt ratio.

Table 10.14 summarizes the pertinent data for the seven alternative capital structures. The values shown for 0, 30, and 60 percent debt ratios were developed in Table 10.13, whereas calculations of similar values for the other debt ratios (10, 20, 40 and 50%) are not shown. Because the coefficient of variation measures the risk relative to the expected EPS, it is the preferred risk measure for use in comparing capital structures. As the firm's financial leverage increases, so does its coefficient of variation of EPS. As expected, an increasing level of risk is associated with increased levels of financial leverage.

The relative risk of the two extremes of the capital structures evaluated in Table 10.13 (debt ratios = 0% and 60%) can be illustrated by showing the probability distribution of EPS associated with each of them. Figure 10.3 shows these two distributions. The expected level of EPS increases with increasing financial leverage, and so does risk, as reflected in the relative dispersion of each of the distributions. Clearly, the uncertainty of the expected EPS, as well as the chance of experiencing negative EPS, is greater when higher degrees of financial leverage are employed.

Further, the nature of the risk-return tradeoff associated with the seven capital structures under consideration can be clearly observed by plotting the expected EPS and coefficient of variation relative to the debt ratio. Plotting the data from Table 10.14 results in Figure 10.4. The figure shows that as debt is substituted for equity (as the debt ratio increases), the level of EPS rises and then begins to fall (graph *a*). The graph demonstrates that the peak earnings per share occurs at a debt ratio of 50 percent. The decline in earnings per share beyond

| TABLE 10.13 | Calculation of EPS for Selected Debt Ratios ($000) for Cooke Company |

Debt Ratio = 0%

Probability of EBIT	0.25	0.50	0.25
EBIT (Table 10.10)	$ 0.00	$100.00	$200.00
Less: Interest (Table 10.12)	0.00	0.00	0.00
Earnings before taxes	$ 0.00	$100.00	$200.00
Less: Taxes ($T = 0.40$)	0.00	40.00	80.00
Net income after taxes	$ 0.00	$ 60.00	$120.00
EPS (25,000 shares, Table 10.11)	$ 0.00	$ 2.40	$ 4.80
Expected EPS[a]		$ 2.40	
Standard deviation of EPS[a]		$ 1.70	
Coefficient of variation of EPS[a]		0.71	

Debt Ratio = 30%

Probability of EBIT	0.25	0.50	0.25
EBIT (Table 10.10)	$ 0.00	$100.00	$200.00
Less: Interest (Table 10.12)	15.00	15.00	15.00
Earnings before taxes	($15.00)	$ 85.00	$185.00
Less: Taxes ($T = 0.40$)	(6.00)[b]	34.00	74.00
Net income after taxes	($ 9.00)	$ 51.00	$111.00
EPS (17,500 shares, Table 10.11)	($ 0.51)	$ 2.91	$ 6.34
Expected EPS[a]		$ 2.91	
Standard deviation of EPS[a]		$ 2.42	
Coefficient of variation of EPS[a]		0.83	

Debt Ratio = 60%

Probability of EBIT	0.25	0.50	0.25
EBIT (Table 10.10)	$ 0.00	$100.00	$200.00
Less: Interest (Table 10.12)	49.50	49.50	49.50
Earnings before taxes	($49.50)	$ 50.50	$150.50
Less: Taxes ($T = 0.40$)	(19.80)[b]	20.20	60.20
Net income after taxes	($29.70)	$ 30.30	$ 90.30
EPS (10,000 shares, Table 10.11)	($ 2.97)	$ 3.03	$ 9.03
Expected EPS[a]		$ 3.03	
Standard deviation of EPS[a]		$ 4.24	
Coefficient of variation of EPS[a]		1.40	

[a]The procedures used to calculate the expected value, standard deviation, and coefficient of variation were presented in Chapter 7.

[b]It is assumed that the firm receives the tax benefit from its loss in the current period.

TABLE 10.14	Expected EPS, Standard Deviation, and Coefficient of Variation for Alternative Capital Structures for Cooke Company		
Capital structure debt ratio	Expected EPS (1)	Standard deviation of EPS (2)	Coefficient of variation of EPS [(2) ÷ (1)] (3)
0%	$2.40	1.70	0.71
10	2.55	1.88	0.74
20	2.72	2.13	0.78
30	2.91	2.42	0.83
40	3.12	2.83	0.91
50	3.18	3.39	1.07
60	3.03	4.24	1.40

that ratio results from the fact that the significant increases in interest are not fully offset by the reduction in the number of common shares outstanding.

If we look at the risk behaviour as measured by the coefficient of variation (graph *b*), we can see that risk increases with increasing leverage. A portion of the risk can be attributed to business risk, but that portion changing in response to increasing financial leverage would be attributed to financial risk.

Clearly, a risk-return tradeoff exists relative to the use of financial leverage. How to combine these risk-return factors into a valuation framework will be addressed later in the chapter. The key point to recognize here is that as a firm

FIGURE 10.3

Probability Distributions

Probability distributions of EPS for debt ratios of 0 and 60% for Cooke Company

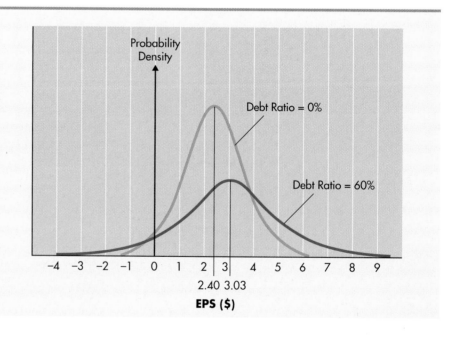

FIGURE 10.4

Expected EPS and Coefficient of Variation of EPS

Expected EPS and coefficient of variation of EPS for alternative capital structures for Cooke Company

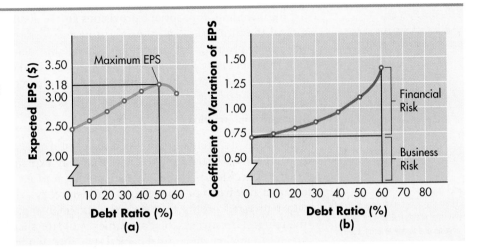

introduces more leverage into its capital structure, it will experience increases in both the expected level of return and the associated risk.

Agency Costs Imposed by Lenders

As noted in Chapter 1, the managers of firms typically act as *agents* of the owners (shareholders). The owners give the managers the authority to manage the firm for the owners' benefit. The *agency problem* created by this relationship extends not only to the relationship between owners and managers, but also to the relationship between owners and lenders.

When a lender provides funds to a firm, the interest rate charged is based on the lender's assessment of the firm's risk. The lender-borrower relationship, therefore, depends on the lender's expectations for the firm's subsequent behaviour. The borrowing rates are, in effect, locked in when the loans are negotiated. After obtaining a loan at a certain rate, the firm could increase its risk by investing in risky projects or by incurring additional debt. Such action could weaken the lender's position in terms of its claim on the cash flow of the firm. From another point of view, if these risky investment strategies paid off, the shareholders would benefit. Because payment obligations to the lender remain unchanged, the excess cash flows generated by a positive outcome from the riskier action would enhance the value of the firm to its owners. In other words, if the risky investments pay off, the owners receive all the benefits; but if the risky investments do not pay off, the lenders share in the costs.

Clearly, an incentive exists for the managers acting on behalf of the shareholders to "take advantage" of lenders. To avoid this situation, lenders impose certain monitoring techniques on borrowers, who as a result incur *agency costs*. The most obvious strategy is to deny subsequent loan requests or to increase the cost of future loans to the firm. Because this strategy is an after-the-fact approach, other controls must be included in the loan agreement. Lenders typically protect themselves by including provisions that limit the firm's ability to significantly alter its business and financial risk. These loan provisions tend to centre on issues such as the minimum level of liquidity, asset acquisitions, executive salaries, and dividend payments.

Hint
Typical loan provisions included in corporate bonds are discussed in Chapter 6.

By including appropriate provisions in the loan agreement, the lender can control the firm's risk and thus be protected from the adverse consequences of this agency problem. Of course, in exchange for incurring agency costs by agreeing to the operating and financial constraints placed on it by the loan provisions, the firm should benefit by obtaining funds at a lower cost.

Asymmetric Information

pecking order
A hierarchy of financing beginning with reinvested profits followed by debt financing and finally external equity financing.

Some recent research has examined the capital structure decisions actually made by companies.[9] There are two views that may explain how the financing (capital structure) decision is made: (1) maintaining a *target capital structure* or (2) following a hierarchy of financing. This hierarchy, called a **pecking order,** begins with reinvested profits followed by debt financing, and finally external equity financing. The surveys of companies indicate that about one-third of firms attempt to implement a target capital structure, while two-thirds follow the pecking order method of financing. Shyam-Sunder and Myers' findings suggest that the pecking order model better explains the debt-equity choice made by companies than the target capital structure model, at least for the mature public firms that they examined.

asymmetric information
The situation in which managers of a firm have more information about operations and future prospects than do investors.

At first glance, on the basis of financial theory, this choice appears to be inconsistent with wealth maximizing goals. However, Stewart Myers explained how "asymmetric information" could account for the pecking order financing preferences of financial managers.[10] **Asymmetric information** results when managers of a firm have more information about operations and future prospects than do investors. Assuming that managers make decisions with the goal of maximizing the wealth of existing shareholders, then asymmetric information can affect the capital structure decisions that managers make.

signal
A financing action by management that is believed to reflect its view of the firm's common share value; generally, debt financing is viewed as a *positive signal* that management believes that the shares are "undervalued," and a new share issue is viewed as a *negative signal* that management believes that the shares are "overvalued."

Suppose, for example, that management has found a valuable investment that will require additional financing. Management believes that the prospects for the firm's future are very good and that the market, as indicated by the firm's current share price, does not fully appreciate the firm's value. In this case, it would be advantageous to current shareholders if management raised the required funds using debt rather than issuing new shares. Using debt to raise funds is frequently viewed as a **signal** that reflects management's view of the firm's share value. Debt financing is a *positive signal* suggesting that management believes that the shares are "undervalued" and therefore a bargain. When the firm's positive future outlook becomes known to the market, the increased value would be fully captured by existing owners, rather than having to be shared with new shareholders.

If, however, the outlook for the firm is poor, management may believe that the firm's shares are "overvalued." In that case, it would be in the best interest of existing shareholders for the firm to issue new common shares. Therefore

9. See, for example, J. Michael Pinegar and Lisa Wilbricht, "What Managers Think of Capital Structure Theory: A Survey," *Financial Management* (Winter 1989), pp. 82–91; R. R. Kamath, "Long-Term Financing Decisions: Views and Practices of Financial Managers of NYSE Firms," *The Financial Review*, 1997, Vol. 32, 350–356; L. Shyam-Sunder and S. Myers, "Testing Static Tradeoff Against Pecking Order Models of Capital Structure," *Journal of Financial Economics*, 1999, Vol. 51, 219–244; and Gishan Dissanaike, Bart M. Lambrecht, and Antonio Saragg, "Differentiating Debt Target from Non-target Firms: An Empirical Study on Corporate Capital Structure," University of Cambridge, JIMS Working Paper No. 18, September 2001.

10. Stewart C. Myers, "The Capital Structure Puzzle," *Journal of Finance* (July 1984), pp. 575–592.

investors often interpret the announcement of a share issue as a *negative signal*—bad news concerning the firm's prospects—and the share price declines. This decrease in share value, along with high underwriting costs for share issues (compared to debt issues), make new common share financing very expensive. When the negative future outlook becomes known to the market, the decreased value would be shared with new shareholders, rather than be fully captured by existing owners.

Because asymmetric information conditions exist from time to time, firms should maintain some reserve borrowing capacity, by keeping debt levels low. This reserve allows the firm to take advantage of good investment opportunities without having to sell common shares at low values or send signals that unduly influence the share price.

The Optimal Capital Structure

So, what *is* an optimal capital structure? To provide some insight into an answer, we will examine some basic financial relationships. It is known that *the value of the firm is maximized when the cost of capital is minimized*. By using a modification of the simple perpetuity, we can define the value of the firm, V, by Equation 10.10:

$$V = \frac{\text{EBIT} \times (1 - T)}{k_a} \tag{10.10}$$

where

$$\text{EBIT} = \text{earnings before interest and taxes}$$
$$T = \text{tax rate}$$
$$k_a = \text{weighted average cost of capital}$$

Clearly, if we assume that EBIT is constant, the value of the firm, V, is maximized by minimizing the weighted average cost of capital, k_a.

Cost Functions

Figure 10.5(a) plots three cost functions—the after-tax cost of debt, k_i; the cost of equity, k_s; and the weighted average cost of capital, k_a—as a function of financial leverage measured by the debt ratio (debt to total assets). The *cost of debt*, k_i, remains low due to the tax shield but slowly increases with increasing leverage to compensate lenders for increasing risk. The *cost of equity, k_s*, is above the cost of debt and increases with increasing financial leverage, but generally increases more rapidly than the cost of debt. The increase in the cost of equity occurs because the shareholders require a higher return as leverage increases, to compensate for the higher degree of financial risk.

The *weighted average cost of capital, k_a*, results from a weighted average of the firm's debt and equity capital costs. At a debt ratio of zero, the firm is 100 percent equity financed. As debt is substituted for equity and as the debt ratio increases, the weighted average cost of capital declines because the debt cost is less than the equity cost ($k_i < k_s$). As the debt ratio continues to increase, the increased debt and equity costs eventually cause the weighted average cost of capital to rise [after point M in Figure 10.5(a)]. This behaviour results in a U-shaped, or saucer-shaped, weighted average cost of capital function, k_a.

Cost Functions and Value

Capital costs and the optimal capital structure

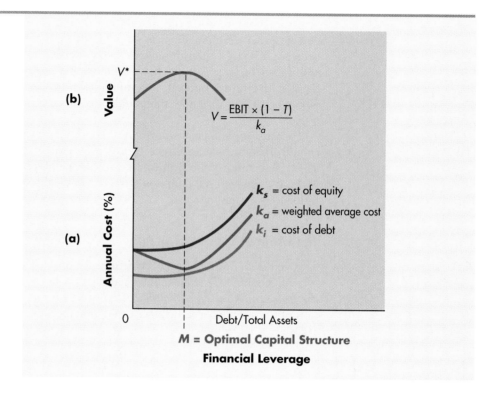

(b)

$$V = \frac{EBIT \times (1 - T)}{k_a}$$

k_s = cost of equity

k_a = weighted average cost

k_i = cost of debt

(a)

M = Optimal Capital Structure

Financial Leverage

A Graphic View of the Optimal Structure

optimal capital structure
The capital structure at which the weighted average cost of capital is minimized, thereby maximizing the firm's value.

Because the maximization of value, V, is achieved when the overall cost of capital, k_a, is at a minimum, the **optimal capital structure** is therefore that at which the weighted average cost of capital, k_a, is minimized. In Figure 10.5(a), point M represents the *minimum weighted average cost of capital*—the point of optimal financial leverage and hence of optimal capital structure for the firm.

Figure 10.5(b) plots the value of the firm resulting from substitution of k_a in Figure 10.5(a) for various levels of financial leverage into Equation 10.10. As shown in Figure 10.5(b), at the optimal capital structure, point M, the value of the firm is maximized at V^*.

Generally, the lower the firm's weighted average cost of capital, the greater the difference between the return on a project and this cost, and therefore the greater the owners' return. Simply stated, minimizing the weighted average cost of capital allows management to undertake a larger number of profitable projects, thereby further increasing the value of the firm.

As a practical matter, there is no way to calculate the exact optimal capital structure point implied by Figure 10.5. Because it is impossible either to know or remain at the precise optimal capital structure, firms generally try to operate in a range that places them near what they believe to be the optimal capital structure. The fact that a company raises financing in lumpy quantities rather than in the exact optimal capital structure percentages causes a company's actual capital structure to change. For example, for a particular year, a company may raise required financing using reinvested profits. This will change the company's capital structure. The next year the company may raise financing using reinvested profits and new debt financing. Again the capital structure will change. *But*, as long as the debt ratio remains within a range of up to 7 percent around the optimal point, a firm, in reality, will be viewed to be operating at the optimal capital structure and will minimize their cost of capital.

Therefore, in Figure 10.5(a), the k_a curve should show a very gradual change at the minimum point (a gradual U-like shape) rather than the very sharp, V-like shape that is shown in the figure. While it is very difficult to determine the exact optimal capital structure *point*, most firms can calculate an optimal *range*. Based on Table 10.9, it seems that the optimal range for many non-financial industries in Canada is a debt ratio of between 55 and 69 percent, with an average of 62 percent. The debt ratios of 31 of the 49 industries shown in the table fall within this range. It is also clear, however, that the optimal debt ratio will vary by industry and company.

IN PRACTICE

Enron Plays Hide and Seek with Debt

Enron Corp.'s December 31, 2000, balance sheet showed long-term debt of $10.2 billion and $300 million in other financial obligations. These figures gave the company a 41 percent ratio of total obligations to total capitalization. That didn't seem out of line for a company in the capital-intensive energy industry.

Yet as the company's financial condition fell apart in the fall of 2001, investors and lenders discovered that Enron's true debt load was far beyond what its balance sheet indicated. By selling assets to perfectly legal special-purpose entities (SPEs), Enron had moved billions of dollars of debt off its balance sheet into subsidiaries, trusts, partnership, and other creative financing arrangements. Former CFO Andrew Fastow claimed that these complex arrangements were disclosed in footnotes and Enron was not liable for repayment of the debts of these SPEs.

Enron's required filing of Form 10–Q with the SEC, on November 19, 2001, told a different story: If its debt were to fall below investment grade, Enron would have to repay those off-balance-sheet partnership obligations. Ironically, its disclosure of about $4 billion in off-balance-sheet liabilities triggered the downgrade of its debt to "junk" status and accelerated debt repayment. Enron's secrecy about its off-balance-sheet ventures led to its loss of credibility in the investment community. Its stock and bond prices slid downward; its market value plunged $35 billion in about a month; and on December 2, 2001, Enron became the largest U.S. company ever to have filed for bankruptcy.

Enron is not alone in its use of off-balance-sheet debt. Most airlines have large aircraft leases structured through off-balance-sheet vehicles, although analysis and investors are aware that the true leverage is higher. **Pacific Gas & Edison**, and **Xerox** have also run into problems from off-balance-sheet debt obligations. Don't expect the Enron debacle to eliminate special-purpose entities, although the SEC has been calling for tighter consolidation rules. Companies like the flexibility that off-balance-sheet financing sources provide, not to mention that such financing makes debt ratios and returns look better.

SOURCE: Peter Bahr, "Causes of Death: Mistrust," *Washington Post* (December 13, 2001), p. E1; Ronald Fink, "What Andrew Fastow Knew," *CFO* (January 1, 2002); and David Henry, "Who Else Is Hiding Debt?" *Business week* (January 28, 2002).

? Review Questions

10–6   What is a firm's *capital structure?* What ratios assess the degree of financial leverage in a firm's capital structure?

10–7   In Canada, most companies have the same capital structure and likely the same optimal capital structure. Do you agree with this statement? Discuss.

10–8   What is the major benefit of debt financing? How does it affect the firm's cost of debt?

10–9   Define *business risk,* and discuss the three factors that affect it. What influence does business risk have on the firm's capital structure decisions? Define *financial risk,* and explain its relationship to the firm's capital structure.

10–10   Briefly describe the *agency problem* that exists between owners and lenders. Explain how the firm must incur *agency costs* for the lender to resolve this problem.

10–11   How does *asymmetric information* affect the firm's capital structure decisions? Explain how and why investors may view the firm's financing actions as *signals.*

10–12   Describe the generally accepted theory concerning the behaviour of the cost of debt, the cost of equity, and the weighted average cost of capital as the firm's financial leverage increases from zero. Where is the *optimal capital structure* under this theory? Where is the optimal capital structure in reality? What is the relationship between the optimal capital structure, cost of capital, and the value of the firm?

10.3   The EBIT–EPS Approach to Capital Structure

EBIT–EPS approach
An approach for selecting the capital structure that maximizes earnings per share over the expected range of earnings before interest and taxes.

The **EBIT–EPS approach** to capital structure involves selecting the capital structure that maximizes earnings per share over the expected range of earnings before interest and taxes. Here the main emphasis is on the effects of various capital structures on *owners' returns.* Because one of the key variables affecting the market value of the firm's shares is its earnings, EPS can be conveniently used to analyze alternative capital structures.

Presenting a Financing Plan Graphically

To analyze the effects of a firm's capital structure on the owners' returns, we consider the relationship between earnings before interest and taxes (EBIT) and earnings per share (EPS). A constant level of EBIT—constant *business risk*—is assumed, to isolate the effect on returns of the financing costs associated with alternative capital structures. EPS is used to measure the owners' returns, which are expected to be closely related to share price.[11]

---

11. The relationship that is expected to exist between EPS and owner wealth is not one of cause and effect. As indicated in Chapter 1, the maximization of profits does not necessarily assure the firm that owners' wealth is also being maximized. Nevertheless, it is expected that the movement of earnings per share will have some effect on owners' wealth, because EPS data constitute one of the few pieces of information investors receive, and they often bid the firm's share price up or down in response to the level of these earnings.

The Data Required

To graph a financing plan, we need to know at least two EBIT–EPS coordinates. The approach for obtaining coordinates can be illustrated by an example.

E x a m p l e ▼ EBIT–EPS coordinates can be found by assuming two EBIT values and calculating the EPS associated with them.[12] Such calculations for three capital structures—debt ratios of 0, 30, and 60 percent—for Cooke Company were presented in Table 10.13. By using the EBIT values of $100,000 and $200,000, the associ- ▲ ated EPS values calculated there are summarized in the table within Figure 10.6.

Plotting the Data

The Cooke Company data can be plotted on a set of EBIT–EPS axes, as shown in Figure 10.6. The figure shows the level of EPS expected for each level of EBIT.

FIGURE 10.6

EBIT–EPS Approach
A comparison of selected capital structures for Cooke Company (data from Table 10.13)

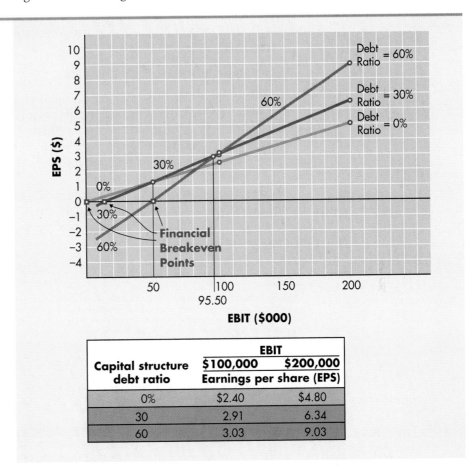

Capital structure debt ratio	EBIT	
	$100,000	**$200,000**
	Earnings per share (EPS)	
0%	$2.40	$4.80
30	2.91	6.34
60	3.03	9.03

12. A convenient method for finding one EBIT–EPS coordinate is to calculate the *financial breakeven point,* the level of EBIT for which the firm's EPS just equals $0. It is the level of EBIT needed just to cover all fixed financial costs—annual interest (I) and preferred share dividends (PD). The equation for the financial breakeven point is

$$\text{Financial breakeven point} = I + \frac{PD}{1-T}$$

where T is the tax rate. It can be seen that when $PD = \$0$, the financial breakeven point is equal to I, the annual interest payment.

financial breakeven point
The level of EBIT necessary just to cover all fixed financial costs; the level of EBIT for which EPS = $0.

For levels of EBIT below the x-axis intercept, a loss (negative EPS) results. Each of the x-axis intercepts is a **financial breakeven point,** where EBIT just covers all fixed financial costs (EPS = $0).

Comparing Alternative Capital Structures

We can compare alternative capital structures by graphing financing plans as shown in Figure 10.6. The following example illustrates this procedure.

Example ▼ Cooke Company's capital structure alternatives were plotted on the EBIT–EPS axes in Figure 10.6. This figure discloses that over certain ranges of EBIT, each capital structure is superior to the others in terms of maximizing EPS. The zero-leverage capital structure (debt ratio = 0%) is superior to either of the other capital structures for levels of EBIT between $0 and $50,000; between $50,000 and $95,500 of EBIT, the capital structure associated with a debt ratio of 30 percent is preferred. At a level of EBIT in excess of $95,500, the capital structure associated with a debt ratio of 60 percent provides the highest earnings per share.[13]

Considering Risk in EBIT–EPS Analysis

When interpreting EBIT–EPS analysis, it is important to consider the risk of each capital structure alternative. Graphically, the risk of each capital structure can be viewed in light of the *financial breakeven point* (EBIT-axis intercept) and the *degree of financial leverage* reflected in the slope of the capital structure line: *The higher the financial breakeven point and the steeper the slope of the capital structure line, the greater the financial risk.*[14]

Further assessment of risk can be performed by using ratios. With increased financial leverage, as measured by the debt ratio, we expect a corresponding decline in the firm's ability to make scheduled interest payments, as measured by the times interest earned ratio.

---

13. An algebraic technique can be used to find the *indifference points* between the capital structure alternatives. This technique involves expressing each capital structure as an equation stated in terms of earnings per share, setting the equations for two capital structures equal to each other, and solving for the level of EBIT that causes the equations to be equal. By using the notation from footnote 12 and letting n equal the number of common shares outstanding, the general equation for the earnings per share from a financing plan is

$$EPS = \frac{(1 - T) \times (EBIT - I) - PD}{n}$$

Comparing Cooke Company's 0 and 30 percent capital structures, we get

$$\frac{(1 - 0.40) \times (EBIT - \$0) - \$0}{25} = \frac{(1 - 0.40) \times (EBIT - \$15) - \$0}{17.50}$$

$$\frac{0.60 \times EBIT}{25} = \frac{0.60 \times EBIT - \$9}{17.50}$$

$$10.50 \times EBIT = 15 \times EBIT - \$225$$

$$\$225 = 4.50 \times EBIT$$

$$EBIT = \$50$$

The calculated value of the indifference point between the 0 and 30 percent capital structures is therefore $50,000, as can be seen in Figure 10.6.

14. The degree of financial leverage (DFL) is reflected in the slope of the EBIT–EPS function. The steeper the slope, the greater the degree of financial leverage, because the change in EPS (y axis) resulting from a given change in EBIT (x axis) will increase with increasing slope and will decrease with decreasing slope.

Example ▼ Reviewing the three capital structures plotted for Cooke Company in Figure 10.6, we can see that as the debt ratio increases, so does the financial risk of each alternative. Both the financial breakeven point and the slope of the capital structure lines increase with increasing debt ratios. If we use the $100,000 EBIT value, the times interest earned ratio (EBIT ÷ interest) for the zero-leverage capital structure is infinity ($100,000 ÷ $0); for the 30 percent debt case, it is 6.67 ($100,000 ÷ $15,000); and for the 60 percent debt case, it is 2.02 ($100,000 ÷ $49,500). Because lower times interest earned ratios reflect higher risk, these ratios support the earlier conclusion that the risk of the capital structures increases with increasing financial leverage. The capital structure for a debt ratio of 60 percent is riskier than that for a debt ratio of 30 percent, which in turn is riskier ▲ than the capital structure for a debt ratio of 0 percent.

Basic Shortcoming of EBIT–EPS Analysis

The most important point to recognize when using EBIT–EPS analysis is that this technique tends to concentrate on *maximizing earnings* rather than maximizing owner wealth. The use of an EPS-maximizing approach generally ignores risk. If investors did not require risk premiums (additional returns) as the firm increased the proportion of debt in its capital structure, a strategy involving maximizing EPS would also maximize owner wealth. Because risk premiums increase with increases in financial leverage, the maximization of EPS *does not* ensure owner wealth maximization. To select the best capital structure, both return (EPS) and risk (via the required return, k_s) must be integrated into a valuation framework consistent with the capital structure theory presented earlier.

? Review Question

10–13 Explain the *EBIT–EPS approach* to capital structure. Include in your explanation a graph indicating the *financial breakeven point*; label the axes. Is this approach consistent with maximization of value? Explain.

10.4 Choosing the Optimal Capital Structure

Creating a wealth maximization framework for use in making capital structure decisions is not easy. Although the two key factors—return and risk—can be used separately to make capital structure decisions, integration of them into a market value context provides the best results. This section describes the procedures for linking the return and risk associated with alternative capital structures to market value to select the best capital structure.

Linkage

To determine its value under alternative capital structures, the firm must find the level of return that must be earned to compensate investors and owners for the risk being incurred. That is, the risk associated with each structure must be linked to the required rate of return. Such a framework is consistent with the overall valuation framework developed in Chapter 8 and applied to capital budgeting decisions in Chapters 12 and 13.

The required return associated with a given level of financial risk can be estimated in a number of ways. Theoretically, the preferred approach would be to first estimate the beta associated with each alternative capital structure and then use the CAPM (see Equation 7.8) to calculate the required return, k_s. A more operational approach involves linking the financial risk associated with each capital structure alternative directly to the required return. Such an approach is similar to the CAPM-type approach demonstrated in Chapter 13 for linking risk and required return (RADR). Here it involves estimating the required return associated with each level of financial risk, as measured by a statistic such as the coefficient of variation of EPS. Regardless of the approach used, one would expect that the required return would increase as the financial risk increases.

Example ▼ Cooke Company, using the coefficients of variation of EPS associated with each of the seven alternative capital structures as a risk measure, estimated the associated required returns. These are shown in Table 10.15. As expected, the estimated required return, k_s, increases with increasing risk, as measured by the ▲ coefficient of variation of EPS.

Estimating Value

The value of the firm associated with alternative capital structures can be estimated by using one of the standard valuation models. If, for simplicity, we assume that all earnings are paid out as dividends, we can use a zero-growth valuation model as developed in Chapter 8. The model, originally stated in Equation 8.11, is restated here with EPS substituted for dividends, because in each year the dividends would equal EPS:

$$P_0 = \frac{\text{EPS}}{k_s} \tag{10.11}$$

TABLE 10.15	Required Returns for Cooke Company's Alternative Capital Structures	
Capital structure debt ratio	Coefficient of variation of EPS (from column 3 of Table 10.14) (1)	Estimated required return, k_s (2)
0%	0.71	11.5%
10	0.74	11.7
20	0.78	12.1
30	0.83	12.5
40	0.91	14.0
50	1.07	16.5
60	1.40	19.0

By substituting the estimated level of EPS and the associated required return, k_s, into Equation 10.11, we can estimate the per share value of the firm, P_0.

Example ▼ Returning again to Cooke Company, we can now estimate the value of its shares under each of the alternative capital structures. Substituting the expected EPS (from column 1 of Table 10.14) and the required returns, k_s (from column 2 of Table 10.15), into Equation 10.11 for each of the alternative capital structures, we obtain the share values given in column 3 of Table 10.16. Plotting the resulting share values against the associated debt ratios, as shown in Figure 10.7, clearly illustrates that the maximum share value occurs at the capital structure
▲ associated with a debt ratio of 30 percent.

Maximizing Value Versus Maximizing EPS

Throughout this text, the goal of the financial manager has been specified as maximizing owner wealth, not profit. Although there is some relationship between the level of expected profit and value, there is no reason to believe that profit-maximizing strategies necessarily result in wealth maximization. It is therefore the wealth of the owners as reflected in the estimated share value that should serve as the criterion for selecting the best capital structure. A final look at Cooke Company will help to highlight this point.

Example ▼ Further analysis of Figure 10.7 clearly shows that although the firm's profits (EPS) are maximized at a debt ratio of 50 percent, share value is maximized at a 30 percent debt ratio. In this case, the preferred capital structure would be the 30 percent debt ratio. The EPS-maximization approach does not provide a similar conclusion because it does not consider risk. Therefore, to maximize owner wealth, Cooke Company should employ the capital structure that
▲ results in a 30 percent debt ratio.

TABLE 10.16	Calculation of Share Value Estimates Associated with Alternative Capital Structures for Cooke Company		
Capital structure debt ratio	Expected EPS (from column 1 of Table 10.14) (1)	Estimated required return, k_s (from column 2 of Table 10.15) (2)	Estimated share value [(1) ÷ (2)] (3)
0%	$2.40	0.115	$20.87
10	2.55	0.117	21.79
20	2.72	0.121	22.48
30	2.91	0.125	23.28
40	3.12	0.140	22.29
50	3.18	0.165	19.27
60	3.03	0.190	15.95

FIGURE 10.7

Estimating Value
Estimated share value and EPS for alternative capital structures for Cooke Company

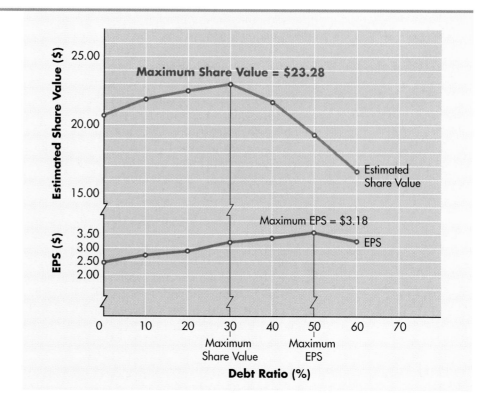

Some Other Important Considerations

Because there is really no practical way to calculate the optimal capital structure, any quantitative analysis of capital structure must be tempered with other important considerations. Numerous additional factors relative to capital structure decisions could be listed; some of the more important factors, categorized by broad area of concern, are summarized in Table 10.17.

? Review Questions

10–14 Do *maximizing value* and *maximizing EPS* lead to the same conclusion about the optimal capital structure? If not, what is the cause?

10–15 How might a firm go about determining its optimal capital structure? In addition to quantitative considerations, what other important factors should a firm consider when it is making a capital structure decision?

TABLE 10.17	Important Factors to Consider in Making Capital Structure Decisions	
Concern	Factor	Description
Business risk	Revenue stability	Firms having stable and predictable revenues can more safely undertake highly levered capital structures than can firms with volatile patterns of sales revenue. Firms with growing sales tend to be in the best position to benefit from added debt because they can reap the positive benefits of leverage, which magnifies the effect of these increases.
	Cash flow	When considering a new capital structure the firm must focus on its ability to generate the necessary cash flows to meet obligations. Cash forecasts reflecting an ability to service debts (and preferred shares) must support any capital structure shift.
Agency costs	Contractual obligations	A firm may be contractually constrained with respect to the type of funds that it can raise. For example, a firm might be prohibited from selling additional debt except when the claims of holders of such debt are made subordinate to the existing debt. Contractual constraints on the sale of additional common shares as well as the ability to distribute dividends might also exist.
	Management preferences	Occasionally, a firm will impose an internal constraint on the use of debt to limit its risk exposure to a level deemed acceptable to management. In other words, due to risk aversion, the firm's management constrains the firm's capital structure at a level that may or may not be the true optimum.
	Control	A management concerned about control may prefer to issue debt rather than (voting) common shares. Under favourable market conditions, a firm that wanted to sell equity could issue *nonvoting shares* or make a *preemptive offering* (see Chapter 6), allowing each shareholder to maintain proportionate ownership. Generally, only in closely held firms or firms threatened by takeover does control become a major concern in the capital structure decision.
Asymmetric information	External risk assessment	The firm's ability to raise funds quickly and at favourable rates depends on the external risk assessments of lenders and bond raters. The firm must therefore consider the potential impact of capital structure decisions both on share value and on published financial statements from which lenders and raters tend to assess the firm's risk.
	Timing	At times when interest rates are low, debt financing might be more attractive; when interest rates are high, the sale of common shares may be more appealing. Sometimes both debt and equity capital become unavailable at what would be viewed as reasonable terms. General economic conditions—especially those of the capital market—can thus significantly affect capital structure decisions.

SUMMARY

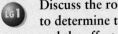 **Discuss the role of breakeven analysis, how to determine the operating breakeven point, and the effect of changing costs on the breakeven point.** Breakeven analysis measures the level of sales necessary to cover total operating costs. The operating breakeven point may be calculated by dividing fixed operating costs by the gross margin, the difference between sales and variable costs, on a per unit or percentage basis. Breakeven can be shown in number of units (Q), total sales, or graphically. The operating breakeven point increases with increased fixed and variable operating costs and decreases with an increase in sale price, and vice versa.

Understand operating, financial, and total leverage and the relationships among them. Operating leverage is the use of fixed operating costs by the firm to magnify the effects of changes in sales on EBIT. The higher the fixed operating costs, the greater the operating leverage. Financial leverage is the use of fixed financial costs by the firm to magnify the effects of changes in EBIT on EPS. The higher the fixed financial costs—typically, interest on debt and preferred share dividends—the greater the financial leverage. The total leverage of the firm is the use of fixed costs—both operating and financial—to magnify the effects of changes in sales on EPS. Total leverage reflects the combined effect of operating and financial leverage.

 Describe the basic types of capital, external assessment of capital structure, and capital structure theory. The two basic types of capital—debt and equity—that make up a firm's capital structure differ with respect to voice in management, claims on income and assets, maturity, and tax treatment. Capital structure can be externally assessed by using financial ratios—debt ratio, times interest earned ratio, and fixed-payment coverage ratio. The capital structure used varies by industry and companies within the industry; however, in 1999, the average debt ratio for non-financial industries in Canada was 62 percent and the times interest earned ratio was 2.70.

Research suggests that there is an optimal capital structure that balances the firm's benefits and costs of debt financing. The major benefit of debt financing is the tax shield. The costs of debt financing include the probability of bankruptcy, caused by business and financial risk; agency costs imposed by lenders; and asymmetric information, which typically causes firms to raise funds in a pecking order of reinvested profits, then debt, and finally external equity financing, to send positive signals to the market and thereby enhance the wealth of shareholders.

 Explain the optimal capital structure using a graphic view of the firm's debt, equity, and weighted average cost of capital functions, and a modified form of the zero-growth valuation model. The zero-growth valuation model can be used to define the firm's value as its after-tax EBIT divided by its weighted average cost of capital. Assuming that EBIT is constant, the value of the firm is maximized by minimizing its weighted average cost of capital (WACC). The optimal capital structure is the one that minimizes the WACC. Graphically, although both debt and equity costs rise with increasing financial leverage, the lower cost of debt causes the WACC to decline and then rise with increasing financial leverage. As a result, the firm's WACC exhibits a U-shape having a minimum value, which defines the optimum capital structure—the one that maximizes owner wealth.

 Discuss the graphical presentation, risk considerations, and basic shortcomings of using the EBIT–EPS approach to compare alternative capital structures. The EBIT–EPS approach can be used to evaluate capital structures in light of the returns they provide the firm's owners and their degree of financial risk. Under the EBIT–EPS approach, the preferred capital structure is the one that is expected to provide maximum EPS over the firm's expected range of EBIT. Graphically, this approach reflects risk in terms of the financial breakeven point and the slope of the capital structure line. The major shortcoming of EBIT–EPS analysis is that by ignoring risk, it concentrates on maximizing earnings rather than owners' wealth.

 Review the return and risk of alternative capital structures and their linkage to market value, and other important capital structure considerations. The best capital structure can be selected from various alternatives by using a valuation model to link return and risk factors. The preferred capital structure would be the one that results in the highest estimated share value—not the highest profits (EPS). Other important nonquantitative factors, such as revenue stability, cash flow, contractual obligations, management preferences, control, external risk assessment, and timing, must also be considered when making capital structure decisions.

(Solutions in Appendix B)

  ST 10–1 **Breakeven point and all forms of leverage** TOR most recently sold 100,000 units at $7.50 each; its variable operating costs are $3 per unit, and its fixed operating costs are $250,000. Annual interest charges total $80,000, and the firm has 8,000 preferred shares outstanding which pay a $5 annual dividend. It currently has 20,000 common shares outstanding. Assume that the firm has a 40 percent tax rate.

    a. At what level of sales in units and sales dollars would the firm break even on operations (i.e., EBIT = $0)?

    b. Calculate the firm's earnings per share (EPS) in tabular form at (1) the current level of sales and (2) a 120,000-unit sales level.

    c. Using the current *$750,000 level of sales as a base,* calculate the firm's degree of operating leverage (DOL).

    d. Using the EBIT *associated with the $750,000 level of sales as a base,* calculate the firm's degree of financial leverage (DFL).

    e. Use the degree of total leverage (DTL) concept to determine the effect (in percentage terms) of a 50 percent increase in TOR's sales *from the $750,000 base level* on its earnings per share.

 ST 10–2 **EBIT–EPS analysis** Newlin Electronics is considering additional financing of $10,000. It currently has $50,000 of 12 percent (annual interest) bonds and 10,000 common shares outstanding. The firm can obtain the financing through a 12 percent (annual interest) bond issue or the sale of 1,000 common shares. The firm has a 40 percent tax rate.

    a. Calculate two EBIT–EPS coordinates for each plan by selecting any two EBIT values and finding their associated EPS.

    b. Plot the two financing plans on a set of EBIT–EPS axes.

    c. On the basis of your graph in **b,** at what level of EBIT does the bond plan become superior to the stock plan?

  ST 10–3 **Optimal capital structure** Hawaiian Macadamia Nut Company has collected the following data with respect to its capital structure, expected earnings per share, and required return.

Capital structure debt ratio	Expected earnings per share	Required return, k_s
0%	$3.12	13%
10	3.90	15
20	4.80	16
30	5.44	17
40	5.51	19
50	5.00	20
60	4.40	22

    a. Compute the estimated share value associated with each of the capital structures using the simplified method described in this chapter (see Equation 10.11).

b. Determine the optimal capital structure based on (1) maximization of expected earnings per share and (2) maximization of share value.

c. Which capital structure do you recommend? Why?

PROBLEMS

WARM-UP **10–1** **Breakeven point—Algebraic**   Kate Rowland wishes to estimate the number of flower arrangements she must sell at $24.95 to break even. She has estimated fixed operating costs of $12,350 per year and variable operating costs of $15.45 per arrangement. How many flower arrangements must Kate sell to break even on operating costs? What will her total sales revenue be at breakeven? Calculate this answer in two different ways.

WARM-UP **10–2** **Breakeven comparisons—Algebraic**   Given the price and cost data shown in the following table for each of the three firms, F, G, and H, answer the following questions.

Firm	F	G	H
Sale price per unit	$ 18.00	$ 21.00	$ 30.00
Variable operating cost per unit	6.75	13.50	12.00
Fixed operating cost	45,000	30,000	90,000

a. What is the operating breakeven point in units and sales dollars for each firm?

b. How would you rank these firms in terms of their risk?

INTERMEDIATE **10–3** **Breakeven point—Algebraic and graphic**   Fine Leather Enterprises sells its single product for $129 per unit. The firm's fixed operating costs are $473,000 annually, and its variable operating costs are $86 per unit.

a. Find the firm's operating breakeven point in units and sales dollars.

b. Label the x axis "Sales (units)" and the y axis "Costs/Revenues ($)," and then graph the firm's sales revenue, total operating cost, and fixed operating cost functions on these axes. In addition, label the operating breakeven point and the areas of loss and profit (EBIT).

INTERMEDIATE **10–4** **Breakeven analysis**   Barry Carter is considering opening a record store. He wants to estimate the number of CDs he must sell to break even. The CDs will be sold for $13.98 each, variable operating costs are $10.48 per CD, and annual fixed operating costs are $73,500.

a. Find the operating breakeven point in CDs.

b. Calculate the total operating costs at the breakeven volume found in **a**.

c. If Barry estimates that at a minimum he can sell 2,000 CDs *per month*, should he go into the record business?

d. How much EBIT would Barry realize if he sells the minimum 2,000 CDs per month noted in **c**?

INTERMEDIATE 10–5 **Breakeven point—Changing costs/revenues**   JWG Company publishes *Creative Crosswords*. Last year the book of puzzles sold for $10 with variable operating cost per book of $8 and fixed operating costs of $40,000. How many books must be sold this year to achieve the breakeven point for the stated operating costs, given the following different circumstances?

a. All figures remain the same as last year.
b. Fixed operating costs increase to $44,000; all other figures remain the same.
c. The selling price increases to $10.50; all costs remain the same as last year.
d. Variable operating cost per book increases to $8.50; all other figures remain the same.
e. What conclusions about the operating breakeven point can be drawn from your answers?

INTERMEDIATE  10–6 **Breakeven analysis**   Molly Jasper and her sister, Caitlin Peters, got into the novelties business almost by accident. Molly, a talented sculptor, would make little figurines as gifts for friends. Occasionally, she and Caitlin would set up a booth at a crafts fair and sell a few of the figurines along with jewellery that Caitlin made. Little by little, demand for the figurines, now called Mollycaits, grew, and the sisters began to reproduce some of the favourites in resin using molds of the originals. The day came when a buyer for a major department store offered them a contract to produce 1,500 figurines of various designs for $10,000. Molly and Caitlin realized that it was time to get down to business. To make bookkeeping simpler, Molly had priced all of the figurines at $8. Variable operating costs amounted to an average of $6 per unit. In order to produce the order, Molly and Caitlin would have to rent industrial facilities for a month, which would cost them $4,000.

a. Calculate Mollycait's operating breakeven point in units and sales dollars.
b. Calculate Mollycait's EBIT on the department store order.
c. If Molly renegotiates the contract at a price of $10, what will the EBIT be?
d. If the store refuses to pay more than $8 per unit, but is willing to negotiate quantity, what quantity of figurines would result in an EBIT of $4,000?
e. At this time, Mollycaits come in 15 different varieties. Whereas the average variable cost per unit is $6, the actual cost varies from unit to unit. What recommendation would you have for Molly and Caitlin with regard to pricing and/or the number and type of units that they offer for sale?

INTERMEDIATE 10–7 **EBIT sensitivity**   Stewart Industries sells its finished product for $9 per unit. Its fixed operating costs are $20,000, and the variable operating cost per unit is $5.

a. Calculate the firm's earnings before interest and taxes (EBIT) for sales of 10,000 units.
b. Calculate the firm's EBIT for sales of 8,000 and 12,000 units, respectively.
c. Calculate the percentage changes in sales (from the 10,000-unit base level) and associated percentage changes in EBIT for the shifts in sales indicated in **b.**
d. On the basis of your findings in **c**, comment on the sensitivity of changes in EBIT in response to changes in sales.

INTERMEDIATE   **10–8** **Degree of operating leverage**   Grey Products has fixed operating costs of $380,000, variable operating costs per unit of $16, and a selling price of $63.50 per unit.

a. Calculate the operating breakeven point in units.

b. Calculate the firm's EBIT at 9,000, 10,000, and 11,000 units, respectively.

c. By using 10,000 units as a base, what are the percentage changes in units sold and EBIT as sales move from the base to the other sales levels used in **b**?

d. Use the percentages computed in **c** to determine the degree of operating leverage (DOL).

e. Use the formula for degree of operating leverage to determine the DOL at 10,000 units.

INTERMEDIATE   **10–9** **Degree of operating leverage—Graphic**   Levin Corporation has fixed operating costs of $72,000, variable operating costs of $6.75 per unit, and a selling price of $9.75 per unit.

a. Calculate the operating breakeven point in units.

b. Compute the degree of operating leverage (DOL) for the following unit sales levels: 25,000, 30,000, 40,000.

c. Graph the DOL figures that you computed in **b** (on the *y* axis) against sales levels (on the *x* axis).

d. Compute the degree of operating leverage at 24,000 units; add this point to your graph.

e. What principle is illustrated by your graph and figures?

INTERMEDIATE   **10–10** **EPS calculations**   Southland Industries has $60,000 of 16 percent (annual interest) bonds outstanding, 1,500 preferred shares paying an annual dividend of $5 per share, and 4,000 common shares outstanding. Assuming that the firm has a 40 percent tax rate, compute earnings per share (EPS) for the following levels of EBIT:

a. $24,600

b. $30,600

c. $35,000

INTERMEDIATE   **10–11** **Degree of financial leverage**   Northwestern Trust has a current capital structure consisting of $250,000 of 16 percent (annual interest) debt and 2,000 common shares. The firm pays taxes at the rate of 40 percent.

a. Using EBIT values of $80,000 and $120,000, determine the associated earnings per share (EPS).

b. Using $80,000 of EBIT as a base, calculate the degree of financial leverage (DFL).

c. Rework parts **a** and **b** assuming that the firm has $100,000 of 16 percent (annual interest) debt and 3,000 common shares.

 INTERMEDIATE   **10–12** **DFL and graphic display of financing plans**   Wells and Associates has EBIT of $67,500. Interest costs are $22,500, and the firm has 15,000 common shares outstanding. Assume a 40 percent tax rate.

a. Use the degree of financial leverage (DFL) formula to calculate the DFL for the firm.

b. Using a set of EBIT–EPS axes, plot Wells and Associates' financing plan.

c. Assuming that the firm also has 1,000 preferred shares paying a $6 annual dividend per share, what is the DFL?

d. Plot the financing plan including the 1,000 shares of $6 preferred stock on the axes used in **b**.

e. Briefly discuss the graph of the two financing plans.

10–13 **Integrative—Multiple leverage measures** Play-More Toys produces inflatable beach balls, selling 400,000 balls a year. Each ball produced has a variable operating cost of $0.84 and sells for $1. Fixed operating costs are $28,000. The firm has annual interest charges of $6,000, preferred share dividends of $2,000, and a 40 percent tax rate.

a. Calculate the operating breakeven point in units and dollars.

b. Calculate the degree of operating leverage (DOL) at sales of $400,000. Explain the meaning of your answers.

c. Calculate the degree of financial leverage (DFL) at sales of $400,000. Explain the meaning of your answers.

d. Calculate the degree of total leverage (DTL) at sales of $400,000. Explain the meaning of your answers.

  10–14 **Integrative—Leverage and risk** Firm R has sales of 100,000 units at $2 per unit, variable operating costs of $1.70 per unit, and fixed operating costs of $6,000. Interest is $10,000 per year. Firm W has sales of 100,000 units at $2.50 per unit, variable operating costs of $1 per unit, and fixed operating costs of $62,500. Interest is $17,500 per year. Assume that both firms are in the 40 percent tax bracket.

a. Compute the degree of operating, financial, and total leverage for firm R. Explain the meaning of your answers.

b. Compute the degree of operating, financial, and total leverage for firm W. Explain the meaning of your answers.

c. Compare the relative risks of the two firms.

d. Discuss the principles of leverage illustrated in your answers.

 10–15 **Integrative—Multiple leverage measures and prediction** Carolina Fastener, Inc., makes a patented marine bulkhead latch that wholesales for $6. Each latch has variable operating costs of $3.50. Fixed operating costs are $50,000 per year. The firm pays $13,000 interest and $7,000 of preferred share dividends per year. At this point, the firm is selling 30,000 latches a year and is taxed at 40 percent.

a. Calculate Carolina Fastener's operating breakeven point in units and sales dollars.

b. Based on the firm's current sales of 40,000 units per year and its interest and preferred dividend costs, calculate its EBIT and EAC.

c. Calculate the firm's degree of operating leverage (DOL). Explain the answer.

d. Calculate the firm's degree of financial leverage (DFL). Explain the answer.

e. Calculate the firm's degree of total leverage (DTL). Explain the answer.

f. Carolina Fastener has entered into a contract to produce and sell an additional 15,000 latches in the coming year. Use the DOL, DFL, and DTL to predict and calculate the changes in EBIT and EAC. Check your work by a simple calculation of Carolina Fastener's EBIT and EAC using the basic information given.

10–16   **Integrative—Breakeven and leverage measures**   Maclauchlan Inc. sells a number
of products whose average selling price is $7.50. The company is planning to
CHALLENGE   produce 100,000 units of the various items. Forecasted operational costs are as
follows:

Depreciation	$175,000
Management salaries	110,000
Factory labour	205,000
Marketing expenses (fixed)	72,000
Direct materials	189,000
Maintenance (50% fixed)	36,000
Direct factory overhead	38,000
Rent	90,000
Total	$915,000

a. Is B/E going to be more or less than 100,000 units? Which costs are fixed
   and variable? Calculate the per unit variable costs. For all remaining questions,
   assume that the fixed costs remain fixed at all levels of production.
b. What is Maclauchlan Inc.'s EBIT at a production volume of 100,000 units?
c. Calculate Maclauchlan Inc.'s breakeven in units and total dollar sales.
d. Calculate the selling price Maclauchlan must charge just to break even at
   production volumes of 100,000, 125,000, and 200,000 units.
e. If Maclauchlan wishes to earn an EBIT that is 10 percent of sales, how many
   units must the company sell?
f. Based on the per unit variable costs calculated in part **a**, and assuming these
   will remain the same, calculate the DOL, DFL, and DTL at a production
   volume of 220,000 units. Maclauchlan has total assets of $925,000 and the
   company has 79,000 common shares outstanding. The average interest rate
   on their outstanding debt is 10 percent. The company's equity ratio is 60
   percent and their tax rate is 20 percent. Prove that the DOL, DFL, and DTL
   calculated are correct.

WARM-UP   10–17   **Various capital structures**   Charter Enterprises currently has $1 million in total
assets and is totally equity financed. It is contemplating a change in capital
structure. Compute the amount of debt and equity that would be outstanding if
the firm were to shift to one of the following debt ratios: 10, 20, 30, 40, 50, 60,
and 90 percent. (*Note:* The amount of total assets would not change.) Is there a
limit to the debt ratio's value?

CHALLENGE   10–18   **Debt and financial risk**   Tower Interiors has made the forecast of sales shown
in the following table. Also given is the probability of each level of sales.

Sales	Probability
$200,000	0.20
300,000	0.60
400,000	0.20

The firm has fixed operating costs of $75,000 and variable operating costs equal to 70 percent of the sales level. The company pays $12,000 in interest per period. The tax rate is 40 percent.

a. Compute the earnings before interest and taxes (EBIT) for each level of sales.
b. Compute the earnings per share (EPS) for each level of sales, the expected EPS, the standard deviation of the EPS, and the coefficient of variation of EPS, assuming that there are 10,000 common shares outstanding.
c. Tower has the opportunity to reduce leverage to zero and pay no interest. This will require that the number of shares outstanding be increased to 15,000. Repeat **b** under this assumption.
d. Compare your findings in **b** and **c**, and comment on the effect of the reduction of debt to zero on the firm's financial risk.

 INTERMEDIATE **10–19**   **EPS and optimal debt ratio**   Williams Glassware has estimated, at various debt ratios, the expected earnings per share and the standard deviation of the earnings per share as shown in the following table.

Debt ratio	Earnings per share (EPS)	Standard deviation of EPS
0%	$2.30	$1.15
20	3.00	1.80
40	3.50	2.80
60	3.95	3.95
80	3.80	5.53

a. Estimate the optimal debt ratio based on the relationship between earnings per share and the debt ratio. You will probably find it helpful to graph the relationship.
b. Graph the relationship between the coefficient of variation and the debt ratio. Label the areas associated with business risk and financial risk.

 INTERMEDIATE **10–20**   **EBIT–EPS and capital structure**   Data-Check is considering two capital structures. The key information is shown in the following table. Assume a 40 percent tax rate.

Source of capital	Structure A	Structure B
Long-term debt	$100,000 at 16% coupon rate	$200,000 at 17% coupon rate
Common equity	4,000 shares	2,000 shares

a. Calculate two EBIT–EPS coordinates for each of the structures by selecting any two EBIT values and finding their associated EPS.
b. Plot the two capital structures on a set of EBIT–EPS axes.
c. Indicate over what EBIT range, if any, each structure is preferred.
d. Discuss the leverage and risk aspects of each structure.
e. If the firm is fairly certain that its EBIT will exceed $75,000, which structure would you recommend? Why?

INTERMEDIATE 10–21   **EBIT–EPS and preferred equity**   Litho-Print is considering two possible capital structures, A and B, shown in the following table. Assume a 40 percent tax rate.

Source of capital	Structure A	Structure B
Long-term debt	$75,000 at 16% coupon rate	$50,000 at 15% coupon rate
Preferred equity	$10,000 with an 18% annual dividend	$15,000 with an 18% annual dividend
Common equity	8,000 shares	10,000 shares

a. Calculate two EBIT–EPS coordinates for each of the structures by selecting any two EBIT values and finding their associated EPS.
b. Graph the two capital structures on the same set of EBIT–EPS axes.
c. Discuss the leverage and risk associated with each of the structures.
d. Over what range of EBIT is each structure preferred?
e. Which structure do you recommend if the firm expects its EBIT to be $35,000? Explain.

   10–22   **Integrative—Optimal capital structure**   Medallion Cooling Systems, Inc., has total assets of $10,000,000, EBIT of $2,000,000, and preferred dividends of $200,000, and is taxed at a rate of 40 percent. In an effort to determine the optimal capital structure, the firm has assembled data on the cost of debt, the number of common shares for various levels of indebtedness, and the overall required return on investment:

INTERMEDIATE

Capital structure debt ratio	Cost of debt, k_d	Number of common shares	Required return, k_s
0%	0%	200,000	12%
15	8	170,000	13
30	9	140,000	14
45	12	110,000	16
60	15	80,000	20

a. Calculate earnings per share for each level of indebtedness.
b. Use Equation 10.11 and the earnings per share calculated in part **a** to calculate a price per share for each level of indebtedness.
c. Choose the optimal capital structure. Justify your choice.

  10–23   **Integrative—Optimal capital structure**   Nelson Corporation has made the following forecast of sales, with the associated probability of occurrence noted.

CHALLENGE

Sales	Probability
$200,000	0.20
300,000	0.60
400,000	0.20

The company has fixed operating costs of $100,000 per year, and variable operating costs represent 40 percent of sales. The existing capital structure consists of 25,000 common shares that have a $10 per share book value. No other capital items are outstanding. The marketplace has assigned the following discount rates to risky earnings per share.

Coefficient of variation of EPS	Estimated required return, k_s
0.43	15%
0.47	16
0.51	17
0.56	18
0.60	22
0.64	24

The company is contemplating *shifting its capital structure* by substituting debt in the capital structure for common equity. The three different debt ratios under consideration are shown in the following table, along with an estimate of the corresponding required interest rate on *all* debt.

Debt ratio	Interest rate on *all* debt
20%	10%
40	12
60	14

The tax rate is 40 percent. The market value of the equity for a levered firm can be found by using the simplified method (see Equation 10.11).
a. Calculate the expected earnings per share (EPS), the standard deviation of EPS, and the coefficient of variation of EPS for the three proposed capital structures.
b. Determine the optimal capital structure, assuming (1) maximization of earnings per share and (2) maximization of share value.
c. Construct a graph (similar to Figure 10.7) showing the relationships in b. (*Note:* You will probably have to sketch the lines, because you have only three data points.)

   10–24   **Integrative—Optimal capital structure**   The board of directors of Morales Publishing, Inc., has commissioned a capital structure study. The company has
  CHALLENGE   total assets of $40,000,000. It has earnings before interest and taxes of $8,000,000 and is taxed at 40 percent.
a. Create a spreadsheet like the one in Table 10.11 showing values of debt and equity as well as the total number of shares, assuming a book value of $25 per share.

% Debt	Total assets	$ Debt	$ Equity	No. of shares @ $25
0%	$40,000,000	$____	$____	_____
10	40,000,000	____	____	_____
20	40,000,000	____	____	_____
30	40,000,000	____	____	_____
40	40,000,000	____	____	_____
50	40,000,000	____	____	_____
60	40,000,000	____	____	_____

b. Given the before-tax cost of debt at various levels of indebtedness, calculate the yearly interest expenses.

% Debt	$ Total debt	Before tax cost of debt, k_d	$ Interest expense
0%	$____	0.0%	$____
10	____	7.5	____
20	____	8.0	____
30	____	9.0	____
40	____	11.0	____
50	____	12.5	____
60	____	15.5	____

c. Using EBIT of $8,000,000, a 40 percent tax rate, and information developed in parts **a** and **b,** calculate the most likely earnings per share for the firm at various levels of indebtedness. Mark the level of indebtedness that maximizes EPS.

% Debt	EBIT	Interest expense	EBT	Taxes	Net income	No. of shares	EPS
0%	$8,000,000	____	____	____	____	____	____
10	8,000,000	____	____	____	____	____	____
20	8,000,000	____	____	____	____	____	____
30	8,000,000	____	____	____	____	____	____
40	8,000,000	____	____	____	____	____	____
50	8,000,000	____	____	____	____	____	____
60	8,000,000	____	____	____	____	____	____

d. Using the EPS developed in part **c,** the estimates of required return, k_s, and Equation 10.11, estimate the value per share at various levels of indebtedness. Mark the level of indebtedness that results in the maximum price per share, P_0.

Debt	EPS	k_s	P_0
0%	——	10.0%	—
10	——	10.3	—
20	——	10.9	—
30	——	11.4	—
40	——	12.6	—
50	——	14.8	—
60	——	17.5	—

e. Prepare a recommendation to the board of directors of Morales Publishing, Inc., that specifies the degree of indebtedness that will accomplish the firm's goal of optimizing shareholder wealth. Use your findings in parts **a** through **d** to justify your recommendation.

10–25 **Integrative—Optimal capital structure**   Country Textiles, which has fixed operating costs of $300,000 and variable operating costs equal to 40 percent of sales, has made the following three sales estimates, with their probabilities noted.

CHALLENGE

Sales	Probability
$ 600,000	0.30
900,000	0.40
1,200,000	0.30

The firm wishes to analyze five possible capital structures—0, 15, 30, 45, and 60 percent debt ratios. The firm's total assets of $1 million are assumed to be constant. Its common equity has a book value of $25 per share, and the firm is in the 40 percent tax bracket. The following additional data have been gathered for use in analyzing the five capital structures under consideration.

Capital structure debt ratio	Before-tax cost of debt, k_d	Required return, k_s
0%	0.0%	10.0%
15	8.0	10.5
30	10.0	11.6
45	13.0	14.0
60	17.0	20.0

a. Calculate the level of EBIT associated with each of the three levels of sales.
b. Calculate the amount of debt, the amount of equity, and the number of common shares outstanding for each of the capital structures being considered.
c. Calculate the annual interest on the debt under each of the capital structures being considered. (*Note:* The before-tax cost of debt, k_d, is the interest rate applicable to *all* debt associated with the corresponding debt ratio.)

d. Calculate the EPS associated with each of the three levels of EBIT calculated in **a** for each of the five capital structures being considered.

e. Calculate the (1) expected EPS, (2) standard deviation of EPS, and (3) coefficient of variation of EPS for each of the capital structures, using your findings in **d.**

f. Plot the expected EPS and coefficient of variation of EPS against the capital structures (x axis) on separate sets of axes, and comment on the return and risk relative to capital structure.

g. Using the EBIT–EPS data developed in **d,** plot the 0, 30, and 60 percent capital structures on the same set of EBIT-EPS axes, and discuss the ranges over which each is preferred. What is the major problem with the use of this approach?

h. Using the valuation model given in Equation 10.11 and your findings in **e,** estimate the share value for each of the capital structures being considered.

i. Compare and contrast your findings in **f** and **h.** Which structure is preferred if the goal is to maximize EPS? Which structure is preferred if the goal is to maximize share value? Which capital structure do you recommend? Explain.

CASE   CHAPTER 10 — Evaluating Tampa Manufacturing's Capital Structure

Tampa Manufacturing, an established producer of printing equipment, expects its sales to remain flat for the next 3 to 5 years due to both a weak economic outlook and an expectation of little new printing technology development over that period. On the basis of this scenario, the firm's management has been instructed by its board to institute programs that will allow it to operate more efficiently, earn higher profits, and, most important, maximize share value. In this regard, the firm's chief financial officer (CFO), Jon Lawson, has been charged with evaluating the firm's capital structure. Lawson believes that the current capital structure, which contains 10 percent debt and 90 percent equity, may lack adequate financial leverage. To evaluate the firm's capital structure, Lawson has gathered the data summarized in the following table on the current capital structure (10% debt ratio) and two alternative capital structures—A (30% debt ratio) and B (50% debt ratio)—that he would like to consider.

	Capital structure[a]		
Source of capital	Current (10% debt)	A (30% debt)	B (50% debt)
Long-term debt	$1,000,000	$3,000,000	$5,000,000
Coupon rate[b]	9%	10%	12%
Common equity	100,000 shares	70,000 shares	40,000 shares
Required return on equity, k_s[c]	12%	13%	18%

[a]These structures are based on maintaining the firm's current level of $10,000,000 of total financing.
[b]Interest rate applicable to *all* debt.
[c]Market-based return for the given level of risk.

Lawson expects the firm's earnings before interest and taxes (EBIT) to remain at its current level of $1,200,000. The firm has a 40 percent tax rate.

Required

a. Use the current level of EBIT to calculate the times interest earned ratio for each capital structure. Evaluate the current and two alternative capital structures using the times interest earned and debt ratios.

b. Prepare a single EBIT–EPS graph showing the current and two alternative capital structures.

c. On the basis of the graph in **b,** which capital structure will maximize Tampa's earnings per share (EPS) at its expected level of EBIT of $1,200,000? Why might this *not* be the best capital structure?

d. Using the zero-growth valuation model given in Equation 10.11, find the market value of Tampa's equity under each of the three capital structures at the $1,200,000 level of expected EBIT.

e. On the basis of your findings in **c** and **d,** which capital structure would you recommend? Why?

WEB EXERCISES   LINKS TO PRACTISE

Visit the following Web sites and complete the suggested exercises. These exercises will allow you to review practical applications of the chapter topics as well as explore the wealth of information regarding managerial finance that is available on the Internet.

www.jaxworks.com/BreakEven.html

www.jaxworks.com/calc6.htm

These links provide two breakeven calculators that allow the user to determine breakeven in units and dollars, generate a breakeven chart, and determine the breakeven point that achieves a stated level of profit. Use these two Web sites to complete some of the problems in the book.

www.globeinvestor.com/static/hubs/quotes.html

Many of the concepts discussed in this chapter can be easily applied to publicly traded companies. The above Web site is a popular source of financial data for Canadian companies.

1. Enter ABX-T in the Enter Symbol area and click on GO. What is the name of this company? Click on Company Snapshot. What does the company do? Click on the Financial Reports link and then Ratios. What is the company's:

   a. debt/equity ratio?

   b. times interest earned ratio?

   c. market-to-book value ratio?

   d. return on common equity?

   e. Click on Quarterly. What is the company's most recent closing price, most recent EPS, the current P/E multiple and market capitalization?

2. Repeat the above for the following symbols: PCA-T, POW-T, T-T, ECA-T, WN-T, or other companies of your choice.
3. Discuss the differences in the use of debt financing by these companies, their ability to cover the required payments, and the impact of the choice of capital structures on the return to the owners of the company.

www.jaxworks.com/zscore2.htm
www.jaxworks.com/zscore3.htm
www.jaxworks.com/calc2a.htm
www.sedar.com/search/search_form_pc_en.htm

The Altman Z-score is widely used to measure the overall financial health of a business. The Z-score considers the financial risk of a company and assesses the chance of bankruptcy. The Z-score model works by calculating five key measures of liquidity and debt for a company based on the following seven financial items: working capital, retained earnings, total assets, market value, total liabilities, sales, and earnings before interest and taxes (EBIT). These financial statement variables are used to calculate various ratios, which are then multiplied by a given weighting. The resulting products are added and a final numerical score determined (the Z-score). This score is used to evaluate the chance that a company will go bankrupt.

The first two Web sites listed provide readings regarding the Altman Z-score. The third Web site provides a worksheet that can be used to calculate the Z-score for a company. The fourth provides a link to the financial statements of publicly traded companies in Canada. Based on the readings, answer the following questions.

1. What ratios are used to determine the Altman Z-score?
2. What weight factor is used to adjust each of the five ratios? What is then done to calculate the Altman Z-score for a company?
3. Who developed the Altman Z-score and what was the development of the model based on? How reliable an indicator of bankruptcy does the Z-score seem to be?
4. Altman developed three ranges for possible Z-scores. What are these ranges, and what do the ranges suggest regarding the financial health of a company?
5. Use the worksheet (the third Web site) to determine the financial health of two publicly traded manufacturing companies in Canada. Some companies to consider include Magna, Linamar, CAE, Bombardier, Algoma, Stelco, Dofasco, Ballard Power, Gennum, Research in Motion, Molson, Biovail, Cinram, Inco, Rothmans, Maax, Vincor, Saputo, Sleeman Breweries, and QLT. Use the fourth Web site listed to link to the financial statements of the selected companies.
6. What does your analysis in part 5 suggest about the selected companies: (a) chance of bankruptcy and (b) optimal capital structures?

11

Dividend Policy

LEARNING GOALS

LG1 Understand cash dividend payment procedures and the role of dividend reinvestment plans.

LG2 Describe the residual theory of dividends and the key arguments with regard to dividend irrelevance and relevance.

LG3 Discuss the key factors involved in formulating a dividend policy.

LG4 Review and evaluate the three basic types of dividend policies.

LG5 Evaluate stock dividends from accounting, shareholder, and company points of view.

LG6 Explain stock splits and common share repurchases and the firm's motivation for undertaking each of them.

11.1 Dividend Fundamentals

Expected cash dividends are a key return variable from which owners and investors determine share value. They represent a source of cash flow to shareholders and provide information about the firm's current and future performance. Because **reinvested profits**—earnings not distributed as dividends—are a form of *internal* financing, the dividend decision can significantly affect the firm's *external* financing requirements, as shown in Chapter 4. In other words, if the firm needs financing, the larger the cash dividend paid, the greater the amount of financing that must be raised externally through borrowing or

reinvested profits
Earnings not distributed as dividends; a form of *internal* financing.

Relishing the Leftovers

After the guests go home, are you glad to see some leftovers in the kitchen (and especially when most of what is left over is the dessert, rather than the vegetables)? If so, you'll understand immediately one of the dividend theories presented in this chapter—the residual theory of dividends, which views dividends as the cash flows remaining available to common shareholders after all acceptable investment opportunities have been undertaken. The size and pattern of the dividends provide information about the firm's current and future performance. Some shareholders want and expect to receive dividends, whereas others are content to see an increase in stock price without receiving dividends. This chapter addresses the issue of whether dividends matter to shareholders and discusses the key aspects of dividend policy.

through the sale of common or preferred shares. (Remember that although dividends are charged to retained earnings, they are actually paid out of cash.) To understand the fundamentals of dividend policy, you first need to understand the procedures for paying cash dividends.

Cash Dividend Payment Procedures

The payment of cash dividends to shareholders is decided by the firm's board of directors. The directors normally meet quarterly or semiannually to determine whether and in what amount dividends should be paid. The past period's financial

Career Key

Accounting personnel will provide the financial data needed by management to make dividend decisions. They will provide the board of directors with the current cash balance and will assist in estimating future cash flows.

performance and future outlook, as well as recent dividends paid, are key inputs to the dividend decision. The payment date of the cash dividend, if one is declared, must also be established. Once declared, the board and company are legally obligated to make the dividend payment. Note, though, there is no obligation to *declare* a dividend, even in cases where a company has been paying dividends for many years. The payment of dividends is at the total discretion of the board of directors.

Amount of Dividends

Career Key

Members of top *management* will provide the background information to help the board establish the best dividend policy. They will need to explain to the board future capital expenditure and financing plans that will affect future dividends.

Whether dividends should be paid and, if so, how large they should be are important decisions that depend primarily on the firm's dividend policy. Many firms pay some cash dividends each period. Most firms have a set policy with respect to the amount of the periodic dividend, but the firm's directors can change this amount at the dividend meeting, based largely on significant increases or decreases in earnings.

Relevant Dates

If the directors of the firm declare a dividend, they also indicate the record and payment dates associated with the dividend. Typically, the directors issue a statement indicating their dividend decision, the record date, and the payment date. This statement is generally provided in a press release and then reported in financial newspapers such as the *Globe and Mail*'s *Report on Business* and the *Financial Post*.

date of record (dividends)
Set by the firm's directors, the date on which all persons whose names are recorded as shareholders receive a declared dividend at a specified future time.

Record Date   All persons whose names are recorded as shareholders on the **date of record,** which is set by the directors, receive a declared dividend at a specified future time. These shareholders are often referred to as *holders of record*.

Due to the time needed to make bookkeeping entries when shares are traded, the shares begin selling **ex dividend** 2 *business days* prior to the date of record. Purchasers of shares selling ex dividend do not receive the current dividend. A simple way to determine the first day on which the stock sells ex dividend is to subtract 2 days from the date of record; if a weekend intervenes, subtract 4 days. Ignoring general market fluctuations, the stock's price is expected to drop by the amount of the declared dividend on the ex dividend date.

ex dividend
Period beginning 2 *business days* prior to the date of record during which a stock is sold without the right to receive the current dividend.

payment date
The actual date on which the firm makes the dividend payment to the holders of record.

Payment Date   The payment date is also set by the directors and is generally a few weeks after the record date. The **payment date** is the actual date on which the firm makes the dividend payment to the holders of record. An example will clarify the various dates and the accounting effects.

Example ▼ At the quarterly dividend meeting of Rudolf Company, a distributor of office products, held June 10, the directors declared an $0.80-per-share cash dividend for holders of record on Monday, June 30. June 10 is termed the declaration date. The firm had 100,000 common shares outstanding. The payment date for the dividend was August 1. Before the dividend was declared, the key accounts of the firm were as follows:

Cash	$200,000	Dividends payable	$ 0
		Retained earnings	1,000,000

When the dividend was declared by the directors, $80,000 of the retained earnings ($0.80 per share × 100,000 shares) was transferred to the dividends payable account. The key accounts thus became

Cash	$200,000	Dividends payable	$ 80,000
		Retained earnings	920,000

Rudolf Company's shares began selling ex dividend 2 *business days* prior to the date of record, which was June 26. This date was found by subtracting 4 days (because a weekend intervened) from the June 30 date of record. Purchasers of Rudolf's stock on June 25 or earlier received the rights to the dividends; those purchasing the stock on or after June 26 do not. Assuming a stable market, Rudolf's common share price was expected to drop by approximately $0.80 per share when it began selling ex dividend on June 26. When the August 1 payment date arrived, the firm makes the dividend payment to the holders of record as of June 30. This produced the following balances in the key accounts of the firm:

Cash	$120,000	Dividends payable	$ 0
		Retained earnings	920,000

▲ The net effect of declaring and paying the dividend was to reduce the firm's total assets (and shareholders' equity) by $80,000.

Dividend Reinvestment Plans

dividend reinvestment plans (DRIPs)
Plans that enable shareholders to use dividends received on the firm's shares to acquire additional full or fractional shares at no transaction (brokerage) cost.

Today many firms offer **dividend reinvestment plans (DRIPs)**, which enable shareholders to use dividends received on the firm's shares to acquire additional shares—even fractional shares—at no transaction (brokerage) cost. Some companies even allow investors to make their *initial purchases* of the firm's shares directly from the company without going through a stockbroker. Under current tax law, cash dividends received (or the amount invested through a DRIP) are taxed as ordinary income. The taxation of dividends was discussed in Chapter 8, with an example provided in Table 8.5 on page 390. Recall, for tax purposes, that the dividend is increased by 25 percent but then a dividend tax credit is allowed that greatly reduces the taxes paid on dividends versus on interest income. When the shares acquired through a DRIP are sold, the proceeds in excess of the original purchase price are taxed as a capital gain.

Many companies that offer DRIPs also offer share purchase plans (SPPs) that allow shareholders to make optional cash contributions, either monthly or quarterly up to some maximum amount, that are then used to purchase additional common shares for the investor. Participation in both DRIPs and SPPs are voluntary; shareholders choose to enroll in the plans.

The benefit of DRIPs and SPPs for investors is that they regularly (every quarter) acquire additional common shares of the company. Over time, with the compounding effect, a very modest initial holding of common shares can become a very large number of shares. The compounding effect is multiplied as a company increases the dividends paid on common shares. In addition, the company assumes all administrative and brokerage fees associated with the plan. The investor receives a statement outlining their dividend payments, shares purchased, and shares held each quarter. The statement also allows investors to mail to the company OCCs that are then used to purchase common shares on the shareholder's behalf. Some companies that offer DRIPs purchase additional common shares for investors at a 5 percent discount to the market price. This incentive may encourage many of the company's individual shareholders to participate in the DRIP.

The benefit of the DRIP and SPP for the company is that they can raise financing avoiding underpricing and flotation costs associated with a public offering of new common shares. In addition, many companies want individuals as shareholders since they are considered more "loyal" investors and will hold the common shares for long periods of time. Also, individuals who own shares are often loyal users of the company's product or services. The DRIP and SPP act as incentives for individuals to become shareholders.

 Numerous companies in Canada offer DRIPs and SPPs. For a list of these companies, see the following Web sites: **www.ndir.com/SI/DRPs.shtml** and **rbcc.royalbank.com/rt/gss.nsf/DRIP+Report?OpenFrameSet**.

? Review Questions

11–1   How do the *declaration date, date of record*, and *holders of record* relate to the payment of cash dividends? What does the term *ex dividend* mean?

11–2   What is a *dividend reinvestment plan*? What benefit is available to plan participants? What is a share purchase plan? Why might companies offer these two plans?

11.2 The Relevance of Dividend Policy

Numerous theories and empirical findings concerning dividend policy have been reported in the financial literature. Although this research provides some interesting insights about dividend policy, capital budgeting and capital structure decisions are generally considered far more important than dividend decisions. In other words, good investment and financing decisions should not be sacrificed for a dividend policy of questionable importance.

A number of key questions have yet to be resolved: Does dividend policy matter? What effect does dividend policy have on share price? Is there a model that can be used to evaluate alternative dividend policies in view of share value? Here we begin by describing the residual theory of dividends, which is used as a backdrop for discussion of the key arguments in support of dividend irrelevance and then those in support of dividend relevance.

The Residual Theory of Dividends

residual theory of dividends
A theory that the dividend paid by a firm should be the amount left over after all acceptable investment opportunities have been undertaken.

One school of thought—the **residual theory of dividends**—suggests that the dividend paid by a firm should be viewed as a *residual*—the amount left over after all acceptable investment opportunities have been undertaken. Using this approach, the firm would treat the dividend decision in three steps as follows:

Step 1   Determine its optimum level of capital expenditures, which would be the level generated by the point of intersection of the investment opportunities schedule (IOS) and marginal cost of capital (MCC) schedule (see Chapter 9).

Step 2   Using the optimal capital structure proportions (see Chapter 10), estimate the total amount of equity financing needed to support the expenditures generated in Step 1.

Step 3   Because the cost of reinvested profits, k_r, is less than the cost of new common shares, k_n, use reinvested profits to meet the equity requirement determined in Step 2. If reinvested profits are inadequate to meet this need, sell new common shares. If the available reinvested profits are in excess of this need, distribute the surplus amount—the residual—as dividends.

Career Key

The *marketing* department would be likely to prefer a no-dividends policy because its capital expenditures proposals would have a better chance of being financed. Marketing's only concern in that case would be that the expected returns of its projects would exceed the marginal cost of capital.

Following this approach, cash dividends are not paid if all of the firm's profits are needed to finance projects. The argument supporting this approach is that it is sound management to be certain that the company has the money it needs to compete effectively and therefore increase share price. This view of dividends tends to suggest that the required return of investors, k_s, is *not* influenced by the firm's dividend policy—a premise that in turn suggests that dividend policy is irrelevant.

Example ▼   Overbrook Industries, a manufacturer of canoes and other small watercraft, has available from the current period's operations $1.8 million that can be retained or paid out in dividends. The firm's optimal capital structure is 30 percent debt and 70 percent equity. Figure 11.1 depicts the firm's marginal cost of capital (MCC) schedule along with three investment opportunities schedules. For each IOS, the level of total new financing or investment determined by the point of intersection of the IOS and the MCC has been noted. For IOS$_1$, it is $1.5 million;

FIGURE 11.1

MCC and IOSs
MCC and IOSs for Overbrook Industries

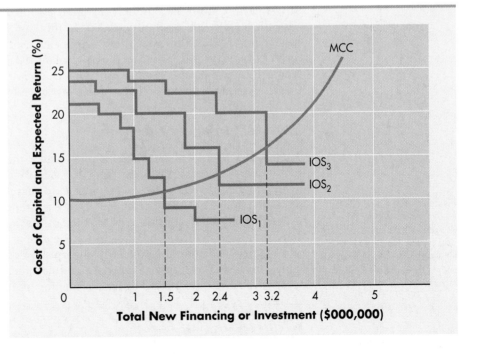

Total New Financing or Investment ($000,000)

TABLE 11.1	Applying the Residual Theory of Dividends to Overbrook Industries for Each of Three IOSs (shown in Figure 11.1)

| | Investment opportunities schedules | | |
Item	IOS_1	IOS_2	IOS_3
(1) New financing or investment (Fig. 11.1)	$1,500,000	$2,400,000	$3,200,000
(2) Reinvested profits available (given)	$1,800,000	$1,800,000	$1,800,000
(3) Equity needed [70% × (1)]	1,050,000	1,680,000	2,240,000
(4) Dividends [(2) − (3)]	$ 750,000	$ 120,000	$ 0[a]
(5) Dividend payout ratio [(4) ÷ (2)]	41.7%	6.7%	0%

[a]In this case, additional new common shares in the amount of $440,000 ($2,240,000 needed−$1,800,000 available) would have to be sold; no dividends would be paid.

for IOS_2, $2.4 million; and for IOS_3, $3.2 million. Although only one IOS will exist in practice, it is useful to look at the possible dividend decisions generated by applying the residual theory in each of the three cases. Table 11.1 summarizes this analysis.

Table 11.1 shows that if IOS_1 exists, the firm will pay out $750,000 in dividends, because only $1,050,000 of the $1,800,000 of available earnings is needed. A 41.7 percent payout ratio results. For IOS_2, dividends of $120,000 (a payout ratio of 6.7%) result. Should IOS_3 exist, the firm would pay no dividends (a 0% payout ratio), because its reinvested profits of $1,800,000 would be less than the $2,240,000 of equity needed. In this case, the firm would have to sell new common shares to meet the requirements generated by the intersection of the IOS_3 and the MCC. Depending on which IOS exists, the firm's dividend would in effect be the residual, if any, remaining after providing the equity financing required to fund all acceptable investments.

Dividend Irrelevance Arguments

The residual theory of dividends implies that if the firm cannot earn a return (IRR) from investment of its earnings that is in excess of cost (MCC), it should distribute the earnings by paying dividends to shareholders. This approach suggests that dividends are irrelevant—that they represent an earnings residual rather than an active decision variable that affects the firm's value. Such a view is consistent with the **dividend irrelevance theory** put forth by Merton H. Miller and Franco Modigliani.[1] M and M's theory shows that in a perfect world (certainty, no taxes, no transactions costs, and no other market imperfections), the value of the firm is unaffected by the distribution of dividends. They argue that the

dividend irrelevance theory
A theory put forth by Miller and Modigliani that, in a perfect world, the value of a firm is unaffected by the distribution of dividends and is determined solely by the earning power and risk of its assets.

---

1. Merton H. Miller and Franco Modigliani, "Dividend Policy, Growth and the Valuation of Shares," *Journal of Business* 34 (October 1961), pp. 411–433.

firm's value is determined solely by the earning power and risk of its assets (investments) and that the manner in which it splits its earnings stream between dividends and internally retained (and reinvested) funds does not affect this value.

However, studies have shown that large dividend changes affect share price in the same direction—increases in dividends result in increased share price, and decreases in dividends result in decreased share price. In response, M and M argue that these effects are attributable not to the dividend itself but rather to the **informational content** of dividends with respect to future earnings. In other words, it is not the preference of shareholders for current dividends (rather than future capital gains) that is responsible for this behaviour. Instead, a change in dividends, up or down, is viewed as a *signal* that management expects future earnings to change in the same direction. An increase in dividends is viewed as a *positive signal* that causes investors to bid up the share price; a decrease in dividends is a *negative signal* that causes a decrease in share price.

M and M further argue that a **clientele effect** exists: A firm attracts shareholders whose preferences with respect to the payment and stability of dividends correspond to the payment pattern and stability of the firm itself. Investors desiring stable dividends as a source of income hold the shares of firms that pay about the same dividend amount each period. Investors preferring to earn capital gains are more attracted to growing firms that reinvest a large portion of their earnings, resulting in a fairly unstable pattern of dividends or no dividends. Because the shareholders get what they expect, M and M argue that the value of their firm's stock is unaffected by dividend policy.

In summary, M and M and other dividend irrelevance proponents argue that, all else being equal, an investor's required return—and therefore the value of the firm—is unaffected by dividend policy for three reasons:

1. The firm's value is determined solely by the earning power and risk of its assets.
2. If dividends do affect value, they do so solely because of their informational content, which signals management's earnings expectations.
3. A clientele effect exists that causes a firm's shareholders to receive the dividends they expect.

These views of M and M with respect to dividend irrelevance are consistent with the residual theory, which focuses on making the best investment decisions to maximize share value. The proponents of dividend irrelevance conclude that because dividends are irrelevant to a firm's value, the firm does not need to have a dividend policy. Although many studies have researched the dividend irrelevance theory, none have been able to fully validate or refute the theory.

Dividend Relevance Arguments

The key argument in support of **dividend relevance theory** is attributed to Myron J. Gordon and John Lintner,[2] who suggest that there is, in fact, a direct relationship between the firm's dividend policy and its market value. Fundamental to

informational content
The information provided by the dividends of a firm with respect to future earnings, which causes owners to bid the price of the firm's shares up or down.

clientele effect
The argument that a firm attracts shareholders whose preferences with respect to the payment and stability of dividends correspond to the payment pattern and stability of the firm itself.

dividend relevance theory
The theory that there is a direct relationship between a firm's dividend policy and its market value.

2. Myron J. Gordon, "Optimal Investment and Financing Policy," *Journal of Finance* 18 (May 1963), pp. 264–272, and John Lintner, "Dividends, Earnings, Leverage, Stock Prices, and the Supply of Capital to Corporations," *Review of Economics and Statistics* 44 (August 1962), pp. 243–269.

bird-in-the-hand argument
The belief, in support of *dividend relevance theory*, that current dividend payments ("a bird in the hand") reduce investor uncertainty and result in a higher value for the firm's shares.

this proposition is their **bird-in-the-hand argument**, which suggests that investors are generally risk averse and attach less risk to current dividends than to future dividends or capital gains. Simply stated, "a bird in the hand is worth two in the bush." Current dividend payments are therefore believed to reduce investor uncertainty, causing investors to discount the firm's earnings at a lower rate and, all else being equal, to place a higher value on the firm's common shares. Conversely, if dividends are reduced or not paid, investor uncertainty will increase, raising the required return and lowering the share's value.

Although many other arguments relating to dividend relevance have been put forward, *numerous empirical studies fail to provide conclusive evidence in support of the intuitively appealing dividend relevance argument*. In practice, however, the actions of financial managers and shareholders alike often tend to support the belief that dividend policy does affect share value. Because our concern centres on the day-to-day behaviour of business firms, the remainder of this chapter is consistent with the belief that *dividends are relevant*—that each firm must develop a dividend policy that fulfills the goals of its owners and maximizes their wealth as reflected in the firm's share price.

? Review Questions

11–3   Describe the *residual theory of dividends*. Does following this approach lead to a stable dividend? Is this approach consistent with dividend relevance? Explain.

11–4   Describe and contrast the basic arguments concerning dividend policy given by: (**a**) Miller and Modigliani (M and M) and (**b**) Gordon and Lintner.

11.3 Factors Affecting Dividend Policy

dividend policy
The plan to be followed when making the dividend decision.

A company's **dividend policy** represents the plan to be followed when making the dividend decision. Companies should develop plans consistent with their financial goals. Before reviewing some types of dividend policies, we discuss the factors involved in developing a dividend policy. These include legal constraints, contractual constraints, internal constraints, the firm's growth prospects, owner considerations, and market considerations.

Legal Constraints

It is illegal for Canadian companies to pay dividends that would reduce the value of the common share account, the direct financing provided by the owners to the company. Dividends can only be paid from earnings: the current year's and the total of prior year's reinvested profits as reflected in retained earnings. To pay dividends in excess of this amount would mean the company was returning to common shareholders their original investment in the company.

net profits rule
Dividends can only be paid from current and past earnings.

When paying dividends, three rules must be followed: (1) the **net profits rule** means that dividends can only be paid from current and past earnings; (2) the

capital impairment rule
Prevents the payment of dividends from the value of common shares on the balance sheet.

insolvency rule
A company cannot pay dividends while insolvent or if the payment of dividends makes the company insolvent.

capital impairment rule prevents the payment of dividends from the value of common shares on the balance sheet; (3) the **insolvency rule** indicates a company cannot pay dividends while insolvent or if the payment of dividends makes the company insolvent.[3] Each of these rules has the same effect: to protect creditors. The rules prevent a company from making payments to common shareholders at the expense of creditors.

Example ▼ Miller Flour company, a large grain processor located in Saskatchewan, had net income after tax of $45,000 for the 2003 fiscal year. The company's shareholders' equity account as of the end of the 2002 fiscal year is presented below:

Miller Flour Company
Shareholders' Equity

Common shares	$300,000
Retained earnings	140,000
Total shareholders' equity	$440,000

What is the maximum amount of dividends that Miller Flour could legally pay? The total of current and past reinvested earnings is $185,000 ($45,000 + $140,000), so this is the maximum dividend that the company could pay in the 2003 fiscal year. Paying more would affect the common share account, and this would be illegal. It would reduce the company's ability to meet its obligations to ▲ creditors.

Based on this discussion, a company can pay a dividend that is more than current earnings. While this may seem odd, in reality it happens regularly. Consider the case where a company incurs a loss in a year. If the company has a long-standing policy of paying dividends, dividends can be paid even though there are no current profits to pay the dividend from. As long as the company has sufficient retained earnings on the balance sheet, a dividend payment may be made. This also assumes, of course, that the company has sufficient cash to make a dividend payment.

Example ▼ If, in the previous example, Miller Company's net income after tax for the 2003 fiscal year was a loss of $20,000, what is the maximum dividend that could be paid? For the 2003 fiscal year, the loss of $20,000 would flow to retained earnings, reducing the balance to $120,000 ($140,000 − $20,000). Therefore, the maximum dividend would be $120,000. In reality, a company would not pay this amount, since it would negatively affect their ability to remain solvent. ▲ Legally, however, Miller could pay this amount in dividends.

Contractual Constraints

Often, the firm's ability to pay cash dividends is constrained by restrictive provisions in a loan agreement. Generally, these constraints prohibit the payment of

---

3. Insolvency occurs when liabilities exceed assets or when a company is not able to pay its bills. The second situation generally occurs well before the first.

cash dividends until a certain level of earnings has been achieved, or they may limit dividends to a certain dollar amount or percentage of earnings. Constraints on dividends help to protect creditors from losses due to the firm's insolvency. The violation of a contractual constraint is generally grounds for a demand of immediate payment by the funds supplier.

Internal Constraints

The firm's ability to pay cash dividends is generally constrained by the amount of excess cash available rather than the level of retained earnings against which to charge them. Although it is possible for a firm to borrow funds to pay dividends, lenders are generally reluctant to make such loans because they produce no tangible or operating benefits that will help the firm repay the loan. Although a firm may have high earnings, its ability to pay dividends may be constrained by a low level of liquid assets (cash and marketable securities).

Example ▼ Miller Flour Company's shareholders' equity account presented earlier indicates that the firm could pay $185,000 in dividends. If the firm has total liquid assets of $50,000 ($20,000 in cash plus marketable securities worth $30,000) and $35,000 of this is needed for operations, the maximum cash dividend the firm **▲** can pay is $15,000 ($50,000 − $35,000).

Growth Prospects

⚠ Hint
Firms that grow very rapidly, such as high-tech firms, cannot afford to pay dividends. Their shareholders are influenced by the possibility of exceptionally higher share price and dividend levels in the future.

The firm's financial requirements are directly related to the anticipated degree of asset expansion. If the firm is in a growth stage, it may need all its funds to finance capital expenditures. Firms exhibiting little or no growth may nevertheless periodically need funds to replace or renew assets.

A firm must evaluate its financial position from the standpoint of profitability and risk to develop insight into its ability to raise capital externally. It must determine not only its ability to raise funds, but also the cost and speed with which financing can be obtained. Generally, a large, mature firm has adequate access to new capital, whereas a rapidly growing firm may not have sufficient funds available to support its numerous acceptable projects. A growth firm is likely to have to depend heavily on internal financing through reinvested profits; it is likely to pay out only a very small percentage of its earnings as dividends. A more stable firm that needs long-term funds only for planned outlays is in a better position to pay out a large proportion of its earnings, particularly if it has ready sources of financing.

Owner Considerations[4]

A company should establish a dividend policy that has a favourable effect on the wealth of the *majority* of owners.

---

4. Theoretically, in an *efficient market*, owner considerations are automatically handled by the pricing mechanism. The logic is as follows. A firm that pays a dividend that is smaller than required by a large number of owners will experience a decline in price because the dissatisfied shareholders will sell their shares. The resulting drop in share price will (as explained in Chapter 8) raise the expected return to investors, which will cause the firm's MCC to rise. As a result—all else being equal—the firm's optimal capital budget will become smaller and the demand for reinvested profits will fall. This decrease should allow the firm to satisfy shareholders by paying the larger dividends that they demand. In spite of this logic, it is helpful to understand some of the important considerations underlying owner behaviour.

One consideration is the *tax status of a firm's owners*. If a firm has a large percentage of wealthy shareholders who are in a high tax bracket, it may decide to pay out a *lower* percentage of its earnings to allow the owners to delay the payment of taxes until they sell the stock. Of course, when the share is sold, if the proceeds are in excess of the original purchase price, the capital gain will be taxed, possibly at a more favourable rate than the one applied to dividend income. Lower income shareholders, however, who need dividend income, will prefer a *higher* payout of earnings.

A second consideration is the *owners' investment opportunities*. A firm should not retain funds for investment in projects yielding lower returns than the owners could obtain from external investments of equal risk. If it appears that the owners have better opportunities externally, the firm should pay out a higher percentage of its earnings. If the firm's investment opportunities are at least as good as similar-risk external investments, a lower payout would be justifiable.

A final consideration is the *potential dilution of ownership*. If a firm pays out a higher percentage of earnings, new equity capital will have to be raised with common shares, which may result in the dilution of both control and earnings for the existing owners. By paying out a low percentage of its earnings, the firm can minimize such possibility of dilution.

Market Considerations

An awareness of the market's probable response to certain types of policies is helpful in formulating a suitable dividend policy. Shareholders are believed to value a *fixed or increasing level of dividends*, as opposed to a fluctuating pattern of dividends. This belief is supported by the research of John Lintner, who found that corporate managers are averse to changing the dollar amount of dividends in response to changes in earnings, particularly when earnings decline.[5] In addition, shareholders are believed to value a policy of *continuous dividend payment*. Because regularly paying a fixed or increasing dividend eliminates uncertainty about the frequency and magnitude of dividends, the earnings of the firm are likely to be discounted at a lower rate. This should result in an increase in the market value of the share and therefore increased owners' wealth.

A final market consideration is the *informational content* of dividends. As indicated earlier, shareholders often view the firm's dividend payment as a *signal* relative to its future success. A stable and continuous dividend is a *positive signal* that conveys to the owners that the firm is in good health. If the firm skips a dividend payment in a given period due to a loss or to very low earnings, shareholders are likely to interpret this as a *negative signal*. The nonpayment of the dividend creates uncertainty about the future, and this uncertainty is likely to result in lower share value. Owners and investors generally construe a dividend payment when a loss occurs as an indication that the loss is merely temporary.

> **⚠ Hint**
> The risk-return concept also applies to the firm's dividend policy. A firm that lets its dividends fluctuate from period to period will be viewed as risky, and investors will require a higher rate of return, which will increase the firm's cost of capital.

? Review Question

11–5   What factors affect dividend policy? Briefly describe each of them.

---

5. John Lintner, "Distribution of Income of Corporations among Dividends, Retained Earnings, and Taxes," *American Economic Review* 46 (May 1956), pp. 97–113.

11.4 Types of Dividend Policies

A company's dividend policy must be formulated with two basic objectives in mind: maximizing the wealth of the firm's owners and providing for sufficient financing. These two interrelated objectives must be fulfilled in light of the previously discussed factors that limit the policy alternatives. Three of the more commonly used dividend policies are described in the following sections. A particular firm's cash dividend policy may incorporate elements of each.

Constant-Payout-Ratio Dividend Policy

dividend payout ratio
Indicates the percentage of each dollar earned that is distributed to the owners in the form of cash; calculated by dividing the firm's cash dividend per share by its earnings per share.

constant-payout-ratio dividend policy
A dividend policy based on the payment of a certain percentage of earnings to owners in each dividend period.

One type of dividend policy occasionally adopted by firms is the use of a constant payout ratio. The **dividend payout ratio**, calculated by dividing the firm's cash dividend per share by its earnings per share, indicates the percentage of each dollar earned that is distributed to the owners in the form of cash. With a **constant-payout-ratio dividend policy**, the firm establishes that a certain percentage of earnings is paid to owners in each dividend period.

The problem with this policy is that if the firm's earnings drop or if a loss occurs in a given period, the dividends may be low or even nonexistent. Because dividends are often considered an indicator of the firm's future condition and status, the firm's stock price may thus be adversely affected by this type of policy.

Example ▼ Peachtree Industries, a miner of potassium, has a policy of paying out 40 percent of earnings in cash dividends. In periods when a loss occurs, the firm's policy is to pay no cash dividends. Peachtree's earnings per share, dividends per share, and average price per share for the past 6 years are shown in the following table.

Year	Earnings/share	Dividends/share	Average price/share
1998	4.50	1.80	50.00
1999	2.00	0.80	46.00
2000	− 1.50	0.00	38.00
2001	1.75	0.70	48.00
2002	3.00	1.20	52.00
2003	−$0.50	$0.00	$42.00

⚠ Hint
Regulated utilities in low-growth areas can use a constant-payout-ratio dividend policy. Their capital requirements are usually low and their earnings are more certain than most firms.

Dividends increased in 2001 and 2002 and decreased in the other years. In years of decreasing dividends, the firm's stock price dropped; when dividends increased, the price of the stock increased. Peachtree's sporadic dividend payments appear to make its owners uncertain about the returns they can expect and the share price fluctuated widely, ending the 6-year period at a level below where
▲ it started.

A constant-payout-ratio dividend policy is only recommended for firms that have a relatively secure revenue source and good cost control, thus ensuring reliable earnings.

Regular Dividend Policy

regular dividend policy
A dividend policy based on the payment of a fixed-dollar dividend in each period.

The **regular dividend policy** is based on the payment of a fixed-dollar dividend in each period. The regular dividend policy provides the owners with generally positive information, thereby minimizing uncertainty. Often, firms using this policy increase the regular dividend once a *proven* increase in earnings has occurred. Under this policy, dividends are almost never decreased.

E x a m p l e ▼ The dividend policy of Woodward Laboratories, a producer of a popular artificial sweetener, is to pay annual dividends of $1 per share until per-share earnings have exceeded $4 for three consecutive years, at which time the annual dividend is raised to $1.50 per share and a new earnings plateau is established. The firm does not anticipate decreasing its dividend unless its liquidity is in jeopardy. Woodward's earnings per share, dividends per share, and average price per share for the past 12 years are shown in the following table.

Year	Earnings/share	Dividends/share	Average price/share
1992	2.85	1.00	35.00
1993	2.70	1.00	33.50
1994	0.50	1.00	33.00
1995	0.75	1.00	33.00
1996	3.00	1.00	36.00
1997	6.00	1.00	38.00
1998	2.00	1.00	38.50
1999	5.00	1.00	42.00
2000	4.20	1.00	43.00
2001	4.60	1.50	45.00
2002	3.90	1.50	46.50
2003	$4.50	$1.50	$47.50

Whatever the level of earnings, Woodward Laboratories paid dividends of $1 per share through 2000. In 2001, the dividend was raised to $1.50 per share because earnings in excess of $4 per share had been achieved for 3 years. In 2001, the firm also had to establish a new earnings plateau for further dividend increases. Woodward Laboratories' average price per share exhibited a stable, ▲ increasing behaviour in spite of a somewhat volatile pattern of earnings.

target dividend-payout ratio
A policy under which the firm attempts to pay out a certain percentage of earnings as a stated dollar dividend, which it adjusts toward a target payout as proven earnings increases occur.

Often, a regular dividend policy is built around a **target dividend-payout ratio**. Under this policy, the firm attempts to pay out a certain percentage of earnings, but rather than let dividends fluctuate, it pays a stated dollar dividend and adjusts it toward the target payout as proven earnings increases occur. For instance, Woodward Laboratories appears to have a target payout ratio of around 35 percent. The payout was about 35 percent ($1 ÷ $2.85) when the dividend policy was set in 1992, and when the dividend was raised to $1.50 in 2001, the payout ratio was about 33 percent ($1.50 ÷ $4.60).

Low-Regular-and-Extra Dividend Policy

low-regular-and-extra dividend policy
A dividend policy based on paying a low regular dividend, supplemented by an additional dividend when earnings are higher than normal.

Some firms establish a **low-regular-and-extra dividend policy,** paying a low regular dividend, supplemented by an additional dividend when earnings are higher than normal in a given period. This additional dividend is called an **extra dividend,** which avoids giving shareholders false expectations that it will be maintained. The use of the "extra" designation is especially common among companies that experience cyclical shifts in earnings.

extra dividend
An additional dividend optionally paid by the firm if earnings are higher than normal in a given period.

By establishing a low regular dividend that is paid each period, the firm gives investors the stable income necessary to build confidence in the firm, and the extra dividend permits them to share in the earnings from an especially good period. Firms using this policy must raise the level of the regular dividend once proven increases in earnings have been achieved. The extra dividend should not be a regular event, or it becomes meaningless. The use of a target dividend-payout ratio in establishing the regular dividend level is advisable.

❓ Review Question

11–6   Describe a constant-payout-ratio dividend policy, a regular dividend policy, and a low-regular-and-extra dividend policy. What are the effects of these policies?

11.5 Other Forms of Corporate Distribution

Three other forms of corporate distributions to shareholders are discussed in this section. First, rather than pay cash dividends, a company may pay a dividend in the form of additional common shares, a stock dividend. Second, stock splits are closely related to stock dividends and give the impression of adding value for shareholders. Finally, over the past 20 years, share repurchases have become quite common and these may be viewed as an alternative way to distribute cash to shareholders.

Stock Dividends

stock dividend
The payment to existing owners of a dividend in the form of common shares.

A **stock dividend** is the payment to existing common shareholders of a dividend in the form of common shares. Often, firms pay stock dividends as a replacement for or a supplement to cash dividends. Although stock dividends do not have a real value, shareholders may perceive them to represent something they did not have before and therefore to have value.

Accounting Aspects

In an accounting sense, the payment of a stock dividend is a shifting of funds between capital accounts rather than a use of funds. When a firm declares a stock dividend, the procedures for announcement and distribution are the same as those described earlier for a cash dividend. The accounting entries associated with the payment of stock dividends are illustrated in the following example.

Example ▼ The current shareholders' equity on the balance sheet of Garrison Corporation, a distributor of prefabricated cabinets, is shown in the following accounts.

Preferred shares	$ 300,000
Common shares (100,000 shares)	900,000
Retained earnings	800,000
Total shareholders' equity	$2,000,000

If Garrison declares a 10 percent stock dividend, 10,000 (10% × 100,000) new common shares are issued. If the prevailing market price of the common shares is $15, the value of the stock dividend is $150,000 (10,000 shares × $15). This amount is transferred from retained earnings to common shares as follows:

Preferred shares	$ 300,000
Common shares (110,000 shares)	1,050,000
Retained earnings	650,000
Total shareholders' equity	$2,000,000

The firm's total shareholders' equity has not changed; funds have only been
▲ *redistributed* among the accounts.

The Shareholder's Viewpoint

The shareholder receiving a stock dividend in reality receives nothing of value. After the dividend is paid, the per-share value of the shareholder's stock decreases in proportion to the dividend in such a way that the market value of his or her total holdings in the firm remains unchanged. The shareholder's proportion of ownership in the firm also remains the same, and *as long as the firm's earnings remain unchanged,* so does his or her share of total earnings. (Clearly, if the firm's earnings and cash dividends increase at the time the stock dividend is issued, an increase in share value is likely to result.) A continuation of the preceding example will clarify this point.

Example ▼ Ms. X owned 10,000 shares of Garrison Corporation's stock. The company's most recent earnings were $220,000, and earnings are not expected to change in the near future. Before the stock dividend, Ms. X owned 10 percent (10,000 shares ÷ 100,000 shares) of the firm's common shares, which were selling for $15 per share. Earnings per share were $2.20 ($220,000 ÷ 100,000 shares). Because Ms. X owned 10,000 shares, her earnings were $22,000 ($2.20 per share × 10,000 shares). After receiving the 10 percent stock dividend, Ms. X has 11,000 shares, which again is 10 percent of the ownership (11,000 shares ÷ 110,000 shares). The market price of the stock can be expected to drop to $13.64 per share [$15 × (1.00 ÷ 1.10)], which means that the market value of Ms. X's holdings is $150,000 (11,000 shares × $13.64 per share). This is the same as the initial value of her holdings (10,000 shares × $15 per share). The earnings per share drops to $2 ($220,000 ÷ 110,000 shares) because the same $220,000 in earnings must now be divided among 110,000 shares. Because Ms. X still owns 10 percent of the company, her share of total earnings is still
▲ $22,000 ($2 per share × 11,000 shares).

In summary, if the firm's earnings remain constant and total cash dividends do not increase, a stock dividend results in a lower per-share market value for the firm's common shares but the same total value. Since the effect of stock dividends, in reality, is nil for both investors and the company, stock dividends rarely occur in Canada's relatively sophisticated financial markets. Investors recognize that there is no real benefit and as a result, there is no point in a company incurring the expenses associated with a stock dividend.

Stock Splits

stock split
A method commonly used to lower the market price of a firm's common shares by increasing the number of shares belonging to each shareholder.

Although not a type of dividend, *stock splits* have an effect on a firm's share price similar to that of stock dividends. A **stock split** is a method commonly used to lower the market price of a firm's common shares by increasing the number of shares held by each shareholder. There is an inverse impact on the two variables. For example, in a 2-for-1 stock split, shareholders receive two shares for each share previously held. At the same time, the market price of the firm's common shares is cut in half. There is no impact on the company's capital structure or on the total value of investors' holdings of common shares.

A company will undertake a stock split when they feel their share price is too high and that reducing the price will increase trading activity and make the shares more attractive for individual investors.

It is not unusual for a stock split to cause a slight increase in the market value of the stock. This is attributable to the informational content of stock splits and the fact that *total* dividends paid commonly increase slightly after a split.[6]

E x a m p l e ▼ Delphi Company, a forest products concern, has 200,000 common shares outstanding. Because the shares are selling at a high market price, the firm has declared a 2-for-1 stock split. The total before- and after-split shareholders' equity is shown in the following table.

Before split	
Common shares (200,000 shares)	$4,400,000
Retained earnings	2,000,000
Total shareholders' equity	$6,400,000

After 2-for-1 split	
Common shares (400,000 shares)	$4,400,000
Retained earnings	2,000,000
Total shareholders' equity	$6,400,000

▲ The insignificant effect of the stock split on the firm's books is obvious.

---

6. Eugene F. Fama, Lawrence Fisher, Michael C. Jensen, and Richard Roll, "The Adjustment of Stock Prices to New Information," *International Economic Review* 10 (February 1969), pp. 1–21, found that the stock price increases after the split announcement, and the increase in stock price is maintained if dividends per share are increased but is lost if dividends per share are *not* increased following the split.

IN PRACTICE

Why Companies Split

Typically, companies announce stock splits when their shares reach a point at which investors consider the shares expensive. In Canada, this often occurs when the share price increases to the $30 to $50 range. Dividing a high-priced share into two or three lower priced shares can increase its marketability by attracting more investors.

"Splits are very important to individual investors, even though you're essentially getting two fives for a 10," suggests a financial analyst. Generally, shares that split have performed very well in the past, so that many investors believe splits indicate that good performance may continue. There is some evidence that this is indeed true. One study showed that over 15 years, a portfolio of 1,275 stocks that split yielded an average return of 19 percent in the first year after the split and 65 percent over 3 years, compared to returns of 11 and 53 percent, respectively, for a similar group of stocks that did not split. In the short term, share prices tend to rise between the time the split is announced and the date of the split. For example, in early May 2002, gold producer Goldcorp Inc. reported healthy earnings, returns, and cash flow, and a 2-for-1 stock split effective May 17, 2002. On May 16, the shares closed trading at $28.15. The next day, the shares closed at $14.55, or $29.10 on a pre-split basis. By May 31, the shares were trading for $18, generating a 27.9 percent return over the 10 trading days following the split.

However, some analysts point out that stocks that split have already risen in price, so that the above-average performance simply reflects an increase in the company's growth and earnings. Splits also signal management's confidence that the upward trend will continue. Companies don't want to split a $50 stock into two shares at $25 and then see the price drop.

Yet sometimes this occurs for reasons outside the company's control. CAE is the world-leading supplier of flight simulators. On July 5, 2002, CAE's common shares split 2-for-1 after the company announced that earnings from continuing operations had increased by 146 percent over two years. On July 4, the shares closed trading at $22.56. The next day, the shares closed at $11.90, or $23.80 pre-split, generating a 5.5 percent, 1-day return. The split seemed to generate a positive result for shareholders. Yet, by late September 2002, CAE shares were trading for less than $4.50, the victim of the terrible bear market that raged in Canada in 2002.

Financial advisors remind investors that a stock split, by itself, is not a reason to buy a stock. As with any stock purchase, you should evaluate the fundamentals of the company, including key ratios, its price/earnings multiple, profit outlook, and industry factors. In terms of a company's underlying value, a stock split is essentially a nonevent.

SOURCES: Daniel Kodlec, "The Dumb Money," *Time*, February 22, 1999. Annual reports of Goldcorp Inc. and CAE.

Common shares can be split in any way desired. For example, the most common share split ratio is 2-for-1, but 3-for-1 and 3-for-2 splits are also usual. Stock splits are most common during a bull market, when the prices of common shares are increasing, and rare during bear markets.

reverse stock split
A method used to raise the market price of a firm's stock by exchanging a certain number of outstanding shares for one new share of stock.

Sometimes a **reverse stock split** is made: A certain number of outstanding shares are exchanged for one new share. For example, in a 1-for-10 split, one new share is exchanged for 10 old shares. Reverse stock splits are initiated when a company's common shares are selling at a very low price (often less than $1) and a company wishes to raise the price to a higher level. Often investors feel shares trading at very low prices (penny stocks) are "too cheap" and thus low-quality, very high-risk investments.

Share Repurchases

Share repurchases occur when a company buys and then retires its own shares. These are sometimes referred to as *share buybacks*. Share repurchases should not be confused with the redemption of long-term debt or preferred shares. Companies have the option of redeeming and retiring these other types of securities; there is no redemption provision associated with common shares. Common shares are a permanent source of financing and will remain outstanding for as long as the company operates, unless the company repurchases the shares.

share repurchase
Company purchase of its own common shares from investors in the stock market; the company then retires the shares.

The basics of a **share repurchase** are simple. First, the company receives permission to repurchase shares from the regulating agency that oversees the operation of the stock exchange that lists the company's shares. In Canada, this is the Toronto Stock Exchange. Second, the company then buys shares from investors through an investment dealer. The company receives the shares which are then retired; the investor receives cash. Over the past 20 years, there has been a tremendous increase in the volume of share repurchases in both Canada and the United States. The next section discusses the two methods used to repurchase common shares.

Types of Share Repurchases

There are two types of share repurchases: open-market offers and fixed-price tender bids. **Open-market share repurchases** are company purchases of their own shares on a stock exchange at the market price. In Canada, these are called normal course issuer bids, and companies must gain approval for these bids from the stock exchange. Open-market repurchases must be completed within one year and are restricted to no more than 5 percent of the shares outstanding. Companies must report to the exchange the number of shares repurchased on a monthly basis. Open-market repurchases are executed at the market price prevailing at the time of the company's order. Over the year the normal course bid is open, there could be numerous market orders, all at substantially different prices.

open-market share repurchases
Company purchases of its own shares on a stock exchange at the market price once approval from the stock exchange is received; termed a *normal course issuer bid* in Canada.

Fixed-price tender bids are offers by a company to purchase a certain percentage of its own shares at a stated price within a specified time period. These are termed substantial issuer bids. Tender bids are generally for much more than 5 percent of the outstanding shares and are open for, generally, no longer than 20 trading days. A tender bid is at a stated price, which is usually at least 20 percent above the market price prior to the announcement of the offer. Tender bids are used when a company wants either to send a strong message to the market that the company's shares are undervalued, or to defeat a hostile takeover by reducing the number of shares outstanding and rewarding shareholders for not tendering their shares to the takeover offer.

fixed-price tender bid
An offer by a company to purchase a certain percentage of its own shares at a stated price that is well above the current market price within a specified time period; termed a substantial issuer bid.

In a **Dutch-auction bid**, a variation of the fixed-price tender bid, a company specifies the number of shares it wishes to repurchase and a range of prices at which it will purchase its shares. Shareholders then choose the number of shares they wish to tender to the bid and the lowest price, within the range established by the company, at which they are willing to sell their shares to the company.

Dutch-auction bid
A variation of the fixed-price tender bid where the company specifies the number of shares it wishes to repurchase and a range of prices at which it will purchase the shares.

Based upon the choices made by tendering shareholders, the company then establishes the lowest price, commonly referred to as the "clearing price," within the range of prices that will result in the company acquiring the maximum number of shares to be purchased under the bid. All shares tendered at or below the clearing price are purchased by the company. Shares tendered above the clearing price are not purchased.

For an open-market repurchase, the seller does not know the company is the buyer of the shares. With a tender offer, the seller knows the company is buying the shares. For examples of both normal course and substantial issuer bids, see the following Web sites: www.celestica.com/cfm/news/index.cfm?Act= Details&PressID=417 and www.cryptologic.com/investor/2001/dec21_2001.html.

Reasons Companies Repurchase Shares

So, why do companies repurchase their own shares? A number of motives have been suggested.

1. Share repurchases reduce the number of common shares outstanding, thereby increasing EPS. Increasing EPS may lead to higher share prices.
2. Repurchases may send a positive signal to the market that the management of the company believes the share price is undervalued.
3. Repurchases may provide price support for a company's common shares if the price has been declining in the market.
4. Share repurchases allow a company to adjust their debt ratio to achieve an optimal capital structure.
5. Stock options have become a significant part of the pay packages of corporate management. To avoid diluting earnings and ownership from the exercise of stock options, a company may repurchase sufficient common shares to offset the exercise of the options.
6. Repurchases act as a defence in the event of an unfriendly takeover offer by reducing the number of publicly traded shares on the market.

Each of these reasons likely applies in some situations when companies repurchase common shares. A seventh reason for share repurchases is the subject of the following section.

Share Repurchases as an Alternative to a Cash Dividend

When common shares are repurchased for retirement, the underlying effect is to distribute cash to the common shareholders who sell their shares to the company. As a result of any repurchase, the participating owners receive cash for their shares. Generally, as long as earnings remain constant, and no additional common shares are issued via other means, the repurchase reduces the number of outstanding shares, raising the earnings per share and therefore the market price per share. In addition, certain owner tax benefits may result.

Only those shareholders who wish to receive cash will participate. Those who do not wish to receive cash (either a dividend or the proceeds from selling) due to tax consequences will hold their shares. The selling shareholders receive cash and any gain on the shares (difference between the selling price and original cost) is a capital gain. In Canada, as shown in Table 8.5, capital gains are taxed more favourably than is dividend income. The shareholders who do not participate in the share repurchase *may* also receive a benefit.

The repurchase of common shares results in a type of *reverse dilution;* earnings per share increase since the number of common shares outstanding is reduced. This *may* result in the market price of the common shares increasing. Thus, a share repurchase may be viewed as an alternative to a cash dividend where both sets of shareholders (participants and non-participants in the repurchase) benefit.

Example ▼ Benton Company, a national sportswear chain, has released the following financial data:

Earnings available for common shareholders	$1,000,000
Number of common shares outstanding	400,000
Earnings per share ($1,000,000 ÷ 400,000)	$2.50
Market price per share	$50
Price/earnings (P/E) ratio ($50 ÷ $2.50)	20

The firm is contemplating using $800,000 of its earnings either to pay cash dividends or to repurchase shares. If the firm pays cash dividends, the amount of the dividend would be $2 per share ($800,000 ÷ 400,000 shares). Due to tax consequences, some shareholders may not wish to receive the dividend. Instead, the company could announce a share repurchase, providing cash to those shareholders wishing to sell. With the repurchase announcement, the share price will likely increase due to the reasons discussed earlier. Assuming the price increases to $51, Benton could acquire 15,686 shares ($800,000 ÷ $51). These shares are retired and 384,314 (400,000 − 15,686) shares remain outstanding.

Earnings per share (EPS) rise to $2.60 ($1,000,000 ÷ 384,314). If the shares still sold at 20 times earnings (P/E = 20), applying the *price/earnings multiple approach* presented in Chapter 8, its market price would rise to $52 per share ($2.60 × 20). The net effect is that the selling shareholders receive the certain $51. The holding shareholders may see the value of their shares increase. This example supports the view that share repurchases provide benefits to both ▲ sets of shareholders and result in higher share prices.

From an accounting perspective, a share repurchase results in a decline in cash. For the equity accounts, the amount paid by the company is first deducted from the value of common shares. But if this amount is more than the proceeds received when the shares were originally sold, the excess is deducted from retained earnings. This process was fully discussed in Chapter 6.

? Review Questions

11-7 What is a *stock dividend?* Why do firms issue stock dividends? Comment on the following statement: "I have a stock that promises to pay a 20 percent stock dividend every year, and therefore it guarantees that I will break even in 5 years."

11-8 What is a *stock split?* What is a *reverse stock split?* Compare a stock split with a stock dividend.

IN PRACTICE   Personal Finance

Banking on Shareholder Returns

The Bank of Montreal, one of the Big 5 Canadian banks and among the top 10 companies in Canada in terms of market capitalization, has paid dividends to its shareholders since 1829, a period of 174 years. In the tough financial environment of 2002, when some companies were reducing or eliminating dividends to save cash, the Bank of Montreal (BMO) announced a dividend increase for the 10th consecutive year. Dividends were increased from $0.53 per share in 1992 to $1.20 for 2002, an average yearly increase of 8.5 percent. In addition, the BMO increased their share repurchase program from $500 million in 2000 to $2 billion in 2001. In total 52 million common shares were repurchased in 2001.

The BMO's dividend policy is to increase dividends "in line with long-term trends in EPS growth, while ensuring that sufficient profits are retained to support anticipated business growth, fund strategic investments, and provide continued support for depositors." They wish to maintain a dividend payout ratio of 30 to 40 percent.

Some feel that dividends are "out of style," and a tax-inefficient way of delivering returns to shareholders. This is the case since dividends are taxed twice, once at the corporate level and again when received by investors. People in this camp feel companies should reinvest profits into the business or pay down debt. "Increasing share prices, not dividends, attract investors," they would say.

For others, the size and pattern of dividends provide information about a firm's current and future performance. Dividend increases send strong signals to investors that a company is confident of its future financial health. "Management believes that the company has enough cash to invest in its growth, pay higher dividends, and buy back shares," they would say. Over time, companies with long histories of dividend increases have maintained the steady earnings growth required to support higher dividend payouts.

Direct payments, like dividends and share repurchases, seem to matter to shareholders in companies like the Bank of Montreal. For example, over the five years to October 31, 2001, the average return on the BMO's common shares was 14.3 percent compared to 5.8 percent on the TSX Index. Said one analyst, "If a company is willing to pay a dividend, then they must actually have the cash in the till." When it comes to dividend policy, that is important!

REFERENCES: *2001 Annual Report*, Bank of Montreal. Richard Blackwell, "List of Dividend-Paying Firms Shrinking," *The Globe and Mail*, February 11, 2002.

11-9   What is the logic behind *repurchasing shares* to distribute excess cash to the firm's owners?

11-10   What methods can be used to repurchase shares? Why do companies repurchase common shares?

SUMMARY

Understand cash dividend payment procedures and the role of dividend reinvestment plans. The cash dividend decision is normally a quarterly decision made by the board of directors that establishes the record date and payment date. Generally, the larger the dividend charged to retained earnings and paid in cash, the greater the amount of financing that must be raised externally. Some firms offer dividend reinvestment plans (DRIP) that allow shareholders to acquire shares in lieu of cash dividends, sometimes at a 5 percent discount to the market price. DRIPs provide benefits to both shareholders and the company.

 Describe the residual theory of dividends and the key arguments with regard to dividend irrelevance and relevance. The residual theory suggests that dividends should be viewed as the earnings left after all acceptable investment opportunities have been undertaken. Dividend irrelevance, which is implied by the residual theory, is argued by Miller and Modigliani using a perfect world wherein information content and clientele effects exist. Gordon and Lintner argue dividend relevance based on the uncertainty-reducing effect of dividends, supported by their bird-in-the-hand argument. Although intuitively appealing, empirical studies fail to provide clear support of dividend relevance. The actions of financial managers and shareholders alike, however, tend to support the belief that dividend policy does affect stock value.

 Discuss the key factors involved in formulating a dividend policy. A firm's dividend policy should maximize the wealth of its owners while providing for sufficient financing. Dividend policy is affected by certain legal, contractual, and internal constraints as well as growth prospects, owner considerations, and market considerations. Legal constraints prohibit corporations from paying out as cash dividends any portion of the common share account; dividends must be paid from earnings: the current year's and the total of past year's reinvested profits. Firms with overdue liabilities or those legally insolvent or bankrupt cannot pay cash dividends. Contractual constraints result from restrictive provisions in the firm's loan agreements. Internal constraints tend to result from a firm's limited excess cash availability. Growth prospects affect the relative importance of retaining earnings rather than paying them out in dividends. The tax status of owners, the owners' investment opportunities, and the potential dilution of ownership are important owner considerations. Finally, market considerations relate to shareholders' pref-

erence for the continuous payment of fixed or increasing streams of dividends and the perceived informational content of dividends.

 Review and evaluate the three basic types of dividend policies. With a constant-payout ratio dividend policy, the firm pays a fixed percentage of earnings out to the owners each period. With this policy, dividends move up and down with earnings, and no dividend is paid when a loss occurs. Under a regular dividend policy, the firm pays a fixed-dollar dividend each period; it increases the amount of dividends only after a proven increase in earnings has occurred. The low-regular-and-extra dividend policy is similar to the regular dividend policy, except that it pays an "extra dividend" in periods when the firm's earnings are higher than normal. The regular and the low-regular-and-extra dividend policies are generally preferred over the constant-payout-ratio dividend policy because their stable patterns of dividends reduce uncertainty.

 Evaluate stock dividends from accounting, shareholder, and company points of view. Occasionally, firms pay stock dividends as a replacement for or supplement to cash dividends. The payment of stock dividends involves a shifting of funds between capital accounts rather than a use of funds. Shareholders receiving stock dividends typically receive nothing of value—the market value of their holdings, their proportion of ownership, and their share of total earnings remain unchanged. Since the effect of stock dividends, in reality, is nil for both investors and the company, stock dividends rarely occur in Canada's relatively sophisticated financial markets.

 Explain stock splits and common share repurchases and the firm's motivation for undertaking each of them. Stock splits are sometimes used to enhance trading activity of a firm's shares by lowering the market price of its shares. A stock split merely involves accounting adjustments—it has no effect on either the firm's cash or its capital structure. Share repurchases can be made in lieu of cash dividend payments to retire outstanding shares and delay the payment of taxes for the shareholders. They involve the actual outflow of cash to reduce the number of outstanding shares and thereby increase earnings per share and the market price per share. Whereas stock repurchases can be viewed as dividend alternatives, stock splits are used to deliberately adjust the market price of shares.

SELF-TEST PROBLEM

(Solution in Appendix B)

ST 11–1 **Share repurchase** The Off-Shore Steel Company has earnings available for common shareholders of $2 million and 500,000 common shares outstanding with a current market price of $60 per share. The firm is currently contemplating paying a $2 per share cash dividend.

a. Calculate the firm's current earnings per share (EPS) and price/earnings (P/E) ratio.

b. If the firm can repurchase at $62 per share, how many shares can be purchased in lieu of making the proposed cash dividend payment?

c. How much will the EPS be after the proposed repurchase? Why?

d. If the shares sell at the old P/E ratio, what will the market price be after repurchase?

e. Compare and contrast the EPS before and after the proposed repurchase.

f. Compare and contrast the shareholders' position under the dividend and repurchase alternatives.

PROBLEMS

 WARM-UP

11–1 **Dividend payment procedures** Wood Shoes, at the quarterly dividend meeting, declared a cash dividend of $1.10 per share for holders of record on Monday, July 10. The firm has 300,000 shares of common stock outstanding and has set a payment date of July 31. Prior to the dividend declaration, the firm's key accounts were as follows:

| Cash | $500,000 | Dividends payable | $ 0 |
| | | Retained earnings | 2,500,000 |

a. Show the entries after the meeting adjourned.

b. When is the *ex dividend* date? What is meant by the term "exdividend"?

c. After the July 31 payment date, what values would the key accounts have?

d. What effect, if any, will the dividend have on the firm's total assets?

e. Ignoring general market fluctuations, what effect, if any, will the dividend have on the firm's stock price on the ex dividend date?

 INTERMEDIATE

11–2 **Dividend payment** Kathy Snow wishes to purchase shares of Countdown Computing, Inc. The company's board of directors has declared a cash dividend of $0.80 to be paid to holders of record on Wednesday, May 12.

a. What is the last day that Kathy can purchase the shares (trade date) in order to receive the dividend?

b. What day does this stock begin trading "ex dividend"?

c. What change, if any, would you expect in the price per share when the stock begins trading on the ex dividend day?

d. If Kathy held the stock for less than one quarter and then sold it for $39 per share, would she achieve a higher investment return by (1) buying the stock *prior to* the ex dividend date at $35 per share and collecting the $0.80 dividend or (2) buying it *on* the ex dividend date at $34.20 per share but not receiving the dividend?

INTERMEDIATE **11–3** **Residual dividend policy**   As president of Young's of Charlottetown, a large clothing chain, you have just received a letter from a major shareholder asking about the company's dividend policy. The shareholder has asked you to estimate the amount of the dividend that you are likely to pay next year. You have not yet collected all the information about the expected dividend payment, but you do know the following:

(1) The company follows a residual dividend policy.

(2) The total capital budget for next year is likely to be one of three amounts, depending on the results of capital budgeting studies that are currently under way. The capital expenditure amounts are $2 million, $3 million, and $4 million.

(3) The forecasted level of reinvested profits next year is $2 million.

(4) The target or optimal capital structure is a debt ratio of 40 percent.

You have decided to respond by sending the shareholder the best information available to you.

a. Describe a *residual dividend policy*.

b. Compute the amount of the dividend (or the amount of new common share financing needed) and the dividend payout ratio for each of the three capital expenditure amounts.

c. Compare, contrast, and discuss the amount of dividends (calculated in **b**) associated with each of the three capital expenditure amounts.

INTERMEDIATE **11–4** **Dividend constraints**   The Howe Company's shareholders' equity account is as follows:

Common shares (400,000 shares)	$2,600,000
Retained earnings	1,900,000
Total shareholders' equity	$4,500,000

The earnings available for common shareholders from this period's operations are $100,000, which have been included as part of the $1.9 million in retained earnings.

a. What is the maximum dividend per share that the firm can pay?

b. If the firm has $160,000 in cash, what is the largest per-share dividend it can pay without borrowing?

c. Indicate the accounts and changes, if any, that will result if the firm pays the dividends indicated in **a** and **b**.

d. Indicate the effects of an $80,000 cash dividend on shareholders' equity.

11–5 Dividend constraints   A firm has $800,000 in common shares, retained earnings of $40,000 (including the current year's earnings), and 25,000 common shares outstanding. In the current year, it has $29,000 of earnings available for the common shareholders.

a. What is the most the firm can pay in cash dividends to each common shareholder?
b. What effect would a cash dividend of $0.80 per share have on the firm's balance sheet entries?
c. If the firm cannot raise any new funds from external sources, what do you consider the key constraint with respect to the magnitude of the firm's dividend payments? Why?

  11–6 Low-regular-and-extra dividend policy   Bennett Farm Equipment Sales, Inc., is in a highly cyclic business. While the firm has a target payout ratio of 25 percent, its board realizes that strict adherence to that ratio would result in a fluctuating dividend and create uncertainty for the firm's shareholders. Therefore, the firm has declared a regular dividend of $0.50 per share per year with extra cash dividends to be paid when earnings justify them. Earnings per share for the last several years are as follows:

Year	EPS
1998	$1.97
1999	2.15
2000	2.80
2001	2.20
2002	2.40
2003	3.00

a. Calculate the payout ratio for each year based on the regular $0.50 dividend and the cited EPS.
b. Calculate the difference between the regular $0.50 dividend and a 25 percent payout for each year.
c. Bennett has established a policy of paying an extra dividend only when the difference between the regular dividend and a 25 percent payout amounts to $1 or more. Show the regular and extra dividends in those years when an extra dividend would be paid. What would be done with the "extra" in years when an extra dividend is not paid?
d. The firm expects that future earnings per share will continue to cycle but remain above $2.20 per share in most years. What factors should be considered in making a revision to the amount paid as a regular dividend? If the firm revises the regular dividend, what new amount should it pay?

  11–7 Alternative dividend policies   A firm has had the earnings per share over the last 10 years, shown in the following table.

Year	Earnings per share
1994	$0.25
1995	0.50
1996	1.80
1997	1.20
1998	2.40
1999	3.20
2000	2.80
2001	3.20
2002	3.80
2003	4.00

a. If the firm's dividend policy were based on a constant payout ratio of 40 percent for all years with positive earnings and 0 percent otherwise, what would be the annual dividend for each year?

b. If the firm had a dividend payout of $1 per share, increasing by $0.10 per share whenever the dividend payout fell below 50 percent for two consecutive years, what annual dividend would the firm pay each year?

c. If the firm's policy were to pay $0.50 per share each period except when earnings per share exceed $3, when an extra dividend equal to 80 percent of earnings beyond $3 would be paid, what annual dividend would the firm pay each year?

d. Discuss the pros and cons of each dividend policy described in **a** through **c**.

CHALLENGE 11–8   **Alternative dividend policies**   Given the earnings per share over the period 1996–2003 shown in the following table, determine the annual dividend per share under each of the policies set forth in **a** through **d**.

Year	Earnings per share
1996	$0.44
1997	1.00
1998	0.60
1999	1.05
2000	0.85
2001	1.20
2002	1.56
2003	1.40

a. Pay out 50 percent of earnings in all years with positive earnings.

b. Pay $0.50 per share and increase to $0.60 per share whenever earnings per share rise above $0.90 per share for two consecutive years.

c. Pay $0.50 per share except when earnings exceed $1 per share, in which case an extra dividend of 60 percent of earnings above $1 per share is paid.

d. Combine policies in **b** and **c**. When the dividend is raised (in **b**), raise the excess dividend base (in **c**) from $1 to $1.10 per share.

e. Compare and contrast each of the dividend policies described in **a** through **d**.

INTERMEDIATE  **11–9**   **Stock dividend—Firm**   Columbia Paper has the shareholders' equity account given below. The firm's common shares have a current market price of $30 per share.

Preferred shares	$100,000
Common shares (10,000 shares)	300,000
Retained earnings	100,000
Total shareholders' equity	$500,000

a. Show the effects on Columbia of a 5 percent stock dividend.
b. Show the effects of (1) a 10 percent and (2) a 20 percent stock dividend.
c. In light of your answers to **a** and **b**, discuss the effects of stock dividends on shareholders' equity.

INTERMEDIATE **11–10**   **Cash versus stock dividend**   Sudbury Tool has the shareholders' equity account given below. The firm's common shares currently sell for $4 per share.

Preferred shares	$ 100,000
Common shares (400,000 shares)	600,000
Retained earnings	320,000
Total shareholders' equity	$1,020,000

a. Show the effects on the firm of a $0.01, $0.05, $0.10, and $0.20 per-share *cash* dividend.
b. Show the effects on the firm of a 1, 5, 10, and 20 percent *stock* dividend.
c. Compare the effects in **a** and **b**. What are the significant differences in the two methods of paying dividends?

INTERMEDIATE **11–11**   **Stock dividend—Investor**   Sarah Warren currently holds 400 shares of Nutri-Foods. The firm has 40,000 shares outstanding. The firm most recently had earnings available for common shareholders of $80,000, and its shares have been selling for $22 per share. The firm intends to retain its earnings and pay a 10 percent stock dividend.
a. How much does the firm currently earn per share?
b. What proportion of the firm does Sarah Warren currently own?
c. What proportion of the firm will Ms. Warren own after the stock dividend? Explain your answer.
d. At what market price would you expect the stock to sell after the stock dividend?
e. Discuss what effect, if any, the payment of stock dividends will have on Ms. Warren's share of the ownership and earnings of Nutri-Foods.

CHALLENGE **11–12**   **Stock dividend—Investor**   Security Data Company has 50,000 common shares outstanding currently selling at $40 per share. The firm most recently had earnings available for common shareholders of $120,000, but it has decided to retain these funds and is considering either a 5 or 10 percent stock dividend in lieu of a cash dividend.
a. Determine the firm's current earnings per share.
b. If Sam Waller currently owns 500 shares, determine his proportion of ownership currently and under each of the proposed stock dividend plans. Explain your findings.

c. Calculate and explain the market price per share under each of the stock dividend plans.

d. For each of the proposed stock dividends, calculate the earnings per share after payment of the stock dividend.

e. What is the value of Sam Waller's holdings under each of the plans? Explain.

f. Should Mr. Waller have any preference with respect to the proposed stock dividends? Why or why not?

INTERMEDIATE

11–13   Stock split—Firm   Growth Industries' current shareholders' equity account is as follows:

Preferred shares	$ 400,000
Common shares (600,000 shares)	2,000,000
Retained earnings	800,000
Total shareholders' equity	$3,200,000

a. Indicate the change, if any, expected if the firm declares a 2-for-1 stock split.

b. Indicate the change, if any, expected if the firm declares a 1-for-1$\frac{1}{2}$ *reverse* stock split.

c. Indicate the change, if any, expected if the firm declares a 3-for-1 stock split.

d. Indicate the change, if any, expected if the firm declares a 6-for-1 stock split.

e. Indicate the change, if any, expected if the firm declares a 1-for-4 *reverse* stock split.

CHALLENGE

11–14   Stock split versus stock dividend—Firm   Mammoth Corporation is considering a 3-for-2 stock split. It currently has the shareholders' equity position shown. The current share price is $120. The most recent period's earnings available for common stock is included in retained earnings.

Preferred shares	$ 1,000,000
Common shares (100,000 shares)	2,000,000
Retained earnings	10,000,000
Total shareholders' equity	$13,000,000

a. What effects on Mammoth would result from the stock split?

b. What change in stock price would you expect to result from the stock split?

c. What is the maximum cash dividend per common share that the firm could pay before and after the stock split?

d. Contrast your answers to **a** through **c** with the circumstances surrounding a 50 percent stock dividend.

e. Explain the differences between stock splits and stock dividends.

CHALLENGE

11–15   Stock dividend versus stock split—Firm   The board of Wicker Home Health Care, Inc., is exploring ways to expand the number of shares outstanding in order to reduce the market price per share to a level that the firm considers more appealing to investors. The options under consideration are a 20 percent stock dividend or a 5-for-4 stock split. At the present time, the firm's equity account and other per share information are as follows:

Common shares (100,000 shares)	1,000,000
Retained earnings	700,000
Total shareholders' equity	$1,700,000
Price per share	$30.00
Earnings per share	$3.60
Dividend per share	$1.08

a. Show the effect on the equity accounts and per share data of a 20 percent stock dividend.
b. Show the effect on the equity accounts and per share data of a 5-for-4 stock split.
c. Which option will accomplish Wicker's goal of reducing current stock price while maintaining a stable level of retained earnings?
d. What legal constraints might encourage the firm to choose a split over a stock dividend?

INTERMEDIATE   11–16   **Share repurchase**   The following financial data on the Bond Recording Company are available:

Earnings available for common shareholders	$800,000
Number of common shares outstanding	400,000
Earnings per share ($800,000 ÷ 400,000)	$2
Market price per share	$20
Price/earnings (P/E) ratio ($20 ÷ $2)	10

The firm is currently contemplating using $400,000 of its earnings to pay cash dividends of $1 per share or repurchasing shares at the investment price.
a. Approximately how many common shares can the firm repurchase at the $21-per-share price using the funds that would have gone to pay the cash dividend?
b. Calculate EPS after the repurchase. Explain your calculations.
c. If the stock still sells at 10 times earnings, how much will the market price be after the repurchase?
d. Compare and contrast the pre- and post-repurchase earnings per share.
e. Compare and contrast the shareholders' position under the dividend and repurchase alternatives. What are the tax implications under each alternative?

CHALLENGE   11–17   **Share repurchase**   Harte Textiles, Inc., a maker of custom upholstery fabrics, is concerned about preserving the wealth of its shareholders during a cyclical downturn in the home furnishings business. The company has maintained a constant dividend payout of $2 tied to a target payout ratio of 40 percent. Management is preparing a share repurchase recommendation to present to the firm's board of directors. The following data have been gathered from the last two years:

	2002	2003
Earnings available for common shareholders	$1,260,000	$1,200,000
Number of shares outstanding	300,000	300,000
Earnings per share	$4.20	$4.00
Market price per share	$23.50	$20.00
Price/earnings ratio	5.6	5.0

a. For 2003, in order to have a $2 per share dividend and meet the 40 percent target payout ratio, how many common shares should the company have outstanding?

b. How many shares would have to be repurchased to have the level of shares outstanding calculated in **a**? If the firm repurchased these shares, what do you expect would happen to the market price per share?

CASE   CHAPTER 11   **Establishing General Access Company's Dividend Policy and Initial Dividend**

General Access Company (GAC) is a fast-growing Internet access provider that initially went public in early 1997. Its revenue growth and profitability have steadily risen since the firm's inception in late 1995. GAC's growth has been financed through the initial common share offering, the sale of bonds in 2000, and the retention of all earnings. Because of its rapid growth in revenue and profits, with only short-term earnings declines, GAC's common shareholders have been content to let the firm reinvest earnings to expand capacity to meet the growing demand for its services. This strategy has benefited most shareholders in terms of stock splits and capital gains. Since the company's initial public offering in 1997, GAC's stock twice has been split 2-for-1. In terms of total growth, the market price of GAC's stock, after adjustment for stock splits, has increased by 800 percent during the seven-year period, 1997–2003.

Because GAC's rapid growth is beginning to slow, the firm's CEO, Marilyn McNeely, believes that its shares are becoming less attractive to investors. Ms. McNeely has had discussions with her CFO, Bobby Rook, who believes that the firm must begin to pay cash dividends. He argues that many investors value regular dividends, and that by beginning to pay them, GAC would increase the demand—and therefore price—for its shares. Ms. McNeely decides that at the next board meeting she will propose that the firm begin to pay dividends on a regular basis.

Ms. McNeely realizes that if the board approves her recommendation, it will have to (1) establish a dividend policy and (2) set the amount of the initial annual dividend. She had Mr. Rook prepare the summary of the firm's annual EPS given in the following table.

Year	EPS
1997	$0.55
1998	0.83
1999	2.20
2000	3.30
2001	3.90
2002	4.10
2003	3.70

Mr. Rook indicates that he expects EPS to remain within 10 percent (plus or minus) of the 2003 value during the next three years. His most likely estimate is an annual increase of about 5 percent.

After much discussion, Ms. McNeely and Mr. Rook agree that she will recommend to the board one of the following types of dividend policies:

1. Constant-payout-ratio dividend policy
2. Regular dividend policy
3. Low-regular-and-extra dividend policy

Ms. McNeely realizes that her dividend proposal will significantly affect the firm's share price and future financing needs and costs. She also knows that she must be sure her proposal is complete and that it fully educates the board with regard to the long-run implications of each policy.

Required

a. Analyze each of the three dividend policies in light of GAC's financial position.
b. Which dividend policy would you recommend? Justify your recommendation.
c. What are the key factors to consider when setting the amount of a firm's initial annual dividend?
d. How should Ms. McNeely go about setting the initial annual dividend she will recommend to the board?
e. In view of your dividend policy recommendation in **b,** how large an initial dividend would you recommend? Justify your recommendation.

WEB EXERCISES   LINKS TO PRACTISE

Visit the following Web sites and complete the suggested exercises. These exercises will allow you to review practical applications of the chapter topics, as well as explore the wealth of information regarding managerial finance that is available on the Internet.

keyword.newswire.ca
www.globeinvestor.com/static/hubs/quotes.html
finance.yahoo.com/?u
Visit the first site above and type "stock split" in the search box and then click on Search by Keyword. Select two press releases by two different companies that

have recently announced splits or use the companies assigned by your instructor. Go to the second site and using the Symbol Lookup find the stock symbol for the company and then determine what the company does. Now, visit the third site and enter the company's symbol in the Enter Symbol box. *Note:* You may have to find the correct symbol for the stock on this site. In the drop-down box click Chart and then Get. Under range, click Max. Now, answer the following questions.

1. What is the company's history of stock splits? How often have they split the stock, and when? Starting with the first split, if an investor held 100 shares, how many shares would they have now?
2. Research the company's share price history for the period before and after the two most recent splits.
   a. Summarize your findings regarding stock price movement.
   b. Do you think the company chose to split the stock at an appropriate price point, and why?
3. Based on your findings in question 2, discuss the rationale for stock splits from the investor's viewpoint and from the company's viewpoint. If you had invested in one of these common shares just before the split, how would you have fared?

www.globeinvestor.com/static/hubs/quotes.html

Visit the above Web site and complete the following:

1. Enter "FL-T" in the Enter Symbol area and click on GO. What is the name of this company? Click on Company Snapshot. What does the company do? Click back in your browser. What is the company's indicated annual dividend and dividend yield? Now click on the Financial Reports link and then Ratios. What is the company's return on common equity? Now click on Quarterly. What is the company's most recent closing price, most recent EPS? The current P/E multiple, and market capitalization?
2. Repeat the above for the following symbols: BCE-T, TA-T, BBD.B-T, AIT-T, CP-T, BMO-T, WN-T, or other companies of your choice.
3. Discuss the differences in the above companies' dividend policies and the impact of the companies' policies on the returns to the owners of the company. Can you draw any conclusions about the relationship between dividends and returns?

keyword.newswire.ca

Visit the above site and type "issuer bid" in the search box and then click on Search by Keyword. Select a press release by a company that has recently announced a normal course issuer bid and another by a company announcing a substantial issuer bid. What do these two companies do? Describe the key features of the bid by each.

keyword.newswire.ca

Visit the above site and type "declares dividend" in the search box and then click on Search by Keyword. Select two press releases by two companies that have recently announced a dividend. Determine the declaration, record, ex-dividend, and payment dates.

INTEGRATIVE CASE 3

O'GRADY APPAREL COMPANY

O'Grady Apparel Company was founded nearly 150 years ago when an Irish merchant named Garrett O'Grady landed in Halifax with an inventory of heavy canvas, which he hoped to sell for tents and wagon covers. Instead, he turned to the sale of harder wearing clothing.

Today, the O'Grady Apparel Company is a small manufacturer of fabrics and clothing whose common shares are traded on the Toronto Stock Exchange. In 2003, the Nova Scotia–based company experienced sharp increases in sales in both domestic and European markets, resulting in record earnings. Sales rose from $15.9 million in 2002 to $18.3 million in 2003 with earnings per share of $3.28 and $3.84, respectively.

The European sales represented 29% of total sales in 2003, up from 24% the year before and only 3% in 1998, 1 year after foreign operations were launched. Although foreign sales represent nearly one-third of total sales, the growth in the domestic market is expected to affect the company most markedly. For 2004, management expects sales to surpass $21 million, and earnings per share are expected to rise to $4.40. (Selected income statement items are presented in Table 1.)

Because of the recent growth, Margaret Jennings, the corporate treasurer, is concerned that available funds are not being used to their fullest. The projected $1,300,000 of internally generated funds for 2004 are expected to be insufficient to meet the company's expansion needs. Management's policy is to maintain the current capital structure proportions of 25% long-term debt, 10% preferred equity, and 65% common equity for at least the next 3 years. In addition, it plans to continue paying out 40% of its earnings as dividends. Total capital expenditures are yet to be determined.

Ms. Jennings has been presented with several competing investment opportunities by division and product managers. However, because funds are limited, choices of

TABLE 1 Selected Income Statement Items

	2001	2002	2003	Projected 2004
Net sales	$13,860,000	$15,940,000	$18,330,000	$21,080,000
Net income after taxes	1,520,000	1,750,000	2,020,000	2,323,000
Earnings per share (EPS)	2.88	3.28	3.84	4.40
Dividends per share	1.15	1.31	1.54	1.76

which projects to accept must be made. The investment opportunities schedule (IOS) is shown in Table 2. To analyze the effect of the increased financing requirements on the weighted average cost of capital (WACC), Ms. Jennings contacted a leading investment banking firm that provided the financing cost data given in Table 3. O'Grady is in the 40% tax bracket.

TABLE 2 Investment Opportunities Schedule (IOS)

Investment opportunity	Expected return (IRR)	Initial investment
A	21%	$400,000
B	19	200,000
C	24	700,000
D	27	500,000
E	18	300,000
F	22	600,000
G	17	500,000

TABLE 3 Financing Cost Data

Long-term debt: The firm can raise $700,000 of additional debt by selling 10-year, $1,000 par value bonds with a 12% annual coupon rate paid semiannually to net $970 after flotation costs. Any debt in excess of $700,000 will have a before-tax cost, k_d, of 18%.

Preferred equity: Preferred shares, regardless of the amount sold, can be issued with a $60 stated value, and a 17% annual dividend rate, and will net $57 per share after flotation costs.

Common equity: The firm expects its dividends and earnings to continue to grow at a constant rate of 15% per year. The firm's shares currently trade for $20 per share. The firm can raise additional funds by selling new common shares, netting $16 per share after discounting and flotation costs.

REQUIRED

a. Calculate the after-tax cost of each source of financing, being sure to include the range of financing the cost applies to.

b. (1) Determine the break points associated with each source of capital.

   (2) Using the break points developed in (1), determine each of the ranges of new financing over which the firm's weighted average cost of capital (WACC) remains constant.

   (3) Calculate the weighted average cost of capital for each range of total new financing.

c. (1) Using your findings in b(3), draw the firm's marginal cost of capital (MCC) schedule and investment opportunities schedule (IOS) on the same graph where the x-axis is dollars and the y-axis is percents.

   (2) Which, if any, of the available investments would you recommend that the firm accept? Explain your answer.

d. (1) Assuming that the specific financing costs do not change, what effect would a shift to a more highly levered capital structure consisting of 50% long-term debt, 10% preferred equity, and 40% common equity have on your previous findings? (*Note:* Rework **b** and **c** using these capital structure weights.)

   (2) Which capital structure—the original one or this one—seems better? Why? If the firm moved from the original capital structure to the new structure, what do you expect would happen to the cost of the three sources of financing? Explain.

e. (1) What type of dividend policy does the firm appear to employ? Does it seem appropriate given the firm's recent growth in sales and profits, and its current investment opportunities?

   (2) Would you recommend an alternative dividend policy? Explain. How would this policy impact the investments recommended in **c** (2)? Recalculate the MCC using your new dividend policy.

PART

5

Long-Term Investment Decisions

Capital Budgeting: Principles and Techniques

LEARNING GOALS

LG1 Discuss the motives for capital budgeting expenditures, the steps in the capital budgeting process, the types of capital budgeting projects, approaches to capital budgeting decisions, and cash flow patterns.

LG2 Introduce the process used to analyze capital budgeting projects, discuss the basic cash flow components of projects, and illustrate how projects are evaluated by comparing the value of a project to its cost.

LG3 Describe the relevant cash flows that are considered in capital budgeting; calculate the initial investment for a project and the change in net working capital; describe the four components of cash inflows—operating income, tax shield from CCA, ITC, and government incentives—and calculate the total cash inflows; and determine the terminal cash flow.

LG4 Describe and illustrate the complete process for calculating the net present value for a capital budgeting project.

LG5 Discuss two other capital budgeting techniques—the payback period and internal rate of return (IRR)—and show how each is calculated.

LG6 Compare the NPV and IRR approaches to capital budgeting, focusing on the conflicting ranking that can occur, and discuss the cross-over rate.

12.1 The Capital Budgeting Decision Process

Long-term investments represent sizable outlays of funds that commit a firm to a course of action. Consequently, the firm needs procedures to analyze and properly select those investments. It must be able to measure relevant cash flows and apply appropriate decision techniques. As time passes, fixed assets may become obsolete or may require an overhaul; at these points, too, financial decisions may be required. **Capital budgeting** is the process of evaluating and selecting long-term investment projects that achieve the goal of owner wealth maximization. Firms typically make a variety of long-term investments, but the most common

capital budgeting
The process of evaluating and selecting long-term investment projects that achieve the goal of owner wealth maximization.

From Dreams to Reality

Every year, with great hope and expectations, businesspeople dream up new plans for expanding, replacing, or renewing the long-term assets they use to run their businesses. These dreams often are the stuff that success is made of, yet they can turn into nightmares for the firm, managers, shareholders, and creditors, if they fail to produce the necessary financial returns. Therefore, besides dreams, companies also need some very down-to-earth consideration of the costs of implementing their dreams and the returns they are likely to reap from these expenditures. This process is called *capital budgeting*. It is an important topic in finance and vital for a company if it is to continue to operate and grow. This chapter explains the principles and techniques of capital budgeting so that dreams that become reality are successes.

🔑 Career Key

The marketing department is extremely involved in the capital budgeting process. New product proposals and production expansion plans must all go through the capital budgeting procedure.

for a manufacturing firm is in *fixed assets*, which include property (land), plant, and equipment. These assets, often referred to as *earning assets*, generally provide the basis for the firm's earnings and cash flow power, and overall value.

Capital budgeting (investment) and financing decisions are treated *separately*. That is, in the analysis of projects, it is assumed that the necessary financing is in place and that this financing's overall cost is used to discount the cash flows associated with the project. The discount rate is the company's cost of capital. This issue was the subject of Chapter 9. In Chapters 12 and 13 we concentrate on fixed asset acquisition. We begin by discussing the motives for capital expenditures.

Capital Expenditure Motives

capital expenditure
An outlay of funds by the firm that is expected to produce benefits over a period of time *greater than* one year.

operating expenditure
An outlay of funds by the firm resulting in benefits received *within* one year.

A **capital expenditure** is an outlay of funds by the firm that is expected to produce benefits over a period of time *greater than* one year. An **operating expenditure** is an outlay resulting in benefits received *within* one year. Fixed asset outlays are capital expenditures, but not all capital expenditures are classified as fixed assets. A $60,000 outlay for a new machine with a usable life of 15 years is a capital expenditure that would appear as a fixed asset on the firm's balance sheet. A $60,000 outlay for advertising that produces benefits over a long period is also a capital expenditure, but advertising would rarely be shown as a fixed asset.[1]

Capital expenditures are made for many reasons. The basic motives for capital expenditures are to expand, replace, or renew fixed assets, or to obtain some other less tangible benefit over a long period. Table 12.1 briefly describes the key motives for making capital expenditures.

Steps in the Process

capital budgeting process
Consists of five distinct but interrelated steps beginning with *proposal generation*, followed by *review and analysis, decision making, implementation,* and *follow-up*.

The **capital budgeting process** consists of five distinct but interrelated steps. It begins with *proposal generation*, followed by *review and analysis, decision making, implementation,* and *follow-up.* Table 12.2 describes these steps. Each step in the process is important. Review and analysis and decision making—steps 2 and 3—consume the majority of time and effort in our discussion of the process, however. Because of their fundamental importance, and because in a course setting we cannot generate ideas or implement and follow up on projects, primary attention is given to review and analysis and decision making.

TABLE 12.1	Key Motives for Making Capital Expenditures

Motive	Description
Expansion	The most common motive for a capital expenditure is to expand the level of operations—usually through acquisition of fixed assets. A growing firm often needs to acquire new fixed assets rapidly, such as the purchase of property and plant facilities.
Replacement	As a firm's growth slows and it reaches maturity, most capital expenditures will be made to replace or renew obsolete or worn-out assets. Each time a machine requires a major repair, the outlay for the repair should be compared to the outlay to replace the machine and the benefits of replacement.
Renewal	Renewal, an alternative to replacement, may involve rebuilding, overhauling, or retrofitting an existing fixed asset. For example, an existing drill press could be renewed by replacing its motor and adding a numeric control system, or a physical facility could be renewed by rewiring and adding air conditioning. To improve efficiency, both replacement and renewal of existing machinery may be suitable solutions.
Other purposes	Some capital expenditures do not result in the acquisition or transformation of tangible fixed assets. Instead, they involve a long-term commitment of funds in expectation of a future return. These expenditures include outlays for advertising, research and development, management consulting, and new products. Other capital expenditure proposals—such as the installation of pollution-control and safety devices mandated by the government—are difficult to evaluate because they provide intangible returns rather than clearly measurable cash flows.

1. Some firms do, in effect, capitalize advertising outlays if there is reason to believe that much of the benefit of the outlay will be received at some future date. The capitalized advertising may appear as a deferred charge such as "deferred advertising expense," which is then amortized over the future. Expenses of this type are often deferred for reporting purposes to increase reported earnings, whereas for tax purposes, the entire amount will be expensed to reduce tax liability.

TABLE 12.2	Steps in the Capital Budgeting Process

Steps (listed in order)	Description
1. Proposal generation	Proposals for capital expenditures are made at all levels within a business organization. To stimulate a flow of ideas, many firms offer cash rewards for proposals that are ultimately adopted. Capital expenditure proposals typically travel from the originator to a reviewer at a higher level in the organization. Clearly, proposals that require large outlays will be much more carefully scrutinized than less costly ones.
2. Review and analysis	Capital expenditure proposals are formally reviewed (1) to assess their appropriateness in light of the firm's overall objectives and plans and, more important, (2) to evaluate their economic validity. The proposed costs and benefits are estimated and then converted into a series of relevant cash flows. Various capital budgeting techniques are applied to these cash flows to measure the investment merit of the potential outlay. In addition, various aspects of the *risk* associated with the proposal are evaluated. Once the economic analysis is completed, a summary report, often with a recommendation, is submitted to the decision maker(s).
3. Decision making	The actual dollar outlay and the importance of a capital expenditure determine the organizational level at which the expenditure decision is made. Firms typically delegate capital expenditure authority on the basis of certain dollar limits. Generally, the board of directors reserves the right to make final decisions on capital expenditures requiring outlays beyond a certain amount. Inexpensive capital expenditures, such as the purchase of a hammer for $15, are treated as operating outlays not requiring formal analysis.[a] Generally, firms operating under critical time constraints with respect to production often give the plant manager the power to make decisions necessary to keep the production line moving.
4. Implementation	Once a proposal has been approved and funding has been made available,[b] the implementation phase begins. For minor outlays, the expenditure is made and payment is rendered. For major expenditures, greater control is required. Often the expenditures for a single proposal may occur in phases, each outlay requiring the signed approval of company officers.
5. Follow-up	Involves monitoring the results during the operating phase of a project. Comparison of actual costs and benefits with those expected and those of previous projects is vital. When actual outcomes deviate from projected outcomes, action may be required to cut the costs, improve benefits, or possibly terminate the project. Analysis of deviations of actual from forecast values provides data that can be used to improve the capital budgeting process, particularly the accuracy of cash flow estimates.

[a]There is a certain dollar limit beyond which outlays are *capitalized* (i.e., treated as a fixed asset) and *amortized* rather than *expensed*. In accounting, the issue of whether to capitalize or expense an outlay is resolved by using the *principle of materiality*, which suggests that any outlays deemed material (i.e., large) relative to the firm's scale of operations should be capitalized, whereas others should be expensed in the current period.

[b]Capital expenditures are often approved as part of the annual budgeting process, although funding will not be made available until the budget is implemented—frequently as long as 6 months after approval.

Follow-up (Step 5) is an important, but often ignored, step in the process. Monitoring a previous investment is a vital part of capital budgeting. Consider that a firm is making a decision now (at time zero) regarding an asset that will generate returns for years into the future. The estimates of these returns are subject to major error. After making the investment in the capital budgeting project, the firm must monitor the returns to determine if the estimated returns are actually achieved. If not, the initial decision may have been incorrect. If the company does not monitor previous capital budgeting decisions, then the capital budgeting process cannot be improved. If the company makes mistakes, then these mistakes must be acknowledged and changes implemented aimed at ensuring the firm improves the accuracy of the cash flow estimates.

Capital Budgeting Terminology

Before developing the concepts, principles, and techniques related to the capital budgeting process, we need to introduce and explain some basic terminology. This section considers four key concepts associated with capital budgeting.

Types of Capital Budgeting Projects

independent projects
Projects whose cash flows are unrelated or independent of one another; the acceptance of one does not eliminate the others from further consideration.

The three most common project types are independent projects, mutually exclusive projects, and replacement projects. **Independent projects** are those whose cash flows are unrelated or independent of one another; the acceptance of one project *does not eliminate* the others from further consideration. If a firm has unlimited funds to invest, all the independent projects that meet its minimum acceptance criterion can be implemented.

For example, a firm with unlimited funds may be faced with three acceptable independent projects: (1) installing air conditioning in the plant, (2) acquiring a small supplier, and (3) purchasing a new computer system. Clearly, the acceptance of any one of these projects does not eliminate the others from further consideration; all three could be undertaken. If the projects were labelled A, B, and C, then the company has eight possible selection alternatives. The company could select project A, or B, or C, or A and B, or A and C, or B and C, or A, B and C, or none of A, B or C. For independent projects, the selection of one project has no impact on the decisions regarding the other projects.

mutually exclusive projects
Projects that compete with one another, so that the acceptance of one eliminates the others from further consideration.

Mutually exclusive projects are those that have the same function and therefore compete with one another. The acceptance of one *eliminates* from further consideration all other similar-function projects. For example, a firm in need of increased production capacity could obtain it by (1) expanding its plant, (2) acquiring another company, or (3) contracting with another company for production. Clearly, the acceptance of one eliminates the need for either of the others. Again, if the projects were labelled A, B, and C, then there are four possible selection alternatives: select project A, or B, or C, or none of the projects.

replacement projects
Projects that involve replacing an existing asset with a new asset.

Another type of mutually exclusive project is a **replacement project**. In this case, a company is considering replacing an existing asset with a new asset. There could be one or ten assets that could be used as the replacement, but, regardless, the firm faces a mutually exclusive decision. If there is a machine that could replace an existing machine, the mutually exclusive decision is to keep the old or replace with the new. If there are three machines, then the decision is similar to that discussed in the previous paragraph.

Unlimited Funds Versus Capital Rationing

unlimited funds
The financial situation in which a firm is able to accept all independent projects that provide an acceptable return.

The availability of funds for capital expenditures affects the firm's decisions. If a firm has **unlimited funds** for investment, making capital budgeting decisions is quite simple: all projects that will provide returns greater than a predetermined level can be accepted.

capital rationing
The financial situation in which a firm has only a fixed number of dollars to allocate among competing capital expenditures.

Typically, though, firms are not in such a situation; they operate instead under **capital rationing**. This means that they have only a fixed number of dollars available for capital expenditures and that numerous projects will compete for these dollars. Therefore the firm must ration its funds by allocating them to projects that will maximize share value. Procedures for dealing with capital rationing are presented in Chapter 13. The discussions that follow in this chapter assume unlimited funds.

Accept/Reject Versus Ranking Approaches

accept/reject approach
The evaluation of capital expenditure proposals to determine whether they meet the firm's minimum acceptance criterion.

ranking approach
The ranking of capital expenditure projects on the basis of some predetermined measure, such as the rate of return.

Two basic approaches to capital budgeting decisions are available. The **accept/reject approach** involves evaluating capital expenditure proposals to determine whether they meet the firm's minimum acceptance criterion. This approach can be used when the firm has unlimited funds, as a preliminary step when evaluating mutually exclusive projects, or in a situation in which capital must be rationed. In all cases, only acceptable projects should be considered.

The second method, the **ranking approach**, involves ranking projects on the basis of some predetermined measure, such as the rate of return. The project with the highest return is ranked first, and the project with the lowest return is ranked last. Only acceptable projects should be ranked. Ranking is useful in selecting the "best" of a group of mutually exclusive projects and in evaluating projects with a view to capital rationing.

Cash Flow Patterns

cash flow pattern
An initial outflow followed by a series of inflows.

Cash flow patterns are the type of cash flows that are expected to be generated by a capital budgeting project. The usual **cash flow pattern** consists of an initial outflow followed by a series of inflows. For example, a firm may spend $10,000 today and as a result expect to receive equal annual cash inflows of $2,000 each year for the next 8 years (an annuity), as depicted on the time line in Figure 12.1.[2] Another type of cash flow pattern is a project that provides unequal annual cash inflows, as depicted in Figure 12.2 on page 557. As was observed in Chapter 5, time value of money concepts are much simpler to apply when the pattern of cash flows is an annuity. An annuity for ten years involves one time value calculation. For a project with three unequal cash flows, three time value calculations are required.

FIGURE 12.1

Cash Flow Pattern for an Annuity
Time line for a project with equal annual cash inflows: an annuity

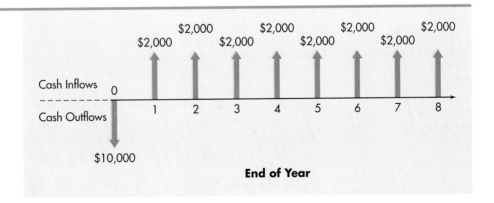

2. Arrows rather than plus or minus signs are frequently used on time lines to distinguish between cash inflows and cash outflows. Upward-pointing arrows represent cash inflows (positive cash flows), and downward-pointing arrows represent cash outflows (negative cash flows).

12–1 What is *capital budgeting*? How do capital expenditures relate to the capital budgeting process? Do all capital expenditures involve fixed assets? Explain.

12–2 What are the key motives for making capital expenditures? Discuss, compare, and contrast them.

12–3 Briefly describe each of the five steps involved in the capital budgeting process.

12–4 Differentiate between each of the following terms: (**a**) independent versus mutually exclusive versus replacement projects; (**b**) unlimited funds versus capital rationing; (**c**) accept/reject versus ranking approaches; (**d**) annuity versus unequal cash flows.

12.2 Basic Capital Budgeting Process

incremental cash flows
The additional cash flows—outflows or inflows—expected to result from a proposed capital expenditure.

To evaluate capital expenditure alternatives, the firm must determine the relevant cash flows, which are the *incremental cash outflows (the amount invested) and subsequent after-tax inflows*. The **incremental cash flows** represent the *additional* cash flows—outflows or inflows—expected to result from a proposed capital expenditure. As noted in Chapter 2, cash flows, rather than accounting figures, are used because cash flows directly affect the firm's ability to pay bills and purchase assets.

Basic Cash Flow Components

The cash flows of any project can include three basic components: (1) the initial investment, (2) operating cash inflows, and (3) the terminal cash flow. All projects—whether for expansion, replacement, renewal, or some other purpose—have the first two components. Some, however, lack the final component, terminal cash flow.

initial investment
The relevant cash outflow required now, at time zero, for a capital budgeting project.

Figure 12.2 depicts the cash flows for a project on a time line. Each of the cash flow components is labelled. The **initial investment** is $50,000 for the proposed project. This is the relevant cash outflow required now, at time zero. The **operating cash inflows**, the incremental after-tax cash inflows resulting from use of the project during its life, gradually increase from $4,000 in the first year to $10,000 in its tenth and final year. These cash inflows are the key benefit associated with investing in a capital project. The components of the incremental cash inflows include increases in operating income generated by the investment project and any tax benefits associated with the project. Both of these components are discussed in detail in Section 12.3. The **terminal cash flow** of $25,000, received at the end of the project's 10-year life, is the after-tax nonoperating cash flow occurring in the final year of the project. It is usually attributable to liquidation of the project. Note that the terminal cash flow does *not* include the $10,000 operating cash inflow for year 10.

operating cash inflows
The incremental after-tax cash inflows resulting from use of a project during its life.

terminal cash flow
The after-tax nonoperating cash flow occurring in the final year of a project, usually attributable to liquidation of the project.

FIGURE 12.2

Cash Flow Components
Time line for major cash flow components

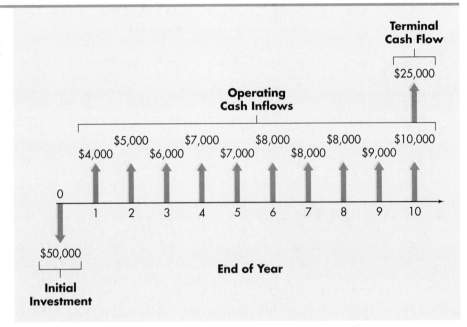

Evaluating Projects

When the relevant cash flows have been determined, an analysis must be completed to evaluate whether a project is acceptable, and to rank projects. A number of techniques are available for performing this analysis. The preferred approaches integrate time value procedures (Chapter 5), risk and return considerations (Chapter 7), and valuation concepts (Chapter 8) to select capital expenditures that are consistent with the firm's goal of maximizing owners' wealth. The approaches that consider all three concepts are referred to as **sophisticated approaches to capital budgeting.** This section focuses on basic valuation techniques to make a decision regarding the merits of investing in a capital budgeting project.

sophisticated approaches to capital budgeting
Capital budgeting techniques that integrate time value procedures, risk and return considerations, and valuation concepts to select capital expenditures that are consistent with the firm's goal of maximizing owners' wealth.

The Value of an Investment Project

In Section 8.1 of Chapter 8, we saw that the value of an asset is based on the present value of the cash flows generated by the asset over its useful life. As we saw in Chapter 8, the discount rate is the return required on the asset that compensates for the risk of the project. What is the required rate of return for capital budgeting projects? For this chapter, the required rate of return is the company's cost of capital. This is the case since, for a capital budgeting project, the company must raise financing to invest in the project. This new financing has an overall cost that, as we saw in Chapter 9, is termed the cost of capital.

As discussed in Chapter 9, the cost of capital reflects the business and financial risk of the company. If the capital budgeting project is in the company's current line of business, the company's cost of capital, by default, reflects the risk of the project. Therefore, discounting the proposed project's cash flows at the company's cost of capital builds into the analysis the requirement that the project provides the minimum required rate of return—the cost of capital. By doing so, the business and financial risk of the project is considered. Therefore, the value of a capital budgeting project to a company is based on the following:

Value of a project (V) = Present value of the asset's incremental after-tax cash inflows

$$V = \sum_{t=1}^{n} CF_t\,(1 - T) \times \text{PVIF}(t \text{ years}, k_a) \tag{12.1}$$

This equation indicates that the cash inflow for year t is calculated after-tax, discounted t periods at the firm's cost of capital, and then summed to all previous and subsequent discounted cash inflows for n periods, the life of the project.

Example ▼ McLaughlin Construction is considering purchasing a hydraulic lift that has a cost of $33,000. The lift will have a life of 8 years and is expected to generate extra (incremental) before-tax cash inflows of $7,500 per year. The company's tax rate is 20 percent and their cost of capital is 13 percent. McLaughlin Construction wonders whether they should purchase the new hydraulic lift. To decide, the first step is to consider the cash flow pattern associated with this project. This can be depicted on a time line like the one shown in Figure 12.1, though for this project, the numbers will change, but the time period is the same. Next, the value of the machine to the company must be determined. The value of the hydraulic lift to McLaughlin Construction is based on the present value of the cash flows the lift will generate over its 8-year life.

The cash flows are $7,500 per year, but this is before-tax. Remember, the cash flow must be considered after-tax since the company will not see any benefits until it has satisfied the government's tax claims. The after-tax cash flow is $6,000 per year [$7,500 × (1 − 0.20)]. To determine the present value of the cash flows, the discount rate that reflects the risk of the project must be used. For McLaughlin Construction this is 13 percent, the company's cost of capital. Therefore, by applying Equation 12.1, the value of the new hydraulic lift to the company is:

$$V = [\$7{,}500 \times (1 - 0.20)] \times \text{PVIFA (8 years, 13\%)}$$
$$= \$6{,}000 \times \text{PVIFA (8 years, 13\%)}$$

Using tables, the present value interest factor for the annuity is 4.799. Using a financial calculator, PMT is $6,000, N is 8, and I is 13 percent. Prior to computing the answer, remember to put 0 in the function not being used, in this case FV. Now press CPT and PV. Using a financial calculator, the answer is $28,793 (ignore the negative sign). Using tables, the answer is $28,794. For problems with larger numbers, the rounding errors when financial tables are used are much greater. For the remainder of capital budgeting, only the results determined using a financial calculator will be provided. The value of the hydraulic lift to McLaughlin Construction is $28,793. This is the present value of the after-tax cash flows discounted at the company's cost of capital, which reflects the risk of the project for the company.

▲

Comparing Value to Cost

The above analysis calculated the value of the asset to the company today (at time 0). This is the case since the cash flows were discounted. The value can now be compared to the initial cost of the asset, which is already at time 0. By subtracting the initial cost of the project (IC) from the value of the project to the company, the **net present value (NPV)** of the project is determined. This is illustrated below in Equation 12.2.

net present value (NPV)
The difference between the value of the project to the company and the project's initial cost.

$$\text{NPV} = (\text{Present value of the after-tax cash inflows}) - (\text{incremental cost})$$

$$\text{NPV} = \left[\sum_{t=1}^{n} CF_t \,(1 - T) \times \text{PVIF}(t \text{ years}, k_a) \right] - IC \tag{12.2}$$

Example ▼ Extending the McLaughlin Construction example, recall that the new hydraulic lift has an incremental cost of $33,000. The value of the lift to the company is $28,793. Therefore, the NPV of the lift is:

$$\text{NPV} = \$28,793 - \$33,000 = -\$4,207$$

This analysis indicates that the cost of the asset is greater than the value of the asset to the company. Therefore, the company should not purchase the new hydraulic lift; the benefits associated with the asset are less than the cost of the asset. Negative NPV projects should *never* be accepted. ▲

The NPV of –$4,207 is the loss the company would incur, discounted to time 0, if they proceeded with the investment. This assumes that all of the forecasts used in the analysis were correct. An alternative way of phrasing the loss is to recognize that the discount rate, the cost of capital, is the required return on the project. Since the NPV is negative, the *expected return* on the project is less than the required return. Therefore, McLaughlin Construction should not acquire the new hydraulic lift.

Extending the Analysis

What happens if some of the variables in the above example are changed? Consider the following independent changes:

1. The company's cost of capital is 11 percent.
2. The expected life of the hydraulic lift is 12 years.
3. The present value of the after-tax cash inflows is $11,070.
4. The new hydraulic lift will replace an existing lift. The book value (unamortized value) of the existing lift is $4,609 but it could be sold for $5,000. The old lift accounted for $7,500 of before-tax cash inflows per year, while the new lift will generate $15,000 in before-tax cash inflows.

For each of these cases, a new NPV must be calculated and McLaughlin Construction must make an accept/reject decision regarding the project.

Changing the Cost of Capital

For the first change, the 11 percent is used as the discount rate rather than 13 percent. This change will increase the present value of the after-tax cash inflows since lower discount rates increase present values. The value of the asset to the company increases to $30,877, so:

$$\text{NPV} = \$30,877 - \$33,000 = -\$2,123$$

Even though the value of the lift to the company increases, the cost is still greater, meaning that the firm should not acquire the asset.

Changing the Life

If the hydraulic lift's expected life is 12 years, cash inflows are received for a longer period of time, which increases the value of the lift to McLaughlin Construction. Using the original cost of capital of 13 percent, the value of the asset to the company increases to $35,506.

$$\text{NPV} = \$35,506 - \$33,000 = +\$2,506$$

Now the value of the lift is greater than its cost, implying that the firm should invest in the asset. Note that the +$2,506 is the value of the lift to McLaughlin, over and above the inital cost, at time 0. The NPV analysis has built in the requirement that the project generates a 13 percent rate of return— McLaughlin's cost of capital. The +$2,506 means that the project has generated a return greater than 13 percent. The expected return for the lift is greater than the required return.

NPV Equals Zero

If the present value of the after-tax cash inflows was $33,000, the NPV is equal to zero; the value of the lift to the company is equal to the cost of the asset.

$$\text{NPV} = \$33,000 - \$33,000 = \$0$$

An NPV of zero indicates that the lift is expected to provide exactly its required rate of return, in this case exactly 13 percent. The company should acquire the lift; it is expected to generate exactly its required rate of return.

Replace an Existing Asset

The fourth scenario is a replacement project. If McLaughlin acquires the new lift, they do not need the old, so it will be sold. The old lift has a book value of $4,609 but a market value of $5,000. Book value is simply the unamortized value of the asset on the company's books. Market value is what a buyer will pay for the old asset. If the company sells the old lift, the cash inflow is the market value, the amount a potential buyer will pay. The incremental cost of the new lift is the $33,000 (purchase price of new) minus $5,000 (proceeds from sale of the old). The new machine is expected to generate incremental cash inflows of $15,000 per year, but the old machine was already generating cash inflows of $7,500 per year. Therefore, the incremental (extra) cash flow is $7,500 per year. The NPV of the project can be calculated using Equation 12.3, which is a slight variation of Equation 12.2:

$$\text{NPV} = (\text{Present value of the incremental after-tax cash inflows}) - (\text{incremental cost})$$

$$\text{NPV} = \left[\sum_{t=1}^{n} ICF_t \, (1 - T) \times \text{PVIF}(t \text{ years}, k_a) \right] - IC \tag{12.3}$$

where ICF is the incremental cash inflows and IC is the incremental cost of the project. Applying this equation to the information for McLaughlin yields:

$$\text{NPV} = (\$15,000 - \$7,500) \times (1 - 0.20) \times \text{PVIFA (8 per, 13\%)} - (\$33,000 - \$5,000)$$

$$\text{NPV} = \$28,793 - \$28,000$$

$$= +\$793$$

The value of the lift is greater than its incremental cost; McLaughlin should replace the existing lift with the new. The project's expected rate of return is greater than the required rate of return.

? Review Questions

12–5   What is meant by the phrase incremental cash flows, and what are the three relevant cash flows considered for capital budgeting projects? When do these three cash flows occur?

12–6   Explain how capital budgeting integrates time value procedures, risk and return considerations, and valuation concepts.

12–7   What is the value of a capital budgeting project to a company based on? What is this value compared to? What is then done?

12–8   Fully explain why a company's cost of capital is important for capital budgeting purposes and how it is used. What is the effect of using the cost of capital to discount the cash flows?

12.3 Calculating Cash Flows

Calculating cash flows, both outflows and inflows, is a critical part of the review and analysis step in the capital budgeting process. This section explains some of the fundamentals associated with calculating cash flows, considers the process of calculating the initial investment in a project, and illustrates how cash inflows are determined.

Relevant Cash Flows

Developing relevant cash flows is most straightforward in the case of *expansion decisions*. In this case, the initial investment, operating cash inflows, and terminal cash flow are merely the after-tax cash outflow and inflows associated with the proposed outlay.

The development of relevant cash flows for *replacement decisions* is a little more involved; the firm must find the *incremental* cash outflows and inflows that will result from the proposed replacement. The initial investment in this case is the difference between the investment needed to acquire the new asset and the proceeds from the sale of the asset being replaced. The operating cash inflows are the difference between the operating cash inflows from the new asset and those from the old asset. The terminal cash flow is the estimated proceeds from the sale of the new asset at the end of its useful life. These relationships are shown in Figure 12.3 and an example was provided at the end of Section 12.2.

Actually, all capital budgeting decisions can be viewed as replacement decisions. Expansion decisions are merely replacement decisions in which all cash

▢─ Career Key

The operations department will submit proposals for the acquisition of new equipment and plants. They will frequently be asked to assist in determining operating cost changes for many capital budget proposals.

FIGURE 12.3

Relevant Cash Flows for Replacement Decisions

Calculation of the three components of relevant cash flow for a replacement decision

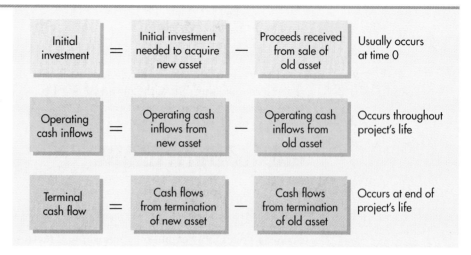

flows from the old asset are zero. In light of this fact, the following discussions emphasize the more general replacement decisions.

Sunk Costs and Opportunity Costs

When estimating the relevant cash flows associated with a proposed capital expenditure, the firm must distinguish between *sunk costs* and *opportunity costs*. These costs are easy to mishandle or ignore, particularly when determining a project's incremental cash flows. **Sunk costs** are cash outlays that have already been made (i.e., past outlays) and therefore have no effect on the cash flows relevant to the current decision. As a result, *sunk costs should not be included in a project's incremental cash flows*. **Opportunity costs** are cash flows that could be realized from the best alternative use of an owned asset. They therefore represent cash flows that will *not be realized* as a result of employing that asset in the proposed project. Because of this, any *opportunity costs should be included as cash outflows* when determining a project's incremental cash flows.

sunk costs
Cash outlays that have already been made (i.e., past outlays) and therefore have no effect on the cash flows relevant to a current decision.

opportunity costs
Cash flows that could be realized from the best alternative use of an owned asset.

Example ▼

⚠ Hint
The concepts of sunk and opportunity costs must be fully understood. Funds already spent are irrelevant to future decisions, but if the opportunity to receive cash inflows is lost due to changing the status of an asset, the lost cash inflows are a relevant cost.

▲

Jankow Equipment is considering converting an old warehouse it owns into a new retail store. Two years ago the company paid a consultant $125,000 to study the market potential associated with establishing a retail store at this location. Currently, Jankow rents the old warehouse to a furniture distributor for storage and Jankow receives $3,500 per month in rent.

The $125,000 is a *sunk cost* because it represents a cash outlay that occurred earlier. It doesn't matter if Jankow converts or does not convert the warehouse, the $125,000 is already spent. The cost is not incremental to the project and *would not be included in the analysis*. The $3,500 per month in rent is an *opportunity cost*. If Jankow converts the warehouse, they lose the opportunity to rent the warehouse. The $3,500 per month *would be included as a cash outlay* in the analysis of the retail store.

Operational and Financial Cash Flows

When calculating cash flows only operational items are considered. Operational items include all items that would affect the calculation of operating income

(EBIT). Financing costs like interest, lease payments, and dividends are ignored. This is the case since, as explained earlier, investment (capital budgeting) and financing decisions are treated separately. For capital budgeting, it is assumed that the financing decisions have already been made and the company has considered all factors that determine their cost of capital. The cost of capital is used to discount the cash flows. If financing costs were also considered within the calculation of the cash flows, these costs would be considered twice: once in the cash flow calculations and again in the discounting process. Therefore, when calculating cash flows:

1. Only incremental amounts are considered; compare the new asset with the old.
2. Ignore sunk costs but include opportunity costs.
3. Only include operational items; ignore financing costs.
4. The cash inflows must be after-tax; the company only receives benefits after paying the appropriate taxes.

Determining the Initial Investment

initial investment
The relevant cash outflows incurred if a capital budgeting project is implemented.

The **initial investment** is the relevant cash outflows incurred if a capital budgeting project is implemented. For all projects, an initial investment occurs now, at time 0. This expenditure marks the beginning of the project's life. For some projects, subsequent investments may also be required. These may be an expenditures that are capitalized or expensed. Regardless, these are costs of the project that must be recognized and then discounted the appropriate period to time zero.

Example ▼ Franklin Freezers is planning to manufacture a new line of products. The company will require a new plant that will take two years to construct. A payment of $750,000 is required now to begin construction, a further $1 million at the end of year 1, and a final payment of $1.5 million at the end of year 2. Each of these is a capital expenditure. In addition, Franklin will have to spend $500,000 in each of years 1 and 2 on development costs that will be treated as operating expenditures and expensed. Franklin's tax rate is 30 percent.

Figure 12.4 provides the relevant cash outflows for this new manufacturing plant for Franklin. Note that the cash outflows for the capital expenditures are shown as the stated amounts, while the cash outflows for the development costs are shown after-tax. Also, to make the various expenditures comparable, the initial investments for years 1 and 2 must be discounted at Franklin's cost of capital for the appropriate number of years to make them comparable to the time 0 ▲ investment.

installation cost
Costs incurred to place equipment or machinery into operation.

incremental cost of a new asset
The total of all costs incurred to get an asset to the point of being able to produce cash inflows for the company, less the proceeds from the sale of an old asset, often the asset being replaced.

The initial investment will also include **installation costs** incurred to place equipment or machinery into operation. The **incremental cost of a new asset** is the total of all costs incurred to get an asset to the point of being able to produce cash inflows for the company, less the proceeds from the sale of an old asset, often the asset being replaced.[3] Occasionally, the asset being replaced may have no value. It may actually cost the company money to dispose of an old asset.

---

3. Depending on the selling price of the old asset, there may be tax implications of the sale. These are generally minor in nature and for most projects can be safely ignored.

FIGURE 12.4

Initial Investment for Franklin Freezers' New Plant

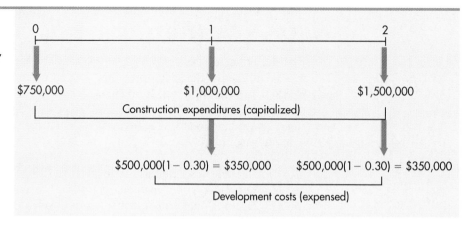

Change in Net Working Capital[4]

Net working capital, as noted in Chapter 3, is the amount by which a firm's current assets exceed its current liabilities. As shown in Chapter 4, if a company invests in assets that increase sales, levels of cash, accounts receivable, inventories, accounts payable, and accruals will also increase. As was noted in Chapter 2, increases in current assets are *uses of cash* (investments). Increases in current liabilities are *sources of cash* (provide financing). As long as the increased sales associated with the project continue, the increased investment in current assets (cash, accounts receivable, and inventories) and increased current liability financing (accounts payable and accruals) would also continue.

The difference between the change in current assets and the change in current liabilities is the **change in net working capital**. Generally, current assets increase by more than current liabilities, resulting in increased net working capital, which would be treated as an initial outflow.[5] If the change in net working capital were negative, it would be shown as an initial inflow. The change in net working capital—whether an increase or a decrease—*is not taxable* because it merely involves a net buildup or reduction of current accounts.

> **change in net working capital**
> The difference between the change in current assets and current liabilities associated with an investment project.

E x a m p l e ▼ Danson Company, a metal products manufacturer, is contemplating expanding its operations. In addition to Danson's acquiring a variety of new capital equipment, financial analysts expect that the changes in current accounts summarized in Table 12.3 will occur and be maintained over the life of the expansion. Current assets are expected to increase by $22,000, and current liabilities are expected to increase by $9,000, resulting in a $13,000 increase in net working capital. In this case, the increase would represent an increased net working capital investment and be treated as a cash outflow when analyzing the project. This outflow will only occur once, at time 0. This outflow will support the increase in sales for the full life of the project. ▲

---

4. Occasionally, this cash outflow is intentionally ignored to enhance the attractiveness of a proposed investment and thereby improve its likelihood of acceptance. Similar intentional omissions and/or overly optimistic estimates are sometimes made to enhance project acceptance. The presence of formal review and analysis procedures should help the firm to ensure that capital budgeting cash flow estimates are realistic and unbiased and that the "best" projects—those making the maximum contribution to owner wealth—are accepted.

5. When net working capital changes, it is assumed to happen at time 0. In practice, the change in net working capital will frequently occur over a period of months, as the project is implemented.

TABLE 12.3	Calculation of Change in Net Working Capital for Danson Company

Current account		Change in balance
Cash	+ $ 4,000	
Accounts receivable	+ 10,000	
Inventories	+ 8,000	
(1) Current assets		+ $22,000
Accounts payable	+ $ 7,000	
Accruals	+ 2,000	
(2) Current liabilities		+ 9,000
Change in net working capital [(1) − (2)]		+ $13,000

Determining the Cash Inflows

As was mentioned earlier, the underlying reason a company invests in a capital project is for the cash inflows the project is expected to generate over its useful life. There are four major components of these cash inflows. Each is discussed below.

Incremental After-Tax Operating Income

Operating income
The principal reason a company considers investing in a fixed asset; operating income may increase because sales increase, costs decrease, or both occur.

Obviously, the principal reason a company considers investing in a fixed asset is the expected increase in operating income. **Operating income** may increase because operating sales increase, operating costs decrease, or both occur. Here the focus is on cash operating sales and costs; non-cash costs are considered in the next section. The following process is used to calculate incremental after-tax operating income:

Incremental sales
less: Incremental operating costs
Incremental operating income
less: Taxes
Incremental after-tax operating income

Many investment projects result in both operating sales and costs increasing. This is the case since when sales increase, costs to produce and sell the product or service will also be incurred. For example, a project that results in incremental sales of $47,000 will also result in costs increasing. If it assumed that cash operating costs are $16,000, the incremental operating income is $31,000 ($47,000 − $16,000). If the tax rate was 22 percent, the incremental after-tax operating income is $24,180 $31,000 × (1 − 0.22). Some fixed assets do not generate sales. Instead, there is a cost to operate the asset. Newer, more efficient versions of the asset may result in operating costs declining. This will result in operating income increasing.

Example ▼ The operating costs for a piece of equipment are $98,000 per year. A more efficient version of the equipment is available and costs only $51,000 per year to operate. To determine the incremental operating income, the process provided above is used, with a focus on the difference between the new and old equipment. The tax rate is 22 percent.

	Current equipment	New equipment	Incremental
Sales	$ 0	$ 0	$ 0
Less: Operating costs	98,000	51,000	– 47,000
Operating income	–$98,000	–$51,000	+$47,000
Less: Taxes (22%)	21,560	11,220	10,340
After-tax operating income	–$76,440	–$39,780	+$36,660

When comparing projects that either increase sales or decrease costs, it should be noted that cost decreases are more valuable than sales increases. This is the case since with sales increases, operating costs must be deducted. Cost decreases fall straight to operating income. This is clear when the incremental after-tax operating incomes for the two examples above are compared. In the first case, sales increased by $47,000, and the incremental after-tax operating income is $24,180. In the second case, operating costs declined and the incremental after-tax operating income is $36,660. Some assets lead to both sales increasing and costs decreasing. This often occurs if production equipment is very old.

Example ▼ Spenceley Automotive is a small manufacturer of specialized car parts. Their current production equipment is 18 years old but could last for many years. Their production is limited to $650,000 of sales per year. Operating costs are 65 percent of sales. Newer, much more efficient and high capacity production equipment is available. With it, Spenceley could produce and sell $1,000,000 of product per year while operating costs would be 41 percent of sales. Spenceley's tax rate is 34 percent. In this example, with both sales increasing and costs declining, the incremental after-tax operating income soars, significantly enhancing the viability of the project, as shown in the following schedule:

	Current equipment	New equipment	Incremental
Sales	$650,000	$1,000,000	+$350.000
Less: Operating costs	442,500	410,000	– 12,500
Operating income	$227,500	$ 590,000	+$362,500
Less: Taxes (34%)	77,350	200,600	+ 123,250
After-tax operating income	$150,150	$ 389,400	+$239,250

Capital Cost Allowance (CCA)

In the above discussion, it was stated that when calculating incremental operating income, non-cash expenses were excluded. In this section, we consider non-cash expenses, with the most visible one being amortization. As discussed in Chapter 2, amortization is the systematic expensing of a portion of the cost of a fixed asset against sales. Expenditures on fixed assets are not expensed; rather they are capitalized and the expenditure is written off over time via the amortization expense. This yearly expense allocates the cost of the asset over its useful life and recognizes that the asset has declined in value. The amortization expense may be used for financial reporting purposes; however, for tax purposes, the Canada Customs and Revenue Agency (CCRA) requires companies to use the capital cost allowance.

capital cost allowance (CCA)
The tax version of amortization, a non-cash expense that increases cash flow.

Capital cost allowance (CCA) is simply the tax version of amortization. When calculating the cash flows for capital budgeting projects, CCA is used since this is the actual amount claimed by the company when filing taxes. CCA is a benefit since it is deducted from income when calculating taxable income, *but*, as a non-cash expense, it reduces taxes but no cash has actually been used. CCA reduces net income but increases cash flow. This concept is illustrated on page 55 in Chapter 2 and again on page 572 in this chapter.

CCA rates
Rates set by the Canada Customs and Revenue Agency (CCRA) that are used to calculate the CCA on an asset class; the rates range from 4 percent to 100 percent.

undepreciated capital cost (UCC)
The undepreciated value of an asset or asset class that is the basis for the amount of CCA that is claimed; also referred to as the book value of an asset.

The CCRA has allocated all assets into various asset classes. All assets in the same class are considered in total for CCA calculation purposes. Table 12.4 provides some examples of assets classes, the applicable CCA rate, and examples of assets that are included in the class. The **CCA rates** range from 4 percent to 100 percent. The dollar amount of CCA that can be charged in any year is based on the **undepreciated capital cost (UCC)** in the asset class multiplied by the CCA rate. CCA is generally calculated based on the declining balance of the UCC. The UCC is the undepreciated value of an asset or asset class on which CCA is charged; also referred to as the book value of an asset.

Example ▼ Tiger Beer acquires a new computer system costing $100,000. Based on the Table 12.4, this is a class 10 asset with a CCA rate of 30 percent. The dollar amount of CCA that can be claimed for the first four years is:

Year	UCC, beginning of year	CCA	UCC, end of year[a]
1	$100,000	$15,000[b]	$85,000
2	$ 85,000	$25,500	$59,500
3	$ 59,500	$17,850	$41,650
4	$ 41,650	$12,495	$29,155

[a]The undepreciated capital cost (UCC) is the asset's book value.

[b]Note that in the year an asset is acquired, only one-half of the allowable CCA can be deducted. This is termed the half-year rule. So, for this example, use 15%, half of the 30% CCA rate.

The benefit of CCA is the tax saving associated with the firm claiming the non-cash expense. This tax saving is termed a tax shield. It is calculated using Equation 12.4 as follows:

$$\text{Tax shield} = \text{CCA} \times \text{tax rate} \qquad (12.4)$$

TABLE 12.4	Capital Cost Allowance Rates

Class	Rate (%)	Examples of assets
Class 1	4	Bridges, buildings, dams, airplane runways, canals, culverts, parking areas
Class 3	5	Buildings acquired before 1988
Class 6	10	Greenhouses, hangars, wood jetties, oil storage tanks, fences
Class 7	15	Canoes, boats, fittings (for ships), engines (for ships), marine railways, scows
Class 8	20	Furniture, radio communications equipment, billboards, calculators
Class 9	25	Aircraft, including furniture, fittings, or equipment attached
Class 10	30	Automobile equipment, computer hardware, feature films, buses
Class 12	100	Cutlery, television commercials, computer software, tableware, uniforms
Class 13	SL[a]	Property that is leasehold interest (CCA depends on type/terms of lease)
Class 14	SL[a]	Patents, franchises, concessions, and licences for a limited period
Class 16	40	Taxicabs, autos for short-term rental, video games, aircraft fittings
Class 17	8	Roads, storage area, sidewalks, telephone or telegraph systems
Class 30	40	Telecommunications spacecraft
Class 33	15	Timber resource property
Class 38	30	Power-generated movable equipment (construction)
Class 39	25	Machinery and equipment in class 43 acquired before February 26, 1992
Class 42	12	Fibre optic cable
Class 43	30	Manufacturing and processing machinery, equipment
Class 44	25	Patents, licences to use patents acquired after April 26, 1993

[a]SL: amortized, on a straight-line basis, over the life of the asset.

In the Tiger Beer example above, if the company's tax rate were 40 percent, the tax shields associated with CCA for the first two years are:

$$\text{Tax shield}_1 = \$15,000 \times 40\% = \$6,000$$
$$\text{Tax shield}_2 = \$25,500 \times 40\% = \$10,200$$

tax shields
The tax savings the firm will experience from being able to claim the CCA on the asset.

▲ The **tax shields** are the tax savings the firm will experience from being able to claim the CCA on the asset.

Putting the First Two Components of Cash Inflows Together

The two sections above provided background material required to be able to calculate cash inflows. Based on this discussion, we are ready to calculate the total cash inflows for a project. To do this, however, we need to expand the process beyond operating income to include the benefit of the tax shield on CCA. The revised process is provided in Table 12.5.

TABLE 12.5	Process Used to Calculate Cash Inflows

		Incremental sales
less:		Incremental operating costs
		Incremental operating income
less:		Taxes
		Incremental after-tax operating income
plus:		Tax shield from CCA
		Incremental after-tax cash inflow

Example ▼ Branch Inc. is trying to determine whether they should purchase a new machine costing $52,000. The machine is a class 8 asset with a CCA rate of 20 percent. The asset will result in sales increasing by $60,000 and operating costs increasing by $25,000 per year. Branch's tax rate is 40 percent. Branch wishes to determine the incremental after-tax cash flows for this project for the first three years of its life. To calculate the incremental after-tax cash flows from the project, the tax shield from CCA is required. So the starting point is to complete the CCA table generating the tax shield for each of the first three years.

Year	UCC, beginning of year	CCA	UCC, end of year	Tax shield
1	$52,000	$5,200[a]	$46,800	$2,080
2	$46,800	$9,360	$37,440	$3,744
3	$37,400	$7,488	$29,912	$2,995

[a]Half-year rule, so use 10%.

Now the cash inflows are calculated using the process provided in Table
▲ 12.5. The results are presented in Table 12.6.

Remaining Components of Cash Inflows

To complete the discussion of the calculation of cash inflows, the remaining two components of the cash inflows must be considered. These are considered in the following sections.

Investment Tax Credit (ITC)

investment tax credit (ITC)
An incentive for businesses in various regions of the country to purchase certain types of fixed assets or undertake certain types of research and development activities; results in a reduction in federal taxes payable.

The **investment tax credit (ITC)** is an incentive for businesses in various regions of the country to purchase certain types of fixed assets or undertake certain types of research and development activities. For 2002, the ITC rate for buildings, machinery, and equipment used in manufacturing and processing, mining, oil and gas, logging, farming, or fishing was 10 percent. This credit only applied for corporations located in the Atlantic provinces and in the Gaspé region of Quebec.

TABLE 12.6   Cash Inflows for the Project

	Year 1	Year 2	Year 3
Incremental sales	$60,000	$60,000	$60,000
Incremental operating cost	$25,000	$25,000	$25,000
Incremental operating income	$35,000	$35,000	$35,000
Tax (40%)	$14,000	$14,000	$14,000
Incremental after-tax operating income	$21,000	$21,000	$21,000
Tax shield from CCA	$ 2,080	$ 3,744	$ 2,995
Incremental after-tax cash inflow	$23,080	$24,744	$23,995

For Canadian controlled private corporations (CCPC) located throughout Canada, an ITC of 35 percent was allowed on the first $2 million of research and development expenditures. For expenditures above $2 million and for non-CCPCs, the ITC rate was 20 percent.

The dollar amount of the ITC can be deducted from *federal taxes payable*. The dollar amount of the ITC is based on the amount of the qualifying expenditure times the ITC rate. So assuming the expenditure is $100,000 and it qualifies for a 20 percent ITC, the dollar amount of the ITC is $20,000 ($100,000 × 20%). This is a direct benefit of the project and must be recognized as a cash flow occurring in year 1.

One minor drawback associated with the ITC is that the dollar amount of the ITC must be deducted from the UCC of the asset for CCA purposes. Therefore, *a company can only claim CCA on the difference between the UCC and the ITC*. So, in the previous example, the UCC for CCA purposes would be $100,000 minus the $20,000 ITC, making the UCC $80,000. The company would then compute CCA based on the $80,000 and the CCA rate.

Example ▼ Recalculate the cash inflows for the Branch Inc. example, assuming the new machine costing $52,000 qualified for a 10 percent ITC. The ITC is $5,200, meaning the UCC for the machine is $52,000 less the ITC of $5,200—$46,800. This is the UCC at the beginning of year 1. The CCA and tax shields are:

Year	UCC, beginning of year	CCA	UCC, end of year	Tax shield
1	$46,800	$4,680	$42,120	$1,872
2	$42,120	$8,424	$33,696	$3,370
3	$33,696	$6,739	$26,957	$2,696

▲ When calculating the cash inflows there are two changes. First, the tax shield from CCA changes in each of the three years. Second, the ITC is a separate component of the cash flows. The results are presented in Table 12.7.

TABLE 12.7 Cash Inflows for the Project with ITC Included

	Year 1	Year 2	Year 3
Incremental sales	$60,000	$60,000	$60,000
Incremental operating cost	$25,000	$25,000	$25,000
Incremental operating income	$35,000	$35,000	$35,000
Tax (40%)	$14,000	$14,000	$14,000
Incremental after-tax operating income	$21,000	$21,000	$21,000
Tax shield from CCA	$ 1,872	$ 3,370	$ 2,696
Plus: ITC	$ 5,200		
Incremental after-tax cash inflow	$28,072	$24,370	$23,696

Comparing the cash flows in the two examples indicates that the benefit of the ITC in the first year more than compensates for the minor loss of tax shield in the subsequent year. The assumption made for the ITC is that it is received when the company's tax return is filed, which is assumed to be at the end of the fiscal year.

Government Incentives

The federal government and all provincial governments provide incentives for business to expand operations or locate a business in particular locations. Since these types of business decisions are capital budgeting projects, the incentives must be included when calculating the cash inflows for a project. Government incentives include cash grants, interest rate buydowns, wage subsidies, rent subsidies, and tax breaks.

cash grants
Direct cash payments by any level of government to the company.

Cash grants are direct cash payments by any level of government to the company. These payments could be made at the beginning of the project and/or at various points in the project's life as the company achieves certain predetermined targets. **Interest rate buydowns** are associated with loans a company negotiates with a lender in order to proceed with a project. The money borrowed is then invested in the project and the government agrees to pay a certain amount of the interest on the loan.

interest rate buydowns
Government payments of interest on a loan on behalf of a company.

Example ▼ Jameson Box Company is considering expanding their plant. This will result in the company hiring an additional 120 employees. The cost of the expansion is $7 million. The provincial government indicates that to enhance the feasibility of the project, the government will pay the first 5 percent of interest on a loan of up to $5 million. A condition of the buydown is that Jameson must negotiate the loan with a major chartered bank and the total amount of the loan must be **▲** invested in the expansion project.

wage and rent subsidies
Payment made by the government to the company's employees or landlord to reduce the effective cost of proceeding with a project.

Wage and rent subsidies are payments made by the government to the company's employees or landlord to reduce the effective cost of proceeding with a project. **Tax breaks** may be reductions in property taxes paid by the company on the land and building where the company locates, or reductions in income taxes the company would have to pay on the profits generated on an operation. Many governments around the world have created "tax-free zones" where all types of taxes are eliminated for a period of time for companies that locate in these areas.

tax breaks
Reductions in the property taxes or reductions in income taxes the company would have to pay on the profits generated on an operation.

Differences Between Cash Inflows and Profitability

This section discusses and illustrates the fundamentals of calculating cash inflows. It is important to remember that the focus of capital budgeting is on cash flows, not profits. Therefore while, in some respects, the process used to calculate both cash inflows and profitability appears similar, at a specified point there is a major difference. Consider the following example.

Example ▼ Fadeon Inc. is evaluating the purchase of a new lathe. The lathe is expected to generate sales of $125,000 per year and incur operating costs of $78,000. CCA on the lathe in year 1 will be $22,000. Fadeon's tax rate is 30 percent. The profit the lathe will generate in year 1 is provided below:

Sales	$125,000
Operating costs	78,000
Operating income	47,000
Less: CCA	22,000
Incremental income before taxes	25,000
Less: Taxes (30%)	7,500
Incremental income after taxes	17,500
Add: CCA	22,000
Incremental after-tax cash inflow	$ 39,500

To adjust the above for cash flows, one alterative is to recognize that CCA, a non-cash expense was deducted from operating income. To calculate cash inflows, CCA should be added back to the bottom line in the above analysis, as was illustrated in Chapter 2 for the Statement of Cash Flows, and as is done above. An alterative is to use the process that was discussed earlier and is provided below:

Sales	$125,000
Operating costs	78,000
Operating income	47,000
Less: Taxes (30%)	14,100
Incremental after-tax operating income	32,900
Tax shield from CCA[a]	6,600
Incremental after-tax cash inflow	$ 39,500

[a]As was shown earlier, a non-cash expense results in tax savings equal to: non-cash expense $\times$ T. For the above $22,000 \times 30\% = \$6,600$.

Note the major difference between the profitability and the cash flow of the asset. The reason for the difference is the non-cash expense, CCA. While the profit on the project in year 1 is only $17,500, the cash inflow is over double at $39,500. This type of difference will always exist when CCA is a significant amount. Readers should understand why there is a difference between profits and cash inflows and be able to calculate cash inflows using both of the above approaches.

Terminal Cash Flows

All investment projects have a finite life. Fixed assets eventually wear out and become obsolete, at which time the project is terminated and the assets liquidated. This may generate terminal cash flows. The proceeds from the sale of the asset are termed the **salvage value**. This is the amount the company receives from the sale of the asset, *less any removal or clean-up costs incurred*. In some cases there may not be any salvage value or there may be a cost associated with terminating a project. The environmental costs of returning a property to its original condition can be very high for some types of projects.

salvage value
The amount received when a project is terminated and an asset is sold.

A second terminal cash flow is associated with the net working capital investment made at the beginning of the project's life. At termination, the sales associated with the project cease, as does the need for the net working capital. Therefore, at termination, the originally invested **net working capital will be recaptured**. As

net working capital recapture
With the termination of a project, the sales associated with the project cease, and the company will recover the originally invested net working capital.

IN PRACTICE

Marketing Sears Canada

For many companies, marketing is a major expenditure that is planned for months in advance of the actual outlay. The benefits of the expenditure are expected to be realized over a number of years. Expenditures on marketing, like all major expenditures, must be carefully analyzed to ensure benefits are realized. As John Wanamaker stated, "I know half the money I spend on advertising is wasted, but I don't know which half." Such a statement for any type of expenditure by a company indicates that more financial analysis is required. If funds are to be committed to any type of investment project, the reason for the total amount of the expenditure must be clear, and the total benefits, the expected cash inflows, estimated.

Sears Canada is an example of a company that seems to have benefited from a close review and analysis of their marketing expenditures. In September 2002, Sears, one of Canada's largest advertisers, announced that they would make a "sea change" in the way they invest their $500 million marketing budget. Prior to 2003, Sears spent 90 percent of the budget, $450 million, on print ads in newspapers. Only 10 percent was spent on television. For 2003, the money spent on television advertising will increase to 30 percent of the marketing budget, or $150 million. The company's goal for 2003 is to have ads on television every week in order to "do brand stories. Television is a better medium for brand building," states Mark Cohen, Sears CEO. While print ads are associated with informing customers of sales, television ads build awareness and interest and encourage customers to visit the store to purchase products that are not on sale.

In addition, Sears Canada was planning to shrink the spending on the ubiquitous Sears catalogues. In 2002, Sears distributed 75 million catalogues. For 2003, this will be reduced to 59 million as the company attempts to send catalogues only to people who buy their products. For 2003, this will result in higher sales and cost savings of $39 million, as the investment in catalogues falls to $143 million from $182 million. The company is also shifting its focus to the Internet, investing the catalogue savings in further developing their Web site. Mr. Cohen indicated that on-line sales were about $200 million per year, with higher margins than in-store sales, and sales are growing by "leaps and bounds." Like many Canadian companies, Sears Canada is investing in their Web site in order to generate higher cash inflows.

Marketing is a major expenditure for many companies. Companies should regularly examine their marketing to ensure it is a positive NPV investment project, that the benefits are greater than the costs, and that very little of the spending is wasted. This may require, as with Sears Canada, a dramatic change in how the money is spent, and a careful analysis of the expected benefits.

REFERENCES: Hollie Shaw, "Sears Faces Off Against Bay on TV," *Financial Post*, September. 27, 2002, FPS; Marina Strauss, "Sears Changing Its Marketing," *The Globe and Mail*, September 27, 2002.

with the original working capital investment, there are no tax consequences of the recapture, since this is an internal reduction of current assets and liabilities.

? Review Questions

12–9   Discuss the differences between the relevant cash flows for an expansion versus a replacement project.

12–10 Distinguish between (**a**) sunk costs and opportunity costs, and (**b**) operational and financial cash flows. Which are included and which are ignored for capital budgeting purposes, and why?

12–11 What is the initial investment of a capital budgeting project, and what type of costs are considered? What is the incremental cost of a new asset?

12–12 What is the change in net working capital and why, and how is it considered when evaluating an investment project? Consider both the beginning and end of a project's life.

12–13 There are four major components of cash inflows for capital budgeting projects. List and fully describe each of these.

12–14 Explain each of the following terms: (**a**) CCA; (**b**) asset class; (**c**) UCC; (**d**) tax shield; (**e**) book value; (**f**) ITC; (**g**) government incentives.

12–15 What is the process used to calculate cash inflows for investment projects?

12.4 Splitting Cash Flows: The Complete Net Present Value Approach

In the previous section, the various components of the initial investment and cash inflows for a capital budgeting project were introduced and discussed. The various components of the inflows are calculated and added to determine the incremental after-tax cash inflow for each year of a project's life. An understanding of cash flows is vital to an understanding of capital budgeting; however, for calculation purposes there are some problems with this approach. The two major problems are discussed next.

Problems with Calculating Cash Inflows Each Year

The first problem is associated with calculating cash inflows for projects with very long lives. In Section 12.3, the process for calculating the tax shield from CCA was discussed. This is a key component of cash inflows. Note, however, that the CCA changes each year, since the dollar amount is based on the declining balance of UCC and a stated percentage rate (the CCA rate). Therefore, for projects with long expected lives, say 25 years, 50 different calculations must be made, just to determine the tax shield. The tax shield must then be added to the after-tax operating income and any other cash inflow components to determine the incremental after-tax cash inflow each year. The cash inflows each year would then have to be discounted back to time 0 for the appropriate number of years at the company's cost of capital. Obviously, this would be a very time-consuming process if done with just a calculator. A computer spreadsheet would greatly speed the process, but even then it is a challenge to structure the analysis.

The second problem is also associated with the tax shield. Since the calculation of CCA is based on the declining balance of UCC, the UCC never reaches zero. As long as there is UCC in the asset class, CCA can be charged on the asset and there is a benefit associated with the project. For example, if a company constructs a new plant (a class 1 asset with a 4% CCA rate) at a cost of $5 million, the plant may be expected to have a useful life of 50 years. The implication is that CCA and tax shields will have to be calculated for 50 years. But even after 50 years, there is still $662,959 of UCC remaining on the plant.[6]

In other words, in order to determine the total benefit of the tax shield from CCA for the plant, the CCA and tax shield will have to be calculated for well over 50 years, and each year's tax shield discounted back to time 0. Again, while not mathematically complicated, it is very time consuming and not the most pleasant way to spend 30 minutes! Also, after analyzing one or two projects, most students would very quickly tire of capital budgeting. But, thankfully, there is a way around this time-consuming process. The present value of the total tax shield on an asset can be calculated by using Equation 12.5 as follows:

$$\text{PV of tax shield from CCA} = C \left[\frac{d \times T}{d + k_a} \right] \left[\frac{1 + (0.5)k_a}{1 + k_a} \right] \tag{12.5}$$

where:

$\quad C =$ Incremental amount of UCC resulting from an asset acquisition
$\quad d =$ CCA rate for the asset
$\quad T =$ Company's tax rate
$\quad k_a =$ Company's cost of capital

Note that the final component of the equation accounts for the half-year rule.

Example ▼ For the plant in the earlier discussion, what is the total present value of the tax shield? The incremental amount of UCC is the construction cost of $5,000,000. If we assume the company's tax rate is 32 percent, and their cost of capital is 10 percent, the present value of the ITC is $436,364 calculated as follows:

$$\text{PV of tax shield} = \$5,000,000 \left[\frac{0.04 \times 0.32}{0.04 + 0.10} \right] \left[\frac{1 + (0.5) \times (0.10)}{1 + 0.10} \right] = \$436,364$$

▲

Note that for a replacement project, the UCC would be reduced by the proceeds received from the sale of the old asset. Also, the UCC would be reduced if the project qualified for an ITC.

Example ▼ Now assume that the new plant replaces an existing plant that is sold as scrap materials raising $300,000. Also, the new building will qualify for a 10 percent ITC. The present value of the total tax shield is based on the incremental amount of UCC added to class 1. By liquidating the existing building and receiving $300,000, the company will have to subtract that amount from the UCC of class 1. The new building will add $5,000,000, so the incremental amount of UCC is $4,700,000. The new building also qualifies for a 10 percent ITC; therefore, the company will receive an ITC of $500,000 ($5,000,000 × 10%). Since the company can only claim CCA on the difference between the UCC and the ITC, C, the

---

6. The equation used to calculate this amount is as follows:

$$\text{UCC}_t = C \times \left(1 - \frac{d}{2} \right) \times (1 - d)^{t-2} \tag{12.6}$$

where: UCC_t is undepreciated capital cost of the asset at the beginning of the year t, C is the original UCC of the asset, d is the CCA rate, and t is the beginning of the year for which the UCC is being calculated.

incremental amount being added to the asset class, is $4,200,000 ($5,000,000 − $300,000 − $500,000). The present value of the total tax shield on the building is $366,545, calculated as follows:

$$\text{PV of tax shield} = \$4,200,000 \left[\frac{0.04 \times 0.32}{0.04 + 0.10}\right]\left[\frac{1 + (0.5) \times (0.10)}{1 + 0.10}\right] = \$366,545$$

Implication of the Analysis

If it is more straightforward to calculate the present value of the total tax shield from CCA using a simple equation, it seems reasonable to calculate the present value of each of the remaining cash inflows separately as well. In other words, the individual components of the cash inflows are considered separate items, the present value of each calculated, and then the present values added together to determine the value of the project to the company. The value is then compared to the initial investment, the NPV calculated, and a decision made regarding the project, as was presented in Section 12.2. This process is illustrated using an example.

Example ▼ Gekkos Toys operates a machine that was purchased five years ago for $510,000 and that now has a book value (UCC) of $104,083. The machine is a class 43 asset with a CCA rate of 30 percent. The current market value of the machine is $100,000. The machine is expected to last 10 more years, at which time it will have no value. A much more efficient version of the machine is now available at a cost of $460,000. The new machine has an expected life of 10 years with no salvage value at that time. It cost Gekkos $95,000 per year to operate the current machine, but due to improved efficiencies, the operating costs for the new machine would fall to $32,000 per year. The new machine is also a class 43 asset. The company's tax rate is 40 percent and their cost of capital is 10 percent. Should Gekkos replace the existing machine with the new model?

To answer this question, the NPV of the proposed project must be calculated. To calculate the NPV, the initial investment and the value of the project to Gekkos must be calculated. The initial investment is the incremental cost of the new machine. If Gekkos Toys buys the new machine, they will pay $460,000. *But*, if they buy the new machine, they will sell the old, raising $100,000. The old machine will be sold since there is no point in having two machines that perform the same function. The incremental cost of the new machine is $360,000 ($460,000 − $100,000).

The value of the project to Gekkos is, as we already know, based on the present value of the cash inflows the project will generate. For the project there are two components of the cash inflows: the incremental after-tax operating income and the tax shield from the CCA based on the incremental amount of UCC added to the asset class. As discussed above, rather than determine the yearly cash inflows, the two components of the incremental after-tax cash flows will be split. The present values of these two items will be analyzed and calculated separately, and added together to determine the present value of the incremental after-tax cash inflows.

The first component of the cash inflows is the incremental operating income which, in this case, is based on the decreased operating costs. The old machine cost $95,000 per year to operate. The new machine costs $32,000 per year, a cost savings of $63,000 per year. This is the incremental operating income. Multiply this amount by (1 – tax rate). The incremental after-tax operating income is $37,800. Note that Gekkos will receive this each year for the 10-year life of the new machine. The $37,800 income is an annuity for 10 periods. Therefore, to calculate the present value of the incremental after-tax income using a financial calculator, $37,800 is the PMT, 10 percent is I (the discount rate), and N is 10. Compute the present value and the answer is $232,265. This is the incremental after-tax operating income. This is shown below as an equation:

$$\text{Present value of incremental after-tax operating income} = (\$95{,}000 - \$32{,}000) = \$63{,}000 \times (1 - 0.40)$$
$$= \$37{,}800 \times \text{PVIFA (10 years, 10\%)}$$
$$= \$232{,}265$$

The second component of the cash inflows is the present value of the tax shield from CCA. Equation 12.5 is used to determine the total present value of the tax shield. The incremental UCC added to the asset class is the incremental cost of the asset. Therefore, applying the equation for the tax shield results in the following:

$$\text{PV of tax shield} = \$360{,}000 \left[\frac{0.30 \times 0.40}{0.30 + 0.10} \right] \left[\frac{1 + (0.5) \times (0.10)}{1 + 0.10} \right] = \$103{,}091$$

The present value of the tax shield is $103,091. You now have the PV of the two components of the cash inflows for the project. These are summed to determine the value of the new machine to Gekkos. This value is $335,356 ($232,265 + $103,091). The NPV of the new machine is:

$$\text{NPV} = (\$232{,}265 + \$103{,}091) - \$360{,}000 = -\$24{,}644$$

The value of the new machine to Gekkos is less than the incremental cost of the machine; therefore, the machine has a negative NPV of –$24,644. This indicates Gekkos should not replace the existing machine: The asset is not expected to generate its required rate of return. Remember, the NPV process builds into the analysis the requirement that the asset provide a return of, at least, its cost of capital. The negative NPV indicates the project does not generate the required return of 10 percent.

Extending the Analysis to Include Other Components

Based on the discussion in Section 12.3, numerous other cash flow components can be associated with a capital budgeting project. This section considers three additional items.

Salvage Value

As discussed in Section 12.3, salvage value is the proceeds the company receives from the sale of an asset at the end of its useful life. How does this impact on the analysis?

Example ▼ In the original discussion of the new machine that Gekkos Toys was considering acquiring, it was stated that the new machine was expected to have no salvage value at the end of its 10-year life. Upon further investigation, it is discovered that the machine will actually have a salvage value of $108,000 at the end of its 10-year life. Now, should Gekkos replace the existing machine with the new model?

There are two impacts of salvage on the analysis. First, the salvage value is a benefit of the project; it is a cash inflow. At the end of year 10, Gekkos will sell this asset, raising $108,000. Since the inflow occurs in the future, it must be discounted at the cost of capital for the appropriate time period using Equation 12.7:

$$S_0 = S_n \times \text{PVIF}(n \text{ years}, k_a\%) \tag{12.7}$$

where S_0 is the present value of the salvage at time 0 and S_n is the salvage value of the asset at the end of year n. Applying this to Gekkos results in the present value of the salvage of:

$$S_0 = \$108,000 \times \text{PVIF (10 years, 10\%)} = \$41,639$$

The second impact of salvage is that a portion of the previously calculated tax shield is lost. The tax shield calculation assumes that the firm will own the asset until it has a zero market value. As it turns out, this is not the case for the new machine Gekkos is analyzing. Gekkos will use the new machine for 10 years at which time it will be worth an estimated $108,000, or $41,639 today. Therefore, Gekkos loses some of the previously calculated tax shield. The amount lost is based on the present value of the salvage, and is calculated using Equation 12.8:

$$\text{PV of tax shield lost} = S_0 \left[\frac{d \times T}{d + k_a} \right] \tag{12.8}$$

Notice that in Equation 12.8, the latter part of the tax shield equation, Equation 12.5, is not used since the half-year rule no longer applies. At the time salvage is realized, year 1 has passed. Applying the equation to the new machine Gekkos is considering results in:

$$\text{PV of tax shield lost} = \$41,639 \left[\frac{0.30 \times 0.40}{0.30 + 0.10} \right] = -\$12,492$$

So the tax shield lost is $12,492 and is a cash outflow. Now there are four components of the cash flows generated by the new machine and the value of the machine to Gekkos is based on the sum of these four amounts. The NPV of the new machine is based on the analysis presented in Table 12.8.

TABLE 12.8 NPV Analysis for the New Machine	
Present value of incremental after-tax operating income	$232,265
PV of tax shield from the incremental CCA	103,091
PV of salvage	41,639
PV of tax shield lost due to salvage	−12,492
Value of new machine	$364,503
Incremental cost of machine	360,000
NPV	$ 4,503

IN PRACTICE

Information Technology's Big Byte

In today's environment, a company's investment in information technology (IT) can entail large capital expenditures. In the rapidly changing IT environment, managers clamour for the latest hardware and software upgrades to keep IT systems current and improve operational efficiencies. The right IT applications, they claim, can save millions in operating costs. Financial managers, on the other hand, struggle to control capital spending while at the same time approving projects that are viable and boost the company's competitive position. Although some of these projects involve the latest hardware and software, many more now focus on leveraging the firm's investment in existing technology by centralizing technology services, integrating the different parts of a company's information systems, and making similar improvements. E-business projects are also on the rise and now account for a growing portion of the total IT budget.

With so much at stake in terms of dollars spent and potential benefits, managers must create a business case that justifies the project and shows how it adds value—no easy task. In addition to measuring dollar benefits in terms of cash inflows, they must attempt to quantify indirect and qualitative benefits. This may be straightforward for systems that increase

sales, but how does the company assign a dollar value to, for example, the increased customer satisfaction generated by a new, easier-to-use customer information system?

During 2001 and 2002, an uncertain economic future meant companies were deferring IT projects and had to choose those that yielded the greatest return and strategic advantage. The director of corporate IT services at La-Z-Boy Inc., a leading manufacturer of upholstered furniture, said, "Previously, we would look primarily at high-level issues. Now, we're not only examining the details of a project but also the underlying assumptions and the business case." IT projects, like all investment projects, are all about results, the projected sales and costs. Recently, La-Z-Boy decided to postpone certain IT projects but moved ahead with strategic technology projects. For example, analysis of a new payroll and human resources system showed that it should lower costs for the entire organization and the project was approved.

REFERENCES: Showwei Chu, "Cognicase Considers Selling European Operations," *The Globe and Mail*, July 29, 2002; Shari Caudron, "The Tao of E-Business," *Business Finance*, September 2001; Sam Greengard, "IT: Luxury or Necessity?," *Industry Week*, December 1, 2001.

In this case the combination of these four cash flows equals $364,503. Therefore, the value of the asset is greater than the incremental cost of the asset, implying that the project has a net present value of $4,503. Remember, this *doesn't* mean that the project generates a rate of return of $4,503. It does mean that the project generates a rate of return greater than the cost of capital, greater than the required rate of return. In this example, the rate of return will be greater than 10 percent, so Gekkos Toys should replace the existing machine with the new machine. ▲

? Review Questions

12–16 What are the problems associated with calculating cash inflows in total for each year of a project's life? How is this problem resolved?

12–17 What is the formula for calculating the tax shield from CCA? What does this formula do? What does this formula assume?

12–18 What process is used to calculate the NPV of an investment project when the incremental cash flows are split into their separate components?

12–19 What impact does salvage value have on the analysis of an investment project?

12.5 Other Capital Budgeting Techniques

NPV is one technique used to evaluate capital budgeting projects. The *payback period and internal rate of return (IRR)* are two other common approaches that are often used.[7] This section discusses and illustrates these two approaches and compares them to the NPV approach. To accomplish this, the following capital budgeting problem will be used.

SRL Metals is a small metal fabricator located in northern Newfoundland. The company is contemplating two investment projects. Both have an initial cost of $25,000 and both have expected lives of five years. Table 12.9 provides the cash flow patterns for these two projects. Note that all components of the cash inflows are considered, including the full value of the tax shield. A simplified example is used in order to focus the discussion on the two techniques. The remainder of this section covers the two other capital budgeting techniques and compares them to the NPV method.

Payback Period

payback period
The length of time in years it takes for a project's yearly incremental after-tax cash inflows to recover the incremental investment in the project.

The **payback period** is the length of time in years it takes for a project's yearly incremental after-tax cash inflows to recover the incremental investment in the project. In the case of an *annuity*, the payback period can be found by dividing the initial investment by the annual cash inflow. When the cash inflows are different amounts each year (a *mixed stream*), the yearly cash inflows must be accumulated until the initial investment is recovered. Although popular, the payback period is generally viewed as an *unsophisticated capital budgeting technique*, because it does *not* explicitly consider the time value of money by discounting cash flows to find present value.

When the payback period is used to make accept/reject decisions, the decision criteria are:

1. For independent projects, if the payback period is *less than* the maximum acceptable payback period, *accept* the project. If the payback period is *greater than* the maximum acceptable payback period, *reject* the project.
2. For mutually exclusive projects, the project with the lower payback period is ranked first (if the period is less than the maximum acceptable value).

---

7. Two other closely related techniques that are sometimes used to evaluate capital budgeting projects are the *average (or accounting) rate of return (ARR)* and the *profitability index (PI)*. The ARR is an unsophisticated technique that is calculated by dividing a project's average profits after taxes by its average investment. Because it fails to consider cash flows and the time value of money, it is ignored here. The PI, sometimes called the *benefit-cost ratio*, is calculated by dividing the present value of cash inflows by the initial investment. This technique, which does not consider the time value of money, is sometimes used as a starting point in the selection of projects under capital rationing. It is discussed more fully in Chapter 13.

| TABLE 12.9 | Cash Flow Patterns for Two Investment Projects |

	Year	Project A	Project B
Initial investment		$25,000	$25,000
Cash inflows[a]:	1	$12,500	$ 4,000
	2	12,500	5,000
	3	4,000	6,500
	4	800	12,500
	5	500	12,500

[a]All components of the cash inflows are included.

The length of the maximum acceptable payback period is determined by management. This value is set *subjectively*, based on a number of factors including, but not limited to, the type of project (expansion, replacement, renewal, etc.), the perceived risk of the project, and the perceived relationship between the payback period and share value. It is simply a value that management feels will, on average, result in good—that is, value-creating—investment decisions. This value will vary from company to company.

Example ▼ We can calculate the payback period for the two projects SRL Metals is evaluating. For both projects, the cash inflows must recoup the $25,000 initial cost. For project A, the first year's cash inflow is $12,500, which is half of the cost. Year 2's cash inflow is also $12,500 and the sum of these two amounts fully recovers the initial investment. So project A's payback period is 2 years.

For project B, the first year's cash flow of $4,000 recovers a very small portion of the initial cost. In year 2, $5,000 is recovered so the cumulative cash inflows are $9,000 ($4,000 + $5,000). For year 3, $6,500 is recovered so the cumulative cash inflows are $15,500 ($9,000 + $6,500). In year 4, the cash inflow is $12,500, so the cumulative amount is $28,000 ($15,500 + $12,500). The payback period is less than 4 years, but more than 3. To recover the $25,000 cost of the project, $9,500 ($15,500 + $9,500 = $25,000) of year 4's cash inflow is required. This is 76 percent ($9,500 ÷ $12,500) of year 4's cash inflow. Therefore the payback period for project B is 3.76 years (3 years plus 76% of year 4).

If SRL's maximum acceptable payback period were 4 years and the projects were independent, both projects would be acceptable. If the projects were mutually exclusive, project A would be selected since it has the shorter payback period. ▲

! Hint
In all three of the decision methods presented in this text, the relevant data are *after-tax cash inflows*. The only relevance of accounting profits is to help determine the incremental after-tax operating income.

! Hint
The payback period indicates to firms taking on projects of high risk how quickly they can recover their investment. In addition, it tells firms with limited sources of capital how quickly the funds invested in a given project will become available for future projects.

The payback period is widely used in reality due to its computational simplicity and its intuitive appeal. By considering cash flows rather than accounting profits, it measures how quickly the firm recovers its initial investment. Because it can be viewed as a measure of *risk exposure*, many firms use the payback period as a decision criterion or as a supplement to sophisticated decision techniques. The longer the firm must wait to recover its invested funds, the greater the possibility of a calamity. Therefore, the shorter the payback period, the lower the firm's exposure to such risk.

Problems with the Payback Period

There are three *major* problems with the payback period as a method of evaluating capital budgeting projects. First, the payback period ignores cash flows that occur after the payback period. When the payback period for project A was calculated, we stopped the analysis at the end of year 2. The problem is that the cash inflows for project A after year 2 decline significantly; total cash inflows over the remaining three years are only $5,300. For project B, the cash inflows in years 3, 4, and 5 total $31,500. By not considering all of the data, we are not fully analyzing the project.

Second, the payback period fails to consider explicitly the time value of money. By simply cumulating cash flows over time, a cash inflow in year 1 is treated the same as a cash inflow in year 4. This is clearly an inappropriate way to analyze a project.[8]

Example ▼ To illustrate this, the NPVs of projects A and B are calculated in Table 12.10. SRL's cost of capital is 10 percent so this is the discount rate used to calculate the value of the two projects to SRL Metals. The NPV analysis clearly indicates that by ignoring time value considerations, SRL would make an incorrect decision by ranking project A ahead of B. Clearly project B creates more value for shareholders; its expected return is greater than project A's. While both projects are acceptable (since both have positive NPVs), B is superior to A. ▲

TABLE 12.10   Calculation of NPVs for Two Investment Projects

Year	Cash inflow Project A	Cash inflow Project B	Present value interest factor (PVIF)[a]	Present value of cash inflow[a] Project A	Present value of cash inflow[a] Project B
1	$1,250	$ 400	0.909	$11,364	$ 3,636
2	$1,250	$ 500	0.826	10,331	4,132
3	$ 400	$ 650	0.751	3,005	4,884
4	$ 80	$1,250	0.683	546	8,538
5	$ 50	$1,250	0.621	310	7,762
Present value of cash inflows				$25,556	$28,952
Less: Initial cost				25,000	25,000
NPV				$ 556	$ 3,952

[a]This is simply the rounded-off time value factors from Table A-3 for 10% and a given year. The figures provided for the present values of the cash inflows were calculated using a financial calculator where the cash inflow is the FV, the appropriate year is N, and 10%, SRL's cost of capital, is I. The PV is computed after inputting 0 into PMT.

---

8. To consider differences in timing *explicitly* in applying the payback method, the *present value payback period* is sometimes used. It is found by first calculating the present value of the cash inflows at the appropriate discount rate and then finding the payback period by using the present value of the cash inflows.

Third, the maximum payback period set by management is merely a subjectively determined number. By using it, a project cannot be evaluated in light of the wealth maximization goal because the method is not based on discounted cash flows. It is not known if the project adds to the firm's value. Instead, the appropriate payback period is simply the maximum acceptable period of time over which management decides that a project's cash flows must equal the initial investment.

In conclusion, the payback period technique could be described as the **fish-and-bait test**: It concentrates on recovering the bait (the initial cost), paying no attention to the size of the fish (PV of all cash inflows). It is a measure of a project's liquidity and capital recovery, rather than the project's ability to generate positive cash flow and increase company value.

fish-and-bait test
A description for the payback period since it concentrates on recovering the bait (the initial cost) paying no attention to the size of the fish (PV of all cash inflows).

Internal Rate of Return (IRR)

internal rate of return (IRR)
The discount rate that equates the present value of the cash inflows with the initial cost of a capital budgeting project; the discount rate that makes the NPV of a project equal to 0.

The **internal rate of return (IRR)** of a capital budgeting project is the discount rate that equates the present value of the cash inflows with the initial cost of the project. In other words, the IRR is the discount rate that makes the NPV of a project equal to 0. The IRR is the expected return of the project. The IRR method is considered a sophisticated capital budgeting technique that has wide appeal in practice. The reason for its wide appeal is that it reduces a capital budgeting project to a single, easily understood number: a percentage return.

A difficulty with IRR is that it is time consuming to calculate by hand. Without a financial calculator or computer spreadsheet, the IRR for a project must be calculated by trial and error. For simple capital budgeting problems, a financial calculator can be used; but for complex problems, a computer spreadsheet is used to calculate the IRR. The equation for IRR is easily extended from Equation 12.3, the calculation of the NPV for a project, as provided in Equation 12.9:

$$\text{NPV} = 0 = \left[\sum_{t=1}^{n} ICF_t (1 - T) \times \text{PVIF}(t \text{ years}, k_a) \right] - IC \tag{12.9}$$

If the IRR for a project is greater than or equal to the company's cost of capital, then the project should be accepted since the NPV of the project will be greater than or equal to 0. If the IRR for a project is less than the company's cost of capital, the project's NPV will be less than 0 and the project is clearly unacceptable.

Calculating the IRR

For a basic capital budgeting project, like those discussed for SRL Metals, the calculation of IRR is not difficult, just time consuming, since a trial-and-error approach must be used. This section considers the process used to calculate IRR. We will start by considering a project where the cash inflows are an annuity.

E x a m p l e ▼ Reconsider the McLaughlin Construction example from Section 12.2. In this example, the company was considering purchasing a new hydraulic lift with a cost of $33,000, a life of 8 years, and incremental after-tax cash inflows of $6,000 per year. To calculate the IRR for this project using a financial calculator, 6,000 is the PMT, 8 is N, the PV is 33,000. Input 0 in FV and compute (CPT) I.

For some calculators, the PV may have to be input as a negative number. In this case, I is 9.17 percent; this is the IRR for the project. To prove it, determine the value of the project to McLaughlin assuming the company's cost of capital was 9.17 percent. The value is $33,000 meaning the NPV is zero. Therefore, the IRR ▲ is 9.17 percent.

If a financial calculator is not available, an approximate answer must be calculated. To do this, first divide the initial cost by the yearly after-tax cash inflow.

Example ▼ For the McLaughlin example, the result is 5.5 ($33,000 ÷ $6,000). This is the payback period. Now, go to Table A-4, the present value interest factors for a $1 annuity (PVIFa) and find, for the life of the project (8 periods), the PVIFa factor closest to the payback period. The factor is between 9 percent and 10 percent, but very close to the 9 percent factor, which is 5.535. The IRR is slightly above 9 percent. A closer approximation can be determined by *interpolation*. Note that the difference between the 9 percent and 10 percent PVIFa factors is 0.200 (5.535 − 5.335). To get to the 5.5 payback period, 0.035 must be deducted from the 9 percent factor. This is 17.5 percent (0.035 ÷ 0.200) of the total difference between the 9 percent and 10 percent factors. Therefore, the IRR is about 9.175 percent. ▲ This result is almost exactly the value determined using the financial calculator.

NPV profile
A table and/or graph that shows the NPV for a project at various discount rates.

When the cash inflows are different amounts each year (a mixed stream), as for the two projects being evaluated by SRL Metals, a different approach to calculating the IRR must be used. This is the NPV profile approach. A **NPV profile** is a table and/or graph that shows the NPV for a project at various discount rates. To illustrate this approach, consider the following example.

Example ▼ We want to calculate the IRR for the two projects being considered by SRL Metals. NPV profiles for the two projects are developed by simply discounting the cash inflows for each of the years at a stated discount rate and determining the NPVs. The outcome of this process for 6 discount rates is provided in Table 12.11.
The data in Table 12.11 can be used to develop NPV profiles on a graph. Figure 12.5 provides the NPV profiles for projects A and B for SRL Metals.

TABLE 12.11 **NPV Profile for Two Investment Projects**[a]

Discount rate (%)	NPV Project A	NPV Project B
0	$5,300	$15,500
5	2,748	9,037
10	556	3,952
12	−235	2,221
14	—	637
16	—	−817

[a]To determine the NPVs, the cash inflows for the two projects are discounted at the stated rate for the appropriate period, summed, and then subtracted from the initial investment. At a 0% discount rate, cash flows over time are equivalent, so the cash inflows are simply added and the initial investment subtracted to calculate NPV.

While the table does not determine the exact IRRs, it can narrow the range. For Project A, based on the NPV, it is clear the IRR is between 10 percent and 12 percent, but closer to 12 percent. (This is why NPVs are not provided for the 14 percent and 16 percent discount rates.) If, for example, 11.5 percent is used as a discount rate, a NPV of –$41 results. Since this is very close to 0, it would be reasonable to conclude that the IRR is a little less than 11.5 percent, say about 11.4 percent. The exact answer is 11.39 percent.

For project B, the IRR is between 14 percent and 16 percent and based on the NPVs, close to 15%. At 15 percent, the NPV is $106, so the IRR is slightly less than 15 percent, say 14.8 percent. The exact IRR is 14.86 percent.[9] A graph drawn to scale, like Figure 12.5, would also allow the analyst to narrow down the correct IRR.

For SRL Metals, we have analyzed the two investment projects using three techniques. The results are summarized below:

	Project A	Project B
Payback period	2 years	3.76 years
NPV (@10%)	$556	$3,952
IRR	11.39%	14.86%

FIGURE 12.5

Net Present Value Profiles for Projects A and B

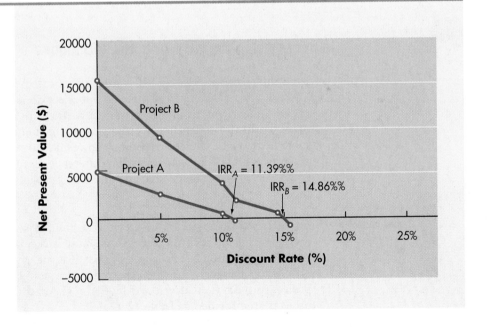

9. Most financial calculators are preprogrammed to calculate IRRs for these simple types of capital budgeting projects through the cash flow (CF) function. The yearly cash inflows are input into the calculator, the initial cost in the PV function (as a negative number), and the IRR computed. To ease the process of determining IRRs, learn how to use your calculator.

What should SRL Metals do? First, given the major problems associated with the payback period technique, the result indicating that project A is superior to B should be ignored. The two sophisticated approaches, NPV and IRR, both give the same result: project B is superior to project A. Project B has a much larger NPV and IRR. This is clearly seen in Figure 12.5. If the projects are mutually exclusive, B is ranked first. If the projects are independent, both are acceptable. Both generate a return greater than SRL's cost of capital as is clear when the values for NPV and IRR are considered.

? Review Questions

12–20 What is the payback period and how is it calculated? Why is it used by companies?
12–21 List and discuss the weaknesses of the payback period.
12–22 What is the internal rate of return of an investment project? How is it calculated?
12–23 How is the IRR used to determine whether a project is acceptable? Why is this approach used?
12–24 Compare the process used to calculate the IRR for a project where the cash inflows are the same amount each year to one where the inflows differ from year to year.
12–25 Do the NPV and IRR approaches always provide the same accept/reject decision for a project? Why is this the case?

12.6 Comparing the NPV and IRR Techniques

Even though both NPV and IRR are sophisticated capital budgeting techniques and will *always* generate the same accept/reject decisions for projects, differences in their underlying assumptions can cause them to *rank* projects differently. In other words, for independent projects, both techniques will always result in the same decisions. Different decisions can result, however, for mutually exclusive projects. This section illustrates the difference, explains why different rankings can occur, and considers which of the two approaches, NPV or IRR, is better to use.

Example ▼ For SRL Metals, based on the previous section, it is very clear that if the projects are independent, both projects A and B are acceptable to the company. If the projects are mutually exclusive, project B is clearly superior to A. Project B's NPV is much higher, as is the expected return, its IRR. Now assume that a third project, project C, is developed by SRL. The cash flows associated with these projects are provided in Table 12.12.

Projects B and C are mutually exclusive projects so they must be ranked. The payback period, NPV, and IRR for project B are already known; they must be calculated for project C. (We will calculate the payback period for practice.) The payback period for C is 1.5 years ($21,250 + $3,750) noting that half ($3,750 ÷ 7,500) of year 2's cash inflow is needed. To calculate the IRR for project C, the NPV profile presented in Table 12.13 for project C is used:

TABLE 12.12	Cash Flow Pattern for Project C	
	Year	Project C
Initial investment		$25,000
Cash inflows:	1	$21,250
	2	7,500
	3	3,000
	4	500
	5	500

TABLE 12.13	NPV Profile for Project C[a]
Discount Rate (%)	Project C
0	$7,750
5	5,435
10	3,422
15	1,656
20	95
21	–196

[a]To determine the NPVs, the cash inflows for the two projects are discounted at the stated rate for the appropriate period, summed, and then subtracted from the initial investment.

The IRR is between 20 percent and 21 percent but closer to 20 percent, say 20.3 percent. The exact IRR is 20.32 percent. Figure 12.6 provides the NPV profiles for both projects B and C. Note that in the process of developing the NPV profile, the NPV of project C was also calculated. What do the various capital budgeting techniques suggest about the two projects? The results are summarized below.

	Project B	Project C
Payback period	3.76 years	1.5 years
NPV (@ 10%)	$3,952	$3,422
IRR	14.86%	20.32%

Based on NPV, project B is superior to C; based on IRR the reverse holds. What should SRL Metals do? To answer this question, we will consider why different rankings can occur.

conflicting rankings
Conflicts in the ranking of projects using the NPV and IRR techniques resulting from differences in the magnitude and timing of cash inflows.

Reason for Different Ranking

Conflicting rankings using the NPV and IRR techniques result from differences in the magnitude and timing of cash inflows. Projects with very large cash

FIGURE 12.6

Net Present Value Profile with Crossover

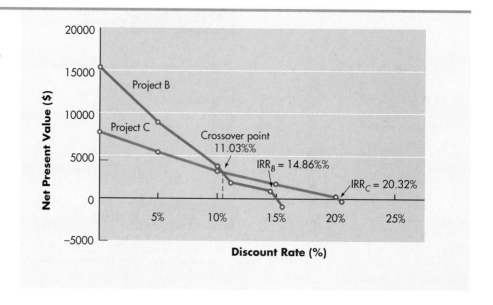

inflows in the early years of a project's life tend to result in high IRRs. The IRR for projects with low cash inflows in the early years and high cash inflows in the later years tend to generate lower IRRs.

The underlying reason for this is the assumption that the two techniques make concerning the reinvestment of a project's cash inflows. The NPV method assumes the project's cash inflows are reinvested at the cost of capital. IRR assumes the cash inflows are reinvested at the IRR. IRR is a *compounded rate of return*, meaning the technique assumes the yearly cash inflows can be reinvested at the IRR and the return compounds over time. In other words, for project C, the IRR method assumes that the $21,250 cash inflow received in year 1 is reinvested by the company to earn a 20.32 percent return. This is an unrealistic assumption for high IRR projects, especially for SRL Metals, given that the company's cost of capital is less than half at 10 percent. If the company cannot reinvest the $21,250 at 20.32 percent, then the true IRR on the project will be much lower.

Since the NPV technique makes a much safer and realistic reinvestment rate assumption, that the cash inflows will be reinvested at the cost of capital, the NPV technique is preferred to the IRR.

Cross-Over Rate

cross-over rate
The discount rate where NPV profiles intersect meaning the NPVs of the two projects are equal, and where the ranking decision for the projects changes.

Another way to compare the NPV and IRR methods is through the use of the **cross-over rate**. Referring again to Figure 12.6, note that the NPV profiles for projects B and C intersect. The intersection point occurs at a discount rate of 11.03 percent, and then the lines quickly diverge in both directions. At the intersection point, the NPVs of the two projects are equal at $3,040 and therefore, a company would be indifferent to the two projects. Also, at this point the ranking decisions for the projects change. If SRL Metal's cost of capital was less than 11.03 percent, project B is preferred. This is clearly seen in Figure 12.6, with the NPV profile of project B being above C when the discount rate is less than

11.03 percent. If the cost of capital is greater than 11.03 percent, project B is preferred. Again, note that the NPV profile for C is above B's in Figure 12.6. For SRL Metals, the cost of capital is 10 percent; therefore project B is ranked ahead of C.

? Review Questions

12–26 For mutually exclusive projects, do the NPV and IRR techniques also provide the same ranking? Explain. Why do the two techniques give different rankings?

12–27 What is the cross-over point and why is it important when ranking projects?

SUMMARY

LG1 **Discuss the motives for capital budgeting expenditures, the steps in the capital budgeting process, the types of capital budgeting projects, approaches to capital budgeting decisions, and cash flow patterns.** Capital budgeting is the process used to evaluate and select capital expenditures consistent with the firm's goal of owner wealth maximization. Capital expenditures are long-term investments made to expand, replace, or renew fixed assets or to obtain some other less tangible benefit. The capital budgeting process contains five distinct but interrelated steps, beginning with proposal generation, followed by review and analysis, decision making, implementation, and follow-up. Capital expenditure proposals may be independent or mutually exclusive. Typically, firms have only limited funds for capital investments and must ration funds among carefully selected projects. To make investment decisions when proposals are mutually exclusive or when capital must be rationed, projects must be ranked; otherwise, accept/reject decisions must be made. Cash flow patterns consist of an initial outflow followed by a series of inflows; the inflows can be either annuities or different amounts each year (mixed streams), or a combination of the two.

LG2 **Introduce the process used to analyze capital budgeting projects, discuss the basic cash flow components of projects, and illustrate** how projects are evaluated by comparing the value of a project to its cost. To evaluate capital budgeting projects, the firm must determine the relevant cash flows, which are the incremental cash outflows (the amount invested) and subsequent after-tax inflows. The cash flows of any project can include three basic components: (1) the initial investment, (2) operating cash inflows, and (3) the terminal cash flow. To evaluate projects, the preferred approaches integrate time value procedures, risk and return considerations, and valuation concepts to select capital expenditures that are consistent with the firm's goal of maximizing owners' wealth. The value of an asset is based on the present value of the cash flows generated by the asset over its useful life. The discount rate used is the return required on the asset that compensates for the risk of the project. For capital budgeting, this is the company's cost of capital. The value of the asset is compared to the initial cost of the asset to determine the net present value (NPV) of the project.

LG3 **Describe the relevant cash flows that are considered in capital budgeting, calculate the initial investment for a project and the change in net working capital, describe the four components of cash inflows—operating income, tax shield from CCA, ITC, and government incentives— and calculate the total cash inflows, and determine the terminal cash flow.** When calculating the relevant cash flows for a capital budgeting project, the following rules must be obeyed: (1) only incremental amounts are considered—compare the new asset with the old; (2) ignore sunk costs but include opportunity costs; (3) only include operational items—ignore financing costs; and (4) the cash inflows must be after-tax—the company only receives benefits after paying the appropriate taxes. The initial investment for a project occurs at time 0 and marks the beginning of the project's life. For some projects, subsequent investments may also be required and these may be capitalized or expensed. Projects that result in sales increasing may also require the investment of working capital—the difference between increases in current assets and current liabilities. There are four major components of the cash inflows: (1) Incremental after-tax operating income, the principal reason a company considers investing in a fixed asset which may result from sales increasing, operating costs decreasing, or both. (2) The tax shield on capital cost allowance (CCA). Since expenditures on fixed assets are capitalized, the expenditure is written off over time by charging CCA. CCA is a benefit since it is deducted from income when calculating taxable income, *but*, as a non-cash expense, it reduces taxes but no cash has actually been used. The benefit of CCA is the tax saving associated with the firm claiming the non-cash expense, which is the tax shield. (3) The investment tax credit (ITC), an incentive for businesses in various regions of the country to make certain expenditures that result in a reduction in federal taxes payable. (4) Government incentives. These four items are the total cash inflows. The terminal cash flow is the combination of the salvage value of the asset and the recapture of working capital.

LG4 **Describe and illustrate the complete process for calculating the net present value for a capital budgeting project.** When calculating cash inflows for individual years, there are two problems. First, since CCA changes each year of a project's life, the tax shield changes. For projects with very long lives, say 25 years, 50 different calculations must be made just to determine the tax shield. The tax shield must then be added to the other cash inflow components and the incremental after-tax cash inflows for each year would then have to be discounted back to time 0. This would

be a very time consuming process. Second, since the UCC never reaches zero, the full value of the tax shield cannot be totally calculated when determining yearly cash inflows. Therefore, Equation 12.5 in the chapter is used to calculate the total present value of the tax shield. The implication is that the individual components of the cash inflows are considered separate items, the present value of each calculated, and then the present values added together to determine the value of the project to the company. The value is then compared to the initial investment, the NPV calculated, and a decision made regarding the project, as was presented earlier. The components include the initial cost, the four components of the inflows, and the terminal value of the project.

LG5 **Discuss two other capital budgeting techniques—the payback period and internal rate of return (IRR)—and show how each is calculated.** NPV is one technique used to evaluate capital budgeting projects. The *payback period* and *internal rate of return (IRR)* are two other common approaches that are often used. The payback period is the length of time in years it takes for a project's yearly incremental after-tax cash inflows to recover the incremental investment in the project. A maximum acceptable payback period is subjectively set by a company to evaluate projects. The payback period is widely used in reality due to its computational simplicity and its intuitive appeal, but there are three problems with this technique. First, the payback period ignores cash flows that occur after the payback period. Second, the payback period fails to explicitly consider the time value of money. Third, the maximum payback period set by management is merely a subjectively determined number. The internal rate of return (IRR) of a capital budgeting project is the discount rate that equates the present value of the cash inflows with the initial cost of the project; it is the expected return of a project. The IRR is the discount rate that makes the NPV of a project equal to 0. The IRR is calculated by developing an NPV profile for a project. The NPV and IRR techniques will always result in the same accept/reject decision for independent projects.

 Compare the NPV and IRR approaches to capital budgeting, focusing on the conflicting ranking that can occur, and discuss the

cross-over rate. Even though both NPV and IRR are sophisticated capital budgeting techniques and will always generate the same accept/reject decisions for projects, differences in their underlying assumptions can cause them to rank mutually exclusive projects differently. Conflicting rankings are due to differences in the magnitude and timing of cash inflows. Projects with very large cash inflows in the early years tend to result in high IRRs. This is because the IRR method assumes the cash inflows are reinvested at the IRR, and the return compounds over time. The NPV method assumes cash inflows are reinvested at the cost of capital. Since the NPV technique makes a much safer and realistic reinvestment rate assumption, the NPV technique is preferred to IRR. The cross-over rate is the discount rate where NPV profiles intersect, meaning the NPVs of the two projects are equal and where the ranking decision for the projects changes.

<hr>

SELF-TEST PROBLEM   **(Solution in Appendix B)**

ST 12–1   Determining cash inflows and calculating NPV   Laidlaw Inc. is evaluating the purchase of a new piece of equipment costing $300,000. The new equipment would replace an existing machine that has a remaining useful life of five years but could be sold today for $50,000. The equipment has a useful life of five years and is a class 10 asset which has a CCA rate of 30 percent. The new equipment qualifies for an investment tax credit of 10 percent. The incremental sales and decreases in operating costs associated with the acquisition of the equipment are provided below. Additional working capital needs associated with the new equipment will be $25,000. At the end of five years, the new equipment is expected to have a salvage value of $35,000. The firm's tax rate is 40 percent and their cost of capital is 18 percent.

Year	Increase in revenue	Decrease in costs
1	$ 85,000	$15,000
2	105,000	5,000
3	100,000	
4	70,000	
5	60,000	

a. Calculate the yearly incremental after-tax cash inflows associated with this machine for the five years of its useful life.
b. If you were required to compute the NPV for this piece of equipment, how would your analysis differ from the process used to solve part **a**? Why would you approach the problem in this manner?
c. Compute the NPV for this piece of equipment. Should Laidlaw purchase this new piece of equipment? Explain.

ST 12–2   All techniques with NPV profile—Mutually exclusive projects   Fitch Industries is in the process of choosing the better of two equal-risk, mutually exclusive, capital expenditure projects—M and N. The relevant cash flows for each project are shown in the following table. The firm's cost of capital is 14 percent.

	Project M	Project N
Initial cost (*IC*)	$28,500	$27,000
Year (*t*)	Cash inflows (*CF*$_t$)	
1	$10,000	$11,000
2	10,000	10,000
3	10,000	9,000
4	10,000	8,000

a. Calculate each project's payback period.
b. Calculate the net present value (NPV) for each project.
c. Calculate the internal rate of return (IRR) for each project using NPV profiles.
d. Summarize the preferences dictated by each measure calculated above, and indicate which project you would recommend. Explain why.
e. Draw the net present value profiles for each project on the same set of axes, and explain the circumstances under which a conflict in rankings might exist.

PROBLEMS

WARM-UP   12–1   NPV   Calculate the net present value (NPV) for the following 20-year projects. Comment on the acceptability of each. Assume that the firm has cost of capital of 14 percent.
a. Initial investment is $10,000; cash inflows are $2,000 per year.
b. Initial investment is $25,000; cash inflows are $3,000 per year.
c. Initial investment is $30,000; cash inflows are $5,000 per year.

WARM-UP   12–2   NPV for varying costs of capital   Dane Cosmetics is evaluating a new fragrance-mixing machine. The machine requires an initial investment of $24,000 and will generate after-tax cash inflows of $5,000 per year for 8 years. For each of the costs of capital listed, (1) calculate the net present value (NPV), (2) indicate whether to accept or reject the machine, and (3) explain your decision.
a. The cost of capital is 10 percent.
b. The cost of capital is 12 percent.
c. The cost of capital is 14 percent.

INTERMEDIATE   12–3   Net present value—Independent projects   Using a 14 percent cost of capital, calculate the net present value for each of the independent projects shown in the following table and indicate whether or not each is acceptable.

	Project A	Project B	Project C	Project D	Project E
Initial cost (*IC*)	$26,000	$500,000	$170,000	$950,000	$80,000
Year (*t*)			Total cash inflows (*CF_t*)		
1	$4,000	$100,000	$20,000	$230,000	$ 0
2	4,000	120,000	19,000	230,000	0
3	4,000	140,000	18,000	230,000	0
4	4,000	160,000	17,000	230,000	20,000
5	4,000	180,000	16,000	230,000	30,000
6	4,000	200,000	15,000	230,000	0
7	4,000		14,000	230,000	50,000
8	4,000		13,000	230,000	60,000
9	4,000		12,000		70,000
10	4,000		11,000		

INTERMEDIATE **12–4** **NPV, with rankings**   Botany Bay, Inc., a maker of ship supplies, is considering four projects. Because of past financial difficulties, the company has a high cost of capital at 15 percent. Which of these projects would be acceptable under those cost circumstances?

	Project A	Project B	Project C	Project D
Initial cost	$50,000	$100,000	$80,000	$180,000
Year (*t*)			Cash inflows (*CF_t*)	
1	$20,000	$35,000	$20,000	$100,000
2	20,000	50,000	40,000	80,000
3	20,000	50,000	60,000	60,000

a. Calculate the NPV of each project using a cost of capital of 15 percent.
b. Rank acceptable projects by NPV.
c. At what approximate cost of capital would all of the projects be acceptable?

INTERMEDIATE **12–5** **Basic capital budgeting process and minimum acceptable NPV**   Musoka Hobbycats is evaluating an investment project with an initial cost of $92,000 and an expected life of 10 years. The incremental sales are expected to be $38,000 per year and the company's operating costs are 48 percent of sales. These are the only benefits of the project. Musoka's cost of capital is 14 percent and the company tax rate is 20 percent.
a. Determine the NPV for this project.
b. For this project to be acceptable,
   i.   What would the expected life of the project have to be?
   ii. What would the initial cost of the project have to be?
   iii. What would the incremental after-tax operating income have to be?
   iv. What would the incremental before-tax operating income have to be?
   v.   What would the incremental sales have to be?
   vi. What would Musoka's cost of capital have to be? Explain each of your answers, indicating why the project is acceptable.

12–6 NPV Simes Innovations, Inc., is negotiating to purchase exclusive rights to manufacture and market a solar-powered toy car. The car's inventor has offered Simes the choice of either a one-time payment of $1,500,000 today or a series of 5 year-end payments of $385,000.

CHALLENGE

a. If Simes has a cost of capital of 9 percent, which form of payment should the company choose?
b. What yearly payment would make the two offers identical in value at a cost of capital of 9 percent?
c. Would your answer to part **a** of this problem be different if the yearly payments were made at the beginning of each year? Show what difference, if any, that change in timing would make to the present value calculation.
d. The after-tax cash inflows associated with this purchase are projected to amount to $250,000 per year for 15 years. Will this factor change the firm's decision as to how to fund the initial investment?

  12–7 Initial investment—Basic calculation Cushing Corporation is considering the purchase of a new grading machine to replace the existing one. The existing machine was purchased 3 years ago at an installed cost of $20,000. The existing machine is expected to have a usable life of at least 5 more years. The new machine costs $35,000 and requires $5,000 in installation costs. The existing machine can currently be sold for $13,500 without incurring any removal or cleanup costs. Both assets have a CCA rate of 20 percent. Calculate the book value of the existing asset and the incremental cost associated with the proposed purchase of a new grading machine.

WARM-UP

  12–8 Incremental operating cash inflows Strong Tool Company has been considering purchasing a new lathe to replace a fully amortized lathe that will last 5 more years. The new lathe is expected to have a 5-year life. The CCA that can be claimed on the new lathe is as follows: $2,000 in year 1; $3,200 in year 2; $1,900 in year 3; and $1,200 in both year 4 and year 5. The firm estimates that the operating revenues and expenses for the new and the old lathes will be as shown in the following table. The firm's tax rate is 40 percent.

INTERMEDIATE

| | New lathe | | Old lathe | |
Year	Sales	Operating expenses	Sales	Operating expenses
1	$40,000	$30,000	$35,000	$25,000
2	41,000	30,000	35,000	25,000
3	42,000	30,000	35,000	25,000
4	43,000	30,000	35,000	25,000
5	44,000	30,000	35,000	25,000

a. Calculate the operating cash inflows associated with each lathe for the 5 years.
b. Calculate the incremental operating cash inflows resulting from the proposed lathe replacement.
c. Depict on a time line the incremental operating cash inflows calculated in **b**.
d. Calculate the value of the new lathe using the cash inflows calculated in **b**. The cost of capital is 10 percent.

12–9 Relevant cash flow pattern fundamentals   For each of the following projects, determine the *relevant cash flows,* classify the cash flow pattern, and depict the cash flows on a time line.

WARM-UP

a. A project requiring an initial investment of $120,000 that generates annual operating cash inflows of $25,000 for the next 18 years. In each of the 18 years, maintenance of the project will require a $5,000 cash outflow.

b. A new machine having an installed cost of $85,000. Sale of the old machine will yield $30,000 after taxes. Operating cash inflows generated by the replacement will exceed the operating cash inflows of the old machine by $20,000 in each year of a 6-year period. At the end of year 6, liquidation of the new machine will yield $20,000 after taxes, which is $10,000 greater than the after-tax proceeds expected from the old machine had it been retained and liquidated at the end of year 6.

c. An asset requiring an initial investment of $2 million that will yield annual operating cash inflows of $300,000 for each of the next 10 years. Operating cash outlays will be $20,000 for each year except year 6, when an overhaul requiring an additional cash outlay of $500,000 will be required. The asset's liquidation value at the end of year 10 is expected to be $0.

  12–10 Expansion versus replacement cash flows   Edison Systems has estimated the cash flows over the 5-year lives for two projects, A and B. These cash flows are summarized in the following table.

WARM-UP

	Project A	Project B
Initial investment	$40,000	$12,000
Year	Operating cash inflows	
1	$10,000	$ 6,000
2	12,000	6,000
3	14,000	6,000
4	16,000	6,000
5	10,000	6,000

a. If project A were actually a *replacement* for project B and if the $12,000 initial investment shown for B was the cash inflow expected from liquidating it, what would be the relevant cash flow for this replacement decision?

b. If projects A and B were completley independent, how can an *expansion decision* such as project A be viewed as a special form of a replacement decision? Explain.

  12–11 Change in net working capital calculation   Samuels Manufacturing is considering the purchase of a new machine to replace one they feel is obsolete. The firm has total current assets of $920,000 and total current liabilities of $640,000. As a result of the proposed replacement, the following *changes* are anticipated in the levels of the current asset and current liability accounts noted.

WARM-UP

Account	Change
Accruals	+ $ 40,000
Marketable securities	0
Inventories	− 10,000
Accounts payable	+ 90,000
Line of credit	0
Accounts receivable	+ 150,000
Cash	+ 15,000

a. Using the information given, calculate the change, if any, in net working capital that is expected to result from the proposed replacement action.

b. Explain why a change in these current accounts would be relevant in determining the initial investment for the proposed capital expenditure.

c. Would the change in net working capital enter into any of the other cash flow components comprising the relevant cash flows? Explain.

  12–12   Calculating initial investment   Vastine Medical, Inc., is considering replacing its existing computer system which was purchased 2 years ago for a cost of $350,000. The system can be sold today for $200,000. The system is a class 10 asset with a CCA rate of 30 percent. A new computer system will cost $500,000 to purchase and install. Replacement of the computer system would not involve any change in net working capital.

WARM-UP

a. Calculate the book value of the existing computer system.

b. Calculate the initial investment associated with the replacement project.

    12–13   Integrative—Complete investment decision   Wells Printing is considering the purchase of a new printing press. The total installed cost of the press is $2.2 million. This outlay would be partially offset by the sale of an existing press. The old press cost $2.1 million 10 years ago, and can be sold currently for $1.2 million. As a result of the new press, sales in each of the next 5 years are expected to increase by $1.6 million, while operating costs are 50 percent of sales. The new press will not affect the firm's net working capital requirements. The CCA rate on the press is 15 percent. The firm's tax rate is 40 percent. Wells Printing's cost of capital is 11 percent.

CHALLENGE

a. Determine the initial investment required by the new press.

b. Determine the incremental after-tax operating income and the tax shield on the new press for the 5-year life of the new press.

c. Determine the payback period.

d. Determine the net present value (NPV) and the internal rate of return (IRR) for the new press.

e. Make a recommendation to accept or reject the new press, and justify your answer.

    12–14   Basic terminology and evaluating projects—Integrative   A firm is considering the following three separate situations.

WARM-UP

Situation A   Build either a small office building or a convenience store on a parcel of land located in a high-traffic area. Adequate funding is available, and both projects are known to be acceptable. The office building requires an initial investment of $620,000 and is expected to provide operating cash inflows of $90,000 per year for 20 years. The convenience store is expected to cost $500,000 and to provide a growing stream of operating cash inflows over its 20-year life. The initial operating cash inflow is $50,000 and will increase by 5 percent each year.

Situation B   Replace a machine with a new one requiring a $60,000 initial investment and providing operating cash inflows of $15,000 per year for the first 5 years. The current value of the old machine is $10,000. At the end of year 5, a machine overhaul costing $20,000 is required. After it is completed, expected operating cash inflows are $10,000 in year 6; $7,000 in year 7; $4,000 in year 8; and $1,000 in year 9, at the end of which the machine will be scrapped for $10,000.

Situation C   Invest in any or all of the four machines whose relevant cash flows are given in the following table. The firm has $500,000 budgeted to fund these machines, all of which are known to be acceptable. Initial investment for each machine is $250,000.

| Year | Operating cash inflows | | | |
	Machine 1	Machine 2	Machine 3	Machine 4
1	$ 50,000	$70,000	$65,000	$90,000
2	70,000	70,000	65,000	80,000
3	90,000	70,000	90,000	70,000
4	−30,000	70,000	90,000	60,000
5	150,000	70,000	−20,000	50,000

For each situation or project, indicate
a. Whether the *situation* is independent or mutually exclusive.
b. Whether the availability of funds is unlimited or if capital rationing exists.
c. Whether accept–reject or ranking decisions are required.
d. Whether each *project's* cash flow pattern is an annuity or a mixed stream.
e. Now assume that the firm's tax rate is 20 percent and for Situation A, the firm's cost of capital is 10 percent. For the office building project, calculate the payback period, NPV, and IRR. For the convenience store, calculate the present value of the after-tax cash inflows for the first five years of the project's life. If you were asked to calculate the NPV and IRR of this project, what would be the easiest way to do this?
f. Assume for Situation B that the cash inflows are after-tax. The firm's cost of capital for this project is 10 percent. Calculate the NPV for Situation B.
g. For Situation C, the cash inflows are after-tax and the company's cost of capital is 10 percent. Determine the payback period, NPV, and IRR for each machine. Develop NPV profiles for all four machines.
   i. If the four machines were independent projects, which should be selected?
   ii. If the four machines were independent, but the company only had $500,000 of funds available, which machines should be selected? Explain
   iii. If the machines were mutually exclusive, which machine should be selected? Explain the reason for your answer.

12–15   **Payback and NPV**   Neil Corporation has three projects under consideration. The cash flows for each of them are shown in the following table. The firm has a 16 percent cost of capital.

INTERMEDIATE

	Project A	Project B	Project C
Initial cost *(IC)*	$40,000	$40,000	$40,000
Year *(t)*		Cash inflows *(CF_t)*	
1	$13,000	$ 7,000	$19,000
2	13,000	10,000	16,000
3	13,000	13,000	13,000
4	13,000	16,000	10,000
5	13,000	19,000	7,000

a. Calculate each project's payback period. Which project is preferred according to this method?
b. Calculate each project's net present value (NPV). Which project is preferred according to this method?
c. Comment on your findings in **a** and **b**, and recommend the best project. Explain your recommendation.

   12–16   **All techniques, conflicting rankings**   Nicholson Roofing Materials, Inc., is considering two mutually exclusive projects, each with an initial investment of $150,000. The company's board of directors has set a 4-year payback requirement and the company's cost of capital is 9 percent. The cash inflows associated with the two projects are as follows:

INTERMEDIATE

		Cash inflows *(CF_t)*	
Year	Project A	Project B
1	$45,000	$75,000
2	45,000	60,000
3	45,000	30,000
4	45,000	30,000
5	45,000	30,000
6	45,000	30,000

a. Calculate the payback period for each project.
b. Calculate the NPV of each project.
c. Calculate the IRR of each project. Develop an NPV profile.
d. Rank the projects using each of the techniques. Make and justify a recommendation.

  12–17   **Payback, NPV, and IRR**   Rieger International is attempting to evaluate the feasibility of investing $95,000 in a piece of equipment having a 5-year life. The firm has estimated the *cash inflows* associated with the proposal as shown in the following table. The firm has a 12 percent cost of capital.

WARM-UP[

Year (t)	Cash inflows (CF_t)
1	$20,000
2	25,000
3	30,000
4	35,000
5	40,000

a. Calculate the payback period for the proposed investment.
b. Calculate the net present value (NPV) for the proposed investment.
c. Calculate the internal rate of return (IRR), rounded to the nearest whole percent, for the proposed investment using an NPV profile.
d. Evaluate the acceptability of the proposed investment using NPV and IRR. What recommendation would you make relative to implementation of the project? Why?

   12–18 **All techniques—Mutually exclusive investment decision**   Pound Industries is attempting to select the best of three mutually exclusive projects. The initial cost and after-tax cash inflows associated with each project are shown in the following table.

CHALLENGE

Cash flows	Project A	Project B	Project C
Initial investment (II)	$60,000	$100,000	$110,000
Cash inflows (CF), years 1–5	$20,000	$ 31,500	$ 32,500

a. Calculate the payback period for each project.
b. Calculate the net present value (NPV) of each project, assuming that the firm has a cost of capital equal to 13 percent.
c. Calculate the internal rate of return (IRR) for each project using an NPV profile.
d. Draw the net present value profile for each project on the same set of axes, and discuss any conflict in ranking that may exist between NPV and IRR.
e. Summarize the preferences dictated by each measure, and indicate which project you would recommend. Explain why.

   12–19 **All techniques with NPV profile—Mutually exclusive projects**   The following two projects of equal risk are alternatives for expanding the firm's capacity. The firm's cost of capital is 13 percent. The cash flows for each project are shown in the following table.

CHALLENGE

	Project A	Project B
Initial cost (IC)	$80,000	$50,000
Year (t)	Cash inflows (CF_t)	
1	$15,000	$15,000
2	20,000	15,000
3	25,000	15,000
4	30,000	15,000
5	35,000	15,000

a. Calculate each project's payback period.

b. Calculate the net present value (NPV) for each project.

c. Calculate the internal rate of return (IRR) for each project using an NPV profile.

d. Draw a net present value profile for each project on the same set of axes, and discuss any conflict in ranking that may exist between NPV and IRR.

e. Summarize the preferences dictated by each measure, and indicate which project you would recommend. Explain why.

WARM-UP **12–20** **Calculating operating income—Sales increase/expense reduction** Vegan Foods has a choice of two projects. Project A will result in sales increasing by $100,000. Project B will result in operating costs decreasing by $100,000. Operating costs are 35 percent of sales and the company's tax rate is 25 percent. Which project generates higher incremental after-tax operating income? Explain why this is the case.

WARM-UP **12–21** **Sunk costs and opportunity costs** Masters Golf Products, Inc., spent 3 years and $1,000,000 to develop its new line of club heads to replace a line that is becoming obsolete. In order to begin manufacturing them, the company will have to invest $1,800,000 in new equipment. The new clubs are expected to generate an increase in operating cash inflows of $750,000 per year for the next 10 years. The company has determined that the existing line could be sold to a competitor for $250,000.

a. How should the $1,000,000 in development costs be classified?

b. How should the $250,000 sale price for the existing line be classified?

c. Depict all of the known relevant cash flows on a time line.

WARM-UP **12–22** **CCA** A firm is evaluating the acquisition of an asset that costs $64,000 and requires $4,000 in installation costs. If this is a class 43 asset, determine the CCA the firm can claim for each of the first 5 years.

WARM-UP **12–23** **Calculating CCA and tax shield** Asto Company just purchased a class 17 asset at a cost of $175,000. Asto Company's tax rate is 26 percent.

a. Calculate the amount of CCA Asto could claim for the first four years of the asset's life.

b. How much tax shield would the company receive each year?

c. Explain what is meant by the term tax shield.

INTERMEDIATE **12–24** **Calculating CCA, ITC, and tax shield** For Asto Company in the above question, assume the class 17 asset being purchased at a cost of $175,000 is replacing another class 17 asset. The current asset has a book value of $33,426, but it could be sold for $22,000. The new asset qualifies for an ITC of 10 percent. For capital budgeting purposes, answer the following questions:

a. What is the incremental cost of the new asset?

b. What is the incremental amount of UCC that will be added to the class 17 asset class?

c. Calculate the amount of CCA and the tax shield from the CCA for the first four years of the asset's life.

INTERMEDIATE **12–25** **Determining operating cash flows** Scenic Tours, Inc., located in Moncton, New Brunswick, is a provider of bus tours throughout the New England area.

The corporation is considering replacing 10 of its older buses. The existing buses were purchased 4 years ago at a total cost of $2,700,000. The new buses would have larger passenger capacity and better fuel efficiency as well as lower maintenance costs. The total cost for 10 new buses is $3,000,000. The old buses could be sold for $1,100,000. The CCA rate on the buses is 30 percent and Scenic Tours tax rate is 40 percent. The following table presents sales and operating expenses for the new and old buses. Use all of the information given to calculate the incremental after-tax cash inflows for the proposed purchase of new buses for 6 years.

	Year					
	1	2	3	4	5	6
With the proposed new buses						
Sales	$1,850,000	$1,850,000	$1,830,000	$1,825,000	$1,815,000	$1,800,000
−Expenses	460,000	460,000	468,000	472,000	485,000	500,000
With the present buses						
Sales	$1,800,000	$1,800,000	$1,790,000	$1,785,000	$1,775,000	$1,750,000
−Expenses	500,000	510,000	520,000	520,000	530,000	535,000

  12–26 **Comparing cash flows and profitability**   Radeon Corp. is considering replacing an existing piece of production equipment. The current equipment generates sales of $1,500,000 per year, while operating costs are $1,050,000. Sales for the new production equipment will total $1,900,000 with costs of $1,100,000. The amortization expense on the old equipment is $35,000 but will be $175,000 on the new. The company's tax rate is 30 percent. Calculate the incremental profitability and cash inflows on the new production equipment for the first year of its life.

INTERMEDIATE LG3 **12–27** **Sunk costs and opportunity costs**   Covol Industries is developing the relevant cash flows associated with the proposed replacement of an existing machine tool with a new technologically advanced one. Given the following costs related to the proposed project, explain whether each would be treated as a *sunk cost* or an *opportunity cost* in developing the relevant cash flows associated with the proposed replacement decision.
a. Covol would be able to use the same tooling, which had a book value of $40,000, on the new machine tool as it had used on the old one.
b. Covol would be able to use its existing computer system to develop programs for operating the new machine tool. The old machine tool did not require these programs. Although the firm's computer has excess capacity available, the capacity could be leased to another firm for an annual fee of $17,000.
c. Covol would have to obtain additional floor space to accommodate the larger new machine tool. The space that would be used is currently being leased to another company for $10,000 per year.
d. Covol would use a small storage facility to store the increased output of the new machine tool. The storage facility was built by Covol at a cost of $120,000 3 years earlier. Because of its unique configuration and location, it is currently of no use to either Covol or any other firm.

e. Covol would retain an existing overhead crane, which it had planned to sell for its $180,000 market value. Although the crane was not needed with the old machine tool, it would be used to position raw materials on the new machine tool.

  12–28   **NPV and IRR**   Benson Designs has prepared the following estimates for a long-term project it is considering. The initial cost is $18,250, and the project is expected to yield after-tax cash inflows of $4,000 per year for 7 years. The firm has a 10 percent cost of capital.

INTERMEDIATE

a. Determine the net present value (NPV) for the project.
b. Determine the internal rate of return (IRR) for the project.
c. Would you recommend that the firm accept or reject the project? Explain your answer.

  12–29   **Relevant cash flows and NPV for a marketing campaign**   Marcus Tube, a manufacturer of high-quality aluminum tubing, has maintained stable sales and profits over the past 10 years. Although the market for aluminum tubing has been expanding by 3 percent per year, Marcus has been unsuccessful in sharing this growth. To increase its sales, the firm is considering an aggressive marketing campaign that centres on regularly running ads in all relevant trade journals and exhibiting products at all major regional and national trade shows. The campaign is expected to require an *annual* tax-deductible expenditure of $150,000 (an expense) over the next 5 years. Sales revenue, as noted in the income statement for 2002 shown below, totalled $20,000,000. If the proposed marketing campaign is not initiated, sales are expected to remain at this level in each of the next 5 years, 2003–2007. With the marketing campaign, sales are expected to rise to the levels shown in the second table for each of the next 5 years; cost of goods sold is expected to remain at 80 percent of sales; general and administrative expense (exclusive of any marketing campaign outlays) is expected to remain at 10 percent of sales; and annual amortization expense is expected to remain at $500,000. Assuming a 40 percent tax rate, determine the incremental after-tax cash flows over the next 5 years associated with the proposed marketing campaign. If Market Tube's cost of capital is 12 percent, should the company proceed with the marketing campaign? Explain.

CHALLENGE

Income Statement
Marcus Tube
for the year ended December 31, 2002

Sales revenue		$20,000,000
Less: Cost of goods sold (80%)		16,000,000
Gross margin		$ 4,000,000
Less: Operating expenses		
General and administrative expense (10%)	$2,000,000	
Amortization expense	500,000	
Total operating expense		2,500,000
Earnings before taxes		$ 1,500,000
Less: Taxes (rate = 40%)		600,000
Net income after taxes		$ 900,000

	Sales Forecast Marcus Tube
Year	Sales revenue
2003	$20,500,000
2004	21,000,000
2005	21,500,000
2006	22,500,000
2007	23,500,000

CHALLENGE

12–30   Integrative—Investment decision   Holliday Manufacturing is considering replacing an existing machine. The new machine costs $1.2 million and requires installation costs of $150,000. The existing machine can now be sold for $185,000. It is 2 years old, cost $800,000 new, and has a $384,000 book value and a remaining useful life of 5 years. If held until the end of 5 years, the machine's market value would be $0. Over its 5-year life, the new machine should reduce operating costs by $350,000 per year. The CCA rate on the machine is 30 percent. The new machine can be sold for $200,000 net of removal and clean up costs at the end of 5 years. An increased investment in net working capital of $25,000 will be needed to support operations if the new machine is acquired. The firm has a 9 percent cost of capital and a 40 percent tax rate.

a. Develop the relevant cash flows needed to analyze the proposed replacement.
b. Determine the net present value (NPV) of the proposal.
c. Determine the internal rate of return (IRR) of the proposal.
d. Make a recommendation to accept or reject the replacement proposal, and justify your answer.
e. What is the highest cost of capital the firm could have and still accept the proposal? Explain.

WARM-UP   **12–31   Book value**   Find the book value for each of the assets shown in the following table, assuming that CCA is being used. (*Note:* See Table 12.4 for the applicable CCA rule.)

Asset	Installed cost	Asset class	Elapsed time since purchase
A	$ 950,000	1	15 years
B	40,000	6	4
C	96,000	8	6
D	350,000	10	1
E	1,500,000	16	9

INTERMEDIATE   **12–32   Integrative—Determining NPV**   Irvin Enterprises has been evaluating an investment project that will use a warehouse the company currently owns but is not using. This project will require an immediate capital expenditure of $1 million for required equipment. The unused warehouse will require very little work in order for the equipment to be put into operation. Irvin has no other intended use for the warehouse but the company has been renting the warehouse for

$70,000 a year. Irvin will also use equipment that was purchased a year ago for $525,000, but which has yet to be used. The equipment is highly technical and over the year the equipment has significantly declined in value. If Irvin were to sell the equipment, the most they would receive is $300,000. The equipment has yet to have any CCA charged against the original purchase price. The incremental operating income for the project is expected to be $355,000 a year for six years, at which time it will increase to $425,000 a year for another six years. At the end of this time, all of the equipment is expected to have a value of only $55,000. Additional working capital requirements related to this new equipment will be $50,000. The CCA rate on the equipment is 30 percent. Irvin's tax rate is 39 percent and their cost of capital is 14 percent.

a. Should Irvin proceed with the new project?

b. If Irvin's cost of capital was not constant over the life of the project, how could this be handled within your analysis?

CHALLENGE 12–33   **Integrative—Determining NPV**   Lombard Company is contemplating the purchase of a new high-speed widget grinder to replace the existing grinder. The existing grinder was purchased 2 years ago at an installed cost of $60,000. The existing grinder is expected to have a usable life of 5 more years. The new grinder costs $105,000 and requires $5,000 in installation costs; it has a 5-year usable life. The existing grinder can currently be sold for $70,000 but removal and cleanup costs will total $42,000. To support the increased business resulting from purchase of the new grinder, accounts receivable would increase by $40,000, inventories by $30,000, and accounts payable by $58,000. At the end of 5 years, the existing grinder is expected to have a market value of zero; the new grinder would be sold to net $29,000 after removal and cleanup costs. Grinders are considered a class 8 asset with a CCA rate of 20 percent. Lombard's tax rate is 40 percent and cost of capital is 12 percent. The estimated operating income over the 5 years for both the new and existing grinder are shown in the following table.

	Operating income before taxes	
Year	New grinder	Existing grinder
1	$43,000	$26,000
2	43,000	24,000
3	43,000	22,000
4	43,000	20,000
5	43,000	18,000

a. Should Lombard replace the existing grinder? Explain.

CHALLENGE 12–34   **Integrative—Determining NPV**   Liam Henby, Assistant to the VP of Finance of Delta Company, has developed an excellent investment proposal that his boss, the VP of Finance, wishes him to analyze. The VP also wants Liam to recommend whether the company should proceed with the project. The VP will take this recommendation to the company's CEO. Liam has approached you to help him complete the task.

The project involves the production of components for the wireless communication business and requires a two-year development period. The project requires the immediate purchase of land costing $600,000. A specialized building will be constructed over the next year with payment of $1.1 million due in exactly one year. Testing will begin at this point and after a year, the machinery required to produce the components will be purchased at a cost of $175,000. Payment is due at the end of the second year. Sales will begin in the third year and, as is usual, sales and expenses will be acknowledged at the end of each year. Beginning in the third year, and running for the next 10 years, sales are expected to amount to $875,000. Expenses are projected to be $325,000. These estimates are the averages of estimates obtained from the marketing staff and the production department.

The project will have a 10-year life, at which time the building will be sold. Proceeds from the sale are expected to be $500,000 but Delta Company will be required to spend $275,000 to complete an environmental clean-up. The machinery will be sold for $50,000. The land on which the building is constructed is expected to appreciate in value at an average rate of 9 percent per year. The CCA rate on the building is 4 percent and is 30 percent on the machinery. Delta Company's cost of capital is 15 percent and the company's tax rate is 40 percent. Note that only one-half of capital gains are taxable.

Analyze this project for Liam Henby and develop the recommendation that Liam should present to the VP of finance. Be sure to provide a complete rationale for your recommendation.

CHALLENGE 12–35 **Integrative—Determining NPV** The Alberta Development Corporation (ADC) is investigating whether they should replace an existing piece of machinery with a technically superior product. The current machine is used to process heavy oil extract and costs $800,000 per year to operate. Its current book value is $125,000 and it could conceivably last an additional 20 years with minimal repairs. Two machines are currently available which meet the specifications set out by ADC's engineers: Machine X costs $500,000, Machine Y $850,000. Both are expected to last for 20 years. The cost of operating Machine X is estimated to be $740,000 per year, while Machine Y is expected to cost $690,000 per year to operate over its economic life.

If the current machine is traded in on Machine X, ADC will receive $50,000 for it. If it is traded in on Machine Y, ADC will receive $75,000. These machines are class 8 assets with a CCA rate of 20 percent. Machine X is anticipated to have a salvage value of $20,000 and Machine Y a salvage value of $75,000 at the end of their respective lives. ADC's marginal rate of tax is 40 percent and their cost of capital is 14 percent.

a. Which machine would you recommend the company purchase? Explain.
b. Assuming that both machines qualify for a 10 percent ITC, how would this change your analysis?
c. If the current machine could no longer be operated, would this change your decision? Explain.

CHALLENGE 12–36 **Integrative—Determining NPV** The Wright Company is contemplating developing and marketing a new, technologically superior product, Zapp, for the spectrum radio systems market. The initial costs of developing and marketing Zapp are estimated to be $1,700,000. Of this total cost, $1,350,000 will be spent immediately and capitalized in CCA class 18 which has a CCA rate of 20 percent. As well, of the $1,350,000 cost, $625,000 qualifies for a 15 percent ITC. The remainder of the project's total cost will be expensed equally in years 2 and 3 of the project's life.

The marketing department estimates that the sales associated with Zapp will begin in one year and will total $425,000 per year. Zapp is expected to generate sales for 25 years. The direct costs of the system are expected to be 24 percent of sales. Other incremental operating costs will be $85,000 per year. The salvage value of the project is expected to be $100,000 at the end of the project's life.

To encourage the establishment of this operation in Prince Edward Island, the provincial government has indicated they are willing to provide a cash grant of $250,000, half payable when the company begins spending on the project, and half on the first anniversary date of the beginning date of the project (i.e., one year's time).

Wright Company's cost of capital is 12 percent, but since the ZAPP project is much riskier than the overall company, the V-P of Finance believes that a higher cost of 15 percent should be used to evaluate the project as this will reflect the greater risk. Wright Company's marginal tax rate is 29 percent. Should Wright Company develop and market Zapp?

CHALLENGE

12–37 Integrative—Determining NPV Atlantic Drydock, located in Georgetown, Prince Edward Island, is considering replacing an existing hoist with one of two newer, more efficient pieces of equipment. The existing hoist is 3 years old, cost $32,000, and has a remaining usable life of 5 years. Hoist A, one of the two possible replacement hoists, costs $40,000 to purchase and $8,000 to install. The other hoist, B, costs $54,000 to purchase and $6,000 to install. Both hoists have 5-year lives and are class 7 assets with CCA rates of 15 percent. The hoists will qualify for a 10 percent ITC.

Increased investments in net working capital will accompany the decision to acquire hoist A or hoist B. Purchase of hoist A would result in a $4,000 increase in net working capital; hoist B would result in a $6,000 increase in net working capital. The projected operating income with each alternative hoist and the existing hoist are given in the following table.

	Operating income before taxes		
Year	With hoist A	With hoist B	With existing hoist
1	$21,000	$22,000	$14,000
2	21,000	24,000	14,000
3	21,000	26,000	14,000
4	21,000	26,000	14,000
5	21,000	26,000	14,000

The existing hoist can currently be sold for $18,000. At the end of 5 years, the existing hoist can be sold to net $1,000. Hoists A and B can be sold to net $1,000. Hoists A and B can be sold to net $12,000 and $20,000, respectively, at the end of the 5-year period. The firm's cost of capital is 14 percent and their tax rate is 26 percent.

a. Should Atlantic Drydock replace the existing hoist? If so, which hoist do you recommend, A or B? Why?

WARM-UP **12–38** **Payback period**   Jordan Enterprises is considering a capital expenditure that requires an initial investment of $42,000 and returns after-tax cash inflows of $7,000 per year for 10 years. The firm has a maximum acceptable payback period of 8 years.
a. Determine the payback period for this project.
b. Should the company accept the project? Why or why not?

WARM-UP **12–39** **Calculating IRR**   Wagner Plows is evaluating the investment in a new computer system with an expected cost of $20,000. The project has a three-year life and the value of the total cash inflows for each year is:

Year	Cash inflow
1	$11,000
2	$9,000
3	$5,800

Using an NPV profile, determine the IRR for this project. Provide both a table and a graph. Provide your answer to the nearest tenth of a decimal point (i.e., 10.1%).

INTERMEDIATE **12–40** **Payback comparisons**   Nova Products has a 5-year maximum acceptable payback period. The firm is considering the purchase of a new machine and must choose between two alternative ones. The first machine requires an initial investment of $14,000 and generates annual after-tax cash inflows of $3,000 for each of the next 7 years. The second machine requires an initial investment of $21,000 and provides an annual cash inflow after taxes of $4,000 for 20 years.
a. Determine the payback period for each machine.
b. Comment on the acceptability of the machines, assuming they are independent projects.
c. Which machine should the firm accept? Why?
d. Do the machines in this problem illustrate any of the criticisms of using payback? Discuss.

INTERMEDIATE **12–41** **Payback period and NPV**   Shell Camping Gear, Inc., is considering two mutually exclusive projects. Each requires an initial investment of $100,000. John Shell, president of the company, has set a maximum payback period of 4 years. The after-tax cash inflows associated with each project are as follows:

Year	Cash inflows (CF_t) Project A	Project B
1	$10,000	$40,000
2	20,000	30,000
3	30,000	20,000
4	40,000	10,000
5	20,000	20,000

a. Determine the payback period of each project. Rank the project.
b. Determine the NPV of each project, and rank the projects using a discount rate of 9 percent.

c. Because they are mutually exclusive, Shell must choose one. Which one should the company invest in?

d. Explain why one of the projects is a better choice than the other one.

INTERMEDIATE 12–42 **IRR—Mutually exclusive projects** Bell Manufacturing is attempting to choose the better of two mutually exclusive projects for expanding the firm's warehouse capacity. The relevant cash flows for the projects are shown in the following table. The firm's cost of capital is 15 percent.

	Project X	Project Y
Initial cost (IC)	$500,000	$325,000
Year (t)	Cash inflows (CF_t)	
1	$100,000	$140,000
2	120,000	120,000
3	150,000	95,000
4	190,000	70,000
5	250,000	50,000

a. Using NPV profiles, calculate the IRR for each of the projects to the nearest decimal.

b. Assess the acceptability of each project based on the IRRs found in a.

c. Which project is preferred, based on the IRRs found in a?

INTERMEDIATE 12–43 **IRR, investment life, and cash inflows** Oak Enterprises has a 15 percent cost of capital. Oak is currently considering a 10-year project that provides annual cash inflows of $10,000 and requires an initial investment of $61,450. (*Note:* All amounts are after taxes.)

a. Determine the IRR of this project. Is it acceptable?

b. Assuming that the cash inflows continue to be $10,000 per year, how many *additional years* would the flows have to continue to make the project acceptable?

c. With the given life, initial investment, and cost of capital, what is the minimum annual cash inflow the firm should accept?

INTERMEDIATE 12–44 **Internal rate of return** For each of the projects shown in the following table, calculate the internal rate of return (IRR) using NPV profiles. In order to be acceptable to a company, in what range would the company's cost of capital have to fall?

	Project A	Project B	Project C	Project D
Initial investment (II)	$90,000	$490,000	$20,000	$240,000
Year (t)	Cash inflows (CF_t)			
1	$20,000	$150,000	$7,500	$120,000
2	25,000	150,000	7,500	100,000
3	30,000	150,000	7,500	80,000
4	35,000	150,000	7,500	60,000
5	40,000	—	7,500	—

| CASE   CHAPTER 12 | Should Clark Upholstery Company Renew or Replace an Existing Machine? |

Bo Humphries, chief financial officer of Clark Upholstery Company, expects the firm's *after-tax operating income* for the next 5 years to be as shown in the following table.

Year	Operating income after taxes
1	$100,000
2	150,000
3	200,000
4	250,000
5	320,000

Bo is beginning to develop the information needed to analyze whether to renew or replace Clark's *only* depreciable asset, a machine that originally cost $230,000 but could now be sold for $20,000. The book value of the machine is $66,293. Bo estimates that at the end of 5 years, the existing machine could be sold for $2,000. The following information is available for Bo to use to determine which of the two alternatives he should recommend to the company's board of directors. Bo wonders whether he should recommend either alternative.

Alternative 1   Renew the existing machine at a total cost of $90,000. The renewed machine would have a 5-year usable life. The CCA rate for the machine is 20 percent and this rate would apply to the total cost of $90,000. Renewing the machine would result in the following projected sales and operating expenses for Clark Upholstery:

Year	Sales	Operating expenses
1	$1,000,000	$801,500
2	1,175,000	884,200
3	1,300,000	918,100
4	1,425,000	943,100
5	1,550,000	968,100

Since the renewed machine would result in increasing sales, an increased investment of $15,000 in net working capital would be required. At the end of 5 years, the machine could be sold to net $8,000.

Alternative 2   Replace the existing machine with a new machine costing $100,000 and requiring installation costs of $10,000. The new machine would have a 5-year usable life. The new machine qualifies for a 10 percent ITC and has a CCA rate of 20 percent. Both of these would apply to the installed price of the new machine. The firm's projected sales and operating expenses if it acquires the machine would be as follows:

Year	Sales	Operating expenses
1	$1,000,000	$764,500
2	1,175,000	839,800
3	1,300,000	914,900
4	1,425,000	989,900
5	1,550,000	998,900

With the new machine, the company would have to change suppliers and would be forced to pay accounts payable in a more timely manner. As a result, the new machine would result in an increased investment of $22,000 in net working capital. At the end of 5 years, the new machine could be sold to net $25,000.

Clark Upholstery's cost of capital is 13 percent and the company tax rate is 25 percent. Should the company replace the existing machine and, if so, which of the two alternatives should Bo recommend? Develop the detailed analysis that Bo will require to present to Clark's board of directors.

WEB EXERCISES LINKS TO PRACTISE

Visit the following Web sites and complete the suggested exercises. These exercises will allow you to review practical applications of the chapter topics as well as explore the wealth of information regarding managerial finance that is available on the Internet.

www-ec.njit.edu/~mathis/interactive/FCCalcIntro.html
www-ec.njit.edu/~mathis/interactive/FCCalcBase4.html
The first Web site provides an introduction to the use of a free "cash flow calculator" that can be used to analyze capital budgeting projects. The calculator can be used to calculate the payback period, net present value, IRR, and effective annual annuity of a project given its cash flow stream. Up to 11 cash flows, both outflows and inflows, can be input into the calculator. The calculator only works for the simpler capital budgeting projects where all benefits are included within the cash inflows.

The link to the calculator itself is at the bottom of the page. Complete problems from the book using this calculator. The second link provides a source of numerous problems that can be used with the calculator. Complete as many problems as you like to reinforce capital budgeting concepts, in particular, the concept of NPV and IRR.

www.bized.ac.uk/virtual/cb
Cameron Balloons manufactures a variety of hot-air balloons, airships, and inflatables. On this Web site you will find complete details about the company, its financial statements, the costs to manufacture balloons, marketing, and their range of products. The Bristol, England–based company is the world's largest

manufacturer of hot-air balloons. They are best known for their special-shape balloons and also the balloons they have made for round-the-world record attempts. Cameron Balloons builds, on average, one balloon a day. Explore the different areas of the site to familiarize yourself with the company.

Now, click on Factory Floor and then Production. Click on Explanations to see how the balloons are produced. Now, return to the previous page and click on Worksheets. Select W2 Investment Decisions. This brings you to a discussion of whether it makes financial sense for Cameron to mechanize the cutting process for the balloon fabric. Read about the situation facing the company and then answer the following questions.

1. Answer the two questions under How Do We Decide?
   a. What advantages might there be from using these new machines?
   b. What disadvantages might there be?
2. Referring to Table 12.1 in your textbook, determine Cameron Balloons' motives for making this type of capital expenditure.
3. In step 2 of the worksheet, the initial costs and the expected cash inflows for the two machines are provided. Is this example an independent or a mutually exclusive project? Why do you think that the inflows from the new machines decline each year?
4. Based on the initial costs and the expected cash inflows for the two machines, calculate the payback period for each machine. Which machine has the shorter payback period? What are the advantages and disadvantages of the payback period as a decision tool? (*Note:* Skip the average rate of return section.)
5. Based on the initial costs and the expected cash inflows for the two machines, calculate the net present value assuming Cameron Balloons' cost of capital is 10 percent. Which machine should the company select based on the NPV? What are the advantages and disadvantages of the NPV method as a decision tool?
6. Now calculate the internal rate of return for the machines. Which machine is preferable? What are the advantages and disadvantages of the NPV method as a decision tool?
7. Summarize your findings and make a recommendation to Cameron's management. Include any qualitative factors you consider important and explain which method you believe is the best for making this investment decision.

www.toolkit.cch.com/text/p06_6100.asp
This Web site considers capital budgeting from the perspective of a small business. Read the first page of the site and then answer the following questions.

1. What is meant by the term major purchase?
2. When completing the analysis of an investment project, are absolute answers calculated? Discuss the risks involved in the process.
3. Do all capital budgeting projects provide a financial payoff?
4. What steps does the site suggest a business should follow when making the ranking decision or the accept/reject decision about a major purchase or project? Briefly discuss the points made on the Web site for each of these steps.

13 Dealing with Project Risk and Other Topics in Capital Budgeting

LEARNING GOALS

LG1 Understand the importance of explicitly recognizing risk in the analysis of capital budgeting projects.

LG2 Discuss breakeven cash flow, sensitivity and scenario analysis, and simulation as behavioural approaches for dealing with risk, and the unique risks facing multinational companies.

LG3 Describe the two basic risk-adjustment techniques in terms of NPV and the procedures for applying the certainty equivalent (CE) approach.

LG4 Review the use of risk-adjusted discount rates (RADRs), portfolio effects, and the practical aspects of RADRs relative to CEs.

LG5 Recognize the problem caused by unequal-lived mutually exclusive projects and the use of annualized net present values (ANPVs) to resolve it.

LG6 Explain the role of real options and the objective of, and basic approaches to, project selection under capital rationing.

LG1

13.1 Introduction to Risk in Capital Budgeting

The capital budgeting techniques introduced in Chapter 12 were applied in an environment where we assumed the risk of the investment project being evaluated was the same as the company's overall risk. Therefore, the cash flows developed using the techniques presented in Chapter 12 were discounted at the company's cost of capital, the discount rate that reflects the business and financial risk of the company. In other words, in Chapter 12, all projects, independent or mutually exclusive, were assumed to be equally risky, and the acceptance and implementation of a project would not change the overall risk of the company.

Getting a Handle on Risk

Every year, millions of visitors pour into casinos or play video lottery terminals, or play the lotteries offered by the federal and provincial governments. All these players are looking for big—or even modest—returns on their gambling dollars. Two key features of gambling, of course, are *uncertainty* and *hope*—the uncertainty of when, if ever, there will be a payoff, and the ongoing hope that it will come with the next quarter, or dollar, or twenty "invested." Although most business investments are not gambles, a similar uncertainty does exist. Managers do all they can to ensure the outcomes of their investments, but despite their best planning and analysis, risk remains because of events outside the company's immediate control. In the previous chapter, we considered capital budgeting projects that had the same level of risk as the overall company. In this chapter, we turn to the issue of how projects with levels of risk different from the overall company are evaluated. We show how risk is incorporated into capital budgeting decisions.

While in reality these types of similar risk projects are quite common, they are not the only kind of capital budgeting project a company must review, analyze, and for which the appropriate accept/reject or ranking decision must be made.

Sometimes a project will be in a different line of business from the firm's current line, or the project's cash flows will have a different level of risk from the company's. The acceptance of such a project will impact the firm's overall risk, though often in a minor way. In this chapter, we assume that the projects being evaluated have different risk characteristics from the overall company. This implies the company cannot analyze the project in exactly the same manner as presented in Chapter 12. The assumption of equal-risk projects is relaxed in order to focus on how a different level of risk is incorporated in the capital budgeting decision process.

Source of Risk

risk
The chance that the inputs into the analysis of an investment project will prove to be wrong.

For capital, **risk** refers to the chance that the inputs into the analysis of an investment project will prove to be wrong. The key inputs are, of course, the various components of the cash flows and the discount rate. If either the estimates for the cash flows or the cost of capital is seriously in error, then the capital budgeting decision made *may* be incorrect. If the cash inflows are overestimated and/or the cost of capital underestimated, then decisions that prove to be very costly for the firm and the shareholders can result. Either occurrence is an example of the adage **GIGO (garbage in, garbage out)**. Poor forecasts result in poor decisions, *no matter how thorough the analysis of the numbers.*

GIGO (garbage in, garbage out)
If cash inflows are overestimated and/or the cost of capital underestimated, then decisions that prove to be very costly for the firm and the shareholders can result; poor forecasts can result in poor capital budgeting decisions.

For an investment project, when we say that the cash inflow for a particular year is expected to be $1,000, we are really saying that based on the range of possible cash inflows and the probability of these cash inflows occurring, we expect the cash inflow to be $1,000. Expected cash inflow estimates are, of course, subject to error. The wider the range of possible inflows, the greater the risk of the expected inflow. Projects with very low positive net present values (NPVs) and a broad range of expected cash inflows are more risky than projects with high NPVs and a narrow range of expected cash inflows.

When analyzing projects, it is useful to consider that for any given firm, positive NPV projects are limited, in some cases very rare. For every positive NPV investment project, it is useful and highly recommended that the personnel involved in the analysis reconsider all aspects of the project to ensure that fore-

TABLE 13.1	Relevant Cash Flows and NPVs for Bennett Company's Projects	
	Project A	Project B
A. Relevant Cash Flows		
Incremental cost	$42,000	$45,000
Year	Operating after-tax cash inflows	
1	$14,000	$28,000
2	14,000	12,000
3	14,000	10,000
4	14,000	10,000
5	14,000	10,000
B. Decision Technique		
NPV @ 10% cost of capital[a]	$11,071	$10,924

[a]From Figure 13.1, calculated using a financial calculator.

casting errors have not occurred. Take a step back and consider what makes the project attractive. Companies must always remember that other people's money is being invested. It might be useful to build into the capital budgeting process a healthy skepticism of positive NPV projects. Companies that do this tend to explicitly recognize and deal with risk and as a result tend to make fewer capital budgeting decisions that destroy company and shareholder wealth.

To illustrate risk concepts, we will assume Bennett Company is analyzing two mutually exclusive projects: A and B. Project A has an incremental cost of $42,000; project B, $45,000. Both projects are expected to have five-year lives and the relevant cash inflows are presented in Table 13.1. Note that the cash inflows include all benefits including incremental operating income, tax shield from CCA, and salvage. Part B of Table 13.1 indicates that by using Bennett Company's cost of capital of 10 percent, project A should be selected since project A's NPV is greater than B's: The expected return from A is greater than B. The cash flows for the two projects are depicted on time lines in Figure 13.1, as is the calculation of the NPV for the two projects. This analysis should be straightforward if Chapter 12 has been completed.

The project evaluation presented in Figure 13.1 assumes the two projects have the same risk as the company. In the following two sections, we use the basic risk concepts presented in Chapter 7 to demonstrate both behavioural and quantitative approaches for explicitly recognizing risk in the analysis of capital budgeting projects.

FIGURE 13.1   **Calculation of NPV for Bennett Company's Capital Expenditure Alternatives**
Time lines depicting the cash flows and NPV calculations for projects A and B

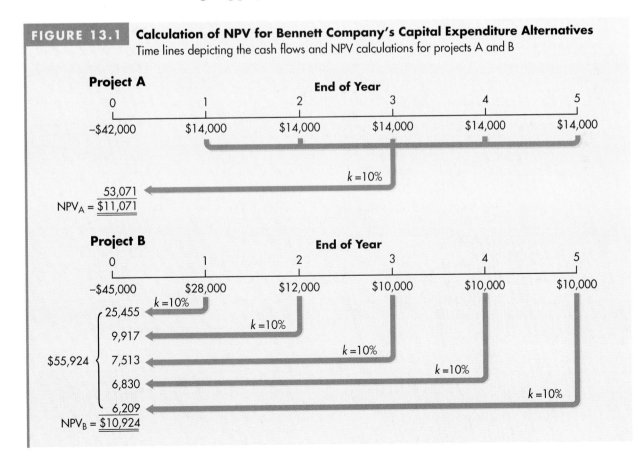

IN PRACTICE

What Happens When Risk Is Not Correctly Recognized?

The word "risk" comes from the early Italian word *risicare*, which means "to dare." During the mad run-up in the high-tech sector in the 1997 to 2000 period, many companies took the idea of *risicare* to a new level. They dared with the takeovers of companies in the high-tech sector, and shareholders paid a heavy price when the sector nosedived in the punishing bear market of 2001–2002. Daring to dream about new opportunities, new business ideas is what capital budgeting is all about. To dare is to create growth and wealth for the company and the common shareholders. But sometimes, the dream becomes a nightmare because the risk of the investment project wasn't well evaluated and considered. The shareholders of numerous companies that purchased other companies, a classic and very costly type of risky capital budgeting project, can attest to the damage that can be done if the risks of takeovers are not correctly evaluated. Two of the many examples of this expensive lesson follow.

In September 2000, Quebecor Inc. and the Caisse de dépôt et placement du Québec purchased Groupe Vidéotron Ltée, paying $5.4 billion for the cable television provider. The winning bid was, as one person knowledgeable about the takeover stated, "far too high" and was motivated to defeat Rogers Communications' initial $4.9 billion bid for the company. Quebecor Inc. is a communications company operating in 17 countries. It is the largest commercial printing company in the world and owns companies in numerous media-related businesses. The Caisse de dépôt manages Quebec's public pension funds. To date, the two organizations have written off over $2.8 billion or almost half of the purchase price due to the declining value of the investment. It is expected that at least another $1.2 billion will be written off. This means that $4 billion of the $5.4 billion purchase price will be lost, implying that the amount paid by the two organizations greatly exceeded Groupe Vidéotron's true value. The capital budgeting process used to justify the initial transaction was badly flawed.

For another example, consider that in October 2002, Nortel Networks sold its optic parts business for US$108 million. While on the surface this might seem like a lot of money, in reality it was a bargain-basement price considering that the sale included assets Nortel bought in 2001 for US$3 billion. A week earlier, Nortel closed another unit of the company, an optical components maker, that was acquired in 2000 for US$1.16 billion. In about 10 days, Nortel removed from the books assets that cost, at least, $4.2 billion. The company received $108 million for these assets, resulting in large writedowns. These transactions, again, reflect very poor capital budgeting analysis, this time for a company that in 2000 was one of the largest high-tech companies in the world.

These two examples illustrate the great damage that can be done to the company and to shareholders if risk is not explicitly recognized or not recognized correctly when analyzing investment projects. In these examples, either the expected cash inflows should have been reduced and/or the discount rate used to evaluate the takeover increased. If either or both of these corrections were made, perhaps many of the takeovers that destroyed shareholder value would not have been undertaken.

REFERENCES: Robert Gibbens, "Caisse, Quebecor May Take Vidéotron Hit," *National Post*, October 12, 2002, FP3; Mathew Ingram, "More to Quebecor Suit Than Meets the Eye," *The Globe and Mail*, September 20, 2002; Mark Evans, "Nortel Casts Off Part of Optical Unit for US$108M," *National Post*, October 8, 2002, FP8; David Akin, "Ultimate Supplier Nortel May Be Out of Demand," *The Globe and Mail*, September 30, 2002.

? Review Questions

13–1 In Chapter 12, what assumption was made concerning the risk of capital budgeting projects? What happens if this assumption doesn't hold? How can the acceptance of a project change the overall risk of a company? Provide an example.

13–2 For capital budgeting, what is meant by the term "risk"? What are the sources of risk?

13–3 What is meant by the phrase "garbage in, garbage out" when applied to capital budgeting? What concept does the phrase reflect?

13.2 Behavioural Approaches for Dealing with Risk

Behavioural approaches can be used to get a "feel" for the level of project risk, whereas *quantitative approaches* allow explicit adjustment of projects for risk. Here we present a few behavioural approaches for dealing with risk in capital budgeting: risk and cash inflows, sensitivity and scenario analysis, and simulation. In addition, some international risk considerations are discussed. We consider quantitative approaches in a later section.

Risk and Cash Inflows

forecasting risk
The possibility that the estimated cash flows are wrong (either too high or low) and, as a result, a wrong decision made.

One of the major components of risk for a project are the projected cash flows. Recognize that many projects have very long expected lives and that forecasting error is a real concern. **Forecasting risk** is the possibility that the estimated cash flows are wrong (either too high or low) and, as a result, a wrong decision made. It is reasonable to assume that cash flow forecasts for six plus years into the future are subject to more forecasting error than forecasts for one to five years into the future. But the NPV analysis implicitly recognizes this through the present value interest factor. Consider that the present value of an expected cash inflow of $1,000 in one year's time, assuming a 12 percent discount rate, is $892.86. The present value of the same $1,000 expected in 10 years' time is only $321.97. So the NPV process implicitly recognizes that the more distant the expected cash inflow, the higher the risk.

Career Key
The *marketing and production* departments will be very involved in this part of the analysis of capital expenditure proposals. Marketing will provide the revenue estimates for the various proposals, while production will provide operating cost data.

For cash flows, risk is associated almost entirely with the cash inflows. The incremental cost of the project is known with virtual certainty since the cash flow occurs now, at time 0. For most capital budgeting projects, the firm will know the cost of the asset and, if a replacement project, the salvage value of the asset being replaced. There is very little—virtually no—risk associated with the incremental cost. If this is the case, then there is little risk associated with any investment tax credit (ITC) or the tax shield from CCA.[1]

---

1. The risk of the tax shield from CCA is associated with the certainty of the discount rate (considered later in the chapter) and the firm's tax rate. Tax rate changes are *entirely* outside the firm's control; therefore, the firm must use the tax rate currently in effect in the analysis of a project. If the tax rate changes in the future, this will affect the tax shield, and other variables, but this is entirely unpredictable. It is a political risk that cannot be controlled.

Risk is associated with the principal reason a company considers investing in a capital budgeting project: the expected increase in operating income. This increase is associated with the expected level of sales, the cost of raw materials, labour costs, factory overhead, selling and administrative expenses, and all other costs that will be affected by the project. The overall expected level of operating income is associated with the interaction of these underlying variables. The other components of the cash flows that are subject to risk include the change in net working capital (since this is based on uncertain sales) and the salvage value of the asset at the end of its useful life. On a present value basis, however, both of these variables are minor: The key component of the cash flows that is subject to significant risk is the incremental operating income.

Therefore, to assess the risk of a proposed capital expenditure, the focus is on the operating income component of the cash inflows. The firm must determine the probability that the operating income will be large enough so the project is acceptable.

Example ▼ Treadwell Tire Company, a tire retailer with a 10 percent cost of capital (k_a), is considering investing in either of two mutually exclusive projects, A or B, each requiring a $10,000 initial investment and expected to provide equal annual incremental after-tax operating incomes (the only relevant cash inflow) over their 15-year lives. For either project to be acceptable, according to the net present value technique, its NPV must be equal to or greater than zero. If we let *CF* equal the annual after-tax cash inflow and *IC* equals the incremental cost, the following condition must be met for projects with annuity cash inflows, such as A and B, to be acceptable:

$$NPV = [CF \times PVIFA_a(k_a, n \text{ years})] - IC = \$0 \qquad (13.1)$$

By substituting $k_a = 10\%$, $n = 15$ years, and $IC = \$10,000$, we can find the **breakeven cash inflow**—the minimum level of after-tax cash inflow necessary for Treadwell's projects to be acceptable:

breakeven cash inflow
The minimum level of after-tax cash inflow necessary for a project to be acceptable, i.e., NPV > $0.

$$[CF \times PVIFA(10\%, 15\text{yrs})] - \$10,000 > \$0$$
$$CF \times (7.606) > \$10,000$$
$$CF > \frac{\$10,000}{7.606} = \underline{\underline{\$1,315}}$$

Note that a financial calculator was used to solve this problem where the $10,000 is the PV, I is 10 percent, and N is 15. Input 0 as the FV and compute (CPT) PMT. The result indicates that for the projects to be acceptable to Treadwell Tire, they must have incremental after-tax operating incomes (cash inflows) of at least $1,315 per year.[2]

Given this breakeven level of cash inflows, the risk of each project could be assessed by determining the probability that the project's cash inflows will equal or exceed this breakeven level. The various statistical techniques that would determine that probability are covered in Chapter 7, Section 7.2. For now, we can simply assume that such a statistical analysis results in the following:

---

2. Note that for the remainder of this chapter, the generic term "cash inflow" will be used. Remember, however, that it is the operating income component that makes cash inflows risky.

Probability of $CF_A > \$1{,}315 \rightarrow 100\%$
Probability of $CF_B > \$1{,}315 \rightarrow\ \ 65\%$

Because project A is certain (100% probability) to have a positive net present value, whereas there is only a 65 percent chance that project B will have a positive NPV, project A is less risky than project B. Of course, the potential level of returns associated with each project must be evaluated in view of the firm's risk preference before the preferred project is selected.

The example clearly identifies risk as it relates to the chance that a project is acceptable, but it does not address the issue of cash flow variability. Even though project B has a greater chance of loss than project A, it might result in higher potential NPVs. Recall from Chapters 7 and 8 that it is the *combination* of risk and return that determines value. Similarly, the worth of a capital expenditure and its impact on the firm's value must be viewed in light of both risk and return. The analyst must therefore consider the *variability* of cash inflows and NPVs to assess project risk and return fully.

Sensitivity and Scenario Analysis

sensitivity analysis
A behavioural approach that uses a number of possible values for a given variable to assess its impact on a firm's return.

Two approaches for dealing with project risk to capture the variability of cash inflows and NPVs are sensitivity analysis and scenario analysis. **Sensitivity analysis**, as noted in Chapter 7, is a behavioural approach that uses a number of possible values for a given variable, such as cash inflows, to assess its impact on the firm's return, measured here by NPV. This technique is often useful in getting a feel for the variability of return in response to changes in a key variable. In capital budgeting, one of the most common sensitivity approaches is to estimate the NPVs associated with pessimistic (worst), most likely (expected), and optimistic (best) cash inflow estimates. The *range* can be determined by subtracting the pessimistic-outcome NPV from the optimistic-outcome NPV.

E x a m p l e ▼   Continuing with Treadwell Tire Company, assume that the financial manager made pessimistic, most likely, and optimistic estimates of the cash inflows for each project. The cash inflow estimates and resulting NPVs in each case are summarized in Table 13.2. Comparing the ranges of cash inflows ($1,000 for project A and $4,000 for B) and, more important, the ranges of NPVs ($7,606 for project A and $30,424 for B) makes it clear that project A is less risky than project B. Given that both projects have the same most likely NPV of $5,212, the assumed risk-averse decision maker may take project A because it has less risk and no possibility of loss. The deciding factor will be the probabilities attached to each of the possible outcomes. If there is only a 10 percent probability of the pessimistic outcome occurring and a 40 percent probability of the optimistic outcome occurring for the two projects, then the decision may swing in favour of project B. ▲

scenario analysis
A behavioural approach that evaluates the impact on return of simultaneous changes in a number of variables.

Scenario analysis, which is a behavioural approach similar to sensitivity analysis but broader in scope, is used to evaluate the impact of various circumstances on the firm's return. Rather than isolating the effect of a change in a single variable, scenario analysis evaluates the impact of simultaneous changes in a number of variables, such as the various components of the cash inflows, the cash outflows, and the cost of capital. For example, the firm could evaluate the

TABLE 13.2	Sensitivity Analysis of Treadwell's Projects A and B	
	Project A	Project B
Initial cost	$10,000	$10,000
	Annual after-tax cash inflows	
Outcome		
Pessimistic	$1,500	$ 0
Most likely	2,000	2,000
Optimistic	2,500	4,000
Range	$1,000	$4,000
	Net present values[a]	
Outcome		
Pessimistic	$1,409	−$10,000
Most likely	5,212	5,212
Optimistic	9,015	20,424
Range	$7,606	$30,424

[a]These values were calculated by using the corresponding annual cash inflows, the 10% cost of capital, and a 15-year life.

Career Key

Information systems analysts will be key to this part of the capital expenditure analysis process. They will design the systems to help complete the sensitivity and scenario analysis and the simulation approach.

impact of both high inflation (scenario 1) and low inflation (scenario 2) on a project's NPV. Or, the firm could consider the impact of different marketing campaigns, selling prices, production processes, or operating or financial structures on cash inflows, outflows, cost of capital, and NPVs. Each scenario will affect the firm's cash inflows, cash outflows, and cost of capital, thereby resulting in different levels of NPV. The decision maker can use these NPV estimates to roughly assess the risk involved with respect to the level of inflation. The widespread availability of computer-based spreadsheet programs (such as *Excel* and *Quattro Pro*) has greatly enhanced the use of both scenario and sensitivity analysis.

Simulation

simulation
A statistically based behavioural approach that applies predetermined probability distributions and random numbers to estimate risky outcomes.

Simulation is a statistically based behavioural approach that applies predetermined probability distributions and random numbers to estimate risky outcomes. By tying the various cash flow components together in a mathematical model and repeating the process numerous times, the financial manager can develop a probability distribution of project returns. Figure 13.2 presents a flowchart of the simulation of the net present value of a project. The process of generating random numbers and using the probability distributions for cash inflows and outflows allows the financial manager to determine values for each of these variables. Substituting these values into the mathematical model results in an NPV. By repeating this process perhaps a thousand times, a probability distribution of net present values is created.

NPV Simulation
Flowchart of a net present
value simulation

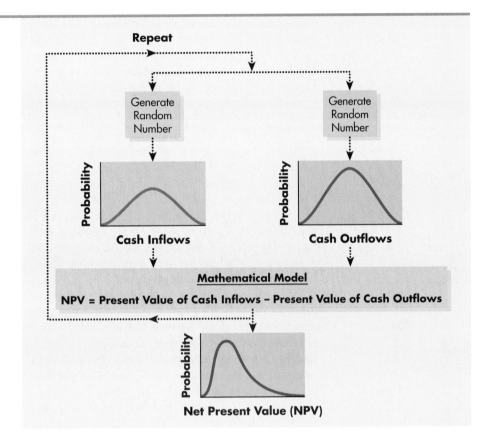

<!-- Repeat -->
<!-- Generate Random Number | Generate Random Number -->
<!-- Probability / Cash Inflows | Probability / Cash Outflows -->
<!-- Mathematical Model -->
<!-- NPV = Present Value of Cash Inflows − Present Value of Cash Outflows -->
<!-- Probability / Net Present Value (NPV) -->

> **! Hint**
> These behavioural approaches may
> seem a bit imprecise to one who has not
> used them. But repeated use and an
> "after-the-fact" review of previous
> analyses improve the accuracy of the
> users.

Although only gross cash inflows and outflows are simulated in Figure 13.2, more sophisticated simulations using individual inflow and outflow components, such as sales volume, sales price, raw material cost, labour cost, selling and administrative expenses, and so on, are quite common. From the distribution of returns, regardless of how they are measured (NPV or IRR), the decision maker can determine not only the expected value of the return but also the probability of achieving or surpassing a given return. The use of computers has made the simulation approach feasible. The output of simulation provides an excellent basis for decision making, because it allows the decision maker to view a continuum of risk-return tradeoffs rather than a single-point estimate.

International Risk Considerations

Although the basic techniques of capital budgeting are the same for purely domestic firms as for multinational companies (MNCs), firms that operate in several countries face risks that are unique to the international arena. Two types of risk are particularly important: exchange rate risk and political risk—including, in the extreme, the risk that assets in foreign countries will be seized by the host government.

Exchange rate risk reflects the danger that an unexpected change in the exchange rate between the Canadian dollar and the currency in which a project's

> **exchange rate risk**
> The danger that an unexpected change
> in the exchange rate between the dollar
> and the currency in which a project's
> cash flows are denominated can reduce
> the market value of that project's cash
> flow.

cash flows are denominated can reduce the market value of that project's cash flow. Although a project's initial investment can usually be predicted with some certainty, the dollar value of future cash inflows can be dramatically altered if the local currency depreciates against the dollar. In the short term, specific cash flows can be hedged by using financial instruments such as currency futures and options. Long-term exchange rate risk can best be minimized by financing the project, in whole or in part, in local currency.

Political risk is much harder to protect against. Once a foreign project is accepted, the foreign government can block the return of profits, seize the firm's assets, or otherwise interfere with a project's operation. The inability to manage political risk after the fact makes it even more important that managers account for political risks before making an investment. They can do so either by adjusting a project's expected cash inflows to account for the probability of political interference or by using risk-adjusted discount rates (discussed later in this chapter) in the capital budgeting decision-making process. In general, it is much better to subjectively adjust individual project cash flows for political risk than to use a blanket adjustment for all projects.

In addition to unique risks that MNCs must face, several other special issues are relevant only for international capital budgeting. One of these special issues is tax law differences between Canada and the country where the project is located. Often, one of the reasons a company locates a project in another country is lower taxes. Because only after-tax cash flows are relevant for capital budgeting, financial managers must carefully account for taxes paid to foreign governments on profits earned within their borders. They must also assess the impact of these tax payments on the parent company's Canadian tax liability, because full or partial credit is generally allowed for foreign tax payments. This issue is discussed in Chapter 17.

A second special issue is transfer pricing. Much of the international trade involving MNCs is, in reality, simply the shipment of goods and services from one of a parent company's wholly owned subsidiaries to another subsidiary located abroad. The parent company therefore has great discretion in setting the **transfer prices,** the prices that subsidiaries charge each other for the goods and services traded between them. The widespread use of transfer pricing in international trade makes capital budgeting in MNCs very difficult unless the transfer prices accurately reflect actual costs and incremental cash flows.

A third special issue in international capital budgeting is that MNCs often must approach international capital projects from a strategic point of view, rather than from a strictly financial perspective. For example, an MNC may feel compelled to invest in a country to ensure continued access, even if the project itself may not have a positive net present value. This motivation was important for Japanese automakers who set up assembly plants in Canada in the 1980s. For much the same reason, U.S. investment in Europe surged during the years before the market integration of the European Community in 1992. MNCs often will invest in production facilities in the home country of major rivals to deny these competitors an uncontested home market. Finally, MNCs may feel compelled to invest in certain industries or countries to achieve a broad corporate objective such as completing a product line or diversifying raw material sources, even when the project's cash flows may not be sufficiently profitable.

transfer prices
Prices that subsidiaries charge each other for the goods and services traded between them.

IN PRACTICE

Kyoto and Risk

The Kyoto Protocol is an international treaty meant to combat the perceived threat of global warming, the so-called greenhouse effect. Greenhouse gases are caused by burning fossil fuels, primarily oil and coal. In fall 2002, the Canadian government agreed to implement the Kyoto Protocol, which called for greenhouse gas emissions in Canada to be lowered to 6 percent below 1990 levels by 2012. For Canada, the impact of Kyoto would be to reduce greenhouse gases by 30 percent below 2002 levels within 10 years. This would require dramatic reductions in the burning of fossil fuels.

It is very uncertain how Canada will achieve this target. This is particularly the case for the energy industry and especially the heavy oil, tar sands projects in Alberta and Saskatchewan. The tar sands are one of the largest deposits of oil in the world and by 2007 will account for about half of Canada's oil output. But its burning generates five to ten times the level of greenhouse gases as conventional oil. How will the development of the greenhouse gas rich oil sands be achieved at the same time that Kyoto is being implemented? This is especially the case when federal politicians suggest that it could take a decade to develop an implementation plan for the Kyoto agreement.

For companies considering investing the billions required to develop the oil sands, these types of inconsistencies create huge uncertainty and therefore risk. For Canadian Natural Resources, one of Canada's largest oil and gas producers, the uncertainty created by Kyoto may mean an oil sands project costing $4.2 billion may be moved to the United States. As a major shareholder said, "with the uncertainty of Kyoto and not knowing what standards we need to meet, there is a risk that the project could be moved." By moving the project, Canadian Natural would reduce its greenhouse gas emissions in Canada by 50 percent.

Studies completed by Canadian Natural indicated that the costs to meet the Kyoto targets ranged from $0.50 to $7 per barrel of oil. These costs reduce the cash inflows for the project, making the project unviable in Canada. This highlights the challenges of making long-term investment decisions in the face of extreme uncertainty. Other Canadian oil companies, including EnCana, Petro-Canada, and Nexen, also indicated that decisions regarding the spending of billions of dollars on oil sands projects have been put in limbo since the announcement to ratify Kyoto was made. As the book was going to press, the Canadian government indicated that the oil companies' costs of meeting the Kyoto Protocol's conditions would be subsidized. This may result in the majority of projects being implemented.

For capital budgeting projects, risk comes in many forms. There can be project and financial risk, but also exchange rate, political, economic, and social risks. Who knew that in 1990 when the United Nations General Assembly began the process of dealing with the perceived threats of global warming, it would eventually affect the risks of major investment projects in the Canadian oil industry? Companies must be constantly on guard to evaluate changing risk when making long-term investment decisions.

REFERENCES: Alan Toulin, "Kyoto to Spark Big Gas Tax Hike," *National Post*, October 4, 2002, FP5; Claudia Cattaneo and Paul Haavardsrud, "Kyoto Could Cost Alberta $4.2B Project," *National Post*, September. 28, 2002, FP1; Claudia Cattaneo, "Canadian National Mulls U.S. Alternative," *National Post*, October 4, 2002, FP5.

❓ Review Questions

13–4 When the various cash flow components associated with a project are considered, which are risky and which have no or very little risk? Explain why this is the case. How is forecasting risk already reflected in cash flows that occur well in the future?

13–5 How can determination of the *breakeven cash inflow* be used to gauge project risk? Explain.

13–6 Briefly describe, compare, and explain how each of the following behavioural approaches can be used to deal with project risk: (a) sensitivity analysis; (b) scenario analysis; and (c) simulation.

13–7 Briefly define and explain how each of the following items that are unique to multinational companies affect their capital budgeting decisions: (a) exchange rate risk; (b) political risk; (c) tax law differences; (d) transfer pricing; and (e) strategic rather than financial viewpoint.

13.3 Risk-Adjustment Techniques

The approaches for dealing with risk that have been presented so far allow the financial manager to get a "feel" for project risk. Unfortunately, they do not provide a quantitative basis for evaluating risky projects. We will now illustrate the two major risk-adjustment techniques using the net present value (NPV) decision method.[3] The NPV decision rule of accepting only those projects with NPVs ≥ \$0 will continue to hold. The basic equation for NPV, first presented in Equation 12.3, is restated below:

$$NPV = \left[\sum_{t=1}^{n} CF_t(1 - T) \times PVIFA(t \text{ years}, k_a) - IC \right] \qquad (13.2)$$

where

$$CF_t = \text{incremental cash inflow in year } t$$
$$IC = \text{incremental cost}$$
$$k_a = \text{cost of capital or discount rate (in percent)}$$
$$n = \text{life of project (in years)}$$

Close examination of Equation 13.2 reveals that because the incremental cost (*IC*), which occurs at time zero, is known with certainty, a project's risk is embodied in the present value of its cash inflows:

$$\sum_{t=1}^{n} CF_t(1 - T) \times PVIFA(t \text{ years}, k_a) \qquad (13.3)$$

Two opportunities to adjust the present value of cash inflows for risk exist: (1) the cash inflows, ICF_t, can be adjusted, or (2) the discount rate, k_a, can be adjusted. Here we describe and compare two techniques—the cash inflow adjustment process, using *certainty equivalents,* and the discount rate adjustment process, using *risk-adjusted discount rates.* In addition, we consider the portfolio effects of project analysis as well as the practical aspects of certainty equivalents and risk-adjusted discount rates.

Certainty Equivalents (CEs)

certainty equivalents (CEs)
Risk-adjustment factors that represent the percent of estimated cash inflow that investors would be satisfied to receive *for certain* rather than the cash inflows that are *possible* for each year.

One of the most direct and theoretically preferred approaches for risk adjustment is the use of **certainty equivalents (CEs),** which represent the percent of estimated

---

3. The IRR could just as well have been used, but because NPV is theoretically preferable, it is used instead.

cash inflow that investors would be satisfied to receive *for certain* rather than the cash inflows that are *possible* for each year. Equation 13.4 presents the basic expression for NPV when certainty equivalents are used for risk adjustment:

$$NPV = (\alpha_t \times CF_t) \times PVIFA(t \text{ years}, R_F) \tag{13.4}$$

where

$$\alpha_t = \text{certainty equivalent factor in year } t \ (0 \le \alpha_t \le 1)$$
$$CF_t = \text{relevant incremental cash inflow in year } t$$
$$R_F = \text{risk-free rate of return}$$

risk-free rate, R_F
The rate of return that one would earn on a virtually riskless investment such as a Government of Canada treasury bill.

The equation shows that a project's incremental cash inflows are first adjusted for risk by converting the expected cash inflows to certain amounts, $\alpha_t \times CF_t$. These certain cash inflows are, in effect, equivalent to "cash in hand," but not at time zero. The second part of the calculation adjusts the certain cash inflows for the time value of money by discounting them at the risk-free rate, R_F. The **risk-free rate, R_F,** is the rate of return that one would earn on a virtually riskless investment such as a Government of Canada treasury bill. It is used to discount the certain cash inflows and should not be confused with a risk-adjusted discount rate. (If a risk-adjusted rate were used, the risk would in effect be counted twice.) Although the process described here of converting risky cash inflows to certain cash inflows is somewhat subjective, the technique is theoretically sound.

Example ▼ Bennett Company wishes to consider risk in the analysis of two projects, A and B. The relevant cash flows for these projects were presented in part A of Table 13.1, and the NPVs, assuming that the projects had equivalent risks, were presented in part B of Table 13.1. Ignoring risk differences and using net present value, calculated using the firm's 10 percent cost of capital, project A was preferred over project B, because its NPV of $11,074 was greater than B's NPV of $10,914.

Now let's assume, however, that on further analysis the firm found that project A was actually more risky than project B. To consider the differing risks, the firm estimated the certainty equivalent factors for each project's cash inflows for each year. Column 2 of Table 13.3 show the estimated values for projects A and B, respectively. Multiplying the risky cash inflows, in column 1, by the corresponding certainty equivalent factors, in column 2, gives the certain cash inflows for projects A and B shown in column 3.

Upon investigation, Bennett's management estimated the prevailing risk-free rate of return, R_F, to be 6 percent. Using that rate to discount the certain cash inflows for each of the projects results in the net present values of $4,544 for project A and $10,152 for B, as shown at the bottom of column 5. Note that as a result of the risk adjustment, project B is now preferred. The usefulness of the certainty equivalent approach for risk adjustment should be quite clear. The only difficulty lies in the need to make subjective estimates of the certainty equivalent
▲ factors.

Risk-Adjusted Discount Rates (RADRs)

A popular approach for risk adjustment involves the use of *risk-adjusted discount rates (RADRs)*. Instead of adjusting the cash inflows for risk, as the certainty equivalent approach does, this approach adjusts the discount rate.[4] Equation

TABLE 13.3	Analysis of Bennett Company's Projects A and B Using Certainty Equivalents

Project A

Year (*t*)	Cash inflows (1)	Certainty equivalent factors[a] (2)	Certain cash inflows [(1) × (2)] (3)	$PVIF_{6\%,t}$[b] (4)	Present value [(3) × (4)] (5)
1	$14,000	0.90	$12,600	0.943	$11,887
2	14,000	0.90	12,600	0.890	11,214
3	14,000	0.80	11,200	0.840	9,404
4	14,000	0.70	9,800	0.792	7,763
5	14,000	0.60	8,400	0.747	6,277
			Present value of cash inflows		$46,545
			− Initial investment		42,000
			Net present value (NPV)		$ 4,544

Project B

Year (*t*)	Cash inflows (1)	Certainty equivalent factors[a] (2)	Certain cash inflows [(1) × (2)] (3)	$PVIF_{6\%,t}$[b] (4)	Present value [(3) × (4)] (5)
1	$28,000	1.00	$28,000	0.943	$26,415
2	12,000	0.90	10,800	0.890	9,612
3	10,000	0.90	9,000	0.840	7,557
4	10,000	0.80	8,000	0.792	6,337
5	10,000	0.70	7,000	0.747	5,231
			Present value of cash inflows		$55,152
			− Initial investment		45,000
			Net present value (NPV)		$10,152

Note: The relevant cash flows for these projects were presented in Table 13.1, and the analysis of the projects using NPV and assuming equal risk was presented in Figure 13.1.

[a] These values were estimated by management; they reflect the risk that managers perceive in the cash inflows.

[b] These are simply the rounded present value interest factors. A financial calculator was used to determine the present values shown.

13.2 is used with one minor adjustment: the discount rate is k_j, the risk-adjusted discount rate, rather than k_a, the company's cost of capital, as noted in Equation 13.5.

---

4. The risk-adjusted discount rate approach can be applied in using the internal rate of return as well as the net present value. If the IRR is used, the risk-adjusted discount rate becomes the cutoff rate that must be exceeded by the IRR for the project to be accepted. In using NPV, the projected cash inflows are merely discounted at the risk-adjusted discount rate.

$$NPV = \sum_{t=1}^{n} CF_t(1 - T) \times PVIFA(t \text{ years, } k_j) \qquad (13.5)$$

risk-adjusted discount rate (RADR)
The rate of return that must be earned on a given project to compensate for the risk of the project.

The **risk-adjusted discount rate (RADR)** is the rate of return that must be earned on a given project to compensate for the risk of the project and ensure that the providers of financing receive a rate of return commensurate with the project's risk. This rate will compensate the providers of both debt and equity capital with their required rate of return. As a consequence, the firm's common share price will increase. The higher the risk of a project, the higher the RADR and therefore the lower the net present value for a given stream of cash inflows. Because the logic underlying the use of RADRs is closely linked to the capital asset pricing model (CAPM) developed in Chapter 7, here we review CAPM, discuss its use in finding RADRs, and describe the application of RADRs.

Review of CAPM

In Chapter 7, the *capital asset pricing model (CAPM)* was used to link the *relevant* risk and return for all assets traded in *efficient markets*. In the development of the CAPM, the *total risk* of an asset was defined as

$$\text{Total risk} = \text{nondiversifiable risk} + \text{diversifiable risk} \qquad (13.6)$$

For assets traded in an efficient market, the *diversifiable risk*, which results from uncontrollable or random events, can be eliminated through diversification. The relevant risk is therefore the *nondiversifiable risk*—the risk for which owners of these assets are rewarded. Nondiversifiable risk for securities is commonly measured by using *beta*, which is an index of the degree of movement of an asset's return in response to a change in the market return.

Using beta, b_j, to measure the relevant risk of any asset j, the CAPM is

$$k_j = R_F + [b_j \times (k_m - R_F)] \qquad (13.7)$$

where

$$
\begin{aligned}
k_j &= \text{required return on asset } j \\
R_F &= \text{risk-free rate of return} \\
b_j &= \text{beta coefficient for asset } j \\
k_m &= \text{return on the market portfolio of assets}
\end{aligned}
$$

In Chapter 7, we demonstrated that the required return on any asset could be determined by substituting values of R_F, b_j, and k_m into the CAPM—Equation 13.7. Any security that is expected to earn in excess of its required return would be acceptable, and those that are expected to earn less than the required return would be rejected.

Using CAPM to Find RADRs

If we assume for a moment that real corporate assets such as computers, machine tools, and special-purpose machinery are traded in efficient markets, the CAPM could be redefined as noted in Equation 13.8:

$$k_{\text{project } j} = R_F + [b_{\text{project } j} \times (k_m - R_F)] \qquad (13.8)$$

The *security market line* (SML)—the graphic depiction of the CAPM—is shown for Equation 13.8 in Figure 13.3. Any project having an IRR falling on or above the SML would be acceptable, because its IRR would equal or exceed the required return, $k_{project}$; any project with an IRR below $k_{project}$ would be rejected. In terms of NPV, any project falling above the SML would have a positive NPV, and any project falling below the SML would have a negative NPV.[5]

Example ▼ Two projects, L and R, are shown in Figure 13.3. Project L has a beta, b_L, and generates an internal rate of return, IRR_L. The required return for a project with risk b_L is k_L. Because project L generates a return greater than that required ($IRR_L > k_L$), project L would be acceptable. Project L would have a positive NPV when its cash inflows are discounted at its required return, k_L. Project R, on the other hand, generates an IRR below that required for its risk, b_R ($IRR_R < k_R$). This project would have a negative NPV when its cash inflows are discounted at its
▲ required return, k_R. Project R should be rejected.[6]

Applying RADRs

Because the CAPM is based upon an assumed efficient market, which does *not* exist for real corporate assets such as plant and equipment, the CAPM is not directly applicable in making capital budgeting decisions. Attention is therefore typically devoted to assessing the *total risk* of a project and using it to determine the risk-adjusted discount rate (RADR), which can be used in Equation 13.5 to find the NPV.

In order not to damage the firm's market value, it must use the correct discount rate when evaluating a project. If a firm discounts a risky project's cash inflows at too low a rate, accepts the project, the firm's market price may drop as investors recognize that the firm has invested in a negative NPV project and has become more risky. On the other hand, if the firm discounts a project's cash inflows at too high a rate, it will reject acceptable projects and not grow as it should. Eventually, the firm's market price may drop because investors, believing that the firm is being overly conservative, will sell their stock, putting downward pressure on the firm's market value.

Unfortunately, there is no formal mechanism for linking total project risk to the level of required return. As a result, most firms subjectively determine the RADR by adjusting their existing required return up or down depending on whether the proposed project is more or less risky, respectively, than the average risk of the firm. This CAPM-type of approach provides a "rough estimate" of project risk and required return because both the project risk measure and the linkage between risk and return are estimates. The following example demonstrates this CAPM-type approach linking project risk and return.

---

5. As noted earlier, whenever the IRR is above the cost of capital or required return (IRR > k), the NPV is positive, and whenever the IRR is below the cost of capital or required return (IRR < k), the NPV is negative. Because by definition the IRR is the discount rate that causes NPV to equal zero and the IRR and NPV always agree on accept–reject decisions, the relationship noted in Figure 13.3 logically follows.

6. If there were a third project with a beta of 1 and an IRR (expected return) of k_m, what should be done? In this case the project's required return is equal to the expected return (IRR = k). The intersection of the risk (beta) and the RADR for the project would be on the SML. This means that the project would have an NPV equal to 0, and therefore should be accepted.

FIGURE 13.3

CAPM and SML
CAPM and SML in capital
budgeting decision making

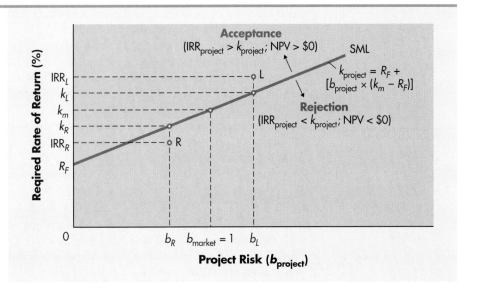

Example ▼ Bennett Company wishes to use the risk-adjusted discount rate approach to determine, according to NPV, whether to implement project A or project B. In addition to the data presented earlier, Bennett's management, after a great deal of analysis, assigned a "risk index" of 1.6 to project A and 1.0 to B. The risk index is merely a numerical scale used to classify project risk—higher index values are assigned to higher risk projects, and vice versa. The CAPM-type relationship used by the firm to link risk, measured by the risk index, and the required return (RADR) is shown in the following table.

	Risk index	Required return (RADR)
	0.0	6% (risk-free rate, R_F)
	0.2	7
	0.4	8
	0.6	9
	0.8	10
Project B →	1.0	11
	1.2	12
	1.4	13
Project A →	1.6	14
	1.8	16
	2.0	18

Note that this table can be easily converted to a graph like Figure 13.3. The one major change for the new graph is that rather than beta being the measure of risk on the x axis, the risk measure is the risk index. Figure 13.4 presents this data in graphical format.

Because project A is riskier than project B (index of 1.6 for A versus 1.0 for B), its RADR of 14 percent is greater than B's RADR of 11 percent. The net present value of each project, using its RADR, is calculated in Figure 13.5. The results clearly show that project B is preferable, because its risk-adjusted NPV of $9,798 is greater than the $6,063 risk-adjusted NPV for project A. This is the same conclusion that resulted from using certainty equivalents in the preceding example. As noted by the NPVs in part B of Table 13.1, when the discount rates are not adjusted for risk, project A would be preferred to project B.

The usefulness of risk-adjusted discount rates should now be clear. The real difficulty of this approach lies in estimating project risk and linking it to the required return (RADR).

Portfolio Effects

As noted in Chapter 7, because investors are not rewarded for taking diversifiable risk, they should hold a diversified portfolio of securities. Because a business firm can be viewed as a portfolio of assets, is it similarly important that the firm maintain a diversified portfolio of assets?

It seems logical that by holding a diversified portfolio the firm could reduce the variability of its cash flows. By combining two projects with negatively correlated cash inflows, the combined cash inflow variability—and therefore the risk—could be reduced.

Are firms rewarded for diversifying risk in this fashion? If they are, the value of the firm could be enhanced through diversification into other lines of business. Surprisingly, the value of the stock of firms whose shares are traded publicly in an efficient marketplace is generally *not* affected by diversification. In other words, diversification is not normally rewarded and therefore is generally not necessary.

Why are firms not rewarded for diversification results? Because investors themselves can diversify by holding securities in a variety of firms; they do not need the firm to do it for them. And investors can diversify more readily—they

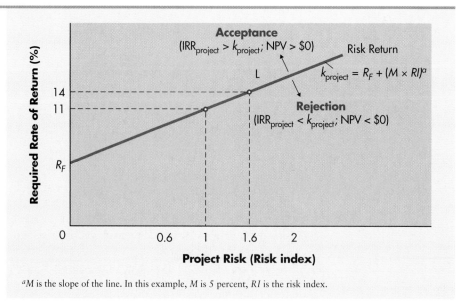

FIGURE 13.4

Risk Index
Use of the risk index in capital budgeting decision making

^a*M* is the slope of the line. In this example, *M* is 5 percent, *RI* is the risk index.

FIGURE 13.5 **Calculation of NPVs for Bennett Company's Capital Expenditure Alternatives using RADRs**

Time lines depicting the cash flows and NPV calculations using RADRs for projects A and B

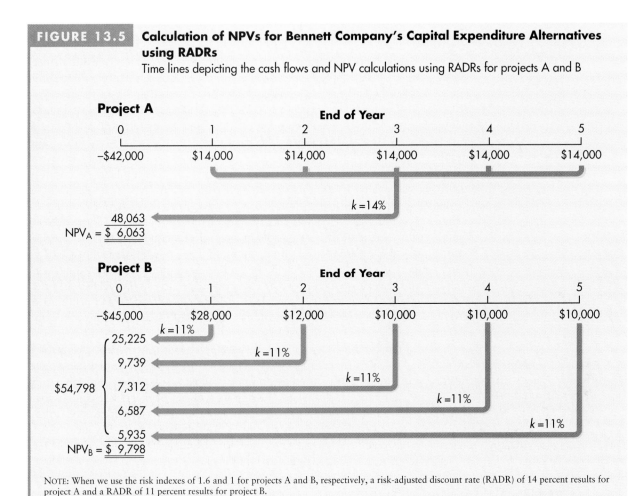

NOTE: When we use the risk indexes of 1.6 and 1 for projects A and B, respectively, a risk-adjusted discount rate (RADR) of 14 percent results for project A and a RADR of 11 percent results for project B.

can make transactions more easily and at a lower cost because of the greater availability of information and trading mechanisms.

Of course, if a firm acquires a new line of business and its cash flows tend to respond more to changing economic conditions (i.e., greater nondiversifiable risk), greater returns would be expected. If, for the additional risk, the firm earned a return in excess of that required (IRR > k), the value of the firm could be enhanced. Also, other benefits such as increased cash, greater borrowing capacity, guaranteed availability of raw materials, and so forth, could result from and therefore justify diversification, in spite of any immediate cash flow impact.

Although a strict theoretical view supports the use of a technique that relies on the CAPM framework, the presence of market imperfections causes the market for real corporate assets to be inefficient. The relative inefficiency of this market, coupled with difficulties associated with measurement of nondiversifiable project risk and its relationship to return, tend to favour the use of total risk to evaluate capital budgeting projects. Therefore, the use of *total risk* as an approximation for the relevant risk does tend to have widespread practical appeal.

CE Versus RADR in Practice

Certainty equivalents (CEs) are the *theoretically preferred* approach for project risk adjustment because they separately adjust for risk and time; they first eliminate risk from the cash flows and then discount the certain cash flows at a risk-free rate. Risk-adjusted discount rates (RADRs), on the other hand, have a major theoretical problem: They combine the risk and time adjustments in a single discount-rate adjustment. Because of the basic mathematics of compounding and discounting, the RADR approach therefore implicitly assumes that risk is an increasing function of time. Rather than demonstrate this implicit assumption, suffice it to say that *CEs are theoretically superior to RADRs.*

However, because of the complexity of developing CEs, *RADRs are more often used in practice.* Their popularity stems from two facts: (1) They are consistent with the general disposition of financial decision makers toward rates of return,[7] and (2) they are easily estimated and applied. The first reason is clearly a matter of personal preference, but the second is based on the computational convenience and well developed procedures involved in the use of RADRs. In practice, risk is often subjectively categorized rather than related to a continuum of RADRs associated with each level of risk, as was illustrated in the preceding example.

Firms often establish a number of *risk classes*, with an RADR assigned to each. Each project is then subjectively placed in the appropriate risk class, and the corresponding RADR is used to evaluate it. This is sometimes done on a division-by-division basis, each division having its own set of risk classes and associated RADRs similar to those in Table 13.4. The use of *divisional costs of capital* and associated risk classes allows the large multidivisional firm to incorporate differing levels of divisional risk into the capital budgeting process and still recognize differences in the levels of individual project risk.

Hint
The use of risk classes is consistent with the concept that risk-averse investors require a greater return for greater risks. In order to increase shareholders' wealth, risky projects must earn greater returns in order to warrant acceptance.

Example ▼ Assume that the management of Bennett Company decided to use a more subjective but practical RADR approach to analyze projects. Each project would be placed in one of four risk classes according to its perceived risk. The classes are ranged from I for the lowest risk projects to IV for the highest risk projects. Associated with each class was an RADR that was appropriate to the level of risk of projects in the class. A brief description of each class, along with the associated RADR, is given in Table 13.4. It shows that lower risk projects tend to involve routine replacement or renewal activities, whereas higher risk projects involve expansion, often into new or unfamiliar activities.

The financial manager of Bennett has assigned project A to Class III and project B to Class II. The cash flows for project A would therefore be evaluated by using a 14 percent RADR, and project B's would be evaluated by using a 10 percent RADR.[8] The net present value of project A at 14 percent was calculated in Figure 13.5 to be $6,063, and the NPV for project B at a 10 percent RADR was shown in Table 13.1 to be $10,924. Clearly, with RADRs based on

---

7. Recall that although NPV was the theoretically preferred evaluation technique, IRR was more popular in actual business practice due to the general preference of businesspeople for rates of return rather than pure dollar returns. The preference for RADRs over CEs is therefore consistent with the preference for IRR over NPV.

8. Note that the 10% RADR for project B using the risk classes in Table 13.4 differs from the 11% RADR used when the risk index of the project was considered. This difference is attributable to the less precise nature of the use of risk classes.

TABLE 13.4	Bennett Company's Risk Classes and RADRs	
Risk class	Description	Risk-adjusted discount rate, RADR
I	*Below-average risk:* Projects with low risk. Typically involve routine replacement without renewal of existing activities.	8%
II	*Average risk:* Projects similar to those currently implemented. Typically involve replacement or renewal of existing activities.	10%[a]
III	*Above-average risk:* Projects with higher than normal, but not excessive, risk. Typically involve expansion of existing or similar activities.	14%
IV	*Highest risk:* Projects with very high risk. Typically involve expansion into new or unfamiliar activities.	20%

[a]This RADR is actually the firm's cost of capital, which was discussed and illustrated in Chapters 9 and 12. It represents the firm's required return on its existing portfolio of projects, which is assumed unchanged with acceptance of the "average risk" project.

the use of risk classes, project B is preferred over project A. As noted earlier, this result is contrary to the preferences shown in Table 13.1, where no attention was given to the differing risk of projects A and B.

? Review Questions

13–8 Explain the concept of *certainty equivalents (CEs)*. How are they used in the risk-adjustment process?

13–9 Describe the logic as well as the basic procedures involved in using *risk-adjusted discount rates (RADRs)*. How does this approach relate to the *capital asset pricing model?* Explain.

13–10 Explain why a firm whose stock is actively traded in the securities markets need not concern itself with diversification. In spite of this, how is the risk of capital budgeting projects frequently measured? Why?

13–11 Compare and contrast CEs and RADRs from both a theoretical and a practical point of view. In practice, how are risk classes often used to apply RADRs? Explain.

13.4 Capital Budgeting Refinements

Refinements must often be made in the analysis of capital budgeting projects to accommodate special circumstances. These adjustments permit the relaxation of certain simplifying assumptions presented earlier. Three areas in which special forms of analysis are frequently needed are: (1) comparison of mutually exclusive projects having unequal lives, (2) recognition of real options, and (3) capital rationing caused by a binding budget constraint.

Comparing Projects with Unequal Lives

The financial manager must often select the best of a group of unequal-lived projects. If the projects are independent, the length of the project lives is not critical. But when unequal-lived projects are mutually exclusive, the impact of differing lives must be considered because the projects do not provide service over comparable time periods. This is especially important when continuing service is needed from the project under consideration. The discussions that follow assume that the unequal-lived, mutually exclusive projects being compared *are ongoing*. If they were not, the project with the highest NPV would be selected.

The Problem

A simple example will demonstrate the basic problem of noncomparability caused by the need to select the best of a group of mutually exclusive projects with differing usable lives.

Example ▼ The AT Company, a regional cable-television company, is evaluating two projects, X and Y. The relevant cash flows for each project are given in the following table. The applicable cost of capital for use in evaluating these equally risky projects is 10 percent.

	Project X	Project Y
Initial investment	$70,000	$85,000
Year	Cash inflows	
1	$28,000	$35,000
2	33,000	30,000
3	38,000	25,000
4	—	20,000
5	—	15,000
6	—	10,000

The net present value of each project at the 10 percent cost of capital using a financial calculator is:

$$\text{NPV}_X = \$81,277 - \$70,000$$
$$= \underline{\$11,277}$$

$$\text{NPV}_Y = \$104,013 - \$85,000$$
$$= \underline{\$19,013}$$

The NPV for project X is $11,277, for project Y $19,013.

Ignoring the differences in project lives, we can see that both projects are acceptable (both NPVs are greater than zero) and that project Y is preferred over project X. If the projects are independent and only one could be accepted, project Y—with the larger NPV—would be preferred. On the other hand, if the projects are mutually exclusive, their differing lives must be considered. Project Y provides 3 more years of service than project X.

The analysis in this example is incomplete if the projects are mutually exclusive (which will be our assumption throughout the remaining discussions). To compare these unequal-lived, mutually exclusive projects correctly, the differing lives must be considered in the analysis; an incorrect decision could result from simply using the above-calculated NPVs to select the best project. Although a number of approaches are available for dealing with unequal lives, here we present the most efficient technique—the annualized net present value (ANPV) approach.

Annualized Net Present Value (ANPV) Approach

annualized net present value (ANPV) approach
An approach to evaluating unequal-lived projects that converts the net present value of unequal-lived, mutually exclusive projects into an equivalent annual amount (in NPV terms).

The **annualized net present value (ANPV) approach** converts the net present value of unequal-lived projects into an equivalent annual amount (in NPV terms) that can be used to select the best project.[9] This net present value based approach can be applied to unequal-lived, mutually exclusive projects by using the following steps:

Step 1   Calculate the net present value of each project j, NPV_j, over its life, n_j, using the appropriate discount rate, k.

Step 2   Divide the net present value of each project having a positive NPV by the present value interest factor for an annuity at the given discount rate and the project's life to get the annualized net present value for each project j, $ANPV_j$, as shown below:

$$ANPV_j = \frac{NPV_j}{PVIFA_{(k\%,\, n_j)}} \qquad (13.9)$$

Step 3   Select the project having the highest ANPV.

E x a m p l e ▼   By using the AT Company data presented earlier for projects X and Y, the three-step ANPV approach can be applied as follows:

Step 1   The net present values of projects X and Y discounted at 10 percent—as calculated in the preceding example for a single purchase of each asset—are
$$NPV_X = \$11,277$$
$$NPV_Y = \$19,013$$

Step 2   Calculate the annualized net present value for each project by applying Equation 13.9 to the NPVs and using a financial calculator:

$$ANPV_X = \frac{\$11,277}{PVIFA(10\%,\ 3yrs)} = \frac{\$11,277}{2.487} = \underline{\underline{\$4,535}}$$

$$ANPV_Y = \frac{\$19,013}{PVIFA(10\%,\ 6yrs)} = \frac{\$19,013}{4.355} = \underline{\underline{\$4,366}}$$

---

9. The theory underlying this as well as other approaches for comparing projects with unequal lives assumes that each project can be repeated in the future for the same initial investment and that each will provide the same expected future cash inflows. Although changing technology and inflation will affect the initial investment and expected cash inflows, the lack of specific attention to them does not detract from the usefulness of this technique.

(*Note:* To make the calculation using a financial calculator, the NPV is the PV, I is 10 percent, and N is the life of the project. Input 0 in FV and compute PMT.)

Step 3   Reviewing the ANPVs calculated in step 2, we can see that project X would be preferred over project Y. Given that projects X and Y are mutually exclusive, project X would be the recommended project because it provides the higher annualized net present value.

▲

Recognizing Real Options

The procedures described in Chapter 12 and thus far in this chapter suggest that to make capital budgeting decisions, we must (1) estimate relevant cash flows, (2) apply an appropriate decision technique such as NPV or IRR to those cash flows, and (3) recognize and adjust the decision technique for project risk. Although this traditional procedure is believed to yield good decisions, a more *strategic approach* to these decisions has emerged in recent years. This more modern view considers any **real options**—opportunities that are embedded in capital projects ("real," rather than financial, asset investments) that enable managers to alter their cash flows and risk in a way that affects project acceptability (NPV). Because these opportunities are more likely to exist in, and be more important to, large "strategic" capital budgeting projects, they are sometimes called *strategic options*.

Some of the more common types of real options—abandonment, flexibility, growth, and timing—are briefly described in Table 13.5. It should be clear from their descriptions that each of these types of options could be embedded in a capital budgeting decision and that explicit recognition of them would probably alter the cash flow and risk of a project and change its NPV.

By explicitly recognizing these options when making capital budgeting decisions, managers can make improved, more strategic decisions that consider in advance the economic impact of certain contingent actions on project cash flow and risk. The explicit recognition of real options embedded in capital budgeting projects will cause the project's *strategic* NPV to differ from its *traditional* NPV as indicated by Equation 13.10.

$$\text{NPV}_{\text{strategic}} = \text{NPV}_{\text{traditional}} + \text{value of real options} \qquad (13.10)$$

real options
Opportunities that are embedded in capital projects that enable managers to alter their cash flows and risk in a way that affects project acceptability (NPV). Also called *strategic options*.

E x a m p l e ▼ Assume that a strategic analysis of Bennett Company's projects A and B (see cash flows and NPVs in Table 13.1) finds no real options embedded in project A and two real options embedded in project B. The two real options in project B are as follows: (1) The project would have, during the first two years, some downtime that would result in unused production capacity that could be used to perform contract manufacturing for another firm, and (2) the project's computerized control system could, with some modification, control two other machines, thereby reducing labour cost, without affecting operation of the new project.

Bennett's management estimated the NPV of the contract manufacturing over the 2 years following implementation of project B to be $1,500 and the NPV of the computer control sharing to be $2,000. Management felt there was a 60 percent chance that the contract manufacturing option would be exercised and only a 30 percent chance that the computer control sharing option would be

TABLE 13.5	Major Types of Real Options
Option type	Description
Abandonment option	The option to abandon or terminate a project prior to the end of its planned life. This option allows management to avoid or minimize losses on projects that turn bad. Explicitly recognizing the abandonment option when evaluating a project often increases its NPV.
Flexibility option	The option to incorporate flexibility into the firm's operations, particularly production. It generally includes the opportunity to design the production process to accept multiple inputs, use flexible production technology to create a variety of outputs by reconfiguring the same plant and equipment, and purchase and retain excess capacity in capital-intensive industries subject to wide swings in output demand and long lead time in building new capacity from scratch. Recognition of this option embedded in a capital expenditure should increase the NPV of the project.
Growth option	The option to develop follow-on projects, expand markets, expand or retool plants, and so on, that would not be possible without implementation of the project that is being evaluated. If a project being considered has the measurable potential to open new doors if successful, then recognition of the cash flows from such opportunities should be included in the initial decision process. Growth opportunities embedded in a project often increase the NPV of the project in which they are embedded.
Timing option	The option to determine when various actions with respect to a given project are taken. This option recognizes the firm's opportunity to delay acceptance of a project for one or more periods, to accelerate or slow the process of implementing a project in response to new information, or to shut down a project temporarily in response to changing product market conditions or competition. As in the case of the other types of options, the explicit recognition of timing opportunities can improve the NPV of a project that fails to recognize this option in an investment decision.

exercised. The combined value of these two real options would be the sum of their expected values.

$$\text{Value of real options for project B} = (0.60 \times \$1,500) + (0.30 \times \$2,000)$$
$$= \$900 + \$600 = \$1,500$$

Substituting the $1,500 real options value along with the traditional NPV of $10,914 for project B (from Table 13.1) into Equation 13.10, we get the strategic NPV for project B.

$$\text{NPV}_{\text{strategic}} = \$10,914 + \$1,500 = \$12,414$$

Bennett Company's project B therefore has a strategic NPV of $12,414, which is above its traditional NPV and now exceeds project A's NPV of $11,071. Clearly, recognition of project B's real options improved its NPV (from $10,914 to $12,414) and causes it to be preferred over project A (NPV of $12,414 for B > NPV of $11,071 for A), which has no real options embedded in it.

It is important to realize that the recognition of attractive real options when determining NPV could cause an otherwise unacceptable project ($\text{NPV}_{\text{traditional}} \leq$

$0) to become acceptable (NPV$_{strategic}$ > $0). The failure to recognize the value of real options could therefore cause management to reject projects that are acceptable. Although doing so requires more strategic thinking and analysis, it is important for the financial manager to identify and incorporate real options in the NPV process. The procedures for doing this efficiently are emerging, and the use of the strategic NPV that incorporates real options is expected to become more commonplace in the future.

Capital Rationing

Firms commonly operate under *capital rationing*—they have more acceptable independent projects than they can fund. *In theory*, capital rationing should not exist. Firms should accept all projects that have positive NPVs (or IRRs ≥ the cost of capital). However, *in practice*, most firms operate under capital rationing. Generally, firms attempt to isolate and select the best acceptable projects subject to a capital expenditure budget set by management. Research has found that management internally imposes capital expenditure constraints to avoid what it deems to be "excessive" levels of new financing, particularly debt. Although failing to fund all acceptable independent projects is theoretically inconsistent with the goal of owner-wealth maximization, here we discuss capital rationing procedures because they are widely used in practice.

The objective of *capital rationing* is to select the group of projects that provides the *highest overall net present value* and does not require more dollars than are budgeted. As a prerequisite to capital rationing, the best of any mutually exclusive projects must be chosen and placed in the group of independent projects. Two basic approaches to project selection under capital rationing are discussed here.

internal rate of return approach
An approach to capital rationing that involves graphing project IRRs in descending order against the total dollar investment, to determine the group of acceptable projects.

investment opportunities schedule (IOS)
The graph that plots project IRRs in descending order against total dollar investment.

Internal Rate of Return Approach

The **internal rate of return approach** involves graphing project IRRs in descending order against the total dollar investment. This graph, which was discussed in more detail in Chapter 9, is called the **investment opportunities schedule (IOS)**. By drawing the cost of capital line and then imposing a budget constraint, the financial manager can determine the group of acceptable projects. The problem with this technique is that it does not guarantee the maximum dollar return to the firm. It merely provides a satisfactory solution to capital rationing problems.

Example ▼ Tate Company, a fast-growing plastics company, is confronted with six projects competing for its fixed budget of $250,000. The initial investment and IRR for each project are as follows:

Project	Initial investment	IRR
A	$ 80,000	12%
B	70,000	20
C	100,000	16
D	40,000	8
E	60,000	15
F	110,000	11

The firm has a cost of capital of 10 percent. Figure 13.6 presents the IOS resulting from ranking the six projects in descending order based on IRRs. According to the schedule, only projects B, C, and E should be accepted. Together they will absorb $230,000 of the $250,000 budget. Projects A and F are acceptable but cannot be chosen because of the budget constraint. Project D is not worthy of consideration, because its IRR is less than the firm's 10 percent cost of capital.

    The drawback of this approach is that there is no guarantee that the acceptance of projects B, C, and E will maximize *total dollar returns* and therefore ▲ owners' wealth.

Net Present Value Approach

net present value approach
An approach to capital rationing that is based on the use of present values to determine the group of projects that will maximize owners' wealth.

The **net present value approach** is based on the use of present values to determine the group of projects that will maximize owners' wealth. It is implemented by ranking projects on the basis of IRRs and then evaluating the present value of the benefits from each potential project to determine *the combination of projects with the highest overall present value*. This is the same as maximizing net present value, in which the entire budget is viewed as the total initial investment. Any portion of the firm's budget that is not used does not increase the firm's value. The unused money can be used to repay debt, invested in marketable securities, or returned to the owners in the form of cash dividends. In these cases, the wealth of the owners may not be enhanced.

E x a m p l e ▼ The group of projects described in the preceding example is ranked in Table 13.6 on the basis of IRRs. The present value of the cash inflows associated with the projects is also included in the table. Projects B, C, and E, which together require $230,000, yield a present value of $336,000. However, if projects B, C, and A were implemented, the total budget of $250,000 would be used, and the present value of the cash inflows would be $357,000. This is greater than the return expected from selecting the projects on the basis of the highest IRRs. Implementing B, C, and A is preferable, because this group of projects maximizes

FIGURE 13.6

Investment Opportunities Schedule
Investment opportunities schedule (IOS) for Tate Company projects

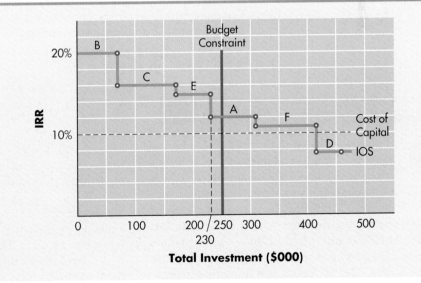

			Present value of
Project	Initial investment	IRR	inflows at 10%
B	$ 70,000	20%	$112,000
C	100,000	16	145,000
E	60,000	15	79,000
A	80,000	12	100,000
F	110,000	11	126,500
D	40,000	8	36,000

TABLE 13.6 Rankings for Tate Company Projects

Cutoff point (IRR < 10%)

the present value for the given budget. *The firm's objective is to use its budget to generate the highest present value of inflows.* Assuming that any unused portion of the budget does not gain or lose money, the total NPV for projects B, C, and E would be $106,000 ($336,000 − $230,000), whereas for projects B, C, and A the total NPV would be $107,000 ($357,000 − $250,000). Selection of projects ▲ B, C, and A will therefore maximize NPV.

? Review Questions

13–12 Explain why a mere comparison of the NPVs of unequal-lived, ongoing, mutually exclusive projects is inappropriate. Describe the *annualized net present value (ANPV)* approach for comparing unequal-lived, mutually exclusive projects.

13–13 What are real options? What are some major types of real options?

13–14 What is the difference between the *strategic* NPV and the *traditional* NPV? Do they always result in the same accept/reject decisions?

13–15 What is *capital rationing?* In theory, should capital rationing exist? Why does it frequently occur in practice?

13–16 Compare and contrast the *internal rate of return approach* and *net present value approach* to capital rationing. Which is better? Why?

SUMMARY

LG1 **Understand the importance of explicitly recognizing risk in the analysis of capital budgeting projects.** Capital budgeting projects can have risk characteristics that are different from the overall firm. These projects must be analyzed in a different manner from projects with the same risk as the firm. Risk refers to the chance that the inputs into the analysis of an investment project will prove to be wrong. The key inputs that are subject to risk are the cash flows and the discount rate. If either of these estimates is incorrect, very costly mistakes can be made. So it is important to incorporate risk considerations in capital budgeting. Various behavioural and quantitative approaches are available for explicitly recognizing risk in the analysis of capital budgeting projects. The acceptance of a project with a level of risk different from the firm impacts the firm's overall risk.

LG2 Discuss breakeven cash flow, sensitivity and scenario analysis, and simulation as behavioural approaches for dealing with risk, and the unique risks facing multinational companies. Risk in capital budgeting is concerned with either the chance that a project will prove unacceptable or, more formally, the degree of variability of cash flows. Finding the breakeven cash inflow and assessing the probability that it will be realized make up one behavioural approach that is used to assess the chance of success. Sensitivity analysis and scenario analysis are also behavioural approaches for dealing with project risk to capture the variability of cash inflows and NPVs. Simulation is a statistically based approach that results in a probability distribution of project returns. It usually requires a computer and allows the decision maker to understand the risk-return tradeoffs involved in a proposed investment. Although the basic capital budgeting techniques are the same for purely domestic and multinational companies, firms that operate in several countries must also deal with both exchange rate and political risks, tax law differences, transfer pricing, and strategic rather than strict financial issues.

LG3 Describe the two basic risk-adjustment techniques in terms of NPV and the procedures for applying the certainty equivalent (CE) approach. The risk of a project whose initial investment is known with certainty is embodied in the present value of its cash inflows, using NPV. The procedure used to calculate this present value provides two opportunities for quantitative risk adjustment: Either the cash inflows or the discount rate can be adjusted for risk. The cash inflow adjustment is called certainty equivalents (CEs) and the discount rate adjustment is called risk-adjusted discount rates (RADRs). CEs are used to adjust the risky cash inflows to certain amounts, which are discounted at a risk-free rate to find the NPV. Although the process of converting risky to certain cash inflows is subjective, the use of CEs is theoretically sound.

LG4 Review the use of risk-adjusted discount rates (RADRs), portfolio effects, and the practical aspects of RADRs relative to CEs. The RADR technique includes a market-based adjustment of the discount rate used to calculate

NPV. The RADR is closely linked to CAPM, but because real corporate assets are generally not traded in an efficient market, the CAPM cannot be applied directly to capital budgeting. Instead, firms develop some CAPM-type of relationship to link a project's risk to its required return, which is used as the discount rate. Often, for convenience, firms will rely on total risk as an approximation for relevant risk when estimating required project returns. RADRs are commonly used in business practice because decision makers prefer rates of return and find them easier to estimate and apply, although CEs are the theoretically superior risk-adjustment technique.

LG5 Recognize the problem caused by unequal-lived mutually exclusive projects and the use of annualized net present values (ANPVs) to resolve it. The problem in comparing unequal-lived mutually exclusive projects is that the projects do not provide service over comparable time periods. The annualized net present value (ANPV) approach is the most efficient method of comparing ongoing mutually exclusive projects having unequal usable lives. It converts the NPVs of unequal-lived projects into an equivalent annual amount—its ANPV—by dividing each project's NPV by the present value interest factor for an annuity at the given cost of capital and project life. The project with the highest ANPV is best.

LG6 Explain the role of real options and the objective of, and basic approaches to, project selection under capital rationing. Real options are opportunities that are embedded in investment projects that allow managers to alter the cash flows and risk in a way that affects a project's NPV. By explicitly recognizing real options, a project's strategic NPV can be calculated. Some of the more common types of real options are abandonment, flexibility, growth, and timing options. The strategic NPV explicitly recognizes the value of real options and thereby improves the quality of the capital budgeting decision. Capital rationing exists when firms have more acceptable independent projects than they can fund. Although, in theory, capital rationing should not exist, in practice it commonly occurs. Its objective is to select from all acceptable projects the group that provides the highest overall net present value and does not require more dollars than are budgeted. The two basic approaches for choosing projects under capital rationing are the internal rate of return approach and the net present value approach. Of these two, the NPV approach better achieves the objective of using the budget to generate the highest present value of inflows.

SELF-TEST PROBLEM   (Solution in Appendix B)

     ST 13–1   **Certainty equivalents and risk-adjusted discount rates**   The CAPM-type relationship linking a risk index to the required return (RADR) and the certainty equivalent factors applicable to CBA Company's mutually exclusive projects A and B follow:

Risk index	Required return (RADR)
0.0 (risk-free rate, R_F)	7.0%
0.2	8.0
0.4	9.0
0.6	10.0
0.8	11.0
1.0	12.0
1.2	13.0
1.4	14.0
1.6	15.0
1.8	16.0
2.0	17.0

	Certainty equivalent factors (α_t)	
Year (t)	Project A	Project B
0	1.00	1.00
1	0.95	0.90
2	0.90	0.85
3	0.90	0.70

The firm is considering two mutually exclusive projects, A and B. Project data are shown in the following table.

	Project A	Project B
Investment cost (*IC*)	$15,000	$20,000
Project life	3 years	3 years
Annual cash inflow (*CF*)	$ 7,000	$10,000
Risk index	0.4	1.8

a. Ignoring any differences in risk and assuming that the firm's cost of capital is 10 percent, calculate the net present value (NPV) of each project.
b. Use NPV to evaluate the projects using *certainty equivalents* to account for risk.
c. Use NPV to evaluate the projects using *risk-adjusted discount rates* to account for risk.
d. Compare, contrast, and explain your findings in **a**, **b**, and **c**.

PROBLEMS

WARM-UP   **13–1**   **Recognizing risk**   Caradine Corp., a media services firm with net income of $3,200,000 last year, is considering several projects.

Project	Initial investment	Details
A	$ 35,000	Replace existing office furnishings.
B	500,000	Purchase digital film-editing equipment for use with several existing accounts.
C	450,000	Develop proposal to bid for a $2,000,000 per year 10-year contract with a potential new client.
D	685,000	Purchase the exclusive rights to market a quality educational television program in syndication to local markets in the United States, a part of the firm's existing business activities.

The media services business is cyclical and highly competitive. The board of directors has asked you, as chief financial officer, to:
a. Evaluate the risk of each proposed project and rank it "low," "medium," or "high."
b. Comment on why you chose each ranking. What makes the project risky?

INTERMEDIATE   **13–2**   **Breakeven cash flows**   Etsitty Arts, Inc., a leading producer of fine cast silver jewellery, is considering the purchase of new casting equipment that will allow it to expand the product line into award plaques. The incremental cost of the equipment is $35,000. The company expects that the equipment will produce steady income throughout its 12-year life.
a. If Etsitty requires a 14 percent return on its investment, what minimum yearly cash inflow would be necessary for the company to go forward with this project?
b. How would the minimum yearly cash inflow change if the company required a 10 percent return on its investment?

INTERMEDIATE   **13–3**   **Breakeven cash inflows and risk**   Pueblo Enterprises is considering investment in either of two mutually exclusive projects, X and Y. Project X requires an initial investment of $30,000; project Y requires $40,000. Each project's cash inflows are 5-year annuities: Project X's inflows are $10,000 per year; project Y's are $15,000. The firm has unlimited funds and, in the absence of risk differences, accepts the project with the highest NPV. The cost of capital is 15 percent.

a. Find the NPV for each project. Are the projects acceptable?
b. Find the *breakeven cash inflow* for each project.
c. The firm has estimated the probabilities of achieving various ranges of cash inflow for the two projects, as shown in the following table. What is the probability that each project will achieve the breakeven cash inflow found in **b**?

Range of cash inflow	Probability of achieving cash inflow in given range	
	Project X	Project Y
$0 to $5,000	0%	5%
$5,000 to $7,500	10	10
$7,500 to $10,000	60	15
$10,000 to $12,500	25	25
$12,500 to $15,000	5	20
$15,000 to $20,000	0	15
Above $20,000	0	10

d. Which project is more risky? Which project has the potentially higher NPV? Discuss the risk-return tradeoffs of the two projects.
e. If the firm wished to minimize the chance of accepting a negative NPV project, which project would you recommend? Which would you recommend if the goal, instead, was achieving the higher NPV?

INTERMEDIATE   **13–4** **Basic sensitivity analysis**   Murdock Paints is in the process of evaluating two mutually exclusive additions to their processing capacity. The firm's financial analysts have developed pessimistic, most likely, and optimistic estimates of the annual cash inflows associated with each project. These estimates are shown in the following table.

	Project A	Project B
Incremental cost (*IC*)	$8,000	$8,000
Outcome	Annual cash inflows (*CF*)	
Pessimistic	$ 200	$ 900
Most likely	1,000	1,000
Optimistic	1,800	1,100

a. Determine the *range* of annual cash inflows for each of the two projects.
b. Assume that the firm's cost of capital is 10 percent and that both projects have 20-year lives. Construct a table similar to that above for the NPVs for each project. Include the *range* of NPVs for each project.
c. Do **a** and **b** provide consistent views of the two projects? Explain.
d. Which project do you recommend? Why?

INTERMEDIATE **13–5** **Sensitivity analysis**   James Secretarial Services is considering the purchase of one of two new personal computers, P and Q. Both are expected to provide benefits over a 10-year period, and each has a required investment of $3,000. The firm uses a 10 percent cost of capital. Management has constructed the following table of estimates of probabilities and annual cash inflows for pessimistic, most likely, and optimistic results.

	Computer P	Computer Q
Initial investment (*II*)	$3,000	$3,000
Outcome	Annual cash inflows (*CF*)	
Pessimistic	$ 500	$ 400
Most likely	750	750
Optimistic	1,000	1,200

    a. Determine the *range* of annual cash inflows for each of the two computers.
    b. Construct a table similar to that above for the NPVs associated with each outcome for both computers.
    c. Find the *range* of NPVs, and subjectively compare the risk of each computer.

INTERMEDIATE **13–6** **Simulation**   Ogden Corporation has compiled the following information on a capital expenditure proposal:
    (1) The projected cash *inflows* are normally distributed with a mean of $36,000 and a standard deviation of $9,000.
    (2) The projected cash *outflows* are normally distributed with a mean of $30,000 and a standard deviation of $6,000.
    (3) The firm has an 11 percent cost of capital.
    (4) The probability distributions of cash inflows and cash outflows are not expected to change over the project's 10-year life.
    a. Describe how the preceding data can be used to develop a simulation model for finding the net present value of the project.
    b. Discuss the advantages of using a simulation to evaluate the proposed project.

INTERMEDIATE **13–7** **Certainty equivalents—Accept–reject decision**   Allison Industries has constructed the following table that gives expected cash inflows and certainty equivalent factors for these cash inflows. These measures are for a new machine with a 5-year life that requires an initial investment of $95,000. The firm has a 15 percent cost of capital, and the risk-free rate is 10 percent.

Year (*t*)	Cash inflows (*CF_t*)	Certainty equivalent factors (α_t)
1	$35,000	1.0
2	35,000	0.8
3	35,000	0.6
4	35,000	0.6
5	35,000	0.2

a. What is the net present value for the machine (unadjusted for risk)?
b. What is the certainty equivalent net present value for the machine?
c. Should the firm accept the project? Explain.
d. Management has some doubts about the estimate of the certainty equivalent factor for year 5. There is some evidence that it may not be any lower than that for year 4. What impact might this have on the decision you recommended in c? Explain.

INTERMEDIATE **13–8** **Certainty equivalents—Mutually exclusive decision**   Kent Manufacturing is considering investing in either of two mutually exclusive projects, C or D. The firm has a 14 percent cost of capital, and the risk-free rate is currently 9 percent. The initial investment, expected cash inflows, and certainty equivalent factors associated with each of the projects are shown in the following table.

	Project C		Project D	
Initial investment (*II*)	$40,000		$56,000	
Year (*t*)	Cash inflows (CF$_t$)	Certainty equivalent factors (α_t)	Cash inflows (CF$_t$)	Certainty equivalent factors (α_t)
1	$20,000	0.90	$20,000	0.95
2	16,000	0.80	25,000	0.90
3	12,000	0.60	15,000	0.85
4	10,000	0.50	20,000	0.80
5	10,000	0.40	10,000	0.80

a. Find the net present value (unadjusted for risk) for each project. Which is preferred using this measure?
b. Find the certainty equivalent net present value for each project. Which is preferred using this risk-adjustment technique?
c. Compare and discuss your findings in a and b. Which, if either, of the projects do you recommend that the firm accept? Explain.

INTERMEDIATE **13–9** **Risk-adjusted discount rates—Basic**   Country Wallpapers is considering investment in one of three mutually exclusive projects, E, F, and G. The firm's cost of capital, k_a, is 15 percent, and the risk-free rate, R_F, is 10 percent. The firm has gathered the following basic cash flow and risk index data for each project.

	Project (*j*)		
	E	F	G
Initial investment (*II*)	$15,000	$11,000	$19,000
Year (*t*)	Cash inflows (CF$_t$)		
1	$ 6,000	$ 6,000	$ 4,000
2	6,000	4,000	6,000
3	6,000	5,000	8,000
4	6,000	2,000	12,000
Risk index (RI$_j$)	1.80	1.00	0.60

a. Find the net present value (NPV) of each project using the firm's cost of capital. Which project is preferred in this situation?
b. The firm uses the following equation to determine the risk-adjusted discount rate, $RADR_j$, for each project j:

$$RADR_j = R_F + [5\% \times RI_j]$$

where

$$R_F = \text{risk-free rate of return}$$
$$RI_j = \text{risk index for project } j$$

Substitute each project's risk index into this equation to determine its RADR.
c. Use the RADR for each project to determine its risk-adjusted NPV. Which project is preferable in this situation?
d. Compare and discuss your findings in **a** and **c**. Which project do you recommend that the firm accept?

13–10 **Integrative—Certainty equivalents and risk-adjusted discount rates**   After a careful evaluation of investment alternatives and opportunities, Masters School Supplies has developed a CAPM-type relationship linking a risk index to the required return (RADR) as shown in the following table.

Risk index	Required return (RADR)
0.0	7.0% (risk-free rate, R_F)
0.2	8.0
0.4	9.0
0.6	10.0
0.8	11.0
1.0	12.0
1.2	13.0
1.4	14.0
1.6	15.0
1.8	16.0
2.0	17.0

The firm is faced with two mutually exclusive projects, A and B. The following are the data the firm has been able to gather about the projects:

	Project A	Project B
Incremental cost (IC)	$20,000	$30,000
Project life	5 years	5 years
Annual cash inflow (CF)	$ 7,000	$10,000
Risk index	0.2	1.4

	Certainty equivalent factors (α_t)	
Year (t)	Project A	Project B
0	1.00	1.00
1	0.95	0.90
2	0.90	0.80
3	0.90	0.70
4	0.85	0.70
Greater than 4	0.80	0.60

All the firm's cash inflows have already been adjusted for taxes.

a. Evaluate the projects using *certainty equivalents*.

b. Evaluate the projects using *risk-adjusted discount rates*.

c. Discuss your findings in **a** and **b**, and explain why the two approaches are alternative techniques for considering risk in capital budgeting.

CHALLENGE 13–11 **Risk-adjusted rates of return vs. certainty equivalents**   Centennial Catering, Inc., is considering two mutually exclusive investments. The company wishes to use two different evaluation methods—certainty equivalents and risk-adjusted rate of return—in its analysis. Centennial's cost of capital is 12 percent and the current risk-free rate of return is 7 percent. Cash flows associated with the two projects are as follows:

	Project X	Project Y
Initial investment	$70,000	$78,000
Year (t)	Cash inflows (CF_t)	
1	$30,000	$22,000
2	30,000	32,000
3	30,000	38,000
4	30,000	46,000

a. Use a certainty equivalent approach to calculate the net present value of each project given the following certainty equivalent factors:

Year	Project X	Project Y
1	0.85	0.95
2	0.90	0.90
3	0.95	0.85
4	0.95	0.80

b. Use a risk-adjusted rate of return approach to calculate the net present value of each project given that Project X has a risk index of 1.20 and Project Y has a risk index of 1.40. Use the following equation to calculate the required project return for each:

$$k_j = R_F + [RI \times (k_a - R_F)]$$

c. Explain why the results of the two approaches may differ from one another. Which project would you choose? Justify your choice.

WARM-UP **13–12 Risk classes and RADR**   Moses Manufacturing is attempting to select the best of three mutually exclusive projects, X, Y, and Z. Though all the projects have 5-year lives, they possess differing degrees of risk. Project X is in Class V, the highest-risk class; project Y is in Class II, the below-average-risk class; and project Z is in Class III, the average-risk class. The basic cash flow data for each project and the risk classes and risk-adjusted discount rates (RADRs) used by the firm are shown in the following tables.

	Project X	Project Y	Project Z
Incremental cost (*IC*)	$180,000	$235,000	$310,000
Year (*t*)	Cash inflows (CF_t)		
1	$80,000	$50,000	$90,000
2	70,000	60,000	90,000
3	60,000	70,000	90,000
4	60,000	80,000	90,000
5	60,000	90,000	90,000

Risk Classes and RADRs

Risk class	Description	Risk-adjusted discount rate (RADR)
I	Lowest risk	10%
II	Below-average risk	13
III	Average risk	15
IV	Above-average risk	19
V	Highest risk	22

a. Find the risk-adjusted NPV for each project.
b. Which, if any, project would you recommend that the firm undertake?

13–13   **Graphing risk, determining equation for the line, calculating NPV**   Preston Lumber has recently calculated the following relationship between the risk index and the required rate of return:

Risk index	Required rate of return
0.0	6%
0.4	8
0.8	10
1.2	12
1.6	14
2.0	16

The firm is evaluating the following mutually exclusive projects which both have four-year lives and require initial investments of $4,000. The annual cash inflows under three operating environments are provided below. All components of the cash inflows are included.

	Project A		Project B	
	Annual cash flows	Probability	Annual cash inflow	Probability
Pessimistic	$-2,000	0.25	$-100	0.20
Most likely	2,000	0.50	1,600	0.50
Optimistic	6,000	0.25	3,000	0.30

a. Graph the relationship between risk and return as suggested by the above data. Be sure to label the axis and indicate the area of risk premium. What is the equation for this line?
b. Calculate the expected cash inflows for both projects.
c. The risk index for project A is 1.4 but only 0.60 for project B. Use the equation determined in **a** to determine the appropriate risk-adjusted discount rate Preston should use to evaluate each project.
d. Which project do you recommend the company select and why?

13–14   **Integrative—Determining NPV**   Mead Computing is considering entering a new line of business: either the SAT or TAT software market. The annual incremental before-tax operating incomes associated with a range of outcomes and the probabilities of the outcomes occurring is presented below:

	SAT		TAT	
Outcome	Incremental operating income	Probability	Incremental operating income	Probability
Optimistic	$24,000	15%	$42,000	10%
Most likely	18,500	60	29,000	70
Pessimistic	11,750	25	3,000	20

Both projects require Mead acquire additional fixed assets. The initial cost for SAT is $42,150 while TAT's initial cost is $56,150. Due to increasing sales, SAT will require Mead invest an additional $12,500 in net working capital while TAT will require an additional $14,000 investment in net working capital. The assets for both projects are class 8 with a CCA rate of 20 percent. The two projects are expected to have five-year lives, when the book value of SAT will be $6,048 while its market value will be $5,000. TAT's book value will be $9,654 while its market value will be $8,000. Mead Computing's tax rate is 40 percent. Based on the risk indexes for the two projects, Mead Company's CFO has determined that the risk-adjusted discount rate for SAT is 13.7 percent and is 16.2 percent for TAT.

a. Calculate the expected operating income for both the SAT and TAT projects.

b. Which project would you recommend the company accept: (i) if the projects were independent; (ii) if the projects were mutually exclusive? Explain the reasons for your answers.

  13–15   **Integrative—Determining NPV**   The Tuna Company is contemplating introducing a new product, Zape, either on a limited scale in New Brunswick or on a broader scale throughout the Maritime provinces. The initial costs of the introductions are $150,000 if Zape is launched only in New Brunswick but $500,000 if a full Maritime provinces launch is undertaken. Both projects qualify for a 10 percent ITC. The assets acquired for the projects are similar and have a CCA rate of 15 percent. Both projects are expected to have productive lives of 15 years. The salvage values are expected to be $43,000 and $122,000 for the New Brunswick and Maritime projects, respectively.

CHALLENGE

The company's management has estimated that the expected incremental before-tax operating income associated with Zape will be $58,000 for the New Brunswick launch but will be $150,000 for the Maritime province wide launch. Both projects will require increased investments in net working capital. For the New Brunswick project it will total $40,000 but a more substantial $125,000 will be required for the Maritime province project. Tuna Company's marginal tax rate is 40 percent. A consultant hired by Tuna Company has suggested that due to different risk profiles, the two projects should be evaluated at different discount rates. The consultant has suggested that 11.5 percent is an appropriate RADR for the New Brunswick launch but due to greater risk, a 13.3 percent RADR should be used for the Maritime province wide launch.

a. Should Zape be introduced? If so, only in New Brunswick or throughout the entire Maritimes?

b. If the SML were used to determine project selection, what additional information is needed? Explain each component.

INTERMEDIATE 13–16   **Unequal lives—ANPV approach**   Evans Industries wishes to select the best of three possible machines, each expected to fulfill the firm's ongoing need for additional aluminum-extrusion capacity. The three machines—A, B, and C—are equally risky. The firm plans to use a 12 percent cost of capital to evaluate each of them. The initial investment and annual cash inflows over the life of each machine are shown in the following table.

	Machine A	Machine B	Machine C
Initial investment (*II*)	$92,000	$65,000	$100,500
Year(*t*)		Cash inflows (*CF*$_t$)	
1	$12,000	$10,000	$ 30,000
2	12,000	20,000	30,000
3	12,000	30,000	30,000
4	12,000	40,000	30,000
5	12,000	—	30,000
6	12,000	—	—

a. Calculate the NPV for each machine over its life. Rank the machines in descending order based on NPV.

b. Use the *annualized net present value (ANPV)* approach to evaluate and rank the machines in descending order based on the ANPV.

c. Compare and contrast your findings in **a** and **b**. Which machine would you recommend that the firm acquire? Why?

INTERMEDIATE **13–17** **Unequal lives—ANPV approach** Portland Products is considering the purchase of one of three mutually exclusive projects for increasing production efficiency. The firm plans to use a 14 percent cost of capital to evaluate these equal-risk projects. The initial investment and annual cash inflows over the life of each project are shown in the following table.

	Project X	Project Y	Project Z
Initial investment (*II*)	$78,000	$52,000	$66,000
Year (*t*)		Cash inflows (*CF*$_t$)	
1	$17,000	$28,000	$15,000
2	25,000	38,000	15,000
3	33,000	—	15,000
4	41,000	—	15,000
5	—	—	15,000
6	—	—	15,000
7	—	—	15,000
8	—	—	15,000

a. Calculate the NPV for each project over its life. Rank the projects in descending order based on NPV.

b. Use the *annualized net present value (ANPV)* approach to evaluate and rank the projects in descending order based on the ANPV.

c. Compare and contrast your findings in **a** and **b**. Which project would you recommend that the firm purchase? Why?

INTERMEDIATE **13–18** **Unequal lives—ANPV approach** JBL Co. has designed a new product sampling system. Management must choose among three alternative courses of action: (1) The firm can sell the design outright to another corporation with payment over 2 years. (2) It can license the design to another manufacturer for a period of 5 years, its likely product life. (3) It can manufacture and market the system itself. The company has a cost of capital of 12 percent. Cash flows associated with each alternative are as follows:

Alternative	Sell	License	Manufacture
Initial investment	$200,000	$200,000	$450,000
Year (t)		Cash inflows (CF_t)	
1	$200,000	$250,000	$200,000
2	250,000	100,000	250,000
3		80,000	200,000
4		60,000	200,000
5		40,000	200,000
6			200,000

a. Calculate the net present value of each alternative and rank the alternatives according to NPV.

b. Calculate the *annualized net present value (ANPV)* of each alternative and rank them accordingly.

c. Why is ANPV preferred over NPV when ranking projects with unequal lives?

INTERMEDIATE **13–19** **Real options and the strategic NPV** Jenny Rene, the CFO of Asor Products, Inc., has just completed an evaluation of a proposed capital expenditure for equipment that would expand the firm's manufacturing capacity. Using the traditional NPV methodology, she found the project unacceptable because

$$\text{NPV}_{\text{traditional}} = -\$1,700 < \$0$$

Before recommending rejection of the proposed project, she has decided to assess whether there might be real options embedded in the firm's cash flows. Her evaluation uncovered the following three options.

Option 1: Abandonment—The project could be abandoned at the end of 3 years, resulting in an addition to NPV of $1,200.

Option 2: Expansion—If the projected outcomes occurred, an opportunity to expand the firm's product offerings further would occur at the end of 4 years. Exercise of this option is estimated to add $3,000 to the project's NPV.

Option 3: Delay—Certain phases of the proposed project could be delayed if market and competitive conditions caused the firm's forecast revenues to develop more slowly than planned. Such a delay in implementation at that point has an NPV of $10,000.

Rene estimated that there was a 25 percent chance that the abandonment option would need to be exercised, a 30 percent chance that the expansion option would be exercised, and only a 10 percent chance that the implementation of certain phases of the project would have to be delayed.

a. Use the information provided to calculate the strategic NPV, $NPV_{strategic}$, for Asor Products' proposed equipment expenditure.

b. Judging on the basis of your findings in part **a**, what action should Rene recommend to management with regard to the proposed equipment expenditures?

c. In general, how does this problem demonstrate the importance of considering real options when making capital budgeting decisions?

INTERMEDIATE **13–20** **Capital rationing—IRR and NPV approaches** Valley Corporation is attempting to select the best of a group of independent projects competing for the firm's fixed capital budget of $4.5 million. The firm recognizes that any unused portion of this budget will earn less than its 15 percent cost of capital, thereby resulting in a present value of inflows that is less than the initial investment. The firm has summarized the key data to be used in selecting the best group of projects in the following table.

Project	Initial investment	IRR	Present value of inflows at 15%
A	$5,000,000	17%	$5,400,000
B	800,000	18	1,100,000
C	2,000,000	19	2,300,000
D	1,500,000	16	1,600,000
E	800,000	22	900,000
F	2,500,000	23	3,000,000
G	1,200,000	20	1,300,000

a. Use the *internal rate of return (IRR) approach* to select the best group of projects.

b. Use the *net present value (NPV) approach* to select the best group of projects.

c. Compare, contrast, and discuss your findings in **a** and **b**.

d. Which projects should the firm implement? Why?

INTERMEDIATE **13–21** **Capital rationing—NPV approach** A firm with a 13 percent cost of capital must select the optimal group of projects from those shown in the following table, given its capital budget of $1 million.

Project	Initial investment	NPV at 13% cost of capital
A	$300,000	$ 84,000
B	200,000	10,000
C	100,000	25,000
D	900,000	90,000
E	500,000	70,000
F	100,000	50,000
G	800,000	160,000

a. Calculate the *present value of cash inflows* associated with each project.
b. Select the optimal group of projects, keeping in mind that unused funds are costly.

| CASE   CHAPTER 13 | Evaluating Cherone Equipment's Risky Plans for Increasing Its Production Capacity |

Cherone Equipment, a manufacturer of electronic fitness equipment, wishes to evaluate two alternative plans for increasing its production capacity to meet the rapidly growing demand for its key product—the Cardiocycle. After months of investigation and analysis, the firm culled the list of alternatives down to the following two plans that would allow it to meet the forecast product demand.

Plan X Use current proven technology to expand the existing plant and semi-automated production line. This plan is viewed as only slightly more risky than the firm's current average level of risk.

Plan Y Install new, just-developed automatic production equipment in the existing plant to replace the current semiautomated production line. Because this plan eliminates the need to expand the plant, it is less expensive than Plan X but is believed to be far more risky due to the unproven nature of the technology.

Cherone, which routinely uses NPV to evaluate capital budgeting projects, has a cost of capital of 12 percent. Currently the risk-free rate of interest, R_F, is 9 percent. The firm decided to evaluate the two plans over a 5-year time period, at the end of which each plan would be liquidated. The before-tax operating income for each of the 5 years for each plan are summarized in the following table:

	Plan X	Plan Y
Incremental cost (*IC*)	$2,700,000	$2,100,000
Year (*t*)	Before-tax operating income	
1	$ 470,000	$ 380,000
2	610,000	700,000
3	950,000	800,000
4	970,000	600,000
5	1,500,000	1,200,000

The CCA rule applicable for each plan is 25 percent. At the end of their 5-year lives, plan A is expected to have a salvage value of $250,000; plan B's salvage value is expected to be $200,000. Cherone's tax rate is 20 percent.

The firm developed additional data that can be used to adjust the two plans for risk. The data, given in the following table, can be used to adjust either the cash inflows using certainty equivalents (CEs) or the discount rate using risk-adjusted discount rates (RADRs). The CEs apply to both the operating income and the salvage value.

	Plan X	Plan Y
Year (t)	Certainty equivalent factors (α_t)	
1	1.00	0.90
2	1.00	0.80
3	0.90	0.80
4	0.90	0.70
5	0.80	0.80
	Risk-adjusted discount rate (RADR)	
	13%	15%

Required

a. Calculate the cash flows for each plan for the first 2 years. Assuming the two plans have the same risk as the firm, calculate the two plans' NPV. What do you recommend Cherone do?

b. Recognizing the differences in plan risk, use the NPV method and each of the following risk-adjustment techniques and the data given earlier to evaluate the acceptability and relative ranking of the two plans.
   (1) Certainty equivalents (CEs).
   (2) Risk-adjusted discount rates (RADRs).

c. Compare and contrast your finding in **a** and **b**. Which plan would you recommend? Did explicit recognition of the risk differences of the plans affect this recommendation?

d. Would your recommendations in **a** and **b** be changed if the firm were operating under capital rationing? Explain.

WEB EXERCISES   LINKS TO PRACTISE

Visit the following Web sites and complete the suggested exercises. These exercises will allow you to review practical applications of the chapter topics as well as explore the wealth of information regarding managerial finance that is available on the Internet.

www.contingencyanalysis.com/_frame/indexfundamentals2.htm
Go to the above Web site which provides an overall discussion of risk, in general. Click on the top link, Risk, and then answer the following questions.

1. How is risk defined, and what are the two components of risk? The Web site provides two examples of risk as defined. Provide another example of risk as defined on the Web site. Do you agree with this definition of risk?

2. Now, scroll down the page and click on Market Risk. Read the definition. What concept relating to the SML does this definition suggest?

3. Now, click on the Capital Asset Pricing Model link and summarize the discussion regarding this model. What are Modern Portfolio Theory, the Capital Market Line, the market portfolio, the risk-free asset, and systematic risk? Why is an understanding of the concept of correlation important for the CAPM?

4. Now click the Back button on your browser and click on the Value at Risk link. What is value at risk (VAR)? How might the concept of VAR be used for capital budgeting decision making?

5. Now go back to the main page and click on Risk Measures. There are nine risk measures discussed in this section. Pick two that you did not discuss above and briefly summarize these measures.

6. Now go back to the main page and click on Risk Intuition. There are seven questions provided. Answer the questions and then consider the results. What can you conclude about your understanding of risk versus the concept of risk as explained by the author of the site? Read the conclusion of the risk intuition quiz. What is enterprise risk management?

7. Return to the main page and again click on Risk Measures. Scroll down the Risk Measures menu in the lower left frame and click on Asset Liability Analysis. Why are statistical risk measures less satisfactory in determining asset risk? Summarize the steps to analyze asset risk.

8. Based on the above work, explain how you would analyze the risk of the following project. The project involves the purchase of automated equipment for a new assembly line. The initial cost of the project is $6,600,000. The expected incremental cash inflows are projected to be the following:

Year 1	$1,280,000
Year 2	$1,640,000
Year 3	$1,820,000
Year 4	$2,030,000
Year 5	$2,450,000

9. For the above project, what types of assumptions would you change to create new cash inflows? Consider various market factors such as timing for the project implementation, inflation, capital costs, and so forth.

www.hbcollege.com/finance/students/capital_bgt_comp.htm
This Web site provides two links. One explains a company's long-term commitment to its capital expenditure program for "maintaining and growing its store base." Review this material and explain how the company incorporates risk in its analysis of investment projects.

The second link provides step-by-step guidelines on both capital budget preparation and analysis. Among the topics presented are: estimating capital expenditures, estimating cash flows, investment analysis tools, using spreadsheets as an analysis aid, and dealing with risk. Read this material to review many of the topics that have been considered in the last two chapters.

GOODTREAD RUBBER COMPANY

Goodtread Rubber Company is a medium-sized tire manufacturer located in southern Ontario, near the hub of the auto-manufacturing industry. The firm's major clients include the big three North American auto producers, but the company also sells to retail stores like Canadian Tire and Wal-Mart. Goodtread Rubber currently has two divisions: The Tire Division manufacturers new tires for the new car market and retailers; the Recap Division manufacturers recapping materials sold to independent tire retreading shops.

Since auto manufacturing moves with the general economy, the Tire Division's earnings are highly correlated with those of other companies. If the Tire Division were operated as a separate company, its beta coefficient would be about 1.60. The sales and profits of the Recap Division, on the other hand, tend to be counter-cyclical: Retread sales boom when people cannot afford to buy new tires. Recap's beta is estimated to be 0.40. Approximately 75 percent of Goodtread's corporate assets are invested in the Tire Division and 25 percent are in the Recap Division.

Goodtread Rubber currently has the opportunity to move away from the tire industry by investing in two separate, independent projects. Both are related to the auto industry, but they do not involve rubber or tires. To make room for the equipment required for the two new projects, Goodtread must remove obsolete equipment from its plant. The company was planning to dispose of this equipment anyway. The current value of the equipment is $75,000 and it will cost the company $20,000 to remove it.

Both of the projects Goodtread is considering will result in sales increasing and additional operating costs being incurred. The pertinent details concerning the two projects have been developed by Goodtread's V.P. of Finance; details are provided below. The estimates are uncertain and both projects are subject to a certain amount of uncertainty. Goodtread Rubber's tax rate is 40 percent.

	Project A	Project B
Incremental sales	$365,000	$590,000
Direct costs (% of sales)	42%	37.5%
Other operating costs	$98,000	$110,500
Required rate of return	14%	18%
Cost of new asset	$415,000	$695,000
Life of project	15 years	20 years
Value of new asset at end of life	$40,000	$30,000
Expected changes in:		
Cash	$30,000	$38,000
Accounts receivable	$90,000	$110,000
Inventory	$130,000	$195,000
Accounts payable	$65,000	$100,000
Grant from government:		
Payable now	$30,000	$35,000
Payable in 1 year's time	$60,000	$70,000
Payable in 2 years' time	$35,000	$45,000
CCA rate	20%	25%
ITC rate	10%	0%

REQUIRED

A. BASED ON THE DATA PROVIDED ABOVE, WHAT IS THE OVERALL BETA OF GOODTREAD RUBBER COMPANY?

b. What discount rate should Goodtread use to evaluate capital budgeting projects? Explain.

c. What would you recommend regarding the two projects? What should Goodtread do? Provide a complete analysis.

d. If the two projects were mutually exclusive, which project should Goodtread invest in? Provide a complete analysis.

PART

6

Working Capital Management

661

14 Working Capital and Management of Current Assets

LEARNING GOALS

LG1 Understand short-term financial management, net working capital, and the related tradeoff between profitability and risk.

LG2 Describe the cash conversion cycle, its funding requirements, and the key strategies for managing it.

LG3 Discuss inventory management: differing views, common techniques, and international concerns.

LG4 Explain the credit selection process and the quantitative procedure for evaluating changes in credit standards.

LG5 Review the procedures for quantitatively considering cash discount changes, other aspects of credit terms, and credit monitoring.

LG6 Understand the management of receipts and disbursements, including float, speeding up collections, slowing payments, cash concentration, zero-balance accounts, and investing in marketable securities.

14.1 Net Working Capital Fundamentals

The firm's balance sheet provides information about the structure of its investments on the one hand and the structure of its financing sources on the other. The structures chosen should consistently lead to the maximization of the value of the owners' investment in the firm.

Important components of the firm's structure include the level of investment in current assets and the use of current liability financing. Figure 14.1 provides a breakdown of the assets and liabilities for non-financial Canadian corporations for 2002. Note that current assets account for 31.7 percent of total assets. Of

Show Me the Money

Managing current assets and
financing the investment in current
assets is a vital task for most businesses. This is particularly the case
for small businesses and for retailers
who have proportionally much larger investments in current assets
than large or manufacturing-oriented businesses. The amount of cash
to hold, accounts receivable policy and management, and decisions
regarding inventory are daily issues for financial managers. So too are
decisions regarding how the investment in these current assets is
financed. Deciding on the mix of financing and short-term financing
are ongoing concerns. Making correct working capital decisions is
vital for a firm to remain solvent and for firm value to increase. But
managing a business's current assets and securing appropriate financing are complex tasks. In this chapter, we look at techniques and
strategies for managing working capital and current assets. We first
discuss the fundamentals of net working capital and then demonstrate
the cash conversion cycle. The balance of the chapter considers the
management of inventory, accounts receivable, and receipts and
disbursements in the context of the cash conversion cycle.

this, accounts receivable are the largest current asset, accounting for 46.1 percent; inventory is next at 37.8 percent; while cash is 16.1 percent of total current assets. Investments, at 13 percent, are a significant component of total
assets. Current liabilities are a surprisingly high portion of total liabilities and
equity. Accounts payable are 16.8 percent of the total and a larger percentage
than long-term debt. Bank loans and short-term paper combined are also larger
than long-term debt. Current liabilities at 13.4 percent of total liabilities and
equity are about the same percentage as current assets. This may be due to the
classification system used in collecting the data. The investments account likely
has a significant amount of short-term items that would increase the current
asset percentage.

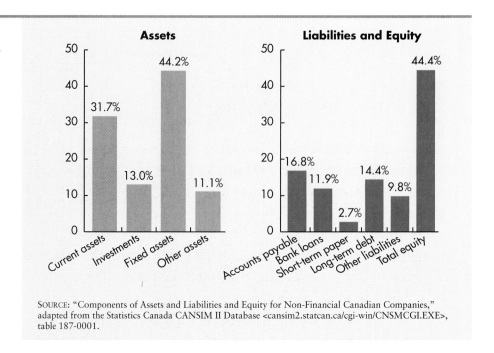

SOURCE: "Components of Assets and Liabilities and Equity for Non-Financial Canadian Companies," adapted from the Statistics Canada CANSIM II Database <cansim2.statcan.ca/cgi-win/CNSMCGI.EXE>, table 187-0001.

FIGURE 14.1

Components of Assets and Liabilities and Equity for Non-financial Canadian Companies

short-term financial management
Management of current assets and current liabilities.

Based on these statistics, it should not be surprising to learn that **short-term financial management**—managing current assets and current liabilities—is one of the financial manager's most important and time-consuming activities. A study of 1,000 companies found that more than one-third of financial management time is spent managing current assets and about one-fourth of financial management time is spent managing current liabilities.[1] This finding is understandable given that decisions in these two areas must be made on a daily basis. In contrast, investment decisions for fixed assets or longer term investments are often made only a few times per year and, while clearly major decisions, likely consume less total time.

The goal of short-term financial management is to manage each of the firm's current assets (inventory, accounts receivable, cash, and marketable securities) and current liabilities (accounts payable, accruals, and short-term loans) to achieve a balance between profitability and risk that contributes positively to the firm's value. Too large an investment in current assets can reduce profitability, whereas too little investment increases liquidity risk: the risk of not being able to repay debts as they come due. Too little current liability financing can reduce profitability, whereas too much increases liquidity risk. These situations generally lead to a reduction in the value of the firm.

For all companies, there is an optimal level of current assets and optimal amount of current liabilities. In reality, as with all things optimal, the difficulty is trying to determine these "ideal" amounts. In the chapter, we first use net working capital to consider the basic relationship between current assets and current liabilities and then use the cash conversion cycle to consider the key aspects of current asset management. In the following chapter, we consider current liability management.

1. Lawrence J. Gitman and Charles E. Maxwell, "Financial Activities of Major U.S. Firms: Survey and Analysis of Fortune's 1000," *Financial Management* (Winter 1985), pp. 57–65.

Net Working Capital

working capital
Current assets, which represent the portion of investment that circulates from one form to another in the ordinary conduct of business.

Current assets, commonly called **working capital,** represent the portion of investment that circulates from one form to another in the ordinary conduct of business. This idea embraces the recurring transition from cash to inventories to receivables and back to cash. As cash substitutes, *marketable securities* are considered part of working capital.

Current liabilities represent the firm's short-term financing, because they include all debts of the firm that come due (must be paid) in 1 year or less. These debts usually include amounts owed to suppliers (accounts payable), employees and governments (accruals), and banks (short-term loans like a line of credit), among others.

net working capital
The difference between the firm's current assets and its current liabilities; can be *positive* or *negative*.

As noted in Chapters 2 and 12, **net working capital** is commonly defined as the difference between the firm's current assets and its current liabilities. When the current assets exceed the current liabilities, the firm has *positive net working capital*. When current assets are less than current liabilities, the firm has *negative net working capital*. The first situation is the more usual one.

The conversion of current assets from inventory to receivables to cash provides the source of cash used to pay the current liabilities. The cash outlays for current liabilities are relatively predictable. When an obligation is incurred, the firm generally knows when the corresponding payment will be due. What is difficult to predict are the cash inflows—the conversion of the current assets to more liquid forms. The more predictable its cash inflows, the less net working capital a firm needs. Because most firms are unable to match cash inflows to outflows with certainty, current assets that more than cover outflows for current liabilities are usually necessary. In general, the greater the margin by which a firm's current assets cover its current liabilities, the better able it will be to pay its bills as they come due.

! Hint
Stated differently, some portion of current assets is usually held to provide liquidity in case it is unexpectedly needed.

The Tradeoff Between Profitability and Risk

profitability
The relationship between revenues and costs generated by using the firm's assets—both current and fixed—in productive activities.

risk (of technical insolvency)
The probability that a firm will be unable to pay its bills as they come due.

technically insolvent
Describes a firm that is unable to pay its bills as they come due.

A tradeoff exists between a firm's profitability and its risk. **Profitability,** in this context, is the relationship between revenues and costs generated by using the firm's assets—both current and fixed—in productive activities. A firm's profits can be increased by (1) increasing revenues or (2) decreasing costs. **Risk,** in the context of short-term financial management, is the probability that a firm will be unable to pay its bills as they come due. A firm that cannot pay its bills as they come due is said to be **technically insolvent.** It is generally assumed that the greater the firm's net working capital, the lower its risk. In other words, the more net working capital, the more liquid the firm and therefore the lower its risk of becoming technically insolvent. Using these definitions of profitability and risk, we can demonstrate the tradeoff between them by considering changes in current assets and current liabilities separately.

Changes in Current Assets

How does changing the level of a firm's current assets affect its risk/return tradeoff? To answer, we will consider the ratio of current assets to total assets. This ratio indicates the *percentage of total assets* that is current. For purposes of illustration, we will assume that the amount of total assets remains

TABLE 14.1 Effects of Changing Ratios on Profits and Risk

Ratio	Change in ratio	Effect on profit	Effect on risk
Current assets / Total assets	Increase	Decrease	Decrease
	Decrease	Increase	Increase
Current liabilities / Total assets	Increase	Increase	Increase
	Decrease	Decrease	Decrease

unchanged.[2] The effects on both (profitability) and risk of an increase or decrease in this ratio are summarized in the upper portion of Table 14.1. When the ratio increases—that is, when current assets increase—profitability decreases. Why? Because current assets are less profitable than fixed assets. Fixed assets are more profitable because they add more value to the product than that provided by current assets. Without fixed assets, the firm could not produce the product.

Risk, however, decreases as the ratio of current assets to total assets increases. The increase in current assets increases net working capital, thereby reducing the risk of technical insolvency. In addition, as you go down the asset side of the balance sheet, the risk associated with the assets increases: Investment in cash and marketable securities is less risky than investment in accounts receivable, inventories, and fixed assets. Accounts receivable investment is less risky than investment in inventories and fixed assets. Investment in inventories is less risky than investment in fixed assets. The nearer an asset is to cash, the less risky it is. The opposite effects on profit and risk result from a decrease in the ratio of current assets to total assets.

Changes in Current Liabilities

Changing the level of a firm's current liabilities also affects its risk/return tradeoff. This can be demonstrated by using the ratio of current liabilities to total assets. This ratio indicates the percentage of total assets that have been financed with current liabilities. Again, assuming that total assets remain unchanged, the effects on both profitability and risk of an increase or decrease in the ratio are summarized in the lower portion of Table 14.1. When the ratio increases, return (profitability) increases. Why? Because the firm uses more of the less expensive current liabilities financing and less long-term financing. Current liabilities are less expensive because only short-term loans have a direct cost. The other current liabilities, especially accounts payable, do not have an interest cost (assuming the company pays them within the credit period). Based on Figure 14.1, the largest component of total current liabilities is no-cost liabilities. However, when the ratio of current liabilities to total assets increases, the risk of technical insolvency also increases, because the increase in current liabilities in turn decreases net working capital. The oppo-

2. In order to isolate the effect of changing asset and financing mixes on the firm's profitability and risk, we assume the level of total assets to be *constant* in this and the following discussion.

Hint It is generally easier to turn receivables into the more liquid asset cash than it is to turn inventory into cash. As we will learn in Chapter 15, the firm can sell its receivables for cash. Inventory has to be sold and then converted to a receivable before it becomes cash.

site effects on profit and risk result from a decrease in the ratio of current liabilities to total assets.

? Review Questions

14–1 Why is *short-term financial management* one of the most important and time-consuming activities of the financial manager? What is *net working capital?*

14–2 What is the relationship between the predictability of a firm's cash inflows and its required level of net working capital? How are net working capital, liquidity, and *risk of technical insolvency* related?

14–3 Why does an increase in the ratio of current to total assets decrease both profits and risk as measured by net working capital? How do changes in the ratio of current liabilities to total assets affect profitability and risk?

14.2 The Cash Conversion Cycle

Central to short-term financial management is an understanding of the firm's cash conversion cycle.[3] This cycle frames discussion of the management of the firm's current assets in this chapter and that of the management of current liabilities in Chapter 15. Here, we begin by demonstrating the calculation and application of the cash conversion cycle.

Calculating the Cash Conversion Cycle

operating cycle (OC)
The time from the beginning of the production process to the collection of cash from the sale of the finished product.

A firm's **operating cycle (OC)** is the time from the beginning of the production process to collection of cash from the sale of the finished product. The operating cycle encompasses two major short-term asset categories: inventory and accounts receivable. It is measured in elapsed time by summing the *average age of inventory (AAI)* and the *average collection period (ACP)*.

$$OC = AAI + ACP \qquad (14.1)$$

Hint
A firm can lower its working capital if it can speed up its operating cycle. For example, if a firm accepts bank credit (like a Visa card), it will receive cash sooner after the sale is transacted than if it has to wait until the customer pays its accounts receivable.

However, the process of producing and selling a product also includes the purchase of production inputs (raw materials) on account, which results in accounts payable. Accounts payable reduce the number of days a firm's resources are tied up in the operating cycle. The time it takes to pay the accounts payable, measured in days, is the *average payment period (APP)*. The operating cycle less the average payment period is referred to as the **cash conversion cycle (CCC)**. It represents the amount of time the firm's resources are tied up. The formula for the cash conversion cycle is

cash conversion cycle (CCC)
The amount of time a firm's resources are tied up; calculated by subtracting the average payment period from the *operating cycle.*

$$CCC = OCC - APP \qquad (14.2)$$

---

3. The conceptual model that is used in this section to demonstrate basic short-term financial management strategies was developed by Lawrence J. Gitman in "Estimating Corporate Liquidity Requirements: A Simplified Approach," *The Financial Review* (1974), pp. 79–88, and refined and operationalized by Lawrence J. Gitman and Kanwal S. Sachdeva in "A Framework for Estimating and Analyzing the Required Working Capital Investment," *Review of Business and Economic Research* (Spring 1982), pp. 35–44.

Substituting the relationship in Equation 14.1 into Equation 14.2, we can see that the cash conversion cycle has three main components, as shown in Equation 14.3: (1) average age of the inventory, (2) average collection period, and (3) average payment period.

$$CCC = AAI + ACP - APP \qquad (14.3)$$

Clearly, if a firm changes any of these time periods, it changes the amount of funds tied up in the day-to-day operation of the firm.

Example ▼ MAX Company, a producer of paper dinnerware, has annual credit sales of $10 million, a cost of goods sold of 75 percent of sales, and purchases that are 65 percent of cost of goods sold. MAX has an average age of inventory (AAI) of 60 days, an average collection period (ACP) of 40 days, and an average payment period (APP) of 35 days. Thus the cash conversion cycle for MAX is 65 days (60 + 40 − 35). Figure 14.2 presents MAX Company's cash conversion cycle as a time line.

The funds MAX has invested in this cash conversion cycle (based on a 365-day year) are:

Inventory = [($10,000,000 × 0.75) ÷ 365] × 60 days	=	$1,232,877
+ Accounts receivable = ($10,000,000 ÷ 365) × 40 days	=	+$1,095,890
− Accounts payable = [($10,000,000 × 0.75 × 0.65) ÷ 365] × 35 days	=	−$ 467,466
Net funds invested in inventory and receivables		$1,861,301

Note that the basic process used to calculate these amounts is based on the ratios used to calculate AAI, ACP, and APP that were discussed in Chapter 3. Total inventory is based on daily inventory times AAI. Accounts receivable are based on daily credit sales times ACP. Accounts payable are based on daily credit purchases times APP.

FIGURE 14.2

Time Line for MAX Company's Cash Conversion Cycle

MAX Company's operating cycle is 100 days, and its cash conversion cycle is 65 days

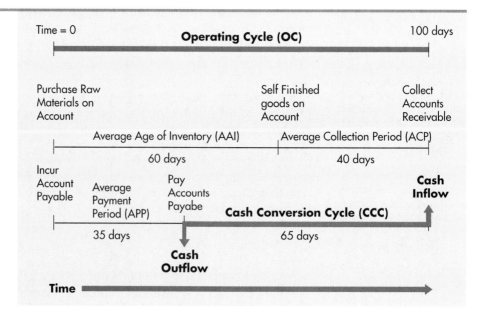

Changes in any of the time periods will change the resources tied up in operations. For example, if MAX could reduce the average collection period on its accounts receivable by 5 days, it would shorten the cash conversion time line and thus reduce the amount of resources MAX has invested in operations. For MAX, a 5-day reduction in the average collection period would reduce the resources invested in the cash conversion cycle by $136,986 [($10,000,000 ÷ 365) × 5]. ▲

Funding Requirements of the Cash Conversion Cycle

operating assets
The difference between the four principal current assets (cash, marketable securities, accounts receivable, and inventory) and accounts payable.

We can use the cash conversion cycle as a basis for discussing how the firm funds its required investment in net current assets. Net current assets are termed operating assets. **Operating assets** are the difference between the four principal current assets (cash, marketable securities, accounts receivable, and inventory) and accounts payable. We first differentiate between permanent and seasonal funding needs and then describe aggressive and conservative seasonal funding strategies.

Permanent Versus Seasonal Funding Needs

permanent funding requirement
A constant investment in operating assets resulting from constant sales over time.

seasonal funding requirement
An investment in operating assets that varies over time as a result of cyclical sales.

If the firm's sales are constant, then its investment in operating assets should also be constant, and the firm will have only a **permanent funding requirement**. If the firm's sales are cyclical, then its investment in operating assets will vary over time with its sales cycles, and the firm will have **seasonal funding requirements** in addition to the permanent funding required for its minimum investment in operating assets.

Example ▼ Nicholson Company holds, on average, $50,000 in cash and marketable securities, $1,250,000 in inventory, and $750,000 in accounts receivable. Nicholson's business is very stable over time, so its current assets can be viewed as permanent. In addition, Nicholson's accounts payable of $425,000 are stable over time. Thus Nicholson has a permanent investment in operating assets of $1,625,000 ($50,000 + $1,250,000 + $750,000 − $425,000). That amount would also equal its permanent funding requirement.

In contrast, Semper Pump Company, which produces bicycle pumps, has seasonal funding needs. Semper has seasonal sales, with its peak sales driven by the summertime purchases of bicycle pumps. Semper holds, at minimum, $25,000 in cash and marketable securities, $100,000 in inventory, and $60,000 in accounts receivable. At peak times, Semper's inventory increases to $750,000, and its accounts receivable increase to $400,000. To capture production efficiencies, Semper produces pumps at a constant rate throughout the year. Thus accounts payable remain at $50,000 throughout the year.

Accordingly, Semper has a permanent funding requirement for its minimum level of operating assets of $135,000 ($25,000 + $100,000 + $60,000 − $50,000) and peak seasonal funding requirements (in excess of its permanent need) of $990,000 [($25,000 + $750,000 + $400,000 − $50,000) − $135,000]. Semper's total funding requirements for operating assets vary from a minimum of $135,000 (permanent) to a seasonal peak of $1,125,000 ($135,000 + $990,000). Figure 14.3 depicts these needs over time. ▲

IN PRACTICE

Current Asset Management: Good for the Heart

Medtronic, a medical technology company, manufactures products to treat patients with heart, vascular, and neurological conditions; diabetes; and Parkinson's disease. The company developed the first implantable heart pacemaker. In October 1999, the company had a strong balance sheet and cash position, but treasurer Gary Ellis was concerned to see the average collection period climbing to 88 days. He moved quickly to regain control of the company's operating cycle, the time from the beginning of the firm's production process to collection of cash from the sale of the finished product. By July 2001, the average collection period was down to 74 days.

Medtronic takes a multi-pronged approach to accounts receivable (A/R) and inventory management. Sales representatives use Palm Pilots to send sales information to headquarters and to receive A/R and inventory data. Such timely communications have helped the company avoid incorrect billing, which had contributed to the buildup of receivables. The sales force has a vested interest in seeing that customers pay their bills and in keeping inventory low: 20 to 30 percent of the sales team's bonus payments are based on A/R and inventory levels.

Because Medtronic generates about 35 percent of total revenue outside North America, the company also has to contend with international receivables, which can take almost twice as long to collect as domestic receivables. In many of the countries in which the company operates, hospital customers are government-run, so the A/R quality and payment period vary from country to country. "In the countries where the average collection period is longer, we tend to have higher prices," says Ellis.

Controlling inventory has been more difficult. Hospitals keep a large supply of different Medtronic products on hand, holding them on consignment and paying as items are used. The company's goal is to get inventory turnover from the current 1.3 to at least 2.0 by changing customer attitudes. "We have to convince hospital staff that they will get the product on a timely basis," Ellis says. If this occurs, the average age of inventory will fall by almost 100 days, from 281 to 183 days.

Ellis also discovered that Medtronic itself was paying bills too promptly. Medtronic subsequently sought and received, from its vendors, longer payment terms and discounts for early payment. The company invests the extra cash generated by more efficient management of its current assets and accounts payable in marketable securities, thereby generating a return on funds that were once invested in current assets.

SOURCES: Susan Kelly, "The Heartbeat of Medtronic," *Treasury & Risk Management*, September 2001, available at **www.treasuryandrisk.com**; "Medtronic at a Glance," **www.medtronic.com**.

Aggressive versus Conservative Seasonal Funding Strategies

aggressive funding strategy
A funding strategy under which the firm funds its seasonal requirements with short-term debt and its permanent requirements with long-term debt.

Short-term funds are typically less expensive than long-term funds. As discussed in Chapter 8, the yield curve is typically upward-sloping. However, long-term funds allow the firm to lock in its cost of funds over a period of time and thus avoid the risk of increases in short-term interest rates. Also, long-term funding ensures that the required funds are available to the firm when needed. Short-term funding exposes the firm to the risk that it may not be able to obtain the funds needed to cover its seasonal peaks. Under an **aggressive funding strategy**, the firm funds its seasonal requirements with short-term debt and its permanent require-

Semper Pump Company's Total Funding Requirements
Semper Pump Company's peak funds need is $1,125,000, and its minimum need is $135,000

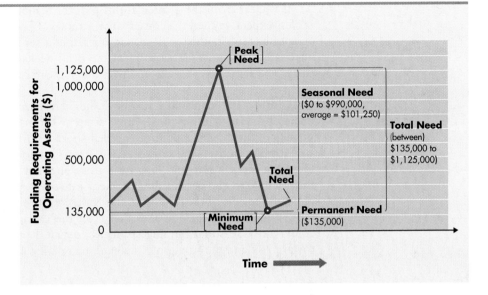

conservative funding strategy
A funding strategy under which the firm funds both its seasonal and its permanent requirements with long-term debt.

ments with long-term debt. Under a **conservative funding strategy**, the firm funds both its seasonal and its permanent requirements with long-term debt.

E x a m p l e ▼   Semper Pump Company has a permanent funding requirement of $135,000 in operating assets and seasonal funding requirements that vary between $0 and $990,000 and average $101,250. If Semper can borrow short-term funds at 6.25 percent and long-term funds at 8 percent, and if it can earn 5 percent on the investment of any surplus balances, then the annual cost of an aggressive strategy for seasonal funding will be

Cost of short-term financing	$= 0.0625 \times \$101,250 =$	$ 6,328.13
+ Cost of long-term financing	$= 0.0800 \times 135,000 =$	10,800.00
− Earnings on surplus balances[4]	$= 0.0500 \times 0 =$	0
Total cost of aggressive strategy		$17,128.13

Alternatively, Semper can choose a conservative strategy, under which surplus cash balances are fully invested. (In Figure 14.3, this surplus will be the difference between the peak need of $1,125,000 and the total need, which varies between $135,000 and $1,125,000 during the year.) The cost of the conservative strategy will be

Cost of short-term financing	$= 0.0625 \times \$ 0 =$	$0
+ Cost of long-term financing	$= 0.0800 \times 1,125,000 =$	90,000.00
− Earnings on surplus balances[5]	$= 0.0500 \times 888,750 =$	44,437.50
Total cost of conservative strategy		$45,562.50

---

4. Because under this strategy the amount of financing exactly equals the estimated funding need, no surplus balances exist.

5. The average surplus balance would be calculated by subtracting the sum of the permanent need ($135,000) and the average seasonal need ($101,250) from the seasonal peak need ($1,125,000) to get $888,750 ($1,125,000 − $135,000 − $101,250). This represents the surplus amount of financing that on average could be invested in short-term vehicles that earn a 5 percent annual return.

▲ It is clear from these calculations that for Semper, the aggressive strategy is far less expensive than the conservative strategy. However, it is equally clear that Semper has substantial peak-season operating-asset needs and that it must have adequate funding available to meet the peak needs and ensure ongoing operations. The aggressive strategy involves much greater liquidity risk.

Clearly, the aggressive strategy's heavy reliance on short-term financing makes it riskier than the conservative strategy because of interest rate swings and possible difficulties in obtaining needed short-term financing quickly when seasonal peaks occur. The conservative strategy avoids these risks through the locked-in interest rate and long-term financing, but it is more costly because of the negative spread between the earnings rate on surplus funds (5% in the example) and the cost of the long-term funds that create the surplus (8% in the example). Where the firm operates, between the extremes of the aggressive and conservative seasonal funding strategies, depends on management's disposition toward risk and the strength of its banking relationships.

Strategies for Managing the Cash Conversion Cycle

A positive cash conversion cycle, as we saw for MAX Company in the earlier example, means the firm must use short-term loans (such as bank loans) to support its operating assets. Loans carry an explicit cost, so the firm benefits by minimizing their use in supporting operating assets. Minimizing the dollar amount of costly short-term financing should be a financial goal for the firm. This goal can be achieved by implementing each of the following operating strategies:

1. *Turn over inventory as quickly as possible* without stockouts that result in lost sales (minimize AAI).
2. *Collect accounts receivable as quickly as possible* without losing sales from high-pressure collection techniques (minimize ACP).
3. *Pay accounts payable as slowly as possible* without damaging the firm's credit rating (maximize APP).
4. *Manage float*, the time it takes to handle and deposit payments, so that it is minimized for payments received from customers but maximized for payments made to suppliers.

Techniques for implementing these four strategies are the focus of the remainder of this chapter and the following chapter.

❓ Review Question

14–4   What is the difference between the firm's *operating cycle* and its *cash conversion cycle*?

14–5   Why is it helpful to divide the funding needs of a seasonal business into its permanent and seasonal funding requirements when developing a funding strategy?

14–6   What are the benefits, costs, and risks of an *aggressive funding strategy* and of a *conservative funding strategy*? Under which strategy is the borrowing often in excess of the actual need?

14–7   Why is it important for a firm to minimize the length of its cash conversion cycle? What strategies can a firm follow to minimize the CCC?

14.3 Inventory Management

The first component of the cash conversion cycle is the average age of inventory. The objective for managing inventory, as noted above, is to turn over inventory as quickly as possible without losing sales from stockouts. The financial manager tends to act as an advisor or "watchdog" in matters concerning inventory; he or she does not have direct control over inventory but does provide input to the inventory management process.

Differing Viewpoints About Inventory Level

Differing viewpoints about appropriate inventory levels commonly exist among a firm's finance, marketing, manufacturing, and purchasing managers. Each views inventory levels in light of his or her own objectives. The *financial manager's* general disposition toward inventory levels is to keep them low, to ensure that the firm's money is not being unwisely invested in excess resources. The *marketing manager*, on the other hand, would like to have large inventories of the firm's finished products. This would ensure that all orders could be filled quickly, eliminating the need for back orders due to stockouts.

The *manufacturing manager's* major responsibility is to implement the production plan so that it results in the desired amount of finished goods of acceptable quality at a low cost. In fulfilling this role, the manufacturing manager would keep raw materials inventories high to avoid production delays. He or she also would favour large production runs for the sake of lower unit production costs, which would result in high finished goods inventories.

The purchasing manager is concerned solely with the raw materials inventories. He or she must have on hand, in the correct quantities at the desired times and at a favourable price, whatever raw materials are required by production. Without proper control, in order to get quantity discounts or in anticipation of rising prices or a shortage of certain materials, the purchasing manager may purchase large quantities of resources than are actually needed at the time.

Common Techniques for Managing Inventory

Numerous techniques are available for effectively managing the firm's inventory. Here we briefly consider four commonly used techniques.

The ABC System

ABC inventory system
Inventory management technique that divides inventory into three groups—A, B, and C—in descending order of importance and level of monitoring, on the basis of the dollar investment in each.

A firm using the **ABC inventory system** divides its inventory into three groups: A, B, and C. This system is based on the 20/80 concept that seems to apply to many multi-product firms. This concept suggests that 20 percent of the firm's products account for 80 percent of the firm's sales, and therefore 80 percent of the investment in inventory. The products within this 20 percent are classified as A items and are actively managed. The B group consists of items that account for the next largest investment in inventory. The C group consists of a large number of items that require a relatively small investment.

The inventory group of each item determines the item's level of monitoring. The A group items receive the most intense monitoring because of the high dollar investment. Typically, A group items are tracked on a perpetual inventory system that allows daily verification of each item's inventory level. B group items are frequently controlled through periodic, perhaps weekly, checking of their levels. C group items are monitored with unsophisticated techniques, such as the **two-bin method**. With the two-bin method, the item is stored in two bins. As an item is needed, inventory is removed from the first bin. When that bin is empty, an order is placed to refill the first bin while inventory is drawn from the second bin. The second bin is used until empty, and so on.

The large dollar investment in A and B group items suggests the need for a better method of inventory management than the ABC system. The EOQ model, discussed next, is an appropriate model for the management of A and B group items.

two-bin method
Unsophisticated inventory-monitoring technique that is typically applied to C group items and involves reordering inventory when one of two bins is empty.

The Economic Order Quantity (EOQ) Model

One of the most common techniques for determining the optimal order size for inventory items is the **economic order quantity (EOQ) model**. The EOQ model considers various costs of inventory and then determines what order size minimizes total inventory cost.

EOQ assumes that the relevant costs of inventory can be divided into *order costs* and *carrying costs*. (The model excludes the actual cost of the inventory item.) Each of them has certain key components and characteristics. **Order costs** include the fixed costs of placing and receiving orders: the cost of writing a purchase order, of processing the resulting paperwork, of receiving an order and checking it against the invoice, and handling the inventory. Order costs are stated in dollars per order. **Carrying costs** are the variable costs per unit of holding an item of inventory for a specific period of time. Carrying costs include storage costs, insurance costs, the costs of deterioration and obsolescence, and the opportunity or financial cost of having funds invested in inventory. These costs are stated in dollars per unit per period.

Order costs decrease as the size of the order increases. Carrying costs, however, increase with increases in the order size. The EOQ model analyzes the tradeoff between order costs and carrying costs to determine the *order quantity that minimizes the total inventory cost*.

economic order quantity (EOQ) model
Inventory management technique for determining an item's optimal order size, which is the size that minimizes the total of its *order costs* and *carrying costs*.

order costs
The fixed costs of placing, receiving, and handling an inventory order.

carrying costs
The variable costs per unit of holding an item in inventory for a specific period of time.

Mathematical Development of EOQ A formula can be developed for determining the firm's EOQ for a given inventory item, where

S = usage in units per period
O = order cost per order
C = carrying cost per unit per period
Q = order quantity in units

The first step is to derive the cost functions order cost and carrying cost. The order cost can be expressed as the product of the cost per order and the number of orders. Because the number of orders equals the usage during the period divided by the order quantity (S/Q), the order cost can be expressed as follows:

$$\text{Order cost} = O \times S/Q \tag{14.4}$$

The carrying cost is defined as the cost of carrying a unit per period multiplied by the firm's average inventory. The average inventory is the order quantity divided by 2 ($Q/2$), because inventory is assumed to be depleted at a constant rate. Thus carrying cost can be expressed as follows:

$$\text{Carrying cost} = C \times Q/2 \tag{14.5}$$

total cost of inventory
The sum of order costs and carrying costs of inventory.

The firm's **total cost of inventory** is found by summing the order cost and the carrying cost. Thus the total cost function is

$$\text{Total cost} = (O \times S/Q) + (C \times Q/2) \tag{14.6}$$

Because the EOQ is defined as the order quantity that minimizes the total cost function, we must solve the total cost function for the EOQ. The resulting equation is

$$\text{EOQ} = \sqrt{\frac{2 \times S \times O}{C}} \tag{14.7}$$

⚠ Hint
The EOQ calculation helps management minimize the total cost of inventory. Lowering order costs will cause an increase in carrying costs and may increase total cost. Likewise, a decrease in total cost may result from reduced carrying costs. The goal, facilitated by using the EOQ calculation, is to lower total cost.

Although the EOQ model has weaknesses, it is certainly better than subjective decision making. Despite the fact that the use of the EOQ model is outside the control of the financial manager, the financial manager must be aware of its utility and must provide certain inputs, specifically with respect to inventory carrying costs.

reorder point
The point at which to reorder inventory, expressed as days of lead time × daily usage.

Reorder Point   Once the firm has determined its economic order quantity, it must determine when to place an order. The **reorder point** reflects the firm's daily usage of the inventory item and the number of days needed to place and receive an order. Assuming that inventory is used at a constant rate, the formula for the reorder point is

$$\text{Reorder point} = \text{days of lead time} \times \text{daily usage} \tag{14.8}$$

For example, if a firm knows that it takes 3 days to place and receive an order, and if it uses 15 units per day of the inventory item, then the reorder point is 45 units of inventory (3 days × 15 units/day). Thus, as soon as the item's inventory level falls to the reorder point (45 units, in this case), an order will be placed at the item's EOQ. If the estimates of lead time and daily usage are correct, then the order will arrive exactly as the inventory level reaches zero. However, lead times and usage rates are not precise, so most firms hold **safety stock** (extra inventory) to prevent stockouts of important items.

safety stock
Extra inventory that is held to prevent stockouts of important items.

Example ▼ MAX Company has an A group inventory item that is vital to the production process. This item costs $1,500, and MAX uses 1,100 units of the item per year. MAX wants to determine its optimal order strategy for the item. To calculate the EOQ, we need the following inputs:

$$\text{Order cost per order} = \$150$$
$$\text{Carrying cost per unit per year} = \$200$$

Substituting into Equation 14.7, we get

$$\text{EOQ} = \sqrt{\frac{2 \times 1{,}100 \times \$150}{\$200}} \simeq \underline{\underline{41}} \text{ units}$$

The reorder point for MAX depends on the number of days MAX operates per year. Assuming that MAX operates 250 days per year and uses 1,100 units of this item, its daily usage is 4.4 units (1,100 − 250). If its lead time is 2 days and MAX wants to maintain a safety stock of 4 units, the reorder point for this item is 12.8 units [(2 × 4.4) + 4]. However, orders are made only in whole units, so the order is placed when the inventory falls to 13 units.

The firm's goal for inventory is to turn it over as quickly as possible without stockouts. Inventory turnover is best calculated by dividing cost of goods sold by average inventory. The EOQ model determines the optimal order size and, indirectly, through the assumption of constant usage, the average inventory. Thus the EOQ model determines the firm's optimal inventory turnover rate, given the firm's specific costs of inventory.

Just-in-Time (JIT) System

just-in-time (JIT) system
Inventory management technique that minimizes inventory investment by having materials arrive at exactly the time they are needed for production.

The **just-in-time (JIT) system** is used to minimize inventory investment. The philosophy is that materials should arrive at exactly the time they are needed for production. Ideally, the firm would have only work-in-process inventory. Because its objective is to minimize inventory investment, a JIT system uses no (or very little) safety stock. Extensive coordination among the firm's employees, its suppliers, and shipping companies must exist to ensure that material inputs arrive on time. Failure of materials to arrive on time results in a shutdown of the production line until the materials arrive. Likewise, a JIT system requires high-quality parts from suppliers. When quality problems arise, production must be stopped until the problems are resolved.

The goal of the JIT system is manufacturing efficiency. It uses inventory as a tool for attaining efficiency by emphasizing quality of the materials used and their timely delivery. When JIT is working properly, it forces process inefficiencies to surface.

Materials Requirement Planning (MRP) System

materials requirement planning (MRP) system
Inventory management technique that applies EOQ concepts and a computer to compare production needs to available inventory balances and determine when orders should be placed for various items on a product's *bill of materials*.

Many companies use a **materials requirement planning (MRP) system** to determine what materials to order and when to order them. MRP applies EOQ concepts to determine how much to order. By means of a computer, it simulates each product's bill of materials, inventory status, and manufacturing process. The *bill of materials* is simply a list of all the parts and materials that go into making the finished product. For a given production plan, the computer simulates materials requirements by comparing production needs to available inventory balances. On the basis of the time it takes for a product that is in process to move through the various production stages and the lead time required to get materials, the MRP system determines when orders should be placed for the various items on the bill of materials.

The advantage of the MRP system is that it forces the firm to consider its inventory needs more carefully. The objective is to lower the firm's inventory investment without impairing production. If the firm's opportunity cost of capital for investments of equal risk is 15 percent, every dollar of investment released from inventory increases before-tax profits by $0.15.

International Inventory Management

International inventory management is typically much more complicated for exporters in general, and for multinational companies in particular, than for purely domestic companies. The production and manufacturing economies of scale that might be expected from selling products globally may prove elusive if products must be tailored for individual local markets, as very frequently happens, or if actual production of goods takes place in factories around the world. When raw materials, intermediate goods, or finished products must be transported long distances—particularly by ocean shipping—there will inevitably be more delays, confusion, damage, theft, and other difficulties to overcome than occur in a one-country operation. The international inventory manager therefore puts a premium on flexibility. He or she is usually less concerned about ordering the economically optimal quantity of inventory than about making sure that sufficient quantities of inventory are delivered where they are needed, when they are needed, and in a condition to be used as planned.

? Review Questions

14–8   What are likely to be the viewpoints of each of the following managers about the levels of the various types of inventory: finance, marketing, manufacturing, and purchasing? Why is inventory an investment?

14–9   Briefly describe each of the following techniques for managing inventory: ABC system, economic order quantity (EOQ) model, just-in-time (JIT) system, and materials requirement planning (MRP) system.

14–10   What factors make managing inventory more difficult for exporters and multinational companies?

14.4 Accounts Receivable Management

The second component of the cash conversion cycle is the average collection period. This period is the average length of time from a sale on credit until the payment becomes usable funds for the firm. The average collection period has two parts. The first part is the time from the sale until the customer mails the payment. The second part is the time from when the payment is mailed until the firm has the collected funds in its bank account. The first part of the average collection period involves managing the credit available to the firm's customers, and the second part involves collecting and processing payments. This section of the chapter discusses the firm's accounts receivable credit management.

The objective for managing accounts receivable is to collect accounts receivable as quickly as possible without losing sales from high-pressure collection techniques. Accomplishing this goal encompasses three topics: (1) credit selection and standards, (2) credit terms, and (3) credit monitoring.

Hint
Some small businesses resolve these problems by selling their accounts receivable to a third party at a discount. Though expensive, this strategy overcomes the problem of not having adequate personnel. It also creates a buffer between the small business and those customers who need a little prodding to stay current.

Credit Selection and Standards

Credit selection involves application of techniques for determining which customers should receive credit. This process involves evaluating the customer's creditworthiness and comparing it to the firm's **credit standards**, its minimum requirements for extending credit to a customer.

credit standards
The firm's minimum requirements for extending credit to a customer.

The Four C's of Credit

four C's of credit
The four key dimensions—character, capacity, capital, and conditions—used by credit analysts to provide a framework for in-depth credit analysis.

One popular credit selection technique is the **four C's of credit**, which provides a framework for the in-depth credit analysis. Because of the time and expense involved, this credit selection method is used for large-dollar credit requests. The four C's are

1. *Character:* The applicant's record of meeting past obligations.
2. *Capacity:* The applicant's ability to repay the requested credit, as judged in terms of financial statement analysis focused on cash flows available to repay debt obligations.
3. *Capital:* The applicant's total assets and net worth (value of common equity). The greater the assets, the more potential security that exists for the credit. Also, growing assets suggests a growing, successful business. High net worth indicates past financial success and a commitment by the shareholders to the company. Net worth can provide a cushion for creditors in times of economic downturns.
4. *Conditions:* Current general and industry-specific economic conditions, and any unique conditions surrounding a specific transaction.

Analysis via the four C's of credit does not yield a specific accept/reject decision, so its use requires an analyst experienced in reviewing and granting credit requests. Application of this framework tends to ensure that the firm's credit customers will pay, without being pressured, within the stated credit terms.

⚠ Hint
Computers are widely used to aid in the credit decision process. Data on each customer's payment patterns are maintained and can be called forth to evaluate requests for renewed or additional credit.

Evaluating Credit Applicants

While the four C's of credit is a good framework for analyzing credit applications, information to base the analysis on is required. One potential source of the information is the applicant. As part of the application process, a company may require that the applicant complete forms providing financial and credit information and references. The application process may also request that the credit applicant provide financial statements for the past few years. They will allow the company to analyze a potential customer's financial position using ratio analysis. The key ratios to focus on for short-term trade credit are liquidity and activity ratios.

A potential problem with this approach to gathering information is that some applicants may not wish to give their financial statements to a supplier. Obviously, very sensitive data is provided in the statements and many managers would not want to divulge this information to suppliers. In this case, a second source of information is required. One such source is D&B (the old Dun & Bradstreet). D&B has developed an extensive database of financial and rating information on thousands of Canadian companies. D&B provides numerous types of reports that allow businesses to assess and manage the risk of doing business with a customer. The key report that D&B provides is "D&B Industry Norms and Key Business Ratios." This report was discussed in Chapter 3.

A second report for analyzing risk is the "D&B Business Information Report." This report provides basic company and historical information, financial information, the company's payment history, and two important ratings. The first rating is the D&B Composite Credit Rating (e.g., 4A3) which gives an indication of creditworthiness. The D&B Rating is divided into two parts. The financial strength code (4A) indicates the amount of the subject's tangible net worth (i.e., the shareholder's funds less any intangible assets). The second number (3) reflects the company's level of risk and is an overall evaluation of creditworthiness. Table 14.2 provides a rating scale for the D&B Composite Credit Rating. For more detail see the following Web sites: **www.dnb.ca/products/businforep.html** and **www.dnb.ca/ram/keys.html**.

The second rating is the D&B Paydex, which gives an overview of how quickly a company has been paying its bills compared to the credit terms offered. An industry Paydex is also provided, when available, so the company can be compared to other companies in its industry. Table 14.2 also provides a rating scale for the Paydex score. Samples of a variety of reports provided by D&B are available at the following Web sites—click on the See a Sample link: **www.dnb.ca/products/businforep.html**, **www.dnb.ca/products/paymentpro.html**, and **www.dnb.ca/products/credcheck.html**.

There is a wealth of information available concerning potential credit customers. To avoid making credit-granting mistakes, it is important companies access as much information as necessary so bad decisions are not made. The amount of information to collect is based on the potential size of the account. The higher the sales that may be made to a potential customer, the greater the cost of a credit-granting mistake, and therefore the more detailed the information that should be collected and analyzed.

Credit Scoring

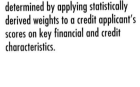

credit scoring
A credit selection method commonly used with high-volume/small-dollar credit requests; relies on a credit score determined by applying statistically derived weights to a credit applicant's scores on key financial and credit characteristics.

Credit scoring is a method of credit selection that is commonly used with high-volume/small-dollar credit requests. It applies statistically derived weights for key financial and credit characteristics to predict whether a credit applicant will pay the requested credit in a timely fashion. Simply stated, the procedure results in a score that measures the applicant's overall credit strength, and the score is used to make the accept/reject decision for granting the applicant credit. Credit scoring is most commonly used by large credit card operations, such as those of banks, oil companies, and department stores. The purpose of credit scoring is to make a relatively informed credit decision quickly and inexpensively, recognizing that the cost of a single bad scoring decision is small. However, if bad debts from scoring decisions increase, then the scoring system must be re-evaluated. For a demonstration of credit scoring, including use of a spreadsheet for that purpose, see the book's Web site at **www.pearsoned.ca/gitman**.

Changing Credit Standards

The firm sometimes will contemplate changing its credit standards in order to improve its returns and create greater value of its owners. To demonstrate,

TABLE 14.2 D&B Credit Rating Scale

Part A: Key to D&B composite credit rating

Estimated financial strength[a]	Composite credit appraisal[b]			
	High	Good	Fair	Limited
5A: $50,000,000 and over	1	2	3	4
4A: $10,000,000 to $49,999,999	1	2	3	4
3A: $1,000,000 to $9,999,999	1	2	3	4
2A: $750,000 to $999,999	1	2	3	4
1A: $500,000 to $749,999	1	2	3	4
BA: $300,000 to $499,999	1	2	3	4
BB: $200,000 to $299,999	1	2	3	4
CB: $125,000 to $199,999	1	2	3	4
CC: $75,000 to $124,999	1	2	3	4
DC: $50,000 to $74,999	1	2	3	4
DD: $35,000 to $49,999	1	2	3	4
EE: $20,000 to $34,999	1	2	3	4
FF: $10,000 to $19,999	1	2	3	4
GG: $5,000 to $9,999	1	2	3	4
HH: up to $4,999	1	2	3	4

[a]The estimated financial strength is based on tangible net worth.

[b]The credit appraisal is based on payment history, the company's financial position, history management, and other general quantitative and qualitative factors.

Part B: Key to Paydex score[a]

Score	Payment[b]
100	Anticipate
90	Discount
80	Prompt
70	Slow to 15
60	Slow to 22
50	Slow to 30
40	Slow to 60
30	Slow to 90
20	Slow to 120
UN	Unavailable

[a]The score is based on the combined individual payment experience of a business, indicating its current payment situation. The higher the score, the more timely the payment history.

[b]*Anticipate* means the customer paid before the invoice was received. *Discount* means the customer paid within the discount period. *Prompt* means the customer paid within the credit terms. *Slow* means the customer paid within the stated number of days after the credit period.

SOURCE: D&B; see www.dnb.ca/ram/keys.html.

⚠ Hint

Relaxing the credit standards and/or credit terms will increase the risk of the firm, but it may also increase the return to the firm. Bad debts and the average collection period will both increase with more lenient credit standards and/or credit terms, but the increased revenue may produce profits that exceed these costs.

consider the following changes and effects on profits expected to result from the *relaxation* of credit standards.

Effects of Relaxation of Credit Standards		
Variable	Direction of change	Effect on profits
Sales volume	Increase	Positive
Investment in accounts receivable	Increase	Negative
Bad debt expenses	Increase	Negative

If credit standards were tightened, the opposite effects would be expected.

Example ▼ Dodd Tool, a manufacturer of lathe tools, is currently selling a product for $10 per unit. Sales (all on credit) for last year were 60,000 units. The variable cost per unit is $6. The firm's total fixed costs are $120,000.

The firm is currently contemplating a *relaxation of credit standards* that is expected to result in the following: a 5 percent increase in unit sales to 63,000 units; an increase in the average collection period from 30 days (its current level) to 45 days; an increase in bad-debt expenses from 1 percent of sales (the current level) to 2 percent. The firm's required return on equal-risk investments (the firm's cost of capital), which is the opportunity cost of tying up funds in accounts receivable, is 15 percent.

To determine whether to relax its credit standards, Dodd Tool must calculate the effect on the firm's additional profit contribution from sales, the cost of the marginal investment in accounts receivable, and the cost of marginal bad debts.

Additional Profit Contribution from Sales   Because fixed costs are "sunk" and thereby unaffected by a change in the sales level, the only cost relevant to a change in sales is variable costs. Sales are expected to increase by 5 percent, or 3,000 units. The profit contribution per unit will equal the difference between the sale price per unit ($10) and the variable cost per unit ($6). The profit contribution per unit therefore will be $4. The total additional profit contribution from sales will be $12,000 (3,000 units × $4 per unit).

Cost of the Marginal Investment in Accounts Receivable   To determine the cost of the marginal investment in accounts receivable, Dodd must find the difference between the cost of carrying receivables under the two credit standards. Because its concern is only with the out-of-pocket costs, *the relevant cost is the variable cost*. The average investment in accounts receivable can be calculated by using the following formula:

$$\text{Average investment in accounts receivable} = \frac{\text{total variable cost of annual sales}}{365 \text{ days}} \times \text{ACP (in days)} \qquad (14.9)$$

The total variable cost of annual sales under the present and proposed plans can be found as follows, using the variable cost per unit of $6:

Total variable cost of annual sales:

Under present plan: ($6 × 60,000 units) = $360,000
Under proposed plan: ($6 × 63,000 units) = $378,000

By substituting the cost and average collection period (ACP) data into Equation 14.9 for each case, we get the following average investments in accounts receivable:

Average investment in accounts receivable:

$$\text{Under present plan: } \frac{\$360,000}{365 \text{ days}} \times 30 \text{ days} = \$29,589$$

$$\text{Under proposed plan: } \frac{\$378,000}{365 \text{ days}} \times 45 \text{ days} = \$46,603$$

The marginal investment in accounts receivable and its cost are calculated as follows:

Cost of marginal investment in accounts receivable:

Average investment under proposed plan	$46,603
− Average investment under present plan	29,589
Marginal investment in accounts receivable	$17,014
× Required return on investment	0.15
Cost of marginal investment in A/R	$ 2,552

The resulting value of $2,552 is considered a cost because it represents the maximum amount that could have been earned on the $17,014 had it been placed in the best equal-risk investment alternative available at the firm's required return on investment of 15 percent.

Cost of Marginal Bad Debts   The cost of marginal bad debts is found by taking the difference between the level of bad debts before and after the proposed relaxation of credit standards.

Cost of marginal bad debts:

Under proposed plan:	(0.02 × $10/unit × 63,000 units) =	$12,600
Under present plan:	(0.01 × $10/unit × 60,000 units) =	6,000
Cost of marginal bad debts		$ 6,600

Note that the bad-debt costs are calculated by using the sale price per unit ($10) to deduct not just the true loss of variable cost ($6) that results when a customer fails to pay its account, but also the profit contribution per unit (in this case $4) that is included in the "additional profit contribution from sales." Thus, the resulting cost of marginal bad debts is $6,600.

Making the Credit Standard Decision   To decide whether to relax its credit standards, the firm must compare the additional profit contribution from sales to the added costs of the marginal investment in accounts receivable and marginal bad debts. If the additional profit contribution is greater than marginal costs, credit standards should be relaxed.

Example ▼ The results and key calculations relating to Dodd Tool's decision whether to relax its credit standards are summarized in Table 14.3. The net addition to total profits resulting from such an action will be $2,848 per year. Therefore, the firm ▲ *should* relax its credit standards as proposed.

The procedures described here for evaluating a proposed change in credit standards is also commonly used to evaluate other changes in the management of accounts receivable. If Dodd Tool had been contemplating tightening its credit standards, for example, the cost would have been a reduction in the profit contribution from sales, and the return would have been from reductions in the cost of the investment in accounts receivable and in the cost of bad debts. Another application of this procedure is demonstrated later in the chapter.

Managing International Credit

Credit management is difficult enough for managers of purely domestic companies, and these tasks become much more complex for companies that operate internationally. This is partly because (as we have seen before) international operations typically expose a firm to *exchange rate risk*. It is also due to the dangers and delays involved in shipping goods long distances and in having to cross at least two international borders.

Exports of finished goods are usually priced in the currency of the importer's local market; most commodities, on the other hand, are priced in U.S. dollars. Therefore, a Canadian company that sells a product in Japan, for example, would have to price that product in Japanese yen and extend credit to a Japanese wholesaler in the local currency (yen). If the yen depreciates against the dollar before the Canadian exporter collects on its accounts receivable, the Canadian company experiences an exchange rate loss; the yen collected are worth fewer

TABLE 14.3 **The Effects on Dodd Tool of a Relaxation of Credit Standards**		
Additional profit contribution from sales		
[3,000 units × ($10 − $6)]		$12,000
Cost of marginal investment in A/R[a]		
Average investment under proposed plan:		
$\dfrac{\$378,000}{365} \times 45$	$46,603	
Average investment under present plan:		
$\dfrac{\$360,000}{365} \times 30$	29,589	
Marginal investment in A/R	$17,014	
Cost of marginal investment in A/R (0.15 × $17,014)		($ 2,552)
Cost of marginal bad debts		
Bad debts under proposed plan (0.02 × $10 × 63,000)	$12,600	
Bad debts under present plan (0.01 × $10 × 60,000)	6,000	
Cost of marginal bad debts		($ 6,600)
Net profit from implementation of proposed plan		$ 2,848

[a]The numerators in the calculation of the average investment in accounts receivable under the proposed and present plans are the total variable costs of annual sales for each of these plans.

dollars than expected at the time the sale was made. Of course, the dollar could just as easily depreciate against the yen, yielding an exchange rate gain to the Canadian exporter. Most companies fear the loss more than they welcome the gain. This issue is discussed more fully in Chapter 17.

For a major currency such as the Japanese yen, the exporter can *hedge* against this risk by using the currency futures, forwards, or options markets, but it is costly to do so, particularly for relatively small amounts. If the exporter is selling to a customer in a developing country, there will probably be no effective instrument available for protecting against exchange rate risk at any price. This risk may be further magnified because credit standards may be much lower (and acceptable collection techniques much different) in developing countries than in North America.

Although it may seem tempting just "not to bother" with exporting, especially for smaller companies, Canada is a trading country and cannot concede export markets to foreign competitors. In 2002, Canadian businesses exported over $400 billion of products to about 200 countries. Exports accounted for 43 percent of Canada's gross domestic product (GDP) versus only 26 percent in 1990. In terms of the percentage of GDP, Canada exports about four times as much as the United States or Japan and is, by far, the biggest exporter in the G7. Canadian companies are active participants in export markets, particularly to the United States. These export sales, if carefully monitored and (where possible) effectively hedged against exchange rate risk, often prove to be very profitable.

This is especially the case where sales are made to the United States, priced in U.S. dollars. It is often the case that U.S. sales are sold at the same price as Canadian sales, but quoted in U.S. dollars. For example, a supplier may quote a Canadian customer a price of $10 per unit. This would be in Canadian dollars. A U.S. customer would receive the same $10 quote, but in this case, it would be in U.S. dollars. Given that a U.S. dollar has been worth, on average, about $1.50 Canadian over the past decade, U.S. sales in U.S. dollars are usually much more profitable for Canadian exporters than are equivalent Canadian sales.

Credit Terms

credit terms
The terms of sale for customers who have been extended credit by the firm.

cash discount
A percentage deduction from the purchase price; available to the credit customer who pays its account within a specified time.

Credit terms are the terms of sale for customers who have been extended credit by the firm. Terms of *net 30* mean the customer has 30 days from the beginning of the credit period (typically *end of month* or *date of invoice*) to pay the full invoice amount. Some firms offer **cash discounts**, percentage deductions from the purchase price for paying within a specified time. For example, terms of *2/10 net 30* mean the customer can take a 2 percent discount from the invoice amount if the payment is made within 10 days of the beginning of the credit period or can pay the full amount of the invoice within 30 days.

A firm's regular credit terms are strongly influenced by the firm's business. For example, a firm selling perishable items will have very short credit terms, because its items have little long-term collateral value; a firm in a seasonal business may tailor its terms to fit the industry cycles. A firm wants its regular credit terms to conform to its industry's standards. If its terms are more restrictive than its competitors', it will lose business; if its terms are less restrictive than its competitors', it will attract poor-quality customers that probably could not pay under the standard industry terms. The bottom line is that a firm should compete on the basis of quality and price of its product and service offerings, not its credit terms. Accordingly, the firm's regular credit terms should match the industry standards, but individual customer terms should reflect the riskiness of the customer.

Cash Discount

Including a cash discount in the credit terms is a popular way to achieve the goal of speeding up collections without putting pressure on customers. The cash discount provides an incentive for customers to pay sooner. By speeding collections, the discount decreases the firm's investment in accounts receivable (which is the objective), but it also decreases the per-unit profit. Additionally, initiating a cash discount should reduce bad debts because customers who take the discount pay the account. The discount should also increase sales volume because customers who take the discount pay a lower price for the product. Accordingly, firms that consider offering a cash discount must perform a benefit–cost analysis to determine whether extending a cash discount is profitable.

Example ▼ MAX Company has an average collection period of 40 days. In accordance with the firm's credit terms of net 30, this period is divided into 32 days until the customers place their payments in the mail (not everyone pays within 30 days) and 8 days to receive, process, and collect payments once they are mailed. MAX is considering initiating a cash discount by changing its credit terms from net 30 to 2/10 net 30. The firm expects this change to reduce the amount of time until the payments are placed in the mail, resulting in an average collection period of 25 days.

As noted earlier in the EOQ example, MAX has a raw material with current annual usage of 1,100 units. Each finished product produced requires 1 unit of this raw material at a variable cost of $1,500 per unit, incurs another $800 of variable cost in the production process, and sells for $3,000 on terms of net 30. MAX estimates that 80 percent of its customers will take the 2 percent discount and that offering the discount will increase sales of the finished product by 50 units (from 1,100 to 1,150 units) per year but will not alter its bad-debt percentage. MAX's opportunity cost of funds invested in accounts receivable is 14 percent. Should MAX offer the proposed cash discount?

An analysis similar to that demonstrated earlier for the credit standard decision, presented in Table 14.4, shows a net loss from the cash discount of $6,747. Thus MAX *should not initiate the proposed cash discount*. However, other discounts may be advantageous. ▲

Cash Discount Period

cash discount period
The number of days after the beginning of the credit period during which the cash discount is available.

The **cash discount period**, the number of days after the beginning of the credit period during which the cash discount is available, can be changed by the financial manager. The net effect of changes in this period is difficult to analyze because of the nature of the forces involved. For example, if a firm were to increase its cash discount period by 10 days (e.g., changing its credit terms from 2/10 net 30 to 2/20 net 30), the following changes would be expected to occur: (1) Sales would increase, positively affecting profit. (2) Bad-debt expenses would

TABLE 14.4   Analysis of Initiating a Cash Discount for MAX Company

Additional profit contribution from sales		
[50 units × ($3,000 − $2,300)]		$35,000
Cost of marginal investment in A/R[a]		
Average investment presently (without discount):		
$\dfrac{\$2,300 \times 1,100 \text{ days}}{365} \times 40 = \dfrac{\$2,530,000}{365} \times 40$	$277,260	
Average investment with proposed cash discount:[b]		
$\dfrac{\$2,300 \times 1,150 \text{ days}}{365} \times 25 = \dfrac{\$2,645,000}{365} \times 25$	181,164	
Reduction in accounts receivable investment	$96,096	
Cost savings from reduced investments in accounts receivable (0.14 × $96,096)[c]		$13,453
Cost of cash discount (0.02 × 0.80 × 1,150 × $3,000)		($55,200)
Net cost from initiation of proposed cash discount		($ 6,747)

[a]In analyzing the investment in accounts receivable, we use the variable cost of the product sold ($1,500 raw materials cost + $800 production cost = $2,300 unit variable cost) instead of the sale price, because the variable cost is a better indicator of the firm's investment.

[b]The average investment in accounts receivable with the proposed cash discount is estimated to be tied up for an average of 25 days instead of the 40 days under the original terms.

[c]MAX's opportunity cost of funds is 14 percent.

decrease, positively affecting profit. (3) The net profit per unit would decrease as a result of more people taking the discount, negatively affecting profit. The difficulty for the financial manager lies in assessing what impact an increase in the cash discount period would have on the firm's investment in accounts receivable. This investment will decrease because of non–discount takers now paying earlier. However, the investment in accounts receivable will increase for two reasons: (1) Discount takers will still get the discount but will pay later and (2) new customers attracted by the new policy will result in new accounts receivable. If the firm were to decrease the cash discount period, the effects would be the opposite of those just described.

Credit Period

credit period
The number of days after the beginning of the credit period until full payment of the account is due.

Changes in the **credit period**, the number of days after the beginning of the credit period until full payment of the account is due, also affect a firm's profitability. For example, increasing a firm's credit period from net 30 days to net 45 days should increase sales, positively affecting profit. But both the investment in accounts receivable and bad-debt expenses would also increase, negatively affecting profit. The increased investment in accounts receivable would result from both more sales and generally slower payment, on average, as a result of the longer credit period. The increase in bad-debt expenses results from the fact that the longer the credit period, the more time available for a firm to fail, making it unable to pay its accounts payable. A decrease in the length of the credit period is likely to have the opposite effects. Note that the variables affected by an increase in the credit period behave in the same way they would have if the credit period standards had been relaxed, as demonstrated earlier in Table 14.3.

Credit Monitoring

credit monitoring
The ongoing review of a firm's accounts receivable to determine whether customers are paying according to the stated credit terms.

The final issue a firm should consider in its accounts receivable management is credit monitoring. **Credit monitoring** is an ongoing review of the firm's accounts receivable to determine whether customers are paying according to the stated credit terms. If they are not paying in a timely manner, credit monitoring will alert the firm to the problem. Slow payments are costly to a firm because they lengthen the average collection period and thus increase a firm's investment in accounts receivable. Two frequently cited techniques for credit monitoring are average collection period and aging of accounts receivable. In addition, a number of popular collection techniques are used by firms.

Average Collection Period

The *average collection period* is the second component of the cash conversion cycle. As noted in Chapter 3, it is the average number of days that credit sales are outstanding. The average collection period has two components: (1) the time from sale until the customer places the payment in the mail and (2) the time to receive, process, and collect the payment once it has been mailed by the customer. The formula for finding the average collection period is

$$\text{Average collection period} = \frac{\text{accounts receivable}}{\text{average credit sales per day}} \qquad (14.10)$$

Assuming receipt, processing, and collection time is constant, the average collection period tells the firm, on average, when its customers pay their accounts.

Knowing its average collection period enables the firm to determine whether there is a general problem with accounts receivable. For example, a firm that has credit terms of net 30 would expect its average collection period (minus receipt, processing, and collection time) to equal about 30 days. If the actual collection period is significantly greater than 30 days, the firm has reason to review its credit operations. If the firm's average collection period is increasing over time, it has cause for concern about its accounts receivable management. A first step in analyzing an accounts receivable problem is to "age" the accounts receivable. By this process the firm can determine whether the problem exists in its accounts receivable in general or is attributable to a few specific accounts.

Aging of Accounts Receivable

aging of accounts receivable
A credit-monitoring technique that uses a schedule that indicates the percentages of the total accounts receivable balance that have been outstanding for specified periods of time.

The **aging of accounts receivable** requires the firm's accounts receivable to be broken down into groups on the basis of the time of origin. The breakdown is typically made on a month-to-month basis, going back 3 or 4 months. The result is a schedule that indicates the percentages of the total accounts receivable balance that have been outstanding for specified periods of time. Its purpose is to enable the firm to pinpoint problems.

If a firm with terms of net 30 has an average collection period (minus receipt, processing, and collection time) of 50 days, the firm will want to age its accounts receivable. If the majority of accounts are 2 months old, then the firm has a general problem and should review its accounts receivable operations. If the aging shows that most accounts are collected in about 35 days and a few accounts are way past due, then the firm should analyze and pursue collection of those specified past-due accounts.

Example ▼ Assume that O'Hare Tools extends credit terms of 30 days to its customers. The firm's December 31, 2002, balance sheet shows $200,000 of accounts receivable. An evaluation of those accounts receivable results in the following breakdown:

Days	Current	0–30	31–60	61–90	Over 90	
Month	December	November	October	September	August	Total
Accounts receivable	$60,000	$40,000	$66,000	$26,000	$8,000	$200,000
Percentage of total	30	20	33	13	4	100

Because O'Hare Tools gives its customers 30 days after the sale is made to pay off their accounts, any December receivables that are still on the firm's books are considered current. All of these sales are within the credit terms. November receivables are between zero and 30 days overdue, October receivables still unpaid are 31 to 60 days overdue, and so on.

The table shows that 30 percent of the firm's receivables are current, 20 percent are 1 month late, 33 percent are 2 months late, 13 percent are 3 months late, and 4 percent are more than 3 months late. Although payment seems generally slow, a noticeable irregularity in these data is the high percentage represented by October receivables. This indicates that some problem may have occurred in October. Investigation may find that the problem can be attributed to the hiring of a new credit manager, the acceptance of a new account that has made a large credit purchase it has not yet paid for, or ineffective collection policy. When such
▲ a discrepancy is found, the analyst should determine its cause.

O⊸ Career Key

Accounting personnel will do the aging of receivables. They will also be helpful in making the determination of whether or not the credit standards of the firm should be changed.

Popular Collection Techniques

A number of collection techniques, ranging from letters to legal action, are employed. As an account becomes more and more overdue, the collection effort becomes more personal and more intense. In Table 14.5 the popular collection techniques are listed, and briefly described, in the order typically followed in the collection process.

? Review Questions

14–11 What is the role of the *four C's of credit* in the credit selection activity? How does a firm evaluate a company based on the four C's? What are the usual sources of the required information?

14–12 Explain why *credit scoring* is typically applied to consumer credit decisions rather than to mercantile credit decisions.

TABLE 14.5   **Popular Collection Techniques**

Technique[a]	Brief description
Letters	After a certain number of days, the firm sends a polite letter reminding the customer of the overdue account. If the account is not paid within a certain period after this letter has been sent, a second, more demanding letter is sent.
Telephone calls	If letters prove unsuccessful, a telephone call may be made to the customer to request immediate payment. If the customer has a reasonable excuse, arrangements may be made to extend the payment period. A call from the seller's attorney may be used.
Personal visits	This technique is much more common at the consumer credit level, but it may also be effectively employed by industrial suppliers. Sending a local salesperson or a collection person to confront the customer can be very effective. Payment may be made on the spot.
Collection agencies	A firm can turn uncollectible accounts over to a collection agency or an attorney for collection. The fees for this service are typically quite high; the firm may receive less than 50 cents on the dollar from accounts collected in this way.
Legal action	Legal action is the most stringent step, an alternative to the use of a collection agency. Not only is direct legal action expensive, but it may force the debtor into bankruptcy without guaranteeing the ultimate receipt of the overdue amount.

[a]Techniques are listed in the order in which they are typically followed in the collection process.

14–13 What are the basic tradeoffs in a *tightening* of credit standards?

14–14 Why are the risks involved in international credit management more complex than those associated with purely domestic credit sales?

14–15 Why do a firm's regular credit terms typically conform to those of its industry?

14–16 Why should a firm actively monitor the accounts receivable of its credit customers? How do the techniques of *average collection period* and *aging of accounts receivable* work?

14.5 Management of Receipts and Disbursements

⚠ Hint
The financial manager of a small business must have a very strong relationship with a commercial banker. Because the small firm cannot afford to hire someone strictly as a manager of receipts and disbursements, the financial manager, who is probably a generalist, needs to rely on the expertise of the commercial banker for the firm's most cost-effective means of managing cash.

As discussed in the previous section, the average collection period (the second component of the cash conversion cycle) has two parts: (1) the time from sale until the customer mails the payment and (2) the receipt, processing, and collection time. The third component of the cash conversion cycle, the average payment period, also has two parts: (1) the time from purchase of goods on account until the firm mails its payment and (2) the receipt, processing, and collection time required by the firm's suppliers. The receipt, processing, and collection time for the firm, both from its customers and to its suppliers, is the focus of receipts and disbursements management.

Float

float
Funds that have been sent by the payer but are not yet usable funds to the payee.

Float refers to funds that have been sent by the payer but are not yet usable funds to the payee. Float is important in the cash conversion cycle because its presence lengthens both the firm's average collection period and its average payment period. However, the goal of the firm should be to shorten its average collection period and lengthen its average payment period. Both can be accomplished by managing float.

Float has three component parts:

mail float
The time delay between when payment is placed in the mail and when it is received.

1. **Mail float** is the time delay between when payment is placed in the mail and when it is received.
2. **Processing float** is the time between receipt of the payment and its deposit into the firm's account.
3. **Clearing float** is the time between deposit of the payment and when spendable funds become available to the firm. This component of float is attributable to the time required for a cheque to clear the banking system.

processing float
The time between receipt of a payment and its deposit into the firm's account.

clearing float
The time between deposit of a payment and when spendable funds become available to the firm.

Some popular techniques for managing the component parts of float to speed up collections and slow down payments are described below.[6]

Speeding Up Collections

Speeding up collections reduces customer collection float time and thus reduces the firm's average collection period, which reduces the investment the firm must make in its cash conversion cycle. In our earlier examples, MAX Company had annual sales of $10 million and 8 days of total collection float (receipt, processing, and collection time). If MAX can reduce its float time to 5 days, it will reduce its investment in the cash conversion cycle by $82,192 ([$10,000,000 ÷ 365 days] × 3 days).

⚠ Hint
One method of accelerating the collection of accounts receivable is to let someone else do the financing for you, such as by using bank credit cards or selling accounts receivable to a third party at a discount. Another method is to change the credit terms: increase the cash discount and shorten the required payment period.

A popular technique for speeding up collection is a lockbox system. A **lockbox system** works as follows: Instead of mailing payments to the company, customers mail payments to a post office box. The firm's bank empties the post office box regularly, processes each payment, and deposits the payments in the firm's account. Deposit slips, along with payment enclosures, are sent (or transmitted electronically) to the firm by the bank so that the firm can properly credit customers' accounts. Lockboxes are geographically dispersed to match the location of the firm's customers. A lockbox system affects all three components of float. Lockboxes reduce mail time and often clearing time by being near the firm's customers. Lockboxes reduce processing time to nearly zero because the bank deposits payments before the firm processes them. Obviously a lockbox system reduces collection float time, but not without a cost; therefore, a firm must perform an economic analysis to determine whether to implement a lockbox system.

lockbox system
A collection procedure in which customers mail payments to a post office box that is emptied regularly by the firm's bank, which processes the payments and deposits them in the firm's account. This system speeds up collection time by reducing processing time as well as mail and clearing time.

Lockbox systems are commonly used by large firms whose customers are geographically dispersed. However, a firm does not have to be large to benefit from a lockbox. Smaller firms can also benefit from a lockbox system. The bene-

---

6. Float, the delay in processing payments, is slowly becoming a thing of the past for many companies. As electronic banking becomes more common among companies, payments are now being made through electronic connections between banks and companies. Now, at the click of a mouse, funds are transferred from the bank account of the paying company and deposited to the bank account of the payee. Float is reduced to nanoseconds!

fit to small firms often comes primarily from transferring the processing of paymetns to the bank.

Slowing Down Payments

Float is also a component of the firm's average payment period. In this case, the float is in the favour of the firm. The firm may benefit by increasing all three of the components of its *payment float*. One popular technique for increasing payment float is **controlled disbursing**, which involves the strategic use of mailing points and bank accounts to lengthen mail float and clearing float, respectively. This approach should be used carefully, though, because longer payment periods may strain supplier relations.

In summary, a reasonable overall policy for float management is (1) to collect payments as quickly as possible, because once the payment is in the mail, the funds belong to the firm, and (2) to delay making payment to suppliers, because once the payment is mailed, the funds belong to the supplier.

Cash Concentration

Cash concentration is the process used by the firm to bring lockbox and other deposits together into one bank, often called the *concentration bank*. Cash concentration has three main advantages. First, it creates a large pool of funds for use in making short-term cash investments. Because there is a fixed-cost component in the transaction cost associated with such investments, investing a single pool of funds reduces the firm's transaction costs. The larger investment pool also allows the firm to choose from a greater variety of short-term investment vehicles. Second, concentrating the firm's cash in one account improves the tracking and internal control of the firm's cash. Third, having one concentration bank enables the firm to implement payment strategies that reduce idle cash balances.

There is a variety of mechanisms for transferring cash from the lockbox bank and other collecting banks to the concentration bank. One mechanism is a **depository transfer cheque (DTC)**, which is an unsigned cheque drawn on one of the firm's bank accounts and deposited in another. For cash concentration, a DTC is drawn on each lockbox or other collecting bank account and deposited in the concentration bank account. Once the DTC has cleared the bank on which it is drawn (which may take several days), the transfer of funds is completed. Most firms currently provide deposit information by telephone to the concentration bank, which then prepares and deposits into its account the DTC drawn on the lockbox or other collecting bank account.

A second mechanism is an **ACH (automated clearinghouse) transfer**, which is a preauthorized electronic withdrawal from the payer's account. A computerized clearing facility (called the *automated clearinghouse*, or *ACH*) makes a paperless transfer of funds between the payer and payee banks. An ACH settles accounts among participating banks. Individual accounts are settled by respective bank balance adjustments. ACH transfers clear in one day. For cash concentrations, an ACH transfer is made from each lockbox or other collecting bank to the concentration bank. An ACH transfer can be thought of as an electronic DTC, but because the ACH transfer clears in one day, it provides benefits over a DTC; however, both banks in the ACH transfer must be members of the clearinghouse.

---

controlled disbursing
The strategic use of mailing points and bank accounts to lengthen mail float and clearing float, respectively.

⚡ Hint
Data on clearing time among banks located in various cities can be developed by the firm itself. It also can be obtained from a major bank's cash management service department or purchased from a firm that sells such information.

cash concentration
The process used by the firm to bring lockbox and other deposits together into one bank, often called the *concentration bank*.

depository transfer cheque (DTC)
An unsigned cheque drawn on one of a firm's bank accounts and deposited in another.

ACH (automated clearinghouse) transfer
Preauthorized electronic withdrawal from the payer's account and deposit into the payee's account via a settlement among banks by the *automated clearinghouse*, or *ACH*.

wire transfer
An electronic communication that, via bookkeeping entries, removes funds from the payer's bank and deposits them in the payee's bank.

A third cash concentration mechanism is a **wire transfer**. A wire transfer is an electronic communication that, via bookkeeping entries, removes funds from the payer's bank and deposits them in the payee's bank. Wire transfers can eliminate mail and clearing float and may reduce processing float as well. For cash concentration, the firm moves funds using a wire transfer from each lockbox or other collecting account to its concentration account. Wire transfers are a substitute for DTC and ACH transfers, but they are more expensive.

It is clear that the firm must balance the costs and benefits of concentrating cash to determine the type and timing of transfers from its lockbox and other

IN PRACTICE

Using the Net to Reduce Working Capital Requirements

Dell Computer has long been recognized for its pioneering supply chain and e-commerce strategies. The direct-to-customer PC company knows how to use technology to manage all aspects of its business, from back-office systems to online ordering. By integrating its various systems, the company continues to provide quality products at low costs, as well as excellent customer service. Its customer relationship management software knows which computers its customers order. Feeding those data to the production planning systems tells manufacturing what components it needs to fill the orders, and supply chain programs send parts forecasts to vendors. Dell requires key suppliers to be linked over the Web so that the process moves forward automatically, keeping Dell's costs, receivables, and inventories very low. As well, the company actively manages their payables to delay payment as long as possible, thereby generating financing for the company.

This was not always the case. For the fiscal year ended February 1, 1996, Dell's average age of inventory (AAI) was 31 days, their average collection period (ACP) was 42 days, and their average payment period (CAPP) was 33 days, meaning the company's cash conversion cycle (CCC) was 40 days. As a result, cash was required to finance the net investment in current assets. For 1996, this amounted to $195 million. While this would be considered very good in some industries, for a leading edge technology company it

was much too high. So Dell's CFO made liquidity re-engineering a company-wide priority. Over six years, the results have been impressive.

For the fiscal year ended February 1, 2002, the company AAI is down to a lean 4 days, the ACP is 29 days, and the APP is 69 days. Dell's CCC is now a *negative* 36 days. In other words, Dell's suppliers not only finance the company's investments in current assets, but also generate surplus financing for the company. For the 2002 fiscal year, this excess cash amounted to an impressive $824 million. As a result, Dell holds huge cash balances; for the 2002 fiscal year, the company held almost $8.3 billion of cash. With these funds, Dell invested in highly liquid, secure marketable securities of various maturities. As such, they have a highly structured investment program that seeks to maximize returns while minimizing risk.

Supply chain software is becoming essential for most companies. It brings together and automates a company's order taking, purchasing, inventory management, and payment processes. A well-designed system shortens product cycle times by helping to anticipate demand, finding suppliers to provide materials on time, and identifying the least costly delivery method and routing.

SOURCES: Dell, various annual reports, available at **www.dell.com**; Brian Milligan, "Supply Chain Software Moves to the Web," *Purchasing*, April 6, 2000.

collecting accounts to its concentration account. The transfer mechanism selected should be the one that is most profitable. (The profit per period of any transfer mechanism equals earnings on the increased availability of funds minus the cost of the transfer system.)

Zero-Balance Accounts

zero-balance account (ZBA)
A disbursement account that always has an end-of-day balance of zero because the firm deposits money to cover cheques drawn on the account only as they are presented for payment each day.

Zero-balance accounts (ZBAs) are disbursement accounts that always have an end-of-day balance of zero. The purpose is to eliminate nonearning cash balances in corporate chequing accounts. A ZBA works well as a disbursement account under a cash concentration system.

ZBAs work as follows: Once all of a given day's cheques are presented for payment from the firm's ZBA, the bank notifies the firm of the total amount of cheques, and the firm transfers funds into the account to cover the amount of that day's cheques. This leaves an end-of-day balance of $0 (zero dollars). The ZBA enables the firm to keep all of its operating cash in an interest-earning account, thereby eliminating idle cash balances. Thus a firm that used a ZBA in conjunction with a cash concentration system would need two accounts. The firm would concentrate its cash from the lockboxes and other collecting banks into an interest-earning account and would write cheques against its ZBA. The firm would cover the exact dollar amount of cheques presented against the ZBA with transfers from the interest-earning account, leaving the end-of-day balance in the ZBA at $0.

A ZBA is a disbursement management tool. As we discussed earlier, the firm would prefer to maximize its payment float. However, some cash managers feel that actively attempting to increase float time on payment is unethical. A ZBA enables the firm to maximize the use of float on each cheque without altering the float time of payments to its suppliers. Keeping all the firm's cash in an interest-earning account enables the firm to maximize earnings on its cash balances by capturing the full float time on each cheque it writes.

Investing in Marketable Securities

Marketable securities are short-term, interest-earning, money market instruments that can easily be converted into cash.[7] Marketable securities are classified as part of the firm's liquid assets. The firm uses them to earn a return on temporarily idle funds. To be truly marketable, a security must have (1) a ready market in order to minimize the amount of time required to convert it into cash and (2) safety of principal, which means that it experiences little or no loss in value over time.

The securities that are most commonly held as part of the firm's marketable-securities portfolio are treasury bills issued by the federal government; certificates of deposit (CDs) issued by chartered banks or trust companies; and various securities issued by corporations. These securities include commercial paper, finance company paper, bankers' acceptances, forward rate agreements, and Euro-deposits. Each of these securities were discussed in Chapter 6. The yields on

---

7. As explained in Chapter 6, the *money market* results from a financial relationship between the suppliers and demanders of short-term funds, that is, marketable securities.

TABLE 14.6	**Yields on Popular Marketable Securities for Various Times to Maturity[a]**		
	Yield for stated maturity		
Security	1-month	3-month	6-month
Certificates of deposit	2.78%	2.88%	
Treasury bills	2.63%	2.69%	2.78%
Commercial paper	2.78%	2.86%	
Bankers' acceptances	2.78%	2.87%	2.94%
Forward rate agreements	NA	3.05%	3.29%
Euro-deposit note:			
US$	1.74%	1.77%	1.76%
C$		2.80%	
Euro		3.21%	
Yen		–0.03%	
Pound		3.88%	

[a]Yields as of October 18, 2002. At this time the Bank of Canada rate was 3% while the prime rate was 4.5%.
SOURCE: Bank of Canada; rates available at **www.bankofcanada.ca/en/interest-look.htm**.

a number of these securities, for various times to maturity, on October 18, 2002, are provided in Table 14.6.

? Review Questions

14–17 What is *float* and what are its three components? Why might the concept of managing float soon be obsolete?

14–18 What are the firm's objectives with regard to collection float and to payment float?

14–19 What are the three main advantages of cash concentration?

14–20 What are three mechanisms of cash concentration? What is the objective of using a zero-balance account (ZBA) in a cash concentration system?

14–21 What two characteristics make a security marketable? Why are the yields on nongovernment marketable securities generally higher than the yields on government issues with similar maturities?

SUMMARY

 LG 1

Understand short-term financial management, net working capital, and the related tradeoff between profitability and risk.

Short-term financial management is focused on managing each of the firm's current assets (inventory, accounts receivable, cash, and marketable securities) and current liabilities (accounts payable, accruals, and notes payable) in a manner that positively contributes to the firm's value. Net working capital is the difference between current assets and current liabilities. Profitability is the relationship between revenues and costs. Risk, in the context of short-term financial decisions, is the probability that a firm will become technically insolvent—unable to pay its bills as they come due. Assuming a constant level of total assets, the higher a firm's ratio of current assets to total assets, the less profitable the firm, and the less risky it is. The converse is also true. With constant total assets, the higher a firm's ratio of current liabilities to total assets, the more profitable and the more risky the firm is. The converse of this statement is also true.

LG2 **Describe the cash conversion cycle, its funding requirements, and the key strategies for managing it.** The cash conversion cycle represents the amount of time a firm's resources are tied up. It has three components: (1) average age of inventory, (2) average collection period, and (3) average payment period. The length of the cash conversion cycle determines the amount of time resources are tied up in the firm's day-to-day operations. The firm's investment in short-term assets often consists of both permanent and seasonal funding requirements. The seasonal requirements can be financed using either a low-cost, high-risk, aggressive financing strategy or a high-cost, low-risk, conservative financing strategy. The firm's funding decision for its cash conversion cycle ultimately depends on management's disposition toward risk and the strength of the firm's banking relationships. To minimize its reliance on negotiated liabilities, the financial manager seeks to (1) turn over inventory as quickly as possible, (2) collect accounts receivable as quickly as possible, (3) pay accounts payable as slowly as possible, and (4) manage mail, processing, and clearing time. Use of these strategies should shorten the cash conversion cycle.

LG3 **Discuss inventory management: differing views, common techniques, and international concerns.** The viewpoints of marketing, manufacturing, and purchasing managers about the appropriate levels of inventory tend to cause higher

inventories than those deemed appropriate by the financial manager. Four commonly used techniques for effectively managing inventory to keep its level low are (1) the ABC system, (2) the economic order quantity (EOQ) model, (3) the just-in-time (JIT) system, and (4) the materials requirement planning (MRP) system. International inventory managers place greater emphasis on making sure that sufficient quantities of inventory are delivered where they are needed, when they are needed, and in the right condition, than on ordering the economically optimal quantities.

LG4 **Explain the credit selection process and the quantitative procedure for evaluating changes in credit standards.** Credit selection and standards are concerned with applying techniques for determining which customers' creditworthiness is consistent with the firm's credit standards. Two popular credit selection techniques are the four C's of credit and credit scoring. To evaluate credit applicants, information to base the analysis on is required. One potential source of the information is the applicant. Another is agencies, such as D&B, that collect financial and rating information on thousands of Canadian companies that can then be used to evaluate the risk of credit applicants. Changes in credit standards can be evaluated mathematically by assessing the effects of a proposed change in profits on sales, the cost of accounts receivable investment, and bad-debt costs.

LG5 **Review the procedures for quantitatively considering cash discount changes, other aspects of credit terms, and credit monitoring.** Changes in credit terms (particularly the initiation of, or a change in, the cash discount) can be quantified in a way similar to that for changes in credit standards. Changes in the cash discount period can also be evaluated using similar methods. Credit monitoring, the ongoing review of customer payment of accounts receivable, frequently involves use of the average collection period and the aging of accounts receivable. A number of popular collection techniques are used by firms.

LG6 **Understand the management of receipts and disbursements, including float, speeding collections, slowing payments, cash concentra-**

tion, zero-balance accounts, and investing in marketable securities. Float refers to funds that have been sent by the payer but are not yet usable funds to the payee. The components of float are mail time, processing time, and clearing time. Float occurs in both the average collection period and the average payment period. One technique for speeding up collections to reduce collection float is a lockbox system. A popular technique for slowing payments to increase payment float is controlled disbursing, which involves strategic use of mailing points and bank accounts. The goal for managing operating cash is to balance the opportunity cost of nonearning balances against the transaction cost of temporary investments. Firms commonly use depository transfer cheques (DTCs), ACH transfers, and wire transfers to transfer lockbox receipts to their concentration banks quickly. Zero-balance accounts (ZBAs) can be used to eliminate nonearning cash balances in corporate chequing accounts. Marketable securities are short-term, interest-earning, money market instruments used by the firm to earn a return on temporarily idle funds. They may be government or non-government issues.

SELF-TEST PROBLEMS   (Solutions in Appendix B)

LG2   **ST 14–1   Cash conversion cycle**   Hurkin Manufacturing Company pays accounts payable on the tenth day after purchase. The average collection period is 30 days, and the average age of inventory is 40 days. The firm currently invests about $18 million on operating-cycle investments. The firm is considering a plan that would stretch its accounts payable by 20 days. If the cost to the firm of investing in assets is 12 percent, what annual savings can it realize by this plan? Assume no discount for early payment of accounts payable.

LG3   **ST 14–2   EOQ analysis**   Thompson Paint Company uses 60,000 gallons of pigment per year. The cost of ordering pigment is $200 per order, and the cost of carrying the pigment in inventory is $1 per gallon per year. The firm uses pigment at a constant rate every day throughout the year.
a. Calculate the EOQ.
b. Determine the total of the plan suggested in **a**.
c. Assuming that it takes 20 days to receive an order once it has been placed, determine the reorder point in terms of gallons of pigment.

LG4   **ST 14–3   Relaxing credit standards**   Regency Rug Repair Company is trying to decide whether it should relax its credit standards. The firm repairs 72,000 rugs per year at an average price of $32 each. Bad-debt expenses are 1 percent of sales, the average collection period is 40 days, and the variable cost per unit is $28. Regency expects that if it does relax its credit standards, the average collection period will increase to 48 days and that bad debts will increase to 1.5 percent of sales. Sales will increase by 4,000 repairs per year. The firm also expects to save $15,000 per year in collection expenses. If the firm's cost of capital is 14 percent, what recommendation would you give the firm? Provide a complete analysis to justify your answer.

PROBLEMS

WARM-UP **14–1** **Cash conversion cycle** American Products is concerned about managing cash efficiently. On the average, inventories have an age of 90 days, and accounts receivable are collected in 60 days. Accounts payable are paid approximately 30 days after they arise. The firm's operating-cycle investments are $30 million per year.
   a. Calculate the firm's operating cycle.
   b. Calculate the firm's cash conversion cycle.
   c. Calculate the amount of resources needed to support the firm's cash conversion cycle.
   d. Discuss how management might be able to reduce the cash conversion cycle.

INTERMEDIATE **14–2** **Changing cash conversion cycle** Camp Manufacturing turns over its inventory 8 times each year, has an average payment period of 35 days, and has an average collection period of 60 days. The firm's operating cycle investments are $3.5 million per year.
   a. Calculate the firm's operating and cash conversion cycles.
   b. Calculate the firm's daily cash operating expenditure. How much in resources must be invested to support its cash conversion cycle?
   c. If the firm pays 14 percent for these resources, by how much would it increase its annual profits by *favourably* changing its current cash conversion cycle by 20 days?

INTERMEDIATE **14–3** **Cash conversion cycle** Harris & Company has an inventory turnover of 12 times each year, an average collection period of 45 days, and an average payment period of 40 days. The firm invests $1 million per year on its operating cycle accounts.
   a. Calculate the firm's operating cycle.
   b. Calculate the firm's cash conversion cycle.
   c. Calculate the amount of negotiated financing required to support the firm's cash conversion cycle.
   d. If the firm's operating cycle were lengthened, without any change in its average payment period (APP), how would this affect its cash conversion cycle and negotiated financing need?

WARM-UP **14–4** **Changes in cash conversion cycles** A firm is considering several plans that affect its current accounts. Given the five plans and their probable results shown in the following table, which one would you favour? Explain.

| | Change | | |
Plan	Average age of inventory	Average collection period	Average payment period
A	+30 days	+20 days	+5 days
B	+20 days	−10 days	+15 days
C	−10 days	0 days	−5 days
D	−15 days	+15 days	+10 days
E	+5 days	−10 days	+15 days

INTERMEDIATE **LG2** **14–5** **Multiple changes in cash conversion cycle**   Garrett Industries turns over its inventory 6 times each year; it has an average collection period of 45 days and an average payment period of 30 days. The firm's annual operating-cycle investment is $3 million.

    a. Calculate the firm's cash conversion cycle, its daily cash operating expenditure, and the amount of resources needed to support its cash conversion cycle.

    b. Find the firm's cash conversion cycle and resource investment requirement if it makes the following changes simultaneously.

      (1) Shortens the average age of inventory by 5 days.

      (2) Speeds up the collection of accounts receivable by an average of 10 days.

      (3) Extends the average payment period by 10 days.

    c. If the firm pays 13 percent for its resource investment, by how much, if anything, could it increase its annual profit as a result of the changes in part **b**?

    d. If the annual cost of achieving the profit in part **c** is $35,000, what action would you recommend to the firm? Why?

INTERMEDIATE **LG2** **14–6** **Changing the cash conversion cycle**   Aspen Jeans, Inc., has collected data about its current operations. The average age of inventory is 55 days; the average collection period is 42 days; and the average payment period is 46 days. The firm has an opportunity cost of short-term financing equal to 9 percent. Annual investments in the operating cycle amount to $4,800,000. Aspen has been offered a contract to produce private label jeans for a large retailer. If the firm takes the contract it will increase operating profits by $35,000 and reduce the average age of inventory to 50 days. However, it will increase the length of the collection period to 65 days. No changes will occur in the payment period or the amount of operating cycle investments.

    a. Calculate Aspen Jeans' current operating and cash conversion cycles.

    b. Recalculate the firm's cycles for the effects that the new contract will produce.

    c. Calculate the change in the cost of financing operating cycle investments.

    d. Compare your results in **c** to the promised additional operating profits. Should the firm accept the contract or not?

INTERMEDIATE **LG2** **14–7** **Aggressive versus conservative seasonal funding strategy**   Dynabase Tool has forecast its total funds requirements for the coming year as shown in the following table.

Month	Amount	Month	Amount
January	$2,000,000	July	$12,000,000
February	2,000,000	August	14,000,000
March	2,000,000	September	9,000,000
April	4,000,000	October	5,000,000
May	6,000,000	November	4,000,000
June	9,000,000	December	3,000,000

    a. Divide the firm's monthly funds requirement into (1) a *permanent* component and (2) a *seasonal* component, and find the monthly average for each of these components.

b. Describe the amount of long-term and short-term financing used to meet the total funds requirement under (1) an *aggressive funding strategy* and (2) a *conservative funding strategy*. Assume that under the aggressive strategy, long-term funds finance permanent needs and short-term funds are used to finance seasonal needs.

c. Assuming that short-term funds cost 12 percent annually and that the cost of long-term funds is 17 percent annually, use the averages found in part **a** to calculate the total cost of each of the strategies described in part **b**.

d. Discuss the risk/return tradeoffs associated with the aggressive strategy and those associated with the conservative strategy.

INTERMEDIATE   14–8   **Aggressive versus conservative financing strategy**   Benitez Industrial Services Corp. has a short-term funds cost of 7 percent and a long-term funds cost of 12 percent. A summary forecast of the company's total assets during the coming year is as follows.

Month	Amount	Month	Amount
January	$ 8,900,000	July	$10,500,000
February	8,500,000	August	10,000,000
March	8,700,000	September	9,600,000
April	9,200,000	October	9,400,000
May	9,800,000	November	9,000,000
June	10,300,000	December	9,000,000

a. Divide the company's financing needs into permanent and seasonal components. Calculate the average seasonal financing need.

b. Determine the financing cost per year of using an aggressive strategy. Calculate the cost per year if a conservative financing strategy is used. Discuss the cost and risk factors involved in each of these strategies.

c. Discuss why virtually no firm follows a conservative strategy. Explain why some may choose a strategy that falls between conservative and aggressive.

INTERMEDIATE 14–9   **Aggressive versus conservative financing strategy**   Marbell International has forecast its seasonal financing needs for the next year as shown in the table below. Assuming that the firm's permanent funds requirement is $4 million, calculate the total annual financing costs using an *aggressive strategy* and those using a *conservative strategy*. Recommend one of the strategies under each of the following conditions:

a. Short-term funds cost 9 percent annually, and long-term funds cost 15 percent annually.

b. Short-term funds cost 10 percent annually, and long-term funds cost 13 percent annually.

c. Both short-term and long-term funds cost 11 percent annually.

Month	Seasonal requirement	Month	Seasonal requirement
January	$ 0	July	$700,000
February	300,000	August	400,000
March	500,000	September	0
April	900,000	October	200,000
May	1,200,000	November	700,000
June	1,000,000	December	300,000

WARM-UP 14–10 **EOQ analysis**   Tiger Corporation purchases 1,200,000 units per year of one component. The fixed cost per order is $25. The annual carrying cost of the item is 27 percent of its $2 cost.

a. Determine the EOQ under the following conditions: (1) no changes, (2) order cost of zero, and (3) carrying cost of zero.

b. What do your answers illustrate about the EOQ model? Explain.

INTERMEDIATE 14–11 **EOQ, reorder point, and safety stock**   Alexis Company uses 800 units of a product per year on a continuous basis. The product has a fixed cost of $50 per order, and its carrying cost is $2 per unit per year. It takes 5 days to receive a shipment after an order is placed, and the firm wishes to hold 10 days' usage in inventory as a safety stock.

a. Calculate the EOQ.

b. Determine the average level of inventory.

c. Determine the reorder point.

b. Indicate which of the following variables change if the firm does not hold the safety stock: (1) order cost, (2) carrying cost, (3) total inventory cost, (4) reorder point, (5) economic order quantity. Explain.

INTERMEDIATE 14–12 **Inventory—The ABC system**   Newton, Inc., has 16 different items in its inventory. The average number of units held in inventory and the average unit cost for each item are listed in the following table. The firm wishes to introduce the ABC system of inventory management. Suggest a breakdown of the items into classifications of A, B, and C. Justify your selection and point out items that could be considered borderline cases.

Item	Average number of units in inventory	Average cost per unit
1	1,800	$ 0.54
2	1,000	8.20
3	100	6.00
4	250	1.20
5	8	94.50
6	400	3.00
7	80	45.00
8	1,600	1.45
9	600	0.95
10	3,000	0.18
11	900	15.00
12	65	1.35
13	2,200	4.75
14	1,800	1.30
15	60	18.00
16	200	17.50

INTERMEDIATE **14–13 Graphic EOQ analysis**   Knoll Manufacturing uses 10,000 units of raw material per year on a continuous basis. Placing and processing an order for additional inventory cost $200 per order. The firm estimates the cost of carrying one unit in inventory at $0.25 per year.

a. What are the annual order costs, carrying costs, and total costs of inventory if the firm orders in quantities of 1,000; 2,000; 3,000; 4,000; 5,000; 6,000; and 7,000 units?

b. Graph the order cost, carrying cost, and total cost (y axis) relative to order quantity (x axis). Label the EOQ.

c. On the basis of your graph, in what quantity would you order? Is this consistent with the EOQ equation? Explain why or why not.

INTERMEDIATE **14–14 Credit scoring**   Clemens Department Store uses credit scoring to evaluate retail credit applications. The financial and credit characteristics considered and weights indicating their relative importance in the credit decision are given in the table that follows. The firm's credit standards are to accept all applicants with credit scores of 80 or more, to extend limited credit on a probationary basis to applicants with scores of greater than 70 and less than 80, and to reject all applicants with scores below 70.

Financial and credit characteristics	Predetermined weight
Credit references	0.25
Education	0.15
Home ownership	0.10
Income range	0.10
Payment history	0.30
Years on job	0.10

The firm currently needs to process three applications that were recently received and scored by one of its credit analysts. The scores for each of the applicants on each of the financial and credit characteristics are summarized in the following table:

	Applicant		
Financial and credit characteristics	A	B	C
	Score (0 to 100)		
Credit references	60	90	80
Education	70	70	80
Home ownership	100	90	60
Income range	75	80	80
Payment history	60	85	70
Years on job	50	60	90

a. Use the data presented to find the credit score for each of the applicants.
b. Recommend the appropriate action for each of the three applicants.

 WARM-UP LG4 **14–15** **Accounts receivable and costs** Randolph Company currently has an average collection period of 45 days and annual credit sales of $1 million.
a. What is the firm's average accounts receivable balance?
b. If the variable cost of each product is 60 percent of sales, what is the average *investment* in accounts receivable?
c. If the equal-risk opportunity cost of the investment in accounts receivable is 12 percent, what is the total opportunity cost of the investment in accounts receivable?

 INTERMEDIATE LG4 **14–16** **Accounts receivable changes without bad debts** Tara's Textiles currently has credit sales of $360 million per year and an average collection period of 60 days. Assume that the price of Tara's products is $60 per unit and that the variable costs are $55 per unit. The firm is considering an accounts receivable change that will result in a 20 percent increase in sales and a 20 percent increase in the average collection period. No change in bad debts is expected. The firm's equal-risk opportunity cost on its investment in accounts receivable is 14 percent.
a. Calculate the additional profit contribution from new sales that the firm will realize if it makes the proposed change.
b. What marginal investment in accounts receivable will result?
c. Calculate the cost of the marginal investment in accounts receivable.
d. Should the firm implement the proposed change? What other information would be helpful in your analysis?

 CHALLENGE LG4 **14–17** **Accounts receivable changes with bad debts** A firm is evaluating an accounts receivable change that would increase bad debts from 2 percent to 4 percent of sales. Sales are currently 50,000 units, the selling price is $20 per unit, and the variable cost per unit is $15. As a result of the proposed change, sales are forecast to increase to 60,000 units.

    a. What are bad debts in dollars currently and under the proposed change?

    b. Calculate the cost of the marginal bad debts to the firm.

    c. Ignoring the additional profit contribution from increased sales, if the proposed changes saves $3,500 and causes no change in the average investment in accounts receivable, would you recommend it? Explain.

    d. Considering *all* changes in costs and benefits, would you recommend the proposed change? Explain.

    e. Compare and discuss your answers in parts **c** and **d**.

 CHALLENGE **14–18** Relaxation of credit standards   Lewis Enterprises is considering relaxing its credit standards to increase its currently sagging sales. As a result of the proposed relaxation, sales are expected to increase by 10 percent from 10,000 to 11,000 units during the coming year; the average collection period is expected to increase from 45 days to 60 days; and bad debts are expected to increase from 1 percent to 3 percent of sales. The sale price per unit is $40, and the variable cost per unit is $31. The firm's required return on equal-risk investments is 25 percent. Evaluate the proposed relaxation, and make a recommendation to the firm.

 CHALLENGE **14–19** Initiating a cash discount   Gardner Company currently makes all sales on credit and offers no cash discount. The firm is considering offering a 2 percent cash discount for payment within 15 days. The firm's current average collection period is 60 days, sales are 40,000 units, selling price is $45 per unit, and variable cost per unit is $36. The firm expects that the change in credit terms will result in an increase in sales to 42,000 units, that 70 percent of the sales will take the discount, and that the average collection period will fall to 30 days. If the firm's required rate of return on equal-risk investments is 25 percent, should the proposed discount be offered?

 CHALLENGE **14–20** Shortening the credit period   A firm is contemplating *shortening* its credit period from 40 to 30 days and believes that as a result of this change, its average collection period will decline from 45 days to 36 days. Bad-debt expenses are expected to decrease from 1.5 percent to 1 percent of sales. The firm is currently selling 12,000 units but believes that as a result of the proposed change, sales will decline to 10,000 units. The sale price per unit is $56, and the variable cost per unit is $45. The firm has a required return on equal-risk investments of 25 percent. Evaluate this decision, and make a recommendation to the firm.

 CHALLENGE **14–21** Lengthening the credit period   Parker Tool is considering lengthening its credit period from 30 to 60 days. All customers will continue to pay on the net date. The firm currently bills $450,000 for sales and has $345,000 in variable costs. The change in credit terms is expected to increase sales to $510,000. Bad-debt expenses will increase from 1 percent to 1.5 percent of sales. The firm has a required rate of return on equal-risk investments of 20 percent.

    a. What additional profit contribution from sales will be realized from the proposed change?

    b. What is the cost of the marginal investment in accounts receivable?

    c. What is the cost of the marginal bad debts?

    d. Do you recommend this change in credit terms? Why or why not?

INTERMEDIATE **14–22**   **Aging accounts receivable**   Burnham Services' accounts receivable totalled $874,000 on August 31, 2002. A breakdown of these outstanding accounts on the basis of the month in which the credit sale was initially made follows. The firm extends 30-day EOM credit terms to its credit customers.

Month of credit sale	Accounts receivable
August 2002	$320,000
July 2002	250,000
June 2002	81,000
May 2002	195,000
April 2002 or before	28,000
Total (August 31, 2002)	$874,000

    a. Prepare an aging schedule for Burnham Services' August 31, 2002, accounts receivable balance.
    b. Using your findings in **a,** evaluate the firm's credit and collection activities.
    c. What are some probable causes of the situation discussed in **b?**

WARM-UP **14–23**   **Inventory investment**   Paterson Products is considering leasing a computerized inventory control system to reduce its average inventories. The annual cost of the system is $46,000. It is expected that with the system the firm's average inventory will decline by 50 percent from its current level of $980,000. The level of stockouts is expected to be unaffected by this system. The firm can earn 20 percent per year on equal-risk investments.
    a. How much of a reduction in average inventory will result from the proposed installation of the computerized inventory control system?
    b. How much, if any, annual savings will the firm realize on the reduced level of average inventory?
    c. Should the firm lease the computerized inventory control system? Explain why or why not.

WARM-UP **14–24**   **Float**   Simon Corporation has daily cash receipts of $65,000. A recent analysis of its collections indicated that customers' payments were in the mail an average of 2.5 days. Once received, the payments are processed in 1.5 days. After payments are deposited, it takes an average of 3 days for these receipts to clear the banking system.
    a. How much collection float (in days) does the firm currently have?
    b. If the firm's opportunity cost is 11 percent, would it be economically advisable for the firm to pay an annual fee of $16,500 to reduce collection float by 3 days? Explain why or why not.

WARM-UP **14–25**   **Lockbox system**   Eagle Industries feels that a lockbox system can shorten its accounts receivable collection period by 3 days. Credit sales are $3,240,000 per year, billed on a continuous basis. The firm has other equally risky investments with a return of 15 percent. The cost of the lockbox system is $9,000 per year.

a. What amount of cash will be made available for other uses under the lockbox system?

b. What net benefit (cost) will the firm realize if it adopts the lockbox system? Should it adopt the proposed lockbox system?

WARM-UP   14–26   **Zero-balance account**   Union Company is considering establishment of a zero-balance account. The firm currently maintains an average balance of $420,000 in its disbursement account. As compensation to the bank for maintaining the zero-balance account, the firm will have to pay a monthly fee of $1,000 and maintain a $300,000 non-interest-earning deposit in the bank. The firm currently has no other deposits in the bank. Evaluate the proposed zero-balance account, and make a recommendation to the firm, assuming that it has a 12 percent opportunity cost.

CASE CHAPTER 14	**Assessing Roche Publishing Company's Cash Management Efficiency**

Lisa Pinto, vice president of finance at Roche Publishing Company, a rapidly growing publisher of college texts, is concerned about the firm's high level of short-term resource investment. She believes that the firm can improve the management of its cash and, as a result, reduce this investment. In this regard, she charged Arlene Bessenoff, the treasurer, with assessing the firm's cash management efficiency. Arlene decided to begin her investigation by studying the firm's operating and cash conversion cycles.

Arlene found that Roche's average payment period was 25 days. She consulted industry data, which showed that the average payment period for the industry was 40 days. Investigation of three similar publishing companies revealed that their average payment period was also 40 days. She estimated the annual costs of achieving a 40-day payment period to be $53,000.

Next, Arlene studied the production cycle and inventory policies. The average age of inventory was 120 days. She determined that the industry standard as reported in a survey done by *Publishing World*, the trade association journal, was 85 days. She estimated the annual costs of achieving an 85-day average age of inventory to be $150,000.

Further analysis showed Arlene that the firm's average collection period was 60 days. The industry average, derived from the trade association data and information on three similar publishing companies, was found to be 42 days—30 percent lower than Roche's. Arlene estimated that if Roche initiated a 2 percent cash discount for payment within 10 days of the beginning of the credit period, the firm's average collection period would drop from 60 days to the 42-day industry average. She also expected the following to occur as a result of the discount: Annual sales would increase from $13,750,000 to $15,000,000; bad debts would fall from 3 percent of sales to 1 percent of sales; and the 2 percent cash discount would be applied to 75 percent of the firm's sales. The firms' variable costs equal 80 percent of sales.

Roche Publishing Company is currently investing $12,000,000 per year in its operating-cycle investment, but it expects that initiating a cash discount will increase its operating-cycle investment to $13,100,000 per year. Arlene's concern was whether the firm's cash management was as efficient as it could be. Arlene knew that the company paid 12 percent annual interest for its resource investment and therefore viewed this value as the firm's required return. For this reason, she was concerned about the resource investment cost resulting from any inefficiencies in the management of Roche's cash conversion cycle.

Required

a. Assuming a constant rate for purchases, production, and sales throughout the year, what are Roche's existing operating cycle (OC), cash conversion cycle (CCC), and resource investment need?
b. If Roche can optimize operations according to industry standards, what would its operating cycle (OC), cash conversion cycle (CCC), and resource investment need to be under these more efficient conditions?
c. In terms of resource investment requirements, what is the annual cost of Roche Publishing Company's operational inefficiency?
d. Evaluate whether Roche's strategy for speeding its collection of accounts receivable would be acceptable. What annual net profit or loss would result from implementation of the cash discount?
e. Use your finding in part **d**, along with the payables and inventory costs given, to determine the total annual cost the firm would incur to achieve the industry level of operational efficiency.
f. Judging on the basis of your findings in parts **c** and **e**, should the firm incur the annual cost to achieve the industry level of operational efficiency? Explain why or why not.

WEB EXERCISE LINKS TO PRACTISE

Visit the following Web sites and complete the suggested exercises. These exercises will allow you to review practical applications of the chapter topics as well as explore the wealth of information regarding managerial finance that is available on the Internet.

www.dnb.ca/products/businforep.html
Visit the above Web site and click on the See a Sample link. Review the report. What information does this report provide to a company analyzing an applicant for credit? Place the mouse on the Payment Trend graph. What information does this graph provide? Evaluate the company's payment history in comparison to the average company in the industry and the lower and higher company in the industry. What information is provided in the Payment Summary and the Current Payment Experience? Based on this Payment Profile Report, would you grant this hypothetical applicant credit if you were the manager of a credit department?

www.dnb.ca/products/paymentpro.html
Visit the above Web site and click on the See a Sample link. Scan the complete report. What information does this report provide to a company analyzing an

applicant for credit? Return to the top of the report. What information is provided in the first section of the report? Place the mouse on the words Record, Trend, Operation, and SIC. What information is provided? Scroll down the report to the next section. What information is provided? Place the mouse on the headings; determine what information is provided in each column.

Scroll down the report. Place the mouse on the word Finance in the Finance section of the report. How often does D&B collect financial statements from companies? What happens if a company does not provide financial statements? What other information is included in this section? Based on the available data, what is the financial strength code for the company? What kinds of information is included in the Public Record section? Scroll down the page to the History section. Place the mouse on the word History. What information is provided in this section? The final section is Operation. What information is provided?

Based on a review of the complete report, would you grant this hypothetical applicant credit if you were the manager of a credit department?

www.treasurypoint.com/products/optimizer_intro.asp
This link provides an online system to help companies optimize their cash management procedures. Answer the following questions regarding this analytical tool.

1. Review the description of the Optimizer and its potential benefits and summarize the application's uses.
2. Click on the Interactive Demos link and then the Scenario 2 link to run the demonstration for investment of cash surpluses. Work through the demonstration for this scenario.
3. What are the three possible solutions for surplus cash investments and their related returns?
4. How do these returns compare with the optimized return?
5. If you were a company treasurer, how would you decide whether to purchase the Optimizer service?
6. Click on the Case Studies link. How would the various companies listed make the decision regarding the purchase of the Optimizer?

retailinteractive.ca/SSG/ri00713e.html
Visit the above Web site and complete the following task.

What is the inventory management cycle? Click on Next at the bottom of the page. Review the various stages of the inventory management cycle and summarize how information technology can lead to significant improvements in the management of inventory.

www.investopedia.com/university/moneymarket
To refresh your memory of the money market, review the nine pages on this site and then take the quiz that is provided on the tenth page. What is the money market, what are the main securities that trade on the money market, and what are the characteristics of these securities?

www.bankofcanada.ca/en/interest-look.htm
Visit the above Web site and update Table 14.6. What has happened to interest rates in the economy since October 18, 2002, the date that the rates provided in the table were collected? What impact would these changes have on a company's portfolio of marketable securities?

15 Management of Current Liabilities

LEARNING GOALS

LG1 Review the key components of a firm's credit terms and the procedures for analyzing them.

LG2 Understand the effects of stretching accounts payable on their cost, and the use of accruals.

LG3 Describe the interest rates and basic types of unsecured bank sources of short-term loans.

LG4 Discuss the basic features of commercial paper and the key aspects of international short-term loans.

LG5 Explain the characteristics of secured short-term loans and the use of accounts receivable as short-term-loan collateral.

LG6 Describe the various ways in which inventory can be used as short-term-loan collateral.

15.1 Spontaneous Liabilities

spontaneous liabilities
Financing that arises from the normal course of business; the two major short-term sources of such liabilities are accounts payable and accruals.

Spontaneous liabilities arise from the normal course of business. The two major spontaneous sources of short-term financing are accounts payable and accruals. As the firm's sales increase, accounts payable increase in response to the increased purchases necessary to produce at higher levels. Also in response to increasing sales, the firm's accruals increase as wages and taxes rise due to greater labour requirements and the increased taxes on the firm's increased earnings. There is normally no explicit cost attached to either of these current liabilities, although they do have certain implicit costs. In addition, both are forms of

Saving for a Rainy Day

In the last chapter we discussed the factors influencing a company's investment in current assets. We also saw that the investment in current assets must be financed. The amount of financing required will vary with

sales. A firm anticipating a seasonal increase in sales will have to build up inventories prior to the expected increase. As the inventory is sold, accounts receivable will increase. Thus, increased financing will be required around the seasonal increase in sales. When a seasonal decrease in sales occurs, inventories will be depleted before the temporary sales decline, and accounts receivable will decrease in the period following. Thus, financing needs will decline. Various strategies exist for financing current assets. Using short-term bank loans to finance a temporary buildup of inventory and accounts receivable until they can be converted to cash is one financing strategy. Other methods include the use of spontaneous sources of financing—accounts payable and accruals—and using long-term financing. In this chapter, we will explain various methods and how these can be used to the firm's advantage.

---

unsecured short-term financing
Short-term financing obtained without pledging specific assets as collateral.

unsecured short-term financing—short-term financing obtained without pledging specific assets as collateral. The firm should take advantage of these "interest-free" sources of unsecured short-term financing whenever possible.

Accounts Payable Management

⚠ Hint
An account payable of a purchaser is an account receivable on the supplier's books. Chapter 14 highlighted the key strategies and considerations involved in extending credit to customers.

Accounts payable are the major source of unsecured short-term financing for business firms. As we saw in Figure 14.1 in the last chapter, accounts payable for the average non-financial company in Canada are 16.8 percent of total liabilities and equity. Accounts payable are a larger percentage of total liabilities and equity than is long-term debt. Accounts payable result from transactions in which merchandise is purchased but no formal note is signed to show the purchaser's liability to the seller. The purchaser in effect agrees to pay the supplier the amount required in accordance with credit terms normally stated on the supplier's invoice. The discussion of accounts payable here is presented from the viewpoint of the purchaser.

Role in the Cash Conversion Cycle

accounts payable management
Management by the firm of the time that elapses between its purchase of raw materials and its mailing payment to the supplier.

The average payment period is the final component of the *cash conversion cycle* introduced in Chapter 14. The average payment period has two parts: (1) the time from the purchase of raw materials until the firm mails the payment and (2) payment float time (the time it takes after the firm mails its payment until the supplier has withdrawn spendable funds from the firm's account). In the preceding chapter, we discussed issues related to payment float time. Here we discuss the management by the firm of the time that elapses between its purchase of raw materials and its mailing payment to the supplier. This activity is **accounts payable management**.

The firm's goal is to pay as slowly as possible without damaging its credit rating. This means that accounts should be paid on the last day possible, given the supplier's stated credit terms. For example, if the terms are net 30, then the account should be paid 30 days from the *beginning of the credit period*, which is typically either the *date of invoice* or the *end of the month (EOM)* in which the purchase was made. This allows for the maximum use of an interest-free loan from the supplier and will not damage the firm's credit rating (because the account is paid within the stated credit terms).

E x a m p l e ▼ In the demonstration of the cash conversion cycle in Chapter 14 (see pages 668–669), MAX Company had an average payment period of 35 days (consisting of 30 days until payment was mailed and 5 days of payment float), which resulted in average accounts payable of $467,466. Thus the daily accounts payable generated by MAX was $13,356 ($467,466/35). If MAX were to mail its payments in 35 days instead of 30, its accounts payable would increase by $66,780 ($13,356 × 5). As a result, MAX's cash conversion cycle would decrease by 5 days, and the firm would reduce its net investment in operations (receivables and inventory) by $66,780. Clearly, if this action did not damage
▲ MAX's credit rating, it would be in the company's best interest.

Analyzing Credit Terms

The credit terms that a firm is offered by its suppliers enable it to delay payments for its purchases. Because the supplier's cost of having its money tied up in merchandise after it is sold is probably reflected in the purchase price, the purchaser is already indirectly paying for this benefit. The purchaser should therefore carefully analyze credit terms to determine the best trade credit strategy. If a firm is extended credit terms that include a cash discount, it has two options—to take the cash discount or to give it up.

Taking the Cash Discount   If a firm intends to take a cash discount, it should pay on the last day of the discount period. There is no direct cost associated with taking a cash discount, but note the indirect cost—the cost of paying prior to the end of the full credit period. For the purposes of our discussion, we will assume the indirect cost is very low and thus can be safely ignored.

Example ▼ Lawrence Industries, operator of a small chain of video stores, purchased $1,000 worth of merchandise on April 30 from a supplier extending terms of 2/10 net 30. If the firm takes the cash discount, it must pay $980 [$1,000 − (0.02 × $1,000)] by May 10, thereby saving $20.
▲

Giving Up the Cash Discount   If the firm chooses to give up the cash discount, it should pay on the final day of the credit period. There is an implicit cost associated with giving up a cash discount. The **cost of giving up a cash discount** is the implied rate of interest paid to delay payment of an account payable for an additional number of days. In other words, the amount is the interest being paid by the firm to keep its money for a number of days. This cost can be illustrated by a simple example. The example assumes that payment will be made on the last possible day (either the final day of the cash discount period or the final day of the credit period).

cost of giving up a cash discount
The implied rate of interest paid to delay payment of an account payable for an additional number of days.

Example ▼ In the preceding example, we saw that Lawrence Industries could take the cash discount on its April 30 purchase by paying $980 on May 10. If Lawrence gives up the cash discount, payment should be made on May 30. To keep its money for an extra 20 days, the firm will give up an opportunity to pay $980 for its $1,000 purchase. In other words, it will cost the firm $20 to delay payment for 20 days. Figure 15.1 shows the payment options that are open to the company.

To calculate the cost of giving up the cash discount, the *true purchase price* must be viewed as the *discounted cost of the merchandise,* which is $980 for Lawrence Industries. The annual percentage cost of giving up the cash discount can be calculated using Equation 15.1:

$$\text{Cost of giving up cash discount} = \frac{CD}{100\% - CD} \times \frac{365}{N} \qquad (15.1)$$

where

$$CD = \text{stated cash discount in percentage terms}$$
$$N = \text{number of days payment can be delayed by giving up}$$
$$\text{the cash discount}$$

Substituting the values for CD (2%) and N (20 days) into Equation 15.1 results in an annualized cost of giving up the cash discount of 37.24% [(2% ÷ 98%) × (365 ÷ 20)].[1]
▲

---

1. This example assumes that Lawrence Industries gives up only one discount during the year, which costs it 2.04 percent for 20 days (i.e., 2% ÷ 98%) or 37.24 percent when annualized. However, if Lawrence Industries *continually* gives up the 2 percent cash discounts, the effect of compounding will cause the annualized cost to rise to 44.59 percent:

Annualized cost when discounts are *continually* given up

$$= \left(1 + \frac{CD}{100\% - CD}\right)^{365/N} - 1 \qquad (15.1a)$$

$$= \left(1 + \frac{2\%}{100\% - 2\%}\right)^{365/20} - 1 = \underline{\underline{44.59\%}}$$

FIGURE 15.1

Payment Options
Payment options for
Lawrence Industries

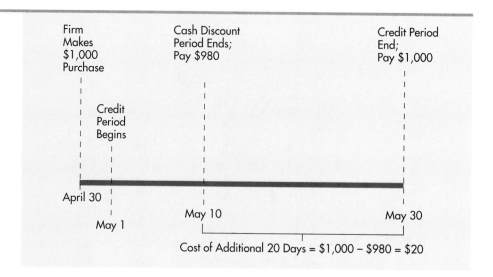

Using the Cost of Giving Up a Cash Discount in Decision Making   The
financial manager must determine whether it is advisable to take a cash discount.
Financial managers must remember that taking cash discounts may represent an
important source of additional profitability.

Example ▼ Mason Products, a large building-supply company, has four possible suppliers,
each offering different credit terms. Otherwise, their products and services are
identical. Table 15.1 presents the credit terms offered by suppliers A, B, C, and D
and the cost of giving up the cash discounts in each transaction. The cost of giving
up the cash discount from supplier A is 37.24 percent; from supplier B, 8.19 percent; from supplier C, 22.58 percent; and from supplier D, 30.42 percent.

  If the firm needs short-term funds, which it can borrow from its bank at an
interest rate of 13 percent, and if each of the suppliers is viewed *separately*,
which (if any) of the suppliers' cash discounts will the firm give up? In dealing
with supplier A, the firm takes the cash discount, because the cost of giving it up
is 37.24 percent, and then borrows the funds it requires from its bank at 13 percent interest. With supplier B, the firm would do better to give up the cash discount, because the cost of this action is less than the cost of borrowing money
from the bank (8.19% versus 13%). With either supplier C or supplier D, the

TABLE 15.1	**Cash Discounts and Associated Costs for Mason Products**	
Supplier	Credit terms	Approximate cost of giving up a cash discount
A	2/10 net 30	37.24%
B	1/10 net 55	8.19
C	3/20 net 70	22.58
D	4/10 net 60	30.42

▲ firm should take the cash discount, because in both cases the cost of giving up the discount is greater than the 13 percent cost of borrowing from the bank.

The example shows that the cost of giving up a cash discount is relevant when one is evaluating a single supplier's credit terms in light of certain *bank borrowing costs*. However, other factors relative to payment strategies may also need to be considered. For example, some firms, particularly small firms and poorly managed firms, routinely give up *all* discounts because they either lack alternative sources of unsecured short-term financing or fail to recognize the implicit costs of their actions.

Effects of Stretching Accounts Payable

stretching accounts payable
Paying bills as late as possible without damaging the firm's credit rating.

A strategy that is often employed by a firm is **stretching accounts payable**—that is, paying bills as late as possible without damaging its credit rating. Such a strategy can reduce the cost of giving up a cash discount.

E x a m p l e ▼ Lawrence Industries was extended credit terms of 2/10 net 30. The cost of giving up the cash discount, assuming payment on the last day of the credit period, was found to be 37.24 percent. If the firm were able to stretch its account payable to 70 days without damaging its credit rating, the cost of giving up the cash discount would be only 12.41 percent $(2\%/98\%) \div [365 \div (70 - 10)]$. Stretching ▲ accounts payable reduces the implicit cost of giving up a cash discount.

Although stretching accounts payable may be financially attractive, it raises an important ethical issue: It may cause the firm to violate the agreement it entered into with its supplier when it purchased merchandise. Clearly, a supplier would not look kindly on a customer who regularly and purposely postponed paying for purchases.

Accruals

accruals
Liabilities for services received for which payment has yet to be made and for which invoice has not been received.

The second spontaneous source of short-term business financing is accruals. **Accruals** are liabilities for services received for which payment has yet to be made and for which invoice has not been received. The most common items accrued by a firm are wages and taxes. Because taxes are payments to the government, their accrual cannot be manipulated by the firm. However, the accrual of wages can be manipulated to some extent. This is accomplished by delaying payment of wages, thereby receiving an interest-free loan from employees who are paid sometime after they have performed the work. The pay period for employees who earn an hourly rate is often governed by union regulations or by provincial law. However, in other cases, the frequency of payment is at the discretion of the company's management.

E x a m p l e ▼ Tenney Company, a large janitorial service company, currently pays its employees at the end of each work week. The weekly payroll totals $400,000. If the firm were to extend the pay period so as to pay its employees 1 week later throughout a year, the employees would in effect be lending the firm $400,000 for a year. If the firm could earn 10 percent annually on invested funds, such a strategy would ▲ be worth $40,000 per year $(0.10 \times \$400,000)$.

? Review Questions

15–1   What are the two major sources of spontaneous short-term financing for a firm? How do their balances behave relative to the firm's sales?

15–2   Is there a cost associated with *taking a cash discount*? Is there any cost associated with *giving up a cash discount*? How do short-term borrowing costs affect the cash discount decision?

15–3   What is "stretching accounts payable"? What effect does this action have on the cost of giving up a cash discount?

15.2 Unsecured Sources of Short-Term Loans

Businesses obtain unsecured short-term loans from two major sources—banks and commercial paper. Unlike the spontaneous sources of unsecured short-term financing, bank loans and commercial paper are negotiated and result from actions taken by the firm's financial manager. Bank loans are more popular because they are available to firms of all sizes; commercial paper is available only to large firms. In addition, international loans can be used to finance international transactions.

Bank Loans

short-term, self-liquidating loan
An unsecured short-term loan in which the use to which the borrowed money is put provides the mechanism through which the loan is repaid.

Banks are a major source of unsecured short-term loans to businesses. The major type of loan made by banks to businesses is the **short-term, self-liquidating loan.** These loans are intended merely to carry the firm through seasonal peaks in financing needs that are due primarily to buildups of inventory and accounts receivable. As inventories and receivables are converted into cash, the funds needed to retire these loans are generated. In other words, the use to which the borrowed money is put provides the mechanism through which the loan is repaid—hence the term *self-liquidating.* Banks lend unsecured, short-term funds in three basic ways: through single-payment notes, lines of credit, and revolving credit agreements. Before we look at these types of loans, we consider loan interest rates.

Loan Interest Rates

prime rate of interest (prime rate)
The lowest rate of interest charged by leading banks on business loans to their most secure business borrowers.

The interest rate on a bank loan can be a fixed or a floating rate, typically based on the prime rate of interest. The **prime rate of interest (prime rate)** is the lowest rate of interest charged by leading banks on business loans to their most secure business borrowers. The prime rate is based on the Bank of Canada rate, the rate the Bank of Canada uses to control inflation and the value of the Canadian dollar in relation to other currencies. The bank rate was discussed in Chapter 6. Actual or expected changes in the Bank of Canada rate trigger changes in the prime rate and all other interest rates in the economy. The difference between the Bank of Canada rate and the prime rate is based on the supply-and-demand relationships for short-term funds.[2] Banks generally determine the rate to be charged

---

2. Since 1980, the prime rate has varied from a record high of 22.75 percent (August 1981) to a low of 3.75 percent (January 2002 through to mid-April 2002). Since 1996, prime has fluctuated from a high of 7.5 percent to a low of 3.75 percent.

to various borrowers by adding a premium to the prime rate to adjust it for the borrower's "riskiness." The premium may be as small as 0.10 percent (10 basis points) or as high as 5 percent to 6 percent (500 to 600 basis points). For most unsecured loans, the premium is usually less than 3 percent.[3]

Fixed- and Floating-Rate Loans   Loans can have either fixed or floating interest rates. On a **fixed-rate loan,** the rate of interest is determined at a set increment above the prime rate on the date of the loan and remains unvarying at that fixed rate until maturity. On a **floating-rate loan,** the increment above the prime rate is initially established, and the rate of interest is allowed to "float," or vary, *as the prime rate varies* until maturity. Generally, the increment above the prime rate will be *lower* on a floating-rate loan than on a fixed-rate loan of equivalent risk, because the lender bears less risk with a floating-rate loan. As a result of the volatile nature of the prime rate during recent years, today *most short-term business loans are floating-rate loans.*

fixed-rate loan
A loan with a rate of interest that is determined at a set increment above the prime rate at which it remains fixed until maturity.

floating-rate loan
A loan with a rate of interest initially set at a stated premium above the prime rate and allowed to "float," or vary, *as the prime rate varies* until maturity.

Method of Computing Interest   Once the *nominal (or stated) annual rate* is established, the method of computing interest is determined. Interest can be paid either when a loan matures or in advance. If interest is paid *at maturity,* the *effective (or true) annual rate*—the actual rate of interest paid—for an assumed 1-year period[4] is equal to:

$$\frac{\text{Interest}}{\text{Amount borrowed}} \qquad (15.2)$$

Most bank loans to businesses require the interest payment at maturity.

When interest is paid *in advance,* it is deducted from the loan so that the borrower actually receives less money than is requested. Loans on which interest is paid in advance are called **discount loans.** The *effective annual rate for a discount loan,* assuming a 1-year period, is calculated as

discount loans
Loans on which interest is paid in advance by being deducted from the amount borrowed.

$$\frac{\text{Interest}}{\text{Amount borrowed} - \text{interest}} \qquad (15.3)$$

Paying interest in advance raises the effective annual rate above the stated annual rate.

Example ▼ Wooster Company, a manufacturer of athletic apparel, wants to borrow $10,000 at a stated annual rate of 10 percent interest for 1 year. If the interest on the loan is paid at maturity, the firm will pay $1,000 (0.10 × $10,000) for the use of the $10,000 for the year. Substituting into Equation 15.2 reveals that the effective annual rate is therefore the stated rate of 10 percent:

$$\frac{\$1,000}{\$10,000} = 10.0\%$$

---

3. Some, generally very large, firms can borrow from their banks at an interest rate slightly below the prime rate. This typically occurs when the borrowing firm either maintains high deposit balances at the bank over time or agrees to pay an upfront fee to "buy down" the interest rate. Below-prime-rate loans are clearly the exception rather than the rule.

4. Effective annual rates (EARs) for loans with maturities of less than 1 year can be found by using the technique presented in Chapter 5 for finding EARs when interest is compounded more frequently than annually. See Equation 5.10.

If the money is borrowed at the same *stated* annual rate for 1 year but interest is paid in advance, the firm still pays $1,000 in interest, but it receives only $9,000 ($10,000 − $1,000). Thus, the effective annual rate in this case is

$$\frac{\$1,000}{\$10,000 - \$1,000} = \frac{\$1,000}{\$9,000} = 11.1\%$$

▲ Paying interest in advance thus makes the effective annual rate (11.1%) greater than the stated annual rate (10.0%).

Single-Payment Notes

single-payment note
A short-term, one-time loan made to a borrower who needs funds for a specific purpose for a short period.

A **single-payment note** can be obtained from a commercial bank by a creditworthy business borrower. This type of loan is usually a one-time loan made to a borrower who needs funds for a specific purpose for a short period. The resulting instrument is a *note*, signed by the borrower, that states the terms of the loan, including the length of the loan and the interest rate. This type of short-term note generally has a maturity of 30 days to one year. The interest charged is usually tied in some way to the prime rate of interest.

Example ▼ Gordon Manufacturing, a producer of rotary mower blades, recently borrowed $100,000 from each of two banks—bank A and bank B. The loans were incurred on the same day, when the prime rate of interest was 9 percent. Each loan involved a 90-day note with interest to be paid at the end of 90 days. The interest rate was set at 1.5 percent above the prime rate on bank A's *fixed-rate note*. Over the 90-day period, the rate of interest on this note will remain at 10.5 percent (9% prime rate + 1.5% increment) regardless of fluctuations in the prime rate. The total interest cost on this loan is $2,589 [$100,000 × (10.5% × 90/365)]. The effective 90-day rate on this loan is 2.589 percent ($2,589/$100,000).

Assuming that the loan from bank A is rolled over each 90 days throughout the year under the same terms and circumstances, and that the interest is not paid but simply accumulated with the note, the effective annual cost of the note is found by using Equation 5.10. Since the cost of the loan is 2.589 percent for 90 days, it is necessary to compound this cost for four periods (the four renewals) and then subtract 1 as follows:

$$\text{Effective annual rate} = (1 + 0.02589)^4 - 1$$
$$= 1.10765 - 1 = 0.10765 = \underline{\underline{10.77\%}}$$

The effective annual rate of interest on the fixed-rate, 90-day note is 10.77 percent.

Bank B set the interest rate at 1 percent above the prime rate on its *floating-rate note*. The rate charged over the 90 days will vary directly with the prime rate. Initially, the rate will be 10 percent (9% + 1%), but when the prime rate changes, so will the rate of interest on the note. For instance, if after 30 days, the prime rate rises to 9.5 percent, and after another 30 days, it drops to 9.25 percent, the firm would be paying 0.822 percent for the first 30 days (10% × 30/365), 0.863 percent for the next 30 days (10.5% × 30/365), and 0.842 percent for the last 30 days (10.25% × 30/365). Its total interest cost would be $2,527 [$100,000 × (0.822% + 0.863% + 0.842%)], resulting in an effective 90-day rate of 2.527 percent ($2,527/$100,000).

Again, assuming the loan is rolled over each 90 days throughout the year under the same terms and circumstances, its effective *annual* rate is 10.65 percent:

$$\text{Effective annual rate} = (1 + 0.02527)^4 - 1$$
$$= 1.10499 - 1 = 0.1050 = \underline{\underline{10.50\%}}$$

Clearly, in this case the floating-rate loan would have been less expensive than the fixed-rate loan due to its generally lower effective annual rate, although this analysis is based on an unknown variable—the prime rate in the future.

Lines of Credit

line of credit
An agreement between a commercial bank and a business specifying the amount of unsecured short-term borrowing the bank will make available to the firm over a given period of time.

A **line of credit** is an agreement between a commercial bank and a business specifying the amount of unsecured short-term borrowing the bank will make available to the firm over a given period of time. It is similar to the agreement under which issuers of bank credit cards, such as MasterCard and Visa, extend preapproved credit to cardholders. A line-of-credit agreement is typically made for a period of 1 year and often places certain constraints on the borrower. It is *not a guaranteed loan* but indicates that if the bank has sufficient funds available, it will allow the borrower to owe it *up to* a certain amount of money. The amount of a line of credit is *the maximum amount the firm can owe the bank* at any point in time.

When applying for a line of credit, the borrower may be required to submit such documents as its cash budget, its pro forma income statement, its pro forma balance sheet, and its recent actual financial statements. If the bank finds the customer acceptable, the line of credit will be extended. The major attraction of a line of credit from a company's perspective is that it provides access to a predetermined maximum amount of funds, when the firm desires. It allows the firm to finance temporary cash shortages, or temporary increases in accounts receivable and/or inventory, without seeking a loan from a bank each time. For most companies, a line of credit is an operational and financial necessity. The major attraction of a line of credit from the bank's point of view is that it eliminates the need to examine the creditworthiness of a customer each time it borrows money.

Interest Rates   The interest rate on a line of credit is normally stated as a floating rate—the *prime rate plus a premium*. If the prime rate changes, the interest rate charged on new *as well as outstanding* borrowing automatically changes. The amount a borrower is charged in excess of the prime rate depends on its creditworthiness. The more creditworthy the borrower, the lower the premium (interest increment) above prime, and vice versa.

operating-change restrictions
Contractual restrictions that a bank may impose on a firm's financial condition or operations as part of a line-of-credit agreement.

Operating-Change Restrictions   In a line-of-credit agreement, a bank may impose **operating-change restrictions,** which give it the right to revoke the line if any major changes occur in the firm's financial condition or operations. The firm is usually required to submit up-to-date, and preferably audited, financial statements for periodic review. In addition, the bank typically needs to be informed of shifts in key managerial personnel or in the firm's operations before changes take place. Such changes may affect the future success and debt-paying ability of the firm and thus could alter its credit status. If the bank does not agree with the proposed changes and the firm makes them anyway, the bank has the right to revoke the line of credit.

Compensating Balances   To ensure that the borrower will be a good customer, many short-term unsecured bank loans—single-payment notes and lines of credit—often require the borrower to maintain, in a chequing account, a **compensating balance** equal to a certain percentage of the amount borrowed. Compensating balances of 10 to 20 percent are frequently required. A compensating balance not only forces the borrower to be a good customer of the bank but may also raise the interest cost to the borrower.

compensating balance
A required chequing account balance equal to a certain percentage of the amount borrowed from a bank under a line-of-credit or revolving credit agreement.

Example ▼

🔲 **Hint**
Sometimes the compensating balance is stated as a percentage of the amount of the line of credit. In other cases, it is linked to both the amount borrowed and the amount of the line of credit.

Estrada Graphics, a graphic design firm, has borrowed $1 million under a line-of-credit agreement. It must pay a stated interest rate of 10 percent and maintain, in its chequing account, a compensating balance equal to 20 percent of the amount borrowed, or $200,000. Thus it actually receives the use of only $800,000. To use that amount for a year, the firm pays interest of $100,000 (0.10 × $1,000,000). The effective annual rate on the funds is therefore 12.5 percent ($100,000 ÷ $800,000), 2.5 percent more than the stated rate of 10 percent.

If the firm normally maintains a balance of $200,000 or more in its chequing account, the effective annual rate equals the stated annual rate of 10 percent because none of the $1 million borrowed is needed to satisfy the compensating balance requirement. If the firm normally maintains a $100,000 balance in its chequing account, only an additional $100,000 will have to be tied up, leaving it with $900,000 of usable funds. The effective annual rate in this case would be 11.1 percent ($100,000 ÷ $900,000). Thus a compensating balance raises the cost of borrowing *only if* it is larger than **▲** the firm's normal cash balance.

Annual Cleanups   To ensure that money lent under a line-of-credit agreement is actually being used to finance seasonal needs, many banks require an **annual cleanup.** This means that the borrower must have a loan balance of zero—that is, owe the bank nothing—for a certain number of days during the year. Insisting that the borrower carry a zero loan balance for a certain period ensures that short-term loans do not turn into long-term loans.

annual cleanup
The requirement that for a certain number of days during the year borrowers under a line of credit carry a zero loan balance (i.e., owe the bank nothing).

All the characteristics of a line-of-credit agreement are negotiable to some extent. Today, banks bid competitively to attract large, well known firms. A prospective borrower should attempt to negotiate a line of credit with the most favourable interest rate, for an optimal amount of funds, and with a minimum of restrictions. Borrowers today frequently pay fees to lenders instead of maintaining deposit balances as compensation for loans and other services. The lender attempts to get a good return with maximum safety. Negotiations should produce a line of credit that is suitable to both borrower and lender.

Revolving Credit Agreements

revolving credit agreement
A line of credit *guaranteed* to a borrower by a commercial bank regardless of the scarcity of money.

A **revolving credit agreement** is nothing more than a *guaranteed line of credit*. It is guaranteed in the sense that the commercial bank assures the borrower that a specified amount of funds will be made available regardless of the scarcity of money. The interest rate and other requirements are similar to those for a line of credit. It is not uncommon for a revolving credit agreement to be for a period greater than 1 year.[5] Because the bank guarantees the availability of funds, a **commitment fee** is normally charged on a revolving credit agreement.[6] This fee often applies to the average unused balance of the credit line. It is normally about 0.5 percent of the *average unused portion* of the funds.

commitment fee
The fee that is normally charged on a *revolving credit agreement;* it often applies to the average unused balance of the borrower's credit line.

Example ▼ REH Company, a major real estate developer, has a $2 million revolving credit agreement with its bank. Its average borrowing under the agreement for the past year was $1.5 million. The bank charges a commitment fee of 0.5 percent. Because the average unused portion of the committed funds was $500,000 ($2 million − $1.5 million), the commitment fee for the year was $2,500 (0.005 × $500,000). Of course, REH also had to pay interest on the actual $1.5 million borrowed under the agreement. Assuming that $160,000 interest was paid on the $1.5 million borrowed, the effective cost of the agreement is 10.83 percent [($160,000 + $2,500)/$1,500,000]. Although more expensive than a line of credit, a revolving credit agreement can be less risky from the borrower's view-
▲ point, because the availability of funds is guaranteed.

Commercial Paper

commercial paper
A form of financing consisting of short-term, unsecured promissory notes issued by firms with a high credit standing.

Commercial paper is a form of financing that consists of short-term, unsecured promissory notes issued by firms with a high credit standing. Generally, only quite large firms of unquestionable financial soundness are able to issue commercial paper. Most commercial paper has maturities ranging from 3 to 270 days. Although there is no set denomination, it is generally issued in multiples of $100,000 or more. A large portion of the commercial paper today is issued by finance companies; manufacturing firms account for a smaller portion of this type of financing. Businesses often purchase commercial paper, which they hold as marketable securities, to provide an interest-earning reserve of liquidity.

Interest on Commercial Paper

Commercial paper is sold at a discount from its *par,* or *face, value.* The interest paid by the issuer of commercial paper is determined by the size of the discount and the length of time to maturity. The actual interest earned by the purchaser is determined by certain calculations, illustrated by the following example.

Example ▼ Bertram Corporation, a large shipbuilder, has just issued $1 million worth of commercial paper that has a 90-day maturity and sells for $980,000. At the end of 90 days, the purchaser of this paper will receive $1 million for its $980,000 investment. The interest paid on the financing is therefore $20,000 on a principal

---

5. A revolving credit agreement may be classified as a form of *intermediate-term financing,* defined as having a maturity of 1 to 7 years. In this text, the intermediate-term financing classification is not used; only short-term and long-term classifications are made. Because many revolving credit agreements are for more than 1 year, they can be classified as a form of long-term financing; however, they are discussed here because of their similarity to line-of-credit agreements.

6. Some banks not only require payment of the commitment fee, but also require the borrower to maintain, in addition to a compensating balance against actual borrowings, a compensating balance of 10 percent or so against the unused portion of the commitment.

Financing Footwear

You won't see "Bennett Footwear Group" on any of the shoes in your closet, but you may own some of its shoe brands, which include Franco Sarto, Danelle, and Zodiac. Bennett designs, imports, and distributes women and children's footwear and also markets its footwear through private-label programs with many key customers. Founded in 1961 as Bennett Importing, the company merged in 1998 with two other footwear companies, positioning the combined enterprise to serve a wide range of footwear markets. The company imports shoes from Italy, Brazil, China, and Portugal. Today Bennett's customers include value-oriented retailers such as Payless ShoeSource and Wal-Mart, as well as many boutiques and even on-line shoe stores.

Although the merger created economies of scale and better market penetration, it also brought Bennett a complex financial structure with too much debt. Bennett also needed funds to grow its business quickly in three areas: (1) to take advantage of the increasing popularity of the Franco Sarto brand, (2) to branch out into men's shoes and accessories, and (3) to expand its private-label products for mass merchandisers.

To deal with their financing problems, Bennett approached CIT Group. CIT Group is a leading source of factoring, financing, and leasing capital and an advisor for companies in more than 30 industries. CIT manages about $50 billion in assets across a diversi-

fied portfolio. Founded in 1908, the company operates in Canada and the United States. They are a leading lender to companies in the apparel and footwear industry.

Bennett and CIT Group worked together to develop a sound program to restructure the company's debt, provide growth capital, and improve liquidity. CIT's industry knowledge and its experience lending to similar companies helped it arrive at a fair value for the inventory and accounts receivable that would serve as loan collateral (security). CIT provided Bennett with a $20 million revolving line of credit secured by inventory, accounts receivable, and trade names, as well as a $6 million three-year term loan.

This financing allowed Bennett to replace debt provided by a former lender and retire $11.5 million of short-term notes. The CIT loans also provided abundant liquidity for Bennett to continue to pursue its aggressive expansion plans for Franco Sarto. With the new line of credit, Bennett had the funds to clean up its balance sheet and keep growing by expanding the popular Franco Sarto line of footwear.

REFERENCES: Case study—Bennett Footwear Group, available at: **www.citcommercialfinance.com/outlooks/ dsp_articles_bennett.asp**; Bennett Footwear Group company overview available at: **company.monster.com/bfg**.

of $980,000. The effective 90-day rate on the paper is 2.04 percent ($20,000/$980,000). To determine the effective annual cost (or rate of return), Equation 15.4 is used, where V is the par value of the discounted security, P is the amount paid, i is the annual yield, and n is the number of days to maturity:

$$V = P \times \left[1 + \frac{i \times n}{365} \right] \tag{15.4}$$

Based on this equation, the effective annual cost of Bertram Corporation's commercial paper is:

$$\$1,000,000 = \$980,000 \times \left[1 + \frac{i \times 90}{365}\right]$$

$$\$1,000,000 = \$980,000 + \frac{\$980,000 \times i \times 90}{365}$$

$$\$20,000 = 241,643.8356i$$

$$i = 0.082766$$

$$i = 8.28\%$$

An interesting characteristic of commercial paper is that its interest cost is *normally* 2 to 4 percent below the prime rate. In other words, firms are able to raise funds more cheaply by selling commercial paper than by borrowing from a commercial bank. The reason is that many suppliers of short-term funds do not have the option, as banks do, of making low-risk business loans at the prime rate. They can invest safely only in marketable securities such as Government of Canada treasury bills and commercial paper. The yields on these marketable securities on October 18, 2002, when the prime rate of interest was 4.5 percent, were about 2.69 percent for 3-month t-bills and about 2.86 percent for 3-month commercial paper (see Table 14.6).

Although the stated interest cost of borrowing through the sale of commercial paper is normally lower than the prime rate, the *overall cost* of commercial paper may not be less than that of a bank loan. Additional costs include the fees paid by most issuers to obtain the bank line of credit used to back the paper, fees paid to obtain third-party ratings used to make the paper more salable, and flotation costs. In addition, even if it is slightly more expensive to borrow from a commercial bank, it may at times be advisable to do so to establish a good working relationship with a bank. This strategy ensures that when money is tight, funds can be obtained promptly and at a reasonable interest rate.

! Hint
Commercial paper is directly placed with investors by the issuer or is sold by dealers in commercial paper. Most of it is purchased by other businesses and financial institutions.

International Loans

In some ways, arranging short-term financing for international trade is no different from financing purely domestic operations. In both cases, producers must finance production and inventory and then continue to finance accounts receivable before collecting any cash payments from sales. In other ways, however, the short-term financing of international sales and purchases is fundamentally different from that of strictly domestic trade.

International Transactions

The important difference between international and domestic transactions is that payments are often made or received in a foreign currency. Not only must a Canadian company pay the costs of doing business in the foreign exchange market, but it also is exposed to *exchange rate risk*. A Canadian-based company that exports goods and has accounts receivable denominated in a foreign currency faces the risk that the Canadian dollar will appreciate in value relative to the foreign currency. The risk to a Canadian importer with foreign-currency-denominated accounts payable is that the dollar will depreciate. Although *exchange rate risk* can often be *hedged* by using currency forward, futures, or options markets, doing so is costly and is not possible for all foreign currencies.

Typical international transactions are large in size and have long maturity dates. Therefore, companies that are involved in international trade generally have to finance larger dollar amounts for longer time periods than companies that operate domestically. Furthermore, because foreign companies may be deemed more risky, some financial institutions are reluctant to lend to Canadian exporters or importers, particularly smaller firms.

Financing International Trade

letter of credit
A letter written by a company's bank to the company's foreign supplier, stating that the bank guarantees payment of an invoiced amount if all the underlying agreements are met.

Several specialized techniques have evolved for financing international trade. Perhaps the most important financing vehicle is the **letter of credit**, a letter written by a company's bank to the company's foreign supplier, stating that the bank guarantees payment of an invoiced amount if all the underlying agreements are met. The letter of credit essentially substitutes the bank's reputation and creditworthiness for that of its commercial customer. A Canadian exporter is more willing to sell goods to a foreign buyer if the transaction is covered by a letter of credit issued by a well-known bank in the buyer's home country.

Firms that do business in foreign countries on an ongoing basis often finance their operations, at least in part, in the local market. A company that has an assembly plant in Mexico, for example, might choose to finance its purchases of Mexican goods and services with peso funds borrowed from a Mexican bank. This not only minimizes exchange rate risk, but also improves the company's business ties to the host community. Multinational companies, however, sometimes finance their international transactions through dollar-denominated loans from international banks. The *Eurocurrency loan markets* allow creditworthy borrowers to obtain financing on very attractive terms.

Transactions Between Subsidiaries

Much international trade involves transactions between corporate subsidiaries. A Canadian company might, for example, manufacture one part in an Asian plant and another part in the United States, assemble the product in Brazil, and sell it in Europe. The shipment of goods back and forth between subsidiaries creates accounts receivable and accounts payable, but the parent company has considerable discretion about how and when payments are made. In particular, the parent can minimize foreign exchange fees and other transaction costs by "netting" what affiliates owe each other and paying only the net amount due, rather than having both subsidiaries pay each other the gross amounts due.

? Review Questions

15–4   How is the *prime rate of interest* relevant to the cost of short-term bank borrowing? What is a *floating-rate loan*?

15–5   How does the *effective annual rate* differ between a loan requiring interest payments *at maturity* and another, similar loan requiring interest *in advance*?

15–6   What are the basic terms and characteristics of a *single-payment note*? How is the *effective annual rate* on such a note found?

15–7   What is a *line of credit*? Describe each of the following features that are often included in these agreements: (**a**) operating change restrictions; (**b**) compensating balance; and (**c**) annual cleanup.

15–8   What is a *revolving credit agreement*? How does this arrangement differ from the line-of-credit agreement? What is a *commitment fee*?

15–9   How is *commercial paper* used to raise short-term funds? Who can issue commercial paper? Who buys commercial paper?

15–10   What is the important difference between international and domestic transactions? How is a *letter of credit* used in financing international trade transactions? How is "netting" used in transactions between subsidiaries?

15.3 Secured Sources of Short-Term Loans

secured short-term financing
Short-term financing (loans) that has specific assets pledged as collateral.

security agreement
The agreement between the borrower and the lender that specifies the collateral held against a secured loan.

When a firm has exhausted its sources of unsecured short-term financing, it may be able to obtain additional short-term loans on a secured basis. **Secured short-term financing** has specific assets pledged as collateral. The *collateral* commonly takes the form of an asset, such as accounts receivable or inventory. The lender obtains a security interest in the collateral through the execution of a **security agreement** with the borrower that specifies the collateral held against the loan. In addition, the terms of the loan against which the security is held form part of the security agreement. They specify the conditions required for the security interest to be removed, along with the interest rate on the loan, repayment dates, and other loan provisions.

Characteristics of Secured Short-Term Loans

Although many people believe that holding collateral as security reduces the risk of a loan, lenders do not usually view loans in this way. Lenders recognize that holding collateral can reduce losses if the borrower defaults, but *the presence of collateral has no impact on the risk of default*. A lender requires collateral to ensure recovery of some portion of the loan in the event of default. What the lender wants above all, however, is to be repaid as scheduled. In general, lenders prefer to make less risky loans at lower rates of interest than to be in a position in which they must liquidate collateral.

Collateral and Terms

Lenders of secured short-term funds prefer collateral that has a duration closely matched to the term of the loan. Current assets—accounts receivable and inventories—are the most desirable short-term loan collateral, because they can normally be converted into cash much sooner than fixed assets. Thus, the short-term lender of secured funds generally accepts only liquid current assets as collateral.

percentage advance
The percentage of the book value of the collateral that constitutes the principal of a secured loan.

Typically, the lender determines the desirable **percentage advance** to make against the collateral. This percentage advance constitutes the principal of the secured loan and is normally between 30 and 100 percent of the book value of the collateral. It varies according to the type and liquidity of collateral.

The interest rate that is charged on secured short-term loans is typically lower than on unsecured short-term loans. For example, the interest rate on a secured line of credit is usually lower than on an unsecured line of credit. The security (collateral) pledged ensures that the company is able to repay all or a very high percentage of the amount borrowed so the bank is willing to lend money at a lower interest rate. The lower rate is usually indicated by a lower premium added to the prime rate. For some types of secured loans, however, a higher rate of interest may be charged. This is often due to the high risk associated with the borrower or with the collateral pledged.

Institutions Extending Secured Short-Term Loans

The primary sources of secured short-term loans to businesses are commercial banks and finance companies. Both institutions deal in short-term loans secured primarily by accounts receivable and inventory. The operations of these institutions were described in Chapter 6.

Only when its unsecured and secured short-term borrowing power from the commercial bank is exhausted will a borrower turn to a finance company for additional secured borrowing. Because the finance company generally ends up with higher risk borrowers, its interest charges on secured short-term loans are usually higher than those of commercial banks.

The Use of Accounts Receivable as Collateral

Two commonly used means of obtaining short-term financing with accounts receivable are *pledging accounts receivable* and *factoring accounts receivable*. Actually, only a pledge of accounts receivable creates a secured short-term loan; factoring really entails the *sale* of accounts receivable at a discount. Although factoring is not actually a form of secured short-term borrowing, it does involve the use of accounts receivable to obtain needed short-term funds.

Pledging Accounts Receivable

A **pledge of accounts receivable** is often used to secure a short-term loan. Because accounts receivable are normally quite liquid, they are an attractive form of short-term loan collateral.

pledge of accounts receivable
The use of a firm's accounts receivable as security, or collateral, to obtain a short-term loan.

The Pledging Process   When a firm requests a loan against accounts receivable, the lender first evaluates the firm's accounts receivable to determine their desirability as collateral. The lender makes a list of the acceptable accounts, along with the billing dates and amounts. If the borrowing firm requests a loan for a fixed amount, the lender needs to select only enough accounts to secure the funds requested. If the borrower wants the maximum loan available, the lender evaluates all the accounts to select the maximum amount of acceptable collateral.

After selecting the acceptable accounts, the lender normally adjusts the dollar value of these accounts for expected returns on sales and other allowances. If a customer whose account has been pledged returns merchandise or receives some type of allowance, such as a cash discount for early payment, the amount of the collateral is automatically reduced. For protection from such occurrences, the lender normally reduces the value of the acceptable collateral by a fixed percentage.

Next, the percentage to be advanced against the collateral must be determined. The lender evaluates the quality of the acceptable receivables and the expected cost of their liquidation. This percentage represents the principal of the loan and typically ranges between 50 and 90 percent of the face value of acceptable accounts receivable. To protect its interest in the collateral, the lender files a **lien,** which is a publicly disclosed legal claim on the collateral. For an example of the complete pledging process, see the book's Web site at **www.pearsoned.ca/gitman.**

lien
A publicly disclosed legal claim on collateral.

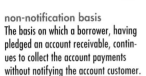

non-notification basis
The basis on which a borrower, having pledged an account receivable, continues to collect the account payments without notifying the account customer.

notification basis
The basis on which an account customer whose account has been pledged (or factored) is notified to remit payment directly to the lender (or factor).

Notification   Pledges of accounts receivable are normally made on a **non-notification basis,** meaning that a customer whose account has been pledged as collateral is not notified. Under the non-notification arrangement, the borrower still collects the pledged account receivable, and the lender trusts the borrower to remit these payments as they are received. If a pledge of accounts receivable is made on a **notification basis,** the customer is notified to remit payment directly to the lender.

Pledging Cost   The stated cost of a pledge of accounts receivable is normally 2 to 5 percent above the prime rate. In addition to the stated interest rate, a service charge of up to 3 percent may be levied by the lender to cover its administrative costs. Clearly, pledges of accounts receivable are a high-cost source of short-term financing.

Factoring Accounts Receivable

factoring accounts receivable
The outright sale of accounts receivable at a discount to a *factor* or other financial institution.

factor
A financial institution that specializes in purchasing accounts receivable from businesses.

Factoring accounts receivable involves selling them outright, at a discount, to a financial institution. A **factor** is a financial institution that specializes in purchasing accounts receivable from businesses. Some commercial banks and finance companies also factor accounts receivable. Although not the same as obtaining a short-term loan, factoring accounts receivable is similar to borrowing with accounts receivable as collateral.

Factoring Agreement   A factoring agreement normally states the exact conditions and procedures for the purchase of an account. The factor, like a lender against a pledge of accounts receivable, chooses accounts for purchase, selecting only those that appear to be acceptable credit risks. Where factoring is to be on a continuing basis, the factor will actually make the firm's credit decisions, because this will guarantee the acceptability of accounts.[7] Factoring is normally done on a *notification basis,* and the factor receives payment of the account directly from the customer. In addition, most sales of accounts receivable to a factor are made on a **non-recourse basis.** This means that the factor agrees to accept all credit risks. Thus, if a purchased account turns out to be uncollectible, the factor must absorb the loss.

non-recourse basis
The basis on which accounts receivable are sold to a factor with the understanding that the factor accepts all credit risks on the purchased accounts.

---

7. The use of credit cards such as MasterCard and Visa by consumers has some similarity to factoring, because the vendor that accepts the card is reimbursed at a discount for purchases made with the card. The difference between factoring and credit cards is that cards are nothing more than a line of credit extended by the issuer, which charges the vendors a fee for accepting the cards. In factoring, the factor does not analyze credit until after the sale has been made; in many cases (except when factoring is done on a continuing basis), the initial credit decision is the responsibility of the vendor, not the factor who purchases the account.

IN PRACTICE

Securitization of Accounts Receivable

Traditionally, corporations raise funds by using either debt or equity capital. The debt could be short-term, like a line of credit or commercial paper, or long-term, like long-term bank loans, bonds and debentures, or mortgages. During the 1980s, securitization started to be used as a method of raising financing. Sometimes referred to as structured financing, this method is now widely used in Canada. Structured financing typically involves converting an income-producing asset to cash. The cash is a source of financing for the company.

Securitization is often used with accounts receivable. This technique takes accounts receivable off the company's balance sheet while generating cash for the company. Financing is raised without issuing either debt or equity. Therefore, securitization can raise financing without affecting the company's capital structure, thus preserving the company's borrowing capacity. In addition, unlike the pledging or factoring of accounts receivable, the financing raised through securitization has a very low cost and can be raised at fixed or floating interest rates.

As an example, Aliant Telecom, the telecommunications company serving all of Atlantic Canada, initiated a securitization agreement in December 2001. Aliant entered into a $150 million accounts receivable securitization agreement with the Bank of Nova Scotia whereby Aliant sold accounts receivable to a securitization trust on a revolving basis. As of September 30, 2002, Aliant had sold $135 million of accounts receivable and had transferred $165 million to the trust.

The short-term financing raised by securitizing their accounts receivable had a lower cost than an issue of commercial paper and was used to retire maturing commercial paper. As part of the securitization agreement, Aliant agreed to refund cash to the trust in case customers defaulted on any of the receivables under securitization. The company also provided surplus receivables in case of default.

In another example, in July 2002, Telus Corporation, the second largest telecommunications company in Canada, announced a securitization agreement to sell approximately $500 million of accounts receivables. About $285 million of the funds raised were added to the company's working capital position, while the remainder were used to retire debt obligation. Telus is required to maintain at least a BBB(low) credit rating or the securitization agreement could be cancelled. In July, Telus was rated BBB(mid) by the Dominion Bond Rating Service (DBRS).

In Canada, the methods used to raise financing are constantly changing as new techniques are developed by financial intermediaries. These new methods can have a number of advantages over the traditional ways of raising funds. The securitization of receivables is a popular and rapidly growing way of raising inexpensive short-term financing.

SOURCES: Aliant Inc., 3rd Quarter Report, September 30, 2002; and "TELUS Arranges $500 Million Accounts Receivable Sale," Telus Coporation press release, July 29, 2002.

Typically, the factor is not required to pay the firm until the account is collected or until the last day of the credit period, whichever occurs first. The factor sets up an account similar to a bank deposit account for each customer. As payment is received or as due dates arrive, the factor deposits money into the seller's account, from which the seller is free to make withdrawals as needed.

In many cases, if the firm leaves the money in the account, a *surplus* will exist on which the factor will pay interest. In other instances, the factor may make *advances* to the firm against uncollected accounts that are not yet due. These advances represent a negative balance in the firm's account, on which interest is charged.

Factoring Cost   Factoring costs include commissions, interest levied on advances, and interest earned on surpluses. The factor deposits in the firm's account the book value of the collected or due accounts purchased by the factor, less the commissions. The commissions are typically stated as a 1 to 3 percent discount from the book value of factored accounts receivable. The *interest levied on advances* is generally 2 to 4 percent above the prime rate. It is levied on the actual amount advanced. The *interest paid on surpluses* is generally between 0.2 and 0.5 percent per month. An example of the factoring process is included on the book's Web site at **www.pearsoned.ca/gitman**.

Although its costs may seem high, factoring has certain advantages that make it attractive to many firms. One is the ability it gives the firm to *turn accounts receivable immediately into cash* without having to worry about repayment. Another advantage of factoring is that it ensures a *known pattern of cash flows*. In addition, if factoring is undertaken on a continuing basis, the firm *can eliminate its credit and collection departments*.

The Use of Inventory as Collateral

Inventory is generally second to accounts receivable in desirability as short-term loan collateral. Inventory normally has a market value that is greater than its book value, which is used to establish its value as collateral. A lender whose loan is secured with inventory will probably be able to sell that inventory for at least book value if the borrower defaults on its obligations.

The most important characteristic of inventory being evaluated as loan collateral is *marketability*, which must be considered in light of its physical properties. A warehouse of *perishable* items, such as fresh peaches, may be quite marketable, but if the cost of storing and selling the peaches is high, they may not be desirable collateral. *Specialized items,* such as fibre-optic cable, are not desirable collateral either, because finding a buyer for them could be difficult. When evaluating inventory as possible loan collateral, the lender looks for items with very stable market prices that have ready markets and that lack undesirable physical properties.

Floating Inventory Liens

floating inventory lien
A secured short-term loan against inventory under which the lender's claim is on the borrower's inventory in general.

A lender may be willing to secure a loan under a **floating inventory lien,** which is a claim on inventory in general. This arrangement is most attractive when the firm has a stable level of inventory that consists of a diversified group of relatively inexpensive merchandise. Inventories of items such as auto tires, screws and bolts, and shoes are candidates for floating-lien loans. Because it is difficult for a lender to verify the presence of the inventory, the lender will generally advance less than 50 percent of the book value of the average inventory. The interest charge on a floating lien is 3 to 5 percent above the prime rate. Commercial banks often require floating liens as extra security on what would otherwise be an unsecured loan. Floating-lien inventory loans may also be available from finance companies. An example of a floating lien is included on the book's Web site at **www.pearsomed.com/gitman**.

Trust Receipt Inventory Loans

A **trust receipt inventory loan** often can be made against relatively expensive automotive, consumer durable, and industrial goods that can be identified by serial number. Under this agreement, the borrower keeps the inventory and the lender may advance 80 to 100 percent of its cost. The lender files a *lien* on all the items financed. The borrower is free to sell the merchandise but is trusted to remit the amount lent, along with accrued interest, to the lender immediately after the sale. The lender then releases the lien on the item. The lender makes periodic checks of the borrower's inventory to make sure that the required amount of collateral remains in the hands of the borrower. The interest charge to the borrower is normally 2 percent or more above the prime rate.

Trust receipt loans are often made by manufacturers' wholly owned financing subsidiaries, known as *captive finance companies,* to their customers. Captive finance companies are especially popular in industries that manufacture consumer durable goods, because they provide the manufacturer with a useful sales tool. For example, General Motors Acceptance Corporation (GMAC), the financing subsidiary of General Motors, grants these types of loans to its dealers. Trust receipt loans are also available through commercial banks and finance companies.

trust receipt inventory loan
A secured short-term loan against inventory under which the lender advances 80 to 100 percent of the cost of the borrower's relatively expensive inventory items in exchange for the borrower's promise to repay the lender, with accrued interest, immediately after the sale of each item of collateral.

Warehouse Receipt Loans

A **warehouse receipt loan** is an arrangement whereby the lender, who may be a commercial bank or finance company, receives control of the pledged inventory collateral, which is stored by a designated agent on the lender's behalf. After selecting acceptable collateral, the lender hires a warehousing company to act as its agent and take possession of the inventory.

Two types of warehousing arrangements are possible. A *terminal warehouse* is a central warehouse that is used to store the merchandise of various customers. The lender normally uses such a warehouse when the inventory is easily transported and can be delivered to the warehouse relatively inexpensively. Under a *field warehouse* arrangement, the lender hires a field warehousing company to set up a warehouse on the borrower's premises or to lease part of the borrower's warehouse to store the pledged collateral. Regardless of which type of warehouse is used, the warehousing company places a guard over the inventory. Only on written approval of the lender can any portion of the secured inventory be released by the warehousing company.

The actual lending agreement specifically states the requirements for the release of inventory. As in the case of other secured loans, the lender accepts only collateral that is believed to be readily marketable and advances only a portion—generally 75 to 90 percent—of the collateral's value. The specific costs of warehouse receipt loans are generally higher than those of any other secured lending arrangements due to the need to hire and pay a warehousing company to guard and supervise the collateral. The basic interest charged on warehouse receipt loans is higher than that charged on unsecured loans, generally ranging

warehouse receipt loan
A secured short-term loan against inventory under which the lender receives control of the pledged inventory collateral, which is stored by a designated warehousing company on the lender's behalf.

from 3 to 5 percent above the prime rate. In addition to the interest charge, the borrower must absorb the costs of warehousing by paying the warehouse fee, which is generally between 1 and 3 percent of the amount of the loan. The borrower is normally also required to pay the insurance costs on the warehoused merchandise. An example of the procedures and costs of a warehouse receipt loan is included on the book's Web site at **www.pearsoned.ca/gitman**.

? Review Questions

15–11 Are secured short-term loans viewed as more risky or less risky than unsecured short-term loans? Why?

15–12 In general, what interest rates and fees are levied on secured short-term loans? Why are these rates generally *higher* than the rates on unsecured short-term loans?

15–13 Describe and compare the basic features of the following methods of using *accounts receivable* to obtain short-term financing: (a) pledging accounts receivable and (b) factoring accounts receivable. Be sure to mention the institutions that offer each of them.

15–14 For the following methods of using *inventory* as short-term loan collateral, describe the basic features of each, and compare their use: (a) floating lien; (b) trust receipt loan; and (c) warehouse receipt loan.

SUMMARY

 Review the key components of a firm's credit terms and the procedures for analyzing them. The major spontaneous source of short-term financing is accounts payable, which are the primary source of short-term funds. Accounts payable result from credit purchases of merchandise. The key features of this form of financing are summarized in part I of Table 15.2. Credit terms may differ with respect to the credit period, cash discount, cash discount period, and beginning of the credit period. The cost of giving up cash discounts is a factor in deciding whether to take or give up a cash discount. Cash discounts should be given up only when a firm in need of short-term funds must pay an interest rate on borrowing that is greater than the cost of giving up the cash discount.

Understand the effects of stretching accounts payable on their cost, and the use of accruals. Stretching accounts payable can lower the cost of giving up a cash discount. This is because the firm can keep its money longer if it gives up the discount. Accruals, which result primarily from wage and tax obligations, are virtually free. The key features of this spontaneous liability are summarized in part I of Table 15.2.

 Describe the interest rates and basic types of unsecured bank sources of short-term loans. Banks are the major source of unsecured short-term loans to businesses. The interest rate on these loans is based on the prime rate of interest plus a risk premium and may be fixed or floating. It should be evaluated by using the effective annual rate. This rate is calculated differently, depending on whether interest is paid when the loan matures or in advance. Bank loans may take the form of a single-payment note, a line of credit, or a revolving credit agreement. The key features of the various types of bank loans are summarized in part I of Table 15.4.

Discuss the basic features of commercial paper and the key aspects of international short-term loans. Commercial paper is an unsecured IOU issued by firms with a high credit standing. The key features of commercial paper are summarized in part II of Table 15.2. International sales and purchases expose firms to exchange rate risk. They are larger and of longer maturity than typical transactions, and can be financed using a letter of credit, by borrowing in the local market, or through dollar-denominated loans from international banks. On transactions between subsidiaries, "netting" can be used to minimize foreign exchange fees and other transaction costs.

Explain the characteristics of secured short-term loans and the use of accounts receivable as short-term loan collateral. Secured short-term loans are those for which the lender requires collateral—typically, current assets such as accounts receivable or inventory. Only a percentage of the

book value of acceptable collateral is advanced by the lender. These loans are more expensive than unsecured loans; collateral does not lower the risk of default, and increased administrative costs result. Both commercial banks and finance companies make secured short-term loans. Both pledging, which is the use of accounts receivable as loan collateral, and factoring, which is the outright sale of accounts receivable at a discount, involve the use of accounts receivable to obtain needed short-term funds. The key features of loans using accounts receivable as collateral are summarized in part III of Table 15.2.

 Describe the various ways in which inventory can be used as short-term loan collateral. Inventory can be used as short-term loan collateral under a floating lien, a trust receipt arrangement, or a warehouse receipt loan. The key features of loans using inventory as collateral are summarized in part III of Table 15.2.

TABLE 15.2   Summary of Key Features of Common Sources of Short-Term Financing

Type of short-term financing	Source	Cost or conditions	Characteristics
I. Spontaneous sources of short-term financing			
Accounts payable	Suppliers of government government	No stated cost except when a cash discount is offered for early payment.	Credit extended on open account for 0 to 120 days. The largest source of short-term financing.
Accruals	Employees and government	Free.	Result because wages (employees) and taxes (government) are paid at discrete points in time after the service has been rendered. Hard to manipulate this source of financing.
II. Unsecured sources of short-term loans			
Bank sources			
(1) Single-payment notes	Commercial banks	Prime plus 0% to 4% risk premium—fixed or floating rate.	A single-payment loan used to meet a funds shortage expected to last only a short period of time.
(2) Lines of credit	Commercial banks	Prime plus 0% to 4% risk premium—fixed or floating rate. Often must maintain 10% to 20% compensating balance and clean up the line annually.	A prearranged borrowing limit under which funds, if available, will be lent to allow the borrower to meet seasonal needs.

(continued)

TABLE 15.2 *(continued)*

Type of short-term financing	Source	Cost or conditions	Characteristics
(3) Revolving credit agreements	Commercial banks	Prime plus 0% to 4% risk premium—fixed or floating rate. Often must maintain 10% to 20% compensating balance and pay a commitment fee of approximately 0.5% of the average unused balance.	A line-of-credit agreement under which the availability of funds is guaranteed. Often for a period greater than one year.
Commercial paper	Business firms—both nonfinancial and financial	Generally 2% to 4% below the prime rate of interest.	An unsecured short-term promissory note issued by the most financially sound firms.

III. Secured sources of short-term loans

Accounts receivable collateral

(1) Pledging	Commercial banks and finance companies	2% to 5% above prime plus up to 3% in fees. Advance 50% to 90% of collateral value.	Selected accounts receivable are used as collateral. The borrower is trusted to remit to the lender on collection of pledged accounts. Done on a non-notification basis.
(2) Factoring	Factors, commercial banks, and finance companies	1% to 3% discount from face value of factored accounts. Interest of 2% to 4% above prime levied on advances. Interest between 0.2% and 0.5% per month earned on surplus balances left with factor.	Selected accounts are sold—generally without recourse—at a discount. All credit risks go with the accounts. Factor will lend (make advances) against uncollected accounts that are not yet due. Factor will also pay interest on surplus balances. Typically done on a notification basis.

Inventory collateral

(1) Floating liens	Commercial banks and finance companies	3% to 5% above prime. Advance less than 50% of collateral value.	A loan against inventory in general. Made when firm has stable inventory of a variety of inexpensive items.
(2) Trust receipts	Manufacturers' captive financing subsidiaries, commercial banks, and finance companies	2% or more above prime. Advance 80% to 100% of cost of collateral.	Loan against relatively expensive automotive, consumer durable, and industrial goods that can be identified by serial number. Collateral remains in possession of borrower, who is trusted to remit proceeds to lender upon its sale.
(3) Warehouse receipts	Commercial banks and finance companies	3% to 5% above prime plus a 1% to 3% warehouse fee. Advance 75% to 90% of collateral value.	Inventory used as collateral is placed under control of the lender either through a terminal warehouse or through a field warehouse. A third party—a warehousing company—guards the inventory for the lender. Inventory is released only on written approval of the lender.

(Solutions in Appendix B)

  ST 15–1   Cash discount decisions   The credit terms for each of three suppliers are shown in the following table.

Supplier	Credit terms
X	1/10 net 55
Y	2/10 net 30
Z	2/20 net 60

a. Determine the cost of giving up the cash discount from each supplier.
b. Assuming that the firm needs short-term financing, recommend whether it would be better to give up the cash discount or take the discount and borrow from a bank at 15 percent annual interest. Evaluate each supplier separately using your findings in part **a**.
c. What impact, if any, would the fact that the firm could stretch its accounts payable (net period only) by 20 days from supplier Z have on your answer in part **b** relative to this supplier?

PROBLEMS

WARM-UP 15–1   Payment dates   Determine when a firm must make payment for purchases made and invoices dated on November 25 under each of the following credit terms.
a. net 30 date of invoice
b. net 30 EOM
c. net 45 date of invoice
d. net 60 EOM

WARM-UP 15–2   Cost of giving up cash discounts   Determine the cost of giving up cash discounts under each of the following terms of sale.
a. 2/10 net 30
b. 1/10 net 30
c. 2/10 net 45
d. 3/10 net 45
e. 1/10 net 60
f. 3/10 net 30
g. 4/10 net 180

INTERMEDIATE 15–3   Credit terms   Purchases made on credit are due in full by the end of the billing period. Many firms extend a discount for payment made in the first part of the billing period. The original invoice contains a type of shorthand notation that explains the credit terms that apply.

a. Write the shorthand expression of credit terms for each of the following.

Cash discount	Cash discount period	Credit period	Beginning of credit period
1%	15 days	45 days	Date of invoice
2	10	30	End of month
2	7	28	Date of invoice
1	10	60	End of month

b. For each of the sets of credit terms in **a**, calculate the number of days until full payment is due for invoices dated March 12.

c. For each of the set of credit terms, calculate the cost of giving up the cash discount.

d. If the firm's cost of short-term financing is 8 percent, what would you recommend in regard to taking the discount or giving it up in each case?

WARM-UP **15–4   Cash discount versus loan**   Erica Stone works in an accounts payable department. She has attempted to convince her boss to take the discount on the 3/10 net 45 credit terms most suppliers offer, but her boss argues that giving up the 3 percent discount is less costly than a short-term loan at 14 percent. Prove to whoever is wrong that the other is correct.

 15–5   Cash discount decisions   Prairie Manufacturing has four possible suppliers, all of whom offer different credit terms. Except for the differences in credit terms, their products and services are virtually identical. The credit terms offered by each supplier are shown in the following table.

INTERMEDIATE

Supplier	Credit terms
J	1/10 net 30
K	2/20 net 80
L	1/20 net 60
M	3/10 net 55

a. Calculate the cost of giving up the cash discount from each supplier.

b. If the firm needs short-term funds, which are currently available from its commercial bank at 16 percent, and if each of the suppliers is viewed *separately*, which, if any, of the suppliers' cash discounts should the firm give up? Explain why.

c. What impact, if any, would the fact that the firm could stretch its accounts payable (net period only) by 30 days from supplier M have on your answer in part **b** relative to this supplier?

WARM-UP **15–6   Changing payment cycle**   Upon accepting the position of chief executive officer and chairman of Reeves Machinery, Frank Cheney changed the firm's weekly payday from Monday afternoon to the following Friday afternoon. The firm's weekly payroll was $10 million, and the cost of short-term funds was 13 percent. If the effect of this change was to delay cheque clearing by one week, what *annual* savings, if any, were realized?

 INTERMEDIATE **15–7   Spontaneous sources of funds, accruals**   When Tallman Haberdashery, Inc., merged with Meyers Men's Suits, Inc., Tallman's employees were switched from a weekly to a bi-weekly pay period. Tallman's weekly payroll amounted to $750,000. The cost of funds for the combined firms is 11 percent. What annual savings, if any, are realized by the change of pay period?

INTERMEDIATE **15–8   Cost of bank loan**   Data Back-Up Systems has obtained a $10,000, 90-day bank loan at an annual interest rate of 15 percent, payable at maturity.
a. How much interest (in dollars) will the firm pay on the 90-day loan?
b. Find the effective 90-day rate on the loan.
c. Annualize your finding in part **b** to find the effective annual rate for this loan, assuming that it is rolled over each 90 days throughout the year under the same terms and circumstances and that the interest is not paid but simply accumulated with the loan.

WARM-UP **15–9   Effective annual rate**   A financial institution made a $10,000, one-year discount loan at 10 percent interest, requiring a compensating balance equal to 20 percent of the face value of the loan. Determine the effective annual rate associated with this loan.

INTERMEDIATE **15–10   Compensating balances and effective annual rates**   Lincoln Industries has a line of credit at The Imperial Bank that requires it to pay 11 percent interest on its borrowing and maintain a compensating balance equal to 15 percent of the amount borrowed. The firm has borrowed $800,000 during the year under the agreement. Calculate the effective annual rate on the firm's borrowing in each of the following circumstances:
a. The firm normally maintains no deposit balances at The Imperial Bank.
b. The firm normally maintains $70,000 in deposit balances at The Imperial Bank.
c. The firm normally maintains $150,000 in deposit balances at The Imperial Bank.
d. Compare, contrast, and discuss your findings in parts **a, b,** and **c.**

INTERMEDIATE **15–11   Compensating balance vs. discount loan**   Weathers Catering Supply, Inc., needs to borrow $150,000 for 6 months. The Eastern Bank has offered to loan the funds at a 9 percent annual rate subject to a 10 percent compensating balance. The Western Bank has offered to lend the funds at a 9 percent annual rate with discount-loan terms. The principal of both loans would be payable at maturity as a single sum.
a. Calculate the effective annual rate of interest on each loan.
b. What could Weathers do that would reduce the effective annual rate on the the Eastern Bank loan?

CHALLENGE **15–12   Integrative—Comparison of loan terms**   Cumberland Furniture wishes to establish a prearranged borrowing agreement with its bank. The bank's terms for a line of credit are 3.30 percent over the prime rate, and each year the borrowing must be reduced to zero for a 30-day period. For an equivalent revolving credit agreement, the rate is 2.80 percent over prime with a commitment fee of 0.50 percent on the average unused balance. With both loans, the required compensating balance is equal to 20 percent of the amount borrowed. The prime rate is currently 8 percent. Both agreements have $4 million borrowing limits. The firm expects on average to borrow $2 million during the year no matter which loan agreement it decides to use.

a. What is the effective annual rate under the line of credit?

b. What is the effective annual rate under the revolving credit agreement? (*Hint:* Compute the ratio of the dollars that the firm will pay in interest and commitment fees to the dollars that the firm will effectively have use of.)

c. If the firm does expect to borrow an average of half the amount available, which arrangement would you recommend for the borrower? Explain why.

INTERMEDIATE    15–13   **Cost of commercial paper**   Commercial paper is sold at a discount. Fan Corporation has just sold an issue of 90-day commercial paper with a face value of $1 million. The firm has received initial proceeds of $978,000.

a. What is the effective annual rate Fan Corporation will pay for financing with commercial paper?

b. If a brokerage fee of $9,612 was paid from the initial proceeds to an investment banker for selling the issue, what effective annual rate will the firm pay?

INTERMEDIATE   15–14   **Accounts receivable as collateral**   Kentville City Castings (KCC) is attempting to obtain the maximum loan possible using accounts receivable as collateral. The firm extends net-30-day credit. The amounts that are owed KCC by its 12 credit customers, the average age of each account, and customer's average payment period are as shown in the following table.

Customer	Account receivable	Average age of account	Average payment period of customer
A	$37,000	40 days	30 days
B	42,000	25	50
C	15,000	40	60
D	8,000	30	35
E	50,000	31	40
F	12,000	28	30
G	24,000	30	70
H	46,000	29	40
I	3,000	30	65
J	22,000	25	35
K	62,000	35	40
L	80,000	60	70

a. If the bank will accept all accounts that can be collected in 45 days or less as long as the customer has a history of paying within 45 days, which accounts will be acceptable? What is the total dollar amount of accounts receivable collateral? (*Note:* Accounts receivable that have an average age greater than the customer's average payment period are also excluded.)

b. In addition to the conditions in part **a,** the bank recognizes that 5 percent of credit sales will be lost to returns and allowances. Also, the bank will lend only 80 percent of the acceptable collateral (after adjusting for returns and allowances). What level of funds would be made available through this lending source?

  15–15   Accounts receivable as collateral   Springer Products wishes to borrow $80,000 from a local bank using its accounts receivable to secure the loan. The bank's policy is to accept as collateral any accounts that are normally paid within 30 days of the end of the credit period, as long as the average age of the account is not greater than the customer's average payment period. Springer's accounts receivable, their average ages, and the average payment period for each customer are shown in the following table. The company extends terms of net 30 days.

INTERMEDIATE

Customer	Account receivable	Average age of account	Average payment period of customer
A	$20,000	10 days	40 days
B	6,000	40	35
C	22,000	62	50
D	11,000	68	65
E	2,000	14	30
F	12,000	38	50
G	27,000	55	60
H	19,000	20	35

a. Calculate the dollar amount of acceptable accounts receivable collateral held by Springer Products.
b. The bank reduces collateral by 10 percent for returns and allowances. What is the level of acceptable collateral under this condition?
c. The bank will advance 75 percent against the firm's acceptable collateral (after adjusting for returns and allowances). What amount can Springer borrow against these accounts?

 15–16   Accounts receivable as collateral, cost of borrowing   Maximum Bank has analyzed the accounts receivable of Scientific Software, Inc. The bank has chosen eight accounts totalling $134,000 that it will accept as collateral. The bank's terms include a lending rate set at prime + 3 percent and a 2 percent commission charge. The prime rate currently is 8.5 percent.

CHALLENGE

a. The bank will adjust the accounts by 10 percent for returns and allowances. It then will lend up to 85 percent of the adjusted acceptable collateral. What is the maximum amount that the bank will lend to Scientific Software?
b. What is Scientific Software's effective annual rate of interest if it borrows $100,000 for 12 months? For 6 months? For 3 months? (Assume that the prime rate remains at 8.5 percent during the life of the loan.)

INTERMEDIATE   **15–17**   **Factoring**   Blair Finance factors the accounts of the Holder Company. All eight factored accounts are shown in the table below, with the amount factored, the date due, and the status as of May 30. Indicate the amounts Blair should have remitted to Holder as of May 30 and the dates of those remittances. Assume that the factor's commission of 2 percent is deducted as part of determining the amount of the remittance.

Account	Amount	Date due	Status on May 30
A	$200,000	May 30	Collected May 15
B	90,000	May 30	Uncollected
C	110,000	May 30	Uncollected
D	85,000	June 15	Collected May 30
E	120,000	May 30	Collected May 27
F	180,000	June 15	Collected May 30
G	90,000	May 15	Uncollected
H	30,000	June 30	Collected May 30

15–18   **Inventory financing**   Raymond Manufacturing faces a liquidity crisis—it needs a loan of $100,000 for 30 days. Having no source of additional unsecured borrowing, the firm must find a secured short-term lender. The firm's accounts receivable are quite low, but its inventory is considered liquid and reasonably good collateral. The book value of the inventory is $300,000, of which $120,000 is finished goods.

CHALLENGE

(1) The Nation Bank will make a $100,000 *trust receipt* loan against the finished goods inventory. The annual interest rate on the loan is 12 percent on the outstanding loan balance plus a 0.25 percent administration fee levied against the $100,000 initial loan amount. Because it will be liquidated as inventory is sold, the average amount owed over the month is expected to be $75,000.

(2) The Bank of PEI will lend $100,000 against a *floating lien* on the book value of inventory for the 30-day period at an annual interest rate of 13 percent.

(3) Citizens' Bank and Trust will loan $100,000 against a *warehouse receipt* on the finished goods inventory and charge 15 percent annual interest on the outstanding loan balance. A 0.5 percent warehousing fee will be levied against the average amount borrowed. Because the loan will be liquidated as inventory is sold, the average loan balance is expected to be $60,000.

a. Calculate the dollar cost of each of the proposed plans for obtaining an initial loan amount of $100,000.

b. Which plan do you recommend? Why?

c. If the firm had made a purchase of $100,000 for which it had been given terms of 2/10 net 30, would it increase the firm's profitability to give up the discount and not borrow as recommended in part **b**? Why or why not?

Selecting Kanton Company's Financing Strategy and Unsecured Short-Term Borrowing Arrangement

Morton Mercado, the CFO of Kanton Company, carefully developed the estimates of the firm's total funds requirements for the coming year. These are shown in the following table.

Month	Total funds	Month	Total funds
January	$1,000,000	July	$6,000,000
February	1,000,000	August	5,000,000
March	2,000,000	September	5,000,000
April	3,000,000	October	4,000,000
May	5,000,000	November	2,000,000
June	7,000,000	December	1,000,000

In addition, Morton expects short-term financing costs of about 10 percent and long-term financing costs of about 14 percent during that period. He developed the three possible financing strategies that follow:

Strategy 1—Aggressive: Finance seasonal needs with short-term funds and permanent needs with long-term funds.
Strategy 2—Conservative: Finance an amount equal to the peak need with long-term funds and use short-term funds only in an emergency.
Strategy 3—Tradeoff: Finance $3,000,000 with long-term funds and finance the remaining funds requirements with short-term funds.

Using the data on the firm's total funds requirements, Morton estimated the average annual short-term and long-term financing requirements for each strategy in the coming year, as shown in the following table.

	Average annual financing		
Type of financing	Strategy 1 (aggressive)	Strategy 2 (conservative)	Strategy 3 (tradeoff)
Short-term	$2,500,000	$0	$1,666,667
Long-term	1,000,000	7,000,000	3,000,000

To ensure that, along with spontaneous financing from accounts payable and accruals, adequate short-term financing will be available, Morton plans to establish an unsecured short-term borrowing arrangement with its bank, National Bank of Canada. The bank has offered either a line of credit or a revolving credit agreement. The terms for a line of credit are an interest rate of 2.50 percent above the prime rate, and the amount borrowed must be reduced to zero for a 30-day period during the year. On an equivalent revolving credit agreement, the interest rate would be 3.00 percent above prime with a commitment fee of 0.50 percent on the average unused balance. Under both loans, a compensating balance equal to 20 percent of the amount borrowed would be required. The prime rate is currently 7 percent. Both the line-of-credit agreement and the revolving credit agreement would have borrowing limits of $1,000,000. For purposes of his analysis, Morton estimates that Kanton will borrow $600,000 on the average during the year, regardless of the financing strategy and loan arrangement it chooses.

Required

a. Determine the total annual cost of the three possible financing strategies.
b. Assuming that the firm expects its current assets to total $4 million throughout the year, determine the average amount of net working capital under each financing strategy. (*Hint:* Current liabilities equal average short-term financing.)
c. Using the net working capital found in part **b** as a measure of risk, discuss the profitability–risk tradeoff associated with each financing strategy. Which strategy would you recommend to Morton Mercado for Kanton Company? Why?
d. Find the effective annual rate under:
    (1) The line-of-credit agreement.
    (2) The revolving credit agreement. (*Hint:* Find the ratio of the dollars that the firm will pay in interest and commitment fees to the dollars that the firm will effectively have use of.)
e. If the firm does expect to borrow an average of $600,000, which borrowing arrangement would you recommend to Kanton? Explain why.

WEB EXERCISE   LINKS TO PRACTISE

Visit the following Web sites and complete the suggested exercises. These exercises will allow you to review practical applications of the chapter topics as well as explore the wealth of information regarding managerial finance that is available on the Internet.

www.expresscs.ca/client-main.htm
www.affacturage.ca/english/faq.htm
The first link is to Express Commercial Services which provides small and medium-sized businesses in Canada with working capital financing. Click on the What Services Does ECS Offer? link. Summarize the services offered. Click the Back button on your browser. Now click on the How Does ECS Provide you with Financing? link. Summarize the discussion of factoring.

Now go to the second Web site provided above. Answers to 10 questions are provided. Review this material. Based on the two sites, what types of companies should factor their receivables? What is the cost? What are the alternatives?

www.cit.com/products_services/index.html
This Web site is a listing of the products and services offered by CIT Group to meet the financing needs of business. The information is listed by industry and alphabetically. Scroll down to the alphabetical listing. Click on the Bulk Sale of

Accounts Receivable link and then the Bulk Sale fact sheet. (Note that this link will open an Acrobat Reader file.) What is the bulk sale of receivables and why would a company use this financing technique?

Go back to the listing of products. Click on the Credit Protection link and then the Credit Protection fact sheet. (Note that this link will open an Acrobat Reader file.) What is the credit protection program, what services are provided, what are the benefits, and how does it work? Why would a company use this service?

Go back to the listing of products. Click on the Factoring link. Describe this program and CIT Group's experience with factoring. Now click on the Facts on Factoring fact sheet. (Note that this link will open an Acrobat Reader file.) Describe the factoring as a financial package and the seven-step factoring cycle. What are the benefits of factoring, why use factoring, and what does it cost? List and describe the five steps in the factoring process. Why would a company use this financing technique? Go back to the main factoring page. Click on the Disguise Case Study link. Describe Disguise and how CIT helped the company finance their investment in working capital.

Go back to the listing of products. Click on the Letters of Credit link. Describe this program and then click on the Purchase Order Financing fact sheet. (Note that this link will open an Acrobat Reader file.) What is purchase order financing, who is eligible for this service, and what is included? Why would a company use this service?

Go back to the listing of products. Click on the Import/Export Factoring link. Describe this program. Why would a company use this service?

strategis.ic.gc.ca/sc_mangb/sources/engdoc/homepage.html
This Web site provides an extensive directory of Canadian financial providers, a powerful search engine of financial providers, information on different types of financing and financial providers, and tips to help you secure financing. Click on the Search for Financing link. Select your province and then click Proceed. Select your region and then Proceed. Make appropriate selection in the five categories listed on the page and then click Proceed. Provide a brief summary of the financing source. Comment on the range of financing alternatives available for the choices made in the five categories.

www.grantthornton.ca/mgt_papers/MIP_template.asp?MIPID=9
This link provides an article, "Sound Cash Management: Managing for Profitability and Survival." Read the article and answer the following questions:
1. Why is proper cash flow management important?
2. What is the objective of sound cash management, and how can this objective be achieved? What determines the optimal level of cash?
3. What policies and procedures should a company follow when managing accounts receivable?
4. What procedures should a company follow to control inventory levels?
5. What policies and procedures should a company follow when managing accounts payable?

INTEGRATIVE CASE 5

CASA DE DISEÑO

In September 2003, Teresa Leal was named treasurer of Casa de Diseño. She decided that she could best orient herself by systematically examining each area of the company's financial operations. She began by studying the firm's short-term financial activities.

Casa de Diseño is located in British Columbia and specializes in a furniture line called "Ligne Moderna." Of high quality and contemporary design, the furniture appeals to the customer who wants something unique for his or her home or apartment. Most Ligne Moderna furniture is built by special order, because a wide variety of upholstery, accent trimming, and colours are available. The product line is distributed through exclusive dealership arrangements with well established retail stores. Casa de Diseño's manufacturing process virtually eliminates the use of wood. Plastic and metal provide the basic framework, and wood is used only for decorative purposes.

Casa de Diseño entered the plastic-furniture market in late 1998. The company markets its plastic furniture products as indoor–outdoor items under the brand name "Futuro." Futuro plastic furniture emphasizes comfort, durability, and practicality, and is distributed through wholesalers. The Futuro line has been very successful, accounting for nearly 40 percent of the firm's sales and profits in 2003. Casa de Diseño anticipates some additions to the Futuro line and also some limited change of direction in its promotion in an effort to expand the applications of the plastic furniture.

Ms. Leal has decided to study the firm's cash management practices. To determine the effects of these practices, she must first determine the current operating and cash conversion cycles. In her investigations, she found that Casa de Diseño purchases all of its raw materials and production supplies on open account. The company is operating at production levels that preclude volume discounts. Most suppliers do not offer cash discounts, and Casa de Diseño usually receives credit terms of net 30. An analysis of Casa de Diseño's accounts payable showed that its average payment period is 30 days. Leal consulted industry data and found that the industry average payment period was 39 days. Investigation of six west coast furniture manufacturers revealed that their average payment period was also 39 days.

Next, Leal studied the production cycle and inventory policies. Casa de Diseño tries not to hold any more inventory than necessary in either raw materials or finished goods. The average inventory age was 110 days. Leal determined that the industry standard, as reported in a survey done by the trade association journal, was 83 days.

Casa de Diseño sells to all of its customers on a net-60 basis, in line with the industry trend to grant such credit terms on specialty furniture. Leal discovered, by aging the accounts receivable, that the average collection period for the firm was 75 days. Investigation revealed that in the industry the same collection period existed where net-60 credit terms were given. Where cash discounts were offered, the collection period was significantly shortened. Leal believed that if Casa de Diseño were to offer credit terms of 3/10 net 60, the average collection period could be reduced by 40 percent.

Casa de Diseño's net investment in the operating-cycle accounts was $26,500,000 per year. Leal considered this expenditure level to be the minimum amount the firm would invest during the fiscal year ended August 31, 2004. Her concern was whether the firm's management of working capital was as efficient as it could be. She knew that the company paid 15 percent annual interest for its investment in working capital. For this reason, she was concerned about the financing cost resulting from any inefficiencies in the management of Casa de Diseño's cash conversion cycle.

REQUIRED

a. Assuming a constant rate for purchases, production, and sales throughout the year, what are Casa de Diseño's existing operating cycle (OC), cash conversion cycle (CCC), and resource investment needs?

b. If Leal can optimize Casa de Diseño's operations according to industry standards, what will Casa de Diseño's operating cycle (OC), cash conversion cycle (CCC), and negotiated financing need be under these more efficient conditions?

c. In terms of resource investment requirements, what is the cost of Casa de Diseño's operational inefficiency?

d. (1) If in addition to achieving industry standards for payables and inventory, the firm can reduce the average collection period by offering 3/10 net 60, what additional savings in resource investment costs would result from the shortened cash conversion cycle, assuming that the level of sales remains constant?

(2) If the firm's sales (all on credit) are $40,000,000 and 45 percent of the customers are expected to take the cash discount, by how much will the firm's annual revenues be reduced as a result of the discount?

(3) If the firm's variable cost of the $40,000,000 in sales is 80 percent, determine the reduction in the average investment in accounts receivable and the annual savings resulting from this reduced investment assuming that sales remain constant.

(4) If the firm's bad-debt expenses decline from 2 percent to 1.5 percent of sales, what annual savings would result, assuming that sales remain constant?

(5) Use your findings in parts (2) through (4) to assess whether offering the cash discount can be justified financially. Explain why or why not.

e. On the basis of your analysis in parts a through d, what recommendations would you offer Teresa Leal?

f. Review for Teresa Leal the key sources of short-term financing, other than accounts payable, that she may consider in order to finance Casa de Diseño's resource investment need calculated in part b. Be sure to mention both unsecured and secured sources.

PART

7

Special Topics in Managerial Finance

16

Hybrid and Derivative Securities

⒧EARNING ⒢OALS

LG1 Differentiate between hybrid and derivative securities and their roles in the corporation.

LG2 Review the basic types of leases, leasing arrangements, the lease-versus-purchase decision, the effects of leasing on future financing, and the advantages and disadvantages of leasing.

LG3 Describe the basic types of convertible securities, their general features, and financing with convertibles.

LG4 Demonstrate the procedures for determining the straight bond value, conversion (or share) value, and market value of a convertible bond.

LG5 Explain the basic characteristics of warrants, the implied price of an attached warrant, and the values of warrants.

LG6 Define options and discuss the basics of calls and puts, options markets, options trading, and the role of call and put options in fund raising.

16.1 An Overview of Hybrids and Derivatives

Chapter 6 described the characteristics of the key securities issued by corporations to raise long-term financing: long-term debt, preferred shares, and common shares. In their simplest form, bonds are pure debt and common shares are pure equity. Preferred shares, on the other hand, are a form of equity that promises to pay fixed periodic dividends that are similar to the fixed contractual interest payments on bonds. Because it blends the characteristics of *both* debt (issued at a stated value, rated for default, traded based on yield, and makes fixed payments to holders) and equity (pay dividends, a permanent source of financing, holders

Outstanding in Their Field

Hybrid corn, which is the dominant type planted in Canada since the 1940s, is the result of crossing two varieties of seed to produce plants with improved quality. Hybrids are common in modern-day agriculture and besides corn, include varieties of sugar beets, alfalfa, barley, rice, wheat, tomatoes, melons, squash, pears, plums, and many flowers. The point of breeding hybrids is to produce offspring that include the best characteristics of the two parent plants. Although you won't find them in fields inspecting their crops, financial engineers are also interested in hybridization, and they have produced securities that combine desirable characteristics of debt and equity. This chapter will look at the various hybrid securities and also at options, a security that is neither debt nor equity. But we'll start the chapter by considering lease financing, a hybrid method of financing the acquisition of fixed assets.

hybrid security
A form of debt or equity financing that possesses characteristics of *both* debt and equity financing.

derivative security
A security that is neither debt nor equity but derives its value from an underlying asset that is often another security; called "derivative" for short.

cannot force bankruptcy), preferred shares are considered a **hybrid security.** Other popular hybrid securities include financial leases, convertible securities, and warrants. Each of these hybrid securities is described in the following pages.

In addition to hybrid securities, this chapter, in the final section, focuses on *options*, a popular **derivative security**—a security that is neither debt nor equity but derives its value from an underlying asset that is often another security. As you'll learn, *derivatives* are not used by corporations to raise funds, but rather serve as a useful tool for managing certain aspects of the firm's risk. In addition, individual and institutional investors use derivatives as an alternative to investing in the underlying financial security on which the derivatives value is based, or to hedge the risk of a portfolio of securities.

? Review Question

16–1   Differentiate between a *hybrid security* and a *derivative security*. How does their use by the corporation differ?

16.2 Leasing

leasing
The process by which a firm can obtain the use of certain fixed assets for which it must make a series of contractual, periodic, tax-deductible payments.

lessee
Has physical control of and uses the assets under a lease contract.

lessor
The owner of an asset that is being leased.

Leasing allows the firm to obtain the use of certain fixed assets for which it must make a series of contractual, periodic, tax-deductible payments. The **lessee** has physical control of and uses the asset under the lease contract; the **lessor** is the owner of the asset. Leasing can take a number of forms.

Basic Types of Leases

The two basic types of leases that are available to a business are *operating* and *financial* leases (often called *capital leases* by accountants).

Operating Leases

operating lease
A *cancellable* contractual arrangement whereby the lessee agrees to make periodic payments to the lessor, often for 5 or fewer years, to obtain the use of an asset; generally, the total payments over the term of the lease are *less* than the lessor's initial cost of the leased asset.

An **operating lease** is normally a contractual arrangement whereby the lessee agrees to make periodic payments to the lessor, often for 5 or fewer years, to obtain the use of an asset. Such leases are generally *cancellable* at the option of the lessee, who may be required to pay a penalty for cancellation. Assets that are leased under operating leases have a usable life that is *longer* than the term of the lease. Usually, however, they would become less efficient and technologically obsolete if leased for a longer period. Computer systems are prime examples of assets whose relative efficiency is expected to diminish as the technology changes. The operating lease is therefore a common arrangement for obtaining such systems, as well as for other relatively short-lived assets such as automobiles and office equipment.

If an operating lease is held to maturity, the lessee at that time returns the leased asset to the lessor, who may lease it again or sell the asset. Normally, the asset still has a positive market value at the termination of the lease. In some instances, the lease contract will give the lessee the opportunity to purchase the leased asset. Generally, the total payments made by the lessee to the lessor are *less* than the lessor's initial cost of the leased asset.

⊙─ Career Key

The *marketing* department will have to determine whether to sell or lease the firm's products. They also will have to understand the lease-vs.-purchase analysis that their prospective customer will be going through in their prepurchase decision process.

Financial (or Capital) Leases

financial (or capital) lease
A *longer-term* lease than an operating lease that is *noncancellable* and obligates the lessee to make payments for the use of an asset over a predefined period of time; the total payments over the term of the lease are *greater* than the lessor's initial cost of the leased asset.

A **financial (or capital) lease** is a *longer-term* lease than an operating lease. Financial leases are *noncancellable* and obligate the lessee to make payments for the use of an asset over a predefined period of time. Financial leases are commonly used for leasing land, buildings, and large pieces of equipment. Examples of equipment that are often leased include: railway cars, aircraft, point-of-sale cash registers, telecommunications and broadcasting equipment, hotel and restaurant equipment, agricultural equipment, buses, and ski lifts and grooming machines. An extensive array of assets are leased by companies.

The noncancellable feature of the financial lease makes it similar to certain types of long-term debt. The lease payment becomes a fixed, tax-deductible expenditure that must be paid at predefined dates. Like debt, failure to make the contractual lease payments can result in bankruptcy for the lessee.

With a financial lease, the total payments over the lease period are *greater* than the lessor's initial cost of the leased asset. In other words, the lessor must receive more than the asset's purchase price to earn its required return on the investment. Technically, under the Canadian Institute of Chartered Accountants (CICA) regulation 3065, "Leases," a financial (or capital) lease is defined as one having one or more of the following elements:

1. The lease transfers ownership of the property to the lessee by the end of the lease term.
2. The lessee has an option to purchase the property at a "bargain price," a price below "fair market value," when the lease expires.
3. The lease term is equal to 75 percent or more of the estimated economic life of the property.
4. At the beginning of the lease, the present value of the lease payments is equal to 90 percent or more of the fair market value of the leased property.

The emphasis in this chapter is on financial leases because they result in inescapable long-term financial commitments by the firm.

Leasing Arrangements

Lessors use three primary techniques for obtaining assets to be leased. The method depends largely on the desires of the prospective lessee.

direct lease
A lease under which a lessor owns or acquires the assets that are leased to a given lessee.

sale-leaseback arrangement
A lease under which the lessee sells an asset for cash to a lessor and then leases back the same asset, making fixed periodic payments for its use.

leveraged lease
A lease under which the lessor acts as an equity participant, supplying only about 20 percent of the cost of the asset, while a lender supplies the balance.

1. A **direct lease** results when a lessor owns or acquires the assets that are leased to a given lessee. In other words, the lessor purchases the asset and the asset is delivered to and then used by the lessee. The lessee did not previously own the assets that it is leasing.
2. In a **sale-leaseback arrangement,** lessors purchase assets already owned by the lessee, and then lease them back to the lessee. This technique is normally initiated by a firm that needs funds for operations. By selling an existing asset to a lessor and then *leasing it back,* the lessee receives cash for the asset immediately while obligating itself to make fixed periodic payments for use of the leased asset.
3. Leasing arrangements that include one or more third-party lenders are **leveraged leases.** Under a leveraged lease, the lessor acts as an equity participant, supplying only about 20 percent of the cost of the asset, and a lender supplies the balance. Leveraged leases have become especially popular in structuring leases of very expensive assets.

maintenance clauses
Provisions normally included in a lease that require one of the parties to maintain the assets and to make insurance and tax payments.

A lease agreement normally specifies whether the lessee is responsible for maintenance of the leased assets. Operating leases normally include **maintenance clauses** requiring the lessor to maintain the assets and to make insurance and tax payments. Financial leases almost always require the lessee to pay maintenance and other costs.

renewal options
Provisions especially common in operating leases that grant the lessee the option to re-lease assets at the expiration of the lease.

purchase options
Provisions frequently included in both operating and financial leases that allow the lessee to purchase the leased asset at maturity, typically for a pre-specified price.

The lessee is usually given the option to renew a lease at its expiration. **Renewal options,** which grant lessees the right to re-lease assets at expiration, are especially common in operating leases, because their term is generally shorter than the usable life of the leased assets. **Purchase options** allowing the lessee to purchase the leased asset at maturity, typically for a prespecified price, are frequently included in both operating and financial leases.

The lessor can be one of a number of parties. In operating leases, the lessor is likely to be the manufacturer's leasing subsidiary. Examples include the finance company subsidiaries of all automative manufacturers (as offered through car dealerships) or of computer and office equipment manufacturers. Financial leases are frequently handled by the leasing subsidiaries of large financial institutions such as commercial banks, life insurance companies, trust companies, pension plans, and investment dealers. In addition, many manufacturers of major pieces of equipment have finance company subsidiaries that arrange leases. Finally, there are many independent leasing companies in Canada that negotiate both operating and financial leases.

The Lease-Versus-Purchase Decision

lease-versus-purchase (or lease-versus-buy) decision
The decision facing firms needing to acquire new fixed assets: whether to lease the assets or to purchase them, using borrowed funds or available liquid resources.

Firms that are contemplating the acquisition of new fixed assets commonly confront the **lease-versus-purchase (or lease-versus-buy) decision.** The alternatives available are (1) lease the assets, (2) borrow funds to purchase the assets, or (3) purchase the assets using available liquid resources. Alternatives 2 and 3, although they differ, are analyzed in a similar fashion; even if the firm has the liquid resources with which to purchase the assets, the use of these funds is viewed as equivalent to borrowing. Therefore, we need to compare only the leasing and purchasing alternatives.

The analysis of the lease-versus-purchase decision is directly associated with the capital budgeting concepts discussed in Chapters 12 and 13. In these chapters we used the net present value (NPV) technique to determine whether an asset should be acquired. If the NPV of the asset was greater than or equal to 0, the asset was expected to generate at least its required rate of return, and therefore should be acquired.

Career Key

Accounting personnel will provide important data and tax insights to the lease-vs.-purchase decision. These analyses will be important to both the purchasing and selling functions of the firm.

The lease-versus-purchase analysis picks up at that point. Here we consider that the value of an asset is in its use, not in its ownership. If an NPV analysis indicates that an asset should be acquired, then the next question is: Should the asset be purchased or leased? So, for this analysis, *we shall assume that the decision to acquire the asset has been made*; we will be considering the method of acquisition.

Cash Flows and Discount Rate Issues

To evaluate whether an asset should be leased or purchased, the cash flows associated with the alternatives must be considered, as must the discount rate to be used. The cash flows that should be considered are:

1. The cost of the asset
2. The yearly lease payments
3. Tax shield from the capital cost allowances that will be charged on the asset

4. Salvage value of the asset at the end of the lease period[1]
5. Tax shield from CCA lost due to salvage
6. Any investment tax credits available on the asset

Also note the cash flows that are *not* included in the analysis. These are the incremental operating income associated with the asset and, for a replacement, the salvage value of the asset being replaced. These cash flows are not considered in the lease-versus-purchase analysis since they would be the same regardless of whether the company leases or purchases. If the company buys the asset, these cash flows are received; if they lease, they are also received.

For costs such as the maintenance and insurance of the asset, their treatment in the analysis is decided by the party who is responsible for making the payment. If the lessee makes the payments, these costs are ignored since the payments would be the same regardless of whether the company purchases or leases the asset. These types of cash flows are not incremental to the analysis, so they can be safely ignored. If the lessor makes one or both of the payments, then they would be a benefit of the lease and must be considered in the analysis.

The discount rate to use to evaluate the lease-versus-purchase question for a lessee is also a vital part of the analysis. If the company leases, consider the situation. The firm is committed to a series of fixed payments, the lease payments must be made before any income accrues to the common shareholders, and if the lease payments are not made, the lessor can reclaim the asset. The obligations associated with a lease are the same as for long-term debt. Both types of financing affect the company's financial risks in the same manner. Therefore, leasing should be viewed as a substitute for long-term debt. The characteristics and accounting treatment for leasing fully supports this claim. As such, the discount rule used to evaluate the lease-versus-purchase decision is the after-tax cost of long-term debt.

Completing a Lease-Versus-Purchase Analysis

To illustrate the technique used to analyze the lease-versus-purchase decision, a problem will be used. The objective is to calculate the NPV of the lease. If the NPV of the lease is positive, then the company should lease the asset; if negative, buy the asset. Since lease payments are required at the beginning of the lease, for present value calculations, an annuity due analysis must be used. Annuity dues were considered in Chapter 5.

Example ▼ After a thorough capital budgeting analysis, Roberts Company, a small machine shop, has decided to acquire a new machine tool that has a cost of $56,000. The life of the machine tool is 10 years, at which time it is expected to have a market value of $8,000. The company could buy the machine tool or arrange for a lease with Canadian Equipment Leasing (CEL). CEL indicates that they will lease the machine tool to Roberts for $7,300 per year, with the first lease payment due

---

1. By including the expected salvage value of the asset at the end of its useful life in the analysis, the cost of exercising the purchase option in a lease agreement can be safely ignored. By including the salvage value in the analysis, the implication is that the firm will not own the asset at the end of the relevant time horizon. This approach means that the two alternatives have the same lives, the term of the lease. Thus, any subsequent cash flows after the lease period are irrelevant.

when the lease agreement is signed. The subsequent nine payments are due on the anniversary dates. At the end of the lease agreement, in ten years, Roberts could buy the machine for $3,000. The machine tool has a CCA rate of 30 percent. Roberts Company's cost of long-term debt is 10 percent and the company's tax rate is 40 percent. Should Roberts Company buy or lease the new machine tool?

To answer this question, the NPV of the lease (NPV_L) must be calculated. If the company leases, they do not have to pay the purchase price, but they do not receive the benefit of the tax shield from CCA, or the salvage. (Also, they do not lose the tax shield due to the salvage.) If they lease, they must make the lease payments but the lease payments are deductible for tax purposes. In either case, at the end of the 10 years, Roberts will no longer have the machine tool. To account for time value issues, the after-tax cost of debt is used. This is 6 percent [$10\% \times (1 - 0.40)$]. The NPV of the lease for Roberts Company is based on the above discussion. Table 16.1 provides the numeric analysis of the problem.

The NPV_L is positive, meaning Roberts *should* lease the new machine tool. Note that this outcome is based on a comparison of the cost of purchasing versus the cost of leasing. The cost of purchasing is $34,884. This is a function of the purchase price ($-$56,000$), plus the present value of the tax shield from CCA ($+$18,138$), plus the present value of the salvage ($+$4,467$), less the tax shield lost due to salvage ($-$1,489$). The cost of leasing is $34,171. The cost of leasing is $713 less than the cost of purchasing and, therefore, is the preferred approach to acquiring the new machine tool.

The techniques illustrated in the Roberts Company example for analyzing the lease-versus-purchase decision are quite straightforward. It is important to recognize that the lower cost of one alternative over the other results from factors such

---

TABLE 16.1   **The Lease-Versus-Purchase Analysis for Roberts Company: Calculate the NPV of the Lease**

$NPV_L =$	Incremental cost	$=$	$+$56,000$
	$-$ PV of tax shield from CCA		
	$\$56,000 \times \left[\dfrac{0.30 \times 0.40}{0.30 + 0.06} \right] \times \dfrac{1.03}{1.06}$	$=$	$-$18,138$
	$-$ PV of salvage		
	$\$8,000 \times PVIF(10 \text{ years, } 6\%)$	$=$	$-$ 4,467$
	$+$ PV of tax shield lost due to salvage		
	$\$4,467 \times \left[\dfrac{0.30 \times 0.40}{0.30 + 0.06} \right]$	$=$	$+$ 1,489$
	$-$ Present value of after-tax lease payments[a]		
	$\$7,300(1 - 0.40) + 7,300(1 - 0.40) \times PVIFA(9 \text{ years, } 6\%) =$		$-$34,171$
	NPV_L	$=$	$+$ 713$

[a]This calculation assumes that the cash outflow associated with the lease payment and the cash inflow associated with the tax savings from the lease payment occur at the same time. If this assumption is not the case, then two separate calculations would have to be made. The first would be the present value of the lease payments, calculated as an annuity due. The second would be the calculation of the tax savings associated with the lease payments ($L \times T$) calculated as an ordinary annuity.

CHAPTER 16   Hybrid and Derivative Securities   **751**

as the differing tax brackets of the lessor and lessee, different tax treatments of leases versus purchases, and differing risks and borrowing costs for the lessor and lessee. Therefore, when making a lease-versus-purchase decision, the firm will find that inexpensive borrowing opportunities, high required lessor returns, and a low risk of obsolescence increase the attractiveness of purchasing. Subjective factors must also be included in the decision-making process. Like most financial decisions, the lease-versus-purchase decision requires some judgment or intuition.

Effects of Leasing on Future Financing

Because leasing is considered a type of financing, it affects the firm's future financing. Lease payments are shown as a tax-deductible expense on the firm's income statement. Anyone analyzing the firm's income statement would probably recognize that an asset is being leased, although the actual details of the amount and term of the lease would be unclear.

capitalized lease
A *financial (capital) lease* that has the present value of all its payments included as an asset and corresponding liability on the firm's balance sheet, as required by accounting regulations.

CICA regulations require explicit disclosure of *financial (capital) lease* obligations on the firm's balance sheet. Such a lease must be shown as a **capitalized lease**, meaning that the present value of all its payments is included as an asset and corresponding liability on the firm's balance sheet. An *operating lease,* on the other hand, need not be capitalized, but its basic features must be disclosed in a footnote to the financial statements. Accounting standards, of course, establish detailed guidelines to be used in capitalizing and disclosing leases.

Example ▼ Lawrence Company, a manufacturer of water purifiers, is leasing an asset with 10 remaining payments of $15,000 per year required. The lease can be capitalized merely by calculating the present value of the lease payments over the remaining life of the lease. If the company could borrow funds at an interest rate of 9 percent and the company's tax rate were 25 percent, then the rate at which the lease payments are discounted would be 6.75 percent [9% × (1 − 0.25)]. The capitalized (present) value of the lease is $106,582 [15,000 × $PVIF_A$ (10 per, 6.75%)]. Note that an annuity due was not used to determine the capitalized amount of the lease since the balance sheet reflects the remaining payments due, not the payments already made. This value would be shown as an asset and corresponding liability on the firm's balance sheet, which should result in an accurate reflection of the firm's true financial position. ▲

Because the consequences of missing a financial lease payment are the same as those of missing an interest or principal payment on debt, a financial analyst must view the lease as a long-term financial commitment of the lessee. The inclusion of each financial (capital) lease as an asset and corresponding liability (i.e., long-term debt) provides for a balance sheet that more accurately reflects the firm's financial status. It thereby permits various types of financial ratio analyses to be performed directly on the statement by any interested party.

Advantages and Disadvantages of Leasing

Leasing has a number of commonly cited advantages and disadvantages that should be considered when making a lease-versus-purchase decision. It is not unusual for a number of them to apply in a given situation.

Advantages

The commonly cited advantages of leasing are as follows:

1. The total cost of leasing may be less than the total cost of owning due to differences in taxation and costs of financing. Lessors with high tax rates and low costs of financing may offer lease rates that are cheaper than the cost of buying for companies with low tax rates and high costs of financing.
2. In a lease arrangement, the firm may *avoid the cost of obsolescence* if the lessor fails to accurately anticipate the obsolescence of assets and sets the lease payment too low. This is especially true in the case of operating leases, which generally have relatively short lives.
3. A lessee *avoids many of the restrictive covenants* that are normally included as part of a long-term loan. Requirements with respect to minimum net working capital, subsequent borrowing, changes in management, and so on are *not* normally found in a lease agreement.
4. In the case of low-cost assets that are infrequently acquired, leasing—especially operating leases—may provide the firm with needed *financing flexibility*. That is, the firm does not have to arrange other financing for these assets.
5. Sale-leaseback arrangements may permit the firm to *increase its liquidity* by converting an *existing* asset into cash, which can then be used as working capital. This can be advantageous for a firm short of working capital or in a liquidity bind.
6. Leasing allows the lessee, in effect, to *depreciate land,* which is prohibited if the land were purchased. Because the lessee who leases land is permitted to deduct the *total lease payment* as an expense for tax purposes, the effect is the same as if the firm had purchased the land and then depreciated it. But since land often increases in value over time, by leasing land the lessee may lose the opportunity for a capital gain on the purchase of the land.
7. Leasing provides *100 percent financing.* Most loan agreements for the purchase of fixed assets require the borrower to pay a portion of the purchase price as a down payment. As a result, the borrower is able to borrow only 90 to 95 percent of the purchase price of the asset. Note, though, since leases require the first payment in advance, less than 100 percent of the cost of the asset is secured.

Disadvantages

The commonly cited disadvantages of leasing are as follows:

1. A lease does not have a stated interest cost. Thus, in many leases the *return to the lessor is quite high,* so the firm might be better off borrowing to purchase the asset.
2. At the end of the term of the lease agreement, the *salvage value* of an asset, if any, is realized by the lessor. If the lessee had purchased the asset, it could have claimed its salvage value. Of course, an expected salvage value when recognized by the lessor results in lower lease payments.
3. Under a lease, the lessee is generally *prohibited from making improvements* on the leased property or asset without the approval of the lessor. If the property were owned outright, this difficulty would not arise. Of course,

IN PRACTICE

Leasing: The New Way to Acquire Assets?

When opening a new business, an owner may choose to lease the equipment and the big-ticket items. When expanding, it may be more attractive to arrange a lease through a leasing company rather than try to negotiate a long-term loan with a bank. When buying an expensive, specialized piece of equipment, the manufacturer may have their own leasing subsidiary that offers favourable terms to the acquiring company, thus presenting an attractive alternative to issuing long-term debt in the capital market.

Many businesses, large and small, are opting to lease rather than purchase and finance equipment. The leasing industry in Canada is large and rapidly growing. The Canadian Finance and Leasing Association estimates that there is over $100 billion of lease financing in place and that about 60 percent of the industry's customers are small and medium-sized businesses. The association estimates that between 22 percent and 25 percent of business investment in new machinery and equipment in Canada is financed by the leasing industry, a tremendous increase from the 5 percent level recorded in the mid-1980s.

Manufacturing companies are among the largest users of equipment lease financing, although service firms such as restaurants, hotels, ski resorts, and microbreweries find it attractive as well. Leasing is particularly appealing to small companies, because their bankers may have tight credit standards on more traditional financing alternatives. When credit markets are tight, small business owners find leasing an attractive alternative since they do not have to buy equipment, which frees up cash for other purposes. In addition to preserving cash, small business owners like being able to leave maintenance to the lessor who owns the equipment.

According to an Equipment Leasing Association survey, the top reasons why small and medium-sized businesses choose to lease rather than buy equipment are to preserve cash flow (cited by 35%), to lock in financing costs (17%), convenience and flexibility of leasing (13%), tax advantages (13%), inclusion of maintenance costs (13%), and ability to afford state-of-the-art technology (9%). With a lease, the company's payments are set at the beginning of the lease term for the life of the lease, so the company is not affected by changes in interest rates. Companies may be able to structure variable payment terms as well, to accommodate seasonal cash flow patterns, and they may also be able to upgrade equipment during the lease term.

Before jumping into lease financing, however, a company must carefully analyze the whole lease package: any down payment required, monthly payments, the responsibilities for maintenance and insurance, and the cost of equipment at the end of the lease. They must know the purchase price, CCA rate, and salvage value of the asset. They must also know their tax rate and the cost of borrowing funds for the long term. Then they should calculate the net present value (NPV) of the lease to determine if leasing or purchasing is the better choice.

SOURCES: Canadian Finance and Leasing Association, 2001–2002 annual report, available at: **www.cfla-acfl.ca**; Mark Henricks, "To Say the Leased," *Entrepreneur*, February 2002; and "Report Sees the Future of the Equipment Leasing and Financing Industry," *Business Wire*, April 5, 2001.

lessors generally encourage leasehold improvements when they are expected to enhance the asset's salvage value.

4. If a lessee leases an *asset that subsequently becomes obsolete*, it still must make lease payments over the remaining term of the lease. This is true even if the asset is unusable.

❓ Review Questions

16–2 What is *leasing?* Define, compare, and contrast *operating leases* and *financial (or capital) leases.* How does CICA Regulation 3065 define a financial (or capital) lease? Describe three methods used by lessors to acquire assets to be leased.

16–3 Describe the process involved in the *lease-versus-purchase decision* process. How are capital budgeting methods applied in this process?

16–4 What type of lease must be treated as a *capitalized lease* on the balance sheet? How does the financial manager capitalize a lease?

16–5 List and discuss the commonly cited advantages and disadvantages that should be considered when making a lease-versus-purchase decision.

16.3 Convertible Securities

conversion feature
An option that is included as part of a long-term debt or a preferred share issue that allows its holder to change the security into a stated number of common shares.

A **conversion feature** is an option that is included as part of a long-term debt or a preferred share issue that allows the holder to change the security into a stated number of common shares. The conversion feature typically enhances the marketability of an issue.

Types of Convertible Securities

Corporate bonds and preferred shares may be convertible into common shares. The most common type of convertible security is the bond. Convertibles normally have an accompanying *call feature*. This feature permits the issuer to retire or encourage conversion of outstanding convertibles when appropriate.

Convertible Bonds

convertible bond
A bond that can be changed into a specified number of common shares.

straight bond
A bond that is nonconvertible, having no conversion feature.

A **convertible bond** can be changed into a specified number of common shares. It is almost always a *debenture*—an unsecured bond—with a call feature. Because the conversion feature provides the purchaser with the possibility of becoming a shareholder on favourable terms, convertible bonds are generally a less expensive form of financing than similar-risk nonconvertible or **straight bonds.** The conversion feature adds a degree of speculation to a bond issue, although the issue still maintains its value as a bond.

Convertible Preferred Shares

convertible preferred shares
Preferred shares that can be changed into a specified number of common shares.

straight preferred shares
Preferred shares that have no conversion feature.

Convertible preferred shares can be changed into a specified number of common shares. They can normally be sold with a lower stated dividend than similar-risk nonconvertible or **straight preferred shares.** The reason is that the convertible preferred holder is assured of the fixed dividend payment associated with a preferred share and also may receive the appreciation resulting from increases in the market price of the underlying common shares. Convertible preferred shares behave much like convertible bonds. The following discussions will concentrate on the more popular convertible bonds.

General Features of Convertibles

Convertible securities are almost always convertible anytime during the life of the security. Occasionally, conversion is permitted only for a limited number of years, say, for 5 or 10 years after issuance of the convertible.

Conversion Ratio

conversion ratio
The ratio at which a convertible security can be exchanged for common shares.

The **conversion ratio** is the ratio at which a convertible security can be exchanged for common shares. The conversion ratio can be stated in two ways.

conversion price
The per-share price that is effectively paid for common shares as the result of conversion of a convertible security.

1. Sometimes the conversion ratio is stated in terms of a given number of common shares. To find the conversion price, which is the per-share price that is effectively paid for common shares as the result of conversion, the par value (not the market value) of the convertible security must be divided by the conversion ratio.

Example ▼ Western Wear Company, a manufacturer of denim products, has outstanding a bond with a $1,000 par value that is convertible into 25 common shares. The bond's conversion ratio is 25. The conversion price for the bond is $40 per share **▲** ($1,000 ÷ 25).

2. Sometimes, instead of the conversion ratio, the conversion price is given. The conversion ratio can be obtained by dividing the *par value* of the convertible by the conversion price.

Example ▼ Mosher Company, a franchiser of seafood restaurants, has outstanding a convertible 20-year bond with a par value of $1,000. The bond is convertible into common shares at a price of $50 per share. The conversion ratio is 20 ($1,000 ÷ **▲** $50).

The issuer of a convertible security normally establishes a conversion ratio or conversion price that sets the conversion price per share at the time of issuance above the current market price of the firm's stock. If the prospective purchasers do not expect conversion ever to be feasible, they will purchase a straight security or some other convertible issue.

Conversion (or Share) Value

conversion (or share) value
The value of a convertible security measured in terms of the market price of the common shares into which it can be converted.

The **conversion (or share) value** is the value of the convertible measured in terms of the market price of the common shares into which it can be converted. The conversion value can be found simply by multiplying the conversion ratio by the current market price of the firm's common shares.

Example ▼ McNamara Industries, a petroleum processor, has outstanding a $1,000 bond that is convertible into common shares at $62.50 a share. The conversion ratio is therefore 16 ($1,000 ÷ $62.50). Because the current market price of the common shares is $65 per share, the conversion value is $1,040 (16 × $65). Because the conversion value is above the bond value of $1,000, conversion is a **▲** viable option for the owner of the convertible security.

Effect on Earnings

contingent securities
Convertibles, warrants, and stock options. Their presence affects the reporting of a firm's earnings per share (EPS).

The presence of **contingent securities,** which include convertibles as well as warrants (described later in this chapter) and stock options (described in Chapter 1 and later in this chapter), affects the reporting of the firm's earnings per share (EPS). Firms with contingent securities that if converted or exercised would dilute (i.e., lower) earnings per share are required to report earnings in two ways—*basic EPS* and *diluted EPS.*

basic EPS
Earnings per share (EPS) calculated without regard to any contingent securities.

Basic EPS are calculated without regard to any contingent securities. It is found by dividing earnings available for common shareholders by the number of common shares outstanding. This is the standard method of calculating EPS that has been used throughout this textbook.

diluted EPS
Earnings per share (EPS) calculated under the assumption that *all* contingent securities that would have dilutive effects are converted into common shares.

Diluted EPS are calculated under the assumption that all contingent securities that would have dilutive effects are converted into common shares. They are found by adjusting basic EPS for the impact of converting all convertibles and exercising all warrants and options that would have dilutive effects on the firm's earnings. This approach treats as common shares *all* contingent securities.

It is calculated by dividing earnings available for common shareholders (adjusted for interest and preferred share dividends that would *not* be paid given assumed conversion of *all* outstanding contingent securities that would have dilutive effects) by the number of common shares that would be outstanding if *all* contingent securities that would have dilutive effects are converted and exercised. Rather than demonstrate these accounting calculations, suffice it to say that firms with outstanding convertibles, warrants, and/or stock options must report basic and diluted EPS on their income statements.

Financing with Convertibles

Using convertible securities to raise long-term funds can help the firm achieve its cost of capital and capital structure goals. There also are a number of more specific motives and considerations involved in evaluating convertible financing.

Motives for Convertible Financing

Convertibles can be used for a variety of reasons. One popular motive is their use as a form of *deferred common share financing*. When a convertible security is issued, both issuer and purchaser expect the security to be converted into common shares at some future point. Because the security is first sold with a conversion price above the current market price of the firm's shares, conversion is initially not attractive. The issuer of a convertible could alternatively sell common shares, but only at or below their current market price. By selling the convertible, the issuer in effect makes a *deferred sale* of common shares. As the market price of the firm's common shares rise to a higher level, conversion may occur. By deferring the issuance of new common shares until the market price of the shares has increased, fewer shares will have to be issued, thereby decreasing the dilution of both ownership and earnings.

⚠ Hint
Convertible securities are advantageous to both the issuer and the holder. The issuer does not have to give up immediate control as it would have to if it were issuing common shares. The holder of a convertible security has the possibility of a future speculative gain.

Another motive for convertible financing is its *use as a "sweetener" for financing*. Because the purchaser of the convertible is given the opportunity to become a common shareholder and share in the firm's future success, *convertibles can be normally sold with lower interest rates than nonconvertibles.* Therefore, from the firm's viewpoint, including a conversion feature reduces the coupon rate on the debt. The purchaser of the issue sacrifices a portion of interest return for the potential opportunity to become a common shareholder. Another important motive for issuing convertibles is that, generally speaking, *convertible securities can be issued with far fewer restrictive covenants than nonconvertibles.* Because many investors view convertibles as equity, the covenant issue is not important to them.

A final motive for using convertibles is to *raise cheap funds temporarily*. By using convertible bonds, the firm can temporarily raise debt, which is typically less expensive than common shares, to finance projects. Once such projects are on line, the firm may wish to shift its capital structure to a less highly levered position. A conversion feature gives the issuer the opportunity, through actions of convertible holders, to shift its capital structure at a future point in time.

Other Considerations

When the price of the firm's common shares rises above the conversion price, the market price of the convertible security will normally rise to a level above its conversion value. When this happens, many convertible holders will not convert, because they already have the market price benefit obtainable from conversion and can still receive fixed periodic interest payments. Because of this behaviour, virtually all convertible securities have a *call feature* that enables the issuer to encourage or *"force" conversion*. The call price of the security generally exceeds the security's par value by a stated premium. Although the issuer must pay a premium for calling a security, the call privilege is generally not exercised until the conversion value of the security is 10 to 20 percent *above the call price*. This type of premium above the call price helps to assure the issuer that the holders of the convertible will convert it when the call is made, instead of accepting the call price.

Unfortunately, there are instances when the market price of a security does not reach a level sufficient to stimulate the conversion of associated convertibles. A convertible security that cannot be forced into conversion by using the call feature is called an **overhanging issue**. An overhanging issue can be quite detrimental to a firm. If the firm were to call the issue, the bondholders would accept the call price rather than convert the bonds. In this case, the firm not only would have to pay the call premium, but would require additional financing to pay off the bonds at their par value. If the firm raised these funds through the sale of equity, a large number of shares would have to be issued due to their low market price. This, in turn, could result in the dilution of existing ownership. The firm could use debt or preferred shares to finance the call, but this use would leave the firm's capital structure no less levered than before the call.

overhanging issue
A convertible security that cannot be forced into conversion by using the call feature.

Determining the Value of a Convertible Bond

The key characteristic of convertible securities that enhances their marketability is their ability to minimize the possibility of a loss while providing a possibility of capital gains. Here we discuss the three values of a convertible bond: (1) the straight bond value, (2) the conversion value, and (3) the market value.

Straight Bond Value

straight bond value
The price at which a convertible bond would sell in the market without the conversion feature.

The **straight bond value** of a convertible bond is the price at which it would sell in the market without the conversion feature. This value is found by determining the value of a nonconvertible bond with similar payments and time to maturity issued by a firm with the same risk. The straight bond value is typically the *floor*, or minimum, price at which the convertible bond would be traded. The straight bond value equals the present value of the bond's coupon and principal payments discounted at the interest rate the firm would have to pay on a nonconvertible bond. This process was fully considered in Chapter 8.

Example ▼ Duncan Company, a southeastern discount store chain, has just sold a $1,000-par-value, 20-year convertible bond with a 12 percent coupon rate paid semiannually. A straight bond could have been sold with a 14 percent coupon interest rate, but the conversion feature compensates for the lower rate on the convertible. The straight bond value of the convertible is calculated as shown:

Period	Payments (1)	Present value interest factor at 7% (2)	Present value [(1) × (2)] (3)
1–40	$ 60[a]	13.332[b]	$799.90
40	1,000	0.067[c]	66.78
		Straight bond value	$866.68

[a]$1,000 at 12% = $120 interest per year ÷ 2 = $60 semiannually.
[b]Present value interest factor for an annuity, *PVIFA*, discounted at 7% for 40 years, from Table A-4, rounded.
[c]Present value interest factor for $1, *PVIF*, discounted at 7% for 40 periods, from Table A-3, rounded.

This value, $866.68, is the minimum price at which the convertible bond is expected to sell. Generally, only in certain instances in which the stock's market price is well below the conversion price will the bond be expected to sell at this ▲ level.

Conversion (or Share) Value

Recall that the *conversion (or share) value* of a convertible security is the value of the convertible measured in terms of the market price of the common shares into which the security can be converted. When the market price of the common shares exceed the conversion price, the conversion (or share) value exceeds the par value. An example will clarify the point.

Example ▼ Duncan Company's convertible bond described earlier is convertible at $50 per share. Each bond can be converted into 20 shares, because each bond has a $1,000 par value. The conversion values of the bond when the shares are selling at $30, $40, $50, $60, $70, and $80 per share are shown in the following table.

Market price of stock	Conversion value
$30	$ 600
40	800
50 (conversion price)	1,000 (par value)
60	1,200
70	1,400
80	1,600

When the market price of the common stock exceeds the $50 conversion price, the conversion value exceeds the $1,000 par value. Because the straight bond value (calculated in the preceding example) is $866.68, the bond will, in a stable environment, never sell for less than this amount, regardless of how low its conversion value is. If the market price per share were $30, the bond would still sell for $866.68—not $600—because its value as a bond would dominate. If the common share price were $60, the bond will sell for more than $1,200, assuming there is still time remaining before conversion. This is the case since the market will price the possibility that the share price will increase beyond $60.

Market Value

market premium
The amount by which the market value exceeds the straight or conversion value of a convertible security.

The market value of a convertible is likely to be greater than its straight value or its conversion value. The amount by which the market value exceeds its straight or conversion value is called the **market premium.** The general relationship of the straight bond value, conversion value, market value, and market premium for Duncan Company's convertible bond is shown in Figure 16.1.

The straight bond value acts as a floor for the security's value up to the point X, where the stock price is high enough to cause the conversion value to exceed the straight bond value.[2] The market premium is attributed to the fact that the convertible gives investors a chance to experience attractive capital gains from increases in the share price while taking less risk. The floor (straight bond value) provides protection against losses resulting from a decline in the share price caused by falling profits or other factors. The market premium tends to be greatest when the straight bond value and conversion (or share) value are nearly equal. Investors perceive the benefits of these two sources of value to be greatest at this point.

Career Key

Information systems analysts will design systems that provide timely information that can be used to monitor and track the market behaviour of the firm's outstanding securities, including convertibles.

? Review Questions

16–6   What is the *conversion feature?* What is a *conversion ratio?* How do convertibles and other *contingent securities* affect EPS? Briefly describe the motives for convertible financing.

---

2. Note that as yields for bonds of comparable risk vary, so too will the floor price (the straight bond value). For example, for the Duncan Company bond, if 3 years elapse and yields on bonds of comparable risk are now 10 percent, the straight bond value will be $1,161.93 and this will act as the floor price, regardless of what has happened to the market price of Duncan's common shares.

FIGURE 16.1

Values and Market Premium

The values and market premium for Duncan Company's convertible bond

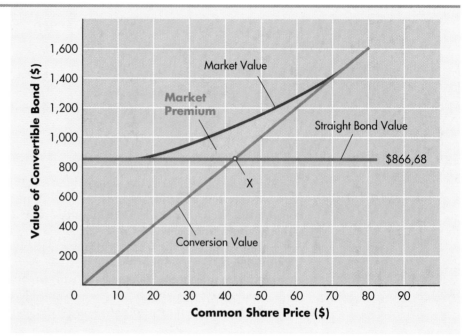

16–7 When the market price of the stock rises above the conversion price, why may a convertible security *not* be converted? How can the *call feature* be used to force conversion in this situation? What is an *overhanging issue*?

16–8 Define the *straight bond value, conversion (or share) value, market value,* and *market premium* associated with a convertible bond, and describe the general relationships among them.

16.4 Warrants

warrant
An instrument that gives its holder the right to purchase a certain number of common shares at a specified price within a certain period of time.

Warrants are similar to share *rights,* which were briefly described in Chapter 6. A **warrant** gives the holder the right to purchase a certain number of common shares at a specified price within a certain period of time. (Of course, holders of warrants earn no income from them until the warrants are exercised or sold.) Warrants also bear some similarity to convertibles in that they provide for the injection of additional equity capital into the firm at some future date.

Basic Characteristics

⚠ Hint
One of the major reasons for tying a warrant or offering a security as a convertible is that, with either of these features, the investor will not require the issuing firm to pay an interest rate that is as high as a security without these features.

Warrants are often attached to debt issues as "sweeteners." When a firm makes a large bond issue, the attachment of warrants may add to the marketability of the issue and lower the required coupon or dividend rate. As sweeteners, warrants are similar to conversion features. Often, when a new firm is raising its initial capital, suppliers of debt will require warrants to permit them to share in whatever success the firm achieves. In addition, established companies sometimes offer warrants with debt or preferred shares to compensate for risk and thereby lower the interest or dividend rate and/or provide for fewer *restrictive covenants*.

Exercise Price

exercise price
The price at which holders of warrants can purchase a specified number of common shares.

The price at which holders of warrants can purchase a specified number of common shares is normally referred to as the **exercise price**. This price is normally set at 10 to 20 percent above the market price of the firm's shares at the time of issuance. Until the market price of the shares exceeds the exercise price, holders of warrants would not exercise them, because they could purchase the stock more inexpensively in the marketplace.

Warrants normally have a life of no more than 5 years, although some have longer lives. Although, unlike convertible securities, warrants cannot be called, their limited life results in holders exercising them when the market price of the common shares is above the exercise price of the warrant.

Warrant Trading

A warrant is *detachable* from the security with which it was sold. This means that the security holder may sell the warrant without selling the security to which it is attached. Many detachable warrants are listed and actively traded on the Toronto Stock Exchange (TSX). Warrants often provide investors with better opportunities for large percentage gains (with increased risk) than the underlying common stock.

Comparison of Warrants to Rights and Convertibles

The similarity between a warrant and a right should be clear. Both result in new equity capital, although the warrant provides for *deferred* equity financing. The life of a right is typically not more than four weeks; a warrant is generally exercisable for a period of years. Rights are issued at a subscription price below the prevailing market price of the stock; warrants are generally issued at an exercise price 10 to 20 percent above the prevailing market price.

Warrants and convertibles also have similarities. The exercise of a warrant shifts the firm's capital structure to a less highly levered position because new common shares are issued without any change in debt. If a convertible bond were converted, the reduction in leverage would be even more pronounced, because common shares would be issued in exchange for a reduction in debt. In addition, the exercise of a warrant provides an influx of new capital; with convertibles, the new capital is raised when the securities are originally issued rather than when converted. The influx of new equity capital resulting from the exercise of a warrant does not occur until the firm has achieved a certain degree of success that is reflected in an increased price for its stock. In this instance, the firm conveniently obtains needed funds.

The Implied Price of an Attached Warrant

implied price of a warrant
The price effectively paid for each warrant attached to a bond.

When attached to a bond, the **implied price of a warrant**—the price that is effectively paid for each attached warrant—can be found by first using Equation 16.1:

$$\text{Implied price of } all \text{ warrants} = \text{price of bond with warrants attached} - \text{straight bond value} \qquad (16.1)$$

The straight bond value is found in a fashion similar to that used in valuing convertible bonds. Dividing the implied price of *all* warrants by the number of warrants attached to each bond results in the implied price of *each* warrant.

Example ▼ Martin Marine Products, a manufacturer of marine drive shafts and propellers, issued a $1,000 par value bond with 20 years to maturity and a 10.5 percent coupon rate paid semiannually. The bond has 15 warrants attached for the purchase of the firm's stock. The bonds were initially sold for their $1,000 par value. When issued, similar-risk straight bonds with 20 years to maturity were selling to yield 11.5 percent. The straight value of the bond is based on the present value of its payments discounted at the 11.5 percent yield on similar-risk straight bonds. This is equal to $922.34.

Substituting the $1,000 price of the bond with warrants attached and the $922.34 straight bond value into Equation 16.1, we get an implied price of *all* warrants of $77.66:

$$\text{Implied price of } all \text{ warrants} = \$1,000 - \$922.34 = \underline{\$77.66}$$

Dividing the implied price of *all* warrants by the number of warrants attached to each bond—15 in this case—we find the implied price of *each* warrant:

$$\text{Implied price of } each \text{ warrant} = \frac{\$77.66}{15} = \underline{\underline{\$5.18}}$$

▲ Therefore, by purchasing Martin Marine Products' bond with warrants attached for $1,000, one is effectively paying $5.18 for each warrant.

The implied price of each warrant is meaningful only when compared to the specific features of the warrant—the number of shares that can be purchased and the specified exercise price. These features can be analyzed in light of the prevailing common share price to estimate the true *market value* of each warrant. Clearly, if the implied price is above the estimated market value, the price of the bond with warrants attached may be too high. If the implied price is below the estimated market value, the bond may be quite attractive. Firms must therefore price their bonds with warrants attached in a way that causes the implied price of its warrants to fall slightly below their estimated market value. Such an approach allows the firm to more easily sell the bonds with a lower coupon rate than would apply to straight debt, thereby reducing its debt service costs.

The Value of Warrants

warrant premium
The difference between the actual market value and theoretical value of a warrant.

Like a convertible security, a warrant has both a market and an intrinsic value. The difference between these values, or the **warrant premium,** depends largely on investor expectations and the ability of investors to get more leverage from the warrants than from the underlying stock.

Intrinsic Value of a Warrant

intrinsic value
The positive difference between the current market price of a firm's common shares and the exercise price of the warrant.

The **intrinsic value** of a warrant is the positive difference between the current market price of a firm's common shares and the exercise price of the warrant. Equation 16.2 provides the equation.

$$IVW = P_0 - E \qquad (16.2)$$

where

IVW = intrinsic value of a warrant
P_0 = current market price of the common shares
E = exercise price of the warrant

The use of Equation 16.2 can be illustrated by the following example.

Example ▼ Dustin Electronics, a major producer of transistors, has outstanding warrants that are exercisable at $40 per share and entitle holders to purchase one common share. The warrants were initially attached to a bond issue to sweeten the bond. The common shares of the firm are currently selling for $45 per share. Substituting P_0 = $45 and E = $40 into Equation 16.2 yields a theoretical warrant value of $5 ($45 − $40). Therefore, the intrinsic value of Dustin's warrants is $5.

If Dustin Electronics' common shares were trading or $38 per share, the intrinsic value of the warrant would be 0. When Equation 16.2 is used, the answer is −$2 ($38 − $40). But a warrant cannot have a negative intrinsic
▲ value. In this case, Dustin Electronics' warrant would have no intrinsic value.

Market Value of a Warrant

The market value of a stock purchase warrant is always above the intrinsic value of the warrant, except at the point of expiry. As the expiry date of a warrant gets nearer, the market value of the warrant declines and approaches its intrinsic value so the difference between the two values is reduced to 0. Also, when the market value of a warrant is very high (the market price of a common share is well above the exercise price of the warrant), the market value of a warrant approaches the intrinsic value. This occurs since investors will try to reduce the risk of large losses on the warrant. Also, as warrant prices increase, the ability to leverage higher percentage returns from investing in warrants disappears.

The general relationship between the intrinsic and market values of Dustin Electronics' warrants is presented graphically in Figure 16.2. The market value of warrants generally exceeds the intrinsic value by the greatest amount when the stock's market price is close to the warrant exercise price per share. In addition, the amount of time until expiration also affects the market value of the warrant. Generally speaking, the more distant the expiration date, the greater the gap between a warrant's market value and its intrinsic value.

Warrant Premium

The *warrant premium*, or amount by which the market value of Dustin Electronics' warrants exceeds the intrinsic value of these warrants, is also shown in Figure 16.2. This premium results from a combination of positive investor expectations, time to warrant expiry, and the ability of the investor with a fixed sum to invest to obtain much larger potential returns (and risk) by trading in warrants rather than the underlying stock. The warrant premium is sometimes termed the time value of the warrant. The warrant premium (WP) is equal to:

$$WP = PW - IVW$$

where PW is the market price of the warrant.

Example ▼ Stan Buyer has $2,880, which he is interested in investing in Dustin Electronics. The firm's stock is currently selling for $45 per share, and its warrants are selling for $8 per warrant. Each warrant entitles the holder to purchase one of Dustin's common shares at $40 per share. Because the stock is selling for $45 per share, the intrinsic warrant value, calculated in the preceding example, is $5 per warrant. The warrant premium of $3 ($8 − $5) results from positive investor expectations, time to expiry and leverage opportunities.

Stan Buyer could invest his $2,880 in either of two ways: He could purchase 64 common shares at $45 per share, or 360 warrants at $8 per warrant, ignoring brokerage fees. If Mr. Buyer purchases the shares and the price rises to $48, his gain is $192 ($3 × 64 shares) or 6.67 percent ($192 ÷ $2,880) on the initial investment. If instead he purchases the warrants and Dustin Electronics' common share price increases to $48, then the warrant will increase by at least $3. If the warrant price were to increase to $12 per warrant, the warrant's intrinsic value would be $8 per share while the premium has increased to $4. Mr. Buyer's gain is $4 per warrant or $1,440 ($4 × 360 warrants) in total. On a percentage basis, the gain is 50 percent ($1,440 ÷ $2,880).

The greater leverage associated with trading warrants should be clear from the example. Of course, because leverage works both ways, it results in greater risk. If the market price of the common shares fell by $3, the loss on the common share investment would be $192. The market price of the warrant may fall to $4 (a $2 intrinsic value and $2 warrant premium) meaning Mr. Buyer would lose

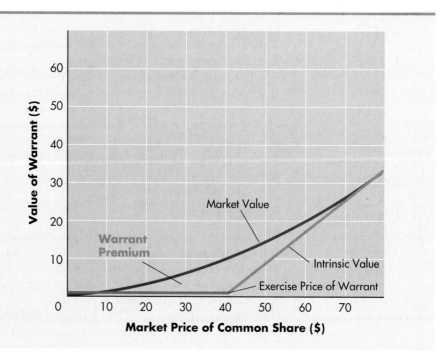

FIGURE 16.2

Values and Warrant Premium

The values and warrant premium for Dustin Electronics' stock purchase warrants

$1,440, or half his investment. Clearly, investing in warrants is more risky than investing in the underlying stock.

? Review Questions

16–9   What are *warrants?* What are the similarities and key differences between the effects of warrants and those of convertibles on the firm's capital structure and its ability to raise new capital?

16–10   What is the *implied price of a warrant?* How is it estimated? To be effective, how should it relate to the estimated *market value* of a warrant?

16–11   What is the general relationship between the intrinsic and market values of a warrant? In what circumstances are these values quite close? What is a *warrant premium?*

16.5 Options

option
An instrument that provides its holder with an opportunity to purchase or sell a specified asset at a stated price on or before a set *expiration date.*

In the most general sense, an **option** can be viewed as an instrument that provides its holder with an opportunity to purchase or sell a specified asset at a stated price on or before a set *expiration date.* Options are probably the most popular type of *derivative security.* Our discussion of options centres on options on common shares. The development of organized options exchanges has created markets in which to trade these options, which are financial securities. Three basic forms of options are rights, warrants, and calls and puts. Rights were discussed in Chapter 6, and warrants were described in the preceding section.

Calls and Puts

call option
An option to *purchase* 100 common shares of a specific company on or before a specified future date at a stated price.

strike price
The price at which the holder of a call option can buy (or the holder of a put option can sell) common shares at any time prior to the option's expiration date.

put option
An option to *sell* 100 common shares on or before a specified future date at a stated price.

option writer
Creates and sells an option contract.

The two most common types of options are calls and puts. A **call option** is an option to *purchase* 100 common shares of a specific company, on or before a specified future date at a stated price. Call options usually have initial lives of 1 to 9 months, occasionally 1 year. The **strike price** is the price at which the holder of the option can buy the shares at any time prior to the option's expiration date; it is generally set at or near the prevailing market price of the common shares at the time the option is created. For example, if a firm's shares are currently selling for $50 per share, a call option created today would likely have a strike price set in the $45 to $55 range. To purchase a call option, a specified price per share must be paid. This is termed the *option premium.*

A **put option** is an option to *sell* 100 common shares on or before a specified future date at a stated strike price. Like the call option, the strike price of the put is set close to the market price of the underlying stock at the time of issuance. The lives and costs of puts are similar to those of calls.

Table 16.2 summarizes the positions of both the buyer and seller of call and put options. Options are created by investors as a way of speculating on the price of a company's common shares or as a way of reducing the risk of an investor's holdings of common shares. The seller of an option is termed the **option writer**. The writer creates the option contract in anticipation that another investor will purchase it.

TABLE 16.2	Positions of the Buyer and Seller of a Call and Put Option
Call option	
Buyer	Pay a premium for *the right to buy* a given quantity of the underlying financial security at the strike price on or before the expiration date.
Seller	Receive a premium and incur *the obligation to sell* a given quantity of the underlying financial security at the strike price on or before the expiration date.
Put option	
Buyer	Pay a premium for *the right to sell* a given quantity of the underlying financial security at the strike price on or before the expiration date.
Seller	Receive the premium and incur *the obligation to buy* a given quantity of the underlying financial security, at the strike price on or before the expiration date.

Option Trading

While options are created by investors, all aspects of option trading are regulated, as is the trading of all other financial securities. In Canada, all option contracts are issued, guaranteed, and cleared by the Canadian Derivatives Clearing Corporation (CDCC). An option contract on a company's common shares is always for 100 shares. Options expire at the close of trading on the third Friday of their month of expiry. Thus, options are standardized and a guarantee that the terms of the option contract will be satisfied is made by the CDCC.

The premium for an option is based on seven factors: 1) the exercise price, 2) the current market price of the common shares, 3) the time to expiry, 4) the volatility of the common shares, 5) the dividend history of the company, 6) interest rate levels, and 7) supply and demand factors. In Canada, options are traded on the common shares of about 75 companies listed on the Toronto Stock Exchange (TSX). The trading of all derivative securities, however, occurs on the Montreal Exchange. For more information on option trading in Canada, see the Web site of the Montreal Exchange at: **www.me.org/accueil_en.php**.

Motives for Trading Options

The most common motive for purchasing call options is the expectation that the market price of the underlying stock will *rise* by more than enough to cover the cost of the option (the option premium) and thereby allow the purchaser of the call to profit.

Example ▼ Cindy Peters believes Wing Enterprises common shares are undervalued. Wing's shares are currently trading for $50. To benefit from her view, Cindy could buy 100 of Wing's common shares paying $50 per share. Excluding commissions, this transaction would cost Cindy $5,000 ($50 × 100 shares). Instead, Cindy could purchase a call option on Wing Enterprises common shares. If Cindy feels that Wing's common shares will increase in price over the next three months, she could buy a call option that expires three months from the current time. If it were September, Cindy would buy a December call option that would expire on the third Friday of December. She must then decide on a strike price.

For a common share trading for $50, there may be options with strike prices ranging from $40 to $60. Assume Wendy decides to buy one December 50 call option on Wing Enterprises common shares. This option contract means Cindy has the option to buy 100 common shares of Wing Enterprises at a price of $50 anytime between now and the third Friday in December. The premium on (price of) options is quoted per share. If this option's premium were $2.50 per share, Cindy would pay the writer of the option contract $250 (she could also pay commissions). Note that the intrinsic value of this option is 0; the current market price and the strike price are the same: $50. But the option has value, due to time: The company's common shares *could* increase between September and the third Friday in December.

For Cindy to break even on this transaction, Wing's common shares must increase to $52.50 per share by the expiry date. If Wing's share price increased to $55 by October 31, then the option will be worth at least $5 per share. The $5 is the difference between the current share price and the strike price ($55 − $50). But there is still time left to the date of expiry. So the option may be trading for $7 per share. To *close her position* in the options on Wing Enterprises, Cindy would write a December $50 call option on Wing and sell it for the current option price of $7 per share. Cindy would receive $700 ($7 × 100 shares). Her gain is $450 ($700 − $250) on a $250 investment or 180 percent ($450 ÷ $250). If she had purchased the shares, Cindy would have made $500 [($55 − $50) × 100 shares], a 10 percent return ($500 ÷ $5,000) on her invested money. The very high potential returns, on modest levels of investment, explain the attraction of option trading.

▲

Note, though, that there is also a very high degree of risk in option trading. If, in the above example, Wing's common share price traded between $47.50 and $50.75 in the period between September and December, and closed trading at $49.75 on the third Friday of December, Cindy would have likely held her position, hoping for the expected increase in share price. As such, she would have ended up losing her $250 investment. Options have high potential returns, but very high risks as well. This, of course, is to be expected, given the risk-return tradeoff that has been considered many times in this book.

Hint

Put and call options are created by *individuals and other firms*. The firm has nothing to do with the creation of these options. Warrants and the convertible features are created by the issuing firm.

Put options are purchased in the expectation that the share price of a given security will *decline* over the life of the option. Purchasers of puts commonly own the shares and wish to protect a gain they have realized since their initial purchase. Buying a put locks in the gain because it enables them to sell their shares at a known price during the life of the option. Investors gain from put options when the price of the underlying stock declines by more than the per-share cost of the option. The logic underlying the purchase of a put is exactly the opposite of that underlying the use of call options.

Example ▼ Assume that Don Kelly pays $325 ($3.25 per share) for a 6-month *put option* on Dante United, a baked goods manufacturer, at a strike price of $40. Don purchased the put option in expectation that the company's share price would drop due to the introduction of a new product line by Dante's chief competitor. By paying $325, Don is assured that he can sell 100 shares of Dante at $40 per share at any time during the next 6 months. The stock price must drop by $3.25 per share by the expiry date to $36.75 per share to cover the cost of the option (ignoring any brokerage fees).

If, on the options expiry date, Dante's common shares were trading for $30 per share, the intrinsic value of the option is $10 per share. Note that Don's net profit on this option contract is $675 [($10 − $3.25) × 100 shares]. Remember, though, if the share price dropped to $30 a few weeks before the options expired, the options would be trading for more than their $10 per share intrinsic value due to time value, and Don's return would be greater.

Because the return would be earned on a $325 investment, this again illustrates the high potential return on investment that options offer. Of course, had the stock price risen above $40 per share, Don would have lost the $325 because there would have been no reason to exercise the option. Had the stock price fallen to between $36.75 and $40 per share, Don probably would have closed his option position to reduce his loss to an amount less than $325.

IN PRACTICE

BCE's Option on Bell Canada

Bell Canada Enterprises (BCE) Inc. is the holding company for Bell Canada, Bell Mobility, Bell ExpressVu and many other companies, including a major stake in CTV, The Globe and Mail, and Sympatico. Bell Canada, the dominant and most vital part of BCE, is the largest telecommunications company in Canada, with major operations in all provinces but particularly in Ontario and Quebec.

In March 1999, BCE sold 20 percent of Bell Canada to Ameritech Corp., a large U.S. telecommunications company, for $5.1 billion. About six months later, in October 1999, Ameritech was acquired by SBC Communications, which also took control of the Bell Canada holding. As part of the original deal, two option contracts were created. First, the owner of the 20 percent stake, SBC, received the right—but not the obligation—to sell the 20 percent stake back to BCE at a 25 percent premium to the market value at the time of the sale. This is a *put option*. The put option was exercisable between July 1, 2002 and December 31, 2002 and for the same period in 2004. If SBC exercised the put option, they had to finance BCE's repurchase of the 20 percent stake for a two-year period.

When the put option was created, BCE also received the right—but not the obligation—to purchase the 20 percent stake in Bell from SBC under the same terms as the put option. This is a *call option*. To exercise the call option, BCE had to arrange for the financing of the repurchase.

On June 28, 2002, BCE announced that they would exercise their call option to buy back the 20 percent stake in Bell Canada for $6.32 billion, a 23.9 percent premium over the amount received in 1999. Michael Sabia, the CEO of BCE, stated that the structure of the deal would maintain BCE's capital structure and that the 20 percent of Bell revenues, earnings, and cash flow was worth the amount paid. This may prove to be correct given that for the December 31, 2001 fiscal year, Bell Canada's revenues were $17.3 billion, assets totalled $27 billion, and cash baseline earnings were $1.2 billion.

This unusual type of option, allowing BCE to reacquire full ownership of Bell Canada, may prove to be the ticket that puts BCE back on track after three years of poor acquisition decisions.

SOURCES: Sean Silcoff, "BCE Pulls Trigger on Bell Stake," *National Post*, June 29, 2002, FPI; Mark Evans, "BCE's Sabia Stands and Delivers," *National Post*, June 29, 2002, FP5; Sean Silcoff, "Bell Buyback 'Probable,' Says Currie," *National Post*, June 13, 2002; and BCE Inc., 2001 annual report.

The Role of Call and Put Options in Fund Raising

Although call and put options are extremely popular investment vehicles, they play *no* direct role in the fund-raising activities of the financial manager. These options are created by investors, not businesses. *They are not a source of financing to the firm.* Institutional investors, whose job it is to invest and manage the savings of individuals, may use call and put options as part of their investment activities to earn a return or to protect or lock in returns already earned on securities.

The presence of options trading on a firm's shares may lead to increased trading activity, but the financial manager has no direct control over this. Buyers of options have neither any say in the firm's management nor any voting rights; only shareholders are given these privileges. Despite the popularity of call and put options as an investment vehicle, the financial manager has very little need to deal with them, especially as part of fund-raising activities.

❓ Review Questions

16–12 What is an *option*? Define *calls* and *puts*. What are the relevant positions of buyers and sellers of call and put options? What role, if any, do call and put options play in the fund-raising activities of the financial manager?

16–13 Describe each of the following concepts regarding options: option writer, strike price, option premium, number of shares per option contract, the CDCC, the role of the Toronto Stock Exchange and Montreal Exchange.

16–14 How does a buyer of a call option make money? How does a seller? How does a buyer of a put option make money? How does a seller? Why would an individual investor buy a call option versus buy the underlying common shares?

SUMMARY

 Differentiate between hybrid and derivative securities and their roles in the corporation. Hybrid securities are forms of debt or equity financing that possess characteristics of both debt and equity financing. Popular hybrid securities include preferred shares, financial leases, convertible securities, and warrants. Derivative securities are neither debt nor equity and derive their value from an underlying asset that is often another security. Options, which are sometimes used by corporations to manage risk, are a popular derivative security.

 Review the basic types of leases, leasing arrangements, the lease-versus-purchase deci- sion, the effects of leasing on future financing, and the advantages and disadvantages of leasing. A lease allows the firm to make contractual, tax-deductible payments to obtain the use of fixed assets. Operating leases are generally 5 or fewer years in term, cancellable, and renewable, and they provide for maintenance by the lessor. Financial leases are longer term, noncancellable, and not renewable, and they require the lessee to maintain the asset. CICA regulations provide specific guidelines for defining a financial (or capital) lease. A lessor can obtain assets to be leased through a direct lease, a sale-leaseback arrangement, or a leveraged lease. The lease-versus-purchase decision can be evaluated by calculating the after-tax cash outflows associated with the leasing and purchasing alternatives. The more desirable alternative is the one that has the lower present value of after-tax cash outflows. CICA regulations require firms to show financial (or capital) leases as assets and corresponding liabilities on their balance sheets; operating leases must be shown in footnotes to the financial statements. A number of commonly cited advantages and disadvantages should be considered when making lease-versus-purchase decisions.

LG3 **Describe the basic types of convertible securities, their general features, and financing with convertibles.** Corporate bonds and preferred shares may both be convertible into common shares. The conversion ratio indicates the number of shares for which a convertible can be exchanged and determines the conversion price. A conversion privilege is almost always available anytime during the life of the security. The conversion (or share) value is the value of the convertible measured in terms of the market price of the common shares into which it can be converted. The presence of convertibles and other contingent securities (warrants and stock options) often requires the firm to report both basic and diluted earnings per share (EPS). Convertibles are used to obtain deferred common shares financing, to "sweeten" bond issues, to minimize restrictive covenants, and to raise cheap funds temporarily. The call feature is sometimes used to encourage or "force" conversion; occasionally, an overhanging issue results.

LG4 **Demonstrate the procedures for determining the straight bond value, conversion (or share) value, and market value of a convertible bond.** The straight bond value of a convertible is the price at which it would sell in the market without the conversion feature. It typically represents the minimum (floor) value at which a convertible bond trades. The conversion value of the convertible is found by multiplying the conversion ratio by the current market price of the underlying common shares. The market value of a convertible generally exceeds both its straight and conversion values, thus resulting in a market premium. The premium, which is largest when the straight and conversion values are

nearly equal, is due to the attractive gains potential from the common shares and the risk protection provided by the straight value of the convertible.

LG5 **Explain the basic characteristics of warrants, the implied price of an attached warrant, and the values of warrants.** Warrants allow their holders to purchase a certain number of common shares at the specified exercise price. Warrants are often attached to debt issues as "sweeteners," generally have limited lives, are detachable, and may be listed and traded on securities exchanges. Warrants are similar to share rights, except that the life of a warrant is generally longer than that of a right, and the exercise price of a warrant is initially set above the underlying share's current market price. Warrants are similar to convertibles, but exercising them has a less pronounced effect on the firm's leverage and brings in new funds. The implied price of an attached warrant can be found by dividing the difference between the bond price with warrants attached and the straight bond value by the number of warrants attached to each bond. The market value of a warrant usually exceeds its intrinsic value, creating a warrant premium. The premium results from positive investor expectations and the ability of investors to get more leverage from trading warrants than from trading the underlying common shares.

LG6 **Define options and discuss the basics of calls and puts, options markets, options trading, and the role of call and put options in fund raising.** An option provides its holder with an opportunity to purchase or sell a specified asset at a stated price on or before a set expiration date. Rights, warrants, and calls and puts are all options. Calls are options to purchase common stock, and puts are options to sell common stock. Options exchanges, such as the Canadian Derivatives Clearing Corporation, provide organized marketplaces in which purchases and sales of both call and put options can be made in an orderly fashion. The options traded on the exchanges are standardized, and the price at which they trade is determined by the forces of supply and demand. Call and put options do not play a direct role in the fund-raising activities of the financial manager.

SELF-TEST PROBLEMS

(Solutions in Appendix B)

ST 16–1 Lease versus purchase Nelson Company is deciding whether it should purchase or lease a new forklift truck that has an expected life of eight years. The truck can be leased for eight years for $17,400 per year, with the first payment due when the lease contract is signed. Nelson could purchase a new forklift for $86,000. The CCA rate on the forklift is 30 percent. The lease includes maintenance costs estimated at $2,000 per year. The salvage value of the forklift truck is estimated to be $4,000 at the end of its useful life. The company's borrowing rate is 15 percent, while their marginal tax rate is 25 percent.

a. What is the present value of the cost of purchasing the new forklift truck? What is the present value of the cost of leasing the new forklift truck? In the analysis of the alternatives, should the maintenance costs be considered and, if so, how? Should Nelson Company lease or purchase the forklift?

b. What do your results imply about the lessor's required rate of return on the lease?

ST 16–2 Finding convertible bond values Mountain Mining Company has an outstanding issue of convertible bonds with a $1,000 par value. These bonds are convertible into 40 shares of common stock. They have an 11 percent annual coupon interest rate paid semiannually and mature in 25 years. The current yield on a straight bond of similar risk is currently 13 percent.

a. Calculate the *straight bond value* of the bond.

b. Calculate the *conversion (or share) values* of the bond when the market price of the common shares is $20, $25, $28, $35, and $50 per share.

c. For each of the share prices given in **b** at what price would you expect the bond to sell? Why?

d. What is the least you would expect the bond to sell for, regardless of the price behaviour of the common shares?

PROBLEMS

WARM-UP   **16–1 Lease cash flows** Given the lease payments and terms shown in the following table, determine the present value of the yearly after-tax lease payments for each firm. Assume that the lease payments are made at the beginning of each year and that the firm is in the 40 percent tax bracket.

Firm	Annual lease payment	Term of lease
A	$100,000	4 years
B	80,000	14
C	150,000	8
D	60,000	25
E	20,000	10

16–2   **Loan interest**   For each of the loan amounts, interest rates, annual payments, and loan terms shown in the following table, calculate the annual interest paid each year over the term of the loan, assuming that the payments are made at the end of each year.

INTERMEDIATE

Loan	Amount	Interest rate	Annual payment	Term
A	$14,000	10%	$ 4,416	4 years
B	17,500	12	10,355	2
C	2,400	13	1,017	3
D	49,000	14	14,273	5
E	26,500	16	7,191	6

 16–3   **Loan payments and interest**   Schuyler Company wishes to purchase an asset costing $117,000. The full amount needed to finance the asset can be borrowed at 14 percent interest. The terms of the loan require equal end-of-year payments for the next 6 years. Determine the total annual loan payment, and break it into the amount of interest and the amount of principal paid for each year. (*Hint:* Use techniques presented in Chapter 5 to find the loan payment.)

INTERMEDIATE

 16–4   **Lease versus purchase**   Doyle Farm Supply, a manufacturer of farm equipment, has offered your company the opportunity to lease or purchase a piece of machinery that has a useful life of 5 years. The asset sells for $40,000 and has a CCA rate of 20 percent. The machinery is expected to have a salvage value of $4,500 at the end of its useful life. At your option, Doyle Farm Supply will guarantee a five-year bank loan at an interest rate of 10 percent, the best rate available, to cover the purchase price. Alternatively, Doyle will lease the asset to your company for five years. The yearly lease payments will be $10,200, with the first payment due when the lease contract is signed.

INTERMEDIATE

a. Having decided to acquire this piece of equipment, what would you recommend regarding the machinery: Should it be purchased or leased? Your company's tax rate is 20 percent.

b. If instead of making yearly payments, you could make monthly lease payment of $850 per month, would this change your recommendation in **a**? Explain.

 16–5   **Lease versus purchase**   Emery Bat and Ball has made the decision to acquire a new lathe, which will replace an existing lathe. The company can purchase or lease the lathe. The existing lathe is currently worth $40,000, while the new lathe will cost $300,000. The new lathe will result in cost savings of $66,500 per year. The new lathe qualifies for a 10 percent ITC and will have a salvage value of $35,000 at the end of its useful life.

CHALLENGE

The CCA rate for lathes is 30 percent and the new lathe is expected to have a life of 12 years. For a 12-year lease, the lease payment would be $40,000, with the first payment due when the lease contract is signed. Emery's tax rate is 40 percent, while their cost of raising long-term debt is expected to be 8 percent. Should the company lease or purchase the new lathe?

CHALLENGE 16–6   **Lease versus purchase**   Shaw Company Ltd. wishes to expand their manufacturing operation by acquiring a $500,000 stamping machine. The CCA rate on the machine is 50 percent and the machine is expected to have a 15-year life. McGuigan Machines, the manufacturer, has offered to lease the machine to Shaw Company. The sales manager of McGuigan Machines indicates to Shaw that since the leasing subsidiary of McGuigan can borrow funds at a very low rate, it is possible for them to offer Shaw an attractive lease rate to secure the machine. For a 15-year lease, the rate would be $50,000 per year, with the first payment due when the lease contract is signed.

Alternatively, Shaw could borrow the $500,000 for 15 years at 10 percent; this would require annual debt repayments of $65,737. At the end of 15 years, the machine could be sold for $20,000. The stamping machine qualifies for an investment tax credit of 10 percent of the cost of the asset. Shaw's tax rate is 30 percent. Since the new stamping machine would result in the creation of four new jobs, Shaw has approached the provincial government regarding financial assistance for the acquisition of the stamping machine. The province has offered a cash grant of $40,000, payable when the machine is acquired, but the grant will be paid only if Shaw purchases the machine.

It has been suggested to Shaw's finance manager that, since the lease rate is over $15,000 per year less than the cost of borrowing the funds required to acquire the stamping machine, Shaw should lease. What would you recommend to Shaw's finance manager: Should they lease or purchase the stamping machine?

INTERMEDIATE 16–7   **Capitalized lease values**   Given the lease payments, terms remaining until the leases expire, and discount rates shown in the following table, calculate the capitalized value of each lease.

Lease	Annual lease payment	Remaining term	Discount rate
A	$ 40,000	12 years	10%
B	120,000	8	12
C	9,000	18	14
D	16,000	3	9
E	47,000	20	11

WARM-UP 16–8   **Conversion price**   Calculate the conversion price for each of the following convertible bonds:
a. A $1,000-par-value bond that is convertible into 20 common shares.
b. A $500-par-value bond that is convertible into 25 common shares.
c. A $1,000-par-value bond that is convertible into 50 common shares.

WARM-UP 16–9   **Conversion ratio**   What is the conversion ratio for each of the following bonds?
a. A $1,000-par-value bond that is convertible into common shares at $43.75 per share.
b. A $1,000-par-value bond that is convertible into common shares at $25 per share.
c. A $600-par-value bond that is convertible into common shares at $30 per share.

WARM-UP 16–10   **Conversion (or share) value**   What is the conversion (or share) value of each of the following convertible bonds?

a. A $1,000-par-value bond that is convertible into 25 common shares. The common shares are currently selling at $50 per share.

b. A $1,000-par-value bond that is convertible into 12.5 common shares. The common shares are currently selling at $42 per share.

c. A $1,000-par-value bond that is convertible into 100 common shares. The common shares are currently selling at $10.50 per share.

WARM-UP 16–11   **Conversion (or share) value**   Find the conversion (or share) value for each of the convertible bonds described in the following table.

Convertible	Conversion ratio	Current market price of common shares
A	25	$42.25
B	16	50.00
C	20	44.00
D	5	19.50

INTERMEDIATE 16–12   **Straight bond value**   Calculate the straight bond value for each of the bonds shown in the following table.

Bond	Par value	Coupon rate (paid semiannually)	Yield on equal-risk straight bond	Years to maturity
A	$1,000	10%	14%	20
B	800	12	15	14
C	1,000	13	16	30
D	1,000	14	17	25

CHALLENGE 16–13   **Determining values—Convertible bond**   Eastern Clock Company has an outstanding issue of convertible bonds with a $1,000 par value. These bonds are convertible into 50 common shares. They have a 10 percent coupon rate paid semiannually and a 20-year maturity. The current yield on straight bonds of similar risk is currently 12 percent.

a. Calculate the *straight bond value* of the bond.

b. Calculate the *conversion (or share) values* of the bond when the market price of the common shares is $15, $20, $23, $30, and $45 per share.

c. For each of the share prices given in b, at what price would you expect the bond to sell? Why?

d. What is the least you would expect the bond to sell for, regardless of the price behaviour of the common shares?

CHALLENGE 16–14   **Determining values—Convertible bond**   Craig's Cake Company has an outstanding issue of 15-year convertible bonds with a $1,000 par value. These bonds are convertible into 80 common shares. They have a 13 percent coupon rate paid semiannually. The current yield on straight bonds of similar risk is 16 percent.

a. Calculate the *straight bond value* of this bond.
b. Calculate the *conversion (or share) values* of the bond when the market price is $9, $12, $13, $15, and $20 per common share.
c. For each of the common share prices given in **b**, at what price would you expect the bond to sell? Why?
d. Graph the straight value and conversion value of the bond for each common share price given. Plot the per-common-share prices on the *x* axis and the bond values on the *y* axis. Use this graph to indicate the minimum market value of the bond associated with each common stock price.

INTERMEDIATE 16–15   Implied prices of attached warrants   Calculate the implied price of *each* warrant for each of the bonds shown in the following table.

Bond	Price of bond with warrants attached	Par value	Coupon rate (paid semiannually)	Yield on equal-risk straight bond	Years to maturity	Number of warrants attached to bond
A	$1,000	$1,000	12%	13%	15	10
B	1,100	1,000	9.5	12	10	30
C	500	500	10	11	20	5
D	1,000	1,000	11	12	20	20

CHALLENGE  16–16   Evaluation of the implied price of an attached warrant   Dinoo Mathur wishes to determine whether the $1,000 price asked for Stanco Manufacturing's bond is fair in light of the intrinsic value of the attached warrants. The $1,000-par, 30-year, 11.5 percent coupon-rate bond pays semiannual interest and has 10 warrants attached for purchase of common shares. The intrinsic value of each warrant is $12.50. The current yield on an equal-risk straight bond is 13 percent.
a. Find the straight value of Stanco Manufacturing's bond.
b. Calculate the implied price of *all* warrants attached to Stanco's bond.
c. Calculate the implied price of *each* warrant attached to Stanco's bond.
d. Compare the implied price for each warrant calculated in **c** to its intrinsic value. On the basis of this comparison, what recommendation would you give Dinoo with respect to the fairness of Stanco's bond price? Explain.

CHALLENGE 16–17   Warrant values   Kent Hotels has warrants that allow the purchase of three common shares at $50 per share. The common share price and the market value of the warrant associated with that price are shown in the following table.

Common share price per share	Market value of warrant
$42	$ 2
46	8
48	9
54	18
58	28
62	38
66	48

a. For each of the common share prices given, calculate the intrinsic warrant value.

b. Graph the intrinsic and market values of the warrant on a set of per-share common share price (x axis)–warrant value (y axis) axes.

c. If the warrant value is $12 when the market price of the common shares is $50, does this contradict or support the graph you have constructed? Explain.

d. Specify the area of *warrant premium*. Why does this premium exist?

e. If the expiration date of the warrants is quite close, would you expect your graph to look different? Explain.

CHALLENGE 16–18 **Common share versus warrant investment** Susan Michaels is evaluating the Burton Tool Company's common shares and warrants to choose the better investment. The firm's shares are currently selling for $50 per share; its warrants to purchase three common shares at $45 per share are selling for $20. Ignoring transactions costs, Ms. Michaels has $8,000 to invest. She is quite optimistic with respect to Burton because she has certain "inside information" about the firm's prospects with respect to a large government contract.

a. How many common shares and how many warrants can Ms. Michaels purchase?

b. Suppose Ms. Michaels purchased the common shares, held them for 1 year, then sold them for $60 per share. What total gain would she realize, ignoring brokerage fees and taxes?

c. Suppose Ms. Michaels purchased warrants and held them for 1 year and the market price of the shares increased to $60 per share. What would be her total gain if the market value of warrants increased to $45 and she sold the warrants (ignoring brokerage fees and taxes)?

d. What benefit, if any, do the warrants provide? Are there any differences in the risk of these two alternative investments? Explain.

CHALLENGE 16–19 **Common shares versus warrant investment** Tom Baldwin can invest $6,300 in the common shares or the warrants of Lexington Life Insurance. The common shares are currently selling for $30 per share. Its warrants, which provide for the purchase of two shares of common stock at $28 per share, are currently selling for $7. The shares are expected to rise to a market price of $32 within the next year, so the expected intrinsic value of a warrant over the next year is $8. The expiration date of the warrant is 1 year from the present.

a. If Mr. Baldwin purchases the common shares, holds them for 1 year, and then sells them for $32, what is his total gain? (Ignore brokerage fees and taxes.)

b. If Mr. Baldwin purchases the warrants and converts them to common shares in 1 year, what is his total gain if the market price of common shares is actually $32? (Ignore brokerage fees and taxes.)

c. Repeat a and b assuming that the market price of the common shares in 1 year is (1) $30 and (2) $28.

d. Discuss the two alternatives and the tradeoffs associated with them.

INTERMEDIATE 16–20 **Options profits and losses** For each of the *100-share option contracts* shown in the following table, use the underlying share price at expiration and other information to determine the amount of profit or loss an investor would have had, ignoring brokerage fees.

Option	Type of option	Cost of option	Strike price	Common share price at expiration
A	Call	$200	$50	$55
B	Call	350	42	45
C	Put	500	60	50
D	Put	300	35	40
E	Call	450	28	26

INTERMEDIATE   LG6   **16–21   Call option**   Carol Krebs is considering buying 100 shares of Sooner Products, Inc., at $62 per share. Because she has read that the firm will likely soon receive certain large orders from abroad, she expects the price of Sooner to increase to $70 per share. As an alternative, Carol is considering the purchase of a call option for 100 shares of Sooner at a strike price of $60. The 90-day option will cost $600. Ignore any brokerage fees or dividends.

a. On a per-share basis, what is the premium on the option? What are the intrinsic value and time value of the option? Provide both on a per-share basis.

b. What will Carol's profit be on the share transaction if its price does rise to $70 and she sells? Provide both a total dollar and a percentage return.

c. Assume that in 60 days, the price of Sooner's common shares increase to $70 per share. Carol wishes to close her option position by selling a call option. If the time value of the option is reduced by $1 per share, how much will Carol earn on the option transaction? Provide both a total dollar and percentage return.

d. At what price must the common shares of Sooner Products be trading for on the expiry date of the option contract for Carol to break even on the option transaction?

e. Compare, contrast, and discuss the relative profit and risk from the common share and the option transactions.

INTERMEDIATE   LG6   **16–22   Put option**   Ed Martin, the pension fund manager for Stark Corporation, is considering purchasing a put option in anticipation of a price decline in the stock of Carlisle, Inc. The option to sell 100 shares of Carlisle, Inc., at any time during the next 90 days at a strike price of $45 can be purchased for $380. The stock of Carlisle is currently selling for $46 per share.

a. On a per-share basis, what is the premium on the option? What are the intrinsic value and time value of the option? Provide both on a per-share basis.

b. Ignoring any brokerage fees or dividends, what profit or loss will Ed make if he buys the option, and Carlisle, Inc., common shares close trading on the expiry date of the option for $46, $44, $40, and $35?

c. What would happen if the price of Carlisle's common shares slowly rose from its initial $46 level to $55 at the end of 90 days? What would happen to the premium on the option?
d. In light of your findings, discuss the potential risks and returns from using put options to attempt to profit from an anticipated decline in share price.

CASE   CHAPTER 16 | **Financing L. Rashid Company's Chemical-Waste-Disposal System**

L. Rashid Company, a rapidly growing chemical processor, needs to raise $3 million in external funds to finance the acquisition of a new chemical-waste-disposal system. After carefully analyzing alternative financing sources, Denise McMahon, the firm's vice-president of finance, reduced the financing possibilities to three alternatives: (1) debt, (2) debt with warrants, and (3) a financial lease. The key terms of each of these financing alternatives follow.

Debt The firm can borrow the full $3 million from the Bank of Alberta. The bank will charge 12 percent annual interest and require annual end-of-year payments of $1,249,047 over the next 3 years. The disposal system has a CCA rate of 20 percent. The firm will pay $45,000 at the end of each year for a service contract that covers all maintenance costs; insurance and other costs will be borne by the firm. The firm plans to keep the equipment and use it beyond its 3-year recovery period.

Debt with Warrants The firm can borrow the full $3 million from a local pension plan. The pension fund will charge 10 percent annual interest and will, in addition, require a grant of 50,000 warrants, each allowing the purchase of two shares of the firm's common shares for $30 per share any time during the next 10 years. L. Rashid's common shares are currently selling for $28 per share, and the warrants are estimated to have a market value of $1 each. The price (market value) of the debt with the warrants attached is estimated to equal the $3 million initial loan principal. The annual end-of-year payments on this loan will be $1,206,345 over the next 3 years. The CCA rate will be the same and maintenance, insurance, and other costs will be the same under this alternative as those described above for the straight debt financing alternative.

Financial Lease The waste-disposal system can be leased from Canadian Equipment Leasing. The lease will require annual payments of $1,200,000 over the next 3 years. The first lease payment is due when the lease is signed. All maintenance costs will be paid by the lessor; insurance and other costs will be borne by the lessee. The lessee will exercise its option to purchase the system for $220,000 at termination of the lease at the end of 3 years.

Denise decided first to determine which of the debt financing alternatives—debt or debt with warrants—would least burden the firm's cash flows over the next 3 years. In this regard, she felt that very few, if any, warrants would be exercised during this period. Once the best debt financing alternative was found,

Denise planned to use a lease-versus-purchase analysis to evaluate it in light of the lease alternative. The firm is in the 40 percent bracket.

Required

a. Under the debt with warrants alternative, find the following:
   (1) Straight debt value.
   (2) Implied price of *all* warrants.
   (3) Implied price of *each* warrant.
   (4) Intrinsic value of a warrant.

b. On the basis of your findings in **a**, do you think the price of the debt with warrants is too high or too low? Explain.

c. Assuming that the firm can raise the needed funds under the specified terms, which debt financing alternative—debt or debt with warrants—would you recommend in view of your findings above? Explain.

d. For the purchase alternative, financed as recommended in **c**, calculate the present value of the cost of purchasing.

e. For the lease alternative, calculate the present value of the cost of leasing.

f. Compare the present values of the costs calculated in **d** and **e**, and determine which would be preferable. Explain and discuss your recommendation.

WEB EXERCISES   LINKS TO PRACTISE

Visit the following Web sites and complete the suggested exercises. These exercises will allow you to review practical applications of the chapter topics as well as explore the wealth of information regarding managerial finance that is available on the Internet.

www.cfla-acfl.ca/glossary.cfm
The above Web site provides a glossary of terms relating to leasing. Define each of the following terms: asset-based financing, asset schedule, bargain purchase option, broker, captive, cash flow–based credit analysis, direct financing lease, economic life, full payout lease, hell-or-high-water clause, lease term, leveraged lease, net lease, stretch lease, trustee, and upgrading.

www.leaseassistant.org
This is the educational Web site of the Equipment Leasing Association (ELA) that provides information on equipment financing and leasing. In 2002, the ELA surveyed small businesses regarding leasing and found that 73 percent of small businesses lease equipment, citing the top three reasons to lease as the ability to manage company growth, take advantage of the latest technology, and improve asset management. Click on Leasing Basics and work through the links to answer the following questions.

1. What are the three ways to finance equipment through leases?
2. Summarize the benefits of leasing equipment. Which would be the most important to you if you were a small business owner? If you were a financial manager at a major corporation?
3. Compare and contrast leases and loans.

Now click on the Informed Decisions link and then How Others Have Leveraged Leasing. Choose one of the cases and answer the following questions based on the information presented.

4. What type of equipment was the company leasing, and why?

5. What benefits did the company achieve through leasing?

www.numa.com/derivs/ref/calculat/cb/calc-cbb.htm

www.numa.com/cgi-bin/numa/calc_cb.pl

The first Web site describes a convertible bond calculator. Read the description of the calculator, the inputs to the calculator, and the outputs. Then go to the second Web site and evaluate the convertible bonds that are discussed in the chapter.

www.stockwarrants.com/SWdemo/Default.htm

This Web site provides detailed coverage and analysis regarding warrants on common shares. A model portfolio consisting of various warrants is developed. The Web site suggests that a disciplined approach to warrant investing can produce returns that considerably exceed those earned on common shares. The Web site provides three tables of warrants. The first table provides a listing of warrants that analysis shows to be most undervalued at current levels. Review the table and select three of the listings. When does the warrant expire? What is the strike price? What is the price of the common shares? What is the intrinsic value of this warrant and what is the premium?

The second table provides the model portfolio. Scroll down to the bottom of the table and review the last three purchases made for the portfolio. Answer the questions above for these three warrants. At the bottom of the table is a summary of the portfolio's performance since the investment strategy was developed. What was the inception date of the portfolio and what was the opening cash position? What is the current value of the portfolio? What was the average yearly return over this period?

The third table is closed positions, all the buys and sells since the portfolio was started. Scan this table. What is your conclusion regarding the success of the strategy, on average? How many winning versus losing trades were made over this period?

www.me.org/accueil_en.php

This is the Web site for the Montreal Exchange. All trading derivative securities in Canada occurs on this exchange.

1. Which companies' options are the most actively traded today?

2. Scroll down the page. Which call option contract is the most actively traded today? Describe the particulars of this option contract. What do the references to series and strike price mean? Fully describe all aspects of this option contract. What is the current price of the company's common shares? If you held the option contract discussed above, would you exercise it today? As a holder of this contract, what would you want to see happen to the company's common share price between now and the expiry of the contract?

3. Scroll down the page. Which put option is the most actively traded today? Answer all of the questions in part 2 for this option contract.

4. Click on the link Equity Derivatives and then Options List. List five companies not considered above that have options that trade on the Montreal Exchange.
5. What are index options and bond options? What do these two types of option contracts allow an investor to do?

17

International Managerial Finance

LEARNING GOALS

LG1 Understand the major factors influencing the financial operations of multinational companies (MNCs).

LG2 Describe the key differences between purely domestic and international financial statements: The consolidation of financial statements and the translation of individual accounts.

LG3 Discuss exchange rate risk and political risk, and explain how MNCs manage them.

LG4 Describe foreign direct investment, investment cash flows and decisions, the factors that influence MNCs' capital structure, and the international debt and equity instruments that are available to MNCs.

LG5 Explain the use of the Eurocurrency market in short-term borrowing and investing (lending) and the basics of cash, credit, and inventory management in international operations.

LG6 Discuss the growth of and special factors relating to international mergers and joint ventures.

LG1

17.1 The Multinational Company and Its Environment

multinational companies (MNCs)
Firms that have international assets and operations in foreign markets and draw part of their total revenue and profits from such markets.

In recent years, as world markets have become significantly more interdependent, international finance has become an increasingly important element in the management of **multinational companies (MNCs)**. These firms, based anywhere in the world, have international assets and operations in foreign markets and draw part of their total revenue and profits from such markets. The principles of managerial finance presented in this text are applicable to the management of MNCs. However, certain factors unique to the international setting tend to complicate the financial management of multinational companies. A simple compari-

"Goodbye—Let Us Know When You Get There"

In the year 1271, at the age of 17, Marco Polo left Venice, Italy. Travelling by ship across the Mediterranean and then by camel across Asia, he reached Cathay—China—more than three years later. Able to speak four languages and having much knowledge of the world from his travels, Polo was warmly received. It was an incredible trip of discovery and it resulted in the opening of trading lanes to the vast, exotic countries of Asia. By the time he returned home 24 years later, Polo had logged about 24,000 kilometres. Today, it is not uncommon for businesspeople to travel that distance in a little over a day. Modern transportation and communication systems have been like steroids (without the risks) in promoting the growth of global business opportunities. This chapter will demonstrate how the principles of managerial finance presented in this book can be applied in the international setting.

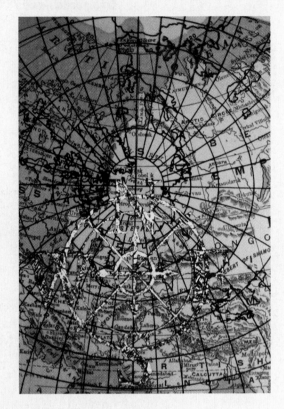

> **⚠ Hint**
>
> One of the reasons that firms have operations in foreign markets is the portfolio concept that was discussed in Chapter 7. Just as it is not wise for the individual investor to put all of his or her investment into the common shares of one firm, it is not wise for a firm to invest in only one market. By having operations in many markets, firms can smooth out some of the cyclical changes that occur in each market.

son between a domestic Canadian firm (firm A) and a Canadian-based MNC (firm B), as illustrated in Table 17.1, indicates the influence of some of the international factors on MNCs' operations.

In the present international environment, multinationals face a variety of laws and restrictions when operating in different countries. The legal and economic complexities existing in this environment are significantly different from those a domestic firm would face. Here we take a brief look at the newly emerging trading blocs in North America, western Europe, South America, and throughout the Americas; GAAT; legal forms of business organization; taxation of MNCs; and financial markets.

TABLE 17.1	International Factors and Their Influence on MNCs' Operations	
Factor	Firm A (domestic)	Firm B (MNC)
Foreign ownership	All assets owned by domestic entities	Portions of equity of foreign investments owned by foreign partners, thus affecting foreign decision making and profits
Multinational capital markets	All debt and equity structures based on the domestic capital market	Opportunities and challenges arise from the existence of different capital markets where debt and equity can be issued
Multinational accounting	All consolidation of financial statements based on one currency	The existence of different currencies and of specific translation rules influences the consolidation of financial statements into one currency
Foreign exchange risks	All operations in one currency	Fluctuations in foreign exchange markets can affect foreign revenues and profits as well as the overall value of the firm

Emerging Trading Blocs: NAFTA, the European Union, Mercosur Group, and FTAA

The development of trading blocs results in economic growth for all countries involved. Trade leads to job creation, it combats poverty, and strengthens economies. With closed borders, every country suffers; this lesson was learned in the Great Depression of the 1930s. Trade is important, not only for wealthy countries like Canada, but also poorer countries like many in Central and South America, as well as Africa and Asia. The countries that often benefit the most from free trade are poorer countries as their goods can enter richer countries' markets tariff-free. As such, they often have a price advantage over the products produced in the home country.

During the early 1990s and into the 21st century, four important trading blocs, centred in the Americas and western Europe, emerged. Chile, Mexico, and several other Latin American countries began to adopt market-oriented economic policies in the late 1980s, forging very close financial and economic ties with Canada and the United States and with each other. In 1988, Canada and the United States negotiated essentially unrestricted trade between their countries. This free-trade zone was extended to include Mexico in late 1992, when the **North American Free Trade Agreement (NAFTA)** was signed by the prime minister of Canada and the presidents of the United States and Mexico. The agreement will soon include Chile, and may eventually include all countries in the Americas. This will be discussed in more detail later in this section.

NAFTA simply mirrors underlying economic reality: The United States is Canada's largest trading partner, and vice versa, while Mexico is the United States' third largest trading partner (after Japan). The volume of trade between the three countries is huge. For example, in 2002, Canada's two-way trade in goods and services with the United States amounted to about $2 billion *per day*,

North American Free Trade Agreement (NAFTA)
The treaty establishing free trade and open markets between Canada, Mexico, and the United States.

or about 78 percent of Canada's total trade in goods and services. Canada's daily trade with all other countries in the world totals about $550 million. So in total, Canada trades about $2.55 billion in goods and services per day. Exports of goods and services account for 43 percent of Canada's gross domestic product (GDP). In 2001, Canada's trade surplus (the excess of exports over imports) stood at a record $64 billion. Obviously, trade is vital for Canada. Canada has an obvious interest in ensuring that current free trade agreements work and in negotiating additional agreements with other countries throughout the world.

European Union (EU)
A significant economic force currently made up of 15 nations that permit free trade within the union.

The **European Union,** or **EU,** has been in existence since 1956. It has a current membership of 15 nations. With a total population estimated at more than 365 million (compared to the population of Canada and the United States of about 320 million) and an overall gross national income parallelling that of the United States, the EU is a significant global economic force. Via a series of major economic, monetary, financial, and legal provisions set forth by the member countries during the 1980s, the countries of western Europe opened a new era of free trade within the union when intraregional tariff barriers fell at the end of 1992. This transformation is commonly called the **European Open Market.**

European Open Market
The transformation of the European Union into a *single* market at year-end 1992.

Although the EU has managed to reach agreement on most of these provisions, debates continue on certain other aspects (some key), including those related to automobile production and imports, monetary union, taxes, and workers' rights. As a result of the Maastricht Treaty of 1991, 11 of the 15 EU nations adopted a single currency, the **euro,** as a continent-wide medium of exchange beginning January 1, 1999. Beginning January 1, 2002, 12 of the 15 EU nations switched to a single set of euro bills and coins, causing the national currencies of all 12 countries participating in **monetary union** to slowly disappear in the following months.

euro
A single currency adopted on January 1, 1999, by 12 of the 15 EU nations, who switched to a single set of euro bills and coins on January 1, 2002.

monetary union
The official melding of the national currencies of the EU nations into one currency, the *euro,* on January 1, 2002.

At the same time that the European Union implemented monetary union (which also involved creating a new European Central Bank), the EU had to deal with a wave of new applicants from eastern Europe and the Mediterranean region. The rapidly emerging new community of Europe offers both challenges and opportunities to a variety of players, including multinational firms. Canadian MNCs today face heightened levels of competition when operating inside the EU. As more of the existing restrictions and regulations are eliminated, huge European MNCs will be created that will be fierce competitors for Canadian (and American) multinationals.

Mercosur Group
A major South American trading bloc that includes countries that account for more than half of total Latin American GDP.

The third major trading bloc that arose during the 1990s is the **Mercosur Group** of countries in South America. Beginning in 1991, the nations of Brazil, Argentina, Paraguay, and Uruguay began removing tariffs and other barriers to intraregional trade. The second stage of Mercosur's development began at the end of 1994, and involved the development of a customs union to impose a common tariff on external trade while enforcing uniform and lower tariffs on intragroup trade. The Mercosur countries represent well over half of total Latin America GDP and, to date, the agreement has been even more successful than its founders had imagined.

While NAFTA and the Mercosur agreement will continue, given the huge volume of trade involved, their long-term fate may depend on negotiations that began in 2001 in Quebec City concerning an Americas-wide free trade agreement. The Quebec meeting was followed, in late 2002, by a meeting in Ecuador attended by representatives from 34 countries in the Americas (North, Central, and South America).

Free Trade Area of the Americas
A trading bloc that would extend the NAFTA and the Mercosur Group to create a free trade zone from the Arctic to Cape Horn.

The purpose of the Ecuador meeting was to outline a time frame to establish the **Free Trade Area of the Americas (FTAA)**. This trading bloc would be an extension of the NAFTA and of the Mercosur Group and would create a free trade area from the Arctic to Cape Horn, the tip of South America. First, though, issues from tariffs on imports to subsidies to business had to be discussed to ensure open borders and a free flow of goods and services between member countries. The objective of the negotiations was to have an agreement in place by 2005, an agreement that would benefit all the citizens of the Americas. Given the new culture of transparency in trade negotiations, many feel these talks will succeed in creating a mammoth free trade zone.

Obviously, the outcome of these negotiations, as well as the reality of the current free trade zones in place around the world, loom large in the plans of any MNC that wishes to access the markets in these areas. Canadian MNCs can benefit from the formation of free trade zones, but only if they are prepared. They must offer a desirable mix of products to a collection of varied consumers and be ready to take advantage of a variety of currencies as well as financial markets and instruments (such as the Euroequities discussed later in this chapter). They must staff their operations with the appropriate combination of local and foreign personnel and, when necessary, enter into joint ventures and strategic alliances.

General Agreement on Tariffs and Trade (GATT)

General Agreement on Tariffs and Trade (GATT)
A treaty that has governed world trade throughout most of the postwar era; it extends free trading rules to broad areas of economic activity and is policed by the *World Trade Organization (WTO)*.

Although it may seem that the world is splitting into a handful of trading blocs, this is less of a danger than it may appear to be, because many international treaties are in force that guarantee relatively open access to at least the largest economies. The most important such treaty is the **General Agreement on Tariffs and Trade (GATT)**. Canada is a signatory to the most recent version of this treaty, which has governed world trade throughout most of the postwar era. The current agreement extends free trading rules to broad areas of economic activity—such as agriculture, financial services, and intellectual property rights—that had not previously been covered by international treaty and were thus effectively off limits to foreign competition.

World Trade Organization (WTO)
International body that polices world trading practices and mediates disputes between member countries.

The 1994 GATT treaty also established a new international body, the **World Trade Organization (WTO)**, to police world trading practices and to mediate disputes between member countries. The WTO began operating in January 1995 and seems to be functioning effectively. In December 2001, the final important nation—the People's Republic of China—was, after years of controversy, granted membership. Now that China's status is resolved, there is an improved chance for stability in world trading patterns, in spite of the stunning collapse of several East Asian economies that began in July 1997. With its recent admittance to the WTO, the long-term economic prognosis for China and the formerly dynamic East Asian markets is much improved.

Legal Forms of Business Organization

foreign subsidiary
An incorporated business established by an MNC that is completely separate from the parent.

An MNC can set up a number of different types of operations in a foreign country. First, if an MNC incorporates a business in a foreign country, it is termed a foreign subsidiary. This **foreign subsidiary** is a legal entity that is completely separate from the parent. Second, if an MNC operates directly within a foreign

branch
A business run by an MNC that is operated directly within a foreign country without incorporating; it is not separate from the parent, but part of the same entity.

foreign affiliate
A foreign corporation in which the MNC owns at least 10 percent of the common shares.

joint venture
A partnership under which the participants have contractually agreed to contribute specified amounts of money and expertise in exchange for stated proportions of ownership and profit.

country without incorporating, the foreign operation is a branch. A **branch** is not separate from the parent; it is part of the same entity. Third, an MNC can establish an operation that is partly owned by the MNC. This could be a foreign affiliate, partnership, or joint venture. A **foreign affiliate** is a foreign corporation in which the MNC owns *at least* 10 percent of the common shares. So, note—*a foreign subsidiary is a foreign affiliate.*

To operate in many foreign countries, it is often essential to enter into joint-venture business agreements with private investors or with government-based agencies of the host country. A **joint venture** is a partnership under which the participants have contractually agreed to contribute specified amounts of money and expertise in exchange for stated proportions of ownership and profit. Joint ventures are common in most of the less developed nations.

The governments of numerous countries, such as Brazil, Colombia, Mexico, and Venezuela in Latin America as well as Indonesia, Malaysia, the Philippines, and Thailand in East Asia, have in recent years instituted new laws and regulations governing MNCs. The basic rule introduced by most of these nations requires that the majority ownership of MNCs' joint-venture projects be held by domestically based investors. In other regions of the world, MNCs will face new challenges and opportunities, particularly in terms of ownership requirements and mergers.

The existence of joint-venture laws and restrictions has implications for the operation of foreign-based subsidiaries. First, majority foreign ownership may result in a substantial degree of management and control by host country participants; this in turn can influence day-to-day operations to the detriment of the managerial policies and procedures that are normally pursued by MNCs. Second, foreign ownership may result in disagreements among the partners as to the exact distribution of profits and the portion to be allocated for reinvestment. Third, operating in foreign countries, especially on a joint-venture basis, can involve problems regarding the remittance of profits. In the past, the governments of Argentina, Brazil, Nigeria, Malaysia, and Thailand, among others, have imposed ceilings not only on the repatriation (return) of capital by MNCs, but also on profit remittances by these firms back to the parent companies. These governments usually cite the shortage of foreign exchange as the motivating factor. Fourth, from a "positive" point of view, it can be argued that MNCs operating in many of the less developed countries benefit from joint-venture agreements, given the potential risks stemming from political instability in the host countries. This issue will be addressed in detail in subsequent discussions.

Taxes

Multinational companies, unlike domestic firms, have financial obligations in foreign countries. One of their basic responsibilities is international taxation—a complex issue because national governments follow a variety of tax policies. The following is a simplified discussion of a *very* complex issue. The very detailed particulars of international corporate taxation are well beyond the scope of this book. Interested readers should consult an international taxation book or the relevant publications provided by chartered accounting firms. In general, from the point of view of a Canadian-based MNC, two major factors must be considered concerning taxation issues.

Taxable Income and Tax Rules[1]

To determine the total taxes to be paid by an MNC, the level of taxable income must be calculated. This can be a complex task. In determining taxable income, it is important to note that every corporation is a resident of at least one country. Most developed countries tax their residents on their worldwide income and tax non-residents on the income earned within the country. Therefore, an MNC based in Canada with a foreign operation may find itself subject to tax *on the same income* both in Canada and in the country where the foreign operation is located. When the same income is taxed twice it is called **double taxation**.

In order to reduce double taxation, many countries have negotiated tax treaties that override domestic law. These treaties place limitations on one country's right to tax residents of the other country. One important limitation is that a company doing business in another country is not subject to tax in that other country unless the company has a *permanent establishment* in that country. Thus, a company can export into a particular country without being subject to income taxes in that country, provided the company does not set up an office or fixed place of business in the country.

In addition to taxing business income, most countries impose withholding taxes on certain types of payments out of the country. Payments subject to withholding taxes include dividends, interest, royalties, and management fees. The tax rate that applies depends on the country involved, but tends to be in the 5 percent to 15 percent range. Since tax treaties normally do not eliminate withholding taxes altogether, double taxation can still occur.

Consider that the income earned by a foreign operation is first taxed as business income. If interest or dividends are then paid to the parent MNC, a withholding tax may apply. In the MNC's home country, the total payment made by the foreign operation is deemed to be income and may be subject to tax. In essence, the foreign subsidiary's earnings may end up being taxed *three times*. To alleviate this burden of excess taxation, most countries offer foreign tax credits. These allow MNCs credit for the taxes paid on income earned in foreign countries and then repatriated to the MNC's home country. Foreign tax credits reduce or eliminate double (or triple) taxation.

The rules, however, are different for dividends received from *foreign affiliates* (foreign corporations in which the MNC owns at least 10 percent of the common shares). Income from an *active business* earned by a foreign affiliate in a *treaty country* (a country with which Canada has a tax treaty) is *exempt* from Canadian tax.

double taxation
A situation where the same income is taxed in two separate countries; to reduce double taxation, many countries have negotiated tax treaties that override domestic law.

Example ▼ Conor Controls is a Canada-based MNC that manufactures heavy machinery. The company has a foreign subsidiary that was financed with equity, in a country with which Canada has a tax treaty. The subsidiary has earnings of $100,000 before local taxes. This is deemed to be active business income. All of the after-tax funds can be paid to the parent as dividends. The applicable taxes consist of a 35 percent foreign income tax rate, and dividend withholding tax of 10 percent.

---

1. We thank Don Wagner of the School of Business at the University of Prince Edward Island for providing us with many of the details in this section.

Subsidiary income before local taxes	$100,000
Foreign income tax at 35%	− 35,000
Dividend declared	$ 65,000
Foreign dividend withholding tax at 10%	− 6,500
Cash dividend payment received by Conor Controls	$ 58,500

While the foreign country has taxed the income and the dividend payment (using a withholding tax), in Canada the dividend income is totally tax exempt. This is the case since the dividend meets the criteria for tax exemption in Canada. The foreign company is an affiliate, operating in a treaty country, and the income was earned by an active business. The total tax burden on Conor Controls' foreign subsidiary would be 35 percent, *if the earnings were not repatriated*. Earnings that are repatriated as dividends are subject to a total tax burden of 41.5 percent [35% business income tax + (65% dividend × 10% dividend withholding tax)].

In the above example, it was assumed that the MNC financed the foreign operation with common equity and was the owner of all or a portion (at least 10%) of the operation. It is also possible for the MNC to finance the foreign operation with debt. This often occurs with joint ventures. When debt financing is used, interest payments may make it possible to reduce the foreign operation's taxable income to zero. When the interest payment is made by the foreign operation to the parent, a withholding tax may apply. The parent company must then declare the interest payment as income in Canada, taxes calculated, and the withholding tax claimed as a tax credit. The following example illustrates these concepts.

Example ▼ Assume Conor Controls' foreign operation was financed with debt rather than equity. The operation's earnings before interest and taxes (EBIT) are $100,000. The foreign operation owes Conor Controls $100,000 of interest. A 10 percent withholding tax applies to interest payments and the Canadian tax rate is 34 percent. The total situation is shown below:

Foreign operations EBIT	$100,000
Interest payment to Conor Controls	$100,000
Taxable income	$ 0
Foreign income tax	$ 0
Withholding tax on interest payment at 10%	$ 10,000
Conor Controls' deemed interest income	$100,000
Canadian taxes at 34%	$ 34,000
Less: Foreign tax credit	$ 10,000
Canadian taxes due	$ 24,000
Total taxes paid	$ 34,000

The effective tax rate on the $100,000 of income earned by Conor Controls' foreign operation is 34 percent, the same rate as if Conor Controls earned the income in Canada. This is a lower tax rate than would be applied if the foreign operation had paid a dividend to Conor Controls.

As is clear from the above discussion and examples, the decision of whether to finance a foreign operation using debt or equity financing is based on the tax rates in the country where the foreign operation is based and in the home country. In countries with very low tax rates, MNCs are more likely to finance a foreign operation with equity since more income will be available for payment as a dividend, which is then exempt from tax (assuming the income is from an active business and it is earned in a treaty country). In countries with high tax rates, debt will likely be the preferred financing method.

The preceding examples clearly demonstrate that the existence of bilateral tax treaties and the subsequent application of tax rules can significantly enhance the overall net funds available to MNCs from their worldwide earnings. Consequently, in an increasingly complex and competitive international financial environment, international taxation is one of the variables that multinational corporations should fully utilize to their advantage.

When an MNC needs a tax rate to make business decisions for the foreign operation, the rate to be used depends on how and whether the MNC repatriates income to the home country. If the MNC finances with debt and pays foreign income as interest in the year it is generated, the home country tax rate will likely apply. For Conor Controls, this rate would be 34 percent. If the MNC finances with equity and pays foreign income as dividends in the year it is generated, then the tax rate used is based on both the income tax and withholding tax. For Conor Controls, this rate would be 41.5 percent. If dividends will not be paid for a long time, the 35 percent tax rate would be the appropriate rate to use.

Financial Markets

Euromarket
The international financial market that provides for borrowing and lending currencies outside their country of origin.

During the last two decades the **Euromarket**—which provides for borrowing and lending currencies outside their country of origin—has grown rapidly. The Euromarket provides multinational companies with an "external" opportunity to borrow or lend funds, with the additional feature of less government regulation.

Growth of the Euromarket

The Euromarket has grown so large for several reasons. First, beginning in the early 1960s, the Russians wanted to maintain their dollar earnings outside the legal jurisdiction of the United States, mainly because of the Cold War. Second, the consistently large U.S. balance-of-payments deficits helped to "scatter" dollars around the world. Third, the existence of specific regulations and controls on dollar deposits in the United States, including interest rate ceilings imposed by the government, helped to send such deposits to places outside the United States.

These and other factors have combined and contributed to the creation of an "external" capital market. Its size cannot be accurately determined, mainly because of its lack of regulation and control. Several sources that periodically estimate its size are the Bank for International Settlements (BIS), Morgan Guaranty Trust, the World Bank, and the Organization for Economic Cooperation and Development (OECD). Today the overall size of the Euromarket is well above $4.0 trillion *net* international lending.

offshore centres
Certain cities or states (including London, Singapore, Bahrain, Nassau, Hong Kong, and Luxembourg) that have achieved prominence as major centres for Euromarket business.

One aspect of the Euromarket is the so-called **offshore centres.** Certain cities or states around the world—including London, Singapore, Bahrain, Nassau, Hong Kong, and Luxembourg—are considered major offshore centres for Euromarket business. The availability of communication and transportation facilities, along with the importance of language, costs, time zones, taxes, and local banking regulations, are among the main reasons for the prominence of these centres.

In recent years, a variety of new financial instruments has appeared in the international financial markets. One is interest rate and currency swaps. Another is various combinations of forward and options contracts on different currencies. A third is new types of bonds and notes—along with an international version of commercial paper—with flexible characteristics in terms of currency, maturity, and interest rate. More details will be provided in subsequent discussions.

Major Participants

The Euromarket is still dominated by the U.S. dollar. However, activities in other major currencies, including the Swiss franc, Japanese yen, British pound sterling, Canadian dollar, and (increasingly) the euro, have in recent years grown much faster than those denominated in the U.S. currency. Similarly, although U.S. financial institutions continue to play a significant role in the global markets, financial giants from Japan and Europe have become major participants in Euromarkets. Canadian financial institutions would be considered minor players.

Following the oil price increases by the Organization of Petroleum Exporting Countries (OPEC) in 1973–1974 and 1979–1980, massive amounts of dollars were placed in various Euromarket financial centres. International banks, in turn, began lending to different groups of borrowers. At the end of 1994, for example, a group of Latin American countries had total borrowings outstanding of about $437 billion. Also, many of the top corporations in the "Tiger economies" of East Asia had huge amounts of foreign-currency–denominated bank debt outstanding when these countries slid into financial crisis in the summer of 1997.

Although developing countries have become a major borrowing group in recent years, the industrialized nations also continue to borrow actively in international markets. Included in the latter group's borrowings are the funds obtained by multinational companies. The multinationals use the Euromarket to raise additional funds as well as to invest excess cash. Both Eurocurrency and Eurobond markets are extensively used by MNCs.

❓ Review Questions

17–1   What are the three important international trading blocs? What is the *European Union* and what is its single new unit of currency? What potential trading bloc is emerging? What is *GATT*?

17–2   What is a *joint venture*? Why is it often essential to use this arrangement? What effect do joint-venture laws and restrictions have on the operation of foreign-based subsidiaries?

17–3   From the point of view of a Canadian-based MNC, what key tax factors need to be considered?

17–4   Discuss the major reasons for the growth of the Euromarket. What is an *offshore centre*? Name the major participants in the Euromarket.

17.2 Financial Statements

Several features differentiate internationally based reports from domestically oriented financial statements. Among these are the issues of consolidation and translation of individual accounts.

Consolidation

At the present time, Canadian accounting rules require the consolidation of financial statements of subsidiaries according to the percentage of ownership by the parent company. Table 17.2 illustrates this point. As indicated, the regulations range from a one-line income-item reporting of dividends to a pro rata inclusion of profits and losses to a full disclosure in the balance sheet and income statement.

Translation of Individual Accounts

Section 1650
The CICA regulation requiring Canadian companies to convert the financial statements of foreign subsidiaries into Canadian dollars for inclusion in the parent company's consolidated financial statements.

integrated foreign subsidiary
An operation that is financially or operationally *interdependent* with the parent company.

Unlike domestic items in the financial statements, international items require translation back into Canadian dollars. Since 1983, all financial statements of Canadian MNCs have had to conform to Section 1650, "Foreign Currency Translation," of the *CICA Handbook*. Under the **Section 1650** regulations, foreign operations must be classified as either integrated or self-sustaining. The choice is made by the MNC and is meant to achieve the overall objective of translation, which is to express financial statements of the foreign operation in Canadian dollars in a manner which best reflects the reporting enterprise's exposure to exchange rate changes.

An **integrated foreign subsidiary** is one that is financially or operationally *interdependent* with the parent company. In this case, the parent company's exposure to exchange rate risk due to the foreign operation's activities is the same as if the parent company had undertaken the operation. For integrated foreign operations, the temporal method of translation of financial statements

TABLE 17.2	Canadian Rules for Consolidation of Financial Statements
Beneficial ownership by parent in subsidiary	Consolidation for financial reporting purposes
0 – < 20%	Deemed a portfolio investment; recognize dividends as received
20 – < 50%	Deemed to be "significant influence," pro rata inclusions of profits and losses
50 – 100%	Full consolidation[a]

[a]Consolidation may be avoided in the case of some majority-owned foreign operations if the parent can convince its auditors that it does not have control of the subsidiaries or if there are substantial restrictions on the repatriation of cash.

SOURCE: Based on Section 3050, "Long-Term Investments," and Section 1590, "Requirements for Consolidation," of the *CICA Handbook*. Refer to any advanced accounting textbook for greater detail.

temporal method
The foreign exchange translation method takes all transactions engaged in by the foreign subsidiary and converts them into Canadian dollars using the exchange rate in effect on the date of the original transaction.

self-sustaining foreign subsidiary
An operation that is financially and operationally *independent* of the parent company.

current rate method
All financial transactions are measured in the currency of the foreign operations and consolidation occurs by converting all balance sheet accounts at the exchange rate in effect at the close of the fiscal year and all income statement accounts at the average exchange rate for the fiscal year.

should be used. The **temporal method** takes all transactions that were measured in a foreign currency and translates them into Canadian dollars using the exchange rate in effect on the date of the original transaction. In effect, the temporal method results in financial statements that are identical to those that would have been produced if the parent company had entered into the same transactions incurred by the foreign operation. Under this method, any exchange rate gains and losses are included in the calculation of net income, and will appear on the income statement.

A **self-sustaining foreign subsidiary** is one that is financially and operationally *independent* of the parent company. In such a case, the parent's exposure to exchange rate risk is limited to the parent's net investment in the subsidiary. Exchange rate changes associated with the subsidiary's operation will have no direct impact on the immediate or short-term cash flows of the parent. As such, the **current rate method** is used to translate the foreign subsidiary's financial statements into Canadian dollars. Under the current rate method, all financial transactions are measured in the currency of the country where the foreign operation is based. Consolidation then occurs by converting all balance sheet accounts at the exchange rate in effect at the close of the fiscal year and all income statement accounts at the average exchange rate for the fiscal year.

Since the exchange rate gains and losses associated with a self-sustaining foreign subsidiary have no direct effect on the activities of the parent, these should not be reflected in the parent's income statement. Instead, they are reported as a separate component of the parent's shareholders' equity. This account is termed the cumulative translation adjustment or foreign currency translation adjustment, and appears on the balance sheet of all Canadian companies with self-sustaining foreign subsidiaries.

? Review Question

17–5   State the rules for consolidation of foreign subsidiaries. Under Section 1650 of the *CICA Handbook,* what are the translation rules for financial statement accounts?

17.3 Risk

The concept of risk clearly applies to international investments as well as to purely domestic ones. However, MNCs must take into account additional factors, including both exchange rate and political risks.

Exchange Rate Risks

exchange rate risk
The risk caused by varying exchange rates between two currencies.

Because multinational companies operate in many different foreign markets, portions of these firms' revenues and costs are based on foreign currencies. To understand the **exchange rate risk** caused by varying exchange rates between two currencies, we examine the relationships that exist among various currencies, the causes of exchange rate changes, and the impact of currency fluctuations.

Relationships Among Currencies

Since the mid-1970s, the major currencies of the world have had a *floating*—as opposed to a *fixed*—relationship with respect to the U.S. dollar and to one another. Among the currencies regarded as being major (or "hard") currencies are the British pound sterling (£), the European Union euro (€), the Japanese yen (¥), the Canadian dollar (C$), and, of course, the U.S. dollar (US$).

foreign exchange rate
The value of two currencies with respect to each other.

The value of two currencies with respect to each other, or their **foreign exchange rate**, is expressed as follows:

$$US\$1 = C\$1.5568$$
$$C\$1 = US\$0.6423$$

Since the U.S. dollar has served as the principal currency of international finance for nearly 60 years, the usual exchange rate quotation in international markets is given as C$1.5568/US$, where the unit of account is the Canadian dollar (C$) and the unit of currency being priced is one U.S. dollar. In this case, it takes 1.5568 Canadian dollars to buy 1 U.S. dollar. Note that the U.S. dollar is the currency that is actually being priced in terms of the Canadian funds needed to buy 1 U.S. dollar. Expressing the exchange rate as US$0.6423/C$ indicates the U.S. dollar price for a Canadian dollar. The Canadian dollar is priced in U.S. funds.

floating relationship
The fluctuating relationship of the values of two currencies with respect to each other.

fixed (or semifixed) relationship
The constant (or relatively constant) relationship of a currency to one of the major currencies, a combination (basket) of major currencies, or some type of international foreign exchange standard.

For the major currencies, the existence of a **floating relationship** means that the value of any two currencies with respect to each other is allowed to fluctuate on a daily basis. On the other hand, many of the nonmajor currencies of the world try to maintain a **fixed (or semifixed) relationship** with respect to one of the major currencies, a combination of major currencies, or some type of international foreign exchange standard.

On any given day, the relationship between any two of the major currencies will contain two sets of figures. One reflects the **spot exchange rate**—the rate on that day. The other indicates the **forward exchange rate**—the rate at some specified future date. The foreign exchange rates given in Figure 17.1 illustrate these concepts. For instance, the figure shows that on Tuesday, November 5, 2002, the spot rate for the British pound was C$2.4341/£ (or £0.4108/C$, as usually stated), and the forward (future) rate was C$2.4128/£ (£0.4145/C$) for 1-year delivery.

spot exchange rate
The rate of exchange between two currencies on any given day.

forward exchange rate
The rate of exchange between two currencies at some specified future date.

In other words, on November 5, 2002, one could execute a contract to take delivery of British pounds in 1 year at a lower dollar price of C$2.4128/£. Note that forward rates are also available for 1-month, 3-month, 6-month, and 2-year contracts. Also note that for the other major currencies (U.S. dollar, euro, and yen) forward exchange rate contracts are also available for transactions 3, 4, and 5 years into the future. For all such contracts, the agreements and signatures are completed on a particular day, but the actual exchange of currencies (say dollars and British pounds) between buyers and sellers will take place on the future date (say, 1 month later).

Figure 17.1 also illustrates the differences between floating and fixed currencies. All the major currencies previously mentioned have spot and forward rates with respect to the Canadian dollar and with each other. Moreover, a comparison of the exchange rates prevailing on November 5, 2002, versus those the previous day, week, or four weeks, indicates that the major currencies' (e.g.,: U.S. dollar and Japanese yen) exchange rates float in relation to the Canadian dollar;

FIGURE 17.1

Exchange Rates (Tuesday, November 5, 2002)

Spot and forward exchange rate quotations

MAJOR CURRENCIES 11.05.02

*Supplied by Royal Bank of Canada – indicative wholesale late afternoon rates. * inverted*

Per US$	Latest	Prev day	Week ago	4 wks ago	% chg on day	% chg in wk	% chg 4 wk
Canada $	1.5568	1.5550	1.5636	1.5963	0.12	-0.43	-2.47
euro*	1.0001	0.9976	0.9834	0.9781	0.25	1.70	2.25
Japan yen	121.83	122.27	122.93	124.30	-0.36	-0.89	-1.98
UK pound*	1.5635	1.5571	1.5569	1.5539	0.41	0.42	0.62
Swiss franc	1.4629	1.4669	1.4900	1.4988	-0.27	-1.82	-2.39
Australia $*	0.5615	0.5616	0.5570	0.5468	-0.02	0.81	2.69
Mexico peso	10.1965	10.1895	10.1845	10.1415	0.07	0.12	0.54
Hong Kong	7.7990	7.7990	7.7991	7.7996	0.00	0.00	-0.01
Singapore $	1.7577	1.7620	1.7695	1.7878	-0.25	-0.67	-1.68
China renminbi	8.2770	8.2773	8.2772	8.2773	0.00	0.00	0.00

Per C$	Latest	Prev day	Week ago	4 wks ago	% chg on day	% chg in wk	% chg 4 wk
US $	0.6423	0.6431	0.6395	0.6264	-0.12	0.44	2.54
euro*	1.5570	1.5513	1.5376	1.5613	0.37	1.26	-0.28
Japan yen	78.26	78.63	78.62	77.86	-0.47	-0.46	0.50
UK pound*	2.4341	2.4213	2.4344	2.4804	0.53	-0.01	-1.87
Swiss franc	0.9397	0.9433	0.9529	0.9389	-0.39	-1.39	0.08
Australia $*	0.8741	0.8732	0.8708	0.8728	0.10	0.37	0.15
Mexico peso	6.5497	6.5527	6.5135	6.3531	-0.05	0.56	3.09
Hong Kong	5.0096	5.0154	4.9879	4.8860	-0.12	0.43	2.53
Singapore $	1.1290	1.1331	1.1317	1.1199	-0.36	-0.24	0.81
China renminbi	5.3167	5.3230	5.2937	5.1853	-0.12	0.43	2.53

FOREIGN EXCHANGE BY COUNTRY

Supplied by BMO Nesbitt Burns Capital Markets – indicative noon rates

Currency	in C$	in US$	Daily % chg	Currency	in C$	in US$	Daily % chg
Antigua,Gr. EC $	0.5828	0.3745	nil	Lebanon (Pound)	0.001029	0.000661	0.02
Argentina (Peso)	0.44085	0.28329	0.57	Luxemb. Euro	1.55530	0.99942	0.39
Austria (Euro)	1.5553	0.9994	0.39	Malaysia (Ringgit)	0.4096	0.2632	nil
Bahamas (Dollar)	1.5562	1.0000	nil	Malta (Lira)	3.7409	2.4038	0.43
Bahrain (Dinar)	4.1279	2.6525	nil	Netherlands (Euro)	1.5553	0.9994	0.39
Barbados (Dollar)	0.7820	0.5025	nil	Neth. Ant. Guilder	0.8743	0.5618	nil
Belgium (Euro)	1.5553	0.9994	0.39	New Zealand $	0.7728	0.4966	-0.06
Bermuda (Dollar)	1.5562	1.0000	nil	Norway (Krone)	0.2115	0.1359	0.48
Brazil (Real)	0.4395	0.2824	-0.79	Pakistan (Rupee)	0.02658	0.01708	0.09
Bulgaria (Lev)	0.780833	0.5018	nil	Panama (Balboa)	1.5562	1.0000	nil
Chile (Peso)	0.002162	0.001389	-0.13	Philippines (Peso)	0.02950	0.01896	0.32
Colombia (Peso)	0.000561	0.000361	0.13	Poland (Zloty)	0.3919	0.2518	0.62
Costa Rica Colon	0.004177	0.002684	-0.04	Portugal (Euro)	1.5553	0.9994	0.39
Cuba (Peso)	0.0741	0.0476	nil	Peru (New Sol)	0.43162	0.27735	-0.14
Cyprus (Pound)	2.7230	1.7498	0.45	Romania (Leu)	0.000046	0.000030	0.07
Czech (Koruna)	0.0504	0.0324	-0.03	Russia (Ruble)	0.048922	0.031437	nil
Denmark (Krone)	0.2093	0.1345	0.38	Saudi Arabia Riyal	0.4150	0.2666	nil
Dominican Rep Peso	0.0841	0.0541	nil	Slovakia (Koruna)	0.0377	0.0242	0.46
Egypt (Pound)	0.3368	0.2165	nil	Slovenia (Tolar)	0.0068	0.0044	0.43
Finland (Euro)	1.5553	0.9994	0.39	S. Africa (Rand)	0.1569	0.1008	-0.11
Greece (Euro)	1.5553	0.9994	0.39	S. Korea (Won)	0.001270	0.000816	-0.56
Guyana (Dollar)	0.00869	0.00559	nil	Spain (Euro)	1.5553	0.9994	0.39
Hong Kong (Dollar)	0.1995	0.1282	nil	Sri Lanka (Rupee)	0.01619	0.01041	nil
Hungary (Forint)	0.00647	0.00416	0.62	Sweden (Krona)	0.1703	0.1094	0.30
India (Rupee)	0.03225	0.02073	0.02	Taiwan (Dollar)	0.04513	0.0290	0.20
Indonesia Rupiah	0.000169	0.000109	0.11	Thailand (Baht)	0.03601	0.0231	0.05
Ireland (Euro)	1.5553	0.9994	0.39	Trinidad & Tob. $	0.2530	0.1626	-0.33
Israel (N Shekel)	0.3291	0.2115	0.34	Turkey (Lira)	0.0000010	0.0000006	2.36
Italy (Euro)	1.5553	0.9994	0.39	Venezuela Bolivar	0.001124	0.00072	3.00
Jamaica (Dollar)	0.03160	0.02030	nil	Spec Draw Right SDR	2.0701	1.3302	0.39
Jordan (Dinar)	2.1977	1.4122	-0.01				
Kuwait (Dinar)	5.1581	3.3146	nil				

FORWARD EXCHANGE RATES

*Supplied by Royal Bank of Canada. Indicative wholesale late afternoon rates. * inverted*

Per US$	Spot	1-mo	3-mo	6-mo	1-yr	2-yr	3-yr	4-yr	5-yr
Canada $	1.5568	1.5584	1.5619	1.5674	1.5782	1.5935	1.6068	1.6199	1.6278
euro*	1.0001	0.9987	0.9960	0.9924	0.9858	0.9743	0.9717	0.9691	0.9717
Japan yen	121.83	121.66	121.36	120.93	119.96	116.74	112.48	107.88	102.98
UK pound*	1.5635	1.5604	1.5546	1.5459	1.5288	1.6252	NA	NA	NA

Per C$	Spot	1-mo	3-mo	6-mo	1-yr	2-yr	3-yr	4-yr	5-yr
US $	0.6423	0.6417	0.6402	0.6380	0.6336	0.6275	0.6224	0.6173	0.6143
euro*	1.5570	1.5563	1.5557	1.5554	1.5558	1.5525	1.5613	1.5698	1.5817
Japan yen	78.26	78.07	77.70	77.15	76.01	73.26	70.00	66.60	63.26
UK pound*	2.4341	2.4317	2.4282	2.4230	2.4128	2.5898	NA	NA	NA

SOURCE: RBC Capital Markets.

the rates change on a constant basis. Other currencies, however, such as the Malaysian ringgit and the Saudi Arabian riyal, are controlled by these contries' governments and do not fluctuate on a daily basis with respect to other currencies. These countries have fixed exchange rates. Some other countries have pegged their exchange rates to the U.S. dollar. For example, the Bahamas and Panama have pegged their exchange rates to the U.S. dollar. In these countries, even though they have their own currencies, U.S. dollars widely circulate.

A final point to note is the concept of changes in the value of a currency with respect to the Canadian dollar or another currency. For the floating currencies, changes in the value of foreign exchange rates are called appreciation or depreciation. For example, Figure 17.1 shows that the value of the Canadian dollar (C$) depreciated against the Mexican peso (MP) from MP 6.5527/C$ on November 4 to MP 6.5497/C$ on November 5. It took slightly fewer MP to buy 1 C$. But over the four weeks to November 5, the C$ appreciated against the MP by 3.09 percent. On November 5, it took 6.5497 MP to buy 1 C$, more than the 6.3531 MP it took 4 weeks earlier. It is also correct to say that over the four weeks the peso depreciated against the dollar, from C$0.1574/MP to C$0.1527/MP by November 5, 2002. It took fewer cents to buy one peso on November 5 than it did four weeks earlier. For the fixed currencies, changes in values are called official *revaluation* or *devaluation,* but these terms have the same meanings as *appreciation* and *depreciation,* respectively.

What Causes Exchange Rates to Change?

Although several economic and political factors influence foreign exchange rate movements, by far the most important explanation for long-term changes in exchange rates is a differing inflation rate between two countries. Countries that experience high inflation rates will see their currencies decline in value (depreciate) relative to the currencies of countries with lower inflation rates.

Example ▼ Assume that the current exchange rate between Canada and the new nation of Farland is 2 Farland Guineas (FG) per Canadian dollar, FG 2.00/C$, which is also equal to C$0.50/FG. This exchange rate means that a basket of goods worth $100 in Canada sells for $100 × FG 2/C$ = FG 200 in Farland, and vice versa (goods worth FG 200 in Farland sell for $100 in Canada).

Now assume that inflation is running at a 25 percent annual rate in Farland but at only a 2 percent annual rate in Canada. In one year, the same basket of goods will sell for 1.25 × FG 200 = FG 250 in Farland, and for 1.02 × $100 = $102 in Canada. These relative prices imply that in 1 year FG 250 will be worth $102, so the exchange rate in 1 year should change to FG 250/$102 = FG 2.45/C$, or C$0.41/FG. In other words, the Farland Guinea will depreciate from FG 2/C$ to FG 2.45/C$, while the dollar will appreciate from C$0.50/FG to C$0.41/FG.
▲

❗ Hint
A firm that borrows money in a developing nation faces the possibility of a double penalty due to inflation. Since many of the loans have floating interest rates, inflation will increase the interest rate on the loan as well as affect the exchange rate of the currencies.

This simple example can also predict what the level of interest rates will be in the two countries. In order to be enticed to save money, an investor must be offered a return that exceeds the country's inflation rate—otherwise there would be no reason to forgo the pleasure of spending money (consuming) today because inflation would make that money less valuable 1 year from now. Let's assume that this *real rate of interest* is 3 percent per year in both Farland and Canada.

TABLE 17.3	Financial Statements for MNC, Inc.'s British Subsidiary

Translation of balance sheet

	12/31/03		12/31/04
Assets	£	C$[a]	C$[b]
Cash	8	20	16
Inventory	60	150	120
Plant and equipment (net)	32	80	64
Total	100	250	200

Liabilities and shareholders' equity

Debt	48	120	96
Paid-in capital	40	100	80
Retained earnings	12	30	24
Total	100	250	200

Translation of income statement

Sales	600	1,500	1,200
Cost of goods sold	550	1,375	1,100
Operating profits	50	125	100

[a]Foreign exchange rate: C$1.00 = £0.40, or £1 = C$2.50

[b]Foreign exchange rate: C$1.00 = £0.50, or £1 = $2.00

Note: This example is simplified to show how the balance sheet and income statement are subject to foreign exchange rate fluctuations. For the applicable rules on the translation of foreign accounts, review the discussion of international financial statements presented earlier.

Using Equation 8.1 (from Chapter 8), we can now reason that the *nominal rate of interest*—quoted market rate, not adjusted for risk—will be approximately equal to the real rate plus the inflation rate in each country, or 3 + 25 = 28 percent in Farland and 3 + 2 = 5 percent in Canada.[2]

Impact of Currency Fluctuations

Multinational companies face exchange rate risks under both floating and fixed arrangements. The case of floating currencies can be used to illustrate these risks. Returning to the Canadian dollar–British pound relationship, we note that the forces of international supply and demand, as well as economic and political elements, help to shape both the spot and forward rates between these two currencies. Because the MNC cannot control much (or most) of these "outside" elements, the company faces potential changes in exchange rates. These changes

---

2. This is an approximation of the true relationship, which is actually multiplicative. The correct formula says that 1 plus the nominal rate of interest, k, is equal to the product of 1 plus the real rate of interest, k^*, and 1 plus the inflation rate, IP; that is, $(1 + k) = (1 + k^*) \times (1 + IP)$. This means that the nominal interest rates for Farland and Canada should be 28.75% and 5.06%, respectively.

can in turn affect the MNC's revenues, costs, and profits as measured in Canadian dollars. For fixed-rate currencies, official revaluation or devaluation, like the changes brought about by the market in the case of floating currencies, can affect the MNC's operations and its dollar-based financial position.

Example ▼

MNC, Inc., a multinational manufacturer of dental drills based in Canada, has a subsidiary in Great Britain that at the end of 2003 had the financial statements shown in Table 17.3. The figures for the balance sheet and income statement are given in the local currency, British pounds (£). Using the foreign exchange rate of £0.40/C$ for December 31, 2003, MNC has translated the statements into Canadian dollars. For simplicity, it is assumed that all the local (the pound) figures are expected to remain the same during 2004. As a result, as of January 1, 2004, the subsidiary expects to show the same British pound figures on 12/31/04 as on 12/31/03. However, because of the decline in the value of the British pound relative to the dollar, from £0.40/C$ to £0.50/C$, the translated dollar values of the items on the balance sheet, along with the dollar profit value on 12/31/04, are lower than those of the previous year. The changes are solely due only to

▲ fluctuations in the foreign exchange rate.

There are additional complexities attached to each individual account in the financial statements. For instance, it is important whether a subsidiary's debt is all in the local currency, all in Canadian dollars, or in several currencies. Moreover, it is important which currency (or currencies) the revenues and costs are denominated in. The risks shown so far relate to what is called the **accounting exposure.** In other words, foreign exchange rate fluctuations affect individual accounts in the financial statements.

A different, and perhaps more important, risk element concerns **economic exposure,** which is the potential impact of foreign exchange rate fluctuations on the firm's value. Given that all future revenues and thus net profits can be subject to foreign exchange rate changes, it is obvious that the *present value* of the net profits derived from foreign operations will have, as a part of its total diversifiable risk, an element reflecting appreciation (revaluation) or depreciation (devaluation) of various currencies with respect to the Canadian dollar.

What can the management of MNCs do about these risks? The actions will depend on the attitude of the management toward risk. This attitude, in turn, translates into how aggressively management wants to hedge (i.e., protect against) the company's undesirable positions and exposures. The money markets, the forward (futures) markets, and the foreign currency options markets can be used—either individually or in combination—to hedge foreign exchange exposures. Further details on certain hedging strategies are described later.

accounting exposure
The risk resulting from the effects of changes in foreign exchange rates on the translated value of a firm's financial statement accounts denominated in a given foreign currency.

economic exposure
The risk resulting from the effects of changes in foreign exchange rates on the firm's value.

Political Risks

Another important risk facing MNCs is political risk. **Political risk** refers to the implementation by a host government of specific rules and regulations that can result in the discontinuity or seizure of the operations of a foreign company. Political risk is usually manifested in the form of nationalization, expropriation, or confiscation. In general, the assets and operations of a foreign firm are taken over by the host government, usually without proper (or any) compensation.

political risk
The potential discontinuity or seizure of an MNC's operations in a host country due to the host's implementation of specific rules and regulations.

macro political risk
The subjection of *all* foreign firms to *political risk* (takeover) by a host country because of political change, revolution, or the adoption of new policies.

micro political risk
The subjection of an individual firm, a specific industry, or companies from a particular foreign country to *political risk* (takeover) by a host country.

Political risk has two basic paths: *macro* and *micro*. **Macro political risk** means that because of political change, revolution, or the adoption of new policies by a host government, *all* foreign firms in the country will be subjected to political risk. In other words, no individual country or firm is treated differently; all assets and operations of foreign firms are taken over wholesale. An example of macro political risk occurred after communist regimes came to power in Russia in 1917, China in 1949, and Cuba in 1959–1960. **Micro political risk,** on the other hand, refers to the case in which an individual firm, a specific industry, or companies from a particular foreign country are subjected to takeover.

IN PRACTICE

Evaluating International Risk Using the O-Factor

Expanding internationally can generate additional revenues from new markets as well as more sources of labour and financing. Financial managers know, however, that doing business overseas is fraught with many types of risk, including exchange rate, political, regulatory, and business environment risks. To help companies decide where to invest and what return on investment to expect, PricewaterhouseCoopers developed its Opacity Index. This analytical model identifies specific incremental borrowing costs related to five key *opacity factors*: legal protections for business, macroeonomic policies, corporate reporting, corruption, and government regulations. *Opacity* refers here to the lack of "clear, accurate, formal, and widely accepted practices."

A country's opacity factor (O-factor) is a composite measure of how these five factors affect the cost of capital and the obstacles to foreign direct investment in a country. The scale ranges from 0 to 150. A lower O-factor means a country is a better location for foreign direct investment. A high O-factor indicates that it is more expensive to operate and raise funds in that country—in effect, that there is a surtax on foreign direct investment (FDI).

What countries are the best places to do business, judging on basis of the Opacity Index? The first Opacity Index, released in early 2001, ranks Singapore first, with the lowest opacity factor (29). And the facts bear this out: Singapore has no tax on FDI. The United States and Chile are next, both with

O-factors of 36. The U.K. is a close fourth with a marginally higher O-factor of 38. At the opposite end of the scale are South Korea (73), Turkey (74), Indonesia (75), Russia (84), and China (87).

The O-factor is used to determine two ratings. The first is the tax equivalent rating, which shows the effect of opacity when viewed as if it imposes a hidden tax. For example, Thailand, with an O-factor of 67, has a tax equivalent rating of 30. This indicates that the lack of opacity in that country is equivalent to levying an additional 30 percent corporate income tax. China's tax equivalent rating is a startling 46. The second rating is the risk premium that indicates the increased cost of borrowing in countries due to opacity. Countries with high O-factors have higher interest rates on long-term debt. For example, Thailand's risk premium is 801, indicating international lenders require an extra 8.01 percent on a debt issue in the country. China's rating of 1,316 implies a premium of 13.16 percent.

Making foreign direct investment decisions is risky. A starting point for managers may be to review the Opacity Index when evaluating the merits of investing in a particular country. In addition to the overall O-factor, managers can look at individual scores for each of the five areas.

SOURCES: Jennifer Caplan, "Why Singapore Is Less Risky Than the U.S.," **CFO.com** (February 14, 2001); Opacity Index Web site at **www.opacityindex.com**.

Examples include the nationalization by a majority of the oil-exporting countries of the assets of the international oil companies in their territories.

Although political risk can take place in any country—including advanced economies like Canada—the political instability of the Third World generally makes the positions of multinational companies most vulnerable there. At the same time, some of the countries in this group have the most promising markets for the goods and services being offered by MNCs. The main question, therefore, is how to engage in operations and foreign investment in such countries and yet avoid or minimize the potential political risk.

Table 17.4 shows some of the approaches that MNCs may be able to adopt to cope with political risk. The negative approaches are generally used by firms in extractive industries such as oil and gas and mining. The external approaches are also of limited use. The best policies MNCs can follow are the positive approaches, which have both economic and political aspects.

In recent years, MNCs have been relying on a variety of complex forecasting techniques whereby "international experts," using available historical data, predict the chances for political instability in a host country and the potential effects on MNC operations. Events in Afghanistan, Pakistan, Indonesia, and India, among others, however, point up the limited use of such techniques and tend to reinforce the usefulness of the positive approaches.

national entry control systems Comprehensive rules, regulations, and incentives introduced by host governments to regulate inflows of *foreign direct investments* from MNCs and at the same time extract more benefits from their presence.

A final point relates to the introduction by most host governments in the last two decades of comprehensive sets of rules, regulations, and incentives. Known as **national entry control systems,** they are aimed at regulating inflows of *foreign direct investments* involving MNCs. They are designed to extract more benefits

---

TABLE 17.4 **Approaches for Coping with Political Risks**

Positive approaches		Negative approaches
Prior negotiation of controls and operating contracts		Licence or patent restrictions under international agreements
Prior agreement for sale	Direct	
Joint venture with government or local private sector		Control of external raw materials
Use of locals in management		Control of transportation to (external) markets
Joint venture with local banks		
Equity participation by middle class	Indirect	Control of downstream processing
Local sourcing		
Local retail outlets		Control of external markets

External approaches to minimize loss

International insurance or investment guarantees

Thinly capitalized firms:

    Local financing

    External financing secured only by the local operation

SOURCE: Rita M. Rodriguez and E. Eugene Carter, *International Financial Management,* 3rd ed. (Englewood Cliffs, NJ: Prentice Hall, 1984), p. 512.

from MNCs' presence by regulating flows of a variety of factors—local ownership, level of exportation, use of local inputs, number of local managers, internal geographic location, level of local borrowing, and the percentages of profits to be remitted and of capital to be repatriated back to parent firms. Host countries expect that as MNCs comply with these regulations, the potential for acts of political risk will decline, thus benefiting MNCs as well.

? Review Questions

17–6   Define *spot* and *forward exchange rates*. Define and compare *accounting exposures* and *economic exposures* to exchange rate fluctuations.

17–7   Explain how differing inflation rates between two countries affect their exchange rates over the long term.

17–8   Discuss *macro* and *micro political risk*. Describe some techniques for dealing with political risk.

17.4 Long-Term Investment and Financing Decisions

Important long-term aspects of international managerial finance include foreign direct investment, investment cash flows and decisions, capital structure, long-term debt, and equity capital. Here we consider the international dimensions of these topics.

Foreign Direct Investment

foreign direct investment (FDI)
The transfer by a multinational firm of capital, managerial, and technical assets from its home country to a host country.

Foreign direct investment (FDI) is the transfer by a multinational firm of capital, managerial, and technical assets from its home country to a host country. The equity participation on the part of an MNC can be 100 percent (resulting in a wholly owned foreign subsidiary) or less (leading to a joint-venture project with foreign participants). In contrast to short-term, foreign portfolio investments undertaken by individuals and companies (such as internationally diversified mutual funds), FDI involves equity participation, managerial control, and day-to-day operational activities on the part of MNCs. Therefore, FDI projects will be subjected not only to business, financial, inflation, and exchange rate risks (as would foreign portfolio investments), but also to the additional element of political risk.

For several decades, U.S.-based MNCs dominated the international scene in terms of both the *flow* and the *stock* of FDI. The total FDI stock of U.S.-based MNCs, for instance, increased from $7.7 billion in 1929 to over $1,245 billion at the end of 2000.

FDI in Canada historically exceeded Canadian corporate FDI abroad. For example, in 1990, FDI in Canada was $130.9 billion while Canadian FDI abroad was $98.4 billion, an FDI surplus of $32.5 billion. By 2001, the figures were $320.9 billion and $389.4 billion, an FDI deficit of $68.5 billion. This swing in FDI balances occurred since 1996, the last year Canada experienced a positive difference in FDI. Over these 12 years, the rate of growth of FDI in Canada was

8.5 percent per year. For Canadian FDI abroad, the growth rate was 13.3 percent per year. For various reasons, Canadian companies are investing more abroad than foreign companies are investing in Canada.

The dollar amount of FDI is impressive when compared to U.S. FDI. In 2000, Canadian FDI abroad was $340.4 billion, which is 27.3 percent of the level recorded by the United States. Given that the Canadian economy is less than 10 percent of the size of the U.S. economy, the level of Canadian FDI abroad is surprisingly high. This, again, shows that the focus of Canadian companies is external, with both trade and FDI data being much higher, on a relative basis, when compared to our larger neighbour to the south.

The largest source of FDI in Canada was the United States, which accounted for 67 percent of the total. The energy and minerals industries attracted the largest portion of the FDI, with these sectors accounting for 21 percent of the total FDI by the end of 2001. The EU's share of FDI in Canada stood at 24 percent of total FDI. The primary destination of Canadian FDI abroad was the United States, accounting for 51 percent of the total by the end of 2001. The finance and insurance sector accounted for 38 percent of the FDI abroad, up sharply from 1992 when it stood at 28 percent.

Investment Cash Flows and Decisions

Measuring the amount invested in a foreign project, its resulting cash flows, and the associated risk is difficult. The returns and NPVs of such investments can significantly vary from the subsidiary's and parent's points of view. Therefore, several factors that are unique to the international setting need to be examined when making long-term investment decisions.

First, elements relating to a parent company's *investment* in a subsidiary and the concept of taxes must be considered. For example, in the case of manufacturing investments, questions may arise as to the value of the equipment a parent may contribute to the subsidiary. Is the value based on the market conditions in the parent country or the local host economy? In general, the market value in the host country is the relevant "price."

The existence of different taxes—as pointed out earlier—can complicate measurement of the *cash flows* to be received by the parent because different definitions of taxable income can arise. There are still other complications when it comes to measuring the actual cash flows. From a parent firm's viewpoint, the cash flows are those that are repatriated from the subsidiary. In some countries, however, such cash flows may be totally or partially blocked. Obviously, depending on the life of the project in the host country, the returns and NPVs associated with such projects can vary significantly from the subsidiary's and the parent's point of view. For instance, for a project of only 5 years' duration, if all yearly cash flows are blocked by the host government, the subsidiary may show a "normal" or even superior return and NPV, although the parent may show no return at all. On the other hand, for a project of longer life, even if cash flows are blocked for the first few years, the remaining years' cash flows can contribute toward the parent's returns and NPV.

Finally, there is the issue of *risk* attached to international cash flows. The three basic types of risk categories are (1) business and financial risks, (2) inflation and exchange rate risks, and (3) political risks. The first category relates to the type of industry the subsidiary is in as well as its financial structure. More

! Hint

The discount rates used by the parent and subsidiary to calculate the NPV will also be different. The parent company has to add in a risk factor based on the possibility of exchange rates changing and the risk of not being able to get the cash out of the foreign country.

details on financial risks are presented later. As for the other two categories, we have already discussed the risks of having investments, profits, and assets/liabilities in different currencies and the potential impacts of political risks.

The presence of the three types of risks will influence the discount rate to be used when evaluating international cash flows. The basic rule is this: The local cost of equity capital (applicable to the local business and financial environments within which a subsidiary operates) is the starting discount rate. To this rate, the risks stemming from exchange rate and political factors would be added; and from it, benefits reflecting the parent's lower capital costs would be subtracted.

Capital Structure

Both theory and empirical evidence indicate that the capital structures of multinational companies differ from those of purely domestic firms. Furthermore, differences are also observed among the capital structures of MNCs domiciled in various countries. Several factors tend to influence the capital structures of MNCs.

International Capital Markets

MNCs, unlike smaller-size domestic firms, have access to the Euromarket (discussed earlier) and the variety of financial instruments available there. Because of their access to the international bond and equity markets, MNCs may have lower long-term financing costs, which result in differences between the capital structures of MNCs and those of purely domestic companies. Similarly, MNCs based in different countries and regions may have access to different currencies and markets, resulting in variances in capital structures for these multinationals.

International Diversification

It is well established that MNCs, in contrast to domestic firms, can achieve further risk reduction in their cash flows by diversifying internationally. International diversification may lead to varying degrees of debt versus equity. Empirically, the evidence on debt ratios is mixed. Some studies have found MNCs' debt proportions to be higher than those of domestic firms. Other studies have concluded the opposite, citing imperfections in certain foreign markets, political risk factors, and complexities in the international financial environment that cause higher agency costs of debt for MNCs.

Country Factors

A number of studies have concluded that certain factors unique to each host country can cause differences in capital structures. These factors include legal, tax, political, social, and financial aspects, as well as the overall relationship between the public and private sectors. Owing to these factors, differences have been found not only among MNCs based in various countries, but also among the foreign subsidiaries of an MNC as well. However, because no one capital structure is ideal for all MNCs, each multinational has to consider a set of global and domestic factors when deciding on the appropriate capital structure for both the overall corporation and its subsidiaries.

Long-Term Debt

As noted earlier, multinational companies have access to a variety of international financial instruments. International bonds are among the most widely used, so we will begin by focusing on them. Next, we discuss the role of international financial institutions in underwriting such instruments. Finally, we consider the use of various techniques by MNCs to change the structure of their long-term debt.

International Bonds

international bond
A bond that is initially sold outside the country of the borrower and often distributed in several countries.

foreign bond
An *international bond* that is sold primarily in the country of the currency of the issue.

Eurobond
An *international bond* that is sold primarily in countries other than the country of the currency in which the issue is denominated.

In general, an **international bond** is one that is initially sold outside the country of the borrower and often distributed in several countries. It is denominated in one of the "hard" currencies like the U.S. or Canadian dollars, euro, British pound, or Japanese yen. When a bond is sold primarily in the country of the currency of the issue, it is called a **foreign bond.** For example, an MNC based in Germany might float a foreign bond issue in the British capital market underwritten by a British syndicate and denominated in British pounds. When an international bond is sold primarily in countries other than the country of the currency in which the issue is denominated, it is called a **Eurobond.** Thus, a Canadian MNC might float a Eurobond in several European capital markets, underwritten by an international syndicate and denominated in U.S. dollars.

The U.S. dollar and the euro continue to be the most frequently used currencies for Eurobond issues, with the euro rapidly increasing in popularity relative to the U.S. dollar. In the foreign bond category, the U.S. dollar and the euro are major choices. Low interest rates, the general stability of the currency, and the overall efficiency of the European Union's capital markets are among the primary reasons for the growing popularity of the euro.

Eurobonds are much more widely used than foreign bonds. These instruments are heavily used, especially in relation to Eurocurrency loans in recent years, by major market participants, particularly corporations. In recent years, many more Canadian companies have been using international bonds to raise financing. The so-called *equity-linked Eurobonds* (i.e., Eurobonds convertible to equity) have found strong demand among Euromarket participants. It is expected that more of these innovative types of instruments will emerge on the international scene in the coming years.

A final point concerns the levels of interest rates in international markets. In the case of foreign bonds, interest rates are usually directly correlated with the domestic rates prevailing in the respective countries. For Eurobonds, several interest rates may be influential. For instance, for a Eurodollar bond, the interest rate will reflect several different rates, most notably the U.S. long-term rate, the Eurodollar rate, and long-term rates in other countries.

The Role of International Financial Institutions

For *foreign bonds,* the underwriting institutions are those that handle bond issues in the respective countries in which such bonds are issued. For *Eurobonds,* a number of financial institutions in the United States, Canada, western Europe, and Japan form international underwriting syndicates. The underwriting costs for Eurobonds are comparable to those for major bond flotations for major companies in the Canadian domestic market. Although U.S. institutions used to dominate the Eurobond scene, recent economic and financial strengths exhibited by some western European (especially U.K. and German) financial firms have led to an erosion of that dominance. Since 1986, a number of European firms have shared with U.S. firms the top positions in terms of acting as lead underwriters of Eurobond issues. However, U.S. investment banks continue to dominate most other international security issuance markets—such as international equity, medium-term note, syndicated loan, and commercial paper markets. U.S. corporations account for well over half of the worldwide securities issues made each year.

To raise funds through international bond issues, many MNCs establish their own financial subsidiaries. Some MNCs, for example, have created subsidiaries in the United States and western Europe, especially in Luxembourg. Such subsidiaries can be used to raise large amounts of funds in "one move," the funds being redistributed wherever MNCs need them. (Special tax rules applicable to such subsidiaries also make them desirable to MNCs.)

Changing the Structure of Debt

As will be more fully explained later, MNCs can use *hedging strategies* to change the structure/characteristics of their long-term assets and liabilities. For instance, multinationals can utilize *interest rate swaps* to obtain a desired stream of interest payments (e.g., fixed rate) in exchange for another (e.g., floating rate). With *currency swaps,* they can exchange an asset/liability denominated in one currency (e.g., the Canadian dollar) for another (e.g., the U.S. dollar). The use of these tools allows MNCs to gain access to a broader set of markets, currencies, and maturities, thus leading to both cost savings and a means of restructuring the existing assets/liabilities. There has been significant growth in such use during the last few years, and this trend is expected to continue.

Equity Capital

Here we look at how multinational companies can raise equity capital abroad. They can sell their shares in international capital markets, or they can use joint ventures, which are sometimes required by the host country.

Equity Issues and Markets

One means of raising equity funds for MNCs is to have the parent's stock distributed internationally and owned by investors of different nationalities. In the 1980s, the world's equity markets became more "internationalized." In other words, although distinct *national* stock markets (such as Toronto, New York, London, and Tokyo) continue to exist and grow, an *international* stock market has also emerged on the global financial scene.

Euroequity market
The capital market around the world that deals in international equity issues; London has become *the* centre of Euroequity activity.

In recent years, the terms **Euroequity market** and "Euroequities" have become widely known. Although a number of capital markets—including New York, Tokyo, Frankfurt, and Zurich—play major roles as hosts to international equity issues, London has become *the* centre of Euroequity activity. In recent years, government sales of state-owned firms to private investors, referred to as *share-issue privatizations,* have accounted for over half of the total volume of Euroequity issues.

With the full financial integration of the European Union, some European stock exchanges still continue to compete with each other. Others have called for more cooperation in forming a single market capable of competing with the New York and Tokyo exchanges. From the multinationals' perspective, the most desirable outcome would be to have uniform international rules and regulations with respect to all the major national stock exchanges. Such uniformity would allow MNCs unrestricted access to an international equity market parallelling the international currency and bond markets.

Joint Ventures

The basic aspects of foreign ownership of international operations were discussed earlier. Worth emphasizing here is that certain laws and regulations enacted by a number of host countries require MNCs to maintain less than 50 percent ownership in their subsidiaries in those countries. For an MNC, for example, establishing foreign subsidiaries in the form of joint ventures means that a certain portion of the firm's total international equity stock is (indirectly) held by foreign owners.

In establishing a foreign subsidiary, an MNC may wish to use as little equity and as much debt as possible, with the debt coming from local sources in the host country or the MNC itself. Each of these actions can be supported: The use of local debt can be a good protective measure to lessen the potential impacts of political risk. Because local sources are involved in the capital structure of a subsidiary, there may be fewer threats from local authorities in the event of changes in government or the imposing of new regulations on foreign business.

In support of the other action—having *more MNC-based debt* in a subsidiary's capital structure—many host governments are less restrictive toward intra-MNC interest payments than toward intra-MNC dividend remittances. The parent firm therefore may be in a better position if it has more MNC-based debt than equity in the capital structure of its subsidiaries.

? Review Questions

17–9   Indicate how NPV can differ depending on whether it is measured from the parent MNC's point of view or from that of the foreign subsidiary when cash flows may be blocked by local authorities.

17–10   Briefly discuss some of the international factors that cause the capital structures of MNCs to differ from those of purely domestic firms.

17–11   Describe the difference between *foreign bonds* and *Eurobonds*. Explain how each is sold, and discuss the determinant(s) of their interest rates.

17–12   What are the long-run advantages of having more *local* debt and less MNC-based equity in the capital structure of a foreign subsidiary?

17.5 Short-Term Financial Decisions

In international operations, the usual domestic sources of short-term financing, along with other sources, are available to MNCs. Included are accounts payable, accruals, bank and nonbank sources in each subsidiary's local environment, and the Euromarket. Our emphasis here is on the "foreign" sources.

The local economic market is a basic source of both short- and long-term financing for a subsidiary of a multinational company. Moreover, the subsidiary's borrowing and lending status, relative to a local firm in the same economy, can be superior, because the subsidiary can rely on the potential backing and guarantee of its parent MNC. One drawback, however, is that most local markets and local currencies are regulated by local authorities. A subsidiary may ultimately choose to turn to the Euromarket and take advantage of borrowing and investing in an unregulated financial forum.

The Euromarket offers nondomestic long-term financing opportunities through Eurobonds. Short-term financing opportunities are available in **Eurocurrency markets.** The forces of supply and demand are among the main factors determining exchange rates in Eurocurrency markets. Each currency's normal interest rate is influenced by economic policies pursued by the respective "home" government. For example, the interest rates offered in the Euromarket on the U.S. dollar are greatly affected by the prime rate inside the United States, and the dollar's exchange rates with other major currencies are influenced by the supply and demand forces in such markets (and in response to interest rates).

Unlike borrowing in the domestic markets, where only one currency and a **nominal interest rate** is involved, financing activities in the Euromarket can involve several currencies and both nominal and effective interest rates. **Effective interest rates** are equal to nominal rates plus (or minus) any forecast appreciation (or depreciation) of a foreign currency relative to the currency of the MNC parent. An example will illustrate the issues involved.

Eurocurrency markets
The portion of the Euromarket that provides short-term, foreign-currency financing to subsidiaries of MNCs.

nominal interest rate
In the international context, the stated interest rate charged on financing when only the MNC parent's currency is involved.

effective interest rate
In the international context, the rate equal to the nominal rate plus (or minus) any forecast appreciation (or depreciation) of a foreign currency relative to the currency of the MNC parent.

Example ▼ A multinational plastics company, International Molding, has subsidiaries in Switzerland (local currency, Swiss franc, Sf) and Japan (local currency, Japanese yen, ¥). On the basis of each subsidiary's forecast operations, the short-term financial needs (in equivalent Canadian dollars) are as follows:

Switzerland: $80 million excess cash to be invested (lent)
Japan: $60 million funds to be raised (borrowed)

On the basis of all the available information, the parent firm has provided each subsidiary with the figures given in the table below for exchange rates and interest rates. (The figures for the effective rates shown are derived by adding the forecast percentage changes to the nominal rates.)

	Currency		
Item	C$	Sf	¥
Spot exchange rates		Sf 1.58/C$	¥125.92/C$
Forecast % change		+1.0%	−2.5%
Interest rates			
Nominal			
Euromarket	4.6%	6.2%	8.5%
Domestic	4.0	5.5	9.0
Effective			
Euromarket	4.6%	7.2%	6.0%
Domestic	4.0	6.5	6.5

From the MNC's point of view, the effective rates of interest, which take into account each currency's forecast percentage change (appreciation or depreciation) relative to the U.S. dollar, are the main considerations in investment and borrowing decisions. (It is assumed here that because of local regulations, a subsidiary is *not* permitted to use the domestic market of *any other* subsidiary.) The relevant question is, where should funds be invested and borrowed?

For investment purposes, the highest available rate of interest is the effective rate for the Swiss franc in the Euromarket. Therefore, the Swiss subsidiary should invest the $80 million in Swiss francs in the Euromarket. To raise funds, the cheapest source *open* to the Japanese subsidiary is the 4.6 percent in the C$ Euromarket. The subsidiary should therefore raise the $60 million in Canadian dollars. These two transactions will result in the most revenues and least costs, respectively.

Several points should be made with respect to the preceding example. First of all, this is a simplified case of the actual workings of the Eurocurrency markets. The example ignores taxes, intersubsidiary investing and borrowing, and periods longer or shorter than a year. Nevertheless, it shows how the existence of many currencies can provide both challenges and opportunities for MNCs. Second, the focus has been solely on accounting values; of greater importance would be the impact of these actions on market value. Third, it is important to note the following details about the figures presented. The forecast percentage change data are those normally supplied by the MNC's international financial managers. Management may, instead, want a *range of forecasts,* from the most likely to the least likely. In addition, the company's management is likely to take a specific position in terms of its response to any remaining exchange rate exposures. If any action is to be taken, certain amounts of one or more currencies will be borrowed and then invested in other currencies in the hope of realizing potential gains to offset potential losses associated with the exposures.

Cash Management

In its international cash management, a multinational firm can respond to exchange rate risks by protecting (hedging) its undesirable cash and marketable securities exposures or by certain adjustments in its operations. The former approach is more applicable in responding to *accounting exposures,* the latter to *economic exposures.* Each of these two approaches is examined here.

Hedging Strategies

hedging strategies
Techniques used to offset or protect against risk; in the international context, these include borrowing or lending in different currencies, undertaking contracts in the forward, futures, and/or options markets, and also swapping assets/liabilities with other parties.

Hedging strategies are techniques used to offset or protect against risk. In international cash management, these strategies include actions such as borrowing or lending in different currencies; undertaking contracts in the forward, futures, and/or options markets; and swapping assets/liabilities with other parties. Table 17.5 briefly outlines some of the major hedging tools available to MNCs. By far the most commonly used technique is to hedge with a forward contract.

To demonstrate how you can use a forward contract to hedge exchange rate risk, assume you are a financial manager for Bombardier Inc., which has just booked a sale of three airplanes worth $100,000,000 to the Swiss national air-

TABLE 17.5	Exchange Rate Risk Hedging Tools	
Tool	**Description**	**Impact on risk**
Borrowing or lending	Borrowing or lending in different currencies to take advantage of interest rate differentials and foreign exchange appreciation/depreciation; can be either on a certainty basis with "up-front" costs or speculative.	Can be used to offset exposures in existing assets/liabilities and in expected revenues/expenses.
Forward contract	"Tailor-made" contracts representing an *obligation* to buy/sell, with the amount, rate, and maturity agreed upon between the two parties; has little up-front cost.	Can eliminate downside risk but locks out any upside potential.
Futures contract	Standardized contracts offered on organized exchanges; same basic tool as a forward contract, but less flexible because of standardization; more flexibility because of secondary market access; has some up-front cost/fee.	Can also eliminate downside risk, plus position can be nullified, creating possible upside potential.
Options	Tailor-made or standardized contracts providing the *right* to buy or to sell an amount of the currency, at a particular price, during a specified time period; has up-front cost (premium).	Can eliminate downside risk and retain unlimited upside potential.
Interest rate swap	Allows the trading of one interest rate stream (e.g., on a fixed-rate Canadian dollar instrument) for another (e.g., on a floating-rate Canadian dollar instrument); fee to be paid to the intermediary.	Permits firms to change the interest rate structure of their assets/liabilities and achieves cost savings due to broader market access.
Currency swap	Two parties exchange principal amounts of two different currencies initially; they pay each other's interest payments, then reverse principal amounts at a preagreed exchange rate at maturity; more complex than interest rate swaps.	All the features of interest rate swaps, plus it allows firms to change the currency structure of their assets/liabilities.
Hybrids	A variety of combinations of some of the preceding tools; may be quite costly and/or speculative.	Can create, with the right combination, a perfect hedge against certain exchange rate exposures.

Note: The participants in these activities include MNCs, financial institutions, and brokers. The organized exchanges include Amsterdam, Chicago, London, New York, Philadelphia, and Zurich, among others. Although most of these tools can be utilized for short-term exposure management, some, such as swaps, are more appropriate for long-term hedging strategies.

line, Swissair. The sale is denominated in Swiss francs (international sales are generally denominated in the customer's currency), and the current spot exchange rate is Sf 1.4175/$ (or, equivalently, $0.7055/Sf). Therefore, you have priced this airplane sale at Sf 141,750,000. If delivery were to occur today, there would be no foreign exchange risk. However, delivery and payment will not occur for 90 days. If this transaction is not hedged, Bombardier will be exposed to significant risk of loss if the Swiss franc depreciates over the next 3 months.

Let us say that between now and the delivery date, the dollar value of the Swiss franc changes from $0.7055/Sf to $0.6061/Sf. Upon delivery of the airplanes, the agreed-upon Sf 141,750,000 will then be worth only $85,914,675 (Sf 141,750,000 × $0.6061/Sf), rather than the $100,000,000 you originally planned for—a foreign exchange loss of over $14 million. If, instead of remaining unhedged, you had sold the Sf 141,750,000 forward 3 months earlier at the

90-day forward rate of $0.7119/Sf offered to you by your bank, you could have locked in a net dollar sale price of $100,911,825 (Sf 141,750,000 × $0.7119/Sf). Of course, if you remained unhedged, and the Swiss franc appreciated, your firm would have experienced a foreign exchange profit for the firm—but most MNCs prefer to make profits through sales of goods and services rather than by speculating on the direction of exchange rates.

Adjustments in Operations

In responding to exchange rate fluctuations, MNCs can give some protection to international cash flows through appropriate adjustments in assets and liabilities. Two routes are available to a multinational company. The first centres on the operating relationships that a subsidiary of an MNC maintains with *other* firms—*third parties*. Depending on management's expectation of a local currency's position, adjustments in operations would involve the reduction of liabilities if the currency is appreciating or the reduction of financial assets if it is depreciating.

For example, if a Canadian-based MNC with a subsidiary in Mexico expects the Mexican currency to *appreciate* in value relative to the Canadian dollar, local customers' accounts receivable would be *increased* and accounts payable would be reduced if at all possible. Because the dollar is the currency in which the MNC parent will have to prepare consolidated financial statements, the net result in this case would be to favourably increase the Mexican subsidiary's resources in local currency. If the Mexican currency were instead expected to *depreciate*, the local customers' accounts receivable would be *reduced* and accounts payable would be increased, thereby reducing the Mexican subsidiary's resources in the local currency.

The second route focuses on the operating relationship a subsidiary has with its parent or with other subsidiaries within the same MNC. In dealing with exchange rate risks, a subsidiary can rely on *intra-MNC accounts*. Specifically, undesirable exchange rate exposures can be corrected to the extent that the subsidiary can take the following steps:

1. In appreciation-prone countries, intra-MNC accounts receivable are collected as soon as possible, and payment of intra-MNC accounts payable is delayed as long as possible.
2. In depreciation-prone countries, intra-MNC accounts receivable are collected as late as possible, and intra-MNC accounts payable are paid as soon as possible.

This technique is known as "leading and lagging," or simply as "leads and lags."

Example ▼ Assume that a Canadian-based parent company, Canadian Motors (CM), both buys parts from and sells parts to its wholly owned Mexican subsidiary, Tijuana Motors (TM). Assume further that CM has accounts payable of $10,000,000 that it is scheduled to pay TM in 30 days and, in turn, has accounts receivable of (Mexican peso) MP 75,900,000 due from TM within 30 days. Because today's exchange rate is MP 7.59/C$, the accounts receivable are also worth $10,000,000. Therefore, parent and subsidiary owe each other equal amounts (though in different currencies), and both are payable in 30 days, but because

TM is a wholly owned subsidiary of CM, the parent has complete discretion over the timing of these payments.

If CM believes that the Mexican peso will depreciate from MP 7.59/C$ to, say, MP 9.00/C$ during the next 30 days, the combined companies can profit by collecting the weak currency (MP) debt immediately, but delaying payment of the strong currency (C$) debt for the full 30 days allowed. If parent and subsidiary do this, and the peso depreciates as predicted, the net result is that the MP 75,900,000 payment from TM to CM is made immediately and is safely converted into $10,000,000 at today's exchange rate, while the delayed $10,000,000 payment from CM to TM will be worth MP 90,000,000 (MP 9.00/C$ × $10,000,000). Thus, the Mexican subsidiary will experience a foreign exchange trading profit of MP 14,100,000 (MP 90,000,000 − MP 75,900,000), whereas the Canadian parent receives the full amount ($10 million) due from TM and therefore is unharmed.

As this example susggests, the manipulation of an MNC's consolidated intracompany accounts by one subsidiary generally benefits one subsidiary (or the parent) while leaving the other subsidiary (or the parent) unharmed. The exact degree and direction of the actual manipulations, however, may depend on the tax status of each country. The MNC obviously would want to have the exchange rate losses in the country with the higher tax rate. Finally, changes in intra-MNC accounts can also be subject to restrictions and regulations put forward by the respective host countries of various subsidiaries.

Credit and Inventory Management

Multinational firms based in different countries compete for the same global export markets. Therefore, it is essential that they offer attractive credit terms to potential customers. Increasingly, however, the maturity and saturation of developed markets is forcing MNCs to maintain and increase revenues by exporting and selling a higher percentage of their output to developing countries. Given the risks associated with the latter group of buyers, as partly evidenced by their lack of a major (hard) currency, the MNC must use a variety of tools to protect such revenues. In addition to the use of hedging and various asset and liability adjustments (described earlier), MNCs should seek the backing of their respective governments in both identifying target markets and extending credit.

Multinationals based in Canada, a number of western European nations, and Japan currently benefit from extensive involvement of government agencies that provide them with the needed service and financial support. In Canada, Export Development Canada (EDC), a Crown corporation, has a mandate to promote and support Canadian exports around the world. The In Practice reading that follows concerns the operation of EDC.

In terms of inventory management, MNCs must consider a number of factors related to both economics and politics. In addition to maintaining the appropriate level of inventory in various locations around the world, a multinational firm is compelled to deal with exchange rate fluctuations, tariffs, nontariff barriers, integration schemes such as the EU, and other rules and regulations. Politically, inventories could be subjected to wars, expropriations, blockages, and other forms of government intervention.

IN PRACTICE

Developing Export Opportunities

Export Development Canada (EDC) is a Canadian Crown corporation. It operates according to commercial principles at arm's length from government, but reports to Parliament. EDC, which has been operating since 1944, is a type of financial institution devoted exclusively to providing trade finance services to support Canadian exporters and investors in 200 markets around the world. Many of these are developing markets that offer a wealth of opportunity for Canadian exporters and investors, but also involve greater risk. EDC helps business assess the long-term potential and manage the increased complexity and risk involved in exporting to these markets. In 2001, EDC supported $45.4 billion in export sales and investments. Without EDC, many of these deals would not have been possible. Nearly 90 percent of EDC's customers are small companies which develop business leads while EDC provides administration and risk management support, such as collections and cash management.

EDC provides Canadian exporters with financing, insurance, and bonding services as well as foreign market expertise to encourage foreign companies to "buy Canadian." Export financing is provided to buyers of Canadian capital goods and services. With export financing in place, an exporter can offer international buyers flexible financing and payment options resulting in a competitive advantage. Financing can be provided as a direct loan, line of credit, or equity investment. Direct loans are a financing arrangement between EDC and a buyer, or a borrower on behalf of a buyer, for a predetermined transaction. Loans usually involve large transactions with long repayment terms. With a line of credit, EDC lends money to foreign purchasers of Canadian goods and services. With the equity program, EDC invests equity in either the Canadian company or a foreign subsidiary of the company.

EDC also provides various types of insurance for exporters. Accounts receivable insurance protects one of the largest assets on many companies' balance sheet. EDC guarantees payment for up to 90 percent of the value of receivables. This insurance protects the exporter if a foreign buyer defaults on payment due to insolvency, the blockage of funds, the refusal of goods by the buyer, or war. Political risk insurance protects an exporter's investments abroad, covering up to 90 percent of the loss. The types of political risk protected include: not being able to convert local earnings into hard currencies or get hard currency out of a country, expropriation of assets, or political violence that destroys or shuts down a business.

EDC's business practices were called into question in October 2002, when a past chairman of EDC revealed the $10.7 billion of EDC's total loan portfolio (loans made to foreign companies to buy Canadian goods) of $21 billion was tied up in customers of just two Canadian companies: Nortel Networks and Bombardier. Such a large exposure to just two industries was viewed to be a very dangerous practice. During 2001 and 2002, Nortel was forced to write off billions in financing they provided to customers, and banks around the world have had to write off billions in loans to telecommunications companies. EDC's shareholders' equity totals $2 billion, but it has also set aside $4.1 billion to cover bad loans. Given that EDC's exposure to Nortel's customers was at least $4 billion, it is possible that much of this amount will have to be used to cover these "single-name exposures."

SOURCES: EDC's Trade Finance Services, available at: **www.edc.ca/index.htm**; Derek DeCloet, "EDC's Pain Could Soon Be Yours," *National Post*, October 18, 2002, FPI; and Ian Jack, "EDC's Exposure to Nortel, Bombardier Draws Fire," *National Post*, October 19, 2002, FP1.

? Review Questions

17–13 What is the *Eurocurrency market*? What are the main factors determining foreign exchange rates in that market? Differentiate between the *nominal interest rate* and *effective interest rate* in this market.

17–14 Discuss the steps to be followed in adjusting a subsidiary's accounts relative to third parties when that subsidiary's local currency is expected to appreciate in value in relation to the currency of the parent MNC.

17–15 Outline the changes to be undertaken in *intra-MNC accounts* if a subsidiary's currency is expected to *depreciate* in value relative to the currency of the parent MNC.

17.6 Mergers and Joint Ventures

The motives for domestic mergers—growth or diversification, synergy, fund raising, increased managerial skill or technology, tax considerations, increased ownership liquidity, and defence against takeover—are all applicable to MNCs' international mergers and joint ventures. Several additional points should also be made.

First, international mergers and joint ventures, especially those involving U.S. firms acquiring Canadian firms, Canadian firms acquiring U.S. firms, and European firms acquiring assets in the United States, increased significantly beginning in the 1980s. MNCs based in western Europe, Japan, and North America are numerous. Moreover, a fast-growing group of MNCs has emerged in the past two decades, based in the so-called newly industrializing countries (which include, among others, Brazil, Argentina, Mexico, Hong Kong, Singapore, South Korea, Taiwan, India, and Pakistan).

Even though many of these companies were hit very hard by the economic problems arising in Asia after July 1997 and following the collapse of the Russian economy in August 1998, top firms from the region have been able to survive and even prosper. Additionally, many Western companies have taken advantage of these economies' weakness to buy into companies that were previously off limits to foreign investors. This has added further to the number and value of international mergers.

Foreign direct investments in North America, the economic engine of the world, have also significantly increased recently. Most of the foreign direct investment is generated between the three North American countries—Canada, the United States, and Mexico—but also comes from six other major countries: Britain, France, the Netherlands, Japan, Switzerland, and Germany. The heaviest investments are concentrated in manufacturing, followed by the petroleum and trade/service sectors. Another trend is the current increase in the number of joint ventures between companies based in Japan and firms domiciled elsewhere in the industrialized world, especially U.S.-based MNCs. Although Japanese authorities continue their discussions and debates with other governments regarding Japan's international trade surpluses as well as perceived trade barriers, mergers and joint ventures continue to take place. In the eyes of some corporate executives, such business ventures are viewed as a "ticket into the Japanese market" as well as a way to curb a potentially tough competitor.

Developing countries, too, have been attracting foreign direct investments in many industries. Meanwhile, during the last two decades, a number of these nations have adopted specific policies and regulations aimed at controlling the inflows of foreign investments, a major provision being the 49 percent ownership limitation applied to MNCs. Of course, international competition among MNCs has benefited some developing countries in their attempts to extract concessions from the multinationals. However, an increasing number of such nations have shown greater flexibility in recent dealings with MNCs, as MNCs have become more reluctant to form joint ventures under the stated conditions. Furthermore, it is likely that as more developing countries recognize the need for foreign capital and technology, they will show even greater flexibility in their agreements with MNCs.

A final point relates to the existence of international holding companies. Places such as Liechtenstein and Panama have long been considered promising spots for forming holding companies because of their favourable legal, corporate, and tax environments. International holding companies control many business entities in the form of subsidiaries, branches, joint ventures, and other agreements. For international legal (especially tax-related) reasons, as well as anonymity, such holding companies have become increasingly popular in recent years.

? Review Question

17–16 What are some of the major reasons for the rapid expansion in international mergers and joint ventures of firms?

SUMMARY

LG 1 **Understand the major factors influencing the financial operations of multinational companies (MNCs).** Four important trading blocs in the Americas and Europe have emerged over the last 15 years: NAFTA (Canada, the United States, Mexico); the European Union (EU); the Mercosur Group in South America; and the FTAA. The EU is becoming even more competitive as it achieves monetary union and most of its members use the euro as a single currency. Free trade among the largest economic powers is governed by the General Agreement on Tariffs and Trade (GATT) and is policed by the World Trade Organization (WTO).

Setting up operations in foreign countries can entail special problems due to the legal form of business organization chosen, the degree of ownership allowed by the host country, and possible restrictions and regulations on the return of capital and profits. Taxation of multinational companies is a complex issue because of the existence of varying tax rates, differing definitions of taxable income, measurement differences, and tax treaties.

The existence and expansion of dollars held outside the United States have contributed to the development of a major international financial market, the Euromarket. The large international banks, developing and industrialized nations, and multinational companies participate as borrowers and lenders in this market.

LG2 **Describe the key differences between purely domestic and international financial statements: the consolidation of financial statements and the translation of individual accounts.** Regulations that apply to international operations complicate the preparation of foreign-based financial statements. Canadian accounting rules require the consolidation of financial statements of subsidiaries according to the percentage of ownership by the parent in the subsidiary. Individual accounts of subsidiaries must be translated back into Canadian dollars using the procedures outlined in Section 1650 of the *CICA Handbook*. Regulations also require that only certain transactional gains or losses from international operations be included in the Canadian parent's income statement.

LG3 **Discuss exchange rate risk and political risk, and explain how MNCs manage them.** Economic exposure from exchange rate risk results from the existence of different currencies and the potential impact they can have on the value of foreign operations. Long-term changes in foreign exchange rates result primarily from differing inflation rates in the two countries. The money markets, the forward (futures) markets, and the foreign currency options markets can be used to hedge foreign exchange exposure. Political risks stem mainly from political instability and from the associated implications for the assets and operations of MNCs. MNCs can employ negative, external, and positive approaches to cope with political risk.

LG4 **Describe foreign direct investment, investment cash flows and decisions, the factors that influence MNCs' capital structure, and the international debt and equity instruments that are available to MNCs.** Foreign direct investment (FDI) involves an MNC's transfer of capital, managerial, and technical assets from its home country to the host country. The investment cash flows of FDIs are subject to a variety of factors, including taxes in host countries, regulations that may block the return (repatriation) of MNCs' cash flow, the usual business and financial risks, risks stemming from inflation and from currency and political actions by host governments, and the application of a local cost of capital.

The capital structures of MNCs differ from those of purely domestic firms because of the MNCs' access to the Euromarket and the financial instruments it offers; the ability to reduce risk in their cash flows through international diversification; and the impact of legal, tax, political, social, and financial factors unique to each host country. MNCs can raise long-term debt through the issuance of international bonds in various currencies. Foreign bonds are sold primarily in the country of the currency of issue; Eurobonds are sold primarily in countries other than the country of the currency in which the issue is denominated. MNCs can raise equity through the sale of their shares in the international capital markets or through joint ventures. In establishing foreign subsidiaries, it may be more advantageous to issue debt than MNC-owned equity.

LG5 **Explain the use of the Eurocurrency market in short-term borrowing and investing (lending) and the basics of cash, credit, and inventory management in international operations.** Eurocurrency markets allow multinationals to invest (lend) and raise (borrow) short-term funds in a variety of currencies and to protect themselves against exchange rate risk exposures. Effective interest rates, which take into account each currency's forecast percentage change relative to the MNC parent's currency, are the main items considered by an MNC in making investment and borrowing decisions. The MNC invests in the currency with the highest effective rate and borrows in the currency with the lowest effective rate. MNCs must offer competitive credit terms and maintain adequate inventories to provide timely delivery to foreign buyers. Obtaining the backing of foreign governments is helpful to the MNC in effectively managing credit and inventory.

LG6 **Discuss the growth of and special factors relating to international mergers and joint ventures.** International mergers and joint ventures, including international holding companies, increased significantly in the last decade. Special factors affecting these mergers include economic and trade conditions and various regulations imposed on MNCs by host countries.

SELF-TEST PROBLEM   **(Solution in Appendix B)**

ST 17–1   **Tax credits**   A Canadian-based MNC has a foreign subsidiary that has earnings before interest and local taxes of $150,000. All the after-tax funds are to be available to be paid to the parent. The applicable taxes consist of a 32 percent foreign income tax rate, a foreign payment withholding tax rate of 8 percent, and a Canadian tax rate of 34 percent. Calculate the net funds available to the parent MNC if:

a. The foreign subsidiary earns active business income, and is in a treaty country, pays no interest, and returns all after-tax funds to the parent MNC through dividends.

b. The foreign subsidiary makes a $150,000 interest payment to the Canadian MNC.

c. Should the foreign operation be financed with debt or equity capital?

PROBLEMS

INTERMEDIATE 17–1   **Tax credits**   A Canadian-based MNC has a foreign subsidiary that earns $250,000 before local taxes, with all the after-tax funds to be available to be paid to the parent. The applicable taxes consist of a 33 percent foreign income tax rate, a foreign payment withholding tax rate of 9 percent, and a Canadian tax rate of 34 percent. Calculate the net funds available to the parent MNC if:

a. The foreign subsidiary earns active business income, is in a treaty country, pays no interest, and returns all after-tax funds to the parent MNC through divdents.

b. The foreign subsidiary makes a $150,000 interest payment to the Canadian MNC.

c. Should the foreign operation be financed with debt or equity capital?

INTERMEDIATE 17–2   **Translation of financial statements**   A Canadian-based MNC has a subsidiary in France (local currency, euro). The balance sheet and income statement of the subsidiary follow. On 12/31/03, the exchange rate is euro 1.50/C$. Assume that the local (euro) figures for the statements remain the same on 12/31/04. Calculate the Canadian dollar–translated figures for the two ending time periods, assuming that between 12/31/03 and 12/31/04 the euro has appreciated against the Canadian dollar by 6 percent.

	Translation of income statement		
	12/31/03		12/31/04
	Euro	C$	C$
Sales	3,000		
Cost of goods sold	2,750	_____	_____
Operating profits	250	_____	_____

	Translation of balance sheet		
Cash	40		
Inventory	300		
Plant and equipment (net)	160	_____	_____
Total	500	_____	_____

	Liabilities and shareholders' equity		
Debt	240		
Paid-in capital	200		
Retained earnings	60	_____	_____
Total	500	_____	_____

CHALLENGE 17–3   **Euromarket investment and fund raising**   A Canadian-based multinational company has two subsidiaries, one in Mexico (local currency, Mexican peso, MP) and one in Japan (local currency, yen, ¥). Forecasts of business operations indicate the following short-term financing position for each subsidiary (in equivalent Canadian dollars):

Mexico: $80 million excess cash to be invested (lent)
Japan: $60 million funds to be raised (borrowed)

The management gathered the following data:

Item	Currency		
	C$	MP	¥
Spot exchange rates		MP 9.18/C$	¥126.7/C$
Forecast % change		+1.5%	+1.0%
Interest rates			
Nominal			
Euromarket	5.0%	6.5%	6.2%
Domestic	4.5	6.1	5.7
Effective			
Euromarket			
Domestic			

Determine the *effective* interest rates for all three currencies in both the Euromarket and the domestic market; then indicate where the funds should be invested and raised. (*Note:* Assume that because of local regulations, a subsidiary is *not* permitted to use the domestic market of *any other* subsidiary.)

CASE   CHAPTER 17   **Assessing a Direct Investment in Chile by Canadian Computer Corporation**

David Smith is Chief Financial Officer for Canadian Computer Corporation (CCC), a successful and rapidly growing manufacturer of personal computers. He has been asked to evaluate an investment project calling for CCC to build a factory in Chile to assemble the company's most popular computer for sale in the Chilean market. David knows that Chile has been a real business success story in recent years—having achieved economic growth rates of over 7 percent per year from 1990 through 2001, even as it made the transition from military dictatorship to democracy—and CCC is eager to invest in this developing economy if an attractive opportunity arises. David's job is to use the information below to see whether this particular proposal meets the company's investment standards.

On the basis of the current Chilean peso (Ps)-to-dollar exchange rate of Ps 500/C$ (assumed value), David calculates that the factory would cost Ps 5,000,000,000 ($10,000,000) to build (including working capital) and would generate sales of Ps 10,000,000,000 ($20,000,000) per year for the first several years. Initially, the factory would import key components from Canada and assemble the computers in Chile using local labour. Smith estimates that half the company's costs will be dollar-denominated components and half will be local currency (peso) costs, but all CCC's revenues will be in pesos. As long as the peso/dollar exchange rate is stable, the company's operating cash flow is expected to equal 20 percent of sales. If, however, the peso were to depreciate relative to the dollar, the company's peso cost of acquiring dollar-denominated components would increase, and its profit margin would shrink because the peso sale prices of its computers would not change.

If CCC made this investment, they would set up a subsidiary in Chile and structure the factory investment so that the subsidiary's capital structure was 60 percent debt and 40 percent equity. Therefore, to finance the Ps 5,000,000,000 factory cost, CCC must obtain Ps 3,000,000,000 ($6,000,000) in debt and Ps 2,000,000,000 ($4,000,000) in equity. The debt can be obtained either by issuing $6,000,000 of dollar-denominated bonds in the Eurobond market at a 6 percent annual rate and then converting the proceeds into pesos or by borrowing the Ps 3,000,000,000 in the Chilean market at a 14 percent annual interest rate. If borrowing is done in dollars, however, the parent company must also service and repay the debt in dollars, even though all project revenues will be in pesos.

For simplicity, assume the parent company decides to contribute the equity capital for the project itself. CCC would do this by contributing $4,000,000 to the subsidiary from its existing resources or from the proceeds of newly issued common shares. This equity financing would then be converted to pesos. (Alternatively, the subsidiary could sell Ps 2,000,000,000 of stock to Chilean investors by listing shares on the Santiago Stock Exchange.) CCC has a 12 percent required return on equity on its dollar-denominated investments.

Required

a. Compute the weighted average cost of capital for this project, assuming that the long-term debt financing is in dollars.

b. Assuming that the peso/dollar exchange rate remains unchanged, compute the present value of the first 5 years of the project's cash flows, using the weighted average cost of capital computed in **a.** What happens to the present value if the dollar appreciates against the peso?

c. Identify the exchange rate risks involved in this project. Given that no forward, futures, or options markets exist for the Chilean peso, how might CCC minimize the exchange rate risk of this project by changes in production, sourcing, and sales? (*Hint:* Exchange rate risk can be minimized either by decreasing dollar-denominated costs, by increasing dollar-denominated revenue, or by doing both.)

d. What are the risks involved in financing this project as much as possible with local funds (pesos)? Which financing strategy—dollar versus peso—would minimize the project's exchange rate risk? Would your answer change if Chile began to experience political instability? What would happen to the attractiveness of the project if Chile joined NAFTA?

WEB EXERCISES   LINKS TO PRACTISE

Visit the following Web sites and complete the suggested exercises. These exercises will allow you to review practical applications of the chapter topics as well as explore the wealth of information regarding managerial finance that is available on the Internet.

europa.eu.int/abc-en.htm
www.euro.ecb.int/en.html
The above are Web sites for the European Union and the European Central Bank. The EU is regularly evaluating new countries for membership. At the time this book was written, the EU had 15 members. How many and which countries are currently in the EU?

At the time this book was written, 12 of the 15 countries had adopted the euro as their currency of exchange. How many and which EU countries are now using the euro? For the EU, what were the perceived benefits of moving to a common currency? Based on your review of this Web site and your understanding of the relationship between Canada and the United States, do you believe it is time that Canada and the United States shared a common currency? Explain the reasons for your answer. How do your reasons compare to those used to support the adoption of the euro? Are the reasons you used to support your answer economic or emotional? Discuss.

www.x-rates.com

This Web site provides currency exchange rates for numerous currencies around the world.

1. What is the current value of the Canadian dollar in relation to the U.S. dollar? To the euro? What has happened to the value of Canadian dollar in relation to the U.S. dollar over the two most recent days?

2. In the table drop-down box, click on Canadian Dollar and click Go. Use the data provided to complete the following table:

Country	Currency	Currency per Canadian dollar	Canadian dollar equivalent
Australia	Dollar	$ _____	$ _____
China	Yuan	_____	_____
EMU	Euro	_____	_____
Great Britain	Pound	_____	_____
India	Rupee	_____	_____
Israel	Shekel	_____	_____
Japan	Yen	_____	_____
Mexico	Peso	_____	_____
Saudi Arabia	Riyal	_____	_____
Singapore	Dollar	_____	_____
South Africa	Rand	_____	_____
South Korea	Won	_____	_____
Taiwan	Dollar	_____	_____
United States	Dollar	_____	_____

3. Now, click the Back button of your browser and, using the Graph box in the middle of the page, select Canadian dollar, American dollar, and 120 days to create a graph. Is the Canadian dollar appreciating or depreciating against the American dollar? What were the lowest and highest values over the 120 trading days? Repeat this for the Canadian dollar and euro.

4. What do the two trends for the Canadian dollar mean for Canadian companies that export products to the U.S. and to countries that use the euro? For products imported from those countries?

www.sedar.com/search/search_form_pc_en.htm

This Web site provides the most recent annual reports for every publicly traded corporation in Canada. Download the annual report for the following three companies and research their international operations: Dofasco Inc., Magna International, and Molson Inc. You may also go to the individual companies' Web sites rather than use the Sedar site to access company information.

1. Provide the following information for each company. You will find this information in the annual report and the notes to the report.
    *   Description of the company. What does the company do?
    *   Total sales, profits, and assets for the most recent two fiscal years.
    *   Current market price, price-earnings ratio, and market capitalization. (Use a Web site like **globeinvestor.com** that provides this type of information.)

- Percent of revenues from overseas operations.
- Number of countries where company does business.
- Number of overseas manufacturing facilities.
- Is the company organized geographically or by product line? (You can usually tell this by the way the company reports segment information.)
- Breakdown of sales, profits, and assets for the most recent fiscal year by geographic region.
2. What is each company's philosophy with regard to selling internationally? For example, does it have local brands or sell the same product worldwide? Do they have foreign subsidiaries, branches, or operations that are partly owned by the MNC?
3. How does the company consolidate their foreign operations in their financial statements? Do they consider their operations as integrated or self-sustaining? What impact has this choice had on their financial results for the most recent fiscal year?
4. How much did the company lose/gain on foreign exchange transactions? (This information is in the notes to the financial statements, in the explanation of other income [charges].)

INTEGRATIVE CASE 6

ORGANIC SOLUTIONS

Organic Solutions (OS), one of the nation's largest plant wholesalers, was poised for expansion. Through strong profitability, a conservative dividend policy, and some recently realized gains in real estate, OS had a strong cash position and was searching for a target company to acquire. The executive members on the acquisition search committee had agreed that they preferred to find a firm in a similar line of business rather than one that would provide broad diversification. This would be their first acquisition, and they preferred to stay in a familiar line of business. Jennifer Morgan, director of marketing, had identified the targeted lines of business through exhaustive market research.

Ms. Morgan had determined that the servicing of plants in large commercial offices, hotels, zoos, and theme parks would complement the existing wholesale distribution business. Frequently, OS was requested by its large clients to bid on a service contract. However, Organic Solutions was neither staffed nor equipped to enter this market. Ms. Morgan was familiar with the major plant service companies in Canada and had suggested Green Thumbs, Inc. (GTI), as an acquisition target because of its significant market share and excellent reputation.

GTI had successfully commercialized a market that had been dominated by small local contractors and in-house landscaping departments. By first winning a contract from one of the largest theme parks in Ontario, GTI's growth in sales had compounded remarkably over its 8-year history.

GTI had also been selected because of its large portfolio of long-term service contracts with several major companies. These contracted clients would provide a captive customer base for the wholesale distribution of OS's plant products.

At the National Horticultural meeting in Victoria this past March, Ms. Morgan and OS's chief financial officer, Jack Levine, had approached the owner of GTI (a closely held corporation) to determine whether a merger offer would be welcomed. GTI's majority owner and president, Herb Merrell, had reacted favourably and subsequently provided financial data including GTI's earnings record and current balance sheet. These figures are presented in Tables 1 and 2.

Jack Levine had estimated that the incremental cash flow after taxes from the acquisition would be $18,750,000 for years 1 and 2; $20,500,000 for year 3; $21,750,000 for year 4; $24,000,000 for year 5; and $25,000,000 for years 6 through 30. He also estimated that the company should earn a rate of return of at least 16 percent on an investment of this type. Additional financial data for 2003 are available in Table 3.

TABLE 1 Green Thumbs, Inc., Earning Record

Year	EPS	Year	EPS
1996	$2.20	2000	$2.85
1997	2.35	2001	3.00
1998	2.45	2002	3.10
1999	2.60	2003	3.30

TABLE 2 Green Thumbs, Inc., Balance Sheet (December 31, 2003)

Assets		Liabilities and equity	
Cash	$ 2,500,000	Current liabilities	$ 5,250,000
Accounts receivable	1,500,000	Mortgage payable	3,125,000
Inventories	7,625,000	Common shares	15,625,000
Land	7,475,000	Retained earnings	9,000,000
Fixed assets (net)	13,900,000		
Total assets	$33,000,000	Total liabilities and equity	$33,000,000

TABLE 3 OS and GTI Financial Data (December 31, 2003)

Item	OS	GTI
Earnings available for common shareholders	$35,000,000	$15,246,000
Number of common shares outstanding	10,000,000	4,620,000
Market price per share	$50	$30[a]

[a]Estimated by Organic Solutions.

REQUIRED

a. What is the maximum price Organic Solutions should offer GTI for a cash acquisition? (*Note:* Assume the relevant time horizon for analysis is 30 years.)

b. If OS planned to sell bonds to finance 80 percent of the cash acquisition price found in part **a,** how might issuance of each of the following bonds impact the firm? Describe the characteristics and pros and cons of each bond.

   (1) Straight bonds.

   (2) Convertible bonds.

   (3) Bonds with warrants attached.

c. If the earnings attributed to GTI's assets grow at a much slower rate than those attributed to OS's premerger assets, what effect might this have on the EPS of the merged firm over the long run?

d. What other merger proposals could OS make to GTI's owners?

e. What impact would the fact that GTI is actually a foreign-based company have on the foregoing analysis? Describe the added regulations, costs, benefits, and risks that are likely to be associated with such an international merger.

Appendix A

Financial Tables

TABLE A-1   Future Value Interest Factors for One Dollar Compounded at k Percent for n Periods:

$$FVIF_{k,n} = (1 + k)^n$$

TABLE A-2   Future Value Interest Factors for a One-Dollar Annuity Compounded at k Percent for n Periods:

$$FVIFA_{k,n} = \sum_{t=1}^{n} (1+k)^{t-1}$$

TABLE A-3   Present Value Interest Factors for One Dollar Discounted at k Percent for n Periods:

$$PVIF_{k,n} = \frac{1}{(1 + k)}$$

TABLE A-4   Present Value Interest Factors for a One-Dollar Annuity Discounted at k Percent for n Periods:

$$PVIFA_{k,n} = \sum_{t=1}^{n} \frac{1}{(1+k)^t}$$

TABLE A-1 Future Value Interest Factors for One Dollar Compounded at *k* Percent for *n* Periods:

$$FVIF_{k,n} = (1 + k)^n$$

Period	1%	2%	3%	4%	5%	6%	7%	8%	9%	10%	11%	12%	13%	14%	15%	16%	17%	18%	19%	20%
1	1.010	1.020	1.030	1.040	1.050	1.060	1.070	1.080	1.090	1.100	1.110	1.120	1.130	1.140	1.150	1.160	1.170	1.180	1.190	1.200
2	1.020	1.040	1.061	1.082	1.102	1.124	1.145	1.166	1.188	1.210	1.232	1.254	1.277	1.300	1.322	1.346	1.369	1.392	1.416	1.440
3	1.030	1.061	1.093	1.125	1.158	1.191	1.225	1.260	1.295	1.331	1.368	1.405	1.443	1.482	1.521	1.561	1.602	1.643	1.685	1.728
4	1.041	1.082	1.126	1.170	1.216	1.262	1.311	1.360	1.412	1.464	1.518	1.574	1.630	1.689	1.749	1.811	1.874	1.939	2.005	2.074
5	1.051	1.104	1.159	1.217	1.276	1.338	1.403	1.469	1.539	1.611	1.685	1.762	1.842	1.925	2.011	2.100	2.192	2.288	2.386	2.488
6	1.062	1.126	1.194	1.265	1.340	1.419	1.501	1.587	1.677	1.772	1.870	1.974	2.082	2.195	2.313	2.436	2.565	2.700	2.840	2.986
7	1.072	1.149	1.230	1.316	1.407	1.504	1.606	1.714	1.828	1.949	2.076	2.211	2.353	2.502	2.660	2.826	3.001	3.185	3.379	3.583
8	1.083	1.172	1.267	1.369	1.477	1.594	1.718	1.851	1.993	2.144	2.305	2.476	2.658	2.853	3.059	3.278	3.511	3.759	4.021	4.300
9	1.094	1.195	1.305	1.423	1.551	1.689	1.838	1.999	2.172	2.358	2.558	2.773	3.004	3.252	3.518	3.803	4.108	4.435	4.785	5.160
10	1.105	1.219	1.344	1.480	1.629	1.791	1.967	2.159	2.367	2.594	2.839	3.106	3.395	3.707	4.046	4.411	4.807	5.234	5.695	6.192
11	1.116	1.243	1.384	1.539	1.710	1.898	2.105	2.332	2.580	2.853	3.152	3.479	3.836	4.226	4.652	5.117	5.624	6.176	6.777	7.430
12	1.127	1.268	1.426	1.601	1.796	2.012	2.252	2.518	2.813	3.138	3.498	3.896	4.334	4.818	5.350	5.936	6.580	7.288	8.064	8.916
13	1.138	1.294	1.469	1.665	1.886	2.133	2.410	2.720	3.066	3.452	3.883	4.363	4.898	5.492	6.153	6.886	7.699	8.599	9.596	10.699
14	1.149	1.319	1.513	1.732	1.980	2.261	2.579	2.937	3.342	3.797	4.310	4.887	5.535	6.261	7.076	7.987	9.007	10.147	11.420	12.839
15	1.161	1.346	1.558	1.801	2.079	2.397	2.759	3.172	3.642	4.177	4.785	5.474	6.254	7.138	8.137	9.265	10.539	11.974	13.589	15.407
16	1.173	1.373	1.605	1.873	2.183	2.540	2.952	3.426	3.970	4.595	5.311	6.130	7.067	8.137	9.358	10.748	12.330	14.129	16.171	18.488
17	1.184	1.400	1.653	1.948	2.292	2.693	3.159	3.700	4.328	5.054	5.895	6.866	7.986	9.276	10.761	12.468	14.426	16.672	19.244	22.186
18	1.196	1.428	1.702	2.026	2.407	2.854	3.380	3.996	4.717	5.560	6.543	7.690	9.024	10.575	12.375	14.462	16.879	19.673	22.900	26.623
19	1.208	1.457	1.753	2.107	2.527	3.026	3.616	4.316	5.142	6.116	7.263	8.613	10.197	12.055	14.232	16.776	19.748	23.214	27.251	31.948
20	1.220	1.486	1.806	2.191	2.653	3.207	3.870	4.661	5.604	6.727	8.062	9.646	11.523	13.743	16.366	19.461	23.105	27.393	32.429	38.337
21	1.232	1.516	1.860	2.279	2.786	3.399	4.140	5.034	6.109	7.400	8.949	10.804	13.021	15.667	18.821	22.574	27.033	32.323	38.591	46.005
22	1.245	1.546	1.916	2.370	2.925	3.603	4.430	5.436	6.658	8.140	9.933	12.100	14.713	17.861	21.644	26.186	31.629	38.141	45.923	55.205
23	1.257	1.577	1.974	2.465	3.071	3.820	4.740	5.871	7.258	8.954	11.026	13.552	16.626	20.361	24.891	30.376	37.005	45.007	54.648	66.247
24	1.270	1.608	2.033	2.563	3.225	4.049	5.072	6.341	7.911	9.850	12.239	15.178	18.788	23.212	28.625	35.236	43.296	53.108	65.031	79.496
25	1.282	1.641	2.094	2.666	3.386	4.292	5.427	6.848	8.623	10.834	13.585	17.000	21.230	26.461	32.918	40.874	50.656	62.667	77.387	95.395
30	1.348	1.811	2.427	3.243	4.322	5.743	7.612	10.062	13.267	17.449	22.892	29.960	39.115	50.949	66.210	85.849	111.061	143.367	184.672	237.373
35	1.417	2.000	2.814	3.946	5.516	7.686	10.676	14.785	20.413	28.102	38.574	52.799	72.066	98.097	133.172	180.311	243.495	327.988	440.691	590.657
40	1.489	2.208	3.262	4.801	7.040	10.285	14.974	21.724	31.408	45.258	64.999	93.049	132.776	188.876	267.856	378.715	533.846	750.353	1051.642	1469.740
45	1.565	2.438	3.781	5.841	8.985	13.764	21.002	31.920	48.325	72.888	109.527	163.985	244.629	363.662	538.752	795.429	1170.425	1716.619	2509.583	3657.176
50	1.645	2.691	4.384	7.106	11.467	18.419	29.456	46.900	74.354	117.386	184.559	288.996	450.711	700.197	1083.619	1670.669	2566.080	3927.189	5988.730	9100.191

USING THE CALCULATOR TO COMPUTE THE FUTURE VALUE OF A SINGLE AMOUNT

Before you begin: Make sure your calculator is set for *one payment per year* and that you are in the end mode for calculations. Also, for any problem where you are only using three time value functions, be sure to put a zero in the time value function that is not being used. An alternative is to clear the memory of the calculator before beginning a time value calculation.

SAMPLE PROBLEM

You place $800 in a savings account at 6 percent compounded annually. What is your account balance at the end of 5 years?

Hewlett-Packard HP 12C, 17 BII, and 19 BII[a]

Inputs:	800	5	6	
Functions:	PV	N	I%YR	FV
Outputs:				1070.58 [b]

---

[a] For the 12C, you would use the n key instead of the N key, and the i key instead of the I%YR key.
[b] The minus sign that precedes the output should be ignored.

TABLE A-1   (Continued)

Period	21%	22%	23%	24%	25%	26%	27%	28%	29%	30%	31%	32%	33%	34%	35%	40%	45%	50%
1	1.210	1.220	1.230	1.240	1.250	1.260	1.270	1.280	1.290	1.300	1.310	1.320	1.330	1.340	1.350	1.400	1.450	1.500
2	1.464	1.488	1.513	1.538	1.562	1.588	1.613	1.638	1.664	1.690	1.716	1.742	1.769	1.796	1.822	1.960	2.102	2.250
3	1.772	1.816	1.861	1.907	1.953	2.000	2.048	2.097	2.147	2.197	2.248	2.300	2.353	2.406	2.460	2.744	3.049	3.375
4	2.144	2.215	2.289	2.364	2.441	2.520	2.601	2.684	2.769	2.856	2.945	3.036	3.129	3.224	3.321	3.842	4.421	5.063
5	2.594	2.703	2.815	2.932	3.052	3.176	3.304	3.436	3.572	3.713	3.858	4.007	4.162	4.320	4.484	5.378	6.410	7.594
6	3.138	3.297	3.463	3.635	3.815	4.001	4.196	4.398	4.608	4.827	5.054	5.290	5.535	5.789	6.053	7.530	9.294	11.391
7	3.797	4.023	4.259	4.508	4.768	5.042	5.329	5.629	5.945	6.275	6.621	6.983	7.361	7.758	8.172	10.541	13.476	17.086
8	4.595	4.908	5.239	5.589	5.960	6.353	6.767	7.206	7.669	8.157	8.673	9.217	9.791	10.395	11.032	14.758	19.541	25.629
9	5.560	5.987	6.444	6.931	7.451	8.004	8.595	9.223	9.893	10.604	11.362	12.166	13.022	13.930	14.894	20.661	28.334	38.443
10	6.727	7.305	7.926	8.594	9.313	10.086	10.915	11.806	12.761	13.786	14.884	16.060	17.319	18.666	20.106	28.925	41.085	57.665
11	8.140	8.912	9.749	10.657	11.642	12.708	13.862	15.112	16.462	17.921	19.498	21.199	23.034	25.012	27.144	40.495	59.573	86.498
12	9.850	10.872	11.991	13.215	14.552	16.012	17.605	19.343	21.236	23.298	25.542	27.982	30.635	33.516	36.644	56.694	86.380	129.746
13	11.918	13.264	14.749	16.386	18.190	20.175	22.359	24.759	27.395	30.287	33.460	36.937	40.745	44.912	49.469	79.371	125.251	194.620
14	14.421	16.182	18.141	20.319	22.737	25.420	28.395	31.691	35.339	39.373	43.832	48.756	54.190	60.181	66.784	111.119	181.614	291.929
15	17.449	19.742	22.314	25.195	28.422	32.030	36.062	40.565	45.587	51.185	57.420	64.358	72.073	80.643	90.158	155.567	263.341	437.894
16	21.113	24.085	27.446	31.242	35.527	40.357	45.799	51.923	58.808	66.541	75.220	84.953	95.857	108.061	121.713	217.793	381.844	656.841
17	25.547	29.384	33.758	38.740	44.409	50.850	58.165	66.461	75.862	86.503	98.539	112.138	127.490	144.802	164.312	304.911	553.674	985.261
18	30.912	35.848	41.523	48.038	55.511	64.071	73.869	85.070	97.862	112.454	129.086	148.022	169.561	194.035	221.822	426.875	802.826	1477.892
19	37.404	43.735	51.073	59.567	69.389	80.730	93.813	108.890	126.242	146.190	169.102	195.389	225.517	260.006	299.459	597.625	1164.098	2216.838
20	45.258	53.357	62.820	73.863	86.736	101.720	119.143	139.379	162.852	190.047	221.523	257.913	299.937	348.408	404.270	836.674	1687.942	3325.257
21	54.762	65.095	77.268	91.591	108.420	128.167	151.312	178.405	210.079	247.061	290.196	340.446	398.916	466.867	545.764	1171.343	2447.515	4987.883
22	66.262	79.416	95.040	113.572	135.525	161.490	192.165	228.358	271.002	321.178	380.156	449.388	530.558	625.601	736.781	1639.878	3548.896	7481.824
23	80.178	96.887	116.899	140.829	169.407	203.477	244.050	292.298	349.592	417.531	498.004	593.192	705.642	838.305	994.653	2295.829	5145.898	11222.738
24	97.015	118.203	143.786	174.628	211.758	256.381	309.943	374.141	450.974	542.791	652.385	783.013	938.504	1123.328	1342.781	3214.158	7461.547	16834.109
25	117.388	144.207	176.857	216.539	264.698	323.040	393.628	478.901	581.756	705.627	854.623	1033.577	1248.210	1505.258	1812.754	4499.816	10819.242	25251.164
30	304.471	389.748	497.904	634.810	807.793	1025.904	1300.477	1645.488	2078.208	2619.936	3297.081	4142.008	5194.516	6503.285	8128.426	24201.043	69348.375	191751.000
35	789.716	1053.370	1401.749	1861.020	2465.189	3258.053	4296.547	5653.840	7423.988	9727.598	12719.918	16598.906	21617.363	28096.695	36448.051	130158.687	*	*
40	2048.309	2846.941	3946.340	5455.797	7523.156	10346.879	14195.051	19426.418	26520.723	36117.754	49072.621	66519.313	89962.188	121388.437	163433.875	700022.688	*	*
45	5312.758	7694.418	11110.121	15994.316	22958.844	32859.457	46897.973	66748.500	94739.937	134102.187	*	*	*	*	*	*	*	*
50	13779.844	20795.680	31278.301	46889.207	70064.812	104354.562	154942.687	229345.875	338440.000	497910.125	*	*	*	*	*	*	*	*

*Not shown due to space limitations.

Texas Instruments BA-35, BAII, BAII Plus[c]

Inputs: 800   5   6

Functions: PV   N   %i   CPT   FV

Outputs: 1070.58 [d]

[c]For the Texas Instruments BAII, you would use the **2nd** key instead of the **CPT** key; for the Texas Instruments BAII Plus, you would use the **I/Y** key instead of the **%i** key.

[d]If a minus sign precedes the output, it should be ignored.

TABLE A-2 Future Value Interest Factors for a One-Dollar Annuity Compounded at k Percent for n Periods: $FVIFA_{k,n} = \sum_{t=1}^{n} (1+k)^{t-1}$

Period	1%	2%	3%	4%	5%	6%	7%	8%	9%	10%	11%	12%	13%	14%	15%	16%	17%	18%	19%	20%
1	1.000	1.000	1.000	1.000	1.000	1.000	1.000	1.000	1.000	1.000	1.000	1.000	1.000	1.000	1.000	1.000	1.000	1.000	1.000	1.000
2	2.010	2.020	2.030	2.040	2.050	2.060	2.070	2.080	2.090	2.100	2.110	2.120	2.130	2.140	2.150	2.160	2.170	2.180	2.190	2.200
3	3.030	3.060	3.091	3.122	3.152	3.184	3.215	3.246	3.278	3.310	3.342	3.374	3.407	3.440	3.472	3.506	3.539	3.572	3.606	3.640
4	4.060	4.122	4.184	4.246	4.310	4.375	4.440	4.506	4.573	4.641	4.710	4.779	4.850	4.921	4.993	5.066	5.141	5.215	5.291	5.368
5	5.101	5.204	5.309	5.416	5.526	5.637	5.751	5.867	5.985	6.105	6.228	6.353	6.480	6.610	6.742	6.877	7.014	7.154	7.297	7.442
6	6.152	6.308	6.468	6.633	6.802	6.975	7.153	7.336	7.523	7.716	7.913	8.115	8.323	8.535	8.754	8.977	9.207	9.442	9.683	9.930
7	7.214	7.434	7.662	7.898	8.142	8.394	8.654	8.923	9.200	9.487	9.783	10.089	10.405	10.730	11.067	11.414	11.772	12.141	12.523	12.916
8	8.286	8.583	8.892	9.214	9.549	9.897	10.260	10.637	11.028	11.436	11.859	12.300	12.757	13.233	13.727	14.240	14.773	15.327	15.902	16.499
9	9.368	9.755	10.159	10.583	11.027	11.491	11.978	12.488	13.021	13.579	14.164	14.776	15.416	16.085	16.786	17.518	18.285	19.086	19.923	20.799
10	10.462	10.950	11.464	12.006	12.578	13.181	13.816	14.487	15.193	15.937	16.722	17.549	18.420	19.337	20.304	21.321	22.393	23.521	24.709	25.959
11	11.567	12.169	12.808	13.486	14.207	14.972	15.784	16.645	17.560	18.531	19.561	20.655	21.814	23.044	24.349	25.733	27.200	28.755	30.403	32.150
12	12.682	13.412	14.192	15.026	15.917	16.870	17.888	18.977	20.141	21.384	22.713	24.133	25.650	27.271	29.001	30.850	32.824	34.931	37.180	39.580
13	13.809	14.680	15.618	16.627	17.713	18.882	20.141	21.495	22.953	24.523	26.211	28.029	29.984	32.088	34.352	36.786	39.404	42.218	45.244	48.496
14	14.947	15.974	17.086	18.292	19.598	21.015	22.550	24.215	26.019	27.975	30.095	32.392	34.882	37.581	40.504	43.672	47.102	50.818	54.841	59.196
15	16.097	17.293	18.599	20.023	21.578	23.276	25.129	27.152	29.361	31.772	34.405	37.280	40.417	43.842	47.580	51.659	56.109	60.965	66.260	72.035
16	17.258	18.639	20.157	21.824	23.657	25.672	27.888	30.324	33.003	35.949	39.190	42.753	46.671	50.980	55.717	60.925	66.648	72.938	79.850	87.442
17	18.430	20.012	21.761	23.697	25.840	28.213	30.840	33.750	36.973	40.544	44.500	48.883	53.738	59.117	65.075	71.673	78.978	87.067	96.021	105.930
18	19.614	21.412	23.414	25.645	28.132	30.905	33.999	37.450	41.301	45.599	50.396	55.749	61.724	68.393	75.836	84.140	93.404	103.739	115.265	128.116
19	20.811	22.840	25.117	27.671	30.539	33.760	37.379	41.446	46.018	51.158	56.939	63.439	70.748	78.968	88.211	98.603	110.283	123.412	138.165	154.739
20	22.019	24.297	26.870	29.778	33.066	36.785	40.995	45.762	51.159	57.274	64.202	72.052	80.946	91.024	102.443	115.379	130.031	146.626	165.417	186.687
21	23.239	25.783	28.676	31.969	35.719	39.992	44.865	50.422	56.764	64.002	72.264	81.698	92.468	104.767	118.809	134.840	153.136	174.019	197.846	225.024
22	24.471	27.299	30.536	34.248	38.505	43.392	49.005	55.456	62.872	71.402	81.213	92.502	105.489	120.434	137.630	157.414	180.169	206.342	236.436	271.028
23	25.716	28.845	32.452	36.618	41.430	46.995	53.435	60.893	69.531	79.542	91.147	104.602	120.203	138.295	159.274	183.600	211.798	244.483	282.359	326.234
24	26.973	30.421	34.426	39.082	44.501	50.815	58.176	66.764	76.789	88.496	102.173	118.154	136.829	158.656	184.166	213.976	248.803	289.490	337.007	392.480
25	28.243	32.030	36.459	41.645	47.726	54.864	63.248	73.105	84.699	98.346	114.412	133.333	155.616	181.867	212.790	249.212	292.099	342.598	402.038	471.976
30	34.784	40.567	47.575	56.084	66.438	79.057	94.459	113.282	136.305	164.491	199.018	241.330	293.192	356.778	434.738	530.306	647.423	790.932	966.698	1181.865
35	41.659	49.994	60.461	73.651	90.318	111.432	138.234	172.314	215.705	271.018	341.583	431.658	546.663	693.552	881.152	1120.699	1426.448	1816.607	2314.173	2948.294
40	48.885	60.401	75.400	95.024	120.797	154.758	199.630	259.052	337.872	442.580	581.812	767.080	1013.667	1341.979	1779.048	2360.724	3134.412	4163.094	5529.711	7343.715
45	56.479	71.891	92.718	121.027	159.695	212.737	285.741	386.497	525.840	718.881	986.613	1358.208	1874.086	2590.464	3585.031	4965.191	6879.008	9531.258	13203.105	18280.914
50	64.461	84.577	112.794	152.664	209.341	290.325	406.516	573.756	815.051	1163.865	1668.723	2399.975	3459.344	4994.301	7217.488	10435.449	15088.805	21812.273	31514.492	45496.094

USING THE CALCULATOR TO COMPUTE THE FUTURE VALUE OF AN ANNUITY

Before you begin: Make sure your calculator is set for *one payment per year* and that you are in the end mode for calculations. Also, for any problem where you are only using three time value functions, be sure to put a zero in the time value function that is not being used. An alternative is to clear the memory of the calculator before beginning a time value calculation.

SAMPLE PROBLEM

You want to know what the future value will be at the end of 5 years if you place five end-of-year deposits of $1,000 in an account paying 7 percent annually. What is your account balance at the end of 5 years?

Hewlett-Packard HP 12C, 17 BII, and 19 BII[a]

Inputs:	1000	5	7	
Functions:	PMT	N	I%YR	FV
Outputs:				5750.74[b]

---

[a]For the 12C, you would use the n key instead of the N key, and the i key instead of the I%YR key.
[b]The minus sign that precedes the output should be ignored.

TABLE A-2 (Continued)

Period	21%	22%	23%	24%	25%	26%	27%	28%	29%	30%	31%	32%	33%	34%	35%	40%	45%	50%
1	1.000	1.000	1.000	1.000	1.000	1.000	1.000	1.000	1.000	1.000	1.000	1.000	1.000	1.000	1.000	1.000	1.000	1.000
2	2.210	2.220	2.230	2.240	2.250	2.260	2.270	2.280	2.290	2.300	2.310	2.320	2.330	2.340	2.350	2.400	2.450	2.500
3	3.674	3.708	3.743	3.778	3.813	3.848	3.883	3.918	3.954	3.990	4.026	4.062	4.099	4.136	4.172	4.360	4.552	4.750
4	5.446	5.524	5.604	5.684	5.766	5.848	5.931	6.016	6.101	6.187	6.274	6.362	6.452	6.542	6.633	7.104	7.601	8.125
5	7.589	7.740	7.893	8.048	8.207	8.368	8.533	8.700	8.870	9.043	9.219	9.398	9.581	9.766	9.954	10.946	12.022	13.188
6	10.183	10.442	10.708	10.980	11.259	11.544	11.837	12.136	12.442	12.756	13.077	13.406	13.742	14.086	14.438	16.324	18.431	20.781
7	13.321	13.740	14.171	14.615	15.073	15.546	16.032	16.534	17.051	17.583	18.131	18.696	19.277	19.876	20.492	23.853	27.725	32.172
8	17.119	17.762	18.430	19.123	19.842	20.588	21.361	22.163	22.995	23.858	24.752	25.678	26.638	27.633	28.664	34.395	41.202	49.258
9	21.714	22.670	23.669	24.712	25.802	26.940	28.129	29.369	30.664	32.015	33.425	34.895	36.429	38.028	39.696	49.152	60.743	74.887
10	27.274	28.657	30.113	31.643	33.253	34.945	36.723	38.592	40.556	42.619	44.786	47.062	49.451	51.958	54.590	69.813	89.077	113.330
11	34.001	35.962	38.039	40.238	42.566	45.030	47.639	50.398	53.318	56.405	59.670	63.121	66.769	70.624	74.696	98.739	130.161	170.995
12	42.141	44.873	47.787	50.895	54.208	57.738	61.501	65.510	69.780	74.326	79.167	84.320	89.803	95.636	101.840	139.234	189.734	257.493
13	51.991	55.745	59.778	64.109	68.760	73.750	79.106	84.853	91.016	97.624	104.709	112.302	120.438	129.152	138.484	195.928	276.114	387.239
14	63.909	69.009	74.528	80.496	86.949	93.925	101.465	109.611	118.411	127.912	138.169	149.239	161.183	174.063	187.953	275.299	401.365	581.858
15	78.330	85.191	92.669	100.815	109.687	119.346	129.860	141.302	153.750	167.285	182.001	197.996	215.373	234.245	254.737	386.418	582.980	873.788
16	95.779	104.933	114.983	126.010	138.109	151.375	165.922	181.867	199.337	218.470	239.421	262.354	287.446	314.888	344.895	541.985	846.321	1311.681
17	116.892	129.019	142.428	157.252	173.636	191.733	211.721	233.790	258.145	285.011	314.642	347.307	383.303	422.949	466.608	759.778	1228.165	1968.522
18	142.439	158.403	176.187	195.993	218.045	242.583	269.885	300.250	334.006	371.514	413.180	459.445	510.792	567.751	630.920	1064.689	1781.838	2953.783
19	173.351	194.251	217.710	244.031	273.556	306.654	343.754	385.321	431.868	483.968	542.266	607.467	680.354	761.786	852.741	1491.563	2584.665	4431.672
20	210.755	237.986	268.783	303.598	342.945	387.384	437.568	494.210	558.110	630.157	711.368	802.856	905.870	1021.792	1152.200	2089.188	3748.763	6648.508
21	256.013	291.343	331.603	377.461	429.681	489.104	556.710	633.589	720.962	820.204	932.891	1060.769	1205.807	1370.201	1556.470	2925.862	5436.703	9973.762
22	310.775	356.438	408.871	469.052	538.101	617.270	708.022	811.993	931.040	1067.265	1223.087	1401.215	1604.724	1837.068	2102.234	4097.203	7884.215	14961.645
23	377.038	435.854	503.911	582.624	673.626	778.760	900.187	1040.351	1202.042	1388.443	1603.243	1850.603	2135.282	2462.669	2839.014	5737.078	11433.109	22443.469
24	457.215	532.741	620.810	723.453	843.032	982.237	1144.237	1332.649	1551.634	1805.975	2101.247	2443.795	2840.924	3300.974	3833.667	8032.906	16579.008	33666.207
25	554.230	650.944	764.596	898.082	1054.791	1238.617	1454.180	1706.790	2002.608	2348.765	2753.631	3226.808	3779.428	4424.301	5176.445	11247.062	24040.555	50500.316
30	1445.111	1767.044	2160.459	2640.881	3227.172	3941.953	4812.891	5873.172	7162.785	8729.805	10632.543	12940.672	15737.945	19124.434	23221.258	60500.207	154105.313	383500.000
35	3755.814	4783.520	6090.227	7750.094	9856.746	12527.160	15909.480	20188.742	25596.512	32422.090	41028.887	51868.563	65504.199	82634.625	104134.500	325394.688	*	*
40	9749.141	12936.141	17153.691	22728.367	30088.621	39791.957	52570.707	69376.562	91447.375	120389.375	*	*	*	*	*	*	*	*
45	25294.223	34970.230	48300.660	66638.937	91831.312	126378.937	173692.875	238384.312	326686.375	447005.062	*	*	*	*	*	*	*	*

*Not shown due to space limitations.

Texas Instruments BA-35, BAII, BAII Plus[c]

Inputs:	1000	5	7		
Functions:	PMT	N	%i	CPT	FV
Outputs:				5750.74[d]	

---

[c]For the Texas Instruments BAII, you would use the 2nd key instead of the CPT key; for the Texas Instruments BAII Plus, you would use the I/Y key instead of the %i key.
[d]If a minus sign precedes the output, it should be ignored.

TABLE A-3 Present Value Interest Factors for One Dollar Discounted at *k* Percent for *n* Periods:

$$PVIF_{k,n} = \frac{1}{(1+k)^n}$$

Period	1%	2%	3%	4%	5%	6%	7%	8%	9%	10%	11%	12%	13%	14%	15%	16%	17%	18%	19%	20%
1	.990	.980	.971	.962	.952	.943	.935	.926	.917	.909	.901	.893	.885	.877	.870	.862	.855	.847	.840	.833
2	.980	.961	.943	.925	.907	.890	.873	.857	.842	.826	.812	.797	.783	.769	.756	.743	.731	.718	.706	.694
3	.971	.942	.915	.889	.864	.840	.816	.794	.772	.751	.731	.712	.693	.675	.658	.641	.624	.609	.593	.579
4	.961	.924	.888	.855	.823	.792	.763	.735	.708	.683	.659	.636	.613	.592	.572	.552	.534	.516	.499	.482
5	.951	.906	.863	.822	.784	.747	.713	.681	.650	.621	.593	.567	.543	.519	.497	.476	.456	.437	.419	.402
6	.942	.888	.837	.790	.746	.705	.666	.630	.596	.564	.535	.507	.480	.456	.432	.410	.390	.370	.352	.335
7	.933	.871	.813	.760	.711	.665	.623	.583	.547	.513	.482	.452	.425	.400	.376	.354	.333	.314	.296	.279
8	.923	.853	.789	.731	.677	.627	.582	.540	.502	.467	.434	.404	.376	.351	.327	.305	.285	.266	.249	.233
9	.914	.837	.766	.703	.645	.592	.544	.500	.460	.424	.391	.361	.333	.308	.284	.263	.243	.225	.209	.194
10	.905	.820	.744	.676	.614	.558	.508	.463	.422	.386	.352	.322	.295	.270	.247	.227	.208	.191	.176	.162
11	.896	.804	.722	.650	.585	.527	.475	.429	.388	.350	.317	.287	.261	.237	.215	.195	.178	.162	.148	.135
12	.887	.789	.701	.625	.557	.497	.444	.397	.356	.319	.286	.257	.231	.208	.187	.168	.152	.137	.124	.112
13	.879	.773	.681	.601	.530	.469	.415	.368	.326	.290	.258	.229	.204	.182	.163	.145	.130	.116	.104	.093
14	.870	.758	.661	.577	.505	.442	.388	.340	.299	.263	.232	.205	.181	.160	.141	.125	.111	.099	.088	.078
15	.861	.743	.642	.555	.481	.417	.362	.315	.275	.239	.209	.183	.160	.140	.123	.108	.095	.084	.074	.065
16	.853	.728	.623	.534	.458	.394	.339	.292	.252	.218	.188	.163	.141	.123	.107	.093	.081	.071	.062	.054
17	.844	.714	.605	.513	.436	.371	.317	.270	.231	.198	.170	.146	.125	.108	.093	.080	.069	.060	.052	.045
18	.836	.700	.587	.494	.416	.350	.296	.250	.212	.180	.153	.130	.111	.095	.081	.069	.059	.051	.044	.038
19	.828	.686	.570	.475	.396	.331	.277	.232	.194	.164	.138	.116	.098	.083	.070	.060	.051	.043	.037	.031
20	.820	.673	.554	.456	.377	.312	.258	.215	.178	.149	.124	.104	.087	.073	.061	.051	.043	.037	.031	.026
21	.811	.660	.538	.439	.359	.294	.242	.199	.164	.135	.112	.093	.077	.064	.053	.044	.037	.031	.026	.022
22	.803	.647	.522	.422	.342	.278	.226	.184	.150	.123	.101	.083	.068	.056	.046	.038	.032	.026	.022	.018
23	.795	.634	.507	.406	.326	.262	.211	.170	.138	.112	.091	.074	.060	.049	.040	.033	.027	.022	.018	.015
24	.788	.622	.492	.390	.310	.247	.197	.158	.126	.102	.082	.066	.053	.043	.035	.028	.023	.019	.015	.013
25	.780	.610	.478	.375	.295	.233	.184	.146	.116	.092	.074	.059	.047	.038	.030	.024	.020	.016	.013	.010
30	.742	.552	.412	.308	.231	.174	.131	.099	.075	.057	.044	.033	.026	.020	.015	.012	.009	.007	.005	.004
35	.706	.500	.355	.253	.181	.130	.094	.068	.049	.036	.026	.019	.014	.010	.008	.006	.004	.003	.002	.002
40	.672	.453	.307	.208	.142	.097	.067	.046	.032	.022	.015	.011	.008	.005	.004	.003	.002	.001	.001	.001
45	.639	.410	.264	.171	.111	.073	.048	.031	.021	.014	.009	.006	.004	.003	.002	.001	.001	.001	*	*
50	.608	.372	.228	.141	.087	.054	.034	.021	.013	.009	.005	.003	.002	.001	.001	.001	*	*	*	*

PVIF is zero to three decimal places.

USING THE CALCULATOR TO COMPUTE THE PRESENT VALUE OF A SINGLE AMOUNT

Before you begin: Make sure your calculator is set for *one payment per year* and that you are in the end mode for calculations. Also, for any problem where you are only using three time value functions, be sure to put a zero in the time value function that is not being used. An alternative is to clear the memory of the calculator before beginning a time value calculation.

SAMPLE PROBLEM

You want to know the present value of $1,700 to be received at the end of 8 years, assuming an 8 percent discount rate.

Hewlett-Packard HP 12C, 17 BII, and 19 BII[a]

Inputs:	1700	8	8	
Functions:	FV	N	I%YR	PV
Outputs:				918.46 [b]

[a]For the 12C, you would use the n key instead of the N key, and the i key instead of the I%YR key.
[b]The minus sign that precedes the output should be ignored.

TABLE A-3 (Continued)

Period	21%	22%	23%	24%	25%	26%	27%	28%	29%	30%	31%	32%	33%	34%	35%	40%	45%	50%
1	.826	.820	.813	.806	.800	.794	.787	.781	.775	.769	.763	.758	.752	.746	.741	.714	.690	.667
2	.683	.672	.661	.650	.640	.630	.620	.610	.601	.592	.583	.574	.565	.557	.549	.510	.476	.444
3	.564	.551	.537	.524	.512	.500	.488	.477	.466	.455	.445	.435	.425	.416	.406	.364	.328	.296
4	.467	.451	.437	.423	.410	.397	.384	.373	.361	.350	.340	.329	.320	.310	.301	.260	.226	.198
5	.386	.370	.355	.341	.328	.315	.303	.291	.280	.269	.259	.250	.240	.231	.223	.186	.156	.132
6	.319	.303	.289	.275	.262	.250	.238	.227	.217	.207	.198	.189	.181	.173	.165	.133	.108	.088
7	.263	.249	.235	.222	.210	.198	.188	.178	.168	.159	.151	.143	.136	.129	.122	.095	.074	.059
8	.218	.204	.191	.179	.168	.157	.148	.139	.130	.123	.115	.108	.102	.096	.091	.068	.051	.039
9	.180	.167	.155	.144	.134	.125	.116	.108	.101	.094	.088	.082	.077	.072	.067	.048	.035	.026
10	.149	.137	.126	.116	.107	.099	.092	.085	.078	.073	.067	.062	.058	.054	.050	.035	.024	.017
11	.123	.112	.103	.094	.086	.079	.072	.066	.061	.056	.051	.047	.043	.040	.037	.025	.017	.012
12	.102	.092	.083	.076	.069	.062	.057	.052	.047	.043	.039	.036	.033	.030	.027	.018	.012	.008
13	.084	.075	.068	.061	.055	.050	.045	.040	.037	.033	.030	.027	.025	.022	.020	.013	.008	.005
14	.069	.062	.055	.049	.044	.039	.035	.032	.028	.025	.023	.021	.018	.017	.015	.009	.006	.003
15	.057	.051	.045	.040	.035	.031	.028	.025	.022	.020	.017	.016	.014	.012	.011	.006	.004	.002
16	.047	.042	.036	.032	.028	.025	.022	.019	.017	.015	.013	.012	.010	.009	.008	.005	.003	.002
17	.039	.034	.030	.026	.023	.020	.017	.015	.013	.012	.010	.009	.008	.007	.006	.003	.002	.001
18	.032	.028	.024	.021	.018	.016	.014	.012	.010	.009	.008	.007	.006	.005	.005	.002	.001	.001
19	.027	.023	.020	.017	.014	.012	.011	.009	.008	.007	.006	.005	.004	.004	.003	.002	.001	*
20	.022	.019	.016	.014	.012	.010	.008	.007	.006	.005	.005	.004	.003	.003	.002	.001	.001	*
21	.018	.015	.013	.011	.009	.008	.007	.006	.005	.004	.003	.003	.003	.002	.002	.001	*	*
22	.015	.013	.011	.009	.007	.006	.005	.004	.004	.003	.003	.002	.002	.002	.001	.001	*	*
23	.012	.010	.009	.007	.006	.005	.004	.003	.003	.002	.002	.002	.001	.001	.001	*	*	*
24	.010	.008	.007	.006	.005	.004	.003	.003	.002	.002	.002	.001	.001	.001	.001	*	*	*
25	.009	.007	.006	.005	.004	.003	.003	.002	.002	.001	.001	.001	.001	.001	.001	*	*	*
30	.003	.003	.002	.002	.001	.001	.001	.001	*	*	*	*	*	*	*	*	*	*
35	.001	.001	.001	.001	*	*	*	*	*	*	*	*	*	*	*	*	*	*
40	*	*	*	*	*	*	*	*	*	*	*	*	*	*	*	*	*	*
45	*	*	*	*	*	*	*	*	*	*	*	*	*	*	*	*	*	*
50	*	*	*	*	*	*	*	*	*	*	*	*	*	*	*	*	*	*

*PVIF is zero to three decimal places.

Texas Instruments BA-35, BAII, BAII Plus[c]

Inputs: 1700   8   8

Functions: FV   N   %i   CPT   PV

Outputs: 918.46 [d]

---

[c]For the Texas Instruments BAII, you would use the 2nd key instead of the CPT key; for the Texas Instruments BAII Plus, you would use the I/Y key instead of the %i key.
[d]If a minus sign precedes the output, it should be ignored.

TABLE A-4   Present Value Interest Factors for a One-Dollar Annuity Discounted at k Percent for n Periods:

$$PVIFA_{k,n} = \sum_{t=1}^{n} \frac{1}{(1+k)^t}$$

Period	1%	2%	3%	4%	5%	6%	7%	8%	9%	10%	11%	12%	13%	14%	15%	16%	17%	18%	19%	20%
1	.990	.980	.971	.962	.952	.943	.935	.926	.917	.909	.901	.893	.885	.877	.870	.862	.855	.847	.840	.833
2	1.970	1.942	1.913	1.886	1.859	1.833	1.808	1.783	1.759	1.736	1.713	1.690	1.668	1.647	1.626	1.605	1.585	1.566	1.547	1.528
3	2.941	2.884	2.829	2.775	2.723	2.673	2.624	2.577	2.531	2.487	2.444	2.402	2.361	2.322	2.283	2.246	2.210	2.174	2.140	2.106
4	3.902	3.808	3.717	3.630	3.546	3.465	3.387	3.312	3.240	3.170	3.102	3.037	2.974	2.914	2.855	2.798	2.743	2.690	2.639	2.589
5	4.853	4.713	4.580	4.452	4.329	4.212	4.100	3.993	3.890	3.791	3.696	3.605	3.517	3.433	3.352	3.274	3.199	3.127	3.058	2.991
6	5.795	5.601	5.417	5.242	5.076	4.917	4.767	4.623	4.486	4.355	4.231	4.111	3.998	3.889	3.784	3.685	3.589	3.498	3.410	3.326
7	6.728	6.472	6.230	6.002	5.786	5.582	5.389	5.206	5.033	4.868	4.712	4.564	4.423	4.288	4.160	4.039	3.922	3.812	3.706	3.605
8	7.652	7.326	7.020	6.733	6.463	6.210	5.971	5.747	5.535	5.335	5.146	4.968	4.799	4.639	4.487	4.344	4.207	4.078	3.954	3.837
9	8.566	8.162	7.786	7.435	7.108	6.802	6.515	6.247	5.995	5.759	5.537	5.328	5.132	4.946	4.772	4.607	4.451	4.303	4.163	4.031
10	9.471	8.983	8.530	8.111	7.722	7.360	7.024	6.710	6.418	6.145	5.889	5.650	5.426	5.216	5.019	4.833	4.659	4.494	4.339	4.192
11	10.368	9.787	9.253	8.760	8.306	7.887	7.499	7.139	6.805	6.495	6.207	5.938	5.687	5.453	5.234	5.029	4.836	4.656	4.486	4.327
12	11.255	10.575	9.954	9.385	8.863	8.384	7.943	7.536	7.161	6.814	6.492	6.194	5.918	5.660	5.421	5.197	4.988	4.793	4.611	4.439
13	12.134	11.348	10.635	9.986	9.394	8.853	8.358	7.904	7.487	7.013	6.750	6.424	6.122	5.842	5.583	5.342	5.118	4.910	4.715	4.533
14	13.004	12.106	11.296	10.563	9.899	9.295	8.745	8.244	7.786	7.367	6.982	6.628	6.302	6.002	5.724	5.468	5.229	5.008	4.802	4.611
15	13.865	12.849	11.938	11.118	10.380	9.712	9.108	8.560	8.061	7.606	7.191	6.811	6.462	6.142	5.847	5.575	5.324	5.092	4.876	4.675
16	14.718	13.578	12.561	11.652	10.838	10.106	9.447	8.851	8.313	7.824	7.379	6.974	6.604	6.265	5.954	5.668	5.405	5.162	4.938	4.730
17	15.562	14.292	13.166	12.166	11.274	10.477	9.763	9.122	8.544	8.022	7.549	7.120	6.729	6.373	6.047	5.749	5.475	5.222	4.990	4.775
18	16.398	14.992	13.754	12.659	11.690	10.828	10.059	9.372	8.756	8.201	7.702	7.250	6.840	6.467	6.128	5.818	5.534	5.273	5.033	4.812
19	17.226	15.679	14.324	13.134	12.085	11.158	10.336	9.604	8.950	8.365	7.839	7.366	6.938	6.550	6.198	5.877	5.584	5.316	5.070	4.843
20	18.046	16.352	14.878	13.590	12.462	11.470	10.594	9.818	9.129	8.514	7.963	7.469	7.025	6.623	6.259	5.929	5.628	5.353	5.101	4.870
21	18.857	17.011	15.415	14.029	12.821	11.764	10.836	10.017	9.292	8.649	8.075	7.562	7.102	6.687	6.312	5.973	5.665	5.384	5.127	4.891
22	19.661	17.658	15.937	14.451	13.163	12.042	11.061	10.201	9.442	8.772	8.176	7.645	7.170	6.743	6.359	6.011	5.696	5.410	5.149	4.909
23	20.456	18.292	16.444	14.857	13.489	12.303	11.272	10.371	9.580	8.883	8.266	7.718	7.230	6.792	6.399	6.044	5.723	5.432	5.167	4.925
24	21.244	18.914	16.936	15.247	13.799	12.550	11.469	10.529	9.707	8.985	8.348	7.784	7.283	6.835	6.434	6.073	5.746	5.451	5.182	4.937
25	22.023	19.524	17.413	15.622	14.094	12.783	11.654	10.675	9.823	9.077	8.422	7.843	7.330	6.873	6.464	6.097	5.766	5.467	5.195	4.948
30	25.808	22.396	19.601	17.292	15.373	13.765	12.409	11.258	10.274	9.427	8.694	8.055	7.496	7.003	6.566	6.177	5.829	5.517	5.235	4.979
35	29.409	24.999	21.487	18.665	16.374	14.498	12.948	11.655	10.567	9.644	8.855	8.176	7.586	7.070	6.617	6.215	5.858	5.539	5.251	4.992
40	32.835	27.356	23.115	19.793	17.159	15.046	13.332	11.925	10.757	9.779	8.951	8.244	7.634	7.105	6.642	6.233	5.871	5.548	5.258	4.997
45	36.095	29.490	24.519	20.720	17.774	15.456	13.606	12.108	10.881	9.863	9.008	8.283	7.661	7.123	6.654	6.242	5.877	5.552	5.261	4.999
50	39.196	31.424	25.730	21.482	18.256	15.762	13.801	12.233	10.962	9.915	9.042	8.304	7.675	7.133	6.661	6.246	5.880	5.554	5.262	4.999

USING THE CALCULATOR TO COMPUTE THE PRESENT VALUE OF AN ANNUITY

Before you begin: Make sure your calculator is set for *one payment per year* and that you are in the end mode for calculations. Also, for any problem where you are only using three time value functions, be sure to put a zero in the time value function that is not being used. An alternative is to clear the memory of the calculator before beginning a time value calculation.

SAMPLE PROBLEM

You want to know what the present value will be of an annuity of $700 per year at the end of each year for 5 years, given a discount rate of 8 percent.

Hewlett-Packard HP 12C, 17 BII, and 19 BII[a]

Inputs:	700	5	8
Functions:	PMT	N	I%YR PV
Outputs:			2794.90 [b]

[a]For the 12C, you would use the n key instead of the N key, and the i key instead of the I%YR key.
[b]The minus sign that precedes the output should be ignored.

TABLE A-4 (Continued)

Period	21%	22%	23%	24%	25%	26%	27%	28%	29%	30%	31%	32%	33%	34%	35%	40%	45%	50%
1	.826	.820	.813	.806	.800	.794	.787	.781	.775	.769	.763	.758	.752	.746	.741	.714	.690	.667
2	1.509	1.492	1.474	1.457	1.440	1.424	1.407	1.392	1.376	1.361	1.346	1.331	1.317	1.303	1.289	1.224	1.165	1.111
3	2.074	2.042	2.011	1.981	1.952	1.923	1.896	1.868	1.842	1.816	1.791	1.766	1.742	1.719	1.696	1.589	1.493	1.407
4	2.540	2.494	2.448	2.404	2.362	2.320	2.280	2.241	2.203	2.166	2.130	2.096	2.062	2.029	1.997	1.849	1.720	1.605
5	2.926	2.864	2.803	2.745	2.689	2.635	2.583	2.532	2.483	2.436	2.390	2.345	2.302	2.260	2.220	2.035	1.876	1.737
6	3.245	3.167	3.092	3.020	2.951	2.885	2.821	2.759	2.700	2.643	2.588	2.534	2.483	2.433	2.385	2.168	1.983	1.824
7	3.508	3.416	3.327	3.242	3.161	3.083	3.009	2.937	2.868	2.802	2.739	2.677	2.619	2.562	2.508	2.263	2.057	1.883
8	3.726	3.619	3.518	3.421	3.329	3.241	3.156	3.076	2.999	2.925	2.854	2.786	2.721	2.658	2.598	2.331	2.109	1.922
9	3.905	3.786	3.673	3.566	3.463	3.366	3.273	3.184	3.100	3.019	2.942	2.868	2.798	2.730	2.665	2.379	2.144	1.948
10	4.054	3.923	3.799	3.682	3.570	3.465	3.364	3.269	3.178	3.092	3.009	2.930	2.855	2.784	2.715	2.414	2.168	1.965
11	4.177	4.035	3.902	3.776	3.656	3.544	3.437	3.335	3.239	3.147	3.060	2.978	2.899	2.824	2.752	2.438	2.185	1.977
12	4.278	4.127	3.985	3.851	3.725	3.606	3.493	3.387	3.286	3.190	3.100	3.013	2.931	2.853	2.779	2.456	2.196	1.985
13	4.362	4.203	4.053	3.912	3.780	3.656	3.538	3.427	3.322	3.223	3.129	3.040	2.956	2.876	2.799	2.469	2.204	1.990
14	4.432	4.265	4.108	3.962	3.824	3.695	3.573	3.459	3.351	3.249	3.152	3.061	2.974	2.892	2.814	2.478	2.210	1.993
15	4.489	4.315	4.153	4.001	3.859	3.726	3.601	3.483	3.373	3.268	3.170	3.076	2.988	2.905	2.825	2.484	2.214	1.995
16	4.536	4.357	4.189	4.033	3.887	3.751	3.623	3.503	3.390	3.283	3.183	3.088	2.999	2.914	2.834	2.489	2.216	1.997
17	4.576	4.391	4.219	4.059	3.910	3.771	3.640	3.518	3.403	3.295	3.193	3.097	3.007	2.921	2.840	2.492	2.218	1.998
18	4.608	4.419	4.243	4.080	3.928	3.786	3.654	3.529	3.413	3.304	3.201	3.104	3.012	2.926	2.844	2.494	2.219	1.999
19	4.635	4.442	4.263	4.097	3.942	3.799	3.664	3.539	3.421	3.311	3.207	3.109	3.017	2.930	2.848	2.496	2.220	1.999
20	4.657	4.460	4.279	4.110	3.954	3.808	3.673	3.546	3.427	3.316	3.211	3.113	3.020	2.933	2.850	2.497	2.221	1.999
21	4.675	4.476	4.292	4.121	3.963	3.816	3.679	3.551	3.432	3.320	3.215	3.116	3.023	2.935	2.852	2.498	2.221	2.000
22	4.690	4.488	4.302	4.130	3.970	3.822	3.684	3.556	3.436	3.323	3.217	3.118	3.025	2.936	2.853	2.498	2.222	2.000
23	4.703	4.499	4.311	4.137	3.976	3.827	3.689	3.559	3.438	3.325	3.219	3.120	3.026	2.938	2.854	2.499	2.222	2.000
24	4.713	4.507	4.318	4.143	3.981	3.831	3.692	3.562	3.441	3.327	3.221	3.121	3.027	2.939	2.855	2.499	2.222	2.000
25	4.721	4.514	4.323	4.147	3.985	3.834	3.694	3.564	3.442	3.329	3.222	3.122	3.028	2.939	2.856	2.499	2.222	2.000
30	4.746	4.534	4.339	4.160	3.995	3.842	3.701	3.569	3.447	3.332	3.225	3.124	3.030	2.941	2.857	2.500	2.222	2.000
35	4.756	4.541	4.345	4.164	3.998	3.845	3.703	3.571	3.448	3.333	3.226	3.125	3.030	2.941	2.857	2.500	2.222	2.000
40	4.760	4.544	4.347	4.166	3.999	3.846	3.703	3.571	3.448	3.333	3.226	3.125	3.030	2.941	2.857	2.500	2.222	2.000
45	4.761	4.545	4.347	4.166	4.000	3.846	3.704	3.571	3.448	3.333	3.226	3.125	3.030	2.941	2.857	2.500	2.222	2.000
50	4.762	4.545	4.348	4.167	4.000	3.846	3.704	3.571	3.448	3.333	3.226	3.125	3.030	2.941	2.857	2.500	2.222	2.000

Texas Instruments BA-35, BAII, BAII Plus[c]

Inputs:	700	5	8		
Functions:	PMT	N	%i	CPT	FV
Outputs:				2794.90[d]	

[c]For the Texas Instruments BAII, you would use the 2nd key instead of the CPT key; for the Texas Instruments BAII Plus, you would use the I/Y key instead of the %i key.
[d]If a minus sign precedes the output, it should be ignored.

Appendix B

Solutions to Self-Test Problems

CHAPTER 1

ST 1-1 **a.** Recommend project 1 since the total impact of project 1 on EPS (in today's dollars) is greater than project 2: $1.32 versus $1.19.

b. Recommend project 1 since if it were implemented, Doyle's common share price will increase to $28.00 which is greater than the $26.50 for project 2. While both projects are acceptable since both result in the share price increasing, the increase with project 1 is greater. If only one project can be implemented, it should be project 1 if share price maximization were Doyle's goal.

c. The current value of common shareholders' interest in Doyle is $195,000,000 (10,000,000 common shares × $19.50). If project 1 were implemented, shareholder value will increase to $308,000,000 (11,000,000 common shares × $28.00). For project 2, shareholder value will increase to $312,700,000 (11,800,000 common shares × $26.50). Project 2 should be recommended.

d. Liam should recommend project 2 as it results in the firm achieving its goal: maximization of shareholder wealth. The goal is to maximize the value of the common shareholders' total interest in the company. This is measured by multiplying the total number of common shares outstanding by the common share price.

e. Project 2 might be the better project because it maximizes cash flows, leading to higher share prices.

CHAPTER 2

ST 2-1 **a.** Current liabilities. The amount is $365,000.

b. Both of these changes will result in total common equity increasing. Recall, common equity consists of both common shares and retained earnings. The sale of common shares generates $40,000 (5,000 shares × $8.00) in cash and reinvested profits are $82,500 ($105,000 − $22,500). Therefore, the total increase in common equity (shareholders' equity) for the 2003 fiscal year would be $122,500. This means that either total assets must increase by $122,500, liabilities decrease by $122,500, or some combination of the two.

c. The long-term debt account would decline by $25,000, so assets must either decline by $25,000, shareholders' equity increase by $25,000, or some combination of the two.

   d. The next impact of parts b and c is to increase total liabilities and shareholders' equity by $97,500 ($122,500 − $25,000). This implies that total assets would increase by this amount, liabilities decrease by $97,500, or some combination of the two.

ST 2-2   a. Yes. Montgomery sold an asset for more than its cost. The capital gain was $141,300 ($260,000 − $112,500 − $6,200). 50% of this capital gain is taxable which is $70,650.

   b. Taxable income is:

EBIT	$180,000
less: Interest expense	42,400
EBT and capital gain	$137,600
plus: Taxable capital gain	70,650
Taxable income	$208,250

   c.

Taxes on first $200,000	@22.16%	$ 44,320
Taxes on remaining $8,250	@31.16%	2,571
Total taxes		$ 46,891
NIAT		$161,359

   d. Montgomery Enterprises is a manufacturer, therefore the company qualifies for the manufacturing and processing deduction. In Quebec, the tax rate was 31.16% for a manufacturer. Therefore, total taxes would be $64,891 ($208,250 × 31.16%) and NIAT would be $143,359.

   e. The tax system "subsidizes" tax deductible expenses for corporations. Therefore, the actual, after-tax cost of the interest expenses was:

   42,400 × (1 − 0.3116) = $29,188

   The "subsidy" was $13,212 ($42,400 × 31.16%)

CHAPTER 3

ST 3-1

Ratio	Too high	Too low
Current ratio = current assets/current liabilities	May indicate poor management of current assets and that the firm is holding excessive cash, accounts receivable, or inventory.	May indicate poor ability to satisfy short-term obligations, that the firm's credit policy is too tight, and/or that inventory is too low and that the firm is missing sales.
Average age of inventory = inventory/average daily COGS	May indicate poor inventory management, excessive inventory, or obsolete inventory.	May indicate lower level of inventory, which may cause stockouts and lost sales.
Times interest earned = earnings before interest and taxes/interest	Implies very high profits, which is never a problem, but could also im;ply that the firm is not using leverage to increase returns to shareholders	May indicate poor ability to pay contractual interest payments and a very high debt level. Ratios less than 1 suggest the possibility of bankruptcy.
Gross margin = gross margin/sales	Indicates the low cost of merchandise sold relative to the sales price; may indicate extremely good control of direct costs (COGS) or noncompetitive pricing and potential lost sales.	Indicates the high cost of the merchandise sold relative to the sales price; may indicate either a low sales price or a high cost of goods sold.
Return on total assets = net income after taxes/total assets		Indicates ineffective management in generating profits with the available assets. Firm may have recently expanded and the assets are not yet generating sales and profits.

ST 3-2

Balance Sheet
O'Keefe Industries
December 31, 2002

Cash	$ 30,000	Accounts payable	$ 120,000
Marketable securities	25,000	Notes payable	160,000^e
Accounts receivable	200,000^a	Accruals	20,000
Inventories	225,000^b	Total current liabilities	$300,000^d
Total current assets	$ 480,000	Long-term debt	$ 576,000^f
Net fixed assets	$ 980,000^c	Shockholders' equity	$ 584,000^g
Total assets	$1,460,000	Total liabilities and	$1,460,000

^{a}Average collection period (ACP) = 40 days
ACP = accounts receivable (A/R)/average sales per day
A/R = ACP × average sales per day
A/R = $1,825,000/365 × 40 days
A/R = $200,000

^{b}Average age of inventory (AAI) = 60 days
AAI = inventory/average COGS per day
Inventory = AAI × average COGS per day
COGS = Sales × (1 – gross margin)
COGS = $1,825,000 × (1 – 0.25)
COGS = $1,368,750
Inventory = 60 days × $1,368,750/365
Inventory = $225,000

^{c}Total asset turnover = 1.25
Total asset turnover = sales/total assets
Total assets = sales/total asset turnover
Total assets = $1,825,000/1.25
Total assets = $1,460,000
Net fixed assets = total assets – total current assets
Net fixed assets = $1,460,000 – $480,000 = $980,000

^{d}Current ratio = 1.60
Current ratio = current assets/current liabilities
1.60 = $480,000/current liabilities
$300,000 = current liabilities

^{e}Notes payable = total current liabilities –
accounts payable – accruals
= $300,000 – $120,000 – $20,000
= $160,000

^{f}Debt ratio = .60
Debt ratio = total liabilities/total assets
.60 = total liabilities/$1,460,000
$876,000 = total liabilities
Total liabilities = current liabilities + long-term debt
$876,000 = $300,000 + long-term debt
$576,000 = long-term debt

^{g}Shareholders' equity = total assets – total liability
Shareholders' equity = $1,460,000 – $876,000
Shareholders' equity = $584,000

CHAPTER 4

ST 4-1   a.

Cash Budget
Carroll Company
April–June

	February	March	April	May	June	July	August
						Accounts receivable at end of June	
Forecast sales	$500	$600	$400	$ 200	$200		
Cash sales (30%)	$150	$180	$120	$ 60	$ 60		
Collections of A/R							
Lagged 1 month [(.7 × .7) = 49%]		245	294	196	98	$ 98	
Lagged 2 months [(.3 × .7) = 21%]			105	126	84	42	$42
						$140 +	$42 = $182
Total cash receipts			$519	$ 382	$242		
Less: Total cash disbursements			600	500	200		
Net cash flow			$ (81)	$(118)	$ 42		
Add: Beginning cash			115	34	(84)		
Ending cash			$ 34	$ (84)	$(42)		
Less: Minimum cash balance			25	25	25		
Required total financing (line of credit)			—	$109	$ 67		
Excess cash balance (marketable securities)			$ 9	—	—		

b. Carroll Company would need a maximum of $109 in financing over the 3-month period.

c.

Account	Amount	Source of amount
Cash	$ 25	Minimum cash balance—June
Line of credit	67	Required total financing—June
Marketable securities	0	Excess cash balance—June
Accounts receivable	182	Calculation at right of cash budget statement

ST 4-2   **a.**

Pro forma Income Statement
Euro Designs, Inc.,
for the year ended December 31, 2003

Sales revenue (given)	$3,900,000
Less: Cost of goods sold (55%)[a]	2,145,000
Gross margin	$1,755,000
Less: Operating expenses (12%)[b]	468,000
Operating earnings	$1,287,000
Less: Interest expense (given)	325,000
Earnings before taxes	$ 962,000
Less: Taxes (40%)	384,800
Net income after taxes	$ 577,200
Less: Cash dividends (given)	320,000
Reinvested profits	$ 257,200

[a]From 2002: CGS/Sales = $1,925,000/$3,500,000 = 55%.
[b]From 2002: Oper. Exp./Sales = $420,000/$3,500,000 = 12%.

b. The percent-of-sales method may underestimate actual 2003 pro forma income by assuming that all costs are variable. If the firm has fixed costs, which by definition would not increase with increasing sales, the 2003 pro forma income would likely be underestimated.

CHAPTER 5

ST 5-1   **a.** *Bank A:*

$$FV_3 = \$10,000 \times FVIF_{4\%/3per} = \$10,000 \times 1.125 = \underline{\underline{\$11,250}}$$
(Calculator solution = $11,248.64)

Bank B:

$$FV_3 = \$10,000 \times FVIF_{4\%/2,2 \times 3yrs} = \$10,000 \times FVIF_{2\%,6per}$$
$$= \$10,000 \times 1.126 = \underline{\underline{\$11,260}}$$
(Calculator solution = $11,261.62)

Bank C:

$$FV_3 = \$10,000 \times FVIF_{4\%/4,4 \times 3yrs} = \$10,000 \times FVIF_{1\%,12per}$$
$$= \$10,000 \times 1.127 = \underline{\underline{\$11,270}}$$
(Calculator solution = $11,268.25)

b. Bank A: $k_{EAR} = (1 + 4\%/1)^1 - 1 = (1 + .04)^1 - 1 = 1.04 - 1 = .04 = \underline{\underline{4\%}}$

Bank B: $k_{EAR} = (1 + 4\%/2)^2 - 1 = (1 + .02)^2 - 1 = 1.0404 - 1 = .0404 = \underline{\underline{4.04\%}}$

Bank C: $k_{EAR} = (1 + 4\%/4)^4 - 1 = (1 + .01)^4 - 1 = 1.040604 - 1 = .040604 = \underline{\underline{4.0604\%}}$

c. Ms. Martin should deal with Bank C: The quarterly compounding of interest at the given 4% rate results in the highest future value as a result of the corresponding highest effective annual rate.

d. *Bank D:*

The EAR for Bank D is:

$e^{.04} - 1 = 1.0408108 - 1$

$\qquad = 0.0408108 = 4.08108\%$

At the end of 3 years, Ms. Martin would have:

$FV_3 = \$10,000 \times FVIF_{4\%,3yrs}$ (continuous compounding)

$\qquad = \$10,000 \times e^{.04 \times 3} = \$10,000 \times e^{.12}$

$\qquad = \$10,000 \times 1.127497$

$\qquad = \underline{\underline{\$11,274.97}}$

This alternative is better than Bank C, because it results in a higher future value because of the use of continuous compounding, which with otherwise identical cash flows always results in the highest future value of any compounding period.

ST 5-2   **a.** On a purely subjective basis, a rational argument could be made for both annuities. The fact that annuity Y's cash flows occur at the end of the year (an *ordinary annuity*) while annuity X's cash flows occur at the beginning of the year (an *annuity due*) favours annuity X, because its beginning-of-year cash flows will have more time to compound than the end-of-year cash flows of annuity Y. On the other hand, it would seem that the extra $1,000 per year in cash flow from annuity Y ($10,000 for annuity Y and $9,000 for annuity X) would outweigh the benefit of annuity X's longer compounding period. As noted in what follows, only after making necessary computations can the more attractive annuity be determined.

b. *Annuity X (annuity due):*

$$FVA_6 = \$9,000 \times FVIFA_{15\%,6yrs} \times (1 + .15)$$
$$= \$9,000 \times 8.754 \times 1.15 = \underline{\underline{\$90,603.90}}$$

(Calculator solution = $90,601.19)

Annuity Y (ordinary annuity):

$$FVA_6 = \$10,000 \times FVIFA_{15\%,6yrs}$$
$$= \$10,000 \times 8.754 = \underline{\underline{\$87,540.00}}$$

(Calculator solution = $87,537.38)

c. Annuity X is more attractive, because its future value at the end of year 6, FVA_6, of $90,601.19 is greater than annuity Y's end-of-year-6 future value, FVA_6, of $87,537.38. The first subjective assessment in **a** was correct. The benefit of receiving annuity X's cash flows at the beginning of the year more than offset the fact that its cash flows are $1,000 less than those of annuity Y, which has end-of-year cash flows. The high interest rate of 15% added to the attractiveness of annuity X (the annuity due), because each of its cash flows earns at this rate for an extra year, thereby enhancing its future value.

ST 5-3   *Alternative A:*

Cash flow stream:

$$PVA_5 = \$700 \times PVIFA_{9\%,5yrs}$$
$$= \$700 \times 3.890 = \underline{\underline{\$2,723}}$$

(Calculator solution = $2,722.76)

Lump sum: $\underline{\underline{\$2,825}}$

Alternative B:

Cash flow stream:

Year (n)	Cash flow (1)	$FVIF_{9\%,n}$ (2)	Present value [(1) × (2)] (3)
1	$1,100	.917	$1,088.70
2	900	.842	757.80
3	700	.772	540.40
4	500	.708	354.00
5	300	.650	195.00
		Present value	$2,935.90

(Calculator solution = $2,935.90)

Lump-sum: $2,800

Conclusion: Alternative B in the form of a cash flow stream is preferred because its present value of $2,935.90 is greater than the other three values.

ST 5-4 $FVA_5 = \$8,000$; $FVIFA_{7\%,5\text{yrs}} = 4.1$; $PMT = ?$

$FVA_n = PMT \times (FVIFA_{k,n})$ [Equation 5.15 or 5.29]

$\$8,000 = PMT \times 4.1$

$PMT = \$8,000/5.751 = \underline{\underline{\$1,951.13}}$

(Calculator solution = $1,951.13)

Judi should deposit $1,951.13 at the end of each of the 5 years to meet her goal of accumulating $8,000 at the end of the fifth year.

CHAPTER 6

ST 6-1 $\$1,000 = \$985.84\left[1 + \dfrac{i(126)}{365}\right]$

$$\$1,000 = \$985.84 + \left[\frac{\$985.84 \times 126\ ^*i}{365}\right]$$

$$\$1,000 - \$985.84 = \$340.31737i$$

$$i = \frac{\$14.16}{\$340.31737}$$

$$i = 4.16\%$$

ST 6-2 $\$75,000,000 = P\left[1 + \dfrac{0.0294 \times 21}{365}\right]$

$P = \$74,873,351.21$

The interest made is the difference between the amount Ferris will pay and the par value; in this case, $126,648.79.

CHAPTER 7

ST 7-1 **a.** Expected return, $\bar{k} = \dfrac{\Sigma \text{Returns}}{3}$ (*Equation 7.2a in footnote 9*)

$$\bar{k}_A = \frac{12\% + 14\% + 16\%}{3} = \frac{42\%}{3} = \underline{\underline{14\%}}$$

$$\bar{k}_B = \frac{16\% + 14\% + 12\%}{3} = \frac{42\%}{3} = \underline{\underline{14\%}}$$

$$\bar{k}_C = \frac{12\% + 14\% + 16\%}{3} = \frac{42\%}{3} = \underline{\underline{14\%}}$$

b. Standard deviation, $\sigma_k = \sqrt{\dfrac{\sum\limits_{i=1}^{n}(k_i - \bar{k})^2}{n-1}}$ (*Equation 7.3a in footnote 10*)

$$\sigma_{k_A} = \sqrt{\frac{(12\% - 14\%)^2 + (14\% - 14\%)^2 + (16\% - 14\%)^2}{3-1}}$$

$$= \sqrt{\frac{4\% + 0\% + 4\%}{2}} = \sqrt{\frac{8\%}{2}} = \underline{\underline{2\%}}$$

$$\sigma_{k_B} = \sqrt{\frac{(16\% - 14\%)^2 + (14\% - 14\%)^2 + (12\% - 14\%)^2}{3-1}}$$

$$= \sqrt{\frac{4\% + 0\% + 4\%}{2}} = \sqrt{\frac{8\%}{2}} = \underline{\underline{2\%}}$$

$$\sigma_{k_C} = \sqrt{\frac{(12\% - 14\%)^2 + (14\% - 14\%)^2 + (16\% - 14\%)^2}{3-1}}$$

$$= \sqrt{\frac{4\% + 0\% + 4\%}{2}} = \sqrt{\frac{8\%}{2}} = \underline{\underline{2\%}}$$

c.

Year	Annual expected returns	
	Portfolio AB	**Portfolio AC**
2003	$(.50 \times 12\%) + (.50 \times 16\%) = 14\%$	$(.50 \times 12\%) + (.50 \times 12\%) = 12\%$
2004	$(.50 \times 14\%) + (.50 \times 14\%) = 14\%$	$(.50 \times 14\%) + (.50 \times 14\%) = 14\%$
2005	$(.50 \times 16\%) + (.50 \times 12\%) = 14\%$	$(.50 \times 16\%) + (.50 \times 16\%) = 16\%$

Over the 3-year period:

$$\bar{k}_{AB} = \frac{14\% + 14\% + 14\%}{3} = \frac{42\%}{3} = \underline{\underline{14\%}}$$

$$\bar{k}_{AC} = \frac{12\% + 14\% + 16\%}{3} = \frac{42\%}{3} = \underline{\underline{14\%}}$$

d. AB is perfectly negatively correlated.
AC is perfectly positively correlated.

e. Standard deviation of the portfolios

$$\sigma_{k_{AB}} = \sqrt{\frac{(14\% - 14\%)^2 + (14\% - 14\%)^2 + (14\% - 14\%)^2}{3 - 1}}$$

$$= \sqrt{\frac{0\% + 0\% + 0\%}{2}} = \sqrt{\frac{0\%}{2}} = \underline{\underline{0\%}}$$

$$\sigma_{k_{AC}} = \sqrt{\frac{(12\% - 14\%)^2 + (14\% - 14\%)^2 + (16\% - 14\%)^2}{3 - 1}}$$

$$= \sqrt{\frac{4\% + 0\% + 4\%}{2}} = \sqrt{\frac{8\%}{2}} = \underline{\underline{2\%}}$$

f. Portfolio AB is preferred, because it provides the same return (14%) as AC but with less risk $[(\sigma_{k_{AB}} = 0\%) < (\sigma_{k_{AC}} = 2\%)]$.

ST 7-2 a. When the market return increases by 10%, the common share's required return would be expected to increase by 15% ($1.50 \times 10\%$). When the market return decreases by 10%, the common share's required return would be expected to decrease by 15% $[1.50 \times (-10\%)]$.

b. $k_j = R_F + [b_j \times (k_m - R_F)]$
   $= 7\% + [1.50 \times (10\% - 7\%)]$
   $= 7\% + 4.5\% = \underline{11.5\%}$

c. The common shares should not be purchased as an investment since the *expected* return on the shares is 11% and this is less than the 11.5% return *required* on the shares.

d. $k_j = 7\% + [1.50 \times (9\% - 7\%)]$
   $= 7\% + 3\% = \underline{10\%}$

   The shares should now be purchased since the *expected* return of 11% is now greater than the *required* return, which has declined to 10% as a result of investors in the marketplace becoming less risk-averse.

CHAPTER 8

ST 8-1 a. $B_0 = I \times (PVIFA_{k_d, n}) + M \times (PVIF_{k_d, n})$
   $I = .08 \times \$1,000 = \$80$
   $M = \$1,000$
   $n = 12$ yrs
   (1) $k_d = 7\%$
   $B_0 = \$80 \times (PVIFA_{7\%, 12yrs}) + \$1,000 \times (PVIF_{7\%, 12yrs})$
   $= (\$80 \times 7.943) + (\$1,000 \times .444)$
   $= \$635.44 + \$444.00 = \underline{\$1,079.44}$

   (Calculator solution = \$1,079.43)
   (2) $k_d = 8\%$
   $B_0 = \$80 \times (PVIFA_{8\%, 12yrs}) + \$1,000 \times (PVIF_{8\%, 12yrs})$
   $= (\$80 \times 7.536) + (\$1,000 \times .397)$
   $= \$602.88 + \$397.00 = \underline{\$999.88}$

   (Calculator solution = \$1,000)

(3) $k_d = 10\%$

$$B_0 = \$80 \times (PVIFA_{10\%,12\text{yrs}}) + \$1,000 \times (PVIF_{10\%,12\text{yrs}})$$
$$= (\$80 \times 6.814) + (\$1,000 \times .319)$$
$$= \$545.12 + \$319.00 = \underline{\$864.12}$$

(Calculator solution = $863.73)

b. (1) $k_d = 7\%$, $B_0 = \$1,079.44$; sells at a *premium*
(2) $k_d = 8\%$, $B_0 = \$999.88 \approx \$1,000.00$; sells at its *par value*
(3) $k_d = 10\%$, $B_0 = \$864.12$; sells at a *discount*

c. $B_0 = \dfrac{I}{2} \times (PVIFA_{k_{d/2},2n}) + M \times (PVIF_{k_{d/2},2n})$

(1) $k_d = 7\%$

$$= \frac{\$80}{2} \times (PVIFA_{7\%/2,2\times12\text{periods}}) + \$1,000 \times (PVIF_{7\%/2,2\times12\text{periods}})$$
$$= \$40 \times (PVIFA_{3.5\%,24\text{periods}}) + \$1,000 \times (PVIF_{3.5\%,24\text{periods}})$$
$$= \$642.33 + \$437.96 = \underline{\$1,080.29}$$

(2) $k_d = 8\%$

$$B_0 = \$40 \times (PVIFA_{4\%,24\text{periods}}) + \$1,000 \times (PVIF_{4\%,24\text{periods}})$$
$$= \$609.88 + \$390.12 = \underline{\$1,000.00}$$

(Calculator solution = $1,000)

(3) $k_d = 10\%$

$$B_0 = \$40 \times (PVIFA_{5\%,24\text{periods}}) + \$1,000 \times (PVIF_{5\%,24\text{periods}})$$
$$= \$551.95 + \$310.07 = \underline{\$862.02}$$

ST 8-2 **a.** $B_0 = \$1,150$

$I = .11 \times \$1,000 = \$110$
$M = \$1,000$
$n = 18$ yrs
$\$1,150 = \$110 \times (PVIFA_{k_d,18\text{yrs}}) + \$1,000 \times (PVIF_{k_d,18\text{yrs}})$

Because if $k_d = 11\%$, $B_0 = \$1,000 = M$, try $k_d = 10\%$.
$B_0 = \$110 \times (PVIFA_{10\%,18\text{yrs}}) + \$1,000 \times (PVIF_{10\%,18\text{yrs}})$
$= (\$110 \times 8.201) + (\$1,000 \times .180)$
$= \$902.11 + \$180.00 = \$1,082.11$

Because $1,082.11 < $1,150, try $k_d = 9\%$.
$B_0 = \$110 \times (PVIFA_{9\%,18\text{yrs}}) + \$1,000 \times (PVIF_{9\%,18\text{yrs}})$
$= (\$110 \times 8.756) + (\$1,000 \times .212)$
$= \$963.16 + \$212.00 = \$1,175.16$

Because the $1,175.16 value at 9% is higher than $1,150, and the $1,082.11 value at 10% rate is lower than $1,150, the bond's yield to maturity must be between 9 and 10%. Because the $1,175.16 value is closer to $1,150, rounding to the nearest whole percent, the YTM is 9%. (By using interpolation, the more precise YTM value is 9.27%.)

Use a calculator to solve it in one easy step. The answer is 9.26%.

b. The calculated YTM of 9.26+% is below the bond's 11% coupon interest rate, because the bond's market value of \$1,150 is above its \$1,000 par value. Whenever a bond's market value is above its par value (it sells at a *premium*), its YTM will be below its coupon interest rate; when a bond sells at *par*, the YTM will equal its coupon interest rate; and when the bond sells for less than par (at a *discount*), its YTM will be greater than its coupon interest rate.

c. $\$1,150 = \$55 \times (PVIFA_{kd,36\text{periods}}) + \$1,000 \times (PVIF_{kd,36\text{periods}})$

$\quad kd = 4.6355\% \times 2$

$\quad\quad = 9.27\%$

ST 8-3 $D_0 = \$1.80/\text{share}$

$\quad\quad k_s = 12\%$

a. *Zero growth:*

$$P_0 = \frac{D_1}{k_s} = \frac{D_1 = D_0 = \$1.80}{.12} = \underline{\underline{\$15/\text{share}}}$$

b. *Constant growth, g = 5%:*

$D_1 = D_0 \times (1 + g) = \$1.80 \times (1 + .05) = \$1.89/\text{share}$

$$P_0 = \frac{D_1}{k_s - g} = \frac{\$1.89}{.12 - .05} = \frac{\$1.89}{.07} = \underline{\underline{\$27/\text{share}}}$$

c. *Variable growth, N = 3, g_1 = 5% for years 1 to 3 and g_2 = 4% for years 4 to ∞:*

$D_1 = D_0 \times (1 + g_1)^1 = \$1.80 \times (1 + .05)^1 = \$1.89/\text{share}$

$D_2 = D_0 \times (1 + g_1)^2 = \$1.80 \times (1 + .05)^2 = \$1.98/\text{share}$

$D_3 = D_0 \times (1 + g_1)^3 = \$1.80 \times (1 + .05)^3 = \$2.08/\text{share}$

$D_4 = D_3 \times (1 + g_2) = \$2.08 \times (1 + .04) = \$2.16/\text{share}$

$$P_0 = \sum_{t=1}^{N} \frac{D_0 \times (1 + g_1)^t}{(1 + k_s)^t} + \left(\frac{1}{(1 + k_s)^N} \times \frac{D_{N+1}}{k_s - g_2} \right)$$

$$\sum_{t=1}^{N} \frac{D_0 \times (1 + g_1)^t}{(1 + k_s)^t} = \frac{\$1.89}{(1 + .12)^1} + \frac{\$1.98}{(1 + .12)^2} + \frac{\$2.08}{(1 + .12)^3}$$

$\quad\quad = [\$1.89 \times (PVIF_{12\%,1\text{yr}})] + [\$1.98 \times (PVIF_{12\%,2\text{yrs}})] + [\$2.08 \times (PVIF_{12\%,3\text{yrs}})]$

$\quad\quad = (\$1.89 \times .893) + (\$1.98 \times .797) + (\$2.08 \times .712)$

$\quad\quad = \$1.69 + \$1.58 + \$1.48 = \$4.75$ (same result using a financial calculator)

$$\left[\frac{1}{(1 + k_s)^N} \times \frac{D_{N+1}}{(k_s - g_2)} \right] = \frac{1}{(1 + .12)^3} \times \frac{D_4 = \$2.16}{.12 - .04}$$

$\quad\quad = (PVIF_{12\%,3\text{yrs}}) \times \frac{\$2.16}{.08}$

$\quad\quad = .712 \times \$27.00 = \$19.22$ (same result using a financial calculator)

$$P_0 = \sum_{t=1}^{N} \frac{D_0 \times (1 + g_1)^t}{(1 + k_s)^t} + \left[\frac{1}{(1 + k_s)^N} \times \frac{D_{N+1}}{k_s - g_2} \right] = \$4.75 + \$19.22$$

$\quad\quad = \$23.97/\text{share}$

CHAPTER 9

ST 9-1   **a.** Cost of debt, k_i (using approximation formula)

$$K_D = \frac{I + \dfrac{\$1,000 - N_d}{n}}{\dfrac{N_d + \$1,000}{2}}$$

$$I = .10 \times \$1,000 = \$100$$
$$N_d = \$1,000 - \$30 \text{ discount} - \$20 \text{ flotation cost} = \$950$$
$$n = 10 \text{ years}$$

$$k_d = \frac{\$100 + \dfrac{\$1,000 - \$950}{10}}{\dfrac{\$950 + \$1,000}{2}}$$

(using a financial calculator)

$$\$50 \times (PVIFA_{kd,20\text{periods}}) + \$1,000 \times (PVIF_{kd,20\text{periods}})$$

$$k_d = 5.415 \times 2 = 10.83\% \text{ (rounded to 10.8\%)}$$
$$k_i = k_d \times (1 - T)$$
$$T = .40$$
$$k_i = 10.8\% \times (1 - .40) = \underline{\underline{6.5\%}}$$

Cost of preferred stock, k_p

$$k_p = \frac{D_p}{N_p}$$

$$D_p = .11 \times \$100 = \$11$$
$$N_p = \$100 - \$4 \text{ flotation cost} = \$96$$

$$k_p = \frac{\$11}{\$96} = \underline{\underline{11.46\%}} \text{ (rounded to 11.5\%)}$$

Cost of retained earnings, k_r

$$D_1 = D_0 (1 + g)$$
$$= \$5.66(1.06)$$
$$= \$6.00$$

$$k_r = k_s = \frac{D_1}{P_0} + g$$

$$= \frac{\$6}{\$80} + 6.0\% = 7.5\% + 6.0\% = \underline{\underline{13.5\%}}$$

Cost of new common stock, k_n

$$k_n = \frac{D_1}{N_n} + g$$

$$D_1 = \$6$$
$$N_n = \$80 - \$2.50 \text{ underpricing} - \$5.50 \text{ flotation cost} = \$72$$
$$g = 6.0\%$$
$$k_n = \frac{\$6}{\$72} + 6.0\% = 8.3\% + 6.0\% = \underline{\underline{14.3\%}}$$

b. (1) Break point, BP

$$BP_{common\ equity} = \frac{AF_{common\ equity}}{w_{common\ equity}}$$

$$AF_{common\ equity} = \$225,000$$
$$w_{common\ equity} = 45\%$$

$$BP_{common\ equity} = \frac{\$225,000}{.45} = \$500,000$$

(2) WACC for total new financing < $500,000

Source of capital	Weight (1)	Cost (2)	Weighted cost [(1) × (2)] (3)
Long-term debt	.40	6.5%	2.6%
Preferred stock	.15	11.5	1.7
Common stock equity	.45	13.5	6.1
Totals	1.00		10.4%

Cost (2) note: $= \dfrac{\$100 + \$5}{\$975} = 10.8\%$

Weighted average cost of capital = 10.4%

(3) WACC for total new financing > $500,000

Source of capital	Weight (1)	Cost (2)	Weighted cost [(1) × (2)] (3)
Long-term debt	.40	6.5%	2.6%
Preferred stock	.15	11.5	1.7
Common stock equity	.45	14.3	6.4
Totals	1.00		10.7%

Weighted average cost of capital = 10.7%

c. IOS data for graph

Investment opportunity	Internal rate of return (IRR)	Initial investment	Cumulative investment
D	16.5%	$200,000	$ 200,000
C	12.9	150,000	350,000
E	11.8	450,000	800,000
A	11.2	100,000	900,000
G	10.5	300,000	1,200,000
F	10.1	600,000	1,800,000
B	9.7	500,000	2,300,000

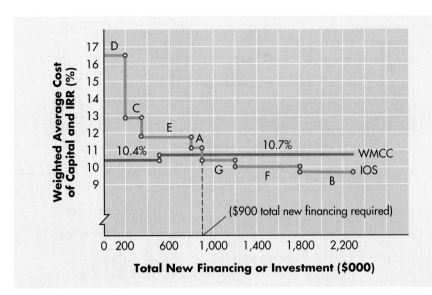

d. Projects D, C, E, and A should be accepted because their respective IRRs exceed the WMCC. They will require $900,000 of total new financing.

CHAPTER 10

ST 10-1   **a.** $Q = \dfrac{FC}{P - VC} = \dfrac{FC}{GM/unit}$

$= \dfrac{\$250,000}{\$7.50 - \$3.00} = \dfrac{\$250,000}{\$4.50} = \underline{\underline{55,556 \text{ units}}}$

$S = \dfrac{FC}{GM\%}$

$= \dfrac{\$250,000}{\$4.50/\$7.50} = \dfrac{\$250,000}{60\%} = \underline{\underline{\$416,667}}$

	+20%	
b. Sales (in units)	100,000	120,000
Sales revenue (units × $7.50/unit)	$750,000	$900,000
Less: Variable operating costs (units × $3.00/unit)	300,000	360,000
Less: Fixed operating costs	250,000	250,000
Earnings before interest and taxes (EBIT)	$200,000	$290,000
	+45%	

Less: Interest	80,000	80,000
Earnings before taxes	$120,000	$210,000
Less: Taxes ($T = .40$)	48,000	84,000
Net income after taxes	$ 72,000	$126,000
Less: Preferred dividends (8,000 shares $\times$ $5.00/share)	40,000	40,000
Earnings available for common	$ 32,000	$ 86,000

Earnings per share (EPS) $32,000/20,000 = $1.60/share $86,000/20,000 = $4.30/share

$$+168.75\%$$

c. $\text{DOL (100,000 units)} = \dfrac{\text{GM\$}}{\text{EBIT}} = \dfrac{\$450,000}{\$200,000} = \underline{\underline{2.25}}$

d. $\text{DFL (100,000 units)} = \dfrac{\text{EBIT}}{\text{EBIT} - I - \dfrac{\text{PD}}{I - T}}$

$$= \dfrac{\$200,000}{\$200,000 - \$80,000 - \dfrac{\$40,000}{1 - 0.40}}$$

$$= \dfrac{200,000}{53,333.33} = \underline{\underline{3.75}}$$

e. $\text{DTL} = \text{DOL} \times \text{DFL}$

$\qquad = 2.25 \times 3.75 = \underline{\underline{8.4375}}$

Using the other DTL formula:

$$\text{DTL} = \dfrac{\text{GM\$}}{\text{EBT} - \dfrac{\text{PD}}{1 - T}} = \dfrac{\$450,000}{\$120,000 - \dfrac{\$40,000}{1 - 40}} = 8.4375$$

If sales increased by 50%, EPS would be expected to increase by 421.875% (8.4375 $\times$ 50%).

ST 10-2

Data summary for alternative plans		
Source of capital	**Plan A (bond)**	**Plan B (common shares)**
Long-term debt	$60,000 at 12% annual interest	$50,000 at 12% annual interest
Annual interest =	.12 $\times$ $60,000 = $7,200	.12 $\times$ $50,000 = $6,000
Common shares	10,000 shares	11,000 shares

a.

	Plan A (bond)		Plan B (shares)	
EBIT[a]	$30,000	$40,000	$30,000	$40,000
Less: Interest	7,200	7,200	6,000	6,000
Net profits before taxes	$22,800	$32,800	$24,000	$34,000
Less: Taxes ($T = .40$)	9,120	13,120	9,600	13,600
Net profits after taxes	$13,680	$19,680	$14,400	$20,400
EPS (10,000 shares)	$1.37	$1.97		
(11,000 shares)			$1.31	$1.85

[a]Values were arbitrarily selected; other values could have been utilized.

	Coordinates	
	EBIT	
	$30,000	$40,000
Financing plan	Earnings per share (EPS)	
A (Bond)	$1.37	$1.97
B (Stock)	1.31	1.85

b.

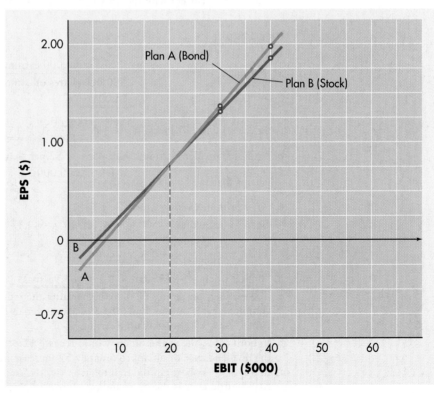

c. The bond plan (Plan A) becomes superior to the stock plan (Plan B) at *around $20,000* of EBIT, as represented by the dashed vertical line in the figure in **b.** (*Note:* The actual point is $19,200, which was determined algebraically by using the technique described in footnote 13 on page 490.)

ST 10-3   **a.**

Capital structure debt ratio	Expected EPS (1)	Required return, k_s (2)	Estimated share value [(1) ÷ (2)] (3)
0%	$3.12	.13	$24.00
10	3.90	.15	26.00
20	4.80	.16	30.00
30	5.44	.17	32.00
40	5.51	.19	29.00
50	5.00	.20	25.00
60	4.40	.22	20.00

b Using the table in **a:**
  (1) Maximization of EPS: *40% debt ratio*, EPS = $5.51/share (see column 1).
  (2) Maximization of share value: *30% debt ratio*, share value = $32.00 (see column 3).
c. Recommend *30% debt ratio*, because it results in the maximum share value and is therefore consistent with the firm's goal of owner wealth maximization.

CHAPTER 11

ST 11-1   **a.** Earnings per share (EPS) = $\dfrac{\$2,000,000 \text{ earnings available}}{500,000 \text{ shares of common outstanding}}$
  = $4.00/share

  Price/earnings (P/E) ratio = $\dfrac{\$60 \text{ market price}}{\$4.00 \text{ EPS}}$ = 15

b. Proposed dividends = 500,000 shares × $2 per share = $1,000,000

  Shares that can be repurchased = $\dfrac{\$1,000,000}{\$62}$ = 16,129 shares

c. *After proposed repurchase:*
  Shares outstanding = 500,000 − 16,129 = 483,871

  EPS = $\dfrac{\$2,000,000}{483,871}$ = $4.13/share

d. Market price = $4.13/share × 15 = $61.95/share

e. The earnings per share (EPS) are higher after the repurchase, because there are fewer common shares outstanding (483,871 shares versus 500,000 shares) to divide up the firm's $2,000,000 of available earnings.

f. In both cases, the shareholders would receive $2 per share—a $2 cash dividend in the dividend case or an approximately $2 increase in share price ($60.00 per share to $61.95 per share) in the repurchase case. (*Note:* The $.05 per share ($2.00 − $1.95) difference is due to rounding.) In reality, it never works this cleanly. The repurchase price may not be $62.00 and the P/E ratio may change. The benefits received by the two groups of shareholders may be very different.

CHAPTER 12

ST 12-1   **a.** Calculate Cash Inflows
Calculate Tax Shield

Year	UCC	CCA	UCC	Tax Shield
1	$220,000	$33,000	$187,000	$13,200
2	$187,000	$56,100	$130,900	$22,440
3	$130,900	$39,270	$91,630	$15,708
4	$91,630	$27,489	$64,141	$10,996
5	$64,141	$19,242	$44,899	$7,697

Calculate Cash Inflows

	YEAR				
	1	2	3	4	5
Incremental sales	$85,000	$105,000	$100,000	$70,000	$60,000
Less: incr operating costs	–$15,000	–$ 5,000	$ 0	$ 0	$ 0
Incremental operating income	100,000	110,000	100,000	70,000	60,000
Less: taxes	40,000	44,000	40,000	28,000	24,000
Increm A/T oper income	60,000	66,000	60,000	42,000	36,000
Plus: tax shield from CCA	13,200	22,440	15,708	10,996	7,697
Other – ITC	30,000				
– working capital	–25,000				25,000
– salvage					35,000
Net After-tax Incremental CFs	$78,200	$88,440	$75,708	$52,996	$103,697

b. Yes, the analysis would differ. Since there are problems with calculating cash inflows each year, especially the tax shield from CCA, the cash inflows are split into their individual components and each analyzed separately. Following this process allows the NPV to be calculated. Note, that the above analysis ignores the benefit associated with the tax shield on almost $45,000 of UCC.

c. The NPV of the project for Laidlaw follows:

NPV of Project:

– Incremental Co: –$300,000 + $50,000	=	–$250,000
+ PV of ITC*		
$300,000 (10%) = $30,000 × PVIF(1 per, 18%)	=	+$ 25,424
– Additional working capital	=	–$ 25,000

+ *PV of incremental after-tax margin*

Yr 1: $100,000(1 − 0.40) × PVIF(1 per, 18%) =	$50,847	
Yr 2: $110,000(1 − 0.40) × PVIF(2 per, 18%) =	$47,400	
Yr 3: $100,000(1 − 0.40) × PVIF(3 per, 18%) =	$36,518	
Yr 4: $ 70,000(1 − 0.40) × PVIF(4 per, 18%) =	$21,663	
Yr 5: $ 60,000(1 − 0.40) × PVIF(5 per, 18%) =	$15,736	
Total PV of incremental after-tax margin	=	$172,164

+ *PV of tax shield from incremental CCA*

$$\$220{,}000 \times \frac{0.30 \times 0.40}{0.30 + 0.18} \times \frac{1.09}{1.18} \qquad = \qquad \$50{,}805$$

+ *PV of Salvage*

$\$35{,}000 \times PVIF(5 \text{ per}, 18\%) \qquad = \qquad \$15{,}299$

− *PV of tax shield lost due to salvage*

$\$15{,}299 \times 0.30 \times 0.40 \qquad = \qquad -\$\ 1{,}836$

+ *Recapture of working capital*

$\$25{,}000 \times PVIF(5 \text{ per}, 18\%) \qquad = \qquad \underline{\$10{,}928}$

NPV $\qquad = \qquad \underline{-\$\ 2{,}206}$

Laidlaw should not purchase the new piece of equipment since the NPV of the project is negative. This means that the value of the project to the company is less than the project's incremental cost; the expected return on the equipment will not cover the cost of the funds invested in the equipment. Note, though that at a slightly lower discount rate, a positive NPV would result for the project.

Note The benefit of the ITC is a reduction in federal taxes payable. Since the company receives the benefit when they file their taxes, it is assumed the company must wait, on average, one year to receive the benefit.

ST 12-2 **a.** Payback period:

Project M: $\dfrac{\$28{,}500}{\$10{,}000} = \underline{2.85 \text{ years}}$

Project N:

Year (t)	Cash inflows (CF$_t$)	Cumulative cash inflows
1	$11,000	$11,000
2	10,000	21,000
3	9,000	30,000
4	8,000	38,000

$$2 + \frac{\$27{,}000 - \$21{,}000}{\$9{,}000} \text{ years}$$

$$2 + \frac{\$6{,}000}{\$9{,}000} \text{ years} = \underline{2.67 \text{ years}}$$

b. Net present value (NPV):

Project M: NPV = $(\$10{,}000 \times PVIFA_{14\%,4yrs}) - \$28{,}500$

$= (\$10{,}000 \times 2.914) - \$28{,}500$

$= \$29{,}140 - \$28{,}500 = \underline{\$640}$

(Calculator solution = $637)

Project N:

Year *(t)*	Cash inflows *(CF_t)* (1)	$PVIF_{14\%,t}$ (2)	Present value at 14% [(1) × (2)] (3)
1	$11,000	.877	$ 9,647
2	10,000	.769	7,690
3	9,000	.675	6,075
4	8,000	.592	4,736
	Present value of cash inflows		$28,148
	− Initial investment		27,000
	Net present value (NPV)		$ 1,148

(Calculator solution = $1,155.18)

c. Internal rate of return (IRR) Calculate using NPV profiles:

	NPV Profile	
Discount rate (%)	NPV Project M	NPV Project N
0	$11,500	$11,000
5	6,960	6,903
10	3,199	3,490
15	50	618
16	−518	99

For project M, the IRR is between 15% and 16% but much closer to 15%. Using a financial calculator, the exact answer is $15.086%, or 15.1% rounded to nearest decimal. For project N, the IRR is slightly greater than 16%, say 16.2%. Using a financial calculator, the exact answer is 16.1935%, or 16.2% rounded to the nearest decimal.

d.

	Project	
	M	N
Payback period	2.85 years	2.67 years[a]
NPV	$637	$1,155[a]
IRR	15.1%	16.2%[a]

[a]Preferred project.

Project N is recommended, because it has the higher NPV. The project also has the shorter payback period, and the higher IRR, which is greater than the 14% cost of capital., but these are incidental reasons to select project N. NPV is the main criterion to use to rank capital budgeting projects.

e. Net present value profiles:

From the NPV profile that follows, it can be seen that the crossover rate is 5.75%. At this discount rate, both projects have a NPV of $6.351. If Fitch Industries' cost of capital was less than 5.75%), project M would be preferred. At rates above 5.75%, project N is preferred. Because the firm's cost of capital is 14%, it can be seen from part d that project N should be selected.

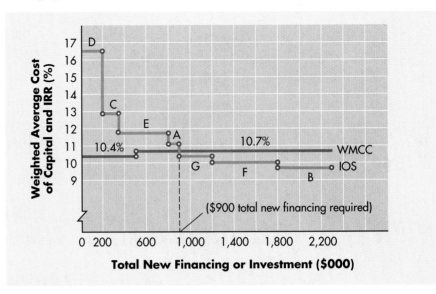

CHAPTER 13

ST 13-1 **a.** $NPV_A = (\$7,000 \times PVIF_{a(10\%,3yrs)}) - \$15,000$
$= \$17,408 - \$15,000 = \underline{\$2,408}$
$NPV_B = (\$10,000 \times PVIF_{a(10\%,3yrs)}) - \$20,000$
$= \$24,869 - \$20,000 = \underline{\$4,869}^*$

*Preferred project, because higher NPV.

b. Project A:

Year (t)	Cash inflows (CF_t) (1)	Certainty equivalent factors (α_t) (2)	Certain CF_t [(1) × (2)] (3)	$PVIF_{7\%,t}{}^a$ (4)	Present value at 7% [(3) × (4)] (5)
1	$7,000	.95	$6,650	.935	$ 6,215
2	7,000	.90	6,300	.873	5,503
3	7,000	.90	6,300	.816	5,143
		Present value of cash inflows			$16,861
	−	Initial investment			15,000
		NPV			$ 1,861*

Project B:

Year (t)	Cash inflows (CF_t) (1)	Certainty equivalent factors (α_t) (2)	Certain CF_t [(1) × (2)] (3)	$PVIF_{7\%,t}{}^a$ (4)	Present value at 7% [(3) × (4)] (5)
1	$10,000	.90	$9,000	.935	$ 8,411
2	10,000	.85	8,500	.873	7,424
3	10,000	.70	7,000	.816	5,714
			Present value of cash inflows		$21,549
		−	Initial investment		20,000
			NPV		$ 1,549

^{a}Values are rounded-off; a financial calculator was used to determine the answer.

*Preferred project, because higher NPV.

c. From the CAPM-type relationship, the risk-adjusted discount rate for project A, which has a risk index of 0.4, is *9%*; for project B, with a risk index of 1.8, the risk-adjusted discount rate is *16%*.

$NPV_A = (\$7,000 \times PVIF_{a(9\%,3yrs)}) - \$15,000$
$= \$17,719 - \$15,000 = \underline{\$2,719}*$
$NPV_B = (\$10,000 \times PVIF_{a(16\%,3per)}) - \$20,000$
$= \$22,459 - \$20,000 = \underline{\$2,459}$

*Preferred project, because higher NPV.

d. When the differences in risk were ignored in **a**, project B is preferred over project A; but when the higher risk of project B is incorporated in the analysis using either certainty equivalents (**b**) or risk-adjusted discount rates (**c**), *project A is preferred over project B.* Clearly, project A should be implemented.

CHAPTER 14

ST 14-1

Basic data		
Time component	Current	Proposed
Average age of inventory (AAI)	40 days	40 days
Average collection period (ACP)	30 days	30 days
Average payment period (APP)	10 days	30 days

Cash conversion cycle (CCC) = AAI + ACP − APP
$CCC_{current}$ = 40 days + 30 days − 10 days = 60 days
$CCC_{proposed}$ = 40 days + 30 days − 30 days = 40 days
Reduction in CCC   20 days

Annual operating cycle investment = $18,000,000
Daily investment = $18,000,000 ÷ 365 = $49,315
Reduction in financing = $49,315 × 20 days = $986,300
Annual profit increase = 12% × $986,300 = $118,356

ST 14-2   a. *Data:*

S = 60,000 gallons

O = $200 per order

C = $1 per gallon per year

Calculation:

$$EOQ = \sqrt{\frac{2 \times S \times O}{C}} = \sqrt{\frac{2 \times 60,000 \times \$200}{\$1}} = \sqrt{24,000,000} = \underline{\underline{4,899 \text{ gallons}}}$$

b. Total cost = $(O \times S/Q) + (C \times Q/2)$

Q = EOQ = 4,899 gallons

Total cost = [$200 × (60,000/4,899)] + [$1 × (4,899/2)]

= ($200 × 12.25) + ($1 × 2,449.5)

= $2,450 + $2,449.5 = $\underline{\$4,899.50}$ = $4,900

c. *Data:*

Lead time = 20 days

Daily usage = 60,000 gallons/365 days

= 164.4 gallons/day

Calculation:

Reorder point = lead time in days × daily usage

= 20 days × 164.4 gallons/day

= $\underline{3,288 \text{ gallons}}$

ST 14-3   **Analysis of the Effects of Easing Collection Efforts on Regency Rug Repair Company**

Additional profit contribution from sales		
[4,000 rugs × ($32 avg. sale price − $28 var. cost)]		$ 16,000
Cost of marginal investment in accounts receivable		
Average investment under proposed plan:		
$\dfrac{(\$28 \times 76,000 \text{ rugs})}{365/48} = \dfrac{\$2,128,000}{365/48}$	$279,847	
Average investment under present plan:		
$\dfrac{(\$28 \times 72,000 \text{ rugs})}{365/40} = \dfrac{\$2,016,000}{365/40}$	220,932	
Marginal investment in A/R	$58,915	
Cost of marginal investment in		
A/R (0.14 × $58,915)		($8,248)
Cost of marginal bad debts		
Bad debts under proposed plan		
(1.5% × $32 × 76,000 rugs)	$ 36,480	
Bad debts under present plan		
(1% × $32 × 72,000 rugs)	23,040	
Cost of marginal bad debts		($13,440)
Annual savings in collection expense		$15,000
Net gain from implementation of proposed plan		$ 9,312

Recommendation: Because a net gain of $9,312 is expected to result from easing collection efforts, *the proposed plan should be implemented.*

CHAPTER 15

ST 15-1 a.

Supplier	Approximate cost of giving up cash discount	
X	$(1\%/99\%) \times [365/(55 - 10)]$	= 8.19%
Y	$(2\%/98\%) \times [365/(30 - 10)]$	= 37.24%
Z	$(2\%/98\%) \times [365/(60 - 20)]$	= 18.62%

b.

Supplier	Recommendation
X	8.19% cost of giving up discount < 15% interest cost from bank; therefore, *give up discount.*
Y	37.24% cost of giving up discount > 15% interest cost from bank; therefore, *take discount and borrow from bank.*
Z	18.62% cost of giving up discount > 15% interest cost from bank; therefore, *take discount and borrow from bank.*

c. Stretching accounts payable for supplier Z would change the cost of giving up the cash discount to

$$(2\%/98\%) \times \{365/(80 - 20) = = \underline{12.41\%}$$

In this case, in light of the 15% interest cost from the bank, the recommended strategy in **b** would be to *give up the discount,* because the 12.41% cost of giving up the discount would be less than the 15% bank interest cost.

CHAPTER 16

ST 16-1 After-tax cost of debt = $15\% \times (1 - 0.25) = 11.25\%$

NPV_L = + Incremental cost   = +$86,000

– PV of tax shield from CCA

$$\$86,000 \times \left[\frac{0.30 \times 0.25}{0.30 + 0.1125} \right] \times \frac{1.05625}{1.1125} \qquad \doteq -\$14,846$$

– PV of Salvage

$\$4,000 \times$ PVIF (8 per, 11.25%)   = –$1,705

+ PV of tax shield lost due to salvage

$$\$1,705 \times \left[\frac{0.30 \times 0.25}{0.30 + 0.1125} \right] \qquad = \quad +\$310$$

– Present value of after-tax lease payments

$\$17,400 (1 - 0.25) + 17,400 (1 - 0.25) \times$ PVIF$_a$ (7 per, 11.25%) = –$74,051

+ Present value of after-tax maintenance costs

$\$2,000 (1 - 0.25) \times$ PVIFa (8 per, 11.25%)   = +$7,651

NPV_L = +$3,359

The present value of the cost of purchasing the new forklift truck = $69,759

The present value of the cost of leasing the new forklift truck = $66,400

The maintenance costs should be considered as either an additional cost of leasing or as a benefit of leasing. The latter technique is used in the above analysis.

The NPV of the lease is $3,359, therefore, Nelson Company should lease the forklift.

b. The lessor's required rate of return on the lease must be less than Nelson's after-tax cost of debt financing. This could be due to a different level of taxation.

ST 16-2 **a.** In tabular form:

Year(s)	Payments (1)	Present value interest factor at 6.5% (2)	Present value
1–50	$ 55[a]	14.725[b]	$809.85
50	1,000	0.043[c]	42.91
		Straight bond value	$852.76

[a]$1,000 at 11% = $110 interest per year ÷ 2 = $55 semiannually
[b]Present value interest factor for an annuity, *PVIFA*, discounted at 6.5% for 50 periods, rounded.
[c]Present value interest factor for $1, *PVIF*, discounted at 6.5% for 50 periods, rounded.

b.

Market price of stock (1)	Conversion ratio (2)	Conversion value [(1) × (2)] (3)
$20	40	$ 800
25 (conversion price)	40	1,000 (par value)
28	40	1,120
35	40	1,400
50	40	2,000

c. The bond would be expected to sell at the higher of the conversion value or straight value. In no case would it be expected to sell for less than the straight value of $852.76. Therefore, if the company's common shares were trading for $20, the bond would sell for its straight value of $852.76, and at common share prices of $25, $28, $35, and $50 the bond would be expected to sell at the associated conversion values (calculated in **b**) of $1,000, $1,120, $1,400, and $2,000, respectively.

These values are the minimum amounts the bond would be expected to trade for. Given that time remains until maturity, the actual price of the bond would be greater than those provided above. The difference is the market premium (time value) as shown in Figure 16.1.

d. The straight bond value of $852.76.

CHAPTER 17

ST 17-1 **a.** Net funds available to the MNC can be calculated as follows:

Subsidiary income before local taxes	$150,000
Foreign income tax at 32%	−48,000
Dividend available to be declared	$102,000
Foreign dividend withholding tax at 8%	−8,160
Net funds available to MNC	$ 93,840

The Canadian parent does not pay any taxes in Canada.

b.

Subsidiary's EBIT	$150,000
Interest payment to parent	150,000
Taxable income	0
Foreign income tax	0
Withholding tax on interest payment (8%)	12,000
MNC's interest income	$150,000
Canadian taxes (34%)	51,000
Less: Foreign tax credit	12,000
Canadian taxes due	39,000
Total taxes paid	$51,000
Net funds available to MNC	$99,000

c. In a. total taxes are $56,160 and the funds available to the Canadian parents are $93,840. In b, total taxes are $51,000 and the funds available are $99,000. In this case, it makes sense for the Canadian parent to fund the foreign operation using debt capital.

Appendix C

Answers to Selected End-of-Chapter Problems

The following list of answers to selected problems and portions of problems is included to provide "check figures" for use in preparing detailed solutions to end-of-chapter problems requiring calculations. For problems that are relatively straightforward, the key answer is given; for more complex problems, answers to a number of parts of the problem are included. Detailed calculations are not shown—only the final and, in some cases, intermediate answers, which should help to confirm whether the correct solution is being developed. Answers to problems involving present and future value were solved by using a financial calculator. For problems containing a variety of cases for which similar calculations are required, the answers for only one or two cases have been included. The only verbal answers included are simple yes-or-no or "choice of best alternative" responses; answers to problems requiring detailed explanations or discussions are not given.

The problems and portions of problems for which answers have been included were selected randomly; therefore, there is no discernible pattern to the choice of problem answers given. The answers given are based on what are believed to be the most obvious and reasonable assumptions related to the given problem; as based on the coverage of the material in the chapter.

CHAPTER 1

1-1	a.	Ms. Harper has unlimited liability: $60,000
	c.	Ms. Harper has limited liability
1-2	b.	$150,000
	f.	No (EVA = –1,045)
1-3	a.	$460,000

CHAPTER 2

2-3		EAC = $29,000
2-4	b.	$27,050
2-5	a.	$1.16
2-8		Preferred: $20/share
		Common: $9.50/share
2-9	a.	EPS = $1.9375
	b.	Total Assets: $926,000
2-12	c.	$1,150,000
2-18	a.	$19,700
	b.	$75,739
2-20	a.	X: $250; Y: $5,000
2-22	b.	NIAT = $198,982
2-23	a.	Taxes payable = $397,646
2-26		$80,000
2-28	b.	$2,256,450
2-29	a.	$81,063

CHAPTER 3

3-3	a.	Average Age of Inventory: 98.85 days
3-7	a.	(2) Times Interest Earned (Pelican) = 62.5
	b.	(2) Profit Margin (Timberland) =13.8%
3-12	a.	Current Ratio: 1.04
		Average Collection Period: 56 days
		Profit Margin: 4.1%
		ROE: 11.3%
3-14	a.	Net Working Capital = +5.45%
		Average Collection Period = –26.19%
		ROA = +39.66%

CHAPTER 4

4-1		August: $92,500
4-2		Accounts Payable, 1-month lag,
		April = $168,000
		Wages and salaries, May = $48,700
		Accounts Payable, 2-month lag,
		June = $146,400
4-4	a.	Ending Cash March: $67,000
	b.	Required total financing April: $37,000
	c.	Line of credit should be at least $37,000 to cover borrowing needs for the month of April.
4-8	a.	NIAT: $216,600
	b.	NIAT: $227,400
4-11	a.	Accounts receivable: $1,440,000
		Net fixed assets: $4,820,000
		Total current liabilities: $2,260,000
		External Funds Required (EFR): $775,000
		Total assets: $9,100,000

| 4-12 | a. | NIAT: $67,500 |
| | c. | EFR: $11,250 |

CHAPTER 5

Solved Using Financial Calculator

5-3		C: 3 years < n< 4 years
5-4		A: $530.66
5-6	a.	(1) $15,457.13
5-10	a.	(1) Annual: $8,811.71
		Semi-annual: $8,954.24
		Quarterly: $9,036.56
5-11	b.	B: 12.6%
		D: 16.99%
5-12		A: $1,197.22
5-15	a.	B: (1) $4,057.59
		(2) $4,544.40
5-19		A: $3,862.84
		B: $138,450.79
		C: $6,956.53
5-22		A: $4,448.63
		D: $80,196.13
5-25		$63.02
5-27	a.	A: $20,838.95
	c.	B
5-32		C: $52,411.34
5-33		A: $109,856.33
5-36		E: $85,292.70
5-40		A: $43,695.28
5-43		A: $1,481.74
		C: $2,623.32
5-45		Future value of retirement home in 20 years = $272,606.52
5-46	b.	$3,764.82

CHAPTER 6

6-1		P = $991.38
6-3	a.	P = $1,289,220,982
6-7	d.	$36,446,958.33
6-9	g.	After-tax interest rate = 4.9%
6-12	c.	iii) 3.81% or 63.5%

CHAPTER 7

7-2		A: 25%
7-4	a.	A: 8%
		B: 20%
7-5	a.	R: 10%
		S: 20%
	b.	R: 25%
		S: 25.5%
7-9	a.	(4) Project 257 CV: .368
		Project 432 CV: .354
7-10	a.	F: 4%
	b.	F:13.38%
	c.	F: 3.345
7-12	b.	Portfolio return: 15.5%
	c.	Standard deviation: 1.638%

7-15	b.	Purchase price = $2,225.84
7-18	a.	18% increase
	b.	9.6% increase
	c.	No change
7-22		A: 8.9%
		D: 15%
7-23	c.	$b = 1.18$
7-24	b.	10%

CHAPTER 8

8-1		Real rate of return = 3.5%
8-3	c.	$26.25
8-5	a.	20 years: 11.5%
8-8		B: $R_f = 12\%$
		D: $R_f = 8\%$
8-11		C: $16,663,96
		E: $14,115.27
8-13	a.	$1,156.47
8-17	b.	(1) $1,256.78
		(3) $815.73
8-28	a.	$k_s = 9.5\%$
8-32	a.	$P_0 = \$34.12$
	c.	$P_0 = \$187.87$
8-38	a.	$k_s = 14.8\%$

CHAPTER 9

9-1	b.	12%
9-3	a.	Net proceeds = $980
	d.	$k_d = 12.26\%$
9-8	b.	6%
	d.	12%
9-13	a.	10.506%
9-20	a.	0 – $600,000: 10.52%
	c.	$1,000,000 and above: 11.71%

CHAPTER 10

10-4	a.	21,000 CDs
	d.	$10,500
10-7	b.	8,000: $12,000
		12,000: $28,000
10-10	a.	$0.375
	c.	$1.935
10-14	a.	DOL: 1.25
		DFL: 1.71
		DTL: 2.14
10-18	b.	Expected EPS = $0.18
10-22	b.	Debt: 60% = $P_0 = \$28.75$
10-25	a.	600,000: $60,000
		900,000: $240,000
		1,200,000: $420,000

CHAPTER 11

11-5	a.	$1.60
11-9	a.	Retained earnings: $85,000

11-11	a.	EPS = $2
	d.	$20 per share
11-16	b.	$2.10
	c.	$21 per share

CHAPTER 12

12-1	a.	$3,246
		–$5,131
		$3,115
12-4	a.	Project A: NPV = –$4,336
		Project B: NPV = $1,118
		Project C: NPV = $7,008
		Project D: NPV = $5,899
	c.	Project A: 9.70%
		Project B: 15.63%
		Project C: 19.44%
		Project D: 17.51%
12-5	a.	–$9,544
		i. 12.67 years
		ii $82,456
		iii $17,636
		iv $22,047
		v $42,398
		vi 11.28%
12-6	b.	$385,604
12-10	a.	Initial Investment: –$28,000
		Year 1: $4,000
		Year 2: $6,000
		Year 3: $8,000
		Year 4: $10,000
		Year 5: $4,000
12-11	a.	ΔNWC = $25,000
12-15	a.	Project A: 3.08 years
		Project B: 3.63 years
		Project C: 2.38 years
	b.	Project A: $2,562
		Project B: –$327
		Project C: $5,451
12-18	a.	Project A: 3.0 years
		Project B: 3.2 years
		Project C: 3.4 years
	b.	Project A: $10,340
		Project B: $10,785.50
		Project C: $4,302.50
	c.	Project A: 20%
		Project B: 17%
		Project C: 15%
12-20		Project A: $48,750
		Project B: $75,000
12-23	a.	Year 1: $7,000
		Year 2: $13,440
		Year 3: $12,365
		Year 4: $11,376
	b.	Year 1: $1,820
		Year 2: $3,494
		Year 3: $3,215
		Year 4: $2,958
12-24	a.	$153,000
	b.	$135,500
	c.	Year 1: $5,420; $1,409
		Year 2: $10,406; $2,706

Year 3: $9,574; $2,489
Year 4: $8,808; $2,290
12-26   Incremental after-tax cash flow = $287,000
12-32   a.   NPV = $52,905
12-34   NPV = –$8,111
12-35   a.   NPV of Machine X = –$111,073
          NPV of Machine Y = –$162,544
     b.   Adjusted NPV of Machine X = –$78,256
          Adjusted NPV of Machine Y = –$106,755
12-36   NPV = –$63,787
12-39   IRR = 15.6%
12-40   a.   Machine 1: 4 years, 8 months
          Machine 2: 5 years, 3 months
12-43   a.   10%
          18.23 years
          $12,244

CHAPTER 13

13-2   a. $6,183.43
13-3   b.   Project X: $8,949.88
          Project Y: $11,933.17
13-4   a.   Project A: $1,600

Project A:	Pessimistic	–$6,297.29
	Most likely	$513.56
	Optimistic	$7,324.41
	Range	$13,621.70

13-7   b.   –$5,573.98
13-8   a.   Project C: $9,069.49
          Project D: $7,940.41
13-9   a.   Project E: $2,129.87
          Project G: $1,136.29
     b.   Project F: 0.15
     c.   Project E: $831.51
13-10   a.   Project A: $5,391.10
      b.   Project A: $7,948.97
13-12   a.   Project Z: –$8,306.04
13-13   b.   Project A:

Project A:	Optimistic	–$500
	Most likely	$1,000
	Pessimistic	$1,500

     c.   Project A: 13%
     d.   Project A: NPV = $1,949
13-15   a.   New Brunswick Project: NPV = $110,242
13-16   a.   Machine A: –$42,663.10
           Machine B: $6,646.58
           Machine C: $7,643.29
13-17   a.   Project X: $2,698.32
13-18   a.   Sell: $177,786.90
      b.   Sell: $105,236.69
13-20   b.   Project C: NPV = $300,000
           Project F: NPV = $500,000
13-21   a.   Project B: $210,000
           Project G: $960,000

CHAPTER 14

14-3   a.   75.42 days
     b.   35.42 days
     c. $97,041
14-6   a.   Current OC = 97 days
          Current CCC = 51 days

     b.   New OC = 115 days
     c.   New CCC = 69 days
          $240,000
14-8   a. $908,333
     b.   Aggressive: $1,083,583
          Conservative: $1,260,000
14-9   a.   Aggressive: $646,500
          Conservative: $780,000
     b.   Aggressive: $571,667
          Conservative: $676,000
          Aggressive: $496,833
          Conservative: $572,000
14-13   a.   1000 units: $2,000.00; $125.00; $2,125.00
          2000 units: $1,000.00; $250.00; $1,250.00
          3000 units: $667.67; $375.00; $1,042.67
          4000 units: $500.00; $500.00; $1000.00
          5000 units: $400.00; $625.00; $1,025.00
          6000 units: $333.33; $750.00; $1,083.33
          7000 units: $285.71; $875.00; $1,160.71
          EOQ = 4000 units
14-14   a.   A: 66.0
          B: 81.5
          C: 76.0
14-15   a. $123,288
      b. $73,973
      c. $8,877
14-23   a. $490,000
      b.   Annual savings = $98,000
      c.   Net savings = $52,000

CHAPTER 15

15-1   b.   December 30
     c.   January 9
15-2   a.   37.24%
     c.   21.28%
15-3   a.   i)   1/15 net 45 day of invoice
          ii) 2/10 net 30 EOM
     b.   iii) 28 days
          iv) 80 days
     c.   i)   12.29%
          iii) 35.47%
15-4   Cost of giving up cash discount = 32.25%
15-5   a.   Supplier K: 12.41%
          Supplier M: 25.09%
15-8   b.   3.70%
      c.   15.64%
15-10   a.   12.94%
15-11   a.   The Eastern Bank: 10.0%
15-13   a.   9.12%
15-14   a.   Total collateral = $200,000
15-16   b.   12 months: 13.5%
15-18   a.   The Bank of P.E.I.: $1,083

CHAPTER 16

16-3   Annual loan payment = $30,087.43
16-4   a. NPV_L = –$3,315
16-6 NPV_L = –$47,708
16-7   Lease A: $272,547.67
          Lease D: $40,500.72

16-9	**b.**	40 shares
16-11		Bond B: $800.00
		Bond C: $880.00
16-14	**a.**	$831.14
		At $12.00: $960
		At $20.00: $1,600
16-16	**c.**	$11.28
16-18	**a.**	160 shares, 400 warrants

16-19	**a.**	$420 or 6.67%
		$900 or 14.29%
16-20		Option B: -$50
		Option D: −$300
		Option E: −$450
16-22	**b.**	At $46: −$380
		At $35: $620

INDEX